WileyPLUS

WileyPLUS is a research-based online environment for effective teaching and learning.

WileyPLUS builds students' confidence because it takes the guesswork out of studying by providing students with a clear roadmap:

- what to do
- how to do it
- if they did it right

It offers interactive resources along with a complete digital textbook that help students learn more. With WileyPLUS, students take more initiative so you'll have greater impact on their achievement in the classroom and beyond.

D1402079

Now available for

Bb
Blackboard

For more information, visit www.wileyplus.com

WileyPLUS

Management
Information
Systems

Moving Business Forward

Second Edition

Management Information Systems

Moving Business Forward

Second Edition

R. Kelly Rainer, Jr.
Brad Prince
Hugh Watson

WILEY

Publisher	Don Fowley
Executive Editor	Beth Lang Golub
Content Manager	Kevin Holm
Production Editor	Tim Lindner
Executive Marketing Manager	Chris Ruel
Marketing Assistant	Marissa Carroll
Design Director	Harry Nolan
Product Designer	Jenny Welter
Editorial Operations Manager	Melissa Edwards
Senior Designer	Maureen Eide
Senior Photo Editor	Lisa Gee
Cover Designer	Jasmine Lee
Senior Content Editor	Wendy Ashenberg
Assistant Editor	Samantha Mandel
Editorial Program Assistant	Katherine Willis
Content Assistant	Helen Seachrist
Production Management Services	Aptara®, Inc.

This book was set in Minion Pro 10/12 by Aptara®, Inc. and printed and bound by Quad Graphics.

This book is printed on acid free paper. ∞

Founded in 1807, John Wiley & Sons, Inc., has been a valued source of knowledge and understanding for more than 200 years, helping people around the world meet their needs and fulfill their aspirations. Our company is built on a foundation of principles that include responsibility to the communities we serve and where we live and work. In 2008, we launched a Corporate Citizenship Initiative, a global effort to address the environmental, social, economic, and ethical challenges we face in our business. Among the issues we are addressing are carbon impact, paper specifications and procurement, ethical conduct within our business and among our vendors, and community and charitable support. For more information, please visit our Web site: www.wiley.com/go/citizenship.

ISBN-13:   978-1-118-44359-0
BRV ISBN: 978-1-118-47768-7

Printed in the United States of America

10 9 8 7 6 5 4

Dear Student,

Why are you here? We are not asking you a philosophical question—that is a different course. We are asking, "Why are you about to spend an entire term learning about information systems? Why are you—an accounting major, or a marketing or management major—being required to study this topic?" You may be asking, "What's in IT for me?" The short answer is that "IT's About Business," and the longer answer is the goal of this book.

Information systems are making the world a very small place and are contributing to rapidly increasing global competition. As a result, organizations are constantly trying to find ways to gain a competitive advantage—by achieving operational excellence, developing new products and services, developing new business models, providing superb customer service, improving decision making, and so on. It should be obvious, then, that an introductory course in information systems is critically important for success in your chosen career.

Rapid advances in information systems mean that, as business students, change will be the only constant you will encounter in today's dynamic digital business environment. We wrote this book for business students of all majors who will soon become business professionals. We have three goals in mind:

1. To help you be immediately successful when you join your organization
2. To help you understand the importance of information systems for individuals, organizations, and society as a whole
3. To enable you to become informed users of your organization's information systems

To accomplish these goals, we have tried to provide the essential, relevant knowledge that you need to understand to effectively use information systems in your careers.

The way we propose to do this is by keeping you *actively involved* in the material. Every section of the chapters has an activity that asks you to do something beyond just reading the textbook that will help you see why the content is useful for your future business career.

We hope you will enjoy this active approach and successfully complete the course with a richer understanding of what's in IT for you.

Kelly Rainer, Brad Prince, and Hugh Watson

Dear Instructor,

We are like you. All of us who teach the introductory course in information systems realize that it is difficult for students to understand the importance and relevance of the topics in the course. As a result, students often memorize the content just before the exam, and then forget it as soon as the exam is over. We all want to engage students at a much deeper level. We know that the best way to accomplish this objective is through *hands-on active learning*, leading to *increased student engagement* in our course content.

Accordingly, active learning and student engagement are key principles of our new book. We recognize the need to actively involve students in problem solving, creative thinking, and capitalizing on opportunities. Every section of every chapter includes extensive hands-on exercises, activities, and mini-cases. End-of-chapter material also includes exercises that require students to use software application tools. Through these activities, we enable students to understand how to *do* something with the concepts they learn, such as meet business goals using information systems, configure products, and use spreadsheets and databases to facilitate problem solving.

The preface on the next page further outlines the goals, features, and support material provided with our new text. We hope you will enjoy teaching with this approach!

Kelly Rainer, Brad Prince, and Hugh Watson

Preface

Chapter Organization

Each chapter contains the following elements:

- **Chapter Outline:** Lists the major concepts covered in each chapter.
- **Learning Objectives:** Provide an overview of the key learning goals that students should achieve after reading the chapter.
- **Chapter-Opening Case:** A short case that focuses on a small or start-up company that is using information systems to solve a business problem. Cases in introductory information systems textbooks typically involve very large organizations. In contrast, our chapter-opening cases demonstrate that small and start-up companies also have business problems that they address using information systems. Students will see that small firms usually have to be quite creative in building and implementing IS solutions, because they do not have MIS departments or large budgets. These small-business cases also add an entrepreneurial flavor to each chapter for students who are planning to start their own businesses.
- **Ruby's Club Internship Case:**
  - At the start of each chapter is a "Ruby's Club internship scenario" that presents a problem at Ruby's Club, a downtown music venue that needs help with redesigning its online presence, overhauling its technological infrastructure, etc. Throughout the semester, the student is presented with problems as if he/she were working as an IT intern for Ruby's Club. Each chapter-opening scenario presents a business problem that the student will be able to solve after reading that chapter.
  - Throughout the chapter are "Ruby's Club Questions" that help students focus on the concepts they will need to solve the Ruby's Club business problem. At the end of each chapter is a "Ruby's Club Internship Assignment" that puts students into the role of an IT Intern. Many assignments are in the form of a business letter that students must address to their employers to solve the problem. Ultimately, this provides students with an opportunity to apply the knowledge they have gained in a business setting, instead of just on their exams.

A supplementary chapter on business writing is available in WileyPLUS for students who need a review.

- **Apply the Concept Activities:** This book's unique pedagogical structure is designed to keep students actively engaged with the course material. Reading material in each chapter subsection is immediately followed by an "Apply the Concept" activity. These activities include links to online videos and articles and other hands-on activities that require students to immediately apply what they have learned. Via WileyPLUS, instructors can assign a section of text along with an Apply the Concept activity and gradable quiz. Each Apply the Concept has the following elements:

  > Background (places the activity in the context of relevant reading material)
  > Activity (a hands-on activity that students carry out)
  > Deliverable (various tasks for students to complete as they perform the activity)
  > Discussion Questions (discussion questions regarding the activity)

Quiz Questions (assignable in WileyPLUS, or available on the Book Companion Site)

- **IT's About Business:** Short cases that demonstrate real-world applications of IT to business. Each case is accompanied by questions relating the case to concepts covered in the chapter. Icons relate these boxes to the specific functional areas.

- **IT's Personal:** Sprinkled throughout the chapters, these short vignettes explain the relevance of MIS concepts to students' daily lives.

- **Before You Go On:** End-of-section reviews prompt students to pause and test their understanding of concepts before moving on to the next section.

- **Examples:** Interspersed throughout the text, these highlight the use (and misuse) of information systems by real-world organizations, thereby illustrating the concepts discussed in the chapter.

- **What's in IT for Me?:** A unique end-of-chapter summary that demonstrates the relevance of each key chapter topic to different functional areas, including accounting, finance, marketing, production/operations management, human resources management, and management information systems. This cross-functional focus makes the book accessible for students from any major.

- **Summary:** Keyed to the Learning Objectives listed at the beginning of the chapter, the summary enables students to review major concepts covered.

- **Discussion Questions and Problem-Solving Activities:** Provide practice through active learning. These exercises are hands-on opportunities to apply the concepts discussed in the chapter.

- **Collaboration Exercises:** Team exercises that require students to take on different functional roles and collaborative to solve business problems. These exercises allow students to get first-hand experience solving business problems using IS tools while also experiencing an authentic business team dynamic.

- **Closing Cases:** Each chapter concludes with two cases about business problems faced by actual companies and how they used IS to solve those issues. The cases are broken down into four parts: a description of the problem, an overview of the IS solution implemented, a presentation of the results of the implementation, and an analysis of key takeaways from the case. Each case is followed by discussion questions, so that students can further explore the concepts presented in the case.

- **Spreadsheet Activity:** Every chapter includes a hands-on spreadsheet project that requires students to practice their Excel skills while using concepts learned in the chapter. Each activity includes deliverables and discussion questions, with multiple choice quiz questions also assignable in WileyPLUS for automatic grading or downloadable through the Book Companion Site. WileyPLUS includes an Excel Lab Manual for students who need introductory coverage or review.

- **Database Activity:** Every chapter includes a hands-on database project that requires students to practice their Access skills while using concepts learned in the chapter. Each activity includes deliverables, quiz questions, and discussion questions. These can be assigned within WileyPLUS for automatic grading. WileyPLUS includes an Access Lab Manual for students who need introductory coverage or review.

- **Glossary:** A study tool that highlights vocabulary within the chapters and facilitates studying.

Key Features

Student Engagement

As discussed in the note addressed to instructors at the beginning of this preface, one of the chief goals of this text is to engage students at a level beyond recognition of key terms. We believe the best way to achieve this goal is through hands-on, active learning that will lead to increased student engagement with the course and its content.

Accordingly, every section of every chapter provides resources that actively involve students in problem solving, creative thinking, and capitalizing on opportunities. Every chapter includes extensive hands-on exercises, activities, and mini-cases, including exercises that require students to solve business problems using Excel and Access.

Cross-Functional Approach

We emphasize the importance of information systems by calling attention in every chapter to how that chapter's topic relates to each business major. Icons guide students to relevant issues for their specific functional area—accounting (ACC), finance (FIN), marketing (MKT), operations management (OM), human resources management (HRM), and management information systems (MIS). Chapters conclude with a detailed summary (entitled 'What's in IT for Me?') of how key concepts in the chapter relate to each functional area. Additionally, each chapter has a collaboration exercise that helps students view the same problem from the perspective of different functional areas.

Diversified and Unique Examples from Different Industries

Extensive use of vivid examples from large corporations, small businesses, and government and not-for-profit organizations enlivens the concepts from the chapter. The examples illustrate everything from the capabilities of information systems, to their cost and justification and the innovative ways that corporations are using IS in their operations. Small businesses have been included in recognition of the fact that many students will work for small-to mid-sized companies, and some will even start their own small business. In fact, some students may already be working at local businesses, and the concepts they are learning in class can be readily observed or put into practice in their part-time jobs. Each chapter constantly highlights the integral connection between business and IS. This connection is especially evident in the chapter-opening and closing cases, the "IT's About Business" boxes, and the highlighted examples.

Successes and Failures

Many textbooks present examples of the successful implementation of information systems, and our book is no exception. However, we go one step beyond by also providing numerous examples of IS failures, in the context of lessons that can be learned from such failures. Misuse of information systems can be very expensive.

Global Focus

An understanding of global competition, partnerships, and trading is essential to success in a modern business environment. Therefore, we provide a broad selection of international cases and examples. We discuss the role of information systems in facilitating export and import, the management of international companies, and electronic trading around the globe. These global examples are highlighted with the global icon.

Innovation and Creativity

In today's rapidly changing business environment, creativity and innovation are necessary for a business to operate effectively and profitably. Throughout our book, we demonstrate how information systems facilitate these processes.

Focus on Ethics

With corporate scandals appearing in the headlines almost daily, ethics and ethical questions have come to the forefront of business people's minds. In addition to devoting an entire chapter to ethics and privacy (Chapter 6), we have included examples and cases throughout the text that focus on business ethics. These examples are highlighted with the ethics icon.

What's New in the Second Edition?

- New chapter on social computing, focusing on how organizations use social computing for business purposes
- New "Plug IT In" on cloud computing, featuring expanded coverage of this important topic
- All new or updated chapter opening and closing cases
- All new or updated "IT's About Business"
- All new or updated examples
- Remodeled student activities that provide a variety of thought-provoking, gradable homework assignments
- New "IT's Personal" vignettes that bring home to students the personal relevance of concepts
- New "Collaboration Exercises" that require students to take on different functional roles and use collaborative software to solve business problems
- Spreadsheet and Database Activities that have been revised to incorporate reviewer feedback
- Remodeled Learning Objectives that clearly define learning goals for each section of book content
- New images and updated interior design that promote visual learning and easy teaching use

Online Supplements

www.wiley.com/college/rainer

Our book also facilitates the teaching of an Introduction to Information Systems course by providing extensive support materials for instructors and students. Visit www.wiley.com/college/rainer to access the Student and Instructor Companion Sites.

Instructor's Manual

The *Instructor's Manual* includes a chapter overview, teaching tips and strategies, answers to all end-of-chapter questions, supplemental mini-cases with essay questions and answers, and experiential exercises that relate to particular topics. It also includes answers and solutions to all spreadsheet and database activities, along with a guide to teaching these exercises, and links to the separate Excel and Access solutions files.

Test Bank

The test bank is a comprehensive resource for test questions. Each chapter contains multiple choice, true/false, short answer, and essay questions. In addition, each chapter includes "Apply Your Knowledge" questions that require more creative thought to answer. Each multiple choice and true/false question is labeled to indicate its level of difficulty: easy, medium, or hard.

The test bank is available for use in Respondus' easy-to-use software. Respondus® is a powerful tool for creating and managing exams that can be printed or published directly to Blackboard, WebCT, Desire2Learn, eCollege, ANGEL, and other learning systems. For more information on Respondus® and the Respondus Test Bank Network, please visit www.respondus.com.

PowerPoint Presentations

The *PowerPoint Presentations* consist of a series of slides for each chapter. The slides are designed around each chapter's content, incorporating key points from the chapter and chapter illustrations as appropriate, as well as real-life examples from the Web. The slides also include links to relevant videos and articles to enhance classroom discussion. They make extensive use of images and video clips.

Student PowerPoints

Posted on the Student Companion Site, these are stripped-down versions of the Instructor slides that students can use for note-taking.

Image Library

All textbook figures are available for download from the Web site. These figures can easily be added to PowerPoint presentations.

Wiley Information Systems Hub

This community Web site is free and open to all instructors who teach an Introduction to IS/MIS course, regardless of book in use. The Hub is topic driven and is a place to ask questions, respond to ideas with comments of your own, share videos, assignments, cases, and news links with other users, and much more. We are delighted to announce David Firth of the University of Montana as the community manager for the site. Please check the Instructor Companion Site for information on how to join.

Updates

(http://wileyinformationsystemsupdates.com)
Weekly updates, harvested from around the Internet by David Firth of the University of Montana, provide you with the latest IT news and issues. These are posted every Monday morning throughout the year at http://wileyinformationsystemsupdates.com/ and feed through to the Wiley Information Systems Hub. They include links to current articles and videos as well as discussion questions to assign or use in class.

BusinessExtra Select

This feature allows instructors to package the text with lab manuals, cases, articles, and other real-world content from sources such as INSEAD, Ivey and Harvard Business School cases, *Fortune*, *The Economist*, and *The Wall Street Journal*. You can combine the book with the content you choose to create a fully customized textbook. For additional information, please visit www.wiley.com/college/bxs.

Practice Quizzes

These multiple choice conceptual questions reinforce knowledge and understanding of basic concepts. They are available in Respondus, the WileyPLUS course, and the Book Companion Site.

WileyPLUS

WileyPLUS

This online teaching and learning environment integrates the entire digital textbook with the most effective instructor and student resources to accommodate every learning style. With WileyPLUS:

- Students achieve concept mastery in a rich, structured environment that is available 24/7.
- Instructors personalize and manage their course more effectively with assessment, assignments, grade tracking, and more.

WileyPLUS can complement the textbook or replace the printed textbook altogether.

For Students

Different learning styles, different levels of proficiency, different levels of preparation—each of your students is unique. WileyPLUS empowers each student to take advantage of his or her strengths.

- Integrated, multimedia resources—including audio and visual exhibits—provide multiple study paths to fit each student's learning preferences and encourage active learning. Resources include
  - > E-book
  - > Minilecture by author for each chapter section
  - > Student PowerPoints for note taking
  - > Video interviews with managers
  - > Lab Manual for Microsoft Office 2010

- WileyPLUS also includes many opportunities for self-assessment. Students can take control of their own learning and practice until they master the material. Resources include
  - > Automatically graded practice questions from the Test Bank
  - > Pre- and postlecture quizzes
  - > Vocabulary flash cards and quizzes

For Instructors

WileyPLUS empowers you with the tools and resources you need to make your teaching as effective as possible.

- You can customize your classroom presentation with a wealth of resources and functionality. You can even add your own materials to your WileyPLUS course. Resources include
  - > PowerPoint presentations
  - > Link to weekly updates
  - > Library of additional "IT's About Business" cases

- With WileyPLUS you can identify students who are falling behind and intervene accordingly, without having to wait for them to come to office hours.

- WileyPLUS simplifies and automates such tasks as assessing student performance, creating assignments, scoring student work, tracking grades, and more.

Acknowledgments

Creating, developing, and producing a text for the introduction to information systems course is a formidable undertaking. Along the way, we were fortunate to receive continuous evaluation, criticism, and direction from many colleagues who regularly teach this course.

We would like to acknowledge the contributions made by the following individuals who participated in focus groups, telesessions, surveys, chapter walkthroughs, class tests, and reviews:

Monica Adya	*Marquette University*
Lawrence Andrew	*Western Illinois University, Macomb*
Orakwue (Bay) Arinze	*Drexel*
Laura Atkins	*James Madison University*
Nick Ball	*Brigham Young University*
Nicholas Barnes	*Nicholls College*
Susan Barzottini	*Manchester CC*
Kristi Berg	*Minot State University*
Andy Borchers	*Lipscomb University*
David Bouchard	*Metropolitan State University*
Dave Bourgeois	*Biola University*
Mari Buche	*Michigan Tech University*

Richard Burkhard	*San Jose State University*
Ashley Bush	*Florida State University*
Donald Carpenter	*Mesa State College*
Teuta Cata	*Northern Kentucky University*
Wendy Ceccucci	*Quinnipiac University*
Susan Chinn	*University of Southern ME, Portland*
Richard Christensen	*Metropolitan State University*
Dmitriy Chulkov	*Indiana University Kokomo*
Phillip Coleman	*Western Kentucky University*
Emilio Collar	*Western CT State University*
Daniel Connolly	*University of Denver*
Lee Cornell	*Minnesota State University, Mankato*
David Croasdell	*University of Nevada, Reno*
Reet Cronk	*Harding University*
Marcia Daley	*Clark, Atlanta*
Donald Danner	*San Francisco State University*
Roy DeJoie	*Purdue, West Lafayette*
Dawna Dewire	*Babson College*
Kevin Duffy	*Wright State*
Lauren Eder	*Rider University*
Ahmed Eshra	*St. John's University*
Roger Finnegan	*Metropolitan State University*
Thomas Fischer	*Metropolitan State University*
Jerry Flatto	*University of Indianapolis*
Jonathan Frankel	*University Massachusetts, Boston*
Judith Gebauer	*University of North Carolina, Wilmington*
Jennifer Gerow	*Virginia Military Institute*
Matt Graham	*University of Maine*
Katie Gray	*University of Texas, Austin*
Penelope (Sue) Greenberg	*Widener University*
Naveen Gudigantala	*University of Portland*
Saurabh Gupta	*University of North Florida*
Bernard Han	*Western Michigan University*
Hyo-Joo Han	*Georgia Southern College*
John Hagle	*Texas State Technical College*
Peter Haried	*University of Wisconsin, LaCrosse*
Ranida Harris	*Indiana University Southeast*
Ranida Harris	*Indiana University Southeast*
Roslin Hauck	*Illinois State University*
Jun He	*University of Michigan, Dearborn*
Richard Herschel	*St. Joseph's University*
Bodgan Hoanca	*University of Alaska*
Mary Carole Hollingsworth	*Georgia Perimeter College, Clarkston Campus*
Terri Holly	*Indian River State College*
Derrick Huang	*Florida Atlantic University*
Maggie Hutchison	*Flagler College*
Mark Hwang	*Central Michigan University*
Lynn Isvik	*Upper Iowa University, Fayette*
Arpan Jani	*University of Wisconsin, River Falls*
Jonathan Jelen	*St. John's University*
Nenad Jukic	*Loyola University*
Stephen Klein	*Ramapo College*
Brian Kovar	*Kansas State University*
Subodha Kumar	*Texas A&M*
Diane Lending	*James Madison University*
Kevin Lertwachara	*Cal Poly San Luis Obispo*
Terry Letsche	*Wartburg College*

Victor Lipe	*Trident Tech*
Chuck Litecky	*Southern Illinois University, Carbondale*
Joan Lumpkin	*Wright State*
Nicole Lytle	*Cal State, San Bernardino*
George Mangalaraj	*Western Illinois University*
Parand Mansouri-Rad	*University of Texas, El Paso*
Michael Martel	*Ohio University*
Nancy Martin	*Southern Illinois University, Carbondale*
Richard McMahon	*University of Houston, Downtown*
Tony McRae	*Collin College*
Vishal Midha	*University of Texas, Pan American*
Esmail Mohebbi	*University West Florida*
Luvai Motiwalla	*University Mass Online*
Mahdi Nasereddin	*Penn State, Berks*
Sandra K. Newton	*Sonoma State University*
Ann O'Brien	*University of Wisconsin, Madison*
Sungjune Park	*University of North Carolina, Charlotte*
Yang Park	*Georgia Southwestern State University*
Alan Peace	*West Virginia University*
Jacqueline Pike	*Duquesne University*
Tony Pittarese	*East Tennessee State University*
Jennifer Pitts	*Columbus State University*
Richard Platt	*University of West Florida*
Larisa Preiser	*Cal Poly, Pomona*
Michelle Ramim	*Nova Southeastern University*
Alison Rampersad	*Lynn University*
Ralph Reilly	*University of Hartford*
Wes Rhea	*Kennesaw State University*
Julio Rivera	*University of Alabama, Birmingham*
Thomas Roberts	*William Patterson University*
Cynthia Ruppel	*Nova Southeastern University*
Russell Sabadosa	*Manchester CC*
Tom Sandman	*Cal State, Sacramento*
Kala Seal	*Loyola Marymount*
Tod Sedbrook	*University of Northern Colorado*
Elaine Seeman	*East Carolina University*
Richard Segall	*Arkansas State University*
Lee Sellers	*EOU—Mt. Hood Metro Center*
Judy Ann Serwatka	*Purdue, North Central*
John Seydel	*Arkansas State University*
Jollean Sinclaire	*Arkansas State University*
Vivek Shah	*Texas State, San Marcos*
Mehrdad Sharbaf	*Loyola Marymount*
Suengjae Shin	*Mississippi State University, Meridian*
Todd Stabenow	*Hawkeye Community College*
Jo Lynne Stalnaker	*University of Wyoming*
Cynthia Stone	*Indiana University*
Nathan Stout	*University of Oklahoma*
Yi Sun	*California State University, San Marcos*
Winston Tellis	*Fairfield University*
Doug Francis Tuggle	*Chapman University*
Wendy Urban	*Temple University*
Darlene de Vida	*Lower Columbia College*
James Villars	*Metropolitan State University*
Padmal Vitharana	*Syracuse University*
Haibo Wang	*Texas A&M International*
Hong Wang	*NC Carolina A&T State University*

June Wei	*University of West Florida*
Melody White	*University of North Texas*
Rosemary Wild	*Cal Poly San Luis Obispo*
Tom Wilder	*Cal State, Chico*
Karen Williams	*University of Texas, San Antonio*
Marie Wright	*Western CT*
Yaquan Xu	*Virginia State University*
Bee Yew	*Fayetteville State University*
Jigish Zaveri	*Morgan State University*
Grace Zhang	*Augusta State University*
Wei Zhang	*University of Massachusetts, Boston*
Zuopeng Zhang	*SUNY, Plattsburgh*
Fan Zhao	*Florida Gulf Coast University*
Robert Zwick	*Yeshiva University*

Special thanks to contributors Dawna Dewire, Joan Lumpkin, Kevin Lertwachara, Roy DeJoie, and Kala Seal for working on the Apply the Concept activities that appear in every chapter. Thanks also to Efrem Mallach for creating the database activities; to Dawna Dewire for writing test questions; to Aditi Mukherjee, Judy Serwatka, and Ranida Harris for working on the Instructor's Manual; and to Terri Holly, Penelope Greenberg, and Aditi Mukherjee for writing quiz questions. We are grateful for the dedication and creativity of all these contributors in helping us craft this new text.

We would like to thank the Wiley team: Beth Lang Golub, Executive Editor; Samantha Mandel, Assistant Editor; Jenny Welter, Product Designer; Wendy Ashenberg, Content Editor; and Chris Ruel, Executive Marketing Manager. We also thank the Content Management team, including Kevin Holm, Content Manager; Jill Spikereit and Tim Lindner, Production Editors; and Dennis Free of Aptara. And thanks to Maureen Eide, Senior Designer; and Lisa Gee, Photo Editor. We would also like to thank Samantha Mandel for managing all the many details of this new text and her skillful and thorough editing of the manuscript.

Brief Contents

Contents

Management
Information
Systems

Moving Business Forward

Second Edition

1 | Introduction to Information Systems

LEARNING OBJECTIVES >>>

1. Identify the reasons why being an informed user of information systems is important in today's world.

2. Describe the various types of computer-based information systems in an organization.

3. Discuss ways in which information technology can affect managers and nonmanagerial workers.

4. Identify positive and negative societal effects of the increased use of information technology.

Warby Parker (www.warbyparker.com) is an online eyewear retailer founded in 2010. The idea for the company was conceived when the firm's founders (MBA students at the time) wondered why glasses—uncomplicated, easily breakable, and mass produced—were typically quite expensive ($500 or more, for example). They felt that they knew why. The optical industry is an oligopoly, meaning that a small number of companies monopolize the business and are making large margins.

Consider, for example, Luxottica (www.luxottica.com), based in Milan, Italy. It owns LensCrafters, Pearle Vision, Sunglass Hut, and the optical shops in Target and Sears. It also owns Ray-Ban, Oakley, and Oliver Peoples. Based on license agreements, it manufactures eyewear for more than 20 top brands, including Chanel, Burberry, Prada, and Stella McCartney. Warby Parker's founders realized that Luxottica had "created the illusion of choice," while in fact they monopolized the industry.

Warby Parker uses the same materials and the same Chinese factories as Luxottica. It then sells its glasses at a lower price because it does not have to pay licensing fees, which can amount to as much as 15 percent of the $100 wholesale cost of a pair of glasses. Warby Parker also does not have to deal with retailers, whose markups can double prices.

© Amanda Rohde/iStockphoto

Warby Parker's business model allows customers to test the company's retro-style glasses via a mail-order, try-it-at-home program. The glasses (including prescription lenses) cost a mere $95, and customers may test up to five frames at a time. On its Web site, Warby Parker even offers a way to upload photos and "try on" frames virtually. Such large-scale individualized shopping experiences have attracted a devoted following among young, trendy professionals and have made the firm a commercial success.

By mid-2011, Warby Parker had sold more than 50,000 pairs of glasses. The company raised $1.5 million from investors in May 2011. Although Warby Parker currently only has a > > >

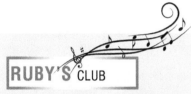

RUBY'S CLUB

Ruby's Club is a small jazz club that opened in 2000 after its owners, Ruben and Lisa, graduated from college. Throughout their college years, they played together in a jazz band and earned business degrees in management and marketing, respectively. They decided to put their collective knowledge together and open their own club.

Ruby's Club has been very successful. However, they realize that they can now be more successful by collecting, analyzing, and using the data that is available to them. To do this, they need to upgrade their infrastructure. This is the perfect time to upgrade everything because they have recently closed for renovation.

Information technology (IT) was not even taught when they were in college, so they have not used much (if any) technology in their club. While they are considering its use as they restructure, they are not sure how much and in what ways they should pursue the use of IT. To help them on this front, they have hired you as an IT intern to help answer many of their questions about technology. They have teamed up with your IT professor and designed questions to go along with the topics you will be learning about in your information systems course. This Internship is designed to accomplish two things. First, it will give them (Ruben and Lisa) the benefit of learning technology in a class that was not offered when they were in school. Second, it will give you the benefit of applying the textbook knowledge you learn to the real world.

As this chapter states, your generation is considered *Homo conexus*. This constant connectivity has to play a role in the restructuring of Ruby's Club. It is your job to help Ruben and Lisa understand exactly how this will look. As you read through the chapters, you will be provided with some discussion questions to help you consider the impact of ISs on Ruby's Club.

small, appointment-only showroom, it will soon be opening a 2,500-square-foot store in New York City.

In addition to enjoying great commercial success, Warby Parker also has a social mission. For every pair of glasses it sells, it provides subsidies to help someone in need buy a pair—although not one of Warby's creations.

The company's success is inspiring competition from more established retailers. For example, in June 2011, the discount fashion site Bluefly (www.bluefly.com) introduced Eyefly (www.eyefly.com), which sells custom, vintage-looking glasses for $99.

Another competitor is Ditto (www.ditto.com), where shoppers use a computer webcam to record a video of their faces and create a virtual, three-dimensional "you." Then, shoppers can virtually try on different frames, look side to side, and blink. Shoppers can solicit feedback from friends on Facebook by sharing shots of their virtual selves wearing different frames.

Sources: Compiled from L. Sanders, "Ditto Lets You Try on Glasses via Webcam," *San Francisco Chronicle*, April 27, 2012; D. Muse, "The New Startup Scene: From Silicon Strip to Silicon Mitten," *Forbes*, December 19, 2011; S. Berfield, "A Startup's New Prescription for Eyewear," *Bloomberg BusinessWeek*, July 4–10, 2011; D. Mau, "Warby Parker vs. Eyefly," *Fashionista*, June 6, 2011; H. Elliot, "The New Model for Retail: Buying Glasses Online," *Forbes*, January 17, 2011; N. Perlroth, "Name You Need to Know in 2011: Warby Parker," *Forbes*, November 22, 2010; www.warbyparker.com, www.eyefly.com, accessed February 18, 2012.

Questions

1. Provide two examples of how Warby Parker uses information technology to support its business model.
2. How might Warby Parker further use information technology to counter large competitors who want to copy their business model? Be specific.

Introduction

Before you proceed, it is important to define information technology and information systems. **Information technology (IT)** relates to any computer-based tool that people use to work with information and to support the information and information-processing needs of an organization. An **information system (IS)** collects, processes, stores, analyzes, and disseminates information for a specific purpose.

IT has far-reaching effects on us as individuals, on organizations, and on our planet. Although this book is largely devoted to the many ways in which IT has transformed modern organizations, you will also learn about the significant impacts of IT on individuals and societies, the global economy, and our physical environment. In addition, IT is making our world smaller, enabling more and more people to communicate, collaborate, and compete, thereby leveling the digital playing field.

When you graduate, either you will start your own business or you will go to work for an organization, whether it is public sector, private sector, for profit, or not for profit. Your organization will have to survive and compete in an environment that has been radically changed by information technology. This environment is global, massively interconnected, intensely competitive, 24/7/365, real time, rapidly changing, and information intensive. To compete successfully, your organization must use IT effectively.

As the Warby Parker case illustrates, small business owners do not need to be experts in technology to be successful. The core competency of Warby Parker's business is not technology. Rather, it is the company's business model. However, the company is effectively using IT to support its business model and thus to create a successful business.

As you read this chapter and this book, keep in mind that the information technologies you will learn about are important to businesses of all sizes. No matter what area of business you major in, what industry you work for, or the size of your company, you will benefit from learning about IT. Who knows? Maybe you will have a great idea and use the tools you learn about in this class to make your dream a reality much the way Warby Parker has!

The modern environment is not only intensely competitive for your organization, but for you as well. You must compete with human talent from around the world. Therefore, you will also have to make effective use of IT.

Accordingly, this chapter begins with a discussion of why you should become knowledgeable about IT. It also distinguishes among data, information, and knowledge, and it differentiates computer-based information systems from application programs. Finally, it considers the impacts of information systems on organizations and on society in general.

1.1 Why Should I Study Information Systems?

You are the most connected generation in history. You have grown up online. You are, quite literally, never out of touch. You use more information technologies (in the form of digital devices) for more tasks, and are bombarded with more information, than any generation in history. The *MIT Technology Review* refers to you as *Homo conexus*. Information technologies are so deeply embedded in your life that your daily routines would be almost unrecognizable to a college student just 20 years ago.

Essentially, you are practicing continuous computing, where you are surrounded with a movable information network. Your network is created by constant cooperation between the digital devices you carry (for example, laptops, media players, and smart phones); the wireline and wireless networks that you access as you move about; and Web-based tools for finding information and communicating and collaborating with other people. Your network enables you to pull information about virtually anything from anywhere, at any time, and to push your own ideas back to the Web, from wherever you are, via a mobile device. Think of everything you do online, often with your phone: register for classes; take classes (and not just at your university); access class syllabi, information, PowerPoints, and lectures; research class papers and presentations; conduct banking; pay your bills; research, shop, and buy products from companies or other people; sell your "stuff"; search for, and apply for, jobs; make your travel reservations (hotel, airline, rental car); have your own blog and post your own podcasts and videocasts to it; have your own page on Facebook; make and upload videos to YouTube; take, edit, and print your own digital photographs; "burn" your own custom-music CDs and DVDs; use RSS feeds to create your personal electronic newspaper; text and tweet your friends and family throughout your day; and many other activities. (*Note:* If any of these terms are unfamiliar to you, do not worry. You will learn about everything mentioned here in detail later in this book.)

The Informed User—You!

So, the question is, Why should you learn about ISs and ITs? After all, you can comfortably use a computer (or other electronic device) to perform many activities, you have been surfing the Web for years, and you feel confident that you can manage any IT application that your organization's management information systems (MIS) department installs. The answer lies in your becoming an **informed user**—that is, a person knowledgeable about information systems and information technology. There are several reasons why you should be an informed user.

In general, informed users tend to get more value from whatever technologies they use. You will enjoy many benefits from being an informed user of IT. First, you will benefit more from your organization's IT applications because you will understand what is "behind" those applications (see Figure 1.1). That is, what you see on your computer screen is brought to you by your MIS department operating "behind" your screen. Second, you will be in a

Media Bakery

Students today are connected by many devices—almost all are wireless.

USERS | MIS

Figure 1.1 IT skills open many doors because IT is so widely used. What do you think is this woman's job?

© Slaomir Fajer/iStockphoto

position to enhance the quality of your organization's IT applications with your input. Third, even as a new graduate, you will quickly be in a position to recommend—and perhaps help select—the IT applications that your organization will use. Fourth, being an informed user will enable you to keep abreast of both new information technologies and rapid developments in existing technologies. In fact, as you will see in the chapter's Closing Case 1, every company today is a technology company, making it even more important for you to be an informed user of information technologies.

Remaining "on top of things" will help you to anticipate the impacts that "new and improved" technologies will have on your organization and to make recommendations on the adoption and use of these technologies. Finally, you will understand how IT can be used to improve your organization's performance and teamwork as well as your own productivity.

Managing the IS function within an organization is no longer the exclusive responsibility of the IS department. Rather, users now play key roles in every step of this process. Our overall objective in this book is for you to be able to immediately contribute to managing the IS function in your organization from your user's perspective. In short, we want to help you become a very informed user!

In addition, if you wish to become an entrepreneur, then being an informed user will help you use IT when you start your own business. IT's About Business 1.1 illustrates how you can build your own apps for your startup company or small business.

IT Offers Career Opportunities

Because IT is vital to the operation of modern businesses, it offers many employment opportunities. The demand for traditional IT staff—programmers, business analysts, systems analysts, and designers—is substantial. In addition, many well-paid jobs exist in areas such as the Internet and electronic commerce (e-commerce), mobile commerce, network security, telecommunications, and multimedia design.

The ISs field includes the people in organizations who design and build information systems, the people who use those systems, and the people responsible for managing those systems. At the top of the list is the chief information officer (CIO).

The CIO is the executive who is in charge of the IS function. In most modern organizations, the CIO works with the chief executive officer (CEO), the chief financial officer

IT's ABOUT BUSINESS 1.1

Businesses Create Their Own Apps

Small business owners are increasingly dependent on mobile applications (apps). According to a 2011 survey by AT&T, about 70 percent of small businesses use mobile apps for operations and almost 40 percent said it would be difficult to survive without them. According to a report published by the Small Business & Entrepreneurship Council in June 2011, mobile apps can help small businesses save about 6 hours of working time per week. The study also estimated that small businesses are saving over 1,095 million hours of working time a year by using mobile apps.

Small business owners who want to create mobile apps—whether to market their products and services to customers or to improve internal productivity—are finding many alternatives to hiring professional programmers. These alternatives include Appsbar (www.appsbar.com), MyAppBuilder (http://myappbuilder.com), AppBreeder (www.appbreeder.com), AppsGeyser (www.appsgeyser.com), Mobile Roadie (www.mobileroadie.com), and AppMakr (www.appmakr.com). Let's look at several examples of small business owners who built their own mobile apps.

- Realtor Nick Galiano wanted to create an app that would let his clients browse his firm's home listings from their mobile phones. Professional software developers estimated that he would have to spend $30,000 for apps that could run on iPhones, BlackBerrys, and Android devices. Then Galiano found Appsbar, a company that builds apps at no charge. Appsbar makes money from advertising placed inside the apps it develops. Not only did Galiano save the $30,000 he would have spent hiring developers for his app, but he saw an increase in business and customer satisfaction.
- Lauren Kay's child care business SmartSitting (www.smartsitting.com) saved about 30 hours of work monthly when she discovered that she could create her own app. She used tools from Zoho (www.zoho.com) to automatically convert the time sheets submitted by her 215 sitters into invoices. These time savings meant monetary savings from $500 to $600 per month.

- Do-it-yourself apps can also be used to create more complex applications for businesses. Greg Taylor, who runs an investment advisory firm called Powerline Advisors, created an app that brings together a wide range of data from five different online sources that could not be found in a single location. These include easily accessible sources such as Yahoo! Finance, in addition to harder-to-find information such as company balance sheets and cash flow statements. He paid programmers about $700 to implement his app and put about 200 hours of "sweat equity" into the app. Taylor updates the data in his app every night and pays a provider called Xignite (www.xignite.com) about $100 per month for corporate financial data. The app integrates the data from different sources, allowing Taylor to gain investment insights because he can more easily see relationships among the different types of financial data. These insights enable him to provide his clients with better investment advice.

Sources: Compiled from K. Casey, "Appsbar Helps SMBs Build Mobile Apps," *InformationWeek*, April 28, 2011; S. Gerber, "Mobile App Development: 10 Tips for Small Business Owners," *Mashable*, April 7, 2011; "AT&T Survey Shows Mobile Apps Integral to Small Business Operations, Remote Workers on the Rise, Facebook Use Growing Rapidly," www.att.com, March 15, 2001; King, R. "DIY Apps Save Small Businesses Time, Money," *Bloomberg BusinessWeek*, February 6, 2012; T. Kuittinen, "U.S. Consumers Shun Games—Mobile Apps Triumphant," *Forbes*, January 13, 2012; B. Tinker, "2011: The Year Mobile Figured Out IT and Vice Versa," *Forbes*, January 2, 2012; www.att.com, www.zoho.com, accessed February 19, 2012.

Questions

1. Why are small businesses becoming so dependent on mobile applications? Provide specific examples to support your answer.
2. Would small businesses be more dependent on mobile applications than large businesses? Why or why not? Explain your answer.
3. Identify and evaluate the advantages and disadvantages of do-it-yourself mobile apps.

Howard Kingsnorth/The Image Bank/Getty Images, Inc.

It's not just students. Today's professionals must be able to use computing technologies to do their job.

(CFO), and other senior executives. Therefore, he or she actively participates in the organization's strategic planning process. In today's digital environment, the IS function has become increasingly important and strategic within organizations. As a result, although the majority of CIOs still rise from the IS department, a growing number are coming up through the ranks in the business units (e.g., marketing, finance, etc.). So, regardless of your college major, you could become the CIO of your organization one day. This is another reason to be an informed user of information systems!

Table 1.1 provides a list of IT jobs along with a description of each one. For further details about careers in IT, see www.computerworld.com/careertopics/careers and www.monster.com.

Career opportunities in IS are strong and are projected to remain strong over the next 10 years. In fact, when *Money Magazine* listed the "fastest growing jobs" in America in 2011, 8 of the top 20 jobs related directly to information technology. These jobs (with their ranks) are as follows:

- Software developer (no. 1)
- Information technology consultant (no. 7)
- Database administrator (no. 8)
- Information technology business analyst (no. 11)
- Business systems analyst (no. 12)
- Software development engineer (no. 13)
- Systems administrator (no. 14)
- Web developer (no. 18)

Not only do IS careers offer strong job growth, but the pay is excellent as well. The Bureau of Labor Statistics, an agency within the U.S. Department of Labor responsible for tracking and analyzing trends relating to the labor market, notes that the median salary for "computer and information systems managers" is approximately $115,000.

Managing Information Resources

Managing information systems in modern organizations is a difficult, complex task. Several factors contribute to this complexity. First, information systems have enormous strategic value to organizations. Firms rely on them so heavily that, in some cases, when these systems are not working (even for a short time), the firm cannot function. (This situation is called "being hostage to information systems.") Second, information systems are very expensive to acquire, operate, and maintain.

A third factor contributing to the difficulty in managing information systems is the evolution of the MIS function within the organization. When businesses first began to use computers in the early 1950s, the MIS department "owned" the only computing resource in the organization: the mainframe. At that time, end users did not interact directly with the mainframe.

In contrast, in the modern organization, computers are located in all departments and almost all employees use computers in their work. This situation, known as *end user computing*, has led to a partnership between the MIS department and the end users. The MIS department now acts as more of a consultant to end users, viewing them as customers. In fact, the main function of the MIS department is to use IT to solve end users' business problems.

As a result of these developments, the responsibility for managing information resources is now divided between the MIS department and the end users. This arrangement raises several important questions: Which resources are managed by whom? What is the role of the MIS department, its structure, and its place within the organization? What

TABLE 1.1 IT Jobs

Position	Job Description
Chief information officer	Highest-ranking IS manager; is responsible for all strategic planning in the organization
IS director	Manages all systems throughout the organization and day-to-day operations of the entire IS organization
Information center manager	Manages IS services such as help desks, hot lines, training, and consulting
Applications development manager	Coordinates and manages new systems development projects
Project manager	Manages a particular new systems development project
Systems manager	Manages a particular existing system
Operations manager	Supervises the day-to-day operations of the data and/or computer center
Programming manager	Coordinates all applications programming efforts
Systems analyst	Interfaces between users and programmers; determines information requirements and technical specifications for new applications
Business analyst	Focuses on designing solutions for business problems; interfaces closely with users to demonstrate how IT can be used innovatively
Systems programmer	Creates the computer code for developing new systems software or maintaining existing systems software
Applications programmer	Creates the computer code for developing new applications or maintaining existing applications
Emerging technologies manager	Forecasts technology trends and evaluates and experiments with new technologies
Network manager	Coordinates and manages the organization's voice and data networks
Database administrator	Manages the organization's databases and oversees the use of database-management software
Auditing or computer security manager	Oversees the ethical and legal use of information systems
Webmaster	Manages the organization's World Wide Web site
Web designer	Creates World Wide Web sites and pages

is the appropriate relationship between the MIS department and the end users? Regardless of who is doing what, it is essential that the MIS department and the end users work in close cooperation.

There is no standard set of choices for how to regulate and divide responsibility for developing and maintaining information resources between the MIS department and end users. Instead, that division depends on several factors: the size and nature of the organization, the amount and type of IT resources, the organization's attitudes toward computing, the attitudes of top management toward computing, the maturity level of the technology, the amount and nature of outsourced IT work, and even the countries in which the company operates. Generally speaking, the MIS department is responsible for corporate-level and shared resources, and the end users are responsible for departmental resources. Table 1.2 identifies both the traditional functions and various new, consultative functions of the MIS department.

So, where do the end users come in? Take a close look at Table 1.2. Under the traditional MIS functions, you will see two functions for which you provide vital input. Under the consultative MIS functions, you will see how the primary responsibility for each function is exercised, and how the MIS department acts as an advisor.

--- BEFORE *YOU GO ON* . . . ---

1. Rate yourself as an informed user. (Be honest; this is not a test!)
2. Explain the benefits of being an informed user of information systems.
3. Discuss the various career opportunities offered in the IT field.

TABLE 1.2 The Changing Role of the IS Department

Traditional Functions of the MIS Department

- Managing systems development and systems project management
  - As an end user, you will have critical input into the systems development process. You will learn about systems development in Chapter 14.

- Managing computer operations, including the computer center

- Staffing, training, and developing IS skills

- Providing technical services

- Infrastructure planning, development, and control
  - As an end user, you will provide critical input about the IS infrastructure needs of your department.

New (Consultative) Functions of the MIS Department

- Initiating and designing specific strategic information systems
  - As an end user, your information needs will often mandate the development of new strategic information systems. You will decide which strategic systems you need (because you know your business needs better than the MIS department), and you will provide input into developing these systems.

- Incorporating the Internet and electronic commerce into the business
  - As an end user, you will be primarily responsible for effectively using the Internet and electronic commerce in your business. You will work with the MIS department to accomplish this task.

- Managing system integration including the Internet, intranets, and extranets
  - As an end user, your business needs will determine how you want to use the Internet, your corporate intranets, and extranets to accomplish your goals. You will be primarily responsible for advising the MIS department on the most effective use of the Internet, your corporate intranets, and extranets.

- Educating the non-MIS managers about IT
  - Your department will be primarily responsible for advising the MIS department on how best to educate and train your employees about IT.

- Educating the MIS staff about the business
  - Communication between the MIS department and the business units is a two-way street. You will be responsible for educating the MIS staff on your business, its needs, and its goals.

- Partnering with business-unit executives
  - Essentially, you will be in a partnership with the MIS department. You will be responsible for seeing that this partnership is one "between equals" and ensuring its success.

- Managing outsourcing
  - Outsourcing is driven by business needs. Therefore, the outsourcing decision largely resides with the business units (i.e., with you). The MIS department, working closely with you, will advise you on technical issues such as communications bandwidth, security, and so on.

- Proactively using business and technical knowledge to seed innovative ideas about IT
  - Your business needs will often drive innovative ideas about how to effectively use information systems to accomplish your goals. The best way to bring these innovative uses of IS to life is to partner closely with your MIS department. Such close partnerships have amazing synergies!

- Creating business alliances with business partners
  - The needs of your business unit will drive these alliances, typically along your supply chain. Again, your MIS department will act as your advisor on various issues, including hardware and software compatibility, implementing extranets, communications, and security.

Apply the Concept 1.1

Background This section pointed out that technology is used to move business forward by connecting the business to its customers, suppliers, partners, etc. Those connections do not just exist to support businesses. Do you realize how connected you are? Computers and information systems have become a part of our everyday life at home. Most of you have a cell phone within reach and have looked at it within the past 5 minutes. No longer is a phone just a phone, it is your connection to family, friends, shopping, driving directions, entertainment (games, movies, music, etc.), and much more.

When you graduate and go to work, most businesses will require you to interface with computer information systems to post transactions or search for information. And just as there are many people working for Apple, Google, AT&T, Verizon, and others making sure your personal network and technology never fails, there are many who work specifically in IT to ensure that business IT is, in fact, moving business forward.

Activity Visit http://www.wiley.com/go/rainer/applytheconcept and click on the link provided for Apply the Concept 1.1. You will be taken to YouTube to learn more about the IT people who work behind the scenes helping IT move business forward. As you watch the video, consider the following questions about all that is involved in the job of an IT manager.

- What is the schedule for an IT manager's work?
- What training does an IT manager need?
- What jobs are available in the IT field?
- Do you know anyone who works directly with IT?
- In which role from the video do you think that person works?

Deliverable

Write a paragraph summary for your professor that explains the major responsibilities of the different positions discussed in the video. Also point out which area you would be most interested in learning more about. Submit your paragraph to your professor.

Quiz questions are assignable in WileyPLUS, and available on the Book Companion Site at http://www.wiley.com/college/rainer.

RUBY'S CLUB QUESTIONS

1. Given that Ruby's customers are college-aged *Homo conexus* users of technology, do you think it will be possible for them to be successful moving into the future without a strong IT strategy?
2. If "informed users" provide more value to a company, can the same be said of "informed customers"?

1.2 Overview of Computer-Based Information Systems

Organizations refer to their MIS functional area by several names, including the MIS Department, the Information Systems Department, the Information Technology Department, and the Information Services Department. Regardless of the name, however, this functional area deals with the planning for—and the development, management, and use of—IT tools to help people perform all of the tasks related to information processing and management. IT relates to any computer-based tool that people use to work with information and to support the information and information-processing needs of an organization.

An IS collects, processes, stores, analyzes, and disseminates information for a specific purpose. It has been said that the purpose of ISs is to get the right information to the right people at the right time in the right amount and in the right format. Because ISs are intended to supply useful information, we need to differentiate between information and two closely related terms: *data* and *knowledge* (see Figure 1.2).

Data items refer to an elementary description of things, events, activities, and transactions that are recorded, classified, and stored but are not organized to convey any specific meaning. Data items can be numbers, letters, figures, sounds, and images. Examples of data items are a collection of numbers (e.g., 3.11, 2.96, 3.95, 1.99, 2.08) and characters (e.g., B, A, C, A, B, D, F, C).

Information refers to data that have been organized so that they have meaning and value to the recipient. For example, a grade point average (GPA) by itself is data, but a student's name coupled with his or her GPA is information. The recipient interprets the meaning and draws conclusions and implications from the information. Consider the examples of data provided in the preceding paragraph. Within the context of a university, the numbers could be GPAs, and the letters could be grades in an Introduction to MIS class.

Knowledge consists of data and/or information that have been organized and processed to convey understanding, experience, accumulated learning, and expertise as they apply to a current business problem. For example, a company recruiting at your school has found over time that students with GPAs over 3.0 have experienced the greatest success in its management program. Based on this accumulated knowledge, that company may decide to interview only those students with GPAs over 3.0. Organizational

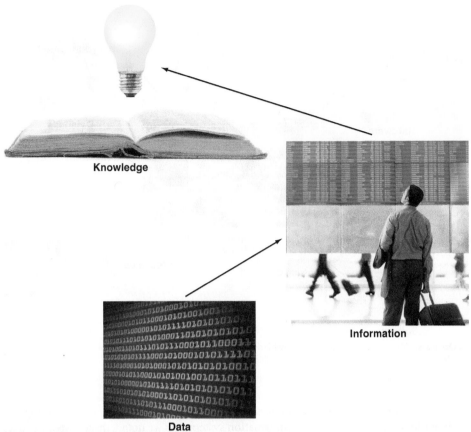

Knowledge

Information

Data

© Chad Reischl/iStockphoto; Exactostock/SuperStock; © Tatiana Popova/iStockphoto

Figure 1.2 Binary Code, the foundation of information and knowledge, is the key to making complex decisions.

knowledge, which reflects the experience and expertise of many people, has great value to all employees.

Consider this example:

Data [No context]	Information [University context]	Knowledge
3.16	3.16 + John Jones = GPA	*Job prospects
2.92	2.92 + Sue Smith = GPA	*Graduate school prospects
1.39	1.39 + Kyle Owens = GPA	*Scholarship prospects
3.95	3.95 + Tom Elias = GPA	
[No context]	[Professional baseball pitcher context]	
3.16	3.16 + Ken Rice = ERA	
2.92	2.92 + Ed Dyas = ERA	*Keep pitcher, trade pitcher, or send pitcher to minor leagues
1.39	1.39 + Hugh Carr = ERA	*Salary/contract negotiations
3.95	3.95 + Nick Ford = ERA	

GPA = grade point average (higher is better)

ERA = earned run average (lower is better); ERA is the number of runs per nine innings accountable to a pitcher

You see that the same data items, with no context, can mean entirely different things in different contexts.

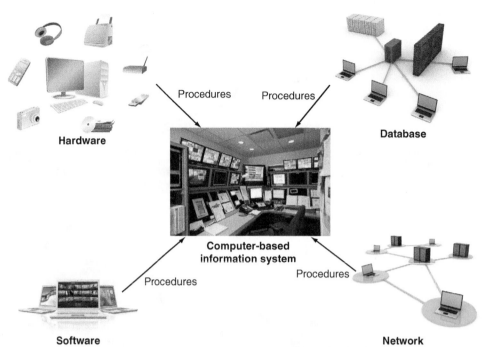

Procedures Procedures

Hardware

Database

Computer-based information system

Procedures

Procedures

Software

Network

© Dzianis Kazlouski/iStockphoto; © Oleksiy Mark/iStockphoto; © Blend_Images/iStockphoto; © Alex Slobodkin/iStockphoto; © Alex Slobodkin/iStockphoto

Figure 1.3 It takes technology (hardware, software, databases, and networks) with appropriate procedures to make a CBIS useful for people.

Now that you have a clearer understanding of data, information, and knowledge, we shift our focus to computer-based information systems. As we noted, these systems process data into information and knowledge that you can use.

A **computer-based information system (CBIS)** is an information system that uses computer technology to perform some or all of its intended tasks. Although not all information systems are computerized, today most are. For this reason, the term *information system* is typically used synonymously with *computer-based information system*. The following are the basic components of computer-based information systems. The first four are called **information technology (IT) components.** Figure 1.3 shows how these four components interact to form a CBIS.

- **Hardware** is a device such as a processor, monitor, keyboard, or printer. Together, these devices accept data and information, process them, and display them.
- **Software** is a program or collection of programs that enable the hardware to process data.
- A **database** is a collection of related files or tables containing data.
- A **network** is a connecting system (wireline or wireless) that permits different computers to share resources.
- **Procedures** are the set of instructions about how to combine hardware, software, databases, and networks in order to process information and generate the desired output.
- *Users* are those individuals who use the hardware and software, interface with it, or utilize its output.

Figure 1.4 shows how these components are integrated to form the wide variety of information systems in an organization. Starting at the bottom of the figure, you see that the IT components of hardware, software, networks (wireline and wireless), and databases form the **information technology (IT) platform.** IT personnel use these components to develop information systems, oversee security and risk, and manage data. These activities cumulatively are called **information technology (IT) services.** The IT components plus IT services comprise the organization's **information technology (IT) infrastructure.** At the top of the pyramid are the various organizational information systems.

TABLE 1.3 Major Capabilities of Information Systems

- Perform high-speed, high-volume, numerical computations

- Provide fast, accurate communication and collaboration within and among organizations

- Store huge amounts of information in an easy-to-access yet small space

- Allow quick and inexpensive access to vast amounts of information, worldwide

- Interpret vast amounts of data quickly and efficiently

- Automate both semiautomatic business processes and manual tasks

Computer-based information systems have many capabilities. Table 1.3 summarizes the most important ones.

Information systems perform these various tasks via a wide spectrum of applications. An **application (app)** is a computer program designed to support a specific task or business process. (A synonymous term is *application program*.) Each functional area or department within a business organization uses dozens of application programs. For instance, the human resources department sometimes uses one application for screening job applicants and another for monitoring employee turnover. The collection of application programs in a single department is usually referred to as a *departmental information system* (also known as a *functional area information system*). For example, the collection of application programs in the human resources area is called the *human resources information system* (*HRIS*). Collections of application programs—that is, departmental information systems—are used in other functional areas as well, such as accounting, finance, marketing, and production/operations. IT's About Business 1.2 illustrates how U.S. railroads are using information systems to improve their operations.

Types of Computer-Based Information Systems

Modern organizations employ many different types of information systems. Figure 1.4 illustrates the different types of information systems that function *within* a single organization,

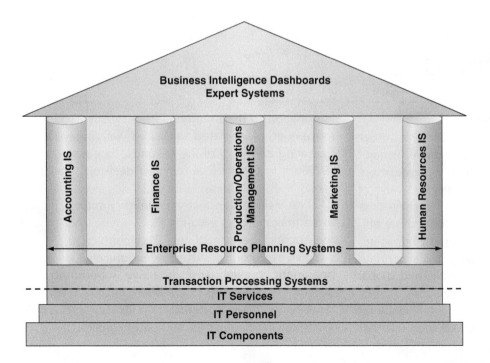

Figure 1.4 How IT components are integrated to form the wide variety of information systems within a single organization.

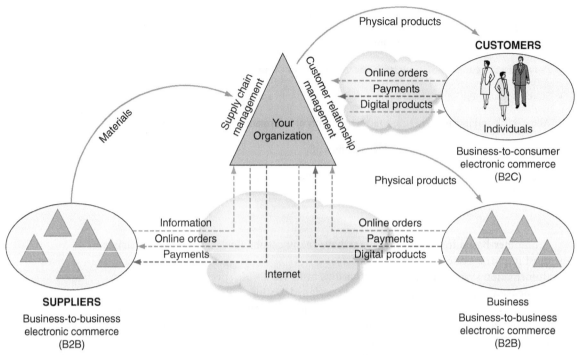

Figure 1.5 The different types of information systems that function among multiple organizations.

and Figure 1.5 shows the different types of information systems that function *among* multiple organizations. You will study transaction processing systems, management information systems, and enterprise resource planning systems in Chapter 11. You will learn about customer relationship management (CRM) systems in Chapter 12 and supply chain management (SCM) systems in Chapter 13.

In the next section, you will learn about the numerous and diverse types of information systems employed by modern organizations. You will also read about the types of support these systems provide.

T's ABOUT BUSINESS 1.2

The Digitization of Railroads

Once a dying industry, railroads have made a major comeback. They are now seeking to operate more trains, carry more freight and passengers, and move at faster speeds than ever before while at the same time lowering their costs. In an effort to become more efficient and safer as well, railroads are rapidly becoming digitized. Major railroads are installing digital communications, sensors, computerized controls, and global positioning receivers on their trains and tracks.

These new types of IT can gather intelligence on location, size, and speed of trains, and then use that information to make automated decisions about train movement. Automated decisions will improve the operating efficiency of the railroads, thus saving money. More importantly, automated decisions may save lives.

The railroad industry is implementing three major digital systems as it moves into the second decade of the 21st century: a positive train control system, electronically controlled pneumatic brakes, and proactive monitoring and detection systems. As you will see, each of these systems brings many potential benefits, but also comes with its own set of issues and controversies.

Positive Train Control

Positive train control (PTC) is essentially a traffic system for trains that utilizes on-board computers, digital communications, and global positioning systems. PTC enables central railroad control stations to see trains' locations. It also enables them to stop trains by remote control if, for example, an engineer fails to obey a signal.

PTC systems are designed to project an electronic safety zone (or buffer) in front of, and behind, trains. The size of a train's buffer space is determined by its length, weight, and braking capabilities. Under this system, if one train were to encroach on another train's buffer zone, the electronic gear on the train whose buffer was invaded would be alerted and its brakes would automatically engage.

In addition to making it safer for trains to operate closer together, such a system would also allow the railroads to retire their light signals, thereby saving themselves a considerable amount of money. However, despite these potential costs savings, there is one distinct advantage to keeping part of the light signal system active. The light signals are connected to an electrical circuit that runs through the rails, so if a break in a rail occurs, the circuit is broken as well. This broken circuit causes the nearest signal to turn red, stopping trains in the vicinity.

The U.S. government has mandated that PTC systems be installed by the end of 2015 on major rail lines used by passenger trains or by trains carrying highly toxic chemicals. At the time of this writing (mid-2012), the major railway companies are still resistant to implementing PTC systems. These companies say that it will cost $13 billion to install and maintain PTC systems, a cost-prohibitive amount of money.

Electronically Controlled Pneumatic Brakes

Another digital development affecting railways is a new kind of brake, known as the electronically controlled pneumatic (or ECP), brake. ECP brakes are controlled by electronic signals instead of air pressure, and therefore engage and release immediately and uniformly. ECP brakes improve train handling, shorten braking distances, lessen wear and tear on railcars, and lower the risk of derailment.

Unfortunately, the cost and technical challenges of implementing ECP brakes are likely to slow down their adoption. For example, trains cannot be comprised of cars with two different kinds of brakes, so replacing the brakes on only some of the nation's 1.6 million freight cars would create a logistical nightmare for the railroads. Further, railroads are already able to shorten braking distances by placing additional locomotives in the middle or rear of freight trains. This solution is temporary, but one that the railroads favor at this time.

Proactive Monitoring and Detection Systems

The railroad industry is also working on methods of predicting, rather than reacting to, equipment problems. Currently, devices such as hot-box detectors beside rail lines measure temperatures as trains go past and spot wheel bearings that have overheated. Once these problems are spotted, trains have to stop to repair the problem.

Railroad companies are also developing digital monitoring systems that can measure stress levels on wheels and other railcar components before serious problems develop. These systems operate through microphones that can pick up the sounds of axle bearings and software algorithms that can then interpret those sounds.

Railroads are also experimenting with putting sensors directly on railcars. These sensors monitor issues such as whether the dome lids on chemical tank cars are open or closed. Chemical companies want this information because lids are supposed to be closed during transit to prevent vandalism. If they received alerts when the lids were open, they could easily detect any breach of the cars. The sensors can also monitor temperatures inside railcars, a feature critical in the case of food shipments.

Sources: Compiled from T. Aspray, "Railroad Stocks Are Still on Track," *Forbes*, January 6, 2012; D. Machalaba, "The Little Engine Really Could," *The Wall Street Journal*, May 23, 2011; R. Lindsey, "Really? You Gotta Let It Go," *Strategic Railroading*, December 7, 2010; F. Roskind, "Positive Train Control Systems Economic Analysis," *Federal Railroad Administration*, July 10, 2009; K. Jones, "Engineer Texted Before Deadly Train Crash," *InformationWeek*, March 3, 2009; www.nscorp.com, www.csx.com, www.up.com, accessed February 19, 2012.

Questions

1. Describe how the three systems discussed in this case can lead to safer railroads. Provide specific examples.

2. What other information technologies could railroads use to improve their performance?

© Sonda Dawes/The Image Works

Data from a coupon center will be connected to marketing and sales, but possibly inventory, accounting, and much more.

Breadth of Support of Information Systems Certain information systems support parts of organizations, others support entire organizations, and still others support groups of organizations. This section addresses all of these systems.

Recall that each department or functional area within an organization has its own collection of application programs, or information systems. These **functional area information systems (FAISs)** are supporting pillars for the information systems located at the top of Figure 1.4: business intelligence systems and dashboards. As the name suggests, each FAIS supports a particular functional area within the organization. Examples are accounting IS, finance IS, production/operations management (POM) IS, marketing IS, and human resources IS.

Consider these examples of IT systems in the various functional areas of an organization. In *finance* and *accounting*, managers use IT systems to forecast revenues and business activity, to determine the best sources and uses of funds, and to perform audits to ensure that the organization is fundamentally sound and that all financial reports and documents are accurate.

In *sales* and *marketing*, managers use information technology to perform the following functions:

- *Product analysis:* developing new goods and services.
- *Site analysis:* determining the best location for production and distribution facilities.
- *Promotion analysis:* identifying the best advertising channels.
- *Price analysis:* setting product prices to obtain the highest total revenues.

Marketing managers also use IT to manage their relationships with their customers.

In *manufacturing*, managers use IT to process customer orders, develop production schedules, control inventory levels, and monitor product quality. They also use IT to design and manufacture products. These processes are called computer-assisted design (CAD) and computer-assisted manufacturing (CAM).

Managers in *human resources* use IT to manage the recruiting process, analyze and screen job applicants, and hire new employees. They also employ IT to help employees manage their careers, to administer performance tests to employees, and to monitor employee productivity. Finally, they rely on IT to manage compensation and benefits packages.

Two information systems support the entire organization: enterprise resource planning systems and transaction processing systems. **Enterprise resource planning (ERP) systems** are designed to correct a lack of communication among the FAISs. As a result, Figure 1.4 shows ERP systems spanning the FAIS. ERP systems were an important innovation because the various FAISs were often developed as stand-alone systems and did not communicate effectively (if at all) with one another. ERP systems resolve this problem by tightly integrating the FAISs via a common database. In doing so, they enhance communications among the functional areas of an organization. For this reason, experts credit ERP systems with greatly increasing organizational productivity.

A **transaction processing system (TPS)** supports the monitoring, collection, storage, and processing of data from the organization's basic business transactions, each of which generates data. For example, when you are checking out of Walmart, each time the cashier swipes an item across the bar code reader, that is one transaction. Definitions of a transaction differ throughout an organization. In accounting, for example, a transaction is anything that changes a firm's chart of accounts. The information system definition of a transaction is broader: A transaction is anything that changes the firm's database. The chart of accounts is only part of the firm's database. Consider a scenario in which a student transfers from one section of an Introduction to MIS course to another section. This move would be a transaction in the university's information system, but not a transaction in the university's accounting department.

The TPS collects data continuously, typically in *real time*—that is, as soon as the data are generated—and provides the input data for the corporate databases. TPSs are considered critical to the success of any enterprise because they support core operations. Significantly, nearly all ERP systems are also TPSs, but not all TPSs are ERP systems. In fact, modern ERP systems incorporate many functions that have previously been handled by the organization's functional area information systems. You study both TPSs and ERP systems in detail in Chapter 11.

ERP systems and TPS function primarily within a single organization. Information systems that connect two or more organizations are referred to as **interorganizational information systems (IOSs)**. IOSs support many interorganizational operations, of which supply chain management is the best known. An organization's **supply chain** is the flow of materials, information, money, and services from suppliers of raw materials through factories and warehouses to the end customers.

Note that the supply chain in Figure 1.5 shows physical flows, information flows, and financial flows. Digitizable products are those that can be represented in electronic form, such as music and software. Information flows, financial flows, and digitizable products go through the Internet, whereas physical products are shipped. For example, when you order a computer from www.dell.com, your information goes to Dell via the Internet. When your transaction is completed (i.e., your credit card is approved and your order is processed), Dell ships your computer to you.

Electronic commerce systems are another type of interorganizational information system. An **electronic commerce (e-commerce) system** enables organizations to conduct transactions, called business-to-business (B2B) electronic commerce, and customers to conduct transactions with businesses, called business-to-consumer (B2C) electronic commerce. (*Note:* You will learn about other types of e-commerce systems in Chapter 9). E-commerce systems are typically Internet based. Figure 1.5 illustrates B2B and B2C electronic commerce.

Support for Organizational Employees. So far you have been concentrating on information systems that support specific functional areas and operations. Now you will learn about information systems that typically support particular employees within the organization.

Clerical workers, who support managers at all levels of the organization, include bookkeepers, secretaries, electronic file clerks, and insurance claim processors. *Lower-level managers* handle the day-to-day operations of the organization, making routine decisions such as assigning tasks to employees and placing purchase orders. *Middle managers* make tactical decisions, which deal with activities such as short-term planning, organizing, and control.

Knowledge workers are professional employees, such as financial and marketing analysts, engineers, lawyers, and accountants. All knowledge workers are experts in a particular subject area. They create information and knowledge, which they integrate into the business. Knowledge workers act as advisors to middle managers and executives. Finally, *executives* make decisions that deal with situations that can significantly change the manner in which business is done. Examples of executive decisions are introducing a new product line, acquiring other businesses, and relocating operations to a foreign country.

Office automation systems (OASs) typically support the clerical staff, lower and middle managers, and knowledge workers. These employees use OASs to develop documents (word processing and desktop publishing software), schedule resources (electronic calendars), and communicate (e-mail, voice mail, videoconferencing, and groupware).

FAISs summarize data and prepare reports, primarily for middle managers, but sometimes for lower-level managers as well. Because these reports typically concern a specific functional area, report generators (RPGs) are an important type of functional area IS.

Business intelligence (BI) systems provide computer-based support for complex, nonroutine decisions, primarily for middle managers and knowledge workers. (They also support lower-level managers, but to a lesser extent.) These systems are typically used with a data warehouse and they enable users to perform their own data analysis. You learn about BI systems in Chapter 5.

TABLE 1.4 Types of Organizational Information Systems

Type of System	Function	Example
Functional area IS	Supports the activities within specific functional area	System for processing payroll
Transaction processing system	Processes transaction data from business events	Walmart checkout point-of-sale terminal
Enterprise resource planning system	Integrates all functional areas of the organization	Oracle, SAP
Office automation system	Supports daily work activities of individuals and groups	Microsoft Office
Management information system	Produces reports summarized from transaction data, usually in one functional area	Report on total sales for each customer
Decision support system	Provides access to data and analysis tools	"What-if" analysis of changes in budget
Expert system	Mimics human expert in a particular area and makes decisions	Credit card approval analysis
Executive dashboard	Presents structured, summarized information about aspects of business important to executives	Status of sales by product
Supply chain management system	Manages flows of products, services, and information among organizations	Walmart Retail Link system connecting suppliers to Walmart
Electronic commerce system	Enables transactions among organizations and between organizations and customers	www.dell.com

Expert systems (ESs) attempt to duplicate the work of human experts by applying reasoning capabilities, knowledge, and expertise within a specific domain. They have become valuable in many application areas, primarily but not exclusively areas involving decision making. For example, navigation systems use rules to select routes, but we do not typically think of these systems as expert systems. Significantly, expert systems can operate as stand-alone systems or be embedded in other applications. We examine ESs in greater detail in "Plug IT In 4."

Dashboards (also called **digital dashboards**) are a special form of IS that supports all managers of the organization. They provide rapid access to timely information and direct access to structured information in the form of reports. Dashboards that are tailored to the information needs of executives are called *executive dashboards*. Chapter 5 provides a thorough discussion of dashboards.

Table 1.4 provides an overview of the different types of organizational information systems.

BEFORE *YOU GO ON . . .*

1. What is a computer-based information system?
2. Describe the components of computer-based information systems.
3. What is an application program?
4. Explain how information systems provide support for knowledge workers.
5. As we move up the organization's hierarchy from clerical workers to executives, how does the type of support provided by information systems change?

Apply the Concept 1.2

Background This section discussed the various functional areas that you will most likely go to work in and the different systems that support them. It should be no surprise that these are the very majors you can choose from in most colleges of business. These four major functional areas are marketing/sales, finance/accounting, manufacturing, and human resources. Often, these different functional areas will use the same database and networks within a company, but they will all use them to support their specific needs. This activity will help you develop a solid understanding of the role of information systems within the different functional areas.

Activity Review the section material that describes the major function of the following departments in most companies: marketing/sales, finance/accounting, manufacturing, and human resources. Then review the basic function of the following types of information systems: transaction processing, management information, and decision support. Once you have a solid understanding of the functional areas and information systems that support them you are ready to move forward with the activity!

Deliverable

Rebuild and complete the chart shown below with the activities that may be completed by each system for each department. To help out, we have pre-filled one item in each type of system. Once you complete your chart, submit it to your professor.

	Transaction Processing	Management Information	Decision Support
Marketing/Sales	Enter sales data		
Accounting/Finance			
Human Resources			Comply with EEOC
Manufacturing		Inventory reporting	

Quiz questions are assignable in WileyPLUS, and available on the Book Companion Site at http://www.wiley.com/college/rainer.

RUBY'S CLUB   QUESTIONS

1. Given that Ruby's is a bar with a small food menu, what type of data do you think this establishment should collect from a single transaction (such as an order for food)?

2. How can Ruby's use data from transactions over a month to help manage inventory?

3. If Ruben and Lisa have transactional data that is organized to create information regarding their customer base, why could knowledge be gained from this that would help them develop a marketing plan?

1.3 How Does IT Impact Organizations?

Throughout this book, you will encounter numerous examples of how IT affects various types of organizations. This section provides an overview of the impact of IT on modern organizations. As you read this section, you will learn how each of these impacts will affect you as well.

IT Will Reduce the Number of Middle Managers

IT makes managers more productive, and it increases the number of employees who can report to a single manager. In these ways, IT ultimately decreases the number of managers and experts. It is reasonable to assume, therefore, that in the coming years organizations will have fewer managerial levels and fewer staff and line managers. If this trend materializes, then promotional opportunities will decrease, making promotions much more competitive. Bottom line: Pay attention in school!

IT Will Change the Manager's Job

One of the most important tasks of managers is making decisions. One of the major consequences of IT has been to change the manner in which managers make many of their decisions. In this way, IT ultimately has changed managers' jobs.

IT often provides managers with near real-time information, meaning that managers have less time to make decisions, making their jobs even more stressful. Fortunately, IT also provides many tools—for example, business intelligence applications such as dashboards, search engines, and intranets—to help managers handle the volumes of information they must deal with on an ongoing basis.

We have been focusing on managers in general in this section. Now, let's focus on you. Because of advances in IT, you will increasingly supervise employees and teams who are geographically dispersed. Employees can work from anywhere at any time, and teams can consist of employees who are literally dispersed throughout the world. Information technologies such as telepresence systems (discussed in Chapter 4) can help you manage these employees even though you do not often see them face to face. For these employees, electronic or "remote" supervision will become the norm. Remote supervision places greater emphasis on completed work and less emphasis on personal contacts and office politics. You will have to reassure your employees that they are valued members of the organization, thereby diminishing any feelings they might have of being isolated and "out of the loop."

Will IT Eliminate Jobs?

One of the major concerns of every employee, part time or full time, is job security. Relentless cost-cutting measures in modern organizations often lead to large-scale layoffs. Put simply, organizations are responding to today's highly competitive environment by doing more with less. Regardless of your position, then, you consistently will have to add value to your organization and to make certain that your superiors are aware of this value.

Many companies have responded to difficult economic times, increased global competition, demands for customization, and increased consumer sophistication by increasing their investments in IT. In fact, as computers continue to advance in terms of intelligence and capabilities, the competitive advantage of replacing people with machines is increasing rapidly. This process frequently leads to layoffs. At the same time, however, IT creates entirely new categories of jobs, such as electronic medical record keeping and nanotechnology.

IT Impacts Employees at Work

Many people have experienced a loss of identity because of computerization. They feel like "just another number" because computers reduce or eliminate the human element that was present in noncomputerized systems.

The Internet threatens to exert an even more isolating influence than computers and television. Encouraging people to work and shop from their living rooms could produce some unfortunate psychological effects, such as depression and loneliness.

IT Impacts Employees' Health and Safety.

Although computers and information systems are generally regarded as agents of "progress," they can adversely affect individuals' health and safety. To illustrate this point, we consider two issues associated with IT: job stress and long-term use of the keyboard.

An increase in an employee's workload and/or responsibilities can trigger *job stress*. Although computerization has benefited organizations by increasing productivity, it has also created an ever-expanding workload for some employees. Some workers feel overwhelmed and have become increasingly anxious about their job performance. These feelings of stress and anxiety can actually diminish rather than improve workers' productivity while jeopardizing their physical and mental health. Management can help to alleviate these problems by providing training, redistributing the workload among workers, and hiring more workers.

On a more specific level, the long-term use of keyboards can lead to *repetitive strain injuries* such as backaches and muscle tension in the wrists and fingers. *Carpal tunnel syndrome* is a particularly painful form of repetitive strain injury that affects the wrists and hands.

Designers are aware of the potential problems associated with the prolonged use of computers. To address these problems, they continually attempt to design a better computing environment. The science of designing machines and work settings that minimize injury and illness is called **ergonomics**. The goal of ergonomics is to create an environment that is safe, well lit, and comfortable. Examples of ergonomically designed products are antiglare screens that alleviate problems of fatigued or damaged eyesight and chairs that contour the human body to decrease backaches. Figure 1.6 displays some sample ergonomic products.

IT Provides Opportunities for People with Disabilities.

Computers can create new employment opportunities for people with disabilities by integrating speech- and vision-recognition capabilities. For example, individuals who cannot type are able to use a voice-operated keyboard, and individuals who cannot travel can work at home.

Going further, adaptive equipment for computers permits people with disabilities to perform tasks they would not normally be able to do. You should note that the Web and graphical user interfaces (e.g., Microsoft Windows) can still make life difficult for people with impaired

(a)

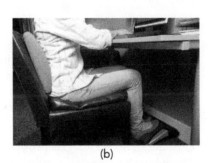

(b)

(c)

(d)

Figure 1.6   Ergonomic products protect computer users.
(a) Wrist support. Media Bakery
(b) Back support. Media Bakery
(c) Eye-protection filter (optically coated glass). Media Bakery
(d) Adjustable foot rest. Media Bakery

vision. Adding audible screen tips and voice interfaces to deal with this problem essentially restores functionality to the way it was before rich, graphical interfaces became standard.

Other devices help improve the quality of life for people with disabilities in more mundane, but useful, ways. Examples are a two-way writing telephone, a robotic page turner, a hair brusher, and a hospital-bedside video trip to the zoo or the museum. Several organizations specialize in IT designed for people with disabilities.

Apply the Concept 1.3

Background This section points out that the whole reason businesses use Information Systems is that they add value to the daily activities. This should not be a surprise to you because you most likely use computers and information systems for the very same reason! Think of five activities that you use your computer for on a regular basis. Most likely many of these activities have to do with school and your classes. However, I would guess that you also use your computer to communicate with friends and family, to find out what movies are showing in theaters this weekend, or to check flights for travel on your next break. Most of us would miss our computers and the information systems we have available through them to help us with these tasks. They add "value" to our lives. The same is true for most business organizations. They depend on computer information systems to complete their daily tasks and to add value to their organization.

Activity Visit http://www.wiley.com/go/rainer/applytheconcept and click on the link provided for Apply the Concept 1.3. It will describe to you how to use a computer to your advantage. Be sure to listen for the reasons or ways that computers provide value to businesses. Consider whether you have seen any of these in your own interactions with a business as a consumer.

Deliverable

Based on the video, list five benefits mentioned for using IS in a business. However, there are many other ways in which a business depends on information systems. Also, name five other benefits an information system can provide. Think of ways you have used IS to interface with a business and the value you have found. Write a short summary (based on the chapter, the video, and your personal experiences) that describes the many ways that computers and IT add value to our lives. Submit this to your instructor.

Quiz questions are assignable in WileyPLUS, and available on the Book Companion Site at http://www.wiley.com/college/rainer.

RUBY'S CLUB   QUESTIONS

1. Ruben and Lisa have always spent hours going through paper receipts trying to determine past sales. They need these figures to know purchase quantities for the products they sell. Given that some of their products have a short shelf life (perishable foods), this needs to be very accurate. In what ways could the capabilities of ISs help them accomplish this task?

2. What type of procedures would Ruben and Lisa need to ensure that the people interacting with the ISs are doing so in an appropriate manner (i.e., correctly inputting data, not using customer data, etc.)?

1.4 Why Are Information Systems Important to Society?

This section explains in greater detail why IT is important to society as a whole. Other examples of the impacts of IT on society appear throughout the book.

IT Affects Our Quality of Life

IT has significant implications for our quality of life. The workplace can be expanded from the traditional 9-to-5 job at a central location to 24 hours a day at any location. IT can provide employees with flexibility that can significantly improve the quality of leisure time, even if it does not increase the total amount of leisure time.

From the opposite perspective, however, IT can also place employees on "constant call" where they are never truly away from the office, even when they are on vacation. In fact, a recent poll revealed that 80 percent of respondents took their laptop computers on their most recent vacations, and 100 percent took their cell phones. Going further, 80 percent did some work while vacationing, and almost all of them checked their e-mail.

Robot Revolution on the Way

Once restricted largely to science fiction movies, robots that can perform practical tasks are becoming more common. In fact, "cyberpooches," nursebots, and other mechanical beings may be our companions before we know it. Around the world, quasi-autonomous devices have become increasingly common on factory floors, in hospital corridors, and in farm fields. In our homes, iRobot (www.irobot.com) produces the Roomba to vacuum our floors, the Scooba to wash our floors, the Dirt Dog to sweep our garages, the Verro to clean our pools, and the Looj to clean our gutters.

Telepresence robots are a recent development in the field of robotics. IT's About Business 1.3 illustrates how organizations use these robots.

 'S ABOUT BUSINESS 1.3

Telepresence Robots

The Business Problem

In our modern digital world, knowledge workers can work from anywhere via a process called *telecommuting*. In fact, a new term, *digital nomad*, has appeared that refers to someone who uses a variety of information technologies such as smartphones, wireless Internet access, and Web-based applications to work remotely from a home, coffee shop, restaurant, airport, airplane, Internet café, or other location.

Digital nomads present a couple of issues for the offices that employ them. First, digital nomads lack a "presence" in their respective offices. Second, it is typically expensive and time-consuming for them to travel to their offices—for example, to attend meetings.

Yet another business issue occurs when a person with a highly desirable skill is needed at a distant location. Examples of individuals with such desirable skills include surgeons, consultants with expertise in a specific industry, salespeople who are well known to high-value clients, and many others.

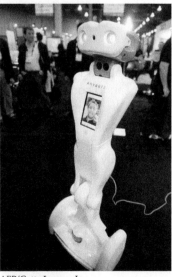

AFP/Gettv Images. Inc.

The telepresence robot provides a solution to all of the issues listed earlier.

The IT Solution

Telepresence robots have been humorously described as a cross between a Segway and Wall-E. These robots are designed to help companies save money on travel and on expensive teleconferencing technology. The robots enable people in remote offices or locations to have a rich communications experience without having to use a complicated videoconferencing system.

A telepresence robot has both a video camera and a video screen embedded in its "head." It also has wheels and can be moved around remotely by computer. It is designed to steer its way clear of obstacles or people.

The robots let a person maintain a consistent connection with co-workers, customers, or clients. The human user controls the robot, located at a remote location, and directs it to move around—for example, around a conference room during a meeting—while broadcasting what is going on to the human it represents. Interestingly, the robots actually break down barriers of awkwardness that people sometimes feel in person-to-person meetings.

Organizations are using telepresence robots for a variety of applications. Consider the following examples:

- Dr. Johns was paged because a man had suffered a stroke and someone had to quickly decide which drug to give him. She hurried, not to the emergency room 200 miles away where the man had been admitted, but to a room in her local hospital. She sat in front of computer monitors, a keyboard, and a joystick that controlled her assistant in the remote emergency room: a telepresence robot.

  She acknowledged the nurse and introduced herself to the patient's grandson, explaining that she would question the patient to determine what drug to give him. The robot's stereophonic hearing conveyed the answers and its hypersensitive camera allowed her to zoom her view of the room in and out, and swing the display left and right.

  By speaking directly with the patient, examining his face and how he controlled his hands, and looking at the cardiac monitor in the emergency room, Dr. Johns was able to assess the stroke with the same accuracy as if she had been physically present. She instructed the nurse to give the patient a particular drug.

- Mike Beltzner, director of Firefox at the Mozilla Corporation, is able to communicate with his programmers in California from his home in Toronto, Canada, by means of a telepresence robot. His telepresence robot swivels his camera eyes back and forth, and Mike can see the entire room. He chats comfortably with the assembled team. When the meeting ends, "Robo-Beltzner" (as his colleagues call him), mingles in the room, chatting. Mike finds that he is getting the same kind of interpersonal connection during the meetings that he would get if he were physically present.

- Chad Evans, a software designer for Phillips Healthcare, is located at his home in Atlanta, Georgia, and his telepresence robot works at the company's headquarters in Santa Monica, California. While he works at his desk in Atlanta, he is visible on the monitor of his robot. His colleagues can see at a glance whether he is available for a chat. When Chad needs to go to a meeting in California or visit a colleague, he drives his robot to a desk or meeting room. If he needs to go to a different floor, someone has to press the elevator buttons for his robot. His robot enables Chad to be as available and transparent to his colleagues as though he were physically present in the office.

- Tom Serani's boss was frustrated that while Tom was on the road, his 20-person sales team working the phones back at company headquarters did not have the same "energy" as when Tom was in the office. As a result, Tom now has a telepresence robot at company headquarters. When he is traveling, Tom can roll his robot up to an office cubicle at headquarters, listen in on a telephone sales pitch, and offer advice. Interestingly, Tom's boss noted that the telepresence robot increased the sales team's energy level to the same level as when Tom was physically in the office.

The Results

Telepresence robots allow much greater flexibility for digital nomads. They provide a flexible view into what is happening in their offices, without requiring money and time to be spent on travel. As you saw in the examples above, companies benefit from valuable employees having a "presence" in the office. Companies also use telepresence robots to connect with people having specialized skills in remote locations.

In the near future, telepresence robots will have artificial intelligence that allows them to do some things on their own. Inevitably, these robots will become "smarter" and more agile. They will not only represent their human users, they will augment them.

Sources: Compiled from K. Terry, "Roomba Maker Sets Sights on Telemedicine," *InformationWeek*, February 2, 2012; D. Bennett, "I'll Have My Robots Talk to Your Robots," *Bloomberg BusinessWeek*, February 21–27, 2011; A. Diana, "12 Advances in Medical Robotics," *InformationWeek*, January 29, 2011; D. Terdiman, "The Telepresence Robots Are Coming," CNET.com, May 18, 2010; J. Markoff, "The Boss Is Robotic, and Rolling Up Behind You," *The*

New York Times, September 4, 2010; www.anybots.com, accessed July 27, 2011.

uestions

1. What are the advantages of a telepresence robot representing you at your office? Provide specific examples to support your answer.

2. What are the disadvantages of a telepresence robot representing you at your office? Provide specific examples to support your answer.

In an example of precision agriculture, Carnegie Mellon University in Pittsburgh has developed self-directing tractors that harvest hundreds of acres of crops around the clock in California. These "robot tractors" use global positioning systems (GPSs) combined with video image processing that identifies rows of uncut crops.

Many robotic devices are also being developed for military purposes. For example, the Pentagon is researching self-driving vehicles and beelike swarms of small surveillance robots, each of which would contribute a different view or angle of a combat zone. The Predator, an unmanned aerial vehicle (UAV), is being used in Iraq, Libya, Pakistan, and Afghanistan.

It probably will be a long time before we see robots making decisions by themselves, handling unfamiliar situations, and interacting with people. Nevertheless, robots are extremely helpful in various environments, particularly environments that are repetitive, harsh, or dangerous to humans.

Improvements in Health Care

IT has brought about major improvements in health care delivery. Medical personnel use IT to make better and faster diagnoses and to monitor critically ill patients more accurately. IT also has streamlined the process of researching and developing new drugs. Expert systems now help doctors diagnose diseases, and machine vision is enhancing the work of radiologists. Surgeons use virtual reality to plan complex surgeries. They also have used a surgical robot to perform long-distance surgery by controlling the robot's movements. In addition, doctors discuss complex medical cases via videoconferencing, and new computer simulations recreate the sense of touch, allowing doctors-in-training to perform virtual procedures without risking harm to an actual patient.

Of the thousands of other applications related to health care, administrative systems are critically important. These systems range from detecting insurance fraud to creating nursing schedules to financial and marketing management.

The Internet contains vast amounts of useful medical information (see www.webmd.com, for example). In an interesting study, researchers at the Princess Alexandra Hospital in Brisbane, Australia, identified 26 difficult diagnostic cases published in the *New England Journal of Medicine*. They selected three to five search terms from each case and then conducted a Google search. The researchers selected and recorded the three diagnoses that Google ranked most prominently and that appeared to fit the symptoms and signs. They then compared these results with the correct diagnoses as published in the journal. They discovered that their Google searches had found the correct diagnosis in 15 of the

1. What are some of the quality-of-life improvements made possible by IT? Has IT had any negative effects on our quality of life?

2. Describe the robotic revolution, and consider its possible implications for humans.

3. Explain how IT has improved health care practices.

26 cases, a success rate of 57 percent. The researchers caution, however, against the dangers of self-diagnosis. They maintain that people should use the information gained from Google and medical Web sites such as WebMD only to participate in their health care by asking questions of their physician.

Apply the Concept 1.4

Background As you have read in this chapter, IS have made a very significant impact on society. In fact, most all of us now use the Internet to communicate with friends, family, and colleagues. E-mail, Facebook, Twitter, text messages, Skype, and all other communication technologies run on and are supported by IS. We can also collaborate in ways that have never before been possible.

For example, what if you needed to plan a vacation with some friends for spring break? Although this may seem simple, you will use search tools, post links, take notes, etc. Why not give it a try?

Activity If you do not have a Google account (that provides access to Gmail, Calendars, Drive, YouTube, etc.), you will need to set one up for this activity. Have your friends do the same and share your usernames (not passwords) with each other.

Now sign into Google Drive (http://drive.google.com) and create a new document. Toward the right-hand side, you will see a "share" button. Click this and add your friends' Google email addresses in the share box. Be sure to give the rights to edit.

Coordinate with them for all of you to sign on at the same time and use the document to type, share links, notes, ideas, etc., and plan your trip! Look up hotels, activities, restaurants, and so on.

Deliverable

Download the document as a PDF when you have your trip all planned out (and are a bit bummed that you are not actually going) to submit to your instructor. In addition, be prepared to discuss some of the benefits of using of Google Drive (or any tool that may become available that would be similar to it). What are some ways in which you could use this tool on campus, at home, or at work?

Quiz questions are assignable in WileyPLUS, and available on the Book Companion Site at http://www.wiley.com/college/rainer.

RUBY'S CLUB QUESTIONS

1. How might a well-designed information system impact Ruby's employees? Specifically, how might it impact Ruben and Lisa? What aspects of running a club would be easier on a computer than on paper?

2. Do you think the addition of an IS would create or eliminate jobs at Ruby's?

In a previous section of this chapter, we discussed how IT supports each of the functional areas of the organization. Here we examine the MIS function.

FOR THE MIS MAJOR

The MIS function directly supports all other functional areas in an organization. That is, the MIS function is responsible for providing the information that each functional area needs in order to make decisions. The overall objective of MIS personnel is to help users improve performance and solve business problems using IT. To accomplish this objective, MIS personnel must understand both the information requirements and the technology associated with each functional area. Given their position, however, MIS personnel must think "business needs" first and "technology" second.

SUMMARY

1. **Identify the reasons why being an informed user of information systems is important in today's world.**

   You will benefit more from your organization's IT applications because you will understand what is "behind" those applications.

   > You will be able to provide input into your organization's IT applications, thus improving the quality of those applications.

   > You will quickly be in a position to recommend, or participate in, the selection of IT applications that your organization will use.

   > You will be able to keep up with rapid developments in existing information technologies, as well as the introduction of new technologies.

   > You will understand the potential impacts that "new and improved" technologies will have on your organization and, therefore, will be qualified to make recommendations concerning their adoption and use.

   > You will play a key role in managing the information systems in your organization.

   > You will be in a position to use IT if you decide to start your own business.

2. **Describe the various types of computer-based information systems in an organization.**

   > Transaction processing systems (TPS) support the monitoring, collection, storage, and processing of data from the organization's basic business transactions, each of which generates data.

   > Functional area information systems (FAISs) support a particular functional area within the organization.

   > Interorganizational information systems (IOSs) support many interorganizational operations, of which supply chain management is the best known.

   > Enterprise resource planning (ERP) systems correct a lack of communication among the FAISs by tightly integrating the functional area ISs via a common database.

   > Electronic commerce (e-commerce) systems enable organizations to conduct transactions with other organizations (called business-to-business (B2B) electronic commerce), and with customers (called business-to-consumer (B2C) electronic commerce).

   > Office automation systems (OASs) typically support the clerical staff, lower and middle managers, and knowledge workers, by enabling them to develop documents (word processing and desktop publishing software), schedule resources (electronic calendars), and communicate (e-mail, voice mail, videoconferencing, and groupware).

   > Business intelligence (BI) systems provide computer-based support for complex, nonroutine decisions, primarily for middle managers and knowledge workers.

   > Expert systems (ESs) attempt to duplicate the work of human experts by applying reasoning capabilities, knowledge, and expertise within a specific domain.

3. **Discuss ways in which information technology can affect managers and nonmanagerial workers.**

   Potential IT impacts on managers:

   > IT may reduce the number of middle managers.

   > IT will provide managers with real-time or near real-time information, meaning that managers will have less time to make decisions.

   > IT will increase the likelihood that managers will have to supervise geographically dispersed employees and teams.

   Potential IT impacts on nonmanagerial workers:

   > IT may eliminate jobs.

   > IT may cause employees to experience a loss of identity.

   > IT may cause job stress and physical problems, such as repetitive stress injury.

4. **Identify positive and negative societal effects of the increased use of information technology.**

   Positive societal effects:

   > IT can provide opportunities for people with disabilities.

   > IT can provide people with flexibility in their work (e.g., work from anywhere, anytime).

   > Robots can take over mundane chores.

   > IT can enable improvements in health care.

   Negative societal effects:

   > IT can cause health problems for individuals.

   > IT can place employees on constant call.

   > IT can potentially misinform patients about their health problems.

>>> CHAPTER GLOSSARY

application (app) A computer program designed to support a specific task or business process.

business intelligence (BI) systems Provide computer-based support for complex, nonroutine decisions, primarily for middle managers and knowledge workers.

computer-based information system (CBIS) An information system that uses computer technology to perform some or all of its intended tasks.

dashboards (or digital dashboards) A special form of IS that supports all managers of the organization by providing rapid access to timely information and direct access to structured information in the form of reports.

data items Elementary descriptions of things, events, activities, and transactions that are recorded, classified, and stored but are not organized to convey any specific meaning.

database A collection of related files or tables containing data.

electronic commerce (e-commerce) system A type of interorganizational information system that enables organizations to conduct transactions, called business-to-business (B2B) electronic commerce, and customers to conduct transactions with businesses, called business-to-consumer (B2C) electronic commerce.

enterprise resource planning (ERP) systems ISs that correct a lack of communication among the FAISs by tightly integrating the functional area ISs via a common database.

ergonomics The science of adapting machines and work environments to people with the goal of creating an environment that is safe, well lit, and comfortable.

expert systems (ESs) Attempt to duplicate the work of human experts by applying reasoning capabilities, knowledge, and expertise within a specific domain.

functional area information systems (FAISs) ISs that support a particular functional area within the organization.

hardware A device such as a processor, monitor, keyboard, or printer. Together, these devices accept data and information, process them, and display them.

information Data that have been organized so that they have meaning and value to the recipient.

information system (IS) Collects, processes, stores, analyzes, and disseminates information for a specific purpose.

information technology (IT) Relates to any computer-based tool that people use to work with information and support the information and information processing needs of an organization.

information technology (IT) components Hardware, software, databases, and networks.

information technology (IT) infrastructure IT components plus IT services.

information technology (IT) platform Formed by the IT components of hardware, software, networks (wireline and wireless), and databases.

information technology (IT) services IT personnel use IT components to perform these IT services: develop information systems, oversee security and risk, and manage data.

informed user A person knowledgeable about information systems and information technology.

interorganizational information systems (IOSs) Information systems that connect two or more organizations.

knowledge Data and/or information that have been organized and processed to convey understanding, experience, accumulated learning, and expertise as they apply to a current problem or activity.

knowledge workers Professional employees, such as financial and marketing analysts, engineers, lawyers, and accountants, who are experts in a particular subject area and create information and knowledge, which they integrate into the business.

network A connecting system (wireline or wireless) that permits different computers to share resources.

office automation systems (OASs) Typically support clerical staff, lower and middle managers, and knowledge workers to develop documents, schedule resources, and communicate.

procedures The set of instructions about how to combine the components of information technology in order to process information and generate the desired output.

software A program or collection of programs that enable the hardware to process data.

supply chain The flow of materials, information, money, and services from suppliers of raw materials through factories and warehouses to the end customers.

transaction processing system (TPS) Supports the monitoring, collection, storage, and processing of data from the organization's basic business transactions, each of which generates data.

>>> DISCUSSION QUESTIONS

1. Describe a business that you would like to start. Discuss how you would use global outsourcing to accomplish your goals.

2. Your university wants to recruit high-quality high school students from your state. Provide examples of (a) the data that your recruiters would gather in this process, (b) the information that your recruiters would process from these data, and (c) the types of knowledge that your recruiters would infer from this information.

3. Can the terms *data*, *information*, and *knowledge* have different meanings for different people? Support your answer with examples.

4. Information technology makes it possible to "never be out of touch." Discuss the pros and cons of always being available to your employers and clients (regardless of where you are or what you are doing).

5. Robots have the positive impact of being able to relieve humans from working in dangerous conditions. What are some negative impacts of robots in the workplace?

6. Is it possible to endanger yourself by accessing too much medical information on the Web? Why or why not? Support your answer.

7. Is the vast amount of medical information on the Web a good thing? Answer from the standpoint of a patient and from the standpoint of a physician.

8. Describe other potential impacts of IT on societies as a whole.

9. What are the major reasons why it is important for employees in all functional areas to become familiar with IT?

10. Refer to the study at Princess Alexandra Hospital (see "Improvements in Health Care"). How do you feel about Google searches finding the correct diagnosis in 57 percent of the cases? Are you impressed with these results? Why or why not? What are the implications of this study for self-diagnosis?

>>> PROBLEM-SOLVING ACTIVITIES

1. Visit some Web sites that offer employment opportunities in IT. Prominent examples are www.dice.com, www.monster.com, www.collegerecruiter.com, www.careerbuilder.com, www.jobcentral.com, www.job.com, www.career.com, www.simplyhired.com, and www.truecareers.com. Compare the IT salaries to salaries offered to accountants, marketing personnel, financial personnel, operations personnel, and human resources personnel. For other information on IT salaries, check *Computerworld*'s annual salary survey.

2. Enter the Web site of UPS (www.ups.com).

   a. Find out what information is available to customers before they send a package.

   b. Find out about the "package tracking" system.

   c. Compute the cost of delivering a $10'' \times 20'' \times 15''$ box, weighing 40 pounds, from your hometown to Long Beach, California (or to Lansing, Michigan, if you live in or near Long Beach). Compare the fastest delivery against the least cost.

3. Surf the Internet for information about the Department of Homeland Security (DHS). Examine the available information, and comment on the role of information technologies in the department.

4. Access www.irobot.com, and investigate the company's robots for education and research. Surf the Web for other companies that manufacture robots, and compare their products with those of iRobot.

>>> COLLABORATION EXERCISE

Background

This chapter has shown the many ways IS have changed business. As you will learn through this course, there are many jobs that have now been created as a result of the growth of IS. Although many positions have been eliminated (such as the typist), others have been created (software developers who write word processing programs).

Activity

Divide your team into the following functional areas: marketing, accounting, finance, human relations, logistics. Do some research as individuals to find out what type of jobs are related to IT for each area. Find some software companies that provide the systems (such as ADP for human resources) and learn about the IT people involved in the organization who support the various departments.

Once everyone has completed the research, meet as a team and have a conversation about the current job market. Work as a team to find open positions related to the areas you have found.

Deliverable

Build a short table that has four columns as shown in the example below. Submit work to your instructor.

Department	IS that Supports	Related IS Positions	Current Job Opening

CLOSING **CASE 1** > Today, Every Company Is a Technology Company

THE BUSINESS >>> PROBLEM

Sixty years into the computer revolution, 40 years into the age of the microprocessor, and 20 years into the rise of the modern Internet, all of the technology required to transform industries through software has been developed and integrated and can be delivered globally. Over 2 billion people now access the Internet via broadband connections. Worldwide, over 5 billion people use cell phones. One billion of those 5 billion cell phone users have smartphones that provide them with instant access to the Internet at all times.

In addition, software programming tools and Internet-based services allow companies in many industries to launch new software-powered startups without investing in new infrastructure or training new employees. For example, in the year 2000 the cost of a business operating a basic Internet application was approximately $150,000 per month. Operating that same application today in Amazon's cloud (discussed in detail in Plug IT In #3) costs about $1,500 per month.

In essence, software is disrupting every industry, and every organization must prepare for this disruption. Numerous companies have attempted to meet the disruption challenge; some have succeeded and some have failed.

SOFTWARE >>> DISRUPTIONS

Let's look at examples of software disruption across several industries. In many of these examples, you can first see where software disrupted the previous market leading companies and then where a new company (or companies) used software to gain a competitive advantage.

- *The book industry:* A dramatic example of software disruption is the fate of Borders bookstore. In 2001, Borders agreed to hand over its online business to Amazon because the bookstore felt that online book sales were nonstrategic and unimportant. Borders filed for bankruptcy in October 2011. That same month, the www.borders.com Web site was replaced with a redirect link to the Barnes & Noble Web site (www.bn.com). In January 2012, Barnes & Noble warned analysts it would lose twice as much money in 2012 than it had previously expected. The company was considering splitting off its growing Nook e-book business from its physical bookstores.

    Today, the world's largest bookseller, Amazon, is a software company. Its core capability is its software engine for selling virtually anything online with no retail stores necessary. Amazon has even reorganized its Web site to promote its Kindle digital books over physical books. Now, even the books themselves are software.

- *The music industry:* Today's dominant music companies are software companies: Apple's iTunes (www.apple.com/itunes), Spotify (www.spotify.com), and Pandora (www.pandora.com). Traditional record labels today exist largely to provide those software companies with content. In mid-2012, the Recording Industry Association of America continues to fight battles over copyright infringement and the illegal download and sharing of digital music files.

- *The video industry:* Blockbuster was the industry leader until disrupted by a software company, Netflix (www.netflix.com). In mid-2012, Netflix has the largest subscriber base of any video service. Blockbuster declared bankruptcy in February 2011 and was acquired by Dish Networks in March 2011.

- *The software industry:* Incumbent software companies such as Oracle and Microsoft are increasingly threatened by software-as-a-service products (e.g., Salesforce.com) and Android, an open-source operating system developed by the Open Handset Alliance (www.openhandsetalliance.com) and led by Google. (We discuss operating systems in Plug IT In #2 and software-as-a-service in Plug IT In #3).

- *The videogame industry:* Today, the fastest growing entertainment companies are videogame makers—again, software. Examples of fast growing videogame companies include:

    o Zynga (www.zynga.com) makes FarmVille and delivers its games entirely online.

    o Rovio (www.rovio.com), the maker of Angry Birds, made almost $100 million in revenue in 2011. The company was nearly bankrupt when it launched Angry Birds on the iPhone in late 2009.

    o Minecraft (www.minecraft.net), another video game delivered only online over the Internet, was first released in 2009. By February 2012, over 5 million people had downloaded it. Interestingly, the creator of Minecraft, Markus Persson, has never spent any money to market his game. Sales grew only by word of mouth.

- *The photography industry:* This industry was disrupted by software years ago. Today it is virtually impossible to buy a mobile phone that does not include a software-powered camera, and photos can be uploaded automatically to the Internet for permanent archiving and global sharing. The previous market leader, Kodak, has been replaced by companies such as Shutterfly (www.shutterfly.com), Snapfish (www.snapfish.com), Flickr (www.flickr.com), and Instagram (www.instagram.com). Kodak declared bankruptcy in January 2012.

- *The marketing industry:* Today's largest direct marketing companies are Facebook (www.facebook.com), Google (www.google.com), Groupon (www.groupon.com), Living Social (www.livingsocial.com), Foursquare (www.foursquare.com), and others. These companies are using software to disrupt the retail marketing industry.

- *The recruiting industry:* LinkedIn (www.linkedin.com) is a fast-growing recruiting company. For the first time, employees can maintain their own resumes on LinkedIn for recruiters to search in real time.

- *The financial services industry:* Software has transformed the financial services industry. Practically every financial transaction is performed by software. And many of the leading innovators in financial services are software companies. For example, Square (https://squareup.com) allows anyone to accept credit card payments with a mobile phone.

Software is also disrupting industries that operate primarily in the physical world. Consider these examples:

- *The automobile industry:* In modern cars, software is responsible for running the engines, controlling safety features, entertaining passengers, guiding drivers to their destinations, and connecting the car to mobile, satellite, and GPS networks. Other software functions in modern cars include Wi-Fi receivers, which turn your car into a mobile hot spot, software, which helps maximize fuel efficiency, and ultrasonic sensors, which enable automatic parallel parking.

    The next step is to network all vehicles together. The creation of software-powered driverless cars is already being undertaken at Google and major car companies.

- Today's leading real-world retailer, Wal-Mart, uses software to power its logistics and distribution capabilities, which it has used to become dominant in its industry.

- *The postal industry:* FedEx, which early in its history took the view that "the information about the package is as important as the package itself," now employs hundreds of developers who build and deploy software products for 350,000 customer sites.

- *The oil and gas industry:* Companies in this industry were early innovators in supercomputing and data visualization and analysis, which are critically important to oil and gas exploration efforts.

- *The agriculture industry:* Agriculture is increasingly powered by software as well, including satellite analysis of soils linked to per-acre seed selection software algorithms. In addition, precision agriculture makes use of automated, driverless tractors controlled by global positioning systems and software.

- *National defense:* Even national defense is increasingly software based. The modern combat soldier is embedded in a web of software that provides intelligence, communications, logistics, and weapons guidance. Software-powered drone aircraft launch airstrikes without putting human pilots at risk. Intelligence agencies perform large-scale data mining with software to uncover and track potential terrorist plots.

THE RESULTS >>>

As you have seen, an increasing number of major businesses and industries are being run on software and delivered as online services—from motion pictures to agriculture to national defense. Regardless of the industry, companies face constant competitive threats from established rivals and entrepreneurial technology companies that are developing disruptive software. These threats will force companies to become more agile in the future and respond to competitive threats more quickly, efficiently, and effectively.

Sources: Compiled from M. De La Merced, "Eastman Kodak Files for Bankruptcy," *The Wall Street Journal*, January 19, 2012; J. Trachtenberg and M. Peers, "Barnes & Noble Seeks Next Chapter," *The Wall Street Journal*, January 6, 2012; "Driverless Car: Google Awarded U.S. Patent for Technology," *BBC News*, December 15, 2011; J. McKendrick, "Five Non-IT Companies That Are Now Indistinguishable from Software Companies," *ZDNet*, December 7, 2011; A. Bleicher, "Five Reasons Every Company Should Act Like a Software Startup," *Forbes*, November 14, 2011; B. Austen, "The End of Borders and the Future of Books," *Bloomberg BusinessWeek*, November 10, 2011; M. Andreessen, "Why Software Is Eating the World," *The Wall Street Journal*, August 20, 2011; J. Knee, "Why Content Isn't King," *The Atlantic*, July/August, 2011; J. Checkler and J. Trachtenberg, "Bookseller Borders Begins a New Chapter...11," *The Wall Street Journal*, February 17, 2011.

Questions

1. If every company is now a technology company, then what does this mean for the company's employees? Discuss your answer and provide specific examples to support your answer.
2. If every company is now a technology company, then what does this mean for every major in a college of business? Discuss your answer and provide specific examples to support your answer.

CLOSING **CASE 2 >** The Arab Spring

The Arab Spring is a wave of demonstrations and protests occurring in the Arab world. Demonstrators have been demanding greater political freedom and an end to autocracy. By mid-2012, there have been revolutions in Tunisia and Egypt, a civil war in Libya, civil uprisings in Bahrain, Syria, and Yemen, major protests in Algeria, Iraq, Jordan, Kuwait, Morocco, and Oman, and minor protests in Lebanon, Mauritania, Saudi Arabia, and Sudan. Protesters have made use of mobile communications, the Internet, and social media to organize, communicate, and raise awareness in the face of state repression and Internet censorship. In this case, we will look at three examples: Tunisia, Egypt, and Syria.

<<< THE PROBLEM

Tunisia. In January 2011, the modern Arab world's first successful popular uprising, called the Jasmine Revolution (named for the national flower), erupted in Tunisia when Mohammed Bouazizi set himself on fire. When he died 18 days later, his story went viral, providing millions of angry young Tunisians with a martyr. Vast numbers of protestors took to the streets, sparking the Jasmine Revolution.

Egypt. In January 2011, another popular uprising broke out in Egypt. In 2010, Khaled Saied, a young man from Alexandria, was beaten to death by the police. Protesters rallied around a Facebook page entitled "We Are All Khaled Saied." Mr. Saied's death became the focal point for Egyptians who had not previously been involved in the protest movement. Beginning on January 25, 2011, millions of protesters from a variety of backgrounds and religions demanded the overthrow of Egyptian President Hosni Mubarak, who had held office since 1981.

Syria. An uprising began in Syria on January 26, 2011, when Hasan Ali Akleh set himself on fire, protesting against the Syrian government. Since that date, the protests have become more widespread and violent. According to the United Nations, by mid-2012 some 8,000 people had been killed and the conflict was ongoing.

Tunisia. The Jasmine Revolution did not need any prominent leaders to rally the protesters or organize the demonstrations. Instead, the revolution was fueled by a steady stream of anonymous text messages and Twitter and Facebook updates. Documents posted on WikiLeaks (see Chapter 6), in which U.S. diplomats had cataloged the corruption at the highest levels of the Tunisian government, deepened the popular rage. Mobile phone videos posted online documented the government's brutal response, including images of police beating and shooting protestors, resulting in at least a hundred deaths. The protesters used the one weapon they understood much better than the government: the Internet. Young Tunisians—educated, multilingual, and knowledgeable about the Internet and social media—devised strategies to evade the government's crude firewalls. Protestors spent several hours each day on Facebook and other social networks. By rendering the state television and radio stations irrelevant, they were able to undermine the regime's propaganda for the first time in many years.

<<< THE ROLE OF INFORMATION TECHNOLOGY

Egypt. In an effort to silence demonstrators, President Mubarak "turned off the Internet." At 12:34 AM on January 28, Egypt's four primary Internet providers—Link Egypt, Vodafone/Raya, Telecom Egypt, and Etisalat Misr—all went "dark." That is, the four providers stopped transmitting all Internet traffic into and out of Egypt. The blackout appeared to be designed to disrupt the organization of the country's protest movement.

"When countries block, we evolve," wrote one activist from the group We Rebuild in a Twitter message on January 28. We Rebuild and other activist groups scrambled to keep the country connected to the outside world, turning to landline telephones, fax machines, and even ham radios to keep information flowing in and out of Egypt.

The activists were successful. On February 2, Egypt's embattled leaders realized that the communications blockage was largely ineffective and indeed counterproductive. The shutdown proved to be more a source of fresh anger than an impediment to the protest movement. Protesters had no trouble gathering larger and larger crowds, culminating with an estimated 250,000 people who assembled in central Cairo on January 29 to demand an end to Mubarak's rule.

Syria. The Internet is playing a major role in the organization and coverage of the protests in Syria. The largest Facebook page in support of the Syrian uprising, called "The Syrian Revolution 2011," has more than 380,000 followers. The page reports on news related to the uprising.

Because the international news media were banned in Syria, the main source of information to the outside world has been private videos, usually taken with mobile phone cameras and uploaded to YouTube and Flickr. Such videos are difficult to verify independently. To add credibility to the videos, protestors often explicitly mention the date and location of the scene and show current newspaper issues.

Activists are organizing protests via Twitter and Facebook and are using Skype and Twitter to communicate because the regime often blocks cell phone transmissions.

For example, Syrian activists are using an iPhone app called "Souria Wa Bas" to disseminate news and information about the conflict. The app, which works on both the iPhone and iPad, includes recent news about opposition groups and their activities, as well as videos, maps, and photos.

THE RESULTS >>>

Tunisia. On January 14, 2011, President Ben Ali was forced into exile.

Egypt. On February 11, 2011, following weeks of determined popular protest and pressures, President Mubarak resigned from office. On June 24, 2012, Egypt's election commission announced that Muslim Brotherhood candidate Mohammed Morsi had won Egypt's presidential election. However, as of mid-2012, the Supreme Council of the Armed Forces remains in power.

Syria. The conflict continues in mid-2012. Some countries have cut ties with the Assad regime including the Gulf States, Libya, Tunisia, Britain, Spain, Turkey, the United States, and Belgium. In addition, the Arab League, Turkey, and most Western powers have imposed severe sanctions on Syria, including bans on trade and transportation, isolating the Assad regime.

Sources: Compiled from J. Peterson, "The Facebook Revolutions: One Year On," *The Daily Caller*, December 18, 2011; J. Harris, "The Year of the Networked Revolution," *The Guardian*, December 13, 2011; A. Hauslohner, "The Revolution's Second Act," *Time*, December 5, 2011; J. Titlow, "How Syrian Protesters Are Using the iPhone to Fuel an Uprising," *ReadWriteWeb*, November 18, 2011; A. Flamand and H. Macleod, "Syria's Protesters Turn to Facebook to Expose 'Citizen Spies,'" *The Guardian*, October 8, 2011; R. Ratnesar, "Not Just the Facebook Revolution," *Bloomberg BusinessWeek*, June 6–12, 2011; R. Mackey, "Social Media Accounts of Protests in Syria," *The New York Times*, April 23, 2011; N. Blanford, "On Facebook and Twitter, Spreading Revolution in Syria," *The Christian Science Monitor*, April 8, 2011; J. Solomon and C. Levinson, "West to Isolate Gadhafi," *Wall Street Journal*, February 26–27, 2011; "The Faces of Egypt's 'Revolution 2.0,'" *CNN.com*, February 21, 2011; "After Egypt, People Power Hits Like a Tsunami," *CNN.com*, February 15, 2011; "Egyptian President Steps Down Amidst Groundbreaking Digital Revolution," *CNN.com*, February 11, 2011; C. Levinson, M. Coker, and J. Solomon, "How Cairo, U.S. Were Blindsided by Revolution," *Wall Street Journal*, February 2, 2011; P. McNamara, "Egypt Lifts Blockade on Internet Service," *Network World*, February 2, 2011; V. Blue, "#Egypt Blocked in China: Is Internet Access a Human Right?" *ZDNet.com*, January 31, 2011; V. Walt, "Tunisia's Nervous Neighbors Watch the Jasmine Revolution," *Time*, January 31, 2011; N. Gohring and R. McMillan, "Without Internet, Egyptians Find New Ways to Get Online," *Computerworld*, January 28, 2011; J. Robertson, "The Day Part of the Internet Died: Egypt Goes Dark," *USA Today*, January 28, 2011; "Tunisia's Revolution Should Be Wake-Up Call to Middle East Autocrats," *Washington Post*, January 15, 2011.

Questions

1. Describe how information technology enabled the Jasmine and Egyptian revolutions.
2. Describe efforts by the Tunisian and Egyptian governments to quell the revolutions. In particular, describe the efforts that were directed at information technology.
3. Discuss how information technology contributed to higher oil prices and higher prices you pay for gasoline.

Ruben and Lisa are seriously considering integrating technology into their club. However, they still need a little convincing because of their lack of experience with computers. Right now, they only have one old computer and it is still running Windows XP. Just last year, they finally decided to have cable Internet installed so they could place product orders quicker. Neither of them is on Facebook or Twitter.

For now, they need to know what types of ISs are available and what they can do with them. With the information in this chapter regarding the different types and uses of ISs, write them a business letter detailing how the use of ISs may help them manage their club on a day-to-day basis. Be sure to include information about the generation they serve and employ (*Homo conexus*) and how they are already connected to and familiar with computers and networks. Finally, submit your letter to your instructor.

SPREADSHEET ACTIVITY

Objective: A spreadsheet is a software tool that allows large amounts of data to be stored, organized, analyzed, and presented in graphical form. A spreadsheet is extremely useful because of its ability to make simple work of a mundane task (such as calculating the average inventory turnover time for 1000 products). Although it is not difficult to calculate averages, the sheer volume of the work makes it very time-consuming. A spreadsheet allows you to create your own "formula" and then apply that formula to all 1000 products at the same time, reducing the amount of work necessary dramatically.

Given these possibilities, you need to take some time to consider the possible applications of a spreadsheet. It is the endless application of the spreadsheet that makes it so powerful. This activity will show you that this tool can be used for a variety of situations and purposes.

Chapter Connection: Data, information, and knowledge are the main focus of this chapter. Spreadsheets are just one of many tools (albeit the most widespread and easily accessible) that can be used to manage data, information, and knowledge.

Activity: As the text introduces the concepts of data, information, and knowledge, this activity will introduce you to the vast possibilities of using spreadsheets to help manage and control data. Unmanaged data will never provide information or knowledge, and so it is imperative to understand not only how to use a spreadsheet but the possibilities of when to use it. Consider the following three examples, and then develop your own ideas about how spreadsheets can be used.

- *Individual:* Money is something everyone has to deal with. A spreadsheet is a great tool to help track and manage personal finances. Someone with a spreadsheet budget can quickly see where his or her money is being spent and make plans for where it will go in the future. With a little creativity and experience, one can quickly create a personal spreadsheet that will help track finances without purchasing a boxed program.

- *Organizations:* It is still the simple things that make a big difference. Companies continue to seek better ways to manage inventory, and often these systems incorporate a spreadsheet. Many supply chain management tools will export data into spreadsheets for analysis. Once in a spreadsheet, charts and graphs can be used to easily display how inventory is being handled.

- *Society:* Every 10 years, the U.S. government performs a census. Much of this information is available to the public. A good deal of interesting information can be gained by placing these data in a spreadsheet. Charts and graphs can be used to analyze population changes, employment rates, demographic information, and trends over time. Spreadsheets can be used to tell a story with this information.

Having read these descriptions, describe to your professor how you might use a spreadsheet to help manage the required maintenance on your vehicle. Think about things like gas mileage, oil changes, expenses, etc. What "math formulas" would you use that a spreadsheet could help with? If it will help, search the Web for "vehicle maintenance spreadsheets" to see what other people do with it!

Deliverable: You will provide a written description that demonstrates the ways a spreadsheet can be used to help keep up with routine maintenance on a vehicle.

Discussion Questions:

1. For data to be turned into information, they often need to be cleaned, organized, calculated, and ultimately presented in some graphical format. Spreadsheets are excellent at all of these. Discuss three tools that help spreadsheets accomplish all of these goals.

2. Students have generated their own ideas for using spreadsheets. Be prepared to discuss your ideas with the class at large. Hopefully, you did not all come up with the same possibilities as other students, and this will help broaden their horizons even more.

Suggested Solution: There is no suggested solution. There is no end to the possible applications of spreadsheet tools. This is the major point of this exercise. It does not teach you anything in particular (although you may learn something); it simply opens your eyes to see that this tool will apply to you sometime. We hope it will make these concepts more real to you as you work through the following exercises.

Quiz questions are assignable in WileyPLUS, and available on the Book Companion Site at http://www.wiley.com/college/rainer.

DATABASE ACTIVITY: INTRODUCTION TO THE DATABASE PROJECT

Objective

How to open and use an existing Access 2010 database, even if you have never done it before.

CHAPTER CONNECTION

All aspects of modern information systems depend on shared databases. Being able to work with them is essential to any manager or knowledge worker of the 21st century. In this chapter, you saw how every department in a modern organization uses information systems. You saw how different departments use them differently: HR staff to recruit, marketing managers to select marketing channels, manufacturing coordinators to develop production schedules. Much of this information is not just for one part of the organization. Order information from sales, for example, goes to manufacturing (if you sell something, it must be produced), purchasing (materials come from suppliers), and accounting (payments, adjustments to inventory values). Linking an organization through a shared database is a major benefit of today's systems.

These uses depend on *data*. You will read more about that later in this course.

However, it is never too early to start thinking about ISs in terms of the data they use. Computers can only work with the data they have. Having the right data is vital to any IS.

PREREQUISITES

None.

Activity

1. Download the **Ch 01 NeTrouble** database from http://www.wiley.com/go/rainer/database and double-click to open it.

2. Familiarize yourself with the parts of the Access window you see. The main ones are shown in Figure 1A.1. (It is from a different database, but the window has the same parts.)

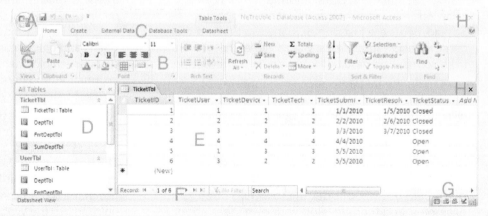

Figure 1A.1 Microsoft Access: Screen shot 1.

The ribbon, A, provides tools to manipulate your data-base. The tools depend on the object you are working with and are organized into groups accessed via tabs (B). The tabs vary with object type, but there will always be a Home tab at the left and a Create tab next to it.

The arrangement of the icons on the ribbon depends on how much space Access has to spread them out. Vary the width of your window to see how the icons rearrange as it becomes narrower. (On most displays, it starts out wide enough for a full array, so making it wider will not change anything.) The sections stay the same, but some tools may lose their labels or disappear under an arrow indicating a pull-down menu when space is tight.

The File tab, letter C, controls the database as a file. You open, close, and save your work here. In Office 2007, this was done via the Office button. Prior releases used a File menu.

The navigation pane, D, lists the objects in the current database. You can choose which types of objects it lists via the pull-down menu that opens when you click the down arrow to the right of "All Tables." Each object type has its own icon. In the screen shot, the spreadsheets represent tables; the green booklets, reports.

Usage Hint: If you see just "Navigation Pane" vertically at the left of the window, click on that text or the » above to expand it. The « at the top of the navigation pane in the screen shot shrinks the pane. That leaves more space for other items.

The main part of the window, E, houses all open objects. The screen shot shows a data table. Each object has a tab with its name at the top. Clicking a tab brings that object to the front. You probably do not see any open tables in your database yet.

The navigation area, F, lets you move through individual records in a database. Here, it shows "1 of 19," corresponding to the highlighted first record of 19 in the table.

Most Access objects can be manipulated in several *views*. A table, for example, has one view (Datasheet view) for reading and editing data, another (Design view) for designing the table itself. You can switch views by clicking the icon at the left of the ribbon (G), by pulling down the menu there, or via the icons at the lower right of the window (also G).

The Access window has two Close boxes (H). The one at the top right of the object area closes the object in front (here, the table TicketTbl). If other objects are open, one of them will now be in front. The Close box at the top right of the window closes the application and exits Access. (It prompts you to save unsaved work first.)

3. Open UserTbl (short for "User Table"). How many records are in it?

Usage Hint: Access can be set to open objects with a single or double click in the navigation pane. If you are using a personal copy, you can set this preference via Options under the File ribbon tab. Click Current Database, then Navigation Options.

4. Sort this table by date of birth: Click in the UserDOB column to select it, then click the top (A to Z) sorting icon in the Sort & Filter section under the ribbon. Who is the oldest user? How old is he or she?

5. Look at the UserDept (User Department) column of the User table. It does not have department names. Instead, it has numbers. Adam is from Department 1, and so on.

6. Open DeptTbl (Department Table). What is the name of Department 1?

7. Open UserRpt (User Report). Adam is listed under that department. Access used his department number to connect his name in the user table with the department name in the department table. This is how relational databases link different types of data. How many users in the Marketing department submitted network trouble tickets? After you find the answer, close the report. Be sure to click the X at the top right of the object area, below the ribbon—not the one at the top right of the entire Access window. Clicking the X at the top right of the entire Access window will exit the Access application.

8. Open UserFrm (User Form). You will see information about the first user, Adam. In the navigation area at the bottom of the window, F in the figure, click on the far right icon to insert a new record. Enter reasonable data. For the user's department, pick any department from the list to the right of the legend "Select department." What department did you pick? Note the User ID number of your new user. Click the New Record icon again to save your work.

Figure 1A.2 Microsoft Access: Screen shot 2.

Usage Hint: Access saves new data in the database as soon as you exit a record. Changes to the design of the database, however, are saved only when you tell it to.

9. Now open TicketTbl. Click in the "New" row of the table. Do not enter anything in the first column; it will be filled automatically with the

next number. In the next column, TicketUser, enter the number of the user you just created. In the next two, TicketDevice and TicketTech, fill in any numbers that are already used in the existing rows of the table. In the next two, enter any dates you want. (If you click on the calendar icon that appears when you select either of those fields, you can use a built-in calendar to select dates.) In the last column, enter any data you want.

10. Open UserRpt again. How many users are in that department now?

Usage Hint: Reports are not automatically updated when data they are based on change. You have to close and reopen them.

Usage Hint: The reason you created a ticket for your new user is that this report shows only users who have submitted trouble tickets. It could have been designed to show all users, whether or not they submitted tickets, but it was not.

11. Open UserQry (User Query) to find all users born after a certain date. Key in 6/6/1986 (June 6, 1986) and click OK. How many users were born after that date?

Deliverable

Submit answers to the eight questions posed in the above activity:

    In step 3: 1 question
    In step 4: 2 questions
    In step 6: 1 question
    In step 7: 1 question
    In step 8: 2 questions
    In step 11: 1 question
(Steps not listed have no questions.)

Quiz Questions

1. True or false: Access puts all the information about something of interest (such as an employee) into a single table.

2. Which of the following information items about a user is *not* given in UserTbl?
    (a) The user's name.
    (b) The user's date of birth.
    (c) The user's e-mail address.
    (d) The user's blood type.

3. If you want to find out a user's age from UserTbl, which of the following is correct?
    (a) There is insufficient information here to determine it.

(b) It can be found by subtracting the date of birth from today's date, dividing the difference in days by 365, and deleting any fractional remainder.

(c) It can be found by subtracting the date of hire from today's date, dividing the difference in days by 365, and deleting any fractional remainder.

(d) It can be found by asking the user or a member of his/her family.

4. The report you looked at in step 7 had all of the following elements, except:
    (a) An overall header at the top, to identify it.
    (b) Number of trouble tickets submitted by each department, below the list of that department's employees.
    (c) Number of trouble tickets submitted by each department, above the list of that department's employees.
    (d) Detail rows with information about each user.

Discussion Questions

1. In step 9 of this activity, you entered a birth date cutoff for the query. User input like this, that determines what data a query returns, is called a *parameter*. Now, suppose you want to book a round trip on an air travel reservation system. List three parameters you must enter into such a system before it can tell you about available flights.

2. The report you used in steps 7 and 8 of this activity included a summary field after each department. It was a simple summary, just a count of users in that department. Suppose this report also contained numeric data, such as user salaries. What other types of department summaries could you have? Are there any summaries, other than the employee count, that you could possibly create from this table as it exists here? (Be creative. Do not worry about whether or not it would make sense to create them. Just ask: Would it be possible?)

3. A university cafeteria checkout system reads the bar code on each item, looks it up in a table, and finds the product description and price. Using this information, it keeps track of the running total. At the end it calculates the total due and compares it to the student's account balance. If the balance is insufficient, it calls a supervisor. Otherwise, it subtracts the cost of the meal from the balance

and prints an itemized receipt showing the remaining balance.

(a) What tables does this database need? (One was mentioned in the description.)

(b) Using paper and pencil or any other tools your instructor specifies, draw the tables as in TicketTbl in the Figure 1A.1. Show columns for all the data in them. Show a few sample rows. Also draw a sample itemized receipt as it might be printed for a student. For each different kind of data item on the receipt, say where it comes from: in the database or as the result of some other calculation.

4. The technician table (TechTbl) lists all the technicians, with their names and other information such as their pay grade (job title). Describe in words how you could find, using the tables in this database, the names of all the users whose problems a given technician worked with. Use the process you have described to find all the users Nancy helped.

2 | Organizational Strategy, Competitive Advantage, and Information Systems

CHAPTER OUTLINE

LEARNING OBJECTIVES >>>

1. Identify effective IT responses to different kinds of business pressures.
2. Describe the strategies that organizations typically adopt to counter Porter's five competitive forces.
3. Describe the characteristics of effective business—IT alignment.

© Julian Rovagnati/iStockphoto

On a Washington, DC, morning, Alison Cohen rides her bicycle to work. She makes the 2-mile trip in 10 minutes—a trip that would otherwise have required a 20-minute subway ride, a 40-minute walk, or a $7 cab ride. Cohen is president of Alta Bicycle Share (www.altabicycleshare.com), the company behind Washington's bicycle-sharing program. Formed in 2010, Alta combines three companies: (1) Alta Planning & Design in Portland, Oregon, designs bike lanes and parks; (2) Montreal's Public Bike System Company owns the credit card processing technology; and (3) Alta itself bids for government contracts and runs operations in three cities in the United States in mid-2012: Washington, DC, area, Boston, and Chicago.

Bicycle sharing is a growing trend among municipalities looking to make their transit systems greener and less congested. Cities buy the bikes and install docking stations where users can rent them with a credit card. Alta maintains the bikes and collects payment, earning either part of the revenue or a flat annual management fee. A day pass costs $5 and an annual pass $75.

In May 2011, Cohen started a bicycle-sharing service in Melbourne, Australia. By July 2011, a staff of 15 full- and part-time employees managed a fleet of 600 bicycles. Also in May 2011, Cohen signed a contract with the Department of Transportation of Washington, DC, and Arlington County, Virginia. The two government entities then built 118 solar-powered docking stations with electronic docking mechanisms that could hold a total of 1,100 bikes.

In June 2011, Cohen expanded the program to Boston, which launched a 600-bike system, sponsored in part by athletic-shoe maker New Balance. Cohen has since submitted proposals for New York City and Vancouver, British Columbia.

In mid-2011, Alta was reportedly earning $3 million in annual revenue and turning a profit. Alta does face competition from B-Cycle (www.bcycle.com), which operates 1,500 bicycles in 11 cities, including Chicago and Denver. **> > >**

RUBY'S CLUB

Ruben and Lisa have a vision that their club will provide a relaxed community atmosphere, with good drinks and good music. However, they operate in a very competitive business environment and feel market pressure to be everything to everyone, even though that is not what they want to be. They feel pressure from their customers to be more technologically advanced, even though they do not see any competitive advantage from it. They also feel a tremendous responsibility (legal and societal pressure) to manage underage consumption of alcohol. However, they are not sure how to respond to these pressures while maintaining their desired atmosphere.

Over the years, they have learned that they not only compete with other clubs and local restaurants, but with the threat of substitute products or services includes theaters, athletic events, parties, and anything else college students choose to do for entertainment. To gain and maintain a solid customer base, they feel they really want a community feel to their club. Like the old Cheers TV show, a place "where everybody knows your name." To achieve this, they are not quite sure what mix of music, drinks, information, networks, data, advertisements, controls, policies, and procedures would position them where they want to be in the market-place. Ruben and Lisa need a solid strategy to help accomplish their vision.

The rent-a-bike phenomenon is also being adopted by the Beijing municipal government. To ease the city's notorious traffic jams, the Beijing China Municipal Commission of Development and Reform is setting up 500 rental kiosks around the city to offer residents the choice of over 20,000 rental bikes.

Sources: Compiled from G. Hesselberg, "B-Cyclists Log Thousands of Trips in Madison," *Wisconsin State Journal*, February 3, 2012; "More Rental Bikes, Subway Lines to Ease Beijing Traffic Congestion," *English.xinhuanet. cn*, January 6, 2012; H. Coster, "New Commute," *Forbes*, June 27, 2011;

P. DeMaio, "The Bike-Sharing Phenomenon," *Carbusters*, February 2009; www.altabicycleshare.com, www.bcycle.com, accessed February 21, 2012.

uestions

1. Describe the problems involved with setting up a bicycle-sharing program in a new city.
2. Describe how information technology can help address these problems.

Introduction

Information systems are critically important in helping organizations respond to business pressures and in supporting organizations' global strategy. As you study this chapter, you will see that any information system can be *strategic*, meaning that it can provide a competitive advantage—if it is used properly.

This chapter also demonstrates the incredible complexity of the information systems employed by a large international company.

Competitive advantage is an advantage over competitors in some measure such as cost, quality, or speed; it leads to control of a market and to larger-than-average profits. Strategy and competitive advantage come in many forms. For example, Alison Cohen used electronic bicycle docking stations and credit card processing machines to automate her bicycle-sharing business. These information technologies have lowered her operating costs and contributed to the success of her startup operation.

Although there are many examples of companies that use technology in more expensive ways, Alta Bicycle demonstrates that an entrepreneurial spirit and a solid understanding of what IT can do for you can provide competitive advantages. As you study this chapter, think of the small businesses in your area that are doing interesting things with IT.

This chapter is important for you for several reasons. First, the business pressures addressed here will affect your organization, but they also will affect you. As a result, you must understand how information systems can help you, and eventually your organization, respond to these pressures.

In addition, acquiring competitive advantage is essential for your organization's survival. Many organizations achieve competitive advantage through the efforts of their employees. Therefore, becoming knowledgeable about strategy and how information systems affects strategy and competitive position will help you throughout your career.

This chapter encourages you to become familiar with your organization's strategy, mission, and goals and to understand its business problems and how it makes (or loses) money. It will help you understand how IT contributes to organizational strategy. Further, it is likely that you will be a member of business–IT committees that decide (among many other things) whether to adopt new technologies and how to use existing technologies more effectively. After studying this chapter, you will be able to make immediate contributions in these committees when you join your organizations.

In this chapter, you will see how information systems enable organizations to respond to business pressures. Next, you will learn how information systems help organizations gain competitive advantages in the marketplace. The chapter with a discussion of business–IT alignment—in other words, how the IT function in an organization supports its strategy.

2.1 Business Pressures, Organizational Responses, and IT Support

Modern organizations compete in a challenging environment. To remain competitive, they must react rapidly to problems and opportunities that arise from extremely dynamic conditions. In this section you examine some of the major pressures confronting modern organizations and the strategies that organizations employ to respond to these pressures.

Business Pressures

The **business environment** is the combination of social, legal, economic, physical, and political factors in which businesses conduct their operations. Significant changes in any of these factors are likely to create business pressures on organizations. Organizations typically respond to these pressures with activities supported by IT. Figure 2.1 illustrates the relationships among business pressures, organizational performance and responses, and IT support. You will learn about three major types of business pressures: market, technology, and societal pressures.

Market Pressures. Market pressures are generated by the global economy, intense competition, the changing nature of the workforce, and powerful customers. Let's look more closely at each of these factors.

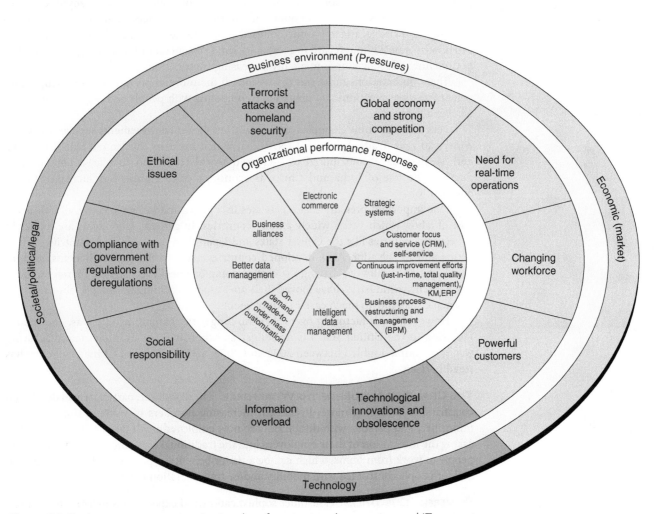

Figure 2.1 Business pressures, organizational performance and responses, and IT support.

GLOBALIZATION. **Globalization** is the integration and interdependence of economic, social, cultural, and ecological facets of life, made possible by rapid advances in IT. In his book *The World Is Flat*, Pulitzer Prize–winning author Thomas Friedman argues that technology is leveling the global competitive playing field, thereby making it "flat."

Friedman identifies three eras of globalization. The first era, Globalization 1.0, lasted from 1492 to 1800. During this era, the force behind globalization was how much muscle, horsepower, or wind power a country could deploy.

The second era, Globalization 2.0, lasted from 1800 to 2000. In this era, the force behind globalization was the emergence of multinational companies—that is, companies that had their headquarters in one country but operated in several countries. In the first half of this era, globalization was driven by falling transportation costs, generated by the development of the steam engine and the railroads. In the second half, the driving force was falling telecommunications costs resulting from the telegraph, telephones, computers, satellites, fiber-optic cable, and the Internet and World Wide Web. The modern global economy began to evolve during this era.

Around the year 2000, the world entered Globalization 3.0. In this era globalization has been driven by the convergence of ten forces that Friedman calls "flatteners." Table 2.1 identifies these forces.

According to Friedman, each era has been characterized by a distinctive focus. The focus of Globalization 1.0 was on countries, the focus of Globalization 2.0 was on companies, and the focus of Globalization 3.0 is on groups and individuals.

As you look at Table 2.1, note that nine of Friedman's ten flatteners directly relate to IT (all except the fall of the Berlin Wall). These flatteners enable individuals to connect, compute, communicate, collaborate, and compete everywhere and anywhere, anytime and all the time; to access limitless amounts of information, services, and entertainment; to exchange knowledge; and to produce and sell goods and services. People and organizations can now operate without regard to geography, time, distance, or even language barriers. The bottom line? Globalization is markedly increasing competition.

These observations make our discussion all the more important for you. Simply put, you and the organizations you join will be competing with people and organizations from all over a flat world.

Let's consider some examples of globalization. Regional agreements such as the North American Free Trade Agreement (NAFTA), which includes the United States, Canada, and Mexico, have contributed to increased world trade and increased competition. Further, the rise of India and China as economic powerhouses has increased global competition.

One important pressure that businesses in a global market must contend with is the cost of labor, which varies widely among countries. In general, labor costs are higher in developed countries like the United States and Japan than in developing countries such as China and El Salvador. Also, developed countries usually offer greater benefits, such as healthcare, to employees, driving the cost of doing business even higher. Therefore, many labor-intensive industries have moved their operations to countries with low labor costs. IT has made such moves much easier to implement.

However, manufacturing overseas is no longer the bargain it once was, and manufacturing in the United States is no longer as expensive. For example, manufacturing wages in China doubled between 2002 and 2008, and the value of China's currency has steadily risen.

THE CHANGING NATURE OF THE WORKFORCE. The workforce, particularly in developed countries, is becoming more diversified. Increasing numbers of women, single parents, minorities, and persons with disabilities are now employed in all types of positions. IT is easing the integration of these employees into the traditional workforce. IT is also enabling people to work from home, which can be a major benefit for parents with young children and for people confronted with mobility and/or transportation issues.

POWERFUL CUSTOMERS. Consumer sophistication and expectations increase as customers become more knowledgeable about the products and services they acquire. Customers

TABLE 2.1 Friedman's Ten Flatteners

- **Fall of the Berlin Wall on November 9, 1989**
  - Shifted the world toward free-market economies and away from centrally planned economies
  - Led to the emergence of the European Union and early thinking about the world as a single, global market

- **Netscape goes public on August 9, 1995**
  - Popularized the Internet and the World Wide Web

- **Development of work-flow software**
  - Enabled computer applications to work with one another without human intervention
  - Enabled faster, closer collaboration and coordination among employees, regardless of their location

- **Uploading**
  - Empowered all Internet users to create content and put it on the Web
  - Led the transition from a passive approach to content to an active, participatory, collaborative approach

- **Outsourcing**
  - Contracting with an outside company to perform a specific function that your company was doing itself and then integrating that work back into your operation (e.g., moving customer call centers to India)

- **Offshoring**
  - Relocating an entire operation, or certain tasks, to another country (e.g., moving an entire manufacturing operation to China)

- **Supply chaining**
  - Technological revolution that led to the creation of networks comprised of companies, their suppliers, and their customers, all of which could collaborate and share information for increased efficiency

- **Insourcing**
  - Delegating operations or jobs within a business to another company that specializes in those operations (e.g., Dell hires FedEx to "take over" Dell's logistics process)

- **Informing**
  - The ability to search for information, best illustrated by search engines

- **The Steroids**
  - Technologies that amplify the other flatteners
  - Enable all forms of computing and collaboration to be digital, mobile, and personal

can use the Internet to find detailed information about products and services, to compare prices, and to purchase items at electronic auctions.

Organizations recognize the importance of customers and have increased their efforts to acquire and retain them. Modern firms strive to learn as much as possible about their customers to better anticipate and address their needs. This process, called *customer intimacy*, is an important component of *customer relationship management* (CRM), an organizationwide effort toward maximizing the customer experience. You will learn about CRM in Chapter 12.

Technology Pressures. The second category of business pressures consists of those pressures related to technology. Two major technology-related pressures are technological innovation and information overload.

TECHNOLOGICAL INNOVATION AND OBSOLESCENCE. New and improved technologies rapidly create or support substitutes for products, alternative service options, and superb quality, as you see in IT's About Business 2.1. As a result, today's state-of-the-art products may be obsolete tomorrow. For example, how fast are new versions of your smartphone being released? How quickly are electronic versions of books, magazines, and newspapers

T'S ABOUT BUSINESS 2.1

Schneider National Simulates Business Operations

Schneider National (www.schneider.com), a $3.7 billion trucking company, is one of the United States's largest freight haulers. The company, headquartered in Green Bay, Wisconsin, employs 13,000 drivers, and operates 10,000 trucks and 33,000 trailers.

With diesel fuel priced around $4 per gallon, Schneider has a strong incentive to send its drivers by the most efficient routes. Designing optimal routes is an incredibly complex problem for a multitude of reasons.

For instance, Schneider drivers can be on the road for between 4 days and 3 weeks at a time, and they need to be back to their homes by a certain date. Government regulations also require that drivers take a certain number of breaks. To further complicate matters, the customers that Schneider serves are only open to receive deliveries during certain hours. So, the company needs to avoid situations where, for example, a driver who lives in Alabama ends his journey in Minnesota. If Schneider does not have any freight for this hypothetical driver to carry on his way home, he would have to drive himself home in an empty truck. This is an expensive waste of truck capacity.

In the past, Schneider has tried to solve the route scheduling problem via pilot projects. The company would select a group of 20 to 200 drivers, have them drive new routes, and test the results. These pilot projects were very expensive and the results were often ambiguous. Often the results gained from a sample of 20 drivers would not "scale up" to the entire company. Further, when Schneider needed to run another experiment to verify its results, its analysts had to run a new pilot project, thereby incurring more costs.

Therefore, Schneider decided to invest in a companywide "tactical planning simulator" that would use software algorithms to mimic the decision making

of human dispatchers across the company. Schneider needed a model that could examine in detail the random variables that affect the efficiency of their thousands of drivers over long periods.

The simulator works by pretending it is assigning freight and gathering orders based on scenarios it is given by Schneider analysts. An example of a given scenario might be adding more drivers in Chicago, having a large customer change the location of its distribution center, or adding an hour in mandated break time for drivers. The simulation produces simulations for the three coming weeks in order to approximate the value of having trucks and drivers in certain locations at certain times. The simulator then runs backward in time for those 3 weeks, checking its results. The simulator does this continually, until it reaches an optimal solution to the scenario. For each 3-week run, the software makes hundreds of thousands of decisions.

Schneider estimates that the simulator has saved the company tens of millions of dollars. For instance, at one point a customer wanted to restrict the number of hours in which Schneider could drop off goods. Schneider ran the problem on its simulator and demonstrated to the customer that limiting the number of hours would cost $600,000 more per year. The customer decided not to limit its hours.

Jetta Productions/Getty Images, Inc.

Another way that the simulator helps Schneider save money is by helping them retain their employees. Drivers frequently burn out and leave the company, but Schneider uses the simulator to determine how many jobs to offer and where to hire drivers.

Sources: Compiled from W. Powell, *Approximate Dynamic Programming*, second edition, John Wiley & Sons, September 27, 2011; H. Coster, "Calculus for Truckers," *Forbes*, September 12, 2011; "Powell Lab Algorithms Help Schneider National Save Millions," *Princeton School of Engineering and Applied Science*, August 26, 2011; "Schneider Streamlines Shipping with Award-Winning Simulator," *Material Handling & Logistics*, August 23, 2010; H. Simao et al., "Approximate Dynamic Programming Captures Fleet Operations for Schneider National, *Interfaces*, July 21, 2010; www.schneider.com, accessed February 21, 2012.

Questions

1. What are potential disadvantages of using the simulator? Provide specific examples to support your answer.

2. Provide examples of how the simulator helps Schneider gain competitive advantage in the trucking industry.

3. Look ahead in this chapter to the discussion of five strategies for competitive advantage. Which strategy (or strategies) does the simulator help Schneider address? Provide examples to support your answer.

---

replacing traditional hard-copy versions? These changes force businesses to keep up with consumer demands.

Consider the Apple iPad (www.apple.com/ipad). Apple released the first iPad in April 2010 and sold 3 million of the devices in 80 days. Rather than taking time to enjoy its success, Apple made its iPad2 available for sale on March 11, 2011, only 11 months later. Apple then released the iPad3 in March 2012.

INFORMATION OVERLOAD. The amount of information available on the Internet doubles approximately every year, and much of it is free. The Internet and other telecommunications networks are bringing a flood of information to managers. To make decisions effectively and efficiently, managers must be able to access, navigate, and utilize these vast stores of data, information, and knowledge. Information technologies, such as search engines (discussed in Chapter 4) and data mining (discussed in Chapter 5), provide valuable support in these efforts.

Societal/Political/Legal Pressures. The third category of business pressures includes social responsibility, government regulation/deregulation, spending for social programs, spending to protect against terrorism, and ethics. This section will explain how all of these elements affect modern businesses.

SOCIAL RESPONSIBILITY. Social issues that affect businesses and individuals range from the state of the physical environment, to company and individual philanthropy, to education. Some corporations and individuals are willing to spend time and/or money to address various social problems. These efforts are known as organizational **social responsibility** or **individual social responsibility**.

One critical social problem is the state of the physical environment. A growing IT initiative, called *green IT*, is addressing some of the most pressing environmental concerns. IT is instrumental in organizational efforts to "go green" in at least four areas.

- Facilities design and management. Organizations are creating more sustainable work environments. Many organizations are pursuing Leadership in Energy and Environmental Design (LEED) certification from the U.S. Green Building Council, a nonprofit group that promotes the construction of environmentally friendly buildings. One impact of this development is that IT professionals are expected to help create green facilities. Consequently, IT personnel have to consider how their computing

Studio Frank/Image Source Limited

In-store comparison shopping is just one way customers are becoming more powerful.

© Maria R.T. Deseo/PhotoEdit.

Although this may be familiar, multitasking will become more complicated when your job depends on it.

decisions influences sustainable design and, in turn, how the building's design influences the IT infrastructure. Green design influences the type of IT devices used and the locations where IT clusters personal computers, people, and servers. IT must become familiar with the metering and monitoring systems used in green buildings and the requirements of buildings' computerized infrastructure.

- Carbon management. As companies try to reduce their carbon footprints, they are turning to IT executives to develop the systems needed to monitor carbon throughout the organization and its supply chain, which can be global in scope. Therefore, IT employees need to become knowledgeable about embedded carbon and how to measure it in the company's products and processes.

  Consider, for example, application development. IT managers will have to ask whether an application will require new hardware to test and run, or how much additional server space (and thus energy) it will require—and how these issues translate into carbon output.

- International and U.S. state environmental laws. IT executives must deal with state laws and international regulations that impact everything from the IT products they buy, to how they dispose of them, to their company's carbon footprint. IT managers must understand environmental compliance issues so they can ask their vendors the right questions regarding specific state, national, and international environmental standards before buying, deploying, and disposing of equipment.

- Energy management. IT executives must understand their entire organization's energy needs for several reasons. First, energy management systems are becoming increasingly sophisticated. To employ these systems effectively and make intelligent consumption decisions, IT personnel must understand the system's complex monitors and sensors. Second, utilities are offering incentives to commercial customers who take certain energy conservation steps, such as enabling computer power management across their networks and designing energy-efficient data centers. Finally, utilities are offering variable rate incentives depending on when companies use electricity and how much they use. These issues require IT systems that can regulate electricity use.

Continuing our discussion of social responsibility, social problems all over the world may be addressed through corporate and individual philanthropy. In some cases, questions arise as to what percentage of contributions actually goes to the intended causes and recipients and what percentage goes to the charity's overhead. Another problem that concerns contributors is that they often exert little influence over the selection of projects their contributions will support. The Internet can help address these concerns and facilitate generosity and connection. Consider the following examples:

- PatientsLikeMe (www.patientslikeme.com), or any of the thousands of message boards dedicated to infertility, cancer, and various other ailments. People use these sites and message boards to obtain information about life-and-death decisions based on volunteered information, while also receiving much-needed emotional support from strangers.

- *GiftFlow* (www.giftflow.org): GiftFlow is a virtual community where you can obtain things you need for free and find people who need the "stuff" you have to give away. GiftFlow connects community organizations, businesses, governments, and neighbors in a network of reciprocity.

- *OurGoods* (www.ourgoods.org): OurGoods enables creative people to help one another produce independent projects. More work is accomplished in networks of shared respect and shared resources than in competitive isolation.

- *Sparked* (www.sparked.com): Sparked is an online "microvolunteering" Web site where large and small organizations list opportunities for people looking to volunteer.

- *Thredup* (www.thredup.com): Thredup is a Web site where parents trade children's clothing and toys.

- *Collaborative Consumption* (www.collaborativeconsumption.com): This Web site is an online hub for discussions about the growing business of sharing, resale, reuse, and barter (with many links to Web sites engaged in these practices).

- *Kiva* (www.kiva.org): Kiva is a nonprofit enterprise that provides a link between lenders in developed countries and entrepreneurs in developing countries. Users pledge interest-free loans rather than tax-deductible donations. Kiva directs 100 percent of the loans to borrowers.

- *DonorsChoose* (www.donorschoose.org): DonorsChoose is an education-oriented Web site that functions entirely within the United States. Users make donations rather than loans. The Web site addresses the huge problem of underfunded public schools.

Still another social problem that affects modern business is the digital divide. The **digital divide** refers to the wide gap between those who have access to information and communications technology and those who do not. This gap exists both within and among countries. IT's About Business 2.2 provides an example of how modern information technologies are enabling the Surui people of the Amazon region in Brazil to bridge the digital divide.

's ABOUT BUSINESS 2.2

The Surui Tribe of the Amazon

 Chief Almir of the Surui tribe of the Brazilian Amazon is using Google to help his tribe maintain its traditional way of life. In 1969, the Surui had their first contact with outsiders, who brought with them disease, violence, and death. Then, loggers arrived and laid waste to the Surui's homeland.

Chief Almir took a leadership role in his tribe at 17 and became the tribe's first member to attend college. In 2006, he fled briefly to the United States when loggers put a bounty on his head. He stumbled upon Google Earth in an Internet café in 2007.

Chief Almir decided that his tribe's survival depended on outreach. His partnership with Google has enabled the tribe to create an online "cultural map" of the Surui with stories from the tribe's elders that are uploaded onto YouTube, as well as a geographical map of their territory created with GPS-equipped smartphones from Google. In 2009, Google employees taught the Surui to use cell phones to record illegal logging on their land.

© David Gunn/iStockphoto

Tribal members can now take photos and videos that are geo-tagged and immediately upload the images to Google Earth. Law enforcement officials can no longer claim ignorance of the problem when evidence of the deforestation is publicly available online. Satellite pictures show that the Surui use of technology is highly effective as the Surui territory is the only remaining intact piece of rainforest in the area.

Chief Almir views his partnership with Google not only as a way to sustain his traditions and his land, but also as an opportunity to teach others about the Surui. Furthermore, the tribe has mounted an ambitious reforestation plan to combat the aggressive logging that is destroying the Surui's 600,000 acres of land.

Smartphones have enabled the tribe to document cleared areas in the forest and form planting plans. The Surui plan to plant 100 million saplings in the next decade. They hope to raise millions of dollars through a United Nations program that gives carbon credits, which can be traded for cash, to countries and tribes that maintain their forests. The money would fund new homes, a hospital, and a school. The Surui have created a word for Google in their language: *ragogmakann*, meaning "the messenger."

Sources: Compiled from "The Most Creative People in Business 2011," *FastCompany*, June, 2011; S. Zwick, "Brazil's Surui Establish First Indigenous Carbon Fund," *Ecosystem Marketplace*, December 3, 2010; R. Butler, "Brazilian Tribe Owns Carbon Rights to Amazon Rainforest Land," *Mongabay.com*, December 9, 2009; R. Butler, "Big REDD," *Washington Monthly*, September 7, 2009; R. Butler, "Amazon Conservation Team Puts Indians on Google Earth to Save the Amazon," *Mongabay.com*, November 14, 2006.

Questions

1. Describe the benefits that all of us gain from the Surui's use of IT.

2. Provide specific examples of how the Surui could make further use of IT to improve their lives.

Many government and international organizations are trying to close the digital divide. As technologies develop and become less expensive, the speed at which the gap can be closed will accelerate.

A well-known project is the One Laptop per Child (OLPC) project (http://one.laptop.org). OLPC is a nonprofit association dedicated to research to develop a very inexpensive laptop—a technology that aims to revolutionize how the world can educate its children.

The first generation of inexpensive laptops appeared in 2007 with a price of $188, which was too high. The second generation of the laptop was scrapped because the price remained too high. The next generation of inexpensive laptops will be a touchscreen tablet computer for schoolchildren in the developing world that uses less power than a light bulb and is unbreakable, waterproof, and one-half the thickness of an iPhone. This computer will be a single sheet of plastic and have a projected price of $75.

COMPLIANCE WITH GOVERNMENT REGULATIONS. Another major source of business pressures is government regulations regarding health, safety, environmental protection, and equal opportunity. Businesses tend to view government regulations as expensive constraints on their activities. In general, government deregulation intensifies competition.

In the wake of 9/11 and numerous corporate scandals, the U.S. government passed many new laws, including the Sarbanes-Oxley Act, the USA PATRIOT Act, the Gramm-Leach-Bliley Act, and the Health Insurance Portability and Accountability Act (HIPAA). Organizations must be in compliance with the regulations contained in these statutes. The process of becoming and remaining compliant is expensive and time consuming. In almost all cases, organizations rely on IT support to provide the necessary controls and information for compliance.

PROTECTION AGAINST TERRORIST ATTACKS. Since September 11, 2001, organizations have been under increased pressure to protect themselves against terrorist attacks. In addition, employees who are in the military reserves have been called up for active duty, creating personnel problems. IT can help protect businesses by providing security systems and possibly identifying patterns of behavior associated with terrorist activities, including cyberattacks (discussed in Chapter 7). See Chapter Closing Case 1 for a look at a software tool developed to combat terrorism.

An example of protection against terrorism is the Department of Homeland Security's US-VISIT program. US-VISIT is a network of biometric-screening systems, such as fingerprint and ocular (eye) scanners, that ties into government databases and watch lists to check the identities of millions of people entering the United States. The system is now operational in more than 300 locations, including major international ports of entry by air, sea, and land.

ETHICAL ISSUES. Ethics relates to general standards of right and wrong. Information ethics relates specifically to standards of right and wrong in information-processing practices. Ethical issues are very important because, if handled poorly, they can damage an organization's image and destroy its employees' morale. The use of IT raises many ethical issues, ranging from monitoring e-mail to invading the privacy of millions of customers whose data are stored in private and public databases. (Chapter 6 covers ethical issues in detail.)

Clearly, then, the pressures on organizations are increasing and organizations must be prepared to take responsive actions if they are to succeed. You will learn about these organizational responses in the next section.

Organizational Responses

Organizations are responding to the various pressures just discussed by implementing IT such as strategic systems, customer focus, make-to-order and mass customization, and e-business. This section explores each of these responses.

Strategic Systems. Strategic systems provide organizations with advantages that enable them to increase their market share and/or profits, to better negotiate with suppliers, and to prevent competitors from entering their markets. As an example, the IT department at Procter & Gamble (P&G; www.pg.com) developed a virtualized environment that the company uses for product design work, product placement research, and consumer feedback studies. P&G utilizes virtual reality models to test design ideas for the next breakthroughs in products such as diapers and cosmetics. Within these "cyberworlds," P&G can rapidly test product performance as well as consumer responses to various kinds of ingredient and packaging choices. Consider how the organizations in IT's About Business 2.3 rely on strategic information systems to carry out their missions more effectively. Pay particular attention to how a strategic information system in one group of organizations can actually harm another group of organizations (see Small Theaters May Go Dark).

IT'S ABOUT BUSINESS 2.3

Two Strategic Information Systems

Sustainability for Hilton Worldwide

Hilton Worldwide is the first major multibrand hospitality company to make sustainability measurement a brand standard. Company management decided to require all of its 3,750 properties to implement LightStay, Hilton's sustainability measurement system, by December 2011.

The LightStay system analyzes performance across 200 operational practices, such as housekeeping, paper-product usage, food waste, chemical storage, air quality, and transportation. LightStay also provides a "meeting impact calculator" that calculates the sustainability impact of any meeting or conference held at any Hilton property. Finally, LightStay also allows Hilton hotels to track sustainability projects, share best practices, and communicate with one another through a dashboard.

Since the introduction of LightStay, Hilton has continuously improved its sustainability and economic performance and has saved more than $74 million in utility costs as a result of the following reductions:

- 6.6% reduction in energy use
- 7.8% reduction in carbon output
- 19% reduction in waste output
- 3.8% reduction in water use

Small Theaters May Go Dark

A strategic information system in one industry may not benefit another industry. In fact, some strategic information systems may have the effect of damaging businesses that cannot keep up.

For the past decade, Hollywood's largest studios have been working on a new production standard for digital motion pictures that could save them $1 billion annually in printmaking fees and shipping costs. Movies in this new format are shipped on hard drives that can hold hundreds of gigabytes of data and are connected to extremely high-definition projectors. To unlock a movie, a distributor sends the theater a code that controls where, when, and how long the theater can play the particular movie.

Unfortunately, many small theater owners cannot afford the expensive new projectors and other equipment that major studios want them to buy. The cost for each theater to play movies in this format is $65,000 to $70,000. Small theater owners note that they would be spending this additional money without incurring any additional revenue. That is, they feel that they cannot pass the cost along to their customers in the form of increased ticket prices.

To induce theaters to purchase the new equipment, celluloid prints (actual hard-copy film) of new movies from major studios will no longer be available in the United States by the end of 2013, according to John Fithian, president of the National Association of Theater Owners.

The largest motion picture chains—Regal Entertainment, AMC Entertainment, and Cinemark Theaters, which account for about half of the $10.2 billion annual revenue pulled in by the U.S. box office—expect to complete the conversion by early 2013. However, Fithian predicts that the United States will lose several thousand screens in small theaters.

Sources: Compiled from N. Leiber, "For Small Theaters, the Digital Future Is Dark," *Bloomberg BusinessWeek*, February 20–26, 2012; "Hilton Worldwide Quantifies Product Sustainability for Global Procurement Operations," *IBM Customer Success Case Study*, January 30, 2012; J. Bruner, "River of Information," *Forbes*, November 7, 2011; G. Hasek, "Hilton LightStay Program Cuts Hotel Energy Use by 6.6%, Saves $74M," *Greenbiz.com*, October 25, 2011; M. Mills, "Entertainment's Tech Boom: The Internet Has Been Assimilated," *Forbes*, May 10, 2011; www.ibm.com, www.hiltonworldwide.com, accessed February 22, 2012.

Questions

1. How does the LightStay system contribute to Hilton's sustainability efforts?

2. Is "going digital" in motion picture production a strategic information system for the motion picture industry? Why or why not? Provide examples to support your answer.

3. Is "going digital" in the motion picture industry a strategic information system for the National Association for Theater Owners? Why or why not? Provide examples to support your answer.

4. Given your answers to Questions 3 and 4 above, what should the motion picture industry do?

5. Can you think of another example where a strategic information system in one company (or industry) can harm another company (or industry)?

Customer Focus. Organizational attempts to provide superb customer service can make the difference between attracting and keeping customers and losing them to competitors. Numerous IT tools and business processes have been designed to keep customers happy. Consider Amazon, for example. When you visit Amazon's Web site anytime after your first visit, the site welcomes you back by name and presents you with information on books that you might like, based on your previous purchases. In another example, Dell guides you through the process of buying a computer by providing information and choices that help you make an informed buying decision.

Make-to-Order and Mass Customization. **Make-to-order** is a strategy of producing customized (made to individual specifications) products and services. The business problem is how to manufacture customized goods efficiently and at a reasonably low cost. Part of the solution is to change manufacturing processes from mass production to mass customization. In mass production, a company produces a large quantity of identical items. In **mass customization**, it also produces a large quantity of items, but it customizes them to fit the needs and preferences of individual customers. Mass customization is simply an attempt to perform make-to-order on a large scale. Body-metrics (www.bodymetrics.com) is an excellent example of mass customization with men's and women's jeans.

EXAMPLE

Well-fitting jeans are notoriously difficult to find. To address this problem, Bodymetrics has partnered with PrimeSense to develop a three-dimensional body-mapping product. The product uses PrimeSense 3D sensors to scan the shapes and curves that make each body unique. The scanner produces a digital replica of each user's size and shape. Customers can try on clothes virtually at a store or in their homes. This scan is then used to provide three services: made-to-measure jeans, body-shape jeans, and online virtual try-on.

With made-to-measure jeans, the scan is used to create a pattern for the jeans, which are hand tailored to the exact lines and contours of the customer's body. The jeans are ready in 3 to 6 weeks, at which time the customer has a final fitting with a Bodymetrics tailor.

Based on its experience with made-to-measure jeans, Bodymetrics has identified three body shapes: straight, semi-curvy, and curvy. Body-shape jeans are specifically designed to fit these different body shapes. After customers are scanned, a Bodymetrics jeans expert helps them determine their body shapes. Customers can then instantly purchase jeans matching their body shapes off the rack in the store.

The online virtual try-on allows customers who have been scanned to try on jeans virtually on their own bodies without physically trying on jeans in a dressing room. The service creates an *avatar* (a three-dimensional graphical representation), which has an amazing resemblance to the customer. Then, the customer can pick various styles of jeans and "virtually see" what the jeans look like on her or his avatar.

Sources: Compiled from S. Laird, "Clothes Shopping With Bodymetrics Lets You Try It On for Virtual Size," *Mashable*, January 9, 2012; "The First Time I Had a Bodymetrics Scan," http://howfayeseesit.wordpress.com, March 23, 2011; L. Talbot, "Bodymetrics: What's Your Jean Shape?" http://lisatalbot.blogspot.com, February 2, 2011; Asmita, "Custom-Fit Jeans with Bodymetrics," www.styleguru.com, January 18, 2007 (*Note:* StyleGuru is a promotional blog.); R. Young, "Turning Tailoring Over to a Computer," *International Herald Tribune*, January 15, 2007; www.bodymetrics.com, www.primesense.com, accessed February 21, 2012.

E-Business and E-Commerce. Doing business electronically is an essential strategy for companies that are competing in today's business environment. **Electronic commerce** (EC or e-commerce) describes the process of buying, selling, transferring, or exchanging products, services, or information via computer networks, including the Internet. **E-business** is a somewhat broader concept. In addition to the buying and selling of goods and services, e-business also refers to servicing customers, collaborating with business partners, and performing electronic transactions within an organization. (Chapter 9 focuses extensively on this topic. In addition, e-commerce applications appear throughout the book.)

You now have a general overview of the pressures that affect companies in today's business environment and the responses that organizations choose to manage these pressures. To plan for the most effective responses, companies formulate strategies. In the new digital economy, these strategies rely heavily on IT, especially strategic information systems. These topics are examined in the next section.

- BEFORE *YOU GO ON . . .*

1. What are the characteristics of the modern business environment?

2. Discuss some of the pressures that characterize the modern global business environment.

3. Identify some of the organizational responses to these pressures. Are any of these responses specific to a particular pressure? If so, which ones?

Apply the Concept 2.1

Background This chapter has described many theories and pointed out that information overload is a very real problem today. The amount of data we can now collect is amazing. Did you know that even your Facebook posts and tweets are data? In fact, the Library of Congress archives Twitter posts after they are 6 months old! What about organizational data? Soon mobile commerce will allow companies to store GPS location, demographic data, and purchase data to create customer profiles that will provide tons of digital data. Businesses will be able to use this in ways that we cannot even imagine today. Companies like IBM, Oracle, SAP, and SAS are leading the way into this world by designing software to help manage this data.

Activity Go to YouTube and search for "IBM Why Data Matters." Look through the list for the following three videos. You may also go to http://www.wiley.com/go/rainer/applytheconcept and click on the links provided for Apply the Concept 2.1.

- Why Data Matters: Context Reveals Answers
- Why Data Matters: Age of Analytics
- Why Data Matters: Extracting Insights, Making Better Decisions

Deliverable

As a consumer, how do you feel about your own privacy given that businesses collect massive amounts of data on your spending habits? How much is too much? At what point would you like to disconnect? Could you? Do you think that people at large have become too dependent on data? Could businesses go back to operating with less knowledge?

Imagine that you were asked to provide a report about this issue to your congressman/congresswoman explaining the direction we are going and whether it is a good thing or not. Write this up in a short report and submit it to your professor.

Go back to http://www.wiley.com/go/rainer/applytheconcept and click on the U.S. Congress link if you want to actually send your letter!

Quiz questions are assignable in WileyPLUS, and available on the Book Companion Site at http://www.wiley.com/college/rainer.

RUBY'S CLUB | QUESTIONS

1. How could IT help Ruby's comply with legal requirements and social responsibilities surrounding the sales of alcohol?
2. Drinks and music never become obsolete, right? How could Ruby's lack of IT create the environment that makes them appear obsolete?
3. The sheer number of possibilities are creating "overload" for Ruben and Lisa before they ever even adopt any specific IT. How can technology be used to help them make a decision about the IT they choose to adopt?

2.2 Competitive Advantage and Strategic Information Systems

A *competitive strategy* is a statement that identifies a business's approach to compete, its goals, and the plans and policies that will be required to carry out those goals.[1] A strategy, in general, can apply to a desired outcome, such as gaining market share. A competitive

[1]Porter, M. E. (1985). *Competitive Advantage.* New York: Free Press.

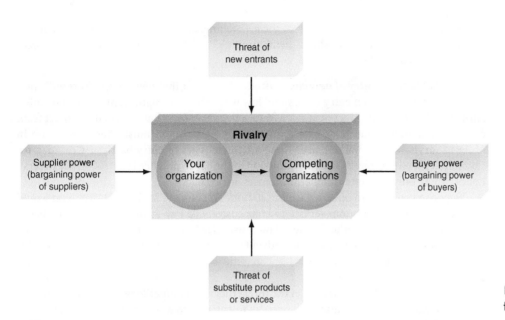

Figure 2.2 Porter's competitive forces model.

strategy focuses on achieving a desired outcome when competitors want to prevent you from reaching your goal. Therefore, when you create a competitive strategy, you must plan your own moves, but you must also anticipate and counter your competitors' moves.

Through its competitive strategy, an organization seeks a competitive advantage in an industry. That is, it seeks to outperform its competitors in a critical measure such as cost, quality, and time-to-market. Competitive advantage helps a company function profitably with a market and generate larger-than-average profits.

Competitive advantage is increasingly important in today's business environment, as you will note throughout the book. In general, the *core business* of companies has remained the same. That is, information technologies simply offer tools that can enhance an organization's success through its traditional sources of competitive advantage, such as low cost, excellent customer service, and superior supply chain management. **Strategic information systems** (SISs) provide a competitive advantage by helping an organization to implement its strategic goals and to improve its performance and productivity. Any information system that helps an organization gain a competitive advantage or reduce a competitive disadvantage qualifies as a SIS.

Porter's Competitive Forces Model

The best-known framework for analyzing competitiveness is Michael Porter's **competitive forces model**.[2] Companies use Porter's model to develop strategies to increase their competitive edge. Porter's model also demonstrates how IT can make a company more competitive.

Porter's model identifies five major forces that can endanger or enhance a company's position in a given industry. Figure 2.2 highlights these forces. Although the Web has changed the nature of competition, it has not changed Porter's five fundamental forces. In fact, what makes these forces so valuable as analytical tools is that they have not changed for centuries. Every competitive organization, no matter how large or small, or what business it is in, is driven by these forces. This observation applies even to organizations that you might not consider competitive, such as local governments. Although local governments are not-for-profit enterprises, they compete for businesses to locate in their districts, for funding from higher levels of government, for employees, and for many other things.

[2]Ibid.

Significantly, Porter concludes that the *overall* impact of the Web is to increase competition, which generally diminishes a firm's profitability.[3] Let's examine Porter's five forces and the ways that the Web influences them.

1. *The threat of entry of new competitors.* The threat that new competitors will enter your market is high when entry is easy and low when there are significant barriers to entry. An **entry barrier** is a product or service feature that customers have learned to expect from organizations in a certain industry. A competing organization must offer this feature in order to survive in the marketplace. There are many types of entry barriers. Consider, for example, legal requirements such as admission to the bar to practice law or a license to serve liquor, where only a certain number of licenses are available.

Suppose you want to open a gasoline station. To compete in that industry, you would have to offer pay-at-the-pump service to your customers. Pay-at-the-pump is an IT-based barrier to entering this market because you must offer it for free. The first gas station that offered this service gained first-move advantage and established barriers to entry. This advantage did not last, however, because competitors quickly offered the same service and thus overcame the entry barrier.

For most firms, the Web *increases* the threat that new competitors will enter the market because it sharply reduces traditional barriers to entry, such as the need for a sales force or a physical storefront. Today, competitors frequently need only to set up a Web site. This threat of increased competition is particularly acute in industries that perform an *intermediation role*, which is a link between buyers and sellers (for example, stock brokers and travel agents), as well as in industries where the primary product or service is digital (for example, the music industry). In addition, the geographical reach of the Web enables distant competitors to compete more directly with an existing firm.

In some cases the Web increases barriers to entry. This scenario occurs primarily when customers have come to expect a nontrivial capability from their suppliers. For example, the first company to offer Web-based package tracking gained a competitive advantage from that service. Competitors were forced to follow.

2. *The bargaining power of suppliers.* Supplier power is high when buyers have few choices from whom to buy and low when buyers have many choices. Therefore, organizations would rather have more potential suppliers so they will be in a stronger position to negotiate price, quality, and delivery terms.

The Internet's impact on suppliers is mixed. On the one hand, it enables buyers to find alternative suppliers and to compare prices more easily, thereby reducing the supplier's bargaining power. On the other hand, as companies use the Internet to integrate their supply chains, participating suppliers prosper by locking in customers.

3. *The bargaining power of customers (buyers).* Buyer power is high when buyers have many choices from whom to buy and low when buyers have few choices. For example, in the past, there were few locations where students could purchase textbooks (typically, one or two campus bookstores). In this situation, students had low buyer power. Today, the Web provides students with access to a multitude of potential suppliers as well as detailed information about textbooks. As a result, student buyer power has increased dramatically.

In contrast, *loyalty programs* reduce buyer power. As their name suggests, loyalty programs reward customers based on the amount of business they conduct with a particular organization (e.g., airlines, hotels, and rental car companies). IT enables companies to track the activities and accounts of millions of customers, thereby reducing buyer power. That is, customers who receive "perks" from loyalty programs are less likely to do business with competitors. (Loyalty programs are associated with customer relationship management, which you will study in Chapter 12.)

4. *The threat of substitute products or services.* If there are many alternatives to an organization's products or services, then the threat of substitutes is high. If there are few alternatives, then the threat is low. Today, new technologies create substitute products very rapidly. For example, customers today can purchase wireless telephones instead of

---

[3]Porter, M. E. (2001, March). "Strategy and the Internet," *Harvard Business Review*, pp. 62–78.

landline telephones, Internet music services instead of traditional CDs, and ethanol instead of gasoline in cars.

Information-based industries experience the greatest threat from substitutes. Any industry in which digitized information can replace material goods (e.g., music, books, and software) must view the Internet as a threat because the Internet can convey this information efficiently and at low cost and high quality.

Even when there are many substitutes for their products, however, companies can create a competitive advantage by increasing switching costs. *Switching costs* are the costs, in money and time, of a decision to buy elsewhere. For example, contracts with smart phone providers typically include a substantial penalty for switching to another provider until the term of the contract expires (quite often, two years). This switching cost is monetary.

As another example, when you buy products from Amazon, the company develops a profile of your shopping habits and recommends products targeted to your preferences. If you switch to another online vendor, it will take time for that company to develop a profile of your wants and needs. In this case, the switching cost involves time rather than money.

5. ***The rivalry among existing firms in the industry.*** The threat from rivalry is high when there is intense competition among many firms in an industry. The threat is low when the competition is among fewer firms and is not as intense.

In the past, proprietary information systems—systems that belong exclusively to a single organization—have provided strategic advantage to firms in highly competitive industries. Today, however, the visibility of Internet applications on the Web makes proprietary systems more difficult to keep secret. In simple terms, when a businessperson sees a competitor's new system online, he or she will rapidly match its features in order to remain competitive. The result is fewer differences among competitors, which leads to more intense competition in an industry.

To understand this concept, consider the highly competitive grocery industry, where Walmart, Kroger, Safeway, and other companies compete essentially on price. Some of these companies have IT-enabled loyalty programs in which customers receive discounts and the store gains valuable business intelligence on customers' buying preferences. Stores use this business intelligence in their marketing and promotional campaigns. (You will learn about business intelligence in Chapter 5.)

Grocery stores are also experimenting with wireless technologies such as radio-frequency identification (RFID, discussed in Chapter 10) to speed the checkout process, track customers through the store, and notify customers of discounts as they pass by certain products. Grocery companies also use IT to tightly integrate their supply chains for maximum efficiency and thus reduce prices for shoppers.

Competition also is being affected by the extremely low variable cost of digital products. That is, once a digital product has been developed, the cost of producing additional "units" approaches zero. Consider the music industry as an example. When artists record music, their songs are captured in digital format. Producing physical products, such as CDs or DVDs, with the songs on them for sale in music stores involves costs. The costs in a physical distribution channel are much higher than the costs involved in delivering the songs over the Internet in digital form.

In fact, in the future companies might give away some products for free. For example, some analysts predict that commissions for online stock trading will approach zero because investors can access the necessary information via the Internet to make their own decisions regarding buying and selling stocks. At that point, consumers will no longer need brokers to give them information that they can obtain themselves, virtually for free.

Porter's Value Chain Model

Organizations use the Porter competitive forces model to design general strategies. To identify specific activities in which they can use competitive strategies for greatest impact, they use Porter's **value chain model** (1985). The value chain model also identifies points where an organization can use IT to achieve competitive advantage (see Figure 2.3).

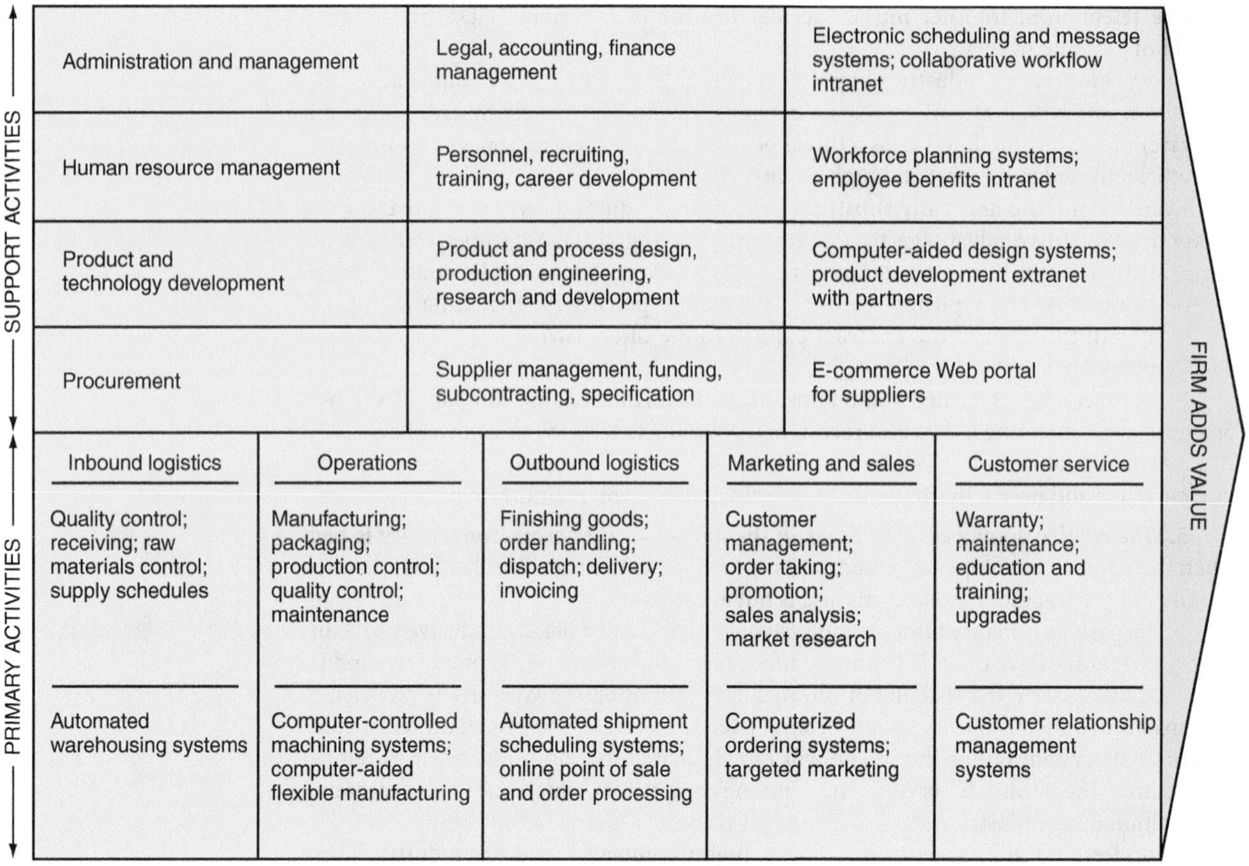

Figure 2.3 Porter's value chain model.

According to Porter's value chain model, the activities conducted in any organization can be divided into two categories: primary activities and support activities. **Primary activities** relate to the production and distribution of the firm's products and services. These activities create value for which customers are willing to pay. Next, you are going to learn about the value chain of a manufacturing company. Keep in mind that other types of firms, such as transportation, health care, education, and retail, have different value chains. The key point is that every organization has a value chain: a sequence of activities through which the organization's inputs, whatever they are, are transformed into more valuable outputs, whatever they are.

In a manufacturing company, for example, primary activities involve purchasing materials, processing the materials into products, and delivering the products to customers. Companies typically perform five primary activities:

Inbound logistics (inputs)

Operations (manufacturing and testing)

Outbound logistics (storage and distribution)

Marketing and sales

Services

Primary activities usually take place in a sequence from 1 to 5. As work progresses in the sequence, value is added to the product in each activity. Specifically, the following steps occur:

1. The incoming materials are processed (in receiving, storage, and so on) in activities called inbound logistics.

2. The materials are used in operations, where value is added by turning raw materials into products.

3. These products are prepared for delivery (packaging, storing, and shipping) in the outbound logistics activities.

4. Marketing and sales sell the products to customers, increasing product value by creating demand for the company's products.

5. Finally, the company performs after-sales service, such as warranty service or upgrade notification, for the customer, adding further value.

The primary activities are buttressed by **support activities**. Unlike primary activities, support activities do not add value directly to the firm's products or services. Rather, as their name suggests, they contribute to the firm's competitive advantage by supporting the primary activities. Support activities consist of the following:

1. The firm's infrastructure (accounting, finance, management)

2. Human resources management

3. Product and technology development (R & D)

4. Procurement

Each support activity can be applied to any or all of the primary activities. In addition, the support activities can also support one another.

A firm's value chain is part of a larger stream of activities, which Porter calls a value system. A **value system**, or an *industry value chain*, includes the suppliers that provide the inputs necessary to the firm along with their value chains. After the firm creates products, these products pass through the value chains of distributors (which also have their own value chains), all the way to the customers. All parts of these chains are included in the value system. To achieve and sustain a competitive advantage, and to support that advantage with information technologies, a firm must understand every component of this value system.

Strategies for Competitive Advantage

Organizations continually try to develop strategies to counter the five competitive forces identified by Porter. You will learn about five of those strategies here. Before we go into specifics, however, it is important to note that an organization's choice of strategy involves trade-offs. For example, a firm that concentrates only on cost leadership might not have the resources available for research and development, leaving the firm unable to innovate. As another example, a company that invests in customer happiness (customer-orientation strategy) will experience increased costs.

Companies must select a strategy and then stay with it, because a confused strategy cannot succeed. This selection, in turn, decides how a company will utilize its information systems. A new information system that can improve customer service but will increase costs slightly will be welcomed at a high-end retailer such as Nordstrom but not at a discount store like Walmart. You learn about the most commonly used strategies in the following paragraphs. Figure 2.4 provides an overview of these strategies.

1. *Cost leadership strategy.* Produce products and/or services at the lowest cost in the industry. An example is Walmart's automatic inventory replenishment system, which enables Walmart to reduce inventory storage requirements. As a result, Walmart stores use floor space only to sell products, and not to store them, thereby reducing inventory costs.

2. *Differentiation strategy.* Offer products, services, or product features that are different from those of your competitor. Southwest Airlines, for example, has differentiated itself as a low-cost, short-haul, express airline. This has proved to be a winning strategy for competing in the highly competitive airline industry. Also, Dell has differentiated itself in the personal computer market through its mass-customization strategy.

3. *Innovation strategy.* Introduce new products and services, add new features to existing products and services, or develop new ways to produce them. A classic example is the introduction of automated teller machines (ATMs) by Citibank. The convenience and cost-cutting features of this innovation gave Citibank a huge advantage over its competitors.

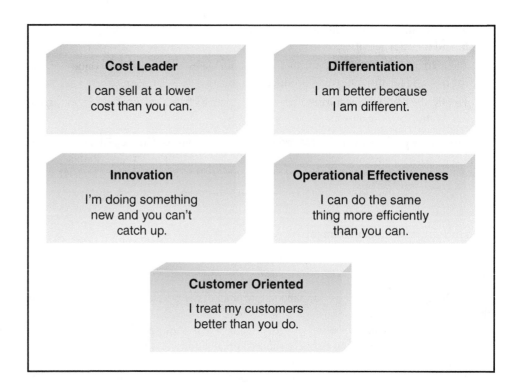

Figure 2.4 Strategies for Competitive Advantage.

Cost Leader

I can sell at a lower cost than you can.

Differentiation

I am better because I am different.

Innovation

I'm doing something new and you can't catch up.

Operational Effectiveness

I can do the same thing more efficiently than you can.

Customer Oriented

I treat my customers better than you do.

BEFORE YOU GO ON . . .

1. What are strategic information systems?
2. According to Porter, what are the five forces that could endanger a firm's position in its industry or marketplaces?
3. Describe Porter's value chain model. Differentiate Porter's competitive forces model and his value chain model.
4. What strategies can companies use to gain competitive advantage?

Like many innovative products, the ATM changed the nature of competition in the banking industry. Today an ATM is a competitive *necessity* for any bank.

4. *Operational effectiveness strategy.* Improve the manner in which internal **business processes** are executed so that a firm performs these activities better than its rivals. Such improvements increase quality, productivity, and employee and customer satisfaction while decreasing time to market.

5. *Customer-orientation strategy.* Concentrate on making customers happy. Web-based systems are particularly effective in this area because they can provide a personalized, one-to-one relationship with each customer.

Apply the Concept 2.2

Background This section has exposed you to Porter's five forces model. This demonstrates the ways that different things influence an organization. The threat of entry of new competitors, bargaining power of suppliers, bargaining power of customers, threat of substitute products or services, and rivalry among existing firms in the industry all have an impact on the outcome of the organization and its ultimate success. Based on this strategic model, there are five strategies presented for competitive advantage: cost leadership, differentiation, innovation, operational effectiveness, and customer orientation.

Walmart is a worldwide company that focuses on a cost-leadership strategy. Go back and review the ways Walmart uses the five forces (or controls them) so that they maintain their position as a worldwide cost leader. Although it may be somewhat easy to apply this to a large global company like Walmart, it is very difficult to think about these concepts as they would apply to small businesses. However, they are just as important to understand.

Activity Visit your favorite restaurant and ask to speak to the manager. In just a few questions, see if the manager has a grasp of the five forces model. Do not ask anything about

Porter, but ask about rivals, substitutes, bargaining power of customers, supplier power, etc. A good manager should be familiar with these concepts whether he or she uses the term *Porter's five forces* or not. Finally, ask what strategy the manager uses and see if you can classify it as a cost leadership, differentiation, innovation, operational effectiveness, and customer orientation strategy.

Deliverable

After your meal is over, write a summary for your instructor that answers the following questions: Does the manager understand all of the forces that impact the business? Are there some forces that the manager needs a better understanding of? Do you see any additional forces at play here? What did you determine the manager's strategy to be?

Quiz questions are assignable in WileyPLUS, and available on the Book Companion Site at http://www.wiley.com/college/rainer.

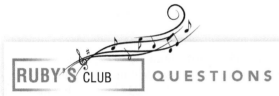

RUBY'S CLUB QUESTIONS

1. In a college town, how strong is the threat of substitute entertainment?
2. Ruben and Lisa's vision for Ruby's is to create a relaxing, community atmosphere. Which strategy do you think best suits their desire? Cost Leader, Differentiator, Innovator, Operational Effectiveness, or Customer Orientation?
3. Which is more powerful for Ruby's? The bargaining power of suppliers or the bargaining power of customers?

2.3 Business–IT Alignment

The "holy grail" of organizations is business–IT alignment, or strategic alignment. **Business–IT alignment** (which we will call "alignment") is the tight integration of the IT function with the strategy, mission, and goals of the organization. That is, the IT function directly supports the business objectives of the organization. There are six characteristics of excellent alignment:

- Organizations view IT as an engine of innovation that continually transforms the business, often creating new revenue streams.
- Organizations view their internal and external customers and their customer service function as supremely important.
- Organizations rotate business and IT professionals across departments and job functions.
- Organizations provide overarching goals that are completely clear to each IT and business employee.
- Organizations ensure that IT employees understand how the company makes (or loses) money.
- Organizations create a vibrant and inclusive company culture.

Unfortunately, many organizations fail to achieve this type of close alignment. In fact, according to a McKinsey & Company survey on IT strategy and spending, only 16 percent of the IT and business executives who participated agreed that their organization had adequate alignment between IT and the business.[4] Given the importance of alignment, why do so many organizations fail to implement this policy? The major reasons are these:

- Business managers and IT managers have different objectives.
- The business and IT departments are ignorant of each other's expertise.
- Communication is lacking.

Put simply, business executives know little about IT, and IT executives understand the technology but do not understand the real needs of the business.

─ BEFORE *YOU GO ON* . . . ─

1. What is alignment?
2. Give examples of alignment regarding student systems at your university. (*Hint:* What are the "business" goals of your university with regard to student registration, fee payment, grade posting, etc.?)

Apply the Concept 2.3

Background As this section has illustrated, corporate strategy and IT strategy must be tightly aligned. For example, if a manager determines that better inventory management is needed, he or she does not necessarily need to go looking for a new point-of-sale system. The manager needs to look for an inventory management system. If you operate in a manufacturing industry, you do not need to implement an electronic health records (EHR) system. Although those are simple examples when you are making these decisions, it becomes imperative that you are very familiar with corporate strategy and available technology to make sure they match up.

Visit http://www.wiley.com/go/rainer/applytheconcept and consider the many options Garmin offers for GPS devices. There are product options that are designed for pilots, automobiles, motorcycles, hikers, anglers (fishermen), and more. If this is all the same technology (GPS), then why can't the company just build one device and sell it to everyone? It is simply because the way the company needs the product to work and the information that the customer needs from it is different depending on what the customer plans to do with it. Although this may be a simple answer, it brings out an important point. Business applications of technology are much the same. Implemented IT must align with business need or it will only be "pretty" technology with no real purpose.

Activity Visit http://www.wiley.com/go/rainer/applytheconcept and click on the link provided for Apply the Concept 2.3. It will take you to SAP's Web site (you may also go directly to http://www.sap.com). SAP is a global enterprise resource planning (ERP) software provider. Have a look at the various industries and solutions that the company offers. Specifically, choose three industries to review. Look for similarities and differences.

Deliverable

Write a small summary for your instructor detailing how this single company provides so many solutions based on its single platform. Be sure to bring IT alignment into your thoughts for your summary.

Quiz questions are assignable in WileyPLUS, and available on the Book Companion Site at http://www.wiley.com/college/rainer.

[4]McKinsey & Company, "IT's Unmet Potential: McKinsey Global Survey Results," *McKinsey Quarterly*, www.mckinseyquarterly.com/ITs_unmet_potential_McKinsey_Global_Survey_Result_2277, accessed August 8, 2011.

1. It seems like Ruby's is in a good position to create Strategic IT alignment since the club can build its IT from the ground up to support its strategy. Do you think it is better to build from scratch, or is it better to have an existing system that you are just updating?

2. How do you think IT alignment could play a role in creating the desired atmosphere for Ruby's Club?

What's in IT for ME?

FOR ALL MAJORS

All of the functional areas of any organization are literally composed of a variety of business processes. Regardless of your major, you will be involved in a variety of business processes from your first day on the job. Some of these processes you will perform by yourself, some will involve only your group or department, and others will involve several (or all) of the organization's functional areas.

It is important for you to be able to visualize processes, understand the inputs and outputs of each process, and identify the "customer" of each process. These capabilities will enable you to make the organization's business processes more efficient and effective. This task generally involves incorporating IT in the process. It is also important for you to appreciate how each process fits into your organization's strategy.

All functional areas in any organization must work together in an integrated fashion in order for the firm to respond adequately to business pressures. These responses typically require each functional area to utilize a variety of information systems. In today's competitive global marketplace, the timeliness and accuracy of these responses is even more critical.

Closely following this discussion, all functional areas must work together for the organization to gain competitive advantage in its marketplace. Again, the functional areas use a variety of strategic information systems to achieve this goal.

You have seen why companies must be concerned with strategic advantage. However, this chapter is particularly important for you for several reasons. First, the business pressures you have learned about affect your organization, but they also affect you as an individual. Thus, it is critical that you understand how information systems can help you, and eventually your organizations, respond to these pressures.

In addition, achieving competitive advantage is essential for your organization's survival. In many cases, you, your team, and all your colleagues will be responsible for creating a competitive advantage. Therefore, having general knowledge about strategy and about how information systems impact the organization's strategy and competitive position will help you in your career.

You also need a basic knowledge of your organization's strategy, mission, and goals, as well as its business problems and how it makes (or loses) money. You now know how to analyze your organization's strategy and value chain, as well as the strategies and value chains of your competitors. You also have acquired a general knowledge of how IT contributes to organizational strategy. This knowledge will help you to do your job better, to be promoted more quickly, and to contribute significantly to the success of your organization.

SUMMARY

1. **Identify effective IT responses to different kinds of business pressures.**

   > *Market pressures:* An example of a market pressure is powerful customers. Customer relationship management systems are an effective IT response that helps companies achieve customer intimacy.

   > *Technology pressures:* An example of a technology pressure is information overload. Search engines and business intelligence applications enable managers to access, navigate, and utilize vast amounts of information.

   > *Societal/political/legal pressures:* An example of a societal/political/legal pressure is social responsibility, such as the state of the physical environment. Green IT is one response that is intended to improve the environment.

2. **Describe the strategies that organizations typically adopt to counter Porter's five competitive forces.**

   Porter's five competitive forces are

   The threat of entry of new competitors

   The bargaining power of suppliers

   The bargaining power of customers (buyers)

   The threat of substitute products or services

   The rivalry among existing firms in the industry

   There are five strategies that organizations typically use to combat Porter's five competitive forces and achieve a competitive advantage.

   > *Cost leadership strategy:* Produce products and/or services at the lowest cost in the industry.

   > *Differentiation strategy:* Offer different products, services, or product features.

   > *Innovation strategy:* Introduce new products and services, put new features in existing products and services, or develop new ways to produce them.

   > *Operational effectiveness strategy:* Improve the manner in which internal business processes are executed so that a firm performs similar activities better than its rivals.

   > *Customer-orientation strategy:* Concentrate on making customers happy.

   Keep in mind that organizations may use more than one strategy to combat each competitive force. For example, to raise barriers to entry for a competitor, an organization might adopt all five of these strategies to make it more difficult for a potential competitor to enter a market.

3. **Describe the characteristics of effective business-IT alignment.**

   Alignment is the tight integration of the IT function with the strategy, mission, and goals of the organization. There are six characteristics of effective alignment:

   > Organizations view IT as an engine of innovation that continually transforms the business.

   > Organizations view customers and customer service as supremely important.

   > Organizations rotate business and IT professionals across departments and job functions.

   > Organizations provide clear, overarching goals for all employees.

   > Organizations ensure that IT employees understand how the company makes (or loses) money.

   > Organizations create a vibrant and inclusive company culture.

>>> CHAPTER GLOSSARY

business environment The combination of social, legal, economic, physical, and political factors in which businesses conduct their operations.

business–IT alignment The tight integration of the IT function with the strategy, mission, and goals of the organization.

business processes Related activities that produce a product or a service of value to the organization, its business partners, and/or its customers.

competitive advantage An advantage over competitors in some measure such as cost, quality, or speed; leads to control of a market and to larger-than-average profits.

competitive forces model A business framework devised by Michael Porter that analyzes competitiveness by recognizing five major forces that could endanger a company's position.

digital divide The gap between those who have access to information and communications technology and those who do not.

e-business Buying and selling of goods and services as well as servicing customers, collaborating with business partners, and performing electronic transactions within an organization.

electronic commerce (EC or e-commerce) The process of buying, selling, transferring, or exchanging products, services, or information via computer networks, including the Internet.

entry barrier Product or service feature that customers expect from organizations in a certain industry; an organization trying to enter this market must provide this product or service at a minimum to be able to compete.

globalization The integration and interdependence of economic, social, cultural, and ecological facets of life, enabled by rapid advances in information technology.

individual social responsibility See **organizational social responsibility**.

make-to-order The strategy of producing customized products and services.

mass customization A production process in which items are produced in large quantities but are customized to fit the desires of each customer.

organizational social responsibility (also called individual social responsibility) Efforts by organizations to solve various social problems.

primary activities Business activities related to the production and distribution of the firm's products and services, thus creating value.

strategic information systems (SISs) Systems that help an organization gain a competitive advantage by supporting its strategic goals and/or increasing performance and productivity.

support activities Business activities that do not add value directly to a firm's product or service under consideration but support the primary activities that do add value.

value chain model Model that shows the primary activities that sequentially add value to the profit margin; also shows the support activities.

value system Includes the producers, suppliers, distributors, and buyers, all with their value chains.

>>> DISCUSSION QUESTIONS

1. Explain why IT is both a business pressure and an enabler of response activities that counter business pressures.

2. What does a flat world mean to you in your choice of a major? In your choice of a career? Will you have to be a lifelong learner? Why or why not?

3. What might the impact of a flat world be on your standard of living?

4. Is IT a strategic weapon or a survival tool? Discuss.

5. Why might it be difficult to justify a strategic information system?

6. Describe the five forces in Porter's competitive forces model and explain how the Internet has affected each one.

7. Describe Porter's value chain model. What is the relationship between the competitive forces model and the value chain model?

8. Discuss the idea that an information system by itself can rarely provide a sustainable competitive advantage.

>>> PROBLEM-SOLVING ACTIVITIES

1. Surf the Internet for information about the Department of Homeland Security. Examine the available information, and comment on the role of information technologies in the department.

2. Experience customization by designing your own shoes at www.nike.com, your car at www.jaguar.com, your CD at www.easternrecording.com, your business card at www.iprint.com, and your diamond ring at www.bluenile.com. Summarize your experiences.

3. Access www.go4customer.com. What does this company do and where is it located? Who are its customers? Which of Friedman's flatteners does this company fit? Provide examples of how a U.S. company would use its services.

4. Enter Walmart China (www.wal-martchina.com/english/index.htm). How does Walmart China differ from your local Walmart (consider products, prices, services, etc.)? Describe these differences.

5. Apply Porter's value chain model to Costco (www.costco.com). What is Costco's competitive strategy? Who are Costco's major competitors? Describe Costco's business model. Describe the tasks that Costco must accomplish for each primary value chain activity. How would Costco's information systems contribute to Costco's competitive strategy, given the nature of its business?

6. Apply Porter's value chain model to Dell (www.dell.com). What is Dell's competitive strategy? Who are Dell's major competitors? Describe Dell's business model. Describe the tasks that Dell must accomplish for each primary value chain activity. How would Dell's information systems contribute to Costco's competitive strategy, given the nature of its business?

7. The market for optical copiers is shrinking rapidly. It is expected that by 2010 as much as 90 percent of all duplicated documents will be done on computer printers. Can a company such as Xerox Corporation survive?

   a. Read about the problems and solutions of Xerox from 2000 to 2010 at www.fortune.com, www.findarticles.com, and www.google.com.

   b. Identify all the business pressures on Xerox.

   c. Find some of Xerox's response strategies (see www.xerox.com, www.yahoo.com, and www.google.com).

   d. Identify the role of IT as a contributor to the business technology pressures (e.g., obsolescence).

   e. Identify the role of IT as a facilitator of Xerox's critical response activities.

>>> COLLABORATION EXERCISE

Background

Imagine that you work for a company based in Atlanta, Georgia. Recent significant growth on the West Coast has made it necessary to open an office there. Because of the time lost in traveling across the country, it has been decided that Web meetings would suffice for 95% of the meetings that would take place.

You and a few colleagues from other departments are given the job of determining which platform would be the best to support your company's upcoming web meetings. There are many companies (Adobe Connect, Webex, Fuze Meeting, etc.) that offer Web-casting type technologies, but each vary in some ways. Obviously, they offer different price packages, but is the one with the lowest cost the best option?

Activity

Work with a team of classmates who are majoring in other areas to determine which online tool will serve the purposes your company has requested. Based on your experiences, what tools will be needed for meetings that each area may have? Are the meeting requirements from Accounting different from HR? What about Finance and Operations?

To accomplish your task, create a new Google document (this will require a Gmail account) and share it with your team members. Be sure that everyone is online at the same time and working together to determine which webcasting solution is the best to meet the needs of your company. Be creative in your document with the use of tables or colors or something to help your reader see how the solution you have chosen fits the criteria requested by your company.

Deliverable

You will now need to submit your work. At the bottom of your report that shows which webcasting solution you have chosen, write a short paragraph explaining how you think this particular online meeting program will support your company. Export the Google Document you created to a pdf and submit this however your professor has required. Be sure to include all the names of group members and the role that each played (which department they represented).

CLOSING **CASE 1** > A Tool to Combat Terrorism and Fight Crime

THE PROBLEM >>> In the months leading up to the terrorist attacks of September 11, 2001 the U.S. government had all the necessary clues to stop al Qaeda perpetrators. The perpetrators were from countries known to harbor terrorists, they entered the United States on temporary visas, they had trained to fly civilian airliners, and they purchased one-way airplane tickets on September 11.

Unfortunately for the workers in the World Trade Center, those clues were located in different databases across many government agencies. An organization like the CIA or FBI has thousands of different databases, each with its own data: financial records, DNA samples, voice and other sound samples, video clips, maps, floor plans, human intelligence reports from all over the world, and many other types of data. Integrating all that data into a coherent whole is extremely difficult. At that time, there was no tool available that enabled government analysts to integrate different types of data located in so many different places.

The origins of Palantir go back to PayPal. Because PayPal was so successful, it attracted criminals who used it to enable money laundering and fraud. By 2000, it was in financial trouble because the antifraud software tools of the time could not keep up with the criminal activity. Each time PayPal analysts caught onto one ploy, the perpetrators changed tactics.

<<< **THE IT SOLUTION**

To deal with these issues, PayPal's analysts built software that could view each transaction as a part of a pattern, rather than as just an entry in a database. This process enabled analysts to spot networks of suspicious accounts and discover patterns missed by the computers. PayPal was then able to freeze suspicious payments before they were processed. The software saved the company hundreds of millions of dollars.

After Ebay acquired PayPal in 2002, PayPal engineers decided to turn PayPal's fraud detection tool into a data analysis system that integrated pattern recognition, artificial intelligence software, and human skills. Palantir (www.palantir.com) was named for the "Seeing Stones" in the *Lord of the Rings* and was initially developed as a software tool employed by the U.S. intelligence community in the war on terrorism. Palantir technology essentially solves intelligence problems that allowed September 11 to take place. That is, Palantir helps law enforcement agencies spot patterns in the huge amounts of data they must analyze every day. Palantir software combs through all available databases, identifies related pieces of information, and integrates everything together in one place.

<<< **THE RESULTS**

Palantir has a customer list that includes the U.S. Department of Defense, the CIA, the FBI, the Army, the Marines, the Air Force, the police departments of New York and Los Angeles, and an increasing number of financial institutions with an interest in detecting bank fraud. Most of Palantir's government work remains classified, but information on some cases has leaked out. In April 2010, security researchers in Canada used Palantir software to crack a spy operation called the Shadow Network that had, among other things, broken into the Indian Defense Ministry and infiltrated the Dalai Lama's e-mail account. Palantir has also been used to unravel child abuse and abduction cases, to find suspects for the murder of a U.S. Immigration and Customs Enforcement special agent, and to uncover bombing networks in Syria, Afghanistan, and Pakistan.

In Afghanistan, the U.S. Special Operations Forces use Palantir to plan assaults. They type a village's name into the system and a map of the village appears, detailing the locations of all reported shooting skirmishes and improvised explosive device (IED) incidents. Using the timeline function, the soldiers can see where the most recent attacks occurred and plot their mission in the village accordingly.

Another good example of Palantir's usefulness comes from the U.S. Marines. They used to spend years gathering fingerprint and DNA evidence from IEDs and trying to match that data against a database of similar information collected from villagers. Usually, by the time they obtained any results, the bombers had disappeared. In contrast, field operatives can now upload fingerprint/DNA evidence from villagers into Palantir and instantly find matches from past attacks.

Wall Street banks are also making good use of Palantir. They are using Palantir technology to search their transaction databases for criminal fraud, trading insights, and even new ways to price mortgages. One of the world's largest banks uses Palantir software to break up a popular scam called BustOut. BustOut involves criminals who steal or purchase access to thousands of people's online identities, and then break into their bank and credit card accounts. After breaking in, the criminals spend weeks biding their time. Once someone on their radar purchases a plane ticket or leaves on holiday, they siphon money out of the accounts as fast as they can while the victim is in transit. The criminals hide their trails by anonymizing their computing activity and disabling alert systems in the bank and credit card accounts. When the bank identifies a small number of compromised accounts, it uses Palantir to uncover the network of thousands of other accounts that have not yet been tapped.

Using Palantir technology, the FBI can now instantly compile thorough dossiers on U.S. citizens. For example, they can integrate surveillance videos with credit card transactions, cell phone records, e-mails, air itineraries, and Web search information. Privacy advocates worry that Palantir will make the FBI and other government agencies even more intrusive consumers of personal data. Another event that caused concern for privacy advocates occurred when a Palantir engineer, exposed by the hacker collective Anonymous for participating in a plot to break into the personal computers of WikiLeaks supporters, was quietly rehired by Palantir after being placed on leave.

Palantir likes to emphasize that the company has developed very sophisticated privacy protection technology. Its software creates audit trails that detail who is privy to certain pieces of information and what they have done with the information. Palantir also has a permission system that ensures that agency workers using their software can access only the data allowed by their clearance level.

Sources: Compiled from A. Vance and B. Stone, "Palantir, the War on Terror's Secret Weapon," *Bloomberg BusinessWeek*, November 22, 2011; "Husky Names Palantir as Software and Consulting Partner," *Oil & Gas Financial Journal*, November 4, 2011; P. Gobry, "Secretive Spy Tech Company Palantir Technologies Raises Another $50 Million," *Business Insider*, May 11, 2011; D. Primack, "Analyze This: Palantir Worth More than $2 Billion," *CNN Money*, May 6, 2011; A. Greenberg, "Palantir Apologizes for WikiLeaks Attack Proposal, Cuts Ties with HB-Gary," *Forbes*, February 11, 2011; D. Storm, "Bank of America Using Three Intelligence Firms to Attack WikiLeaks," *Computerworld*, February 9, 2011; S. Gorman, "How Team of Geeks Cracked the Spy Trade," *Wall Street Journal*, September 4, 2009; www.palantir.com, accessed February 16, 2012.

Questions

1. Palantir states that it has privacy protection technology. Is this technology sufficient to protect against the misuse of Palantir technology? Why or why not? Provide specific examples to support your answer.
2. Describe possible applications of Palantir in the health care industry.

CLOSING **CASE 2** > The Information Technology Behind the World's Largest Airline

THE BUSINESS >>> PROBLEM

In 2011, United Airlines and Continental Airlines merged to form the world's largest airline. When buying Continental, United promised investors $1.2 billion in new revenue and cost savings.

Unfortunately, merging airlines is extremely difficult, largely because of the enormous number of processes that can be different between two airlines. Three major challenges that arose after the United/Continental merger were (1) integrating both airlines' flight information systems, (2) integrating both airlines' passenger information systems, and (3) reconciling both airlines' speedup-slowdown algorithms (an algorithm is a mathematical formula).

THE IT >>> SOLUTIONS

Flight Information Systems. Integrating United and Continental's flight information systems was a major strategic challenge. One worry was that data would become corrupted during the integration of two systems, resulting in the loss of vital flight information such as destinations, arrival times, flight numbers, or plane locations.

In August 2010, the integration team decided that United's existing flight information system, Unimatic, would be better able to handle the size of the merged airline's fleet than Continental's system. With that decision, a second team, composed of computer technicians and operations center managers, created an exhaustive list of tests and contingency plans to ensure that the data could be combined without causing a catastrophe. The airline's emergency operations center was fully staffed for the data cutover.

For the final test in late October 2011, the team had an empty Continental 737 fly from Houston to El Paso and back, just to test that the operations center could successfully track the flight. The team asked the pilots to pretend to have a mechanical problem and return to the gate. That event successfully appeared on the system. Then the team asked the pilots to change the flight number and reroute the plane to Austin to see if that event appeared in the system. It did. Encouraged by the dress rehearsal, the team set a date for the data integration.

On November 2, 2010, just after midnight when there would be relatively few flights in the air, technicians took Unimatic offline. They began inserting Continental's data into Unimatic. For the next hour, as the technicians updated and tested the software, the operations center tracked the airline's flights manually. That manual process would become impossible when air traffic rose to daytime levels, and the airline had plans for a mass cancellation the next morning if the system did not operate as planned.

At 1:23 AM, Unimatic went back online. There were a few small glitches—planes that had crossed the international dateline during the outage had an extra 24 hours added to their arrival time—but otherwise everything had worked.

The Passenger Information Systems. At the time of the merger, the passenger information system was divided between both airlines' databases. The integration team had to integrate not only the two databases, but also both airlines' Web sites and loyalty programs. The team decided to adopt Continental's passenger services system, called Shares.

Shares had several advantages over United's old passenger information system, Apollo. Shares was more flexible and easier to customize (for instance, it was capable of asking travelers whether they would like to purchase an upgrade or extra legroom). On the flipside, Shares was less intuitive to use than Apollo, and United veterans struggled to learn it. All the dry runs proceeded smoothly, and just after New Year's Day in 2011, United agents handled all of the Continental flights at Los Angeles International Airport without a problem.

Speedup-Slowdown Algorithms. One critical issue for airlines is communicating to pilots when they should speed up, slow down, and take a different route. Both airlines used a different algorithm to determine when a plane should go faster to make up for a late departureand when (to the eternal disappointment of its passengers) it should not go faster. Flying faster burns more fuel, and fuel is expensive. But, being late is also expensive. Customers who miss connections have to be rebooked and sometimes put up in hotels, flight crews have to be paid for the extra time, and ground crews sit idle when planes are late.

The speedup-slowdown algorithm analyzes all these factors (and more) and decides when the cost of being late outweighs the cost of speed. United and Continental's algorithms were different and did not always agree. The integration team spent many hours developing a new algorithm that combined the best features of each airline's original algorithm.

Solving these three integration problems (and there were many other problems) was vital in order for the merger to clear its biggest regulatory hurdle: getting a single operating certificate from the Federal Aviation Administration. By the time the certificate was awarded on November 30, 2011, more than 500 employees had spent 2 years working on the integration. Along the way, they reduced the 440 instructions manuals that governed everything taking place before, during, and after a flight down to 260.

<<< THE RESULTS

Sources: Compiled from D. Bennett, "Marriage at 30,000 Feet," *Forbes*, February 6–12, 2012; G. Karp, "United Continental Merger Still to be Sealed," *Star Tribune*, December 28, 2011; H. Martin, "Working Out 2,000 Details of a Merger," *Los Angeles Times*, December 3, 2011; B. Mutzabaugh, "Merger Milestone: United, Continental Now Single Airline to FAA," *USA Today*, November 30, 2011; "United, Continental Merge Frequent Flyer Programs," *Washington Post*, October 16, 2011; S. Carey and J. Nicas, "United Feeling Merger Pains," *Wall Street Journal*, September 27, 2011; I. Schneider, "Merged United-Continental Has Windows 7 to Consider," *InformationWeek*, May 4, 2010; www.united.com, accessed February 13, 2012.

Questions

1. Provide two specific examples of why it was so important for United and Continental to integrate their information systems to ensure the success of the merger.

2. Provide two specific examples of difficulties the companies experienced in integrating their information systems.

Ruben and Lisa seriously need to understand their market. To help them, search the Web in your local area for bars, clubs, theaters, restaurants, and athletic events, and then do an analysis of the types of entertainment Ruby's Club will compete against. Rate each as to whether their strategy is cost leadership, differentiation, innovation, operational effectiveness, or customer orientation. Make notes about how they communicate with their customers. Do they use Facebook? Twitter? Email? Traditional mail? Flyers on campus? How do they advertise themselves to their customers?

Finally, provide Ruben and Lisa (submit to your instructor) a competitive grid similar to the table below that is based on the information presented in this chapter. Use the competition in your local area as the basis for your discussion and provide suggestions on how to accomplish their vision (relaxing community atmosphere) by some combination of the strategies outlined in this chapter. Be sure to discuss IT alignment in your submission.

Competition Name	Cost Leader	Innovation	Differentiation	Operational Effectiveness	Customer Orientation
Local Business 1			This club is different because it focuses on beer and country music.		
Local Business 2	This club is just cheap. Cheap cover, cheap drinks, etc.				

SPREADSHEET ACTIVITY

Objective: Strategic information systems are designed to help create some type of competitive advantage. This activity teaches you that something as simple as sorting and filtering within a spreadsheet can be a form of a strategic information system in that it will help make strategic decisions.

Chapter Connection: Porter's five forces are demonstrated in this activity. The two most focused on are the bargaining power of customers and industry rivalry. These will be evaluated in the activity by working with multiple pages within one workbook. Each page will provide a different comparison that will provide new/different information.

Activity: There are many factors that play a role in determining the final cost of a product. There are even more decisions that play into which options

are chosen for a given product. Often, strategic information systems are used to help create competitive advantage. The recreational vehicle (RV) industry is no exception. Companies try to fit as many options into a camper as they can without dramatically increasing the weight, sacrificing the durability of the unit, or driving manufacturing costs so high that the price is uncompetitive. Industry innovations quickly become standard, customer desires change as gas prices go up and down, and businesses are left to sort everything out.

Visit http://www.wiley.com/go/rainer/spreadsheet and find the links provided for Chapter 2. The first link will be a video about sorting and filtering within spreadsheets. It will explain the process and how something this simple can be used to help make strategic decisions. Then click on the second link to download the file for this activity "MIS–Chapter 2.xlsx." It includes a customer survey regarding RV options and customer preferences as well as a list of competitive offerings and prices.

Then sort and filter the information based on criteria given to you by your professor. By sorting and filtering, you are creating information from your data (the raw facts). You will then use this information to make strategic business decisions to help your RV company create a competitive advantage within the marketplace.

Deliverable: The final product will be a spreadsheet filtered to show rank of the organization among different criteria relative to their competition. Once you have filtered and ranked the data, you will make suggestions as to the best course of action that will provide the strongest possible competitive advantage for the company. This recommendation will come in the form of a business letter.

Discussion Questions:

1. Too often, information systems are viewed as complicated computer programs that are difficult to understand. However, spreadsheets can provide much of the needed functionality. At what point is it cost-effective to purchase a more legitimate program than to use simple tools found within a spreadsheet?

2. Given the fact that information systems are there to support decisions, why do you think many opt for more expensive systems than the relatively easy-to-use spreadsheet?

Quiz questions are assignable in WileyPLUS, and available on the Book Companion Site at http://www.wiley.com/college/rainer.

DATABASE ACTIVITY: CREATING TABLES

Objective

In this activity, you will learn how to create Access tables from an existing design. The construction of any database begins with creating its data tables. If you cannot create tables, you cannot create a database. Even if you use a database that someone else has created, knowing where the tables come from will help you understand what you can do with it and why it sometimes behaves in ways that you might otherwise not expect.

The database has to be designed first, of course. You will do that in the Chapter 3 activity if your instructor assigns it. Here we have done the design for you, so you can "get your hands dirty" early in the course.

CHAPTER CONNECTION

Competitive advantage and strategic information systems depend on high-quality data. The tables in a database determine what can be done with it. Understanding how its tables determine what a database can do will help you figure out what strategic systems your company can develop or how its databases must change to support the systems it needs.

PREREQUISITES

None.

Activity

1. In this activity, which you will find online at http://www.wiley.com/go/rainer/database, you will create a database of university departments and courses from scratch. You will create database tables, tell Access how they are related to each other, and enter data into them. You will use similar tables in future Access activities.

The following database diagram (a type of diagram called an *entity-relationship diagram*, as you will learn in Chapter 3) describes part of the data for a university. Specifically, this part of the database will store data about four *entities*: departments, courses, students, and grades.

The lines in the diagram tell us that:

- Each department can have several courses, but might not have any.
- Each course belongs to exactly one department.
- Each course can have several students, but might not have any. (This would be a temporary situation when registration starts.)

- Each student in the course receives one grade.
- Each student can take several courses, but might not be registered for any (yet).
- Each course gives that student one grade.

This information is contained in four tables. You will create the two on the left of the ERD, the Department and Course tables. The first, the department table, will contain the same data that we see here on a spreadsheet:

	A	B	C	D
1	**Name**	**Prefix**	**Space**	**Created On**
2	English	ENL	2500	2/9/1894
3	History	HIS	3500	8/1/1892
4	Physics	PHY	4000	9/1/1892
5	Economics	ECO	2000	3/1/1926
6	Languages	LAN	2300	4/15/1918
7				

2. To create the department table, start by launching Access. Click "Blank database" at the upper left of the "Available Templates" section of its opening window. At the lower right, name this database Activity2.accdb (or as your instructor specifies). Then click Create.

3. You will see the *Datasheet view* of the new table, with no data. You could start by entering column names and data in this view. If you do this, Access will make assumptions about your data. Its assumptions are usually correct, but they are wrong often enough to cause problems that are easier to avoid now than fix later. There are also things you cannot do in this view. So, switch to *Design view* by clicking the "drafting tools" icon at the top left corner.

Usage Hint: Most Access objects can be manipulated in three, four, or more views. The icon shows the view that Access designers thought you are most likely to want next. If you want a different view, you can click the triangle under the drafting tools icon to drop down a menu of icons or click on one of the icons at the bottom right corner of the window, which shows all available views.

4. Before changing views, Access requires you to name your new table. Name it DeptTbl and click "OK." The ending "Tbl" identifies it as a table, distinguishing it from other things called "Dept" (such as, for example, a department list) that you might create later.

Usage Hint: Some people put the letters that identify the object type at the start of its name: TblDept, for example. That groups objects of each type in

an alphabetical list. Here, it is a matter of personal preference unless your instructor specifies otherwise. This project will put the letters that identify the object type at the end of its name.

5. Access has already created the first field of your table, a unique identifier called "ID." It was not on the spreadsheet, but a true database needs it. The *AutoNumber* data type will assign a different number to every department, ensuring you will be able to tell them apart even if two have the same name. (This is why schools give students unique ID numbers.) In a database, such a unique identifier is called a *primary key*. Access indicates primary keys by key icons to the left of their names in Design view. Change the name of this field from ID to DeptID, to avoid later confusion with primary keys of other tables.

6. Enter the name of the next column, DeptName, below DeptID. If you tab to the next field, you will see that Access automatically sets its data type to Text. Because department names are text strings, leave that alone. You can describe it in the third column if you want. (Your instructor may have requirements for this.)

Usage Hint: Both these names begin with "Dept." This helps us tell department names from student or instructor names outside the context of their tables.

7. The next row, which will become the next column of the table in Datasheet view, gives the three-letter prefix that applies to that department's courses. Call it DeptPrefix. It is of data type Text too. In the Description column, enter "Three upper-case letters." This will help people who use the database know what to enter there.

8. The fourth column of the database table will say how many square feet of office space the department uses. So, in the fourth row, enter the name DeptSpace. This time, click the down arrow at the right of its Data Type field to drop down a menu of data types. Select Number.

Usage Hint: You can also key in the word "Number." As soon as you enter "n" Access will complete the word because no other data types start with that letter.

9. The fifth data column will say when the department was created. (This is needed because university tradition calls for departments to march into graduation ceremonies in order of creation, oldest first.) Call this field DeptCreated. Change its data type to Date/Time. In the Field Properties pane in the lower part of the window, click the blank area

to the right of the word "Format." In the menu of date/time formats that drops down, select Medium Date.

At this point your table definition should look like this:

All Access Objects	⊙ «	DeptTbl		
Search...	🔎	**Field Name**	**Data Type**	**Description**
Tables	⊼	DeptID	AutoNumber	
▦ DeptTbl		DeptName	Text	
		DeptPrefix	Text	Three upper-case letters
		DeptSpace	Number	Square feet
		DeptCreated	Date/Time	When department was created

10. Now, click on the Datasheet icon at the top left of the window to return to Datasheet view and enter data. Access will prompt you to save the table. Answer "Yes." (Answering "No" would leave the table in Design view.)

Usage Hint: If you are defining a large data table, do not wait until it is all done to save your work. Click the File ribbon tab and choose Save, or click the diskette icon at the top left of the window, every few minutes.

11. In Datasheet view, click in the first row under DeptName to begin entering data for the first department. Enter the name "English," the prefix "ENG," an area of 2500 square feet, and a creation date of September 2, 1894. Access automatically gave the first department a DeptID of 1. Your table should now look like this:

All Access Objects	⊙ «	DeptTbl					
Search...	🔎	DeptID ▾	DeptName ▾	DeptPrefix ▾	DeptSpace ▾	DeptCreatec ▾	Click to Add
Tables	⊼	1	English	ENG	2500	02-Sep-1894	
▦ DeptTbl		*	(New)				

12. When you see this, you realize that the area should be formatted with a comma after the thousands digit. Select the DeptSpace column, or any data in it. Make the Fields ribbon tab active and select Standard format from the Format pull-down menu in the Formatting section.

Usage Hint: Another way to do this is to click the Apply Comma Number Format icon (looks like a comma) in the Formatting section. That format also

puts two decimal places after the integer part of the number. We do not want decimal places here, so click the Decrease Decimals icon (shows two zeroes with an arrow pointing to one zero) twice to get rid of them.

Usage Hint: A third option is to return to Design view, select DeptSpace, click in the Format row of the Field Properties panel, click the down arrow at the far right of that row to pull down the menu of formats, and select Standard format. Then return to Datasheet view. That is overkill for comma formatting, but you need to do it if the option you want is not in the ribbon.

13. Continue to add the remainder of the data shown in the above spreadsheet. If your instructor gives you different or additional requirements, follow them.

14. Now create the Course table, as shown in the following spreadsheet. Start by clicking the Create tab above the ribbon. In that ribbon click the leftmost icon, Table. Then continue as before, naming this table CourseTbl. Include a primary key, even though it is not shown in the spreadsheet. Be sure to give the CourseDept field data type Number, to match the AutoNumber data type of the primary key in DeptTbl. Select data types for the other fields based on your understanding of their content. (A real database, rather than showing the instructor's name here, would have a link to a faculty table.)

15. The key characteristic of a database, which differentiates it from a file with information about one real-world entity, is that the tables in it are associated with each other. Look at the Course table. It does not show directly that the first course is taught by the English department. It doescontain, however, the department key "1." That key identifies a row in the Department table.

◇	A	B	C	D	E	F	G
1	**CrsDept**	**CrsNum**	**CrsTitle**	**CrsProf**	**CrsRoom**	**CrsDays**	**CrsStart**
2	1	101	English Literature	Barker	McCosh 150	MWF	9:00
3	1	307	Chaucer	Robertson	Mahoney 301	MW	1:00
4	2	131	Asian History	Zhang	Healey 310	TR	1:00
5	2	225	World War II	Freedman	Healey 312	MWF	10:00
6	3	215	Quantum Mechanics	Wheeler	Palmer 242	MWF	11:00
7	4	101	Macroeconomics	Doody	Higgins 120	W	6:00
8	5	207	French Short Story	Malraux	Charlton 202	TR	11:30
9	5	321	Spanish Poetry	Garcia	Wexler 431	TR	8:30
10							

That row gives us the prefix ENG to create the complete identifier "ENG 307," the full name of the department ("English") if we need it, and anything else we want to know about the department.

Creating a column with department codes in the Courses table makes it possible for Access to connect the two tables. But what if we enter, say, 55, into a CourseDept field when we mean 5? Access will gladly accept the data, but later it will not be able to find a department to match it. That is because it does not know, yet, that these two fields are meant to match.

Now we have to tell it to make that connection. To do that, first close the tables, saving them if prompted. Then, click the Database Tools tab on the ribbon. On that ribbon click "Relationships," left of center. In the Show Tables dialogue box, shift-click the unselected table to select both of them, click Add, and close the box.

16. To tell Access about the connection, drag CourseDept in the Course table onto DeptID in the Department table. You will see a dialogue box with a check-box to "Enforce Referential Integrity." This means that Access will check that every CourseDept in the Course table matches an existing DeptID in the Department table: it will not let you assign a course to Department 55 unless Department 55 exists. Check this box and click Create.

If you carried out the previous steps correctly, you will see a line between these two data fields. It will have a "1" by DeptTbl and a ∞ (infinity) symbol by CourseTbl. This means the two are in a many-to-one relationship: a department can have many courses, but each course is in only one department. It should look like this:

If this did not happen, the most common reasons are:

- **You got a line between the two, but there are no symbols at its ends.** You did not check "Enforce Referential Integrity." Double-click the line to edit it (or right-click

and select Edit Relationship), check the box, and OK the change.

- **"The database engine could not lock table '[name]' because it is already in use by another person or process."** A table is still open. Cancel the request, bring the open table to the front by clicking its tab, close it (saving if asked), and repeat.

- **"Microsoft Office Access can't create this relationship and enforce referential integrity."** At least one CourseDept does not match a DeptID. Check that CourseDept is of data type Number and all values in that column are correct. If you used data from this activity, check your tables against the data here. If you used other data, such as your instructor's, check the tables against that data. If you used your own, confirm that all CourseDept values match DeptID values. Then repeat the process.

Deliverable

Your database file with the above two tables, their data, and the relationship.

Usage Hint: Access 2010 can give database files the file name extension *.mdb* (works with any recent Access release) or *.accdb* (works with Access 2007 and later). While it is open, Access 2010 creates a temporary file having the same name but extension *.laccdb*. This *lock file* prevents other programs from changing a database while it is in use. It goes away when you close the database. If you submit a database while it is open, it is easy to submit the lock file by mistake. The easiest way to avoid that error is to close the database first. If you send it while it is open, be sure you send the right file. A lock file will be of no use to your instructor.

Quiz Questions

1. True or false: If a field has data type AutoNumber, it will never have the same value in two rows of the table.

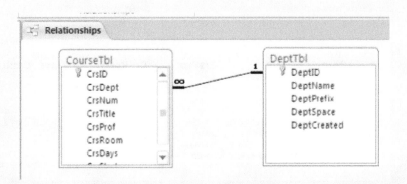

2. Which of the following is *not* a valid Access data type?
   - (a) Text
   - (b) Date/Time
   - (c) Color
   - (d) Number

3. True or false: You must use the Description field in a table's Design view to describe what each field of the table is for.

4. True or false: To enter data into a table, you use Datasheet view.

Discussion Questions

1. A primary key, such as DeptID in this activity, identifies a single row of a database table uniquely. It must meet two conditions: every row of the table has to have one, and they must all be different. Would the three-letter prefix that a department uses for its courses be a suitable primary key? Why or why not?

2. Use Access online help and/or the search engine of your choice to learn the difference between Text and Memo data types. Explain, to a nontechnical reader, when to use each.

3. Suppose the English department changes its name to English Literature and its course prefix to ENL. The Department table is updated to reflect these changes. What changes must be made to the Course table in order to update all the course listings?

3 | Data and Knowledge Management

LEARNING OBJECTIVES >>>

1. Discuss ways that common challenges in managing data can be addressed using data governance.

2. Explain how to interpret relationships depicted in an entity-relationship diagram.

3. Discuss the advantages and disadvantages of relational databases.

4. Explain the elements necessary to successfully implement and maintain data warehouses.

5. Describe the benefits and challenges of implementing knowledge management systems in organizations.

© Tom England/iStockphoto

Databases come in all shapes and sizes. As you will see in this chapter, a database consists of attributes, entities, tables, and relationships. The purpose of a database can differ greatly depending on the nature of the business.

Take, for example, Dennis Rollins, owner of a small car lot in Bowdon, Georgia. Dennis needed an effective way to manage the data surrounding his car lot. A solid online presence can be difficult to achieve for small used car dealers because there are so many makes and models of cars to sell and so many online outlets through which to advertise. In order to manage his data himself, Dennis would need at least one database to help manage inventory and at least one other database to allow his customers to view product information. In addition, Dennis would need to hire a full-time employee to manage Internet sales. Adding two databases and a full-time employee was far beyond Dennis' capacity, so he needed an easier solution.

That easier solution came in the form of Dealer Car Search (http://dealercarsearch.com). Dealer Car Search specializes in

creating car dealer Web sites. The company offers products for small businesses, dealers, and dealer chains. However, the database maintained by Dealer Car Search is what truly makes the company so successful. It is the key to its customers' experiences because it provides the data entry capabilities, analysis capabilities, reporting, and search features needed by all parties.

Now, when Dennis has a new vehicle to sell, he can enter his data just once onto his customer page on Dealer Car Search. With the data entered once (no data redundancy), it automatically appears on his Web site (http://rollinsautomotive.com) and other car sites (such as http://autotrader.com). Dealer Car Search also supplies Dennis with an inventory management system that provides a view of his inventory with reports to help him determine his pricing. If Dennis changes a price or updates any other information, the change automatically appears on all other sites. **> > >**

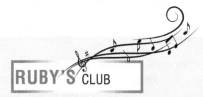

RUBY'S CLUB

Data collection has always been important to Ruben and Lisa. However, their form of data collection was to keep up with paper receipts from cover charges, drinks, food, etc. They mainly did this to create financial statements. However, they also know that their data collection is incomplete because many people pay with cash and no itemized receipt is printed. Therefore, often the best they can do is a general statement of costs and sales. They have no way to measure and track individual sales, customers, products, and the like.

In fact, they have never been able to track sales to customers, weeknight, band (type of music playing), and so on. Even more important, they do not know very much about their customers. Why do they come? What do they like? What do they wish was better? What are the most popular drink items? How do people rate their overall experience? Which drink and food items are most popular and at what time of the night? How can they best reach their customer base? Facebook? Twitter? E-mail?

The only way to answer these questions is to have data that can be analyzed to create information. The only way to capture the data in an organized format is to use a database. And the only way to have a structured database is to start by laying out the outline of that database. This process is called "normalization and entity relationship modeling."

The result? The database (provided by Dealer Car Search) offers Dennis a one-stop solution. It provides inventory management, Internet advertising, mobile apps, performance reporting, lead management, and much more.

Therefore, for Dealer Car Search, Rollins Automotive, and Rollin's customers, this application of a database provides a seamless experience that is beneficial for all parties involved.

Sources: Compiled from http://dealercarsearch.com, http://rollinsautomotive.com, accessed February 29, 2012.

Questions

1. Why is Dealer Car Search's database largely responsible for its success?
2. Why didn't Dennis Rollins just build his own database using Access? Support your answer.

Introduction

"Big Data" represents a very real problem that every business faces. This problem becomes even more pronounced when you consider the vast increases in the amount of data that organizations capture and store. The opening case describes the numerous problems caused by Big Data, the solutions that organizations are employing to manage these data, several good results, and a few poor results. The important idea to realize here is that Big Data will continue to get "bigger," and organizations will have to find ever-more creative solutions to manage it.

Between 2006 and 2010, the amount of digital information created, captured, and replicated each year added about 18 million times as much information as currently exists in all the books ever written. Images captured by billions of devices around the world, from digital cameras and camera phones to medical scanners and security cameras, comprise the largest component of this digital information.

We are accumulating data and information at a frenzied pace from such diverse sources as company documents, e-mails, Web pages, credit card swipes, phone messages, stock trades, memos, address books, and radiology scans. New sources of data and information include blogs, podcasts, videocasts (think of YouTube), digital video surveillance, and radio frequency identification (RFID) tags and other wireless sensors (discussed in Chapter 10). We are awash in data that we have to make sense of and manage. To deal with the growth and the diverse nature of digital data, organizations must employ sophisticated techniques for information management.

Information technologies and systems support organizations in managing—that is, acquiring, organizing, storing, accessing, analyzing, and interpreting—data. As you noted in Chapter 1, when these data are managed properly, they become *information* and then *knowledge*. Information and knowledge are valuable organizational resources that can provide a competitive advantage. This chapter will examine the processes whereby data are transformed first into information and then into knowledge.

Few business professionals are comfortable making or justifying business decisions that are not based on solid information. This is especially true today, when modern information systems make access to that information quick and easy. For example, we have technology that formats data in a way that managers and analysts can easily understand. Consequently, these professionals can access these data themselves and analyze them according to their needs, using a variety of tools. The result is useful information. Executives can then apply their experience to use this information to address a business problem, thereby producing knowledge. Knowledge management, enabled by information technology, captures and stores knowledge in forms that all organizational employees can access and apply, thereby creating the flexible, powerful "learning organization."

Clearly, data and knowledge management are vital to modern organizations. But, why should *you* learn about them? The reason is that you will have an important role in the development of database applications. The structure and content of your organization's **database**, a group of logically related files that stores data and the associations among them, depends on how users (you) look at your business activities. For example, when database developers in the firm's MIS group build a database, they use a tool called entity-relationship (ER) modeling. This tool creates a model of how users view a business activity. When you understand how to create and interpret an ER model, then you can evaluate whether the developers have captured your business activity correctly.

Keep in mind that decisions about data last longer, and have a broader impact, than decisions about hardware or software. If decisions concerning hardware are wrong, then the equipment can be replaced relatively easily. If software decisions turn out to be incorrect, they can be modified, though not always painlessly or inexpensively. Database decisions, in contrast, are much harder to undo. Database design constrains what the organization can do with its data for a long time. Remember that business users will be stuck with a bad database design, and not the database programmers, who will quickly move on to their next projects. This is why it is so important to get database designs right the first time—and you will be playing a key role in these designs.

Regarding relational databases, when you know how data are stored in tables, then you know what types of data you have available for analysis and decision making. Of course, your familiarity with data warehouses will serve the same purpose. Also, understanding relational databases will help you work with database developers in defining a new database or suggesting improvements to an existing one. It is one thing for you to say to a database developer, "I wish I could get this information from the database." It is quite another thing to say, "If you could add this column of data to Table A and this other column of data to Table B, then I could get this information from the database." Database developers enjoy responding to specific, knowledgeable requests from users!

In addition, you might want to create a small, personal database using a software product such as Microsoft Access. In that case, you will want to know at least the basics of the product.

After the data are stored in your organization's databases, they must be accessible to users in a form that helps users make decisions. Organizations accomplish this objective by developing data warehouses. You should become familiar with data warehouses because they are invaluable decision-making tools.

You will also make extensive use of your organization's knowledge base to perform your job. For example, when you are assigned a new project, you will likely research your firm's knowledge base to identify factors that contributed to the success of previous, similar projects.

You begin this chapter by examining the multiple problems involved in managing data and the database approach that organizations use to solve those problems. You will then see how database management systems enable organizations to access and use the data stored in the databases. Next, you study data warehouses and data marts and how you use them for decision making. You finish the chapter by taking a look at knowledge management.

3.1 Managing Data

IT applications require data. Data should be of high quality, meaning that they should be accurate, complete, timely, consistent, accessible, relevant, and concise. Unfortunately, however, the process of acquiring, keeping, and managing data is becoming increasingly difficult.

The Difficulties of Managing Data

Because data are processed in several stages and often in several places, they are frequently subject to problems and difficulties. Managing data in organizations is difficult for many reasons.

First, the amount of data increases exponentially with time. Much historical data must be kept for a long time, and new data are added rapidly. For example, to support millions of customers, large retailers such as Walmart have to manage many terabytes of data. IT's About Business 3.1 illustrates how Scale Computing helps small businesses manage their data storage needs.

IT'S ABOUT BUSINESS 3.1

A Data Storage Startup Saves Small Businesses Big Money

Scale Computing (www.scalecomputing.com) targets small companies with its line of data storage devices. The company's strategy is to trim their clients' costs by giving them the capacity they need at a cost they can afford.

HP (www.hp.com), Dell (www.dell.com), and EMC (www.emc.com) prefer to sell storage in large amounts suitable for huge corporations. Although the giant storage manufacturers do make small storage units as well, Scale Computing can deliver equal storage performance by substituting expensive hardware with software.

 Typical storage units have physical controllers (a type of computer) that divide data up among different hard drives. Scale Computing eliminates the controllers by using software to divide the data. Scale's devices also use slower, cheaper hard drives that work together to retrieve data as quickly as a similar number of faster, more expensive hard drives. For example, a hospital that might pay up to $60,000 for 12 terabytes of storage from one of the big storage vendors, would only need to pay Scale $33,000 for the same amount of storage.

In the past, small businesses had to estimate how much storage capacity they would need in the future. If they guessed too high, they overpaid for storage. If they guessed too low, they had to buy additional storage devices. Each additional storage device bought in this way adds complexity to small information technology departments.

With Scale's equipment, small companies can simply buy extra nodes that work together. Scale says that any extra terabytes of storage typically cost half of what the competition charges. For example, the GEO Foundation (www.geofoundation.org),

a network of five charter schools in Indiana and Colorado, saved $15,000 immediately by using Scale's equipment rather than that of a major storage vendor, and will save another $21,000 when the organization adds more storage in 2012.

© Steve Cole/iStockphoto

Scale Computing's next move is to further cut its clients' hardware costs. A software update will turn Scale's physical storage units into servers, eliminating the need for that physical equipment. Scale says that its software will decrease the cost of a typical 12-terabyte datacenter by more than half, to approximately $50,000.

Scale has 600 customers around the world. The company has yet to turn a profit, but has raised $31 million in venture capital.

Sources: Compiled from J. Colao, "Thanks for the Memory," *Forbes*, February 27, 2012; D. Hill, "Scale Computing: New Twists to Scale-Out Storage for the Mid-Market," *Network Computing*, January 27, 2012; B., Nelson, J. Colao, and M. Mallet, "American's Most Promising Companies 2011," *Forbes*, November 30, 2011; www.scalecomputing.com, accessed February 11, 2012.

Questions

1. What are some of the advantages that Scale Computing offers small companies?

2. If you are a large company with extensive storage needs, would you consider Scale Computing? Why or why not?

In addition, data are also scattered throughout organizations and are collected by many individuals using various methods and devices. These data are frequently stored in numerous servers and locations and in different computing systems, databases, formats, and human and computer languages.

Another problem is that data come from multiple sources: internal sources (for example, corporate databases and company documents), personal sources (for example, personal thoughts, opinions, and experiences), and external sources (for example, commercial databases, government reports, and corporate Web sites). Data also come from the Web, in the form of clickstream data. **Clickstream data** are those data that visitors and customers produce when they visit a Web site and click on hyperlinks (described in Chapter 4). Clickstream data provide a trail of the users' activities in the Web site, including user behavior and browsing patterns.

Adding to these problems is the fact that new sources of data, such as blogs, podcasts, videocasts, and RFID tags and other wireless sensors, are constantly being developed. As you saw in the chapter-opening case, data degrades over time. For example, customers move to new addresses or change their names, companies go out of business or are bought, new products are developed, employees are hired or fired, and companies expand into new countries.

Data are also subject to *data rot*. Data rot refers primarily to problems with the media on which the data are stored. Over time, temperature, humidity, and exposure to light can cause physical problems with storage media and thus make it difficult to access the data. The second aspect of data rot is that finding the machines needed to access the data can be difficult. For example, it is almost impossible today to find 8-track players. This means that a library of 8-track tapes has become relatively worthless, unless you have a functioning 8-track player or you convert the tapes to a modern medium such as CD.

Data security, quality, and integrity are critical, yet they are easily jeopardized. In addition, legal requirements relating to data differ among countries as well as industries, and they change frequently.

Another problem arises from the fact that, over time, organizations have developed information systems for specific business processes, such as transaction processing, supply chain management, customer relationship management, and other processes. Information systems that specifically support these processes impose unique requirements on data, which results in repetition and conflicts across an organization. For example, the marketing function might maintain information on customers, sales territories, and markets that duplicates data within the billing or customer service functions. This situation produces inconsistent data in the enterprise. Inconsistent data prevent a company from developing a unified view of core business information—data concerning customers, products, finances, and so on—across the organization and its information systems.

Two other factors complicate data management. First, federal regulations (for example, Sarbanes-Oxley) have made it a top priority for companies to better account for how information is being managed with their organizations. Sarbanes-Oxley requires that (1) public companies evaluate and disclose the effectiveness of their internal financial controls and (2) independent auditors for these companies agree to this disclosure. The law also holds CEOs and CFOs personally responsible for such disclosure. If their companies lack satisfactory data management policies and fraud or a security breach occurs, the company officers could be held personally responsible and face prosecution.

Second, companies are drowning in data, much of which is unstructured. As you have seen, the amount of data is increasing exponentially. To be profitable, companies must develop a strategy for managing these data effectively.

Because of these numerous problems, data are difficult to manage. As a result, organizations are turning to data governance.

Data Governance

Data governance is an approach to managing information across an entire organization. It involves a formal set of business processes and policies that are designed to ensure that data are handled in a certain, well-defined fashion. That is, the organization follows unambiguous rules for creating, collecting, handling, and protecting its information. The objective is to make information available, transparent, and useful for the people authorized to access it, from the moment it enters an organization, until it is outdated and deleted.

One strategy for implementing data governance is master data management. **Master data management** is a process that spans all organizational business processes and applications. It provides companies with the ability to store, maintain, exchange, and synchronize a consistent, accurate, and timely "single version of the truth" for the company's core master data.

Master data are a set of core data, such as customer, product, employee, vendor, geographic location, and so on, that span the enterprise information systems. It is important to distinguish between master data and transaction data. *Transaction data*, which are generated and captured by operational systems, describe the activities, or transactions, of the business. In contrast, master data are applied to multiple transactions and are used to categorize, aggregate, and evaluate the transaction data.

Let's look at an example of a transaction: You (Mary Jones) purchase one Samsung 42-inch plasma television, part number 1234, from Bill Roberts at Best Buy, for $2,000, on April 20, 2011. In this example, the master data are "product sold," "vendor," "salesperson," "store," "part number," "purchase price," and "date." When specific values are applied to the master data, then a transaction is represented. Therefore, transaction data would be, respectively, "42-inch plasma television," "Samsung," "Bill Roberts," "Circuit City," "1234," "$2,000," and "April 20, 2011."

An example of master data management is the city of Dallas, Texas, which implemented a plan for digitizing public and private records, such as paper documents, images, drawings, and video and audio content, that are maintained by the city. The master database can be accessed by any of the 38 government departments that have appropriate access. The city is integrating its financial and billing processes with its customer relationship management program. (You will learn about customer relationship management in Chapter 12.)

How will Dallas utilize this system? Imagine that the city experiences a water-main break. Before it implemented the system, repair crews had to search City Hall for records that were filed haphazardly. Once the workers found the hard-copy blueprints, they would take them to the site and, after going over them manually, would decide on a plan of action. In contrast, the new system delivers the blueprints wirelessly to the laptops of crews in the field, who can magnify or highlight areas of concern to generate a quick response. This process reduces the time it takes to respond to an emergency by several hours.

Along with data governance, organizations use the database approach to efficiently and effectively manage their data. You turn your attention to the database approach in the next section.

— BEFORE YOU GO ON . . . —

1. What are some of the difficulties involved in managing data?
2. Define *data governance, master data,* and *transactional data.*

Apply the Concept 3.1

Background The amount of data we create today is absolutely mind boggling. EMC is a global company that focuses on helping organizations manage their data. Recently, the company sponsored a study to determine exactly how big the "digital universe" is and what its projected growth looks like. There are some amazing findings in this study that point to a dramatic growth in data and in increase in virtual data centers. In the future (as it is now) it will be possible to run your information systems in data centers that do not even operate on your own premises.

Activity Go to http://www.wiley.com/go/rainer/applytheconcept and click on the link for Apply the Concept 3.1. It will take you to a YouTube video titled "IDC Study:

Digital Universe: Sponsored by EMC." Watch this 5-minute video and consider the trends. Specifically, consider the difference in IT growth and IT professionals to work in the area and the amount of data that is not secure or only minimally secure. Now imagine that your parents own their own business. It is successful, but struggling under pressure to upgrade IT services for their employees and customers. What could you say that would help them look ahead to the future rather than staying in the past?

Deliverable

Write an e-mail to your parents to explain to them what is likely to happen over the next 10 years. What do you think they should do to plan for the next 10 years? What qualities should they look for in new employees? What training should they submit current employees to? What should the purpose of data governance be in their 10-year plan?

Submit your e-mail to your instructor.

Quiz questions are assignable in WileyPLUS, and available on the Book Companion Site at http://www.wiley.com/college/rainer.

RUBY'S CLUB QUESTIONS

1. How many sources of information can you think of for Ruby's Club?
2. Even though Ruby's Club is not subject to Sarbanes-Oxley legal documentation requirements, can you think of any reasons why it would be a good idea for the club to operate up to these standards?

3.2 The Database Approach

From the time of the first computer applications in business (mid-1950s) until the early 1970s, organizations managed their data in a *file management environment*. This environment evolved because organizations typically began automating one application at a time. These systems grew independently from one another, without overall planning. Each application required its own data, which were organized in a data file.

A data file is a collection of logically related records. Therefore, in a file management environment, each application has a specific data file related to it, containing all the data records needed by the application. Over time, organizations developed numerous applications, each with an associated, application-specific data file.

For example, you can relate to a situation where most of your information is in your university's central database, but a club to which you belong has its own files, the athletics department has separate files for student athletes, and your instructors may maintain grade data on their personal computers. It is easy for your name to be misspelled in one of these databases or files but not in others. If you move, your address might be updated correctly in one database or file but not in others.

Using databases eliminates many problems that arose from previous methods of storing and accessing data, such as file management systems. Databases are arranged so that one set of software programs—the database management system—provides all users with access to all the data. (You will study database management systems later in this chapter.) This system minimizes the following problems:

- *Data redundancy:* The same data are stored in many places.
- *Data isolation:* Applications cannot access data associated with other applications.
- *Data inconsistency:* Various copies of the data do not agree.

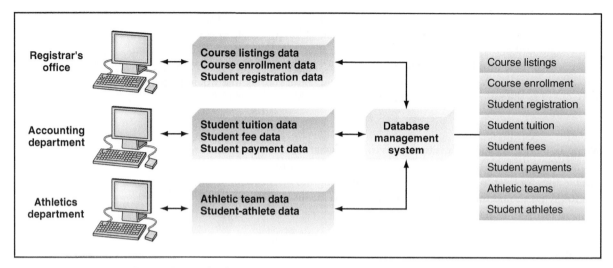

Figure 3.1 A database management system (DBMS) provides access to all data in the database.

In addition, database systems maximize the following issues:

- *Data security:* Because data are "put in one place" in databases, there is a potential for losing a lot of data at once. Therefore, databases have extremely high security measures in place to deter mistakes and attacks. (You will learn about information security in Chapter 7.)

- *Data integrity:* Data meet certain constraints, such as no alphabetic characters in a Social Security number field.

- *Data independence:* Applications and data are independent of one another (that is, applications and data are not linked to each other, meaning that all applications are able to access the same data).

Figure 3.1 illustrates a university database. Note that university applications from the registrar's office, the accounting department, and the athletics department access data through the database management system.

A database can contain vast amounts of data. To make these data more understandable and useful, they are arranged in a hierarchy. In the next section, you will become familiar with the data hierarchy. You will then see how databases are designed.

The Data Hierarchy

Data are organized in a hierarchy that begins with bits and proceeds all the way to databases (see Figure 3.2). A **bit** (*bi*nary dig*it*) represents the smallest unit of data a computer can process. The term *binary* means that a bit can consist only of a 0 or a 1. A group of eight bits, called a **byte**, represents a single character. A byte can be a letter, a number, or a symbol. A logical grouping of characters into a word, a small group of words, or an identification number is called a **field**. For example, a student's name in a university's computer files would appear in the "name" field, and her or his Social Security number would appear in the "Social Security number" field. Fields can also contain data other than text and numbers. A field can contain an image, or any other type of multimedia. Examples are a motor vehicle department's licensing database containing a person's photograph and a field containing a voice sample to authorize access to a secure facility; and in the Apple iTunes Store, a song is a field in a record, with other fields giving the song's title, its price, and the album of which it is part.

A logical grouping of related fields, such as the student's name, the courses taken, the date, and the grade, comprises a record. A logical grouping of related records is called a **file** or a **table**. For example, the records from a particular course, consisting of course number,

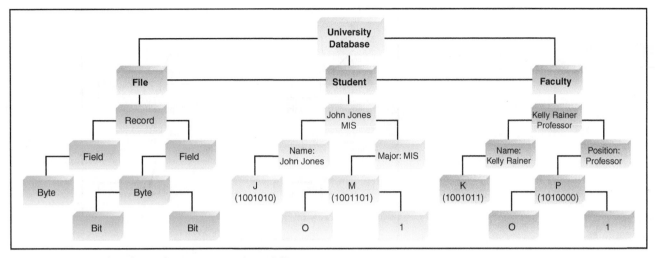

Figure 3.2 Hierarchy of data for a computer-based file.

professor, and students' grades, would constitute a data file for that course. A logical grouping of related files would constitute a *database*. Using the same example, the student course file could be grouped with files on students' personal histories and financial backgrounds to create a student database.

Now that you have seen how data are arranged in a database, you will learn about how today's organizations design their databases. You will focus on entity-relationship (ER) modeling and normalization procedures.

Designing the Database

To be valuable, a database must be organized so that users can retrieve, analyze, and understand the data they need. A key to designing an effective database is the data model. A **data model** is a diagram that represents entities in the database and their relationships. An entity is a person, place, thing, or event—such as a customer, an employee, or a product—about which information is maintained. Entities can typically be identified in the user's work environment. A **record** generally describes an entity. An instance of an entity is a specific, unique representation of the entity. For example, an instance of the entity STUDENT would be a particular student.

Each characteristic or quality of a particular entity is called an *attribute*. For example, if our entities were a customer, an employee, and a product, entity attributes would include customer name, employee number, and product color.

Every record in a file must contain at least one field that uniquely identifies that record so that it can be retrieved, updated, and sorted. This identifier field is called the **primary key**. For example, a student record in a U.S. university would use a unique student number as its primary key. (*Note:* In the past, your Social Security number served as the primary key for your student record. However, for security reasons, this practice has been discontinued.) In some cases, locating a particular record requires the use of secondary keys. A **secondary key** is another field that has some identifying information but typically does not identify the file with complete accuracy. For example, the student's major might be a secondary key if a user wanted to find all students in a particular major field of study. It should not be the primary key, however, because many students can have the same major.

Entity-Relationship Modeling. Designers plan and create the database through the process of **entity-relationship modeling**, using an **entity-relationship (ER) diagram**. There are many approaches to ER diagramming. You will see one particular approach here, but there are others. The good news is that if you are familiar with one version of ER diagramming, then you will be able to easily adapt to any other type of ER diagramming.

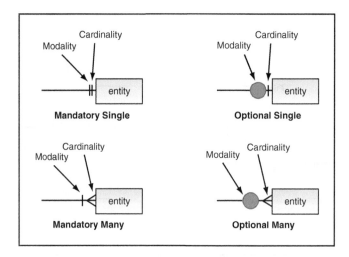

Figure 3.3 Relationships between entities reflecting business rules.

ER diagrams consist of entities, attributes, and relationships. Entities are pictured in boxes, and relationships are shown in diamonds. The attributes for each entity are listed, and the primary key is underlined.

Relationships illustrate an association between two entities. A relationship has a name that is a verb. Cardinality and modality are the indicators of the business rules in a relationship. *Cardinality* refers to the maximum number of times an instance of one entity can be associated with an instance in the related entity. *Modality* refers to the minimum number of times an instance of one entity can be associated with an instances in the related entity. Cardinality can be 1 or Many, and its symbol is placed on the outside of the relationship line, closest to the entity. Modality can be 1 or 0, and its symbol is placed on the inside of the relationship line, next to the cardinality symbol. Figure 3.3 shows the cardinality and modality symbols. Figure 3.4 shows an ER diagram.

As defined earlier, an **entity** is something that can be identified in the users' work environment. For example, consider student registration at a university. Students register for courses and register their cars for parking permits. In this example, STUDENT, PARKING PERMIT, CLASS, and PROFESSOR are entities, as shown in Figure 3.4.

Entities of a given type are grouped in **entity classes**. In our example, STUDENT, PARKING PERMIT, CLASS, and PROFESSOR are entity classes. An **instance** of an entity class is the representation of a particular entity. Therefore, a particular STUDENT (James Smythe, 145-89-7123) is an instance of the STUDENT entity class; a particular parking permit (91778) is an instance of the PARKING PERMIT entity class; a particular class (76890) is an instance of the CLASS entity class; and a particular professor (Margaret Wilson, 115-65-7632) is an instance of the PROFESSOR entity class.

Entity instances have **identifiers**, which are attributes that are unique to that entity instance. For example, STUDENT instances can be identified with Student Identification Number; PARKING PERMIT instances can be identified with Permit Number; CLASS instances can be identified with Class Number; and PROFESSOR instances can be identified with Professor Identification Number. These identifiers (or primary keys) are underlined on ER diagrams, as in Part (b) of Figure 3.4.

Entities have **attributes**, or properties, that describe the entity's characteristics. In our example, examples of attributes for STUDENT are Student Name and Student Address. Examples of attributes for PARKING PERMIT are Student Identification Number and Car Type. Examples of attributes for CLASS are Class Name, Class Time, and Class Place. Examples of attributes for PROFESSOR are Professor Name and Professor Department. (Note that each course at this university has one professor—no team teaching.)

Why is Student Identification Number an attribute of both the STUDENT and PARKING PERMIT entity classes? That is, why do we need the PARKING PERMIT entity class? If you consider all interlinked university systems, the PARKING PERMIT entity class is needed for other applications, such as fee payments, parking tickets, and external links to the state Department of Motor Vehicles.

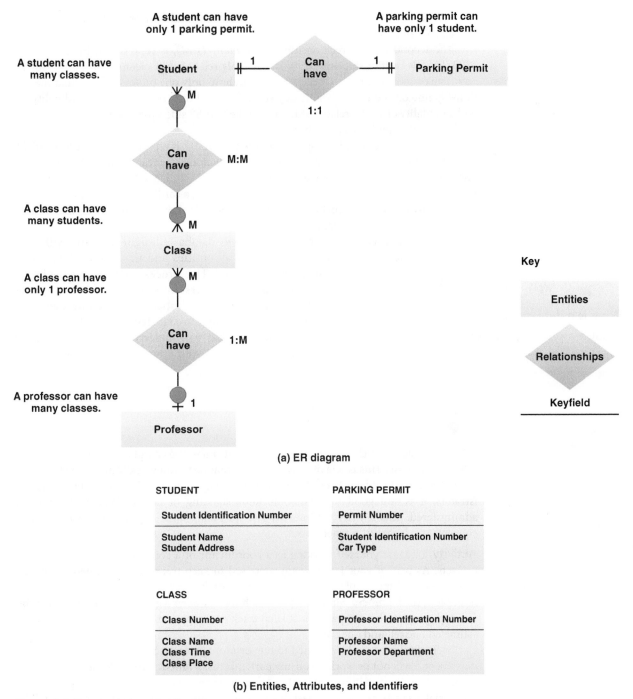

A student can have
only 1 parking permit.

A parking permit can
have only 1 student.

A student can have
many classes.

Student

1 Can
have 1 Parking Permit

1:1

M

Can
have M:M

A class can have
many students.

M

Class

A class can have
only 1 professor.

M

Can
have 1:M

A professor can have
many classes.

1

Professor

Key

Entities

Relationships

Keyfield

(a) ER diagram

STUDENT

Student Identification Number

Student Name
Student Address

PARKING PERMIT

Permit Number

Student Identification Number
Car Type

CLASS

Class Number

Class Name
Class Time
Class Place

PROFESSOR

Professor Identification Number

Professor Name
Professor Department

(b) Entities, Attributes, and Identifiers

Figure 3.4 Entity-relationship diagram model.

Entities are associated with one another in relationships, which can include many entities. (Remember that relationships are noted by diamonds on ER diagrams.) The number of entities in a relationship is the degree of the relationship. Relationships between two items are called *binary relationships*. There are three types of binary relationships: one-to-one, one-to-many, and many-to-many.

In a *one-to-one (1:1)* relationship, a single-entity instance of one type is related to a single-entity instance of another type. Figure 3.4a shows STUDENT–PARKING PERMIT as a 1:1 relationship. The relationship means that a student can have a parking permit, but does not need to have to have one. (Clearly, if a student does not have a car, then he or she will not need a parking permit.) Note that the relationship line on the PARKING PERMIT side shows zero or one—that is, a cardinality of 1 and a modality of 0. On the STUDENT side of the relationship, only one parking permit can be assigned to one student. Note that the relationship line on the STUDENT side shows one and only one—that is, a cardinality of 1 and a modality of 1.

The second type of relationship, *one-to-many (1:M)*, is represented by the CLASS–PROFESSOR relationship in Figure 3.4(a). This relationship means that a professor can have one or more courses, but each course can have only one professor. Note that the relationship line on the PROFESSOR side shows one and only one—that is, a cardinality of 1 and a modality of 1. The relationship line on the CLASS side shows one or many—that is, a cardinality of Many and a modality of 1.

The third type of relationship, *many-to-many (M:M)*, is represented by the STUDENT–CLASS relationship in Figure 3.4(a). This M:M relationship means that a student can have one or more courses, and a course can have one or more students. Note that the relationship line on the STUDENT side shows one or more—that is, a cardinality of Many and a modality of 1. Further, the relationship line of the CLASS side shows one or more—that is, a cardinality of Many and a modality of 1.

ER modeling is valuable because it allows database designers to talk with users throughout the organization to ensure that all entities and the relationships among them are represented. This process underscores the importance of taking all users into account when designing organizational databases. Notice that all entities and relationships in our example are labeled in terms that users can understand. Now that you understand how a database is designed, you can turn your attention to database management systems.

BEFORE *YOU GO ON . . .*

1. What is a data model?
2. What is a primary key? A secondary key?
3. What is an entity? An attribute?

Apply the Concept 3.2

Background This section has exposed you to the complicated job of designing a database. This is one of those concepts that just cannot really be grasped until you work through a problem. Even though very few people go on to become database administrators, it is still good to have some understanding of how a database is built and administered. This activity will present you with a scenario and then you will apply the concepts you have just learned about.

Activity Imagine yourself working as a coordinator of a company with several ongoing projects. As part of your job, you are supposed to keep track of its commercial projects, employees, and the employees' participation in each project. Usually, a project will have multiple team members, but some projects have not been assigned to any team member. For each project, the company must keep track of the project's title, description, location, estimated budget, and due date.

Each employee can be assigned to one or more projects. Some employees can also be on leave and will not be working on any particular assignment. Project leaders usually need to know the following information about their team members: name, address, phone number, Social Security number, highest degree attained, and his/her expertise (for example, IS, accounting, marketing, and finance).

You have been asked by your manager to conceptually design a database that can help the company keep track of the information described in this scenario. To begin, you need to identify entity classes and their attributes and determine (or create) primary key attribute(s) for each entity class. In addition, you will need to identify foreign key attribute(s) and establish relationships among the entity classes you have identified.

Deliverable

Develop your conceptual design and present your instructor with your entity classes and their attributes. Also be sure to identify the primary key attribute(s). Present a drawing similar to the one in the text if your instructor requires it.

Quiz questions are assignable in WileyPLUS, and available on the Book Companion Site at http://www.wiley.com/college/rainer.

RUBY'S CLUB QUESTIONS

1. If the bartender, cover charge clerk, and chef all kept separate spreadsheets to keep up with customers, purchases, and payments, what type of data problems do you see they could have?

2. How could a networked database help to alleviate some of the problems in the first question?

3.3 Database Management Systems

A **database management system (DBMS)** is a set of programs that provide users with tools to add, delete, access, modify, and analyze data stored in one location. An organization can access the data by using query and reporting tools that are part of the DBMS or by using application programs specifically written to access the data. DBMSs also provide the mechanisms for maintaining the integrity of stored data, managing security and user access, and recovering information if the system fails. Because databases and DBMSs are essential to all areas of business, they must be carefully managed.

There are a number of different database architectures, but we focus on the relational database model because it is popular and easy to use. Other database models (for example, the hierarchical and network models) are the responsibility of the MIS function and are not used by organizational employees. Popular examples of relational databases are Microsoft Access and Oracle.

The Relational Database Model

Most business data—especially accounting and financial data—traditionally were organized into simple tables consisting of columns and rows. Tables allow people to compare information quickly by row or column. In addition, items are easy to retrieve by finding the point of intersection of a particular row and column.

The **relational database model** is based on the concept of two-dimensional tables. A relational database generally is not one big table—usually called a *flat file*—that contains all of the records and attributes. Such a design would entail far too much data redundancy. Instead, a relational database is usually designed with a number of related tables. Each of these tables contains records (listed in rows) and attributes (listed in columns).

These related tables can be joined when they contain common columns. The uniqueness of the primary key tells the DBMS which records are joined with others in related tables. This feature allows users great flexibility in the variety of queries they can make. Despite these features, however, this model has some disadvantages. Because large-scale databases can be composed of many interrelated tables, the overall design can be complex and therefore have slow search and access times.

Consider the relational database example about students shown in Figure 3.5. The table contains data about the entity called students. Attributes of the entity are student name, undergraduate major, grade point average, and graduation date. The rows are the records on Sally Adams, John Jones, Jane Lee, Kevin Durham, Juan Rodriguez, Stella Zubnicki, and Ben Jones. Of course, your university keeps much more data on you than our example shows. In fact, your university's student database probably keeps hundreds of attributes on each student.

Query Languages. Requesting information from a database is the most commonly performed operation. **Structured query language (SQL)** is the most popular query language used to request information. SQL allows people to perform complicated searches by using relatively simple statements or key words. Typical key words are SELECT (to specify a desired attribute), FROM (to specify the table to be used), and WHERE (to specify conditions to apply in the query).

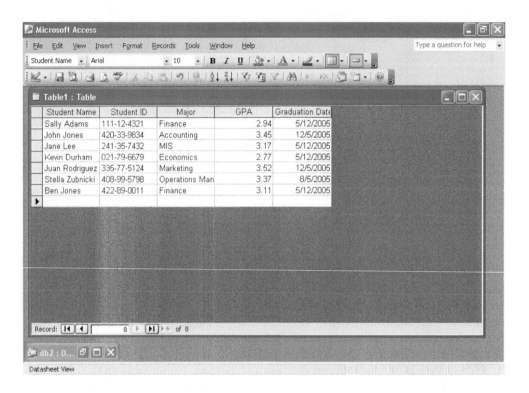

Figure 3.5 Example of a student database.

To understand how SQL works, imagine that a university wants to know the names of students who will graduate cum laude (but not magna or summa cum laude) in May 2012. The university IS staff would query the student relational database with an SQL statement such as SELECT Student Name, FROM Student Database, WHERE Grade Point Average > 3.40 and Grade Point Average < 3.60. The SQL query would return: John Jones and Juan Rodriguez.

Another way to find information in a database is to use **query by example (QBE)**. In QBE, the user fills out a grid or template (also known as a *form*) to construct a sample or description of the data desired. Users can construct a query quickly and easily by using drag-and-drop features in a DBMS such as Microsoft Access. Conducting queries in this manner is simpler than keying in SQL commands.

Data Dictionary. When a relational model is created, the **data dictionary** defines the format necessary to enter the data into the database. The data dictionary provides information on each attribute, such as its name, whether it is a key or part of a key, the type of data expected (alphanumeric, numeric, dates, and so on), and valid values. Data dictionaries can also provide information on how often the attribute should be updated; why it is needed in the database; and which business functions, applications, forms, and reports use the attribute.

Data dictionaries provide many advantages to the organization. Because they provide names and standard definitions for all attributes, they reduce the chances that the same attribute will be used in different applications but with a different name. In addition, data dictionaries give organizations an inventory of their data resources, making it possible to manage that resource more effectively.

Normalization. To use a relational database management system effectively, the data must be analyzed to eliminate redundant data elements. **Normalization** is a method for analyzing and reducing a relational database to its most streamlined form for minimum redundancy, maximum data integrity, and best processing performance. When data are *normalized*, attributes in the table depend only on the primary key.

As an example of normalization, consider an automotive repair garage. This business takes orders from customers who want to have their cars repaired. In this example, ORDER, PART, SUPPLIER, and CUSTOMER are entities. There can be many PARTS in an ORDER, but each PART can come from only one SUPPLIER. In a nonnormalized relation called ORDER (see Figure 3.6), each ORDER would have to repeat the name, description, and price of each PART needed to complete the ORDER, as well as the name and address of each SUPPLIER. This relation contains repeating groups and describes multiple entities.

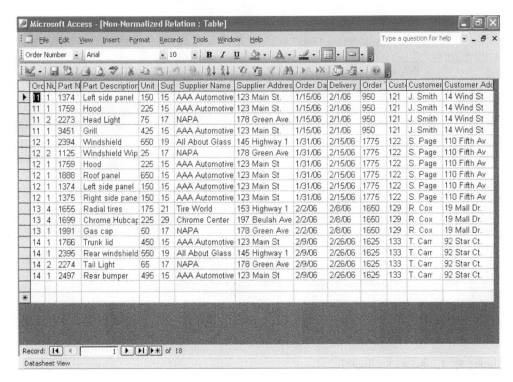

Figure 3.6 Nonnormalized relation.

For example, consider the table in Figure 3.6 and notice the very first column (labeled Order). This column contains multiple entries for each order—four rows for Order 11, six rows for Order 12, and so on. These multiple rows for an order are called repeating groups. The table in Figure 3.6 also contains multiple entities: ORDER, PART, SUPPLIER, and CUSTOMER. When you normalize the data, you want to eliminate repeating groups and have normalized tables, each containing only one entity.

You might think that four entities would mean four normalized tables. (The ORDER, SUPPLIER, and CUSTOMER tables are shown in Figure 3.7(a), and the PART table is shown in Figure 3.7(b).) But, to fully normalize the data in this example, you must create an extra table, called ORDERED-PARTS. This table (see Figure 3.7(b)) contains the particular parts, and how many of each part are in a particular order.

The normalization process, illustrated in Figure 3.8, breaks down the relation, ORDER, into smaller relations: ORDER, SUPPLIER, and CUSTOMER (Figure 3.7(a)) and ORDERED PARTS and PART (Figure 3.7(b)). Each of these relations describes a single entity. This process is conceptually simpler, and it eliminates repeating groups. For example, consider an order at the automobile repair shop. The normalized relations can produce the order in the following manner (see Figure 3.8).

- The ORDER relation provides the Order Number (the primary key), Order Date, Delivery Date, Order Total, and Customer Number.

- The primary key of the ORDER relation (Order Number) provides a link to the ORDERED PARTS relation (the link numbered 1 in Figure 3.8).

- The ORDERED PARTS relation supplies the Number of Parts information to ORDER.

- The primary key of the ORDERED PARTS relation is a composite key that consists of Order Number and Part Number. Therefore, the Part Number component of the primary key provides a link to the PART relation (the link numbered 2 in Figure 3.8).

- The PART relation supplies the Part Description, Unit Price, and Supplier Number to ORDER.

- The Supplier Number in the PART relation provides a link to the SUPPLIER relation (the link numbered 3 in Figure 3.8).

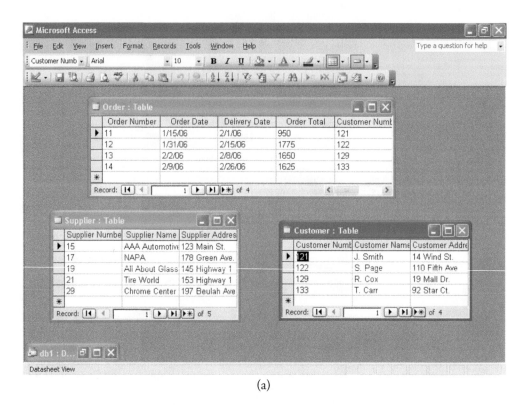

(a)

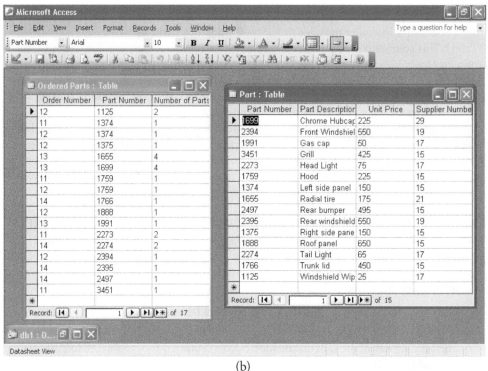

(b)

Figure 3.7 Smaller relationships broken down from the nonnormal relations. (a) Order, Supplier, Customer. (b) Ordered Parts, Part.

- The SUPPLIER relation provides the Supplier Name and Supplier Address to ORDER.
- The Customer Number in ORDER provides a link to the CUSTOMER relation (the link numbered 4 in Figure 3.8).
- The CUSTOMER relation supplies the Customer Name and Customer Address to ORDER.

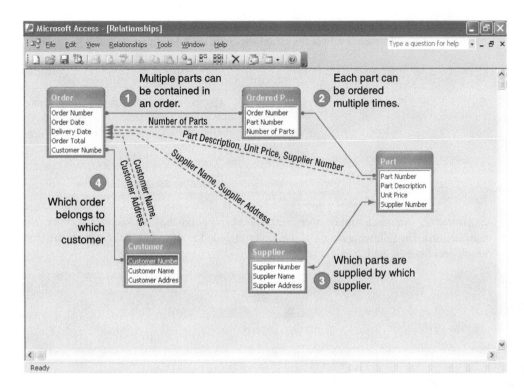

Figure 3.8 How normalized relations produce the order.

Databases in Action

It is safe to say that almost all organizations have one or more databases. Further, there are numerous interesting database applications. This chapter's Closing Case 2 describes how databases can provide the foundation for many functions in an organization.

Organizations implement databases to efficiently and effectively manage their data. However, because databases typically process data in real time (or near real time), it is not practical to allow users access to the databases. After all, the data will change while the user is looking at it! As a result, data warehouses have been developed that allow users to access data for decision making. You will learn about data warehouses in the next section.

— BEFORE *YOU GO ON . . .*

1. What are the advantages and disadvantages of relational databases?
2. What are the benefits of data dictionaries?
3. Describe how structured query language works.

Apply the Concept 3.3

Background This section has shown some of the issues with traditional filing systems. Redundancy is one of them and is a huge problem in data management because anytime there is redundancy there is a possibility to introduce error. If you have one customer listed two ways in your database, how do you know it is not two separate people? What would it do to your data analysis to have incorrect data?

Activity As was stated in Apply the Concept 3.2, there are times when the best way to learn something is to do it. Consider the following tables and scenarios and see if you can find the problems based on what you have learned in this section about normalization and problems within databases.

Scenario 1. A retail store decides to create a relational database to help keep track of its customers. The following is one of the tables included in this database.

Customer ID	First Name	Last Name	Income	Phones
1	John	Smith	$20,000	756-1111, 756-9111, 756-8400
2	Jane	Summers	$35,000	756-1000, 756-4567
3	Joe	Saunders	$30,000	756-6111
4	Jen	Smithson	$45,000	756-0094, 756-0924

Scenario 2. An office supply store creates a relational database to keep track of its sales transactions. The following is one of the tables included in the relational database the store employees have created.

Customer ID	First Name	Last Name	Customer Phone	Order Number	Order Date	Item Description	Quantity	Unit Price	Shipped
1	Kara	Liu	756-1111	1	01/02/10	Staplers	2	$18.99	Y
1	Kara	Liu	756-1111	1	01/02/10	Pens	20	$5.79	N
2	Kevin	Lawrence	756-1000	2	01/03/10	Staplers	5	$18.99	N
3	Kimberly	Long	756-6111	3	01/05/10	Pens	35	$5.79	Y

Deliverable

For Scenario 1, describe what potential problems might arise if the store continues to store its customer information in this table. Be sure to use the terminology presented in this section with your answer. What changes would you make to improve the design of this table?

For Scenario 2, describe any potential problems that may arise if the store continues to store its sales information in this table. Again, look through the terms presented in this section for your answer. What changes would you recommend to this business owner in regard to this database design?

Submit your answers to your professor.

Quiz questions are assignable in WileyPLUS, and available on the Book Companion Site at http://www.wiley.com/college/rainer.

RUBY'S CLUB | **QUESTIONS**

1. Given the type of information Ruben and Lisa want to find in their data, what advantages would they find in a relational database over multiple flat files (spreadsheets)?

2. What safety precautions could Ruben and Lisa implement for customers with a relational database? For example, a bartender may recognize that he has sold five shots to a particular customer and refuse to serve that person more out of concern for his or her health. If that customer had purchased these from different bartenders, could this have occurred?

3. What are the implications of a serve/no serve decision (due to overindulgence) from the customer viewpoint and Ruby's Club?

3.4 Data Warehouses and Data Marts

Today, the most successful companies are those that can respond quickly and flexibly to market changes and opportunities. A key to this response is the effective and efficient use of data and information by analysts and managers. The problem is providing users with access to corporate data so that they can analyze it to make better decisions. Let's look at an example. If the manager of a local bookstore wanted to know the profit margin on used books at her store, she could find out from her database, using SQL or QBE. However, if she needed to know the trend in the profit margins on used books over the last 10 years, she would have a very difficult query to construct in SQL or QBE.

This example illustrates several reasons why organizations are building data warehouses and/or data marts. First, the bookstore's databases have the necessary information to answer the manager's query, but this information is not organized in a way that makes it easy for her to find what she needs. Second, the organization's databases are designed to process millions of transactions per day. Therefore, complicated queries might take a long time to answer and might degrade the performance of the databases. Third, transactional databases are designed to be updated. This update process requires extra processing. Data warehouses and data marts are read-only, and the extra processing is eliminated because data already in the data warehouse are not updated. Fourth, transactional databases are designed to access a single record at a time. Data warehouses are designed to access large groups of related records.

As a result of these problems, companies are using a variety of tools with data warehouses and data marts to make it easier and faster for users to access, analyze, and query data. You will learn about these tools in Chapter 5: Business Intelligence.

Describing Data Warehouses and Data Marts

In general, data warehouses and data marts support business intelligence (BI) applications. As you will see in Chapter 5, business intelligence is a broad category of applications, technologies, and processes for gathering, storing, accessing, and analyzing data to help business users make better decisions. A **data warehouse** is a repository of historical data that are organized by subject to support decision makers in the organization.

Because data warehouses are so expensive, they are used primarily by large companies. A **data mart** is a low-cost, scaled-down version of a data warehouse that is designed for the end-user needs in a strategic business unit (SBU) or a department. Data marts can be implemented more quickly than data warehouses, often in less than 90 days. Further, they support local rather than central control by conferring power on the using group. Typically, groups that need a single or a few BI applications require only a data mart, rather than a data warehouse.

The basic characteristics of data warehouses and data marts include the following:

- *Organized by business dimension or subject.* Data are organized by subject (for example, by customer, vendor, product, price level, and region). This arrangement is different from transactional systems where data are organized by business process, such as order entry, inventory control, or accounts receivable.

- *Use online analytical processing.* Typically, organizational databases are oriented toward handling transactions. That is, databases use **online transaction processing** (OLTP), where business transactions are processed online as soon as they occur. The objectives are speed and efficiency, which are critical to a successful Internet-based business operation. Data warehouses and data marts, which are not designed to support OLTP but to support decision makers, use online analytical processing. *Online analytical processing (OLAP)* involves the analysis of accumulated data by end users.

- *Integrated.* Data are collected from multiple systems and are integrated around subjects. For example, customer data may be extracted from internal (and external) systems and integrated around a customer identifier so that a comprehensive view of the customer is created.

- *Time variant.* Data warehouses and data marts maintain historical data (i.e., it includes time as a variable). Unlike transactional systems, where only recent data (such as for the last day, week, or month) are maintained, a warehouse or mart may store years of data. Historical data are needed to detect deviations, trends, and long-term relationships.
- *Nonvolatile.* Data warehouses and data marts are nonvolatile—no one can change or update the data. Nonvolatility means that the warehouse or mart reflects history, which is critical for trend analysis. Warehouses and marts are updated, but through IT-controlled load processes rather than by users.
- *Multidimensional.* Typically the data warehouse or mart uses a multidimensional data structure. Recall that relational databases store data in two-dimensional tables. In contrast, data warehouses and marts store data in more than two dimensions. For this reason, the data are said to be stored in a **multidimensional structure**. A common representation for this multidimensional structure is the *data cube*.

The data in data warehouses and marts are organized by *business dimensions*, which are the edges of the data cube and are subjects such as product, geographic area, and time period. If you look ahead briefly to Figure 3.11 for an example of a data cube, you see that the product dimension is comprised of nuts, screws, bolts, and washers; the geographic area dimension is comprised of east, west, and central; and the time period dimension is comprised of 2008, 2009, and 2010. Users can view and analyze data from the perspective of these business dimensions. This analysis is intuitive because the dimensions are in business terms, easily understood by users.

A Generic Data Warehouse Environment

The environment for data warehouses and marts includes the following:

- Source systems that provide data to the warehouse or mart
- Data integration technology and processes that are needed to prepare the data for use
- Different architectures for storing data in an organization's data warehouse or data marts
- Different tools and applications for the variety of users (you will learn about these tools and applications in Chapter 5)
- Metadata, data quality, and governance processes that are in place to ensure that the warehouse or mart meets its purposes

Figure 3.9 shows a generic data warehouse/data mart environment. Let's drill down into the component parts.

Source Systems. There is typically some "organizational pain" (i.e., business need) that motivates the development of BI capabilities in a firm. Working backward, this pain leads to information requirements, BI applications, and source system data requirements. The data requirements can require only a single source system, as in the case of a data mart, or hundreds of source systems, as in the case of an enterprisewide data warehouse.

A variety of source systems can be used. Possibilities include operational/transactional systems, enterprise resource planning (ERP) systems, Web site data, third-party data (e.g., customer demographic data), and more. The trend is to include more types of data (e.g., sensing data from RFID tags). These source systems often use different software packages (e.g., IBM, Oracle) and store data in different formats (e.g., relational, hierarchical).

A common source for the data in data warehouses is the company's operational databases, which can be relational databases. To differentiate between relational databases and multidimensional data warehouses and marts, suppose your company has four products—nuts, screws, bolts, and washers—that have been sold in three territories—East, West, and Central—for the previous three years—2008, 2009, and 2010. In a relational database, these sales data would look like Figures 3.10(a), (b), and (c). In a multidimensional database, these data would be represented by a three-dimensional matrix (or data cube), as shown in Figure 3.10. You would say that this matrix represents sales *dimensioned by* products and

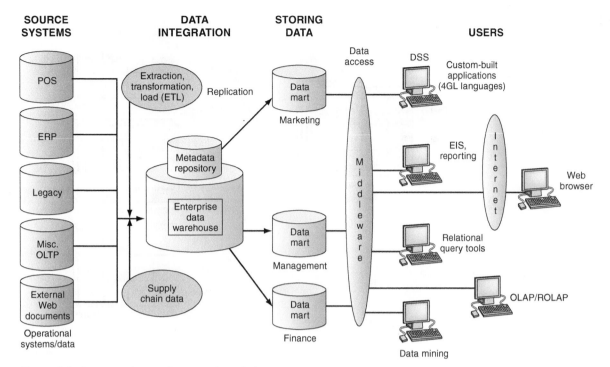

SOURCE SYSTEMS | DATA INTEGRATION | STORING DATA | USERS

Figure 3.9 Data warehouse framework and views.

regions and year. Notice that in Figure 3.10(a) you can see only sales for 2008. Therefore, sales for 2009 and 2010 are presented in Figures 3.10(b) and 3.10(c), respectively. Figures 3.12(a), (b), and (c) show the equivalence between these relational and multidimensional databases.

Many source systems have been in use for years and contain "bad data" (e.g., missing or incorrect data) and are poorly documented. As a result, data profiling software should be used at the beginning of a data warehousing project to better understand the data. For example, data profiling software can provide statistics on missing data, identify possible primary and foreign keys, and reveal how derived values (e.g., column 3 = column 1 + column 2) are calculated. Subject area database specialists (e.g., marketing, human resources) can also help in understanding and accessing the data in source systems.

Other source systems issues must be addressed. Often there are multiple systems that contain some of the same data and the best system must be selected as the source.

(a) 2009

Product	Region	Sales
Nuts	East	50
Nuts	West	60
Nuts	Central	100
Screws	East	40
Screws	West	70
Screws	Central	80
Bolts	East	90
Bolts	West	120
Bolts	Central	140
Washers	East	20
Washers	West	10
Washers	Central	30

(b) 2010

Product	Region	Sales
Nuts	East	60
Nuts	West	70
Nuts	Central	110
Screws	East	50
Screws	West	80
Screws	Central	90
Bolts	East	100
Bolts	West	130
Bolts	Central	150
Washers	East	30
Washers	West	20
Washers	Central	40

(c) 2011

Product	Region	Sales
Nuts	East	70
Nuts	West	80
Nuts	Central	120
Screws	East	60
Screws	West	90
Screws	Central	100
Bolts	East	110
Bolts	West	140
Bolts	Central	160
Washers	East	40
Washers	West	30
Washers	Central	50

Figure 3.10 Relational databases.

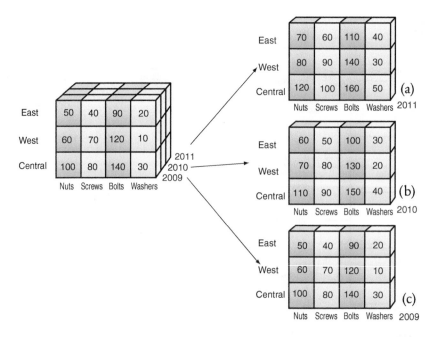

Figure 3.11 Data cube.

Organizations must also decide how granular (i.e., detailed) the data should be. For example, are daily sales figures needed or are data at the individual transaction level needed? The conventional wisdom is that it is best to store data at a highly granular level because the data are likely to be requested at some point.

Data Integration. It is necessary to extract data from source systems, transform it, and load it into a data mart or warehouse. This is often called ETL, but the term *data integration* is increasingly used because of the growing number of ways that source system data can be handled. For example, in some cases, data are extracted, loaded into a mart or warehouse, and then transformed (i.e., ELT rather than ETL).

Data extraction can be performed by handwritten code (e.g., SQL queries) or by commercial data integration software. Most companies ultimately use commercial software. It makes it relatively easy to specify the tables and attributes in the source systems that are to be used, map and schedule the movement of the data to the target (e.g., a data mart or warehouse), make the required transformations, and ultimately load the data.

The data are transformed to make them more useful. For example, data from different systems may be integrated around a common key, such as a customer identification number. This is the approach taken with customer data in order to have a 360-degree view of all interactions with customers (discussed in Chapter 12). For example, think of a bank. Customers may go to a branch, bank online, use an ATM, have a car loan, and more. The systems for these touchpoints (the numerous ways that organizations interact with customers, such as e-mail, the Web, direct contact, the telephone, etc.) are typically separate. To analyze and fully understand how customers are using the bank, it is necessary to integrate the data from the various source systems in a data mart or warehouse.

Other kinds of transformations are also made. For example, format changes to the data may be required, such as using *male* and *female* to denote gender, as opposed to 0 and 1 or M and F. Aggregations may be performed, say on sales figures, so that queries can use the summaries rather than recalculating them each time. Data cleansing software may be used to "clean up" the data, such as eliminating duplicate records (e.g., for the same customer).

Data are loaded into the warehouse or mart during a "load window." This window (i.e., the period for loading new data) is getting smaller as companies seek to have ever-fresher data in their warehouses. Many companies have moved to real-time data warehousing where data are moved (using data integration processes) from source systems to the data warehouse or mart almost immediately. For example, within 15 minutes of a purchase at Walmart, the details of the sale are in a warehouse and available for analysis.

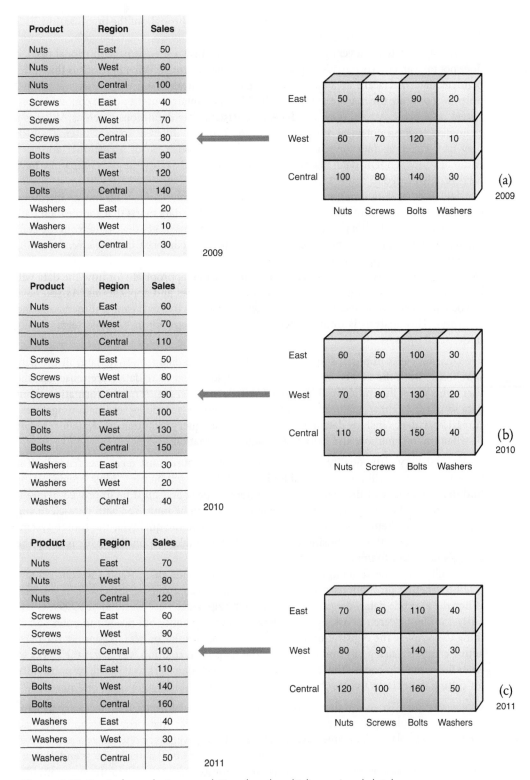

Product	Region	Sales
Nuts	East	50
Nuts	West	60
Nuts	Central	100
Screws	East	40
Screws	West	70
Screws	Central	80
Bolts	East	90
Bolts	West	120
Bolts	Central	140
Washers	East	20
Washers	West	10
Washers	Central	30

2009

	Nuts	Screws	Bolts	Washers
East	50	40	90	20
West	60	70	120	10
Central	100	80	140	30

(a) 2009

Product	Region	Sales
Nuts	East	60
Nuts	West	70
Nuts	Central	110
Screws	East	50
Screws	West	80
Screws	Central	90
Bolts	East	100
Bolts	West	130
Bolts	Central	150
Washers	East	30
Washers	West	20
Washers	Central	40

2010

	Nuts	Screws	Bolts	Washers
East	60	50	100	30
West	70	80	130	20
Central	110	90	150	40

(b) 2010

Product	Region	Sales
Nuts	East	70
Nuts	West	80
Nuts	Central	120
Screws	East	60
Screws	West	90
Screws	Central	100
Bolts	East	110
Bolts	West	140
Bolts	Central	160
Washers	East	40
Washers	West	30
Washers	Central	50

2011

	Nuts	Screws	Bolts	Washers
East	70	60	110	40
West	80	90	140	30
Central	120	100	160	50

(c) 2011

Figure 3.12 Equivalence between relational and multidimensional databases.

Storing the Data. A variety of possible architectures can store decision support data. The most common architecture is *one central enterprise data warehouse*, without data marts. Most organizations use this approach, as the data in the warehouse is accessed by all users and is the *single version of the truth*.

Another architecture is *independent data marts*. With this architecture, data are stored for a single or a few applications, such as in marketing or finance. Limited thought is given to how the data might be used for other applications and throughout the organization. This is a very application-centric approach to storing data.

This approach is not very good. Although it may meet a specific organizational need, it does not take an enterprisewide approach to data management. What happens is that independent data marts are created throughout the organization by various organizational units. Not only are the marts expensive to build and maintain, but they often contain inconsistent data. For example, they may have inconsistent data definitions (such as, What is a customer? Is one a potential or current customer?) or use different source systems (which may have different data for what should be the same, such as for a customer address). Although independent data marts are an organizational reality, larger companies have increasingly moved to data warehouses.

Still another data warehouse architecture is the *hub and spoke*. With this architecture, data are stored in a central data warehouse with dependent data marts that source their data from the central repository. Because the dependent data marts get their data from the central repository, the data in the dependent data marts still comprise the *single version of the truth* for decision support purposes.

The dependent data marts store the data in a format appropriate for how the data will be used and for providing faster response times to queries and applications. As you have learned, users can view and analyze data from the perspective of business dimensions and measures. This analysis is intuitive because the dimensions are in business terms, easily understood by users.

Metadata. It is important to maintain data about the data (i.e., metadata) in the data warehouse. Both the IT personnel who operate and manage the data warehouse and the users who access the warehouse's data need metadata. IT personnel need information about data sources; database, table, and column names; refresh schedules; and data usage measures. Users' needs include data definitions; the report/query tools that are available; report distribution information; and help desk contact information.

Data Quality. The quality of the data in the warehouse must meet users' needs. If it does not, the data will not be trusted and ultimately will not be used. Most organizations find that the quality of the data in source systems is poor and must be improved before it can be used in the data warehouse. Some of the data can be improved with data-cleansing software, but the better, long-term solution is to improve the quality at the source system level. This requires that the business owners of the data take responsibility for making the changes necessary to improve the quality of the data.

To illustrate a need to improve data quality, a large hotel chain wanted to conduct targeted marketing promotions using zip code data collected during the check-in process. When the zip code data were profiled, many of the zip codes were found to be 99999. Obviously, the clerks were not asking customers for their zip codes but needed to enter something to complete the registration process. A short-term solution was to conduct the marketing campaign using city and state data. The long-term solution was to get the clerks to enter the actual zip codes. The latter required the hotel managers to take the responsibility for getting their clerks to enter better data.

Governance. To ensure that BI is meeting organizational needs, it is necessary to have governance to plan and control BI activities. This requires that people, committees, and processes be in place. Companies that are effective in BI governance often have a senior-level committee made up of vice-presidents and directors who ensure that the business and BI strategies are in alignment; prioritize projects; and allocate resources. Then there is a middle management–level committee that oversees the various projects in the BI portfolio and sees that the projects are being completed effectively and efficiently. Lower-level operational committees perform tasks such as creating data definitions and identifying and solving data problems. All these committees require the collaboration and contributions of business and IT personnel.

Users. Once the data are in a data mart or warehouse, access is possible. This access begins the process of receiving business value from BI; everything else constitutes creating BI infrastructure.

Potential BI users are many, including IT developers; frontline workers; analysts; information workers; managers and executives; and suppliers, customers, and regulators. Some of these users are *information producers* in that they primarily create information for others. IT developers and analysts typically are in this category. On the other hand, some users are *information consumers*, including managers and executives, because they consume information created by others.

Companies have reported hundreds of successful data-warehousing applications. For example, you can read client success stories and case studies at the Web sites of vendors such as NCR Corp. (www.ncr.com) and Oracle (www.oracle.com). For a more detailed discussion, visit the Data Warehouse Institute (http://tdwi.org). The benefits of data warehousing include the following:

- End users can access needed data quickly and easily via Web browsers because these data are located in one place.

- End users can conduct extensive analysis with data in ways that may not have been possible before.

- End users can obtain a consolidated view of organizational data.

These benefits can improve business knowledge, provide competitive advantage, enhance customer service and satisfaction, facilitate decision making, and streamline business processes. IT's About Business 3.2 demonstrates the benefits of data warehousing to the state of Michigan.

T'S ABOUT BUSINESS 3.2

A Data Warehouse Provides Value for the State of Michigan

In a tight economic climate, state governments are looking closely at methods to save money. For instance, the state of Michigan tried to increase savings by consolidating 40 data centers into 3 and consolidating state data into a data warehouse. The data warehouse contained data from the Department of Community Health, the state police, the department of corrections, the department of natural resources, the court administration office, and many other state agencies.

The Michigan state data warehouse serves 10,000 users from 21 different state agencies. For the first time in Michigan state history, users of the data warehouse can analyze data across Michigan state agencies. Previously, state data had resided in silos for each separate state agency. Analysis of the data in the data warehouse has provided the following interesting results:

- By accessing motor vehicle records and hunting and fishing licenses, the state located parents who were behind (or had never paid) child support.

- The Michigan Department of Treasury increased the number of tax returns they review from 6,000 in the old paper-

© Felix Alim/iStockphoto

based system to 452,000 in 2011.

- The Michigan Department of Treasury can now use data to look at ways of revising the state tax code to make Michigan more attractive to business.

- The state can use birth records in the data warehouse to identify children born to Medicaid parents and enroll them in the same managed care plan as their parents.

- For patients with diabetes, the data warehouse tracks their treatment plans and treatment received, and can deliver a year's health history to a new physician if a patient moves.

- The data warehouse helps the Department of Health and Human Services determine the best placement for foster children. If the department receives an emergency call to relocate a child, it can search its data on foster families, which is tied to geographical mapping data, and find an appropriate home within the same neighborhood or school district to minimize the child's disruption.

- The data warehouse revealed that the state's lead poisoning prevention program was far less effective than previously thought by the Michigan Department of Health and Human Services. In response, department personnel then began going door to door in the most affected regions to warn residents of the danger, test residents who had not already been tested, and arrange for corrective measures.

What is the bottom line? Let's only consider Medicaid in Michigan. Michigan's Medicaid program has a $14 billion budget, with almost 2 million clients. The data warehouse is saving the Michigan Medicaid system $1 million each business day, as measured by Michigan's Department of Community Health. The state achieved these savings by billing Medicaid patients' existing insurance plans when they had them, using death records to recover payments made to clients who died, and reducing fraud.

Other states can follow Michigan's lead and develop their own data warehouses. In that way, they too will be able to gain added efficiency and effectiveness in state government.

Sources: Compiled from T. Groenfeldt, "Big Data Saves Michigan $1 Million Each Business Day," *Forbes*, January 11, 2012; T. Groenfeldt, "Michigan Saves $1 Million Per Business Day with Data Warehouse," *WTN News*, October 5, 2011; "State of Michigan Serves as National Model for Better Healthcare," *Ingenix.com*, accessed February 25, 2012; "State of Michigan Data," www.michigan.gov, accessed February 28, 2012.

Questions

1. Why is it so important for organizations to integrate data that is currently stored in silos? Provide examples from the state of Michigan's experience to support your answer.

2. What are some potential disadvantages of consolidating Michigan's data into one data warehouse?

BEFORE YOU GO ON . . .

1. Differentiate between data warehouses and data marts.
2. Describe the characteristics of a data warehouse.
3. What are three possible architectures for data warehouses and data marts in an organization?

Despite their many benefits, data warehouses do have problems. First, they can be very expensive to build and to maintain. Second, incorporating data from obsolete mainframe systems can be difficult and expensive. Finally, people in one department might be reluctant to share data with other departments.

Apply the Concept 3.4

Background Section 3.4 has shown you how that databases, data warehouses, and data marts are used to help organizations keep up with how fast the market changes. Another difficulty is that technology itself is changing so fast that it is hard to keep up with what is possible. Many organizations are at a point where they know they need to upgrade systems, but the possible technology options are so many they do not know which one will carry them the farthest into the future.

Activity Visit http://www.wiley.com/go/rainer/applytheconcept and click on the link provided for Apply the Concept 3.4. It will take you to a YouTube video titled "UNC Data Warehouse" by user "ibmhealthcare." This video will show an example of how University of North Carolina (UNC) brought multiple systems together in one data warehouse and improved project proposals and usability of the system. As you watch the video, think about the data now available that was not accessible before the university's data warehouse was built. Also, consider the different systems that support your university or college compared to the (somewhat) synchronized system at UNC.

Deliverable

List some of the challenges in implementing data warehouses at the UNC Health System. Also list the benefits the UNC Health System gained from its data warehouse. Now list the multiple systems you imagine your school has and what advantages they could receive from a single centralized system rather than multiple systems.

Quiz questions are assignable in WileyPLUS, and available on the Book Companion Site at http://www.wiley.com/college/rainer.

3.5 Knowledge Management

As noted throughout this text, data and information are critically important organizational assets. Knowledge is a vital asset as well. Successful managers have always used intellectual assets and recognized their value. But these efforts were not systematic, and they did not ensure that knowledge was shared and dispersed in a way that benefited the overall organization. Moreover, industry analysts estimate that most of a company's knowledge assets are not housed in relational databases. Instead, they are dispersed in e-mail, word processing documents, spreadsheets, and presentations on individual computers. This arrangement makes it extremely difficult for companies to access and integrate this knowledge. The result frequently is less-effective decision making.

Concepts and Definitions

Knowledge management (KM) is a process that helps organizations manipulate important knowledge that is part of the organization's memory, usually in an unstructured format. For an organization to be successful, knowledge, as a form of capital, must exist in a format that can be exchanged among persons. In addition, it must be able to grow.

Knowledge. In the information technology context, knowledge is distinct from data and information. As you learned in Chapter 1, data are a collection of facts, measurements, and statistics; information is organized or processed data that are timely and accurate. Knowledge is information that is *contextual*, *relevant*, and *useful*. Simply put, knowledge is *information in action*. **Intellectual capital** (or **intellectual assets**) is another term for knowledge.

To illustrate with an example, a bulletin listing all the courses offered by your university during one semester would be considered data. When you register, you process the data from the bulletin to create your schedule for the semester. Your schedule would be considered information. Awareness of your work schedule, your major, your desired social schedule, and characteristics of different faculty members could be construed as knowledge, because it can affect the way you build your schedule. You see that this awareness is contextual and relevant (to developing an optimal schedule of classes) as well as useful (it can lead to changes in your schedule). The implication is that knowledge has strong experiential and reflective elements that distinguish it from information in a given context. Unlike information, knowledge can be exercised to solve a problem.

Numerous theories and models classify different types of knowledge. Here you will focus on the distinction between explicit knowledge and tacit knowledge.

Explicit and Tacit Knowledge. **Explicit knowledge** deals with more objective, rational, and technical knowledge. In an organization, explicit knowledge consists of the policies, procedural guides, reports, products, strategies, goals, core competencies, and IT infrastructure of the enterprise. In other words, explicit knowledge is the knowledge that has been codified (documented) in a form that can be distributed to others or transformed into a process or a strategy. A description of how to process a job application that is documented in a firm's human resources policy manual is an example of explicit knowledge.

In contrast, **tacit knowledge** is the cumulative store of subjective or experiential learning. In an organization, tacit knowledge consists of an organization's experiences, insights, expertise, know-how, trade secrets, skill sets, understanding, and learning. It also includes the organizational culture, which reflects the past and present experiences of the organization's people and processes, as well as the organization's prevailing values. Tacit knowledge is generally imprecise and costly to transfer. It is also highly personal. Finally, because it is unstructured, it is difficult to formalize or codify, in contrast to explicit knowledge. A salesperson who has worked with particular customers over time and has come to know their needs quite well would possess extensive tacit knowledge. This knowledge is typically not recorded. In fact, it might be difficult for the salesperson to put into writing.

Knowledge Management Systems

The goal of knowledge management is to help an organization make the most effective use of the knowledge it has. Historically, management information systems have focused on capturing, storing, managing, and reporting explicit knowledge. Organizations now realize they need to integrate explicit and tacit knowledge in formal information systems. **Knowledge management systems (KMSs)** refer to the use of modern information technologies—the Internet, intranets, extranets, databases—to systematize, enhance, and expedite intrafirm and interfirm knowledge management. KMSs are intended to help an organization cope with turnover, rapid change, and downsizing by making the expertise of the organization's human capital widely accessible. IT's About Business 3.3 describes a new type of knowledge management at Quora.

'S ABOUT BUSINESS 3.3

A Web Site for Gathering Subjective Knowledge

Two decades after the invention of the World Wide Web, vast areas of knowledge and experience are still not online, let alone searchable. "Ninety percent of the information people have is still in their heads and not on the Web," says one of Quora's cofounders. Quora's other cofounder calls it "experiential knowledge." Wikipedia (www.wikipedia.org) has amazing breadth and scope, but there is only so much that any encyclopedia, limited to verifiable facts about discrete nouns, can capture within the entire database of human knowledge. On the other end of the "knowledge" spectrum, Web sites such as Facebook and Twitter allow people to describe their lives and to make personal observations. However, it is very difficult on such networks to separate informed opinions from speculation.

Quora (www.quora.com), a question-and-answer (Q&A) Web site, straddles the space between the two approaches—the objective (Wikipedia) and the subjective (social networks). Other Q&A sites include Yahoo!

Answers (http://answers.yahoo.com) and WikiAnswers (http://wiki.answers.com). Yahoo! Answers is the leading Q&A site, with 204 million unique visitors worldwide in November 2011. But few searches can be satisfied with Yahoo! Answers, where the questions are often silly and the replies are often conflicting or flat-out inaccurate. Many replies tend to be guesswork offered by people with little or no knowledge of the subject at hand.

On Quora's Web site, you can get started with the page—framed as a question—about getting started on Quora. Or you can begin by sifting through random questions that are displayed in the center of the screen. On the top of the Quora homepage is a large search bar. Using key words, you can find questions that others have already posed or choose topics to follow so that the Web site can begin serving up queries more suited to your interests. You can also start following people. That way, the questions that people you are following ask, the answers they get, and the questions they follow will show up in your feed. You can also vote "up" answers that you think are helpful, and vote "down" those that are not. All of your activity shows up in your feed.

Quora offers several advantages over other Q&A sites, including the following:

- Real names are mandatory, so there is a heavy social cost to acting the fool. Real names increase the quality of answers and reduce bad behavior and flaming. Quora does allow anonymous posts, however, which helps when asking about a personal health issue, for example, or responding about your own experience as a fellow sufferer.

- Many Web sites provide only one viewpoint at a time on a particular issue, meaning that the user has to search for referencing articles or scan through many comments to find a counterpoint. Quora allows both point and counterpoint to coexist at an equal level in a discussion.

- Quora encourages answers that are thorough and in-depth. In Quora's community, the most valued responses reflect honest intelligence and wisdom.

- Users can vote an answer up or down, the better to push quality to the top and frivolous or poorly conceived answers to the bottom (if not off the page entirely). Users can also deem an answer "not helpful"—a signal to the Quora team or one of the site's hundred-plus volunteers that perhaps they should consider deleting it.

- Unlike on Facebook, everything users write can be trimmed, corrected, or otherwise edited by one of the rigorous volunteers. Volunteers often send answers back to their authors marked up with suggested edits. Questions, too, can get extensively reworded.

Quora's goal is to capture as much subjective knowledge as possible. By creating an environment for members to post questions, answer questions, and rate the quality of others' answers, Quora is building a searchable repository of information while it also builds a community. Quora hopes to attract so many users that its subjective, experiential, inherent knowledge will construct a comprehensive picture of the world.

Despite these admirable goals, one major complaint about Quora has emerged. Veteran members have noted a declining quality associated with the rapid growth in Quora membership. Both founders acknowledge that the average quality of answers on Quora has declined significantly. The site was flooded with so many new members at the start of 2011—a 500 percent increase in just one month—that at one point in mid-January 2011, half of Quora's users had been on the site for two weeks or less. Quora's "old hands" felt that the newcomers posed unintelligent questions. Even worse, the newcomers pushed up other users' answers even when those answers were tangential and not helpful.

Another problem with Quora is the large gaps in its knowledge areas, which is only to be expected as the Web site is relatively young, having emerged in 2009. One example of a knowledge gap is that Quora has brilliant entries for high-tech startups but almost no entries for Hollywood.

Despite these shortcomings, in mid-2012 approximately 300,000 people were visiting Quora's Web site each month. Quora has not yet earned any revenue. But, if Quora can fulfill its vision of getting experts to engage in conversation and thus generate searchable and authoritative answers to many thousands of questions, then it may someday grab more page views than Wikipedia by filling in gaps that no encyclopedia could ever address.

Sources: Compiled from N. Robertson, "Five Reasons Why Quora Matters to Marketers," *Marketingprofs.com*, June 14, 2011; G. Rivlin, "Does Quora Really Have All the Answers?" *Wired*, April 26, 2011; M. Lowman, "The Mystery Behind Quora," *BostInnovation*, February 1, 2011; S. Goodson, "Why Is Quora Exploding?" *Forbes*, January 11, 2011; M. Ingram, "Can Quora Survive Its Growing Popularity?" *GigaOm*, January 9, 2011; C. Arthur and J. Kiss, "Quora: The Hottest Question-and-Answer Website You've Probably Never Heard Of," *The Guardian*, January 5, 2011; M. Siegler, "Quora Signups Exploded in Late December," *TechCrunch*, January 5, 2011; Q. Hardy, "What Does Quora Know?" *Forbes*, November 18, 2010; www.quora.com, accessed February 26, 2012.

Questions

1. Compare and contrast Quora to knowledge management systems in individual organizations. Could a Quora-type knowledge management system be used inside an organization? Why or why not? Support your answer.

2. Provide examples of how Quora can fill in the gaps in its searchable knowledge base.

Organizations can realize many benefits with KMSs. Most importantly, they make **best practices**, the most effective and efficient ways of doing things, readily available to a wide range of employees. Enhanced access to best-practice knowledge improves overall organizational performance. For example, account managers can now make available their tacit knowledge about how best to handle large accounts. The organization can then use this knowledge to train new account managers. Other benefits include improved customer service, more efficient product development, and improved employee morale and retention.

At the same time, however, implementing effective KMSs presents some challenges. First, employees must be willing to share their personal tacit knowledge. To encourage this behavior, organizations must create a knowledge management culture that rewards employees who add their expertise to the knowledge base. Second, the knowledge base must be continually maintained and updated. New knowledge must be added, and old, outdated knowledge must be deleted. Finally, companies must be willing to invest in the resources needed to carry out these operations.

The KMS Cycle

A functioning KMS follows a cycle that consists of six steps (see Figure 3.13). The reason the system is cyclical is that knowledge is dynamically refined over time. The knowledge in an effective KMS is never finalized because the environment changes over time and knowledge must be updated to reflect these changes. The cycle works as follows:

1. *Create knowledge.* Knowledge is created as people determine new ways of doing things or develop know-how. Sometimes external knowledge is brought in.

2. *Capture knowledge.* New knowledge must be identified as valuable and be represented in a reasonable way.

3. *Refine knowledge.* New knowledge must be placed in context so that it is actionable. This is where tacit qualities (human insights) must be captured along with explicit facts.

4. *Store knowledge.* Useful knowledge must then be stored in a reasonable format in a knowledge repository so that others in the organization can access it.

5. *Manage knowledge.* Like a library, the knowledge must be kept current. It must be reviewed regularly to verify that it is relevant and accurate.

6. *Disseminate knowledge.* Knowledge must be made available in a useful format to anyone in the organization who needs it, anywhere and anytime.

— BEFORE *YOU GO ON . . .* —

1. What is knowledge management?
2. What is the difference between tacit knowledge and explicit knowledge?
3. Describe the knowledge management system cycle.

Figure 3.13 The knowledge management system cycle.

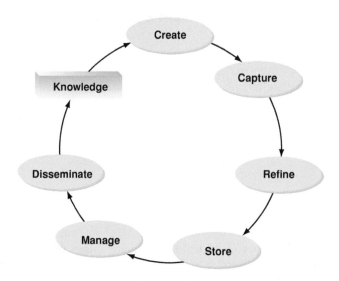

Apply the Concept 3.5

Background As you have already learned in this text, data are captured, stored, analyzed, and shared to create knowledge within organizations. This knowledge is exposed in meetings when colleagues are interpreting the information they received from the latest report, when presentations are given, through e-mail among co-workers, etc. The problem many organizations face is that there are massive amounts of knowledge created and shared, but it is not stored in a centralized, searchable format.

Activity Visit http://www.wiley.com/go/rainer/applytheconcept and click on the links provided for Apply the Concept 3.5. They will take you to two YouTube videos. First is "Discover What You Know" by user "porterken" and second is "Lee Bryant—Knowledge Management" by user "usnowfilm." Each of these illustrate the importance of capturing knowledge within an organization so that it may be shared with the right person at the right time to help support making the right decision.

Deliverable

Write a short paragraph or two to discuss the challenges faced by companies when they attempt to implement a knowledge management system. How many of these are technical and how many are social? Also, discuss the ways that companies can use Web 2.0 technologies to help capture and share knowledge. Submit this to your instructor.

Quiz questions are assignable in WileyPLUS, and available on the Book Companion Site at http://www.wiley.com/college/rainer.

RUBY'S CLUB QUESTIONS

1. Explicit and tacit knowledge are two very different animals. Explicit knowledge is defined as knowledge that is easily captured. Tacit knowledge is more difficult to manage. Think of the bartender who works for Ruben and Lisa. What are some examples of explicit and tacit knowledge he/she may acquire over time?

2. Can you think of any ways to capture the tacit knowledge from a bartender and pass it on to another new employee?

What's in IT for ME?

FOR THE ACCOUNTING MAJOR

The accounting function is intimately concerned with keeping track of the transactions and internal controls of an organization. Modern databases enable accountants to perform these functions more effectively. Databases help accountants manage the flood of data in today's organizations so that they can keep their firms in compliance with the standards imposed by Sarbanes-Oxley.

Accountants also play a role in cost justifying the creation of a knowledge base and then auditing its cost-effectiveness. In addition, if you work for a large CPA company that provides management services or sells knowledge, you will most likely use some of your company's best practices that are stored in a knowledge base.

FOR THE FINANCE MAJOR

Financial managers make extensive use of computerized databases that are external to the organization, such as CompuStat or Dow Jones, to obtain financial data on organizations in their industry. They can use these data to determine if their organization meets industry benchmarks in return on investment, cash management, and other financial ratios.

Financial managers, who produce the organization's financial status reports, are also closely involved with Sarbanes-Oxley. Databases help these managers comply with the law's standards.

FOR THE MARKETING MAJOR

Databases help marketing managers access data from the organization's marketing transactions, such as customer purchases, to plan targeted marketing campaigns and to evaluate the success of previous campaigns. Knowledge about customers can make the difference between success and failure. In many databases and knowledge bases, the vast majority of information and knowledge concerns customers, products, sales, and marketing. Marketing managers regularly use an organization's knowledge base, and they often participate in its creation.

FOR THE
PRODUCTION/OPERATIONS MANAGEMENT MAJOR

Production/operations personnel access organizational data to determine optimum inventory levels for parts in a production process. Past production data enable production/operations management (POM) personnel to determine the optimum configuration for assembly lines. Firms also collect quality data that inform them not only about the quality of finished products but also about quality issues with incoming raw materials, production irregularities, shipping and logistics, and after-sale use and maintenance of the product.

Knowledge management is extremely important for running complex operations. The accumulated knowledge regarding scheduling, logistics, maintenance, and other functions is very valuable. Innovative ideas are necessary for improving operations and can be supported by knowledge management.

FOR THE
HUMAN RESOURCES MANAGEMENT MAJOR

Organizations keep extensive data on employees, including gender, age, race, current and past job descriptions, and performance evaluations. HR personnel access these data to provide reports to government agencies regarding compliance with federal equal opportunity guidelines. HR managers also use these data to evaluate hiring practices, evaluate salary structures, and manage any discrimination grievances or lawsuits brought against the firm.

Databases help HR managers provide assistance to all employees as companies turn over more and more decisions about health care and retirement planning to the employees themselves. The employees can use the databases for help in selecting the optimal mix among these critical choices.

HR managers also need to use a knowledge base frequently to find out how past cases were handled. Consistency in how employees are treated not only is important, but it also protects the company against legal actions. In addition, training for building, maintaining, and using the knowledge system sometimes is the responsibility of the HR department. Finally, the HR department might be responsible for compensating employees who contribute their knowledge to the knowledge base.

SUMMARY

1. **Discuss ways that common challenges in managing data can be addressed using data governance.**

   The following are three common challenges in managing data:

   > Data are scattered throughout organizations and are collected by many individuals using various methods and devices. These data are frequently stored in numerous servers and locations and in different computing systems, databases, formats, and human and computer languages.

   > Data come from multiple sources.

   > Information systems that support particular business processes impose unique requirements on data, which results in repetition and conflicts across an organization.

   One strategy for implementing data governance is master data management. Master data management provides companies with the ability to store, maintain, exchange, and synchronize a consistent, accurate, and timely "single version of the truth" for the company's core master data. Master data management consistently manages data gathered from across an organization, consistently manages data from multiple sources, and consistently manages data across business processes in an organization.

2. **Explain how to interpret relationships depicted in an entity-relationship diagram.**

   See Figure 3.4 and its accompanying explanation for a demonstration of interpreting relationships in an ER diagram.

3. **Discuss the advantages and disadvantages of relational databases.**

   Relational databases allow people to compare information quickly by row or column. In addition, items are easy to retrieve by finding the point of intersection of a particular row and column. On the other hand, large-scale relational databases can be composed of many interrelated tables, making the overall design complex with slow search and access times.

4. **Explain the elements necessary to successfully implement and maintain data warehouses.**

   To successfully implement and main a data warehouse, an organization must:

   > Link source systems that provide data to the warehouse or mart.

   > Prepare the necessary data for the data warehouse using data integration technology and processes.

   > Decide on an appropriate architecture for storing data in the data warehouse or data mart.

   > Select the tools and applications for the variety of organizational users.

   > Ensure that metadata, data quality, and governance processes are in place to ensure that the data warehouse or mart meets its purposes.

5. **Describe the benefits and challenges of implementing knowledge management systems in organizations.**

   Organizations can realize many benefits with KMSs.

   > Best practices are readily available to a wide range of employees.

   > Improved customer service;

   > More efficient product development;

   > Improved employee morale and retention.

   Challenges to implementing KMSs include:

   > Employees must be willing to share their personal tacit knowledge;

   > Organizations must create a knowledge management culture that rewards employees who add their expertise to the knowledge base

   > The knowledge base must be continually maintained and updated.

   > Companies must be willing to invest in the resources needed to carry out these operations.

   Organizations can use knowledge management to develop best practices, to establish the most effective and efficient ways of doing things, and to make these practices readily available to a wide range of employees. Other benefits of knowledge management include improved customer service, more efficient product development, and improved employee morale and retention.

   A functioning KMS follows a cycle that consists of six steps: create knowledge, capture knowledge, refine knowledge, store knowledge, manage knowledge, and disseminate knowledge.

attribute Each characteristic or quality describing a particular entity.

best practices The most effective and efficient ways to do things.

bit A binary digit—that is, a 0 or a 1.

byte A group of eight bits that represents a single character.

clickstream data Data collected about user behavior and browsing patterns by monitoring users' activities when they visit a Web site.

data dictionary Collection of definitions of data elements; data characteristics that use the data elements; and the individuals, business functions, applications, and reports that use this data element.

data governance An approach to managing information across an entire organization.

data mart A low-cost, scaled-down version of a data warehouse that is designed for the end-user needs in a strategic business unit (SBU) or a department.

data model Definition of the way data in a DBMS are conceptually structured.

data warehouse A repository of historical data that are organized by subject to support decision makers in the organization.

database A group of logically related files that stores data and the associations among them.

database management system (DBMS) The software program (or group of programs) that provides access to a database.

entity A person, place, thing, or event about which information is maintained in a record.

entity classes Groupings of entities of a given type.

entity-relationship (ER) diagram Document that shows data entities and attributes and relationships among them.

entity-relationship (ER) modeling The process of designing a database by organizing data entities to be used and identifying the relationships among them.

explicit knowledge The more objective, rational, and technical types of knowledge.

field A grouping of logically related characters into a word, a small group of words, or a complete number.

file A grouping of logically related records.

identifiers Attributes that are unique to an entity instance.

instance A particular entity within an entity class.

intellectual capital (or **intellectual assets**) Other terms for knowledge.

knowledge management (KM) A process that helps organizations identify, select, organize, disseminate, transfer, and apply information and expertise that are part of the organization's memory and that typically reside within the organization in an unstructured manner.

knowledge management systems (KMSs) Information technologies used to systematize, enhance, and expedite intra- and inter-firm knowledge management.

master data A set of core data, such as customer, product, employee, vendor, geographic location, and so on, that spans an enterprise's information systems.

master data management A process that provides companies with the ability to store, maintain, exchange, and synchronize a consistent, accurate, and timely "single version of the truth" for the company's core master data.

multidimensional structure Storage of data in more than two dimensions; a common representation is the *data cube*.

normalization A method for analyzing and reducing a relational database to its most streamlined form for minimum redundancy, maximum data integrity, and best processing performance.

online transaction processing (OLTP) Processing of business transactions online as soon as they occur.

primary key The identifier field or attribute that uniquely identifies a record.

query by example (QBE) Database language that enables the user to fill out a grid (form) to construct a sample or description of the data wanted.

record A grouping of logically related fields.

relational database model Data model based on the simple concept of tables in order to capitalize on characteristics of rows and columns of data.

secondary key An identifier field or attribute that has some identifying information but typically does not identify the file with complete accuracy.

structured query language (SQL) Popular relational database language that enables users to perform complicated searches with relatively simple instructions.

table A grouping of logically related records.

tacit knowledge The cumulative store of subjective or experiential learning, which is highly personal and hard to formalize.

>>> DISCUSSION QUESTIONS

1. Explain the difficulties involved in managing data.

2. What are the problems associated with poor-quality data?

3. What is master data management? What does it have to do with high-quality data?

4. Explain why master data management is so important in companies that have multiple data sources.

5. Describe the advantages of relational databases.

6. Explain why it is important to capture and manage knowledge.

7. Compare and contrast tacit knowledge and explicit knowledge.

1. Access various employment Web sites (e.g., www. monster.com and www.dice.com) and find several job descriptions for a database administrator. Are the job descriptions similar? What are the salaries offered in these positions?

2. Access the Web sites of several real estate companies. Find the sites that take you through a step-by-step process for buying a home, that provide virtual reality tours of homes in your price range and location, that provide mortgage and interest rate calculators, and that offer financing for your home. Do the sites require that you register to access their services? Can you request that an e-mail be sent to you when properties in which you might be interested become available?

3. It is possible to find many Web sites that provide demographic information. Access several of these sites and see what they offer. Do the sites differ in the types of demographic information they offer? If so, how? Do the sites require a fee for the information they offer? Would demographic information be useful to you if you wanted to start a new business? If so, how and why?

4. The Internet contains many Web sites that provide information on financial aid resources for students. Access several of these sites. Do you have to register to access the information? Can you apply for financial aid on the sites, or do you have to request paper applications that you must complete and return?

5. Draw an entity-relationship diagram for a small retail store. You wish to keep track of the product name, description, unit price, and number of items of that product sold to each customer. You also wish to record customer name, mailing address, and billing address. You must track each transaction (sale) as to date, product purchased, unit price, number of units, tax, and total amount of the sale.

6. Draw the entity-relationship diagram for the following patient appointment system. The business rules of this system are the following:

    A doctor can be scheduled for many appointments but might not have any scheduled at all. Each appointment is scheduled with exactly one doctor. A patient can schedule one or more appointments. One appointment is scheduled with exactly one patient. An appointment must generate exactly one bill, and a bill is generated by only one appointment. One payment is applied to exactly one bill, and one bill can be paid off over time by several payments. A bill can be outstanding, having nothing yet paid on it at all. One patient can make many payments, but a single payment is made by only one patient. Some patients are insured by an insurance company. If they are insured, they can only carry insurance with one insurance company. An insurance company can have many patients carry their policies. For patients who carry insurance, the insurance company will make payments, with each single payment made by exactly one insurance company.

7. Access the Web sites of IBM (www.ibm.com), Sybase (www.sybase.com), and Oracle (www.oracle.com), and trace the capabilities of their latest data management products, including Web connections.

8. Enter the Web site of the Gartner Group (www.gartner. com). Examine the company's research studies pertaining to data management. Prepare a report on the state of the art.

9. Calculate your personal digital footprint at http://www. wiley.com/go/rainer/problemsolving.

10. Diagram a knowledge management system cycle for a fictional company that sells customized T-shirts to students.

>>> COLLABORATION EXERCISE

Background

Imagine that you and a few colleagues are given the job of determining designing a database for a pet store. The manager has asked that the following data be collected. Of course, there are multiple attributes for each of these entities. Your team has been tasked with outlining the specific data required to make this database a reality.

- Customer data
- Product data
- Employee data
- Financial data
- Vendor data
- Sales data
- Inventory data
- Building data
- Other data (specify)

Recall from the chapter that an entity-relationship diagram (ER diagram) displays the data that would be contained within multiple tables as well as the relationships between those tables.

Activity

Divide into teams as instructed by your professor. Then equally divide the team by functional area. You will need some operations, marketing, accounting, human resources, management, etc., representatives on your team. Decide which functional area should work with the entities listed above.

Independently define the attributes for each entity. Once you complete this individual task, work with your group to find relationships among the attributes. You may have to add or remove or change some to reconcile the data you would collect in the individual tables.

Build your ER Diagram using Google Docs. If you are not familiar with Google Drawings, visit http://www.wiley.com/ go/rainer/collaboration and click on the link for Chapter 3 Collaboration Exercise. It will take you to a YouTube and search for "Introduction to Google Drawing" by "logontolearn."

Deliverable

Submit your group's ER Diagram to your instructor to review.

CLOSING **CASE 1** > Big Data

Organizations and individuals need to process an unimaginably vast amount of data that is growing ever more rapidly. According to the IDC Digital Universe study, in 2011 the world generated 1.8 zettabytes of data. (A zettabyte is one trillion gigabytes, the equivalent of the information on 250 billion DVDs.) Furthermore, the amount of data produced worldwide is increasing by 50 percent each year. Analysts have coined the term *Big Data* for the super-abundance of data available today. Big data generally consists of the following:

- Traditional enterprise data—examples include customer information from customer relationship management systems, transactional enterprise resource planning data, Web store transactions, general ledger data.

- Machine-generated/sensor data—examples include smart meters, manufacturing sensors, equipment logs, trading systems data.

- Social data—examples include customer feedback comments, microblogging sites such as Twitter, social media sites such as Facebook.

THE PROBLEM >>> Big Data makes it possible to do many things that were previously impossible: e.g., spot business trends more rapidly and accurately, prevent disease, track crime, etc. Big Data, properly analyzed, can reveal valuable patterns and information that were previously hidden because of the amount of work required to discover them. Leading corporations, such as Walmart and Google, have been able to process Big Data for years, but they have had to do so at great expense. Today's commodity hardware, cloud computing (see Plug IT In #3), and open source software bring Big Data processing within budget for most organizations.

The problems with Big Data fall into three general categories: volume, velocity, and variety.

- *Volume:* Irrespective of the source, structure, format, and frequency of data, data is always valuable. If a certain kind of data seems to have no value today, it is because we have not yet been able to analyze it effectively. For example, several years ago when Google began harnessing satellite imagery, capturing street views, and then sharing this geographical data for free, few people understood its value at that time. Today, we recognize that such data is incredibly valuable.

    Consider machine-generated data, which is produced in much larger quantities than nontraditional data. For instance, sensors in a single jet engine can generate 10 terabytes of data in 30 minutes. With more than 25,000 airline flights per day, the daily volume of data from just this single source is incredible. Smart electrical meters, sensors in heavy industrial equipment, and telemetry from automobiles add to the volume problem.

- *Velocity:* The rate at which data flows into an organization is rapidly increasing. Velocity is critically important because it increases the speed of the feedback loop between a company and its customers. For example, the Internet and mobile technology mean that online retailers are able to compile histories not just on final sales, but on their customers' every click and interaction. Companies that are able to quickly utilize that information—for example, by recommending additional purchases—gain competitive advantage.

- *Variety:* Traditional data formats tend to be relatively well described and change slowly. Examples of traditional data include financial market data, point-of-sale transactions, and many others. In contrast, nontraditional data formats change rapidly. Nontraditional data formats include satellite imagery, broadcast audio streams, digital music files, Web page content, scans of government documents, and comments on social networks.

The first step for many organizations toward managing Big Data was to integrate information silos into a database environment and then to develop data warehouses for decision making. After completing this step, many organizations turned their attention to the business of information management—helping to make sense of their proliferating data. In recent years, Oracle, IBM, Microsoft, and SAP have spent billions of dollars all together buying software firms that specialize in data management and business intelligence. (You will learn about business intelligence in Chapter 5.)

<<< THE IT SOLUTION

Many organizations are turning to NoSQL databases (think of them as "not only SQL" databases) to process Big Data. These databases provide an alternative when a firm does not have traditional, structured data that fits neatly into the rows and columns of relational databases.

NoSQL databases can handle unstructured data and inconsistent or missing data. Many products utilize NoSQL databases, including Cassandra (http://cassandra.apache.org), CouchDB (http://couchdb.apache.org), MongoDB (www.mongodb.org), and Hadoop (http://hadoop.apache.org). As of mid-2012, Hadoop was receiving the most attention.

Hadoop is a software platform that stores and manages large volumes of structured and unstructured data. Clickstream and social media applications are driving much of the demand for Hadoop, with particular emphasis on MapReduce. MapReduce is a data-processing approach supported on Hadoop (and other software packages) that is ideal for processing big volumes of these new data types. MapReduce breaks a Big Data problem into subproblems, distributes those onto hundreds or thousands of servers, then combines the results to come up with an answer to the overarching data problem.

At the turn of the twentieth century, new flows of information through channels such as the telegraph and telephone supported mass production. Today, the availability of abundant data from a myriad of sources enables companies to cater to small niche markets (and even individual customers) anywhere in the world.

<<< THE RESULTS

Some industries have led the way in their ability to gather and exploit data. Consider these industry examples:

- Credit card companies monitor every purchase and can accurately identify fraudulent ones, using rules derived from analyzing billions of transactions.

- Insurance companies can analyze data in such a way as to spot suspicious claims.

- Mobile phone companies analyze subscribers' calling patterns to determine whether most of their frequent contacts are on a rival network. If that rival network is offering an attractive promotion that might cause that subscriber to defect, he or she can be offered an incentive to stay.

- Retailers effectively analyze customer transactions to tailor promotions. Retailers also watch online sales and marketing trends, and closely monitor and analyze social media comments about their products, brands, and the companies themselves.

- The oil industry examines seismic data before drilling new wells in order to increase the likelihood that oil companies will find oil and not a "dry hole."

Unfortunately, despite years of effort, law enforcement and intelligence agencies' databases are not particularly well integrated with each other. For instance, in the healthcare industry, large-scale efforts to computerize health records have hit bureaucratic, technological, and ethical roadblocks.

Despite these difficulties, stories of effective data management in organizations abound. As just one example, let's look at Nestlé. Nestlé sells more than 100,000 products in 200 countries, using 550,000 suppliers. Previously, the company was not using its huge buying power effectively because its databases had severe problems. Nestlé found that of its 9 million records of vendors, customers, and materials, about one-half were obsolete or duplicated and about one-third of the remainder was inaccurate or incomplete. The company overhauled its databases, improving the quality of its data. With the improved data, its American operation was able to save $30 million per year on just one ingredient (vanilla). Savings and improved efficiency such as Nestle experienced will continue to become the norm for companies around the world, leading to improved decision making and competitive success.

Sources: Compiled from S. Lohr, "The Age of Big Data," *The New York Times*, February 11, 2012; "Volume, Velocity, Variety: What You Need to Know About Big Data," *O'Reilly Media*, January 19, 2012; E. Dumbill, "Five Big Data Predictions for 2012," *O'Reilly Media*, December 14, 2011; "IDC Digital University Study 2011," http://www.emc.com/collateral/demos/microsites/emc-digital-universe-2011/index.htm, 2011; J. Enriquez, "The Glory of Big Data," *Popular Science*, November, 2011; R. Pacella, "Where Data Lives," *Popular Science*, November, 2011; D. McCafferty, "The Big Data Conundrum," *CIO Insight*, November 9, 2010; D. Henschen, "Big Data," *InformationWeek*, October 10, 2011; M. Korn and S. Tibken, "Fumbling Over Data," *The Wall Street Journal*, October 3, 2011; R. King, "Getting a Handle on Big Data with Hadoop," *Bloomberg BusinessWeek*, September 7, 2011; D. Henschen, "What's at Stake in the Big Data Revolution?" *InformationWeek*, August 18, 2010; S. Nunziata, "Business Analytics: Turning IP into Opportunity," *CIO Insight*, August 17, 2010; D. Henschen, "The Big Data Era: How Data Strategy Will Change," *InformationWeek*, August 7, 2010; M. Loukides, "What Is Data Science?" *O'Reilly Media*, June 2, 2010; "Data, Data Everywhere," *The Economist*, February 25, 2010; D. Bollier, "The Promise and Peril of Big Data," *The Aspen Institute*, January 1, 2010; T. Davenport, J. Harris, and R. Morison, "Analytics at Work: Smarter Decisions, Better Results," *Harvard Business Press*, 2010; "Big Data—It's Not Just for Google Anymore," *AMD White Paper*, 2010; www.nestle.com, www.ibm.com, accessed February 19, 2011.

Questions

1. Is Big Data really a problem on its own, or are the use, control, and security of the data the true problem? Provide specific examples to support your answer.
2. What are the implications of having incorrect data points in your Big Data? What are the implications of incorrect or duplicated customer information? How valuable are decisions that were made based on faulty information derived from incorrect data?

CLOSING **CASE 2** > Kayak Uses QuickBase for Global Collaboration

THE PROBLEM >>> Kayak, a travel Web site (www.kayak.com), wished to provide as-complete-as-possible real-time information on the pricing and availability of flights, hotels, automobile rentals, and other travel options to the thousands who visit their Web site each day. Although a large majority of its customer service, operations, and system development work occurs within the United States, Kayak still needed an efficient way to coordinate and collaborate with employees and business partners in Europe, India, and China. The company lacked the ability to update and exchange huge spreadsheets among dozens of people worldwide.

Another key area that Kayak had to address was their response time to customer feedback. The company received many messages from customers each day, and considered this feedback to be an early predictor of the feelings of its customer base. For instance, if there was a travel provider who was performing poorly or if Kayak's user interface on Safari browsers was not functioning properly, the company needed to be aware of these issues as soon as possible.

With such a diverse range of customer issues to address, Kayak's philosophy was (and is) that every Kayak employee is a customer service representative. However, Kayak was impeded from fulfilling this philosophy because it still lacked an efficient method to quickly get customer feedback to the appropriate employees so that they could respond in a timely manner.

Kayak selected QuickBase as its IT solution to their above issues. QuickBase (http:// quickbase.intuit.com) is a Web-based collaborative database application that allows developers and users to create their own custom applications without writing any computer code. QuickBase also enables Kayak to create customer applications that match their preexisting business processes and then integrate those processes with their existing systems. That way, Kayak can centralize important data on the Web.

<<< **THE IT SOLUTION**

As a Web-based database, QuickBase improves the way Kayak's distributed teams collaborate. Kayak's teams can now share information among members, customers, and business partners in real time. QuickBase also saves Kayak teams time by automating administrative tasks. For instance, e-mail notifications and reminders keep team members informed and help them stay on track. QuickBase also allows Kayak to set custom roles and permissions to determine each team member's level of access to data, so that team members only see database information to which they have been granted access.

Now, Kayak users can import data from an existing application, or add, edit, and delete data directly in QuickBase by filling in simple, customizable forms. These data processes automatically update Kayak's online database in real time, so regardless of when or where Kayak's business teams work, they have accurate, up-to-date information that is easily accessible in one central location.

Best of all, QuickBase is hosted by Intuit (www.intuit.com), which means that Kayak does not need to buy, deploy, or maintain an information technology infrastructure. Therefore, Kayak does not need to maintain an information systems department, which saves the company a great deal of time and money.

Kayak uses QuickBase to help manage its global internal and external systems developers who build and maintain its Web site. QuickBase provides a central repository where all team members can check in with their latest status, issues, questions, and other collaborative communications. Hundreds of Kayak employees share this information around the clock and around the world. Since 2009, Kayak has completed over 100 projects with outside developers using QuickBase.

<<< **THE RESULTS**

Kayak also uses QuickBase to create a sophisticated customer service application. When a customer message arrives, QuickBase can automatically analyze its contents and route it to a Kayak customer service representative for immediate attention. This automatic routing allows customer representatives to specialize—so one representative might field questions about passwords, while another fields questions about credit cards, and still another fields questions about hotel sales. Once routed, QuickBase tracks all questions and answers. The representative receives the question, clicks the link, and goes to the QuickBase record where he or she sees complete details about the issue, including the thread history. This customer service application is so innovative that Kayak has applied for a patent on it.

Sources: Compiled from R. Wang, "How Intuit Uses Cloud Computing," *Forbes*, February 9, 2012; "QuickBase Helps Kayak Coordinate Global Teams and Manage Customer Feedback," *QuickBase Customer Success Story*, http://intuit.quickbase.com, accessed February 26, 2012; B. Ives, "Shareable Databases: Intuit QuickBase Bringing Desktop Database Users into Enterprise 2.0," *The App Gap*, February 17, 2009.

Questions

1. Describe the many ways that Kayak uses QuickBase. Is QuickBase just a database management system, or is it something more? Support your answer.

2. How can Kayak, a Web-based company, operate without an information systems department? (*Hint:* See Plug IT In 3.) What are the advantages and disadvantages of operating this way?

It is important for Ruben and Lisa (on the front end) to determine the structure of their database. As you have learned in the chapter, this structure is called an entity-relationship (ER) model and is illustrated by an ER diagram. They would like to collect Customer Name, Drinks and/or Food Purchased by customer, Sale Amount, Payment Method, Date and Time of Transaction, Drinks sold by Time, Food sold by Time, Time from entrance or last purchase (i.e., how long it took a customer to buy the first drink), Drink Ingredients Used, Food Ingredients Used, Band Playing, and Genre for starters.

Ultimately, Ruben and Lisa want a system to capture data on the way out the door for an "Exit Survey." It would be simple and only include a couple of items, but a quick rating of the overall experience by users would be worth a lot for the club's planning process. They really feel these data items could be combined in various ways to give them very useful information. For now, these two business owners just need help getting the structure right. Take these items and create an appropriate ER diagram and submit it to Ruben and Lisa (your professor).

SPREADSHEET ACTIVITY

Objective: Normalization is taught in this chapter. Often, normalization begins when organizations are ready to transition from a large spreadsheet to a multidimensional database. This exercise will have you work your way through this transition.

Chapter Connection: *Primary key, secondary key, and attributes:* These terms are a bit abstract until you have to make these determinations yourself. The process of normalization is best when it is practiced. Spreadsheets provide the perfect opportunity.

Activity: When schools first began keeping digital records of students, they used a spreadsheet to manage the data. It did not take long before it was obvious that the spreadsheet alone was not sufficient to manage this information. The problem was that the spreadsheet recorded each student as a single event. Every time someone accessed the page to update a grade, contact information, receipt of payment, or class enrollment, that person had to access the main page to make changes. This meant that everyone had access to everything. The registrar could see financial information and the bursar could see academic information.

A database, no doubt, is more suited for this type of application and the normalization process will prepare the spreadsheet for conversion. Visit http://www.wiley.com/go/rainer/spreadsheet and download the spreadsheet for this exercise (MIS—Chapter 3.xlsx). Carefully choose a primary key according to the definitions provided in this chapter. Look for data that will uniquely identify each student. Perhaps this will be a student number or a combination of the student's last and first name. Whatever you decide, normalize the data and allow the primary key to tie the information together from one sheet to another. Your normalized spreadsheet will have multiple sheets rather than one single sheet. Perhaps you will have student information, financial information, academic enrollment, major, grades, etc. Take the single sheet and move the data into multiple sheets. Be sure to copy your primary keys onto each page so that the data can be reconciled.

Deliverable: The final product will be a normalized spreadsheet that is much easier to understand and update and that is ready to be converted to a database.

Discussion Questions:

1. Even though this exercise is about normalization for a database, is it also helpful to have data normalized in a spreadsheet? Why or why not?

2. What are the differences in spreadsheets and databases when it comes to data manipulation?

Quiz questions are assignable in WileyPLUS, and available on the Book Companion Site at http://www.wiley.com/college/rainer.

DATABASE ACTIVITY:

Objective

Just as every house begins with an architectural drawing, every database must begin with a data model. In this activity, you will develop the most common type of data model: an *entity-relationship diagram* (ERD).

CHAPTER CONNECTION

Section 2 of this chapter introduces you to data modeling, specifically entity-relationship diagramming, as part of learning about database management. This activity applies those concepts.

Understanding the structure of a database is a good guide to developing it. It reduces the chances of errors that will be difficult to correct later on. In addition, professional database developers communicate with ERDs when they design a database for business needs. The ERD defines what the database will be. Knowing their language will improve your chances of getting a database that meets your needs.

PREREQUISITES

Read the following material before proceeding on to the activity. Reading this chapter will also put the activity in perspective.

ERD Styles

The ERD style that the book uses is one of many. They are similar but differ in details. If you learn one, you will be able to understand an ERD in another, much as an English speaker from London can converse with someone from New York. Some differences among versions follow:

- The name of an entity may be shown outside its box (usually just above it, as in part b of the figure in the book) or inside it (as in part a of the figure).
- The attributes of an entity may be shown in a separate box (as in the figure in the book), within its box, or in ovals surrounding the box and connected to it.
- An entity's primary key may be in bold type; starred; underlined; or if the name of the entity is outside the box, in a separate part of the box (as in part b of the figure in the book).

- Foreign keys can be shown in italics or set off in any other way that is not the same as the one used for primary keys, not identified at all, or not shown at all. In this last case, the lines connecting entities convey the relationship information.
- Relationships can be described in diamonds on the lines (as in part a of the figure in the book), in text next to the lines, or not described in the ERD.

When relationships are described once, the direction of the description is not always clear. In the figure, does "Can have" between Class and Professor mean "a class can have a professor" or "a professor can have a class?" It does not say. That is why some diagramming methods describe each relationship twice, once for each direction.

- When a relationship has "one" at one end, there may be a short line across the relationship line (as in part a of the figure in the book) or no symbol at all. In that case, the information is conveyed by the absence of crows' feet.

ERD Symbols

An ERD shows the kind of relationship two entities have by symbols at the ends of the line that connects the entities. Each end of each line has two symbols.

The symbol all the way at the end of the line defines the *maximum cardinality* of the relationship: How many of that entity can there be? Rather than an exact count, the options are simply *1* or *many*, because that is all that matters in most database designs. A maximum of 1 is indicated by a short line across the line that connects the entities. A maximum of more than 1 is indicated by "crows' feet": three lines spreading out like the toes on a bird's foot.

Further away from that symbol is a symbol for minimum cardinality: What is the smallest valid number of this entity that there can be? Here, the choices are 0 (there does not have to be one) and 1 (there must be at least one). Zero is shown by a circle. You can think of it as representing the digit 0 or the first letter of the word *optional*. A short line across the line that connects the entities means a minimum of 1. This is the same symbol as is used to indicate a maximum of 1, but there is no possible confusion because they are in different places.

The four possible combinations of these two pairs of symbols, and their meanings, are as follows:

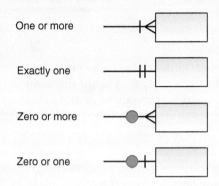

One or more

Exactly one

Zero or more

Zero or one

Suppose you have a database with information about students and their computers. Each computer belongs to exactly one student. A student, however, may have more than one computer—or may not have any. That *one-to-many relationship* would be shown this way:

A relationship in which both entities have a maximum cardinality of *one* is called a *one-to-one* relationship. If one of the entities has a maximum cardinality of *many*, it is called a *one-to-many* (or *many-to-one*) relationship. If they both do, it is called a *many-to-many* relationship.

Associative Entities

Because foreign keys only work in one direction at a time, a many-to-many relationship requires a new table between the two entities. For example, consider a school database. There is a many-to-many relationship between students and courses: each student can take more than one course, and each course can have more than one student. A database cannot show that directly. A row of the course table cannot have a foreign key for students, because there can be more than one. A row of the student table cannot have a foreign key for courses either, because there can also be more than one. The solution is to put a third entity between them. Each row in it reflects one student taking one course. Its ERD would look like this:

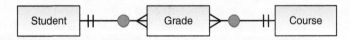

In this example, that entity also stores each student's grade in that course, and takes its name from this. The grade cannot be in the student table, because students may earn different grades in different courses. It cannot be in the course table, because

different students in the same course may earn different grades. It has to go in a table that describes that unique combination of student and course.

The circle symbols in this ERD fragment shows that a student might not be in any courses and that a course might not have any students. This would be the situation before students register for courses. It also shows that, if there is a record in the Grade table, it goes with exactly one student, no more and no less, and with exactly one course, also no more and no less. Finally, it shows that a student may be in more than one course and that a course may have more than one student. Be sure you understand how the ERD shows these things.

Sales databases usually have a Line Item table that works this way. (The ORDERED-PARTS table in Section 3.3 is an example of this.) Each order can be for many products. Each product can appear in many orders. Each row of this table is for one product in one order. In this case, the additional data in that entity is the quantity of the item in the order.

An entity that goes in the middle of a many-to-many relationship is called an *associative entity*. As a minimum, it contains two foreign keys: one for each connection. Often, as in these two examples, it also carries data. When an associative entity carries data, an ERD must show it. If it exists only to make the many-to-many relationship work and has no data of its own, some ER diagramming approaches show it but others do not.

An associative entity, like any other entity, needs a primary key. Neither foreign key is unique, so they will not work. Suppose Susan is registered for English 307. The foreign key that identifies Susan is not unique in the Grades table, because she has other courses.. The one that identifies English 307 is not unique either, because other students also take it. However, Susan is only registered for it once, so the combination of Susan and English 307 *is* unique. Such a primary key, a unique combination of columns that are not unique individually, is called a *composite* key. To avoid dealing with composite keys, associative entities can be given separate primary keys such as sequence numbers. They do not mean anything, but they satisfy the requirement that every table must have a primary key.

Activity

1. Read the following description of a business situation:

    A university needs a database to record student information. You know the following:

    - The database will store information on departments, courses, sections, and students.
    - Each department can teach many courses.
    - Each course is taught by one department.
    - Each course can have many sections.

- Each section belongs to one course.
- Each section has many students.
- Each student enrolls in many sections.

2. Draw an ERD for a database that will convey the information in the above description. Use the graphics program of your choice, or paper and pencil. (People who draw ERDs for a living use specialized graphics programs that have the required shapes built in and that can enforce the rules of entity-relationship diagramming.)

- Show all relationships among entities. For each end of each relationship, use ERD symbols to show both the minimum cardinality (0 or 1; that is, can it be absent or must there be one?) and the maximum cardinality (1 or many). Use a short line across the relationship line to show a maximum cardinality of 1, as in the book.
- Show the primary key of each entity in a separate area at the top of the entity box, as in the figure in the book.
- Show all the foreign keys in each entity. Underline them.
- Show at least three attributes of each entity, based on your understanding of the situation described. If you cannot think of three, show all you have.

Deliverable

Your completed ER diagram.

Quiz Questions

1. Which of the following is *not* a possible type of relationship between database entities as shown in an ERD?
   (a) One to one
   (b) Many to many
   (c) Two to one
   (d) Many to one

2. True or false: A many-to-one relationship requires an associative entity.

3. An associative entity has a primary key and at least this many foreign keys:
   (a) 0
   (b) 1
   (c) 2
   (d) 3

4. The *attributes* of an entity are
   (a) The data items that describe it in a database
   (b) The names it can be called by
   (c) The foreign keys in its database record
   (d) The date and time it was entered into the database, and the user ID of the person who entered it

Discussion Questions

1. Why is it important for people who are not database specialists to be familiar with ER concepts and diagramming?

2. Where does an ERD show the attributes of an entity?

3. What ERD symbols indicate a many-to-one relationship?

4 | Telecommunications and Networking

LEARNING OBJECTIVES >>>

1. Compare and contrast the two major types of networks.
2. Describe the wireline communications media and transmission technologies.
3. Describe the most common methods for accessing the Internet.
4. Explain the impact that networks have had on business and everyday life for each of the six major categories of network applications.

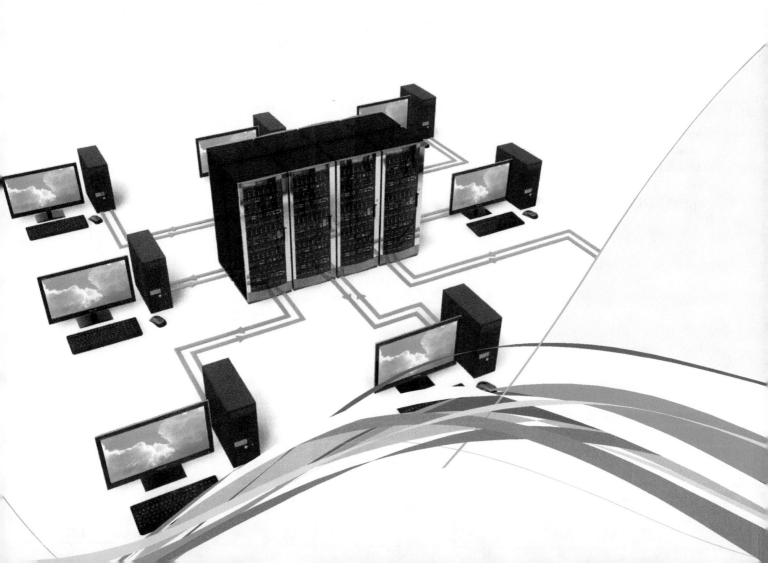

Sometimes, using the right network can make all the difference. What is the right network? Well, it depends. As an organization grows, its network will need to change and evolve to meet its new needs. This is exactly the case with Studio G, an architecture firm in San Jose, California. When the firm had just been founded, it had only two employees and they needed only two lines to communicate with their customers. However, as the business grew, Studio G needed a better communication solution.

Solving the communication problem should be simple. Just add more telephone lines, right? Not quite. Studio G did not have a receptionist, so they needed some type of networked phone system that could route calls and help customers reach the appropriate contact. The only type of system capable of routing calls in this way is a private branch exchange (PBX). A PBX is a telephone exchange that serves a particular business or office, as opposed to a telephone exchange operated by a telephone company for several businesses or for the public. A PBX makes connections among the internal telephones of a private organization and connects them to the public switched telephone network.

© rzdeb/iStockphoto

As their networked phone system provider, Studio G chose Cisco's Small Business Unified Communications Series. Cisco's system provides excellent flexibility in routing calls and voice mails, transferring calls, etc. Also, the system provided these functions without the owners having to pay for a receptionist.

What is the result? Studio G is now able to keep pace with their larger competitors because of their ability to communicate with their customers at a fraction of the cost spent by other organizations. Kelly Simcox, owner of Studio G Architects, Inc. said "We have grown substantially . . . [and] are competing for projects against firms that are substantially larger than ours."

As we can see, in this situation, the right telecommunication solution was not the age-old telephone line. In fact, it was a computerized networking solution that utilized Web **> > >**

RUBY'S CLUB

The network at Ruby's Club has consisted of digital subscriber line (DSL) and a computer. This is not much of a local area network (LAN) at all. To accomplish their desires of a collecting data from different customer contact points (such as cover charge, food and/or drink purchases, exit questionnaire), they will need multiple computers or devices connected to their network. Additionally, to create the community atmosphere they desire, they want to offer wireless Internet access to their customers so they never feel out of touch.

This will require lots of networking hardware on both the internal wired LAN and the public wireless LAN. To make matters more difficult, Ruben and Lisa know nothing about establishing a network. They did not even install their own DSL line . . . it was connected by their local telephone company. All they know is how to turn it on and the right phone number to call when they have a problem. Establishing and maintaining a LAN that connects employees and customers, while providing adequate security for all parties, will be quite an undertaking. However, they believe the benefits of establishing this network will far outweigh the costs.

Because you are learning about telecom and networks, it will be very helpful for you to share this information with them with a recommendation on how to build out their network!

technology and high-speed Internet. Many similar solutions are available today for small businesses to help them communicate with their customers in more efficient ways. As you have seen in this case, networking solutions will continue to allow small businesses to compete on a more level playing field with their larger competitors, which may have significant ramifications for the customer in terms of pricing and available options.

Sources: Compiled from "Small Architecture Firm Keeps Pace with Large Competitors," *Cisco Customer Case Study*, 2011; www.cisco.com, accessed March 11, 2012.

Questions

1. As a business grows, why do its communication network needs grow?
2. What advantages does the Cisco system provide for Studio G?

Introduction

You need to know three fundamental points about network computing. First, computers do not work in isolation in modern organizations. Rather, they constantly exchange data with one another. Second, this exchange of data—facilitated by telecommunications technologies—provides companies with a number of very significant advantages. Third, this exchange can take place over any distance and over networks of any size.

Without networks, the computer on your desk would be merely another productivity-enhancement tool, just as the typewriter once was. The power of networks, however, turns your computer into an amazingly effective tool for accessing information from thousands of sources, thereby making both you and your organization more productive. Regardless of the type of organization (profit/not-for-profit, large/small, global/local) or industry (manufacturing, financial services, healthcare), networks in general, and the Internet in particular, have transformed—and will continue to transform—the way we do business.

Networks support new ways of doing business, from marketing to supply chain management to customer service to human resources management. In particular, the Internet and private intranets—networks located within a single organization—have an enormous impact on our lives, both professionally and personally. In fact, for all organizations, having an Internet strategy is no longer just a source of competitive advantage. Rather, it is necessary for survival.

Computer networks are essential to modern organizations, for many reasons. First, networked computer systems enable organizations to be more flexible so they can adapt to rapidly changing business conditions. Second, networks enable companies to share hardware, computer applications, and data across the organization and among different organizations. Third, networks make it possible for geographically dispersed employees and work groups to share documents, ideas, and creative insights. This sharing encourages teamwork, innovation, and more efficient and effective interactions. In addition, networks are a critical link between businesses, their business partners, and their customers.

Clearly, networks are essential tools for modern businesses. But, why do *you* need to be familiar with networks? The simple fact is that if you operate your own business or work in a business, you cannot function without networks. You will need to communicate rapidly with your customers, business partners, suppliers, employees, and colleagues. Until about 1990, you would have used the postal service or telephone system with voice or fax capabilities for business communication. Today, however, the pace of business is much faster—almost real time. To keep up with this incredibly fast pace, you will need to use computers, e-mail, the Internet, cell phones, and mobile devices. Further, all of these technologies will be connected via networks to enable you to communicate, collaborate, and compete on a global scale.

Networking and the Internet are the foundation for commerce in the twenty-first century. Recall that one important objective of this book is to help you become an informed user of information systems. A knowledge of networking is an essential component of modern business literacy.

You begin this chapter by learning what a computer network is and identifying the various types of networks. You then study network fundamentals and follow by turning your attention to the basics of the Internet and the World Wide Web. You conclude the chapter by seeing the many network applications available to individuals and organizations—that is, what networks help you do.

4.1 What Is a Computer Network?

A **computer network** is a system that connects computers and other devices (e.g., printers) via communications media so that data and information can be transmitted among them. Voice and data communication networks are continually becoming faster—that is, their bandwidth is increasing—and cheaper. **Bandwidth** refers to the transmission capacity of a network; it is stated in bits per second. **Broadband** refers to network transmission capacities ranging from approximately 1 million bits per second (megabits/sec) to as much as 20 megabits/sec with fiber-to-the-home (discussed later in this chapter). You are familiar with certain types of broadband connections, such as **digital subscriber line (DSL)** and cable to your homes and dorms. DSL and cable fall within the range of transmission capacity mentioned here and thus are defined as broadband connections.

The various types of computer networks range from small to worldwide. They include (from smallest to largest) personal area networks (PANs), local area networks (LANs), metropolitan area networks (MANs), wide area networks (WANs), and the Internet. PANs are short-range networks—typically a few meters—used for communication among devices close to one person. PANs can be wired or wireless. (You will learn about wireless PANs in Chapter 10.) MANs are relatively large computer networks that cover a metropolitan area. MANs fall between LANs and WANs in size. WANs typically cover large geographic areas and can span the entire planet.

Local Area Networks

Regardless of their size, networks represent a compromise among three objectives: speed, distance, and cost. Organizations can generally have any two of the three. To cover long distances, organizations can have fast communication if they are willing to pay for it, or cheap communication if they are willing to accept slower speeds. A third possible combination of the three trade-offs is fast, cheap communication with distance limitations. This is the idea behind local area networks.

A **local area network (LAN)** connects two or more devices in a limited geographical region, usually within the same building, so that every device on the network can communicate with every other device. Most LANs today use Ethernet (discussed later in this chapter). Figure 4.1 illustrates an Ethernet LAN that consists of four computers, a server, and a printer, all of which connect via a shared cable. Every device in the LAN has a *network interface card* (NIC) that allows the device to physically connect to the LAN's communications medium. This medium is typically unshielded twisted-pair wire (UTP).

Although it is not required, many LANs have a **file server** or **network server**. The server typically contains various software and data for the network. It also houses the LAN's network operating system, which manages the server and routes and manages communications on the network.

Wide Area Networks

When businesses have to transmit and receive data beyond the confines of the LAN, they use wide area networks. Interestingly, the term *wide area network* did not even exist until local area networks appeared. Before that time, what we call a wide area network today was simply called a "network."

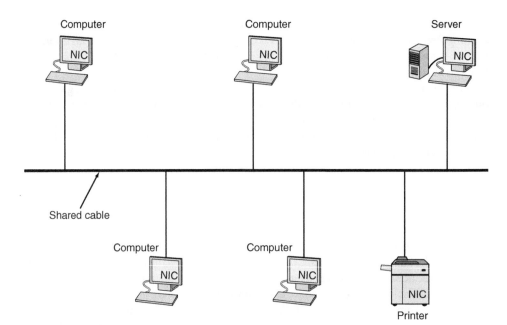

Figure 4.1 An Ethernet LAN.

A **wide area network (WAN)** is a network that covers a large geographic area. WANs typically connect multiple LANs. WANs generally are provided by common carriers such as telephone companies and the international networks of global communications services providers. WANs have large capacity, and they typically combine multiple channels (for example, fiber-optic cables, microwave, and satellite). The Internet is an example of a WAN.

WANs also contain routers. A **router** is a communications processor that routes messages from a LAN to the Internet, across several connected LANs, or across a wide area network such as the Internet.

Enterprise Networks

Organizations today have multiple LANs and may have multiple WANs, which are interconnected to form an **enterprise network**. Figure 4.2 displays a model of enterprise computing. Note that the enterprise network in the figure has a **backbone network**. Corporate backbone networks are high-speed central networks to which multiple smaller networks (such as LANs and smaller WANs) connect. The LANs are called *embedded LANs* because they connect to the backbone WAN.

BEFORE YOU GO ON . . .

1. What are the primary business reasons for using networks?

2. What is the difference between LANs and WANs?

3. Describe an enterprise network.

Figure 4.2 An enterprise network.

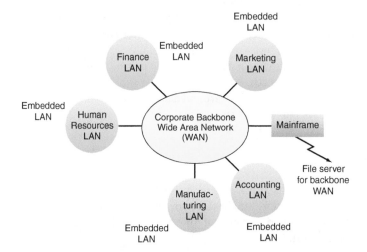

Apply the Concept 4.1

Background This section has introduced you to the different types of networks that connect businesses around the world. Because of this, today's organizations are spread out over many geographic locations. Often headquarters are in one city and various branches are in other cities. Many times, employees even work from home and do not have a physical office to go to. The computer network is the technology that allows all of this to happen. For a network to function, a few components are required. In this activity, you will place these components in the appropriate places to create a computer network.

Activity Consider the following company called JLB TechWizards and potential network components.

JLB TechWizards Locations

1. *Headquarters:* This international company manufactures and sells computer equipment; the firm also services equipment it has sold. The company's headquarters are in Chicago, Illinois, and offices there include marketing, accounting, HR, and manufacturing. Each office has a number of PCs that connect with a main server in an IS. All offices are closely located and share data and printers.

2. *Offshore manufacturing:* A new manufacturing facility is opening in Hong Kong and needs to be connected 24/7 to company headquarters. There are 30 terminals at this plant. Inventory, orders, and schedules are shared during the workday at both locations.

3. *Sales force:* JLB TechWizards has about 15 technicians who service equipment sold within the United States. Each technician has a laptop that needs to connect off and on to the database (at headquarters) about 3 hours each day for checking inventory and entering repairs and orders. Technicians are constantly on the road to small, mountainous, rural cities and need to be able to check inventory whether in a hotel or at a customer site. Each evening technicians must log on for updates and to post daily activity. You may want to include multiple options so they can always connect!

4. *Employees from home:* JLB TechWizards has a number of employees that work from home part time on flextime. These employees need a fast, secure connection because some are dealing with financial data and the main computer and its databases at headquarters. They all live within 20 miles of their workplace.

Components

1. *Network:* LAN, MAN, WAN
2. *Connection:* direct connection (in-house), dial-up, Internet
3. *Interface devices:* network interface card (Ethernet or wireless), server, routers, DSL/cable
4. *Channel:* twisted pair (UTP-Cat3 or 5), fiber, wireless, satellite, or tower)

Deliverable

From the lists above, indicate which components are needed to connect JLB TechWizards employees to a database that is located at the company's headquarters. Without this, they will not be able to do their jobs and answer customer-related questions. (You may need multiple components for each group.) If you are not familiar with any of the terms, review the text for more information.

Submit your list of required components to your professor.

Quiz questions are assignable in WileyPLUS, and available on the Book Companion Site at http://www.wiley.com/college/rainer.

1. Which type of network would best suit the needs of Ruby's Club? A LAN, a MAN, or a WAN? Why?
2. What type of wired connections would you recommend to Ruben and Lisa within their club? Be sure to pick something that is widely used so it will be easy to find support.

4.2 Network Fundamentals

In this section, you will learn the basics of how networks actually operate. You will then distinguish between analog and digital signals and explain how modems enable computer networks to "translate" among them. You follow by studying wireline communications media, which enable computers in a network to transmit and receive data. You conclude this section by looking at network protocols and types of network processing.

Analog and Digital Signals

Networks transmit information with two basic types of signals, analog and digital. **Analog signals** are continuous waves that transmit information by altering the characteristics of the waves. Analog signals have two parameters, *amplitude* and *frequency*. For example, all sounds—including the human voice—are analog, traveling to human ears in the form of waves. The higher the waves (or amplitude), the louder the sound; the more closely packed the waves, the higher the frequency or pitch. In contrast, **digital signals** are discrete pulses that are either on or off, representing a series of *bits* (0s and 1s). This quality allows digital signals to convey information in a binary form that can be interpreted by computers. Figure 4.3 illustrates both analog and digital signals.

The function of a **modem** is to convert digital signals to analog signals—a process called *modulation*—and analog signals to digital signals—a process called *demodulation*. (The name *modem* is a contraction of *modulator-demodulator*.) Modems are used in pairs. The modem at the sending end converts a computer's digital information into analog

Figure 4.3 Analog and digital signals.

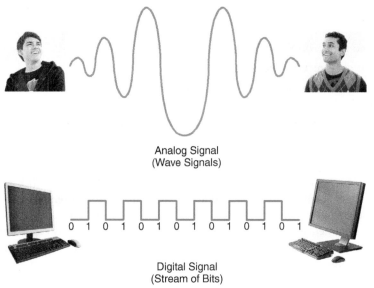

Analog Signal
(Wave Signals)

0 1 0 1 0 1 0 1 0 1 0 1 0 1 0 1

Digital Signal
(Stream of Bits)

Fancy/Image Source; Media Bakery; © Zoonar/Dmitry Rukhle/Age Fotostock America, Inc.

signals for transmission over analog lines, such as telephone lines. At the receiving end, another modem converts the analog signal back into digital signals for the receiving computer. There are three types of modems: dial-up modems, cable modems, and DSL modems.

The U.S. public telephone system was originally designed as an analog network to carry voice signals or sounds in an analog wave format. In order for this type of circuit to carry digital information, that information must be converted into an analog wave pattern by a *dial-up modem*. Dial-up modems have transmission speeds of up to 56 kilobytes per second (Kbps).

Cable modems are modems that operate over coaxial cable—for example, cable TV. They offer broadband access to the Internet or corporate intranets. Cable modem speeds vary widely. Most providers offer bandwidth between 1 and 6 million bits per second (Mbps) for downloads (from the Internet to a computer) and between 128 and 768 thousand bits per second (Kbps) for uploads. Cable modem services share bandwidth among subscribers in a locality. That is, the same cable line connects to many households. Therefore, when large numbers of neighbors access the Internet at the same time, cable speeds can decrease significantly during those times.

DSL (discussed later in this chapter) *modems* operate on the same lines as voice telephones and dial-up modems. DSL modems always maintain a connection, so an Internet connection is immediately available.

Communications Media and Channels

Communicating data from one location to another requires some form of pathway or medium. A **communications channel** is such a pathway and is comprised of two types of media: cable (twisted-pair wire, cable, or fiber-optic cable) and broadcast (microwave, satellite, radio, or infrared).

Cable media or **wireline media** use physical wires or cables to transmit data and information. Twisted-pair wire and coaxial cables are made of copper, and fiber-optic cable is made of glass. The alternative is communication over **broadcast media** or **wireless media**. The key to mobile communications in today's rapidly moving society is data transmissions over electromagnetic media—the "airwaves." In this section you will study the three wireline channels. Table 4.1 summarizes the advantages and disadvantages of each of these channels. You will become familiar with wireless media in Chapter 10.

Twisted-Pair Wire. Twisted-pair wire is the most prevalent form of communications wiring; it is used for almost all business telephone wiring. **Twisted-pair wire** consists of

TABLE 4.1 Advantages and Disadvantages of Wireline Communications Channels

Channel	Advantages	Disadvantages
Twisted-pair wire	Inexpensive Widely available Easy to work with	Slow (low bandwidth) Subject to interference Easily tapped (low security)
Coaxial cable	Higher bandwidth than twisted-pair Less susceptible to electromagnetic interference	Relatively expensive and inflexible Easily tapped (low to medium security) Somewhat difficult to work with
Fiber-optic cable	Very high bandwidth Relatively inexpensive Difficult to tap (good security)	Difficult to work with (difficult to splice)

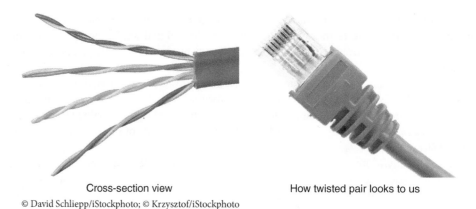

Figure 4.4 Two views of twisted-pair wire.

Cross-section view   How twisted pair looks to us

© David Schliepp/iStockphoto; © Krzysztof/iStockphoto

strands of copper wire twisted in pairs (see Figure 4.4). It is relatively inexpensive to purchase, widely available, and easy to work with. However, it also has some significant disadvantages. Specifically, it is relatively slow for transmitting data, it is subject to interference from other electrical sources, and it can be easily tapped by unintended receivers for gaining unauthorized access to data.

Coaxial Cable. **Coaxial cable** (Figure 4.5) consists of insulated copper wire. It is much less susceptible to electrical interference than is twisted-pair wire and it can carry much more data. For these reasons, it is commonly used to carry high-speed data traffic as well as television signals (thus the term *cable TV*). However, coaxial cable is more expensive and more difficult to work with than twisted-pair wire. It is also somewhat inflexible.

Fiber Optics. **Fiber-optic cable** (Figure 4.6) consists of thousands of very thin filaments of glass fibers that transmit information via light pulses generated by lasers. The fiber-optic cable is surrounded by cladding, a coating that prevents the light from leaking out of the fiber.

Fiber-optic cables are significantly smaller and lighter than traditional cable media. They also can transmit far more data, and they provide greater security from interference and tapping. As of 2011, optical fiber had reached data transmission rates of more than 50 trillion bits (terabits) per second in laboratory experiments. Fiber-optic cable is typically used as the backbone for a network, whereas twisted-pair wire and coaxial cable connect the backbone to individual devices on the network.

Network Protocols

Computing devices that are connected to the network must access and share the network to transmit and receive data. These devices are often referred to as *nodes* of the network. They work together by adhering to a common set of rules and procedures—known as a **protocol**—that enable them to communicate with one another. The two major protocols are the Ethernet and Transmission Control Protocol/Internet Protocol.

Figure 4.5 Two views of coaxial cables.

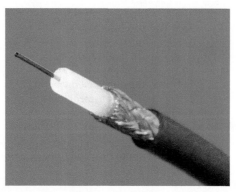

Cross-section view   How coaxial cable looks to us

GIPhotoStock/Photo Researchers; © Piotr Malczyk/iStockphoto

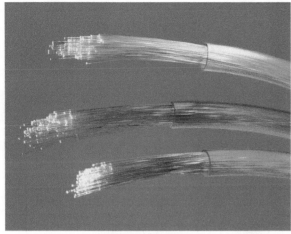

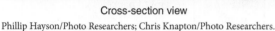

| Cross-section view | How fiber-optic cable looks to us |

Phillip Hayson/Photo Researchers; Chris Knapton/Photo Researchers.

Figure 4.6 Two views of fiber-optic cables.

Ethernet. A common LAN protocol is **Ethernet**. Most large corporations use 10-gigabit Ethernet, where the network provides data transmission speeds of 10 gigabits (10 billion bits) per second. However, 100-gigabit Ethernet is becoming the standard.

Transmission Control Protocol/Internet Protocol. The **Transmission Control Protocol/Internet Protocol (TCP/IP)** is the protocol of the Internet. TCP/IP uses a suite of protocols, the main ones being the Transmission Control Protocol (TCP) and the Internet Protocol (IP). The TCP performs three basic functions: (1) It manages the movement of packets between computers by establishing a connection between the computers, (2) it sequences the transfer of packets, and (3) it acknowledges the packets that have been transmitted. The **Internet Protocol (IP)** is responsible for disassembling, delivering, and reassembling the data during transmission.

Before data are transmitted over the Internet, they are divided into small, fixed bundles of data called *packets*. The transmission technology that breaks up blocks of text into packets is called **packet switching**. Each packet carries the information that will help it reach its destination—the sender's IP address, the intended receiver's IP address, the number of packets in the message, and the number of the particular packet within the message. Each packet travels independently across the network and can be routed through different paths in the network. When the packets reach their destination, they are reassembled into the original message.

It is important to note that packet-switching networks are reliable and fault tolerant. For example, if a path in the network is very busy or is broken, packets can be dynamically ("on the fly") rerouted around that path. Also, if one or more packets does not get to the receiving computer, then only those packets need to be resent.

Why do organizations use packet switching? The main reason is to achieve reliable end-to-end message transmission over sometimes unreliable networks that may have transient (short-acting) or persistent (long-acting) faults.

The packets use the TCP/IP protocol to carry their data. TCP/IP functions in four layers (see Figure 4.7). The *application layer* enables client application programs to access the other layers, and it defines the protocols that applications use to exchange data. One of these application protocols is the **Hypertext Transfer Protocol (HTTP)**, which defines how messages are formulated and how they are interpreted by their receivers. The *transport layer* provides the application layer with communication and packet services. This layer includes TCP and other protocols. The *Internet layer* is responsible for addressing, routing, and packaging data packets. The IP is one of the protocols in this layer. Finally, the *network interface layer* places packets on, and receives them from, the network medium, which can be any networking technology.

Two computers using TCP/IP can communicate even if they use different hardware and software. Data sent from one computer to another proceed downward through all four layers, beginning with the sending computer's application layer and going through its network interface layer. After the data reach the receiving computer, they travel up the layers.

Email: Sending a Message via SMPT (Simple Mail Transfer Protocol)	Application	Email: Message received
Break Message into packets and determine order	Transport	Packets reordered and replaced (if lost)
Assign sending and receiving IP addresses and apply to each packet	Internet	Packets routed through internal network to desired IP address
Determine path across network/Internet to intended destination	Network Interface	Receipt of packets

Figure 4.7 The four layers of the TCP/IP.

© CostinT/iStockphoto

TCP/IP enables users to send data across sometimes unreliable networks with the assurance that the data will arrive in uncorrupted form. TCP/IP is very popular with business organizations because of its reliability and the ease with which it can support intranets and related functions.

Let's look at an example of packet-switching across the Internet. Figure 4.8 illustrates a message being sent from New York City to Los Angeles over a packet-switching network. Note that the different colored packets travel by different routes to reach their destination in Los Angeles, where they are reassembled into the complete message.

Types of Network Processing

Organizations typically use multiple computer systems across the firm. **Distributed processing** divides processing work among two or more computers. This process enables computers in different locations to communicate with one another via telecommunications links. A common type of distributed processing is client/server processing. A special type of client/server processing is peer-to-peer processing.

Client/Server Computing. **Client/server computing** links two or more computers in an arrangement in which some machines, called **servers**, provide computing services for user PCs, called **clients**. Usually, an organization performs the bulk of its processing or application/data storage on suitably powerful servers that can be accessed by less powerful

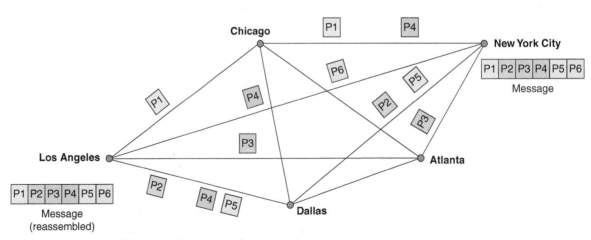

Figure 4.8 Packet switching.

client machines. The client requests applications, data, or processing from the server, which acts on these requests by "serving" the desired commodity.

Client/server computing leads to the ideas of "fat" clients and "thin" clients. As discussed in "Plug IT In 2," *fat clients* have large storage and processing power and therefore can run local programs (such as Microsoft Office), if the network is down. In contrast, *thin clients* may have no local storage and limited processing power. Thus, they must depend on the network to run applications. For this reason, they are of little value when the network is not functioning.

Peer-to-Peer Processing.
Peer-to-peer (P2P) processing is a type of client/server distributed processing where each computer acts as *both* a client and a server. Each computer can access (as assigned for security or integrity purposes) all files on all other computers.

There are three basic types of peer-to-peer processing. The first accesses unused CPU power among networked computers. A well-known application of this type is SETI@home (http://setiathome.ssl.berkeley.edu). These applications are from open-source projects and can be downloaded at no cost.

The second form of peer-to-peer is real-time, person-to-person collaboration, such as Microsoft SharePoint Workspace (http://office.microsoft.com/en-us/sharepoint-workspace). This product provides P2P collaborative applications that use buddy lists to establish a connection and allow real-time collaboration within the application.

The third peer-to-peer category is advanced search and file sharing. This category is characterized by natural-language searches of millions of peer systems. It enables users to discover other users, not just data and Web pages. One example of this category is BitTorrent.

BitTorrent (www.bittorrent.com) is an open-source, free, peer-to-peer file-sharing application that is able to simplify the problem of sharing large files by dividing them into tiny pieces, or "torrents." BitTorrent addresses two of the biggest problems of file sharing: (1) downloading bogs down when many people access a file at once, and (2) some people leech, meaning they download content but refuse to share. BitTorrent eliminates the bottleneck by enabling all users to share little pieces of a file at the same time—a process called *swarming*. The program prevents leeching because users must upload a file while they download it. This means that the more popular the content, the more efficiently it zips over a network.

BEFORE *YOU GO ON . . .*

1. Compare and contrast the three wireline communications channels.
2. Describe the various technologies that enable users to send high-volume data over any network.
3. Describe the Ethernet and TCP/IP protocols.
4. Differentiate between client/server computing and peer-to-peer processing.

Apply the Concept 4.2

Background This section covers network channels, protocols, and other fundamentals. These computer networks are the way in which most business workers receive and share information with customers, suppliers, and fellow employees. These networks work because they adhere to a common set of rules called a protocol. Two common protocols are Ethernet and Transmission Control Protocol/Internet Protocol (TCP/IP). Ethernet is used more for a LAN within an office. TCP/IP is the protocol of the Internet. This exercise is aimed at helping you understand how TCP/IP and packet switching work and the benefits of their use.

Chances are you have used the Internet for research, for e-mail, or to share photos with friends. The Internet would not function without a network. In fact, it is the largest network in the world because it allows us to communicate and share information all over the world. For all of us to be able to share files over this vast network, some standards are needed for the messages sent. The standard currently used is TCP/IP.

Activity Visit http://www.wiley.com/go/rainer/applytheconcept and click on the links provided for Apply the Concept 4.2. It will take you to two YouTube videos. The first is "IS 300: Packet Switching and the Internet (I)" and the second is "IS 300: Packet Switching and the Internet (II)." Both are by user "uwis300." You will see that for TCP/IP to function, a number of components are involved. Be sure to pay attention to the following components and their functions:

Address	Router
Ports 80 and 25	Packet
Firewall	Web browser
Proxy	Paths of the packets
Network interface	Web server

Deliverable

Using the information from the videos and your text, draw a flowchart showing the steps that a homework assignment sent via e-mail would take from your computer to your professor. Be sure to use the components listed above in your drawing.

Submit your drawing to your professor.

Quiz questions are assignable in WileyPLUS, and available on the Book Companion Site at http://www.wiley.com/college/rainer.

RUBY'S CLUB   QUESTIONS

1. What networking model should work best for the employees of Ruby's Club? A client/server or peer-to-peer network? What aspects cause you to make this choice?

2. If the client/server method is chosen, do you think the data should be stored on the client or the server? Defend your view.

4.3 The Internet and the World Wide Web

The **Internet ("the Net")** is a global WAN that connects approximately 1 million organizational computer networks in more than 200 countries on all continents, including Antarctica, and features in the daily routine of almost 2 billion people. Participating computer systems include smart phones, PCs, LANs, databases, and mainframes.

The computers and organizational nodes on the Internet can be of different types and makes. They are connected to one another by data communications lines of different speeds. The primary network connections and telecommunications lines that link the nodes are referred to as the backbone. For the Internet, the backbone is a fiber-optic network that is operated primarily by large telecommunications companies.

As a network of networks, the Internet enables people to access data in other organizations and to communicate, collaborate, and exchange information seamlessly around the world, quickly and inexpensively. Thus, the Internet has become a necessity for modern businesses.

The Internet grew out of an experimental project of the Advanced Research Project Agency (ARPA) of the U.S. Department of Defense. The project began in 1969 as the *ARPAnet*. Its purpose was to test the feasibility of a WAN over which researchers, educators, military personnel, and government agencies could share data, exchange messages, and transfer files.

Today, Internet technologies are being used both within and among organizations. An **intranet** is a network that uses Internet protocols so that users can take advantage of familiar applications and work habits. Intranets support discovery (easy and inexpensive browsing and search), communication, and collaboration inside an organization. For the numerous uses of intranets, see www.intranetjournal.com.

In contrast, an **extranet** connects parts of the intranets of different organizations. In addition, it enables business partners to communicate securely over the Internet using virtual private networks (VPNs, explained in Chapter 7). Extranets offer limited accessibility to the intranets of participating companies, as well as necessary interorganizational communications. They are widely used in the areas of business-to-business (B2B) electronic commerce (see Chapter 9) and supply chain management (SCM; see Chapter 13).

No central agency manages the Internet. Instead, the cost of its operation is shared among hundreds of thousands of nodes. Thus, the cost for any one organization is small. Organizations must pay a small fee if they wish to register their names, and they need to have their own hardware and software to operate their internal networks. The organizations are obliged to move any data or information that enter their organizational network, regardless of the source, to their destination, at no charge to the senders. The senders, of course, pay the telephone bills for using either the backbone or regular telephone lines.

Accessing the Internet

The Internet may be accessed in several ways. From your place of work or your university, you can access the Internet via your organization's LAN. A campus or company backbone connects all of the various LANs and servers in the organization to the Internet. You can also log onto the Internet from your home or on the road, using either wireline or wireless connections.

Connecting via an Online Service. You can also access the Internet by opening an account with an Internet service provider. An **Internet service provider (ISP)** is a company that provides Internet connections for a fee. Large ISPs include America Online (www.aol.com), Juno (www.juno.com), Earthlink (www.earthlink.com), and NetZero (www.netzero.net). In addition, many telephone providers and cable companies sell Internet access, as do computer companies such as Microsoft. To use this service you need a modem and standard communication software. To find a local ISP, access www.thelist.com. There, you can search by your telephone area code for an ISP that services your area.

ISPs connect to one another through **network access points (NAPs)**. NAPs are exchange points for Internet traffic. They determine how traffic is routed. NAPs are key components of the Internet backbone. Figure 4.9 shows a schematic of the Internet. The white links at the top of the figure represent the Internet backbone; the brown dots where the white links meet are the NAPs.

Connecting via Other Means. There have been several attempts to make access to the Internet cheaper, faster, and easier. For example, terminals known as Internet kiosks have been located in such public places as libraries and airports (and even in convenience stores in some countries) for use by people who do not have their own computers. Accessing the Internet from smart phones and iPads is common, and fiber-to-the-home (FTTH) is growing rapidly. FTTH involves connecting fiber-optic cable directly to individual homes. This system initially was restricted to new residential developments, but it is rapidly spreading. Table 4.2 summarizes the various means that you can use to connect to the Internet.

Addresses on the Internet. Each computer on the Internet has an assigned address, called the **Internet Protocol (IP) address**, that distinguishes it from all other computers.

© Mark Stay/iStockphoto.

Figure 4.9 Internet (backbone in white).

TABLE 4.2 Internet Connection Methods

Service	Description
Dial-up	Still used in the United States where broadband is not available.
DSL	Broadband access via telephone companies.
Cable modem	Access over your cable TV coaxial cable. Can have degraded performance if many of your neighbors are accessing the Internet at once.
Satellite	Access where cable and DSL are not available.
Wireless	Very convenient, and WiMAX will increase the use of broadband wireless.
Fiber-to-the-home (FTTH)	Expensive and usually only placed in new housing developments.

The IP address consists of numbers, in four parts, separated by dots. For example, the IP address of one computer might be 135.62.128.91. You can access a Web site by typing this number in the address bar of your browser.

Currently, there are two IP addressing schemes. The first scheme, IPv4, is the most widely used. IP addresses using IPv4 consist of 32 bits, meaning that there are 2^{32} possibilities for IP addresses, or 4,294,967,295 distinct addresses. Note that the IP address in the preceding paragraph (135.62.128.91) is an IPv4 address. At the time that IPv4 was developed, there were not as many computers needing addresses as there are today. Therefore, a new IP addressing scheme has been developed, called IPv6.

IP addresses using IPv6 consist of 128 bits, meaning that there are 2^{128} possibilities for distinct IP addresses, which is an unimaginably large number. IPv6, which is replacing IPv4, will accommodate the rapidly increasing number of devices that need IP addresses, such as smart phones.

IP addresses must be unique so computers on the Internet know where to find one another. The Internet Corporation for Assigned Names (ICANN) (www.icann.org) coordinates these unique addresses throughout the world. Without that coordination, we would not have one global Internet.

Because the numeric IP addresses are difficult to remember, most computers have names as well. ICANN accredits certain companies called *registrars* to register these names, which are derived from a system called the **domain name system (DNS)**. **Domain names** consist of multiple parts, separated by dots, that are read from right to left. For example, consider the domain name *business.auburn.edu*. The rightmost part of an Internet name is its *top-level domain (TLD)*. The letters *edu* in business.auburn.edu indicate that this is an educational site. The following are popular U.S. TLDs:

com	commercial sites
edu	educational sites
mil	military government sites
gov	civilian government sites
org	organizations

To finish our domain name example, *auburn* is the name of the organization (Auburn University), and *business* is the name of the particular machine (server) within the organization to which the message is being sent.

In other countries, the country name or designator is the TLD. For example, *de* stands for Germany, *it* for Italy, and *ru* for Russia. In essence, every country decides for itself whether to use TLDs. Moreover, those countries that use TLDs do not necessarily follow the

U.S. system. For example, the United Kingdom uses *.co* where the U.S. uses *.com* and *.ac* (for academic) where the U.S. uses *.edu*. In contrast, many other non-U.S. Web sites use U.S. TLDs, especially *.com*.

The Future of the Internet

Consumer demand for content delivered over the Internet is increasing at 60 percent per year. In 2010, monthly traffic across the Internet totaled roughly 8 exabytes (1 exabyte is equivalent to 50,000 years of DVD-quality data). Many experts are now concerned that Internet users will experience brownouts from three factors: (1) the increasing number of people who work online, (2) the soaring popularity of Web sites such as YouTube that require large amounts of bandwidth, and (3) the tremendous demand for high-definition television delivered over the Internet. These brownouts will lead to computers going offline for several minutes at a time. Researchers assert that if Internet bandwidth is not improved rapidly, then within a few years (see this chapter's Closing Case 1) the Internet will be able to function only at a much reduced speed.

Even today, the Internet sometimes is too slow for data-intensive applications such as full-motion video files (movies) or large medical files (X-rays). In addition, the Internet is unreliable and is not secure. As a result, Internet2 has been developed by more than 200 U.S. universities collaborating with industry and government. **Internet2** develops and deploys advanced network applications such as remote medical diagnosis, digital libraries, distance education, online simulation, and virtual laboratories. Internet2 is designed to be fast, always on, everywhere, natural, intelligent, easy, and trusted. Internet2 is not a separate physical network from the Internet. For more detail, see www.internet2.edu.

The World Wide Web

Many people equate the Internet with the World Wide Web. However, they are not the same thing. The Internet functions as a transport mechanism, whereas the World Wide Web is an application that uses those transport functions. Other applications, such as e-mail, also run on the Internet.

The **World Wide Web (The Web, WWW, or W3)** is a system of universally accepted standards for storing, retrieving, formatting, and displaying information via a client/server architecture. The Web handles all types of digital information, including text, hypermedia, graphics, and sound. It uses graphical user interfaces (GUIs), so it is very easy to navigate.

Organizations that wish to offer information through the Web must establish a *home page*, which is a text and graphical screen display that usually welcomes the user and provides basic information on the organization that has established the page. In most cases, the home page will lead users to other pages. All the pages of a particular company or individual are collectively known as a **Web site**. Most Web pages provide a way to contact the organization or the individual. The person in charge of an organization's Web site is its *Webmaster*. (*Note: Webmaster* is a gender-neutral title.)

To access a Web site, the user must specify a **uniform resource locator (URL)**, which points to the address of a specific resource on the Web. For instance, the URL for Microsoft is http://www.microsoft.com. Recall that HTTP stands for hypertext transport protocol. The remaining letters in this URL—www.microsoft.com— indicate the domain name that identifies the Web server that stores the Web site.

Users access the Web primarily through software applications called **browsers**. Browsers provide a graphical front end that enables users to point-and-click their way across the Web, a process called *surfing*. Web browsers became a means of universal access because they deliver the same interface on any operating system under which they run. As you see in IT's About Business 4.1, companies are pouring resources into improving their browsers.

> ### BEFORE YOU GO ON . . .
>
> 1. Describe the various ways that you can connect to the Internet.
> 2. Identify the parts of an Internet address.
> 3. What are the functions of browsers?
> 4. Describe the difference between the Internet and the World Wide Web.

IT'S ABOUT BUSINESS 4.1

Browser Competition Heats Up

Companies are investing increasing amounts of resources in browsers, which are the programs through which users access content on the Web. The credit for this trend of increased investments (which is highly beneficial to the consumer) goes to two parties. The first party is Google, whose big plans for its Chrome browser (www.google.com/chrome) have forced Microsoft to pay fresh attention to its own browser, Internet Explorer (IE). Previously, Microsoft had all but stopped efforts to enhance IE after the company won the last browser war by defeating Netscape.

 The European Union (EU) is the second party responsible for increased investments in Web browsers. Starting in March 2010, the EU required personal computer manufacturers to offer their Europe-based customers more freedom to choose. This requirement originated as part of an antitrust settlement with Microsoft. Under the new regime, when European purchasers boot up their computers for the first time, they will be presented with a screen that lists a dozen browsers (all free) in random order. Users can then download any of these browsers and start surfing the Web.

When considering the subject of Web browsers, users should bear in mind the business reasons for companies to provide free Web browsers. Chrome, for instance, is a key part of Google's strategy to make computer users comfortable with cloud computing (discussed in Plug IT In 3). The objective of Chrome is to convince users to spend less money and time on programs that they have to license from software companies (e.g., from Microsoft), and to instead use free data and services such as Google Docs, which resides on servers and storage systems on the Internet. In this way, Chrome—which is available in versions for Windows, Mac, and Linux—is designed to drive user dependency on Google's own ad-driven services.

In order for this strategy to work, the browser (in this case, Chrome) has to be good. It turns out that Chrome *is* good—Chrome 17 is fast, takes up little space on users' hard drives, and offers advanced support for HTML5. Chrome Instant even has your Web page ready to read before you finish typing in the Web address!

© Cagri Ozgur/iStockphoto

There are other good browsers out there, however. Mac users, for instance, can use Apple's own browser, Safari 5.1.2 (www.apple.com/safari), which is excellent. Safari is also available in a Windows version. Safari 5.1.2 mostly adds support for OS X Lion (Apple's latest version of its OS X operating system). Both Mac and Windows users of Safari get the added bonus of a Reading List panel, which provides a personal to-do list that you can edit.

Another excellent browser is Mozilla Firefox 11 (www.mozilla.com/en-US/firefox/fx/), a next-generation descendant of Netscape. Maintained by an open-source community, Firefox is not affiliated with any one corporation and is noted for its constant creative innovation. It is available for Windows, Macs, and Linux systems. Firefox benefits from a well-developed application base that includes thousands of add-ons for everything from speeding up YouTube downloads to StumbleUpon, which helps users discover and share Web sites that match their interests.

Another good browser choice is Opera 11.60 (www.opera.com), created by the Norwegian company Opera Software. Like Firefox, Opera 11.60 is available in Windows, Mac, and Linux versions. Opera is fast, HTML5 compliant, and provides features such as Opera Turbo, which speeds up weak Internet connections. Users occasionally encounter a Web site that does not cooperate with Opera, but that situation is becoming quite rare.

Finally, there is Microsoft Internet Explorer 9 (www.microsoft.com/IE9). IE 9 contains many enhancements, including additional security features and HTML5 compliance. Microsoft has promised that IE 9 will run faster than the previous IE version.

Regardless of which browser users select, they should take into consideration issues of security and privacy. Every company brags about its Web browser's security features, but there is truly no such thing as a "secure browser," because that would imply 100 percent security (in Chapter 7, you will learn that 100 percent security is impossible). Furthermore, browsing privacy can never be truly guaranteed. All browsers offer "private" or "incognito" modes, but for the most part such settings only prevent people looking at your computer from seeing the Web sites you have browsed. They do not stop those sites from keeping records of your visits.

In light of these issues, different browsers have taken different approaches to security and privacy. IE9 offers Tracking Protection, which allows users to subscribe to block lists, so that advertising networks do not have access to your data (and therefore cannot exchange data) about your browsing habits.

Firefox offers the Do Not Track header tag. This feature is analogous to the phone-based Do Not Call lists, indicating your preference to the advertiser. In a test run by PC Magazine's, however, this Firefox feature did not block interactions with third-party advertisers. In mid-2012, Chrome, Opera, and Safari have yet to implement any tracking protection.

As of February 2012, usage statistics, courtesy of StatCounter (www.statcounter.com), for the major desktop browsers were as follows:

Microsoft IE	35.7 percent
Google Chrome	30 percent
Mozilla Firefox	25 percent
Apple Safari	7 percent
Opera	2.3 percent

Sources: Compiled from M. Muchmore, "Browser Wars," *PC Magazine,* March 14, 2012; "Internet Browser Software Review," TopTenReviews, May 2011; R. Jaroslovsky, "Browser Wars: The Sequel," Bloomberg BusinessWeek, March 8, 2010.

Questions

1. Given that all browsers are free, what features do the major browser companies focus on to gain competitive advantage?

2. Which browser do you use? Why? Provide examples of why you use this particular browser.

Apply the Concept 4.3

Background This section has introduced you to the difference in the Internet and the World Wide Web. Additionally, it has shown that the Internet is the largest network in the world and it would not function without domain names and IP addresses. Domain names work much like the address book on your phone. It is much easier to remember the name of the person you want to call than to remember that person's specific number. You typically open your address book and click a name and it calls the related number.

Domain names are similar to this in that the Internet actually runs on IP addresses (strings of numbers) and we use domain names to point to them. When you type a domain name, there is an "address book" (technically called a domain name server) on the Web that finds the right string of numbers to direct your request to.

Activity HowStuffWorks.com has a nice explanation of how this domain-naming system works. Visit http://www.wiley.com/go/rainer/applytheconcept and click on the link provided for Apply the Concept 4.3. It will take you to the How Stuff Works site and the page on How Domain Name Servers Work. Read this section of content as well as the content in the chapter that explains domain name servers.

Deliverable

Write an e-mail to your best friend explaining how excited you are (and if you are not excited just fake it…) that you have learned how a domain name server works. Consider the following questions as you prepare your e-mail:

1. What is the function of a domain name server?

2. What are three top-level domains?

3. What is the country code for Germany?

4. How many bits are in IPv4? Give an example of IPv4.

5. How many bits are in IPv6? Give an example of IPv6.

Send the email to your instructor (and your friend if you are really excited!).

Quiz questions are assignable in WileyPLUS, and available on the Book Companion Site at http://www.wiley.com/college/rainer.

RUBY'S CLUB   QUESTIONS

1. What is the difference in the Internet and an Intranet? How can Ruby's use the strengths of each to better serve its customers and make its vision a reality?

2. Ruben and Lisa want to build a new Web site. Do you think they should host it locally or use a Web hosting service? What hardware and connectivity would they need to support a locally run Web site?

4.4 Network Applications

Now that you have a working knowledge of what networks are and how you can access them, the key question is, How do businesses use networks to improve their operations? This section addresses that question. Stated in general terms, networks support businesses and other organizations in all types of functions.

This section will explore numerous network applications, including discovery, communication, collaboration, e-learning and distance learning, virtual universities, and telecommuting. These applications, however, are merely a sampling of the many network applications currently available to users. Even if these applications formed an exhaustive list today, they would not do so tomorrow when something new will be developed. Further, placing network applications in categories is difficult because there will always be borderline cases. For example, the difference between chat rooms (in the communications category) and teleconference (in the collaboration category) is only one of degree.

Discovery

The Internet enables users to access or discover information located in databases all over the world. By browsing and searching data sources on the Web, users can apply the Internet's discovery capability to areas ranging from education to government services to entertainment to commerce. Although having access to all this information is a great benefit, it is critically important to realize that there is no quality assurance for information on the Web. The Web is truly democratic in that *anyone* can post information to it. Therefore, the fundamental rule about information on the Web is "User beware!"

In addition, the Web's major strength—the vast stores of information it contains—also presents a major challenge. The amount of information on the Web can be overwhelming, and it doubles approximately each year. As a result, navigating through the Web and gaining access to necessary information are becoming more and more difficult. To accomplish these tasks, people increasingly are using search engines, directories, and portals.

Search Engines and Metasearch Engines. A **search engine** is a computer program that searches for specific information by key words and then reports the results. A search engine maintains an index of billions of Web pages. It uses that index to find pages

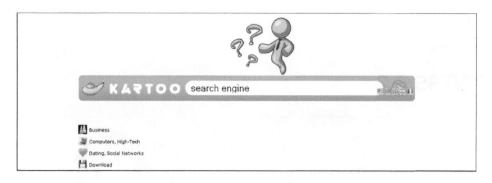

Figure 4.10 The KartOO home page (www.kartoo.com).

that match a set of user-specified keywords. Such indexes are created and updated by *web-crawlers*, which are computer programs that browse the Web and create a copy of all visited pages. Search engines then index these pages to provide fast searches.

In mid-2010, three search engines accounted for almost all searches in the United States: Google (www.google.com, 65.5 percent), Yahoo (www.yahoo.com, 16.8 percent), and Microsoft Network (now called Bing, www.msn.com, 11.8 percent). In addition, there is an incredible number of other search engines that are quite useful, many of which perform very specific searches (see an article on "The Top 100 Alternative Search Engines" that appeared on www.readwriteweb.com). The leading search engine in China is Baidu, with 64 percent of the Chinese market.

For an even more thorough search, you can use a metasearch engine. **Metasearch engines** search several engines at once and then integrate the findings to answer users' queries. Examples are Surf-wax (www.surfwax.com), Metacrawler (www.metacrawler.com), Mamma (www.mamma.com), KartOO (www.kartoo.com), and Dogpile (www.dogpile.com). Figure 4.10 illustrates the KartOO home page.

One interesting search engine is known as Summly. IT's About Business 4.2 explains how Summly works.

Publication of Material in Foreign Languages. Not only is there a huge amount of information on the Internet, but it is written in many different languages. How, then, do you access this information? The answer is that you use an *automatic translation* of Web pages. Such translation is available to and from all major languages, and its quality is improving with time. Some major translation products are Microsoft's Bing translator (http://www.microsofttranslator.com) and Google (www.google.com/language_tools) (see Figure 4.11), as well as products and services available at Trados (www.trados.com).

Should companies invest their time and resources to make their Web sites accessible in multiple languages? The answer is, absolutely. In fact, multilingual Web sites are now a competitive necessity because of the global nature of the business environment. Companies

Figure 4.11 Google Translate.

IT'S ABOUT BUSINESS 4.2

A New Search Engine

When Nick D'Alosio was 12, he created an app called SongStumblr, which used Bluetooth to let users know what people nearby were listening to. Next, he taught himself the basics of artificial intelligence (AI) software and built an app called Facemood, which updates you on the emotional state of your friends by monitoring their Facebook status. Over the next 3 years, Nick earned about $30,000 from profits from one-time sales of his apps, netting about $1.50 for each app download after deducting Apple's 30 percent share of the profits. By age 15, he had set up his own company (his mother had to sign all legal documents because he was underage).

In 2011, while studying for a history exam, he grew frustrated with the huge amount of text that showed up on Google search results. To save himself time, he wrote a program that summarized content in an easily digestible preview. He used his flair for languages—he was studying Latin, Mandarin, and French at the time—to create a program that would extract the most relevant sentences out of long text. Microsoft Word already had a summarizing tool that ran on a "linear" algorithm that searched for the most frequent keywords sequentially, but Nick figured he could do better with a genetic algorithm that could choose important sentences as a human does. Therefore, he created a program that detects the topic of a text and uses that information to determine what metrics to apply. Then, the program will use those metrics to determine, for example, if numbers are more important than descriptive words, and extract critical sentences accordingly.

Nick realized that his program could be used as much more than just a personal study tool. It could be used as a service for media companies, financial institutions, law firms, or any organization having to extract key points from huge amounts of data. For example, if you visit a Web site with lots of information, Summly (the name of the app) will give you a more user-friendly version of the information in 3 to 5 bullet points. Summly works especially well with news articles, because it bullet points the main headlines. Summly also gives you key words for the article.

© Oleksiy Mark/iStockphoto

D'Alosio spent the summer of 2011 honing his knowledge of AI and writing computer code. He contacted a linguistics researcher at MIT's Semantics Lab and paid him $250 to analyze his algorithm. The researcher's conclusion: Summly constructed summaries in a way that was 40 percent more similar to the process humans use than its competitors. This finding was enough validation for D'Alosio to release a free app (then called Trimit), which ran on an iPhone and received regular updates as he refined it. He set up a Web site and a demo video of the app on YouTube. A patent search revealed that, while similar apps existed in the market, none featured the trained AI component or tie-in to the iPhone that Trimit could boast.

Shortly after the app's release, two investment funds contacted d'Alosio via his Web site. One was Horizons Ventures, whose founder and manager had seen a story about Trimit on TechCrunch (a technology blog) and was interested in the technology behind the app. After thoroughly examining D'Alosio's app, Horizons bought a 25 percent stake in the product for $300,000 in September 2011.

Over the course of the next 3 months, Summly was downloaded 130,000 times. The downloads were free in order to build name recognition for the product.

You might ask, if the downloads are free, how does D'Alosio plan to make a profit? Rather than make money from users, he plans to license Summly to media and financial companies, Web browsers, and search engines. He will charge these outlets either a regular subscription fee or a fee for every 1,000 summaries. He has yet to set the exact pricing on his product.

D'Alosio is currently hiring full-time programmers who will train his genetic algorithm to mimic choices made by humans. This process is tedious and time-consuming, and involves reading thousands and thousands of Web articles (such as Wikipedia, movie reviews, and Quora answers), choosing the three to five most important sentences, and feeding them into the algorithm.

D'Alosio believes his product will be successful because search interfaces like Google have not changed in many years, despite a dramatic increase in the amount of content available on the Web. He believes that he has developed an entirely new type of search engine that can revolutionize the search-engine field.

Sources: Compiled from P. Olson, "Search Engine Wunderkind," *Forbes*, March 12, 2012; J. Wakefield, "British Designer of Summly App Hits Jackpot," *BBC News*, December 28, 2011; M. Kirkpatrick, "Summly: New App Helps You Read All Your Bookmarked Links in Minutes," *ReadWriteWeb*, December 13, 2011; P. Olson, "Teenage Programmer Backed by Hong Kong Billionaire Li Ka Shing," *Forbes*, December 13, 2011; C. Bonnington, "Teen's IOS App Uses Complex Algorithms to Summarize the Web," *Wired*, December 13, 2011; www.summly.com, accessed March 2, 2012.

Questions

1. Go to http://itunes.apple.com/us/app/summly/id488689465?mt=8) and watch the demo video. What are the advantages of the Summly app? Do you see any disadvantages in using the product?

2. Has D'Alosio actually created a new kind of search engine? Why do you say that? Support your answer.

---

increasingly are looking outside their home markets to grow revenues and attract new customers. When companies are disseminating information around the world, getting that information correct is essential. It is not enough for companies to translate Web content. They must also localize that content and be sensitive to the needs of the people in local markets.

To reach 80 percent of the world's Internet users, a Web site needs to support a minimum of ten languages: English, Chinese, Spanish, Japanese, German, Korean, French, Italian, Russian, and Portuguese. At 20 cents and more per word, translation services are expensive. Companies supporting ten languages can spend $200,000 annually to localize information and another $50,000 to maintain the Web sites. Translation budgets for major multinational companies can run in the millions of dollars. Many large companies use Systran S.A. (www.systransoft.com) for high-quality machine translation services.

Portals. Most organizations and their managers encounter information overload. Information is scattered across numerous documents, e-mail messages, and databases at different locations and systems. Finding relevant and accurate information is often time-consuming and may require users to access multiple systems.

One solution to this problem is to use portals. A **portal** is a Web-based, personalized gateway to information and knowledge that provides relevant information from different IT systems and the Internet using advanced search and indexing techniques. After reading the next section, you will be able to distinguish among four types of portals: commercial, affinity, corporate, and industrywide.

A **commercial (public) portal** is the most popular type of portal on the Internet. It is intended for broad and diverse audiences and offers routine content, some of it in real time (for example, a stock ticker). Examples are Lycos (www.lycos.com) and Microsoft Network (www.msn.com).

In contrast, an **affinity portal** offers a single point of entry to an entire community of affiliated interests, such as a hobby group or a political party. Your university most likely has an affinity portal for its alumni. Figure 4.12 displays the affinity portal for the University of West Georgia. Other examples of affinity portals are www.techweb.com and www.zdnet.com.

As the name suggests, a **corporate portal** offers a personalized, single point of access through a Web browser to critical business information located inside and outside an organization. These portals are also known as *enterprise portals*, *information portals*, and *enterprise information portals*. In addition to making it easier to find needed information, corporate portals offer customers and employees self-service opportunities.

Whereas corporate portals are associated with a single company, an **industrywide portal** serves entire industries. An example is TruckNet (www.truck.net), a portal for the trucking industry and the trucking community, including professional drivers, owner/

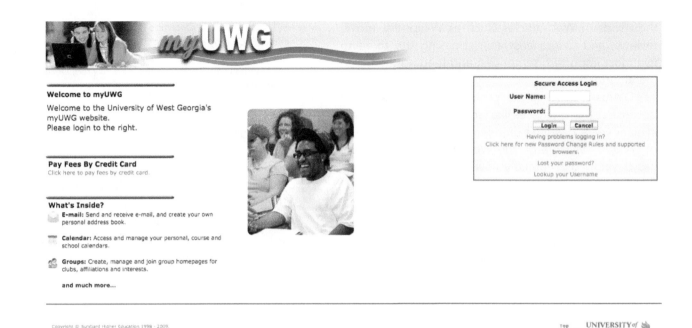

Figure 4.12 University of West
Georgia affinity portal.
(Courtesy of University of West Georgia.)

operators, and trucking companies (see Figure 4.13). TruckNet provides drivers with personalized Web-based e-mail, access to applications to leading trucking companies in the United States and Canada, and access to the Drivers Round Table, a forum where drivers can discuss issues of interest. The portal also provides a large database of trucking jobs and general information related to the trucking industry.

These four types of portals are differentiated by the audiences they serve. Another type, the mobile portal, is distinguished by its technology. A **mobile portal** is accessible from mobile devices, although any of the four portals just discussed can be accessed by mobile devices. Mobile devices are typically wireless, so you will study them in detail in Chapter 10.

Communication

The second major category of network applications is communication. There are many types of communication technologies, including e-mail, call centers, chat rooms, and voice. You learn about each one in this section. You will see another type of communication, blogging, in Chapter 8.

Electronic Mail. Electronic mail (e-mail) is the largest-volume application running over the Internet. Studies have found that almost all companies conduct business transactions via e-mail, and the vast majority confirm that e-mail is tied to their means of generating revenue. In fact, for many users, e-mail has all but replaced the telephone.

Figure 4.13 The TruckNet
portal.
Courtesy of the *Truck.net* copyright

Web-Based Call Centers. Effective personalized customer contact is becoming an important aspect of Web-based customer support. Such service is provided through *Web-based call centers*, also known as *customer care centers*. For example, if you need to contact a software vendor for technical support, you will usually be communicating with the vendor's Web-based call center, using e-mail, a telephone conversation, or a simultaneous voice/Web session. Web-based call centers are sometimes located in foreign countries such as India. Such *offshoring* is an important issue for U.S. companies.

For several reasons, some U.S. companies are moving their call center operations back to the United States. First, they feel that they have less control of their overseas call center operations. They must depend on the vendor company, ensuring that it can uphold their standards, such as quality of service. Second, language difficulties can occur. Third, companies that manage sensitive information can run the risk of breaching customer confidentiality. Finally, the vendor company's call center representatives typically work with many companies. As a result, they may not deliver the same level of customer services that is required.

Electronic Chat Rooms. *Electronic chat* refers to an arrangement whereby participants exchange conversational messages in real time. A **chat room** is a virtual meeting place where many people (in fact, anyone) come to chat. Chat programs allow you to send messages to people who are connected to the same channel of communication at the same time. Anyone can join in the conversation. Messages are displayed on your screen as they arrive, even if you are in the middle of typing a message.

There are two major types of chat programs. The first type is Web based, which allows you to send messages to Internet users by using a Web browser and visiting a Web chat site (for example, http://messenger.yahoo.com). The second type is e-mail based (text only) and is called *Internet Relay Chat (IRC)*. A business can use IRC to interact with customers, provide online experts for answers to questions, and so on.

Voice Communication. When people need to communicate with one another from a distance, they use the telephone more frequently than any other communication device. With the plain old telephone service (POTS), every call opened up a dedicated circuit for the duration of the call. A dedicated circuit connects you to the person with whom you are talking and is devoted only to your call. In contrast, as you saw earlier in this chapter, the Internet divides data into packets, which traverse the Internet in random order and are reassembled at their destination.

With **Internet telephony**, also known as **voice-over Internet protocol** or **VoIP**, phone calls are treated as just another kind of data. That is, your analog voice signals are digitized, sectioned into packets, and then sent over the Internet. In the past, to utilize VoIP you needed a computer with a sound card and a microphone. Today, however, you do not need special phones or headsets for your computer.

VoIP can reduce your monthly phone bills. However, packet switching can cause garbled communications. For example, if the packets of a message arrive out of order, that is not a problem when you are sending an e-mail or transmitting a photo. Correctly reassembling the packets of a voice message, however, can garble the message. Fortunately, this is less of a problem than in the past, because VoIP software continues to improve and typical communications links are much faster. So, although VoIP is not perfect, it is ready for prime time.

Skype (www.skype.com) provides several VoIP services for free: voice and video calls to users who also have Skype, instant messaging, short message service, voice mail, one-to-one and group chats, and conference calls with up to nine people (see Figure 4.14). As of mid-2010, the most current version of Skype for Windows was version 5.5. Skype 5.5 offers full-screen, high-definition video calling, Skype Access (to access WiFi hotspots), call transfer to a Skype contact on a mobile or landline, improved quality of calls, and ease of use. In addition, it offers other functions for which users pay. For example, SkypeOut allows you to make calls to landline phones and mobile phones. SkypeIn provides a number that your friends can call from any phone and you pick up the call in Skype.

Vonage (www.vonage.com) also provides VoIP services, but for a fee (approximately $25 per month). With Vonage you make and receive calls with your existing home phone

Figure 4.14 Skype 5.5 interface.
Courtesy of Skype.

through your broadband Internet connection. Your phone actually connects to Vonage instead of an actual phone company. The person whom you are calling does not need to have Vonage or even an Internet connection.

Unified Communications. In the past, organizational networks for wired and wireless data, voice communications, and videoconferencing operated independently, and the IT department managed each network separately. This arrangement increased costs and reduced productivity.

Unified communications (UC) simplifies and integrates all forms of communications—voice, voice mail, fax, chat, e-mail, instant messaging, short message service, presence (location) services, and videoconferencing—on a common hardware and software platform. *Presence services* enable users to know where their intended recipients are and if they are available, in real time.

UC unifies all forms of human and computer communications into a common user experience. For example, UC allows an individual to receive a voice mail message and then read it in his or her e-mail inbox. In another example, UC enables users to seamlessly collaborate with another person on a project, regardless of where the users are located. One user could quickly locate the other user by accessing an interactive directory, determine if that user were available, engage in a text messaging session, and then escalate the session to a voice call, or even a video call, all in real time.

Collaboration

The third major category of network applications is collaboration. An important feature of modern organizations is that people collaborate to perform work. **Collaboration** refers to efforts by two or more entities—that is, individuals, teams, groups, or organizations—who work together to accomplish certain tasks. The term **work group** refers specifically to two or more individuals who act together to perform some task.

Workflow is the movement of information as it flows through the sequence of steps that make up an organization's work procedures. Workflow management makes it possible to pass documents, information, and tasks from one participant to another in a way that is governed by the organization's rules or procedures. Workflow systems are tools for automating business processes.

If group members are in different locations, they constitute a **virtual group (team)**. Virtual groups conduct *virtual meetings*—that is, they "meet" electronically. **Virtual collaboration** (or *e-collaboration*) refers to the use of digital technologies that enable organizations or individuals to collaboratively plan, design, develop, manage, and research products, services, and innovative applications. Organizational employees frequently collaborate—virtually with one another. In addition, organizations collaborate virtually with customers, suppliers, and other business partners to improve productivity and competitiveness.

One type of collaboration is *crowdsourcing*, which refers to outsourcing a task to an undefined, generally large group of people in the form of an open call. Let's look at some examples of crowdsourcing on college campuses.

- *Crowdsourcing help desks:* IT help desks are a necessary service on college campuses because students depend on their computers and Internet access to complete their school work and attend class online. At Indiana University at Bloomington, new IT help desks use crowdsourcing to alleviate the cost and pressure of having to answer so many calls. Students and professors post their IT problems on an online forum, where other students and amateur IT experts answer them.

- *Recruitment:* In 2010, Champlain College in Vermont instituted a Champlain For Reel program, inviting students to share via YouTube videos their experiences at the school and how they benefited from their time there. The YouTube channel serves to recruit prospective students and even updates alumni on campus and community events.

- *Scitable* (www.nature.com/scitable) combines social networking and academic collaboration. Through crowdsourcing, students, professors, and scientists discuss problems, find solutions, and swap resources and journals. It is a free site that lets each individual user turn to crowdsourcing for answers even while helping others.

- *The Great Sunflower Project:* Gretchen LeBuhn, an associate biology professor at San Francisco State University, needed help with her studies of honeybees, but she had limited grant money, so she contacted gardening groups around the country. Through this crowdsourcing strategy, LeBuhn ultimately created a network of more than 25,000 gardeners and schools to assist with her research. She then sent these participants seeds for plants that attract bees. In return, the participants recorded honeybee visits and activity for her on her Web site.

Collaboration can be *synchronous*, meaning that all team members meet at the same time. Teams may also collaborate *asynchronously* when team members cannot meet at the same time. Virtual teams, whose members are located throughout the world, typically must collaborate asynchronously.

A variety of software products are available to support all types of collaboration. Among the most prominent are Microsoft SharePoint Workspace, Google Docs, IBM Lotus Quickr, and Jive. In general, these products provide online collaboration capabilities, work-group e-mail, distributed databases, bulletin whiteboards, electronic text editing, document management, workflow capabilities, instant virtual meetings, application sharing, instant messaging, consensus building, voting, ranking, and various application development tools.

These products also provide varying degrees of content control. Wikis, Google Docs, Microsoft SharePoint Workspace, and Jive provide for shared content with *version management*, whereas Microsoft SharePoint Workspace and IBM Lotus Quickr offer *version control*. Products that provide version management track changes to documents and provide features to accommodate multiple people working on the same document at the same time. In contrast, version-control systems provide each team member with an account that includes a set of permissions. Shared documents are located in shared directories. Document directories are often set up so that users must check out documents before they can edit them. When one team member checks out a document, no other member can access it. Once the document has been checked in, it becomes available to other members.

In this section, we review the major collaboration software products. We then shift our attention to two tools that support collaboration—electronic teleconferencing and videoconferencing.

Microsoft SharePoint. Microsoft's SharePoint product (www.microsoft.com/Sharepoint/default.mspx) provides shared content with version control. SharePoint supports document directories and has features that enable users to create and manage surveys, discussion forums, wikis, member blogs, member Web sites, and workflow. It also has a rigorous permissions structure, which allows organizations to control users' access based on their organizational role, team membership, interest, security level, or other criteria.

One company that has used SharePoint effectively is Continental Airlines. When new federal regulations regarding long runway delays went into effect, Continental responded by implementing a SharePoint system that puts various aspects of flight operations—aircraft status, pilots, crews, and customer care—on the same page. Using the system, the 135 general managers at the airline's domestic airports fill out a 16-page form online. The form includes the names and numbers of airport workers, from the airport authority to the person who drives the stairs to planes waiting on the runway. The general managers have to specify how they would manage delays of an hour, two hours, and two-and-one-half hours. The Sharepoint system includes a dashboard for Continental's centralized system operations center. People in the center can use the dashboard to find information about delays quickly and to communicate with pilots, crews, and dispatchers to decide what to do to mitigate any delays.

Google Docs. Google Docs (http://docs.google.com) is a free Web-based word processor, spreadsheet, and presentation application. It enables users to create and edit documents online while collaborating with other users. In contrast to Microsoft SharePoint Workspace, Google Docs allows multiple users to open, share, and edit documents at the same time.

IBM Lotus Quickr. IBM's Lotus Quickr (www.ibm.com/lotus/quickr) product provides shared content with version control in the form of document directories with check-in and check-out features based on user privileges. Quickr provides online team spaces where members can share and collaborate by utilizing team calendars, discussion forums, blogs, wikis, and other collaboration tools for managing projects and other content.

Compagnie d'Enterprises (CFE), one of Belgium's largest construction companies, has put the collaboration tools of Quickr to good use. Construction projects require many parties to collaborate effectively. When these projects are conducted on a global scale and the parties are scattered throughout the world, the projects become incredibly complex. CFE needed to tap its best resources for its projects, regardless of where those resources were located. The company was using e-mail to share documents with suppliers and clients, but this process resulted in version-control errors and security vulnerabilities. To eliminate these problems, CFE deployed Quickr with its centralized document libraries and version control. The software reduced both the volume of large attachments sent through e-mail and the impact of those e-mails on the system. As a result, project teams were able to work more efficiently.

Jive. Jive's (www.jivesoftware.com) newest product, Clearspace, uses Web collaboration and communication tools such as forums, wikis, and blogs to allow people to share content with version management, via discussion rooms, calendars, and commotion lists. For example, Nike originally used Clearspace Community to run a technical support forum on Nike Plus (http://nikerunning.nike.com), a Web site where runners track their miles and calories burned using a sensor in their shoes. The company soon noticed that runners were also using the forum to meet other athletes. In response, Nike expanded its forum to include a section where runners could meet and challenge one another to races. Since that time, 40 percent of visitors to the site who did not own the Nike Plus sensor ended up buying the product.

Electronic Teleconferencing. **Teleconferencing** is the use of electronic communication technology that enables two or more people at different locations to hold a simultaneous conference. There are several types of teleconferencing. The oldest and simplest is a telephone conference call, where several people talk to one another from multiple locations. The biggest disadvantage of conference calls is that they do not allow the participants to

Marketwire/Newscom

Figure 4.15 Telepresence system.

communicate face to face. In addition, participants in one location cannot see graphs, charts, and pictures at other locations.

To overcome these shortcomings, organizations are increasingly turning to video tele-conferencing, or videoconferencing. In a **videoconference**, participants in one location can see participants, documents, and presentations at other locations. The latest version of videoconferencing, called *telepresence*, enables participants to seamlessly share data, voice, pictures, graphics, and animation by electronic means. Conferees can also transmit data along with voice and video, which allows them to work together on documents and to exchange computer files.

Several companies are offering high-end telepresence systems. For example, Hewlett-Packard's Halo system (www.hp.com), Cisco's TelePresence 3000 (www.cisco.com), and Polycom's HDX (www.polycom.com) use massive high-definition screens up to eight feet wide to show people sitting around conference tables (see Figure 4.15). Telepresence systems also have advanced audio capabilities that let everyone talk at once without canceling out any voices. Telepresence systems can cost up to $400,000 for a room, with network management fees ranging up to $18,000 per month. Financial and consulting firms are quickly adopting telepresence systems. For example, the Blackstone Group (www.blackstone.com), a private equity firm, has 40 telepresence rooms around the world, and Deloitte & Touche has 12.

Let's look at two other organizations that use telepresence systems.

The telepresence system of international law firm DLA Piper (www.dlapiper.com) saves the company approximately $1 million per year in travel costs and lost productivity. The firm realizes these savings by rescheduling half of its in-person board meetings as telepresence conferences and relying on at least two attorneys per week to use telepresence rather than travel. Making it possible for globally based attorneys to work closely together via telepresence helps drive home the reality that the firm has offices all over the world and therefore should have an international focus. This benefit of telepresence cannot be quantified in terms of dollars and cents.

The insurance giant MetLife (www.metlife.com) is using telepresence in three dedicated conference rooms in Chicago, New York, and New Jersey and is expanding the system to other offices nationally and internationally. MetLife has experienced a direct cost savings as well as better employee time efficiency. Further, telepresence is helping the company meet its "green initiative" goal of reducing its carbon emissions by 20 percent. Interestingly, one MetLife executive noted that when the company uses telepresence for meetings, employees who would not normally be asked to travel to headquarters now have the opportunity to make presentations and get valuable exposure to company executives.

E-Learning and Distance Learning

E-learning and distance learning are not the same thing, but they do overlap. **E-learning** refers to learning supported by the Web. It can take place inside classrooms as a support to conventional teaching, such as when students work on the Web during class. It also can take place in virtual classrooms, in which all coursework is done online and classes do not meet face-to-face. In these cases, e-learning is a part of distance learning. **Distance learning (DL)** refers to any learning situation in which teachers and students do not meet face-to-face.

Today, the Web provides a multimedia interactive environment for self-study. Web-enabled systems make knowledge accessible to those who need it, when they need it, anytime, anywhere. For this reason, e-learning and DL can be useful both for formal education and for corporate training. IT's About Business 4.3 illustrates how high school students are using e-learning and distance learning to take advanced placement (AP) classes online.

IT'S ABOUT BUSINESS 4.3

Massive Open Online Courses

Massive Open Online Courses—known as MOOCs—are a tool for democratizing higher education. Hundreds of thousands of students around the world who lack access to elite universities have been embracing MOOCs as a way to acquire sophisticated skills and high-paying jobs without having to pay tuition or secure a college degree.

Consider Stanford University's experience. In fall 2011, 160,000 students in 190 countries enrolled in a single AI course offered by Stanford. An additional 200 registered for the course on campus. A few weeks into the semester, attendance for the on-campus course decreased to about 30, as students decided to watch online videos instead of physically attending the class. The course gave rise to its own community, including a Facebook group, online discussions among participants, and volunteer translators who made the course available in 44 languages.

The 23,000 students who completed the course received a PDF file (suitable for framing) by e-mail showing their percentile score. However, the file did not contain the name "Stanford University." A total of 248 students, none from Stanford, earned grades of 100 percent.

Besides the AI course, Stanford offered two other MOOCs in fall 2011—Machine Learning (104,000 registered, 13,000 completed the course), and Introduc-

tion to Databases (92,000 registered, 7,000 completed the course). In Spring 2012, Stanford offered 13 MOOCs, including Anatomy, Cryptography, Game Theory, and Natural Language Processing.

On February 13, 2012, the Massachusetts Institute of Technology, which had been posting course materials online for 10 years, opened registration for its first MOOC, a circuits and electronics course. The course served as a prototype for the university's MITx project, which will eventually offer a wide range of courses and some sort of credential for those who complete them.

Several factors enabled the creation of MOOCs, including improved technology and the rapidly increasing costs of traditional universities. MOOCs are highly automated, with computer-graded assignments and exams. Nonetheless, MOOCs offer many opportunities for social interaction. The Stanford MOOCs, for example, offered virtual office hours and online discussion forums where students could ask and answer questions—and vote on which questions were important enough to filter up to the professors.

One Stanford professor noted that in a classroom, when a professor asks a question to the class, one student answers and the others do not get a chance to participate. On the other hand, in an online environment with embedded quizzes, *everyone* has to try to answer the questions. If they do not know the answer to the questions, they can go back and listen to the lecture over and over until they do. The professor noted that MOOCs allow students to work at their own pace and keep practicing until they master the content.

A student in one of Stanford's Fall 2011 MOOCs had not been a technology major, nor did she follow a technological career path. She studied psychology at the University of Pittsburgh and was a physician's assistant in charge of the presurgical ward at New York Downtown Hospital. She took the Stanford MOOC on technology in order to better understand her husband's career (he was a developer at Foursquare). Despite the fact that she did not initially take the class to affect her own job, she has since used her new software skills to automate some of the routine tasks she performs at work, such as keeping track of which patients require follow-up before surgery. Her skills also help her communicate with the information technology specialists installing electronic medical records systems at the hospital.

In what some academicians see as a threat to higher education, some MOOCs now offer an informal credential (although such a credential, in most cases, is not free). The provost at Stanford notes that there are many issues to consider with MOOCs, from questions of copyright of course materials to implications for Stanford's accreditation if the university provides an official credential for these courses.

One of the professors who taught Stanford's first MOOC cofounded Udacity (www.udacity.com), a for-profit startup that offers a variety of MOOCs. Nor is Udacity the only such startup—Udemy (www.udemy.com), founded in 2010, is a similar startup with backing from the founders of Groupon (www.groupon.com). Both sites plan to monetize their students' skills and obtain their permission to sell leads to recruiters, thereby helping them to find jobs. Both companies will have detailed records on thousands of students who have learned new skills, and many of those students will want to make those skills known to potential employers. For example, if a recruiter were searching for the top one hundred people in a certain geographic area who have knowledge about machine learning, Udacity and Udemy would be able to provide that information for a fee.

Sources: Compiled from T. Lewin, "Instruction for Masses Knocks Down Campus Walls," *The New York Times*, March 4, 2012; B. Sheridan and B. Greeley, "Computer Coding: Not for Geeks Only," *Bloomberg BusinessWeek*, January 26, 2012; L. Chamberlin and T. Parish, "MOOCs: Massive Open Online Courses or Massive and Often Obtuse Courses?" *eLearn Magazine*, August 2011; I. de Waard, "Explore a New Learning Frontier: MOOCs," *Learning Solutions Magazine*, July 25, 2011; R. Kop, "The Challenges to Connectivist Learning on Open Online Networks: Learning Experiences During a Massive Open Online Course," *International Review of Research in Open and Distance Learning*, v. 12, no. 3, 2011; K. Masters, "A Brief Guide to Understanding MOOCs," *The Internet Journal of Medical Education*, v. 1, no. 2, 2011; E. Fuller, "Top 10 Benefits of a College Degree," *Christian Science Monitor*, October 2010; www.udacity.com, www.stanford.edu, www.mit.edu, accessed February 25, 2012.

Questions

1. Discuss possible quality control issues with MOOCs. For each issue that you list, please also describe how you would go about solving the problem.

2. What are some specific examples of the impact that MOOCs could have on traditional higher education? Please explain your answer.

3. Would you be willing to enroll in a MOOC as a full-time student at your university? Would you be willing to enroll in a MOOC after you graduate? Why or why not?

There are many benefits to e-learning. For example, online materials can deliver very current content that is of high quality (created by content experts) and consistent (presented the same way every time). It also gives students the flexibility to learn at any place, at any time, and at their own pace. In corporate training centers that use e-learning, learning time generally is shorter, which means that more people can be trained within a given timeframe. This system reduces training costs as well as the expense of renting facility space.

Despite these benefits, e-learning has some drawbacks. For one, students must be computer literate. Also, they may miss the face-to-face interaction with instructors. In addition, accurately assessing students' work can be problematic because instructors really do not know who completed the assignments.

E-learning does not usually replace the classroom setting. Rather, it enhances it by taking advantage of new content and delivery technologies. Advanced e-learning support environments, such as Blackboard (www.blackboard.com), add value to traditional learning in higher education.

Virtual Universities

Virtual universities are online universities in which students take classes via the Internet at home or an off-site location. A large number of existing universities offer online education of some form. Some universities, such as the University of Phoenix (www.phoenix.edu), California Virtual Campus (www.cvc.edu), and the University of Maryland (www.umuc.edu), offer thousands of courses and dozens of degrees to students worldwide, all online. Other universities offer limited online courses and degrees but use innovative teaching methods and multimedia support in the traditional classroom.

Telecommuting

Knowledge workers are being called the distributed workforce, or digital nomads. This group of highly prized workers is now able to work anywhere and anytime, a process called **telecommuting**. Distributed workers are those who have no permanent office at their companies, preferring to work at home offices, in airport lounges or client conference rooms, or on a high school stadium bleacher. The growth of the distributed workforce is driven by globalization, extremely long commutes to work, rising gasoline prices, ubiquitous broadband communications links (wireline and wireless), and powerful laptop computers and computing devices.

Telecommuting has a number of potential advantages for employees, employers, and society. For employees, the benefits include reduced stress and improved family life. In addition, telecommuting offers employment opportunities for housebound people such as single parents and persons with disabilities. Employer benefits include increased productivity, the ability to retain skilled employees, and the ability to attract employees who do not live within commuting distance.

However, telecommuting also has some potential disadvantages. For employees, the major disadvantages are increased feelings of isolation, possible loss of fringe benefits, lower pay (in some cases), no workplace visibility, the potential for slower promotions, and lack of socialization. In addition, telecommuting employees often have difficulties "training" their families to understand that they are at work even though they are physically at home. Families have to understand that they should not disturb the telecommuter for anything that they would not have disturbed him or her about in a "real" office. The major disadvantages to employers are difficulties in supervising work and potential data security problems.

BEFORE YOU GO ON . . .

1. Discuss the network applications that you studied in this section and the tools and technologies that support each one.

2. Identify the business conditions that have made videoconferencing more important.

3. Differentiate between e-learning and distance learning.

4. Describe virtual universities.

5. What is telecommuting? Do you think you would like to telecommute? Why or why not?

Apply the Concept 4.4

Background This section has shown that the three big applications of a network are discovery, communication, and collaboration. *Discovery* occurs when you find information in other places that is useful to you. *Communication* occurs when you send information to another person that is helpful to them and *collaboration* exists when two or more people work on information together at the same time. Corporate networks (intranets) attempt to accomplish this within an organization by making data accessible to employees in different departments. You will learn more about this in Chapter 10: Information Systems Within the Organization.

Because the Internet has opened the door for more employees to work from a distance (telecommuting), there have been a number of tools built to support discovery, communication, and collaboration online. Many of these tools are mentioned in the text of this chapter (Microsoft SharePoint, Google Docs, etc.).

Activity Visit http://www.wiley.com/go/rainer/applytheconcept and click on the links provided for Apply the Concept 4.4. First is the Web site for Fuze Meeting and second are some video tutorials that may be helpful if you have never used this type of system before. Fuze Meeting also offers apps for many mobile devices. Have a look to better understand the platforms that exist to support this type of communication and collaboration.

Deliverable

Describe an imaginary situation where you may have a online group meeting where the purpose was to design an advertising scheme for a new product. In your description, be sure to outline how the Fuze Meeting software would support discovery, communication, and collaboration. Are there any of these three that are more or less supported than others?

Submit your write-up to your professor.

Quiz questions are assignable in WileyPLUS, and available on the Book Companion Site at http://www.wiley.com/college/rainer.

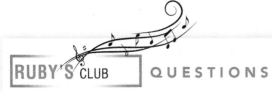

RUBY'S CLUB QUESTIONS

1. How can Ruby's Club capitalize on network tools such as e-mail, chat, or instant messaging?
2. What type of workflow projects could help streamline the operations for Ruby's Club?

What's in IT for ME?

FOR THE ACCOUNTING MAJOR

Accounting personnel use corporate intranets and portals to consolidate transaction data from legacy systems to provide an overall view of internal projects. This view contains the current costs charged to each project, the number of hours spent on each project by individual employees, and an analysis of how actual costs compare to projected costs. Finally, accounting personnel use Internet access to government and professional Web sites to stay informed on legal and other changes affecting their profession.

FOR THE FINANCE MAJOR

Corporate intranets and portals can provide a model to evaluate the risks of a project or an investment. Financial analysts use two types of data in the model: historical transaction data from corporate databases via the intranet and industry data obtained via the Internet. In addition, financial services firms can use the Web for marketing and to provide services.

FOR THE MARKETING MAJOR

Marketing managers use corporate intranets and portals to coordinate the activities of the sales force. Sales personnel access corporate portals via the intranet to discover updates on pricing, promotion, rebates, customer information, and information about competitors. Sales staff can also download and customize presentations for their customers. The Internet, particularly the Web, opens a completely new marketing channel for many industries. Just how advertising, purchasing, and information dispensation should occur appears to vary from industry to industry, product to product, and service to service.

FOR THE
PRODUCTION/OPERATIONS MANAGEMENT MAJOR

Companies are using intranets and portals to speed product development by providing the development team with three-dimensional models and animation. All team members can access the models for faster exploration of ideas and enhanced feedback. Corporate portals, accessed via intranets, enable managers to carefully supervise their inventories as well as real-time production on assembly lines. Extranets are also proving valuable as communication formats for joint research and design efforts among companies. The Internet is also a great source of cutting-edge information for POM managers.

FOR THE
HUMAN RESOURCES MANAGEMENT MAJOR

Human resources personnel use portals and intranets to publish corporate -policy manuals, job postings, company telephone directories, and training classes. Many companies deliver online training obtained from the Internet to employees through their intranets. Human resources departments use intranets to offer employees health care, savings, and benefit plans, as well as the opportunity to take competency tests online. The Internet supports worldwide recruiting efforts; it can also be the communications platform for supporting geographically dispersed work teams.

FOR THE MIS MAJOR

As important as the networking technology infrastructure is, it is invisible to users (unless something goes wrong). The MIS function is responsible for keeping all organizational networks up and running all the time. MIS personnel, therefore, provide all users with an "eye to the world" and the ability to compute, communicate, and collaborate anytime, anywhere. For example, organizations have access to experts at remote locations without having to duplicate that expertise in multiple areas of the firm. Virtual teaming allows experts physically located in different cities to work on projects as though they were in the same office.

SUMMARY

1. **Compare and contrast the two major types of networks.**

The two major types of networks are local area networks (LANs) and wide area networks (WANs). LANs encompass a limited geographic area and are usually composed of one communications medium. In contrast, WANs encompass a broad geographical area and are usually composed of multiple communications media.

2. **Describe the wireline communications media and channels.**

Twisted-pair wire, the most prevalent form of communications wiring, consists of strands of copper wire twisted in pairs. It is relatively inexpensive to purchase, widely available, and easy to work with. However, it is relatively slow for transmitting data, it is subject to interference from other electrical sources, and it can be easily tapped by unintended receivers.

Coaxial cable consists of insulated copper wire. It is much less susceptible to electrical interference than is twisted-pair wire and it can carry much more data. However, coaxial cable is more expensive and more difficult to work with than twisted-pair wire. It is also somewhat inflexible.

Fiber-optic cables consist of thousands of very thin filaments of glass fibers that transmit information via light pulses generated by lasers. Fiber-optic cables are significantly smaller and lighter than traditional cable media. They also can transmit far more data, and they provide greater security from interference and tapping. Fiber-optic cable is often used as the backbone for a network, whereas twisted-pair wire and coaxial cable connect the backbone to individual devices on the network.

3. **Describe the most common methods for accessing the Internet.**

Common methods for connecting to the Internet include dial-up, DSL, cable modem, satellite, wireless, and fiber to the home.

4. **Explain the impact that networks have had on business and everyday life for each of the six major categories of network applications.**

> *Discovery* involves browsing and information retrieval, and provides users the ability to view information in databases, download it, and/or process it. Discovery tools include search engines, directories, and portals.

Discovery tools enable business users to efficiently find needed information.

> Networks provide fast, inexpensive *communications*, via e-mail, call centers, chat rooms, voice communications, and blogs. Communications tools provide business users with a seamless interface among team members, colleagues, business partners, and customers.

> *Collaboration* refers to mutual efforts by two or more entities (individuals, groups, or companies) who work together to accomplish tasks. Collaboration is enabled by workflow systems. Collaboration tools enable business users to collaborate with colleagues, business partners, and customers.

> *E-learning* refers to learning supported by the Web. Distance learning refers to any learning situation in which teachers and students do not meet face-to-face. E-learning provides tools for business users to enable their lifelong learning.

> *Virtual universities* are online universities in which students take classes via the Internet at home or an off-site location. Virtual universities make it possible for students to obtain degrees while working full time, thus increasing their value to their firms.

> *Telecommuting* is the process whereby knowledge workers are able to work anywhere and anytime. Telecommuting provides flexibility for employees, with many benefits and some drawbacks.

>>> CHAPTER GLOSSARY

affinity portal A Web site that offers a single point of entry to an entire community of affiliated interests.

analog signals Continuous waves that transmit information by altering the amplitude and frequency of the waves.

backbone networks High-speed central networks to which multiple smaller networks (such as LANs and smaller WANs) connect.

bandwidth The transmission capacity of a network, stated in bits per second.

broadband A transmission speed ranging from approximately one megabit per second up to several terabits per second.

broadcast media (also called **wireless media**) Communications channels that use electromagnetic media (the "airwaves") to transmit data.

browsers Software applications through which users primarily access the Web.

cable media (also called **wireline media**) Communications channels that use physical wires or cables to transmit data and information.

chat room A virtual meeting place where groups of regulars come to "gab" electronically.

client/server computing Form of distributed processing in which some machines (servers) perform computing functions for end-user PCs (clients).

clients Computers, such as users' personal computers, that use any of the services provided by servers.

coaxial cable Insulated copper wire; used to carry high-speed data traffic and television signals.

collaboration Mutual efforts by two or more individuals who perform activities in order to accomplish certain tasks.

commercial (public) portal A Web site that offers fairly routine content for diverse audiences; offers customization only at the user interface.

communications channel Pathway for communicating data from one location to another.

computer network A system that connects computers and other devices via communications media so that data and information can be transmitted among them.

corporate portal A Web site that provides a single point of access to critical business information located inside and outside of an organization.

digital signals A discrete pulse, either on or off, that conveys information in a binary form.

digital subscriber line (DSL) A high-speed, digital data-transmission technology using existing analog telephone lines.

distance learning (DL) Learning situations in which teachers and students do not meet face-to-face.

distributed processing Network architecture that divides processing work between two or more computers, linked together in a network.

domain name system (DNS) The system administered by the Internet Corporation for Assigned Names (ICANN) that assigns names to each site on the Internet.

domain names The name assigned to an Internet site, consisting of multiple parts, separated by dots, which are translated from right to left.

e-learning Learning supported by the Web; can be done inside traditional classrooms or in virtual classrooms.

enterprise network An organization's network composed of interconnected multiple LANs and WANs.

Ethernet A common local area network protocol.

extranet A network that connects parts of the intranets of different organizations.

fiber-optic cable A communications medium consisting of thousands of very thin filaments of glass fibers, surrounded by cladding, that transmit information via light pulses generated by lasers.

file server (also called **network server)** A computer that contains various software and data files for a local area network and contains the network operating system.

Hypertext Transport Protocol (HTTP) The communications standard used to transfer pages across the WWW portion of the Internet; defines how messages are formulated and transmitted.

industrywide portal A Web-based gateway to information and knowledge for an entire industry.

Internet (The Net) A massive global WAN that connects approximately 1 million organizational computer networks in more than 200 countries on all continents, including Antarctica, and features in the daily routine of almost 2 billion people. Participating computer systems include smart phones, PCs, LANs, databases, and mainframes.

Internet Protocol (IP) A set of rules responsible for disassembling, delivering, and reassembling packets over the Internet.

Internet Protocol (IP) address An assigned address that uniquely identifies a computer on the Internet.

Internet service provider (ISP) A company that provides Internet connections for a fee.

Internet telephony (Voice-over Internet Protocol or VoIP) The use of the Internet as the transmission medium for telephone calls.

Internet2 A new, faster telecommunications network that deploys advanced network applications such as remote medical diagnosis, digital libraries, distance education, online simulation, and virtual laboratories.

intranet A private network that uses Internet software and TCP/IP protocols.

local area network (LAN) A network that connects communications devices in a limited geographical region, such as a building, so that every user device on the network can communicate with every other device.

metasearch engine A computer program that searches several engines at once and integrates the findings of the various search engines to answer queries posted by users.

mobile portal A Web site that is accessible from mobile devices.

modem Device that converts signals from analog to digital and vice versa.

network access points (NAPs) Computers that act as exchange points for Internet traffic and determine how traffic is routed.

network server (see **file server**)

packet switching The transmission technology that divides blocks of text into packets.

peer-to-peer (P2P) processing A type of client/server distributed processing that allows two or more computers to pool their resources, making each computer both a client and a server.

portal A Web-based personalized gateway to information and knowledge that provides information from disparate information systems and the Internet, using advanced search and indexing techniques.

protocol The set of rules and procedures governing transmission across a network.

router A communications processor that routes messages from a LAN to the Internet, across several connected LANs, or across a wide area network such as the Internet.

search engine A computer program that searches for specific information by key words and reports the results.

servers Computers that provide access to various network services, such as printing, data, and communications.

synchronous optical network (SONET) An interface standard for transporting digital signals over fiber-optic lines; allows the integration of transmissions from multiple vendors.

telecommuting A work arrangement whereby employees work at home, at the customer's premises, in special workplaces, or while traveling, usually using a computer linked to their place of employment.

teleconferencing The use of electronic communication that allows two or more people at different locations to have a simultaneous conference.

Transmission Control Protocol/Internet Protocol (TCP/IP) A file transfer protocol that can send large files of information across sometimes unreliable networks with assurance that the data will arrive uncorrupted.

twisted-pair wire A communications medium consisting of strands of copper wire twisted together in pairs.

unified communications Common hardware and software platform that simplifies and integrates all forms of communications—voice, e-mail, instant messaging, location, and videoconferencing—across an organization.

uniform resource locator (URL) The set of letters that identifies the address of a specific resource on the Web.

videoconference A virtual meeting in which participants in one location can see and hear participants at other locations and can share data and graphics by electronic means.

virtual collaboration The use of digital technologies that enable organizations or individuals to collaboratively plan, design, develop, manage, and research products, services, and innovative information systems and electronic commerce applications.

virtual group (team) A work group whose members are in different locations and who meet electronically.

virtual universities Online universities in which students take classes via the Internet at home or an off-site location.

Voice-over Internet Protocol (VOIP; see **Internet telephony)**

Web site Collectively, all of the Web pages of a particular company or individual.

wide area network (WAN) A network, generally provided by common carriers, that covers a wide geographic area.

wireless media (see **broadcast media**)

wireline media (see **cable media**)

work group Two or more individuals who act together to perform some task, on either a permanent or temporary basis.

workflow The movement of information as it flows through the sequence of steps that make up an organization's work procedures.

World Wide Web (The Web, WWW, or **W3)** A system of universally accepted standards for storing, retrieving, formatting, and displaying information via a client/server architecture; it uses the transport functions of the Internet.

>>> DISCUSSION QUESTIONS

1. What are the implications of having fiber-optic cable to everyone's home?

2. What are the implications of BitTorrent for the music industry? For the motion picture industry?

3. Discuss the pros and cons of P2P networks.

4. Should the Internet be regulated? If so, by whom?

5. Discuss the pros and cons of delivering this book over the Internet.

6. Explain how the Internet works. Assume you are talking with someone who has no knowledge of information technology (in other words, keep it very simple).

7. How are the network applications of communication and collaboration related? Do communication tools also support collaboration? Give examples.

8. Search online for the article from *The Atlantic:* "Is Google Making Us Stupid?" *Is* Google making us stupid? Support your answer.

>>> PROBLEM-SOLVING ACTIVITIES

1. Calculate how much bandwidth you consume when using the Internet every day. How many e-mails do you send daily and what is the size of each? (Your e-mail program may have e-mail file size information.) How many music and video clips do you download (or upload) daily and what is the size of each? If you view YouTube often, surf the Web to find out the size of a typical YouTube file. Add up the number of e-mail, audio, and video files you transmit or receive on a typical day. When you have calculated your daily Internet usage, determine if you are a "normal" Internet user or a "power" Internet user. What impact does network neutrality have on you as a "normal" user? As a "power" user?

2. Access several P2P applications, such as SETI@home. Describe the purpose of each application, and indicate which ones you would like to join.

3. Access http://ipv6.com and www.ipv6news.info and learn about more advantages of IPv6.

4. Access www.icann.org and learn more about this important organization.

5. Set up your own Web site using your name for the domain name (for example, KellyRainer).
   - Explain the process for registering a domain.
   - Which top-level domain will you use and why?

6. Access www.icann.org and obtain the name of an agency or company that can register a domain for the TLD that you selected. What is the name of that agency or company?

7. Access the Web site for that agency or company (in question 6) to learn the process that you must use. How much will it initially cost to register your domain name? How much will it cost to maintain that name in the future?

8. You plan to take a two-week vacation in Australia this year. Using the Internet, find information that will help

you plan the trip. Such information includes, *but is not limited to*, the following:

a. Geographical location and weather conditions at the time of your trip

b. Major tourist attractions and recreational facilities

c. Travel arrangements (airlines, approximate fares)

d. Car rental; local tours

e. Alternatives for accommodation (within a moderate budget) and food

f. Estimated cost of the vacation (travel, lodging, food, recreation, shopping, etc.)

g. Country regulations regarding the entrance of your dog

h. Shopping

i. Passport information (either to obtain one or to renew one)

j. Information on the country's language and culture

k. What else do you think you should research before going to Australia?

9. From your own experience or from the vendor's information, list the major capabilities of Lotus Notes/Domino. Do the same for Microsoft Exchange. Compare and contrast the products. Explain how the products can be used to support knowledge workers and managers.

10. Visit Web sites of companies that manufacture telepresence products for the Internet. Prepare a report. Differentiate between telepresence products and videoconferencing products.

11. Access Google (or YouTube) videos and search for "Cisco Magic." This video shows Cisco's next-generation telepresence system. Compare and contrast it with current telepresence systems.

12. Access the Web site of your university. Does the Web site provide high-quality information (right amount, clear, accurate, etc.)? Do you think a high-school student who is thinking of attending your university would feel the same way?

13. Compare and contrast Google Sites (www.google.com/sites) and Microsoft Office Live (www.liveoffice.com). Which site would you use to create your own Web site? Explain your choice.

14. Access the Web site of the Recording Industry Association of America (www.riaa.com). Discuss what you find there regarding copyright infringement (that is, downloading music files). How do you feel about the RIAA's efforts to stop music downloads? Debate this issue from your point of view and from the RIAA's point of view.

15. Research the companies involved in Internet telephony (Voice-over IP). Compare their offerings as to price, necessary technologies, ease of installation, and so on. Which company is the most attractive to you? Which company might be the most attractive for a large company?

16. Access some of the alternative search engines at http://www.wiley.com/go/rainer/problemsolving. Search for the same terms on several of the alternative search engines and on Google. Compare the results on breadth (number of results found) and precision (results are what you were looking for).

17. Second Life (www.secondlife.com) is a three-dimensional, online world built and owned by its residents. Residents of Second Life are avatars who have been created by real people. Access Second Life, learn about it, and create your own avatar to explore this world. Learn about the thousands of people who are making "real-world" money from operations in Second Life.

18. Access Microsoft's Bing translator (http://www.microsofttranslator.com) or Google (www.google.com/language_tools) translation pages. Type in a paragraph in English and select, for example, English-to-French. When you see the translated paragraph in French, copy it into the text box, and select French-to-English. Is the paragraph that you first entered the same as the one you are looking at now? Why or why not? Support your answer.

>>> COLLABORATION EXERCISE

Background

Napster was initially created as a music-sharing site where users would copy songs off of CDs they had purchased and then share them with other users. It was wildly popular in spite of the fact that the majority of users' at the time were connected via dial-up networks. It could take up to an hour to download a 3 MB music file over an old 56K modem! Eventually it became so big that it caught the eye of the music industry, which began a series of lawsuits against the heaviest

users. Today, the music industry operates off of multiple "subscription"-type sites that have legalized digital music.

Activity

Work with a group to imagine the type of data sharing you may experience on the job. Divide your group into functional areas. What kind of files would benefit from a centralized file sharing site? This would not necessarily be a database, but large files that are easier stored and shared through file sharing services—things like handbooks, catalogs, manuals, etc., that are often too large to e-mail. For the functional area you are assigned, search the Web for different files that are too large for e-mail and download them. Once everyone in your group has his or her files (make sure they are all public files), upload them into a single group file sharing service. You can use Dropbox, LimeWire, or whatever you want. Most will offer a free trial account you can use.

Deliverable

Share your folder with your instructor with an accompanying document explaining what documents have been placed there from each department. Include an explanation of your experience as a group of using the Web for discovery, communication, and collaboration.

CLOSING **CASE 1 >** The Network Neutrality Wars

Although the steady progress of communications technologies has resulted in bandwidth commensurate with user traffic on most Web sites in 2011, the explosion of streaming video and mobile technologies is beginning to cause bandwidth problems. The Internet was designed to transmit content such as e-mails and Web pages. Media items being transmitted through the Web today, such as high-definition movies, are several magnitudes greater in size than the Internet was originally designed to handle. To further compound this problem, there are now more than 50 million smart phone users in the United States, many of whom use the Internet to stream video content to their phones. This means that the number of users uploading large content such as videos has skyrocketed within the past few years.

 In a widely cited estimate, Cisco Systems (www.cisco.com) predicted that Internet traffic will triple by 2014, increasing to 64 exabytes (1 exabyte is 1 million terabytes) a month. To provide a reference point, monthly traffic in 2006 was 5 exabytes, enough to store every word ever spoken. Moreover, by 2014, more than 90 percent of Internet traffic will consist of video uploads, downloads, and streaming. As startling as Cisco's statistics may sound, market researcher Infonetics (www.infonetics.com) contends that Cisco's numbers may be conservative. Infonetics proposed several possible scenarios of how Internet development could unfold, one frightening example of which is that Internet backbone carriers might cease upgrading their technologies, leaving consumers with slow connections and hindering Internet innovation.

 This potential issue with Internet bandwidth is as much about economics as technology. Currently, consumers can send 1-kilobyte e-mails or watch the latest 30-gigabyte movie on their large-screen televisions for the same monthly broadband fee. Unlike the system used for power and water bills where higher usage equals higher fee, monthly broadband fees are not tied to bandwidth usage.

 A study from Juniper Networks (www.juniper.net) highlights this "revenue-per-bit" problem. The report predicts that Internet revenue for carriers such as AT&T (www.att.com) and Comcast (www.comcast.com) will grow by 5 percent per year through 2020. At the same time, Internet traffic will increase by 27 percent annually, meaning that carriers will have to increase their bandwidth investment by 20 percent per year just to keep up with demand. Under this model, the carriers' business models will break down by 2014, because their total necessary investment will come to exceed revenue growth.

 Few industry analysts expect carriers to stop investing in new capacity, but analysts agree that a financial crunch is coming. As Internet traffic soars, analysts expect the revenue per megabit to fall from 43 cents in 2010 to just 2 cents in 2014. These figures translate into a far lower return on investment. Although carriers can find ways to increase their capacity, it will be difficult for them to reap any revenue benefits from doing so.

 The heart of the problem is that, even if the technology is up to the task of shipping huge amounts of data, no one is sure how to pay for these technologies. One possible solution is to eliminate network neutrality.

<<< THE PROBLEM

A POSSIBLE >>> SOLUTION

Network neutrality is the current model under which Internet service providers (ISPs) are required to operate. Under this model, ISPs must allow customers equal access to content and applications, regardless of the source or nature of the content. That is, Internet backbone carriers must treat all Web traffic equally on a first-come, first-serve basis.

Telecommunications and cable companies want to eliminate network neutrality. Instead, they want to charge differentiated prices based on the amount of bandwidth consumed by the content that is being delivered over the Internet. These companies believe that differentiated pricing is the most equitable method by which they can finance necessary investments in their network infrastructures.

To bolster the argument in favor of differentiated pricing, ISPs point to the enormous amount of bandwidth required to transmit pirated versions of copyrighted materials over the Internet. In fact, Comcast (the second largest ISP in the United States) reported in 2010 that illegal file sharing of copyrighted material was consuming 50 percent of its network capacity. In 2008, the company slowed down transmission of BitTorrent (www.bittorrent.com) files, which are frequently used for piracy and illegal sharing of copyrighted materials. In response, the Federal Communications Commission (FCC) ruled that Comcast had to stop slowing down peer-to-peer traffic. Comcast then filed a lawsuit challenging the FCC's authority to enforce network neutrality.

ISPs further contend that mandating net neutrality will hinder U.S. international competitiveness by decreasing innovation and discouraging capital investments in new network technologies. According to this scenario, ISPs will be unable to handle the exploding demand for Internet and wireless data transmission.

In April 2010, a federal appeals court ruled in favor of Comcast, declaring that the FCC did not have the authority to regulate how an ISP manages its network. This ruling favored differentiated pricing of transmissions over the Internet and was a major blow to network neutrality.

Meanwhile, proponents of network neutrality are petitioning Congress to regulate the industry to prevent network providers from adopting strategies similar to Comcast. They argue that the risk of censorship increases when network providers can selectively block or slow access to certain content, such as access to competing low-cost services such as Skype and Vonage. They also assert that a neutral network encourages everyone to innovate without needing permission from phone companies, cable companies, or other authorities, and that the neutral Internet has helped to create many new businesses.

Most analysts expect that those users who consume the most data eventually will have to pay more, most likely in the form of tiered pricing plans. Americans, however, have never had to contend with limits on the amount of data they upload and download, so there may be some pushback from users.

THE EARLY >>> RESULTS

Despite the fact that the court ruled against network neutrality in April 2010, on December 21, 2010, the FCC approved network neutrality rules that prohibited broadband providers from blocking customer access to legal Web content. The new rules bar wireline-based broadband providers—but not mobile broadband providers—from "unreasonable discrimination" against Web traffic. In January 2011, Verizon filed a legal appeal challenging the FCC's authority to enforce these new rules. As of mid-2012, the battle over network neutrality is still ongoing.

MORE RECENT >>> RESULTS FOR WIRELESS USERS

U.S. wireless networks have already moved in the direction of tiered-pricing plans. In June 2010, for example, AT&T discontinued its all-you-can-use $30 a month data plan and announced tiered-pricing plans for its mobile consumers.

One iPhone user related his story. For 4 years, he had been doing the same things on his iPhone: checking e-mail, listening to Pandora Internet radio, using Google Maps, browsing the Web, and shopping online. He averaged about 1.76 gigabytes of data per month in 2011. In January 2012, however, he surpassed a limit set by AT&T (his wireless carrier). AT&T sent an e-mail to him, suggesting that he consider using Wi-Fi when possible for applications that use the highest amounts of data, such as streaming video apps, remote Web camera apps, and other high-bandwidth uses. To say that he was unhappy would be an understatement. He promptly began searching wireless plans at competing companies.

There is little, if any, agreement on what constitutes excessive data usage. An NPD Connected Intelligence (www.connected-intelligence.com) study of 700 Android smartphone users found that these users utilized 724 megabytes per month on AT&T's network, 1.7 gigabytes on T-Mobile's network, 902 megabytes on Verizon Wireless' network, and 1.2 gigabytes on Sprint's network.

On October 1, 2011, AT&T started slowing speeds for the 5 percent of their unlimited-plan users who use the most bandwidth. AT&T subscribers on tiered plans do not see bandwidth limitations. They just have to pay for more data if they go over the data limit in their plans. AT&T new data plans offer 300 megabytes for $20 per month, 3 gigabytes for $30, and 5 gigabytes for $50. New customers are no longer allowed to sign up for unlimited plans anymore. The AT&T model may foreshadow the direction that many Internet and cable providers will need to take in the future in order to remain profitable in the face of skyrocketing bandwidth demands.

Sources: J. Hamilton, "AT&T Must Give Shareholders Net Neutrality Vote," *Bloomberg*, February 14, 2012; W. Plank, "Confessions of an iPhone Data Hog," *The Wall Street Journal*, January 27, 2012; J. Engebretson, "Verizon Confirms It Will Appeal Newly Published Net Neutrality Rules Soon," *Connected Planet*, September 27, 2011; E. Wyatt, "House Votes Against 'Net Neutrality'," *The New York Times*, April 8, 2011; L. Segall, "Verizon Challenges FCC Net Neutrality Rules," *CNN Money*, January 21, 2011; K. Corbin, "Net Neutrality 2011: What Storms May Come," *Internet News*, December 30, 2010; C. Albanesius, "What Do the FCC's Net Neutrality Rules Mean for You?" *PC Magazine*, December 22, 2010; G. Gross, "FCC Approves Compromise Net Neutrality Rules," *Network World*, December 21, 2010; P. Burrows, "Will Video Kill the Internet, Too?" *Bloomberg BusinessWeek*, December 6–12, 2010; J. Nocera, "The Struggle for What We Already Have," *New York Times*, September 4, 2010; C. Miller, "Web Plan Is Dividing Companies," *New York Times*, August 11, 2010; A. Schatz and S. Ante, "FCC Web Rules Create Pushback," *Wall Street Journal*, May 6, 2010; www.comcast.com, www.att.com, accessed March 13, 2012.

Questions

1. How do you feel about the net neutrality issue? Do you believe heavier bandwidth users should pay for more bandwidth? Do you believe wireless carriers should operate under different rules than wireline carriers? Please explain your answer.
2. Evaluate your own bandwidth usage. (For example, do you upload and download large files, such as movies?) If network neutrality were to be eliminated, what would the impact be for you?
3. Should businesses monitor network usage? Do see a problem with employees using company-purchased bandwidth for personal use? Please explain your answer.

CLOSING **CASE 2** > Marriott's Corporate Portal

Marriott International operates more than 3,500 hotel properties worldwide under its portfolio of brands, including Marriott Hotels & Resorts, JW Marriott, Renaissance, Edition, Autograph Collection, and Courtyard by Marriott. The properties fall into the following categories: luxury, collections, lifestyle and boutique, signature, select service, and extended stay.

Until 2011, Marriott used a "one size fits all" approach for its advertising, marketing, and branding efforts in different locations, despite the fact that independent franchisers own most of its properties. For years, regardless of location or brand, each property was offered the exact same (low) level of marketing support.

As a result of this policy, each Marriott property was largely responsible for its own marketing efforts, meaning that there was little consistency from location to location, or brand to brand. Furthermore, many properties did not have the funds to support their own marketing efforts. Finally, to compound the problem even further, Marriott had no easy

<<< THE PROBLEM

method set up for sharing of marketing materials between corporate headquarters and the various properties.

As customer attitudes and preferences changed, Marriott realized that its corporate marketing practices needed to evolve as well. Consequently, the company launched a rebranding effort to tailor its marketing and branding decisions to each unique brand and target market. To fully implement this shift in strategy, the company needed a better way to share and leverage its marketing assets. Therefore, it created a user-friendly online corporate portal to manage the creation, distribution, and review of marketing practices and material, as well as to support its new brand standards.

THE IT >>> SOLUTION

To help address its marketing concerns, Marriott International deployed BrandWorks, an automated online marketing portal, in all of its locations. BrandWorks makes it quick, easy, and cost-effective for each of the company's properties to create their own customized marketing materials. Marriot hotels, advertising agencies, and marketing managers use the portal to share and/or download stock photography, view brand standards and guidelines, download marketing templates, and use document wizards to create customized marketing material.

With BrandWorks, Marriott is able to offer different programs and strategies to each of its distinct brands to better appeal to their respective target audiences (for instance, leisure travelers and business travelers use very different criteria when deciding which hotel to stay in). Using BrandWorks, Marriott compiled a comprehensive catalog of updated brand guidelines, templates, strategies, and materials so that its promotions and marketing activities could be implemented properly and cost-effectively across all of its markets and in multiple languages.

Marriott also deployed a centralized offer-management system in BrandWorks. This system allows its properties worldwide to create Marriott rewards offers and deals, and then promote them on the Marriott Web site and in other marketing channels.

BrandWorks also has built-in tracking capabilities to report on promotional programs, as well as automated analyses to identify which offers, programs, and marketing campaigns are most successful. In 2012, Marriott integrated social media strategies for all its brands and properties into the portal.

THE RESULTS >>>

BrandWorks enabled Marriott to improve information sharing and collaboration among its global locations and corporate teams. Internal users can report on total log-ins, the number of documents currently in the system based on brand and category, and the number of offers created and disseminated through each marketing channel. This data enables the company to determine what marketing information to activate for each brand and for each audience, and thereby deliver a better customer experience, educate global properties on brand, ensure consistency across locations and languages, and enable executives to make better decisions.

The offer management system within BrandWorks enables Marriott users to deliver revenue-generating offers to customers more rapidly. Because BrandWorks has built-in capabilities to tailor its offers to distinct audiences, demographics, and marketing channels, more than three times as many offers have been submitted through the portal than were submitted without it.

Other Marriott departments have started to use BrandWorks as well. For example, the HR department has begun posting its presentations on the portal. The food and beverage department also posts its menus to the portal, as well as information on group sales and event management.

From 2009 to 2011, user log-ins to Marriott's increased by 186 percent, while the amount of marketing material distributed through the portal more than doubled. In 2011 alone, more than 6,000 users from Marriott properties, corporate headquarters, and regional departments logged in to BrandWorks. The users came from 70 countries and territories, and represented 16 different brands. They accessed BrandWorks remotely through any Internet browser using desktops, laptops, tablets, and smart phones.

Sources: Compiled from S. Brier, "How Marriott Got Marketing Right," *Baseline Magazine*, January 17, 2012; S. Brier, "Marriott Saves Estimated $9.2 Million in Marketing Costs with Online Portal," *Hospitality Technology*,

December 19, 2011; T. McQuilken, "Marriott Brings Marketing to Next Level with BrandWorks," *Hotel Business*, September 21, 2011; "Case Study: Marriott International," *Excella Consulting*, accessed February 28, 2012; www.marriott.com, accessed February 29, 2012.

Questions

1. Provide examples of the advantages BrandWorks brought to Marriott's franchisees.
2. Provide examples of how BrandWorks could be used for functional areas of Marriott other than marketing.

RUBY'S CLUB   INTERNSHIP ASSIGNMENT

Ruben and Lisa have lots of questions and they need lots of answers. For now, it would be helpful if they understood the difference between DSL, cable, and fiber connections. They are especially interested in the upfront cost of installation, speed, and monthly fee. In addition, they need to know how to wire their building. What cable medium would be best for them to use to wire their building for network access?

Finally, look at the hardware requirements for running a Web site. Compare this with the fees charged by a hosting company and give Ruben and Lisa a suggestion on whether they should include a Web server (and faster Internet connection) when they are designing their LAN.

SPREADSHEET ACTIVITY: BUILDING CHARTS AND TABLES

Objective: Creating charts and graphs is a really nice skill for you to develop. Visual data can be shared more quickly, comprehended more easily, and displayed much more cleanly than simply numbers in a spreadsheet. This activity will require you to build both charts and tables to present data surrounding network speeds.

Chapter Connection: As you learn about network connections and speeds, this exercise will show you how to do an analysis on your own. It is possible that your Internet connection is not providing the speeds you are paying for! This tool is also useful when your Internet does not seem to be running as quickly as it should. Knowing how to test the speed will help you determine where the possible problem could be.

Prerequisites: There are no prerequisites for this activity.

Activity: Calculating return on investment (ROI) is extremely difficult when it comes to ROI for information systems. For example, when network administrators sense a strain on their network (from network diagnostics or user complaints), they may look into upgrading their network.

To get a feel for the type of information someone might see, create your own spreadsheet of data while watching your Internet connection at home. If you are not at home regularly, choose a computer in a convenient location and test the speed there. Go to http://www.wiley.com/go/rainer/spreadsheet and look for the link provided for Chapter 4. This link will take you to "speedtest.net" and the network test will be on the home page asking you to "Begin Test." The test will take only a few minutes. In a new spreadsheet, create columns for the following:

- Date
- Time
- Ping speed
- Upload speed

- Download speed
- Test location (not your location, but the host of the test)

Collect this data for a week, preferably three times a day (i.e., morning, afternoon, and evening). Once you have your 15 data points, create a chart that shows the change in bandwidth available over time. This is exactly what a network administrator might see when trying to determine if it is necessary to upgrade the system. Additionally, calculate the average, minimum, and maximum for each day and for the entire week. Place this data in a chart for quick reference.

Back at http://www.wiley.com/go/rainer/spreadsheet you will also find a short video on creating charts and graphs to help you create your final product.

Deliverable: The deliverable will be a line chart that shows data speeds over time.

Note: There is no correct answer, but there are wrong answers if you do not collect enough data or do not create the chart appropriately.

Discussion Questions:

1. What is it about a chart that makes it easier to comprehend than raw numbers?
2. Is it possible for charges and graphs to depict real data in a way that misleads the viewer?

Quiz questions are assignable in WileyPLUS, and available on the Book Companion Site at http://www.wiley.com/college/rainer.

DATABASE ACTIVITY: REPORTS I

Objective

In this activity, you will learn how to create an Access report, with grouping and summaries. A database is not useful if you can't get information out of it. Reports are one way users get information from a database. Reports can connect data from several tables, organize it, sort it, group it, summarize it and more. Once designed, a report can be run as needed, reflecting the database content as of that instant.

CHAPTER CONNECTION

Companies must monitor their network performance to make sure it's reliable, secure, and free of performance bottlenecks. Reports such as those in this activity help them do this.

The database in this activity tracks network problems. Users who notice problems submit "trouble tickets." These describe the problem and, later, its resolution. They identify the user who submitted the it, the equipment involved, and the technician who fixed it.

Management can use reports derived from this database to identify problem devices and vendors, to evaluate technician performance, to identify users who are helpful in finding problems or who report non-existent ones, and more.

PREREQUISITES

None.

Activity:

In this activity, which you will find online at http://www.wiley.com/rainer/go/database, you'll take a database and create multi-level reports from it. You will add summary fields to this report and reformat it to improve its appearance.

1. Download the **Ch 04 NeTrouble** database from http://www.wiley.com/rainer/go/database and open it. (You saw this database earlier if you did the Chapter 1 activity. This version does not include the report, query or form you used there. Here, you'll create other reports from the same underlying data.)
2. To create a new report, click the Create tab over the ribbon.
3. The section labeled "Reports" offers several reporting tools. We'll use the Report Wizard, a compromise between the Report button (which doesn't offer much control) and Report Design (which forces us to do all the "heavy lifting" ourselves, without the head start that the Wizard can provide). Click on it.
4. The first screen lets us choose which tables we'll base our report on and which fields from those tables we want to use. (It also lets us base the report on queries. A query creates a temporary table, so for this purpose they're the same. You'll create reports based on queries in later activities.) Our report will list trouble tickets by

user, so start by selecting the UserTbl table. from the pull-down list under the Tables/Queries heading.

5. The left box shows all fields in the selected table. To move a field into the report, select it and click ">." It moves into the right box. If you move a field you don't want, "<" moves it back. ">>"moves all the fields of that table into the report. This is useful when you want most of them, since ">>" followed by one or two "<" can be faster than moving all those you want individually. Finally, "<<" moves everything in this table out of the report and back to the table so you can start over.

Here, move the user's name into the report.

6. Next, select DeptTbl, move DeptName into the report.

7. Finally, select the TicketTbl table. Move TicketSubmitted, TicketResolved and TicketStatus into the report. Click Next.

8. This is the panel where you structure your report. Choose each of the three tables, one after another, and see how the report organization changes. For this report, select "by DeptTbl" and click Next.

9. We don't need any more grouping levels. Click Next.

10. Within each category, choose to sort the tickets by when they were submitted. Pull down the first sorting menu and select TicketSubmitted. Click Next.

11. Leave the layout unchanged here. Click Next.

12. (Number not used in Access 2010 version of activity; there's another step here in Access 2007.)

13. Change the title of the report to DeptRpt. Then click Finish and see the result.

Usage Hint: If you see "###" in any of the fields, the reason is almost certainly that the standard field width isn't wide enough to show the data. Switch to Layout view by clicking the second icon from the right in the lower right corner of the window, click in each field that has this problem to select it, and make it

wide enough to see the data. You may have to move column headers to keep them aligned with the data. Or, click on the data and shift-click on the heading to select them both, then make them wider together.

14. Our second report will add summary fields to this report. First, make a copy of the report so your instructor can see the version without summary fields. Right-click on the report in the navigation panel at the left of the Access window and select Copy. Then click Paste in the ribbon. (It's under the Home tab, so click that tab if it's not already selected.) Name the new report SumDeptRpt and confirm.

15. Open SumDeptRpt and select Layout view. Make sure the Design tab is selected, and click Group & Sort from the Grouping & Totals section.

Usage Hint: Access calls any kind of summary a "total." If you want an arithmetic total, you must ask for a sum. We'll use the term "summary" rather than "total" here to avoid this common source of confusion, but you'll see "total" on Access screens.

16. A new panel will open up at the bottom of the window. Its top row starts "Group on DeptID" and ends with "More" and a triangle pointing to the right. That word "more" hides many options. Click the triangle to see them.

17. We want to count the number of tickets each department submits. Pull down the triangle next to "with no totals." The first option lets us summarize TicketSubmitted, TicketStatus or TicketResolved. We should count TicketSubmitted since every trouble ticket has a value in this field. Next, select either count. (They would be different if we counted a field that is blank for some tickets. Therefore, if we had selected TicketResolved or TicketStatus, we would use Count Records so that records that are blank in this field would be counted.) Check boxes to show the grand total and department totals in the group footer. When you click the triangle again to release the dialogue box, you'll see department totals after each department with the grand total at the bottom. Your report should start like this:

DeptRpt				
DeptName	UserName	TicketSubmitted	TicketResolved	TicketStatus
Marketing				
	Adam			
		1/1/2011	1/5/2010	Closed
		5/5/2011		Open
	Betty			
		10/10/2010	10/11/2010	Closed
		2/2/2011	2/6/2010	Closed

4

If we had wanted to total by user, we would have clicked on the "More" triangle at that level in the panel at the bottom of the window.

Close your report, saving your changes.

18. Now we'll improve the appearance of this report. Make a copy of SumDeptRpt. Call it FmtDeptRpt, open it, and go to Layout view. (Layout changes can also be made in Design view. Design view gives more control over some aspects of the layout, but Layout view can often suffice and gives immediate visual feedback when you make a change. It's preferable when it will do the job.)

19. First, change the column headings. Access sets them to the names of the database fields. However, database field names are for developers. Report headings should be for people who will read the report. Select each, just as in a word processor, and change them to read "Department," "User," "Date Submitted," "Date Resolved" and "Status." Change the main report heading to "Trouble Tickets by Department and User." Shrink the width of the User column to bring the data elements closer together. Click "Logo" in the ribbon (Design tab, Header/Footer section), find a suitable picture, and insert. (By default, Access puts logos in the main heading area.) Switch to Report view. Your report should now start like this:

Trouble Tickets by Department and User				
Department	User	Date Submitted	Date Resolved	Status
Marketing				
	Adam			
		1/1/2011	1/5/2010	Closed
		5/5/2011		Open
	Betty			
		10/10/2010	10/11/2010	Closed
		2/2/2011	2/6/2010	Closed
		4		
Accounting				

20. Now it's your turn. Develop a report that shows trouble tickets by device ID. Group devices by name (category). Within a name, group by ticket status: Closed, Open or Cancelled. Provide counts for each category and for the entire report. Edit column headings and report title to be meaningful to business-oriented readers of the report. Name your report "DeviceRpt," and be sure to save it when you're done.

As with other aspects of Access, many videos on creating reports are available on the Web. You can find them by searching for "Access report," "Access report tutorial," or any similar string on a video hosting site such as YouTube, or using the general search engine of your choice while restricting its answers to videos.

Deliverables

Your database with the four reports as specified above. Your instructor may add additional requirements.

Quiz Questions

1. A report shows the content of the database as of:
   A. The time the report is run (opened).
   B. The time the report was designed.
   C. The time the user looks at the report.
   D. The time the user keys into the Report Effective Time field.

2. True or false: A report can contain information from no more than two tables.

3. True or false: Report design can only be changed in Design mode.

Discussion Questions

1. Suppose you own or manage a restaurant. You have a typical restaurant computer system in which servers enter orders, which the kitchen uses to prepare orders, and which later creates bills and processes payments. Describe three reports that this system could prepare for your use. Draw, using paper and pencil, the top of each: header, column headings, a few lines of sample data, and the first summary field.

2. Your instructor may have received a report with a class roster soon after the term started. It is based on two tables: a class table that lists the student IDs of everyone in the class, and a student table that gives the name, major, GPA, and so on for each student. Students are normally listed alphabetically by family name. (It's also based on a query, which

finds only students in this class, but that's a separate topic.)

A. Discuss two ways this list could be organized, besides the usual order by name.

B. Discuss two summaries that this report, organized either in its usual way or in one of the above two ways (your choice), could have.

3. Your e-mail program has an address list. Each entry in it includes an e-mail address. Some entries also include the sender's real name. A few may have other information. Describe a report that could be produced from this list and other information that your e-mail program stores. Give it at least one summary field. Draw its first few rows.

5 | Business Intelligence

LEARNING OBJECTIVES >>>

1. Explain different ways in which IT supports managerial decision making.
2. Provide examples of different ways that organizations make use of BI.
3. Explain the value that different BI applications provide to large and small businesses.
4. Offer examples of how businesses and government agencies can use different BI applications to analyze data.
5. Explain how your university could use CPM to effect solutions to two campus problems.

If you were in the business of supplying heating oil in the northeastern United States, would it be useful to know if a big winter snowstorm was likely to arrive with subzero temperatures in Massachusetts the following month? If you were a firefighter in the backcountry of California and knew that the odds of intense Santa Anna winds would increase dramatically in 3 weeks, how would you react? If you were a Home Depot manager, wouldn't you want to have snow shovels in stock if there was going to be a large snowstorm? If you worked in the Federal Emergency Management Agency, would you want to get a 30-day advance warning of the next hurricane?

Although there is widespread use of satellite imaging and computer modeling in the field of meteorology, the founders of EarthRisk Technologies (www.earthrisktech.com), a 2010 startup, say it is still nearly impossible to use current weather forecasting models to make anything more than the most general predictions about weather more than 2 weeks away.

© Vitalina Rybakova/iStockphoto

EarthRisk has implemented weather forecasting software to estimate the likelihood of extreme weather events 30 to 40 days in advance. The founders emphasize that EarthRisk provides information that helps its clients make decisions of value.

EarthRisk draws on 60 years of weather data to identify conditions that could lead to big temperature swings weeks later. The weather events that precede a hot or cold stretch are like dominoes toppling in sequence. The company's software predicts the probability of each domino falling over and sells that information to energy companies that want to lock in fuel prices before periods of peak demand.

EarthRisk's next project is to detect Atlantic hurricanes days in advance by analyzing conditions such as ocean temperatures, sea level pressures, and vertical wind shear. The > > >

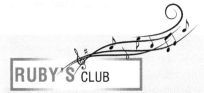

RUBY'S CLUB

As Ruben and Lisa prepare to reopen Ruby's Club for business, they need to establish some measurements to help them stay on track. They have a goal of a $300,000 net profit for their first year after their grand "reopening." This is an increase from $150,000 the previous year. To achieve this, they have to deal with one of the biggest problems they face—shrinkage.

Shrinkage occurs when a bartender pours someone a little more alcohol than the drink recipe calls for, gives someone a free drink, or accidentally spills some alcohol on the floor. The result is that a bottle of alcohol that (for example) should provide enough alcohol to make 40 drinks only actually brings in money for 30 drinks. This shrinkage may not seem like much, but on a large scale (including food items) it can make a huge difference.

What Ruben and Lisa need is data and decision support. This chapter refers to this as business intelligence. They need to know how to set and measure monthly and weekly goals to know whether or not they are on track to make their overall goal of $300,000 net profit when they reopen.

company also wants to make its software intuitive enough to be used by nonmeteorologists at insurance companies and other businesses.

Sources: B. Bigelow, "EarthRisk Figures Odds in Long-Range Forecasts of 'Extreme Weather,'" *Xconomy*, January 25, 2012; D. Rice, "Team Seeks to Provide More Advance Warning on Hurricanes," *USA Today*, October 11, 2011; J. Tozzi, "Weather Seer," *Bloomberg BusinessWeek*, September 26–October 2, 2011; G. Robbins, "EarthRisk Seeks Business Niche Spotting Severe Weather," *San Diego Union Tribune*, August 2011; www.earthrisktech.com, accessed February 27, 2012.

uestions

1. What impact will EarthRisk have on the business model of The Weather Channel? If you were a Weather Channel executive, what would you do to counter the threat of EarthRisk?
2. Provide examples of other organizations to whom long-range weather forecasts would be valuable.

Introduction

Business intelligence (BI) is a broad category of applications, technologies, and processes for gathering, storing, accessing, and analyzing data to help business users make better decisions. BI applications enable decision makers to quickly ascertain the status of a business enterprise by examining key information. Managers need current, timely, and accurate information that their current systems often cannot provide. Implementing BI applications can generate significant benefits throughout a company, supporting important decisions about the firm's overall business goals.

Consider these examples:

- The low-budget Oakland A's of major-league baseball analyzed data to develop new statistics to discover undervalued players. The team's analysis was described in a 2003 book by Michael Lewis, *Moneyball*, which was made into a 2011 movie starring Brad Pitt.
- Retailers such as Walmart and Kohl's analyze sales, pricing, and economic, demographic, and weather data to tailor product selections at particular stores and determining the timing of price markdowns.
- Shipping companies, such as UPS, analyze data on truck delivery times and traffic patterns to fine-tune routing.
- Online dating services, such as Match.com, constantly analyze their Web listings of personal characteristics, reactions, and communications to improve their algorithms for matching individuals on dates.

This chapter describes information systems that support *decision making*. We begin by reviewing the manager's job and the nature of modern managerial decisions. This discussion will help you to understand why managers need computerized support. You then learn about the concepts of business intelligence for supporting individuals, groups, and entire organizations.

It is impossible to overstate the importance of BI to you. Recall from Chapter 1 that the essential goal of information systems is to provide the right information to the right person in the right amount at the right time in the right format. In essence, BI achieves this goal. BI systems provide business intelligence that you can act on in a timely fashion.

It is also impossible to overstate the importance of your input into the BI process within an organization, for several reasons. First, you (the user community) will decide what data should be stored in your organization's data warehouse. You will then work closely with the MIS department to obtain these data.

Going further, you will use your organization's BI applications, probably from your first day on the job. With some BI applications, such as data mining and decision support systems, you will decide how you want to analyze the data (user-driven analysis). With other BI applications such as dashboards, you will decide which data you want to see and in which format. Again, you will work closely with your MIS department to ensure that the dashboard meets your needs.

Much of this chapter is concerned with large-scale BI applications. However, you should keep in mind that smaller organizations, and even individual users, can implement small-scale BI applications as well. For example, Excel spreadsheets provide some BI functions, as do SQL queries of a database.

The most popular BI tool by far is Excel. For years, BI vendors "fought" against the use of Excel. Eventually, however, they decided to "join it" by designing their software so that it interfaces with Excel. How does this process work? Essentially, users download plug-ins that add functionality (e.g., the ability to list the top 10 percent of customers, based on sales) to Excel (or any of the Microsoft Office products). This process can be thought of as creating "Excel on steroids." Excel then connects to the vendor's application server—which provides additional data-analysis capabilities—which in turn connects to a back-end database, such as a data mart or warehouse. This arrangement gives Excel users the functionality and access to data that are typical of sophisticated BI products, while allowing users to work with a familiar client: Excel.

Microsoft has made similar changes to its product line. In particular, Excel can now be used with MS SQL Server (a database product), and it can be utilized in advanced BI applications, such as dashboards and data mining/predictive analysis.

After you finish this chapter, you will have a basic understanding of decision making, the business intelligence process, and BI applications in organizations today. This knowledge will enable you to immediately and confidently provide input into your organization's BI processes and applications. Further, the hands-on exercises in this chapter will familiarize you with the actual use of BI software. These exercises will enable you to use your organization's BI applications to effectively analyze data and thus make better decisions. Enjoy!

5.1 Managers and Decision Making

Management is a process by which an organization achieves its goals through the use of resources (people, money, materials, and information). These resources are considered to be *inputs*. Achieving the organization's goals is the *output* of the process. Managers oversee this process in an attempt to optimize it. A manager's success is often measured by the ratio between inputs and outputs for which he or she is responsible. This ratio is an indication of the organization's productivity.

The Manager's Job and Decision Making

To appreciate how information systems support managers, you must first understand the manager's job. Managers do many things, depending on their position in the organization, the type and size of the organization, the organization's policies and culture, and the personalities of the managers themselves. Despite these variations, however, all managers perform three basic roles:

1. *Interpersonal roles:* figurehead, leader, liaison
2. *Informational roles:* monitor, disseminator, spokesperson, analyzer
3. *Decisional roles:* entrepreneur, disturbance handler, resource allocator, negotiator[1]

Early information systems primarily supported the informational roles. In recent years, information systems have been developed that support all three roles. In this chapter, you will focus on the support that IT can provide for decisional roles.

Media Bakery; © Sigrid Olsson/Photo Alto/Age Fotostock; Image Source Limited; Artiga Photo/Masterfile

[1]*Mintzberg*, H. (1973). *The Nature of Managerial Work.* New York: Harper & Row.

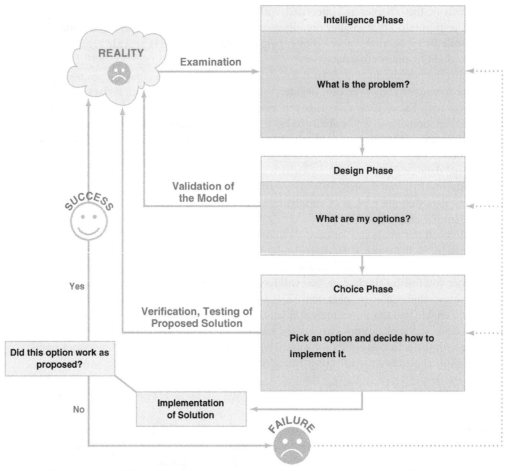

Figure 5.1 The process and phases of decision making.

Media Bakery; © Sigrid Olsson/Photo Alto/Age Fotostock; Image Source Limited; Artiga Photo/Masterfile

A **decision** refers to a choice among two or more alternatives that individuals and groups make. Decisions are diverse and are made continuously. Decision making is a systematic process. Economist Herbert Simon described decision making as composed of three major phases: intelligence, design, and choice.[2] Once the choice is made, the decision is implemented. Figure 5.1 illustrates this process, indicating which tasks are included in each phase. Note that there is a continuous flow of information from intelligence to design to choice (bold lines), but at any phase there may be a return to a previous phase (broken lines).

This model of decision making is quite general. Undoubtedly, you have made decisions where you did not construct a model of the situation, validate your model with test data, or conduct a sensitivity analysis. The model we present here is intended to encompass all of the conditions that might occur when making a decision. For some decisions, some steps or phrases may be minimal, implicit (understood), or absent.

The decision-making process starts with the *intelligence phase*, in which managers examine a situation and identify and define the problem or opportunity. In the *design phase*, decision makers construct a model for the situation. They do this by making assumptions that simplify reality and by expressing the relationships among all the relevant variables. Managers then validate the model by using test data. Finally, decision makers set criteria for evaluating all of the potential solutions that are proposed. The *choice phase* involves selecting a solution or course of action that seems best suited to resolve the problem. This solution (the decision) is then implemented. Implementation is successful if the proposed solution solves the problem or seizes the opportunity. If the solution fails, then the process returns to the previous phases. Computer-based decision support assists managers in the decision-making process.

[2]Simon, H. A. (1977). *The New Science of Management Decision Making.* Upper Saddle River, NJ: Prentice Hall.

Why Managers Need IT Support

Making good decisions is very difficult without solid information. Information is vital for each phase and activity in the decision-making process. Even when information is available, however, decision making is difficult because of the following trends:

- The *number of alternatives* is constantly *increasing* from innovations in technology, improved communications, the development of global markets, and the use of the Internet and e-business. A key to good decision making is to explore and compare many relevant alternatives. The more alternatives that exist, the more a decision maker needs computer-assisted searches and comparisons.

- Most decisions must be made *under time pressure*. It is often not possible to process information manually fast enough to be effective.

- Because of increased uncertainty in the decision environment, decisions are becoming more complex. It is usually necessary to *conduct a sophisticated analysis* in order to make a good decision.

- It is often necessary to rapidly access remote information, consult with experts, or conduct a group decision-making session, all without incurring large expenses. Decision makers can be situated in different locations, as can the information. Bringing them all together quickly and inexpensively can be a major challenge.

These trends create major difficulties for decision makers. Fortunately, as you will see throughout this chapter, a computerized analysis can be of enormous help.

What Information Technologies Are Available to Support Managers?

In addition to discovery, communication, and collaboration tools (Chapter 4) that provide indirect support to decision making, several other information technologies have been successfully used to support managers. As noted, these technologies are collectively referred to as business intelligence (BI). BI is closely linked to data warehousing, which provides the data needed for BI. You will now learn about additional aspects of decision making to place our discussion of BI in context. You will first look at the different types of decisions that managers face.

A Framework for Computerized Decision Analysis

To better understand BI, you will note that various types of decisions can be placed along two major dimensions: problem structure and the nature of the decision.[3] Figure 5.2 provides an overview of decision making along these two dimensions.

Problem Structure. The first dimension of decision making is *problem structure*, where decision-making processes fall along a continuum ranging from highly structured to highly unstructured (see the left column in Figure 5.2). *Structured decisions* refer to routine and repetitive problems for which standard solutions exist, such as inventory control. In a structured problem, the first three phases of the decision process—intelligence, design, and choice—are laid out in a particular sequence, and the procedures for obtaining the best (or at least a good enough) solution are known. Two basic criteria that are used to evaluate proposed solutions are minimizing costs and maximizing profits. These types of decisions are candidates for decision automation.

At the other extreme of problem complexity are unstructured decisions. These are "fuzzy," complex problems for which there are no cut-and-dried solutions. An unstructured problem is one in which there is no standardized procedure for carrying out any of the three phases. In such a problem, human intuition and judgment often play an important role in making the decision. Typical unstructured problems include planning new service offerings, hiring an executive, and choosing a set of research and development (R&D) projects

[3]Gorry, G. A., & Scott Morton, M. S. (1971). "A Framework for Management Information Systems," *Sloan Management Review, 13*(1), pp. 55–70.

for the coming year. Although BI cannot make unstructured decisions, it can provide information that assists decision makers.

Located between structured and unstructured problems are *semistructured* problems, in which only some of the decision process phases are structured. Semistructured problems require a combination of standard solution procedures and individual judgment. Examples of semistructured problems are evaluating employees, setting marketing budgets for consumer products, performing capital acquisition analysis, and trading bonds.

The Nature of Decisions. The second dimension of decision support deals with the *nature of decisions*. All managerial decisions fall into one of three broad categories:

1. *Operational control:* executing specific tasks efficiently and effectively
2. *Management control:* acquiring and using resources efficiently in accomplishing organizational goals
3. *Strategic planning:* the long-range goals and policies for growth and resource allocation

These categories are displayed along the top row of Figure 5.2.

Note: Strategic decisions define the context in which management control decisions are made. In turn, management control decisions define the context in which operational control decisions are made.

The Decision Matrix. The decision matrix. The three primary classes of decision types and the three broad categories of the nature of decisions can be combined in a decision-support matrix that consists of nine cells, as diagrammed in Figure 5.2. Lower-level managers perform tasks in cells 1 and 4, but not 7 because operational managers are not expected to make strategic decisions. The tasks in cells 2, 5, and 8 are usually the responsibility of middle-managers and professional staff. Finally, the tasks in cells 6 and 9 are generally carried out by senior executives while cell 3 is empty because senior executives are not involved in day-to-day operational tasks.

Computer Support for Structured Decisions. Examples of computer support that might be used for the nine cells in the matrix are displayed in the right-hand column of Figure 5.2. Structured and some semistructured decisions, especially of the operational and management control type, have been supported by computers since the 1950s. Decisions of this type are made in all functional areas, but particularly in finance and operations management.

	Operational Control	Management Control	Strategic Planning	IS Support
Structured	Accounts receivable, order entry `1`	Budget analysis, short-term forecasting, personnel reports, make-or-buy analysis `2`	`3`	MIS, statistical models (management science, financial, etc.)
Semistructured	Production scheduling, inventory control `4`	Credit evaluation, budget preparation, plant layout, project scheduling, reward systems design `5`	Building a new plant, mergers and acquisitions, planning (product, quality assurance, compensation, etc.) `6`	Decision support systems, business intelligence
Unstructured	`7`	Negotiating, recruiting an executive, buying hardware, lobbying `8`	New technology development, product R&D, social responsibility planning `9`	Decision support systems, expert systems, enterprise resource planning, neural networks, business intelligence, big data

Figure 5.2 Decision support framework. Technology is used to support the decisions shown in the column at the far right.

Problems that lower-level managers encounter on a regular basis typically have a high level of structure. Examples are capital budgeting (for example, replacement of equipment), allocating resources, distributing merchandise, and controlling inventory. For each type of structured decision, prescribed solutions have been developed, which often include mathematical formulas that can often be used. This approach is called *management science* or *operations research*, and it is executed with the aid of computers.

Apply the Concept 5.1

Background If you look back through this section you will see that Henry Mintzberg's 1973 book, *The Nature of Managerial Work*, was referenced when the three basic roles of a manager were presented. This text focuses on the decisional role because that is the one most supported by information systems. Professor Mintzberg's work goes much farther than just the decisional role.

Activity Visit http://www.wiley.com/go/rainer/applytheconcept and click on the link provided for Apply the Concept 5.1. It will take you to a YouTube video titled "Data Driven Decision Making" by user "minnetonka schools." This video mentions a strategic plan, operational control, and decisional control. As you watch the video, be sure to watch for these key points and to see how they are supported by data.

Deliverable

Write a short paper (a couple of paragraphs is plenty) for your professor detailing how Minnetonka Schools uses data to make better decisions. Also ask a few teachers to see if your school has any similar data systems that allow this type of decision making. If it does not, what would you recommend (from the student perspective) that would help you be successful? Submit this paper to your instructor.

Quiz questions are assignable in WileyPLUS, and available on the Book Companion Site at http://www.wiley.com/college/rainer.

BEFORE *YOU GO ON . . .*

1. Describe the decision-making process proposed by Simon.

2. You are registering for classes next semester. Apply the decision-making process to your decision about how many and which courses to take. Is your decision structured, semistructured, or unstructured?

3. Consider your decision-making process when registering for classes next semester. Explain how information technology supports (or does not support) each phase of this process.

RUBY'S CLUB QUESTIONS

1. Discuss how the three roles of a manager (interpersonal, informational, and decisional) might play out as Ruben and Lisa tackle shrinkage. Will bartenders become defensive? Should they share financial information? How much should they monitor the bartenders?

2. Which of the four reasons why a manager needs IT support do you feel is most applicable in this situation? Is it that the number of alternatives is increasing? Time pressure? Uncertainty? Or the need to bring remote individuals and data into the picture?

3. Is the shrinkage problem a structured, semistructured, or unstructured situation? If it is structured, what controls may be put in place to handle it? If it is unstructured, what policies might be instituted to help reign in the problem?

4. Does this situation fall into operational control, management control, or strategic planning? Or does it fall into all three?

5. In what ways could IT provide help to Ruben and Lisa as they try to make their $300,000 net profit and control shrinkage?

5.2 What Is Business Intelligence?

To provide users with access to corporate data, many organizations are implementing data warehouses and data marts, which you learned about in Chapter 3. Users analyze the data in warehouses and marts using a wide variety of BI tools. Many vendors offer integrated packages of these tools under the overall label of "business intelligence (BI)" software. Major BI vendors include SAS (www.sas.com), Hyperion (www.hyperion.com, now owned by Oracle), Business Objects (www.businessobjects.com, now owned by SAP), Information Builders (www.informationbuilders.com), SPSS (www.spss.com, now owned by IBM), and Cognos (www.ibm.com/cognos).

As has been shown, BI is vital to modern decision making and organizational performance. Let's now consider in greater detail the technical foundation for BI and the wide variety of ways that BI can be used.

The term *business intelligence* is relatively new. Business and IT analyst Howard Dresner coined the term in 1989 while he was an analyst at Gartner, a market research firm. The term is especially popular in industry, where it is used as an umbrella term that encompasses all decision support applications.

BI encompasses not only applications but also technologies and processes. It includes both "getting data in" (to a data mart or warehouse) and "getting data out" (through BI applications).

In addition, a significant change is taking place within the BI environment. In the past, organizations used BI only to support management. Today, however, BI applications are increasingly available to front-line personnel (e.g., call center operators), suppliers, customers, and even regulators. These groups rely on BI to provide them with the most current information.

The Scope of Business Intelligence

The use of BI in organizations varies considerably. In smaller organizations, BI may be limited to Excel spreadsheets. In larger ones, BI is often enterprisewide, and it includes applications such as data mining/predictive analytics, dashboards, and data visualization. It is important to recognize that the importance of BI to organizations continues to grow. It is not an exaggeration to say that for many firms, BI is now a requirement for competing in the marketplace, as illustrated in IT's About Business 5.1.

 S ABOUT BUSINESS 5.1

Analytics in the National Basketball Association

Six high-definition cameras are positioned within the Oracle Arena, home of the National Basketball Association's Golden State Warriors. The system is part of SportVU (www.sportvu.com) a player-tracking system from Stats (www.stats.com). Data from the cameras, collected 25 times per second, is analyzed by SportVU's proprietary algorithms.

The software deciphers and identifies every dribble and pass, based only on optical movement of the ball and its relative distance to the players.

Stats thought that the NBA would be an excellent venue for its SportVU system for several reasons. First, with its consistent scoring, there would be enough data points in a game that teams would be

© pagadesign/iStockphoto

interested to see the results. Second, the NBA games are played in a relatively confined space (a regulation NBA court is only 94 feet by 50 feet), meaning that it is relatively easy to film players. Finally, the NBA is a $4 billion industry that would have money to spare on an analytics system.

Unfortunately for Stats, NBA teams had already had access to play-by-play data for decades. This data consisted of simple, textual rundowns that efficiently mapped how a game played out. A brief scan of a one-page printout as the coach was running into the locker room at halftime, and he could determine intermediate-level metrics such as assist-to-field-goal ratio and turnovers-per-minute.

As a result, the system was a difficult sell to the NBA, but four teams signed on to be charter members: the Houston Rockets, the Dallas Mavericks, the San Antonio Spurs, and the Oklahoma City Thunder. The Golden State Warriors signed on later.

The system has provided these teams with many previously unknown metrics. For example, the system revealed that for the Warriors' first 14 home games at Oracle Arena, guards Monta Ellis and Stephen Curry accounted for nearly 60 percent of the team's entire ball possession. Curry, the team's point guard, had achieved 937 touches of the ball over those games, compared to 948 for Ellis, the team's leading scorer. More interesting for the Warriors was seeing that the team had a 51.5 percent shooting percentage off passes from Ellis compared to 44.6 percent from Curry.

The system provided other interesting insights for all five teams as well. These insights included points per touch, catch-and-shoot field-goal percentage, secondary assists per game, and even how physically far apart players were from their defenders during the game.

Golden State did have a .477 winning percentage after implementing SportVU, compared to .395 before they deployed the system. In addition, SportVU clients San Antonio, Dallas, and Oklahoma City represent three of the eight Western Conference playoff teams. The most successful NBA franchise in history, the Boston Celtics, recently signed on as the sixth SportVU-equipped team.

Concluding that the SportVU system has contributed to the success of these teams is premature in mid-2012. Stats is planning on adding features to its SportVU system, including near real-time functionality, so that the tracking data can be synchronized to the play-by-play data in less than 30 seconds. This new functionality will provide a close representation and analysis of on-court play almost as it is happening.

Sources: Compiled from S. Wickersham, "Can NBA Teams Harness a Deluge of Next-Level Numbers?" *ESPN the Magazine*, June 27, 2011; E. Malinowski, "Hoops 2.0: Inside the NBA's Data-Driven Revolution," *Wired*, April 18, 2011; "NBA Teams that Have Analytics Department," *nbastuffer.com*, accessed February 27, 2012; www.sportvu.com, www.stats.com, accessed February 27, 2012.

Questions

1. How do you think an NBA player would feel about SportVU? Pro or con? Support your answer.

2. How do you think an NBA coach would feel about SportVU? Pro or con? Support your answer.

3. How do you think an NBA team's front office would feel about SportVU? Pro or con? Support your answer.

4. Do the constituencies represented in the first three questions differ in how you think they would feel about SportVU? If so, why? If not, why not?

Not all organizations use BI in the same way. For example, some organizations employ a single or a few applications, while others utilize enterprisewide BI. The following subsections examine three specific BI targets that represent different levels of change:

- The development of a single or a few related BI applications
- The development of infrastructure to support enterprisewide BI
- Support for organizational transformation

These targets differ in terms of their focus; scope; level of sponsorship, commitment, and required resources; technical architecture; impact on personnel and business processes; and benefits.

The Development of a Single or a Few Related BI Applications. This BI target is often a point solution for a departmental need, such as campaign management in marketing. Sponsorship, approval, funding, impacts, and benefits typically occur at the departmental level. For this target, organizations usually create a data mart to store the necessary data. Organizations must be careful that the mart—an "independent" application—does not become a "data silo" that stores data that are inconsistent with and cannot be integrated with data used elsewhere in the organization.

The Development of Infrastructure to Support Enterprisewide BI.
This BI target supports current and future BI needs. A crucial component of BI at this level is an enterprise data warehouse. Because it is an enterprisewide initiative, senior management often provides sponsorship, approval, and funding. In addition, the impacts and benefits are felt throughout the organization.

An example of this target is the 3M Corporation. Traditionally 3M's various divisions had operated independently and had utilized separate decision support platforms. Not only was this arrangement costly, but it also prevented 3M from integrating the data and presenting a "single face" to its customers. Thus, for example, sales representatives did not know whether or how business customers were interacting with other 3M divisions. The solution was to develop an enterprise data warehouse that enabled 3M to operate as an integrated company. As an added benefit, the cost of implementing this system was covered by savings resulting from the consolidation of the various platforms.

Support for Organizational Transformation.
With this target, BI is used to fundamentally transform the ways in which a company competes in the marketplace. BI supports a new business model and it enables the business strategy. Because of the scope and importance of these changes, critical elements such as sponsorship, approval, and funding originate at the highest organizational levels. The impact on personnel and processes can be significant, and the benefits are organizationwide.

Harrah's Entertainment provides a good example of this BI target. Traditionally, Harrah had managed its various properties as "independent fiefdoms." Then, in the early 1990s, gambling on riverboats and Indian reservations became legal. Harrah's senior management perceived this as an opportunity to expand the company's properties. In addition, the company decided to implement a new business model that would enable it to operate all of these properties in an integrated way. At the heart of this model was the collection and use of customer data and the creation of a customer loyalty program, known as Total Rewards, that encouraged customers to play across all of Harrah's casinos. To implement this strategy, Harrah's had to create a BI infrastructure (a data warehouse) that collected data from casino, hotel, and special event systems (e.g., wine-tasting weekends) across the various customer touchpoints (e.g., slot machines, table games, and Internet). Harrah's used these data to reward loyal customers and reach out to them in personal and appealing ways—for example, through promotional offers created using BI. As a result, the company became a leader in the gaming industry.

Nonprofit organizations also use BI to transform the way they operate. As you see in IT's About Business 5.2, Marwell Wildlife uses BI to transform the organization's conservation efforts.

T'S ABOUT BUSINESS 5.2

Using Analytics to Save the Grevy's Zebra

Marwell Wildlife (www.marwell.org.uk) is an international conservation charity and zoo based in Hampshire, England, that works to preserve the wild population of Grevy's zebra. This species of zebra is on the endangered species list, with a wild population of only 2,500. Marwell relies heavily on analytics software from IBM to aid in its conservation efforts. The software allows Marwell to analyze information from the field, including data from aerial surveys, camera traps, and radio collars. This analysis gives the conservation group a crucial understanding of both the threats facing the zebras and the policies that could help the zebra population to recover organically.

Some of the most important data available to Marwell comes from a survey of nomadic herdsmen in northern Kenya, the area where most of the remaining Grevy's zebras live. People in the local pastoral communities are able to provide valuable information to Marwell because they have such an in-depth knowledge about the landscape and its wildlife.

To extract information from the local communities, field researchers from Marwell and other organizations partnering in the survey spent a month in remote areas of Kenya, conducting a questionnaire-based survey. These field researchers gathered information about the distribution of the zebra population and threats to zebras, and learned about the attitudes of the people of the region toward the zebra.

The survey confirmed what conservationists have long recognized—that the needs of the local human population can conflict with those of an endangered species. An obvious example of this conflict is the fact that local herdsmen were hunting the zebras, but there were also more subtle manifestations of this conflict. The zebras live in dry areas near herdsmen who raise livestock, so the zebras often compete with livestock for water and pasture space.

The researchers also analyzed their data for insights into human practices and attitudes that may have an impact on the zebra population. The IBM analytics software enabled them to examine multiple variables affecting attitudes, such as education level and whether or not people had been previously exposed to conservation efforts, to better understand the reasons behind people's various attitudes and beliefs.

Some of the patterns the researchers uncovered did not relate to the zebras, but rather to the humans sharing their habitat. Marwell researchers discovered that herdsmen saw benefits from living close to the zebras. For example, zebras can point the way to pastures in dry years and they attract tourists, which boosts the economy. The researchers further found that zebras are hunted not just for their meat, but also for medicine. Zebra fat is highly valued by the pastoral communities as a treatment for illnesses ranging from headaches to tuberculosis. Most of the survey respondents said that they would be glad to switch to conventional medicines if they were available. These findings show promising opportunities to make changes that have the potential to benefit people and zebras.

Sources: Compiled from M. Behan, "Analytics Helps Save an Endangered Species," *Baseline Magazine*, July 28, 2011; "Marwell Wildlife Uses Analytics in the Conservation of Endangered Species," *IBM Case Study*, April 5, 2011; A. Bridgwater, "IBM Predictive Analytics Software Helps Save Grevy's Zebra," *ComputerWeekly.com*, September 15, 2010; www.marwell.org.uk, accessed February 26, 2012.

Questions

1. What other types of data could Marwell analyze to better understand the problem of the Grevy's zebra?

2. What advantages does the IBM software provide to Marwell in its goal to save endangered species? Are there other advantages not mentioned in this case? Provide specific examples.

In Chapter 3, you studied the basics of data warehouses and data marts. In this section, you have seen how important data warehouses and marts are to the different ways that organizations use BI. In the next section, you will learn how the user community can analyze the data in warehouses and marts, how the results of these analyses are presented to users, and how organizations can use the results of these analyses.

BEFORE *YOU GO ON . . .*

1. Define BI.
2. Discuss the breadth of support provided by BI applications to organizational employees.
3. Identify and discuss the three basic targets of BI.

Apply the Concept 5.2

Background You have read in this section about how data can be used to provide business intelligence. Google Analytics is a tool that provides just such data to help businesses make decisions about their website. The information is captured by Google and then presented to create business intelligence. However, Google only provides the data in graphs and charts. It is still up to the business to make informed decisions based on the information they find.

By looking at this application, you should begin to see how data must be captured, categorized, and be flexible for reporting. The video illustrates the dimensions of a cube without calling it a cube, mentions a data warehouse as the repository of all the data, and shows "drill down" without calling it such.

Activity Visit http://www.wiley.com/go/rainer/applytheconcept and click on the link provided for Apply the Concept 5.2. It will take you to a YouTube video titled "Google Analytics for Business Intelligence" by user "clicksharpmarketing." By watching this video, you should begin to see how data must be captured, be categorized, and be flexible for reporting. The video illustrates the dimensions of a cube without calling it a cube, mentions a data warehouse as the repository of all the data, and shows "drill down" without calling it such.

Based on the terms that were introduced in the video, answer the following:

1. What is a bounce rate?
2. What is the difference between a visit and a new visit?
3. Define the three main categories of Web traffic.
4. What is the concept of a key word, and how is it used by Google Analytics?

Deliverable

Write an email to your best "imaginary" friend who is also a Web designer. Explain these terms in the email to help him/her know how to analyze results from their Web sites. Submit your "email" to your professor.

Quiz questions are assignable in WileyPLUS, and available on the Book Companion Site at http://www.wiley.com/college/rainer.

RUBY'S CLUB QUESTIONS

1. BI tools allow better decisions to be made by presenting information to the right person at the right time. Imagine a scenario where the bartender has a computer screen that monitors the club's collections vs. its sales. What would keep this system from working properly?
2. How would you collect information to make this a reality?

5.3 Business Intelligence Applications for Data Analysis

A good strategy to study the ways in which organizations use BI applications is to consider how the users analyze data, how the results of their analyses are presented to them, and how managers and executives implement these results. Recall from Chapter 3 that the data are stored in a data warehouse or data mart. The user community analyzes these data using a variety of BI applications. The results of these analyses can be presented to users via other BI applications. Finally, managers and executives put the overall results to good use. You will become familiar with data analysis, presentation, and use in depth in the next three sections.

A variety of BI applications for analyzing data are available. They include multidimensional analysis (also called online analytical processing, or OLAP), data mining, and decision support systems.

Multidimensional Analysis or Online Analytical Processing

Some BI applications include **online analytical processing (OLAP)** capabilities, also referred to as **multidimensional data analysis.** OLAP involves "slicing and dicing" data stored in a dimensional format, drilling down the data to greater detail, and aggregating the data.

Consider our example from Chapter 3. Recall Figure 3.10 showing the data cube. The product is on the x-axis, geography is on the y-axis, and time is on the z-axis. Now, suppose you want to know how many nuts the company sold in the West region in 2009. You would slice and dice the cube using nuts as the specific measure for product, West as the measure for geography, and 2009 as the measure for time. The value(s) in the cell(s) that remain after our slicing and dicing is (are) the answer to our question. You might also want to know how many nuts were sold in January 2009; this is an example of drilling down. Alternatively, you might want to know how many nuts were sold during 2008–2010, which is an example of aggregation, also called "rollup."

Data Mining

Data mining refers to the process of searching for valuable business information in a large database, data warehouse, or data mart. Data mining can perform two basic operations: (1) predicting trends and behaviors and (2) identifying previously unknown patterns. BI applications typically provide users with a view of what has happened. Data mining helps to explain why it is happening, and it predicts what will happen in the future.

Regarding the first operation, data mining automates the process of finding predictive information in large databases. Questions that traditionally required extensive hands-on analysis can now be answered directly and quickly from the data. A typical example of a predictive problem is *targeted marketing*. Data mining can use data from past promotional mailings to identify those people who are most likely to respond favorably to future mailings. Another example of a predictive problem is forecasting bankruptcy and other forms of default.

Data mining can also identify previously hidden patterns in a single step. For example, it can analyze retail sales data to discover seemingly unrelated products that people often purchase together. The classic example is beer and diapers. Data mining found that young men tend to buy beer and diapers at the same time when they shop at a convenience store.

One significant pattern-discovery operation is detecting fraudulent credit card transactions. After you use your credit card for a time, a pattern emerges of the typical ways you use your card—the places you use your card, the amount you spend, and so on. If your card is stolen and used fraudulently, this usage is often different from your pattern. Data mining tools can discern this difference and bring this issue to your attention.

Numerous data mining applications are used in business and in other fields. According to a Gartner report (www.gartner.com), most of the Fortune 1000 companies worldwide currently use data mining, as the following representative examples illustrate. Note that in most cases the intent of data mining is to identify a business opportunity in order to create a sustainable competitive advantage.

- *Retailing and sales:* Predicting sales, preventing theft and fraud, and determining correct inventory levels and distribution schedules among outlets. For example, retailers such as AAFES (stores on military bases) use Fraud Watch from SAP (www.sap.com) to combat fraud by employees in their 1,400 stores.

- *Banking:* Forecasting levels of bad loans and fraudulent credit card use, predicting credit card spending by new customers, and determining which kinds of customers will best respond to (and qualify for) new loan offers.

- *Manufacturing and production:* Predicting machinery failures, and finding key factors that help optimize manufacturing capacity.

- *Insurance:* Forecasting claim amounts and medical coverage costs, classifying the most important elements that affect medical coverage, and predicting which customers will buy new insurance policies.

- *Policework:* Tracking crime patterns, locations, and criminal behavior; identifying attributes to assist in solving criminal cases.

- *Health care:* Correlating demographics of patients with critical illnesses, and developing better insights on how to identify and treat symptoms and their causes.

- *Marketing:* Classifying customer demographics that can be used to predict which customers will respond to a mailing or buy a particular product.

Decision Support Systems

Decision support systems (DSS) combine models and data in an attempt to analyze semi-structured and some unstructured problems with extensive user involvement. **Models** are simplified representations, or abstractions, of reality. DSS enable business managers and analysts to access data interactively, to manipulate these data, and to conduct appropriate analyses.

Decision support systems can enhance learning and contribute to all levels of decision making. DSS also employ mathematical models. In addition, they have the related capabilities of sensitivity analysis, what-if analysis, and goal-seeking analysis, which you will learn about next. You should keep in mind that these three types of analysis are useful for any type of decision support application. For example, Excel supports them.

Sensitivity Analysis. *Sensitivity analysis* is the study of the impact that changes in one or more parts of a decision-making model have on other parts. Most sensitivity analyses examine the impact that changes in input variables have on output variables.

Most models include two types of input variables: decision variables and environmental variables. "What is our reorder point for these raw materials?" is a decision variable (internal to the organization). "What will the rate of inflation be?" is an environmental variable (external to the organization). The output in this example would be the total cost of raw materials. The point of a sensitivity analysis is usually to determine the impact of environmental variables on the result of the analysis.

Sensitivity analysis is extremely valuable because it enables the system to adapt to changing conditions and to the varying requirements of different decision-making situations. It provides a better understanding of the model and the problem that the model purports to describe.

What-If Analysis. A model builder must make predictions and assumptions regarding the input data, many of which are based on the assessment of uncertain futures. The results depend on the accuracy of these assumptions, which can be highly subjective. *What-if analysis* attempts to predict the impact of a change in the assumptions (input data) on the proposed solution. For example, what will happen to the total inventory cost *if* the originally assumed cost of carrying inventories is not 10 percent but 12 percent? In a well-designed BI system, managers themselves can interactively ask the computer these types of questions as many times as needed.

Goal-Seeking Analysis. *Goal-seeking analysis* represents a "backward" solution approach. It attempts to find the value of the inputs necessary to achieve a desired level of output. For example, let's say that an initial BI analysis predicted a profit of $2 million. Management might want to know what sales volume would be necessary to generate a profit of $3 million. To find out, the company would perform a goal-seeking analysis.

However, managers cannot simply press a button that says "increase sales." Some action(s) will be necessary to make the sales increase possible. The action(s) could be to lower prices, to increase research and development, to provide a higher commission rate for the sales force, to increase advertising, to take some other action, or to implement some combination of these actions. Whatever the action is, it will cost money, and the goal-seeking analysis must take this into account.

BEFORE *YOU GO ON . . .*

1. Describe multidimensional analysis and construct a data cube with information from IT's About Business 5.1. (*Hint:* You must decide which three business dimensions you would like to analyze in your data cube.)

2. What are the two basic operations of data mining?

3. What is the purpose of decision support systems?

Apply the Concept 5.3

Background This section has shown that data is more abundant today than ever before. One thing we are learning is that there is much we can know that we do not know. In fact, there are many questions that we do not even know should be asked! This is the purpose of data mining. It uses computers and software to look into large databases searching out trends that can become the foundation for future business planning.

Activity Visit http://www.wiley.com/go/rainer/applytheconcept and click on the link provided for Apply the Concept 5.3. It will take you to a video about data mining. As you watch, consider the following questions:

1. What is the goal of data mining?

2. What is classification?

3. What is clustering?

4. How does a person know if a model is right?

Now go to Walmart and look around the store. How did the company determine which items would be on an end cap (the end of an aisle)? Who decided how high to put the Cheerios and where to put the Lucky Charms? Why is the milk in the back of the store? How much of the layout do you think was determined by past data mining?

Deliverable

Write a newspaper article titled "I Was Data Mined By Walmart—Why I Buy Too Much" for your professor that details the answers to the four questions above and that presents your thoughts from your visit to Walmart. Submit this to your instructor.

Quiz questions are assignable in WileyPLUS, and available on the Book Companion Site at http://www.wiley.com/college/rainer.

RUBY'S CLUB | QUESTIONS

1. Ruben and Lisa hope to use Excel as their decision support tool. Which analysis would be best suited for their goal and shrinkage problem? The what-if analysis? The goal-seeking analysis? Or the sensitivity analysis? Or, do you think it would be a combination of all three?

2. What tools can you find in Excel that would support these analyses? (*Hint:* Google "Sensitivity Analysis Excel.")

5.4 Business Intelligence Applications for Presenting Results

The results of the types of data analyses you just learned about can be presented with dashboards and data visualization technologies. Today, users increasingly rely on data that are real time or almost real time. Therefore, you will note a discussion of real-time BI in this section.

Dashboards

Dashboards evolved from executive information systems, which were information systems designed specifically for the information needs of top executives. However, as you saw in this chapter's opening case, today all employees, business partners, and customers can use digital dashboards.

A **dashboard** provides easy access to timely information and direct access to management reports. It is very user friendly and is supported by graphics. Of special importance, it enables managers to examine exception reports and drill down into detailed data. Table 5.1 summarizes the various capabilities that are common to many dashboards. In addition,

TABLE 5.1 The Capabilities of Dashboards

Capability	Description
Drill down	The ability to go to details, at several levels. Can be done through a series of menus or by clicking on a drillable portion of the screen.
Critical success factors (CSFs)	The factors most critical for the success of business. Can be organizational, industry, departmental, or for individual workers.
Key performance indicators (KPIs)	The specific measures of CSFs.
Status access	The latest data available on KPIs or some other metric, often in real time.
Trend analysis	Short-term, medium-term, and long-term trend of KPIs or metrics, which are projected using forecasting methods.
Exception reporting	Reports that highlight deviations larger than certain thresholds. Reports may include only deviations.

some of the capabilities discussed in this section are now part of many BI products, as illustrated in Figure 5.3.

One outstanding example of a dashboard is the "Bloomberg." Bloomberg LLP (www.bloomberg.com), a privately held company, provides a subscription service that sells financial data, software to analyze these data, trading tools, and news (electronic, print, TV, and radio). All of this information is accessible through a color-coded Bloomberg keyboard that displays the desired information on a computer screen, either the user's or one that Bloomberg provides. Users can also set up their own computers to access the service without a Bloomberg keyboard. The subscription service plus the keyboard is called the "Bloomberg." It literally represents a do-it-yourself dashboard, because users can customize their information feeds as well as the look and feel of those feeds (see Figure 5.4).

Figure 5.3 Sample performance dashboard.

© NAN104/iStockphoto

Bloomberg via Getty Images, Inc.

Figure 5.4 The Bloomberg Terminal is a specific set of hardware and software used by financial professionals on trading floors around the world.

In another example, Figure 5.5 shows a human resources dashboard/scorecard developed by iDashboards, one of the leading BI software vendors. At a glance, users can see employee productivity, hours, team, department, and division performance in graphical, tabular, summary, and detailed form. The selector box to the left enables the user to easily change between specific analysts to compare their performance.

A unique and interesting application of dashboards to support the informational needs of executives is the Management Cockpit. Essentially, a Management Cockpit is a strategic management room containing an elaborate set of dashboards that enable top-level decision makers to pilot their businesses better. The goal is to create an environment that encourages more efficient management meetings and boosts team performance via effective communication. To help achieve this goal, the dashboard graphically displays key performance indicators and information relating to critical success factors on the walls of a meeting room, called the Management Cockpit Room (see Figure 5.6). The cockpitlike arrangement of instrument panels and displays helps managers visualize how all the different factors in the business interrelate.

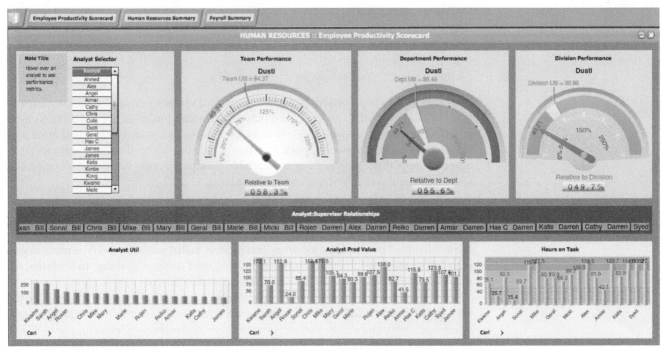

Courtesy of iDashboards

Figure 5.5 A human resource dashboard/scorecard.

Figure 5.6 Management
Cockpit.

The Management Cockpit is a registered trademark of SAP, created by Professor M. Georges.

Within the room, the four walls are designated by color: Black, Red, Blue, and White. The Black Wall displays the principal success factors and financial indicators. The Red Wall measures market performance. The Blue Wall projects the performance of internal processes and employees. The White Wall indicates the status of strategic projects. The Flight Deck, a six-screen, high-end PC, enables executives to drill down to detailed information. External information needed for competitive analyses can easily be imported into the room.

Board members and other executives hold meetings in the Cockpit Room. Managers also meet there with the comptroller to discuss current business issues. For this purpose, the Management Cockpit can implement various what-if scenarios. It also provides a common basis for information and communication. Finally, it supports efforts to translate a corporate strategy into concrete activities by identifying performance indicators.

Data Visualization Technologies

After data have been processed, they can be presented to users in visual formats such as text, graphics, and tables. This process, known as data visualization, makes IT applications more attractive and understandable to users. Data visualization is becoming more and more popular on the Web for decision support. A variety of visualization methods and software packages that support decision making are available. Two particularly valuable applications are geographic information systems and reality mining.

Geographic Information Systems.
A **geographic information system (GIS)** is a computer-based system for capturing, integrating, manipulating, and displaying data using digitized maps. Its most distinguishing characteristic is that every record or digital object has an identified geographical location. This process, called *geocoding*, enables users to generate information for planning, problem solving, and decision making. In addition, the graphical format makes it easy for managers to visualize the data.

Today, relatively inexpensive, fully functional PC-based GIS packages are readily available. Representative GIS software vendors are ESRI (www.esri.com), Intergraph (www.intergraph.com), and Pitney Bowes Mapinfo (www.pbinsight.com/welcome/mapinfo). In addition, both government sources and private vendors provide diversified commercial GIS data. Some of these GIS packages are free—for example, CD-ROMs from Mapinfo and downloadable material from www.esri.com and http://data.geocomm.com.

There are countless applications of GISs to improve decision making in both the public and private sectors. For example, IT's About Business 5.3 shows how SecureAlert uses electronically transmitted location data and data visualization in its monitoring system.

'S ABOUT BUSINESS 5.3

SecureAlert

SecureAlert (www.securealert.com) works with law enforcement agencies around the United States to track about 15,000 ex-convicts, all of whom wear electronic, location-reporting ankle cuffs. To accomplish this task, SecureAlert must collect and analyze billions of global positioning system (GPS) signals transmitted by the cuffs each day. Technicians at SecureAlert's monitoring center watch computer screens filled with multicolored dots moving about digital maps. Each dot represents someone on parole or probation wearing one of the company's cuffs.

The more traditional part of the work consists of ensuring that people under house arrest stay in their houses. However, advances in the way information is collected and analyzed mean that SecureAlert is not just watching. The company says that it can actually predict when a crime is about to be committed.

Using data from the ankle cuffs and other sources, SecureAlert identifies patterns of suspicious behavior. A person convicted of domestic violence, for example, might get out of jail and set up a law-abiding routine. Quite often, however, SecureAlert's technology sees such people backslide and start visiting locations frequented by their victims. If the convict gets too close to these locations for comfort, an alarm goes off at SecureAlert and a flashing siren appears on SecureAlert screens. At this time, the system can call an offender through a two-way cellphone attached to the ankle cuff to ask what the person is doing, or set off a 95-decibel audio device as a warning to others. More typically, the company will notify probation officers or police about the suspicious activity and have them investigate.

SecureAlert emphasizes that if a parolee wearing an ankle cuff wanders out-of-bounds, there is always a human in the process to make a judgment call. The company says that it is always tuning its monitoring systems to balance between "crying wolf" and "catching serious situations." SecureAlert's innovative use of information technology saves law enforcement agencies a great deal of time and money, while also contributing to the prevention of crime.

© alengo/iStockphoto

Sources: Compiled from "New GPS Device to Help Warn Domestic Violence Victims About Abusers," *CBS New York*, November 1, 2011; "Trinidad & Tobago Interested in Electronic Tagging Programme," *Antigua Observer*, October 24, 2011; A. Vance, "New Analytics Technology Is Predicting What You're About To Do Next," *Bloomberg BusinessWeek*, September 12–18, 2011; D. Randall, "Oh, That? That's My Pal," *Forbes*, September 4, 2008; www.securealert.com, accessed February 27, 2012.

Questions

1. Discuss the privacy implications of the SecureAlert system.
2. What are the weaknesses of the SecureAlert system? Provide specific examples to support your answer.

Reality Mining. One important emerging trend is the integration of GISs and global positioning systems (GPSs, discussed in Chapter 10). Using GISs and GPSs together can produce an interesting new type of technology, called **reality mining**. Reality mining allows analysts to extract information from the usage patterns of mobile phones and other wireless devices.

Real-Time Business Intelligence

Until recently, BI has focused on the use of historical data. This focus has changed with the emergence of technology for capturing, storing, and using real-time data. Real-time BI enables users to employ multidimensional analysis, data mining, and decision support-systems to analyze data in real time. In addition, it helps organizations to make decisions and to interact with customers in new ways as presented in IT's About Business 5.4.

IT'S ABOUT BUSINESS 5.4

Catalina Marketing

Catalina Marketing (www.catalinamarketing.com) pro-vides precision marketing capabilities to manufactur- ers, retailers, and health providers. The company's marketing systems enable the delivery of the right message to the right audience in the right environment so clients can successfully build their brands. In this way, Catalina helps clients develop deeper, more productive consumer relationships.

Catalina manages the evolving purchase histories of more than 75 percent of U.S. shoppers. The company uses the transaction-level data to help clients develop customized, measurable campaigns to acquire, maximize, and retain their most valuable consumers. Catalina clients include manufacturers such as Coca-Cola, Kellogg's, Kraft Foods, and Procter & Gamble, and retailers such as Kmart, Kroger, Ralph's, Safeway, Stop & Shop, Target, and Winn-Dixie.

Catalina's in-store network consists of 50,000 food, drug, and mass-merchant locations worldwide. In the United States, Catalina is installed in more than 26,000 locations. In addition, Catalina's CouponNetwork.com is one of the world's largest consumer couponing sites.

Catalina's primary database holds more than 2.5 petabytes of data and adds data on more than 300 mil-lion transactions per week. When you pay with a loyalty card at any one of 50,000 member grocery, drug, or mass-merchandise retail stores in the United States, Germany, and Japan, insights derived from Catalina's database trigger promotions and offers based on your past purchases. Catalina's point-of-sale printers at checkout lanes produce coupons that are handed to customers along with their receipts within seconds of the transactions.

To deliver its data analytics results in a timely fash-ion, Catalina pioneered in-database processing with Netezza (www.netezza.com). *In-database pro-cessing* means that data analytics software runs *inside* a database or data warehouse. This process eliminates the time, effort, and expense of moving large data sets from an enterprise database or data warehouse to a separate data analytics software application. In-database processing meant that Catali-na moved its scoring of purchase-behavior models into the Netezza data warehouse for faster processing.

For Catalina, in-database processing was the only way to solve a productivity challenge. Catalina's data warehouse is roughly the same size as the enterprise data warehouses at Walmart and Bank of America. The company uses it to analyze what consumers buy, the pattern of items they buy together, and how these pur-chase patterns vary by geography, market area, chain, store, and zip code. Most importantly for Catalina and its clients, these analyses predict and reveal the power of promotions, delivered through coupons, to change purchasing behavior.

Catalina captures transactions and delivers cou-pons in real time no matter which store a customer is shopping in. As a result, Catalina can support multitrip "threshold" promotions that were never before possi-ble. For example, a retail chain or manufacturer might offer $10 off your next shopping trip if you buy 10 products from a specific manufacturer within three months. In this example, Catalina delivers up-to-the-minute customer status information to all retail loca-tions. And, customers earn an incentive instantaneously, no matter which store they are in, as soon as they meet the purchase threshold.

Without data-driven analyses, redemption rates on coupons are around 1 percent. With basic target-ing, such as giving buyers of diet soda or dog food coupons for alternative brands, redemption rates rise to 6 to 10 percent. Using historical purchase-behavior data and the sophisticated predictive models that Catalina uses, redemption rates are as high as 25 percent.

Sources: Compiled from D. Henschen, "Oracle Analytics Package Expands In-Database Processing Options," *InformationWeek*, February 8, 2012; D. Henschen, "At the Cutting Edge of 'Big Data'," *InformationWeek*, September 19, 2011; J. Vijayan, "Need for 'Big Data' Analytics Drives Vendors' Acquisitions," *Computerworld*, March 4, 2011; www.catalinamarketing.com, www.netezza.com, accessed February 27, 2012.

Questions

1. Why is the timely delivery of coupons tailored to customers' purchase histories so important to Catalina's client companies? Provide specific examples to support your answer.

2. Discuss privacy concerns that could come from Catalina's use of customers' purchase histories. Provide examples to support your answer.

Apply the Concept 5.4

Background This section discusses visualization tools to help understand the information that is contained in data. This is important because it is easier and much quicker to glance at a graph than it is to look at a page full of numbers. MicroStrategy is a company that specializes in dashboards and products that help with data visualization. Recently, the company has also offered iPad and iPhone apps to allow data to be accessible on mobile devices. Taking things a step further, MicroStrategy now can create a conference room that allows sharing of graphs and charts over devices to a large TV or projector in the meeting room.

Activity Visit http://www.wiley.com/go/rainer/applytheconcept and click on the link provided for Apply the Concept 5.4. It will take you to a YouTube video titled "MicroStrategy Mobile Integrates with Apple TV" by user "microstrategybi." This video demonstrates how the company's product not only allows a single user to analyze data visually, but that user can easily share his or her view of the data with others in a conference room with minimal setup. You may also want to visit MicroStrategy's Web site as mentioned in the video for more information (this link is also provided at http://www.wiley.com/go/rainer/applytheconcept).

Deliverable

Write an imaginary request to your boss to install a system like this in your boardroom. Be sure to point out what is so significant of visual, instant, on-demand information sharing. Because you know your boss is skeptical of everything, go ahead and address the following concern as well: "Given that strategy cannot change instantaneously, why do we need information on a minute-by-minute basis?"

Submit your request to your professor.

Quiz questions are assignable in WileyPLUS, and available on the Book Companion Site at http://www.wiley.com/college/rainer.

RUBY'S CLUB QUESTIONS

1. Dashboards are very nice, but seem very complex to create. Do you think graphs and charts in Excel could be as effective as the elaborate dashboard examples provided in the chapter?

2. What type of chart do you think would be beneficial in tackling the problem of shrinkage? Would it be a bar chart? Pie chart? Line chart? How could this be developed in Excel?

5.5 Business Intelligence in Action: Corporate Performance Management

Corporate performance management (CPM) is involved with monitoring and managing an organization's performance according to *key performance indicators* (KPIs) such as revenue, return on investment (ROI), overhead, and operational costs. For online businesses, CPM includes additional factors such as the number of page views, server load, network traffic, and transactions per second. BI applications allow managers and analysts to analyze data to obtain valuable information and insights concerning the organization's KPIs.

— BEFORE YOU GO ON . . . —

1. What is corporate performance management?
2. How do BI applications contribute to corporate performance management?

Apply the Concept 5.5

Background Key performance indicators (KPIs) are defined by management as the key ratios or numbers that it needs to watch to be sure the company is staying on track according to the managers' strategy. Once these are determined (often through data mining), dashboards can be created so that management can look at and understand current trends and performance measures.

Activity Visit http://www.wiley.com/go/rainer/applytheconcept and click on the link provided for Apply the Concept 5.5. It will take you to a YouTube video titled "Introduction to Dashboards" by user "asutraining." Also visit the site mentioned in the video (also provided at http://www.wiley.com/go/rainer/applytheconcept) and look at the dashboard descriptions. At the time of this writing, the "factbook" (on the left-hand side of the Web site) was in the public domain. Click on this link and look through the data. As you watch the video and review the Web site, consider the following questions:

1. Why does Arizona State University (ASU) have a procedure in place to grant access to its dashboards?
2. Would you be able to get access?
3. How important is the use of color in a dashboard?
4. Why a summary page and a data page?

Deliverable

Write a small report to the vice president of academic affairs at ASU (do not send it of course) that details of your findings. Outline the past trends, the current situations, and the future possibilities for the vice-president. Explain how the dashboard proved helpful in your report. Submit it to your instructor.

Quiz questions are assignable in WileyPLUS, and available on the Book Companion Site at http://www.wiley.com/college/rainer.

What's in for ME?

FOR THE ACCOUNTING MAJOR

BI is used extensively in auditing to uncover irregularities. It is also used to uncover and prevent fraud. CPAs use BI for many of their duties, ranging from risk analysis to cost control.

FOR THE FINANCE MAJOR

People have been using computers for decades to solve financial problems. Innovative BI applications have been created for activities such as making stock market decisions, refinancing bonds, assessing debt risks, analyzing financial conditions, predicting business failures, forecasting financial trends, and investing in global markets.

FOR THE MARKETING MAJOR

Marketing personnel utilize BI in many applications, from planning and executing marketing campaigns to allocating advertising budgets to evaluating alternative routings of salespeople. New marketing approaches such as targeted marketing and database marketing are heavily dependent on IT in general and on data warehouses and BI applications in particular.

FOR THE

PRODUCTION/OPERATIONS MANAGEMENT MAJOR

BI supports complex operations and production decisions, from inventory control to production planning to supply chain integration.

FOR THE

HUMAN RESOURCES MANAGEMENT MAJOR

Human resources personnel use BI for many of their activities. For example, BI applications can find résumés of applicants posted on the Web and sort them to match needed skills and to support management succession planning.

FOR THE MIS MAJOR

MIS provides the data infrastructure used in BI. MIS personnel are also involved in building, deploying, and supporting BI applications.

SUMMARY

1. **Explain different ways in which IT supports managerial decision making.**

When making a decision, either organizational or personal, the decision maker goes through a three-step process: intelligence, design, and choice. When the choice is made, the decision is implemented.

Several information technologies have been successfully used to directly support managers. Collectively, they are referred to as business intelligence information systems. Figure 5.2 provides a matrix that shows how technology supports the various types of decisions that managers must make.

2. **Provide examples of different ways that organizations make use of BI.**

> *The development of a single or a few related BI applications.* This BI target is often a point solution for a departmental need, such as campaign management in marketing. A data mart is usually created to store necessary data.

> *The development of infrastructure to support enterprise-wide BI.* This target supports current and future BI needs. A critical component is an enterprise data warehouse.

> *Support for organizational transformation.* With this target, BI is used to fundamentally change how a company competes in the marketplace. BI supports a new business model and enables the business strategy.

3. **Explain the value that different BI applications provide to large and small businesses.**

Users have a variety of BI applications available to help them analyze data. These applications include multidimensional analysis, data mining, and decision support systems.

Multidimensional analysis, also called online analytical processing (OLAP), involves "slicing and dicing" data stored in a dimensional format, drilling down to greater data detail, and aggregating data. Data mining refers to the process of searching for valuable business information in a large database, data warehouse, or data mart. Decision support systems (DSS) combine models and data in an attempt to analyze semistructured and some unstructured problems with extensive user involvement. (The examples of using each application at your university, we leave to you.)

4. **Offer examples of how businesses and government agencies can use different BI applications to analyze data.**

A dashboard provides easy access to timely information and direct access to management reports. A geographic information system (GIS) is a computer-based system for capturing, integrating, manipulating, and displaying data using digitized maps. Reality mining analyzes information extracted from the usage patterns of mobile phones and other wireless devices. (Examples of how these technologies might be used by businesses and government agencies, we leave to you.)

5. **Explain how your university could use CPM to effect solutions to two campus problems.**

CPM is involved with monitoring and managing an organization's performance according to key performance indicators (KPIs) such as revenue, return on investment (ROI), overhead, and operational costs. (An example of how your university might use CPM, we leave to you.)

>>> CHAPTER GLOSSARY

business intelligence A broad category of applications, technologies, and processes for gathering, storing, accessing, and analyzing data to help business users make better decisions.

corporate performance management The area of business intelligence involved with monitoring and managing an organization's performance, according to key performance indicators (KPIs) such as revenue, return on investment (ROI), overhead, and operational costs.

dashboard A BI application that provides rapid access to timely information and direct access to management reports.

data mining The process of searching for valuable business information in a large database, data warehouse, or data mart.

decision A choice among two or more alternatives that individuals and groups make.

decision support systems (DSS) Business intelligence systems that combine models and data in an attempt to solve semistructured and some unstructured problems with extensive user involvement.

geographic information system A computer-based system for capturing, integrating, manipulating, and displaying data using digitized maps.

management A process by which organizational goals are achieved through the use of resources.

models (in decision making) Simplified representations, or abstractions, of reality.

online analytical processing (OLAP) (or multidimensional data analysis) A set of capabilities for "slicing and dicing" data using dimensions and measures associated with the data.

reality mining Extraction by analysts of information from the usage patterns of mobile phones and other wireless devices.

>>> DISCUSSION QUESTIONS

1. Your company is considering opening a new factory in China. List several typical activities involved in each phase of the decision (intelligence, design, and choice).

2. Recall that data mining found that young men tend to buy beer and diapers at the same time when they shop at a convenience store. Now that you know this relationship exists, can you provide a rationale for it?

3. American Can Company announced that it was interested in acquiring a company in the health maintenance organization (HMO) field. Two decisions were involved in this act: (1) the decision to acquire an HMO and (2) the decision of which HMO to acquire. How can the company use BI to assist it in this endeavor?

4. Discuss the strategic benefits of BI systems.

5. Will BI replace business analysts? (*Hint:* See W. McKnight, "Business Intelligence: Will Business Intelligence Replace the Business Analyst?" *DMReview*, February 2005).

>>> PROBLEM-SOLVING ACTIVITIES

1. The city of London (United Kingdom) charges an entrance fee for automobiles and trucks into the central city district. About a thousand digital cameras photograph the license plate of every vehicle passing by. Computers read the plate numbers and match them against records in a database of cars for which the fee has been paid for that day. If the computer does not find a match, the car owner receives a citation by mail. Examine the issues pertaining to how this process is accomplished, the mistakes it can make, and the consequences of those

mistakes. Also examine how well the system is working by checking press reports. Finally, relate the process to business intelligence.

2. Enter www.cognos.com and visit the demos on the right side of the page. Prepare a report on the various features shown in each demo.

3. Enter www.fico.com and find products for fraud detection and risk analysis. Prepare a report.

4. Enter www.teradatastudentnetwork.com (TSN) (you will need a password) and find the paper titled "Data Warehousing Supports Corporate Strategy at First American Corporation" (by Watson, Wixom, and Goodhue). Read the paper and answer the following questions:

   a. What were the drivers for the data warehouse/business intelligence project in the company?

   b. What strategic advantages were realized?

   c. What were the critical success factors for the project?

5. Access http://www.wiley.com/go/rainer/problemsolving to find the video of Hans Rosling's presentation. Comment on his data visualization techniques.

6. Enter www.visualmining.com. Explore the relationship between visualization and business intelligence. See how business intelligence is related to dashboards.

7. Access http://www.wiley.com/go/rainer/problemsolving. Identify all types of business intelligence software. Join a discussion group about topics discussed in this chapter. Prepare a report.

8. Visit the sites of some GIS vendors (such as www.mapinfo.com, www.esri.com, or www.autodesk.com). Download a demo. What are some of the most important capabilities and applications?

9. Analyze Microsoft Virtual Earth (www.microsoft.com/virtualearth) as a business intelligence tool. (*Hint:* Access http://www.wiley.com/rainer/go/problemsolving. What are the business intelligence features of this product?

>>> COLLABORATION EXERCISE

Background

In this chapter a company named MicroStrategy has come up multiple times. This business offers many products for business use that are intended to help companies manage and interpret their data. One of these products is a free tool called "MicroStrategy Cloud Personal" where you can upload your own data and let MicroStrategy software create reports for you. Go to http://www.wiley.com/go/rainer/collaboration and click the link provided. It will take you to Microstrategy's Web site explaining some "cloud" tools available for personal data analysis.

Activity

Work with a team to create data on the money you spend on food for a week. Have each team member create 10 rows of data in a spreadsheet. You will first have to agree on the type of data you will create and the column titles so everyone's data will match up. Once you all create your data points, combine them into one spreadsheet and upload it into the MicroStrategy Personal Cloud.

Deliverable

Share your work with your teammates. Let everyone on the team have some time to look through the data and then compile a report for your professor based on the data your team put together. Be sure to include images of your graphs and reports. Is there anything in this analysis that surprises you? Did you determine if you should change any habits based on this work?

CLOSING **CASE 1** > Procter & Gamble Uses Analytics in Novel Ways

Procter & Gamble (www.pg.com), the world's largest consumer products company with $79 billion in sales and 127,000 employees, manages massive streams of data in order to effectively operate its global business. The company has been forecasting its profits on a monthly basis for about 40 years, trying to predict components such as sales, commodity prices, and exchange rates. Before P&G deployed new information technologies, decisions took weeks or months, because data had to be manually gathered, collated, and channeled through various committees before reaching high-level company executives.

<<< **THE PROBLEM**

THE IT >>> SOLUTION

Today, P&G uses high-speed networks, data visualization, and high-speed analysis on multiple streams of data and information. More efficient software and increased computing power has vastly increased the amount of real-time data that P&G can process compared to what IT could do previously. In order to make better, faster decisions, P&G implemented the information technologies Business Sphere, the Immersion Lab, and the Handshake Room.

P&G implemented Business Sphere early in 2011. Business Sphere is an umbrella technology that integrates 14 different technologies from multiple vendors. The room contains two huge monitors, which give the executives a visual of the 4 billion times each day that P&G products are used in more than 80 countries.

In the Immersion Lab, another information technology employed by P&G, managers work in a mock hotel room where they try out many different mobile devices, building confidence that their employees can work anywhere on any type of phone or tablet.

In the Handshake Room, P&G solves customers' business problems and makes sales. The Handshake Room provides virtual store simulations with two screens along one wall. One of the screens, about 8 feet square, shows blank store shelves onto which can be projected three-dimensional images of any P&G product that a manager might want to stock in any size or label configuration. Another monitor shows store interiors of big retailers such as Walmart and Safeway. P&G can insert any new store display into these views so buyers can observe the display's look and its effect on store flow.

THE RESULTS >>>

P&G's executives hold their meetings in the Business Sphere at the company's headquarters. In four clicks on a tablet computer, they can change the image on a screen from a view of a world map to a graph of toothpaste prices in India with a sales comparison that shows local brands are gaining market share. A few clicks on another computer can bring up a view of shampoo sales in Australia, which renders it immediately apparent that P&G will need to sell 585,000 more cases of shampoo for sales just to break even. Yet another view might indicate big opportunities for hair care in Germany and pet food in the United States.

One of the great advantages of the Business Sphere is that from day 1, it enabled managers in some 40 locations worldwide to see the exact same data. This data consistency meant that everyone can recognize and agree upon target countries, regions, or products for particular attention. Everyone can also easily judge the company's progress against its strategic plan and inroads made against the competition, in some cases even down to individual retailers.

The Business Sphere also enables P&G executives and managers to make decisions in minutes based on data provided. All information about sales is now decided at the executive level each week and production is viewed in near real time worldwide. The company is also increasing the amount of data collected by a factor of seven.

The Immersion Lab allows P&G managers to test various information technologies to ensure that they will work on whatever device an employee prefers. P&G analysts are also testing various tools that could allow employees to collaborate more effectively, such as wikis (discussed in detail in Chapter 8) for project management.

In the Handshake Room, P&G analysts ask customers to present a business problem. The analysts use the technology in the room to present a solution to the problem, and often make a sale on the spot.

Sources: Compiled from C. Murphy, "How to Get One Version of the Truth," *InformationWeek*, November 7, 2011; D. Henschen, "P&G Turns Analysis into Action," *InformationWeek*, September 14, 2011; Q. Hardy, "The Matrix of Soap," *Forbes*, August 22, 2011; Q. Hardy, "At Procter & Gamble Toothpaste is Data," *Forbes*, August 3, 2011; www.pg.com, accessed February 25, 2012.

Questions

1. Why is the Business Sphere so important to P&G executives? Provide examples to support your answer.
2. Why is the Handshake Room so important in gaining new business for P&G? Provide examples to support your answer.

CLOSING **CASE 2** > Predictive Policing

In the city of Santa Cruz, California, there were 160 car thefts and 495 burglaries in 2011. For a city of 60,000, those numbers are average. Nonetheless, the Santa Cruz police force (SCPD) faces significant challenges. Since 2001, the SCPD has had to lay off 10 of its 104 officers, despite a citywide population growth in the city of 5,500 people. Therefore, the department now has to do more with less.

<<< **THE PROBLEM**

Since 2001, property crime in Santa Cruz decreased by 29 percent and violent crime decreased by 39 percent. At the end of 2011, both types of crime were at their lowest levels since 1973, when the collection of systematic nationwide data was instituted. Many factors—for example, an aging population and increased incarceration rates—have contributed to these decreases. However, most criminologists believe the major reason for these decreases to be the intelligence now available to the SCPD based on data analysis.

On July 1, 2011, the SCPD changed the way it fights crime. The department began using a new information system that provides intelligence to the police about when and where future crimes were most likely to take place and how officers could be deployed to prevent those crimes. The information system consists of a sophisticated algorithm (software) that analyzes large sets of data. This approach is called predictive policing.

<<< **THE IT SOLUTION**

The algorithm is based on one used by seismologists to predict earthquakes. It targets property crime such as home burglaries, car break-ins, and vehicle thefts. Such crimes tend to cluster and spread in a way that is similar to tremors after a large earthquake.

The algorithm identifies hot spots, which are 500-foot-by-500-foot areas at the highest risk for property crimes. The SCPD then divides the city into five regions, with at least one car on duty in each. Officers pick up their hot spot maps at the roll call meeting that precedes each shift. Each map contains a hot spot. Above each map is a set of statistics: the probability that a crime will take place in that hot spot that day; the two hour-long windows when that potential crime is most likely to occur; and the likelihood that the crime will be a property crime.

Before the software was implemented, individual officers had to decide where and how to focus their time when on patrol based on their own limited experience of the area. After the implementation, officers were able to clearly identify hot spots based on the maps they received and then make a concerted effort to heavily patrol those areas.

The impacts of the new information system on crime in Santa Cruz are promising, although it is too early for them to be conclusive. By the end of July 2011, property crime was down 27 percent from the year before, an impressive drop, particularly given the 25 percent rise in the first 6 months of the year. Furthermore, seven criminals had been discovered inside the hot spots.

<<< **THE RESULTS**

One afternoon at a hot spot, two women were detained after they were caught looking into cars in a triple-decker parking garage. One had an outstanding warrant out for her arrest for previous possession of methamphetamines and the other was caught in possession of meth on the site. At another hot spot, police officers stopped a man for suspicious behavior. When they searched him, they found stolen goods from a burglary that had taken place nearby a few days before. These arrests point to the effectiveness of the SCPD's new predictive policing system.

Predictive policing saves Santa Cruz money. For every crime prevented by the police, they save the costs they would have incurred of processing and booking the perpetrators, detaining them if need be prior to trial, trying them in court, and housing them in correctional institutions postconviction.

When predictive policing was first introduced in Santa Cruz in July 2011, some police officers thought it sounded like "voodoo magic." Relying on mathematics and statistics to combat property crime ran counter to many officers' ideas of police work. Some officers took it as an affront to their skills. Others were concerned that it would mean extra work. However, many officers came around when they realized that driving through a 500-by-500-foot hot spot during an hour-long window requires very little effort in, for quite a lot of result out. This favorable result-to-effort ratio perfectly exemplifies the impact of intelligence systems on various organizations, businesses, and government operations. Small, directed efforts, guided and informed by intelligence systems, can bring about great change.

Sources: Compiled from B. Gourley, "Predictive Policing with Big Data," *Cloud Computing Journal*, February 26, 2012; L. Eldridge, "Predictive Policing Is Not 'Minority Report'...At Least Not Yet," *PoliceOne.com*, January 13, 2012; R. King, "IBM Analytics Help Memphis Cops Get 'Smart,'" *Bloomberg BusinessWeek*, December 5, 2011; K. Thompson, "The Santa Cruz Experiment," *Popular Science*, November, 2011; L. Brokaw, "Predictive Policing: Working the Odds to Prevent Future Crimes," *Sloan Management Review*, September 12, 2011; J. Rubin, "Stopping Crime Before It Starts," *The Los Angeles Times*, August 21, 2011; E. Goode, "Sending the Police Before There's a Crime," *The New York Times*, August 15, 2011; www.cityofsantacruz.com, accessed February 26, 2012.

Questions

1. What are the advantages of predictive policing to the city of Santa Cruz? Provide specific examples.
2. What are potential disadvantages of predictive policing to the city of Santa Cruz? To the SCPD? Provide specific examples.
3. Which of the following choices best describes predictive policing? (1) A way to catch criminals; (2) a way to prevent crimes from happening; or (3) both? Support your answer.

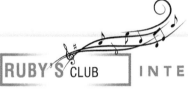

RUBY'S CLUB   INTERNSHIP ASSIGNMENT

Go to http://www.wiley.com/go/rainer/rubysclub and look for the links provided for Chapter 5. You will find Ruben and Lisa's spreadsheet from last year as well as some video tutorials that deal with using Excel for a goal-seeking analysis.

The spreadsheet includes data on cover sales, food sales, and drink sales for each week. It also provides information on the type of music (genre, band, DJ, etc.) that was playing and what other type of events may have been going on that week.

Your task will be to use Excel as a platform for creating BI and to provide Ruben and Lisa with projected profit margin that will be required to meet their goals depending on their level of sales. This will then determine how closely they need to monitor shrinkage.

Assume that total sales (drink+food+cover) are $425000 for their first year back open. To achieve the $300,000 net profit goal, what will their profit margin have to be? Compare this to the profit margin from their last year open (net profit was $150,000 and sales data is in the spreadsheet). Will they need to be more efficient with regard to shrinkage? If so, how much?

Finally, write a business letter to Ruben and Lisa to help them understand their sales and profit margin goals for the coming year. Submit your spreadsheet along with your letter.

SPREADSHEET ACTIVITY: LINKING SHEETS WITH FORMULAS

Objective: The objective of this activity is to help you understand that while spreadsheets are powerful, an interconnected workbook is even more so. You will learn how to write formulae that use information contained in different pages to help tie the workbook together.

Chapter Connection: Even though the opening case makes the point that spreadsheets are antiquated and often not able to keep up with the vast amounts of data needed to run an organization, spreadsheets still occupy an important place in smaller organizations. This activity brings business intelligence to the smaller mom-and-pop organizations.

Activity: As you have seen, business intelligence is a huge concept. It can, however, also apply in much smaller ways to everyday business. Business intelligence can help small mom-and-pop organizations in tremendous ways. Consider the following example.

Ted is a 45-year-old full-time accountant. He loves his job and has had quite a successful career. He also takes great pride in working with his hands. Specifically, he has always enjoyed working with wood and making small rocking horses for children. For years he just made these for family and friends, but lately he has decided to start selling his work. The accountant side of him has kept detailed records of his inventory, costs, sales, hours, profits, losses, and so on. Now it is time to take his workbook and create business intelligence out of it.

Ted's spreadsheet contains some basic information but no formulas. Notes describe what he has done and the decisions he wants to make. You can download the spreadsheet from http://www. wiley.com/go/rainer/spreadsheet (look for Chapter 5 links). Specifically, Ted wants to know how much he has invested in each rocking horse. His time,

materials, advertising, and other costs will definitely make a difference in his final price. Keep in mind that the point of this spreadsheet is to provide business intelligence. Although spreadsheet skills are required, they are the means to the end of helping Ted set appropriate prices.

Deliverable: The final product will be a spreadsheet with Ted's data calculated to provide business intelligence in a small business scenario.

Discussion Questions:

1. How does algebra play a role in writing formulas?

2. What happens to your data if you build a formula off of a previously incorrect formula?

3. If formulas are set up to predict or forecast (such as in regression), how many scenarios could be calculated?

Quiz questions are assignable in WileyPLUS, and available on the Book Companion Site at http://www.wiley.com/college/rainer.

DATABASE ACTIVITY: USING PIVOT TABLES

Objective

To learn how to turn a database into a *pivot table*, which is a structured representation of the database content that lets you observe the relationships of any data field, or group of data fields, to others.

CHAPTER CONNECTION

In this chapter, you read how information systems can be used for better decisions. Most of what you read discussed specialized tools for organizing and presenting data. These are found mostly in medium-large organizations and up. What's a small business to do?

Even a small business can use a database management system (DBMS) to organize and store information. In this module, we will see one way to use an Access database to support decision making: the pivot table.

This is a small-scale example of business intelligence (section 5.2) and a BI application (section 5.3).

PREREQUISITES

None.

Activity

In this activity, which you will find online at http://www.wiley.com/go/rainer/database, you will use a sales database for a group of computer stores. You will analyze it for differences among stores, for trends, and to see how the group could improve sales.

1. Download the **Ch 05 CarlaComputerStores** database from http://www.wiley.com/go/rainer/database and open it.

2. Open the OrderQry query by clicking on it in the Navigation Pane at the left of the Access window.

Usage Hint: If you do not see the navigation pane, but the words "Navigation Pane" run vertically at the far left of the window, click on those words or on the » above them to expand it.

Usage Hint: Depending on how your copy of Access is set up, navigation pane items may open with a single or double click. If a single click does not work, double-click. If you are using your own copy, you can set this preference in Options under the File tab. In the Current Database section, click "Navigation Options... ."

You will see what looks like a table with information about every sale since in this database. (Its first few rows are shown below.) As you will learn in the Chapter 10 activity, this "table" is not stored in the database. It is created as needed by combining data from other tables in a *query*. Those other tables are listed under Tables in the navigation pane. You can see how they are related to each other by clicking "Relationships" in the Database Tools ribbon.

OrderQry		
StoreCity ▾	CustName ▾	OrderPrice ▾
Atlanta	Alice	$399.00
Atlanta	Alice	$438.99
Atlanta	Alice	$958.98
Atlanta	Alice	$1,737.98
Atlanta	Emily	$788.97
Atlanta	Emily	$549.94
Atlanta	Gladys	$1,137.97

These tables are a simplified version of what a real store would use. For example, a real database would include order date and method of payment. However, this database has purchase history: what each customer bought, when, at what store, and with what other items. That is what we will use here.

3. To analyze customer spending, look at this query in Pivot Table view. Select that view from the drop-down View menu at the left of the Home ribbon, or click the second icon from the left at the bottom right of the window.

Usage Hint: Access often provides multiple ways to do something. It usually does not matter which you choose. As you use Access more, you will develop preferences. They do not have to be the same as anyone else's.

4. A windoid labeled "Pivot Table Field List" floats above the main Access window. It lists all the fields in the query, plus other items that can be derived from them. You will drag these into sections of the pivot table pane to analyze the data.

Usage Hint: If you do not see the Field List windoid, click the Field List icon in the Show/Hide section toward the left end of the ribbon, under the Design tab.

Let's see if there are differences in order size among stores. Drag OrderPrice into the main area of the pane, labeled "Drop Totals or Detail Fields Here."

5. You will see all the order amounts in the central section of the pivot table. It is useless by itself. In terms of Chapter 1 concepts, it is data, not information. To organize them by store, drag StoreCity into the "Drop Row Fields Here" area at the left of the pane.

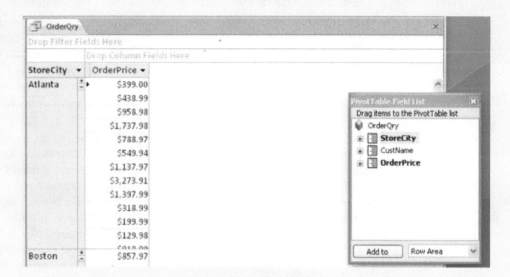

6. We want to see the average order size for each store. Select the OrderPrice column by clicking on its header. Then click the AutoCalc icon on the Design ribbon (Σ, the uppercase Greek letter sigma, a common mathematical symbol for summation). From the drop-down menu, select Average. You will see each store's average order size below the list of orders.

Usage Hint: The overall average is labeled "Grand Total." In everyday language, a "total" is what you get when you add several numbers. Access refers to that concept as a *sum*. To Access, a "total" is any summary calculation: sum, average, count, or any of the others listed under the AutoCalc icon.

Which city has the highest average sales? The lowest?

7. Suppose we only care about averages, not individual sales. To hide the details, select that column again and click "Hide Details" in the Show/Hide area at the left of the Design ribbon. "Show Details" in the same section will toggle them back on. You can hide or show details for one store by clicking "−" (hide) or "+" (show) under the store's city.

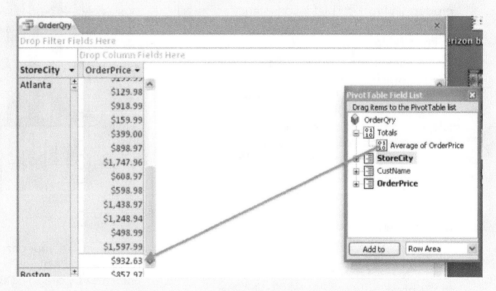

StoreCity ▼	Average of OrderPrice
Atlanta	$932.63
Boston	$832.86
Chicago	$871.29
Denver	$989.55
Grand Total	$898.81

8. This is called a "pivot table" because you can *pivot* data from the top to the left and vice versa to make it easier to analyze. Drag the StoreCity label from its current position, above the city names, to the "Drop Column Fields Here" area at the top of the table. Hide and show details. See how the display changes.

Usage Hint: If you get an error message when you move the label, delete one of the totals and re-create it. To delete a total, right-click it in the field list and select Delete, the only item in the drop-down menu that appears..

9. Select Show Details, if they are not already showing, to display order prices. Select it by clicking OrderPrice near the top of any city column. Under AutoCalc, display the sum and the count. One store has the highest total sales but the smallest average sale. Why?

10. Close the query, saving changes when prompted.

11. We want to analyze our sales by city. Open ItemsQry. The TotPrice column in this table is not in the database. It is a calculated field: it is derived on the fly by multiplying the price of the product (in ProductTbl, for consistency across all orders) and the quantity in a given order. Switch to Pivot Table view.

Usage Hint: If you are curious about how calculated fields work, switch to Design View of the query and look at the rightmost column in the lower pane. You will have to make the column wider to see the entire formula, but it is not complicated.

   Now, move TotPrice into the main section of the pivot table pane and StoreCity into the Row Fields section. Select TotPrice in the pivot table, add its sum, and click Hide Details in the Show/Hide section of the ribbon.

12. It seems that Boston sold more during the period than any of the other stores. To find out why, we must *drill down* into the data. (Drilling down is central to most data analysis.) Add ProdCategory to the pivot table as a column field. What you get should look like this:

StoreCity	ProdCategory	Sum of TotPrice
Atlanta	CPU	$7,889.00
	Display	$2,851.00
	Memory	$959.87
	Portable	$4,891.00
	Printer	$2,419.89
	Storage	$2,439.68
	Total	$21,450.44
Boston	CPU	$10,085.00

Usage Hint: If your product categories ended up to the left of the city names, just select its name at the top of the column and drag it to the right until a thick blue line shows up to the right of the StoreCity column. Then release your mouse button.

13. You realize that this table is not easy to interpret. A chart would be better. Choose Pivot Chart view from the drop-down menu at the left end of the ribbon, or click the Pivot Chart icon at the bottom right of the Access window. Add a legend with the tool in the Show/Hide section of the Design ribbon.

14. You now realize that this is not the ideal chart design. It tells us that Atlanta, for example, got more revenue from CPUs than from memory, but anyone who knows computers would expect that. We would like to know how Atlanta compares with other stores in terms of memory revenue. Click Switch Row/Column in the Active Field section of the Design ribbon. You should get a chart whose lower left corner looks like this:

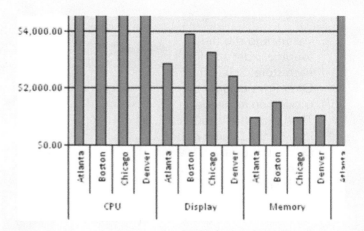

Usage Hint: If your chart does not look like this, try returning to Pivot Table view, swapping categories and cities by dragging one column past the other, and returning to the chart. You may have to switch chart row and columns again.

15. From the part of this chart above the screen shot, we see that Chicago's CPU sales are a concern. Before calling the Chicago store manager, however, we need to do more research. Go back to PivotTable view and drag ProdDescrip into the row field area. Each category will be broken down by product. To see only products in the CPU category, click the down arrow next to ProdCategory to get a list of categories to filter. Uncheck everything except CPU and confirm.

Usage Hint: Rather than unchecking all the categories except the one we care about, it is easier to uncheck everything by clicking "All," then check "CPU."

16. Now look at the chart again. The Chicago store did not sell any SuperCPUs! Its sales of the three slower models are more or less in line with expectations. We do not know the reason for this, of course. Maybe there are few gamers and graphic artists in the store's sales area. (These are two major markets for top-of-the-line systems.) Maybe the Chicago store ran a promotion for these during an earlier period and most of its potential customers bought one then. Maybe a competitor is running such a promo now. We do know, however, what we want to ask when we call the Chicago store manager.

17. Close your database, saving changes when prompted.

Deliverable

1. Your database, with the most recent pivot table and chart.

2. Answers to the questions in items 6 and 9 above, in the form specified by your instructor.

Quiz Questions

1. In step 6, which store had the highest average order amount?

   (a) Atlanta

   (b) Boston

   (c) Chicago

   (d) Denver

2. A pivot table is a way of looking at this type of Access object:

   (a) Query

   (b) Table

   (c) Form

   (d) Either A or B

   (e) Either B or C

3. The central section of the pivot table pane contains this type of information:

   (a) Names of pivot table categories

   (b) Summary data for pivot table cells

   (c) Individual data elements from the database, but not totals

   (d) Links to the underlying Access tables

4. If a pivot table has only one column (that is, it has categories down the left but none across the top), then:

   (a) You can create categories across the top by dragging categories from the side.

   (b) You can create categories across the top by dragging new table fields into the "Drag Colum Fields Here" area.

   (c) You can analyze data in that column without having fields across the top.

   (d) All of the above are correct.

Discussion Questions

1. How could pivot tables be useful for someone in the kind of job you hope to have after you graduate? (Say what that job is.)

2. Describe a business decision for which pivot tables would *not* be helpful. Explain why you don't think they would help with it.

3. Suppose you worked for a large chain of photo stores. Your database has millions of rows with a few dozen columns in each, but its structure is much like this one. Would that change your approach to using pivot tables? If so, how? (Assume your computer is fast enough that the database size does not cause slow response times. In practice, that might not be true.)

Additional Resources

The ten-minute video at http://www.wiley.com/rainer/go/database is an excellent resource for this activity. As you watch it, keep in mind that Access has many ways to do almost anything. Matthew MacDonald does not always do things exactly as we did here. You can do them as he does them, as described here, and often in other ways as well.

6 | Ethics and Privacy

CHAPTER OUTLINE

LEARNING OBJECTIVES >>>

1. Describe the four categories of ethical issues related to information technology.

2. Discuss potential threats to the privacy of personal data stored in different locations.

You probably never thought of yourself as a lawbreaker, right? Most likely you would not go into a music store and steal a CD or DVD, or go into a bookstore and steal a book. But would you download something that you had not purchased? Would you copy a picture from someone else's Web site and claim it for your own? Would you download an article and try to customize it so that it did not appear to be plagiarized?

These issues are becoming more and more important as we move into the 21st century. Social networks are making it very easy to share and reshare information. So, who owns information that gets posted on the Internet? Consider one social network, Pinterest. Pinterest is a small business with only about 20 employees. It is primarily a technology company that provides infrastructure and software to users so that they can "pin" things they like. Realizing that many users would likely try to "pin" pictures or ideas that were not their own, they pre-empted the problem by writing into their user agreement that users could only pin pictures or ideas that were their own original work. Sounds simple enough, right?

Wrong. What happens when Pinterest users pin ideas that are not theirs? Pinterest is a small business and does not have the personnel to police every pin that its users make. And, of course, many Pinterest users do not adhere to the terms of the user agreement. So, given the facts of the case, who is at fault? Is Pinterest at fault? The company will revoke access if it catches users downloading copyrighted third-party material, but it does not have the manpower to effectively police this. Or, are the users who agree not to steal intellectual property but do so anyway the ones who are truly at fault? **> > >**

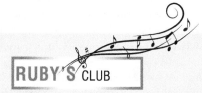

RUBY'S CLUB

Ruben and Lisa have never developed an ethics and privacy statement for their club. Honestly, they never thought they would need one. But with the new information systems that will collect customer data and establish memberships, they realize it is now imperative that they develop a statement of this type.

Ruben and Lisa have both seen privacy statements. They get them in the mail from their credit card companies and agree to them anytime they create their own memberships online. However, they have never really paid attention to them and now have a lot of questions about their own statements.

Obviously, they know they need to deal with how they will handle the privacy of online information. But they are unsure of how to deal with ethical issues in their club. Should they use their information systems to track the number of alcoholic beverages their customers purchase? If they do, is it ethical to limit a customer? Should they request a release form to continue to sell drinks after a certain point?

Use the information in this chapter to help them make these decisions.

Pinterest is just an example of a site that suffers from this dilemma. All social media sites have similar agreements and also experience a host of intellectual property issues. Is the main issue here that people do not care about user agreements? Do you think there will eventually be a legal "crackdown" in social media over ethical issues like there was with Napster a few years ago?

Sources: Compiled from T. Poletti, "Is Pinterest the Next Napster?" *The Wall Street Journal*, March 14, 2012; A. Prakash, "Exploring the Ethics of Pinterest," www.ohmyhandmade.com, March 14, 2012; www.pinterest.com, accessed March 9, 2012.

Questions

1. Who is at fault for the third-party copyright violations enabled by Pinterest? Pinterest or its users?
2. Compare the ethics of "pinning" on Pinterest with downloading music files on Napster. Do you think that Pinterest will face the same fate as Napster? Why or why not?

Introduction

You will study two major issues in this chapter: ethics and privacy. Both issues are closely related to IT and raise significant questions. For example, consider Chapter Closing Case 2. Are the actions of the Samwer brothers ethical? The answer to this question is not straightforward. In fact, IT has made finding answers to these questions even more difficult.

You will encounter numerous ethical and privacy issues in your career, many of which will involve IT in some manner. This chapter will give you insights into how to respond to these issues. Further, it will help you to make immediate contributions to your company's code of ethics and its privacy policies. You will also be able to provide meaningful input concerning the potential ethical and privacy impacts of your organization's information systems on people inside and outside the organization.

For example, suppose your organization decides to adopt Web 2.0 technologies (presented in Chapter 8) to include business partners and customers in new product development. You will be able to analyze the potential privacy and ethical implications of implementing these technologies.

6.1 Ethical Issues

Ethics refers to the principles of right and wrong that individuals use to make choices that guide their behaviors. Deciding what is right or wrong is not always easy or clear-cut. Fortunately, many frameworks are available to help us make ethical decisions.

Ethical Frameworks

There are many sources for ethical standards. Here we consider four widely used standards: the utilitarian approach, the rights approach, the fairness approach, and the common good approach. There are many other sources, but these four are representative.

The *utilitarian approach* states that an ethical action is the one that provides the most good or does the least harm. The ethical corporate action would be the one that produces the greatest good and does the least harm for all affected parties—customers, employees, shareholders, the community, and the environment.

The *rights approach* maintains that an ethical action is the one that best protects and respects the moral rights of the affected parties. Moral rights can include the rights to make one's own choices about what kind of life to lead, to be told the truth, not to be injured, and to a degree of privacy. Which of these rights people are actually entitled to—and under what circumstances—is widely debated. Nevertheless, most people acknowledge that individuals are entitled to some moral rights. An ethical organizational action would be one

© AlexMax/iStockphoto

All ethical frameworks attempt to balance good for all. (*Source:* maxstockphoto/Shutterstock)

Figure 6.1 General framework for ethical decision making.

that protects and respects the moral rights of customers, employees, shareholders, business partners, and even competitors.

The *fairness approach* posits that ethical actions treat all human beings equally, or, if unequally, then fairly, based on some defensible standard. For example, most people might believe it is fair to pay people higher salaries if they work harder or if they contribute a greater amount to the firm. However, there is less certainty regarding CEO salaries that are hundreds or thousands of times larger than those of other employees. Many people question whether this huge disparity is based on a defensible standard or whether it is the result of an imbalance of power and hence is unfair.

The *common good approach* highlights the interlocking relationships that underlie all societies. This approach argues that respect and compassion for all others is the basis for ethical actions. It emphasizes the common conditions that are important to the welfare of everyone. These conditions can include a system of laws, effective police and fire departments, health care, a public educational system, and even public recreation areas.

If we combine these four standards, we can develop a general framework for ethics or ethical decision making (Figure 6.1). This framework consists of five steps:

- Recognize an ethical issue.
  - Could this decision or situation damage someone or some group?
  - Does this decision involve a choice between a good and bad alternative?
  - Is this issue about more than what is legal? If so, how?
- Get the facts.
  - What are the relevant facts of the situation?
  - Do I know enough to make a decision?
  - Which individuals and/or groups have an important stake in the outcome?
  - Have I consulted all relevant persons and groups?
- Evaluate alternative actions.
  - Which option will produce the most good and do the least harm? (the utilitarian approach)
  - Which option best respects the rights of all stakeholders? (the rights approach)
  - Which option treats people equally or proportionately? (the fairness approach)
  - Which option best serves the community as a whole, and not just some members? (the common good approach)
- Make a decision and test it.
  - Considering all the approaches, which option best addresses the situation?
- Act and reflect on the outcome of your decision.
  - How can I implement my decision with the greatest care and attention to the concerns of all stakeholders?
  - How did my decision turn out, and what did I learn from this specific situation?

Now that we have created a general ethical framework, we will focus specifically on ethics in a corporate environment.

Ethics in the Corporate Environment

Many companies and professional organizations develop their own codes of ethics. A **code of ethics** is a collection of principles that are intended to guide decision making by members of the organization. For example, the Association for Computing Machinery (www.acm.org), an organization of computing professionals, has a thoughtful code of ethics for its members.

Keep in mind that different codes of ethics are not always consistent with one another. Therefore, an individual might be expected to conform to multiple codes. For example, a person who is a member of two large professional computing-related organizations may be

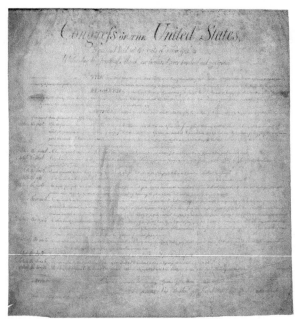

© Photri Images/SuperStock

The Bill of Rights is basically a legalized set of ethical standards. (*Source:* © Photri Images/SuperStock)

required by one organization to comply with all applicable laws and at the same time be required by the other organization to refuse to obey unjust laws.

Fundamental tenets of ethics include responsibility, accountability, and liability. **Responsibility** means that you accept the consequences of your decisions and actions. **Accountability** refers to determining who is responsible for actions that were taken. **Liability** is a legal concept that gives individuals the right to recover the damages done to them by other individuals, organizations, or systems.

Before you go any further, it is very important that you realize that what is *unethical* is not necessarily *illegal*. For example, a bank's decision to foreclose on a home can be technically legal, but it can raise many ethical questions. In many instances, then, an individual or organization faced with an ethical decision is not considering whether to break the law. As the foreclosure example illustrates, however, ethical decisions can have serious consequences for individuals, organizations, and society at large.

In recent years we have witnessed a large number of extremely poor ethical decisions, not to mention outright criminal behavior. During 2001 and 2002, three highly publicized fiascos occurred at Enron, WorldCom, and Tyco, respectively. At each company, executives were convicted of various types of fraud for using illegal accounting practices. These actions led to the passage of the Sarbanes-Oxley Act in 2002. Sarbanes-Oxley requires publicly held companies to implement financial controls and company executives to personally certify financial reports.

 More recently, the subprime mortgage crisis exposed unethical lending practices throughout the mortgage industry. The crisis also highlighted pervasive weaknesses in the regulation of the U.S. financial industry as well as the global financial system. It ultimately contributed to a deep recession in the global economy.

Improvements in information technologies have generated a new set of ethical problems. Computing processing power doubles about every two years, meaning that organizations are more dependent than ever before on their information systems. Organizations can store increasing amounts of data at decreasing cost, enabling them to store more data on individuals for longer periods of time. Computer networks, particularly the Internet, enable organizations to collect, integrate, and distribute enormous amounts of information on individuals, groups, and institutions. As a result, ethical problems are arising concerning the appropriate collection and use of customer information, personal privacy, and the protection of intellectual property, as IT's About Business 6.1 illustrates.

 IT'S ABOUT BUSINESS 6.1

Carrier IQ

Carrier IQ is a mobile software company that provides diagnostic analysis of smartphones to the wireless industry. The company produces software installed on over 150 million smartphones that logs everything their users do, from what Web sites they visit to what they say in their text messages. The software is a diagnostic tool that wireless carriers say plays a crucial role in helping them assess and troubleshoot their networks.

The problem with Carrier IQ was

© pictafolio/iStockphoto

that users did not initially know that the tracking application was on their smartphones. When security researchers drew attention to it at the end of 2011, privacy and security concerns exploded.

Interestingly, Carrier IQ's own privacy policy states, "When Carrier IQ's products are deployed, data gathering is done in a way where the end user is informed or involved." This policy statement is particularly interesting because the Carrier IQ tool runs without the knowledge of users and appears to be difficult, if not impossible, to uninstall.

On November 12, 2011, Android developer Trevor Eckhart stated in a post on http://androidsecuritytest.com that Carrier IQ was logging information such as location without notifying users or allowing them to opt out. That logged information included keystrokes, an inclusion that potentially violated U.S. federal law. On November 16, 2011, Carrier IQ sent Eckhart a cease-and-desist letter claiming he was making "false allegations" and infringing upon copyright by posting Carrier IQ training documents on his Web site. In response, Eckhart sought and received the backing of user rights advocacy group Electronic Frontier Foundation (EFF; www.eff.org).

On November 18, 2011, Eckhart published a YouTube video in which he showed Carrier IQ software in the act of logging as plain text, a variety of keystrokes. Included in the demonstration were clear text captures of passwords to otherwise secure Web sites, and activities performed when the cellular network was disabled. The video of the demonstration showed Carrier IQ's software processing keystrokes, browser data, and text messages' contents, but the video did not show that the information was transmitted.

On November 23, 2011, Carrier IQ backed down and apologized. In the statement of apology, Carrier IQ denied allegations of keystroke logging and other forms of tracking, and offered to work with the EFF.

Carrier IQ stated that the core purpose of its tool is to uncover broad trends across a network. Its software, for example, can help carriers find out where calls are dropping and why, and zero in on device glitches. For instance, if a specific handset has a battery life problem, Carrier IQ's tool can help find out why.

Sprint (www.sprint.com) said it uses Carrier IQ to uncover network problems. Sprint says that CarrierIQ collects enough information for them to understand "the customer experience" with devices on their network and to have an idea of how to address any connection problems. Sprint says that it does not, and in fact does not have the ability to, look at the contents of messages, photos, videos, etc., using the Carrier IQ tool.

One privacy advocate stated that Carrier IQ "does not seem as nefarious as incompetent, but that may not be enough to allay the legitimate concerns of the public." He went on to state that the enormous amount of data stored by the Carrier IQ tool on smartphones would be a "gold mine to a hacker."

On December 2, 2011, the controversy made its way into the courts. A lawsuit was filed in the U.S. District Court for the Northern District of California against Carrier IQ and phone makers Samsung and HTC, claiming that Carrier IQ's app violates customer privacy. Class-action lawsuits against Carrier IQ have been filed by the U.S. Department of Justice, the Federal Trade Commission, Massachusetts, and Missouri as well.

Sources: Compiled from J. Vijayan, "AT&T, Sprint Confirm Use of Carrier IQ Software on Handsets," *Computerworld*, December 1, 2011; D. Gross, "Fallout Continues Over Smartphone Tracking App," *CNN*, December 2, 2011; C. Albanesius, "Carrier IQ Controversy Results in Class-Action Suits," *PC Magazine*, December 2, 2011; M. Peckham, "Carrier IQ 'Wiretap' Debacle: Much Ado about Something?" *Time*, December 1, 2011; D. Goldman, "Carrier IQ: Your Phone's Secret Recording Device," *CNN Money*, December 1, 2011; A. Greenberg, "Phone 'Rootkit' Maker Carrier IQ May Have Violated Wiretap Law in Millions of Cases," *Forbes*, November 30, 2011; D. Kravets, "Researcher's Video Shows Secret Software on Millions of Phones Logging Everything," *Wired*, November 29, 2011; S. Shankland, "Carrier IQ Apologizes, Drops Threat to Security Researcher," *CNET News*, November 25, 2011; "The Rootkit of All Evil—CIQ," *MIT Technology Review*, November 17, 2011; R. Holly, "How Much of Your Phone Is Yours?" *Geek.com*, November 15, 2011; www.carrieriq.com, accessed March 14, 2012.

Questions

1. Describe the ethical implications of Carrier IQ software.

2. Describe the privacy implications of Carrier IQ software.

Ethics and Information Technology

All employees have a responsibility to encourage ethical uses of information and information technology. Many of the business decisions you will face at work will have an ethical dimension. Consider these decisions you might have to make:

- Should organizations monitor employees' Web surfing and e-mail?
- Should organizations sell customer information to other companies?

- Should organizations audit employees' computers for unauthorized software or illegally downloaded music or video files?

The diversity and ever-expanding use of IT applications have created a variety of ethical issues. These issues fall into four general categories: privacy, accuracy, property, and accessibility.

1. *Privacy issues* involve collecting, storing, and disseminating information about individuals.

2. *Accuracy issues* involve the authenticity, fidelity, and accuracy of information that is collected and processed.

3. *Property issues* involve the ownership and value of information.

4. *Accessibility issues* revolve around who should have access to information and whether they should have to pay for this access.

Table 6.1 lists representative questions and issues for each of these categories. In addition, Online Appendix W6.1 presents 14 ethics scenarios for you to consider. These scenarios will provide a context for you to consider situations that involve ethical or unethical behavior.

Many of the issues and scenarios we have examined, such as photo tagging and geotagging, involve privacy as well as ethics. In the next section, you will learn about privacy issues in more detail.

— BEFORE *YOU GO ON* . . . —

1. What does a code of ethics contain?
2. Describe the fundamental tenets of ethics.

TABLE 6.1 A Framework for Ethical Issues

- **Privacy Issues**
  - What information about oneself should an individual be required to reveal to others?
  - What kind of surveillance can an employer use on its employees?
  - What types of personal information can people keep to themselves and not be forced to reveal to others?
  - What information about individuals should be kept in databases and how secure is the information there?

- **Accuracy Issues**
  - Who is responsible for the authenticity, fidelity, and accuracy of the information collected?
  - How can we ensure that the information will be processed properly and presented accurately to users?
  - How can we ensure that errors in databases, data transmissions and data processing are accidental and not intentional?
  - Who is to be held accountable for errors in information and how should the injured parties be compensated?

- **Property Issues**
  - Who owns the information?
  - What are the just and fair prices for its exchange?
  - How should we handle software piracy (copying copyrighted software)?
  - Under what circumstances can one use proprietary databases?
  - Can corporate computers be used for private purposes?
  - How should experts who contribute their knowledge to create expert systems be compensated?
  - How should access to information channels be allocated?

- **Accessibility Issues**
  - Who is allowed to access information?
  - How much should companies charge for permitting accessibility to information?
  - How can accessibility to computers be provided for employees with disabilities?
  - Who will be provided with equipment needed for accessing information?
  - What information does a person or an organization have a right to obtain, under what conditions, and with what safeguards?

Apply the Concept 6.1

Background As you move into the business world, you need to be aware of the current trends and happenings dealing with the four areas of concern presented in Section 6.1 (privacy, property, accuracy, and accessibility). It is important that you are aware of these issues as you move into the business world because these are the exact issues you will have to deal with.

Activity Review various articles in mainstream, business, and IS/IT-related sources and identify articles with an IT ethical issue in the article. Mainstream sources might include *Time* magazine, *Newsweek*, and the local newspaper. Business sources might include the *Wall Street Journal* and *BusinessWeek*. IS/IT-related sources might include *Infoweek*, *InfoWorld*, and *Computerworld*.

Review (scan for the main topic) at least two articles from a mainstream source, a business source, and an IS/IT-related source, and then classify the articles based upon the four categories of ethical issues (privacy, property, accuracy, and accessibility) found in Section 6.1. Note that more than one category may apply to the same article.

Deliverable

Create a table to submit to your professor that identifies the following:

- Article's title
- Source of the article (mainstream, business, or IS/IT-related)
- Ethical category or categories in the article (they may fall into multiple areas)
- Summary of the article's main points
- Submit your report to your instructor.

Quiz questions are assignable in WileyPLUS, and available on the Book Companion Site at http://www.wiley.com/college/rainer.

RUBY'S CLUB QUESTIONS

1. Which framework do you think is the best for Ruby's Club: utilitarian, rights, fairness, or the common good? Why do you feel this way?

2. How do the concepts of responsibility, accountability, and liability play into the number of drinks an individual has consumed? At what point does Ruby's become responsible for the condition in which a customer leaves the club?

3. Because purchase does not necessarily equal consumption (perhaps the person is buying drinks for a friend), should Ruby's limit the number of drinks a customer can purchase?

6.2 Privacy

In general, **privacy** is the right to be left alone and to be free of unreasonable personal intrusions. **Information privacy** is the right to determine when, and to what extent, information about you can be gathered and/or communicated to others. Privacy rights apply to individuals, groups, and institutions.

The definition of privacy can be interpreted quite broadly. However, court decisions in many countries have followed two rules fairly closely:

1. The right of privacy is not absolute. Privacy must be balanced against the needs of society.

2. The public's right to know supersedes the individual's right of privacy.

These two rules illustrate why determining and enforcing privacy regulations can be difficult. The right to privacy is recognized today in all U.S. states and by the federal government, either by statute or common law.

Rapid advances in information technologies have made it much easier to collect, store, and integrate data on individuals in large databases. On an average day, you generate data about yourself in many ways: surveillance cameras on toll roads, in public places, and at work; credit card transactions; telephone calls (landline and cellular); banking transactions; queries to search engines; and government records (including police records). These data can be integrated to produce a **digital dossier**, which is an electronic profile of you and your habits. The process of forming a digital dossier is called **profiling**.

Data aggregators, such as LexisNexis (www.lexisnexis.com) and Acxiom (www.acxiom.com), are good examples of profiling. These companies collect public data such as real estate records and published telephone numbers, in addition to nonpublic information such as Social Security numbers, financial data, and police, criminal, and motor vehicle records. They then integrate these data to form digital dossiers on most adults in the United States. They ultimately sell these dossiers to law enforcement agencies and companies that conduct background checks on potential employees. They also sell them to companies that want to know their customers better, a process called *customer intimacy*.

However, data on individuals can be used in more controversial manners. For example, a controversial new map in California identifies the addresses of donors who supported Proposition 8, the referendum that outlawed same-sex marriage in California (see www.eightmaps.com). Gay activists created the map by combining Google's satellite mapping technology with publicly available campaign records that listed Proposition 8 donors who contributed $100 or more. These donors are outraged, claiming that the map invades their privacy and could expose them to retribution.

Electronic Surveillance

According to the American Civil Liberties Union (ACLU), tracking people's activities with the aid of computers has become a major privacy-related problem. The ACLU notes that this monitoring, or **electronic surveillance**, is rapidly increasing, particularly with the emergence of new technologies. Electronic surveillance is conducted by employers, the government, and other institutions.

In general, employees have very limited legal protection against surveillance by employers. The law supports the right of employers to read their employees' e-mail and other electronic documents and to monitor their employees' Internet use. Today, more than three-fourths of organizations are monitoring employees' Internet usage. In addition, two-thirds use software to block connections to inappropriate Web sites, a practice called *URL filtering*. Further, organizations are installing monitoring and filtering software to enhance security by stopping malicious software and to increase productivity by discouraging employees from wasting time.

In one organization, the chief information officer (CIO) monitored about 13,000 employees for three months to determine the type of traffic they engaged in on the network. He then forwarded the data to the chief executive officer (CEO) and the heads of the human resources and legal departments. These executives were shocked at the questionable Web sites the employees were visiting, as well as the amount of time they were spending on those sites. The executives quickly made the decision to implement a URL filtering product.

Surveillance is also a concern for private individuals regardless of whether it is conducted by corporations, government bodies, or criminals. Users in the United States are still struggling to define the appropriate balance between personal privacy and electronic surveillance, especially when threats to national security are involved.

Personal Information in Databases

Modern institutions store information about individuals in many databases. Perhaps the most visible locations of such records are credit-reporting agencies. Other institutions that store personal information include banks and financial institutions; cable TV, telephone, and utilities companies; employers; mortgage companies; hospitals; schools and universities; retail establishments; government agencies (such as the Internal Revenue Service, your state, your municipality); and many others.

© Pamela Moore/iStockphoto

Electronic surveillance of employees is legal, but not of customers. But would you do it if you could make money from the information?

There are several concerns about the information you provide to these record keepers. Some of the major concerns are these:

- Do you know where the records are?
- Are the records accurate?
- Can you change inaccurate data?
- How long will it take to make a change?
- Under what circumstances will personal data be released?
- How are the data used?
- To whom are the data given or sold?
- How secure are the data against access by unauthorized people?

Information on Internet Bulletin Boards, Newsgroups, and Social Networking Sites

Every day you see more and more *electronic bulletin boards*, *newsgroups*, *electronic discussions* such as chat rooms, and *social networking sites* (discussed in Chapter 8). These sites appear on the Internet, within corporate intranets, and on blogs. A *blog*, short for *Weblog*, is an informal, personal journal that is frequently updated and intended for general public reading. How does society keep owners of bulletin boards from disseminating information that may be offensive to readers or simply untrue? This is a difficult problem because it involves the conflict between freedom of speech on one hand and privacy on the other. This conflict is a fundamental and continuing ethical issue in U.S. society.

There is no better illustration of the conflict between free speech and privacy than the Internet. Many Web sites contain anonymous, derogatory information on individuals, who typically have little recourse in the matter. Approximately one-half of U.S. firms use the Internet in examining job applications, including searching for individuals on Google and on social networking sites. Consequently, derogatory information that can be found on the Internet can harm your chances of being hired. This problem has become serious enough that a company called Reputation Defender (www. reputationdefender.com) will search for damaging content online and destroy it on behalf of clients.

Social networking sites can also present serious privacy concerns. IT's About Business 6.2 takes a look at privacy problems arising as the U.S. government mines publicly available data on the Internet.

Privacy Codes and Policies

Privacy policies or **privacy codes** are an organization's guidelines for protecting the privacy of its customers, clients, and employees. In many corporations, senior management

IT'S ABOUT BUSINESS 6.2

Government Mines Publicly Available Internet Data

The Intelligence Advanced Research Projects Activity (IARPA; www.iarpa.gov) of the U.S. government is developing a project aimed at mining the vast resources of the Internet to predict the behavior of large groups of humans. IARPA utilizes automated data collection to gather publicly accessible data such as Web search queries, Twitter messages, Facebook entries, blog entries, Internet traffic flow, digital location trails generated by cell phones, financial market indicators, traffic webcams, and changes in Wikipedia entries. IARPA then utilizes this data to focus on patterns of communication, consumption, and population movement. IARPA's automated system will operate without human supervision. Its scope will not be limited to political and economic events, but will also explore the ability to predict pandemics and other types of widespread contagion.

A similar project by the Defense Advanced Research Projects Agency (DARPA), aims to automatically identify insurgent social networks in Afghanistan. DARPA argues that its analyses can expose terrorist cells and other groups not based in a particular country by tracking their meetings, rehearsals, and sharing of material and money transfers.

 Arguments rage on about the IARPA and DARPA projects between those who feel that the projects can provide valuable insights and those who feel that such projects may give governments an unprecedented "Big Brother" surveillance ability. On the pro side, a computer scientist at the MIT Media Laboratory opined that the result of IARPA and DARPA would probably be a much better understanding of what is going on in the world and how well local governments handle difficult situations, enabling them to improve their performance (e.g., the reactions of New Orleans and the state of Louisiana in

the aftermath of Hurricane Katrina). A physicist at the University of Notre Dame also noted that there is a huge amount of predictive power in such data, which could allow governments

© alengo/iStockphoto

to spot trends quickly and therefore operate more efficiently and effectively.

However, on the con side, advocates of privacy rights worry that public data and the related analysis techniques can be adapted for clandestine "total information" operation. They feel that these techniques can be used as easily against political opponents in the United States as they can against threats from foreign countries. The main worry is that the growth of data mining techniques is quickly outpacing the ability of scientists and government officials to think through questions of privacy and ethics.

Sources: E. Montalbano, "FBI Seeks Data-Mining App for Social Media," *InformationWeek*, January 26, 2012; S. Weinberger, "The Spy Who Tweeted Me: Intelligence Community Wants to Monitor Social Media," *Wired*, September 2011; J. Markoff, "Government Aims to Build a 'Data Eye in the Sky'," *The New York Times*, October 10, 2011; E. Montalbano, "Intelligence Agencies Seek Tools to Predict Global Events," *InformationWeek*, August 25, 2011; www.iarpa.gov, accessed March 11, 2012.

Questions

1. Discuss the ethical implications of the IARPA and DARPA projects.

2. Discuss the privacy implications of the IARPA and DARPA projects.

has begun to understand that when an organization collects vast amounts of personal information, it must be protected. In addition, many organizations give their customers some voice in how their information is used by providing them with opt-out choices. The **opt-out model** of informed consent permits an entity to collect personal information

TABLE 6.2 Privacy Policy Guidelines: A Sampler

- **Data Collection**
  - Data should be collected on individuals only for the purpose of accomplishing a legitimate business objective.
  - Data should be adequate, relevant, and not excessive in relation to the business objective.
  - Individuals must give their consent before data pertaining to them can be gathered. Such consent may be implied from the individual's actions (e.g., applications for credit, insurance, or employment).

- **Data Accuracy**
  - Sensitive data gathered on individuals should be verified before they are entered into the database.
  - Data should, where and when necessary, be kept current.
  - The file should be made available so the individual can ensure that the data are correct.
  - If there is disagreement about the accuracy of the data, the individual's version should be noted and included with any disclosure of the file.

- **Data Confidentiality**
  - Computer security procedures should be implemented to ensure against unauthorized disclosure of data. These procedures should include physical, technical, and administrative security measures.
  - Third parties should not be given access to data without the individual's knowledge or permission, except as required by law.
  - Disclosures of data, other than the most routine, should be noted and maintained for as long as the data are maintained.
  - Data should not be disclosed for reasons incompatible with the business objective for which they are collected.

until the individual specifically requests that the data not be collected. Privacy advocates prefer the **opt-in model** of informed consent, which prohibits an entity from collecting any personal information unless the individual specifically authorizes it.

One privacy tool currently available to consumers is the Platform for Privacy Preferences (P3P), a protocol that automatically communicates privacy policies between an electronic commerce Web site and visitors to that site. P3P enables visitors to determine the types of personal data that can be extracted by the Web sites they visit. It also allows visitors to compare a Web site's privacy policy to the visitors' preferences or to other standards, such as the Federal Trade Commission's (FTC) Fair Information Practices Standard or the European Directive on Data Protection.

Table 6.2 provides a sampling of privacy policy guidelines. The last section in Table 6.2, Data Confidentiality, refers to security, which you will explore in Chapter 7. It is important to note that all the good privacy intentions in the world are useless unless they are supported and enforced by effective security measures.

International Aspects of Privacy

As the number of online users has increased globally, governments throughout the world have enacted a large number of inconsistent privacy and security laws. This highly complex global legal framework is creating regulatory problems for companies. Approximately 50 countries have some form of data-protection laws. Many of these laws conflict with those of other countries, or they require specific security measures. Other countries have no privacy laws at all.

The absence of consistent or uniform standards for privacy and security obstructs the flow of information among countries, which is called *transborder data flows*. The European Union (EU), for one, has taken steps to overcome this problem. In 1998 the European

Community Commission (ECC) issued guidelines to all its member countries regarding the rights of individuals to access information about themselves. The EU data-protection laws are stricter than U.S. laws and thus could create problems for multinational corporations, which could face lawsuits for privacy violation.

The transfer of data in and out of a nation without the knowledge of either the authorities or the individuals involved raises a number of privacy issues. Whose laws have jurisdiction when records are stored in a different country for reprocessing or retransmission purposes? For example, if data are transmitted by a Polish company through a U.S. satellite to a British corporation, which country's privacy laws control the data, and when? Questions like these will become more complicated and frequent as time passes. Governments must make an effort to develop laws and standards to cope with rapidly changing information technologies in order to solve some of these privacy issues.

The United States and the EU share the goal of privacy protection for their citizens, but the United States takes a different approach. To bridge the different privacy approaches, the U.S. Department of Commerce, in consultation with the EU, developed a "safe harbor" framework to regulate the way that U.S. companies export and handle the personal data (such as names and addresses) of European citizens. See www.export.gov/safeharbor.

BEFORE YOU GO ON . . .

1. Describe the issue of privacy as it is affected by IT.
2. Discuss how privacy issues can affect transborder data flows.

Apply the Concept 6.2

Background This section has defined *privacy* as the right to be left alone and to be free of unreasonable personal intrusions. Information privacy is the right to determine when, and to what extent, information about you can be gathered and/or communicated to others. And we are in control, right?

If so, then why do people seem to always fear big government. Now that the entire world is connected by the Internet, it seems inevitable that people will fear the "big brother" of the government spying on us and invading our privacy. However, as this section points out, the law usually allows the right of society to have information over an individual's right to privacy.

In 2002 the movie *Minority Report* presented a future time where a special police group was able to predict when and where crimes were going to happen. This group could arrest criminals before they committed the crime. Additionally, in 2008 a movie titled *Eagle Eye* showed a computer system becoming so smart that it chose to abide by the Constitution even if it meant having the president of the United States killed.

Activity Movie night! If you have not seen the movies mentioned above, have a movie night and watch them from the perspective of privacy and information security. Talk to your friends about the movies and get their thoughts on these issues.

Deliverable

Summarize the movies and illustrate the privacy concerns they present. In your summary, attempt to answer the following question: At what point has data collection gone too far? When will consumers wake up and realize what is being stored? Will the government ever go as far as the movies present?

Submit your thoughts to your professor.

Quiz questions are assignable in WileyPLUS, and available on the Book Companion Site at http://www.wiley.com/college/rainer.

RUBY'S CLUB QUESTIONS

1. If privacy needs must be balanced against society's need to know information, at what point should Ruby's inform a customer's friends (on Facebook or Twitter) that the customer is about to leave the club a little too intoxicated?

2. With their new network, Ruben and Lisa hope to offer wireless Internet access. However, they are concerned about whether or not they should block certain Web sites. In particular, they want to be sure their customers are not using their network to download offensive material. Although it may not be illegal content, it may not be appropriate or representative of the atmosphere they want to present in their club. What are your thoughts?

What's in iT for ME?

FOR THE ACCOUNTING MAJOR

Public companies, their accountants, and their auditors have significant information security responsibilities. Accountants are now being held professionally and personally responsible for reducing risk, eliminating fraud, increasing the transparency of transactions, and ensuring compliance with generally accepted accounting principles (GAAP). Regulatory agencies such as the SEC and the Public Company Accounting Oversight Board (PCAOB) require accounting departments to monitor information security, fraud prevention and detection, and internal controls over financial reporting. Forensic accounting, a combination of accounting and information security, is one of the most rapidly expanding areas in accounting today.

FOR THE FINANCE MAJOR

Because information security is essential to the success of modern organizations, it is no longer just the concern of the CIO. As a result of global regulatory requirements and the passage of Sarbanes-Oxley, responsibility for information security lies with the CEO and the chief financial officer (CFO) as well. Consequently, all aspects of the security audit, including the security of information and information systems, are key concerns for financial managers.

FOR THE MARKETING MAJOR

Marketing professionals have new opportunities to collect data about their customers—for example, through business-to-consumer electronic commerce (discussed in Chapter 9). Business ethics clearly mandate that these data should be used only within the company and should not be sold to anyone else. Marketers do not want to be sued for invasion of privacy over data collected for the marketing database.

Customers expect their data to be properly secured. However, profit-motivated criminals want that data. Therefore, marketing managers must analyze the risks of their operations. Failure to protect corporate and customer data will cause significant public relations problems and outrage customers. Customer relationship management (discussed in Chapter 12) operations and tracking customers' online buying habits can expose unencrypted data to misuse or result in privacy violations.

FOR THE

PRODUCTION/OPERATIONS MANAGEMENT MAJOR

POM professionals decide whether to outsource (or offshore) manufacturing operations. In some cases, these operations are sent overseas to countries that do not have strict labor laws. This situation raises serious ethical questions. For example, is it ethical to hire employees in countries with poor working conditions in order to reduce labor costs?

FOR THE

HUMAN RESOURCES MANAGEMENT MAJOR

Ethics are critically important to HR managers. HR policies explain the appropriate use of information technologies in the workplace. Questions such as these arise: Can employees use the Internet, e-mail, or chat systems for personal purposes while at work? Is it ethical to monitor employees? If so, how? How much? How often? HR managers must formulate and enforce such policies while at the same time maintaining trusting relationships between employees and management.

FOR THE MIS MAJOR

Ethics might be more important for MIS personnel than for anyone else in the organization, because these individuals have control of the information assets. They also have control over a huge amount of personal information on all employees. As a result, the MIS function must be held to the highest ethical standards. In fact, as you will see in the chapter-closing case about Terry Childs, regardless of what he actually did, what one thinks of what he did, and whether his conviction was justified, a person in his situation has the opportunity to behave improperly, and should not.

SUMMARY

1. **Describe the four categories of ethical issues related to information technology.**

The major ethical issues related to IT are privacy, accuracy, property (including intellectual property), and accessibility to information. Privacy may be violated when data are held in databases or transmitted over networks. Privacy policies that address issues of data collection, data accuracy, and data confidentiality can help organizations avoid legal problems.

2. **Discuss potential threats to the privacy of personal data stored in different locations.**

Threats to privacy include advances in information technologies, electronic surveillance, and personal information in databases, Internet bulletin boards, newsgroups, and social networking sites. The personal threat in Internet bulletin boards, newsgroups, and social networking sites is that you might post too much information about yourself that many unknown people can see.

>>> CHAPTER GLOSSARY

accountability A tenet of ethics that refers to determining who is responsible for actions that were taken.

code of ethics A collection of principles that are intended to guide decision making by members of the organization.

digital dossier An electronic description of you and your habits.

electronic surveillance Tracking people's activities with the aid of computers.

ethics The principles of right and wrong that individuals use to make choices to guide their behaviors.

information privacy The right to determine when, and to what extent, information about you can be gathered and/or communicated to others.

liability A legal concept that gives individuals the right to recover the damages done to them by other individuals, organizations, or systems.

opt-in model A model of informed consent that prohibits an entity from collecting any personal information unless the individual specifically authorizes it.

opt-out model A model of informed consent that permits an entity to collect personal information unless the individual specifically requests that the data not be collected.

privacy The right to be left alone and to be free of unreasonable personal intrusions.

privacy codes (see **privacy policies**)

privacy policies (also known as **privacy codes**) An organization's guidelines for protecting the privacy of customers, clients, and employees.

profiling The process of forming a digital dossier.

responsibility A tenet of ethics whereby you accept the consequences of your decisions and actions.

>>> DISCUSSION QUESTIONS

1. In 2008, the Massachusetts Bay Transportation Authority (MBTA) obtained a temporary restraining order barring three Massachusetts Institute of Technology (MIT) students from publicly displaying what they claimed to be a way to get "free subway rides for life." Specifically, the 10-day injunction prohibited the students from revealing vulnerabilities of the MBTA's fare card. The students were scheduled to present their findings in Las Vegas at the DEFCON computer hacking conference. Were the students' actions legal? Were their actions ethical? Discuss your answer from the perspective of the students and then from the perspective of the MBTA.

2. Frank Abagnale, the criminal played by Leonardo DiCaprio in the motion picture *Catch Me If You Can*, ended up in prison. However, when he left prison, he went to work as a consultant to many companies on matters of fraud.

   a. Why do companies hire perpetrators (if caught) as consultants? Is this a good idea?

   b. You are the CEO of a company. Discuss the ethical implications of hiring Frank Abagnale as a consultant.

>>> PROBLEM-SOLVING ACTIVITIES

1. An information security manager routinely monitored the Web surfing done by her company's employees. She discovered that many employees were visiting the "sinful six" Web sites. (*Note:* The sinful six are Web sites with material related to pornography, gambling, hate, illegal activities, tastelessness, and violence.) She then prepared a list of the employees and their surfing histories and gave the list to management. Some managers punished their employees. Some employees, in turn, objected to the monitoring, claiming that they should have a right to privacy.

   a. Is monitoring of Web surfing by managers ethical? (It is legal.) Support your answer.

   b. Is employee Web surfing on the "sinful six" ethical? Support your answer.

   c. Is the security manager's submission of the list of abusers to management ethical? Why or why not?

   d. Is punishing the abusers ethical? Why or why not? If yes, then what types of punishment are acceptable?

   e. What should the company do in this situation? (*Note:* There is a variety of possibilities here.)

2. Access the Computer Ethics Institute's "Ten Commandments of Computer Ethics" at the Web site of the Computer Professionals for Social Responsibility: http://www.wiley.com/go/rainer/problemsolving. Study these ten rules and decide if any others should be added.

3. Access the Association for Computing Machinery's code of ethics for its members at http://www.wiley.com/go/rainer/problemsolving. Discuss the major points of this code. Is this code complete? Why or why not? Support your answer.

4. Access www.eightmaps.com. Is the use of data on this Web site illegal? Unethical? Support your answer.

5. The Electronic Frontier Foundation (www.eff.org) has a mission of protecting rights and promoting freedom in the "electronic frontier." Review the organization's suggestions about how to protect your online privacy and summarize what you can do to protect yourself.

6. Access your university's guidelines for ethical computer and Internet use. Are there limitations as to the types of Web sites that you can visit and the types of material you can view? Are you allowed to change the programs on the lab computers? Are you allowed to download software from the lab computers for your personal use? Are there rules governing the personal use of computers and e-mail?

7. Access "The Core Rules of Netiquette" at http://www.wiley.com/go/rainer/problemsolving. What do you think of this code of ethics? Should it be expanded? Is it too general?

8. Access www.cookiecentral.com and www.epubliceye.com. Do these sites provide information that helps you protect your privacy? If so, then explain how.

9. Do you believe that your university should be allowed to monitor e-mail sent and received on university computers? Why or why not? Support your answer.

>>> COLLABORATION EXERCISE

Background

We all receive privacy statements each day. But how many of us read them? Do you actually read every statement you agree to when you click the "I Agree" button? Periodically it is a good idea to skim over these to know exactly what you agree with when you check the box. It is even more important to study revisions to see what has changed when the company sends out a new and updated version.

Activity

Work with your team to research various privacy statements. Use popular sites like Facebook, Google, Twitter, LinkedIn, Pinterest, etc., as your main sources of information.

For example, in 2012 Google updated its privacy and information sharing policy and would not allow anyone

to opt out of it. You either agreed to Google's policy or you stopped using Google. What about Facebook and its privacy statements? Have each team member analyze a company and report back to the team. In most cases, you will be able to find Web sites that have already analyzed and put together histories of privacy issues.

Deliverable

Work with your team to prepare a short paper that highlights the major issues and trends you have found. Do you think companies are moving toward protecting customers' data? Do you think customers are becoming smarter about what they share? Do social media have the best interest of their users in mind? Put some thought into these issues, prepare your paper, and submit it to your professor.

CLOSING **CASE 1** > Google and China

THE PROBLEM >>> Google wished to open a search page in China, but in order to do so, it looked like the company would need to accept censorship by the Chinese government. Google wanted to comply with government regulations so that it could expand its business to China, but Google did not wish to compromise the usefulness or appeal of its Web site's search function.

ATTEMPTS AT >>>
A SOLUTION

On January 27, 2006, Google launched its China-based search page (www.google.cn). Google hoped that its decision to create a search engine in the .cn domain—one that followed the Chinese government's rules of censorship—would lead to a level playing field with Baidu, the leading Chinese search engine. Baidu was launched in 2000, and therefore would compete directly with google.cn.

Unfortunately, even as Google rolled out its google.cn Web address, there were indications that its compromise on censorship would not satisfy the Chinese government. For example, unexplained outages of its Web site occurred, but Baidu did not experience any outages.

Not long after Google received its operating license in December 2005, the Chinese government declared that the license was no longer valid. They stated that it was not clear whether Google's activities made it an Internet service or a news portal. (Foreigners are forbidden by the Chinese government from operating news portals in China.) Google then began an 18-month long negotiation to restore its license, which it finally received in June 2007. The negotiation was resolved in secret.

In 2007, Google was granted a valuable concession. Chinese users had only to type "g.cn" and they would go to the google.cn site. By then, however, many Chinese Web users had written off Google as an unwelcome outsider with less than reliable service.

Google had a firm policy against storing personal data inside China in order to avoid a situation in which the government could demand that Google turn over that data. Therefore, the company did not offer a number of its key services for local Chinese users—no Gmail, no Blogger, no Picasa, no YouTube.

As Chinese employees were hired, it took some time for some of them to adjust to the Google style. For instance, many were uncomfortable with Google's worldwide policy that employees initiate and pursue independent projects during 20 percent of their work time. Engineers had to be told by a visiting Google executive that they did not need permission to do a 20 percent project.

However, the most pressing concern of Google's Chinese engineers was their lack of access to Google's production code. Google was a collaborative company that wanted its engineers around the world to innovate on its existing products and create exciting new ones. The company empowered them to do so by giving them access to its production code base. Without this access, Chinese engineers were limited in what they could do and felt that their lack of access sent a message that they were second-class employees. Suspicion lingered that the Google executives behind this no-access policy had intentionally placed rigid restrictions on Google's employees in China as a form of corporate civil disobedience against Google's cooperation with Chinese government censors.

Google's success in China depended in part on having a government relations point person who could navigate the problems associated with preserving Google's values without offending Chinese officials. Google's first such point person was experienced in the ways of Chinese bureaucracies, but did not speak English and seemed to fail to appreciate issues from Google's perspective.

Her tenure at Google ended when she took it upon herself to give iPods to Chinese officials. She charged the iPods to Google and another executive approved the charge. In Chinese business culture, such gifts are routine, but the act unambiguously violated Google policy, not least because it was an explicit violation of the U.S. Foreign Corrupt Practices Act.

To replace their first (unsuccessful) government liaison, Google chose a three-person, all-female government relations team. However, as it turned out, they had their hands full fending off Chinese government directives. For example, a demand might come from a government ministry to take down 10 items. Google would typically take down seven and hope that the compromise resolved the matter. Then, after a few days or weeks, Google would quietly restore links it had censored. Every 5 months, Google's policy review committee in China would meet to make sure it was filtering the minimum it could possibly get away with.

Google executives began to think that the company's great China compromise was not working because of the heavy censorship. A turning point came in 2008, the year China hosted the summer Olympics. In the months before the Games, China apparently decided to increase its restrictions on Web content. It demanded that, in addition to censoring google.cn search results, Google also purge objectionable links from the Chinese-language version of Google.com. That was unacceptable to Google. Complying with these demands would mean that Google was acting as an agent of repression to Chinese-speaking people all over the world, including in the United States. Other search engines, including Microsoft, agreed to such demands. But Google stalled, hoping that after the Olympics the Chinese would back off their demands. However, they did not and the demands for more censorship became both broader in scope and more frequent.

Then, a new problem arose involving Google Suggest, a Google search feature that instantly offers fully developed search queries when users type just a few characters or words into the search box. This innovation was first offered in China after Google's search team realized that, because of difficulties associated with typing Chinese characters, Chinese users generally entered shorter queries into the search box. But, Chinese officials discovered that in many instances, the suggestions offered by Google were related to sexual matters. Google China executives tried to explain that apparently someone had spammed keywords to artificially boost the popularity of sex sites in Google Suggest. The officials were not impressed and told Google that the company "would be punished."

At the end of 2009, Google was hacked and some of the company's more closely guarded intellectual property was stolen. The hack was geographically tied to China and both the sophistication of the attack and the nature of its targets pointed to the Chinese government itself as an instigator of, or a party to, the attack. Even worse, the attackers had penetrated the Gmail accounts of Chinese dissidents and human rights activists. All their contacts, their plans, and their most private information had fallen into the hands of the intruders.

<<< THE RESULTS

On January 10, 2010, Google's top executives decided to shut down google.cn. The company decided that it would no longer carry out censorship on behalf of the Chinese government. Google subsequently stopped offering Web search on google.cn, and instead directed Web goers to a search site based in Hong Kong that is not subject to government censorship requirements. For users in mainland China, the Hong Kong search site, along with other Google services such as Gmail, suffers frequent service disruptions.

In 2012, Google has acknowledged that it cannot afford to miss out on the world's biggest Internet market and has renewed its push to expand in China. One goal is to introduce its Android Market to China. The Android Market offers thousands of mobile applications to users of Android-powered smartphones and tablets, but is not available in China despite the fact that it powers some 60 percent of all Chinese smartphones. Google is trying to win over Chinese consumers with services that do not require official censorship, such as Shihui. Shihui helps people search Chinese sites that offer discounts at local stores.

Google's move comes at a pivotal time for China's Internet industry. Despite the prevalence of government censorship, the Web is increasingly an outlet for Chinese citizens to share information and express discontent, even about the government. Twitter-like microblogging services such as Sina Corporation's Weibo have become popular platforms for sharing opinions and information about controversial topics, even as Google has been on the sidelines.

Perhaps the most telling change is that in 2011, China renewed Google's license to operate a Web site in the country.

Sources: Compiled from S. Li and B. Womack, "Google China Business Grows, 'Continues to Thrive' Alegre Says," *Bloomberg BusinessWeek*, January 24, 2012; J. Maragioglio, "Google Renews Expansion Efforts in China," *Mobiledia*, January 13, 2012; A. Efrati and L. Chao, "Google Softens Tone on China," *The Wall Street Journal*, January 12, 2012; M. Brian, "Google Gains China Internet License Renewal, Still Avoids Search Censorship," *TheNextWeb*, September 7, 2011; S. Levy, "Inside Google's China Misfortune," *CNN*, April 15, 2011; S. LaFraniere and D. Barboza, "China Tightens Censorship of Electronic Communications," *The New York Times*, March 21, 2011; D. MacMillan, "Google's Quixotic China Challenge," *Bloomberg BusinessWeek*, March 25, 2010.

QUESTIONS

1. Google's informal corporate motto is "Don't Be Evil." Discuss this motto in light of Google's decision to stop censoring its search results on behalf of the Chinese government.

2. Discuss Google's decision to stop censoring its search results in China in terms of the ethical framework at the beginning of this chapter.

Closing CASE 2 > Attack of the Dot Clones

THE PROBLEM >>>

Fab (www.fab.com) is a highly successful flash-deal Web site for designer goods. Launched in June 2011, Fab had sales of $20 million in its first six months. The company's CEO attributed Fab's success to the authenticity of its products, its refusal to offer knock-offs, and the fact that its offerings consisted of objects and design products that could not be found elsewhere.

Six months after Fab launched, other sites began to create knock-offs of their products. An e-commerce design Web site called Bamarang (www.bamarang.de) opened for business in Germany, the United Kingdom, France, Australia, and Brazil. Like Fab, Bamarang offers discounts of up to 70 percent on designer goods. The layout, color scheme, and typefaces of their Web site closely resemble Fab. Bamarang even has a shot of an Eames chair as the background photo for its sign-in page, just as Fab does.

Bamarang is the creation of German brothers Oliver, Marc, and Alexander Samwer. This brotherly trio has hit upon a wildly successful business model: identify promising U.S. Internet businesses and then clone them internationally. Since starting their first "dot clone" (a German version of eBay) in 1999, they have duplicated Airbnb, eHarmony, Pinterest, and other high-profile businesses for the international market. In total, they have launched more than 100 companies. Their Zappos clone, Zalando, now dominates six European markets and is estimated to be worth $1 billion by *Financial Times Deutschland*.

The Samwers' base of operations is a startup business incubator in Berlin called Rocket Internet. Rocket launches companies, hires staff, and provides marketing and design support, search engine optimization, and day-to-day management until startups can take over for themselves.

<<< A POTENTIAL SOLUTION

The Samwers launched their clone of eBay, called Alando, in early 1999. Four months after Alando's launch, eBay bought the company for $53 million—and the Samwers became Germany's first Internet millionaires.

In November 2008, Groupon went live in Chicago and shortly after became one of the fastest growing Internet businesses ever. In January 2010, the Samwers launched a Groupon knockoff called CityDeal. Within 5 months it was the top deal-of-the-day Web site in the United Kingdom, France, Spain, Italy, Ireland, the Netherlands, Switzerland, Austria, Poland, Finland, Denmark, Sweden, and Turkey.

Groupon could have fought CityDeal in the marketplace. Groupon could also have filed an intellectual property lawsuit, although the chances of the company winning would have been very slim. Companies cannot be patented and trademarks apply only within the countries where they are registered. Perhaps taking the path of least resistance, in May 2010, Groupon bought its German clone for 14 percent of Groupon's shares. (In March 2012, Rocket owned 6 percent of Groupon, a stake worth about $1 billion.)

Wrapp (www.wrapp.com) is a European startup that partners with retailers to allow users to give gifts to their friends through Facebook. Unsurprisingly, the Samwers launched DropGifts, a clone of Wrapp, in February 2012. Unlike Groupon, Wrapp responded in the offensive. The company is planning on adding new territories much faster than it had previously planned and it hope is to gain first mover advantages in important markets. In order to fund its rapid growth, Wrapp is turning back to investors for additional funding.

The Wrapp management team feels that the best defense against copycats is to do a better job. It thinks that it has stronger existing relationships with retailer partners than the copycats and that it has more big partnerships on the way.

But what about Fab? On February 21, 2012, the company announced its acquisition of a German non-Samwer facsimile, Casacanda. The Fab CEO said that Casacanda is less of a copycat and more a group of people who came up with a similar idea to Fab's.

<<< THE RESULTS

The Samwers are revered among young German entrepreneurs for putting Berlin's startup scene on the map. On the other hand, they are despised for giving Germany a reputation as the copycat capital of Europe.

There are several indications of the Samwers' image problem. In summer 2011, a Berlin startup called 6Wunderkinder called for an anticopycat revolution in that city. In January 2012, about 20 Rocket employees, some of them close allies of the Samwers, announced that they were leaving to launch a rival startup factory, called Project A Ventures, focusing on backing original ideas. In February 2012, Russian entrepreneur Yuri Milner, an investor in Facebook, Zynga, and Twitter, pulled out of a plan to invest in Rocket. The German media speculated that it was because of the Samwers' reputation.

Despite their questionable image, the Samwers say that they are not necessarily copycats. They say that they take an idea already on the Internet and "make it better." Groupon's CEO went so far as to say that "An idea for a company is the easy part, and execution is the hard part." He said that the Samwers were the best operators had had ever seen.

Sources: Compiled from B. Johnson, "Exclusive: Wrapp CEO Goes Toe-to-Toe with Samwer Bros.," *GigaOM.com*, March 7, 2012; C. Winter, "The German Website Copy Machine," *Bloomberg BusinessWeek*, March 5–11, 2012; M. Cowan, "Inside the Clone Factory: The Story of Germany Samwer Brothers," *Wired*, March 2, 2012; B. Johnson, "Now Samwer Bros Clone Fab and Target European Rollout," *GigaOM.com*, January 25, 2012; "Attack of the Clones," *The Economist*, August 6, 2011.

Questions

1. Discuss the ethics of the Samwers' business model. Now discuss the legality of the Samwers' business model. Compare the two discussions.
2. What are some alternatives that companies might use to combat dot clones?
3. Discuss the ethical implications of the statement from Groupon's CEO that the Samwers are superb operators, not simply copycats.

To complete this assignment, Ruben and Lisa need suggestions on developing their Ethics and Privacy Statement. Search Google (or another search engine) for clubs in your local area and see if they have an Ethics and Privacy Statement online. Can you tell if they take the utilitarian, rights, fairness, or common good approach to ethics? What seems to be the norm for clubs? Do any of them deal with the ethics of monitoring alcohol consumption?

Finally, prepare a statement for Ruben and Lisa to use as their rough draft as they prepare their own Ethics and Privacy Statement. Submit it to your professor.

SPREADSHEET ACTIVITY

PROTECTING INFORMATION IN A SPREADSHEET

Objective: You will learn how to lock and protect spreadsheets to keep private information protected. You will also learn the difference between a "protected" spreadsheet and a secure database.

Chapter Connection: Ethics are a difficult subject in information systems. The tighter you keep a system, the less useful it is. However, the more freely you allow people to access data, the more privacy issues you have on your hands. The object of this exercise is to help establish the necessary balance between ethics, privacy, and data usefulness.

Activity: Recently, a fraternity on campus made plans to host a party with a sorority and took reservations for T-shirt orders. One of the members was an MIS student who had set up a Google Survey for the orders and had exported all of the data into a spreadsheet. The data included name, address, shirt size, address, phone number, and so on. The university has asked the fraternity to keep this data confidential due to problems in the past.

Specifically, a year earlier, the same data were stored in an unsecured spreadsheet that was e-mailed around the fraternity. One of the fraternity brothers took some of the information and used it to exploit and make fun of a physically larger sorority sister. To ensure that this does not happen again, the university is asking the fraternity to show evidence that the spreadsheet is locked and will only be seen by those approved to deliver the T-shirts within the fraternity and the sorority.

As a member of those approved by the university to manage this information, your job is to take the data collected by the Google Survey and move private information to the private page and lock it so that it cannot be used to exploit any member of either fraternity or sorority. You will need to use your own judgment to determine which information needs to be moved to the private, locked page of the spreadsheet.

Go to http://www.wiley.com/go/rainer/spreadsheet to download the Excel file you will need. Then watch the accompanying video to learn how to make a spreadsheet secure.

Deliverable: The final product will be a spreadsheet with the survey data in a spreadsheet with the single page of data divided between a secure page and an "open" page.

Discussion Questions:

1. How can a spreadsheet be helpful if it is so easy to secure and hack?

2. Are Google spreadsheets more secure than Excel spreadsheets?

3. If a sheet needs to be "very hidden," then why not go ahead and delete it?

Quiz questions are assignable in WileyPLUS, and available on the Book Companion Site at http://www.wiley.com/college/rainer.

DATABASE ACTIVITY:

Objective

In this activity, you will learn how to select only the useful rows of a table, hiding the others, and sort a table on any column in it. A database is useless if you cannot get information out of it. Access offers many ways to do that. Some are simple but limited. Others are more capable but require more work. Filtering and sorting a table are at the low end but are still often useful. We will start with them here, and go on to more complex (but more capable) methods in later activities.

CHAPTER CONNECTION

All organizations keep critical information in databases. Security and privacy considerations govern who can access that database and what they are allowed to see there. This means being able to see some parts of a database but not others. Hence, the way people select parts of a database to see is closely connected to privacy and security considerations. Discussion questions 1 and 2 at the end of this activity go into this connection more deeply.

PREREQUISITES

None.

Activity

In this activity, which you will find online, you will learn how to filter and sort an Access table to zero in on exactly the rows you want. The techniques are simple, but will be useful often.

The database you may have used with the Chapter 4 activity has information a company might use to track problems with network equipment. Its central element is the *trouble ticket*. A ticket is submitted by a user, who works in a department, and refers to a device (item of network equipment). A ticket is initially open. It is assigned to a technician, may go to "in process" or "on hold" (if there is any delay in resolving it), and is eventually closed or canceled. That database has five tables: users, departments, technicians, devices, and trouble tickets. You can see how they are connected in the NeTrouble database on the Web site. Choose the Database Tools tab above the ribbon, and click on the relationship map.

1. Download and open the **Ch 06 NetSimple** database from http://www.wiley.com/rainer/go/database. It has one table with the same information as in NeTrouble, minus some columns (such as

employee date of birth and date of hire) to save screen space.

   This is usually a poor way to organize a database. It violates the normalization rules you learned in Chapter 3. However, this "flat file" data structure is common; it is not always bad and it is where filtering works best.

2. Suppose you want to see the trouble tickets for all your routers. Open TroubleTbl in NetSimple. Make sure it is in Datasheet view. (It should open that way.) The second column of the table, DeviceName, gives the type of device.

3. Pull down the triangle to the right of the column name by clicking on it. You will see a list of all the different devices in the table, sorted alphabetically.

   (You will see entries for both "Router," which is correct, and "Rooter," a misspelling. The chance of this sort of error is one reason that a flat file database is not a good idea for anything but the simplest data storage requirements.)

4. You will also see two entries in the table above the list of types: one that reads "Select All" and one that refers to blank (empty) cells in the datasheet. At this point all the boxes are checked. Click Select All to uncheck all the boxes. Then click "Bridge" and OK.

5. All the rows have gone away except for those with Bridge in the DevName column—that is, except for all the trouble tickets that refer to bridges. You will see a small funnel next to the triangle in that column. It means the data you see are filtered on the content of that column.

6. Click the Home tab above the ribbon. In the Sort & Filter section toward the right side of the ribbon, Toggle Filter (a funnel icon) will be highlighted. Click it a few times to see what it does.

7. You can filter for more than one column at a time. Pull down the filtering menu for the Department column. It shows only the departments that are now visible—that is, those that reported a problem with a bridge. Since HR did not report any problems with bridges, HR is not in the list.

   Now, click Marketing. The Marketing box will be unchecked. So will the Select All box because all the choices are no longer selected. Click OK. Trouble tickets from Marketing are now hidden, leaving those from all other departments. Both columns show funnels next to their triangles.

The Toggle Filter button in the ribbon alternates between both filters on and both off. If you want to turn one of them off while leaving the other on, you must clear it individually in its column.

5. To sort the visible trouble tickets by the date they were submitted, pull down the sorting and filtering menu of the TicketSubmitted column. Choose Sort Newest to Oldest and click OK. The table now shows the trouble tickets with the newest at the top. This is useful if you need to find out about the latest problems.

Usage Hint: You can also sort by selecting a column and clicking one of the icons on the left side of the Sort & Filter section of the Home ribbon. The top icon sorts in ascending order; the middle one sorts in descending order; and the last one clears any existing sorts on that column. This may be faster if the Home ribbon is already selected, but probably is not if you are working with a different ribbon.

6. Select the TicketSubmitted column of the table by clicking on its heading. Pull down its Sort & Filter menu and move your mouse pointer to Date Filters. (The type of filters you get here depends on the data type of the column you are working with.) Another menu will come out from the side of the main menu. Select After . . ., the fourth entry. In the dialogue box that appears, enter 3/1/2011.

7. Close this database, being sure to save your work.

Usage Hint: If you open your database again at this point, it may seem that your sort and filters disappeared. They did not. They were saved with the database. They are just not applied. Clicking Toggle Filters will reactivate them.

8. Now, download and open the **Ch 06 NeTrouble** database from the Web site. (You may have used a similar database in the Chapter 4 activity.) It is a better way to structure the trouble reporting data. However, as you will see, it is more awkward to filter on a multiple-table database. That is why we will learn about other query techniques for such databases later, in the Chapter 10 activity. To get the same result that was so easy to get above, proceed as follows:

9. Open DeviceTbl. Find the Bridge row or rows. Because this table is short, you can scan it by eye in a couple of seconds. Record its primary key (DeviceID, its first column) and close it.

10. Open the TicketTbl. Find its Device column. Filter that column for the device key or keys you just recorded. This will select the trouble tickets for all bridges.

   This is a lot of work to get a result that you obtained more easily the first time—and you only needed to use two tables, not seven or eight.

That is one downside of multiple-table databases versus flat files. Their business advantages still outweigh their drawbacks. You will see how to get around those difficulties by using other query tools in future activities.

11. Close this database, being sure to save your work.

Deliverables

1. Your Ch 06 NetSimple database, with the filters you applied.
2. Your Ch 06 NeTrouble database, with the filters you applied.

Quiz Questions

1. True or false: Clicking on a Sort icon, with a table column selected, does exactly the same as selecting the corresponding Sort option from that column's pull-down filtering menu.

2. Consider the filter you applied to the single-table database in activity steps 3 to 5 above. Could you have used the same basic method, but checking different boxes, to select

   (a) All devices other than bridges?

   (b) All devices that are either bridges or switches?

   (c) All devices that are routers or rooters, to include misspellings?

   (d) Any of the above?

3. True or false: You apply a filter to a database table, close the database, then reopen it. When you look at that table in Datasheet view, its rows will still be filtered as they were.

4. he Sort & Filter section of the ribbon is found under which ribbon tab?

   (a) Home

   (b) Create

   (c) Database Tools

   (d) Datasheet

Discussion Questions

1. Suppose you have the five-table version of this database (NeTrouble) and have been asked to analyze the distribution of trouble tickets by department. You understand the difficulty of doing this, as you did it for a different problem in activity steps 8 to 10, and are willing to put up with that. However, for privacy reasons, you are not allowed to access the user table. Would this be a problem? Why or why not? If it would, suggest a solution.

2. Sometimes a person should see only certain rows of a table. Student access to grades is one example: you may see your own rows, but not those of other students. One way to make this happen is to

create a copy of the table, filter for rows this person should *not* see, select them all, delete them, and then clear the filter to show the remaining rows. (This would have to be done automatically, or by someone who is allowed to see the entire table.) The result can then be e-mailed to the student, plugged into a Web page template, etc.

Think of two other situations where access to a table must be controlled on a row basis. Would this solution work for each of them? Why or why not?

3. The filtering menu of a column shows all data values in that column with check boxes. Rows containing checked values will remain visible when the filter is applied. Other rows will be hidden, but can be shown by clearing the filter or toggling it off. More complex criteria can be applied by selecting [____] Filters, where the blank specifies the data type of the column (e.g., text) and providing any parameters as in activity step 6 above.

Choose any column of any table that contains text data. Select Text Filters from the drop-down menu. Consider the eight types of filters in the submenu that appears. Think of two situations in which those eight types do not meet the filtering needs. Be specific in explaining what these situations call for that they cannot handle.

7 | Information Security

LEARNING OBJECTIVES >>>

1. Give one specific example of each of the five factors that are contributing to the increasing vulnerability of information resources.

2. Compare and contrast human mistakes and social engineering by way of specific examples.

3. Describe negative consequences that might result from at least three different kinds of deliberate attacks on information systems.

4. Assess how you might employ each of the three risk mitigation strategies in the context of your owning a home.

5. Identify the three major types of controls that organizations can use to protect their information resources.

Picture your graduation day. You have finally completed your undergraduate degree. You initially looked for a job, but you have since decided that you want to start your own business. You pitch your idea to your best friend and ask him/her to join you in a new business venture. Because your degree is in marketing, you would like to start a small promotions business. You and your new business partner develop a solid business strategy, get a small business loan from the bank to purchase your computer equipment, and then head over to the courthouse to set up your new Limited Liability Corporation.

Two years later, things could not have turned out better! Hard work, late nights, and social media exposure has landed your business quite a few clients. The two computers you purchased with your small business loan (one for you and one for your business partner) have turned out to be invaluable. In fact, you now realize more than ever how much you depend on your computers and how lost your business would be without them. You wonder if your antivirus software is up-to-date and if there is anything else you should be doing to protect your critical business data, especially your clients' data. But, you are too busy to research these issues and you just trust that everything will be OK.

You and your partner have never had computers this nice. Fast processors, big monitors, and plenty of memory (all purchased with business intent of course) make for much better computers than either of you have at home. Naturally you both use your computers for personal work as well. Why not, right?

But then, suddenly, your business partner's computer starts to slow down dramatically. Your machine is identical to his, but yours runs much faster. Your partner takes his computer back to Best Buy to have the Geek Squad look it over. The technician determines that malware has infected his computer so thoroughly that the hard drive must be replaced. Additionally, **> > >**

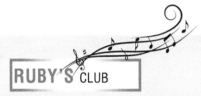

RUBY'S CLUB

Ruben and Lisa are very excited about their new Web site and the opportunity to sell merchandise online. However, it seems that every day they hear of an attack where credit card information has been stolen; disgruntled employees have shared passwords and made customer data vulnerable; computers physically stolen from behind locked doors; fire creating loss of data; and other situations where customer information has been compromised. They really feel stuck between a "rock and a hard place" because they are experiencing immense pressure to move into the e-commerce realm, yet they are very concerned about information security by doing so!

They want to know what kind of threats are really out there and which ones are legitimate for them as a nightclub? In what ways would Ruby's make itself vulnerable to cybercrime by adding e-commerce to its Web site? How many of these threats can be avoided by having a third party (such as Amazon, Yahoo, Google, or PayPal) provide e-commerce tools that provide some level of security and confidence, but how much does Ruby's need? How much training do employees need to truly create a secure environment for their customers and their private information?

the data on his hard drive cannot be recovered and he has not backed up any of his files (not even the business data).

Now, you have problems. Lost data may result in lost (certainly irritated) customers. In addition, you will have to spend time and money recreating that data.

How could your partner's unprotected Web surfing have resulted in so much lost data? The fact is that even though you both consider yourselves somewhat tech savvy, neither of you ever took steps to protect your computers. You just assumed that a malware infection would never happen to you.

Now, what would you say if you knew that you are not alone? A recent report by GFI Software showed that over 40 percent of small- to medium-sized businesses (SMBs) reported a security breach that resulted from an employee visiting a Web site that hosted malware. Amazingly, even though 40 percent of SMBs have experienced this problem, 55 percent reported that preventing this from happening again was not a priority! Furthermore, 70 percent of the respondents do NOT have any policy about Web use at work and say that Web use is not a problem!

As you can see from this case, security on computers and information systems is vital to avoid losing business relationships and significant amounts of time and money. There are many third-party companies that provide security solutions (see for example, GFI Software at www.gfi.com), but you are responsible for seeking out their services and implementing security controls on your own systems and customer data. If you do not prioritize security measures, you expose your computer and your files to potentially irrevocable damage from thousands of malware systems and viruses.

Sources: Compiled from "GFI Software Survey: 40% of SMBs Have Suffered a Security Breach Due to Unsafe Web Surfing," *Enhanced Online News*, October 12, 2011; "Small Businesses Hacked But Still Not Taking Precautions: Survey Says," *The Huffington Post*, November 7, 2011; www.gfi.com, accessed March 8, 2012.

Questions

1. What security controls should you and your business partner have adopted *at a minimum*?
2. How important are backup plans and file backup procedures to small businesses?
3. Why is it important to protect customer information in businesses of any size?

As you saw in this case, information security controls are essential to all businesses, regardless of size. In addition, a solid backup plan is critical to information security. As you consider this case, think about the devastating impact that a security breach would have on a small business. The loss of important data about the business, coupled with the loss of customer data, could shut the business down.

Introduction

Information security is closely related to IT and raises significant questions. For example, how do organizations show due diligence in protecting sensitive, classified information? Is the cause of security breaches in organizations managerial, technological, or some combination of both? How should organizations protect their information more effectively? The most important question raised in this chapter, however, is whether it is possible to secure the Internet. The answer to this question affects every one of us.

The answers to these and other questions are not clear. As you learn about information security in the context of information technology, you will acquire a better understanding of these issues, their importance, their relationships, and their trade-offs.

Information technologies, properly used, can have enormous benefits for individuals, organizations, and entire societies. So far, you have learned about diverse ways in which IT has made businesses more productive, efficient, and responsive to consumers. You have explored areas such as medicine and philanthropy in which IT has improved people's health and well-being. Unfortunately, information technologies can also be misused, often with devastating consequences. Consider the following:

- Individuals can have their identities stolen.

- Organizations' customer information can be stolen, leading to financial losses, erosion of customer confidence, and legal action.
- Countries face the threat of cyberterrorism and cyberwarfare. Cyberwarfare is a critical problem for the U.S. government. In fact, President Barack Obama's 2009 stimulus package contained billions of dollars to upgrade the government's digital defenses.

In fact, the misuse of information technologies has come to the forefront of any discussion of IT. For example, the Ponemon Institute (www.ponemon.org), a research firm, found that organizations spent an average of $7.20 million for each security breach in 2011.

The study measured the direct costs of a data breach, such as hiring forensic experts, notifying customers, setting up telephone hotlines to field queries from concerned or affected customers, offering free credit monitoring subscriptions, and discounts for future products and services. The study also measured more intangible costs of a breach, such as the loss of business from increased customer turnover (known as *customer churn*) and decreases in customer trust.

According to the study, employee negligence caused many of the data breaches. This finding confirms that organizational employees are a weak link in information security. As a result, it is very important for you to learn about information security so that you will be better prepared when you enter the workforce.

7.1 Introduction to Information Security

Security can be defined as the degree of protection against criminal activity, danger, damage, and/or loss. Following this broad definition, **information security** means protecting an organization's information and information systems (known as an organization's *information resources*) from unauthorized access, use, disclosure, disruption, modification, or destruction. Clearly, information and information systems can be compromised by deliberate criminal actions and by anything that can impair the proper functioning of an organization's information systems.

Before you continue, let's look at these key terms. Organizations have huge amounts of information and numerous information systems that are subject to many threats. A **threat** to an information resource is any danger to which a system may be exposed. The **exposure** of an information resource is the harm, loss, or damage that can result if a threat compromises that resource. An information resource's **vulnerability** is the possibility that the system will suffer harm by a threat.

A number of factors are contributing to the increasing vulnerability of organizational information resources, making it much more difficult to secure them. Before you learn about these factors, they are listed here:

George Doyle/Image Source Limited

Human mistakes such as unattended equipment often leave resources vulnerable to theft.

- Today's interconnected, interdependent, wirelessly networked business environment
- Smaller, faster, cheaper computers and storage devices
- Decreasing skills necessary to be a computer hacker
- International organized crime taking over cybercrime
- Lack of management support

The first factor is the evolution of the information technology resource from mainframe only to today's highly complex, interconnected, interdependent, wirelessly networked business environment. The Internet now enables millions of computers and computer networks to freely and seamlessly communicate with one another. Organizations and individuals are exposed to a world of untrusted networks and potential attackers. A *trusted network*, in general, is any network within your organization. An *untrusted network*, in general, is any network external to your organization. In addition, wireless technologies enable employees to compute, communicate, and access the Internet anywhere and anytime. Significantly, wireless is an inherently nonsecure broadcast communications medium.

The second factor reflects the fact that modern computers and storage devices (e.g., thumb drives or flash drives) continue to become smaller, faster, cheaper, and more portable, with greater storage capacity. These characteristics make it much easier to steal or lose a computer or storage device that contains huge amounts of sensitive information. Also, many more people are able to afford powerful computers and connect inexpensively to the Internet, thus increasing the target size of an attack on information assets.

The third factor is that the computing skills necessary to be a hacker are *decreasing*. The reason is that the Internet contains information and computer programs (called *scripts*) that users with few skills can download and use to attack any information system connected to the Internet. (Security experts can also use these scripts for legitimate purposes, such as testing the security of various systems.)

The fourth factor is that international organized crime is taking over cybercrime. Cybercrime refers to illegal activities taking place over computer networks, particularly the Internet. VeriSign's iDefense Security Intelligence Services (http://idefense.com) provides security information to governments and Fortune 500 companies. VeriSign states that groups of well-organized criminals have taken control of a global billion-dollar crime network. The network, powered by skillful hackers, targets known software security weaknesses. These crimes are typically nonviolent but quite lucrative. For example, the losses from armed robberies average hundreds of dollars and those from white-collar crimes average tens of thousands of dollars. In contrast, losses from computer crimes average hundreds of thousands of dollars. In fact, the 2011 Norton Cybercrime Report estimates the total cost of cybercrime at $388 billion per year. Also, these crimes can be committed from anywhere in the world, at any time, effectively providing an international safe haven for cybercriminals. Computer-based crimes cause billions of dollars in damages to businesses each year, including the costs to repair information systems and the costs of lost business.

The fifth and final factor is lack of management support. For the entire organization to take security policies and procedures seriously, senior managers must set the tone. Ultimately, however, lower-level managers may be even more important. These managers are in close contact with employees every day and thus are in a better position to determine whether employees are following security procedures.

BEFORE YOU GO ON . . .

1. Define information security.
2. Define a threat, an exposure, and a vulnerability.
3. Why are the skills needed to be a hacker decreasing?

Apply the Concept 7.1

Background This section has taught you about the importance of information security when doing business over the Web. It is important to note that the chain is only as strong as its weakest link. Therefore, while you may have been careful to maintain security across your network, if your business partners do not, then as your information passes over their networks it will be at risk.

Activity Visit http://www.wiley.com/go/rainer/applytheconcept and click on the link to VeriSign's Web site. As you read over this page, keep in mind that VeriSign is a company that is in the business of protecting Web sites and Web users and that is something that we all appreciate. In fact, it is likely that you feel some level of comfort when you see the VeriSign symbol on an e-commerce site.

Deliverable

After reading the article, write a paragraph from VeriSign to potential business that explains the following questions:

1. What are the five steps that occur when a browser connects to a secure Web site?

2. What is an SSL certificate and how does it fit in the five steps mentioned in question 1?

3. What are the normal visual cues that a connection is secure and what is the extended verification that is seen on some sites?

4. What are the benefits of using VeriSign to both the merchant and the customer?

Submit your paragraph to your instructor.

Quiz questions are assignable in WileyPLUS, and available on the Book Companion Site at http://www.wiley.com/college/rainer.

RUBY'S CLUB   QUESTIONS

1. Describe the ways Ruby's Club is vulnerable to security threats based on the nature of its business.

2. Based on the current operating environment, do you think it is acceptable for Ruben and Lisa to continue to operate without upgrading their IS because they are afraid of security issues? If they are too afraid, where will their business be in another 5 years with no information system?

7.2 Unintentional Threats to Information Systems

Information systems are vulnerable to many potential hazards and threats, as you see in Figure 7.1. The two major categories of threats are unintentional threats and deliberate threats. In this section you will learn about unintentional threats. The next section addresses deliberate threats.

Unintentional threats are those acts with no malicious intent. Human errors are unintentional and represent a serious threat to information security.

Human Errors

Organizational employees span the breadth and depth of the organization, from mail clerks to the CEO, and across all functional areas. There are two important points to be made about employees. First, the higher the level of employee, the greater the threat the employee poses to information security. This situation exists because higher-level employees typically have greater access to corporate data and enjoy greater privileges on organizational information systems. Second, employees in two areas of the organization pose significant threats to information security: human resources and information systems. Human resources employees generally have access to sensitive personal information about all employees. Likewise, information systems employees not only have access to sensitive organizational data, but they also often control the means to create, store, transmit, and modify that data.

Other employees include contract labor, consultants, and janitors and guards. Contract labor, such as temporary hires, may be overlooked in information security. However, these employees often have access to the company's network, information systems, and information assets. Consultants, while technically not employees, do work for the company. Depending on the nature of their work, these people may also have access to the company's network, information systems, and information assets.

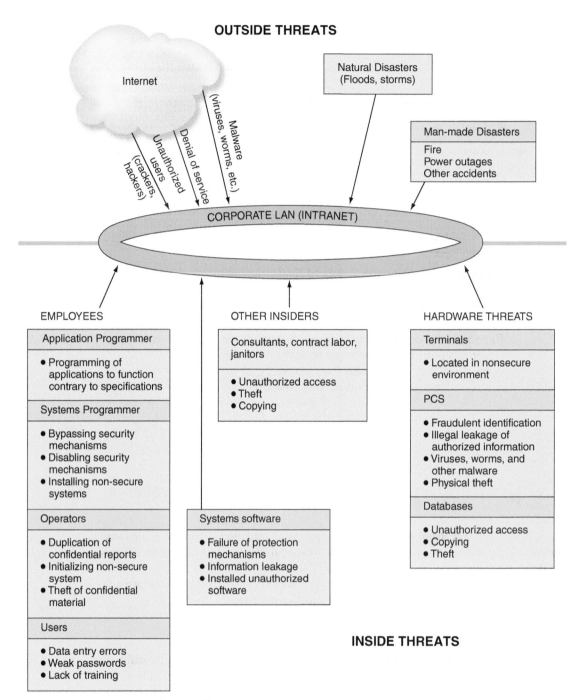

OUTSIDE THREATS

Internet

Unauthorized users (crackers, hackers)

Denial of service

Malware (viruses, worms, etc.)

Natural Disasters (Floods, storms)

Man-made Disasters
Fire
Power outages
Other accidents

CORPORATE LAN (INTRANET)

EMPLOYEES

Application Programmer
- Programming of applications to function contrary to specifications

Systems Programmer
- Bypassing security mechanisms
- Disabling security mechanisms
- Installing non-secure systems

Operators
- Duplication of confidential reports
- Initializing non-secure system
- Theft of confidential material

Users
- Data entry errors
- Weak passwords
- Lack of training

OTHER INSIDERS

Consultants, contract labor, janitors
- Unauthorized access
- Theft
- Copying

Systems software
- Failure of protection mechanisms
- Information leakage
- Installed unauthorized software

HARDWARE THREATS

Terminals
- Located in nonsecure environment

PCS
- Fraudulent identification
- Illegal leakage of authorized information
- Viruses, worms, and other malware
- Physical theft

Databases
- Unauthorized access
- Copying
- Theft

INSIDE THREATS

Figure 7.1 Security threats.

Janitors and guards are the most frequently ignored people in information security. Companies might outsource their security and janitorial services, meaning that, although these individuals technically are not employees, they nevertheless do work for the company. Moreover, they are usually present when most—if not all—other employees have gone home. They typically have keys to every office and nobody questions their presence in even the most sensitive parts of the building. In fact, an article from the Winter 1994 edition of *2600: The Hacker Quarterly* described how to get a job as a janitor for the purpose of gaining physical access to an organization.

Human errors or mistakes by employees pose a large problem as the result of laziness, carelessness, or a lack of awareness concerning information security. This lack of awareness

TABLE 7.1 Human Mistakes

Mistake	Description and Examples
Carelessness with laptops	Losing laptops, misplacing laptops, leaving them in taxis, and so on.
Carelessness with computing devices	Losing or misplacing these devices, or using them carelessly so that malware is introduced into an organization's network.
Opening questionable e-mails	Opening e-mails from someone unknown, or clicking on links embedded in e-mails (see "Phishing Attacks" later in this chapter).
Careless Internet surfing	Accessing questionable Web sites; can result in malware and/or alien software being introduced into the organization's network.
Poor password selection and use	Choosing and using weak passwords (see "Strong Passwords" later in this chapter).
Carelessness with one's office	Unlocked desks and filing cabinets when employees go home at night; not logging off the company network when gone from the office for any extended period of time.
Carelessness using unmanaged devices	Unmanaged devices are those outside the control of an organization's IT department and company security procedures. These devices include computers belonging to customers and business partners, computers in the business centers of hotels, and computers in Starbucks, Panera Bread, and so on.
Carelessness with discarded equipment	Discarding old computer hardware and devices without completely wiping the memory; includes computers, cell phones, Blackberries, and digital copiers and printers.
Careless monitoring of environment	These hazards, which include dirt, dust, humidity, and static electricity, are harmful to the safe operation of computing equipment.

comes from poor education and training efforts by the organization. Human mistakes manifest themselves in many different ways, as you see in Table 7.1.

The human errors that you have just studied are unintentional on the part of the employee. However, employees can also make unintentional mistakes as a result of actions by an attacker. Attackers often employ social engineering to induce individuals to make unintentional mistakes and disclose sensitive information.

Social Engineering

In a **social engineering** attack, the perpetrator uses social skills to trick or manipulate a legitimate employee into providing confidential company information such as passwords. The most common example of social engineering occurs when the attacker impersonates someone else on the telephone, such as a company manager or information systems employee. The attacker claims to have forgotten the password and asks the legitimate employee to provide a password to use. Other common exploits include posing as an exterminator, an air conditioning technician, or a fire marshal. Examples of social engineering abound.

In one company, a perpetrator entered a company building wearing a company ID card that looked legitimate. He walked around and put up signs on bulletin boards saying, "The help desk telephone number has been changed. The new number is 555-1234." He then exited the building and began receiving

Blend/Image Source Limited.

Who is real and who is engaged in social engineering? Can you tell?

© Creasource/Corbis

Piracy is theft. Would you steal a DVD?

calls from legitimate employees thinking they were calling the company help desk. Naturally, the first thing the perpetrator asked for was user name and password. He now had the information necessary to access the company's information systems.

Two other social engineering techniques include tailgating and shoulder surfing. *Tailgating* is a technique designed to allow the perpetrator to enter restricted areas that are controlled with locks or card entry. The perpetrator follows closely behind a legitimate employee and, when the employee gains entry, asks the person to "hold the door." *Shoulder surfing* occurs when a perpetrator watches the employee's computer screen over that person's shoulder. This technique is particularly successful in public areas such as airports and commuter trains and on airplanes.

--- BEFORE *YOU GO ON* . . . ---

1. What is an unintentional threat to an information system?
2. Provide other examples of social engineering attacks.

Apply the Concept 7.2

Background Sensitive information is generally stored in a safe location both physically and digitally. However, as this section has discussed, there are often unintentional threats that result from careless mistakes. Employees often use USB drives to take information home. Although the information may be completely legal for them to have, the USB drive makes it easy to lose or copy onto unauthorized machines. In fact, any device that stores information can become a threat to information security—backup drives, CDs, DVDs, and even printers!

Printers?! Because people can "copy" information? Not quite. Continue the activity to find out more!

Activity Go to http://www.wiley.com/go/rainer/applytheconcept and click on the link provided for Apply the Concept 7.2. You will find an article about how the hard drive in a printer sometimes stores images of all the documents that have been copied. In the past when these printers are discarded their hard drives have not been erased, leaving medical records, police reports, and other private information in a vulnerable state.

Visit your library (school or local) and local copy center (Kinkos, Staples, Office Max, etc.) and see if their copiers, hard drives are ever cleaned to erase sensitive information. Find out if they even have a policy in place that would require this information to be erased or not.

Deliverable

Create a table that lists the locations you visited, if they ever clean their hard drives, and if they have a policy. Submit your table to your professor.

Quiz questions are assignable in WileyPLUS, and available on the Book Companion Site at http://www.wiley.com/college/rainer.

RUBY'S CLUB QUESTIONS

1. To which of the social engineering methods do you think Ruby's is most vulnerable?
2. Given the threat that small USB-powered storage devices make it easy to store information, what type of policy could Ruby's implement to avoid information being stolen?

7.3 Deliberate Threats to Information Systems

There are so many types of deliberate acts that a brief list is provided here for your convenience:

- Espionage or trespass
- Information extortion
- Sabotage or vandalism
- Theft of equipment or information
- Identity theft
- Compromises to intellectual property
- Software attacks
- Alien software
- Supervisory control and data acquisition (SCADA) attacks
- Cyberterrorism and cyberwarfare

Espionage or Trespass

Espionage or trespass occurs when an unauthorized individual attempts to gain illegal access to organizational information. It is important to distinguish between competitive intelligence and industrial espionage. Competitive intelligence consists of legal information-gathering techniques, such as studying a company's Web site and press releases and attending trade shows. In contrast, industrial espionage crosses the legal boundary.

Information Extortion

Information extortion occurs when an attacker either threatens to steal, or actually steals, information from a company. The perpetrator demands payment for not stealing the information, for returning stolen information, or for agreeing not to disclose the information.

Sabotage or Vandalism

Sabotage and vandalism are deliberate acts that involve defacing an organization's Web site, possibly causing the organization to lose its image and its customers to experience a loss of confidence. One form of online vandalism is a hacktivist or cyberactivist operation. These are cases of high-tech civil disobedience to protest the operations, policies, or actions of an organization or government agency.

Theft of Equipment and Information

Computing devices and storage devices are becoming smaller yet more powerful with vastly increased storage (e.g., laptops, Blackberries, personal digital assistants, smart phones, digital cameras, thumb drives, and iPads). As a result, these devices are becoming easier to steal and easier for attackers to use to steal information.

Table 7.1 points out that one type of human mistake is carelessness with laptops. In fact, such carelessness often leads to laptops being stolen. The cost of a stolen laptop includes the loss

FSTOP/Image Source Limited.

Software attacks are frustrating, can be embarrassing, and often stop productivity.

of data, the loss of intellectual property, laptop replacement, legal and regulatory costs, investigation fees, and lost productivity.

One form of theft, known as *dumpster diving*, involves the practice of rummaging through commercial or residential trash to find information that has been discarded. Paper files, letters, memos, photographs, IDs, passwords, credit cards, and other forms of information can be found in dumpsters. Unfortunately, many people never consider that the sensitive items they throw in the trash may be recovered. Such information, when recovered, can be used for fraudulent purposes.

Dumpster diving is not necessarily theft, because the legality of this act varies. Because dumpsters are usually located on private premises, dumpster diving is illegal in some parts of the United States. Even in these cases, however, the relevant laws are enforced with varying degrees of rigor.

Identity Theft

Identity theft is the deliberate assumption of another person's identity, usually to gain access to his or her financial information or to frame him or her for a crime. Techniques for obtaining information include the following:

- Stealing mail or dumpster diving
- Stealing personal information in computer databases
- Infiltrating organizations that store large amounts of personal information (e.g., data aggregators such as Acxiom, www.acxiom.com)
- Impersonating a trusted organization in an electronic communication (**phishing**)

Recovering from identity theft is costly, time-consuming, and difficult. Victims also report problems in obtaining credit and obtaining or holding a job, as well as adverse effects on insurance or credit rates. In addition, victims state that it is often difficult to remove negative information from their records, such as their credit reports.

Anyone's personal information can be compromised in other ways. For example, an identity can be uncovered just from examining searches in a search engine. The ability to analyze all searches by a single user can enable a criminal to identify who the user is and what he or she is doing. As just one example, the *New York Times* tracked down a particular person based solely on her AOL searches.

Compromises to Intellectual Property

Protecting intellectual property is a vital issue for people who make their livelihood in knowledge fields. **Intellectual property** is the property created by individuals or corporations that is protected under *trade secret*, *patent*, and *copyright* laws.

A **trade secret** is an intellectual work, such as a business plan, that is a company secret and is not based on public information. An example is a corporate strategic plan. A **patent** is a document that grants the holder exclusive rights on an invention or process for 20 years. **Copyright** is a statutory grant that provides the creators of intellectual property with ownership of the property for the life of the creator plus 70 years. Owners are entitled to collect fees from anyone who wants to copy the property. It is important to note that these are definitions under U.S. law. There is some international standardization, but it is far from total. Therefore, differences may be found between U.S. law and other countries' laws.

The most common intellectual property related to IT deals with software. The U.S. Federal Computer Software Copyright Act (1980) provides protection for *source* and *object code* of computer software, but the law does not clearly identify what is eligible for protection. For example, copyright law does not protect similar concepts, functions, and general features such as pull-down menus, colors, and icons. However, copying a software program without making payment to the owner—including giving a disc to a friend to install on his or her computer—is a copyright violation. Not surprisingly, this practice, called **piracy**, is a major problem for software vendors. The global trade in pirated software amounts to billions of dollars.

Software Attacks

Software attacks have evolved from the outbreak era—during which malicious software (**malware**) tried to infect as many computers worldwide as possible—to the profit-driven, Web-based attacks of today. Cybercriminals are heavily involved with malware attacks to make money, and they use sophisticated, blended attacks typically via the Web. Table 7.2 shows a variety of software attacks. You will see that software attacks are grouped into three categories: remote attacks needing user action; remote attacks needing no user action; and software attacks by programmers during the development of a system. IT's About Business 7.1 provides an example of a software attack.

TABLE 7.2 Types of Software Attacks

Type	Description
(1) Remote Attacks Needing User Action	
Virus	Segment of computer code that performs malicious actions by attaching to another computer program.
Worm	Segment of computer code that performs malicious actions and will replicate or spread, by itself (without requiring another computer program).
Phishing Attack	Phishing attacks use deception to acquire sensitive personal information by masquerading as official-looking e-mails or instant messages.
Spear Phishing Attack	Phishing attacks target large groups of people. In spear phishing attacks, the perpetrators find out as much information about an individual as possible to improve their chances that phishing techniques will be able to obtain sensitive, personal information.
(2) Remote Attacks Needing No User Action	
Denial-of-Service Attack	Attacker sends so many information requests to a target computer system that the target cannot handle them successfully and typically crashes (ceases to function).
Distributed Denial-of-Service Attack	An attacker first takes over many computers, typically by using malicious software. These computers are called *zombies*, or *bots*. The attacker uses these bots (which form a *botnet*) to deliver a coordinated stream of information requests to a target computer, causing it to crash.
(3) Attacks by Programmer Developing a System	
Trojan Horse	Software programs that hide in other computer programs and reveal their designed behavior only when they are activated.
Back Door	Typically, a password, known only to the attacker, that allows him or her to access a computer system at will, without having to go through any security procedures (also called a *trap door*).
Logic Bomb	Segment of computer code that is embedded within an organization's existing computer programs and is designed to activate and perform a destructive action at a certain time or date.

"Anonymous" Attacks the Vatican

 "Anonymous" is an elusive hacker movement that has carried out Internet attacks on well-known organizations such as Sony and PBS. Anonymous first gained widespread notoriety with an attack on the Church of Scientology in 2008 and has carried out hundreds of cyberstrikes since then. The group has targeted law enforcement agencies, Internet security companies, and opponents of the whistle-blower Web site WikiLeaks.

In August 2011, Anonymous attacked the Vatican. The campaign against the Vatican involved hundreds of people, some with hacking skills and some without. A core group of participants openly encouraged support for the attack using YouTube, Twitter, and Facebook. Others searched for vulnerabilities on the Vatican Web site. When that failed, they enlisted amateur recruits to flood the site with traffic, hoping it would crash. The attack, even though it was unsuccessful, provides insight into the recruiting, reconnaissance, and warfare tactics used by Anonymous.

The Vatican attack was initially organized by hackers in South America and Mexico before spreading to other countries, and it was timed to coincide with Pope Benedict XVI's visit to Madrid in August 2011 for World Youth Day. Hackers first tried to take down a Web site that the Catholic Church had set up to promote the pope's visit, handle registrations, and sell merchandise. Anomymous's goal—according to YouTube messages delivered by an Anonymous spokesperson—was to disrupt the event. The YouTube videos that were posted included a verbal attack on the pope. One video even called on volunteers to "prepare your weapons, my dear brothers, for this August 17th to Sunday August 21st, we will drop anger over the Vatican."

The hackers spent weeks spreading their message via their own Web site and via social sites such as Twitter and Flickr. Their Facebook page called on volunteers to download free attack software and implored them to "stop child abuse" by joining in the cause. This message featured split-screen images of the pope seated on a gilded throne on one side and starving African children on the other. It also linked to articles about abuse cases and blog posts itemizing the church's assets.

It took 18 days for the hackers to recruit enough people to launch their attack. Then, the reconnaissance phase of the mission began. A core group of approximately 12 skilled

© Nikada/iStockphoto

hackers spent three days poking around the church's World Youth Day Web site, looking for common security holes that could let them inside. Probing for such loopholes used to be tedious and slow, but the emergence of automated scanning software to locate security weaknesses made the process much simple and quicker.

In this case, the scanning software failed to turn up any vulnerabilities on the World Youth Day Web page. So, the hackers turned to a brute-force attack—a distributed denial-of-service attack (DDoS) that clogs a Web site with data requests until it crashes. Even unskilled supporters could take part in this attack from their computers or smartphones.

Over the course of the campaign's final 2 days, Anonymous enlisted as many as a thousand people to download attack software, or directed them to custom-built Web sites that allowed them to participate in the campaign using their smartphones. Visiting a particular Web address caused the phones to instantly start flooding the target Web site with hundreds of data requests each second, without needing any special software.

On the first day of the DDoS, the church site experienced 28 times its normal amount of traffic, rising to 34 times the normal amount of traffic on the following day. Hackers involved in the attack, who did not identify themselves, stated via Twitter that the 2-day effort succeeded in slowing the Web site's performance and made the page unavailable in several countries.

Imperva (www.imperva.com), the firm hired by the Vatican to counter the attack, denied that the Web site's performance was affected and said that the company's technologies had successfully defended the World Youth Day site against the attack. Imperva said that the Vatican's defenses held strong because it had invested in the infrastructure needed to repel cyberattacks.

Following this unsuccessful attack, Anonymous moved on to other targets, including an unofficial site about the pope, which the hackers were briefly able to deface. Hacker movements such as Anonymous are now able to gain widespread membership through the Internet and represent a serious threat to Web sites and organizations.

Sources: Compiled from M. Schwartz, "Anonymous Leaves Clues in Failed Vatican Attack," *InformationWeek*, February 29, 2012; R.

Vamosi, "Report: Anonymous Turns to Denial of Service Attacks as a Last Resort," *Forbes*, February 28, 2012; A. Greenberg, "WikiLeaks Tightens Ties to Anonymous in Leak of Stratfor E-Mails," *Forbes*, February 27, 2012; M. Liebowitz, "'Anonymous' Vatican Cyberattack Revealed by Researchers," *MSNBC*, February 27, 2012; N. Perlroth and J. Markoff, "In Attack on Vatican Web Site, a Glimpse of Hackers' Tactics," *The New York Times*, February 26, 2012; www.imperva.com, accessed February 29, 2012.

Questions

1. Describe the various components of Anonymous's traditional attack method. Which aspects are of most concern to security companies?

2. Describe the distributed denial-of-service attack that Anonymous used on the Vatican.

Another type of software attack uses scareware. Scareware is a type of malware designed to trick victims into purchasing and downloading useless and potentially dangerous software. IT's About Business 7.2 provides an example of two criminals who made a fortune with scareware.

IT'S ABOUT BUSINESS 7.2

Scareware

Sam Jain and Daniel Sundin were masters of social engineering who built an illegal empire by frightening people into handing over their money in exchange for low-quality software.

In August 2003, Jain and Sundin took advantage of the Blaster worm, a worm that had quickly compromised hundreds of thousands of computers and caused consumer panic. During the first 4 days of the Blaster epidemic, some 40,000 computer users called Microsoft for support. By playing off the general panic, Jain and Sundin were able to exploit a vast audience via manipulative ad campaigns. They founded a scareware company called Innovative Marketing, Inc., or IMI, based solely around this enterprise.

Here is how IMI worked. The company started by producing a subpar security software product. Then they deployed pop-up ads that announced fake alerts about problems on users' hard drives—for example, "you

have 284 severe system threats." These pop-ups prompted customers to download a free trial of IMI's software or pay $39.95 for the "full-featured version" of IMI's software. Once installed, the trial versions pumped more ads into the users' Web browsers, which urged

© Stephen Zabel/iStockphoto

users to purchase the "full-featured version." The ploy was quite ironic: Jain and Sundin exploited consumer fears of viruses in order to perpetrate what was, in effect, another virus—and victims paid for the privilege.

The IMI scheme was quite successful, as it quickly became a sophisticated enterprise with hundreds of employees and offices on four continents. IMI had telephone support centers in Ohio, Argentina, and India, and marketed its products under more than 1,000 different brand names and in at least nine languages. From 2002 to 2008, IMI turned profits of hundreds of millions of dollars.

Over time, IMI also became an innovation hub. The company was constantly experimenting and tweaking its security software packages, which ranged from antivirus programs to registry cleaners to firewall software. The company also refined its marketing techniques by sending customers ads for a variety of products and then conducting sophisticated statistical analyses to see which approach was the most effective.

One highly successful marketing technique that emerged from this research was the "scanner method." A pop-up ad would offer users a "free scan" of their supposedly infected hard drive. Once the phony scanner announced its (always alarming) results, it provided a link to IMI's software. This advertising method proved to be quite effective social hacking. Because potential customers had already invested time in the "scan" and been duly frightened by it, they were much more likely to purchase the software.

Leading advertising networks banned IMI, so the company set up a series of fake online ad agencies that placed banners on popular Web sites such as *The Economist*, eHarmony, and Major League Baseball. IMI embedded these ads with hidden computer code so that if someone from inside the hosting site's offices looked at the ads, they would see appeals from mainstream companies such as Travelocity, Priceline, and Weight Watchers. But, if regular users viewed the ads, they saw ads for used cars or diet pills. When consumers clicked on these ads, they were redirected to Web sites selling antivirus software, or even worse, "antivirus software" would automatically download to their computers.

One challenge IMI faced was dodging angry customers who were demanding their money back. The company's goal was to avoid refunding any money while preventing customers from calling their credit card companies, which would endanger IMI's banking relationships. Customers were not upset that the company's software was ineffective—most customers had no way of knowing that. But, in many cases, customers' existing antivirus software would flag IMI applications as malware. This made IMI applications difficult to install and slowed computer speeds to a crawl. IMI therefore set up call centers to provide support in multiple languages, usually by instructing customers to uninstall their other antivirus software. This trick mollified users, as it returned computer speeds to normal. The IMI applications still provided no actual service to customers, but upsetting warnings from legitimate antivirus software stopped showing up, leaving nervous customers with the impression that their new purchase had done its job.

Today, Jain and Sundin's whereabouts are unknown and there are warrants out for both of their arrests. With IMI apparently out of action, a new generation of scareware is rising to take its place. The most promising venues for these new scareware programs are social networking sites, where misleading posts on Facebook and Twitter can snare unwary users.

Sources: Compiled from B. Wallace, "How Two Scammers Built an Empire Hawking Sketchy Software," *Wired*, October 2011; M. Schwartz, "FBI Breaks Up Two Big Scareware Rings," *InformationWeek*, June 23, 2011; J. Blum, "International Computer Scam Disrupted After $72 Million Lost," *Bloomberg BusinessWeek*, June 22, 2011; R. McMillan, "Alleged $100 Million Scareware Sellers Facing Charges," *PC World*, May 27, 2010; D. Kennedy, "The Proliferation of Scareware Hits Home," *Forbes*, March 16, 2010.

Questions

1. Explain the difference between scareware and other types of cyberattacks.

2. Describe methods that organizations can use to combat scareware.

Alien Software

Many personal computers have alien software (also called *pestware*) running on them that the owners do not know about. Alien software is clandestine software that is installed on a computer through duplicitous methods. **Alien software** is typically not as malicious as viruses, worms, or Trojan horses, but it does use up valuable system resources. In addition, it can report on your Web surfing habits and other personal behavior.

The vast majority of pestware is **adware**—software designed to help pop-up advertisements appear on your screen. Adware is so common because it works. According to advertising agencies, for every 100 people who delete such an ad, three click on it. This "hit rate" is extremely high for Internet advertising.

Spyware is software that collects personal information about users without their consent. Two types of spyware are addressed here: keystroke loggers and screen scrapers.

Keystroke loggers (also called *keyloggers*) record keystrokes and record Internet Web browsing history. The purposes range from criminal (e.g., theft of passwords and sensitive personal information such as credit card numbers) to annoying (e.g., recording Internet search history for targeted advertising).

Companies have attempted to counter key loggers by switching to other forms of input for authentication. For example, all of us have been forced to look at wavy, distorted letters and type them correctly into a box. That string of letters is called a CAPTCHA and it is a test. The point of CAPTCHA is that reading those distorted letters is something that computers cannot do accurately (yet). The fact that you can transcribe them means that you are probably not a software program run by an unauthorized person, such as a spammer. As a result, attackers have turned to *screen scrapers* (or *screen grabbers*), software that records a continuous "movie" of a screen's contents rather than simply recording keystrokes.

Spamware is pestware that is designed to use your computer as a launch pad for spammers. **Spam** is unsolicited e-mail, usually for the purpose of advertising for products and services. When your computer is used this way, e-mails from spammers appear to come from you. Even worse, spam will be sent to everyone in your e-mail address book.

Not only is spam a nuisance, but it wastes time and money. Spam costs U.S. companies billions of dollars per year. These costs come from productivity losses, clogged e-mail systems, additional storage, user support, and antispam software. Spam can also carry viruses and worms, making it even more dangerous.

Cookies are small amounts of information that Web sites store on your computer, temporarily or more or less permanently. In many cases, cookies are useful and innocuous. For example, some cookies store passwords and user IDs that you do not have to retype every time you load a new page at the Web site that issued the cookie. Cookies are also necessary if you want to shop online, because they are used for your shopping carts at various online merchants.

Tracking cookies, however, can be used to track your path through a Web site, the time you spend there, what links you click on, and other details that the company wants to record, usually for marketing purposes. Tracking cookies can also combine this information with your name, purchases, credit card information, and other personal data, to develop an intrusive profile of your spending habits.

Most cookies can be read only by the party that created them. However, some companies that manage online banner advertising are, in essence, cookie-sharing rings. These companies can track information such as which pages you load and which ads you click on. They then share this information with their client Web sites (which may number in the thousands). For a cookie demonstration, see http://cookiedemo.com.

Supervisory Control and Data Acquisition (SCADA Attacks)

SCADA refers to a large-scale, distributed, measurement and control system. SCADA systems are used to monitor or to control chemical, physical, or transport processes such as oil refineries, water and sewage treatment plants, electrical generators, and nuclear power plants. Essentially, SCADA systems provide the link between the physical world and the electronic world.

SCADA systems consist of multiple sensors, a master computer, and communications infrastructure. The sensors connect to physical equipment and read status data such as the open/closed status of a switch or a valve, as well as measurements such as pressure, flow, voltage, and current. By sending signals to equipment, sensors control that equipment, such as opening or closing a switch or valve or setting the speed of a pump.

The sensors are connected in a network, and each sensor typically has an Internet (Internet Protocol, or IP) address. (You studied about IP addresses in Chapter 4.) If an attacker can gain access to the network, he or she can disrupt the power grid over a large area or disrupt the operations of a large chemical plant. Such actions could have catastrophic results.

BEFORE *YOU GO ON . . .*

1. Why has the theft of computing devices become more serious over time?
2. What are the three types of software attacks?
3. Define *alien software*.
4. What is a SCADA system?

Cyberterrorism and Cyberwarfare

With both **cyberterrorism** and **cyberwarfare**, attackers use a target's computer systems, particularly via the Internet, to cause physical, real-world harm or severe disruption, usually to carry out a political agenda. Cyberterrorism and cyberwarfare range from gathering data to attacking critical infrastructure (via SCADA systems). The two types of attacks are discussed synonymously here, even though cyberterrorism typically is carried out by individuals or groups, whereas cyberwarfare involves nations. Following are examples of cyberattacks against Estonia and the Republic of Georgia.

EXAMPLE

In 2007, a 3-week wave of massive distributed denial-of-service (DDoS) cyberattacks against the Baltic country of Estonia disabled the Web sites of government ministries, political parties, newspapers, banks, and companies. One of the most wired societies in Europe, Estonia is a pioneer of e-government. As a result, the country is highly vulnerable to cyberattack. In the early phase of the DDoS attack, some perpetrators were identified by their IP addresses. Many of these addresses were Russian and some of them were from Russian state institutions.

In August 2008, Russian troops entered the Republic of Georgia's province of South Ossetia to crush a Georgian attempt to control a breakaway by that region. DDoS attacks on Georgian Web sites were apparently synchronized with the Russian invasion. The cyberattack shut down the Web site of the Georgian president, Mikheil Saakashvilli, for 24 hours and defaced the Georgian parliament Web site with images of Adolf Hitler. Saakashvilli blamed Russia for the attacks, but the Russian government denied the charges.

Terrorist groups around the world have expanded their activities on the Internet, increasing the sophistication and volume of their videos and messages, in an effort to recruit new members and raise money. In response, the U.S. military is expanding its offensive capabilities to attack terrorists' Web sites, rather than just monitor them.

Apply the Concept 7.3

Background It is sad that there are many people out there who are proud of the fact that they can take advantage of others. Fraud, espionage, information extortion, identity theft, cyberterrorism, spamming, phishing, pharming, and many other deliberate acts have created a world where we must always confirm the identity and validity of those we share information with.

Activity Go to http://www.wiley.com/go/rainer/applytheconcept and click on the link provided for Apply the Concept 7.3. It will take you to a video about foreign lotteries. This scam has taken advantage of many elderly simply because they are not aware that scams exist! After watching the video, search the Web for other scams that involve Craigslist, Ebay, and any other site you may find.

Deliverable

Imagine that you are the owner of a site such as Craigslist. Write a memo to your users (both buyers and sellers) explaining your intention to run a "clean" site where all parties are safe.

In your memo, give your own definition of fraud for your users' information. Include expectations of ethical behavior and legal transactions. Submit this memo to your professor.

Quiz questions are assignable in WileyPLUS, and available on the Book Companion Site at http://www.wiley.com/college/rainer.

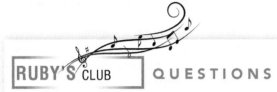

RUBY'S CLUB | **QUESTIONS**

1. Given the stories in the chapter, what are some scenarios where someone might use USB drives to access Ruby's private customer data?

2. Because Ruby's is being redesigned, where should "back office" operations be housed to help deter theft of equipment?

7.4 What Organizations Are Doing to Protect Information Resources

Why is it so difficult to stop cybercriminals? Table 7.3 lists the major difficulties involved in protecting information. Because organizing an appropriate defense system is so important to the entire enterprise, it is one of the major responsibilities of any prudent CIO as well as the functional managers who control information resources. In fact, IT security is the business of *everyone* in an organization.

TABLE 7.3 The Difficulties in Protecting Information Resources

Hundreds of potential threats exist.

Computing resources may be situated in many locations.

Many individuals control information assets.

Computer networks can be located outside the organization and are thus difficult to protect.

Rapid technological changes make some controls obsolete as soon as they are installed.

Many computer crimes are undetected for a long period of time, so it is difficult to learn from experience.

People tend to violate security procedures because the procedures are inconvenient.

The amount of computer knowledge necessary to commit computer crimes is usually minimal. As a matter of fact, one can learn hacking, for free, on the Internet.

The cost of preventing hazards can be very high. Therefore, most organizations simply cannot afford to protect against all possible hazards.

It is difficult to conduct a cost–benefit justification for controls before an attack occurs because it is difficult to assess the value of a hypothetical attack.

Another reason why it is difficult to protect information resources is that the online commerce industry is not particularly willing to install safeguards that would make it harder to complete transactions. It would be possible, for example, to demand passwords or personal identification numbers for all credit card transactions. However, these requirements might discourage people from shopping online. Also, there is little incentive for companies like AOL to share leads on criminal activity either with one another or with the FBI. For credit card companies, it is cheaper to block a stolen credit card and move on than to invest time and money on a prosecution.

Despite these difficulties, the information security industry is battling back. Companies are developing software and services that deliver early warnings of trouble on the Internet. Unlike traditional antivirus software, which is reactive, early-warning systems are proactive, scanning the Web for new viruses and alerting companies to dangers.

Organizations spend a great deal of time and money protecting their information resources. Before doing so, they perform risk management.

Risk is the probability that a threat will impact an information resource. The goal of **risk management** is to identify, control, and minimize the impact of threats. In other words, risk management seeks to reduce risk to acceptable levels. Risk management encompasses three processes: risk analysis, risk mitigation, and controls evaluation.

Risk analysis is the process by which an organization assesses the value of each asset being protected, estimates the probability that each asset will be compromised, and compares the probable costs of the asset's being compromised with the costs of protecting that asset. Organizations perform risk analysis to ensure that their information systems' security programs are cost effective. The risk analysis process prioritizes the assets to be protected based on each asset's value, its probability of being compromised, and the estimated cost of its protection. The organization then considers how to mitigate the risk.

In **risk mitigation**, the organization takes concrete actions against risks. Risk mitigation has two functions: (1) implementing controls to prevent identified threats from occurring and (2) developing a means of recovery should the threat become a reality. Several risk mitigation strategies may be adopted by organizations. The three most common are risk acceptance, risk limitation, and risk transference.

- **Risk acceptance:** Accept the potential risk, continue operating with no controls, and absorb any damages that occur.
- **Risk limitation:** Limit the risk by implementing controls that minimize the impact of the threat.
- **Risk transference:** Transfer the risk by using other means to compensate for the loss, such as by purchasing insurance.

In controls evaluation, the organization examines the costs of implementing adequate control measures against the value of those control measures. If the costs of implementing a control are greater than the value of the asset being protected, then control is not cost effective. In the next section, you will study the various controls that organizations use to protect their information resources.

─ BEFORE YOU GO ON . . . ─

1. Describe several reasons why it is difficult to protect information resources.
2. Compare and contrast risk management and risk analysis.

Apply the Concept 7.4

Background The heart of information systems is the data used in processing transactions and making business decisions. However, often this data is private information about individuals and companies. It is important that this data and information be used wisely and protected. The Federal Trade Commission (FTC) has established a set of Fair Information Practices Principles as guidelines for government agencies' collection and use of personal information. These same guidelines also should be a basis for business use of data.

Activity Go to http://www.wiley.com/go/rainer/applytheconcept and click on the link provided for Apply the Concept 7.4. This link will take you to a Web page where you can review the Fair Information Practices Principles for protecting America's consumers. As you read over this document, pay attention to the five key points of the guidelines. Once you are familiar with them, go back to http://www.wiley.com/go/rainer/applytheconcept and click on the second link. It will take you to a YouTube video titled "Ordering Pizza in the Future" video by user "dedots."

Deliverable

Build a table that has the key points of the Fair Information Practices in one column and how this video met or broke each point. Submit this to your professor.

Quiz questions are assignable in WileyPLUS, and available on the Book Companion Site at http://www.wiley.com/college/rainer.

RUBY'S CLUB QUESTIONS

1. A risk analysis is crucial for Ruby's. Is the e-commerce part of the club's site crucial to its business plan? If not, should the club accept the risk and go with its e-commerce plans? Should Ruben and Lisa limit the risk by simply displaying products but only selling them at their nightclub? Or should they transfer the risk and use a third-party company to run the e-commerce of the site?

2. Ruben and Lisa should be familiar with the "penetration attack" given that they sell alcohol and are often tested by the Beverage Control Board to see if they will sell alcohol to minors. How could they use this same concept and test their own security against intentional and unintentional threats?

7.5 Information Security Controls

To protect their information assets, organizations implement **controls**, or defense mechanisms (also called *countermeasures*). **Information security controls** are designed to protect all of the components of an information system, including data, software, hardware, and networks. Because there are so many diverse threats, organizations utilize layers of controls, or defense-in-depth.

Controls are intended to prevent accidental hazards, deter intentional acts, detect problems as early as possible, enhance damage recovery, and correct problems. Before you study controls in more detail, it is important to emphasize that the single most effective control is user education and training, leading to increased awareness of the vital importance of information security on the part of every organizational employee. As you have learned in this chapter, an organization's employees are its greatest information security risk. In fact, the fastest way to build a botnet is to attack individual employees. Once a botnet has been established, it is difficult to combat it. However, IT's About Business 7.3 shows a company that has been successful in thwarting botnets.

How to Fight a Botnet

FireEye (www.fireeye.com) defends corporations and governments against targeted malicious software. FireEye's clients include Fortune 500 companies and members of the U.S. intelligence community. FireEye is one of the world's most effective private cybercrime fighters.

FireEye's software examines the entire life cycle of malicious software (or "malware"): how the malware operates in a network, what the malware is looking for, which servers delivered the malware, and from which control servers the malware receives its orders. Since 2005, FireEye has deflected some of the world's most destructive online attacks, including Aurora, the attack originating in China that targeted Google and other technology firms in 2009; coreflood, the botnet that had been stealing millions of dollars from global bank accounts since the mid-2000s and possibly earlier; and Zeus, a program that used personal information to steal hundreds of millions of dollars from financial institutions in 2007.

Let's look at the confrontation between FireEye and the Rustock botnet. Rustock is the most advanced botnet the Web had ever seen. It reeled people in by putting out spam that advertised for fake drugs, online pharmacies, and Russian stocks. Then, from 2007 to 2011, Rustock quietly and illegally took control of over a million computers around the world. Symantec, a computer security company, found that Rustock generated as many as 44 billion spam e-mails per day, or about 47.5 percent of the total number of junk e-mails sent per day worldwide. Although the perpetrators behind the Rustock botnet were not yet identified at that time, profits from it were thought to be in the millions of dollars.

For months, FireEye worked together with Microsoft and Pfizer to plot a counterattack. Microsoft and Pfizer got involved because Rustock was selling fake Viagra, a Pfizer product, as well as sham lotteries using the Microsoft logo. Working from FireEye's intelligence, in March 2011 U.S. Marshals stormed seven Internet data centers across the United States where Rustock had hidden its 96 command servers. Microsoft lawyers and technicians and computer forensics experts also participated in the raids. A team deployed to the Netherlands confiscated an additional two Rustock command servers.

Although the operation was executed flawlessly, Rustock was still able to fight back. From an unknown location, the botmaster remotely sneaked back into its network, locked out Microsoft's technicians, and began to erase files. Clearly, the Rustock masterminds did not want anyone seeing what was inside their hard drives. After some difficulty, the Microsoft technicians were able to regain control of their servers. However, the data that was erased in the 30 minutes that it took the Microsoft technicians to regain control of their servers may now be lost forever.

As FireEye and its partner companies analyzed Rustock's equipment, they discovered that much of it was leased to customers with addresses in Azerbaijan. Forensic analysis of the captured servers pointed Rustock's opponents to Moscow and St. Petersburg. Rustock had used the name Cosma2k to conduct business on the Internet and had a WebMoney account (www.webmoney.com) under the name Vladimir Alexandrovich Shergin. No one knows whether Shergin was a real name or an alias. But, WebMoney was able to inform investigators that "Shergin" had listed an address in a small city outside Moscow.

On April 6, 2011, Microsoft delivered its first status report in its lawsuit against Rustock to the federal court in Seattle. On June 14, Microsoft then published notices in Moscow and St. Petersburg newspapers, detailing its allegations against the botnet spammer. The notices urged the perpetrators of Rustock to respond to the charges or risk being declared guilty. Microsoft also offered (and is still offering) $250,000 for information about the identity of the person or persons operating the botnet. Unfortunately, the Rustock perpetrators have still not been caught and security experts believe that over 600,000 computers around the world are still infected with Rustock malware.

Sources: Compiled from K. Higgins, "Microsoft Offers $250,000 for Rustock Botnet Operator Identity," *InformationWeek*, July 19, 2011; "Microsoft Offers Reward for Information on Rustock," *The Official Microsoft Blog*, July 18, 2011; C. Stewart, "Botnet Busters," *Bloomberg BusinessWeek*, June 20–26, 2011; "Spammers Sought After Botnet Takedown," *BBC News*, March 25, 2011; M. Schwartz, "Microsoft, Feds Knock Rustock Botnet Offline," *InformationWeek*, March 18, 2011; N. Wingfield, "Spam Network Shut Down," *The Wall Street Journal*, March 18, 2011; M. Hickens, "Prolific Spam

Network Is Unplugged," *The Wall Street Journal*, March 17, 2011; "Operation b107—Rustock Botnet Takedown," *Microsoft Malware Protection Center*, March 17, 2011; www.fireeye.com, accessed March 5, 2012.

Questions

1. Describe why it was so important for law enforcement officials to capture all 96 Rustock command servers at one time.

2. If the perpetrators of Rustock are ever caught, will it be possible to prove that the perpetrators were responsible for the malware? Why or why not? Support your answer.

The three major types of controls are physical controls, access controls, and communications controls. Figure 7.2 illustrates these controls. In addition to applying controls, organizations plan for business continuity in case of a disaster and audit their information resources.

Physical Controls

Physical controls prevent unauthorized individuals from gaining access to a company's facilities. Common physical controls include walls, doors, fencing, gates, locks, badges, guards, and alarm systems. More sophisticated physical controls include pressure sensors, temperature sensors, and motion detectors. One weakness of physical controls is that they can be inconvenient to employees.

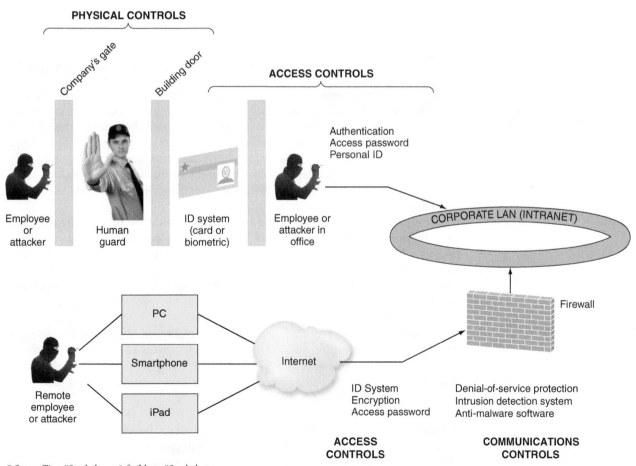

© Sergey Titov/iStockphoto; © fatihhoca/iStockphoto.

Figure 7.2 Where defense mechanisms are located.

Guards deserve special mention because they have very difficult jobs for at least two reasons. First, their jobs are boring and repetitive and generally do not pay well. Second, if they do their jobs thoroughly, other employees harass them, particularly if their being conscientious slows up the process of entering a facility.

Organizations also put other physical security considerations in place. Such controls limit users to acceptable log-in times and locations. These controls also limit the number of unsuccessful log-in attempts and they require all employees to log off their computers when they leave for the day. In addition, computers are set to automatically log off the user after a certain period of disuse.

Access Controls

Access controls restrict unauthorized individuals from using information resources. These controls involve two major functions: authentication and authorization. **Authentication** determines the identity of the person requiring access. After the person is authenticated (identified), authorization is applied. **Authorization** determines which actions, rights, or privileges the person has, based on verified identity.

Authentication. To authenticate (identify) authorized personnel, an organization can use one or more of the following methods: something the user is, something the user has, something the user does, and/or something the user knows.

Something the user is (also known as **biometrics**), is an authentication method that examines a person's innate physical characteristics. Common biometric applications are fingerprint scans, palm scans, retina scans, iris recognition, and facial recognition. Of these, fingerprints, retina scans, and iris recognition provide the most definitive identification. The following example shows how powerful biometrics can be for identification purposes.

EXAMPLE The Biometric Identification Project of India

India has vast numbers of anonymous poor citizens. As a result, the nation is deploying its Unique Identification Project, also known as Aadhaar, which means "the foundation" in several Indian languages. The goal of the Unique Identification Project is to issue identification numbers linked to the fingerprints and iris scans of every single person in India. This process will ultimately encompass some 1.2 billion people who speak more than 300 languages and dialects. The biometrics and the Aadhaar identification number will serve as a verifiable, portable, and unique national ID.

This project seeks to remedy a key problem with the poor. The existence of many poor Indian citizens is not officially acknowledged by the government because they lack birth certificates and other official documentation. Therefore, these citizens are not able to access government services to which they are entitled. For example, in mid-2012, less than half of Indian households have an associated bank account. The rest of households are "unbanked" and must stash their savings in cash around their homes.

Aadhaar kicked off the ground in September 2010, when officials armed with iris scanners, fingerprint scanners, digital cameras, and laptops began registering the first few villagers and Delhi slum dwellers. By 2014, the government plans to have 600 million people entered into its biometric database.

Each individual record is between 4 and 8 megabytes, meaning that the database will ultimately hold some 20 petabytes. The unprecedented scale of the Aadhaar database will make managing it extraordinarily difficult. Therefore, one of the most important tasks is to ensure that each record in the database is matched to one and only one person. For this process, Aadhaar must check all 10 fingerprints and both irises of each person against those of everyone else. Using 10 prints and both irises boosts the accuracy rate to 99 percent. However, in a country the size of India, 99 percent accuracy means that 12 million people could end up with faulty records.

Additionally, Aadhaar faces enormous physical and technical challenges: reaching millions of illiterate Indians who have never seen a computer, persuading them to have their irises scanned, ensuring that their scanned information is accurate, and safeguarding the resulting massive amounts of data. Another problem is that civil libertarians object to the project on privacy grounds.

As an example of the impact of this project, consider Kiran, a poor citizen of India. She thinks she is 32, but she is not sure. She has no birth certificate or ID of any kind—no driver's license, no voting card, nothing at all to document her existence. When she was 24, she left her home in a destitute farming village and ended up in a Delhi slum. She and her children were among the first to have their personal information entered into the Aadhaar system.

The first thing Kiran plans to use her Aadhaar number for, she says, is to obtain a city government card that will entitle her to subsidized groceries. "I've tried very hard to get one before but they wouldn't give it to me because I couldn't prove I live in Delhi." In sum, the Aadhar project should allow millions of poor Indian citizens to access government services that previously were out of reach to them.

Sources: Compiled from "World's Biggest Biometric ID Scheme Forges Ahead," *BBC News India*, February 12, 2012; M. Magnier, "India's Biometric ID Number Plan Divided by Bureaucracy," *Los Angeles Times*, January 28, 2012; B. Turbeville, "Cashless Society: India Implements First Biometric ID Program for All of Its 1.2 Billion Residents," *Infowars.com*, January 12, 2012; V. Beiser, "Identified," *Wired*, September 2011; www.iaadhaar.com, accessed February 29, 2012.

Questions

1. Describe the problems that India is facing in implementing this biometric identification system.
2. Describe the benefits that India hopes to gain in implementing the biometric identification system.
3. Describe the benefits that the biometric identification system should provide to India's impoverished citizens.

Something the user has is an authentication mechanism that includes regular identification (ID) cards, smart ID cards, and tokens. *Regular ID cards,* or *dumb cards,* typically have the person's picture, and often his or her signature. *Smart ID cards* have a chip embedded in them with pertinent information about the user. (Smart ID cards used for identification differ from smart cards used in electronic commerce [see Chapter 9]. Both types of card have embedded chips, but they are used for different purposes). *Tokens* have embedded chips and a digital display that presents a log-in number that the employees use to access the organization's network. The number changes with each log-in.

Something the user does is an authentication mechanism that includes voice and signature recognition. In **voice recognition**, the user speaks a phrase (e.g., his or her name and department) that has been previously recorded under controlled, monitored conditions. The voice recognition system matches the two voice signals. In **signature recognition**, the user signs his or her name, and the system matches this signature with one previously recorded under controlled, monitored conditions. Signature recognition systems also match the speed of the signature and the pressure of the signature.

Something the user knows is an authentication mechanism that includes passwords and passphrases. Passwords present a huge information security problem in all organizations.

All users should use strong passwords so that the password cannot easily be discovered. Strong passwords have the following characteristics:

- They should be difficult to guess.
- They should be longer rather than shorter.
- They should contain uppercase letters, lowercase letters, numbers, and special characters.
- They should not be a recognizable word.
- They should not be the name of anything or anyone familiar, such as family names or names of pets.
- They should not be a recognizable string of numbers, such as a Social Security number or birthday.

Unfortunately, strong passwords are irritating. If the organization mandates longer (stronger) passwords and/or frequent password changes, they become more difficult to remember, causing employees to write them down. What is needed is a way for a user to create a strong password that is easy to remember. A passphrase can help, either by being a password itself or by helping you create a strong password.

A **passphrase** is a series of characters that is longer than a password but can be memorized easily. Examples of passphrases are "may the force be with you always," "go ahead make my day," "live long and prosper," and "a man's got to know his limitations." A user can turn a passphrase into a strong password in this manner. Start with the last passphrase above, and use the first letter of each word. You will have amgtkhl. Then capitalize every other letter, to have AmGtKhL. Then add special characters and numbers, to have 9AmGtKhL//*. Now you have a strong password that you can remember.

Many organizations are using *multifactor authentication* (more than one type of authentication) to more efficiently and effectively identify authorized users. This type of authentication is particularly important when users are logging in from remote locations.

Single-factor authentication, which is notoriously weak, commonly consists simply of a password. Two-factor authentication consists of a password plus one type of biometric identification (e.g., a fingerprint). Three-factor authentication is any combination of three authentication methods. You should keep in mind that stronger authentication is more expensive and can be irritating to users as well.

Authorization. Once users have been properly authenticated, then the rights and privileges that they have on the organization's systems are established, a process called *authorization*. Companies use the principle of least privilege for authorization purposes. A **privilege** is a collection of related computer system operations that can be performed by users of the system. **Least privilege** is a principle that users be granted the privilege for some activity only if there is a justifiable need to grant this authorization.

Communications Controls

Communications (network) controls secure the movement of data across networks. Communications controls consist of firewalls, anti-malware systems, whitelisting and blacklisting, encryption, virtual private networking (VPN), secure socket layer (SSL), and employee monitoring systems.

Firewalls. A **firewall** is a system that prevents a specific type of information from moving between untrusted networks, such as the Internet, and private networks, such as your company's network. Put simply, firewalls prevent unauthorized Internet users from accessing private networks. All messages entering or leaving your company's network pass through a firewall. The firewall examines each message and blocks those that do not meet specified security rules. Firewalls filter network traffic according to categories of activities likely to cause problems, whereas anti-malware systems filter traffic according to a database of specific problems.

Firewalls range from simple, for home use, to very complex for organizational use. Figure 7.3a shows a basic firewall for a home computer. In this case, the firewall is

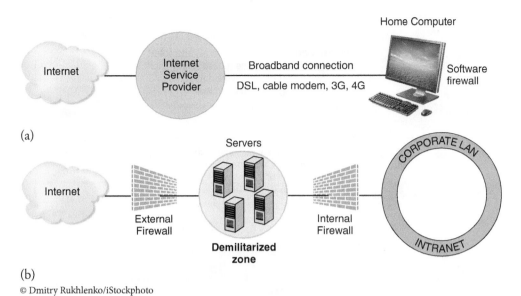

(a)

(b)

© Dmitry Rukhlenko/iStockphoto

Figure 7.3 (a) Basic firewall for home computer. (b) Organization with two firewalls and demilitarized zone.

implemented as software on the home computer. Figure 7.3b shows an organization that has implemented an external firewall, which faces the Internet, and an internal firewall, which faces the company network. Corporate firewalls typically consist of software running on a computer dedicated to the task. A **demilitarized zone (DMZ)** is located between the two firewalls. Messages from the Internet must first pass through the external firewall. If they conform to the defined security rules, then they are sent to company servers located in the DMZ. These servers typically handle Web page requests and e-mail. Any messages designated for the company's internal network (e.g., its intranet) must pass through the internal firewall, again with its own defined security rules, to gain access to the company's private network.

The danger from viruses and worms is so severe that many organizations are placing firewalls at strategic points *inside* their private networks. In this way, if a virus or worm does get through both the external and internal firewalls, then the internal damage may be contained.

Anti-malware Systems. **Anti-malware systems (antivirus software)**, also called AV, are software packages that attempt to identify and eliminate viruses, worms, and other malicious software. This software is implemented at the organizational level by the information systems department. Hundreds of AV software packages are currently available. Among the best known are Norton Antivirus (www.symantec.com), McAfee Virusscan (www.mcafee.com), and Trend Micro PC-cillin (www.trendmicro.com).

Anti-malware systems are generally reactive. They work by creating definitions, or signatures, of various types of malware, and then updating these signatures in their products. The anti-malware software then examines suspicious computer code to see if it matches a known signature. If it does, then the anti-malware software will remove it. This is the reason why organizations update their malware definitions so often. (See Chapter Closing Case 2.)

Because malware is such a serious problem, the leading vendors are rapidly developing anti-malware systems that function proactively as well as reactively. These systems evaluate behavior rather than relying on signature matching. In theory, therefore, it is possible to catch malware before it can infect systems.

Whitelisting and Blacklisting. A report by the Yankee Group (www.yankeegroup.com), a technology research and consulting firm, stated that 99 percent of organizations had anti-malware systems installed, but 62 percent of companies still suffered successful malware attacks. As you have noted, anti-malware systems are usually reactive, and malware continues to infect companies.

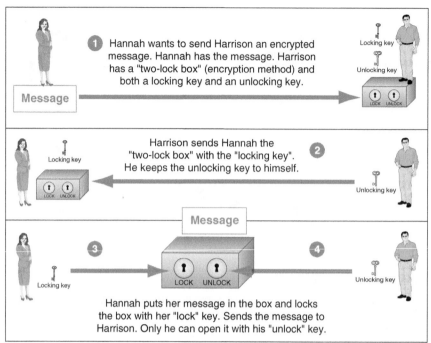

1. Hannah wants to send Harrison an encrypted message. Hannah has the message. Harrison has a "two-lock box" (encryption method) and both a locking key and an unlocking key.

Message

Locking key

Unlocking key

LOCK UNLOCK

2. Harrison sends Hannah the "two-lock box" with the "locking key". He keeps the unlocking key to himself.

Locking key

LOCK UNLOCK

Unlocking key

Message

3.   4.

Locking key

LOCK UNLOCK

Unlocking key

Hannah puts her message in the box and locks the box with her "lock" key. Sends the message to Harrison. Only he can open it with his "unlock" key.

Figure 7.4 How public key encryption works. (Omnisec AG.)

Courtesy of Brad Prince.

One solution to this problem is whitelisting. **Whitelisting** is a process in which a company identifies the software that it will allow to run and does not try to recognize malware. Whitelisting permits acceptable software to run and either prevents anything else from running or lets new software run in a quarantined environment until the company can verify its validity.

Whereas whitelisting allows nothing to run unless it is on the whitelist, **blacklisting** allows everything to run unless it is on the blacklist. A blacklist, then, includes certain types of software that are not allowed to run in the company environment. For example, a company might blacklist peer-to-peer file sharing on its systems. In addition to software, people, devices, and Web sites can also be whitelisted and blacklisted.

Encryption. When organizations do not have a secure channel for sending information, they use encryption to stop unauthorized eavesdroppers. **Encryption** is the process of converting an original message into a form that cannot be read by anyone except the intended receiver.

All encryption systems use a key, which is the code that scrambles, and then decodes, the messages. The majority of encryption systems use public-key encryption. **Public-key encryption**—also known as *asymmetric encryption*—uses two different keys: a public key and a private key (see Figure 7.4). The public key (locking key) and the private key (unlocking key) are created simultaneously using the same mathematical formula or algorithm. Because the two keys are mathematically related, the data encrypted with one key can be decrypted by using the other key. The public key is publicly available in a directory that all parties can access. The private key is kept secret, never shared with anyone, and never sent across the Internet. In this system, if Hannah wants to send a message to Harrison, she first obtains Harrison's public key (locking key), which she uses to encrypt her message (put the message in the "two-lock box"). When Harrison receives Hannah's message, he uses his private key to decrypt it (open the box).

Although this system is adequate for personal information, organizations doing business over the Internet require a more complex system. In such cases, a third party, called a **certificate authority**, acts as a trusted intermediary between companies. As such, the certificate authority issues digital certificates and verifies the worth and integrity of the certificates. A **digital certificate** is an electronic document attached to a file certifying that the file is from the organization it claims to be from and has not been modified from its original format. As you can see in Figure 7.5, Sony requests a digital certificate from VeriSign, a certificate authority, and uses this certificate when doing business with Dell. Note that the digital certificate contains an identification number, the issuer, validity dates, and the requester's public key. For examples of certificate authorities, see www.entrust.com, www.verisign.com, www.cybertrust.com, www.secude.com, and www.thawte.com.

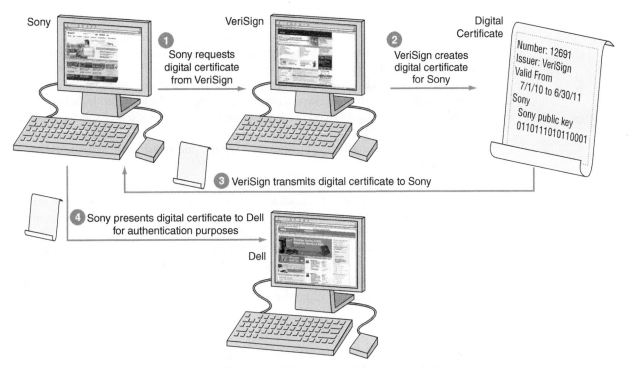

Figure 7.5 How digital certificates work. Sony and Dell, business partners, use a digital certificate from VeriSign for authentication.

Virtual Private Networking. **A virtual private network (VPN)** is a private network that uses a public network (usually the Internet) to connect users. As such, VPNs integrate the global connectivity of the Internet with the security of a private network and thereby extend the reach of the organization's networks. VPNs are called "virtual" because they have no separate physical existence. They use the public Internet as their infrastructure. They create a *virtual private* network by using log-ins, encryption, and other techniques to enhance privacy.

VPNs have several advantages. First, they allow remote users to access the company network. Second, they allow flexibility. That is, mobile users can access the organization's network from properly configured remote devices. Third, organizations can impose their security policies through VPNs. For example, an organization may dictate that only corporate e-mail applications are available to users when they connect from unmanaged devices.

To provide secure transmissions, VPNs use a process called tunneling. **Tunneling** encrypts each data packet to be sent and places each encrypted packet inside another packet. In this manner, the packet can travel across the Internet with confidentiality, authentication, and integrity. Figure 7.6 illustrates a VPN and tunneling.

Figure 7.6 Virtual private network and tunneling.

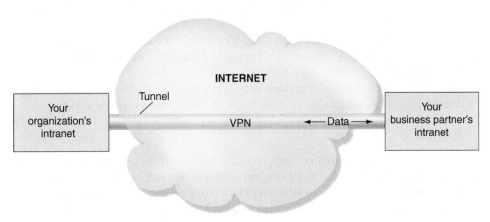

Secure Socket Layer (SSL). **Secure socket layer**, now called **transport layer security (TLS)**, is an encryption standard used for secure transactions such as credit card purchases and online banking. TLS encrypts and decrypts data between a Web server and a browser end to end.

TLS is indicated by a URL that begins with https rather than http, and it often includes a small padlock icon in the browser's status bar. Using a padlock icon to indicate a secure connection and placing this icon in a browser's status bar, are artifacts of specific browsers. Other browsers use other icons (e.g., a key that is either broken or whole). The important thing to remember here is that browsers usually provide visual confirmation of a secure connection.

Employee Monitoring Systems. Many companies are taking a proactive approach to protecting their networks from what they view as one of their major security threats, namely employee mistakes. These companies are implementing **employee monitoring systems**, which monitor their employees' computers, e-mail activities, and Internet surfing activities. These products are useful to identify employees who spend too much time surfing on the Internet for personal reasons, who visit questionable Web sites, or who download music illegally. Vendors that provide monitoring software include SpectorSoft (www.spectorsoft.com) and Websense (www.websense.com).

Business Continuity Planning

An important strategy for organizations is to be prepared for any eventuality. A critical element in any security system is a business continuity plan, also known as a disaster recovery plan. Large businesses have these plans. For you as an individual, or for a small business, a plan for backing up your important data will serve. For example, Carbonite (www.carbonite.com) will provide unlimited data backup for a home or home office for $59 per year. For small businesses, Carbonite offers 50 gigabytes of backup for $229 per year and 500 gigabytes for $599 per year.

Business continuity is the chain of events linking planning to protection and to recovery. The purpose of the business continuity plan is to provide guidance to people who keep the business operating after a disaster occurs. Using this plan, employees prepare for, react to, and recover from events that affect the security of information assets and the subsequent restoration to normal business operations. The plan helps to ensure that critical business functions continue.

In the event of a major disaster, organizations can employ several strategies for business continuity. These strategies include hot sites, warm sites, and cold sites. A **hot site** is a fully configured computer facility, with all services, communications links, and physical plant operations. A hot site duplicates computing resources, peripherals, telephone systems, applications, and workstations. A **warm site** provides many of the same services and options of the hot site. However, a warm site typically does not include the actual applications the company needs. A warm site does include computing equipment such as servers, but it often does not include user workstations. A **cold site** provides only rudimentary services and facilities, such as a building or room with heating, air conditioning, and humidity control. This type of site provides no computer hardware or user workstations. The point of a cold site is that it takes care of long lead-time issues. Building or even renting space takes a long time. Installing high-speed communication lines, often from two or more carriers, takes a long time. Installing high-capacity power lines takes a long time. By comparison, buying and installing servers should not take a particularly long time.

Hot sites reduce risk to the greatest extent, but they are the most expensive option. Conversely, cold sites reduce risk the least, but they are the least expensive option.

Information Systems Auditing

Companies implement security controls to ensure that information systems work properly. These controls can be installed in the original system or they can be added after a system is in operation. Installing controls is necessary but not sufficient to provide adequate security. In addition, people responsible for security need to answer questions such as these: Are all controls installed as intended? Are they effective? Has any breach of security occurred? If so, what actions are required to prevent future breaches?

These questions must be answered by independent and unbiased observers. Such observers perform the task of *information systems auditing*. In an IS environment, an **audit** is an examination of information systems, their inputs, outputs, and processing.

Types of Auditors and Audits. The two types of auditors and audits are internal and external. IS auditing is usually a part of accounting *internal auditing,* and it is frequently performed by corporate internal auditors. An *external auditor* reviews the findings of the internal audit as well as the inputs, processing, and outputs of information systems. The external audit of information systems is frequently a part of the overall external auditing performed by a certified public accounting (CPA) firm.

IS auditing considers all potential hazards and controls in information systems. It focuses on topics such as operations, data integrity, software applications, security and privacy, budgets and expenditures, cost control, and productivity. Guidelines are available to assist auditors in their jobs, such as those from ISACA (formerly the Information Systems Audit and Control Association, www.isaca.org).

How Is Auditing Executed? IS auditing procedures fall into three categories: (1) auditing around the computer, (2) auditing through the computer, and (3) auditing with the computer.

Auditing around the computer means verifying processing by checking for known outputs using specific inputs. This approach is best used in systems with limited outputs. In *auditing through the computer,* inputs, outputs, and processing are checked. Auditors review program logic and test data. *Auditing with the computer* means using a combination of client data, auditor software, and client and auditor hardware. This approach allows the auditor to perform tasks such as simulating payroll program logic using live data.

- **BEFORE** *YOU GO ON . . .*
  1. What is the single most important information security control for organizations?
  2. Differentiate between authentication and authorization. Which one of these always comes first?
  3. Compare and contrast whitelisting and blacklisting.
  4. What is the purpose of a disaster recovery plan?
  5. What is information system auditing?

Apply the Concept 7.5

Background Security controls are designed to protect all components of an information system, including data, software, hardware, and networks. Because there are so many diverse threats, organizations utilize layers of controls. One area discussed in the book is public key encryption. This method of encryption requires a public key and a private key. The public key is shared and used to encrypt a message that only the individual's private key can decrypt.

Activity Go to http://www.wiley.com/go/rainer/applytheconcept and click on the link provided for Apply the Concept 7.5. It will take you to a YouTube titled "SSL Explained" by user "pyroblue." This video introduces you to the inventors of public key encryption as well as the method that it uses to work. After watching this video, visit HowStuffWorks.com (or click the second link for Apply the Concept 7.5 on the Apply the Concept link page) and read the article titled "How Encryption Works".

Deliverable

Write an e-mail to an elderly person (or just anyone who may be hesitant to share his or her credit card online) that explains how the public key encryption works. Discuss the benefits of public key encryption (two keys) over private key encryption (one key). Submit this to your professor.

Quiz questions are assignable in WileyPLUS, and available on the Book Companion Site at http://www.wiley.com/college/rainer.

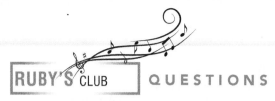

RUBY'S CLUB QUESTIONS

1. What security controls should Ruben and Lisa put in place to help ensure the safety of sensitive customer information?

2. Should Ruben and Lisa put these controls in place, or should they hire a third-party vendor to put them in place?

What's in 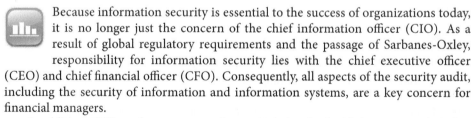 for ME?

FOR THE ACCOUNTING MAJOR

Public companies, their accountants, and their auditors have significant information security responsibilities. Accountants are now being held professionally responsible for reducing risk, ensuring compliance, eliminating fraud, and increasing the transparency of transactions according to generally accepted accounting principles (GAAP). The Securities and Exchange Commission (SEC) and the Public Company Accounting Oversight Board (PCAOB), among other regulatory agencies, require information security, fraud prevention and detection, and internal controls over financial reporting. Forensic accounting, a combination of accounting and information security, is one of the most rapidly growing areas in accounting today.

FOR THE FINANCE MAJOR

Because information security is essential to the success of organizations today, it is no longer just the concern of the chief information officer (CIO). As a result of global regulatory requirements and the passage of Sarbanes-Oxley, responsibility for information security lies with the chief executive officer (CEO) and chief financial officer (CFO). Consequently, all aspects of the security audit, including the security of information and information systems, are a key concern for financial managers.

In addition, CFOs and treasurers are increasingly involved with investments in information technology. They know that a security breach of any kind can have devastating financial effects on a company. Banking and financial institutions are prime targets for computer criminals. A related problem is fraud involving stocks and bonds that are sold over the Internet. Finance personnel must be aware of both the hazards and the available controls associated with these activities.

FOR THE MARKETING MAJOR

Marketing professionals have new opportunities to collect data on their customers (e.g., through business-to-consumer electronic commerce). Customers expect their data to be properly secured. However, profit-motivated criminals want that data. Therefore, marketing managers must analyze the risk of their operations. Failure to protect corporate and customer data will cause significant public relations problems and make customers very angry. Customer relationship management (CRM) operations and tracking customers' online buying habits can expose data to misuse (if they are not encrypted) or result in privacy violations.

FOR THE
PRODUCTION/OPERATIONS MANAGEMENT MAJOR

Every process in a company's operations—inventory purchasing, receiving, quality control, production, and shipping—can be disrupted by an information technology security breach or an IT security breach at a business partner. Any weak link in supply chain management or enterprise resource management systems puts the entire chain at risk. Companies may be held liable for IT security failures that affect other companies.

FOR THE
HUMAN RESOURCES MANAGEMENT MAJOR

HR managers have responsibilities to secure confidential employee data. In addition, they must ensure that all employees explicitly verify that they understand the company's information security policies and procedures.

FOR THE MIS MAJOR

The MIS function provides the security infrastructure that protects the organization's information assets. This function is critical to the success of the organization, even though it is almost invisible until an attack succeeds. All application development, network deployment, and introduction of new information technologies have to be guided by IT security considerations. MIS personnel must customize the risk-exposure security model to help the company identify security risks and prepare responses to security incidents and disasters.

Senior executives of publicly held companies look to the MIS function for help in meeting Sarbanes-Oxley requirements, particularly in detecting "significant deficiencies" or "material weaknesses" in internal controls and remediating them. Other functional areas also look to the MIS function to help them meet their security responsibilities.

SUMMARY

1. **Give one specific example of each of the five factors that are contributing to the increasing vulnerability of information resources.**

   The five factors are as follows:

   > Today's interconnected, interdependent, wirelessly networked business environment

   >> Example: the Internet

   > Smaller, faster, cheaper computers and storage devices

   >> Examples: netbooks, thumb drives, iPads

   > Decreasing skills necessary to be a computer hacker

   >> Example: information system hacking programs circulating on the Internet

   > International organized crime taking over cybercrime

   >> Example: Organized crime has formed transnational cybercrime cartels. Because it is difficult to know exactly where cyberattacks originate, these cartels are extremely hard to bring to justice.

   > Lack of management support

   >> Example: Suppose that your company spent $10 million on information security countermeasures last year and experienced no successful attacks on information resources. Shortsighted management might conclude that the company could spend less during the next year and obtain the same results. Bad idea.

2. **Compare and contrast human mistakes and social engineering by way of specific examples.**

   Human mistakes are unintentional errors. However, employees can also make unintentional mistakes because of actions by an attacker, such as social engineering. *Social engineering* is an attack in which the perpetrator uses social skills to trick or manipulate a legitimate employee into providing confidential company information.

   An example of a human mistake is tailgating. An example of social engineering is when an attacker calls an employee on the phone and impersonates a superior in the company.

3. **Describe negative consequences that might result from at least three different kinds of deliberate attacks on information systems.**

The types of deliberate attacks are as follows:

> *Espionage or trespass* occurs when an unauthorized individual attempts to gain illegal access to organizational information.

> *Information extortion* occurs when an attacker either threatens to steal, or actually steals, information from a company. The perpetrator demands payment for not stealing the information, for returning stolen information, or for agreeing not to disclose the information.

> *Sabotage and vandalism* are deliberate acts that involve defacing an organization's Web site, possibly causing the organization to lose its image and experience a loss of confidence by its customers because of sabotage or vandalism.

> Computing devices and storage devices are becoming smaller yet more powerful with vastly increased storage, making these devices easier and more valuable to *steal*.

> *Identity theft* is the deliberate assumption of another person's identity, usually to gain access to his or her financial information or to frame him or her for a crime.

> *Protecting intellectual property* is a vital issue for people who make their livelihood in knowledge fields. Protecting intellectual property is particularly difficult when that property is in digital form.

> *Software attacks* occur when malicious software penetrates a computer system. Today, these attacks are typically profit driven and Web based.

> *Alien software* is clandestine software that is installed on a computer through duplicitous methods. Alien software uses valuable system resources and can report on your Web surfing habits and other personal behavior.

> Supervisory control and data acquisition (SCADA) refers to a large-scale, distributed measurement and control system. SCADA systems are used to monitor or to control chemical, physical, or transport processes. A *SCADA attack* attempts to compromise such a system in order to cause damage to the real-world processes that the system controls.

> With both *cyberterrorism* and *cyberwarfare,* attackers use a target's computer systems, particularly via the Internet, to cause physical, real-world harm or severe disruption, usually to carry out a political agenda.

4. **Assess how you might employ each of the three risk mitigation strategies in the context of your owning a home.**

The three risk mitigation strategies are the following:

> With *risk acceptance*, the organization accepts the potential risk, continues operating with no controls, and absorbs any damages that occur. If you own a home, you may decide not to insure it. Thus, you are practicing risk acceptance. Clearly, this is a bad idea.

> With *risk limitation*, the organization limits the risk by implementing controls that minimize the impact of threats. As a homeowner, you practice risk limitation by putting in an alarm system or by cutting down weak trees near your house.

> With *risk transference*, the organization transfers the risk by using other means to compensate for the loss, such as by purchasing insurance. The vast majority of homeowners practice risk transference by purchasing insurance on their houses and contents.

5. **Identify the three major types of controls that organizations can use to protect their information resources.**

Physical controls prevent unauthorized individuals from gaining access to a company's facilities. Common physical controls include walls, doors, fencing, gates, locks, badges, guards, and alarm systems. More sophisticated physical controls include pressure sensors, temperature sensors, and motion detectors.

Access controls restrict unauthorized individuals from using information resources. These controls involve two major functions: authentication and authorization. Authentication determines the identity of the person requiring access. As an example, authentication can be established with biometrics. After the person is authenticated (identified), authorization is applied. Authorization determines which actions, rights, or privileges the person has, based on verified identity. As an example, authorization is based on least privilege.

Communications (network) controls secure the movement of data across networks. Communications controls consist of firewalls, anti-malware systems, whitelisting and blacklisting, encryption, virtual private networking (VPN), secure socket layer (SSL), and vulnerability management systems.

>>> CHAPTER GLOSSARY

access controls Controls that restrict unauthorized individuals from using information resources and are concerned with user identification.

adware Alien software designed to help pop-up advertisements appear on your screen.

alien software Clandestine software that is installed on a computer through duplicitous methods.

anti-malware systems (antivirus software) Software packages that attempt to identify and eliminate viruses, worms, and other malicious software.

audit An examination of information systems, their inputs, outputs, and processing.

authentication A process that determines the identity of the person requiring access.

authorization A process that determines which actions, rights, or privileges the person has, based on verified identity.

back door (also known as *trap door*) Typically a password, known only to the attacker, that allows the attacker to access the system without having to go through any security procedures.

biometrics The science and technology of authentication (i.e., establishing the identity of an individual) by measuring the subject's physiologic or behavioral characteristics.

blacklisting A process in which a company identifies certain types of software that are not allowed to run in the company environment.

certificate authority A third party that acts as a trusted intermediary between computers (and companies) by issuing digital certificates and verifying the worth and integrity of the certificates.

cold site A backup location that provides only rudimentary services and facilities.

communications (network) controls Controls that deal with the movement of data across networks.

controls Defense mechanisms (also called *countermeasures*).

cookies Small amounts of information that Web sites store on your computer, temporarily or more or less permanently.

copyright A grant that provides the creator of intellectual property with ownership of it for the life of the creator plus 70 years.

cybercrime Illegal activities executed on the Internet.

cyberterrorism Can be defined as a premeditated, politically motivated attack against information, computer systems, computer programs, and data that results in violence against noncombatant targets by subnational groups or clandestine agents.

cyberwarfare War in which a country's information systems could be paralyzed from a massive attack by destructive software.

demilitarized zone (DMZ) A separate organizational local area network that is located between an organization's internal network and an external network, usually the Internet.

denial-of-service attack A cyberattack in which an attacker sends a flood of data packets to the target computer, with the aim of overloading its resources.

digital certificate An electronic document attached to a file certifying that this file is from the organization it claims to be from and has not been modified from its original format or content.

distributed denial-of-service (DDoS) A denial-of-service attack that sends a flood of data packets from many compromised computers simultaneously.

employee monitoring systems Systems that monitor employees' computers, e-mail activities, and Internet surfing activities.

encryption The process of converting an original message into a form that cannot be read by anyone except the intended receiver.

exposure The harm, loss, or damage that can result if a threat compromises an information resource.

firewall A system (either hardware, software, or a combination of both) that prevents a specific type of information from moving between untrusted networks, such as the Internet, and private networks, such as your company's network.

hot site A fully configured computer facility, with all information resources and services, communications links, and physical plant operations, that duplicates a company's computing resources and provide near real-time recovery of IT operations.

identity theft Crime in which someone uses the personal information of others to create a false identity and then uses it for some fraud.

information security Protecting an organization's information and information systems from unauthorized access, use, disclosure, disruption, modification, or destruction.

information systems controls The procedures, devices, or software aimed at preventing a compromise to a system.

intellectual property The intangible property created by individuals or corporations that is protected under trade secret, patent, and copyright laws.

keystroke loggers (keyloggers) Hardware or software that can detect all keystrokes made on a compromised computer.

least privilege A principle that users be granted the privilege for some activity only if there is a justifiable need to grant this authorization.

logic bomb Segments of computer code embedded within an organization's existing computer programs.

malware malicious software such as viruses and worms.

network controls (*see* **communications controls**).

passphrase A series of characters that is longer than a password but that can be memorized easily.

passwords Private combinations of characters that only the user should know.

patent A document that grants the holder exclusive rights on an invention or process for 20 years.

phishing attack An attack that uses deception to fraudulently acquire sensitive personal information by masquerading as an official-looking e-mail.

physical controls Controls that restrict unauthorized individuals from gaining access to a company's computer facilities.

piracy Copying a software program (other than freeware, demo software, etc.) without making payment to the owner.

privilege A collection of related computer system operations that can be performed by users of the system.

public-key encryption (also called *asymmetric encryption*) A type of encryption that uses two different keys: a public key and a private key.

risk The likelihood that a threat will occur.

risk acceptance A strategy in which the organization accepts the potential risk, continues to operate with no controls, and absorbs any damages that occur.

risk analysis The process by which an organization assesses the value of each asset being protected, estimates the probability that each asset might be compromised, and compares the probable costs of each being compromised with the costs of protecting it.

risk limitation A strategy in which the organization limits its risk by implementing controls that minimize the impact of a threat.

risk management A process that identifies, controls, and minimizes the impact of threats, in an effort to reduce risk to manageable levels.

risk mitigation A process whereby the organization takes concrete actions against risks, such as implementing controls and developing a disaster recovery plan.

risk transference A process in which the organization transfers the risk by using other means to compensate for a loss, such as by purchasing insurance.

SCADA (Supervisory Control and Data Acquisition) Large-scale, distributed, measurement and control systems used to monitor or to control chemical, physical, or transport processes.

secure socket layer (SSL) (also known as *transport layer security*) An encryption standard used for secure transactions such as credit card purchases and online banking.

security The degree of protection against criminal activity, danger, damage, and/or loss.

signature recognition The user signs his or her name, and the system matches this signature with one previously recorded under controlled, monitored conditions.

social engineering Getting around security systems by tricking computer users inside a company into revealing sensitive information or gaining unauthorized access privileges.

spam Unsolicited e-mail.

spamware Alien software that uses your computer as a launch platform for spammers.

spyware Alien software that can record keystrokes and/or capture passwords.

strong passwords Passwords that are difficult to guess; longer rather than shorter; contain uppercase and lowercase letters, numbers, and special characters; and are not a recognizable word or string of numbers.

threat Any danger to which an information resource may be exposed.

trade secret Intellectual work, such as a business plan, that is a company secret and is not based on public information.

transport layer security (TLS) (*see* **secure socket layer**).

trap doors (*see* **back door**).

Trojan horse A software program containing a hidden function that presents a security risk.

tunneling A process that encrypts each data packet to be sent and places each encrypted packet inside another packet.

virtual private network (VPN) A private network that uses a public network (usually the Internet) to securely connect users by using encryption.

virus Malicious computer code that can attach itself to (or "infect") other computer programs without the owner of the program being aware of the infection.

voice recognition The user speaks a phrase that has been previously recorded under controlled, monitored conditions, and the voice recognition system matches the two voice signals.

vulnerability The possibility that an information resource will suffer harm by a threat.

warm site A site that provides many of the same services and options of a hot site but does not include the company's applications.

whitelisting A process in which a company identifies acceptable software and permits it to run, and either prevents anything else from running or lets new software run in a quarantined environment until the company can verify its validity.

worm Destructive computer code that replicates itself without requiring another program to provide a safe environment for replication.

>>> DISCUSSION QUESTIONS

1. Why are computer systems so vulnerable?

2. Why should information security be of prime concern to management?

3. Is security a technical issue? A business issue? Both? Support your answer. *Hint:* Read Kim Nash, "Why Technology Isn't the Answer to Better Security," *CIO* (www.cio.com), October 15, 2008.

4. Compare information security in an organization with insuring a house.

5. Why are authentication and authorization important to e-commerce?

6. Why is cross-border cybercrime expanding rapidly? Discuss possible solutions.

7. Discuss why the Sarbanes-Oxley Act is having an impact on information security.

8. What types of user authentication are used at your university and/or place of work? Do these authentication measures seem to be effective? What if a higher level of authentication were implemented? Would it be worth it, or would it decrease productivity?

9. Why are federal government authorities so worried about SCADA attacks?

1. A critical problem is assessing how far a company is legally obligated to go in order to secure personal data. Because there is no such thing as perfect security (i.e., there is always more that can be done), resolving this question can significantly affect cost.

   a. When are security measures that a company implements sufficient to comply with its obligations?

   b. Is there any way for a company to know if its security measures are sufficient? Can you devise a method for any organization to determine if its security measures are sufficient?

2. Assume that the daily probability of a major earthquake in Los Angeles is .07 percent. The chance of your computer center being damaged during such a quake is 5 percent. If the center is damaged, the average estimated damage will be $4.0 million.

   a. Calculate the expected loss in dollars.

   b. An insurance agent is willing to insure your facility for an annual fee of $25,000. Analyze the offer and discuss whether to accept it.

3. Enter www.scambusters.org. Find out what the organization does. Learn about e-mail frauds and Web site scams. Report your findings.

4. Visit http://www.wiley.com/go/rainer/problemsolving (to visit the website of the Department of Homeland Security). Search the site for "National Strategy to Secure Cyberspace," and write a report on the agency's agenda and accomplishments to date.

5. Enter www.alltrustnetworks.com and other vendors of biometrics. Find the devices they make that can be used to control access into information systems. Prepare a list of products and major capabilities of each.

6. Software piracy is a global problem. Access the following Web sites: www.bsa.org and www.microsoft.com/piracy. What can organizations do to mitigate this problem? Are some organizations dealing with the problem better than others are?

7. Investigate the Sony Playstation Network hack that occurred in April 2011.

   a. What type of attack was it?

   b. Was the success of the attack because of technology problems at Sony, management problems at Sony, or a combination of both? Provide specific examples to support your answer.

   c. Which Sony controls failed?

   d. Could Sony have prevented the hack? If so, how?

   e. Discuss Sony's response to the hack.

   f. Describe the damages that Sony incurred from the successful hack.

>>> COLLABORATION EXERCISE

Background

This chapter has shown the importance of information security. The "What's in IT for Me?" section illustrated the different ways each business area needs to be aware of security. In some cases there are government regulations, in others there are strategic, logistical, or technical reasons for needing security.

Activity

Divide your team into functional areas. Assign one person to each of the following: vice-president of accounting, vice-president of finance, vice-president of human resources, and vice-president of production. Imagine that your chief executive officer (CEO) is really having a hard time understanding why you need to invest in a chief information officer (CIO) to oversee your information systems. Right now each department is doing its own thing and managing its own systems. Everyone needs help and direction from an expert and the group of vice presidents has agreed that you need a CIO.

Deliverable

Write an executive summary that accompanies an imaginary full report. The imaginary report would include a full description of how the CIO would help each functional area, so the executive summary will include the highlights of what this position would mean to you. Have each team member research from his or her respective position why you need a CIO to help maintain information security. Finally, submit your executive summary to your professor. For help formatting your executive summary, search Google for "Executive Summary Template." You will find many examples there to help you.

CLOSING **CASE 1** > Compliance

THE PROBLEM >>>   Modern businesses face an incredible array of regulatory and compliance requirements. Various problems and scandals have forced political leaders and entire industries to introduce new laws, regulations, and industry standards (for example, Sarbanes-Oxley [SOX], the Health Insurance Portability and Accountability Act [HIPAA], the Payment Card Industry Data Security Standard [PCI DSS], the European Union Privacy Directive, and many others). Therefore, governance, risk management, and compliance (GRC) solutions have become increasingly important to all organizations.

GRC involves almost every part of any organization, including business operations, security, and IT assets. Moreover, new information technologies—including mobile computing, cloud computing, and social media—have made it more difficult than ever to keep data secure and comply with government and industry requirements. To make matters even more difficult, as systems and organizations become more interconnected, firms need to be able to track where data originates, where it travels, where it is stored, and who has access to it. Enterprises must therefore be able to provide constant real-time protection for applications, files, and data.

In addition, organizations must often deal with the foreign corrupt practices, differing business practices of contractors and third-party providers, obtaining background checks in other countries, and many other issues. The ability to track internal transactions and processes is only one part of the problem. GRC typically spans an entire supply chain.

SOLUTIONS >>>   Although many organizations have constructed GRC frameworks—with applications designed to monitor, report, and provide alerts about compliance activities—gaps and potential hazards still exist. Many organizations deal with potential problems by writing a policy, procedure, or prohibition. Unfortunately, employees often violate policies and undermine procedures. As a result, GRC must focus on many key areas: information security, privacy, threat and risk analysis, compliance with government regulations and industry requirements, enforcement strategies, internal audits, and others.

Let's look at some examples of organizations that are making progress with their GRC obligations:

- Sallie Mae (www.salliemae.com), the world's leading provider of student planning and loans, manages more than 10 million student loans valued at $268 billion. Altogether, about 10,000 employees and contractors handle documents and oversee business processes. Consequently, Sallie Mae must monitor 162 different compliance rules and regulations, including SOX, Federal Information Security Management Act (FISMA), Federal Financial Institutions Examination Council (FFIEC), Gramm-Leach-Bliley Act (GLBA), PCI DSS, and Fair and Accurate Credit Transactions Act (FACTA).

   Building an automated compliance model was critically important to Sallie Mae. In the past, the company stored records in a variety of systems and files, including massive spreadsheets. Today, the company uses SailPoint IdentityIQ (www.sailpoint.com) to oversee a role-based access management framework. The system provides visibility into user-access privileges and provides complete oversight into identity data. Managers work with a finite set of defined roles rather than a huge number of individual users. All the information is visible via a dashboard.

   This approach has yielded benefits, particularly as employees use laptops, smartphones, tablets, and other mobile tools to exchange data. IdentityIQ manages virtual private networks (VPNs), tokens, and other authentication tools. The system also allows the company to provide access to social networking sites for authorized employees on an exception basis.

   The results have been impressive. Although the number of controls increased from 800 to 2,500 from 2009 to 2011, Sallie Mae was able to cut overall GRC expenses by 40 percent.

- Tognum America (www.tognumamerica.com) manufactures engines used in boats, military systems, and off-highway equipment. The firm ships products to dozens of countries and must cope with numerous regulations and restrictions, including U.S. Customs requirements, export controls, sanctions, and embargo lists that change on a regular basis. A breach could result in fines or loss of business.

  In the past, the company relied on spreadsheets and manual processes to keep track of compliance issues related to incoming and outgoing shipments. These manual processes contained a huge risk of human error. The company now relies on SAP BusinessObjects' Global Trade Services (GTS) (www.sap.com) system to automate its GRC processes. The system checks the latest restriction lists, which sometimes change between the receipt of an order and shipment of that order.

  However, Tognum faces additional challenges. Orders stream in via a number of networks and systems. In some cases, customers call the company directly. In other instances, distributors enter orders, or employees place an order from a computer located in the office or from a mobile device in the field. The GTS system tracks all the orders and provides a real-time view of any issues or problems. It simplifies the process of achieving the highest level of compliance.

  Since implementing the GTS system, Tognum America has boosted compliance ratings by more than 15 percent to the current level of more than 95 percent. The company has also achieved the added benefit of reducing invoicing discrepancies by 80 percent.

- CardSmith (www.card-smith.com) provides electronic payment and transaction processing systems used primarily by colleges and universities. The firm manages cashless payment cards for nearly 150 schools. Students rely on the cards to purchase meals, supplies, and other campus goods. Parents transfer money into the accounts as necessary, making it essential that they have the highest level of trust in the system.

  The payment cards—in many cases multiuse smartcards that also provide access control for dorms and other areas—require tight oversight and adherence to a number of regulatory and compliance issues, including PCI DSS, GLBA, the Patriot Act, and the Credit Card Accountability, Responsibility, and Disclosure (CARD) Act of 2009.

  As a result, CardSmith turned to Hosting.com (www.hosting.com), a hosted security solution that provides a variety of protection and reporting tools that meet the PCI Council's Data Security Standard. The system handles host intrusion detection, vulnerability management, monitoring and testing, and PCI DSS security scanning.

  CardSmith has to secure computers, point-of-sale terminals, and mobile payment terminals; use encryption, and protect logs from tampering. For example, the Hosting system maintains snapshots of logs, which are written and recorded in real time.

  CardSmith controls and manages data flowing to and from smartphones, tablet devices, and other mobile tools. As a result, students can securely check their account balances using these devices, as data travels across wireless networks in an encrypted state.

  CardSmith is also pushing for tamper-proof terminals at universities and health care provider locations, and the use of tokens as a substitute for sending actual card numbers. The result is that the company sees very little fraud and has achieved very high levels of compliance.

- The Northern Ireland Civil Service (NICS) takes a broad approach to GRC. The government organization has more than 25,000 civil servants delivering key services and economic and social policy data to government ministers and citizens throughout the country. Protecting sensitive data and records while adhering to regulatory requirements, including the United Kingdom's Data Protection and Freedom of Information Acts, is vital for NICS.

  NICS data resides in documents and systems that span 11 government departments in more than 250 locations. Using Hewlett-Packard (www.hp.com) TRIM records management software, NICS has built a single virtual data repository known as Records Northern Ireland (NI). The system contains both structured and unstructured data, including more than 9 million documents and information about e-mail accounts, network devices, and hard disks. It allows the agency to control who may access the information; the system also tracks documents and how they are used and shared.

The Records NI system makes it easier to find needed information. The system has helped NICS achieve a much higher level of compliance while improving workflows.

RESULTS >>> Companies and application vendors are increasingly focusing on merging the information technology and business aspects of GRC. Although authentication, passwords, robust reporting, monitoring, and other controls are an important part of GRC, systems must integrate technology, process controls, and risk management. These are the three cornerstones of effective GRC.

An effective GRC framework finds ways to capture and establish ownership of information. GRC also cuts across multiple entities, including shareholders, stakeholders, investors, and insurers. Balancing productivity with protection is essential. Ultimately, effective GRC revolves around well-defined processes, the right tools and technologies; it also ensures that employees and partners are trustworthy and educated about the risks inherent in today's business environment.

Unfortunately, technology, by its nature, advances faster than the ability to provide an appropriate framework. As a result, organizations today face enormous, continuing GRC challenges as firms try to keep abreast of advances in technology.

Sources: Compiled from J. Goodchild, "12 Tips for Implementing GRC," *CIO*, February 23, 2012; E. Savitz, "Managing Cloud Risks," *Forbes*, October 25, 2011; S. Greengard, "Navigating the GRC Maze," *Baseline Magazine*, September 30, 2011; J. Buchanan, "Cloud Computing: 4 Tips for Regulatory Compliance," *CIO*, August 8, 2011; D. Woods, "Compliance in the Best-of-Breed Cloud," *Forbes*, July 20, 2010; C. Dunlap, "Trends in Identity and Access Management," *Forbes*, April 27, 2010; www.salliemae.com, www.tognumamerica.com, www.card-smith.com, accessed March 5, 2012.

Questions

1. Describe the GRC problem that all organizations face. What is the relationship between information technology and the GRC problem? Provide specific examples of this relationship.
2. In the examples in this case, all the organizations used external vendors to help them achieve GRC compliance. Why did these organizations use external vendors? Why didn't they manage the GRC problem in-house? Support your answer with examples.

CLOSING **CASE 2 >** Computer Espionage

THE PROBLEM >>> At an American oil company, hackers obtained a network administrator password, intercepted help-desk queries, and infiltrated private accounts. With that high-level network access, the hackers copied thousands of confidential e-mails—including those of top executives—and transmitted them to China in massive files late at night.

By the time the FBI informed the company of suspicious network traffic, Chinese firms had outbid the oil company on several acquisitions by just a few thousand dollars. It could have been far worse. For months, malicious software had been penetrating further into the company's information systems and had accessed computers that controlled oil-drilling and pipeline operations. Simply put, the hackers could have completely disabled the oil company.

Security analysts state that this is just one incident in an ongoing, aggressive campaign of electronic espionage that costs U.S. firms billions of dollars, endangers U.S. military secrets, and threatens to erode our technological edge. Electronic espionage combines elements of white-collar crime, international spying, and even acts of war. Such attacks are called advanced persistent threats (APTs).

Well-financed teams of hackers that U.S. intelligence agencies believe are backed by foreign governments now constitute a major national security risk. The hackers use tactics that are difficult to trace and choose targets within U.S. infrastructure, government, and military. News sources have identified APT victims that include Google, Morgan Stanley, Dow Chemical, Symantec, Northrop Grumman, and Lockheed Martin.

In February 2011, a security firm called McAfee (www.mcafee.com) released a report describing a series of network infiltrations originating from locations in China and aimed at six global oil, gas, and petrochemical companies (ExxonMobil, Royal Dutch Shell, British Petroleum, Marathon Oil, Conoco Phillips, and Baker Hughes). Instead of trying to identify vulnerabilities in these firms' security systems, the APTs focused on exploiting the one area that is impossible to control—the vulnerabilities of company employees. The hackers found personal information about the oil companies' executives on social networking Web sites. They then created e-mails aimed at enticing the executives to click on a poisoned link. (This attack technique is called "spear phishing.") When victims clicked on these links, they were redirected to a Web site where malicious software loaded onto their computers.

In spring 2011, secret U.S. State Department cables obtained by WikiLeaks and made public by Reuters detailed a widespread digital spying operation linked to China's People's Liberation Army. According to the cables, the operation targeted not only U.S. government and private industry, but also high-level European officials. The Chinese hackers even managed to remotely activate the computer microphones and Web cameras of French officials so they could listen to and look at everything from office gossip to high-level diplomatic planning sessions.

In August 2011, a report from McAfee detailed hacks into 72 public and private computer networks in 14 countries. McAfee warned of "the biggest transfer of wealth in terms of intellectual property in history." These findings establish that hacking is a major international security problem.

The best approach once an intrusion is detected is for companies and individuals not to tip their hands until they are ready to respond with a serious defense. Countermeasures usually involve first identifying as many infected computers as possible by looking for suspicious software on hard drives and then tracking which computers have been contacting suspicious host servers. The response team then attempts to immediately pull as many infected computers as possible off the network by any means necessary. In some cases, this process involves literally pulling a cable out of the computer. Often it is impossible to know whether all the malicious software has been successfully removed. **<<< POSSIBLE SOLUTIONS**

In 2009 the Obama administration created the U.S. Cyber Command, which are executive orders signed by President Obama that give the U.S. military the all-clear to use weapons that can perform tasks ranging from espionage to the crippling of an enemy's electrical grid.

Despite this measure, the government can unfortunately go only so far to protect the networks of private companies. In 2011, the Department of Defense launched a pilot program with the defense industrial base that helps contractors improve security and share information about emerging forms of malicious software.

Plausible deniability is precisely what makes digital espionage such an effective tool. Digital espionage is difficult to detect and impossible to prove, and therefore cannot be used to justify retaliation. Digital security experts call this the attribution problem. At most, security personnel might know the immediate computer involved in hacking a company or government agency, but most often they do not even know that. Even if security personnel know that a particular computer is involved in an attack, security personnel do not know who controls that computer. It could be another hacked computer somewhere that someone else is controlling. **<<< THE RESULTS**

Private industry and government agencies are understandably reluctant to reveal any information about breaches. Most U.S. companies, however, remain vulnerable to security breaches and are naïve about the extent of the problem. Even with countermeasures, most security experts believe that keeping capable and determined attackers out of a system is impossible. One expert says, "If you want to talk about really confidential stuff in e-mail, you've got to understand that if you've got a real sophisticated adversary, they're reading it. It's not only that you're only as secure as the weakest link in your network. In an interconnected world, you're only as secure as the weakest link in the global chain of information."

Sources: Compiled from S. Gorman, "Chinese Hackers Suspected in Long Term Nortel Breach," *The Wall Street Journal*, February 14, 2012; M. Riley and S. Pearson, "China-Based Hackers Target Law Firms to Get Secret Deal Data," *Bloomberg*, January 31, 2012; A. Piore, "The Secret War," *Popular Mechanics*, January, 2012; S. Gorman, "China Hackers Hit U.S. Chamber," *The Wall Street Journal*, December 21, 2011; S. Martin, "Federal Panel Warns that China's Accounting, Computer Espionage Bear Watching," *Emerging Money*, November 16, 2011; M. Riley and A. Vance, "The Code War," *Bloomberg BusinessWeek*, July 25–31, 2011; F. Rashid, "Northrup Grumman, L-3 Communications Hacked Via Cloned RSA SecureID Tokens," *eWeek*, June 2, 2011; S. Gorman, "Cyber Combat: Act of War," *The Wall Street Journal*, May 31, 2011; J. Markoff and D. Barboza, "Researchers Trace Data Theft to Intruders in China," *The New York Times*, April 5, 2010; L. Whitney, "U.S. Cyber Command Prepped to Launch," *CNET News*, March 23, 2010; D. Gelernter, "Welcome to Cold War II," *Forbes*, April 3, 2009.

Questions

1. If the security experts are correct and organizations have no way to fully protect their information assets, then what should an organization do to protect those assets?
2. Go to Wikipedia (www.wikipedia.org) and look up "mutually assured destruction." Apply what you learn there to this case. That is, does cyberwarfare fit in the "mutually assured destruction" category? Why or why not?

RUBY'S CLUB · INTERNSHIP ASSIGNMENT

Ruben and Lisa have decided to go with a third party to handle their e-commerce transactions. They do not want to store any customer payment information on their Web site. Although they realize they are losing some money on each transaction in fees to the e-commerce provider, they consider this fee cost-effective "risk transfer" for them.

Specifically, they are considering the Google Checkout, Amazon Stores, eBay Stores, Yahoo Business, and PayPal as viable options. They feel that their customers would recognize these companies and feel confident in their transactions by associating with them.

As their intern, they want you to research these five options and provide them feedback on each. Which provides the easiest method of integrating e-commerce into their own new Web site? Which currently has largest customer base? Which one are customers most comfortable with? Have they had any recent security breaches? If so, how did they handle them and what were the ramifications to their customer (the company they provided the e-commerce tools to and the customers of that company)?

After you do your research, write Ruben and Lisa a letter (in business format) and make a suggestion as to the one you feel would best suit their needs.

SPREADSHEET ACTIVITY: RISK ANALYSIS WITH A SPREADSHEET

Objective: This activity will bring together the ideas of security and formula writing in a spreadsheet. Upon completion, you will be able to take data presented in written form, translate it into numbers, create formulas, and then rank security issues based on the spreadsheet you create.

Chapter Connection: Security issues are not all created equal. Some are frequent and inexpensive to overcome; others are rare and costly. Intentional and unintentional threats must be dealt with. But as a network manager, how do you know what deserves the most resources? Given that you never know where the next threat will come from, how will you allocate resources? This activity will bring this discussion to a spreadsheet and help you apply your math and spreadsheet skills to this very "real-world" situation.

Activity: Consider the following situation. You are the network manager at a local bank. A number of security issues must be dealt with. However, like everyone else, you have limited resources. You only have $10,000 in your budget to allocate to security. This money can be spent on hardware, software, training, or anything else you deem worthy of this money. Here is a list of potential threats.

- *Malware:* If malware ends up installed on a computer in the system, it could easily spread to the other machines without anyone knowing it is there. The expense of repairing the machines and restoring data are minimal when compared to the cost of rebuilding trust in the consumer. Estimated total cost of marketing and repairing customer trust: $25,000. Probability of occurring: 35 percent. Cost of preventative maintenance and training: $3,500.

- *Careless employees:* Judy has to run to the restroom. Because she trusts everyone she works with, she walks away from her computer without locking it. When she is away from her desk and her computer is unlocked, Johnny walks in. No one thinks anything about Johnny on Judy's computer because he is the local "computer guru" even though he is a janitor. While Judy is away and Johnny is on her computer, he transfers a total of $7,500 from over 150 total accounts by running a script in the computer system. When Judy returns, she sees Johnny on the computer and thanks him for watching it, laughing about how she accidentally left it unlocked. Probability of occurring: 5 percent. Cost of preventative maintenance and training: $2,000.

- *Cloud computing:* Banks rely on many software packages to accomplish their goals. Not the least of these are the many packages run by the home office. These are accessed over the Internet, and private data are transferred back and forth. A hacker who is able to hack into the local system would by default have access to the cloud. The cost of this is monumental. Customer data from across the nation would be compromised. Having a backup of all data is imperative. Keeping employees trained on using the system, avoiding social engineering, changing passwords, and other issues are paramount to help protect the home office and the local office. Total potential loss: $2.5 million. Probability of occurrence: 2.5 percent. Cost of preventative maintenance and training: $7,000.

- *Fire:* This is always a threat. If a fire breaks out, it could be devastating. Loss of technology equipment alone would run close to $20,000. Loss of records would be almost unrecoverable. However, the chance of fire is relatively low. At a 2 percent chance of fire, this is a minimal concern. The cost of preventative maintenance is not cheap. Sprinklers have to be inspected, fire retardant material must be tested, and fire extinguishers must be replaced. Total preventative maintenance cost is $1,500. However, the total potential loss is a devastating $250,000.

Given that most people agree that risk (R) is equal to the consequence (C) multiplied by the probability of occurrence (P):

$$R = C*P$$

Create a spreadsheet that calculates this formula. Then use your estimated risk to figure the return on security investment (ROSI) that most consider to be equal to risk avoided (R; hopefully it will be avoided by the investment) divided by the cost of preventative maintenance (PM).

$$ROSI = R/PM$$

This number represents the "impact" of an investment and can be used to help determine how to create a budget so that the return is maximized. The higher the number, the more of the risk is covered by the investment. Use this number to prioritize where to make security investments.

Because your budget is only $10,000, you will need to determine where to spend your money. According to this scenario, total coverage would cost $14,000. Use the ROSI to recommend a budget. Also provide your spreadsheet for justification of the budget.

Deliverable: The final product will be a spreadsheet formula, ranking, and presentation of a suggested budget.

Discussion Questions:

1. Discuss the advantages and disadvantages of building a formula once and copying it to multiple rows or columns.

2. Discuss the importance of taking verbal or written clues and being able to build a spreadsheet. Is a spreadsheet the ultimate combination of math and business?

3. Given that no one has unlimited resources, is it possible to ever cover all the bases and ensure security? What type of agreement must there be between the business and the consumer for this situation to exist and be acceptable?

Quiz questions are assignable in WileyPLUS, and available on the Book Companion Site at http://www.wiley.com/college/rainer.

DATABASE ACTIVITY: TABLES II

Objective

Information systems need checks to catch errors in the entry of data. Errors can lead to bad decisions, producing the wrong products, ordering too much or too little, sending one group messages meant for another, and more. If you develop a database for yourself or your team, you should check for as many errors as you can. When you use a database, you can form an opinion of its reliability by seeing how it checks its inputs.

Not all errors can be caught, of course. If a street address is entered as 63 instead of 36 Elm, a database cannot tell it is wrong. Many errors can be caught, however. You will learn a few of the methods here using the following features of Microsoft Access:

- Default values
- Range checks
- Value checks against a list

CHAPTER CONNECTION

Security includes keeping bad data out of databases. Checking data as entered can prevent many errors and some mischief. Here, you will see how Access checks data as it is entered. Other database management systems work in much the same way.

PREREQUISITES

Before you begin this activity, you will need to familiarize yourself with and practice three concepts in this activity: default values, validation checks based on a range of valid data, and validation checks against a list. The following sections introduce these concepts and provide practice in dealing with them. Read these sections and complete the brief practice items before moving to the larger activity.

DEFAULT VALUES

A *default value* is the value of a data item if no other value is entered. Say an Ohio college attracts primarily students from the Dayton area. Most of its applicants have home phones in area code 937. A database could pre-enter 937 as the area code of new applicants. The work-study student who enters applicant information into a database can change it for those with different home phone area codes, but having it saves time and reduces errors.

To enter a default value for a field in an Access table:

1. Open the table in Design view.
2. Select the field for which you want to specify a default value.
3. Find the Default Value row in the Field Properties pane, under the General tab.
4. Click on the right side of this row and key in the desired value, as shown in Figure 7A.1.

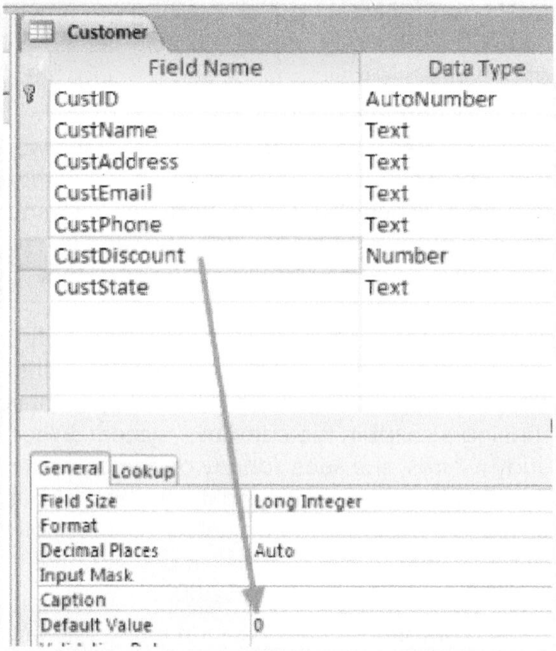

Figure 7A.1

Usage Hint: You can also assign default values and perform validation checks on fields in forms instead of in tables. In the form's Layout or Design view, open its Property Sheet, select a field, select the Data or All tab on the Property Sheet, and continue as above. The check will be applied only to data entered via that form. Checks entered in table definitions are applied to all data entered in any way.

5. Go to Datasheet view to confirm that the default value was entered correctly. You should see the value in the bottom (New) row of the table. If you enter a default value in a form, you will not see it in the table's Datasheet view, but you will see it if you enter a new record via the form.

RANGE CHECKS

Database designers often need to make sure data are in an allowable range. For example, the quantity of something in an order must be greater than zero, or the year of birth of a pupil entering kindergarten in September 2012 might have to be 2007.

This, by the way, shows one reason for putting checking in a form rather than in the table on which the form is based. Suppose an occasional student born outside the usual year enters kindergarten. The school principal might have a different form, in which a new student's year of birth can be 2006, 2007 or 2008. Supervisors can often override data checks that apply to the workers they supervise.

To enter a range check for a field in an Access table:

1. Open the table in Design view.

2. Select the field for which you want to enter a range check.

3. In the Field Properties pane below the list of fields, under the General tab, find the Validation Rule row.

4. In the right side of this row, enter an expression that will evaluate to True or False, and is True for valid data. For example, the expression ">5" (without quotation marks) means the value entered in the field must be greater than 5. The data the user enters is implied to the left of the ">."

These comparison operators are used in validation expressions:

= (equal to) Seldom useful by itself. If a database designer knows what a value must be, why require a user to enter it?

> (greater than)

< (less than)

>= (greater than or equal to)

<= (less than or equal to)

<> (less than or greater than; that is, *not* equal to)

In addition, these are often useful in validation and other expressions:

AND requires *both* the condition on its left and the condition on its right to be met. ">= 0 AND <=10" requires a value of at least zero but not over ten.

OR requires *either* the condition on its left or the one on its right, possibly both, to be met. "<5 OR >50" excludes numbers from 5 to 50 but allows all others. (Be sure you understand why the expression means this.)

BETWEEN . . . AND . . . means just what you would think. "BETWEEN 0 AND 10" is another way to write the condition that was used as an example for AND.

IS NULL lets you leave a field blank. Some versions of Access will not let you leave one blank if it has a validation rule, because blank data does not satisfy the rule. If you want to allow the field to be left empty, write "IS NULL OR . . ." where the rest of the rule is whatever you want as validation if anything at all is entered.

If you want to use a date in a condition, enclose it between #s. ">=#1/1/2010#" (without quotation marks) will accept any date in 2010 or later.

Instead of an actual date, you can write "DATE()" to mean today's date. ">DATE()" will accept any date in the future. This can be useful, for example, for delivery date estimates. It does not guarantee that the order will arrive then, but it prevents a company from promising to deliver something last week.

There is more. For example, you could make sure an account number consists of a letter followed by five digits, the last of which is even. Once you understand how validation rules work, you can read up on the rest if you need to.

5. Optionally, but a good practice, enter an error message in the right side of the Validation Text row. Access will display it to the user if the test fails. A few suggestions:

- Make messages informative. Say "Quantity must be greater than zero," not "Quantity error."

- Do not try to be funny. It is nearly impossible to do this well. Even a genuinely funny message loses its humor after someone has seen it five (or fifty) times.

- Do not insult the user. (The user might be your boss.)

- Do not end the message with an exclamation point. "Must be from 1 to 5" is fine. "Must be from 1 to 5!" is scolding. Nobody likes to be scolded.

If you do not provide a message, Access will display the rule that the data did not satisfy in a standard message format. Some users will be able to figure out the problem from this, but many nontechnical people will find it confusing.

6. Test your work by going to Datasheet view, entering sample data values, and confirming that valid ones are accepted but invalid ones are not. Pick values that provide good tests. Try values at the limits: if a number is supposed to be *less than* 10, not *less than or equal to* 10, make sure 10 is rejected.

Usage Hint: Access does not apply validation checks to default values. This can lead to problems when a user changes a default, realizes that the change was in error, and tries to change it back. If there are both a default and a validation rule for the same field, be sure the validation rule allows the default value. That way, users can restore the default value if they change it by mistake.

CHECKING VALUES AGAINST A LIST

Sometimes there is no simple formula to define valid data, but there is a list of valid values. For example, you might require a state code in a U.S. postal address to be one of the 50+ two-letter codes that the U.S. Postal Service recognizes or you might require a department name to match one of the departments in your company.

The simplest way to handle this is to list them in the rule. The expression "IN (a, b, c, . . .)" does this. This evaluates as True if the entered value is a, b, c, up to as many as you have. (Replace a, b, c, and so on with the valid values.) If items are text, put them in quotation marks. A rule to see if a location is one of your firm's offices might look like this:

IN ("Boston", "Paris", "Sydney", "Santiago")

Usage Hint: If you are in North America, you were taught that commas go inside quotation marks in English writing. That does not apply to Access functions!

Longer lists should be in tables. (This is a flexible concept that can do more than reduce data entry errors.) To get a pull-down list with all valid values:

1. Create a new table with one field. Give it the same data type as the field whose data you want to validate. Enter all valid data values into this column. Save the table, giving it a suitable name, and close it. You can change it whenever the list of valid data values changes.

2. Open the table that contains the field you want to check against this list. In Design view, select that field. Select its Data Type column and change its data type to "Lookup Wizard …"

3. On the first page of the wizard, tell it you want to look up values in a table or query.

4. On the next page, select the table you just created.

5. On the next page, select the only column this table has and move it to the right-hand pane by clicking the ">" symbol. Click "Next" a few times until the wizard exits Figure 7A.2.

6. A value list created this way lets the user select values from a pull-down list. It also lets the user enter a value that is not in the list. If you want to prevent that, while this field is still selected, click the Lookup tab in the Field Properties pane. Change "Limit to list" to Yes via the down arrow at the right of the row. (If you do not do this now, you can do it later.)

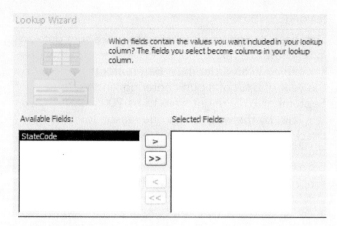

Figure 7A.2

Usage Hint: If you do this with a table that already contains data, you may have to re-enter the data in the column you were working with. In that case, make sure to keep a record of it, or have some other way to re-create it, before you confirm all the steps in closing the wizard.

7. Switch to Datasheet view to confirm that the field behaves correctly.

8. You can click the Database Tools ribbon tab and look at the relationship map. If it does not show the new table, click Show Table and add it to the map. You will see a link between the new table and the table that contains the data to be validated against it.

Activity

1. Download the **Ch 07 CustOrder** database from http://www.wiley.com/rainer/go/database and open it. It has tables for customers, orders, line items and products. Its structure resembles the example in Section 3.3 of the book. The Ordered Parts table there corresponds to the line item table here.

2. Open the Line Item table and specify a default value of 1 for Quantity.

3. Open the Customer table and enter a default value of 0 for customer discount. Also, for the same field, add a rule to limit the discount to a range of 0 to 25. (If this column was formatted as a percentage, you would have to enter the upper limit as 0.25, not 25. Access can display fractions as percentages, but that is just for display. It treats them as fractions internally and validates them that way. Here, however, because the column is not formatted as a percentage, use 25.) Enter an error message to display if a user tries to enter a value outside this range.

4. In the Order table, add a validation rule to the order date: it must be no later than today. (The limiting value, today, is allowable.)

5. Create a table CountryList with one column: countries from which you expect orders. Enter ten countries into it, including your home country, the other countries in the sample data, and enough others of your choice to make ten. Link the table to the Country field in the Customer table. The user should be allowed to enter a new country in the Customer table if a customer's country is not in the list. (Because you are doing this to a table that already has data in it, you will have to re-enter the country names when you are done. If you cannot figure them out from the city names, write them down first.)

Deliverable

Your completed database, with the above changes.

Quiz Questions

1. True or false: A person entering data into an Access database can change a field from its default value to a different value.

2. In which of the following places can you specify a default value for a data element?

   2.1. In a table, in Datasheet view

   2.2. In a table, in Design view

   2.3. In a report

   2.4. In a form

   Choose one of the following four answers, (a) through (d):

   (a) 2.2

   (b) 2.2 and 2.4

   (c) 2.1 and 2.4

   (d) 2.2 and 2.3

3. Which of the following validation rules will allow only dates between July 13 and December 16, 2011 (including both endpoints)?

   (a) >#7/12/2011# AND <#12/17/2011#

   (b) BETWEEN #7/13/2011 AND #12/16/2011#

   (c) >=#7/13/2011# AND <=#12/16/2011#

   (d) All of the above

4. If a validation rule has no validation text, which of the following will happen?

   (a) The rule will not be applied. Any data can be entered without checking.

   (b) The rule will be applied to Number and Date data, but not to Text data.

   (c) The rule will be applied, but the error message may not be informative.

   (d) The rule will be applied to new data, but not to data that someone changes later.

Discussion Questions

1. How would you write a validation rule to permit a data value to be either 0 or any number from 5 through 10?

2. What is the purpose of Validation Text in an Access table definition?

3. How would you write a validation rule that requires a data value to be one of the six letters A, B, C, D, F or I?

8 | Social Computing

LEARNING OBJECTIVES >>>

1. Describe six Web 2.0 tools and the two major types of Web 2.0 sites.

2. Describe the benefits and risks of social commerce to companies.

3. Identify the methods used for shopping socially.

4. Discuss innovative ways to use social networking sites for advertising and market research.

5. Describe how social computing improves customer service.

6. Discuss different ways in which human resource managers make use of social computing.

7. Discuss the advantages and disadvantages of crowdsourcing to organizations.

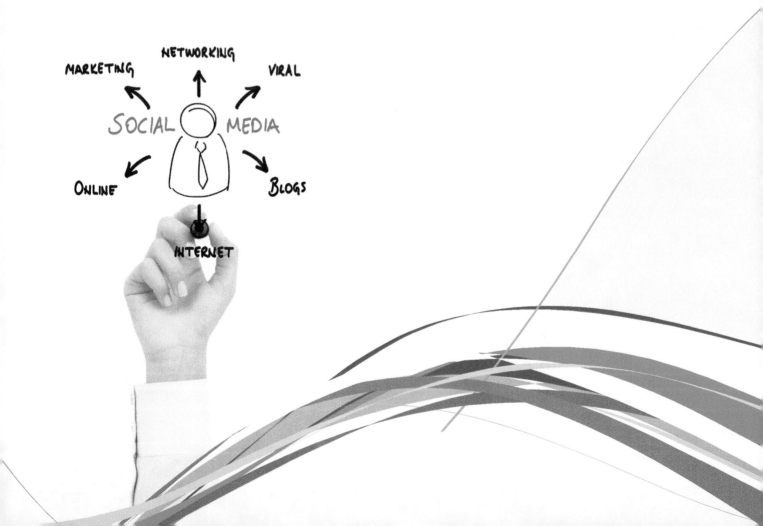

© Courtney Keating/iStockphoto

Lisa Keiling owns a tanning salon in Wedowee, Alabama, that does very well from January to May. Unfortunately, during the rest of the year the demand for tanning beds is extremely low. In fact, the demand is so low that Lisa decided to try some new strategies. She tried a small hunting/fishing shop in a room where a tanning bed had been. Even though Wedowee is a small town with lots of hunting and fishing, that idea did not work well. Then, Lisa decided to sublease part of her space to add a hairdressing room in the back. This idea generated a lot of extra revenue and became a very important part of her business.

During the months where tanning was minimal, Lisa's main income was revenue that came from the leased space to the hairdresser, but she still needed help to make it through the slow times. After searching around for small business ideas, she found a machine that would cut out vinyl designs that could be placed on cups, purses, bowls, plates, frames, or any hard surface. With this machine, she could customize just about anything that she could imagine! She purchased it and began learning to use it.

Once she became good at producing vinyl designs, she wondered how to get the word out. She knew she needed to use the Internet, but she did not feel comfortable building a Web site herself. Then, Lisa realized that she was very familiar with Facebook. Because she had lived in this area for a long time and already had many "friends" on Facebook, the site was a natural fit to advertise for her new business. Lisa first created an account for her company. As she designed each new product, she simply posted a picture of it on Facebook, "liked" it herself from her personal page, and other people did the same. Her new creations were going viral and getting the word out in small-town Wedowee, and she was getting new business!

For Lisa, the vinyl designs business and Facebook saved her business in the winter months. You can visit her Facebook page and see that she is very active online every day. Her page has given her customers a place to contact her and it has **> > >**

RUBY'S CLUB

Ruby's Club introduced their Web site only five years ago. Since then, it has been a very basic Web 1.0 site, containing static information that has changed very little over the course of the years. Now, with the rise of Web 2.0 technology and the growing skills of Internet users, it seems natural that Ruben and Lisa can use this technology to reach their customers.

Although they are aware of this technology, neither of them is very experienced with it. Ruben only joined Facebook last year because he was trying to learn more about a band that was coming to perform at the club. He has not explored it much from a business standpoint and really does not know what is possible. And Twitter is not even on their radar yet.

In addition, they want to explore options such as blogs, wikis, and other Web 2.0 material. But where do they go? What should they hope to accomplish?

given her a way to sell her product without people having to come to her store.

Currently, she is exploring the addition of a Web site to streamline the ordering process. This Web site would be synced with her Facebook page, and serve to give customers a single place for orders. She hopes that all of her efforts will continue to make her business a success, with the custom gift shop as her main source of income and the tanning salon providing only supplemental income.

Sources: Compiled from authors' personal interviews with Lisa Keiling.

uestions

1. What other actions could Lisa take on Facebook to "get the word out" about her custom gifts?
2. Does Lisa really need a Web site for her business, or is her Facebook page sufficient? Hint: Can she take orders via her Facebook page?

Introduction

Humans are social individuals, and thus human behavior is innately social. Humans, therefore, typically orient their behavior around other members of their community. As a result, people are sensitive to the behavior of those around them and many of their decisions are influenced by their social context.

Traditional information systems support organizational activities and business processes and concentrate on cost reduction and increases in productivity. In a variation of this traditional model, **social computing** is a type of IT that combines social behavior and information systems to create value. Social computing concentrates on improving collaboration and interaction among people and on user-generated content. In social computing, social information is not anonymous, but is significant precisely because it is linked to particular individuals, who are in turn linked to their own networks of individuals.

Social computing makes socially produced information available to all. This information may be provided directly, as when users rate a movie (for example, at Rotten Tomatoes), or provided indirectly, as with Google's PageRank algorithm, which sequences search results.

In social computing, users, rather than organizations, produce, control, use, and manage content via interactive communications and collaboration. As a result, social computing is transforming power relationships in organizations. Employees and customers are empowered by their ability to use social computing to organize themselves. Thus, social computing can influence those in power to listen to the concerns and issues of ordinary people. Organizational customers and employees are joining this social computing phenomenon, with serious consequences for most organizations.

Most governments and companies in modern developed societies are not prepared for the new social power of the masses. Today, managers, executives, and government officials can no longer control the conversation around policies, products, and other issues.

In the new world of business and government, organizational leaders will have to demonstrate authenticity, even-handedness, transparency, good faith, and humility. If they do not, customers and employees may distrust them, to potentially disastrous effect. For example, customers who do not like a product or service can quickly broadcast their disapproval. Another example is that prospective employees do not have to take their employers at their word for what life is like at their companies—they can find out from people who already work there. A final example is that employees now have many more options to start their own companies, which could compete with their former companies.

As you see from these examples, the world is becoming more democratic and reflective of the will of ordinary people, enabled by the power of social computing. On the one hand, social power can help keep a company vital and can enable customers and employee activists to become a source of creativity, innovation, and new ideas that will move a company forward. On the other hand, companies that show insensitivity toward customers or employees quickly find themselves on a downward slide. Consider the following examples:

- Hershey faced public relations problems in August 2011 when 400 college students revolted, walking off their jobs. These students were hired through a U.S. State Department-sponsored foreign-exchange program, and they did not like the stress of working in a candy-packing factory, sometimes on all-night shifts. The students, who came from China, Nigeria, Turkey, and Ukraine, were excellent communicators and used YouTube, Facebook, and other tools to bring attention to their plight.

- Adidas came under attack in New Zealand when fans of the country's hugely popular national rugby team were outraged to learn that Adidas team jerseys were being sold for significantly more at home than in other countries. Fans found this information by researching product prices in New Zealand and the United States online. Armed with this information, fans organized protests. Soon, national news programs picked up coverage of the protest and of Adidas's slow response to the consumer outrage. Customers started returning Adidas clothing to stores in disgust, and employees felt so threatened by the populace that they removed Adidas's logos from their company vehicles.

- In the Netherlands in 2011, a social media campaign against bankers' bonuses focused on the Amsterdam-based company ING. Bank customers began threatening en masse to withdraw deposits. In response, CEO Jan Hommen voluntarily waived his own upcoming $1.8 million bonus and then ordered all company directors to do the same.

Organizations today are using social computing in a variety of innovative ways, including marketing, customer relationship management, human resource management, and others. In fact, so many organizations are competing to use social computing in as many new ways as possible that an inclusive term for the use of social computing in business has emerged: *social commerce*. Because social computing is facilitated by Web 2.0 tools and sites, you begin this chapter by examining these technologies. You then turn your attention to a diverse number of social commerce activities, including shopping, advertising, market research, customer relationship management, human resource management, and crowd-sourcing. You conclude the chapter by studying the risks and concerns associated with social computing.

When you complete this chapter, you will have a thorough understanding of social computing and the ways in which modern organizations use it. You will be familiar with the advantages and disadvantages of social computing and the risks and rewards it can bring to your organization. For example, most of you already have pages on social networking sites, so you are familiar with the benefits and drawbacks of such sites. This chapter will enable you to apply this knowledge to your organization's efforts in the social computing arena. You will be in a position to contribute to your organization's policies on social computing. You will also be able to help your organization design its own strategy for social computing.

Significantly, social computing can help you start your own business. For example, many entrepreneurs have developed successful businesses on Facebook (see this chapter's opening case).

As we noted earlier, social computing is facilitated by Web 2.0 tools and sites. In the next section, you will learn about Web 2.0 tools such as AJAX, tagging, really simple syndication, blogs, microblogs, and wikis. You will also learn about two major types of Web 2.0 sites, social networking sites and mashups.

8.1 Web 2.0

The World Wide Web, which you learned about in Chapter 4, first appeared in 1990. Web 1.0 was the first generation of the Web. We did not use this term in Chapter 4 because there was no need to say "Web 1.0" until Web 2.0 emerged.

The key developments of Web 1.0 were the creation of Web sites and the commercialization of the Web. Users typically had minimal interaction with Web 1.0 sites. Rather, they passively receive information from those sites.

Web 2.0 is a popular term that has proved difficult to define. According to Tim O'Reilly, a noted blogger, **Web 2.0** is a loose collection of information technologies and applications, plus the Web sites that use them. These Web sites enrich the user experience by encouraging user participation, social interaction, and collaboration. Unlike Web 1.0 sites, Web 2.0 sites are not so much online places to visit as Web locations that facilitate information sharing, user-centered design, and collaboration. Web 2.0 sites often harness collective intelligence (for example, wikis); deliver functionality as services, rather than packaged software (for example, Web services); and feature remixable applications and data (for example, mashups). Web 2.0 has also been defined as a new digital ecosystem, with characteristics of creativity, connectivity, collaboration, convergence, and community.

AJAX

Most Web 2.0 applications have rich, user-friendly interfaces based on AJAX. **AJAX** is a Web development technique that enables portions of Web pages to reload with fresh data instead of requiring the entire Web page to reload. This process speeds up response time and increases user satisfaction.

Tagging

A **tag** is a keyword or term that describes a piece of information—for example, a blog, a picture, an article, or a video clip. Users typically choose tags that are meaningful to them. Tagging allows users to place information in multiple, overlapping associations rather than in rigid categories. For example, a photo of a car might be tagged with "Corvette," "sports car," and "Chevrolet." Tagging is the basis of *folksonomies*, which are user-generated classifications that use tags to categorize and retrieve Web pages, photos, videos, and other Web content.

One specific form of tagging, known as *geo-tagging*, refers to tagging information on maps. For example, Google Maps allows users to add pictures and information, such as restaurant or hotel ratings, to maps. Therefore, when users access Google Maps, their experience is enriched because they can see pictures of attractions, reviews, and things to do, all related to the map location they are viewing.

Really Simple Syndication (RSS)

Really Simple Syndication (RSS) allows you to receive the information you want (customized information), when you want it, without having to surf thousands of Web sites. RSS allows anyone to syndicate (publish) his or her blog, or any other content, to anyone who has an interest in subscribing. When changes to the content are made, subscribers receive a notification of the changes and an idea of what the new content contains. Subscribers can then click on a link that will take them to the full text of the new content.

For example, CNN.com provides RSS feeds for each of its main topic areas, such as world news, sports news, technology news, and entertainment news. NBC uses RSS feeds to allow viewers to download the most current version of shows such as *Meet the Press* and *NBC Nightly News.*

You can find thousands of Web sites that offer RSS feeds at Syndic8 (www.syndic8.com) and NewsIsFree (www.newsisfree.com). Figure 8.1 illustrates how an RSS can be searched and how RSS feeds can be located.

To use RSS, you can utilize a special news reader that displays RSS content feeds from Web sites you select. Many such readers are available, several of them for free. Examples are AmphetaDesk (www.disobey.com/amphetadesk) and Pluck (www.pluck.com). In addition, most browsers have built-in RSS readers. For an excellent RSS tutorial, visit www.mnot.net/rss/tutorial.

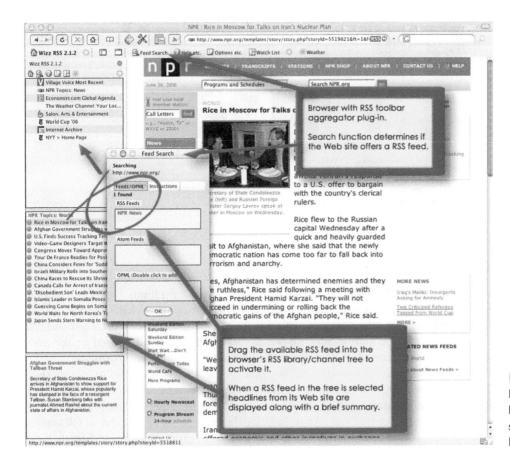

Browser with RSS toolbar aggregator plug-in.

Search function determines if the Web site offers a RSS feed.

Drag the available RSS feed into the browser's RSS library/channel tree to activate it.

When a RSS feed in the tree is selected headlines from its Web site are displayed along with a brief summary.

Figure 8.1 The Web site of National Public Radio (NPR) with RSS toolbar aggregator and search function. (Courtesy of NPR. Used with permission.)

Blogs

A weblog (blog for short) is a personal Web site, open to the public, in which the site creator expresses his or her feelings or opinions via a series of chronological entries. *Bloggers*—people who create and maintain blogs—write stories, convey news, and provide links to other articles and Web sites that are of interest to them. The simplest method of creating a blog is to sign up with a blogging service provider, such as www.blogger.com (now owned by Google), www.xanga.com (see Figure 8.2), and www.sixapart.com. The **blogosphere** is the term for the millions of blogs on the Web.

Many companies listen to consumers in the blogosphere who express their views on the companies' products. In marketing, these views are called *consumer-generated media*. For example, Nielsen (www.nielsen-online.com) "mines" the blogosphere to provide information for its clients in several areas. Nielsen helps clients find ways to serve potential markets, ranging from broad-based to niche markets. The company also helps clients detect false rumors before these rumors appear in the mainstream press and gauges the potency of a marketing push or the popularity of a new product.

Although blogs can be very useful, they also have shortcomings. Perhaps the primary value of blogs is their ability to bring current, breaking news to the public in the fastest time possible. Unfortunately, in doing so, bloggers sometimes cut corners and their blogs can be inaccurate. Regardless of their various problems, blogs have transformed the ways in which people gather and consume information.

Microblogging

Microblogging is a form of blogging that allows users to write short messages (or capture an image or embedded video) and publish them. These messages can be submitted via text messaging from mobile phones, instant messaging, e-mail, or just over the Web. The

Figure 8.2 Xanga organizes blogs by common content (dating, beauty, food, and more) to help readers find multiple blogs on one website.

content of a microblog differs from that of a blog because of the limited space per message (usually up to 140 characters). The most popular microblogging service is Twitter.

Twitter is a free microblogging service that allows its users to send messages and read other users' messages and updates, known as **tweets**. Tweets are displayed on the user's profile page and delivered to other users who have signed up to receive them.

Twitter is becoming a very useful business tool. It allows companies to quickly share information with people interested in their products, thereby creating deeper relationships with their customers. Businesses also use Twitter to gather real-time market intelligence and customer feedback. As an individual user, you can use Twitter to tell companies about your experience with their business, offer product ideas, and learn about great offers.

For a great example of a company using Twitter to get closer to customers, look ahead to IT's About Business 12.1.

Wikis

A **wiki** is a Web site made up entirely of content posted by users. Wikis have an "edit" link on each page that allows any user to add, change, or delete material, fostering easy collaboration.

Wikis take advantage of the combined input of many individuals. Consider Wikipedia (www.wikipedia.org), an online encyclopedia which is the largest wiki in existence. Wikipedia contains more than 3.4 million articles in English, which get a combined total of nearly 500 million views every day. Wikipedia relies on volunteer administrators who enforce a neutral point of view and encourage users to delete copy displaying clear bias. Nevertheless, there are still major debates over the reliability and accuracy of Wikipedia articles. Many educators will not allow students to cite references from Wikipedia because Wikipedia content is of uncertain origin. Moreover, Wikipedia does not provide any quality assessment or fact checking by experts. Therefore, academics and others still have major concerns about the accuracy of user-provided content.

Organizations use wikis in several ways. In project management, for example, wikis provide a central repository for capturing constantly updated product features and specifications, tracking issues, resolving problems, and maintaining project histories. In addition, wikis enable companies to collaborate with customers, suppliers, and other business partners on projects. Wikis are also valuable in knowledge management. For example, companies use wikis to keep enterprisewide documents, such as guidelines and frequently asked questions, accurate and current.

© esolla/iStockphoto

A wiki allows open contribution to a document.

Social Networking Web Sites

A **social network** is a social structure composed of individuals, groups, or organizations linked by values, visions, ideas, financial exchange, friendship, kinship, conflict, or trade. **Social networking** refers to activities performed using social software tools (e.g., blogging) or social networking features (e.g., media sharing).

A social network can be described as a map of all relevant links or connections among the network's members. Such a map of all relevant links or connections for one member is that person's **social graph**. Mark Zuckerberg of Facebook originally coined this term to refer to the social network of relationships among users of Facebook. The idea was that Facebook would take advantage of relationships among individuals to offer a richer online experience.

Social networks can also be used to determine the social capital of individual participants. **Social capital** refers to the number of connections a person has within and between social networks.

Participants congregate on *social networking Web sites* where they can create their own profile page for free and on which they can write blogs and wikis; post pictures, videos, or music; share ideas; and link to other Web locations they find interesting. Social networkers chat using instant messaging and Twitter and tag posted content with their own key words, making content searchable and facilitating interactions and transactions. Social networkers converse, collaborate, and share opinions, experiences, knowledge, insights, and perceptions with each other. Through these sites, users are able to find like-minded people online, either to pursue an interest or a goal or just to establish a sense of community among people who may never meet in the real world.

Table 8.1 shows the variety of online social networking platforms. Social networking web sites allow users to upload their content to the Web in the form of text, voice, images, and videos.

© Logorilla/iStockphoto

Social networking allows convenient connections to those of similar interest.

TABLE 8.1 Categories of Social Networking Web Sites

Socially oriented: Socially focused public sites, open to anyone

- Facebook (www.facebook.com)
- Google Orkut (www.orkut.com)
- Google+ (https://plus.google.com)
- Hi5 (www.hi5.com)

Professional networking: Focused on networking for business professionals

- LinkedIn (www.linkedin.com)

Media sharing

- *Netcasting* includes podcasting (audio) and videocasting (audio and video). For example, educational institutions use netcasts to provide students with access to lectures, lab demonstrations, and sports events. In 2007, Apple launched iTunes U, which offers free content provided by major U.S. universities such as Stanford and MIT.
- *Web 2.0 media* sites allow people to come together and share user-generated digital media, such as pictures, audio, and video.
  - Video (Amazon Video on Demand, YouTube, Hulu, Facebook)
  - Music (Amazon MP3, Last.fm, Rhapsody, Pandora, Facebook, iTunes)
  - Photographs (Photobucket, Flickr, Shutterfly, Picasa, Facebook)

Communication

- *Blogs*: Blogger, LiveJournal, Open Diary, TypePad, WordPress, Vox, Expression Engine, Xanga
- *Microblogging/Presence applications*: Twitter, Plurk, Tumblr, Yammer, Qaiku

Collaboration: Wikis (Wikimedia, PBworks, Wetpaint)

Social bookmarking (or *social tagging*): Focused on helping users store, organize, search, and manage bookmarks of Web pages on the Internet

- Delicious (www.delicious.com)
- StumbleUpon (www.stumbleupon.com)
- Google Reader (http://reader.google.com)
- CiteULike (www.citeulike.com)

Social news: Focused on user-posted news stories that are ranked by popularity based on user voting

- Digg (www.digg.com)
- Chime.in (http://chime.in)
- Reddit (www.reddit.com)

Events: Focused on alerts for relevant events, people you know nearby, etc.

- Eventful (www.eventful.com)
- Meetup (www.meetup.com)
- Foursquare (www.foursquare.com)

Virtual meeting place: Sites that are essentially three-dimensional worlds, built and owned by the residents (the users)

- Second Life (www.secondlife.com)

Interesting New Social Networks

- Empire Avenue (www.empireavenue.com) is a social exchange network where members invest virtual currency in people and brands that interest them.
- Color (www.color.com) is a free mobile app that creates an instant social network based on users' locations and proximity to others. Users can instantly share images, videos, and text conversations with others nearby.
- Foursquare (http://foursquare.com) is a location-based mobile service that enables participants to share their location with friends by checking in via a smartphone app.
- Hunch (www.hunch.com) maps people's interests by asking them a series of questions. The site creates a "taste graph," which tracks everything that a user likes and dislikes.

Online Marketplaces for Microjobs

- For example, TaskRabbit (www.taskrabbit.com) and Zaarly (www.zaarly.com) enable people to farm out chores to a growing number of temporary personal assistants. Thousands of unemployed or under-employed workers use these sites. The part-time or full-time tasks are especially popular with stay-at-home moms, retirees, and students. Workers choose their jobs and negotiate their own rates.

Enterprise Social Networks

Business-oriented social networks can be public, such as LinkedIn.com. As such, they are owned and managed by an independent company.

However, an increasing number of companies have created their own in-house, private social networks for their employees, former employees, business partners, and/or customers. Such networks are considered to be "behind the firewall" and are often referred to as *corporate social networks*. By establishing these networks, companies enable connections among employees that allow them to establish virtual teams, bring new employees up to speed, improve collaboration, and increase employee retention by creating a sense of community. Employees are able to interact with their coworkers on a level that is typically absent in large organizations or when people work remotely.

Corporate social networks are used for many processes, including

- Networking and community building, both inside and outside an organization
- Crowdsourcing: gathering ideas, insights, and feedback from crowds
- Social collaboration: collaborative work and problem solving using wikis, blogs, instant messaging, collaborative office, and other special-purpose Web-based collaboration platforms; for example, see Laboranova (www.laboranova.com)
- Social publishing: employees and others creating either individually or collaboratively, and posting contents—photos, videos, presentation slides, and documents—into a member's or a community's accessible-content repository such as YouTube, Flickr, SlideShare, and DocStoc
- Social views and feedback
- Social intelligence and social analytics: monitoring, analyzing, and interpreting conversations, interactions, and associations among people, topics, and ideas to gain insights. Social intelligence is useful for examining relationships and work patterns of individuals and groups and for discovering people and expertise

Think about IBM. With more than 426,000 employees across 170 countries, more than 100,000 contractors, and a broad range of business partners and customers, IBM has no choice but to be a social business. In fact, IBM has become the largest corporate consumer of social technologies. On any given day, 50 percent of IBMers regularly work away from traditional IBM offices. About 12 percent work at home and another 20 percent are mobile workers.

To enable its social networking, IBM has deployed Social Blue (formerly Beehive), an internal social networking site that gives IBM employees a rich connection to the people they work with on both a personal and a professional level. Social Blue helps employees make new connections, track current friends and coworkers, and renew contacts with people they have worked with in the past. When employees join Social Blue, they get a profile page. They can use the status message field and the free-form "About Me" section of their profile page to let other people at IBM know where they are and what they are doing.

Employees can also use Social Blue to post photos, create lists, and organize events. If users are hosting an event, they can create an event page in Social Blue and invite people to attend.

Users can create top-five lists, called "hive fives," to share their thoughts on any topic they are passionate about. Social Blue also comes in handy when preparing for conference calls. If users do not know the other people on the call, they can check out the participants' Social Blue profiles before the call and find out if they have current interests, either work related or recreational, or if they have colleagues in common.

In addition to social goals, the Social Blue team created the site to help IBM employees meet the challenge of building relationships that are vital to working in large, distributed enterprises. Social Blue helps project leaders find people with the right skills for their project.

Mashups

A **mashup** is a Web site that takes different content from a number of other Web sites and mixes them together to create a new kind of content. The launch of Google Maps is credited with providing the start for mashups. A user can take a map from Google, add his or her own data, and then display a map mashup on his or her Web site that plots crime scenes, cars for sale, or anything else. (See Figure 8.3.)

There are many examples of mashups (for a complete list of mashups, see www.programmableweb.com):

- Craigslist developed a dynamic map of all available apartments in the United States that are listed on Craigslist (www.housingmaps.com).

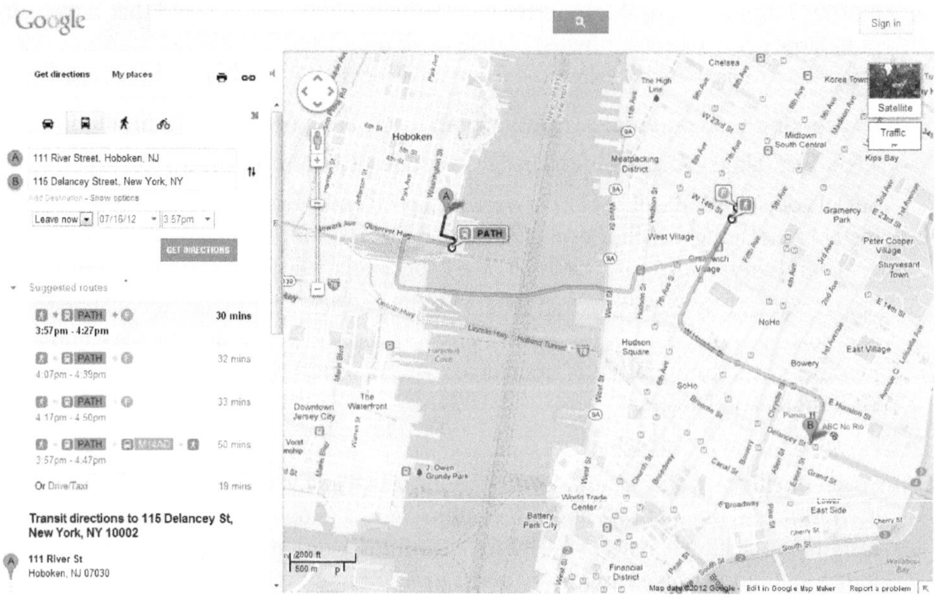

Figure 8.3 GoogleMaps (www. googlemaps.com) is a classic example of a Mashup. In this case, GoogleMaps is pulling in information from public transportation web sites to provide the customer with transit directions.

— BEFORE YOU GO ON . . . —

1. Differentiate among blogs, microblogs, and wikis.
2. What are the differences between public and private social networking sites?

• Everyblock.com is a mashup of Web services that integrates content from newspapers, blogs, and government databases to enable citizens of cities such as Chicago, New York, and Seattle to find out what is happening in their neighborhoods. Available information includes crime information, restaurant inspections, and local photos posted on Flickr.

Apply the Concept 8.1

Background This section differentiates Web 1.0 and Web 2.0 by describing them as (1.0) places to visit versus (2.0) places to interact and share information. Whether you have thought of it in these terms or not, you are familiar with these differences. No doubt you are much more accustomed to Web 2.0 now, and businesses have begun integrating information sharing on their public sites.

Activity Visit http://www.wiley.com/go/rainer/applytheconcept and click on the link for Apply the Concept 8.1. This video will give you a good explanation of Web 2.0 technologies. Take notes of the different things that Web 2.0 makes available and then click on the second link provided. It will take you to a CNN Money Web page that provides a rank order list of the Fortune 500. Look at the Web sites of the top 10 and identify the Web 2.0 technologies that they employ on their site.

Deliverable

Prepare a table similar to the one shown below that identifies the following about the Fortune 10 (or 20):

• The company's name
• The company's rank
• The type of company (e.g., retail, consulting services, communications, etc.)
• A list of the Web 2.0 technologies/applications that are being used by each company

- A brief description of the ways that each of the Web 2.0 technologies/applications is being used by the company

Company Name	Company Rank	Industry	Web 2.0 Technologies Used

Submit your work to your professor with a note about any trends you find in your analysis.

Quiz questions are assignable in WileyPLUS, and available on the Book Companion Site at http://www.wiley.com/college/rainer.

RUBY'S CLUB QUESTIONS

1. Search for RSS feeds and see how most people use them. Are they for advertising? Newsletters? Articles? New products? Promotions?

2. Are there any bars or clubs in your area that use RSS feeds? What seems to be their purpose?

3. Blogs allow for posts and comments. Although it creates a space for interaction, comments and praise, it also allows for negative comments. Is a blog something Ruby's could benefit from? Can you find other bars/clubs that use blogs? How do they seem to be incorporated into their strategy?

8.2 Fundamentals of Social Computing in Business

Social computing in business, or **social commerce,** refers to the delivery of electronic commerce activities and transactions through social computing. Social commerce also supports social interactions and user contributions, allowing customers to participate actively in the marketing and selling of products and services in online marketplaces and communities. With social commerce, individuals can collaborate online, get advice from trusted individuals, find goods and services, and then purchase them. Here are a few examples of social commerce:

- Disney allows people to book tickets on Facebook without leaving the social network.
- PepsiCo gives a live notification when its customers are close to physical stores (grocery, restaurants, gas stations) that sell Pepsi products. Then PepsiCo sends them coupons and discount information using Foursquare.
- Mountain Dew attracts video game lovers and sport enthusiasts via Dewmocracy contests. The company also uses the most dedicated community members to contribute ideas.

TABLE 8.2 Potential Benefits of Social Commerce

Benefits to Customers

- Better and faster vendor responses to complaints, because customers can air their complaints in public (on Twitter, Facebook, and YouTube) and because of crowdsourcing complaints
- Customers can assist other customers (e.g., in online forums)
- Customers' expectations can be met more fully and quickly
- Customers can easily search, link, chat, and buy while staying on a social network's page

Benefits to Businesses

- Can test new products and ideas quickly and inexpensively
- Learn a lot about their customers
- Identify problems quickly and alleviate customer anger
- Learn about customers' experiences via rapid feedback
- Increase sales when customers discuss products positively on social network site
- Create better marketing campaigns and brand awareness
- Use low-cost user-generated content, for example, in marketing campaigns
- Get free advertising through viral marketing
- Identify influential brand advocates and reward them

- Levi's advertises on Facebook by enabling consumers to populate a "shopping cart" based on what their friends think they would like.
- Wendy's uses Facebook and Twitter to award $50 gift cards to those who have the funniest and quirkiest responses to various challenges.

There are many potential benefits of social commerce. Table 8.2 shows potential benefits to customers and to vendors.

Using social computing does have risks. It is risky to allow a product, brand, or company to appear on social computing Web sites where content is user generated and not edited or filtered. In this process, companies must be willing to accept negative reviews and feedback. In fact, negative reviews and feedback can be some of the most valuable information that a company receives.

Companies using social computing are always concerned with negative posts. For example, when a company creates a Facebook business page, by default the site allows other members of the Web site—potentially including disgruntled customers or unethical competitors—to post notes on the firm's Facebook wall or comment on what the firm has posted.

But, if the company turns off the feature that lets others write on its Wall, people may wonder what the company is afraid of. The company will also be eliminating its opportunity to have great customer conversations take place, perhaps marketing the firm's products and services better than it could do. Further, the company could delete posts, but that only encourages the post author to scream louder about being censored.

Another risk is the 20–80 rule of thumb, which posits that a minority of individuals (20 percent) contribute most of the content (80 percent) to blogs, wikis, social computing Web sites, etc. For example, in an analysis of thousands of submissions over a three-week time frame to news voting site Digg, the *Wall Street Journal* reported that one-third of the stories that made it to Digg's homepage were submitted by 30 contributors (out of 900,000 registered members). Other risks of social computing include the following:

- Information security concerns
- Invasion of privacy
- Violation of intellectual property and copyright
- Employees' reluctance to participate
- Data leakage of personal information or corporate strategic information

- Poor or biased quality of users' generated content
- Cyberbullying/cyberstalking and employee harassment

Consider Rosetta Stone (www.rosettastone.com), which produces software for language translation. To get the most mileage possible out of social computing, Rosetta Stone has a strategy to control its customer interaction on Facebook. The strategy involves both human intervention and software to help monitor the firm's Facebook presence. Specifically, the software helps to monitor Wall posts and respond to them constructively.

Fans of facebook.com/RosettaStone who post questions on its Wall are likely to get a prompt answer because the Facebook page is integrated with customer service software from Parature (www.parature.com). The software scans Wall posts and flags those that require a company response, as opposed to those that represent fans of the company talking among themselves. Rosetta Stone customer service representatives are also able to post responses to the Wall that are logged in the Parature issue tracking database.

Companies are engaged in many types of social commerce activities, which include shopping, advertising, market research, customer relationship management, human resource management, and crowdsourcing. In the next sections of this chapter, you will learn about each social commerce activity.

BEFORE *YOU GO ON . . .*

1. Differentiate between electronic commerce and social commerce.
2. Describe the potential benefits of social commerce to customers and vendors.
3. Why are companies so worried about negative posts on social networking sites? Link your answer to the capabilities of social computing.
4. Describe several risks associated with social computing.

Apply the Concept 8.2

Background This section has described many concerns about social computing. Among these concerns are privacy, security, copyright (and other intellectual property right issues), poor quality content, etc. However, social computing is also too valuable to ignore! It truly is a double-edged sword.

Then again, social computing did not create negative customer opinions; it just gave them a platform to share from (right next to the positive opinions). It is creating a world where things are more transparent. Companies must truly seek the customers' good or they will be "outed" by social computing as greedy.

Activity Visit http://www.wiley.com/go/rainer/applytheconcept and click on the link provided for Apply the Concept 8.2. This will take you to a blog article about a negative video that was published on YouTube about Nestle. It went viral and their legal team asked for the video to be removed. The article goes on to discuss different methods for dealing with this negative publicity on social networks.

Also click on the second link provided for Apply the Concept 8.2. This is a story of a FedEx driver who threw a fragile package over a fence. This video also went viral, but FedEx did not ask for it to be removed.

Consider the two approaches to handling the risks involved in social computing. Which do you think is better?

Deliverable

Write a paragraph summarizing what you have learned from these videos. Write three rules for dealing with negative publicity in your summary. Submit your work to your professor.

Quiz questions are assignable in WileyPLUS, and available on the Book Companion Site at http://www.wiley.com/college/rainer.

1. Would it be reasonable for Ruby's to allow their patrons to easily post comments about bands, drinks, food, etc., on their Web site? What if someone said something negative?

2. Social computing comes with many risks as noted here in the text. What additional risks would be associated with alcohol sales and social media?

3. What if one of Ruby's customers tagged a photo (on Ruby's social media page) of someone else who appeared extremely intoxicated? On the drive home, the intoxicated customer was in an accident but the breath test indicated a blood alcohol level within the legal limit. Should the content on Ruby's social site be available for use in court against the consumer who caused the accident? The business didn't tag the photo or authorize the "tag." Is Ruby's liable?

8.3 Social Computing in Business: Shopping

Social shopping is a method of electronic commerce that takes all of the key aspects of social networks—friends, groups, voting, comments, discussions, reviews, etc.—and focuses them on shopping. Social shopping helps shoppers connect with each other based on tastes, location, age, gender, and so forth.

The nature of shopping is changing, especially for brand-name clothes and related items. For example, popular brands such as Gap, Shopbop, InStyle, and Lisa Klein are joining communities on Stylehive (www.stylehive.com) to help promote the season's latest fashion collections. Shoppers are using sites like ThisNext (www.thisnext.com) to create profiles and blog about their favorite products in social communities. By tagging each item, everything becomes searchable. This process means that your search within these Web sites can yield results targeted to you.

There are several methods to shop socially. You will learn about each of them in the next section.

Ratings, Reviews, and Recommendations

Prior to a purchase, customers typically collect information such as what brand to buy, from which vendor, and at what price. Online customers do this by using shopping aids such as comparison agents and looking at Web sites such as Epinions (www.epinions.com). Today, customers also use social networking to guide them in purchase decisions. They resort to ratings, reviews, and recommendations from friends, fans, followers, and experienced customers.

Ratings, reviews, and recommendations are usually available in social shopping. In addition to seeing what is already posted, shoppers also have an opportunity to contribute their own ratings and reviews and discuss those from others. (See Figure 8.4.) The ratings and reviews come from the following:

- Customer ratings and reviews: either integrated into the vendor's Web page, a social network page, a customer review site, or in customer feeds (e.g., Amazon, iTunes, Buzzillions, Epinions).

- Expert ratings and reviews: views from an independent authority (e.g., see Metacritic).

- Sponsored reviews: paid-for reviews (e.g., SponsoredReviews, PayPerPost).

- Conversational marketing: individuals converse via e-mail, blog, live chat, discussion groups, and tweets. Monitoring these conversations yields rich data for market research and customer service.

For example, Maui Jim (www.mauijim.com), the sunglass company, used favorable word-of-mouth marketing as a key driver of sales for the company. Recently, the company

Cars   Books   Movies   Music   Computers & Software   Electronics   Gifts   Home & Garden   Kids & Family   Office Supply   Sports   Travel   More...

Home > Media > Videos & DVDs > Pinocchio

Pinocchio

★★★★☆ 28 consumer reviews | ✍ Write a Review

Average Rating: Excellent

		Where Can I Buy It?		Compare all Prices
5 stars	▇▇▇ 19			
4 stars	▇ 7	$6.99	Smart Buy	See It ➤
3 stars	▎2			
2 stars		$1.99	Lowest Price	See It ➤
1 star				
📘 🔴+1 📧 Ask friends for feedback		$7.95	Third Lowest Price	See It ➤

No image available

Compare Prices | **Read Reviews (28)** | **View Details**

Highest Rated Review by the Community

"When You Wish Upon a Star..."
★★★★★ Jun 05 '00

Pros: classic with great characters and songs
Cons: one bad word, but it's used in the other sense

Summary: After the astoundingly successful "Snow White and the Seven Dwarfs," the Disney animation crew set to work on Walt Disney's second full-length animated feature. The result was an enduring tale that still inspires people to dare to dream, while reminding ... read more

by bilbopooh
TOP REVIEWER
in Movies

✍ Write a Review   Sort by: Date   Rating

Very, very good, but not without flaws
★★★★☆ Apr 12 '09

by dolphinboy

Pros: Interesting characters, colorful palette, excellent animation
Cons: I have a minor quibble with one message portrayed.

Summary: This review is for Disney's seventieth anniversary re-release of their classic telling of the 1883 story by Carlo Collodi. It was actually released on February 7, 1940, making it only sixty-nine years old. This release comes with a DVD version, ... read more

Figure 8.4 Epinions (www.epinions.com) is a web site that allows customers to rate anything from cars to music. In this screenshot, customers review a popular children's film.

used Bazaarvoice's Ratings & Reviews to allow customers to contribute 5-point ratings and authentic product reviews on the company's entire line of sunglasses and accessories. In effect, Maui Jim wanted to extend customers' word-of-mouth reviews across the Web.

Maui Jim wants its customers to share their candid opinions on the style, fit, and performance of all sunglass models. The reviews are integrated into its Web site search function to ensure that customers searching for a particular product will see that product's rating in the search results. The company has seen a huge positive response to its ratings efforts.

Social recommendation Web sites such as ShopSocially (www.shopsocially.com), Blippy (www.blippy.com), and Swipely (www.swipely.com) encourage conversations about purchases. The product recommendations come from users' friends and acquaintances and arguably are more trustworthy than reviews by strangers.

ThisNext (www.thisnext.com) is a Web site where people recommend their favorite products to others. The site blends two powerful elements of real-world shopping: word-of-mouth recommendations from trusted sources and the ability to browse products in a way that naturally leads to discovery. IT's About Business 8.1 discusses another Web site of this type, Pinterest (www.pinterest.com) in detail.

IT'S ABOUT BUSINESS 8.1

Pinterest

Social networks originated with blogging tools such as Blogger and WordPress, where users had to write an entire blog post to express themselves. Then Twitter and Facebook emerged, and a simple status update was all that was required to share a thought on the Web. These Web sites then discovered even simpler ways to share—for example, retweeting the updates of others and "liking" Web pages on Facebook. Tumblr, now one of the largest blogging platforms, also fits the trend. Not only is the site largely used to share images, but realigning the posts of others is a primary activity on the site.

Social sharing itself now involves less effort and is more visual; "people-centric" recommendations are being augmented by "topic-centric" networks. This means that while Facebook lets you explore the Web through information shared by friends, newer social networks organize content by topics of interest.

Flipboard (http://flipboard.com), 2011's hit news app, is an example of these trends, organizing content by both topics and the "stuff" your friends enjoy. Flipboard turns the news into a more visual experience on your iPad, personalizing your experience by highlighting links shared by your online connections and topics that you find interesting.

Pinterest (www.pinterest.com) is 2012's hottest new app. The Web site is a visual social network that organizes images by topic and lets you reshare with just one click. Pinterest lets users create online scrapbooks to share images of projects or coveted products. The site is a kind of visual bulletin—or inspiration—board. Users, who currently must request an invitation to join Pinterest, create boards with categories like "Books I Love" or "Beautiful Places" or "Products That Save Me Time." Users can then link images from Web sites (using a Pinterest browser bookmark) or upload images from their computers and "pin" the images to the boards. As with Twitter, users can follow other users, and Pinterest images can be repinned and shared.

Pinterest has a devoted base of users—most of them female—who enjoy "pinning" items they find around the Web. Although clothing, home décor, and recipes dominate the site, inspirational quotes and humor are also popular topics for users to add to their pinboards.

According to comScore, unique visitors to Pinterest increased 400 percent from September 2011 to December 2011. In January 2012, Pinterest attracted 11 million visitors, who spent nearly 100 minutes on the site in that month. And in February 2012, analysts noted that Pinterest drove more visitors to third-party Web sites than Google+, YouTube, and LinkedIn combined.

Pinterest's problem, however, is that the site in not sure how it is going to make money. This situation is not unusual for an Internet startup. After watching the growth of Facebook and Twitter—both of which grew quickly at first without a traditional business model—Pinterest cofounder Ben Silbermann is following the same path and plans to worry about money-making details later.

Generating revenue from social networking sites, which are usually free to users, has historically been a challenge. Options for Pinterest include selling targeted advertising and data on users' interests. Unfortunately, neither option is original and both run the risk of alienating Pinterest users.

Retailers are looking to piggyback off the popularity of Pinterest. Bergdorf Goodman, a unit of the Neiman Marcus Group, has begun actively trying to develop a following for its high-end clothing and accessories on Pinterest. Lands' End Canvas added a widget to its product pages, making it easier for users to immediately pin or repost images to their Pinterest profiles.

Etsy.com, an online crafts marketplace with over 50,000 Pinterest followers, is using Pinterest's price display feature. This means that when Pinterest users "pin" for example, an Etsy chair on a board for their followers to see, the image of the chair will automatically include the chair's title and a banner showing the price.

Pinterest has also been helpful to small businesses. Consider The Wedding Chicks (www.weddingchicks.com). The four-year-old online retailer of wedding-party gifts said Pinterest brings its Web site more than double the traffic that Facebook and Twitter do. In addition, Warby-Parker (www.warbyparker.com), an eyewear brand sold online, has seen a 400 percent increase from October 2011 to February 2012 in the number of visitors to its Web site that come directly from Pinterest. Finally in October 2011, UncommonGoods (www.uncommongoods.com), an online gift retailer, began noticing traffic coming to its Web site from Pinterest. In March 2012, traffic from Pinterest to the UncommonGoods Web site has rivaled traffic from Facebook.

Sources: Compiled from K. Bischoff, "Winning the Mommy Market—Our StumbleUpon vs. Pinterest vs. Facebook Experiment," *Forbes*, March 8, 2012; D. Donston-Miller, "Pinterest: Why Your Company Should Take An Interest," *InformationWeek*, March 6, 2012; T. Watson, "Pinterest and the Hype Factor," *Forbes*, February 24, 2012; S. Needleman, "Start-Ups Follow Pinterest's Lead," *The Wall Street Journal*, February 23, 2012; S. Needleman and P. Tam, "The Rite of Web Passage—Huge Traffic, No Revenue," *The Wall Street Journal*, February 16, 2012; P. Cashmore, "Why Pinterest Is 2012's Hottest Website," CNN Tech, February 6, 2012; www.pinterest.com, accessed March 7, 2012.

Questions

1. Describe two other ways in which Pinterest could generate revenue without alienating its users.

2. Are Facebook and Pinterest competitors? Why or why not? Support your answer.

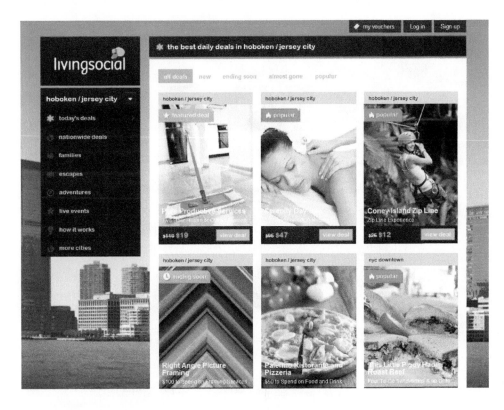

Figure 8.5 LivingSocial (www.livingsocial.com) is a popular example of a group shopping web site.

Group Shopping

Group-shopping Web sites such as Groupon (www.groupon.com) and LivingSocial (www.livingsocial.com, see Figure 8.5) offer major discounts or special deals during a short time frame. Group buying is closely associated with special deals (flash sales).

For example, LivingSocial asks people to sign up for a deal at a restaurant, spa, or an event in a given city. You can click on "today's deal" or on "past deal" (some past deals can still be active). The deals are e-mailed to anyone who signs up with LivingSocial. If you like it, you click on an icon and receive the deal the next day. After you buy the deal, you get a unique link to share with your friends. If you find three or more people willing to buy that specific deal using your link, then your deal is free.

Vinobest is a French wine merchant that uses Facebook for group buying/flash deals. The company offers expert oenologist opinions and sommelier selections for group-buying deals on wine. Vinobest offers active pricing—the more people who buy, the cheaper the wine.

Individuals can also shop together virtually in real time. In this process, shoppers log on to a Web site, contact their friends and family, and then they all shop online together at the same time. Some real-time shopping providers, such as DoTogether (www.dotogether.com) and Wet Seal (www.wetseal.com), have integrated their shopping service right into Facebook. You log in to Facebook, install the firm's app, and invite your friends to join you on your virtual retail shopping experience.

Shopping Communities and Clubs

Shopping clubs host sales for their members that last just a few days and usually feature luxury brands at heavily discounted prices. Club organizers host three to seven sales per day, usually via e-mail messages that entice club members to shop at more than 70 percent off retail—but quickly, before the product runs out.

Luxury brands effectively partner with online shopping clubs, as they offer a means to dispose of special-run, sample, overstock, or liquidation goods, while the relative exclusivity of the clubs avoids diminishing a brand's image. Other examples include Beyond the Rack (www.beyondtherack.com), Gilt Groupe (www.gilt.com), Rue La La (www.ruelala.com), and One King's Lane (www.onekingslane.com).

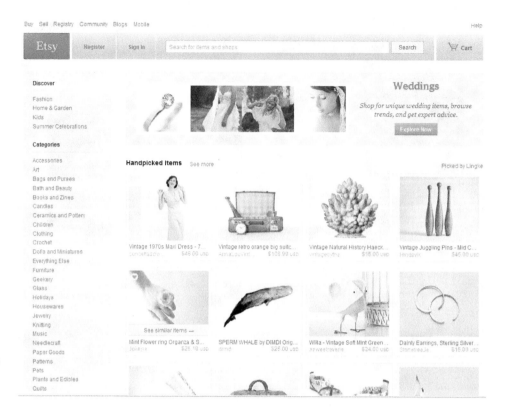

Figure 8.6 Etsy (www.etsy.com) is a social marketplace for all handmade or vintage items.

Kaboodle (www.kaboodle.com) is another example of a shopping community. Kaboodle is a free service that lets users collect information from the Web and store it on a Kaboodle list that can be shared with others. Kaboodle simplifies shopping by making it easier for people to find items they want in a catalog and by allowing users to share recommendations with one another using Kaboodle lists and groups. Kaboodle lists can also be used for planning vacations, sharing research for work and school, sharing your favorite bands with friends, and basically everything else you might want to collect and share information about.

The "Our Add" Kaboodle button simplifies the online shopping experience because once you have it, you simply click on it whenever you see a product anywhere online and you will automatically upload a snapshot of the item, its price and other product information, and a link that sends you to where to buy it to one of your Kaboodle lists. Then, you can find it again any time you want.

Social Marketplaces and Direct Sales

Social marketplaces act as online intermediaries that harness the power of social networks for introducing, buying, and selling products and services. A social marketplace should enable the marketing of members' own creations (see Etsy in Figure 8.6). Other examples include

- Craigslist (www.craigslist.com) provides online classifieds in addition to supporting social activities such as meetings and events
- Fotolia (www.fotolia.com) is a social marketplace for the community of creative people who enjoy sharing, learning, and expressing themselves through images, forums, and blogs; members provide royalty-free stock images that other individuals and professionals can legally buy and share
- Flipsy (www.flipsy.com) can be used by anyone to list, buy, and sell books, music, movies, and games

Peer-to-peer Shopping Models

Peer-to-peer shopping models are the high-tech version of old-fashioned bazaars and bartering systems. Individuals use these models to sell, buy, rent, or barter online. For example, many Web sites have emerged to facilitate online sharing. SnapGoods created a community of people who rent goods to people in need, usually for the short term. SnapGoods helps these people connect over the Internet.

All of the sites encourage **collaborative consumption**—that is, peer-to-peer sharing or renting. This trend is the result of the recession, but it has a green aspect as well. One of collaborative consumption's most surprising benefits, however, turns out to be social. In an era when we may not know our neighbors that well, sharing things—even with strangers we have just met online—allows us to make meaningful connections. Some people share cars and others invite travelers to stay in their homes for free. The following example shows the benefits of collaborative consumption.

BEFORE *YOU GO ON . . .*

1. Why are ratings, reviews, and recommendations so important in social shopping?
2. Why do companies selling on shopping clubs have to pay attention to protecting their brands?
3. How is peer-to-peer shopping related to sustainability (i.e., the green movement)?

EXAMPLE Collaborative Consumption

An entirely new generation of businesses is emerging, created by the intersection of the economic crisis, environmental concerns, and the maturation of the social computing. These firms facilitate the sharing of cars, clothing, couches, apartments, tools, meals, and even skills. The basic characteristic of these sharing marketplaces is that they extract value out of the "stuff" we already have.

The premise of collaborative consumption is simple: Access to goods and skills is more important than ownership of them. There are three types of collaborative consumption:

- Product-service systems that facilitate the sharing or renting of a product (e.g., car sharing)
- Redistribution markets, which enable the reownership of a product (e.g., Craigslist)
- Collaborative lifestyles in which assets and skills can be shared (e.g., coworking spaces)

Consider our second most expensive asset, our cars. Across the United States, Canada, and Western Europe, the average person uses his or her car only 8 percent of the time. In fact, cars are the ultimate expensive, underutilized commodity. In 2000, Zipcar started convincing city dwellers that they could enjoy the perks of access without the expense of actually owning a car. Zipcar, however, is hampered by the cost of expanding and maintaining its fleet, a cost (in mid-2012) of some $90 million per year.

Competitors are emerging with business models that might be more efficient than Zipcar's. Companies like RelayRides (http://relayrides.com), Zimride (www.zimride.com), Spride (www.spride.com), and Getaround (www.getaround.com) do not own any cars—they simply enable the sharing of autos owned by individuals. For example, the average person who allows his or her car to be rented at RelayRides makes $250 per month. Some users are making enough on RelayRides to make their entire car payment. And because RelayRides has a $1 million insurance policy covering both sides during each reservation, it is low risk.

There are environmental benefits to car sharing as well. When people's mobility costs shift from being fixed (ownership) to variable (renting), they make more efficient decisions about when they actually need to drive. Research has shown that the average car sharer drives 40 percent less than the average owner.

German car manufacturer Daimler is taking car sharing seriously. Its Car2Go (www.car2go.com) service is similar to Zipcar's, except that it does not require a reservation or a two-way trip. Car2Go's mobile app allows a person walking down the street in a city to locate a Smart car on that block, access it immediately via a windshield card reader and PIN number, drive it anywhere locally, and leave it there for someone else to use. The fuel-efficient Smart car has a 100-watt solar roof, which powers the car's telematics and its battery.

Daimler is also developing an app called Car2Gether (www.car2gether.com), which matches local drivers with people looking for a ride. Riders submit a request to a driver of any type of car, and both profiles are linked to their Facebook pages and Twitter feeds. After the ride, both driver and rider rate each other.

The challenge that worries everyone in the sharing space is trust. Sharing only really works when there is reputation involved. Most sharing platforms try to combat this issue by building a self-policing community. Almost all platforms require profiles for both parties and feature community rating systems.

Startups like TrustCloud (http://trustcloud.com) would like to become the portable reputation system for the Web. The company has built an algorithm to collect (if you choose to opt in) your online "data exhaust"—the trail you leave as you engage with others on Facebook, LinkedIn, Twitter, commentary-filled sites like TripAdvisor, and others—and calculate your reliability, consistency, and responsiveness. The result is a contextual badge that you carry to any Web site, a trust rating similar to the credit rating you have in the "offline" world.

Of course, Facebook is already collecting a huge amount of your data exhaust on its own site. As a result, Facebook has the potential to become the arbiter of online trust.

Collaborative consumption has the potential to be extremely disruptive to existing organizations. For example, if "the people formerly known as "consumers" began consuming 10 percent less and sharing 10 percent more, the effect on the margins of traditional corporations is going to be disproportionately greater.

Sources: Compiled from D. Sacks, "The Sharing Economy," *Fast Company*, May, 2011; www.car2go.com, http://trustcloud.com, accessed March 30, 2012.

Questions

1. What are some potential disadvantages of car sharing?
2. Describe how collaborative consumption can be disruptive to traditional organizations.

 Apply the Concept 8.3

Background Social shopping is nothing new. This section defines it as taking the key aspects of social networks (groups, reviews, discussions, etc.) and focusing these aspects on shopping. People have done this for years offline just through general conversation.

Today, most consumers do a lot of research before they make a purchase by reading the reviews other customers have purchase. Recently, however, the validity of reviews has been questioned. While you learn about social shopping, you should also be aware of the potential fraud that takes place online.

Activity Go to http://www.wiley.com/go/rainer/applytheconcept and click on the link for Apply the Concept 8.3. This will take you to an article from the *New York Times* that was published on January 26th, 2012, titled "For $2 a Star, an Online Retailer Gets 5-star Product Reviews."

Talk to five of your friends about this and get their feedback. How did they respond to the fact that product ratings may not be legitimate? Ask them the following questions:

- What star rating do you require to consider a product?
- Do you read reviews or just look at stars?
- If you read reviews, do you read only the good, only the bad, or a mixture?
- Do you rely on reviews more than a third-party company such as *Consumer Reports*?

Summarize your conversations in a couple of paragraphs and present it to your professor. Keep these thoughts in mind as you progress through the rest of this chapter.

Quiz questions are assignable in WileyPLUS, and available on the Book Companion Site at http://www.wiley.com/college/rainer.

8.4 Social Computing in Business: Marketing

Marketing may be defined as the process of building profitable customer relationships by creating value for customers and capturing value in return. Advertising and market research are two marketing processes where social computing is particularly useful. In this section, you learn about social computing in advertising and market research.

Advertising

Social advertising represents advertising formats that make use of the social context of the user viewing the ad. Social advertising is the first form of advertising to leverage user dynamics such as peer pressure, friend recommendations and likes, and other forms of social influence.

Advertising is considered by many to be the answer to the challenge of making money off social networking sites and social commerce sites. Advertisers have long noted the large number of visitors on social networks and the amount of time they spend there. As a result, they are willing to pay to place ads and run promotions on social networks. Advertisers now place ads on all major social networking Web sites.

Most ads in social commerce are branded content paid by advertisers. These ads come in two major categories: social ads and social apps. Social advertisements are ads placed in paid-for media space on social media networks.

Social apps are branded online applications that support social interactions and user contributions (e.g., Nike+).

Viral marketing (word of mouth) is especially effective with social networking. For example, Stormhoek Vineyards (www.stormhoek.com) first offered a free bottle of wine to bloggers. About 100 of them posted voluntary comments about the winery on their own blogs within six months. Most had positive comments that were read by their readers and by other bloggers.

Other innovative ways to advertise in social media:

- Use a company Facebook page, including a store that attracts fans and lets them "meet" other customers. Then advertise in your Facebook store.
- Tweet business success stories to your customers.
- Integrate ads into YouTube videos.
- Add a Facebook "Like" button with its sponsored story to your product (e.g., Gatorade brand scored 1.2 million conversations in six months using their "Mission Control" campaign).
- Mercedes-Benz launched a "Tweet Race," which challenged four teams to drive across the country to Dallas, Texas, where the 2011 Super Bowl was played in February 2011. Each team collected Twitter followers with the help of a celebrity coach. Each tweet or retweet earned the team points, as did other activities, such as photographing other Mercedes cars during the road trip. Whichever team had the most points by the end of the trip was declared the winner.
- Facebook has a feature called the "sponsored story." When a member chats with friends and one of them indicates that he or she "checked into" a place or "like it," say at Starbucks, a boxed "sponsored story" will appear with the logo of Starbucks (fee paid to Facebook). Furthermore, the name Starbucks will also appear in the user's news feed (another fee paid to Facebook). The users have the option to delete the boxed advertisement.

For an interesting example of aggressive social advertising, you need look no further than YouTube. IT's About Business 8.2 illustrates how YouTube is increasing its ad revenue in an incredible number of areas.

YouTube Is Redefining the Entertainment Business

When cable television emerged, it provided special-interest channels that the existing, traditional television networks (ABC, CBS, and NBC) did not offer. In addition, new cable channels such as CNN and ESPN were underestimated when they debuted. On cable today, special-interest channels such as kitesurfing channels, snow skiing channels, piano channels, etc., are no longer offered. Business model limitations mean that those channels are not going to appear in traditional media, either television networks or cable networks.

YouTube is exploiting this gap. It is utilizing its vast customer base (some 500 million viewers per month) to help define a new way for content creators to reach an audience. The concept is intriguing, but actually implementing the idea proved to be challenging for YouTube.

When it was first created, YouTube suffered from a reputation problem. Advertisers worried that their brands might end up next to a lowbrow home video. Therefore, YouTube needed to create a business model that was unique to video. The site built a multitude of ad products crafted around the way people actually used their Web site. With the help of these new ad products, many of the activities regularly performed by YouTube users—starting their experience at the home page, searching for a video, visiting a channel, watching a movie trailer, or watching a music video—were translated into appropriate advertising opportunities. Google has predicted that by 2015, 50 percent of display ads on YouTube will include video, while 75 percent will have a social component.

The new ad products have begun to attract major brand advertisers to the Web site. Consider the Philadelphia Cream Cheese product at Kraft Foods. The brand manager of the product learned that YouTube is a haven for how-to videos about cooking. He came up with the "Real Women of Philadelphia" competition and hired Food Network star Paula Deen to be the master of ceremonies. On the launch day of the eight-month campaign, Kraft bought all of the advertising space on YouTube's home page, which cost more than $375,000. In a video embedded in the ad, Deen invited women to invent Philly cream cheese recipes and cast themselves in their

© Alex Gumerov/iStockphoto

own videos as TV professionals. The goal was to drive viewers to Philly's Real Women community, which included Kraft's YouTube channel. The launch video was seen by 51 million people. Ten million of those people watched the entire video to the end, and almost 100,000 clicked through to the Philly cream cheese Web site. In addition to the recipe views, Real Women helped boost Philly's revenue by 5 percent, the first increase in five years.

Promoted videos, which are video ads featured prominently on YouTube's search-results page, share prime space with the types of content that a particular user has searched for in the past. However, research studies have shown that these ads triple brand awareness, even without further action or follow-up on the part of the viewer.

YouTube has also found a method to overhaul the way ads are consumed and sold on its site. This process, called TrueView, gives viewers the option to skip an ad entirely, but charges advertisers a premium if their content is chosen and watched the entire way through.

YouTube started its Partner program in 2007 to encourage audience-attracting producers to create more and better content. Under this program, YouTube sells ads against its videos and gives audience-attracting producers more than half the revenue gained. In mid-2012, YouTube had recruited more than 10,000 partners to the program. Analysts estimate that the top 300 to 400 partners earned their living from content they produced for YouTube.

In December 2011, YouTube released Personalized Channels, which tries to replicate for video the predictive experience that Pandora creates for music.

YouTube has had great success with globally broadcast live concerts that the North America-only sites Hulu and Netflix cannot match. In November 2010, just before the release of Bon Jovi's greatest-hits album and international tour, the band gave an intimate concert in a 2,100-person venue in New York's Times Square and streamed it live via YouTube around the world. The YouTube team globally marketed the show and let Bon Jovi use YouTube's new moderator tool to give fans an opportunity to interact by helping to pick the concert's song list. After this YouTube marketing campaign, Bon Jovi's greatest-hits album debuted in the top five in more than 20 markets around the world.

Google acquired YouTube (www.youtube.com) in 2006 for $1.65 billion, less than 20 months after the Web site was founded. Since that time, YouTube has often been referred to as "Google's folly." Despite this moniker, in mid-2012 Google is the world's largest video platform. YouTube's success is largely from its strategy of cultivating its vibrant community.

Google believes that YouTube is emerging as the first global TV station. Video delivered via the Internet is creating a world with hundreds of thousands of "TV channels," and YouTube is helping people build these next-generation networks. Not only has YouTube created the largest online video community in the world, it is shaping the way video is produced, distributed, and monetized.

YouTube is realizing increasing amounts of revenue. Google does not break out specific numbers for YouTube, but financial analysts who cover the company estimate that YouTube's revenue has increased from somewhere between $100 million and $250 million in 2008 to approximately $1 billion in 2010.

Skeptics of YouTube's business model persist. They believe that YouTube still needs Hollywood content if it is to compete with Hulu and Netflix—services that YouTube dwarfs in size and global scope. Hollywood producers, however, still view YouTube primarily as a great promotion platform rather than a home for their content.

Take a look at YouTube's initiatives to expand programming and ad formats.

YouTube Content

Original Content: YouTube shares ad revenue with top content creators.

Examples: *The Annoying Orange*, Next New Networks, Machinma, Nigahiga, The *Young Turks*

Concerts: Live streaming concerts have drawn between 5 and 10 million live views. YouTube teamed up with Vevo and American Express in 2010 for its Unstaged series.

Examples: Bon Jovi, U2, The National, Alicia Keys, Arcade Fire, John Legend & The Roots

Sports: IPL, a cricket league in India, pulled in 55 million views during its first season on YouTube.

Examples: IPL and Major League Baseball

How To: YouTube has given rise to a generation of teaching stars. Michelle Phan's tutorial on Lady Gaga's "Poker Face" look has received 24 million views and paved the way for Phan's deals with Colgate, Lancome, and others.

Examples: Michelle Phan (makeup), Sal Khan (Khan Academy), ViewDo (guitar)

Movies/TV: YouTube tries to offer longer-form content not available elsewhere. World Wrestling Entertainment (WWE; www.wwe.com) posts full episodes of Friday Night Smackdown to YouTube 24 hours after airing them on TV. WWE's executive vice-president of digital media says that WWE is making six figures per month in ad revenue.

Examples: *Striker*, Sundance Film Festival, BBC Channels 4 and 5

Advertising as Content: To promote its Trivial Pursuit: Bet You Know It edition, Hasbro ads pit users against YouTube stars, generating more than 250 million views.

Examples: Kraft (Paula Deen), Hasbro, *The Last Exorcism*

YouTube's Sources of Revenue

Home Page: The YouTube Homepage Roadblock allows brands to own the homepage for 24 hours with a 100 percent share. The homepage averages 50 million impressions and over 18 million unique daily visitors. Therefore, the home page enables brands to have a big impact on a concentrated audience.

Examples: Verizon, Hasbro, Kraft, Dreamworks, Fox

Promoted Videos: Like sponsored ads on Google, promoted videos pop up around search results.

Advertisers pay only when users click "Play."

Examples: Evian, Panasonic, Stouffer's, Wrigley, Maybelline

Content ID: To prevent hosting illegally posted videos, YouTube learned how to identify them, a process called Content ID. YouTube then alerts copyright owners—including early adopter CBS—and they decide whether to take down the video or sell ads against it.

Examples: CBS, Lionsgate (*Mad Men*), Sony

Click-to-Buy: Call-to-action spots with videos can transform viewers into consumers. For example, Monty

Python videos directed viewers to the troupe's DVDs on Amazon, increasing sales by 23,000 percent.

Examples: Cee Lo Green (iTunes), Monty Python (Amazon)

Branded Channels: YouTube gives brands a lot of latitude. The CEO of the Visionaire Group says that YouTube gives his company the flexibility to engage the user in a way that no other outlet does.

Examples: Lionsgate (*The Expendables*), Samsung, Tipp-Ex

Display: Google predicts that digital billboards will add more video and become more social in the next few years, turning into a $50 billion industry.

Examples: Blizzard Entertainment, HTC, Absolut, Volvo

Sources: Compiled from A. Knapp, "Indie Hip-Hop Star Destorm Power on YouTube and the Future of Music," *Forbes*, March 1, 2012; H. Shaughnessy, "YouTube Creators and the Rise of Social Entertainment," *Forbes*, February 21, 2012; A. Knapp, "Meredith Valiando Is Bringing YouTube to Concert Halls," *Forbes*, February 18, 2012; H. Shaughnessy, "Where Is the Big Time Headed? RockStar, Comic, Actor, and the Story of the Social Brand," *Forbes*, February 1, 2012; J. Perez, "YouTube to Boost Original, Professional Programming," *CIO*, October 29, 2011; D. Jeffrey, "Viacom Tells Court YouTube Deliberately Violated Copyrights," *Bloomberg BusinessWeek*, October 18, 2011; A. Efrati, "YouTube Goes Professional," *The Wall Street Journal*, October 4, 2011; D. Sacks, "Blown Away," *Fast Company*, February 2011; F. Gillette, "On YouTube, Seven-Figure Views, Six-Figure Paychecks," *Bloomberg BusinessWeek*, September 23, 2010; T. Claburn, "YouTube Promises 15 Minutes of Fame," *InformationWeek*, July 29, 2010; E. Williams, "The YouTube Dilemma," *Bloomberg BusinessWeek*, March 18, 2009; www.youtube.com, accessed March 8, 2012.

uestions

1. Describe YouTube's basic model for revenue generation.

2. If you were the CEO of a television network, how would you combat YouTube?

Market Research

Traditionally, marketing professionals used demographics compiled by market research firms as one of their main tools to identify and target potential customers. Obtaining this information was time-consuming and costly, as marketing professionals had to ask potential customers to provide it. Today, however, members of social networks provide this information voluntarily on their pages! (Think about all the information that you provide on your favorite social networking Web sites.) Because of the open nature of social networking, merchants can easily find their customers, see what they do online, and see who their friends are.

This information provides a new opportunity to assess markets in near real time. Word of mouth has always been one of the most powerful marketing methods—more often than not, people use products that their friends like and recommend. Social media sites can provide this type of data on numerous products and services.

Companies are utilizing social computing tools to get feedback from customers. This trend is referred to as *conversational marketing*. These tools enable customers to supply feedback via blogs, wikis, online forums, and social networking sites. Again, customers are providing much of this feedback to companies voluntarily and for free.

Social computing not only generates faster and cheaper results than traditional focus groups, but also fosters closer customer relationships. For example, Dell Computer operates a feedback Web site called IdeaStorm, where it allows customers to suggest and vote on improvements in its offerings (see Figure 8.7).

Retailers know that customers, especially the younger ones, want to be heard, and they also want to know whether others agree with them. Retailers are opening up their Web sites to customers, letting them post product reviews, ratings, and in some cases photos and videos.

The result is that customer reviews are emerging as a prime place for online shoppers to visit. Approximately one-half of consumers consult reviews before making an online purchase, and almost two-thirds of consumers are more likely to purchase from a site if it has ratings and reviews.

For example, Del Monte (www.delmonte.com), through its "I Love My Dog" program, gathers data from pet owners that can help shape its marketing decisions. Its private social

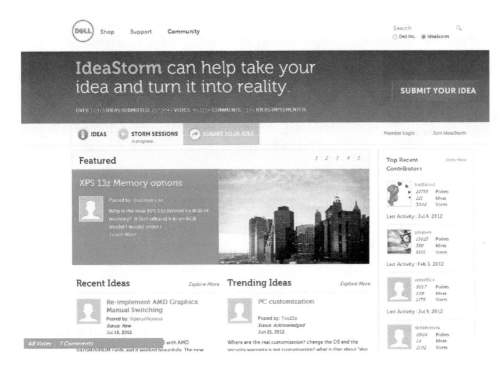

Figure 8.7 Customers share their ideas and feedback with Dell via IdeaStorm (www.ideastorm.com).

network helps Del Monte make decisions about products, test-market campaigns, understand buying preferences, and generate discussions about new items and product changes.

Using social computing for market research is not only a tool for businesses. Customers enjoy the capabilities that social computing offers when they are shopping as well. In IT's About Business 8.3, you see how social computing helps shoppers perform market research to find the car they want on Cars.com.

IT'S ABOUT BUSINESS 8.3

Buying a Vehicle Takes Work!

Cars.com, a business unit of Classified Ventures (www.classifiedventures.com), serves approximately 10 million car shoppers per month. The company knows that comparing features on automobiles can be confusing to buyers. To make a wise buying decision, customers must compare many different types of information, including performance specifications, a variety of high-tech systems, and numerous safety features. As a result, the Web site of Cars.com (www.cars.com) integrates different types of data from different sources and presents it in a way that customers can use to shop for vehicles, compare features, read reviews, and obtain price quotes directly from dealerships.

To help customers understand and use all the information on its Web site, the company is integrating

Web 2.0 technology wherever it adds value and streamlines customer interactions. Cars.com is turning Web 2.0 into a competitive advantage. The company provides sophisticated Web capabilities and mobile tools that make it easier for customers to find, view, and extract the information they need to make a buying decision. Cars.com recognizes that a seamless experience on its Web site equals clicks, which equals revenue. The company earns revenue from online classified ads place by automakers, dealers, and private-party sellers. It also sells banner advertisements and provides lead-generation services.

Cars.com offers comprehensive pricing information, photo galleries, buying guides, side-by-side comparison tools, original editorial content, expert car reviews, and other relevant content from auto manufacturers, user-generated content from customers themselves such as ratings of cars, and others. The company's Web site contains online portals for dealers, employees, and customers.

The company's Web site contains many useful Web 2.0 tools. A few examples include the following:

- A tool focused on helping dealers list used vehicles at an optimal price when they place a classified ad.

- A tool that provides information about inventory levels, buying trends, and other factors.

- A tool offers customers live data about incentives. When a potential buyer visits the Cars.com configuration tool and clicks through various automobiles and options, he or she sees the specific manufacturer and dealer incentives and rebates that currently exist—matched to the specific vehicle and exact configuration. This capability eliminates the problems associated with clicking to a different part of the Web site and manually searching for the information. The company notes that this feature increases the "stickiness" factor of the Web site. (Stickiness refers to the amount of time spent on a Web site by a visitor.)

Cars.com is also using social media such as Facebook and Twitter to further integrate content and offerings. The company wants to increase its visibility, while making information more accessible and useful to a larger audience.

The company also offers iPhone, Android, and BlackBerry mobile apps, and it has implemented a mobile Web site that is optimized for mobile phone browsers. Approximately 25 percent of the firm's total online traffic arrives through mobile devices.

Sources: Compiled from B. Upbin, "Forbes Panel Tracks Footprints of the Elusive Customer," *Forbes*, February 7, 2012; S. Greengard, "Cars.com Drives Performance," *Baseline Magazine*, June 14, 2011; H. Elliot, "Common Car-Buying Mistakes," *Forbes*, May 9, 2011; www.cars.com, accessed February 22, 2012.

Questions

1. Is it possible for the Cars.com Web site to provide too much information to its customers? If so, how could providing too much information hurt the company?

2. What other Web 2.0 functionality could Cars.com include on its Web site to provide additional information for visitors to the company's Web site?

Conducting Market Research Using Social Networks

Customer sentiment expressed on Twitter, Facebook, and other such sites represent an incredibly valuable source of information for companies. Customer activities on social networking sites generate huge amounts of data that must be analyzed, so that management can conduct better marketing campaigns, product design, and service offerings. The monitoring, collection, and analysis of socially generated data, and the resultant strategic decisions are combined in a process known as **social intelligence**.

For example, Wendy's International (www.wendys.com) uses software to sift through over 500,000 customer messages the fast-food chain collects each year. Using Clarabridge (www.clarabridge.com) text analytics software, Wendy's analyzes comments from its online notes, e-mails, receipt-based surveys, and social media. Before, the company used a combination of spreadsheets and keyword searches to review comments in what it describes as a slow and expensive manual approach. The new software enables Wendy's to track customer experiences at the store level within minutes.

Social networks provide excellent sources of valuable information for market research. Here you see illustrative examples of how to use Facebook, Twitter, and LinkedIn for market research.

Using Facebook for Market Research. There are several ways to use Facebook for market research. See the following examples:

- Get feedback from your Facebook fans (and their friends if possible) on advertising campaigns, market research, etc. It is like having a free focus group.

- Test market your messages. Provide two or three options and ask fans which one they prefer and why.

- Use Facebook for survey invitations (i.e., to recruit participants). Essentially, turn Facebook into a giant panel and ask Facebook users to participate in a survey. Facebook offers a self-service model for displaying ads, and ads can be invitations to take a survey. Facebook also allows you to target your audience very specifically based on traditional demographic models (age, gender, etc.).

Using Twitter for Market Research. Your customers, your prospects, and industry thought leaders all use Twitter, making it a rich source of instantly updated information. See the following examples:

- Visit Twitter Search (www.twitter.com/search). Enter a company's Twitter name. Not only can you follow what companies are saying, you can also follow what everyone is saying to them. Monitoring@ replies to your competitors and their employees will help you develop your own Twitter strategy by allowing you to see (a) what they are doing and more importantly (b) what people think about it. You can also see the company's response.

- Take advantage of the tools that enable you to find people in the industries they operate in. Use search.twitter.com to monitor industry-specific keywords. Check out Twellow (www.twellow.com). This site automatically categorizes a Twitter user into one to three industries based on that person's bio and tweets.

- Want to see what topic is on most people's minds today? Look at the chart on TweetStats (www.tweetstats.com). It will show you the most frequently used words so you can be a part of those conversations.

- An increasing number of companies are utilizing Twitter to solicit information from customers and interact with them. Examples include Dell (connecting with customers), JetBlue (learning about customers), Teusner Wines (gathering feedback, sharing information), and Pepsi (fast response time in dealing with complaints).

Using LinkedIn for Market Research. Post a question (e.g., solicit advice) regarding the topic or issue you are interested in. You may get a better result if you go to a specific LinkedIn group.

For example, let's take a look at how Mountain Dew uses social computing for market research. The company has always appealed to consumers who were looking for high-caffeine beverages. However, the brand wanted to unite all of its customers into one community with its Dewmocracy contests, which let consumers pick the newest flavor.

Several brands have used social networks to help them choose new flavors, but Mountain Dew is expanding its scale from the most dedicated fans to the public at large. The first step of its market research involved sending seven flavors of soda to 50 Dew fanatics, who were also given cameras and told to debate and show their like or dislike for the brand on a video. The cameras were a great idea because it made the social media effort more personable. Rather than just looking at static images or tweets, Dew fans could see like-minded Dew fanatics in action. After narrowing the seven flavors to three, based in part on the videos, Mountain Dew turned to its Dew Labs Community, a 4,000-person group of passionate soda fans. Those fans then created nearly every element of the three sodas, including color, name, packaging, and marketing campaigns. After that process was complete, the three flavors were made available in stores for a limited time, with the general public electing a winner via online voting. The Dewmocracy campaign used Facebook, Twitter, and You-Tube to unite consumers through a common interest.

BEFORE YOU GO ON . . .

1. What is social advertising?
2. Describe several ways to advertise in social media.
3. Why are the social aspects of market research so valuable to market researchers?
4. Define *social intelligence*.
5. Describe several ways to conduct market research on social networking sites.

Apply the Concept 8.4

Background This section focused on the ways that some businesses use social advertising to create a competitive advantage. They allow customers to share product information and make purchases right in the social network. You have probably received some note on a social network that asked you to share with five of your friends. This type of social commerce is here to stay, but just how many people can you really reach with this type of virtual word-of-mouth marketing?

For example, imagine you want to know how many users could be reached at the third level of friends away from the initial group when the initial group consists of 100 people and each person shares the message with 3 people. For this example, assume that each person shares with another unique individual. Level 1 is the initial 300 people. Level 2 is the initial 300 multiplied by 300. This equals 900 customers. This group of 900 customers shares with 3 more people. So at the third level, there is the potential to reach 2700 customers. The table below demonstrates this concept.

Level	100 Share with 2	100 Share with 3	200 Share with 4	200 Share with 5
1	200	300	800	
2	400	900		
3	800	2,700		

Activity Build and complete your own table just to see how quickly social commerce can help sell products. Label your columns as shown in the table above. Finally, use the table you build to determine how many initial contacts a company has to make to reach over 12,000 people at the third level assuming that each user shares with 4 people.

Deliverable

Complete your table down to the fifth level for all four columns and submit this to your instructor. Include a paragraph answering the question above about determining how many initial contacts are needed to reach the 12,000 mark at the third level.

Submit your table and paragraph to your instructor.

Quiz questions are assignable in WileyPLUS, and available on the Book Companion Site at http://www.wiley.com/college/rainer.

RUBY'S CLUB QUESTIONS

1. Social advertising would be easy to get going. Are there any clubs in your area that engage in social advertising? How do they do it? Does it work?

2. If Ruben and Lisa post a survey after a big night to learn more about who was there and what they thought about it, how could they ensure that they only received comments from people who were actually there?

3. Should survey results be posted for the public to see or kept private?

8.5 Social Computing in Business: Customer Relationship Management

The customer service profession has undergone a significant transformation, both in the way that customer service professionals do business and the way that customers adapt to interacting with companies in a newly connected environment. Social computing has vastly altered both the expectations of customers and the capabilities of corporations in the area of customer relationship management.

How Social Computing Improves Customer Service

Customers are now incredibly empowered. Companies are closely monitoring social computing because they are mindful of the negative comments posted by social network members, but also because they see an opportunity to involve customers proactively to reduce problems by improved customer service.

Empowered customers know how to use the wisdom and power of crowds and communities to their benefit. These customers choose how they interact with companies and brands, and they have elevated expectations. These customers are participatory and have active involvement with businesses, not just as purchasers, but also as advocates and influencers as well. As a result, businesses must respond to customers quickly and accurately. Fortunately, social computing provides many opportunities for businesses to do just that, thereby giving businesses the opportunity to turn disgruntled customers into champions for the firm. Consider the following examples:

- Qantas airlines (www.qantas.com.au) had a policy that required large musical instruments to be stored in the cargo hold, sometimes causing damage to the instruments. After suffering $1,200 in damage to his saxophone, Jamie Oehlers of Australia organized a Facebook campaign to persuade the airline to reverse the policy. When one person complains, he or she typically gets a nice letter, but company policy will most likely not change. But when more than 8,700 people joined forces on Facebook (including members of national symphony orchestras), posting stories and pictures of instruments that had been damaged in the cargo hold and saying they would boycott the airline, Qantas had to listen carefully. The airline announced that they had listened to their customers and changed the policy. The new policy allows small musical instruments as carry-on baggage.

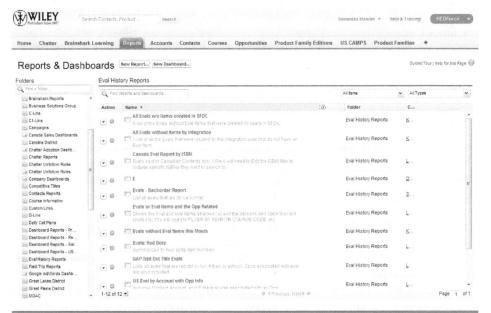

Figure 8.8 Salesforce.com is a powerful customer relationship management tool that allows companies to track business opportunities. This is an example of different customer reports that can be pulled from Salesforce in the version used by John Wiley & Sons.

- Safeway, a large grocery chain, has a customer club. Members can receive in-store discounts. Members also receive e-mails with coupons and a description of what is on sale as well as an online newsletter with health news and recipes, shopping tips, etc. To extend this service, Safeway invites you to become a Facebook fan and follow the company on Twitter. This way you will be the first to know about exclusive promotions and savings. Plus, you are able to connect and share with other Safeway shoppers.

  You can also visit the company's blog, "Today at Safeway!" Team members post items from the floral department, the bakery department, and other departments throughout the stores. You can hear from Safeway's experts on nutrition, environmental sustainability, and more. The Safeway blog is a free way to promote active discussion among the Safeway community. All comments are moderated by Safeway and will not be posted if they contain offensive language, private or personal information, hateful or violent content, personal attacks, self-serving or promotion of goods, Web sites, or services. Members are asked to post only original content.

- Best Buy is a large appliances retailer that wanted to be a source for customers beyond their experience in stores. The company developed a unique way to connect with customers through their Twitter's @twelpforce account to provide real-time customer service.

  Best Buy empowered the "blue shirt" members of its Geek Squad tech support service and corporate employees to staff its @twelpforce, and any Best Buy employee working on company time can provide answers by using an @ reply to the customer. About 4,000 employees signed up to answer questions. By tagging their tweets with Twelpforce, the answer is sent through the @twelpforce account, allowing anyone to search the feed for topics they are researching. Between December 15, 2010, and February 1, 2011, @twelpforce provided over 38,000 answers to customer inquiries.

- In December 2010, Groupon featured a discount to a restaurant delivery service in Tokyo for the New Year. The promotion was wildly successful as more than 500 "Groupons" were sold. Unfortunately, the restaurant was not prepared for the success and was unable to accommodate all the orders. Deliveries were late and many of them were in terrible condition.

Andrew Mason, the CEO of Groupon, took on the responsibility. He acknowledged that he contracted to an organization that was not prepared to deal with the volume of the Groupon promotion. Groupon refunded money back to the customers who bought the coupons and gave away vouchers for future business. Groupon also created a video that featured a public apology about the incident. It was sincere and informative, explaining exactly what happened and holding nothing back.

BEFORE *YOU GO ON . . .*

1. Describe how social computing has changed customer service.

2. How do empowered customers change the power relationships in an organization?
   Hint: Refer to this chapter's Introduction.

 Apply the Concept 8.5

Background Social Customer Relationship Management is about using social networks to maintain loyal relationships. One company that is very good at doing that is ZAGG (Zealous About Great Gadgets). ZAGG makes and sells accessories for mobile devices such as smartphones and tablets. To help sell its products, the company has developed one of the best social customer relationship management plans around.

When ZAGG develops a new product, the company not only posts notes about this product on its social networking page, but also involves customers. For example, when ZAGG was releasing its ZAGGFolio for the iPad, the company allowed fans to vote on the colors of the new product.

ZAGG is also good at monitoring the social network to watch for product issues. It is not uncommon for someone to complain and then receive feedback from a ZAGG employee regarding this issue. Not only does the company maintain that customer, but it also develops a sense of trust with all its customers who feel they would be given the same treatment.

Activity Go to http://www.wiley.com/go/rainer/applytheconcept and click on the link to ZAGG's Web site. Near the top of the page, you see a link to their Facebook page. Visit this and review their timeline. Look for customer complaints and see how the company deals with them. Do you find a customer representative present on the social networking site? Are there any competitions? Polls? Give-aways? Can you reverse engineer the company's social customer relationship management methodology?

Now imagine that you are a marketing manager and have been asked to help develop a strategy for using Facebook to help manage customer relationships. Is there anything you can use from the text and what you have seen here?

Deliverable

Create a list of the top 10 ideas you have for ways to engage in social customer relationship management. If they are not your own ideas, reference the source. However, it will be better for you to synthesize both the chapter material and what you have seen at ZAGG's Web site and to develop your own ideas.

Quiz questions are assignable in WileyPLUS, and available on the Book Companion Site at http://www.wiley.com/college/rainer.

RUBY'S CLUB | **QUESTIONS**

1. Ruben and Lisa feel a deep sense of responsibility in taking care of their customers even if their customers do not take care of themselves. A dead customer is not profitable! How might they employ tools in social networks to help their customers make good decisions regarding alcohol consumption, driving, etc.?

2. How might customers feel about a club recommending that they not drive home based on comments their friends made on a social network?

8.6 Social Computing in Business: Human Resource Management

Human resources (HR) departments in many organizations use social computing applications mainly in the areas of recruiting and training. For example, Deloite Touche Tohmatsu set up a social network to assist its HR managers in downsizing and regrouping teams.

Recruiting

Both recruiters and job seekers are moving to online social networks as new recruiting platforms. Enterprise recruiters are scanning online social networks, blogs, and other social resources to identify and find information about potential employees. If job seekers are online and active, there is a good chance that they will be seen by recruiters. In addition, on social networks there are many passive job seekers—people who are employed but would take a better job if it appeared. So, it is important that both active and passive job seekers maintain profiles online that truly reflect them. IT's About Business 8.4 takes a look at the difficulties of the online recruiting process and provides some tips when you are looking for a job yourself.

So You Want to Find a Job

The Problem

Let's say you want to find a job. Like the majority of job hunters, you will probably conduct your search almost exclusively online. Together, the most popular employment Web sites, such as Monster (www.monster.com) and CareerBuilder (www.careerbuilder.com), now list some 5.2 million openings in the United States and 1 million in the United Kingdom. Approximately 88 percent of entry-level positions in the United States are now listed only online.

Using a job site has clear advantages for you: It is the cheapest, fastest, and most efficient way to connect employers and potential employees. Unfortunately, the clear advantages of these sites have led to a runaway success that the sites are sometimes unequipped to handle. Luckily for you, there are new competitors poised to fix those problems.

The key issue for the companies that own the job sites is that the sites are neither as cheap nor as efficient as they once were. Job hunters such as yourself send these companies too many resumes for them to process effectively. Combined with the economic downturn, this inundation of resumes may lead you to feel that your applications are ending up in a "black hole." For example, Starbucks attracted 7.6 million job applicants in 2011 for 65,000 corporate and retail job openings, and Procter & Gamble received nearly 1 million applications in 2011 for 2,000 available positions.

To add to your difficulty in finding a job, many employers have downsized their recruiting staffs in recent years, so they cannot keep up with the flood of applications produced by the job sites' sorting applications. Even if they try to replace human recruiters with software to sift applications, that has serious down sides as well. If their sorting algorithm is too rigid, it can yield irrelevant results that waste time and money. Not only that, but less-qualified candidates can game the system by loading their resumes with the correct keywords. Finally, sorting applications removes any human interaction (e.g., actual human job interviews) that can signal a good fit between candidate and position.

A Variety of Solutions

 In response to these problems, a number of new job-search startups are moving beyond traditional job sites. These companies

© Alex Slobodkin/iStockphoto

are trying to create better-targeted matching systems that reduce the possibility of gaming the system and that leverage social networking trends.

Beyond Credentials (www.beyondcredentials.com) is using specialized algorithms to shrink the applicant pool to a more manageable, higher-quality size, looking for young professionals with good grades from good schools. The firm also works only with employers offering a minimum $30,000 starting salary, room for advancement, and working environments that Beyond Credentials staffers say that they would want for themselves. Invited applicants have a personal pitch page that can even include video.

Beyond Credentials eases the problem of high volume of resumes (detrimental to both yourself and recruiters) and improves the quality and appropriateness of candidates. Northwestern Mutual and other firms are willing to pay to use the site. Beyond Credentials charges $5,000 annually for one recruiter to use the site and $1,000 more per additional recruiter. The company added 3,500 employers during the last six months of 2011.

Older, experienced workers, who are more choosy, want job sites to work better. Therefore, many companies are working on job sites that aim for greater responsiveness, even if the feedback is computer generated. Recruitment-technology consultants Taleo (www.taleo.com) and Kenexa (www.kenexa.com) offer software platforms that can track the entire hiring process and notify applicants at "touchpoints": when an application is received, for example, or passed on to a manager.

In perhaps the most dramatic shift in the online employment business, job searchers are turning away from traditional sites and turning toward social networks such as LinkedIn and Facebook, where many feel more comfortable and in control. Applicants such as yourself have helped LinkedIn raise its market share in job search from 4.7 percent in 2010 to a projected 12.2 percent by 2013. That shift is why, in 2011, Simply Hired (www.simplyhired.com) integrated social networking into its search process to allow job seekers to integrate their networks with Simply Hired's job listings, making contacts and referrals to target companies easier. Jobvite (www.jobvite.com) helps client companies by integrating social networking with the personal referrals that employers prefer. Clients' employees are allowed to send their online "friends" a "jobvite" to apply for an opening.

Fortune 500 companies are also using social networking in their hiring. Forty-two percent of them now have a Facebook or LinkedIn page. Further, Jobvite's annual survey found that the percentage of recruiters who plan to hire through social media increased to 89 percent in 2011.

So, how are Monster and CareerBuilder responding? They are trying to imitate and surpass their competitors. Both claim that they are not just job sites anymore but instead offer an array of products, some with social-networking features. In June 2011, Monster introduced an application to let Facebook users create separate professional networks, which eventually can be used by client employers—imitating and competing with BranchOut (www.branchout.com). Both Monster and CareerBuilder have moved quickly to transfer their apps to mobile, which is particularly important in Asia, where job hunting is done on mobile phones rather than desktop computers.

The job search industry is extremely competitive, with the lines between company offerings blurring. For example, in September 2011 Taleo announced a linkage with LinkedIn, allowing LinkedIn users to fill out online applications with their LinkedIn data and giving recruiters access to LinkedIn profiles, all with a single click of a mouse. In another example, CareerBuilder is offering new software and products, including one that looks much like Jobvite.

The Results

The bottom line for all job sites is that they do not want to produce 2,000 candidates, but rather 20 great candidates. However, there is enormous overlap in what different sites offer, with each borrowing from the others. In mid-2012, innovative technologies had increased job sites' revenues. Questions remain as to whether or not the job sites are making the process more effective for job seekers. However, career coaches offer valuable tips to help you find a job.

The most important secret to making online job search sites work for you: Use them sparingly. When looking for a job, it is too easy to spend all day on your keyboard, combing through listings, trying endless search filters, and sending your résumé into black holes. Job coaches say to spend your time this way: 80 percent of your day networking and directly contacting the people in charge of jobs you want. Ten percent of your time should go to headhunters. Spend only the remaining 10 percent of your time online.

Here is how to make your time online count. To start with, you should be on LinkedIn. LinkedIn is an incredibly powerful job search tool.

Next, access the Google-like job aggregators, Indeed (www.indeed.com) and SimplyHired (www.simplyhired.com). Both list millions of jobs. Both sites also make it easy to narrow your search using filters. These filters include title, company name, location, and many others. Indeed allows you to search within a specific salary range. SimplyHired lets you sort for friendly, socially responsible, and even dog-friendly workplaces.

Spend a little time playing with search commands. Both sites have advanced search options. Try plugging in the name of a company you might want to work for or an advanced degree that qualifies you for specialized work. For example, you could enter "CFA" if you are a certified financial analyst or "LEED" if you are a building engineer with expertise in environmental efficiency.

SimplyHired has a useful tool called "Who do I know." If you are on LinkedIn, this tool will instantly display your LinkedIn contacts with connections to various job listings. Who do I know also syncs with Facebook.

One more trick to using the aggregators: Have them deliver listings to your inbox. Set up an e-mail alert that delivers new job postings to you via e-mail each day.

Also look for niche sites that are specific to your field. For technology-related jobs, for instance, www.dice.com has a strong reputation. For nonprofit jobs, try www.idealist.org. For government jobs, the U.S. government's site is an excellent resource: www.usajobs.com.

One more great online resource: Craigslist. It is one site the aggregators do not tap. Craigslist's focus is local listings, and it is especially useful for entry-level jobs and would-be interns.

Beyond locating listings for specific jobs, career coaches say job sites can be a resource for key words and phrases that you can pull from job descriptions and include in your résumé, letters, and e-mails. Use the language from a job description in your cover letter.

Web sites like Vault (www.vault.com), Monster.com, and CareerBuilder.com are useful, but you have only so much time. These sites do offer some helpful career tips. Vault, in particular, offers very useful career guides.

The bottom line: It is critically important to extend most of your efforts *beyond* online search. There is just too much competition online.

Sources: Compiled from T. Team, "LinkedIn Looks to Hitch Ride from Mobile Ads," *Forbes*, February 14, 2012; R. Silverman, "No More Resumes, Say Some Firms," *The Wall Street Journal*, January 24, 2012; L. Weber, "Your Resume vs. Oblivion," *The Wall Street Journal*, January 24, 2012; S. Adams, "Secrets of Making the Most of Job Search Websites," *Forbes*, January 18, 2012; G. Anders, "The Rare Find," *Bloomberg BusinessWeek*, October 17–23, 2011; J. Francis, "Facebook Joins Labor Department in Online Job-Search Project," *Bloomberg BusinessWeek*, October 20, 2011;, F. Russo "The New Online Job Hunt," *Time*, October 3, 2011; S. Adams, "Unemployment: The Good News, the Bad News, and What to Do About It," *Forbes*, April 1, 2011; K. Jones, "Online Job Searches Rise as Economy Slides," *InformationWeek*, January 26, 2009; www.monster.com, www.careerbuilder.com, www.jobvite.com, www.simplyhired.com, www.beyondcredentials.com, accessed March 5, 2012.

Questions

1. What are the advantages of using online job sites when you look for your first job?
2. What are the disadvantages of using online job sites when you look for your first job?

BEFORE *YOU GO ON . . .*

1. Describe the impact of social computing on the recruitment process. (*Note:* There are pros and cons in this process.)
2. Describe the impact of social computing on looking for a job. Again, there are pros and cons in this process.

Training

Several companies use virtual worlds for training purposes. For example, Cisco uses its virtual campus in Second Life for product training and executive briefings. IBM runs management and customer interaction training sessions in Second Life as well.

Apply the Concept 8.6

Background Social human resource management is changing the way we search and apply for jobs and make hiring decisions. Going digital was a natural step but it was an awkward step. When position announcements went from the bulletin board and local newspaper to Monster.com, the result was overwhelming. However, we are too connected today to go back. We live in a connected world and you will no doubt use social networks to find and apply for jobs.

This section has already given a good description of how to get connected to professional sites. Many of you are already on the personal social networks, but are unaware of how to use these to get a job.

Activity Visit http://www.wiley.com/go/rainer/applytheconcept and click on the first link provided for Apply the Concept 8.6. This will take you to LinkedIn, a professional social network. Create a profile there that includes the college you currently attend. Connect to your classmates as they also complete this activity. You never know when you will need to call on one of these relationships.

Next, visit the other links provided (SimplyHired, Monster.com, and Indeed.com) and see which ones will allow you to connect your LinkedIn profile. As you connect these professional sites, think of the differences in a professional social network and a personal social network.

Write a journal entry for today, the day you established yourself online in professional, social HR networks. In your journal entry, give yourself advice on the types of connections you should look for, whether or not you want personal friends connected to your professional network, and how to keep your personal network separate.

Quiz questions are assignable in WileyPLUS, and available on the Book Companion Site at http://www.wiley.com/college/rainer.

RUBY'S CLUB   QUESTIONS

1. Ruben will need some help with all of his new IT. Where should he look to post a job?
2. What tools are available to help sort through applicants? Ruben received over 300 applications and does not have time to go through all of them to find the top 20 people.

8.7 Crowdsourcing

Suppose an organization has a problem it needs to solve. Why not offer the problem to a crowd to determine whether their collective knowledge and wisdom can come up with a solution? This process, called **crowdsourcing**, involves taking a job traditionally performed by an employee or a consultant and outsourcing it to an undefined group of people in the form of an open call. Crowdsourcing harnesses crowds to solve problems, innovate, and get work done. Crowdsourcing embraces freelancers, volunteers, customers, and low-paid amateurs to create content, solve problems, and perform research and development. Crowdsourcing presumes that a large number of enthusiasts can outperform a small group of experienced professionals.

Crowdsourcing provides many potential benefits to organizations. First, problems can be explored at relatively low cost, and often very quickly. Second, many times crowds solve problems for free. Third, the organization can tap a wider range of talent than might be present in its own organization. Fourth, by listening to the crowd, organizations gain first-hand insight on their customers' desires. Finally, crowdsourcing taps into the global world of ideas, helping companies work through a rapid design process. Can crowds really outperform experts employed by a company? (See Figure 8.9.) Let's look at some examples where they have done so.

- Procter & Gamble (P&G) uses InnoCentive (www.innocentive.com), where company researchers post their problems. P&G offers cash rewards to problem solvers.
- At defense contractor HCL Technologies (www.hcltech.com), crowdsourcing provides the foundation for strategic business planning. More than 8,000 employees review internal business plans to create transparency across business units and open up the strategic planning process across the company. The process has provided more honest assessments and better overall business analysis. As a result, HCL has changed its strategic focus from providing application support to providing strategic services to its clients.

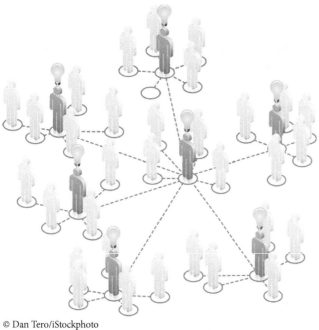

© Dan Tero/iStockphoto

Figure 8.9 Crowdsourcing.

- TrendHunter (www.trendhunter.com) provides the Trend Report, which focuses on insight, predictions, market research, fashion, design, pop culture, retail, and e-commerce. These reports are used by CEOs, entrepreneurs, and the media. To create the 2011 annual Trend Report, TrendHunter crowdsourced the trends and filtered the response. According to the company, in preparing its report, it made use of the collective insights of 40,000 trend hunters, 92,000 crowdsourced articles, and 360,000 page views of data.

- Until a few years ago, book publishers had to rely on stock photography for many of the images used in their books. These photos were taken by professional photographers and were quite expensive. Today, high-quality digital cameras cost less than $1,000 and, with available photo-editing software, amateur photographers can create images that almost match those of the professionals. The amateurs can upload their pictures to image-sharing Web sites such as iStockphoto (www.istockphoto.com), where interested parties can license and download the images for $1 to $5 per image, which is a fraction of the price of a regular stock photo. Because overhead costs are extremely low, iStockphoto can make a profit while still sharing part of the revenue with the pictures' creators.

There are many questions and concerns about crowdsourcing. Here are some of these concerns:

- How accurate is the content created by nonexperts in the crowd? How is accuracy maintained?

- How is crowd-created content being updated? How can companies be sure the content is relevant?

- Should the crowd be limited to only experts? How would a company go about doing that?

- The crowd may submit too many ideas, with most being worthless. If this happens, it can cost too much money to evaluate all of the ideas. For example, during the BP oil spill in 2010, there were over 20,000 suggestions submitted on how to stem the flow of oil. The problem was very technical, so there were many poor suggestions. Despite the fact that BP was under severe time constraints, it had to evaluate all of the ideas.

- Content contributors may violate copyrights, intentionally or unintentionally.

- The quality of decisions depends on the composition of the crowd. The best decisions may come if the crowd is made up of diverse opinions and ideas. But, in many cases, companies do not know the makeup of the crowd in advance.

Despite the many questions and concerns about crowdsourcing, the process does have great value. IT's About Business 8.5 shows an innovative use of crowdsourcing with online gamers.

BEFORE *YOU GO ON . . .*

1. Define crowdsourcing.
2. Describe the potential benefits of crowdsourcing.
3. Describe the concerns with crowdsourcing.

When you work in a team on a class project, are you crowdsourcing? Why or why not?

IT'S ABOUT BUSINESS 8.5

Scientific Discoveries via Crowdsourcing and Online Gamers

Players of the online game, Foldit (fold.it/portal), helped to discover an enzyme involved in the reproduction of AIDS in rhesus monkeys. In just three weeks, the gamers deciphered the structure of a retrovirus protein that has stumped scientists for over a decade. The discovery added to the understanding of the disease and raised hope that games could help in other research.

Scientists had been trying to understand the structure of this enzyme for years, but had previously been unable to find the right protein structure through other techniques, such as computer simulations. Proteins can be folded into many different shapes, and the Foldit game encourages players to try various combinations, guided by the kind of human intuition and reasoning that computers cannot yet match.

Foldit was developed by the Center for Game Science at the University of Washington. In addition to trying to solve problems directly, university researchers are collecting data on people's pattern-recognition and puzzle-solving techniques, which the researchers will try to re-create in computer models. Other folding games under way include one to explore the H2N2 flu virus.

Others have tried applying the game approach to scientific or business problems. InnoCentive (www.innocentive.com) organizes contests that it bills as "challenges," usually with a corporate sponsor that puts up prize money. The hard part is formulating the problem in a specific form with very clear rules. Players have to know what the rules are and what they are going to get if they succeed with the challenge.

InnoCentive runs a number of scientifically oriented challenges. For example, Life Technologies (www.lifetechnologies.com), the manufacturer of a DNA sequencing machine that has been miniaturized to the size of a laser printer, has been working with InnoCentive on a series of seven $1 million challenges for improvements in the device's speed and accuracy.

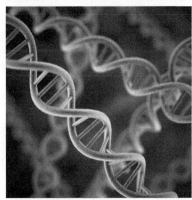
© Andrey Prokhorov/iStockphoto

InnoCentive also hosts more business-oriented challenges. One example is a $5,000 prize for suggesting a "unique way to package and differentiate a new microbrew beer." Other InnoCentive challenges have included helping NASA gather ideas related to astronaut health and performance and soliciting ideas for the response to last year's BP oil spill in the Gulf of Mexico.

Sources: Compiled from D. Mukherjee, "Could Collaboration Cure Cancer?" *Forbes,* December 16, 2011; D. Carr, "Online Gamers Crack AIDS Mystery," *InformationWeek,* October 10, 2011; "U.S. Gamers Crack Puzzle in AIDS Research that Stumped Scientists for Years," *Fox News,* September 19, 2011; F. Khatib et al. "Crystal Structure of a Monomeric Retroviral Protease Solved By Protein Folding Game Players," *Nature Structural and Molecular Biology,* 2011; www.innocentive.com, accessed March 10, 2012.

Questions

1. Why is crowdsourcing so valuable in solving difficult problems?
2. What are the disadvantages of crowdsourcing?

Apply the Concept 8.7

Background Crowdsourcing is sort of like taking your problems, throwing them onto the mosh pit at a concert, and hoping they will stay on top for a perfect body surf. The issue is that sometimes they get dropped and stomped on. While crowdsourcing at times can be very profitable, the text brings up many excellent concerns about this method of problem solving.

These concerns are very much like the issues presented by open source software. Open-Source systems are just that—open. You can modify, customize, change, improve, or do anything to the software you want as long as you share it with the general community for someone else to build on. Closed systems, on the other hand (such as Microsoft), are editable. You must wait on the developer to offer upgrades, patches, or fixes.

Activity Go to http://www.wiley.com/go/rainer/applytheconcept and click on the link provided. It will take you to a Wikipedia article that discusses open versus closed source system development. Read this article as a close comparison to crowdsourcing. Many of the concerns will be the same.

Now imagine that you are the mayor of a large city that is going to make drastic changes to its public transportation. Bus routes will be redrawn, technology will be upgraded, payment methodologies will be changed, policies rewritten, etc. Given the governmental nature of this project, it may seem best to handle it completely "in-house" and not allow the public to play any role in the decision making. But as it is a public transportation system, perhaps the "crowd" could make some good decisions.

Deliverable

Imagine the topics that would need to be addressed for this type of project and build a list of things you feel would be better crowdsourced and the ones you feel would be better kept "in-house." Give a short explanation with each item on your list.

Quiz questions are assignable in WileyPLUS, and available on the Book Companion Site at http://www.wiley.com/college/rainer.

What's in ▮T▮ for ME?

FOR THE ACCOUNTING MAJOR

Audit teams use social networking technologies internally to stay in touch with team members who are working on multiple projects. These technologies serve as a common channel of communications. For example, an audit team manager can create a group, include his or her team members as subscribers, and then push information regarding projects to all members at once. Externally, these technologies are useful in interfacing with clients and other third parties for whom the firm and its staff provide services.

FOR THE FINANCE MAJOR

Many of the popular social networking sites have users who subscribe to finance-oriented subgroups. Among these groups are finance professionals who collaborate and share knowledge as well as nonfinancial professionals who are potential clients.

FOR THE MARKETING MAJOR

Social computing tools and applications enable marketing professionals to become closer to their customers in a variety of ways, including blogs, wikis, ratings, and recommendations. Marketing professionals now receive almost real-time feedback on products.

FOR THE

PRODUCTION/OPERATIONS MANAGEMENT MAJOR

Social computing tools and applications allow production personnel to "enlist" business partners and customers in product development activities.

FOR THE

HUMAN RESOURCES MANAGEMENT MAJOR

Social networks offer tremendous benefits to human resources professionals. HR personnel can perform a great deal of their recruiting activities by accessing such sites as LinkedIn. They can also check out potential new hires by accessing a large number of social networking sites. Internally, HR personnel can utilize private, internal social networks for employee expertise and experience in order to find the best person for a position or project team.

FOR THE MIS MAJOR

The MIS department is responsible for two aspects of social computing usage: (1) monitoring employee usage of social computing applications while at work, both time and content, and (2) developing private, internal social networks for company employees and then monitoring the content of these networks.

SUMMARY

1. **Describe six Web 2.0 tools and two major types of Web 2.0 sites.**

   AJAX is a Web development technique that enables portions of Web pages to reload with fresh data instead of requiring the entire Web page to reload.

   A *tag* is a key word or term that describes a piece of information (for example, a blog, a picture, an article, or a video clip).

   Really Simple Syndication (RSS) allows you to receive the information you want (customized information), when you want it, without having to surf thousands of Web sites.

   A *weblog* (*blog* for short) is a personal Web site, open to the public, in which the site creator expresses his or her feelings or opinions with a series of chronological entries. Companies are using blogs in different ways. Some companies listen to the blogosphere for marketing purposes. Others open themselves up to the public for input into their processes and products.

   A *wiki* is a Web site on which anyone can post material and make changes to already posted material. Wikis

   foster easy collaboration and they harness the collective intelligence of Internet users.

   Social networking Web sites allow users to upload their content to the Web in the form of text (for example, blogs), voice (for example, podcasts), images, and videos (for example, videocasts).

   A *mashup* is a Web site that takes different content from a number of other Web sites and mixes them together to create a new kind of content.

2. **Describe the benefits and risks of social commerce to companies.**

   Social commerce refers to the delivery of electronic commerce activities and transactions through social computing.

   Benefits of social commerce to customers include the following: better and faster vendors' response to complaints; customers can assist other customers; customers' expectations can be met more fully and quickly; customers can easily search, link, chat, and buy while staying in the social network's page.

Benefits of social commerce to vendors include the following: can test new products and ideas quickly and inexpensively; learn much about their customers; identify problems quickly and alleviate anger; learn from customers' experiences with rapid feedback; increase sales when customers discuss products positively on social network site; create better marketing campaigns and brand awareness; use low-cost user-generated content, for example in marketing campaigns; get free advertising through viral marketing; identify influential brand advocates and reward them.

Risks of social computing include information security concerns; invasion of privacy; violation of intellectual property and copyright; employees' reluctance to participate; data leakage of personal information or corporate strategic information; poor or biased quality of users' generated content; cyberbullying/cyberstalking and employee harassment.

3. **Identify the methods used for shopping socially.**

Social shopping is a method of electronic commerce that takes all of the key aspects of social networks—friends, groups, voting, comments, discussions, reviews, etc.—and focuses them on shopping.

Methods for shopping socially include what other shoppers say; group shopping; shopping communities and clubs; social marketplaces and direct sales; and peer-to-peer shopping.

4. **Discuss innovative ways to use social networking sites for advertising and market research.**

Social advertising represents advertising formats that employ the social context of the user viewing the ad.

Innovative ways to advertise in social media include the following: create a company Facebook page; tweet business success stories to your customers; integrate ads into YouTube videos; add a Facebook "Like" button with its sponsored story to your product; use sponsored stories.

Using Facebook for market research: get feedback from your Facebook fans (and their friends if possible) on advertising campaigns, market research, etc.; test market your messages; use Facebook for survey invitations.

Using Twitter for market research: use Twitter Search; use Twellow; look at the chart on TweetStats.

Using LinkedIn for market research: post a question (e.g., solicit advice) regarding the topic or issue you are interested in.

5. **Describe how social computing improves customer service.**

Customers are now incredibly empowered. Companies are closely monitoring social computing because they are mindful of the negative comments posted by social network members, but also because they see an opportunity to involve customers proactively to reduce problems by improved customer service.

Empowered customers know how to use the wisdom and power of crowds and communities to their benefit. These customers choose how they interact with companies and brands, and they have elevated expectations. These customers are participatory and have active involvement with businesses, not just as purchasers, but also as advocates and influencers. As a result, businesses must respond to customers quickly and accurately. Fortunately, social computing provides many opportunities for businesses to do just that, thereby giving businesses the opportunity to turn disgruntled customers into champions for the firm.

6. **Discuss different ways in which human resource managers make use of social computing.**

Recruiting: Both recruiters and job seekers are moving to online social networks as new recruiting platforms. Enterprise recruiters are scanning online social networks, blogs, and other social resources to identify and find information about potential employees. If job seekers are online and active, there is a good chance that they will be seen by recruiters. In addition, on social networks there are many passive job seekers—people who are employed but would take a better job if it appeared. So, it is important that both active and passive job seekers maintain profiles online that truly reflect them.

Training: Several companies use virtual worlds for training purposes. For example, Cisco uses its virtual campus in Second Life for product training and executive briefings. IBM runs management and customer interaction training sessions in Second Life as well.

7. **Discuss the advantages and disadvantages of crowdsourcing to organizations.**

Crowdsourcing is the process of taking a job traditionally performed by an employee or a consultant and outsourcing it to an undefined group of people in the form of an open call.

Crowdsourcing potential benefits to organizations: problems can be explored at relatively low cost and often very quickly; many times crowds solve problems for free; the organization can tap a wider range of talent than it has in its own organization; organizations gain firsthand insight on their customers' desires; crowdsourcing taps into the global world of ideas, helping companies work through a rapid design process.

Concerns with crowdsourcing include the following: the accuracy of the results; the relevance of the results; the quality of the results; should the crowd be limited to only experts and how does a company do that; crowd may submit too many ideas, and it costs too much money to evaluate all of the ideas; content contributors may violate copyrights, intentionally or unintentionally.

>>> CHAPTER GLOSSARY

AJAX A Web development technique that allows portions of Web pages to reload with fresh data rather than requiring the entire Web page to reload.

blog (weblog) A personal Web site, open to the public, in which the site creator expresses his or her feelings or opinions with a series of chronological entries.

blogosphere The term for the millions of blogs on the Web.

collaborative consumption Peer-to-peer sharing or renting.

crowdsourcing The process of taking a job traditionally performed by an employee or consultant and outsourcing it to an undefined group of people in the form of an open call.

mashup Web site that takes different content from a number of other Web sites and mixes them together to create a new kind of content.

microblogging A form of blogging that allows users to write short messages (or capture an image or embedded video) and publish them.

Really Simple Syndication (RSS) A technology that allows users to receive the information they want, when they want it, without having to surf thousands of Web sites.

social advertising Advertising formats that make use of the social context of the user viewing the ad.

social capital The number of connections a person has within and between social networks.

social commerce The delivery of electronic commerce activities and transactions through social computing.

social computing A type of information technology that combines social behavior and information systems to create value.

social graph A map of all relevant links or connections for one member of a social network.

social intelligence The monitoring, collection, and analysis of socially generated data and the resultant strategic decisions.

social marketplaces These act as online intermediaries that harness the power of social networks for introducing, buying, and selling products and services.

social network A social structure composed of individuals, groups, or organizations linked by values, visions, ideas, financial exchange, friendship, kinship, conflict, or trade.

social networking Activities performed using social software tools (e.g., blogging) or social networking features (e.g., media sharing).

social shopping A method of electronic commerce that takes all of the key aspects of social networks—friends, groups, voting, comments, discussions, reviews, etc.—and focuses them on shopping.

tag A keyword or term that describes a piece of information.

tweet Messages and updates posted by users on Twitter.

Twitter A free microblogging service that allows its users to send messages and read other users' messages and updates.

Web 2.0 A loose collection of information technologies and applications, plus the Web sites that use them.

Web 2.0 media Any Web site that provides user-generated media content and promotes tagging, rating, commenting, and other interactions among users and their media contributions.

weblog (see blog)

wiki A Web site on which anyone can post material and make changes to other material.

>>> DISCUSSION QUESTIONS

1. How would you describe Web 2.0 to someone who has not taken a course in information systems?

2. If you were the CEO of a company, would you pay attention to blogs about your company? Why or why not? If yes, would you consider some blogs to be more important or more reliable than are others? If so, which ones? How would you find blogs relating to your company?

3. Do you have a page on a social networking Web site? If yes, why? If no, what is keeping you from creating one? Is there any content that you definitely would *not* post on such a page?

4. How can an organization best employ social computing technologies and applications to benefit its business processes?

5. What factors might cause an individual, an employee, or a company to be cautious in the use of social networks?

6. Why are advertisers so interested in social networks?

7. What sorts of restrictions or guidelines should firms place on the use of social networks by employees? Are social computing sites a threat to security? Can they tarnish a firm's reputation? If so, how? Can they enhance a firm's reputation? If so, how?

8. Why are marketers so interested in social networks?

9. Why are human resource managers so interested in social networks?

1. Enter www.programmableweb.com and study the various services that the Web site offers. Learn how to create mashups and then propose a mashup of your own. Present your mashup to the class.

2. Go to Amazon's Mechanical Turk Web site (www.mturk.com). View the available Human Intelligence Tasks (HITs). Are there any HITs that you would be interested in to make some extra money? Why or why not?

3. Access Pandora (www.pandora.com). Why is Pandora a social networking site?

4. Access ChatRoulette (www.chatroulette.com). What is interesting about this social networking site?

5. Using a search engine, look up the following:
   - *Most popular or most visited blogs.* Pick two and follow some of the posts. Why do you think these blogs are popular?
   - *Best blogs* (try www.bloggerschoiceawards.com). Pick two and consider why they might be the "best blogs."

6. Research how to be a successful blogger. What does it take to be a successful blogger? What time commitment might be needed? How frequently do successful bloggers post?

7. Design a mashup for your university. Include the purpose of the mashup, sources of data, and intended audience.

Background

This chapter has shown that there are many positives associated with social computing as well as many negatives. However, in spite of the negatives, it is something that you will have to deal with as a job applicant, employee, or business manager.

In some cases, you will need to develop your own social tools. To give you some experience with this, this collaboration exercise will have you create a social network for a small business venture.

Activity

You are cofounder of a local bicycle shop and need some publicity. To help with this, you have decided to sponsor an annual bike race in your local area. There is already a runner's club and you hope to draw some athletes to the bike race from that group.

You have a support team from all departments working with you. Your team (classmates) should consist of someone from marketing, logistics, finance, and legal.

Visit http://www.wiley.com/go/rainer/collaboration and click on the link provided. It will take you to the home page for Ning, a company that allows you to create your own social network. Using the trial period, build a social community to promote your bike race. Be sure to mark your calendar and cancel your subscription if you want to before you are charged!

Invite your friends to join the network and give you feedback on what your team has created. Have them ask questions about the plan, legal issues, pricing, organization, etc.

Deliverable

Send an invitation to your professor to join your social community. With the invitation, send an explanation of what your team has accomplished and how the different areas have contributed.

CLOSING **CASE 1** > Facebook Commerce

THE PROBLEM >>> With almost 1 billion members, Facebook is a very desirable Web site on which to advertise, sell, and conduct other social commerce activities. Facebook's size alone is enough to attract the attention of all companies. Clearly, Facebook offers opportunities for companies to reach out to customers and conduct business transactions. However, what is the best way to take advantage of Facebook's size (customers are already there) to do business?

A VARIETY OF >>>
SOLUTIONS Facebook commerce (or f-commerce) refers to commerce executed on, or influenced by, the Facebook platform. Two major types of F-commerce are emerging, commerce-on Facebook and commerce-off Facebook. *Commerce-on Facebook* is a type of electronic commerce

in which the transaction occurs inside Facebook, specifically the purchase of goods and/or services inside Facebook with a credit card or other valid monetary system. *Commerce-off Facebook* (which occurs on other Web sites) is a type of electronic commerce that takes advantage of Facebook's Open Graph, allowing shoppers to sign in to Facebook from any online Web site with any computing device (e.g., laptop, netbook, phone).

Commerce-on Facebook.
Facebook Stores, Facebook Credits, and Complete Selling Through Facebook are three types of commerce-on Facebook.

FACEBOOK STORES. Facebook Stores occur in a variety of formats and are not limited to traditional retailers. There are many examples. The P&G Pampers F-Store, powered by Amazon WebStore, sold 1,000 diapers packs direct to consumers in less than one hour after the store "went live." ASOS became Europe's first fully integrated F-store allowing consumers to complete purchases without ever leaving Facebook. Delta Airlines launched Delta Ticket Counter, allowing consumers to book and pay for flights inside Facebook.

FACEBOOK CREDITS. Facebook Credits are just like tokens at an arcade or amusement park. Credits are a secure way to play games and buy virtual and digital goods on Facebook. You can buy credits using your credit card, PayPal, mobile phone, or other payment methods. Warner Brothers allows consumers to use Facebook credits to stream movies in Facebook for 30 Facebook credits ($3) Complete Selling through Facebook per movie.

COMPLETE SELLING THROUGH FACEBOOK. 1-800-Flowers has pioneered a selling process that never takes the user away from Facebook. Shoppers can select products, options, see delivery dates, and even include a personal message without interrupting their Facebook experience. However, 1-800-Flowers does not take full advantage of the social environment. It does not, for example, provide an easy way to ask a relative what Mom's favorite flowers are or what her zip code is.

Delta Airlines has built a complete ticketing system into its Facebook page, and while the airline allows the user to promote Delta by posting a general message on his or her Wall, it does not do much to help the user share details with friends involved in the trip, something that a Send Button could do nicely.

1-800-Flowers and Delta do their selling via *Facebook apps*. The primary advantage of using an app is screen real estate. iFrame content is restricted to the 520 pixel-wide middle page column, while an app can control the left most 760 pixels, a 46% increase in visible selling space. The disadvantage of apps is that they are more difficult to maintain and they may stress smaller budgets within businesses lacking Facebook development expertise.

Commerce-off Facebook.
There are several examples of Commerce-off Facebook. Merchant integration with Facebook works in four ways: Facebook-enabled Web sites, Facebook in-store retail, Facebook-initiated selling, and Facebook check-in deals.

FACEBOOK-ENABLED WEB SITES: These are traditional Web sites and e-commerce sites that integrate with Facebook to offer customers a Facebook experience while shopping or researching purchases. Brands can bring the Facebook experience to their Web sites, tapping users' connections and interests to support the purchasing process. The simplest examples involve using social plugins, which are short code snippets that ping Facebook's network for information about the user visiting the brand's site. Social plugins include the Like Button, Send Button, Subscribe Button, Recommendations, Login Button, and many others.

The Like Button is the most common plugin and is usually regarded as a content-sharing device. However, when it is used in conjunction with a product page, it can provide peer support by displaying the names and profile images of people who have Liked the product. Most appealing for brands is the fact that it also highlights any of the user's Facebook friends who have Liked the product.

A more sophisticated approach uses Facebook's Open Graph application programmer interface to retrieve the Likes and interests of the user, as well as those of his or her friends. There is a permission screen involved and every friend's privacy settings are individually respected.

Amazon offers a "Tap into Your Friends" option. After the permission screen, the user is taken to an Amazon page showing the upcoming birthdays of Facebook friends and their Amazon Wish List if they have one. Amazon uses a user's friends' profile data, which often includes favorite books and music, to make gift suggestions.

Log in to www.TripAdvisor.com with Facebook Connect and users have a personalized experience that allows them to see their friends' travel recommendations, thereby socializing their travel planning and purchases. The Levi's Friend Store allows shoppers to browse their friends' "likes" by product category.

FACEBOOK IN-STORE RETAIL. In this program, brick-and-mortar retailers integrate with Facebook to offer customers a Facebook experience while shopping in their stores. Macy's Magic Fitting Room is a Facebook-connected fitting room equipped with a camera-enhanced 72-inch mirror and an iPad that allows customers to try on clothes and then share the experience with their Facebook friends.

FACEBOOK-INITIATED SELLING. Businesses can set up a storefront for free on their Facebook pages. They start the shopping process on Facebook and then have the customer jump to their e-commerce pages at some point in the process to complete the purchase process.

For example, Lady Gaga's Facebook store takes users on a rather abrupt transition. Users can browse products on her Facebook page, but any click takes them to the product page at www.bravadousa.com, a licensed merchandise marketer and fulfillment service. The Facebook branding is gone, and the look and feel changes completely. A new window opens that makes any Facebook multitasking (e.g., chat) cumbersome. Apparently, a page with over 30 million Likes can get away with this. Justin Bieber has the exact same arrangement.

Best Buy keeps shoppers in the Facebook environment a bit longer and takes advantage of its social features while they are there. Best Buy's store app is labeled "Shop + Share." Users can search or browse for products. When they find something that interests them, they have two options: Ask Friends or Shop Now. Ask Friends leads to a Wall post asking about the product. Interestingly, Best Buy makes Ask Friends much more noticeable than Shop Now, which takes the user to the product page at www.bestbuy.com for the shopping cart and checkout process.

FACEBOOK "CHECK-IN DEALS." This program allows local retailers to drive traffic to their stores by offering special discounts to consumers who check in to their location with Facebook Places on their mobile phones. In a promotion, The Gap leveraged check-in deals by offering a free pair of blue jeans to the first 10,000 consumers who checked in at Gap stores. Mazda U.K. offered a 20 percent discount off the Mazda X5 for Check-in Deals when Facebook Places launched in the United Kingdom.

THE RESULTS >>>

F-commerce is still in its infancy and barely survived its birth. In 2007, Facebook tried Project Beacon, which collected e-commerce activity on third-party sites and announced a user's purchases on his or her friends' news feed. Facebook quickly withdrew from that privacy nightmare but its poor reputation for freely dispersing user data still deters f-commerce. Many Facebook users have become so accustomed to Facebook's aggressive data-sharing policies that they automatically assume the worst. A JWT study (www.jwt.com) found that some 75 percent of people have concerns about Facebook privacy and security.

Experienced e-commerce managers also see problems with Facebook itself. Facebook does have relatively slow page loads and smaller page size because of Facebook's advertising and navigation. Analysts wonder why customers would bother shopping through Facebook when a faster and better experience is only a browser tab away, at the e-commerce Web site of a vendor. Facebook advertising is also an issue. No matter how you structure your f-commerce store, the user will still be served targeted Facebook ads during the buying process.

Many web marketers question the social nature of shopping itself, and there is considerable opinion that people visit Facebook to catch up with their friends and not to be sold products. After all, the average Facebook user is connected to 130 friends and 80 interest groups and makes his or her preferences known through rich profiles and by posting 90 pieces of content per month. Facebook users spend 700 billion minutes per month in an active, relaxed environment where word of mouth is built into every click. However, the good news for businesses on that front, from the JWT study, is that 48 percent of millennials (aged 20 to 33) would like to see the places where they shop give them the ability to buy directly on Facebook.

In January 2012, P&G announced that the company was scaling back its $10 billion annual ad budget (mostly in traditional media) to take advantage of free impressions offered by Facebook in the form of Likes and status updates. Then in May 2012, General Motors canceled its entire $10 million Facebook ad budget. The two decisions were made for different reasons: GM was not convinced that Facebook ads are effective and P&G was looking for free media advertising efficiencies.

Some industry analysts are pointing out that advertising on Facebook is not as effective for some advertisers as advertising on search engine Web sites. The reason is that people searching for information on purchase decisions are better targets for ads than people checking out messages from friends. Further, these analysts have fundamental doubts about whether advertising on Facebook is a good idea because the process interrupts personal conversations with impersonal branding.

WordStream (www.wordstream.com), a search marketing management company, compared advertising on Google with advertising on Facebook. WordStream's findings suggest that Facebook is a much less effective ad medium than Google. Let's take a look at the findings.

Total Reach

Facebook: 51 percent of all Internet users
Google: 90 percent of all Internet users

First Quarter Revenues, 2012

Facebook: $1.06 billion, down 6.5 percent (compared with first quarter, 2011)
Google: $2.9 billion, up one percent (compared with first quarter, 2011)

Click-Through Rates

Facebook: 0.051 percent
Google: 0.4 percent
Average: 0.1 percent

The click-through rate of an advertisement is the number of clicks on an ad divided by the number of times the ad is shown, expressed as a percentage. The average click through rate for an ad on the Internet in general is 0.1 percent. That is, an ad that is shown 10,000 times on the Internet in general would be clicked on 10 times. If an ad is shown 10,000 times on Facebook, it would be clicked on 5 times. Correspondingly, an ad shown 10,000 times on Google would be clicked on 40 times. Google ads receive 8 times as many clicks as ads on Facebook, a definite competitive advantage.

Regardless of the pros and cons of f-commerce, there is one overwhelming fact. Facebook is where the customers are, and they should be able to buy wherever and whenever they like. Today, over two-thirds of companies use Facebook to drive customers to their e-commerce sites, 44 percent use Facebook apps for product launches and promotions, and 26 percent build e-commerce applications (e.g., a Web store) on Facebook itself.

Sources: H. Elliott, "GM Retools: Goodbye Facebook, Hello Manchester United," *Forbes*, May 31, 2012; J. Edwards, "Here's the Real Reason GM Pulled $10 Million in Ads from Facebook," *Business Insider*, May 29, 2012; J. Edwards, "Facebook's Worst Nightmare: After GM, Here's How the Other Dominoes Could Fall," *Business Insider*, May 15, 2012; J. Edwards, "Data: Google Totally Blows Away Facebook on Ad Performance," *Business Insider*, May 15, 2012; J. Corpus, "F-Commerce for Hollywood: Turning Fans into Customers," *Forbes*, September 19, 2011; J. Ente, "The Beginner's Guide to Facebook Commerce," *Mashable*, July 14, 2011; E. Savitz, "Attention Facebook Shoppers: Get Ready for F-Commerce," *Forbes*, June 27, 2011; T. McMullen, "Attention Facebook Shoppers: Get Ready for F-Commerce," *Forbes*, June 27, 2011; J. Hird, "101 Examples of F-Commerce," *EConsultancy*, May 19, 2011; J. Diner, "F-Commerce, the Arrival of the Facebook Consumer," *ClickZ.com*, May 10, 2011; M. Lazerow, "Facebook Takes People-Centric Ads to the Next Level," *Ad Age Digital*, January 27, 2011; www.facebook.com, accessed February 9, 2012.

Questions

1. What are the advantages for a business conducting commerce on Facebook? The disadvantages?
2. What are the advantages for customers conducting commerce on Facebook? The disadvantages?

CLOSING **CASE 2** > Social Computing at Starbucks

THE PROBLEM >>> Starbucks is the world's largest coffee house with over 16,000 stores in 50 countries. In addition, Starbucks sells coffee in its online store (www.starbucksstore.com).

Starting in 2007, the company's operating income declined sharply, from over $1 billion in 2007, to $504 million in 2008, and $560 million in 2009. These decreases were not only the result of the economic slowdown, but were also the result of increased competition (for example, from Green Mountain Coffee Roasters).

THE SOLUTION >>> To increase its revenue, Starbucks decided to emphasize its social computing strategies. The company focused on the needs, wants, and likes of existing customers and building on those relationships in order to gain new customers.

Starbucks's major social computing activities centered on its private site, My Starbucks Idea, and on Facebook. The company further launched a presence on all of the other major social networks as well. My Starbucks Idea is a forum for consumers to make suggestions, ask questions, and vent their frustrations. This community of about 200,000 registered members can discuss ideas and collaborate on creating new ones. The consumer-generated ideas range from thoughts on rewards cards, eliminating paper cups, ways to foster community within the brick-and-mortar Starbucks locations, and requests to revive drink flavors. The brand keeps the community in the loop with its "Ideas in Action" blog, where staffers write about new developments and announce community contest winners. The blog also provides statistics on ideas generated by category (over 105,000 by January 2012). The company may provide incentives for idea generation. For example, in June 2010, Starbucks offered $20,000 for ideas on the reuse of its cups.

Facebook. Over 19 million people like Starbucks on Facebook. The company offers an excellent online purchasing experience on Facebook and also offers mobile commerce as well.

Fully integrated into Facebook, Starbucks practices social commerce, known as f-commerce. Users can reload their (virtual) Starbucks mobile card with a payment card in order to pay for drinks with their cell phones or load cash onto the Starbucks plastic payment card. Users can also surprise their Facebook friends by reloading their friends' cards.

Starbucks started using social commerce on Facebook in 2007 and since then has actively used Facebook events, discussions, and notes in conjunction with well-coordinated ad campaigns to drive traffic both to its physical and online stores.

Starbucks has been active in the conversational aspects of social marketing through posts on its Wall and information for fans via news feeds—whether it is content, questions, or updates aimed at stimulating discussion about the brand. Also, Starbucks has invested in advertising in engagement ads on Facebook's homepage and elsewhere on Facebook to drive traffic to its page.

LinkedIn. Starbucks has a profile on the site with almost 40,000 followers. It provides business data about the company, shows new hires (managerial positions), and advertises open managerial positions.

Twitter. In January 2011, there were over 1 million followers (Follow@starbucks) on Twitter organized in some 18,000 lists. Each "list" has its own followers and tweets. Whenever the company has some new update or campaign, it ignites a conversation on Twitter. Therefore, the news appears on Twitter before anywhere else.

YouTube and Flickr. Starbucks runs campaigns and has a presence on both sites (www.youtube.com/starbucks and www.flickr.com/starbucks). The sites offer a selection of videos and photos for view.

Starbucks Digital Network. Starbucks Digital Network offers exclusive content to all of its in-store customers. It is designed for all major mobile devices. The network's content features news, entertainment, business, health, and even local neighborhood information channels. Foursquare and LinkedIn have already signed partnership deals with the network, along with the *New York Times*, iTunes, and WSJ.com.

Starbucks turned revenue around by effectively bridging the digital and physical worlds. In 2010, their operating income almost tripled (to $1.437 billion) and so did the stock price. Earnings are projected to double by 2013. In addition, the company's social computing initiatives were rewarded in 2008 by Forrester Research with a Groundswell Award, recognizing it as an excellent example of using social computing to embrace customers.

<<< **THE RESULTS**

Sources: Compiled from R. Stickney, "Starbucks Warns of Facebook Gift Card Scam," *NBC San Diego*, October 18, 2011; M. Walsh, "Starbucks Surpasses 10 Million Fans, Closing in on Lady Gaga," *Media Post*, July 15, 2010; M. Stelzner, "How Starbucks Engages Millions of Facebook Fans," *Social Media Examiner*, May 20, 2010; P. Marsden, "Starbucks F-Commerce + M-Commerce = New Gold Standard," *Social Commerce Today*, May 7, 2010; E. York, "Starbucks Gets Its Business Brewing Again with Social Media," *Advertising Age*, February 22, 2010; www.starbucks.com, www.facebook.com/#!/Starbucks, accessed May 20, 2012.

Questions

1. Compare and contrast Starbucks' marketing strategies across the various social networking sites.
2. Describe possible disadvantages of Starbucks' use of social computing in its marketing efforts. Provide specific examples to support your answer. (*Hint:* See "Starbucks Warns of Facebook Gift Card Scam.")

RUBY'S CLUB | INTERNSHIP ASSIGNMENT

The end-of-section discussion questions have already asked you to consider many facets of Web 2.0 and social media. RSS feeds, Facebook, Twitter, blogs, etc., provide multiple ways for businesses to connect with their customers. How are other bars/clubs using these tools? If you have not searched this to answer the section questions, search now and see what you can find.

Remember that Ruby's strategy is to create a relaxing "community" environment where customers come for nice music and good drinks. Can these social outlets help them

create this? Will there be more privacy issues brought up than this is worth?

Finally, write a letter to Ruben and Lisa explaining the different social outlets and how they may use them in their grand reopening to help promote their club. Do not take for granted that they are familiar with each social network and how it works. Remember: Ruben is a "newbie" when it comes to Facebook and does not even have a Twitter account! Submit this letter to Ruben and Lisa via your professor.

SPREADSHEET ACTIVITY

Objective: When someone uses the phrase "social network," we generally think of MySpace or Facebook. However, many online tools allow people to collaborate and work together on projects. Google Docs is one of these. This activity will introduce the Google Spreadsheet Survey tool.

Chapter Connection: Although Google Spreadsheets are not social networks like Facebook and MySpace, they are definitely examples of Web 2.0. They allow multiple people to work together and collaborate on many projects. The Google Spreadsheet Survey tool

is no exception. It allows for the easy collection and sharing of data.

Activity: Consider the following scenario. You are the marketing officer for "Students for Better Campus Lunches" and have been charged with a campuswide survey to find out how people feel about the current food offerings and their desires for future possibilities. You decide to use a Google Form because the data are automatically saved in a Google Spreadsheet and will be easy for you to analyze. The following questions have been recommended. You will likely need to reword some of these so they will fit a multiple-choice question format. You also may want to have a couple of open-ended questions to allow for comments.

1. How often do you eat on campus?
2. Which meals do you eat?
3. Are you satisfied with the current choices?
4. What cuisines would you like to see more of?
5. What do you think we could do without?
6. Is eating on campus too expensive?
7. Do you have any general recommendations for food on campus?

To complete this exercise, you will need to create a Google account if you do not already have one. Then log in to http://docs.google.com and create a new form. Go to the Google Docs Web site and watch the tutorials on how to create Google Forms. Or simply search Google for "Google Form Videos" and have a look at the tutorials.

Once you have created your form, have some friends complete your survey and have a look at the

data in your spreadsheet. Export this spreadsheet as a Microsoft Excel file and submit it to your professor.

Deliverables: The final product will be a workable survey/form built in Google Docs and the spreadsheet that it creates.

Discussion Questions:

1. Discuss the advantages and disadvantages of using this type of tool. For example, how do you know how many times someone completes the survey? Given this lack of control, in how many situations would this truly be useful?
2. If you were to embed a Google Form into another Web page, do you think you should tell people that your form was created on a Google site? Should you explain the security levels available? How much do you want them to know about how easily they could take and retake the survey?

Quiz questions are assignable in WileyPLUS, and available on the Book Companion Site at http://www.wiley.com/college/rainer.

DATABASE ACTIVITY: FORMS I

Objective

In this activity, you will learn how to use forms that select columns of interest from one or more related tables, to view or to enter new data. So far we have entered all our data directly into our tables and looked at them that way too (or in reports). We opened tables in Datasheet view, selected a row, and keyed in the data or examined it. In this activity, you will learn a better way to enter or view data.

Working with one table at a time is not ideal for two main reasons:

1. Understanding information in a meaningful way often means looking at more than one table. Registering for a new course may involve a registration table, a student table, a course table, and perhaps others.
2. Looking at a table shows all its columns. A real table may have hundreds of columns. Most database uses do not need all, or even most, of them. Grouping those needed for one purpose will not be ideal for a different one.

Using forms solves both of these problems. In this activity, you will see how.

CHAPTER CONNECTION

The unifying characteristic of social network applications is that users, not site owners, provide the content. For this to work, the interfaces they use must hide the underlying complexity of the database. Forms can do this.

PREREQUISITES

None.

Activity

In this activity, which you will find online, you will learn about creating forms with the Form tool and the Form Wizard. You will create complex forms, using up to three tables.

1. Download and open the Ch 08 PhotoNet database from http://www.wiley.com/go/rainer/database. It contains three tables: members, photos, and comments. Each comment is by a member, about a photo posted by a member. (They may be the same—that is, a member may comment on his or her own photo.) Open the relationship map, under the Database Tools ribbon tab, to see how they are related.

2. We will start with a one-table form to provide a user-friendly data entry environment. To create a form based on the Member table, open it and make sure it is in front so Access will know which table to base the form on. Then click the "Create" ribbon tab, find the Forms section, and click "Form." A simple form based on MemberTbl will show up.

3. The form will be in Layout view. In the Chapter 9 activity you will learn to modify a form in this view. Here, just close the form. When prompted, name it NewMemberFrm.

4. Open it again. It will be in Form view, showing data for Member 1. Use the navigation tools at the bottom to move through the rows of MemberTbl. Tool tips on each symbol tell what it does. You can also enter a record number in the field that says "*n* of *m*," where *n* is the number of the current record (table row) and *m* is the number of records in the table.

5. Enter a new record by first clicking the far right icon in the navigation area at the bottom of the form. Enter yourself as a new member, with today's date as your joining date. Fill the other fields with data of your choice.

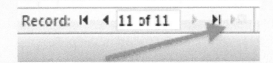

6. Suppose we want to see all of a member's photos. PhotoTbl lists them by MemberID. People do not know members by their IDs. We use names in the real world, handles on most Web sites. These are in MemberTbl. So, a form to show a member's handle and photos must use two tables. To create this form, again click the "Create" ribbon tab. This time, select the Form Wizard. If your window is not wide enough for Access to display its label, it is the icon in that section with the wizard's wand sprinkling magic dust.

7. The Wizard asks you to select tables and columns for this form. First, select MemberTbl from the Tables/Queries pull-down list. When its fields are showing, move MemberHandle to the right panel ("Selected Fields") by selecting it and clicking ">." Then select PhotoTbl from the pull-down list, and move PhotoTitle and PhotoLink into the form. Then click "Next."

8. Because we want to list each member with his or her photos, view it by MemberTbl. (If we view by photo, the form will treat member data as an extension of photo data.) Click "Next."

9. A Datasheet view of the subform means that, within each member form, the member's photos will be listed in an embedded datasheet. Select this option, and click "Next."

10. Title the main form "Photos by Member" and the subform "Photo List." Select "Open the form to view or enter information," and click "Finish" to see the form you created.

11. You will see a form with Member 1's photos. The navigation tools at the bottom of the subform go through them. Those at the bottom of the entire window go through members. As you change members, the subform changes to show each one's photos. To enter a new photo, find the desired member and add it to the subform. Access will enter the correct MemberID in PhotoTbl. Confirm this: Enter a new photo for the first user, then open PhotoTbl. Your new item will be at the end, with that user's MemberID.

12. If a member forgets to add a photo link, the post should display a photo of the founder's dog. To make this happen, do either (a) or (b) in the following list. Method a, using the table, will enter this link whenever a new member is added in any way. Method b, using the form, will enter it only when a new member is added via this form.

(a) Open PhotoTbl in Design view. Select the PhotoLink row. Enter "http://www.wiley.com/go/rainer/database" (*with* the quotation marks) in the Default Value row as shown in the following screen shot. Close the table.

Field Name	Data Type	
PhotoID	AutoNumber	
PhotoMember	Number	Prima
PhotoDatePosted	Date/Time	Wher
PhotoDateTaken	Date/Time	Wher
PhotoLink	Hyperlink	Link t
PhotoTitle	Text	
PhotoSubject	Text	As gi
PhotoCamera	Text	Optic
PhotoExposure	Text	Optic
PhotoInfo	Text	Any i

Field Properties

General | Lookup

Format
Caption
Default Value
Validation Rule

(b) Open the Photos by Member form in either Design or Layout view. (Layout view is shown in the following screen shot, but either one works as well as the other.) In either view, click the "Design" tab. Then click the "Property Sheet" icon at the far right. On that sheet, select its "Data" tab. Enter "http://www.wiley.com/go/rainer/database" (*with the* quotation marks) in the Default Value row. Then return to Form view. The property sheet will vanish, because it is not usable in Form view. This URL will be in the "New" row of the table. Because it is a default, not a fixed value, a user can replace it with a real link.

Usage Hint: An Access object's property sheet describes it in full. It is the "go-to place" for when all other attempts to change something about an object fail, to set precise dimensions that cannot be set as accurately by dragging on the screen, or to change some object characteristics that are not visible anywhere else.

13. The third form, to show members, photos, and comments, is more complex. Because both PhotoTbl and CommentTbl link to MemberTbl (the first for who posted a photo, the second for who commented on it) and to each other (as each comment is about a photo), the Form Wizard cannot figure out their connections. We must do this form in stages. First, we will create a *subform* to show photos and their comments. Then, we will put it into a form with member information. For the subform, use the Form Wizard as before using all three tables, organizing it by PhotoTbl. You will see member data treated as part of the comment data. This time, in what was step 9 (above), choose the "Tabular" format. Save this as PhotoSubform.

14. Again using Form Wizard, create a form from only MemberTbl, with MemberName and MemberHandle. Go to Design view. With the mouse, grab the Form Footer (bottom of the form) by its top edge and drag it down to make as much space as possible for the subform.

15. Select the Design ribbon, and click "Subform" in the Controls section. (It is probably at the bottom of the left column of three small icons, but Access will sometimes rearrange ribbons to fit the window. Mouse around until you get a Subform/Subreport tool tip.) The mouse pointer will become a 1 when you move it to the form design area. Drag it over the space you created when you

expanded the form to create a rectangle where the subform will go.

16. Click the "Property Sheet" icon at the right of the ribbon, or double-click the edge of the rectangle you just drew. (Hitting the edge takes precise positioning.) The first row under the Data tab reads "Source Object." Pull down the menu of possible source objects via the down arrow at the right of that row, and select "PhotoSubform." It will appear in the rectangle.

17. Switch to Form view and see what you created. You probably feel that you can improve its layout. In a real situation, you would. In the Chapter 9 activity, you will learn how. For now, close your database, saving it if prompted.

Deliverables

Your three forms, as described in the problem.

Quiz Questions

1. Consider the following four statements:

    i. You can edit the relationships among database tables.

    ii. You can see the contents of more than one table at a time.

    iii. You can set a default value for a data field.

    iv. You are not distracted by data fields you do not need for what you are doing.

    Which of the preceding statements describe(s) the advantages of using Access forms over using a table directly?

    (a) Only (ii)

    (b) Both (ii) and (iv)

    (c) Both (ii) and (iii)

    (d) All of the listed items are advantages of Access forms over using a table directly.

2. True or False? When table relationships are simple, the Form Wizard can figure out which rows of one table are associated with a row in another table.

3. True or False? The Form button in the Access Create ribbon can create a form that uses data from more than one table.

4. Which of the following *cannot* be done in the Form Wizard?

   (a) Selecting tables on which to base the form being designed

   (b) Selecting a design theme/color scheme for the form being designed

   (c) Selecting totals to be placed in the form being designed

   (d) None of the above (All three can be done in the Form Wizard.)

Discussion Questions:

1. Consider the on-screen grade report you get at the end of each term. It is a form, although your school's course information system probably does not use Access. It is based on tables that contain student information such as your name, course information such as full course titles, and a table with grades that connects your record in the student table to the records of your courses in the course table.

   Suppose you were designing this form in the Form Wizard. Describe, in words, the steps you would go through. Invent table names and column names as necessary.

2. Go to http://www.wiley.com/go/rainer/database (Digital Photography Review). At the top, click "Forums." Select any camera type forum from the menu that drops down. In the list of threads for that forum, select any thread with at least ten messages (in the rightmost column of the thread listing). You will see that replies to other messages are listed, indented, under the message to which they reply. A long thread can have many levels of indentation.

   What additional information must be added to the CommentTbl of this activity's database to make this possible? (Ignore the complexities of actually displaying things this way, whether in an Access form or anywhere else. It takes a lot of programming to make it work. Just discuss the information a program would need in order to do this at all.)

3. A city tax department has a table of real estate properties and a table of property owners. A property belongs to only one owner. An owner may own more than one property. Using paper and pencil (or other tools that your instructor may specify), draw a form it could use to show all of one owner's properties. Make reasonable assumptions about the columns in both tables.

9 | E-Business and E-Commerce

LEARNING OBJECTIVES >>>

1. Describe the six common types of electronic commerce.

2. Describe the various online services of business-to-consumer (B2C) commerce, providing specific examples of each.

3. Describe the three business models for business-to-business electronic commerce.

4. Identify the ethical and legal issues related to electronic commerce, providing examples.

When Matt Lauzon was a senior at Babson College in Wellesley, Massachusetts, he created an interesting business plan. He developed a Web site, Gemvara (www.gemvara.com), which makes it possible for consumers to design custom, high-end jewelry without ever having to visit a jewelry store.

To find varied opinions and advice about his business plan, Lauzon signed 50 brick-and-mortar jewelers to a network that let their clients customize items both in their stores and online. He discovered that customers were very excited about the experience of customizing from home, because they had more control over the design process. Lauzon's business plan concentrated on the concept of electronic commerce for what Lauzon calls "Generation Me."

Gemvara's 1,500 products can be customized into more than 1 billion variations. Each design is made to order by integrating the customer's vision with gemstones, precious metals, and processes.

Lauzon launched Gemvara in February 2011. Since that time, the Web site has experienced double-digit monthly revenue growth, received more than 1 million page views per month, and enjoyed an average order price of approximately $1,000.

© Antagin/iStockphoto

Lauzon attributes much of his company's success to its Zappos-like customer service, which is available 24/7 via phone, e-mail, or live chat. He notes that establishing trust between his company and customers, especially for expensive purchases like fine jewelry, is essential. Approximately 45 percent of Gemvara's customers have never purchased a piece of jewelry online before, and 24/7 customer service goes a long way toward overcoming the trust barrier. **> > >**

RUBY'S CLUB

Ruben and Lisa are ready to implement e-business on their Website. They intend to sell hats, shirts, bracelets, necklaces, shot glasses, tumblers, coffee mugs, special event T-shirts, and other paraphernalia. They do not need a complicated site because they will only sell around 20 items.

They have decided to use PayPal as the payment mechanism. It appears that PayPal provides a nice set of e-commerce tools that they can integrate into their site. Additionally, many people already have a PayPal account. This will allow them to tap into an exiting set of customers without having to develop their own platform. It will also give them instant credibility in the online marketplace.

Given their decision, they want you to learn about the e-commerce market. Use this chapter's material to help them understand how they can use these tools to create an online retail store. By the end, they hope you can give them an idea of the concerns they may face as they move to this system. Also, they want some specific directions on implementing PayPal on their site.

Sources: "America's Most Promising Companies: Gemvara," *Forbes*, November 30, 2011; L. Indvik, "How Gemvara Is Changing the Way Fine Jewelry Is Bought Online," *Mashable*, March 27, 2011; J. Holland, "The Bling King," *Entrepreneur*, March, 2011; www.gemvara.com, accessed March 2, 2012.

Questions

1. Access the Gemvara Web site. What are its strengths? Its weaknesses? Would you design and purchase jewelry on the site? Why or why not?

2. Search out other Web sites who are Gemvara competitors. Discuss each site's strengths and weaknesses. In light of your findings, do you think Gemvara will ultimately be successful long term? Why or why not?

3. How would a traditional brick-and-mortar jewelry store compete against Gemvara and other similar Web sites?

Introduction

One of the most profound changes in the modern world of business is the emergence of electronic commerce, also known as e-commerce (EC). E-commerce is transforming all business functional areas and their fundamental tasks, from advertising to paying bills. Its impact is so widespread that it is affecting almost every organization. This means that, regardless of where you land a job, your organization likely will be practicing electronic commerce.

Electronic commerce influences organizations in many significant ways. First, it increases an organization's reach, defined as the number of potential customers to whom the company can market its products. In fact, e-commerce provides unparalleled opportunities for companies to expand worldwide at a small cost, to increase market share, and to reduce costs. By utilizing electronic commerce, many small businesses can now operate and compete in market spaces once dominated by larger companies.

Another major impact of electronic commerce has been to remove many of the barriers that previously impeded entrepreneurs seeking to start their own businesses. E-commerce offers amazing opportunities for you to open your own business by developing an e-commerce Web site. IT's About Business 9.1 shows you how one person used e-commerce to start an extremely successful business.

'S ABOUT BUSINESS 9.1

Finding a Doctor Right Now

ZocDoc (www.zocdoc.com) is a Web site that allows patients to make doctors' appointments, much in the same way that Open Table (www.opentable.com) allows customers to make dinner reservations. ZocDoc allows patients to read verified reviews written by real patients, find doctors in their vicinity who accept their insurance, and instantly book appointments with local medical professionals online or via the free iPhone or Android app.

ZocDoc is free for patients, but

© Sean Locke/iStockphoto

doctors pay a $250 monthly fee to be in their database. ZocDoc's software catalogs each physician's insurance plans and appointment calendars. It also sends checkup reminders to patients. On their 50th birthdays, ZocDoc members receive an e-mail that reads: "There was recently a 13% drop in new cases [of colon cancer] . . . because more people are getting colonoscopies."

In addition to driving patients to the doctor more frequently, ZocDoc helps patients select the doctor that is right for them. Patients are asked to rate their experience, and most do so via comments and one-to-five star ratings in three categories—overall recommendation, bedside manner, and wait time.

It was difficult to get ZocDoc off the ground. Days before debuting ZocDoc at a technology conference in San Francisco, the Web site's founder had only three names in his database of doctors. In desperation, he staked out the waiting room of a practice with five doctors. The doctors finally agreed to join his list, giving him enough names to fill out a scroll-down menu. He also dug into his savings to pay for salespeople to recruit doctors and for computer programmers to write code to integrate ZocDoc software with the myriad of different back-office systems in doctors' offices.

ZocDoc is now in 15 cities, including New York, San Francisco, and Dallas. In 2011, available appointments posted on ZocDoc.com increased by 120 percent to 6.6 million, while unique visits to the Web site increased by 500 percent to 1 million per month. For example, the New York Eye & Ear Infirmary estimates that the practice's 120 doctors who have signed up with ZocDoc have gained 9,000 new patients in just over 2 years.

Sources: V. Barret, "What the Patient Ordered," *Forbes*, February 27, 2012; S. Lohr, "Lessons from ZocDoc, a Health Tech Start-up That Works," *New York Times*, January 30, 2012; Z. Moukheiber, "Is ZocDoc the Fastest Growing Health Information Technology Company?" *Forbes*, August 8, 2011; C. Meyers, "ZocDoc Sweeps the Nation, Revolutionizing Doctor-Patient Relationships," *TheNextWeb*, June 2, 2011; www.zocdoc.com, accessed February 11, 2012.

uestions

1. Describe ZocDoc's business model.
2. What are the disadvantages of ZocDoc's business model for the company? For the patients?

Electronic commerce is also drastically changing the nature of competition, because of the development of new online companies, new business models, and the diversity of EC-related products and services. Recall your study of competitive strategies in Chapter 2, particularly the impact of the Internet on Porter's five forces. You learned that the Internet can both endanger and enhance a company's position in a given industry.

This chapter's Closing Case 1 shows you that e-commerce has fundamentally altered the nature of competition in the futures markets and stock markets. Despite all the advantages of e-commerce, the Flash Crash demonstrates that the reliance on computers (and thus on e-commerce) can lead to disaster if the process is not properly monitored by humans.

It is important for you to have a working knowledge of electronic commerce because your organization almost certainly will be employing e-commerce applications that affect the firm's strategy and business model. This knowledge will make you more valuable to your organization and will enable you to quickly contribute to e-commerce applications in your functional area. As you read What's In IT For Me? at the end of the chapter, envision yourself performing the activities discussed in your functional area.

Going further, you may decide to become an entrepreneur and start your own business. In this case, it is even more essential for you to understand electronic commerce, because e-commerce, with its broad reach, will probably be critical for your business to survive and thrive.

In this chapter, you will discover the major applications of e-business and will be able to identify the services necessary for its support. You then study the major types of electronic commerce: business-to-consumer (B2C), business-to-business (B2B), consumer-to-consumer (C2C), business-to employee (B2E), and government-to-citizen (G2C). You conclude by examining several legal and ethical issues that have arisen as a result of the rapid growth of e-commerce.

9.1 Overview of E-Business and E-Commerce

Any entrepreneur or company that decides to practice electronic commerce must develop a strategy to do so effectively. The first step is to determine exactly *why* you want to do business over the Internet using a Web site. There are several reasons for employing Web sites:

- To sell goods and services
- To induce people to visit a physical location
- To reduce operational and transaction costs
- To enhance your reputation

A Web site can accomplish any of these goals. Unless a company (or you) has substantial resources, however, it is difficult to accomplish all of them at the same time. The appropriate Web site for achieving each goal will be somewhat different. As you set up your Web site, you must consider how the site will generate and retain traffic, as well as a host of other issues. The point here is that, when you are studying the various aspects of electronic commerce, keep the strategy of the organization or entrepreneur in mind and you will have a good idea as to the type of Web site to use.

This section examines the basics of e-business and e-commerce. First, you define these two concepts and then become familiar with pure and partial electronic commerce. You then take a look at the various types of electronic commerce. Next, you focus on e-commerce mechanisms, which are the ways that businesses and people buy and sell over the Internet. You conclude this section by considering the benefits and limitations of e-commerce.

Definitions and Concepts

Electronic commerce (**EC** or **e-commerce**) describes the process of buying, selling, transferring, or exchanging products, services, or information via computer networks, including the Internet. **Electronic business** (e-business) is a somewhat broader concept. In addition to the buying and selling of goods and services, **e-business** refers to servicing customers, collaborating with business partners, and performing electronic transactions within an organization.

Electronic commerce can take several forms depending on the degree of digitization involved. The *degree of digitization* is the extent to which the commerce has been transformed from physical to digital. This concept can relate to both the product or service being sold and the delivery agent or intermediary. In other words, the product can be either physical or digital, and the delivery agent can be either physical or digital.

In traditional commerce, both dimensions are physical. Purely physical organizations are referred to as **brick-and-mortar organizations.** (You may also see the term *bricks-and-mortar.*) In contrast, in *pure EC* all dimensions are digital. Companies engaged only in EC are considered **virtual** (or **pure-play**) **organizations.** All other combinations that include a mix of digital and physical dimensions are considered *partial* EC (but not pure EC). **Clicks-and-mortar organizations** conduct some e-commerce activities, yet their primary business is carried out in the physical world. A common alternative to the term *clicks-and-mortar* is *clicks-and-bricks.* You will encounter both terms. Therefore, clicks-and-mortar organizations are examples of partial EC. E-commerce is now so well established that people generally expect companies to offer this service in some form.

Purchasing a shirt at Walmart Online or a book from Amazon.com is partial EC because the merchandise, although bought and paid for digitally, is physically delivered by FedEx or UPS. In contrast, buying an e-book from Amazon.com or a software product from Buy.com is pure EC because the product itself as well as its delivery, payment, and transfer are digital. To avoid confusion, we use the term *electronic commerce* to denote both pure and partial EC.

Types of E-Commerce

E-commerce can be conducted between and among various parties. In this section, you will identify the six common types of e-commerce and learn about three of them—C2C, B2E, and e-government—in detail. You then consider B2C and B2B in separate sections because they are very complex.

- **Business-to-consumer electronic commerce (B2C).** In B2C, the sellers are organizations and the buyers are individuals. You learn about B2C electronic commerce in Section 9.2.

- **Business-to-business electronic commerce (B2B).** In B2B transactions, both the sellers and the buyers are business organizations. The vast majority of EC volume is of this type. You will learn more about B2B electronic commerce in Section 9.3. Figure 1.5 also illustrates B2B electronic commerce.

- **Consumer-to-consumer electronic commerce (C2C).** In C2C (also called customer-to-customer), an individual sells products or services to other individuals. The major strategies for conducting C2C on the Internet are auctions and classified ads.

In dozens of countries, C2C selling and buying on auction sites are exploding. Most auctions are conducted by intermediaries such as eBay (www.ebay.com). Consumers can also select general sites such as www.auctionanything.com, a company that sells software and services that help individuals and organizations conduct their own auctions. In addition, many individuals are conducting their own auctions.

The major categories of online classified ads are similar to those found in print ads: vehicles, real estate, employment, pets, tickets, and travel. Classified ads are available through most Internet service providers (AOL, MSN, etc.), at some portals (Yahoo!, etc.), and from Internet directories and online newspapers. Many of these sites contain search engines that help shoppers narrow their searches. Craigslist (www.craigslist.org) is the largest online classified ad provider.

Internet-based classified ads have one big advantage over traditional types of classified ads: They provide access to an international, rather than a local, audience. This wider audience greatly increases both the supply of goods and services and the number of potential buyers. It is important to note that the value of expanded geographic reach depends greatly on what is being bought or sold. For example, you might buy software from a company located 1,000 miles away from you, but you would not buy firewood from someone at such a distance.

- **Business-to-employee (B2E).** In B2E, an organization uses EC internally to provide information and services to its employees. For example, companies allow employees to manage their benefits and to take training classes electronically. In addition, employees can buy discounted insurance, travel packages, and tickets to events on the corporate intranet. They also can order supplies and materials electronically. Finally, many companies have electronic corporate stores that sell the company's products to its employees, usually at a discount.

- **E-government.** E-government is the use of Internet technology in general and e-commerce in particular to deliver information and public services to citizens (called government-to-citizen or G2C EC) and to business partners and suppliers (called government-to-business or G2B EC). G2B EC is much like B2B EC, usually with an overlay of government procurement regulations. That is, G2B EC and B2B EC are similar conceptually. However, the functions of G2C EC are conceptually different from anything that exists in the private sector (e.g., B2C EC).

- E-government is also an efficient way of conducting business transactions with citizens and businesses and within the governments themselves. E-government makes government more efficient and effective, especially in the delivery of public services. An example of G2C electronic commerce is electronic benefits transfer, in which governments transfer benefits, such as Social Security and pension payments, directly to recipients' bank accounts.

- **Mobile commerce (m-commerce).** The term *m-commerce* refers to e-commerce that is conducted entirely in a wireless environment. An example is using cell phones to shop over the Internet. You will learn about m-commerce in Chapter 10.

Each type of EC is executed in one or more business models. A **business model** is the method by which a company generates revenue to sustain itself. Table 9.1 summarizes the major EC business models.

TABLE 9.1 E-Commerce Business Models

Online direct marketing	Manufacturers or retailers sell directly to customers. Very efficient for digital products and services. Can allow for product or service customization. (www.dell.com)
Electronic tendering system	Businesses request quotes from suppliers. Uses B2B with a reverse auction mechanism.
Name-your-own-price	Customers decide how much they are willing to pay. An intermediary tries to match a provider. (www.priceline.com)
Find-the-best-price	Customers specify a need; an intermediary compares providers and shows the lowest price. Customers must accept the offer in a short time or may lose the deal. (www.hotwire.com)
Affiliate marketing	Vendors ask partners to place logos (or banners) on partner's site. If customers click on logo, go to vendor's site, and buy, then vendor pays commissions to partners.
Viral marketing	Receivers send information about your product to their friends.
Group purchasing (e-coops)	Small buyers aggregate demand to get a large volume; then the group conducts tendering or negotiates a low price.
Online auctions	Companies run auctions of various types on the Internet. Very popular in C2C, but gaining ground in other types of EC. (www.ebay.com)
Product customization	Customers use the Internet to self-configure products or services. Sellers then price them and fulfill them quickly (*build-to-order*). (www.jaguar.com)
Electronic marketplaces and exchanges	Transactions are conducted efficiently (more information to buyers and sellers, lower transaction costs) in electronic marketplaces (private or public).
Bartering online	Intermediary administers online exchange of surplus products and/or company receives "points" for its contribution, and the points can be used to purchase other needed items. (www.bbu.com)
Deep discounters	Company offers deep price discounts. Appeals to customers who consider only price in their purchasing decisions. (www.half.com)
Membership	Only members can use the services provided, including access to certain information, conducting trades, etc. (www.egreetings.com)

Major E-Commerce Mechanisms

Businesses and customers can buy and sell on the Internet through a number of mechanisms. The most widely used are electronic catalogs, electronic auctions, e-storefronts, e-malls, and e-marketplaces.

Catalogs have been printed on paper for generations. Today, however, they are available on CD-ROM and the Internet. Electronic catalogs consist of a product database, directory and search capabilities, and a presentation function. They are the backbone of most e-commerce sites.

An **auction** is a competitive process in which either a seller solicits consecutive bids from buyers or a buyer solicits bids from sellers. The primary characteristic of auctions is that prices are determined dynamically by competitive bidding. Electronic auctions (e-auctions) generally increase revenues for sellers by broadening the customer base and shortening the cycle time of the auction. Buyers generally benefit from e-auctions because they can bargain for lower prices. In addition, they do not have to travel to an auction at a physical location.

The Internet provides an efficient infrastructure for conducting auctions at lower administrative costs and with many more involved sellers and buyers. Individual consumers and corporations alike can participate in auctions. The two major types of auctions are forward and reverse.

Forward auctions are auctions that sellers use as a channel to many potential buyers. Usually, sellers place items at sites for auction and buyers bid continuously for them. The highest bidder wins the items. Both sellers and buyers can be individuals or businesses. The popular auction site eBay.com is a forward auction.

In **reverse auctions**, one buyer, usually an organization, wants to buy a product or a service. The buyer posts a request for quotation (RFQ) on its Web site or on a third-party site. The RFQ provides detailed information on the desired purchase. The suppliers study the RFQ and then submit bids electronically. Everything else being equal, the lowest-price bidder wins the auction. The reverse auction is the most common auction model for large purchases (in terms of either quantities or price). Governments and large corporations frequently use this approach, which may provide considerable savings for the buyer.

Auctions can be conducted from the seller's site, the buyer's site, or a third party's site. For example, eBay, the best-known third-party site, offers hundreds of thousands of different items in several types of auctions. Overall, more than 300 major companies, including Amazon.com and Dellauction.com, offer online auctions.

An *electronic storefront* is a Web site that represents a single store. An *electronic mall*, also known as a *cybermall* or *e-mall*, is a collection of individual shops under one Internet address. Electronic storefronts and electronic malls are closely associated with B2C electronic commerce. You study each one in more detail in Section 9.2.

An electronic marketplace (e-marketplace) is a central, virtual market space on the Web where many buyers and many sellers can conduct e-commerce and e-business activities. Electronic marketplaces are associated with B2B electronic commerce. You learn about electronic marketplaces in Section 9.3.

Electronic Payment Mechanisms

Implementing EC typically requires electronic payments. **Electronic payment systems** enable buyers to pay for goods and services electronically, rather than writing a check or using cash. Payments are an integral part of doing business, whether in the traditional manner or online. Traditional payment systems have typically involved cash and/or checks.

In most cases, traditional payment systems are not effective for EC, especially for B2B. Cash cannot be used because there is no face-to-face contact between buyer and seller. Not everyone accepts credit cards or checks, and some buyers do not have credit cards or checking accounts. Finally, contrary to what many people believe, it may be *less* secure for the buyer to use the telephone or mail to arrange or send payments, especially from another country, than to complete a secured transaction on a computer. For all of these reasons, a better way is needed to pay for goods and services in cyberspace. This better method is electronic payment systems. Let's now take a closer look at four types of electronic payment: electronic checks, electronic credit cards, purchasing cards, and electronic cash.

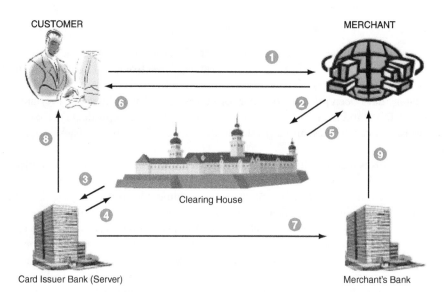

CUSTOMER

MERCHANT

Clearing House

Card Issuer Bank (Server)

Merchant's Bank

Figure 9.1 How e-credit cards work. (The numbers 1-9 indicate the sequence of activities.)

Electronic Checks

Electronic checks (e-checks) are similar to regular paper checks. They are used primarily in B2B. A customer who wishes to use e-checks must first establish a checking account with a bank. Then, when the customer buys a product or a service, he or she e-mails an encrypted electronic check to the seller. The seller deposits the check in a bank account and funds are transferred from the buyer's account into the seller's account.

Like regular checks, e-checks carry a signature (in digital form) that can be verified (see www.authorize.net). Properly signed and endorsed e-checks are exchanged between financial institutions through electronic clearinghouses. (See www.eccho.org and www.troygroup. com for details.)

Electronic Cards

There are a variety of electronic cards. These cards are used for different purposes, and include electronic credit cards, virtual credit cards, purchasing cards, stored-value money cards, and smart cards.

Electronic credit cards allow customers to charge online payments to their credit card account. These cards are used primarily in B2C and in shopping by small-to-medium enterprises (SMEs). Here is how e-credit cards work (see Figure 9.1).

- Step 1: When you buy a book from Amazon, for example, your credit card information and purchase amount are encrypted in your browser. This way the information is safe while it is "traveling" on the Internet to Amazon.

- Step 2: When your information arrives at Amazon, it is not opened. Rather, it is transferred automatically (in encrypted form) to a *clearinghouse*, where it is decrypted for verification and authorization.

- Step 3: The clearinghouse asks the bank that issued you your credit card (the card issuer bank) to verify your credit card information.

- Step 4: Your card issuer bank verifies your credit card information and reports this to the clearinghouse.

- Step 5: The clearinghouse reports the result of the verification of your credit card to Amazon.

- Step 6: Amazon reports a successful purchase and amount to you.

- Step 7: Your card issuer bank sends funds in the amount of the purchase to Amazon's bank.

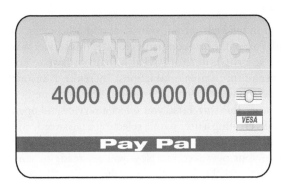

Figure 9.2 Example of virtual credit card.

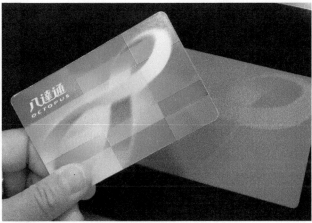

Mike Clarke/AFP/Getty Images/NewsCom

Figure 9.3 Example of purchasing card.

- Step 8: Your card issuer bank notifies you (either electronically or in your monthly statement) of the debit on your credit card.
- Step 9: Amazon's bank notifies Amazon of the funds credited to its account.

Virtual credit cards allow customers to shop online (see Figure 9.2). These cards are for a single use. The goal is to thwart criminals by using a different, random card number every time you shop online. A virtual number is good only on the Web site where you make your purchase. An online purchase made with a virtual card number shows up on your bill just like any other purchase.

Purchasing cards are the B2B equivalent of electronic credit cards (see Figure 9.3). In some countries, purchasing cards are the primary form of payment between companies. Unlike credit cards, where credit is provided for 30 to 60 days (for free) before payment is made to the merchant, payments made with purchasing cards are settled within a week.

Stored-value money cards allow you to store a fixed amount of prepaid money and then spend it as necessary. These cards are used to pay for photocopies in your library, for transportation, and for telephone calls. Each time you use the card, the amount is reduced by the amount you spent. Figure 9.4 shows a New York City Metro (subway and bus) card.

Smart cards contain a chip that can store a considerable amount of information—more than a hundred times that of a stored-value money card (see Figure 9.5). Smart cards are frequently multipurpose—that is, you can use them as a credit card, a debit card, a

© Clarence Holmes Photography/Alamy Limited

Figure 9.4 The New York City Metro Card.

© MARKA/Alamy Limited

Figure 9.5 Smart cards are frequently multipurpose.

stored-value money card, or a loyalty card. Smart cards are ideal for *micropayments*, which are small payments of a few dollars or less.

Person-to-Person Payments

Person-to-person payments enable two individuals, or an individual and a business, to transfer funds without using a credit card. One of the first companies to offer this service was PayPal (an eBay company). An attractive security feature of PayPal is that you have to put only enough money in the account to cover any upcoming transactions. Therefore, if anyone should gain access to your account, that person will not have access to all of your money.

Person-to-person payment services work this way. First, you select a service and open up an account. Basically, this process entails creating a user name, selecting a password, and providing the service with a credit card or bank account number. Next, you transfer funds from your credit card or bank account to your new account. Now you are ready to send money to someone over the Internet. You access the service—for example, PayPal—with your user name and password, and you specify the e-mail address of the person to receive the money, along with the dollar amount that you want to send. The service then sends an e-mail to the payee's e-mail address. The e-mail contains a link back to the service's Web site. When the recipient clicks on the link, he or she is taken to the service. There, the recipient is asked to set up an account to which the money that you sent will be credited. The recipient can then credit the money from this account to either a credit card or a bank account. The service charges the payer a small amount, roughly $1 per transaction.

Benefits and Limitations of E-Commerce

Few innovations in human history have provided as many benefits to organizations, individuals, and society as e-commerce has. E-commerce benefits organizations by making national and international markets more accessible and by lowering the costs of processing, distributing, and retrieving information. Customers benefit by being able to access a vast number of products and services, around the clock. The major benefit to society is the ability to easily and conveniently deliver information, services, and products to people in cities, rural areas, and developing countries.

Despite all these benefits, EC has some limitations, both technological and nontechnological, that have restricted its growth and acceptance. One major technological limitation is the lack of universally accepted security standards. Also, in less-developed countries, telecommunications bandwidth often is insufficient and accessing the Web is expensive. Nontechnological limitations include the perceptions that EC is insecure, has unresolved legal issues, and lacks a critical mass of sellers and buyers. As time passes, the limitations, especially the technological ones, will diminish or be overcome.

BEFORE *YOU GO ON . . .*

1. Define e-commerce and distinguish it from e-business.
2. Differentiate among B2C, B2B, C2C, and B2E electronic commerce.
3. Define *e-government*.
4. Discuss forward and reverse auctions.
5. Identify some benefits and limitations of e-commerce.

Apply the Concept 9.1

Background Today there are many companies who specialize in making e-commerce a reality for small businesses. Amazon, Yahoo, PayPal, and others offer services that provide all a small business needs to sell product and accept payment over the Internet. In fact, it seems that many consumers prefer for their transactions to go through these larger global companies because they trust these companies' security.

Activity Go to http://www.wiley.com/go/rainer/applytheconcept and click on the link provided for Apply the Concept 9.1. This will take you to PayPal's Web site. Click on the business tab at the top of the page. At the time of this writing there were lots of links at the bottom of that page that described the services they offered. Review the payment options described in the text and see how many of them PayPal offers to its customers.

Deliverable

Build a table that lists in one column the payment mechanism discussed in this section, the PayPal equivalent in a second column, and a discussion of how it is similar or why PayPal does not offer this type of payment in a third. Your table will look something like this:

Payment Types	PayPal Equivalent	Description

Quiz questions are assignable in WileyPLUS, and available on the Book Companion Site at http://www.wiley.com/college/rainer.

RUBY'S CLUB | **QUESTIONS**

1. Ruby's Club is definitely not a pure e-commerce business. Its main product is entertainment, and the owners simply want to sell their brand via hats, t-shirts, and other paraphernalia. To what degree can they digitize the entertainment aspect of their product?
2. In what ways might Ruby's utilize B2B or B2C E-commerce?

9.2 Business-to-Consumer (B2C) Electronic Commerce

B2B EC is much larger than B2C EC by volume, but B2C EC is more complex. The reason is that B2C involves a large number of buyers making millions of diverse transactions per day with a relatively small number of sellers. As an illustration, consider Amazon, an online retailer that offers thousands of products to its customers. Each customer purchase is relatively small, but Amazon must manage that transaction as if that customer were its most important one. Each order must be processed quickly and efficiently, and the products must be shipped to the customer in a timely manner. In addition, returns must be managed. Multiply this simple example by millions, and you get an idea of the complexity of B2C EC. Overall, B2B complexities tend to be more business related, whereas B2C complexities tend to be more technical and volume related.

This section addresses the primary issues in B2C EC. We begin by studying the two basic mechanisms that customers utilize to access companies on the Web: electronic storefronts and electronic malls. In addition to purchasing products over the Web, customers also access online services. Therefore, the next section covers several online services, such as banking, securities trading, job searching, and travel. The complexity of B2C EC creates two major challenges for sellers: channel conflict and order fulfillment.

We examine these two topics in detail. Finally, companies engaged in B2C EC must "get the word out" to prospective customers. This section concludes with a look at online advertising.

Electronic Storefronts and Malls

For several generations, home shopping from catalogs, and later from television shopping channels, has attracted millions of customers. Today, shopping online offers an alternative to catalog and television shopping. **Electronic retailing (e-tailing)** is the direct sale of products and services through electronic storefronts or electronic malls, usually designed around an electronic catalog format and/or auctions.

Like any mail-order shopping experience, e-commerce enables you to buy from home and to do so 24 hours a day, 7 days a week. However, EC offers a wider variety of products and services, including the most unique items, often at lower prices. Furthermore, within seconds, shoppers can access very detailed supplementary product information. In addition, they can easily locate and compare competitors' products and prices. Finally, buyers can find hundreds of thousands of sellers. Two popular online shopping mechanisms are electronic storefronts and electronic malls.

Electronic Storefronts. As noted earlier, an **electronic storefront** is a Web site that represents a single store. Hundreds of thousands of electronic storefronts can be found on the Internet. Each one has its own uniform resource locator (URL), or Internet address, at which buyers can place orders. Some electronic storefronts are extensions of physical stores such as Hermes, The Sharper Image, and Walmart. Others are new businesses started by entrepreneurs who discovered a niche on the Web (e.g., Restaurant.com and Alloy.com). Manufacturers (e.g., www.dell.com) and retailers (e.g., www.officedepot.com) also use storefronts. IT's About Business 9.2 illustrates how Macy's is expanding its online presence.

IT'S ABOUT BUSINESS 9.2

Macy's Increases Its Online Presence

Macy's has more than 800 store locations in 45 states and is rapidly growing its online business. Its e-commerce business has become increasingly important and continues to expand. In fiscal years 2008, 2009, and 2010, Macy's online sales increased by 30 percent, 20 percent, and 29 percent, respectively. Macy's e-commerce group oversees Web sites such as www.macys.com and www.bloomingdales.com. The overall goals of the group are to make Macy's Web sites the main contact interface for all of their Internet-using customers and to drive customer traffic into their physical stores.

In January 2011, Macy's announced that it was adding more than 700 new positions over the next two years to support the growth of its online business. The company's strategy for its online business is to provide a multichannel opportunity for its customers that enables them to shop seamlessly in stores, online, and via mobile devices. The company is also building an online fulfillment center in West Virginia and expanding its existing fulfillment center in Tennessee.

Macy's is using Splunk (www.splunk.com) to support its e-commerce initiatives. Splunk is a company founded to make machine data directly accessible to business users without their having to go through their information technology department as intermediaries. Splunk's software enables Macy's to monitor, report, and analyze its historical data and its live click-stream data from the Web.

© sturti/iStockphoto

Macy's also uses Splunk software to proactively identify network and systems issues that could lead to its Web site crashing, which would prevent customers from researching products or buying online. For example, late in 2010, Splunk alerted Macy's technicians to a problem that would have been catastrophic to online operations if it had not been addressed quickly. The technicians solved the problem within 30 minutes without any downtime for the Web site. This would not have been possible before Macy's starting using Splunk,

as its technicians formerly used a manual process to react to problems once they had already occurred. It often took Macy's technicians 48 hours to resolve a problem. These long delays in restoring Web site connectivity resulted in dollar losses and damage to the company's brand.

In addition to proactively preventing downtimes, another key benefit of the Splunk software is that it enables Macy's to gather a variety of data that executives and analysts can use to determine how Macy's Web sites are being utilized by customers. The software is useful throughout the year and is especially valuable during the Christmas shopping season.

Macy's uses other tools to help keep its online operations operating smoothly. One tool, DynaTrace Software, enables the store to test the performance of new e-commerce applications that they deploy. Macy's integrates DynaTrace with an application from Coradiant called TruSight. These integrated applications allow company analysts to examine Web site performance from the perspective of users by providing real-time visibility into the performance and availability of Web applications. The applications do this by capturing and measuring information on user transactions as they happen. Macy's integrated software has helped it identify user problems not being reported to the company's customer service department. For example, during the 2010 holiday shopping season, DynaTrace and TruSight enabled analysts to find a sign-in issue during the online checkout process that could have potentially had a major negative impact on online operations and customer satisfaction.

Sources: Compiled from T. Henschen, "Splunk Answers Business Demand for Big Data Analysis," *InformationWeek,* January 12, 2012; T. Groenfeldt, "Security Data is Big Data and a Business Advantage," *Forbes,* December 14, 2011; T. Taulli, "Splunk: Patience Can Make Billions," *Forbes,* April 12, 2011; B. Violino, "Macy's Ramps Up Online Operations," *Baseline Magazine,* January 27, 2011; www.macys.com, www.splunk.com, www.dynatrace.com accessed February 24, 2012.

Questions

1. Why is it so important that the Macy's Web sites function as optimally as possible?

2. What is the relationship between Macy's Web sites and increasing customer traffic in their physical stores?

Electronic Malls

Whereas an electronic storefront represents a single store, an **electronic mall**, also known as a *cybermall* or an *e-mall*, is a collection of individual shops grouped under a single Internet address. The basic idea of an electronic mall is the same as that of a regular shopping mall: to provide a one-stop shopping place that offers a wide range of products and services. A cybermall may include thousands of vendors. For example, Microsoft Shopping (now Bing shopping, www.bing.com/shopping) includes tens of thousands of products from thousands of vendors.

There are two types of cybermalls. In the first type, known as *referral malls* (for example, www.hawaii.com), you cannot buy anything. Instead, you are transferred from the mall to a participating storefront. In the second type of mall (for example, http://shopping.google.com), you can actually make a purchase (see Figure 9.6). At this type of mall, you might shop from several stores, but you make only one purchase transaction at the end. You use an *electronic shopping cart* to gather items from various vendors and then pay for them all together in a single transaction. The mall organizer, such as Google!, takes a commission from the sellers for this service.

Online Service Industries

In addition to purchasing products, customers can also access needed services via the Web. Selling books, toys, computers, and most other products on the Internet can reduce vendors' selling costs by 20 to 40 percent. Further reduction is difficult to achieve because the products must be delivered physically. Only a few products, such as software or music, can be digitized and then delivered online for additional savings. In contrast, services, such as

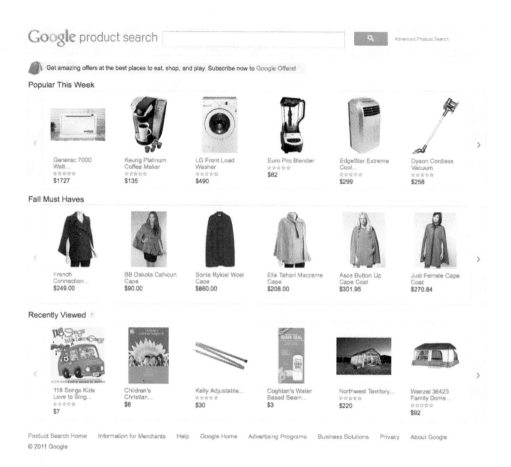

Figure 9.6 Electronic malls include products from many vendors.

buying an airline ticket and purchasing stocks or insurance, can be delivered entirely through e-commerce, often with considerable cost reduction. Not surprisingly, then, online delivery of services is growing very rapidly, with millions of new customers being added each year.

One of the most pressing EC issues relating to online services (as well as in marketing tangible products) is **disintermediation**. Intermediaries, also known as middlemen, have two functions: (1) They provide information and (2) they perform value-added services such as consulting. The first function can be fully automated and most likely will be assumed by e-marketplaces and portals that provide information for free. When this occurs, the intermediaries who perform only (or primarily) this function are likely to be eliminated. This process is called disintermediation.

In contrast, performing value-added services requires expertise. Unlike the information function, then, this function can be only partially automated. Thus, intermediaries who provide value-added services not only are likely to survive, but they may actually prosper. The Web helps these employees in two situations: (1) when the number of participants is enormous, as with job searches, and (2) when the information that must be exchanged is complex.

In this section, you will examine some leading online service industries: banking, trading of securities (stocks, bonds), job matching, travel services, and online advertising.

Cyberbanking. *Electronic banking*, also known as **cyberbanking**, involves conducting various banking activities from home, at a place of business, or on the road instead of at a physical bank location. Electronic banking has capabilities ranging from paying bills to applying for a loan. For customers, it saves time and is convenient. For banks, it offers an inexpensive alternative to branch banking—for example, about 2 cents cost per transaction versus $1.07 at a physical branch. It also enables banks to attract remote customers. In addition to regular banks with added online services, **virtual banks**, which are dedicated solely to Internet transactions, are emerging. An example of a virtual bank is First Internet Bank of Indiana (www.firstib.com) (see Figure 9.7).

Figure 9.7 First Internet Bank of Indiana.

International banking and the ability to handle trading in multiple currencies are critical for international trade. Transfers of electronic funds and electronic letters of credit are important services in international banking. An example of support for EC global trade is provided by TradeCard, in conjunction with MasterCard. TradeCard is an international company that provides a secure method for buyers and sellers to make digital payments anywhere on the globe (see the demo at www.tradecard.com). In another example, banks and companies such as Oanda (www.oanda.com) provide conversions of more than 160 currencies.

Online Securities Trading.

Emarketer.com estimates that some 40 million people in the United States use computers to trade stocks, bonds, and other financial instruments. In fact, several well-known securities companies, including E*Trade, Ameritrade, and Charles Schwab, offer only online trading. In Korea, more than half of stock traders are already using the Internet for that purpose. Why? Because it is cheaper than is a full-service or discount broker. On the Web, investors can find a considerable amount of information regarding specific companies or mutual funds in which to invest (for example, http://money.cnn.com and www.bloomberg.com).

For example, let's say you have an account with Scottrade. You access Scottrade's Web site (www.scottrade.com) from your personal computer or your Internet-enabled mobile device, enter your account number and password to access your personalized Web page, and then click on "stock trading." Using a menu, you enter the details of your order—buy or sell, margin or cash, price limit, market order, and so on. The computer informs you of the current "ask" and "bid" prices, much as a broker would do over the telephone. You can then approve or reject the transaction.

The Online Job Market.

The Internet offers a promising new environment for job seekers and for companies searching for hard-to-find employees. Thousands of companies and government agencies advertise available positions, accept resumes, and take applications via the Internet.

Job seekers use the online job market to reply online to employment ads, to place resumes on various sites, and to use recruiting firms (for example, www.monster.com, www.simplyhired.com, www.linkedin.com, and www.truecareers.com). Companies that have jobs to offer advertise these openings on their Web sites, and they search the bulletin boards of recruiting firms. In many countries, governments must advertise job openings on the Internet.

Travel Services.

The Internet is an ideal place to plan, explore, and arrange almost any trip economically. Online travel services allow you to purchase airline tickets, reserve hotel rooms, and rent cars. Most sites also offer a fare-tracker feature that sends you e-mail messages about low-cost flights. Examples of comprehensive online travel services are Expedia.com, Travelocity.com, and Orbitz.com. Online services are also provided by all major airline vacation services, large conventional travel agencies, car rental agencies, hotels (e.g., www.hotels.com), and tour companies. In a variation of this process, Priceline.com allows you to set a price you are willing to pay for an airline ticket or hotel accommodations. It then attempts to find a vendor that will match your price.

One costly problem that e-commerce can cause is "mistake fares" in the airline industry. For example, over the weekend of May 4–6, 2007, United Airlines offered a $1,221 fare for a U.S.-to-New Zealand round-trip in business class. This price was incorrect; the actual price was higher. By the time United noticed the mistake and pulled the fare, however, hundreds of tickets had been sold, thanks in part to online travel discussion groups.

Online Advertising. *Advertising* is the practice of disseminating information in an attempt to influence a buyer–seller transaction. Traditional advertising on TV or in newspapers is impersonal, one-way mass communication. In contrast, direct-response marketing, or telemarketing, contacts individuals by direct mail or telephone and requires them to respond in order to make a purchase. The direct-response approach personalizes advertising and marketing. At the same time, however, it can be expensive, slow, and ineffective. It can also be extremely annoying to the consumer.

Internet advertising redefines the advertising process, making it media rich, dynamic, and interactive. It improves on traditional forms of advertising in a number of ways. First, Internet ads can be updated any time at minimal cost and therefore can be kept current. In addition, these ads can reach very large numbers of potential buyers all over the world. Further, they are generally cheaper than radio, television, and print ads. Finally, Internet ads can be interactive and targeted to specific interest groups and/or individuals.

Advertising Methods. The most common online advertising methods are banners, pop-ups, and e-mail. Banners are simply electronic billboards. Typically, a **banner** contains a short text or graphical message to promote a product or a vendor. It may even contain video clips and sound. When customers click on a banner, they are transferred to the advertiser's home page. Banner advertising is the most commonly used form of advertising on the Internet (see Figure 9.8).

A major advantage of banners is that they can be customized to the target audience. If the computer system knows who you are or what your profile is, it might send you a banner that is supposed to match your interests. A major disadvantage of banners is that they can convey only limited information because of their small size. Another drawback is that many viewers simply ignore them.

Pop-up and pop-under ads are contained in a new browser window that is automatically launched when you enter or exit a Web site. A **pop-up ad** appears in front of the current browser window. A **pop-under ad** appears underneath the active window; when users close the active window, they see the ad. Many users strongly object to these ads, which they consider intrusive. Modern browsers let users block pop-up ads, but this feature must be used with caution because some Web sites depend on pop-up capabilities to present content other than advertising. For example, when you log on to your Verizon e-mail page, you also see a brief (one line each) summary of recent news stories. If you hover your mouse over one of them, you get a pop-up window with an extended summary (a few paragraphs) of that story. Another example is the WebCT Vista software for online instruction, where discussion group posts appear in pop-up windows. Blocking pop-ups would make the first of these two examples less useful and would eliminate important functionality from the second example.

E-mail is emerging as an Internet advertising and marketing channel. It is generally cost-effective to implement and provides a better and quicker response rate than other

© MARKA/Alamy Limited

Figure 9.8 When customers click on a banner ad, they are transferred to the vendor's home page.

advertising channels. Marketers develop or purchase a list of e-mail addresses, place them in a customer database, and then send advertisements via e-mail. A list of e-mail addresses can be a very powerful tool because the marketer can target a group of people or even individuals.

As you have probably concluded by now, there is a potential for misuse of e-mail advertising. In fact, some consumers receive a flood of unsolicited e-mail, or *spam*. **Spamming** is the indiscriminate distribution of electronic ads without the permission of the receiver. Unfortunately, spamming is becoming worse over time.

Two important responses to spamming are permission marketing and viral marketing. **Permission marketing** asks consumers to give their permission to voluntarily accept online advertising and e-mail. Typically, consumers are asked to complete an electronic form that asks what they are interested in and requests permission to send related marketing information. Sometimes, consumers are offered incentives to receive advertising.

Permission marketing is the basis of many Internet marketing strategies. For example, millions of users periodically receive e-mails from airlines such as American and Southwest. Users of this marketing service can ask to be notified of low fares from their hometown or to their favorite destinations. Significantly, they can easily unsubscribe at any time. Permission marketing is also extremely important for market research (for example, search for "Media Metrix" at www.comscore.com).

In one particularly interesting form of permission marketing, companies such as Clickdough.com, ExpressPaidSurveys.com, and CashSurfers.com have built customer lists of millions of people who are happy to receive advertising messages whenever they are on the Web. These customers are paid $0.25 to $0.50 an hour to view messages while they do their normal surfing.

Viral marketing refers to online word-of-mouth marketing. The strategy behind viral marketing is to have people forward messages to friends, family members, and other acquaintances suggesting they "check this out." For example, a marketer can distribute a small game program embedded with a sponsor's e-mail that is easy to forward. The marketer releases only a few thousand copies, with the expectation that the recipients in turn will forward the program to many more thousands of potential customers. In this way, viral marketing enables companies to build brand awareness at a minimal cost without having to spam millions of uninterested users.

Issues in E-Tailing

Despite e-tailing's increasing popularity, many e-tailers continue to face serious issues that can restrict their growth. Perhaps the two major issues are channel conflict and order fulfillment.

Clicks-and-mortar companies may face a conflict with their regular distributors when they sell directly to customers online. This situation, known as **channel conflict**, can alienate the distributors. Channel conflict has forced some companies to avoid direct online sales. For example, Walmart, Lowe's, and Home Depot would rather have customers come to their stores. Therefore, although all three companies maintain e-commerce Web sites, their sites place more emphasis on providing information—products, prices, specials, and store locations—than on online sales.

Channel conflict can arise in areas such as pricing and resource allocation—for example, how much money to spend on advertising. Another potential source of conflict involves the logistics services provided by the offline activities to the online activities. For example, how should a company handle returns of items purchased online? Some companies have completely separated the "clicks" (the online portion of the organization) from the "mortar" or "bricks" (the traditional bricks-and-mortar part of the organization). However, this approach can increase expenses and reduce the synergy between the two organizational channels. As a result, many companies are integrating their online and offline channels, a process known as **multichanneling**. IT's About Business 9.3 shows how the online channel is causing problems for brick-and-mortar retailers. On the other hand, eBay sees great potential in the hybrid online/offline shopping experience, as you see in IT's About Business 9.4.

IT's ABOUT BUSINESS 9.3

What To Do About Showrooming?

A Pew Research (www.pewresearch.org) survey showed that during the 2011 holiday season, 52 percent of shoppers with smartphones walked into brick-and-mortar retail stores, saw products that interested them, and did at least some research on their phones. Nineteen percent of them ultimately made their purchases online. This comparison process is called "showrooming."

"Showrooming" occurs when shoppers come into a store to see a product in person, only to buy it from a rival online, frequently at a lower price. This process is presenting a worsening problem for brick-and-mortar retailers, including Target, Best Buy, Walmart, Barnes & Noble, and many others. At the same time, showrooming is an advantage for Amazon and other online retailers.

On December 10, 2011, Amazon released its Price Check app, which has served to make showrooming even more widespread. With the Price Check app, Amazon gives customers an additional 5 percent discount (up to $5) on up to three qualifying products if the customer has checked the price of those items while shopping in a physical retail store. Eligible categories of products included electronics, toys, music, sporting goods, and DVDs. Using this new Amazon app, shoppers can price check in four ways: by scanning a bar code, by snapping a photo of the product, by saying the product's name, or by typing in a search query.

Traditional retailers like Target and Walmart are playing catch-up in online retailing, which is becoming an increasingly important avenue for sales. Analysts estimate that Target and Walmart's Web sites currently account for only a paltry 1 to 2 percent of their annual sales. To demonstrate the growing importance of having a strong online presence, in 2011, brick-and-mortar store sales increased 4.1 percent during the holiday shopping season, while online sales increased by 15 percent during the same period. Further, although online sales represent only 8 percent of total sales, that figure is up from just 2 percent in 2000. Therefore, it is crucially important for Target and Walmart to become more attractive to their customers online.

As a further example of revenue loss from a poor online presence, Target had a disappointing 2011 Christmas season, with sales at stores that had been open one year or more increasing by only 1.7 percent, about half of what analysts expected. The company said sales were particularly disappointing in electronics, movies, books, and music—products whose sales have migrated most significantly to the Internet.

In fall 2011, Target relaunched and upgraded its Web site, which had been operated by Amazon for the last decade. In the past when Target's site had been operated by Amazon, the site had crashed several times, most notably when shoppers rushed to buy a special line of items made by Italian fashion house Missoni.

Lessons From IT Failures

Therefore, Target asked suppliers for help in limiting showrooming. In January 2012, Target sent a letter to its vendors, suggesting that they create special products for Target so that they could set themselves apart from their competitors and shield themselves from the price comparisons that have become so easy for shoppers to perform on their computers and smartphones. Where special products are not possible, Target asked its suppliers to help it match rivals' prices. Target also said that it might create a subscription service that would give shoppers a discount on regularly purchased merchandise. Vendors are likely to try to meet Target's requests because it is a very large retail chain.

Some analysts noted that Target's new tactics are unlikely to reverse the showrooming trend, because the tactics will not address the root problems that they and other traditional retailers are facing. Online-only retailers have significantly lower labor costs and, at least for the time being, do not collect sales tax in most states, which makes them very appealing to their customers. More importantly, sites such as Amazon are based on an entirely different business model than are traditional retailers. That is, Amazon can sell products so cheaply because it uses its other profitable business units—such as cloud data storage and fees it charges merchants to sell on its Web site—to subsidize the rest of its businesses. Traditional retailers that do not use this model are unable to match Amazon's low prices, thereby putting them at a fundamental disadvantage. In addition, consumer preferences in general are moving to online venues.

As successful and unshakable as companies like Walmart and Target may seem today, it remains to be seen whether low price points at online retailers will spell ruin for their more traditional business models. Traditional retailers will have to offer customers a truly exceptional shopping and buying experience to have a hope of competing in the marketplace.

Sources: Compiled from N. Potter, "'Showrooming': People Shopping in Stores, Then Researching by Cell Phone, Says Pew Survey," *ABC News*, January 31, 2012; A. Zimmerman, "Showdown Over 'Showrooms'," *The Wall Street Journal*, January 23, 2012; J. Milliot, "The Amazon Price Check App and the Battle Over 'Showrooming'," *Publishers Weekly*, December 9, 2011; T. Novellino, "The Amazon App Attack," *Portfolio.com*, December 8, 2011; E. Straub, "Browse at a Bookstore, Buy at Amazon: The Evil of Showrooming," *Time*, December 8, 2011; A. Chang, "Retail Groups Lash Out After Amazon Announces Price Check App Promotion," *The Los Angeles Times*, December 7, 2011; A. Chang, "Amazon Giving Shoppers Up to $15 for Using Its Price Check App," *The Los Angeles Times*, December 6, 2011; www.target.com, www.pewresearch.org, accessed February 28, 2012.

Questions

1. What else could Target and other brick-and-mortar retailers do to combat showrooming? Provide examples of IT solutions and non-IT solutions that were not discussed in this case.

2. Do you practice showrooming? If so, why? Do you showroom only to compare prices? List other reasons why shoppers might practice showrooming.

3. Are there other categories of goods other than the ones mentioned in this case that might lend themselves to showrooming? Provide specific examples to support your answer.

IT'S ABOUT BUSINESS 9.4

The Future of Shopping

Once a retail pioneer, by late 2011 eBay (www.ebay.com) had become an auction wasteland with outdated technology. In order to save the company, John Donahoe, eBay's new CEO, completely remodeled the company's business practices. He removed layers of bureaucracy between management and engineers, opened up Pay-Pal to outside developers, created a beta-lab Web site that consumers could experiment with and comment on, and invested in new electronic commerce technology. Donahoe also worked to reduce eBay's dependence on auctions as source of revenue. By mid-2012, only 24 percent of revenue of eBay's revenue came from auctions, down from 35 percent in previous years.

Donahoe also shifted eBay's focus as a Web site. He saw that the increased use of mobile devices was blurring the lines between online and offline shopping and wanted to put eBay at the center of the hybrid online/offline shopping experience. According to research firm Forrester Research, the financial opportunity of this hybrid experience dwarfs the space of simple e-commerce (i.e., browsing and buying online), which represents just 9 percent of all retail sales. Donahoe's vision for eBay's future is for the company to deliver to its customers the ability to shop wherever they want, however they want, for the best price, and with the greatest convenience.

How did eBay go about accomplishing this goal and transitioning into a hybrid online/offline shopping experience? The retailer followed the progression below:

© franckreporter/iStockphoto

Step 1: eBay bought RedLaser. RedLaser is a company whose technology allows consumers to scan bar codes, vehicle identification numbers, gift cards, asset tags, and QR codes with their mobile devices.

 Step 2: eBay bought Milo (www.milo.com), a company that makes the inventory of offline stores viewable online 24/7. While Milo had

been able to land major retailers for its inventory network, the company was still a relatively small player. eBay had the designers and developers who could help Milo with its technical challenges. EBay also had more than 30 million sellers and merchants in its marketplace, many of whom had offline inventory that Milo could tap. As a result, Milo's technology could help eBay list far more products than ever before possible.

 Step 3: eBay bought GSI Commerce (www. gsicommerce.com). GSI commerce is a company that builds e-commerce platforms for several hundred offline retailers. The company concentrates on customer care and interactive marketing for its clients. With this purchase, eBay was able to improve its online customer interactions, strengthen its customer relationships, and provide superior customer service.

Step 4: eBay bought Where (www.where.com). Where builds location-based mobile apps for every major mobile device platform, including Android, iPhone, and BlackBerry, and boasts some 4 million active users per month. Where shows local listings for restaurants, bars, merchants, and events, and suggests places and deals for you based on your location and past behavior. The absorption of Where into eBay allowed eBay customers to shop from any location. Further, Where enabled eBay to suggest additional products to customers based on their location.

 Step 5: eBay bought Fig Card (http://figcard. com, bought by PayPal in 2011). Fig Card allows merchants to accept payments from mobile devices in stores by using a simple USB device that plugs into the cash register or point-of-sale terminal. All the consumer needs to participate is the Fig app on their smartphone. Once consumers set up their payment information and designate PayPal as a payment option, Fig Card is also able to integrate with PayPal. This new functionality allowed eBay to expand the options that its customers could use to pay for purchases.

Step 6: eBay already owns PayPal (www.paypal.com). eBay wants every transaction to end with PayPal.

Consider these scenarios:

- Imagine that you have met your girlfriend for lunch and you are admiring her new handbag. You take a picture of her purse with your smartphone. Your smartphone then uses an eBay app to reveal all of the boutiques within a 3-mile radius that have the same color and style bag in stock right then. The app also tells you the prices of the bag you are looking for at each store. You then decide which store has your ideal combination of price and location, and you order the bag via your phone. After lunch, you visit that store, and bypass the checkout lines because you show the salesperson your digital receipt on your phone.

- The local Starbucks "sees" you (i.e., senses your smartphone's location) when you are two blocks away and wants to give you a dollar for your next Frappuccino. Starbucks puts the one dollar into your PayPal account, where it sits until it expires in one hour.

- What about that new Canon camera you are thinking about, but are not yet ready to purchase? Scan its bar code (or RFID tag or QR code) into your PayPal "wish list," which PayPal is prototyping in early 2012. Then, when you walk by a retailer who has the camera in stock, that store can make you a special pricing offer that is better than you have found anywhere else.

Here is the model: eBay + RedLaser + Milo + GSI + PayPal + Fig Card + Where = Success!

Recall that eBay's new CEO wants to establish a complete shopping experience for the company's customers. With each piece of the puzzle, eBay has made it easier, faster, and more convenient for its customers to shop. Furthermore, the company's customers have more choices than ever before and many of those choices are relevant to where the customer is located. eBay's new model appears to be working. The company says that, although all the pieces are not yet integrated, it still facilitated nearly $4 billion in mobile transactions in 2011.

Sources: Compiled from R. Kim, "With X.Commerce, eBay Eyes a Bigger Prize as Sales Enabler," *GigaOM*, October 12, 2011; D. Sacks, "How Jack Abraham Is Reinventing eBay," *Fast Company*, June 22, 2011; L. Rao, "eBay Closes $2.4 Billion Acquisition of GSI Commerce," *TechCrunch*, June 20, 2011; S. Kirsner, "eBay Buys Mobile Payments Start-up Fig Card, Second Boston Acquisition in April," *Boston.com*, April 28, 2011; www.milo.com, www.ebay.com, accessed March 20, 2012.

Questions

1. What are the advantages of eBay's hybrid shopping experience vision for the customer?

2. What are potential disadvantages of eBay's hybrid shopping experience vision for the customer?

The second major issue confronting e-commerce is order fulfillment, which can create problems for e-tailers as well. Any time a company sells directly to customers, it is involved in various order fulfillment activities. It must perform the following activities: quickly find the products to be shipped; pack them; arrange for the packages to be delivered speedily to the customer's door; collect the money from every customer, either in advance, by COD, or by individual bill; and handle the return of unwanted or defective products.

It is very difficult to accomplish these activities both effectively and efficiently in B2C, because a company has to ship small packages to many customers and do it quickly. For this reason, companies involved in B2C activities often experience difficulties in their supply chains.

In addition to providing customers with the products they ordered and doing it on time, order fulfillment provides all related customer services. For example, the customer must receive assembly and operation instructions for a new appliance. In addition, if the customer is not happy with a product, an exchange or return must be arranged. (Visit www.fedex.com to see how returns are handled via FedEx.)

In the late 1990s, e-tailers faced continuous problems in order fulfillment, especially during the holiday season. These problems included late deliveries, delivering wrong items, high delivery costs, and compensation to unhappy customers. For e-tailers, taking orders over the Internet is the easy part of B2C e-commerce. Delivering orders to customers' doors is the hard part. In contrast, order fulfillment is less complicated in B2B. These transactions are much larger, but they are fewer in number. In addition, these companies have had order fulfillment mechanisms in place for many years.

BEFORE *YOU GO ON . . .*

1. Describe electronic storefronts and malls.
2. Discuss various types of online services, such as cyberbanking, securities trading, job searches, travel services, and so on.
3. Discuss online advertising, its methods, and its benefits.
4. Identify the major issues relating to e-tailing.
5. What are spamming, permission marketing, and viral marketing?

Apply the Concept 9.2

Background At this point in your "buying" career, you have probably bought something online, gone to an auction site and possibly won a bid, and engaged in some form of online banking. Your generation is very comfortable with the retail side of e-commerce. In the midst of this, you have probably created an account with a few vendors and received some e-mail advertisements. No doubt you have also seen some pop-up ads promoting products when you search for certain items.

Another thing that has changed is that companies now want you to do their advertising for them. The text refers to this as viral marketing.

Activity Go to http://www.wiley.com/go/rainer/applytheconcept and click on the link provided for Apply the Concept 9.2. It will take you to a video on viral marketing. Now imagine that you work for a BBQ restaurant that also has a catering business. The owner has never done much with e-mail and she is looking for you to help develop a viral marketing plan for the restaurant.

Deliverable

Write an e-mail that the business owner can ask her patrons to share with others. Be sure to develop an incentive for the customers to share and for those who receive the e-mail to share it with others. Put some thought into this based on your own experience. Try to create a "use and share" feeling in the e-mail. Submit the e-mail to your instructor.

Quiz questions are assignable in WileyPLUS, and available on the Book Companion Site at http://www.wiley.com/college/rainer.

1. Would it make sense for Ruby's Club to have a presence in an electronic mall? Why or why not?

2. How might Ruby's use multichannelling as most of the club's online customers would also be in the same geographical area?

9.3 Business-to-Business (B2B) Electronic Commerce

In *business to business (B2B)* e-commerce, the buyers and sellers are business organizations. B2B comprises about 85 percent of EC volume. It covers a broad spectrum of applications that enable an enterprise to form electronic relationships with its distributors, resellers, suppliers, customers, and other partners. Organizations can use B2B to restructure their supply chains and their partner relationships.

B2B applications utilize any of several business models. The major models are sell-side marketplaces, buy-side marketplaces, and electronic exchanges.

Sell-Side Marketplaces

In the **sell-side marketplace** model, organizations attempt to sell their products or services to other organizations electronically from their own private e-marketplace Web site and/or from a third-party Web site. This model is similar to the B2C model in which the buyer is expected to come to the seller's site, view catalogs, and place an order. In the B2B sell-side marketplace, however, the buyer is an organization.

The key mechanisms in the sell-side model are electronic catalogs that can be customized for each large buyer and forward auctions. Sellers such as Dell Computer (www.dellauction.com) use auctions extensively. In addition to conducting auctions from their own Web sites, organizations can use third-party auction sites, such as eBay, to liquidate items. Companies such as Ariba (www.ariba.com) are helping organizations to auction old assets and inventories.

The sell-side model is used by hundreds of thousands of companies. It is especially powerful for companies with superb reputations. The seller can be either a manufacturer (for example, Dell or IBM), a distributor (for example, www.avnet.com), or a retailer (for example, www.bigboxx.com). The seller uses EC to increase sales, reduce selling and advertising expenditures, increase delivery speed, and lower administrative costs. The sell-side model is especially suitable to customization. Many companies allow their customers to configure their orders online. For example, at Dell (www.dell.com), you can determine the exact type of computer that you want. You can choose the type of chip (for example, Itanium 2), the size of the hard drive (for example, 1 terabyte), the type of monitor (for example, 22-inch flat screen), and so on. Similarly, the Jaguar Web site (www.jaguar.com) allows you to customize the Jaguar you want. Self-customization greatly reduces any misunderstandings concerning what customers want and it encourages businesses to fill orders more quickly.

Buy-Side Marketplaces

The **buy-side** marketplace is a model in which organizations attempt to buy needed products or services from other organizations electronically. A major method of buying goods and services in the buy-side model is the reverse auction.

The buy-side model uses EC technology to streamline the purchasing process. The goal is to reduce both the costs of items purchased and the administrative expenses involved in purchasing them. In addition, EC technology can shorten the purchasing cycle time. Procurement includes purchasing goods and materials as well as sourcing (finding goods), negotiating with suppliers, paying for goods, and making delivery arrangements. Organizations now use the Internet to accomplish all of these functions.

Purchasing by using electronic support is referred to as e-procurement. **E-procurement** uses reverse auctions, particularly group purchasing. In **group purchasing**, multiple buyers combine their orders so that they constitute a large volume and therefore attract more seller attention. In addition, when buyers place their combined orders on a reverse auction, they can negotiate a volume discount. Typically, the orders of small buyers are aggregated by a third-party vendor, such as the United Sourcing Alliance (www.usa-llc.com).

Electronic Exchanges

Private exchanges have one buyer and many sellers. Electronic marketplaces (e-marketplaces), called **public exchanges** or just **exchanges**, are independently owned by a third party and connect many sellers and many buyers. Public exchanges are open to all business organizations. They frequently are owned and operated by a third party. Public exchange managers provide all the necessary information systems to the participants. Thus, buyers and sellers merely have to "plug in" in order to trade. B2B public exchanges are often the initial point for contacts between business partners. Once the partners make contact, they may move to a private exchange or to private trading rooms provided by many public exchanges to conduct their subsequent trading activities.

Some electronic exchanges deal in direct materials and others in indirect materials. *Direct materials* are inputs to the manufacturing process, such as safety glass used in automobile windshields and windows. *Indirect materials* are those items, such as office supplies, that are needed for maintenance, operations, and repairs (MRO). There are three basic types of public exchanges: vertical, horizontal, and functional. All three types offer diversified support services, ranging from payments to logistics.

Vertical exchanges connect buyers and sellers in a given industry. Examples of vertical exchanges are www.plasticsnet.com in the plastics industry and www.papersite.com in the paper industry.

Vertical exchanges are frequently owned and managed by a *consortium*, a term for a group of major players in an industry. For example, Marriott and Hyatt own a procurement consortium for the hotel industry, and ChevronTexaco owns an energy e-marketplace. The vertical e-marketplaces offer services that are particularly suited to the community they serve.

Horizontal exchanges connect buyers and sellers across many industries and are used primarily for MRO materials. Examples of horizontal exchanges are TradersCity (www.traderscity.com), Globalsources (www.globalsources.com), and Alibaba (www.alibaba.com).

In *functional exchanges*, needed services such as temporary help or extra office space are traded on an "as-needed" basis. For example, Employease (www.employease.com) can find temporary labor by searching employers in its Employease Network.

BEFORE *YOU GO ON . . .*

1. Briefly differentiate between the sell-side marketplace and the buy-side marketplace.

2. Briefly differentiate among vertical exchanges, horizontal exchanges, and functional exchanges.

Apply the Concept 9.3

Background Many businesses today engage in both B2B and B2C. As is described in this text, in a B2B relationship the customer is another business, but in B2C the customer is the end consumer. The methodologies for managing and engaging these two different customers are very different. Therefore, the customer relationship management (CRM) tools used must serve different purposes on the B2C side (many customers) than the B2B side (few large customers).

Activity Go to http://www.wiley.com/go/rainer/applytheconcept and click on the link provided for Apply the Concept 9.3. It will take you to a Web site that discusses the differences between B2C and B2B. Also read over the second article linked on the Apply the Concept page of links. Once you feel like you have a good grasp on the difference, search the Web for some different CRM tools that support B2C and B2B.

Imagine that your senior marketing manager has created a task force to select a CRM tool. You operate in a B2C environment, but the options the manager has given the task force to choose between are all B2B software packages! Write an e-mail that delicately shows the manager the difference between these two and that explains that the products he/she has selected will not work for your company. Be careful how you say it—managers do not like to hear that they are wrong!

Submit your e-mail to your professor.

Quiz questions are assignable in WileyPLUS, and available on the Book Companion Site at http://www.wiley.com/college/rainer.

RUBY'S CLUB QUESTIONS

1. Ruby's suppliers have offered electronic data processing (EDP) for years. However, Ruben and Lisa have always placed their orders via the telephone. How might EDP help them?

2. Should they continue with B2B business as usual or go ahead and upgrade now? What data might be available for them via EDP that they do not currently have access to?

9.4 Ethical and Legal Issues in E-Business

Technological innovation often forces a society to reexamine and modify its ethical standards. In many cases, the new standards are incorporated into law. In this section, you will learn about two important ethical considerations—privacy and job loss—as well as various legal issues arising from the practice of e-business.

Ethical Issues

Many of the ethical and global issues related to IT also apply to e-business. Here you will learn about two basic issues: privacy and job loss.

By making it easier to store and transfer personal information, e-business presents some threats to privacy. First, most electronic payment systems know who the buyers are. It may be necessary, then, to protect the buyers' identities. Businesses frequently use encryption to provide this protection.

Another major privacy issue is tracking. For example, individuals' activities on the Internet can be tracked by cookies (discussed in Chapter 7). Cookies store your tracking history on your personal computer's hard drive, and any time you revisit a certain Web site, the server recognizes the cookie. In response, antivirus software packages routinely search for potentially harmful cookies.

In addition to compromising individual privacy, the use of EC may eliminate the need for some of a company's employees, as well as brokers and agents. The manner in which these unneeded workers, especially employees, are treated can raise ethical issues: How should the company handle the layoffs? Should companies be required to retrain employees for new positions? If not, how should the company compensate or otherwise assist the displaced workers?

Legal and Ethical Issues Specific to E-Commerce

Many legal issues are related specifically to e-commerce. When buyers and sellers do not know one another and cannot even see one another, there is a chance that dishonest people will commit fraud and other crimes. During the first few years of EC, the public witnessed many such crimes. These illegal actions ranged from creating a virtual bank that disappeared along with the investors' deposits to manipulating stock prices on the Internet. Unfortunately, fraudulent activities on the Internet are increasing. In the following section, you explore some of the major legal issues that are specific to e-commerce.

Fraud on the Internet. Internet fraud has grown even faster than Internet use itself. In one case, stock promoters falsely spread positive rumors about the prospects of the companies they touted in order to boost the stock price. In other cases, the information provided might have been true, but the promoters did not disclose that they were paid to talk up the companies. Stock promoters specifically target small investors who are lured by the promise of fast profits.

Stocks are only one of many areas where swindlers are active. Auctions are especially conducive to fraud, by both sellers and buyers. Other types of fraud include selling bogus investments and setting up phantom business opportunities. Because of the growing use of e-mail, financial criminals now have access to many more people. The U.S. Federal Trade Commission (FTC, www.ftc.gov) regularly publishes examples of scams that are most likely to be spread via e-mail or to be found on the Web. Later in this section, you will see some ways in which consumers and sellers can protect themselves from online fraud.

Domain Names. Another legal issue is competition over domain names. Domain names are assigned by central nonprofit organizations that check for conflicts and possible infringement of trademarks. Obviously, companies that sell goods and services over the Internet want customers to be able to find them easily. In general, the closer the domain name matches the company's name, the easier the company is to locate.

A domain name is considered legal when the person or business who owns the name has operated a legitimate business under that name for some time. Companies such as Christian Dior, Nike, Deutsche Bank, and even Microsoft have had to fight or pay to get the domain name that corresponds to their company's name. Consider the case of Delta Air Lines. Delta originally could not obtain the Internet domain name delta.com because Delta Faucet had purchased it first. Delta Faucet had been in business under that name since 1954 and therefore had a legitimate business interest in the domain name. Delta Air Lines had to settle for delta-airlines.com until it bought the domain name from Delta Faucet. Delta Faucet is now at deltafaucet.com. Several cases of disputed domain names are already in court.

Cybersquatting. **Cybersquatting** refers to the practice of registering or using domain names for the purpose of profiting from the goodwill or the trademark that belongs to someone else. The Anti-Cybersquatting Consumer Protection Act (1999) permits trademark owners in the United States to sue for damages in such cases.

However, some practices that could be considered cybersquatting are not illegal, although they may well be unethical. Perhaps the more common of these practices is "domain tasting." Domain tasting lets registrars profit from the complex money trail of pay-per-click advertising. The practice can be traced back to the policies of the organization responsible for regulating Web names, the Internet Corporation for Assigned Names and Numbers (ICANN) (www.icann.org) (see Figure 9.9). In 2000, ICANN established the "create grace period," a five-day period during which a company or person can claim a domain name and then return it for a full refund of the $6 registry fee. ICANN implemented this policy to allow someone who mistyped a

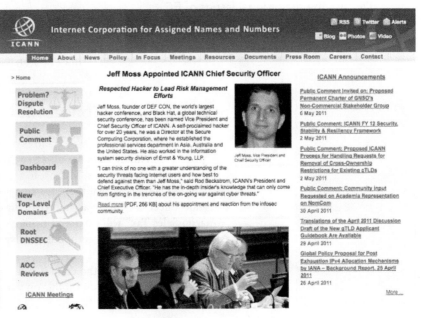

Figure 9.9 Internet Corporation for Assigned Names and Numbers (ICANN) Web site (*Source*: www.icann.org).

domain to return it without cost. In some cases, companies engage in cybersquatting by registering domain names that are very similar to their competitors' domain names in order to generate traffic from people who misspell Web addresses.

Domain tasters exploit this policy by claiming Internet domains for five days at no cost. These domain names frequently resemble those of prominent companies and organizations. The tasters then jam these domains full of advertisements that come from Yahoo! and Google. Because this process involves zero risk and 100 percent profit margins, domain tasters register millions of domain names every day—some of them over and over again. Experts estimate that registrants ultimately purchase less than 2 percent of the sites they sample. In the vast majority of cases, they use the domain names for only a few days to generate quick profits.

Taxes and Other Fees. In offline sales, most states and localities tax business transactions that are conducted within their jurisdiction. The most obvious example is sales taxes. Federal, state, and local authorities now are scrambling to create some type of taxation policy for e-business. This problem is particularly complex for interstate and international e-commerce. For example, some people claim that the state in which the *seller* is located deserves the entire sales tax (in some countries, it is a value-added tax, or VAT). Others contend that the state in which the *server* is located also should receive some of the tax revenues.

In addition to the sales tax, there is a question about where—and in some cases, whether—electronic sellers should pay business license taxes, franchise fees, gross-receipts taxes, excise taxes, privilege taxes, and utility taxes. Furthermore, how should tax collection be controlled? Legislative efforts to impose taxes on e-commerce are opposed by an organization named the Internet Freedom Fighters. So far, their efforts have been successful. As of mid-2011, the United States and several other countries had placed a ban on imposing a sales tax on business conducted on the Internet. In addition, buyers were exempt from any tax on Internet access.

Copyright. Recall from Chapter 6 that intellectual property is protected by copyright laws and cannot be used freely. This point is significant because many people mistakenly believe that once they purchase a piece of software, they have the right to share it with others. In fact, what they have bought is the right to *use* the software, not the right to *distribute* it. That right remains with the copyright holder. Similarly, copying material from Web sites without permission is a violation of copyright laws. Protecting intellectual property rights in e-commerce is extremely difficult, however, because it involves hundreds of millions of people in some 200 countries with differing copyright laws who have access to billions of Web pages.

BEFORE *YOU GO ON . . .*

1. List and explain some ethical issues in EC.
2. Discuss the major legal issues of EC.
3. Describe buyer protection and seller protection in EC.

Apply the Concept 9.4

Background Amazon.com is a well-known online retailer. In fact, it is one of a kind in many ways. It failed to turn a profit for many years and now competes with Apple, Google, and Microsoft, some of the biggest names in the tech sector.

But did you know that there is a huge controversy surrounding Amazon? The retailer does not collect sales tax in all states. No big deal, right? Not exactly. A quick Web search for "Amazon Sales Tax" will no doubt bring you up to speed quickly on the issue. Of course, Amazon sees this as their competitive advantage and has used its power to influence state governments.

On the other side of the coin, if you purchase something online and do not pay sales tax, you are supposed to submit this on your income tax statement and pay taxes then. But do you?

Activity Go ahead and search the Web to see if Amazon collects sales tax in your state. If the company doesn't, it is likely that the issue has been raised. How do you feel if Amazon does have fulfillment centers in your state (therefore it operates in your state and should collect sales tax) and it charges you tax when it doesn't charge others? What if a business in your state uses Amazon's fulfillment services and does not collect sales tax? Should Amazon's partnership with the company in your state require it to collect tax on every purchase in your state?

Deliverable

Think all of this over for a while. Taxes are an issue that will not go away soon and technology is only going to make this situation more and more difficult as we move forward. Ultimately, write a letter to your congressman on this issue. Submit your letter to your professor.

Quiz questions are assignable in WileyPLUS, and available on the Book Companion Site at http://www.wiley.com/college/rainer.

RUBY'S CLUB QUESTIONS

1. What ethical and legal information can you find on PayPal's site?
2. If Ruby's uses PayPal, who do you think would be responsible for any errors? What should Ruben and Lisa do if PayPal's Code of Ethics is different from what they consider ethical?

What's in  for ME?

FOR THE ACCOUNTING MAJOR

Accounting personnel are involved in several EC activities. Designing the ordering system and its relationship with inventory management requires accounting attention. Billing and payments are also accounting activities, as are determining cost and profit allocation. Replacing paper documents with electronic means will affect many of the accountant's tasks, especially the auditing of EC activities and systems. Finally, building a cost-benefit and cost-justification system to determine which products/services to take online and creating a chargeback system are critical to the success of EC.

FOR THE FINANCE MAJOR

The worlds of banking, securities and commodities markets, and other financial services are being reengineered because of EC. Online securities trading and its supporting infrastructure are growing more rapidly than any other EC activity. Many innovations already in place are changing the rules of economic and financial incentives for financial analysts and managers. Online banking, for example, does not recognize state boundaries, and it may create a new framework for financing global trades. Public financial information is now accessible in seconds. These innovations will dramatically change the manner in which finance personnel operate.

FOR THE MARKETING MAJOR

A major revolution in marketing and sales is taking place because of EC. Perhaps its most obvious feature is the transition from a physical to a virtual marketplace. Equally important, however, is the radical transformation to one-on-one advertising and sales and to customized and interactive marketing. Marketing channels are being combined, eliminated, or recreated. The EC revolution is creating new products and markets and significantly altering existing ones. Digitization of products and services also has implications for marketing and sales. The direct producer-to-consumer channel is expanding rapidly and is fundamentally changing the nature of customer service. As the battle for customers intensifies, marketing and sales personnel are becoming the most critical success factor in many organizations. Online marketing can be a blessing to one company and a curse to another.

FOR THE
PRODUCTION/OPERATIONS MANAGEMENT MAJOR

EC is changing the manufacturing system from product-push mass production to order-pull mass customization. This change requires a robust supply chain, information support, and reengineering of processes that involve suppliers and other business partners. Suppliers can use extranets to monitor and replenish inventories without the need for constant reorders. In addition, the Internet and intranets help reduce cycle times. Many production/operations problems that have persisted for years, such as complex scheduling and excess inventories, are being solved rapidly with the use of Web technologies. Companies can now use external and internal networks to find and manage manufacturing operations in other countries much more easily. Also, the Web is reengineering procurement by helping companies conduct electronic bids for parts and subassemblies, thus reducing cost. All in all, the job of the progressive production/operations manager is closely tied in with e-commerce.

FOR THE
HUMAN RESOURCES MANAGEMENT MAJOR

HR majors need to understand the new labor markets and the impacts of EC on old labor markets. Also, the HR department may use EC tools for such functions as procuring office supplies. Moreover, becoming knowledgeable about new government online initiatives and online training is critical. In addition, HR personnel must be familiar with the major legal issues related to EC and employment.

FOR THE MIS MAJOR

The MIS function is responsible for providing the information technology infrastructure necessary for electronic commerce to function. In particular, this infrastructure includes the company's networks, intranets, and extranets. The MIS function is also responsible for ensuring that electronic commerce transactions are secure.

SUMMARY

1. **Describe the six common types of electronic commerce.**

   In *business-to-consumer* (B2C) electronic commerce, the sellers are organizations and the buyers are individuals. In *business-to-business* (B2B) electronic commerce, the sellers and the buyers are businesses. In *consumer-to-consumer* (C2C) electronic commerce, an individual sells products or services to other individuals. In *business-to-employee* (B2E) electronic commerce, an organization uses EC internally to provide information and services to its employees. *E-government* is the use of Internet technology in general

   and e-commerce in particular to deliver information and public services to citizens (called government-to-citizen or G2C EC) and business partners and suppliers (called government-to-business or G2B EC). *Mobile commerce* refers to e-commerce that is conducted entirely in a wireless environment. We leave the examples of each type to you.

2. **Describe the various online services of business-to-consumer (B2C) commerce, providing specific examples of each.**

Electronic banking, also known as cyberbanking, involves conducting various banking activities from home, at a place of business, or on the road instead of at a physical bank location.

Online securities trading involves buying and selling securities over the Web.

Online job matching over the Web offers a promising environment for job seekers and for companies searching for hard-to-find employees. Thousands of companies and government agencies advertise available positions, accept resumes, and take applications via the Internet.

Online travel services allow you to purchase airline tickets, reserve hotel rooms, and rent cars. Most sites also offer a fare-tracker feature that sends you e-mail messages about low-cost flights. The Internet is an ideal place to plan, explore, and arrange almost any trip economically.

Online advertising over the Web makes the advertising process media-rich, dynamic, and interactive.

We leave the examples to you.

3. **Describe the three business models for business-to-business electronic commerce.**

In the *sell-side marketplace* model, organizations attempt to sell their products or services to other organizations electronically from their own private e-marketplace Web site and/or from a third-party Web site. Sellers such as Dell Computer (www.dellauction.com) use sell-side auctions extensively. In addition to auctions from their own Web sites, organizations can use third-party auction sites, such as eBay, to liquidate items.

The *buy-side marketplace* is a model in which organizations attempt to buy needed products or services from other organizations electronically.

E-marketplaces, in which there are many sellers and many buyers, are called *public exchanges*, or just exchanges. Public exchanges are open to all business organizations. They frequently are owned and operated by a third party. There are three basic types of public exchanges: vertical, horizontal, and functional. *Vertical exchanges* connect buyers and sellers in a given industry. *Horizontal exchanges* connect buyers and sellers across many industries. In *functional exchanges*, needed services such as temporary help or extra office space are traded on an "as-needed" basis.

4. **Identify the ethical and legal issues related to electronic commerce, providing examples.**

E-business presents some threats to privacy. First, most electronic payment systems know who the buyers are. It may be necessary, then, to protect the buyers' identities with encryption. Another major privacy issue is tracking, where individuals' activities on the Internet can be tracked by cookies.

The use of EC may eliminate the need for some of a company's employees, as well as brokers and agents. The manner in which these unneeded workers, especially employees, are treated can raise ethical issues: How should the company handle the layoffs? Should companies be required to retrain employees for new positions? If not, how should the company compensate or otherwise assist the displaced workers?

We leave the examples to you.

>>> CHAPTER GLOSSARY

auction A competitive process in which either a seller solicits consecutive bids from buyers or a buyer solicits bids from sellers, and prices are determined dynamically by competitive bidding.

banner Electronic billboards, which typically contain a short text or graphical message to promote a product or a vendor.

brick-and-mortar organizations Organizations in which the product, the process, and the delivery agent are all physical.

business model The method by which a company generates revenue to sustain itself.

business-to-business electronic commerce (B2B) Electronic commerce in which both the sellers and the buyers are business organizations.

business-to-consumer electronic commerce (B2C) Electronic commerce in which the sellers are organizations and the buyers are individuals; also known as e-tailing.

business-to-employee electronic commerce (B2E) An organization using electronic commerce internally to provide information and services to its employees.

buy-side marketplace B2B model in which organizations buy needed products or services from other organizations electronically, often through a reverse auction.

channel conflict The alienation of existing distributors when a company decides to sell to customers directly online.

clicks-and-mortar organizations Organizations that do business in both the physical and digital dimensions.

consumer-to-consumer electronic commerce (C2C) Electronic commerce in which both the buyer and the seller are individuals (not businesses).

cyberbanking Various banking activities conducted electronically from home, a business, or on the road instead of at a physical bank location; also known as *electronic banking*.

cybersquatting Registering domain names in the hope of selling them later at a higher price.

disintermediation Elimination of intermediaries in electronic commerce.

e-government The use of electronic commerce to deliver information and public services to citizens, business partners, and suppliers of government entities, and those working in the public sector.

electronic business (e-business) A broader definition of electronic commerce, including buying and selling of goods and services, and servicing customers, collaborating with business partners, conducting e-learning, and conducting electronic transactions within an organization.

electronic commerce (EC or e-commerce) The process of buying, selling, transferring, or exchanging products, services, or information via computer networks, including the Internet.

electronic mall A collection of individual shops under one Internet address; also known as a *cybermall* or an *e-mall*.

electronic marketplace A virtual market space on the Web where many buyers and many sellers conduct electronic business activities.

electronic payment systems Computer-based systems that allow customers to pay for goods and services electronically, rather than writing a check or using cash.

electronic retailing (e-tailing) The direct sale of products and services through storefronts or electronic malls, usually designed around an electronic catalog format and/or auctions.

electronic storefront The Web site of a single company, with its own Internet address, at which orders can be placed.

e-procurement Purchasing by using electronic support.

e-wallets Software components in which a user stores secured personal and credit card information for one-click reuse.

exchanges (see **public exchanges**)

forward auctions Auctions that sellers use as a selling channel to many potential buyers; the highest bidder wins the items.

group purchasing The aggregation of purchasing orders from many buyers so that a volume discount can be obtained.

mobile commerce (m-commerce) Electronic commerce conducted in a wireless environment.

multichanneling A process in which a company integrates its online and offline channels.

permission marketing Method of marketing that asks consumers to give their permission to voluntarily accept online advertising and e-mail.

person-to-person payments A form of electronic cash that enables the transfer of funds between two individuals, or between an individual and a business, without the use of a credit card.

pop-under ad An advertisement that is automatically launched by some trigger and appears underneath the active window.

pop-up ad An advertisement that is automatically launched by some trigger and appears in front of the active window.

public exchanges (or exchanges) Electronic marketplaces in which there are many sellers and many buyers, and entry is open to all; frequently owned and operated by a third party.

reverse auctions Auctions in which one buyer, usually an organization, seeks to buy a product or a service, and suppliers submit bids; the lowest bidder wins.

sell-side marketplace B2B model in which organizations sell to other organizations from their own private e-marketplace and/or from a third-party site.

smart cards Cards that contains a microprocessor (chip) that enables the card to store a considerable amount of information (including stored funds) and to conduct processing.

spamming Indiscriminate distribution of e-mail without the receiver's permission.

stored-value money cards A form of electronic cash on which a fixed amount of prepaid money is stored; the amount is reduced each time the card is used.

viral marketing Online word-of-mouth marketing.

virtual banks Banking institutions dedicated solely to Internet transactions.

virtual (or pure play) organizations Organizations in which the product, the process, and the delivery agent are all digital.

>>> DISCUSSION QUESTIONS

1. Discuss the major limitations of e-commerce. Which of these limitations are likely to disappear? Why?

2. Discuss the reasons for having multiple EC business models.

3. Distinguish between business-to-business forward auctions and buyers' bids for RFQs.

4. Discuss the benefits to sellers and buyers of a B2B exchange.

5. What are the major benefits of G2C electronic commerce?

6. Discuss the various ways to pay online in B2C. Which method(s) would you prefer and why?

7. Why is order fulfillment in B2C considered difficult?

8. Discuss the reasons for EC failures.

9. Should Mr. Coffee sell coffeemakers online? *Hint:* Take a look at the discussion of channel conflict in this chapter.

10. In some cases, individuals engage in cybersquatting so that they can sell the domain names to companies expensively. In other cases, companies engage in cybersquatting by registering domain names that are very similar to their competitors' domain names in order to generate traffic from people who misspell Web addresses. Discuss each practice in terms of its ethical nature and legality. Is there a difference between the two practices? Support your answer.

1. Assume you are interested in buying a car. You can find information about cars at numerous Web sites. Access five Web sites for information about new and used cars, financing, and insurance. Decide which car you want to buy. Configure your car by going to the car manufacturer's Web site. Finally, try to find the car from www.autobytel.com. What information is most supportive of your decision-making process? Write a report about your experience.

2. Compare the various electronic payment methods. Specifically, collect information from the vendors cited in this chapter and find additional vendors using Google.com. Pay attention to security level, speed, cost, and convenience.

3. Conduct a study on selling diamonds and gems online. Access such sites as www.bluenile.com, www.diamond.com, www.thaigem.com, www.tiffany.com, and www.jewelryexchange.com.

   a. What features do these sites use to educate buyers about gemstones?

   b. How do these sites attract buyers?

   c. How do these sites increase customers' trust in online purchasing?

   d. What customer service features do these sites provide?

4. Access www.nacha.org. What is NACHA? What is its role? What is the ACH? Who are the key participants in an ACH e-payment? Describe the "pilot" projects currently underway at ACH.

5. Access www.espn.com. Identify at least five different ways the site generates revenue.

6. Access www.queendom.com. Examine its offerings and try some of them. What type of electronic commerce is this? How does this Web site generate revenue?

7. Access www.ediets.com. Prepare a list of all the services the company provides. Identify its revenue model.

8. Access www.theknot.com. Identify the site's revenue sources.

9. Access www.mint.com. Identify the site's revenue model. What are the risks of giving this Web site your credit and debit card numbers, as well as your bank account number?

10. Research the case of www.nissan.com. Is Uzi Nissan cybersquatting? Why or why not? Support your answer. How is Nissan (the car company) reacting to the www.nissan.com Web site?

11. Enter www.alibaba.com. Identify the site's capabilities. Look at the site's private trading room. Write a report. How can such a site help a person who is making a purchase?

12. Enter www.grubhub.com. Explore the site. Why is the site so successful? Could you start a competing site? Why or why not?

13. Enter www.dell.com, go to "Desktops," and configure a system. Register to "My Cart" (no obligation). What calculators are used there? What are the advantages of this process as compared with buying a computer in a physical store? What are the disadvantages?

14. Enter www.checkfree.com and www.lmlpayment.com to identify their services. Prepare a report.

15. Access various travel sites such as www.travelocity.com, www.orbitz.com, www.expedia.com, www.kayak.com, and www.pinpoint.com. Compare these Web sites for ease of use and usefulness. Note differences among the sites. If you ask each site for the itinerary, which one gives you the best information and the best deals?

16. Access www.outofservice.com, and answer the musical taste and personality survey. When you have finished, click on "Results" and see what your musical tastes say about your personality. How accurate are the findings about you?

17. **Tips for Safe Electronic Shopping**

    - Look for reliable brand names at sites such as Walmart Online, Disney Online, and Amazon. Before purchasing, make sure that the site is authentic by entering the site directly and not from an unverified link.

    - Search any unfamiliar selling site for the company's address and phone and fax numbers. Call up and quiz the employees about the seller.

    - Check out the vendor with the local Chamber of Commerce or Better Business Bureau (www.bbbonline.org). Look for seals of authenticity such as TRUSTe.

    - Investigate how secure the seller's site is by examining the security procedures and by reading the posted privacy policy.

    - Examine the money-back guarantees, warranties, and service agreements.

    - Compare prices with those in regular stores. Too-low prices are too good to be true and some catch is probably involved.

    - Ask friends what they know. Find testimonials and endorsements on community Web sites and well-known bulletin boards.

- Find out what your rights are in case of a dispute. Consult consumer protection agencies and the National Consumer League's Fraud Center (www. fraud.org).

- Check Consumerworld (www.consumerworld.org) for a collection of useful resources.
- For many types of products, www.resellerratings.com is a useful resource.

>>> COLLABORATION EXERCISE

Background

Converting a business from bricks-and-mortar to e-business is a rather complicated task. At the turn of the 20th century (the early 1900s) Sears & Roebuck was the dominant force to deal with. This company's business model (mailing out a catalog, receiving payment and orders, processing, fulfillment) was years ahead of the local "general store." Search Wikipedia for more information on the history of Sears and to better understand the mail-order catalog model.

Activity

Divide your team into the following positions: consumer, order processing, accounts receivable, product fulfillment, shipping, inventory, and sales. Now given your responsibility, work through a catalog order that includes five different items. To make it easier, imagine that full payment is received. Begin with the consumer and have each person write down on a piece of paper the information each needs at every stage. For example, the consumer will hand two pieces of paper to the order processing person: one will be the order and the other will be the payment. Then the order processing person will notify others in the group by creating a new piece of paper with new information. They will also keep a copy for themselves. As this order moves through the "company," you will see how much paper and information is generated by traditional business.

Deliverable

As a team, write a summary of your experience that compares e-commerce to traditional commerce. Did anyone make a mistake when transferring the information? How could computer information systems (and therefore e-commerce) have helped make the process flow better?

Submit your paper to your instructor.

CLOSING **CASE 1** > The Flash Crash

THE PROBLEM >>>

On May 6, 2010, the U.S. stock market experienced a crash in which the Dow Jones Industrial Average lost almost 9 percent of its total value, only to recover those losses within minutes. It was the second-largest point swing—1,010.14 points—and the biggest one-day point decline—998.5 points—on an intraday basis in the history of Dow Jones. This crash became known as the Flash Crash.

That day, the market was already under pressure as a result of a massive debt crisis in Greece. Then, an automated sale of a large block of futures touched off a chain reaction of events. A futures contract is an agreement, traded on an exchange, to buy or sell assets—particularly commodities or shares of stock—at a fixed price but to be delivered and paid for later. After the automated sale, a mutual fund's computer program began selling $4.1 billion of futures contracts.

Normally, a sale of this size would take place over as many as 5 hours. In this case, however, the sell algorithm installed on the mutual fund's computer placed 75,000 contracts on the market in 20 minutes. The algorithm was programmed to execute the trade "without regard to price or time," which meant that it continued to sell even as prices rapidly dropped.

Many of the contracts sold by the algorithm were purchased by high-frequency traders (HFTs). HFTs are computerized traders who buy and sell at high speed. They account for a large percentage of overall trading in today's markets. The HFT programs detected that they had amassed excessive "long" positions, meaning that they purchased a large amount of stock with the expectation that its price would rise. They immediately began to sell these stocks aggressively, which in turn caused the mutual fund's algorithm to accelerate its selling. As the HFT and mutual fund programs traded contracts back and forth, they created a "hot potato" effect, where contracts changed hands 27,000 times in 14 seconds. Despite this frenzied trading, however, only 200 contracts were actually bought or sold. In most cases, the same contracts moved back and forth between the mutual funds and the HFTs in microseconds.

The only buy orders originated from automated systems, which were submitting orders known as "stub quotes." Stub quotes are offers to buy stocks at prices so low that the purchasers are unlikely to ever be the only buyers of that stock. However, during the flash crash, the stub quotes were the only offers from buyers. When the only offer to buy available is a penny-priced stub quote, a market order, by definition, will buy the stock at that price. In this respect, automated trading systems will follow their algorithms regardless of the outcome. This process caused shares of some prominent companies, such as Procter & Gamble and Accenture, to trade down as low as a penny per share. Significantly, human involvement probably would have prevented these orders from executing at absurdly low prices.

The U.S. Securities and Exchange Commission (SEC) responded to the crash by instituting circuit breakers on all stocks in the S&P 500 stock index. Circuit breakers halt trading in a stock for 5 minutes if the price moves by 10 percent or more in a 5-minute period. After a short time, the SEC expanded the circuit breakers to include a broader range of stocks. However, no one knows for sure if the circuit breakers can prevent future "flash crashes."

<<< **A STOPGAP SOLUTION**

Lawmakers are also proposing another possible solution: enacting a small tax on each equity trade. Such a tax would likely discourage some high-frequency trading, slow the market's overall pace, and raise billions of dollars in revenue for the federal government. Some of the tax revenues could be used to enhance the SEC's monitoring efforts.

The circuit breakers are now in place as a (hopeful) preventative measure for future market crashes. However, the Flash Crash raises a larger question about the stock market. In recent years, the market has grown exponentially faster and more diverse than it was before. The primary venue for stock trading is no longer the New York Stock Exchange, but rather computer servers run by companies around the world. This diversity has made stock trading cheaper, which benefits both institutional and individual investors. Unfortunately, it has also made it more difficult to ensure an orderly market.

<<< **THE RESULTS**

One study says flash events actually happen routinely, at speeds so fast that they do not register on regular market records. Such flash events could have troubling consequences for market stability. The study analyzed 5 years of stock market trades between 2006 and 2011 that occurred faster than 950-milliseconds, and found 18,520 crashes and spikes. These trades happened so quickly that human traders could not react. In addition, those trades fell into patterns that did not fit market patterns observed at slower time scales. The study concluded that ultrahigh-frequency trading has created a new world, one where the usual rules do not apply and the computer algorithms that run the trading are only dimly understood by humans (even those humans who created the algorithms).

Circuit breakers or not, traders are still trying to find ways to trade even faster. One new computer chip built specifically for high-frequency trading can make trades in .000000074 seconds, and a proposed $300 million transatlantic cable is being built just to shave .0006 seconds off transaction times between New York City and London.

A major danger for the financial industry is that regulators, politicians, and industry leaders—already distracted by the major challenge of reforming Wall Street in the wake of the broader credit crisis of 2008—will shrug off the Flash Crash as an aberration requiring no fundamental rethinking of how human, machine, and market interact. Left unchecked, Wall Street's computer models will remain susceptible to unpredictable disasters, and there is every possibility that flash crashes will happen again.

Sources: Compiled from B. Keim, "Nanosecond Trading Could Make Markets Go Haywire," *Wired*, February 16, 2012; M. Millar, "'Lightning Fast Future Traders Working in Nanoseconds," *BBC News*, November 17, 2011; L. Salamone, "On Wall Street, the Race to Zero Continues," *HPC Wire*, September 27, 2011; "New $300 Million Transatlantic Cable Makes Stock Trades 6 Milliseconds Faster," *Public Intelligence*, September 14, 2011;

E. Macbride, "Flash Crash Update: Why the Multi-Asset Meltdown Is a Real Possibility," *Forbes*, March 2, 2011; T. McCabe, "When the Speed of Light Is Too Slow: Trading at the Edge," Kurzweilai.net, November 11, 2010; Spicer, J. "Special Report: Globally, the Flash Crash Is No Flash in the Pan," *Reuters*, October 15, 2010; E. Lambert, "The Truth About the Flash Crash," *Forbes*, October 1, 2010; S. Schaefer, "Dissecting the Flash Crash," *Forbes*, October 1, 2010; L. Mearian, "Regulators Blame Computer Algorithm for Stock Market 'Flash Crash,'" *Computerworld*, October 1, 2010; G. Bowley, "Lone $4.1 Billion Sale Led to 'Flash Crash' in May," *New York Times*, October 1, 2010; S. Patterson, "Letting the Machines Decide," *Wall Street Journal*, July 13, 2010; N. Mehla, "The Machines That Ate the Market," *Bloomberg BusinessWeek*, May 20, 2010; S. Patterson, "How the 'Flash Crash' Echoed Black Monday," *Wall Street Journal*, May 17, 2010; L. Harris, "How to Prevent Another Trading Panic," *Wall Street Journal*, May 12, 2010; E. Wyatt, "Regulators Vow to Find Way to Stop Rapid Dives," *New York Times*, May 10, 2010; S. Patterson and T. Lauricella, "Did a Big Bet Help Trigger 'Black Swan' Stock Swoon?" *Wall Street Journal*, May 10, 2010; A. Lucchetti, "Exchanges Point Fingers Over Human Hands," *Wall Street Journal*, May 9, 2010.

Questions

1. Do you think information technology has made it easier to do business? Or has IT only raised the bar on what is required to be able to do business in the 21st century? Support your answer with specific examples.

2. With the rise of electronic commerce, what do you think will happen to those without computer skills, Internet access, computers, smart phones, and so on? Will they be able to survive and advance by hard work?

CLOSING **CASE 2** > Kickbucks to Shop!

THE PROBLEM >>>

The biggest challenge facing retailers in America is getting people to enter their stores. Conversion rates (converting shoppers into customers who make a purchase) in the virtual world (online shopping) are between 0.5 percent and 3 percent. Conversion rates in the physical world range from 20 percent to as high as 95 percent. So, if foot traffic is so important, then why don't companies reward people for visiting their stores? The answer is that they don't even know that you came through the door.

THE IT >>>
SOLUTION

To solve this disconnect, Cyriac Roeding built a smartphone-optimized rewards program that offers customers discounts and promotions simply for entering retail stores—a model he describes as "the physical-world equivalent of an online click." His company, Shopkick (www. shopkick.com), through its Shopkick mobile application, delivers "kickbucks" rewards to all registered iPhone and Android users who enter a participating retail location. Kickbucks can be collected and redeemed across any partner store and turned into gift cards, discounts, song downloads, movie tickets, Facebook Credits, or even charitable donations.

Shopkick does not rely on GPS triangulation. Instead, the company uses a patent-pending device located in each participating store. The box, which costs retailers less than $100 and is roughly the size of a paperback book, plugs into any power outlet. It emits an audio signal that is undetectable to the human ear, but is automatically picked up by a smartphone's internal microphone, thereby qualifying the owner of that smartphone to earn kickbucks. Because the audio signal's range is limited to the perimeter of the store, users must physically enter the location in order for their phones to pick up the signal. Further, because detection occurs via the mobile device, consumers retain control over the privacy of their presence information.

Retailers decide how many kickbucks a shopper receives for entering their businesses. Retailers can leverage the Shopkick app to deliver special offers, such as discounts on specific merchandise.

Shopkick also extends beyond retail. In partnership with brands including Kraft Foods and Procter & Gamble, Shopkick offers smaller rewards for scanning product bar codes, which extends the network to about 230,000 additional stores nationwide.

Shopkick receives a small commission fee for each kickbuck a customer earns. If a shopper makes a purchase after using the app, Shopkick claims a percentage of that transaction as well.

After reading this case, it may appear to you that Shopkick is similar to Loopt (acquired by Green Dot, www.greendot.com), and Foursquare (https://foursquare.com). However, Shopkick differs from these sites in that it is not a social networking tool. Shopkick is an app built around the act of shopping, not around letting your friends know where you are.

<<< THE RESULTS

Over 1,000 individual U.S. retail outlets and over 100 shopping centers now employ Shopkick's services. Shopkick has partnered with Best Buy, Macy's, Target, Sports Authority, Crate & Barrel, and the mall operator company Simon Property Group. Retailers credit Shopkick with increasing their customer traffic.

For example, sporting goods chain Sports Authority has deployed the app in more than 100 of its U.S. locations. In late 2010, the chain doubled, and sometimes tripled, kickbucks rewards to determine the potential effect on walk-ins. The promotion increased Shopkick user walk-in growth from 50 to 70 percent.

Shopkick is expanding the core capabilities of its model. As the app improves, retailer offers will probably become more sophisticated as well, with kickbucks awards and promotions eventually targeting consumers according to age, gender, geography, shopping frequency, or purchase history.

Sources: E. Lee and B. Evangelista, "Shopkick Rides Surge in Shopping with Cell Phones," *San Francisco Chronicle*, February 1, 2012; T. Geron, "Shopkick Teams Up with Visa for In-Store Rewards," *Forbes*, November 21, 2011; C. Miller, "Visa and Shopkick Give Rewards for Making Purchases," *The New York Times*, November 21, 2011; T. Geron, "Why So Many Shopkick Users 'Walk Around' in Stores," *Forbes*, August 4, 2011; J. Ankeny, "The Rebirth of Retail," *Entrepreneur*, March, 2011; B. Stone and B. Sheridan, "The Retailer's Clever Little Helper," *Bloomberg BusinessWeek*, August 26, 2010; www.shopkick.com, accessed March 21, 2012.

Questions

1. If you were the CEO of Shopkick, in what direction would you expand your service next? Provide specific examples to support your answer.
2. Do you see any potential disadvantages of Shopkick for the consumer? For the retailer? Provide examples to support your answer.
3. As Shopkick's app improves, what effects will tailored offers from retailers have on shopper habits and on the stores making the offers?

RUBY'S CLUB   INTERNSHIP ASSIGNMENT

Determine the type of e-commerce (pure vs. partial) Ruby's Club will engage in. Then look at the tools that PayPal offers through its Business Payment Solutions. Give Ruben and Lisa some feedback on exactly what options they have for their Web site based on your decisions and research. Give examples of how other businesses in the same category (again pure vs. partial) conduct business. How can PayPal support this model? What benefits will Ruby and Lisa receive from using PayPal? What potential ethical and legal problems might they face?

Finally, provide instructions on how they can implement this payment mechanism. Determine which of the business solutions is the best for Ruben and Lisa's needs and gather the instructions on how to implement this system. Finally, let them know the percentage PayPal will take from each transaction, but present it as an opportunity cost to quickly and safely provide e-commerce on their site. Be sure to reference any training materials payPal may offer.

SPREADSHEET ACTIVITY: BUILDING CHARTS AND GRAPHS

Objective: Graphs and charts are helpful tools within most spreadsheet applications. This activity will place you in a business scenario where graphs and charts are extremely helpful in determining customer patterns and preferences.

Chapter Connection: E-business and e-commerce are much more than simply buying and selling via the Internet. Amazon.com is a perfect example of a company that has leveraged the power of the Web to make product suggestions to customers and help them find the right product. This activity builds on this concept and applies spreadsheet tools to help provide this type of business data and make it useful even in a traditional bricks-and-mortar scenario.

Activity: Go to Amazon.com (or go to http://www.wiley.com/go/rainer/spreadsheet and click on the link to Amazon there) and search for a Coleman Sundome 10 X 10 tent. At the time of this writing, customers are shown items that are frequently purchased with the tent, items that customers often buy with it (but not as frequently as the other group), and finally a list of related products. This type of information is very helpful to consumers, especially when combined with customer ratings.

Another type of feedback provided by Amazon.com is the list of items that are most frequently purchased after shopping for a particular item. This type of information is invaluable to consumers and can only be provided in an online environment. Walmart cannot tell customers what most people buy when they are standing in the aisle, so consumers are blind and have to make a choice based on either information they found before they arrived or what is said on the box.

Imagine that you work for a small bookstore. You would like to post a chart next to a book showing that it is one of the more popular books purchased or possibly to direct someone to a more popular book (that you also sell). Search Amazon.com for three books (pick your own genre) and find Amazon's "Customers who bought this item also bought" section. You may have to search for more than three books to find this section because it is not listed on every page. Collect the 5-star rating and total number of ratings (4.5/5 stars by 1135 reviewers) for the main book and for the 5 competing books and place it in a spreadsheet. You will use different columns for each of these as shown in the table below. Be sure to also include the data from your original book.

	5-Star Rating	Total Ratings
Main book 1	4.5	568
Customers also bought 1	3.5	789
Customers also bought 2	4.0	156
Customers also bought 3	2.7	45
Customers also bought 4	4.5	9
Customers also bought 5	5	12

Once your data collection is complete, you will have data for each of the three books in a spreadsheet. The table above illustrates what the data may look like for one of these books. Use the tools provided in Microsoft Excel to create at least three different types of charts based on your data. Take each chart and copy and paste it in a Word document that you could place on the shelf in your bookstore to help drive customers to the right product. If you need some help with charts, watch the tutorials that are linked at http://www.wiley.com/go/rainer/spreadsheet.

Deliverable: The final product will be five separate Word documents that the owner of the small bookstore could place on the shelf in front of a product. The chart will show the percentage of Amazon.com customers who buy that product as well as what other books they purchase. The final documents demonstrate how traditional businesses can leverage the power of e-business and e-commerce in their stores with public information.

Discussion Questions:

1. Given the complexity of e-business and e-commerce, is it something that everyone should engage in? Is the future of business to have a Web site and sell everything online? Will there always be a place for traditional brick-and-mortar stores?

2. Online shopping provides many advantages to consumers. Other than the example provided in this exercise, what other ways can you think of that will help traditional businesses leverage the power of online tools for their in-store customers?

Quiz questions are assignable in WileyPLUS, and available on the Book Companion Site at http://www.wiley.com/college/rainer.

DATABASE ACTIVITY: FORMS II

Objective

In this activity, you will learn how to create a three-table form directly, using the Form Wizard, and how to improve the appearance of your forms. You were introduced to forms in the Chapter 8 activity. There, you created three forms: one based on a single table, one based on two tables, and one based on three tables where you had to create a subform yourself to deal with complex table relationships. Here, you will extend what you know to more complex form design issues.

CHAPTER CONNECTION

This chapter of the book is about electronic commerce. E-commerce runs on forms. With the knowledge you will gain here, you will be able to develop forms that need only be connected to the Web and a database to be used in that area.

PREREQUISITES

Chapter 8 activity (Forms I).

Activity

In this activity, which you will find online at http://www.wiley.com/go/rainer/database, you will work with a new database to create more advanced types of forms.

1. Download the **Ch 09 ItemSales** database from http://www.wiley.com/co/rainer/database and open it. A store might use a database like this. It has data on items it sells, their manufacturers, and the distributors from which it gets them. A distributor may supply items from several manufacturers. The relationship map, accessed via the Database Tools ribbon, shows the table relationships.

2. The first form will show all three tables. Open the Form Wizard. From DistTbl, select the distributor's name, city, and state. (You should not have any trouble figuring out the correct column names for these.) From MfrTbl, select the manufacturer's name and country. From ProdTbl, select the item number, name, shipping weight, and selling price. Organize the form by DistTbl and specify "Form with subform(s)."

3. Finish creating the form as you did in the previous activity. Save the form as DistForm. Save its subforms as MfrSubform and ProdSubform. Open it to enter data.

4. You will see that there are two subforms inside the main form here. This is how the Form Wizard creates a three-table form. Although the lower one is not nested physically within the upper one, it behaves as though it is. When you move through the manufacturers supplied by the first distributor, in the upper subform, the lower subform changes to show each manufacturer's products.

5. This form looks exactly as the wizard created it. Now we will change its appearance. Repeat the form creation process, this time naming your form DistForm2, its subforms MfrSubform2 and ProdSubform2. Open it in Layout view to make changes.

Usage Hint: You might wonder, Why not just make a copy of the form? You could. You would have to make copies of the subforms, too. Then, you would have to open the forms and change their source data to refer to the copies. It is easier to create a new set.

6. Let's start with labels:

   (a) The form header shows the form's name in the database, DistForm2. Click on it to edit and change it to "Distributors with Manufacturers and Products" (without quotation marks). This may make its box several lines deep. If it does, drag its right edge with your mouse far enough to the right to fit the header on one line. Then drag its bottom edge up as far as possible without covering any of the text.

   (b) Click in the field names in the top portion of the form and change them to "Distributor," "City" and "State." The original names were chosen for database developers. These names make more sense to the people who will use this form.

   (c) Shrink those fields vertically to one line each.

   (d) If you are used to an earlier version of Access, you may know that you cannot adjust one field without changing the others unless you remove the layout controls. This is no longer necessary in Access 2010. You can adjust the fields now. So, shrink the State field in width until it is about the right size for a few letters. Shrink the City field until it is long enough for a long city name. Then select the State field and its label (click one, then shift-click the other) together so they will move as a unit and position them to the right of the city field.

Usage Hint: It can be hard to get the City and State fields to line up precisely. Design view has a grid to make this easier, but most things are easier done in Layout view. In that view, you can open the form's Property Sheet, under the Arrange ribbon tab. Click a field whose position is OK—say, the City field. Note the value of its Top attribute (under the Property Sheet's Format tab). To align other fields with it, select them, and set their Top to that value.

Another option is to use the alignment tools in the Arrange ribbon in Design view. They are fine, but their behavior can be nonintuitive. Try them if you want. There is an Undo button if you do not like the result.

(e) Edit the labels of the two subforms to read "Manufacturer" and "Product" in full. (This sometimes works better in Design view than in Layout view.) Using the Font tools under either the Format or the Home ribbon tab, make them bold and increase their size to 14 points.

(f) Shrink the fields ProdID and ProdPrice to reasonable widths for their contents. (You have to grab the column divider in the header row, not further down.) Then adjust the subform widths to what is now required. Also, move them up to use some of the space freed up when you put the distributor's city and state on a single line. (Forms that are unnecessarily spread out are hard to use and can take up an annoyingly large amount of screen space when several windows are open.)

(g) Find a picture on the Web and download it. Click Logo in the Format ribbon, navigate to the picture, and select it. It will appear in your form's header. Move it to the right of the text.

(h) Go to Design view if you are not already in it. Click the Rectangle tool in the Controls section of the Design ribbon. (You may have to scroll the set of icons down to see it.) You will see other tools that are not in Layout view, too. Draw a rectangle around all the distributor data at the top of the form.

(i) Switch back to Form view and admire your creation. At work, you might do more. You know about some of the tools you could use. Close the form, saving if prompted.

7. Your third form will be one that a firm could use to review customer orders. Download the **Ch 09 DaffyDonuts** database from http://www.wiley.com/go/rainer/database. It has four tables: customers, products, orders, and line items. You can see their relationships in the relationship map of the database. (It resembles the example in Section 3.3 of the book, minus its supplier table. Its Line Item table is called Ordered Parts there.)

8. Open the Form Wizard and create a form using all four tables. Organize it by customer. Show all the customer information except CustomerID, order date and total, line item quantity, and product name and price. Use Tabular form for the Order subform (the first one), Datasheet form for the line item/product subform (the second).

9. Open the form in Layout view and improve its arrangement as you did earlier.

10. This form could be used by customers. Customers need instructions. To put them on the form, go to Design view. (Layout view will not do this.) Choose either the Label or the Text Box tool from the Design ribbon, the second or third item from the left in the Controls section. The mouse pointer becomes crosshairs. Draw a rectangle in any free space on the form. (You can move form elements to free up space.) Enter any text in it—we are not practicing instruction writing. In Form view, confirm that your "instructions" show up.

11. It can be hard to remember customer names or key them in without error. Access offers two ways to make it unnecessary. One, a *list box*, restricts selections to data in the list. We will use that here. The other, a *combo box*, lets users enter a new value in addition to those.

To begin, make room for the box where the CustName field is now. In Design view, delete it and its label. If any other fields move up to fill its space, select them and move them back down.

12. To create a list box, go to Design view and the Design ribbon. Click the downward triangle with the line over it at the right of the Controls section to confirm that Use Control Wizards is selected. If it is not, select it. Then click the List Box tool, shown in the figure, on the ribbon. (You may have to scroll the list up or down, or display the entire set via the same downward triangle with the line over it, to see this tool. You can also identify it by holding the mouse over it to see its tool tip.)

Draw a rectangle with the crosshairs where the customer name field used to be. Make it wide enough for a couple of data fields, deep enough for a few rows.

13. In the first step of the wizard, select "Find a record on my form based on the value I selected in my

list box," as this is what you want to do. Click Next.

14. Because you will pick a customer name, select CustTbl as the source of the values if it is not already selected. (This depends on your form design. Access may or may not have enough information to figure that out.) Click Next if necessary to advance to the next step.

15. Move CustID and CustName into the Selected Fields pane. You will need CustID to identify the correct record uniquely, CustName for people to read. Click Next.

16. Make sure the box to hide the key column is checked—your users do not need customer numbers—and expand the field width to permit longer names in the future. Click Next.

17. Choose the label Customer Name. Click Finish.

18. Go to Form view. You will see customer names in the list box, with scroll bar and arrows to move through the list. Select a customer name, and his or her orders will appear below it. Select one of that customer's orders, and its line items will appear in the bottom subform.

19. If necessary, move other fields out of the way of your list box. Close this form, saving if prompted. Name it CustOrderForm.

Deliverable

The two databases, ItemSales and DaffyDonuts, with their new forms.

Quiz Questions

1. True or false: In a list box, if you do not see the value you want, you can enter it.

2. To draw a new rectangle on a form, you would use
   (a) Form view
   (b) Layout view
   (c) Design view
   (d) Pivot chart view

3. True or false: In creating a form with subforms with the Form Wizard, all the data fields on the subforms must be in the tables that are chosen for the form.

4. In formatting data fields in Layout mode, the tools in the ribbon do all of the following *except*
   (a) Highlight text
   (b) Change text size
   (c) Change font
   (d) Put text in italics

Discussion Questions

1. The last form above was described as being used to review customer orders. Therefore, its users do not need to be able to change order data. A company's order entry personnel, or customers directly, could use a similar form to enter new orders. They would first enter information such as date about a new order, then its line items. Discuss where one or more additional list boxes and/or combo boxes might be helpful for this new purpose. (Do not add them to the data base. Just discuss where you would and what they would do.)

2. Search the Web for information on form usability. (The phrase "ease of use" can be useful in your search strings.) Find four guidelines for easy-to-use forms. For each guideline, state whether the forms you developed here follow it, do not follow it, or it does not apply. (Your answers can differ for the two forms.) If they do not follow it, say what would have to change to follow it. If they do not apply, explain why.

3. If you were a market analyst for DaffyDonuts and wanted to analyze which of your products sell best in different stores and at different times, what additional data might you want that is not in the second form you developed here? Suggest three items. Do not limit your thinking to what is in the tables of this database but not on the form. Think more broadly. Discuss how you might use each of the additional data fields.

10 | Wireless, Mobile Computing, and Mobile Commerce

LEARNING OBJECTIVES >>>

1. Identify advantages and disadvantages of each of the four main types of wireless transmission media.

2. Explain how businesses can use technology employed by short-range, medium-range, and long-range networks, respectively.

3. Provide a specific example of how each of the five major m-commerce applications can benefit a business.

4. Describe technologies that underlie pervasive computing, providing examples of how businesses can utilize each one.

5. Explain how the four major threats to wireless networks can damage a business.

© B Christopher/Alamy Limited

Have you ever gone into a restaurant, had a great time, and enjoyed a wonderful meal, only to find out that the restaurant does not accept credit cards? Naturally, you do not have enough cash on you and so you have to walk to the nearest ATM. Why, you ask yourself, would a business not accept credit cards? Some businesses do not accept credit cards simply because they do not want to pay fees to the credit card companies (fees start from at least 2.75 percent of the transaction price). For other businesses, they do not accept credit cards for technological and logistical reasons. Such was the case for Tony Adams.

Chef (and owner) Tony Adams runs a mobile restaurant in Orlando, Florida (see http://bigwheeltruckmenu.com and http://bigwheelprovisions.com). Tony prides himself on his original recipes based on fresh locally sourced foods, often from the local farmers market. His Web site proudly advertises that "Local Is Lovely."

Tony sells his food from a food truck, and his location changes daily. He needed a mobile connection to accept credit card payments. Tony first tried a mobile app that allowed him to type in credit card numbers, but the app was cumbersome and did not allow him to customize his menus every day in the way that he needed. Also, he still had to total each order on paper or with a calculator and then use the app only for accepting a credit card. He needed a much quicker way to calculate total amounts and accept credit card payments.

Then he heard about Square (http://squareup.com). Square offers an iPad point-of-sale (POS) system that allows Tony to customize his menus daily. As he logs in his menu items, Tony creates his POS for the day. Each item gets its own button so he only has to tap the menu items to total each order. Square also offers a small device (it looks like a square) that plugs into the headphone jack of the iPad (and will also work on an iPhone). About the size of a postage stamp, this little > > >

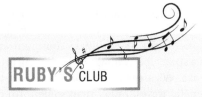

RUBY'S CLUB

Imagine this scenario. A customer arrives at Ruby's Club and is catching up with some friends. Rather than leaving the conversation and going to the bar, he gets out his smart phone, goes to Ruby's mobile site, and places a drink order. Payment is made on PayPal's mobile site. The completed order information, including an order ID, is transmitted to the bartender and the customer at the same time. Customers also receive a reminder that they will have to show their ID when they pick up the order, or it will not be delivered and their money will not be refunded.

In just a few minutes, customers receive a text message that their drink is ready. They approach the "Web order" end of the bar, show their text message and their ID, and pick up their drink.

Is this feasible? What technology should Ruby's use to deliver this wireless content? Ruben and Lisa have already discussed a Wi-Fi network, but they wonder what other alternatives might allow this type of interaction with their customers.

gadget allows you to swipe the magnetic stripe of a credit card to enter the numbers into the POS. The result for Tony is a POS system that offers a quicker transaction for himself and his customers.

Do not confuse what Tony is doing with mobile payments. Tony is using technology to accept credit cards in a mobile environment. In fact, he is not alone in this. This technology has opened the door for many mobile vendors to begin accepting credit cards with their iPads and iPhones. Mobile payments (meaning that someone makes a payment with a mobile phone rather than a debit/credit card) are an option for Tony's consumers who use Square's app called "Square Card Case." This app allows two

Square users to connect app-to-app, complete a transaction, and not even have to swipe a credit card.

Sources: Compiled from http://squareup.com, http://squareup.com/register, http://bigwheelprovisions.com, http://bigwheeltruckmenu.com, accessed March 20, 2012.

Questions

1. Other than efficiency, what are additional advantages for Tony in his use of Square?
2. Describe possible disadvantages of the Square app for Tony.

Introduction

The old, traditional working environment that required users to come to a wired computer was ineffective and inefficient. The solution was to build computers that are small enough to carry or wear and can communicate via wireless networks. The ability to communicate anytime and anywhere provides organizations with a strategic advantage by increasing productivity and speed and improving customer service. **Wireless** is a term that is used to describe telecommunications in which electromagnetic waves, rather than some form of wire or cable, carry the signal between communicating devices such as computers, smart phones, and iPads.

Before you continue, it is important to distinguish between the terms *wireless* and *mobile*, because they can mean different things. The term *wireless* means exactly what it says: without wires. In contrast, *mobile* refers to something that changes its location over time. Some wireless networks, such as MiFi (discussed later in this chapter), are also mobile. Others, however, are fixed. For example, microwave towers form fixed wireless networks.

Wireless technologies enable individuals and organizations to conduct mobile computing, mobile commerce, and pervasive computing. These terms are defined here, and then each one is discussed in detail later in the chapter.

Mobile computing refers to a real-time, wireless connection between a mobile device and other computing environments, such as the Internet or an intranet. *Mobile commerce*—also known as *m*-commerce—refers to e-commerce (EC) transactions conducted with a mobile device. *Pervasive computing*, also called *ubiquitous computing*, means that virtually every object has processing power with wireless or wired connections to a global network.

Wireless technologies and mobile commerce are spreading rapidly, replacing or supplementing wired computing. In fact, Cisco (www.cisco.com) predicts that the volume of mobile Web traffic will double every year until 2013. As illustrated in this chapter's first closing case, there is a huge battle underway to provide you with a mobile, digital wallet and to enable you to get rid of your physical wallet altogether, including all of the credit and debit cards you have in it. Billions of dollars are at stake, further highlighting the importance of wireless to you and your organizations.

Almost all (if not all) organizations utilize wireless computing. Therefore, when you begin your career, you likely will be assigned a company smart phone and a wirelessly enabled computer. Clearly, then, it is important for you to learn about wireless computing not only because you will be using wireless applications but also because wireless computing will be so important to your organization. In your job, you will be involved with customers who conduct wireless transactions, with analyzing and developing mobile commerce applications, and with wireless security. And the list goes on.

Simply put, an understanding of wireless technology and mobile commerce applications will make you more valuable to your organization. When you look at "What's In IT For Me?" at the end of this chapter, envision yourself performing the activities discussed in your functional area. An understanding of wireless technology can also help you start and grow your own business, as illustrated in the chapter opening case.

The wireless infrastructure upon which mobile computing is built may reshape the entire IT field. The technologies, applications, and limitations of mobile computing and mobile commerce are the focus of this chapter. You begin the chapter by learning about wireless devices and wireless transmission media. You continue by examining wireless computer networks and wireless Internet access. You then look at mobile computing and mobile commerce, which are made possible by wireless technologies. Next, you turn your attention to pervasive computing and conclude the chapter by familiarizing yourself with a critical component of the wireless environment—namely, wireless security.

10.1 Wireless Technologies

Wireless technologies include both wireless devices, such as smart phones, and wireless transmission media, such as microwave, satellite, and radio. These technologies are fundamentally changing the ways organizations operate.

Individuals are finding wireless devices convenient and productive to use, for several reasons. First, they can make productive use of time that was formerly wasted—for example, while commuting to work on public transportation. Second, because they can take these devices with them, their work locations are becoming much more flexible. Third, wireless technology enables them to schedule their working time around personal and professional obligations.

Wireless Devices

Wireless devices provide three major advantages to users:

- They are small enough to easily carry or wear.
- They have sufficient computing power to perform productive tasks.
- They can communicate wirelessly with the Internet and other devices.

Modern *smart phones* provide capabilities that include cellular telephony, Bluetooth, Wi-Fi, a digital camera for images and video, global positioning system (GPS), an organizer, a scheduler, an address book, a calculator, access to e-mail and Short Message Service (SMS, sending and receiving short text messages up to 160 characters in length), instant messaging, text messaging, an MP3 music player, a video player, Internet access with a full-function browser, and a QWERTY keyboard.

One downside of smart phones is that people can use them to copy and pass on confidential information. For example, if you were an executive at Intel, would you want workers snapping pictures of their colleagues with your secret new technology in the background? Unfortunately, managers think of these devices as phones, not as digital cameras that can transmit wirelessly. New jamming devices are being developed to counter the threat. Some companies, such as Samsung (www.samsung.com), have recognized the danger and have banned the devices from their premises altogether. Regardless of any disadvantages, cell phones, and particularly smart phones, have far greater impact on human society than most of us realize, as you see in the following example.

EXAMPLE The Power of Cell Phones

The lack of banks in Africa has long constrained the flow of capital and economic growth on that continent. In the past, most banks considered the costs of expanding branch networks too high and the return from poorer customers too low. In addition, Africa seemed to represent a low number of potential bank customers relevant to its size, as the African Development Bank (ADB; www.afdb.org) estimated that only 20 percent of African families have bank accounts. However, in a new report, the ADB estimated that a consumer class—defined as those who have $2 to $10 a day to spend—has grown to about 300 million people across the African continent. At the same time, mobile phone subscriptions in Africa have increased from 90 million in 2005 to 333 million in 2010, according to the United Nations.

To give an example of the difficulty caused by the lack of African banks, even in South Africa, the continent's richest economy, rural residents rely on taxi drivers to transfer cash between towns. The drivers typically take a 10 percent cut of the total amount of cash that they ferry. South Africa's largest bank, Standard Bank (www.standardbank.co.za), is now breaking away from its main business model of drawing customers to its branches and ATMs and moving toward a low-cost mobile phone banking model that is based on proximity to people. That is, rather than have a small number of banks located only in South Africa's larger towns and cities, Standard Bank is opening bank shops in far more numerous locations.

In mid-2012, Standard Bank has opened 10,000 "bank shops," mostly in predominately black townships. The sites range from street-side convenience stores to taverns. A bank shop offers minimal banking services at lower fees than a regular bank branch.

Consider Mavis Nonkongozelo, a preschool teacher who banks at the Five Sisters convenience store in Khayelitsha Township in South Africa. She walks up to the store with her mobile phone and her cash. With a few taps on her cell phone, Mavis connects to the Standard Bank's network. The clerk accepts a 20-rand bill (about US $2.94) and then taps on her own cell phone. The money is credited to Ms. Nonkongozelo's special no-fee account. Ms. Nonkongozelo was not able to save money before Standard arrived in her township. Now, she has 240 rand in her account. She says that it is safer for her to walk to the convenience store than to take a longer walk to the nearest ATM, where, in her high-crime neighborhood, she would run the risk of being mugged.

In Kenya, Western Union teamed up with M-Pesa, a unit of Kenyan telecommunications firm Safaricom (www.safaricom.co.ke), to conduct money transfers with other parts of the world via mobile phones. In mid-2012, M-Pesa has over 14 million customers. Consider Moses Githua, a Kenyan with no steady job and no access to a bank. Githua uses M-Pesa to deposit any money that he earns into a "digital wallet," where it sits until he is ready to use it. This process allows him to keep his savings beyond the reach of thieves. In addition to helping Kenyans safely save money, M-Pesa also allows Kenyans who have left the country to send money back home.

Sources: Compiled from B. Greeley and E. Ombok, "In Kenya, Keeping Cash Safe on a Cell Phone," *Bloomberg BusinessWeek*, September 12–18, 2011; P. Wonacott, "Banking Via a Cell-phone and a Shack," *The Wall Street Journal*, June 13, 2011; www.afdb.org, www.standardbank.com.za, www.safaricom.com.ke, accessed March 22, 2012.

William Andrew/Photographer's Choice/ Getty Images, Inc.

1. Discuss the importance of bank shops to lower-income people in Africa (and anywhere else for that matter).

2. What are the disadvantages of bank shops to the bank? To the bank's customers?

Yet the latest version of cell phones—smart phones—can cause problems despite all their advantages. The following example demonstrates how smart phones can disrupt the court system.

EXAMPLE Smart Phones in Court

Smart phones are now present in U.S. jury boxes, raising serious questions about juror impartiality and the ability of judges to control courtrooms. A Reuter's legal analysis found that jurors' forays onto the Internet via smart phones have resulted in dozens of mistrials, appeals, and overturned verdicts.

For decades, courts have instructed jurors not to seek information about cases outside of the evidence introduced at trial, and jurors are routinely warned not to communicate about a case with anyone before they reach a verdict. Today, however, jurors can, with a few clicks on their smart phones, look up definitions of legal terms on Wikipedia, view crime scenes via Google Earth, and communicate on their Facebook pages.

The consequences can be significant. In September 2010, for example, a Florida court overturned the manslaughter conviction of a man charged with killing his neighbor, citing the jury foreman's use of an iPhone to look up the definition of *prudent* in an online dictionary. That same month, the Nevada Supreme Court granted a new trial to a defendant convicted of sexually assaulting a minor, because the foreman had used his smart phone to search online for information about the types of physical injuries suffered by young victims of sexual assaults.

Courts are exploring ways to keep jurors "unplugged." Some judges now confiscate all smart phones from jurors when they enter a courtroom. In 2009, California updated its civil jury instructions to bar jurors from "all forms of electronic communication." From a different perspective, some legal experts argue that rather than try to stifle jurors from pursuing information on the Internet, courts need to figure out how to help them do so in a responsible way.

Sources: Compiled from S. Eder, "Jury Files: The Temptation of Twitter," *The Wall Street Journal*, March 12, 2012; "Juries and the Internet: Justice Online," *The Guardian*, January 3, 2011; "As Jurors Go Online, U.S. Trials Go Off Track," *Reuters*, December 8, 2010.

Wireless Transmission Media

Wireless media, or broadcast media, transmit signals without wires. The major types of wireless media are microwave, satellite, radio, and infrared. Table 10.1 lists the advantages and disadvantages of each type.

TABLE 10.1 Advantages and Disadvantages of Wireless Media

Channel	Advantages	Disadvantages
Microwave	High bandwidth Relatively inexpensive	Must have unobstructed line of sight Susceptible to environmental interference
Satellite	High bandwidth Large coverage area	Expensive Must have unobstructed line of sight Signals experience propagation delay Must use encryption for security
Radio	High bandwidth Signals pass through walls Inexpensive and easy to install	Creates electrical interference problems Susceptible to snooping unless encrypted
Infrared	Low to medium bandwidth Used only for short distances	Must have unobstructed line of sight

Microwave. **Microwave transmission** systems transmit data via electromagnetic waves. These systems are used for high-volume, long-distance, line-of-sight communication. *Line-of-sight* means that the transmitter and receiver are in view of each other. This requirement creates problems because Earth's surface is curved rather than flat. For this reason, microwave towers usually cannot be spaced more than 30 miles apart.

Clearly, then, microwave transmissions offer only a limited solution to data communications needs, especially over very long distances. In addition, microwave transmissions are susceptible to environmental interference during severe weather such as heavy rain and snowstorms. Although long-distance microwave data communications systems are still widely used, they are being replaced by satellite communications systems.

Satellite. **Satellite transmission** systems make use of communication satellites. Currently, there are three types of satellites circling Earth: geostationary (GEO), medium-earth-orbit (MEO), and low-earth-orbit (LEO). Each type has a different orbit, with the GEO being farthest from Earth and the LEO the closest. In this section, you examine the three types of satellites and then discuss two major satellite applications: Global positioning systems and Internet transmission via satellites. Table 10.2 compares and contrasts the three types of satellites.

As with microwave transmission, satellites must receive and transmit data via line-of-sight. However, the enormous *footprint*—the area of Earth's surface reached by a satellite's transmission—overcomes the limitations of microwave data relay stations. The most basic rule governing footprint size is simple: The higher a satellite orbits, the larger its footprint. Thus, medium-earth-orbit satellites have a smaller footprint than geostationary satellites, and low-earth-orbit satellites have the smallest footprint of all. Figure 10.1 compares the footprints of the three types of satellite.

In contrast to line-of-sight transmission with microwave, satellites use *broadcast* transmission, which sends signals to many receivers at one time. So, even though satellites are line-of-sight like microwave, they are high enough for broadcast transmission, thus overcoming the limitations of microwave.

TYPES OF ORBITS. *Geostationary earth orbit (GEO) satellites* orbit 22,300 miles directly above the equator. These satellites maintain a fixed position above Earth's surface because, at their altitude, their orbital period matches the 24-hour rotational period of Earth. For this reason, receivers on Earth do not have to track GEO satellites. GEO satellites are excellent for sending television programs to cable operators and for broadcasting directly to homes.

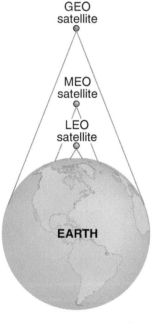

Figure 10.1 Comparison of satellite footprints. (Courtesy of Kelly Rainer.)

TABLE 10.2 Three Basic Types of Telecommunications Satellites

Type	Characteristics	Orbit	Number	Use
GEO	• Satellites stationary relative to point on Earth • Few satellites needed for global coverage • Transmission delay (approximately .25 second) • Most expensive to build and launch • Longest orbital life (many years)	22,300 miles	8	TV signal
MEO	• Satellites move relative to point on Earth • Moderate number needed for global coverage • Requires medium-powered transmitters • Negligible transmission delay • Less expensive to build and launch • Moderate orbital life (6–12 years)	6,434 miles	10–12	GPS
LEO	• Satellites move rapidly relative to point on Earth • Large number needed for global coverage • Requires only low-power transmitters • Negligible transmission delay • Least expensive to build and launch • Shortest orbital life (as low as 5 years)	400–700 miles	Many	Telephone

One major limitation of GEO satellites is that their transmissions take a quarter of a second to send and return. This brief pause, one kind of **propagation delay**, makes two-way telephone conversations difficult. Also, GEO satellites are large and expensive, and they require substantial amounts of power to launch.

Medium-earth-orbit (MEO) satellites are located about 6,000 miles above Earth's surface. MEO orbits require more satellites to cover Earth than GEO orbits because MEO footprints are smaller. MEO satellites have two advantages over GEO satellites: They are less expensive and they do not have an appreciable propagation delay. However, because MEO satellites move with respect to a point on Earth's surface, receivers must track these satellites. (Think of a satellite dish slowly turning to remain oriented to a MEO satellite).

Low-earth-orbit (LEO) satellites are located 400 to 700 miles above Earth's surface. Because LEO satellites are much closer to Earth, they have little, if any, propagation delay. Like MEO satellites, however, LEO satellites move with respect to a point on Earth's surface and therefore must be tracked by receivers. Tracking LEO satellites is more difficult than tracking MEO satellites because LEO satellites move much more quickly than MEO satellites relative to a point on Earth.

Unlike GEO and MEO satellites, LEO satellites can pick up signals from weak transmitters. This characteristic makes it possible for satellite telephones to operate via LEO satellites, because they can operate with less power and smaller batteries. Another advantage of LEO satellites is that they consume less power and cost less to launch than GEO and MEO satellites.

At the same time, however, the footprints of LEO satellites are small, which means that many of them are required to cover the planet. For this reason, a single organization often produces multiple LEO satellites, known as *LEO constellations*. Two examples are Iridium and Globalstar.

Iridium (www.iridium.com) has placed a LEO constellation in orbit that consists of 66 satellites and 12 in-orbit spare satellites. The company maintains that it provides complete satellite communications coverage of Earth's surface, including the polar regions. Globalstar (www.globalstar.com) also has a LEO constellation in orbit.

GLOBAL POSITIONING SYSTEMS. The **global positioning system** (**GPS**) is a wireless system that utilizes satellites to enable users to determine their position anywhere on Earth. GPS is supported by 24 MEO satellites that are shared worldwide. The exact position of each satellite is always known because the satellite continuously broadcasts its position along with a time signal. By using the known speed of the signals and the distance from three satellites (for two-dimensional location) or four satellites (for three-dimensional location), it is possible to find the location of any receiving station or user within a range of 10 feet. GPS software can also convert the user's latitude and longitude to an electronic map.

Most of you are probably familiar with GPS in automobiles, which "talks" to drivers when giving directions. Figure 10.2 illustrates two ways for drivers to obtain GPS information in a car: a dashboard navigation system and a GPS app (in this case, TomTom; www.tomtom.com) on an iPhone.

Commercial use of GPS for activities such as navigating, mapping, and surveying has become widespread, particularly in remote areas. Cell phones in the United States now must have a GPS embedded in them so that the location of a person making an emergency call (for example, 911, known as **wireless 911**) can be detected immediately.

Three other global positioning systems are either planned or operational. The Russian GPS, *GLONASS*, was completed in 1995. However, the system fell into disrepair with the collapse of the Soviet economy. In 2010, however, GLONASS achieved 100 percent coverage of Russian territory. The European Union GPS, *Galileo*, has an anticipated completion date of 2015. China expects to complete its GPS, *Beidou*, by 2020.

INTERNET OVER SATELLITE (IoS). In many regions of the world, Internet over Satellite (IoS) is the only option available for Internet connections because installing the necessary cables is either too expensive or physically impossible. IoS enables users to access the Internet via GEO satellites from a dish mounted on the side of their homes. Although IoS makes the Internet available to many people who otherwise could not access it, it has its drawbacks. Not only do GEO satellite transmissions entail a propagation delay, but they also can be disrupted by environmental influences such as thunderstorms.

Radio. **Radio transmission** uses radio-wave frequencies to send data directly between transmitters and receivers. Radio transmission has several advantages. First, radio waves travel easily through normal office walls. Second, radio devices are fairly inexpensive and easy to install. Third, radio waves can transmit data at high speeds. For these reasons, radio increasingly is being used to connect computers to both peripheral equipment and local area networks (LANs; discussed in Chapter 4).

Figure 10.2 Obtaining GPS information in an automobile. (*Source:* Image Source.)

Dashboard GPS

TomTom app on iPhone

As with other technologies, however, radio transmission also has its drawbacks. First, radio media can create electrical interference problems. Also, radio transmissions are susceptible to snooping by anyone who has similar equipment that operates on the same frequency.

Another problem with radio transmission is that when you travel too far away from the source station, the signal breaks up and fades into static. Most radio signals can travel only 30 to 40 miles from their source. However, *satellite radio* overcomes this problem. **Satellite radio** (or digital radio) offers uninterrupted, near CD-quality transmission that is beamed to your radio, either at home or in your car, from space. In addition, satellite radio offers a broad spectrum of stations, including many types of music, news, and talk.

XM Satellite Radio and Sirius Satellite Radio were competitors that launched satellite radio services. XM broadcast its signals from GEO satellites, while Sirius used MEO satellites. In July 2008, the two companies merged to form Sirius XM (www.siriusxm.com). Listeners subscribe to the service for a monthly fee.

INFRARED. The final type of wireless transmission is infrared transmission. **Infrared** light is red light that is not commonly visible to human eyes. Common applications of infrared light are found in remote control units for televisions, VCRs, and DVD and CD players. In addition, like radio transmission, infrared transceivers are used for short-distance connections between computers and peripheral equipment and local area networks. A *transceiver* is a device that can transmit and receive signals.

— BEFORE *YOU GO ON . . .* —

1. Describe the most common types of wireless devices.
2. Describe the various types of transmission media.

Apply the Concept 10.1

Background As stated in this section, mobile communication has changed our world quicker than any other technology. This rapid change has created many challenges for businesses. While it seems obvious that mobile communications are helpful, knowing exactly when to adopt new technology is difficult. Today, most employees and consumers alike expect mobile ready content.

Activity Visit http://www.wiley.com/go/rainer/applytheconcept and click on the link provided for Apply the Concept 10.1. It will take you to an article that details some of the ways technology has changed the accounting practice. You will see that adopting technology is a much greater decision than just jumping on the latest bandwagon. Learning to watch trends will help you to be able to determine when the newest technology is worth it and when the next generation may be a better fit. Either way, IT expenditures are very expensive and difficult to rationalize if you are only considering return on investment (ROI).

Deliverable

Write a summary based on your own understanding of technology trends in the accounting field. Also, talk to your accounting professors (or friends that major in accounting) to see if the trends that were identified in 2008 have actually come to pass. The video mentions USB thumb drives being on every keychain. Are they still? Have we moved to a new technology thanks to being connected everywhere all the time?

Submit your summary to your instructor.

Quiz questions are assignable in WileyPLUS, and available on the Book Companion Site at http://www.wiley.com/college/rainer.

1. What qualities of wireless transmission via radio waves would make it most ideal for Ruby's Club?
2. Which business models would work best with satellite transmissions?

10.2 Wireless Computer Networks and Internet Access

You have learned about various wireless devices and how these devices transmit wireless signals. These devices typically form wireless computer networks, and they provide wireless Internet access. Next, you will categorize wireless networks by their effective distance: short range, medium range, and wide area.

Short-Range Wireless Networks

Short-range wireless networks simplify the task of connecting one device to another, and they eliminate wires and enable users to move around while they use the devices. In general, short-range wireless networks have a range of 100 feet or less. In this section, you consider three basic short-range networks: Bluetooth, ultra-wideband (UWB), and near-field communications (NFC).

Bluetooth. **Bluetooth** (www.bluetooth.com) is an industry specification used to create small personal area networks. A **personal area network** is a computer network used for communication among computer devices—for example, telephones, personal digital assistants, and smart phones—located close to one person. Bluetooth 1.0 can link up to eight devices within a 10-meter area (about 30 feet) with a bandwidth of 700 kilobits per second (Kbps) using low-power, radio-based communication. Bluetooth 2.0 can transmit up to 2.1 megabits per second (Mbps) and, at greater power, up to 100 meters. Ericsson, the Scandinavian mobile handset company that developed this standard, called it Bluetooth after the tenth-century Danish King Harald Blatan (*Blatan* means "Bluetooth"). Ericsson named the standard after Blatan because he unified previously separate islands into the nation of Denmark.

Common applications for Bluetooth are wireless handsets for cell phones and portable music players. Advantages of Bluetooth include low power consumption and the fact that it uses omnidirectional radio waves—that is, waves that are emitted in all directions from a transmitter. For this reason, you do not have to point one Bluetooth device at another for a connection to occur.

Ultra-Wideband. **Ultra-wideband (UWB)** is a high-bandwidth wireless technology with transmission speeds in excess of 100 Mbps. This very high speed makes UWB a good choice for applications such as streaming multimedia from, say, a personal computer to a television.

Time Domain (www.timedomain.com), a pioneer in UWB technology, has developed many UWB applications. One interesting application is the PLUS Real-Time Location System (RTLS). An organization can utilize PLUS to locate multiple people and assets simultaneously. Employees, customers, and/or visitors wear the PLUS Badge Tag. PLUS Asset Tags are placed on equipment and products. PLUS is extremely valuable for health care environments, where real-time location of caregivers (e.g., doctors, nurses, technicians) and mobile equipment (e.g., laptops, monitors) is critical.

Near-Field Communications. **Near-field communications (NFC)** has the smallest range of any short-range wireless networks. It is designed to be embedded in mobile devices such as cell phones and credit cards. For example, using NFC, you can swipe your device or card within a few centimeters of POS terminals to pay for items (see this chapter's Closing Case 1). NFC also has many other interesting uses. For example, IT's About Business 10.1 shows how NFC technology helps travelers in Japan.

IT'S ABOUT BUSINESS 10.1

Near-Field Communications Helps Travelers in Japan

 Japan's smart phones are called *keitai*. On their keitai, Japanese subscribers have a high-resolution camera, a projector, and near-field communication (NFC) capability. For example, a Japanese woman uses her keitai to scan a QR code at a Tokyo bus stop. A timetable appears instantly on her screen, along with the estimated arrival time of the next bus. When her bus arrives, she uses her keitai to pay by simply waving it close to the payment terminal in the front of the bus.

Because the keitai are NFC equipped, they can function as boarding passes/tickets for trains, airplanes, and events. They also allow users to check into hotels and will even serve as an electronic room key. Keitai also act as electronic wallets (e-wallets). With up to 50,000 yen credit input into a keitai over the Internet, customers use their keitai to buy groceries at convenience stores, pay taxi drivers, and purchase goods from Japan's ubiquitous vending machines.

Japan's leading airline, All Nippon Airways (ANA), has been using e-wallets to compete with the country's fast trains for several years. As one ANA spokesperson said, "The major drawback of flying compared to train travel is, of course, the time spent at the airport."

With ANA's all-in-one keitai ticket and boarding pass, passengers can arrive and board their planes within 15 minutes. This service, called SKiP, uses an e-wallet technology developed by communications company NTT.

Keitai are also equipped with GPS technology, which makes them very useful navigation tools. The Total Navigation site on a keitai shows three-dimensional maps and directions on the screen. If a user is holding the phone while navigating, it will vibrate to alert the driver to upcoming turns.

Keitai also help visitors cope with the Japanese language. For example, menus in Japanese restaurants are invariably only in Japanese. Using a keitai, a visitor can take a picture of a potential meal and the phone describes in English what the meal actually is. This is a valuable tool for many restaurants, because Japan looks to foreign tourists for needed revenue. Other applications allow users to bring up menus, reviews, and translations by other users simply by focusing the phone's mobile camera at the restaurant itself.

In Kyoto, the Hyatt Regency offers an iPhone rental service that pinpoints guests' locations and beams target text, video, and graphics to inform, help, and guide them around the area. The hotel also augments this service with advice and suggestions from the concierge.

The keitai are also equipped with augmented reality (AR). AR apps know where users are and beam location-relevant information to their phones. This information is viewed superimposed on the camera viewfinder on the phone's screen. AR apps in Japan also add tagging and social networking. Like other AR apps, your keitai calculates your position, then, using the camera, displays location-specific information graphically on top of your real-world view.

Interestingly, individuals and businesses can add their own information to these AR apps. They point the phone's camera at the landscape, adding "tags" that can include text, images, and sound that can be picked up by others in the area later. Tags can translate into coupons from businesses or travel trips from friends and colleagues.

Sources: Compiled from M. Fitzpatrick, "Near Field Communication Transforms Travel in Japan," *BBC News*, April 28, 2011; S. Clark, "NTT Adds New Mobile Marketing Capabilities to Japan's

Osaifu-Keitai Mobile Wallet Service," *Near Field Communications World*, June 16, 2010; S. Toto, "Separate Keitai: Meet Japan's Sexiest New Handset," *TechCrunch*, February 5, 2010; "Japanese Cell Phone Culture," www.japaneselifestyle.com.au, accessed February 13, 2012.

Questions

1. As the Japanese travel industry creates more applications of technology for travel,

what assumptions is it making about tourists?

2. Which of these apps would you find most useful? Provide specific examples of the app(s) and the way(s) in which you would use them.

3. Do you see any problem with the social networking aspect of AR apps? Support your answer.

Medium-Range Wireless Networks

Medium-range wireless networks are the familiar wireless local area networks (WLANs). The most common type of medium-range wireless network is Wireless Fidelity, or Wi-Fi. WLANs are useful in a variety of settings, some of which may be challenging.

Wireless Fidelity (Wi-Fi). **Wireless fidelity (Wi-Fi)** is a medium-range WLAN, which is a wired LAN but without the cables. In a typical configuration, a transmitter with an antenna, called a **wireless access point**, connects to a wired LAN or to satellite dishes that provide an Internet connection. Figure 10.3 displays a wireless access point. A wireless access point provides service to a number of users within a small geographical perimeter (up to a couple of hundred feet), known as a **hotspot**. Supporting a larger number of users across a larger geographical area requires multiple wireless access points. To communicate wirelessly, mobile devices, such as laptop PCs, typically have a built-in wireless network interface capability.

Wi-Fi provides fast and easy Internet or intranet broadband access from public hotspots located at airports, hotels, Internet cafés, universities, conference centers, offices, and homes (see Figure 10.4). Users can access the Internet while walking across a campus, to their office, or through their homes. In addition, users can access Wi-Fi with their laptops, desktops, or PDAs by adding a wireless network card. Most PC and laptop manufacturers incorporate these cards in their PCs.

The Institute of Electrical and Electronics Engineers (IEEE) has established a set of standards for wireless computer networks. The IEEE standard for Wi-Fi is the 802.11 family. As of mid-2012, there are four standards in this family: 802.11a, 802.11b, 802.11g, and 802.11n. (802.11ac is a new standard under development that will provide very high bandwidth.)

Today, many WLANs use the 802.11n standard, which can transmit up to 600 Mbps and has a range of about 800 feet. There are many 802.11n products. One example is Netgear's (www.netgear.com) RangeMax Wireless-N router.

The major benefits of Wi-Fi are its low cost and its ability to provide simple Internet access. It is the greatest facilitator of the wireless Internet—that is, the ability to connect to the Internet wirelessly.

Corporations are integrating Wi-Fi into their strategies. For example, Starbucks, McDonald's, Panera, and Barnes & Noble offer customers Wi-Fi in many of their stores, primarily for Internet access. The airlines are also getting in on the Wi-Fi act, as you see in IT's About Business 10.2.

Courtesy of Brad Prince

Figure 10.3 Wireless access point.

Figure 10.4 Starbucks' patrons using Wi-Fi. (*Source:* © Marianna Day Massey/Zuma Press.)

IT's ABOUT BUSINESS 10.2

Airlines Turn to Wi-Fi

After years of using drop-down televisions and expensive seat-back monitors, airlines now hope to entertain passengers on the screens that the travelers bring with them. The airlines are providing Wi-Fi, movies, and TV shows that can be viewed on travelers' smart phones, tablets, and laptops. Despite their current economic difficulties, airlines are investing heavily in Wi-Fi capabilities. The airlines hope that this upfront investment will help them tap into a new source of revenue as they attract customers who need to be online while traveling.

By the time of this writing in mid-2012, over 1,300 aircraft offer Internet access to passengers. The Internet connection can be accessed at any point above 10,000 feet, the federal minimum altitude for using portable electronics. By 2013, over half of all passenger planes will be connected to the Internet. At least four companies are competing to provide Wi-Fi service to aircraft.

Five major U.S. carriers—Delta, American, AirTran, Alaska Airlines, and Virgin America—got into the wireless-providing business early. They signed contracts with Gogo (www.gogoair.com), the early option for in-flight Wi-Fi, and are now locked into contracts for a service that is quickly being bested by a number of rivals. Gogo beams its connection from cellular towers on the ground to antennas on the plane. But, the service is limited to the continental United States and Alaska, and does not include live television.

Gogo's competitors plan to offer expanded services and more features, but they have not yet proven themselves. Their promised services rely on satellites, which require heavier receivers that take longer to install than Gogo's receivers. Row 44 (http://row44.com), the Wi-Fi provider to Southwest Airlines, and Panasonic Avionics (www.mascorp.com), another in-flight Wi-Fi provider, offer global Wi-Fi via satellite; by the end of 2012, they plan to stream live news and sports channels to flyers' devices.

ViaSat (www.viasat.com) aims to launch more powerful in-flight Wi-Fi with the newest satellite technology—called Ka band—by late 2012. Ka band's competitive advantage is its higher bandwidth, which can service at least 10 times as many users as other in-flight Wi-Fi providers without affecting download speed. Gogo has announced plans to switch to Ka band by 2013 in the United States and to become a global Wi-Fi provider by 2015.

In the fall of 2012, Delta launched its on-demand service on 16 aircraft, offering $4 movies and $1 TV shows for flyers' laptops. American offers the same functions on 15 aircraft. Both airlines are running national ad campaigns focused on their in-flight connectivity. Southwest charges $5 a flight for Row 44 Wi-Fi. Gogo charges $5 to $13 for Wi-Fi based on flight time and offers 15 minutes of Wi-Fi for $2. On the other hand, Virgin Atlantic plans to replace its seat-back touch screens with high-definition screens and to offer an enhanced Gogo Wi-Fi service that is four times as fast.

Not surprisingly, passengers are unhappy with the cost of in-flight Wi-Fi access. Only about 7 percent of passengers currently avail themselves of the service. Although competition among in-flight Wi-Fi providers will drive prices down over time, in-flight Wi-Fi will not be an effective revenue-producing technology for airlines until prices drop.

Sources: Compiled from N. Trajos, "More Airlines Add Wi-Fi, But Travelers Balk at Paying," *USA Today*, January 16, 2012; J. Nicas, "Playing the Wireless Card: Airlines Rush to Add Wi-Fi," *The Wall Street Journal*, October 11, 2011; www.gogoair.com, http://row44.com, www.mascorp.com, www.viasat.com, accessed March 20, 2012.

Questions

1. Would you use in-flight Wi-Fi if you had to pay the prices listed in this case? Why or why not?
2. How much would you pay to use in-flight Wi-Fi? (Your answer can be $0.)
3. What are the potential dangers of using in-flight Wi-Fi services?

Although Wi-Fi has become extremely popular, it is not without problems. Three factors are preventing the commercial Wi-Fi market from expanding even further: roaming, security, and cost.

- At this time, users cannot roam from hotspot to hotspot if the hotspots use different Wi-Fi network services. Unless the service is free, users have to log on to separate accounts and, where required, pay a separate fee for each service. (Some Wi-Fi hotspots offer free service, while others charge a fee.)

- Security is the second barrier to greater acceptance of Wi-Fi. Because Wi-Fi uses radio waves, it is difficult to shield from intruders.

- The final limitation to greater Wi-Fi expansion is cost. Even though Wi-Fi services are relatively inexpensive, many experts question whether commercial Wi-Fi services can survive when so many free hotspots are available to users.

WI-FI DIRECT. Until late 2010, Wi-Fi required the presence of a wireless antenna at the center of a hotspot and ad-hoc connections among individual computers or other devices were somewhat limited. Because of these limitations, organizations have typically used Wi-Fi for communications of up to about 800 feet, and they have used Bluetooth for shorter, ad hoc connections.

Wi-Fi Direct is a new iteration of Wi-Fi. It enables peer-to-peer communications, so devices can connect directly. Wi-Fi Direct enables users to transfer content among devices, even without a wireless antenna. It can connect pairs or groups of devices at Wi-Fi speeds of up to 250 Mbps and at distances of up to 800 feet. Further, devices with Wi-Fi Direct can broadcast their availability to other devices just as Bluetooth devices can. Finally, Wi-Fi Direct is compatible with the more than 1 billion Wi-Fi devices currently in use.

Wi-Fi Direct will probably challenge the dominance of Bluetooth in the area of device-to-device networking. It offers a similar type of connectivity but with greater range and much faster data transfer.

MIFI. MiFi is a small, portable wireless device that provides users with a permanent Wi-Fi hotspot wherever they go. Thus, users are always connected to the Internet. The range of the MiFi device is about 10 meters. Developed by Novatel, the MiFi device is also called an intelligent mobile hotspot. Accessing Wi-Fi through the MiFi device allows up to five persons to be connected at the same time, sharing the same connection.

MiFi provides broadband Internet connectivity anywhere there is 3G cellular network coverage. MiFi also allows users to use voice-over-IP technology to make free (or cheap) calls, both locally and internationally. One drawback with MiFi is the cost, both for acquiring it and for using it.

SUPER WI-FI. Super Wi-Fi is a term coined by the U.S. Federal Communications Commission (FCC) to describe a wireless network proposal that creates long-distance wireless Internet connections. (The use of the trademark "Wi-Fi" in the name has been criticized because Super Wi-Fi is not based on Wi-Fi technology.) Regardless, Super Wi-Fi uses the lower-frequency white spaces between television channel frequencies. These lower frequencies allow the signal to travel further and penetrate walls better than normal Wi-Fi frequencies.

Super Wi-Fi is already in use in Houston, Texas, and Wilmington, North Carolina. The technology threatens cell phone carriers' 3G technology and it could be used to bring broadband wireless Internet access to rural areas.

WIRELESS MESH NETWORKS. **Mesh networks** use multiple Wi-Fi access points to create a wide area network that can be quite large. Mesh networks could have been included in the long-range wireless section, but you see them here because they are essentially a series of interconnected local area networks.

Around the United States, public wireless mesh programs have stalled and failed (for example, in Philadelphia, in Boston, and on Long Island, New York). Service providers that partnered with cities to maintain the systems are dropping out, largely because the projects' costs are escalating and the revenue models are unclear. However, San Jose, California, is building a new "municipal Wi-Fi" network that shows promise, as the following example illustrates.

EXAMPLE Municipal Wi-Fi in San Jose, California

Municipal wireless networks (also called municipal Wi-Fi) were supposed to turn an entire city into a wireless access zone, in order to provide universal wireless access to the Internet. Cities attempted to provide municipal Wi-Fi via wireless mesh networks, using hundreds of wireless access points often located on utility poles. Unfortunately, municipal wireless networks did not work as planned. They proved to be expensive to install and maintain. Further, they often did not provide adequate bandwidth for users to access the Internet.

A new downtown Wi-Fi network being built in San Jose, California, could indicate a new beginning for the ill-fated and brief "muni Wi-Fi" attempts over the last decade. San Jose's network is scheduled to be deployed in the summer of 2012.

The city's goal is not to provide wireless Internet for all residents throughout the city. Instead, their goal is to replace an aging early municipal Wi-Fi network and make Wi-Fi available to all residents within the context of certain key municipal infrastructure applications. For instance, the new Wi-Fi network will support mobile Wi-Fi users in the city's parking guidance system, which can feed near real-time information about the location of empty spaces in the network of city-owned parking garages. It will also be used to support an expanding population of wireless parking meters. Both processes will generate city revenues, creating a sustainable foundation for the network's operations. This revenue generation is the basis for offering free, pervasive, high-bandwidth Wi-Fi connectivity as an end-user amenity in the 1.5-square-mile downtown area.

Sources: Compiled from J. Cox, "San Jose Wi-Fi Net Could Mark Rethinking of 'Muni Wi-Fi',"
Network World, March 13, 2012; http://www.sanjoseca.gov/, accessed March 21, 2012.

Despite these problems, there are many examples of successful mesh-network applications. Consider the following:

- U.S. military forces are using wireless mesh networks to connect their laptops in field operations.

- Electric meters are now being placed on residences to transfer their readings to the central office for billing, without the need for human readers or the need to connect the meters with cables.

- The LEO Iridium constellation operates as a mesh network, with wireless links among adjacent satellites. Calls between two satellite phones are routed through the mesh, from one satellite to another across the constellation, without having to go through an Earth-based station. As a result, the signal travels a shorter distance, reducing any transmission lag. In addition, the constellation can operate with fewer Earth stations.

Wide-Area Wireless Networks

Wide-area wireless networks connect users to the Internet over a geographically dispersed territory. These networks typically operate over the licensed spectrum—that is, they use portions of the wireless spectrum that are regulated by the government. In contrast, Bluetooth and Wi-Fi operate over the unlicensed spectrum and are therefore more prone to interference and security problems. In general, wide-area wireless network technologies fall into two categories: cellular radio and wireless broadband.

Cellular Radio. **Cellular telephones (cell phones)** provide two-way radio communications over a cellular network of base stations with seamless handoffs. Cellular telephones differ from cordless telephones, which offer telephone service only within a limited range through a single base station attached to a fixed landline—for example, within a home or an office.

The cell phone communicates with radio antennas, or towers, placed within adjacent geographic areas called *cells* (see Figure 10.5). A telephone message is transmitted to the local cell—that is, the antenna—by the cell phone and then is passed from cell to cell until it reaches the cell of its destination. At this final cell, the message either is transmitted to the receiving cell phone or it is transferred to the public switched telephone system to be transmitted to a wireline telephone. This is why you can use a cell phone to call other cell phones as well as standard wireline phones.

Until early 2011, large cell towers have been a "given" for cellular technology. The following example introduces an exciting new technology from Alcatel-Lucent (www.alcatel-lucent.com) that aims to replace these towers.

Cellular technology is quickly evolving, moving toward higher transmission speeds and richer features. The technology has progressed through several stages:

- *First generation (1G)* cellular used analog signals and had low bandwidth (capacity).

- *Second generation (2G)* uses digital signals primarily for voice communication; it provides data communication up to 10 Kbps.

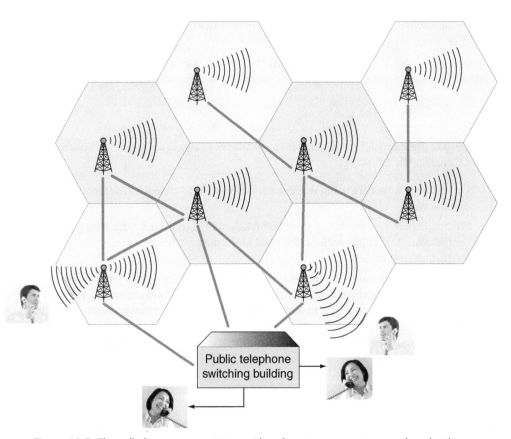

Figure 10.5 The cell phone communicates with radio antennas, or towers, placed within adjacent geographic areas called *cells*. (*Sources:* Image Source; Anthony Lee/OJO Images/ Getty Images, Inc.)

Example lightRadio

The global wireless industry is spending $210 billion per year to operate its networks and $50 billion per year to upgrade them. Despite all that spending and pressure on consumers to curb their data usage, the networks are fighting a losing battle. Mobile data usage is expected to grow 30 times by 2015 and 500 times by 2020. With a combination of miniaturization and cloud technology (discussed in Plug IT In 3), lightRadio might be able to help wireless carriers keep pace with their customers.

A lightRadio is a 2.3-inch cube that contains all of the components of a cell tower. Alcatel-Lucent's engineers stripped out all the heavy power equipment that controls cell towers and moved it to centralized stations. Consequently, the lightRadio cubes are small enough to be deployed virtually anywhere and almost inconspicuously—for example, on top of bus station awnings, on the sides of buildings, and on lampposts.

Not only are lightRadio cubes much smaller and less conspicuous than cell towers, they also are 30 percent more efficient. Wireless carriers can assess live data about who is using the cubes and then adjust the antennas' directional beams to maximize their potential. For example, antennas may be pointed in one direction as people are coming to work in the morning and in another direction when they are going home. In addition, the cubes contain multigenerational antennas that can relay 2G, 3G, and 4G network signals (discussed next), all from the same cube.

Each lightRadio cube powers about a two-block radius, so in urban areas they can be deployed throughout the city and stacked in stadiums or other areas that need extra capacity. In rural areas, they can be deployed on top of existing cell towers.

Sources: Compiled from S. Portlock, "Bell Labs' lightRadio Cube Has Big First Year, Wows Crowds at Mobile Congress," *The Star Ledger* (www.nj.com/starledger), February 29, 2012; D. Goldman, "The Tiny Cube That Could Cut Your Phone Bill," *CNNMoney*, March 21, 2011; C. Babcock, "Alcatel Lucent Shrinks Cell Phone Towers," *InformationWeek*, February 7, 2011; www.alcatel-lucent.com, accessed May 11, 2011.

- *2.5G* uses digital signals and provides voice and data communication up to 144 Kbps.
- *Third generation (3G)* uses digital signals and can transmit voice and data up to 384 Kbps when the device is moving at a walking pace, 128 Kbps when it is moving in a car, and up to 2 Mbps when it is in a fixed location. 3G supports video, Web browsing, and instant messaging.

Third-generation cellular service does have disadvantages. Perhaps the most fundamental problem is that cellular companies in North America use two separate technologies: Verizon and Sprint use Code Division Multiple Access (CDMA), while Cingular and others use Global System for Mobile Communications (GSM). CDMA companies are currently using *Evolution-Data Optimized* (*EV-DO*) technology, which is a wireless broadband cellular radio standard.

In addition, 3G is relatively expensive. In fact, most carriers limit how much information you can download and for what the service can be used. For instance, some carriers prohibit downloading or streaming audio or video. If you go beyond the limits, the carriers reserve the right to cut off your service.

- *Fourth generation (4G)* is still under development and is not one defined technology or standard. The International Telecommunications Union has specified speed requirements for 4G: 100 Mbps (million bits per second) for high-mobility communications such as cars and trains, and 1 Gbps (billion bits per second) for low-mobility communications such as pedestrians. A 4G system is expected to provide a secure all-IP (Internet Protocol)-based mobile broadband system to all types of mobile devices. Many of the current "4G" offerings do not meet the ITU specified speeds, but they call their service 4G nonetheless. See the "IT's Personal" article below for more information.

Wireless Broadband or WiMAX. Worldwide Interoperability for Microwave Access, popularly known as WiMAX, is the name for IEEE Standard 802.16. WiMAX has a wireless access range of up to 31 miles, compared to 300 feet for Wi-Fi. WiMAX also has a data-transfer rate of up to 75 Mbps. It is a secure system, and it offers features such as voice and video. WiMAX antennas can transmit broadband Internet connections to antennas on homes and businesses miles away. The technology can therefore provide long-distance broadband wireless access to rural areas and other locations that are not currently being served.

BEFORE *YOU GO ON . . .*

1. What is Bluetooth? What is a WLAN?
2. Describe Wi-Fi, cellular service, and WiMAX.

IT'S PERSONAL: WIRELESS AND MOBILE

What the GSM3GHSDPA+4GLTE???

This chapter explains the many mobile platforms that are available to you as a consumer. There are cellular, Bluetooth, Wi-Fi, satellite, and other wireless options available. That seems simple enough to understand. But within the cellular area, things get confusing because there are so many acronyms used by the telecommunication companies these days. Have you ever wondered if Verizon 3G was equivalent to AT&T 3G? What about 4G and 4G LTE? Of course, most people assume that 4G is faster than 3G, but how much so?

Once, Apple released an update to its mobile operating system (iOS), and suddenly AT&T started showing 4G on the iPhone rather than 3G! That was with no phone upgrade! Pretty nice, right? Wrong. In this instance, it was just a change in terminology rather than a change in technology. The speed of the 3G/4G network had not changed. (Note: AT&T "4G LTE" is a different technology and does offer significantly higher speeds than AT&T 3G or 4G.)

Actual connection speeds are described in bit rates, meaning how many bits (1's or 0's) you can move in one second. If you see a speed described as 1.5 Mbps, this translates to 1.5 million bits per second. That sounds like a tremendous rate, but knowing the bits per second is only part of understanding the actual speed you will experience. This is because connection speed and throughput speed are different. Actual throughput will always be less than connection speed.

It works much like your car. Your car is probably capable of driving over 100 mph. However, you are "throttled down" by various speed limits so much that you never reach your potential speed. Your actual speed varies depending on the route you take and the limits imposed along that route. So even though AT&T, Verizon, Sprint, and others boast incredible wireless speeds ("Up to 20 Mbps!"), they will always say "up to" because they know that you will never actually download a file at that rate.

The best way to see actual speeds of the networks is to go to your local wireless store and run a speed test using the demo model they have on display. This will give you first-hand experience of the actual throughput speed you can expect from their network. This number is much more realistic and will mean more to you than understanding the terms 3G, 4G, 4G LTE, etc.

Here is how you do the test: First, make sure the unit is only connected to a cellular network (not Wi-Fi). Then go to http://speedtest.net and click "Begin Test." I just ran this test from my iPhone 4S on AT&T's 4G (not 4G LTE) network. My download speed was 3.80 Mbps and my upload speed was 1.71 Mbps. These numbers are more informative than any name they are given (3G, 4G, etc.) because you see exactly what you can expect out of your wireless connection. Run this test at competing stores (AT&T, Verizon, Sprint, T-Mobile, etc.) and you will have real data to compare. As names change, you can always run a test to find the facts.

Apply the Concept 10.2

Background Many cellular phones today have many radios in them. Both the iPhone 5 and the Galaxy S3 have has three different radio transceivers and one radio receiver. They are Cellular (4G LTE, 4G, or 3G depending on your carrier), Bluetooth, Wi-Fi, and GPS (the one that only receives). With all of these radios in a small mobile device, the possibilities of connectivity are nearly endless. For this activity, let's focus on Bluetooth.

As described in the chapter, it is used for short range, personal area networks. Many people use Bluetooth networks for sound via wireless headphones, speakerphones, car stereos, or speakers. The author personally uses an iPhone and four different radio transmitters to play music in his car. First, a Verizon MiFi provides a 3G data connection (so the author does not go over his AT&T quota). This 3G is shared with his iPhone over a Wi-Fi connection. This is done to stream Pandora music over Bluetooth to an FM transmitter that sends the signal to the factory FM radio. So at one time, the author is using cellular, Wi-Fi, Bluetooth, and FM just to listen to Pandora radio.

However, Bluetooth can also be used to make the iPhone a remote for a keynote presentation, a display for a heart rate monitor, body activity monitor, sleep monitor, blood pressure monitor, or to connect to devices such as Google Glasses (search Google for this—it's awesome!).

Activity Research the different Bluetooth devices for business purposes. How many of these are viable? What industries are more likely to use them? What positions within the industries are likely to need small personal area networks for employees? How many devices can work with both Bluetooth and Wi-Fi?

Deliverable

Build a table that lists the different Bluetooth technologies you have found and that shows their potential applications. Try to find at least five different technologies and uses if you can. Submit your work to your instructor.

Quiz questions are assignable in WileyPLUS, and available on the Book Companion Site at http://www.wiley.com/college/rainer.

RUBY'S CLUB QUESTIONS

1. For Ruby's Club, what is a significant difference in the way Bluetooth operates compared to infrared transmission that would make it more feasible for Ruben and Lisa's choice of technology?

2. Obviously, Ruben and Lisa want to create a WLAN with some type of wireless technology. Based on the options discussed in Section 10.2, which one do you think would be the most worthwhile? Keep in mind that for it to be useful to customers, devices must be compatible with the club's network.

10.3 Mobile Computing and Mobile Commerce

In the traditional computing environment, users come to a computer, which is connected with wires to other computers and to networks. Because these networks need to be linked by wires, it is difficult or even impossible for people on the move to use them. In particular, salespeople, repair people, service employees, law enforcement agents, and utility workers can be more effective if they can use IT while in the field or in transit. Thus, mobile computing was designed for workers who travel outside the boundaries of their organizations as well as for anyone traveling outside his or her home.

Mobile computing refers to a real-time connection between a mobile device and other computing environments, such as the Internet or an intranet. This innovation is revolutionizing how people use computers. It is spreading at work and at home; in education, health care, and entertainment; and in many other areas.

Mobile computing has two major characteristics that differentiate it from other forms of computing: mobility and broad reach. *Mobility* means that users carry a device with them and can initiate a real-time contact with other systems from wherever they happen to be. *Broad reach* refers to the fact that when users carry an open mobile device, they can be reached instantly, even across great distances.

These two characteristics, mobility and broad reach, create five value-added attributes that break the barriers of geography and time: ubiquity, convenience, instant connectivity, personalization, and localization of products and services. A mobile device can provide information and communication regardless of the user's location (*ubiquity*). With an Internet-enabled mobile device, users can access the Web, intranets, and other mobile devices quickly and easily, without booting up a PC or placing a call via a modem (*convenience* and *instant connectivity*). A company can customize information and send it to individual consumers as a short message service (SMS) (*customization*). And, knowing a user's physical location helps a company advertise its products and services (*localization*). Mobile computing provides the foundation for mobile commerce (m-commerce).

Mobile Commerce

In addition to affecting our everyday lives, mobile computing is also transforming the way organizations conduct business by allowing businesses and individuals to engage in mobile commerce. As you saw at the beginning of this chapter, **mobile commerce** (or m-commerce) refers to electronic commerce (EC) transactions that are conducted in a wireless environment, especially via the Internet. Like regular EC applications, m-commerce can be transacted via the Internet, private communication lines, smart cards, and other infrastructures. M-commerce creates opportunities for businesses to deliver new services to existing customers and to attract new customers. To see how m-commerce applications are classified by industry, see www.wirelessresearch.eu.

The development of m-commerce is driven by the following factors:

- *Widespread availability of mobile devices.* By mid-2012, more than 5 billion cell phones were in use throughout the world. Experts estimate that within a few years about 70 percent of cell phones in developed countries will have Internet access. Going further, as already discussed in this chapter, cell phones are spreading even more quickly in developing countries. Thus, a potential mass market is developing for mobile computing and m-commerce.

- *Declining prices.* The price of wireless devices is declining and will continue to decline.

- *Bandwidth improvement.* To properly conduct m-commerce, you need sufficient bandwidth for transmitting text, voice, video, and multimedia. Wi-Fi, 4G cellular technology, and WiMAX provide the necessary bandwidth.

Mobile computing and m-commerce include many applications. These applications result from the capabilities of various technologies. You will examine these applications and their impact on business activities in the next section.

Mobile Commerce Applications

Mobile commerce applications are many and varied. The most popular applications include location-based applications, financial services, intrabusiness applications, accessing information, and telemetry. The rest of this section examines these various applications and their effects on the ways people live and do business.

An interesting twist on mobile applications has emerged, called a mobile extension. Mobile applications are Internet applications that run on smart phones and other mobile devices. Mobile applications help users connect to Internet services more commonly accessed on desktop or laptop computers. As you see in IT's About Business 10.3, mobile extensions are different from mobile applications.

ᵀ'ˢ ABOUT BUSINESS 10.3

Mobile Extensions

The 100,000 or so user forum members of Bigfishtackle. com (www.bigfishtackle.com), a Web site for fishing enthusiasts, like to share information about where "the big ones are biting." Naturally, they want to do that in real time from their mobile phones. Accordingly, in 2007 Bigfishtackle began reformatting its Web site for easy readability on smaller mobile device screens.

Midway through the reformatting process, however, Bigfishtackle discovered dotMobi (http://mtld.mobi/), a Dublin, Ireland, company that sells .mobi domain names, as well as tools for creating a mobile-optimized Web experience. Now, Bigfishtackle.mobi (www.bigfishtackle. mobi) gives its forum members viewing, browsing, and posting functionalities on their mobile devices that function just like the desktop Web experience, but that are specifically designed for small mobile phone screens.

The .mobi designation does not indicate a separate Web site from bigfishtackle.com. Instead, it is a mobile-optimized extension of the original Web site. To use the .mobi extension, Bigfishtackle did not have to change its URL. In fact, companies can change items on their .mobi sites, and those changes will integrate with their regular Web sites in real time.

The success of the iPhone and the Android smart phones created a rapidly growing market for mobile apps, but with that success came new challenges, especially for app developers. App developers do not receive full proceeds from their apps because app stores will take part of their revenue stream. Also, the app must undergo testing and certification procedures before it can appear on a virtual store shelf. But the biggest challenge for app developers and app stores is how to get an app noticed when it becomes available. At the Apple store, for example, an app has to fight for attention against more than 500,000 other apps.

Also, even if consumers do find an app, will they use it? As mobile phone users download an increasing number of apps, concerns are growing about the potential for app overload.

Many analysts feel that in the long run, mobile extension Web sites could prove to offer greater business benefits than mobile apps. In fact, many small business owners would rather spend their time and money enhancing their core Web sites (which also enhances their mobile extension sites at the same time), than trying to build a separate mobile app.

Diego Cervo/Blend Images/ Getty Images, Inc.

The best part for small businesses is that they do not need an IT department to develop a .mobi Web site. For example, dotMobi's goMobi (http://gomobi. info) tool enables business owners to use simple drag-and-drop methods to turn their desktop Web site into a mobile Web site. In addition, with dotMobi's free mobiReady.com (http://ready.mobi) service, owners can test their mobile extensions to see how they will look from the perspective of different mobile devices. These tools may well enable mobi sites to become more prevalent in the future.

Sources: Compiled from D. OShea, "Business in Motion," *Entrepreneur*, March 2011; http://mtld.mobi/, http://gomobi.info, http://ready.mobi, accessed March 20, 2012.

Questions

1. How do .mobi Web site extensions differ from mobile apps?
2. What are the advantages of mobile apps compared to mobile extensions?
3. What are the advantages of mobile extensions compared to mobile apps?

Location-Based Applications and Services. M-commerce B2C applications include location-based services and location-based applications. Location-based mobile commerce is called **location-based commerce (or L-commerce)**.

Location-based services provide information that is specific to a given location. For example, a mobile user can (1) request the nearest business or service, such as an ATM or a restaurant; (2) receive alerts, such as a warning of a traffic jam or an accident; and (3) find a friend. Wireless carriers can provide location-based services such as locating taxis, service personnel, doctors, and rental equipment; scheduling fleets; tracking objects such as packages and train boxcars; finding information such as navigation, weather, traffic, and room schedules; targeting advertising; and automating airport check-ins.

Consider, for example, how location-based advertising can make the marketing process more productive. Marketers can use this technology to integrate the current locations and preferences of mobile users. They can then send user-specific advertising messages concerning nearby shops, malls, and restaurants to consumers' wireless devices.

Financial Services. Mobile financial applications include banking, wireless payments and micropayments, money transfers, wireless wallets, and bill-payment services. The bottom line for mobile financial applications is to make it more convenient for customers to transact business regardless of where they are or what time it is. Harried customers are demanding such convenience.

In many countries, banks increasingly offer mobile access to financial and account information. For example, Citibank (www.citibank.com) alerts customers on their digital cell phones about changes in their account information.

If you took a taxi ride in Frankfurt, Germany, you could use your cell phone to pay the taxi driver. Such very small purchase amounts (generally less than $10) are called *micropayments*.

Web shoppers historically have preferred to pay with credit cards. Because credit card companies sometimes charge fees on transactions, however, credit cards are an inefficient way to make very small purchases. The growth of relatively inexpensive digital content, such as music (for example, iTunes), ring tones, and downloadable games, is driving the growth of micropayments, as merchants seek to avoid paying credit card fees on small transactions.

Ultimately, however, the success of micropayment applications will depend on the costs of the transactions. Transaction costs will be small only when the volume of transactions is large. One technology that can increase the volume of transactions is wireless mobile wallets. Various companies offer **mobile wallet (m-wallet)** technologies that enable cardholders to make purchases with a single click from their mobile devices. Chapter Closing Case 1 discusses mobile wallets in detail.

In China, SmartPay allows users to use their mobile phones to pay their phone bills and utility bills, buy lottery tickets and airline tickets, and make other purchases. SmartPay launched 172.com (see www.172.com), a portal that centralizes the company's mobile, telephone, and Internet-based payment services for consumers. The portal is designed to provide a convenient, centralized source of information for all these transactions.

Intrabusiness Applications. Although business-to-consumer (B2C) m-commerce gets considerable publicity, most of today's m-commerce applications actually are used *within* organizations. In this section, you will see how companies use mobile computing to support their employees.

Mobile devices increasingly are becoming an integral part of workflow applications. For example, companies can use nonvoice mobile services to assist in dispatch functions— that is, to assign jobs to mobile employees, along with detailed information about the job. Target areas for mobile delivery and dispatch services include transportation (e.g., delivery of food, oil, newspapers, cargo; courier services; tow trucks; taxis), utilities (e.g., gas, electricity, phone, water); field service (e.g., computer, office equipment, home repair); health care (e.g., visiting nurses, doctors, social services); and security (e.g., patrols, alarm installation).

Accessing Information. Mobile portals and voice portals are designed to aggregate and deliver content in a form that will work within the limited space available on mobile devices. These portals provide information anywhere and anytime to users.

A **mobile portal** aggregates and provides content and services for mobile users. These services include news, sports, and e-mail; entertainment, travel, and restaurant information; community services; and stock trading. The world's best-known mobile portal—i-mode from NTT DoCoMo (www.nttdocomo.com)—has more than 40 million subscribers, primarily in Japan. Major players in Europe are Vodafone, O2, and T-Mobile. Some traditional portals—for example, Yahoo, AOL, and MSN—have mobile portals as well.

A **voice portal** is a Web site with an audio interface. Voice portals are not Web sites in the normal sense because they can also be accessed through a standard phone or a cell phone. A certain phone number connects you to a Web site, where you can request information verbally. The system finds the information, translates it into a computer-generated voice reply, and tells you what you want to know. Most airlines provide real-time information on flight status this way.

An example of a voice portal is the voice-activated 511 travel-information line developed by Tellme.com. It enables callers to inquire about weather, local restaurants, current traffic, and other handy information. In addition to retrieving information, some sites provide true interaction. For example, iPing (www.iping.com) is a reminder and notification service that allows users to enter information via the Web and receive reminder calls. This service can even call a group of people to notify them of a meeting or conference call.

Telemetry Applications. **Telemetry** is the wireless transmission and receipt of data gathered from remote sensors. Telemetry has numerous mobile computing applications. For example, technicians can use telemetry to identify maintenance problems in equipment. As another example, doctors can monitor patients and control medical equipment from a distance.

Car manufacturers use telemetry applications for remote vehicle diagnosis and preventive maintenance. For instance, drivers of many General Motors cars use its OnStar system (www.onstar.com) in numerous ways. IT's About Business 10.4 describes two telemetry applications.

I**T**'S ABOUT BUSINESS 10.4

Telemetry in Action

U.S. Xpress Enterprises

U.S. Xpress Enterprises (www.usxpress.com) is one of the largest private trucking companies. Through a device installed in the cabs of its 10,000 truck fleet, the company can track where drivers are, how many times they have braked hard in the last few hours, whether they texted customers saying they would be late, and for how long they rested.

U.S. Xpress can use these data points to track particular issues that are important to the company. For instance, it pays particular attention to the fuel economy of each driver. Truckers generally keep their engines running and the air-conditioning on after they have pulled over for the night. If a driver has a 10-hour break, the company decided that the truck's air-conditioning system should be set at 70 degrees for the first 2 hours so the driver can go to sleep. After that, the company would like the air-conditioning to go back up to 78 or 79 degrees. Through these new guidelines, and importantly, having the ability to track compliance, U.S. Xpress has lowered its annual fuel consumption by 62 gallons per truck, thereby saving a total of $24 million per year.

© Ales Veuscek/iStockphoto

Another item tracked by U.S. Xpress systems are drivers' tweets and blog posts. The company has a sentiment dashboard that monitors how the truckers are feeling. If managers see that the truckers strongly dislike a software application or a policy, they can respond with a new software application or new policies in a few hours. For U.S. Xpress, this monitoring process is a key tool in its driver retention initiatives. (Driver turnover is a chronic problem in the trucking business.)

IRhythm Technologies

IRhythm Technologies (www.irhythmtech.com), a medical device manufacturer, makes a type of oversize, plastic bandage called the Zio Patch. This product helps doctors detect cardiac problems before they become fatal. The Zio Patch is designed to be plastered to patients' chests for 2 weeks. During this time, it measures patients' heart activity. Then, the patients mail the Zio Patch back to IRhythm's offices, where a technician feeds the information gathered by the Patch into Amazon's cloud computing service.

IRhythm's analytic software divides the 14-day periods into chunks and analyzes them using algorithms. Unusual activity is flagged and sent to physicians. For quality control of the Zio Patch itself, IRhythm uses Splunk. Splunk's system monitors the strength of the patch's recording signals, whether heat affects its adhesiveness to the skin, and for how long patients actually wear the device.

The advantage of the waterproof Zio Patch is that it can be worn for an extended period compared to rival products. Rival products are typically much larger, and can only be worn for a couple of days. In addition, rival products often need to be removed when patients sleep or shower—which happens to be when heart abnormalities often occur. The 14 days of constant wear allowed by Zio Patch produces a large amount of data that therefore catches trends that competitor products miss.

Sources: Compiled from A. Vance, "New Analytics Technology Is Predicting What You're About To Do Next," *Bloomberg BusinessWeek*, September 12–18, 2011; www.usxpress.com, www.irhythmtech.com, accessed March 18, 2012.

Questions

1. Describe other examples of how telemetry applications can be useful to the trucking and health care industries.

2. Are there disadvantages to using telemetry technology in the trucking industry? In the health care industry? Provide examples to support your answer.

An interesting telemetry application for individuals is an iPhone app called Find My iPhone. Find My iPhone is a part of the Apple iCloud (www.apple.com/icloud). Find My iPhone provides several very helpful telemetry functions. If you lose your iPhone, there are two ways to see its approximate location on a map: You can sign into the Apple iCloud from any computer or you can use the Find My iPhone app on another iPhone, iPad, or iPod touch.

If you have left your iPhone somewhere you remember, you can write a message and display it on your iPhone's screen. The message might say, "Left my iPhone. Please call me at 301-555-1211." Your message appears on your iPhone, even if the screen is locked. And, if the map shows your iPhone is nearby—perhaps in your office under a pile of papers—you can tell Find My iPhone to play a sound that overrides the volume or silent setting.

If you left your iPhone in a public place, you may want to protect its contents. You can remotely set a four-digit passcode lock to prevent people from using your iPhone, accessing your personal information, or tampering with your settings.

You can initiate a remote wipe (erase all contents) to restore your iPhone to its factory settings. If you eventually find your iPhone, you can connect it to your computer and use iTunes to restore the data from your most recent backup.

If you have lost your iPhone and do not have access to a computer, you can download the Find My iPhone app to a friend's iPhone, iPad, or iPod touch and sign in to access all the Find My iPhone features.

- BEFORE *YOU GO ON . . .* -

1. What are the major drivers of mobile computing?
2. Describe mobile portals and voice portals.
3. Describe wireless financial services.
4. List some of the major intrabusiness wireless applications.

Apply the Concept 10.3

Background George Santayana (1863–1952) was a philosopher who said that "Those who cannot remember the past are condemned to repeat it." This has been reworded into several general statements about the importance of understanding history.

NTT DoCoMo is a Japanese cell phone service provider who dominated the market until around 1999 when its growth began to plateau. Only offering phone services seemed to be tapering off. At this time the company launched a new service (called i-Mode) that allowed users to access limited Internet data and offered customized apps. (See http://www.wiley.com/go/rainer/applytheconcept and click on the first link listed for Apply the Concept 10.3 for more information on i-Mode.) However, the Internet connection and apps were most (if not only) available on nonsmart phones.

Activity Visit http://www.wiley.com/go/rainer/applytheconcept and click on the second link for Apply the Concept 10.3 and look at the growth chart that NTT DoCoMo presents. Notice how the complexity of the activities grows as you move toward the upper right-hand corner of the chart. Think about standard nonsmart phones in this market (the major product NTT DoCoMo had to offer). Would they stand a chance at helping moving customers into the life and behavior assistance areas? Although DoCoMo was ahead of its time with i-Mode, the rest of the market (bandwidth accessibility, cell phone computing power, etc.) was not ready to move forward with this model of cell phone usage.

Deliverable

Imagine that you are the Senior VP of R&D for Google's Android division. Given NTT DoCoMo's above example of a good idea with mismatched technology, write a memo to your team explaining that you have decided to hold off on sending your latest Android updates to market. You feel you have an excellent product that the market is just not ready for. It is more advanced than the devices and the bandwidth can support. Use this example to show that in some cases the first to the market is not the winner. All the pieces of the puzzle have to come together to make a successful product launch. If you like, put together a table that shows how your strongest competitor (the Apple iPhone) has evolved alongside the available technology (a big factor in its success).

Submit your memo to your professor.

Quiz questions are assignable in WileyPLUS, and available on the Book Companion Site at http://www.wiley.com/college/rainer.

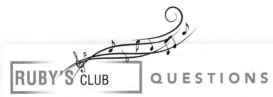

RUBY'S CLUB QUESTIONS

1. Ruben and Lisa's idea for the mobile ordering of drinks is a form of location-based m-commerce. What other advantages (aside from mobile ordering and paying for drinks) can you think of that Ruben and Lisa can tap into?

2. Mobile commerce offers five value-added attributes that break the barriers of geography and time: ubiquity, convenience, instant connectivity, personalization, and localization of products and services. Which of these do you think is most important for Ruben's idea of the mobile ordering system?

10.4 Pervasive Computing

A world in which virtually every object has processing power with wireless or wired connections to a global network is the world of **pervasive computing** (or **ubiquitous computing**). Pervasive computing is invisible "everywhere computing" that is embedded in the objects around us—the floor, the lights, our cars, the washing machine, our cell phones, our clothes, and so on.

For example, in a *smart home*, your home computer, television, lighting and heating controls, home security system, and many appliances can communicate with one another via a home network. You can control these linked systems through various devices, including your pager, cell phone, television, home computer, PDA, and even your automobile. One of the key elements of a smart home is the *smart appliance*, an Internet-ready appliance that can be controlled by a small handheld device or a desktop computer via a home network, either wireline or wireless. Two technologies provide the infrastructure for pervasive computing: radio-frequency identification and wireless sensor networks.

Media Bakery

Key fobs are a simple example of how wireless technologies have changed our lives.

Radio-Frequency Identification

Radio-frequency identification (**RFID**) technology allows manufacturers to attach tags with antennas and computer chips on goods and then track their movement through radio signals. There are many uses for RFID tags, as you see in IT's About Business 10.5.

T'S ABOUT BUSINESS 10.5

BP Uses Wireless Technologies

BP (www.bp.com) launched a wide-ranging information technology initiative in 2009. The initiative, which BP calls "Track and Trace," involves deploying a web of networked RFID tags, cellular phones, and GPS devices to monitor key assets around the world. Its goals were to improve safety and compliance. Another goal was to save money by reducing BP's asset loss and theft, employee downtime, and material waste.

Track and Trace relies on a wide range of sensing technologies that had to be customized for the project. The technologies had to be safe to use around oil and gas and be able to survive harsh conditions—from arctic cold to desert heat to Gulf humidity. For example, BP worked with a vendor partner to develop a GPS tracking device for pipeline inspectors, who often work alone in hazardous, remote conditions. The vendor had

to shrink its standard device and ensure that it would not emit sparks, making it safe for use around combustible materials. Track and Trace technologies also had to be practical on a massive scale to influence the operations of a company with around 80,000 employees, thousands of facilities around the world, and millions of pieces of field equipment.

When the Deepwater Horizon oil rig exploded in 2010, killing 11 people and spewing oil into the Gulf of Mexico for 87 days, BP faced one of the industry's biggest and costliest oil cleanups in history. When the incident occurred, Track and Trace enabled BP to respond quickly in managing the cleanup, primarily through alerting spill responders about what equipment they had to work with and what condition the rig was in. BP deployed RFID-tagged Wave Gliders (self-powered robots that float around collecting data on air and water quality) in the Gulf of Mexico, and tagged skimmers and other key assets across four U.S. Gulf states.

Another example of Track and Trace's usefulness is the role it played when BP had to perform routine refinery maintenance at the firm's Gelsenkirchen (GSK) refinery in Germany. To accomplish this process, BP had to place RFID tags on 100,000 blinds at the refinery. GSK technicians must work section by section, sealing off one area before proceeding to the next. To do that, they use what is called a blind to close off pipe ends at the flange. Blinds must be inserted and removed in a precise sequence. Engineers use Track and Trace to track the blinds with handheld readers. SAP software analyzes the data from Track and Trace to automatically determine which flanges should be blinded, and when.

In another Track and Trace project, BP outfitted oil trucks in Alaska with cellular equipment that transmits data to BP through the AT&T cellular network or, as a backup, through Iridium's satellites. The system monitors driver activity and sends alerts through e-mail and text about a suspected accident or unsafe activity such as speeding or hard braking. The system monitors about 900 trucks and generates roughly 500,000 messages per week.

Sources: Compiled from T. Team, "BP Goes for Public Relations Makeover to Get Beyond Gulf Spill," *Forbes*, February 7, 2012; P. McDougall, "Asset Tracking Aids Huge BP Cleanup," *InformationWeek*, September 19, 2011; C. Swedberg, "BP Uses RFID Sensors to Track Pipe Corrosion," *RFID Journal*, January 31, 2011; www.bp.com, accessed March 11, 2012.

Questions

1. How did Track and Trace technologies help BP to effectively manage the catastrophic oil spill in the Gulf of Mexico?

2. What other uses might BP have for wireless sensor technologies?

RFID was developed to replace bar codes. A typical bar code, known as the *Universal Product Code (UPC)*, is made up of 12 digits that are batched in various groups. The first digit identifies the item type, the next 5 digits identify the manufacturer, and the next 5 identify the product. The last digit is a check digit for error detection. Bar codes have worked well, but they have limitations. First, they require a line of sight to the scanning device. This system works well in a store, but it can pose substantial problems in a manufacturing plant or a warehouse or on a shipping/receiving dock. Second, because bar codes are printed on paper, they can be ripped, soiled, or lost. Third, the bar code identifies the manufacturer and product but not the actual item. Two systems are being developed to replace bar codes: *QR (for quick response) codes* and RFID systems. Figure 10.6 shows bar codes, QR codes, and an RFID tag.

A QR code is a two-dimensional code, readable by dedicated QR readers and camera phones. QR codes have several advantages over bar codes:

- QR codes can store much more information than bar codes.
- Data types stored in QR codes include numbers, text, URLs, and even Japanese characters.
- The size of QR codes is small because these codes store information horizontally and vertically.
- QR codes are more resistant to damage than bar codes.
- QR codes can be read from any direction or angle, so the possibility of a failure in reading a QR code is reduced.

RFID systems use tags with embedded microchips, which contain data, and antennas to transmit radio signals over a short distance to RFID readers. The readers pass the data over a network to a computer for processing. The chip in the RFID tag is programmed with information that uniquely identifies an item. It also contains information about the item such as its location and

Figure 10.6 Bar codes, RFID tags, and QR codes. (*Sources:* © Patrick Duinkerke/iStockphoto; © raphotography/iStockphoto; Media Bakery.)

Figure 10.7 Small RFID tag. (*Source:* © Ecken, Dominique/ Keystone Pressedienst/Zuma Press.)

where and when it was made. Figure 10.7 shows an RFID reader and an RFID tag on a pallet.

There are two basic types of RFID tags: active and passive. *Active RFID tags* use internal batteries for power and they broadcast radio waves to a reader. Because active tags contain batteries, they are more expensive than passive RFID tags and can be read over greater distances. Active tags, therefore, are used for more expensive items. *Passive RFID tags* rely entirely on readers for their power. They are less expensive than active tags and can be read only up to 20 feet. They are generally applied to less-expensive merchandise. Problems with RFID include expense and the comparatively large size of the tags. RFID tags can also speed up grocery shopping, as the following example shows.

EXAMPLE

Shoppers are using a system called Scan It in about half of the supermarket chain owner Ahold USA's (www.ahold.com) Stop & Shop and Giant supermarkets in the northeastern United States. Using this system, shoppers scan and bag their own groceries as they navigate the aisles, while a screen keeps a running total of their purchases. About a dozen times per shopping trip, the device lets out a "Ka-ching" as an electronic coupon appears on the screen. When finished selecting items, Scan It shoppers either go to a self-checkout station to upload their bill and pay, or hand the scanner to a cashier. If shoppers scan an unwanted item by accident, they simply select "Remove" from the menu option, scan the item again, and the item is removed from their cart and their total payment due.

Ahold has found that shoppers who use the Scan It system spend about 10 percent more in its stores than the average customer. Therefore, the company is now testing ways for customers to download Scan It software directly into their smart phones. They are also exploring ways for customers to use their smart phones to pay.

Sources: Compiled from A. Zimmerman, "Check Out the Future of Shopping," *The Wall Street Journal*, May 18, 2011; www.ahold.com, accessed March 21, 2012.

Wireless Sensor Networks

Wireless sensor networks (WSNs) are networks of interconnected, battery-powered, wireless sensors called *motes* (analogous to nodes) that are placed into the physical environment. The motes collect data from many points over an extended space. Each mote contains processing, storage, and radio-frequency sensors and antennas. Each mote "wakes up" or activates for a fraction of a second when it has data to transmit. It then relays those data to its nearest neighbor. So, instead of every mote transmitting its data to a remote computer at a base station, the data are moved mote by mote until they reach a central computer where they can be stored and analyzed. An advantage of a wireless sensor network is that if one mote fails, then another one can pick up the data. This process makes WSNs very efficient and reliable. Also, if the network requires more bandwidth, it is easy to boost performance by placing new motes when and where they are required.

The motes provide information that enables a central computer to integrate reports of the same activity from different angles within the network. Therefore, the network can determine with much greater accuracy information such as the direction in which a person is moving, the weight of a vehicle, and the amount of rainfall over a field of crops.

There are many applications of wireless sensors. Nest Labs (www.nest.com) produces a "digital thermostat" that combines sensors and Web technology. The thermostat senses not only air temperature, but also the movements of people in a house, their comings and goings, and adjusts room temperatures accordingly to save energy.

Placing sensors in all kind of products makes the products "smart." Smart equipment includes sensors in bridges and oil rigs that alert their human minders when they need repairs, before equipment failure occurs. Sensors in jet engines produce data in real time on the operating performance of the engines. Sensors in fruit and vegetable cartons can track location and "sniff" the produce, warning in advance of spoilage, so shipments can be rerouted or rescheduled.

In Dubuque, Iowa, IBM has started on a long-term project with the local government to use sensors, software, and the Internet to improve the city's use of water, electricity, and transportation. In a pilot project in 2011, digital water meters were installed in 151 homes, with software monitoring water use and patterns, informing residents about ways to consume less and alerting them to likely leaks. The savings in the pilot study translated into decreasing water use by 65 million gallons per year in the entire city.

A very useful application of sensors is to use them in smart electrical meters, thus forming a smart grid. Smart meters monitor the usage of electricity and transmit that data to the utility company. IT's About Business 10.6 shows the advantages of smart meters in Brazil.

---- **BEFORE** *YOU GO ON . . .* ----

1. Define *pervasive computing*, *RFID*, and *wireless sensor networks*.

2. Provide two specific business uses of RFID technology.

IT's ABOUT BUSINESS 10.6

Brazil Uses Smart Meters

Reading electricity meters can be a dangerous job in Brazil, as AES Electropaulo (www. aeselectropaulo.com.br) meter readers well know.

Robson Dourado, a São Paulo meter reader, says residents of São Paulo's Morro do Indio slum watch him carefully as he makes his rounds, worried that he will see rogue wires siphoning away power illegally.

Electricity theft is rampant across much of Latin America, so much so that statisticians have devised a formula that uses the stolen wattage to measure the size of a country's informal economy. In some parts of Brazil, as much as 20 percent of electricity is stolen. To combat the problem and avoid violent encounters,

utilities are using smart meters. The devices, which cost $150 to $400 each, allow power companies to monitor power usage remotely and in real time. The meters can detect unusually heavy demand, which may signal an illegal hookup. They can also shut off service to households and businesses that do not pay their bills.

The devices remove the human factor from meter reading, so customers can no longer collude with dishonest meter readers to cheat the power company.

Smart meters are the perfect solution, says the chief technology officer of a Rio de Janeiro-based utility that has installed more than 150,000 of the devices. He says, "They save us money, they are easy to install, and they require little maintenance." One Brazilian government official believes the meters may save utility companies as much as $4.7 billion per year.

© Kenneth Chung/iStockphoto

Sales of smart meters in South America and Latin America are expected to generate $24 billion in revenue through 2020, two-thirds of it in Brazil. Estimates are that Brazilian utility companies may install as many as 63.5 million smart meters by 2020, while Mexico may install some 22.4 million, Argentina some 4.9 million, and Chile some 3.2 million over the same time.

In Rio de Janeiro, utility companies are taking advantage of preparations for the 2014 World Cup soccer championship and the 2016 Olympic Games to deploy the meters. Before August 2011, about 80 percent of electricity in Tabajara and Morro dos Cabritos, two particularly violent slums, was stolen through illegal connections. After police established a constant presence in the slums in 2011, a utility company installed 50,000 smart meters. Electricity theft has dropped to zero since that time, proving the efficacy of the new technology.

Sources: Compiled from S. Nielsen, "Smart Meters Help Brazil Zap Electricity Theft," *Bloomberg BusinessWeek*, March 8, 2012; "Latin America's First Smart Grid Project Now Complete," *SmartGridNews*, December 22, 2011; "Brazil Will Adopt Smart Meters," *Gulfnews.com*, October 30, 2011; J. St. John, "Echelon Partners Up to Break into Brazil's Smart Meter Market," *Greentechmedia*, October 13, 2011; J. St. John, "Brazil: The Next Hot Smart Meter Market," *GigaOM.com*, November 24, 2010; www.aeselectropaulo.com.br, accessed March 20, 2012.

Questions

1. If smart meters are installed in large numbers, then what happens to the meter readers? Do you see problems with this scenario?

2. Besides deterring theft, what other advantages might a smart meter provide to a utility company? To a homeowner? To a business?

Apply the Concept 10.4

Background Pervasive computing exists when the world around us becomes more connected in a digital manner. Refrigerators could text you if the door is not fully shut. The thermostat is connected to the Internet so you can turn the temperature down after you leave home and realize you forgot to set it. The alarm system (this is not new) calls the police, fire department, and you when there is a problem.

Activity Visit http://www.wiley.com/go/rainer/applytheconcept and click on the link for Apply the Concept 10.4. This will take you to a video about "Sixth Sense Technology" by "Pranav Mistry." Dr. Mistry's research goes one step further than pervasive computing and attempts to completely blend the physical and digital world. Anything can be a screen, no keyboard or mouse is required, and information is automatically displayed when it recognizes something in the physical world and has relevant information to share.

Deliverable

Describe a typical day for a pediatrician when this technology becomes a production scale reality. How will the office visit be handled? Will there be paper charts? Computerized charts? What about diagnosis? What if the computer system could see what the doctor sees and help with a diagnosis? What if the computer system could record the patient encounter so as to provide evidence in a malpractice situation? Would this be beneficial or would this "pervasive" technology become "invasive"?

Submit your description to your professor.

Quiz questions are assignable in WileyPLUS, and available on the Book Companion Site at http://www.wiley.com/college/rainer.

RUBY'S CLUB | QUESTIONS

1. How might Ruby's Club utilize telemetry to measure and account for its problem with shrinkage (the problem of a bartender pouring a little more alcohol than the customer paid for)?

2. Is there a mobile portal that could help Ruben and Lisa reach their customers?

10.5 Wireless Security

Clearly, wireless networks provide numerous benefits for businesses. However, they also present a huge challenge to management—namely, their inherent lack of security. Wireless is a broadcast medium, and transmissions can be intercepted by anyone who is close enough and has access to the appropriate equipment. There are four major threats to wireless networks: rogue access points, war driving, eavesdropping, and radio-frequency jamming.

A *rogue access point* is an unauthorized access point to a wireless network. The rogue could be someone in your organization who sets up an access point meaning no harm but fails to inform the IT department. In more serious cases, the rogue is an "evil twin"— someone who wishes to access a wireless network for malicious purposes.

In an evil twin attack, the attacker is in the vicinity with a Wi-Fi-enabled computer and a separate connection to the Internet. Using a hotspotter—a device that detects wireless networks and provides information on them (see www.canarywireless.com)—the attacker simulates a wireless access point with the same wireless network name, or SSID, as the one that authorized users expect. If the signal is strong enough, users will connect to the attacker's system instead of the real access point. The attacker can then serve them a Web page asking for them to provide confidential information such as user names, passwords, and account numbers. In other cases, the attacker simply captures wireless transmissions. These attacks are more effective with public hotspots (for example, McDonald's and Starbucks) than with corporate networks.

War driving is the act of locating WLANs while driving (or walking) around a city or elsewhere. To war drive or walk, you simply need a Wi-Fi detector and a wirelessly enabled computer. If a WLAN has a range that extends beyond the building in which it is located, then an unauthorized user might be able to intrude into the network. The intruder can then obtain a free Internet connection and possibly gain access to important data and other resources.

Eavesdropping refers to efforts by unauthorized users to access data that are traveling over wireless networks.

In *radio-frequency (RF) jamming*, a person or a device intentionally or unintentionally interferes with your wireless network transmissions.

As you see, wireless systems can be difficult to secure. Plug IT In 6 discusses a variety of techniques and technologies that you should implement to help you avoid these threats.

— BEFORE *YOU GO ON* . . . —

1. Describe the four major threats to the security of wireless networks.

2. Which of these threats is the most dangerous for a business? Which is the most dangerous for an individual? Support your answers.

Apply the Concept 10.5

Background For many of us, our life information lives within our smart phones. Contacts, pictures, e-mail, driving directions, entertainment, communication, and soon even our wallets (probably the car keys too). However, as we put more and more information on our phones, we are also putting ourselves at risk for a dramatic loss of information.

Activity Visit http://www.wiley.com/go/rainer/applytheconcept and click on the first link for Apply the Concept 10.5. This will provide some information about security issues for mobile phones. Then take a look at the article at the second link that illustrates how Google has committed to ensuring the safety of apps that are loaded onto Android devices. Finally, read over the article at the last link about the centralized database that the major phone system carriers have agreed to develop to help crack down on phone theft.

Deliverable

Build a table that shows the advantages and disadvantages of keeping lots of personal information on your phone. Additionally, describe the decision of locking the phone (and the convenience you give up for that) or leaving it unlocked. Consider the information that is available if it is left open. At the same time, consider how long it would take to keep it password protected. Once you develop your list, consider if you personally want to change any habits.

Submit your table to your professor.

Quiz questions are assignable in WileyPLUS, and available on the Book Companion Site at http://www.wiley.com/college/rainer.

RUBY'S CLUB QUESTIONS

1. Wireless security is going to be very important at Ruby's Club. Ruben and Lisa only want customers who have paid the cover fee to be able to access the network. What ideas can you give them to help manage this need?
2. How do hotels and restaurants handle this problem? Would their model work for Ruby's Club?

What's in IT for ME?

FOR THE ACCOUNTING MAJOR

Wireless applications help accountants to count and audit inventory. They also expedite the flow of information for cost control. Price management, inventory control, and other accounting-related activities can be improved with the use of wireless technologies.

FOR THE FINANCE MAJOR

Wireless services can provide banks and other financial institutions with a competitive advantage. For example, wireless electronic payments, including micropayments, are more convenient (anywhere, anytime) than traditional means of payment, and they are less expensive. Electronic bill payment from mobile devices is becoming more popular, increasing security and accuracy, expediting cycle time, and reducing processing costs.

FOR THE MARKETING MAJOR

Imagine a whole new world of marketing, advertising, and selling, with the potential to increase sales dramatically. Such is the promise of mobile computing. Of special interest for marketing are location-based advertising as well as the new opportunities resulting from pervasive computing and RFIDs. Finally, wireless technology also provides new opportunities in sales force automation (SFA), enabling faster and better communications with both customers (CRM) and corporate services.

FOR THE
PRODUCTION/OPERATIONS MANAGEMENT MAJOR

Wireless technologies offer many opportunities to support mobile employees of all kinds. Wearable computers enable off-site employees and repair personnel working in the field to service customers faster, better, and less expensively. Wireless devices can also increase productivity within factories by enhancing communication and collaboration as well as managerial planning and control. In addition, mobile computing technologies can improve safety by providing quicker warning signs and instant messaging to isolated employees.

FOR THE
HUMAN RESOURCES MANAGEMENT MAJOR

Mobile computing can improve HR training and extend it to any place at anytime. Payroll notices can be delivered as SMSs. In addition, wireless devices can make it even more convenient for employees to select their own benefits and update their personal data.

FOR THE MIS MAJOR

MIS personnel provide the wireless infrastructure that enables all organizational employees to compute and communicate anytime, anywhere. This convenience provides exciting, creative, new applications for organizations to cut costs and improve the efficiency and effectiveness of operations (for example, to achieve transparency in supply chains). Unfortunately, as you saw earlier, wireless applications are inherently insecure. This lack of security is a serious problem with which MIS personnel must contend.

SUMMARY

1. **Identify advantages and disadvantages of each of the four main types of wireless transmission media.**

Microwave transmission systems are used for high-volume, long-distance, line-of-sight communication. One advantage is the high volume. A disadvantage is that microwave transmissions are susceptible to environmental interference during severe weather such as heavy rain and snowstorms.

Satellite transmission systems make use of communication satellites, and they receive and transmit data via line-of-sight. One advantage is that the enormous footprint—the area of Earth's surface reached by a satellite's transmission—overcomes the limitations of microwave data-relay stations. Like microwaves, satellite transmissions are susceptible to environmental interference during severe weather.

Radio transmission systems use radio-wave frequencies to send data directly between transmitters and receivers. An advantage is that radio waves travel easily through normal office walls. A disadvantage is that radio transmissions are susceptible to snooping by anyone who has similar equipment that operates on the same frequency.

Infrared light is red light that is not commonly visible to human eyes. Common applications of infrared light are in remote-control units for televisions, VCRs, and DVD and CD players. An advantage of infrared is that it does not penetrate walls and so does not interfere with other devices in adjoining rooms. A disadvantage is that infrared signals can be easily blocked by furniture.

2. **Explain how businesses can use technology employed by short-range, medium-range, and long-range networks, respectively.**

Short-range wireless networks simplify the task of connecting one device to another, eliminating wires and enabling users to move around while they use the devices. In general, short-range wireless networks have a range of 100 feet or less. Short-range wireless networks include Bluetooth, ultra-wideband, and near-field communications. A business application of ultra-wideband is the PLUS Real-Time Location System from Time Domain. Using PLUS, an organization can locate multiple people and assets simultaneously.

Medium-range wireless networks include Wireless Fidelity (Wi-Fi) and mesh networks. *Wi-Fi* provides fast and easy Internet or intranet broadband access from public hotspots located at airports, hotels, Internet cafés, universities, conference centers, offices, and homes. *Mesh networks* use multiple Wi-Fi access points to create a wide area network that can be quite large.

Wide-area wireless networks connect users to the Internet over geographically dispersed territory. They include cellular telephones and wireless broadband. *Cellular telephones* provide two-way radio communications over a cellular network of base stations with seamless handoffs. *Wireless broadband* (WiMAX) has a wireless access range of up to 31 miles and a data-transfer rate of up to 75 Mbps. WiMAX can provide long-distance broadband wireless access to rural areas and remote business locations.

3. **Provide a specific example of how each of the five major m-commerce applications can benefit a business.**

Location-based services provide information specific to a location. For example, a mobile user can (1) request the nearest business or service, such as an ATM or restaurant; (2) receive alerts, such as a warning of a traffic jam or an accident; and (3) find a friend. With *location-based advertising*, marketers can integrate the current locations and preferences of mobile users. They can then send user-specific advertising messages about nearby shops, malls, and restaurants to wireless devices.

Mobile financial applications include banking, wireless payments and micropayments, money transfers, wireless wallets, and bill-payment services. The bottom line for mobile financial applications is to make it more convenient for customers to transact business regardless of where they are or what time it is.

Intrabusiness applications consist of m-commerce applications that are used *within* organizations. Companies can use nonvoice mobile services to assist in dispatch functions—that is, to assign jobs to mobile employees, along with detailed information about the job.

When it comes to *accessing information*, mobile portals and voice portals are designed to aggregate and deliver content in a form that will work within the limited space available on mobile devices. These portals provide information anywhere and anytime to users.

Telemetry is the wireless transmission and receipt of data gathered from remote sensors. Company technicians can use telemetry to identify maintenance problems in equipment. Car manufacturers use telemetry applications for remote vehicle diagnosis and preventive maintenance.

4. **Describe technologies that underlie pervasive computing, providing examples of how businesses can utilize each one.**

Pervasive computing is invisible and everywhere computing that is embedded in the objects around us. Two technologies provide the infrastructure for pervasive computing: *radio-frequency identification* (RFID) and *wireless sensor networks* (WSNs).

RFID is the term for technologies that use radio waves to automatically identify the location of individual items equipped with tags that contain embedded microchips. WSNs are networks of interconnected, battery-powered, wireless devices placed in the physical environment to collect data from many points over an extended space.

5. **Explain how the four major threats to wireless networks can damage a business.**

The four major threats to wireless networks are rogue access points, war driving, eavesdropping, and radio-frequency jamming. A *rogue access point* is an unauthorized access point to a wireless network. *War driving* is the act of locating WLANs while driving around a city or elsewhere. *Eavesdropping* refers to efforts by unauthorized users to access data that are traveling over wireless networks. *Radio-frequency jamming* occurs when a person or a device intentionally or unintentionally interferes with wireless network transmissions.

>>> CHAPTER GLOSSARY

Bluetooth Chip technology that enables short-range connection (data and voice) between wireless devices.

cellular telephones (cell phones) Phones that provide two-way radio communications over a cellular network of base stations with seamless handoffs.

Global Positioning System (GPS) A wireless system that uses satellites to enable users to determine their position anywhere on earth.

hotspot A small geographical perimeter within which a wireless access point provides service to a number of users.

infrared A type of wireless transmission that uses red light not commonly visible to human eyes.

location-based commerce (l-commerce) Mobile commerce transactions targeted to individuals in specific locations, at specific times.

mesh networks Networks composed of multiple Wi-Fi access points that create a wide area network that can be quite large.

microwave transmission A wireless system that uses microwaves for high-volume, long-distance, point-to-point communication.

mobile commerce (or m-commerce) Electronic commerce transactions that are conducted with a mobile device.

mobile computing A real-time connection between a mobile device and other computing environments, such as the Internet or an intranet.

mobile portal A portal that aggregates and provides content and services for mobile users.

mobile wallet (m-wallet) A technology that allows users to make purchases with a single click from their mobile devices.

near-field communications (NFC) The smallest of the short-range wireless networks that is designed to be embedded in mobile devices such as cell phones and credit cards.

personal area network A computer network used for communication among computer devices close to one person.

pervasive computing (or **ubiquitous computing**) A computer environment where virtually every object has processing power with wireless or wired connections to a global network.

propagation delay Any delay in communications from signal transmission time through a physical medium.

radio-frequency identification (RFID) technology A wireless technology that allows manufacturers to attach tags with antennas and computer chips on goods and then track their movement through radio signals.

radio transmission Uses radio-wave frequencies to send data directly between transmitters and receivers.

satellite radio (or **digital radio**) A wireless system that offers uninterrupted, near CD-quality music that is beamed to your radio from satellites.

satellite transmission A wireless transmission system that uses satellites for broadcast communications.

telemetry The wireless transmission and receipt of data gathered from remote sensors.

ubiquitous computing (see **pervasive computing**)

ultra-wideband (UWB) A high-bandwidth wireless technology with transmission speeds in excess of 100 Mbps that can be used for applications such as streaming multimedia from, say, a personal computer to a television.

voice portal A Web site with an audio interface.

wireless Telecommunications in which electromagnetic waves carry the signal between communicating devices.

wireless 911 911 emergency calls made with wireless devices.

wireless access point An antenna connecting a mobile device to a wired local area network.

Wireless Fidelity (Wi-Fi) A set of standards for wireless local area networks based on the IEEE 802.11 standard.

wireless local area network (WLAN) A computer network in a limited geographical area that uses wireless transmission for communication.

wireless sensor networks (WSNs) Networks of interconnected, battery-powered, wireless sensors placed in the physical environment.

>>> DISCUSSION QUESTIONS

1. Discuss how m-commerce can expand the reach of e-business.

2. Discuss how mobile computing can solve some of the problems of the digital divide.

3. List three to four major advantages of wireless commerce to consumers and explain what benefits they provide to consumers.

4. Discuss the ways in which Wi-Fi is being used to support mobile computing and m-commerce. Describe the ways in which Wi-Fi is affecting the use of cellular phones for m-commerce.

5. You can use location-based tools to help you find your car or the closest gas station. However, some people see location-based tools as an invasion of privacy. Discuss the pros and cons of location-based tools.

6. Discuss the benefits of telemetry in health care for the elderly.

7. Discuss how wireless devices can help people with disabilities.

8. Some experts say that Wi-Fi is winning the battle with 3G cellular service. Others disagree. Discuss both sides of the argument and support each one.

9. Which of the applications of pervasive computing do you think are likely to gain the greatest market acceptance over the next few years? Why?

>>> PROBLEM-SOLVING ACTIVITIES

1. Investigate commercial applications of voice portals. Visit several vendors, e.g. Microsoft and Nuance (links to both websites are available via http://www.wiley.com/go/rainer/problemsolving). What capabilities and applications do these vendors offer?

2. Using a search engine, try to determine whether there are any commercial Wi-Fi hotspots in your area. (*Hint:* Access http://www.wiley.com/rainer/go/problemsolving.)

3. Examine how new data-capture devices such as RFID tags help organizations accurately identify and segment their customers for activities such as targeted marketing. Browse the Web, and develop five potential new applications not listed in this chapter for RFID technology. What issues would arise if a country's laws mandated that such devices be embedded in everyone's body as a national identification system?

4. Investigate commercial uses of GPS. Start with www.neigps.com. Can some of the consumer-oriented products be used in industry? Prepare a report on your findings.

5. Access www.bluetooth.com. Examine the types of products being enhanced with Bluetooth technology. Present two of these products to the class and explain how they are enhanced by Bluetooth technology.

6. Explore www.nokia.com. Prepare a summary of the types of mobile services and applications Nokia currently supports and plans to support in the future.

7. Enter www.ibm.com. Search for "wireless e-business." Research the resulting stories to determine the types of wireless capabilities and applications IBM's software and hardware support. Describe some of the ways these applications have helped specific businesses and industries.

8. Research the status of 3G and 4G cellular service by visiting the links available via http://www.wiley.com/go/rainer/problemsolving. Prepare a report on the status of 3G and 4G based on your findings.

9. Enter Pitney-Bowes Business Insight (www.pbinsight.com). Click on "MapInfo Professional," then click on the "Resources" tab, then on the "Demos" tab. Look for the location-based services demos. Try all the demos. Summarize your findings.

10. Enter www.packetvideo.com. Examine the demos and products and list their capabilities.

11. Enter www.onstar.com. What types of *fleet* services does OnStar provide? Are these any different from the services OnStar provides to individual car owners? (Play the movie.)

12. Access an article about "The Internet of Things" at http://www.wiley.com/go/rainer/problemsolving. What is "the internet of things"? What types of technologies are necessary to support it? Why is it important?

>>> COLLABORATION EXERCISE

Background

Greenway Medical Technologies sells electronic health record (EHR) software. Part of the company's product allows physicians to access patient records from their mobile devices. Many doctors love the flexibility of being able to share information quickly and easily with colleagues for a second opinion. They also appreciate the ability to catch up on charts from home, the road, the train, etc.

Activity

Divide your team into the following positions: patient, doctor, nurse, business administrator, and IT director. Once your position is determined, do a little research on the idea of EHRs and mobile devices. Try to find and develop a

"platform" for a conversation about the advantages and disadvantages of this product.

Once everyone has completed the research, meet as a team and have a conversation about implementing this at your local office. Stay in the role you were assigned and cast your vote for or against the implementation of the EHRs that allows mobile access.

Deliverable

Submit your teams, voting results. Be sure to provide some background as to who voted which way and what the rationale was. Even if everyone agreed, explain yourselves so it is clear that you have had a serious discussion.

Submit your team's vote and explanation to your instructor.

CLOSING **CASE 1** > The Battle for the Mobile Wallet

THE PROBLEM >>> Customers today are in more of a hurry than ever before. To satisfy them and keep their business, retailers are looking for strategies to speed up the checkout process and improve the overall customer experience. One strategy is to use customers' smart phones as a replacement for credit and debit cards. Instead of swiping a plastic card at the checkout counter, consumers merely wave their phones a few inches above a payment terminal. This process uses a contact-free technology called near-field communications (NFC).

The technology described in the preceding paragraph, known as the mobile wallet, is already being installed on millions of phones in both the United States and overseas.

However, wide adoption of this technology in the United States is being hindered by a major battle among large corporations.

In one camp are the established credit card companies such as MasterCard, Visa, and American Express, in alliance with the banks that actually issue the cards to customers. The goal of these businesses is to maintain their traditional position at the center of any payment system and to continue to collect fees from merchants. However, they are facing intense competition from the other camp, which consists of technology companies such as Google and PayPal whose goal is to become major players in the new payment system. In addition, Apple and the mobile carriers such as Verizon, AT&T, and T-Mobile form a third camp that wants to collect fees through its own control of the phones. Adding to the competitive mix are individual companies such as Starbucks that are developing proprietary mobile wallet technologies.

In the middle of this corporate battleground are the retailers, who may yet be the deciding factor in determining who wins the payment battle. Retailers have to install terminals that accept mobile payments in order to take advantage of mobile wallet technology. Additionally, consumer advocates are concerned that a mobile system would bring higher fees, which would ultimately be borne by the customers.

The stakes in this competition are enormous because the small fees generated every time consumers swipe their cards add up to tens of billions of dollars of annual revenue in the United States alone. This revenue, of course, goes straight into the pocket of whoever controls the payment system. Before any company makes money, all of them need to sort out what role each one will play and who will collect the lucrative transaction fees from retailers.

Mobile Phone Carriers. In 2010, three of the four big mobile phone service providers—AT&T, T-Mobile, and Verizon, but not Sprint—along with Discover (www.discovercard.com) and Barclays Bank (www.barclays.co.uk)—formed a joint venture named Isis. Their intention was to create a new payment network that included both credit card companies and card-issuing banks. Isis creates a digital wallet into which customers of card-issuing banks can easily move their accounts. Consumers would interface with Isis through a mobile app, which would give them access to multiple credit and debit accounts. Retailers would participate by offering targeted offers to loyal members through Isis, while product companies and brands could also offer discounts to customers who opt in.

<<< **A VARIETY OF SOLUTIONS**

Credit Card Issuers. All three-card issuers have mobile wallet applications: MasterCard has MasterCard PayPass (which is integrated into Google Wallet), Visa has the payWave mobile wallet, and American Express has American Express Serve (with Sprint).

The credit card companies claim that their mobile applications enable consumers to make online payments quickly, without having to enter card numbers and billing addresses over and over. For example, a smart phone game could allow players to buy add-ons, such as new weapons or extra ammunition, by clicking a Visa logo. A caterer might be able to e-mail a bill with a button that allows a client to pay with one click. Payers would authorize the transaction simply by entering a name and password.

Technology Companies. In May 2011, Google released a free Android app called the Google Wallet. The wallet securely stores multiple credit cards or a Google prepaid card linked to your credit card. Google also introduced Google Offers, a location-based service that delivers daily, targeted, Groupon-like deals to the Google Wallet. The wallet also allows people to register their store loyalty cards and gift cards in the app.

Interestingly, if future models of the Apple iPhone incorporate NFC, the iPhone may route payments through Apple's iTunes store, which already has 200 million accounts tied to credit cards. Apple iTunes could therefore be transformed into mobile wallets. Both Google Wallet and Apple iTunes, however, would need access to smart phone chips and to merchants' terminals. Apple could solve this problem by manufacturing its own smart phone chips, but Google could not because it makes only software for Android smart phones, not the phones themselves.

PayPal demonstrated its Cloud Wallet in 2011, which does not use near-field communications. The only thing customers need to do to use the wallet is to enter a phone number and PIN at the register. PayPal is also integrating check-in capabilities with its mobile application and location-based services, so that smart phone users can identify nearby stores or restaurants.

Individual Companies. In January 2011, Starbucks (www.starbucks.com) announced that customers could use a bar code app on their phones to buy coffee in almost 7,000 of its stores. This is the first major pay-by-phone initiative in the United States. Customers can download the free Starbucks Card app and hold their phones in front of a scanner at Starbucks cash registers. The money is subtracted from customers' Starbucks accounts, which they can connect to their credit cards or, on iPhones, to PayPal funds. Customers can also use the Starbucks app to check their balances, find nearby stores, and earn stars to qualify for free drinks.

THE RESULTS >>> In December 2011, Verizon blocked its customers from installing Google Wallet on their smart phones. Verizon said that Google Wallet is not currently secure to use on its phones because of technical issues, and they are working with Google to iron those issues out.

Despite this public statement, industry analysts say Verizon's move is likely related to its plan to team up with rival carriers AT&T and T-Mobile on the mobile payments venture Isis. Google is working with MasterCard, Citigroup, and Sprint Nextel Corporation on its Google Wallet. Meanwhile, Visa is developing another digital wallet.

The battle for the transaction fees from your mobile wallet is ongoing, and the results will be several years in arriving. However, the potential for large revenue streams is real, because mobile wallets have clear advantages. For example, which are you more likely to have with you at any given moment—your phone or your wallet? Also, keep in mind that if you lose your phone, it can be located on a map and remotely deactivated. Plus, your phone can be password protected. Your wallet cannot do these things.

Sources: Compiled from K. Kelleher, "PayPal's Bid for the Digital Wallet Looks Strong," CNN Money, March 21, 2012; A. Efrati and A. Troianovski, "War Over the Digital Wallet," *The Wall Street Journal*, December 7, 2011; B. Reed, "Verizon Cites Security Issue for Nixing Google Wallet," *Network World*, December 6, 2011; D. Goldman, "Verizon Blocks Google Wallet," *CNN Money*, December 6, 2011; C. Iozzio, "The Cash Killer," *Popular Science*, November, 2011; F. Graham, "Will NFC Make the Mobile Wallet Work?" *BBC News*, October 27, 2011; K. Boehret, "Google Mobile App Aims to Turn Phones Into Wallets," *The Wall Street Journal*, September 21, 2011; T. Duryee, "PayPal's Response to Google's Payment Plans," *AllThingsD.com*, September 15, 2011; M. Hachman, "Is Google Wallet What Mobile Payments Need to Succeed?" *PC Magazine*, May 27, 2011; B. Reed, "Google Wallet: Five Things You Need to Know," *Network World*, May 26, 2011; R. Kim, "Isis: Respect the Carriers; We'll Be Key to NFC Success," *GigaOM*, May 6, 2011; S. Marek, "AT&T, Verizon Wireless and T-Mobile Backpedal on Isis Joint Venture," *FierceWireless*, May 4, 2011; R. Sidel and S. Raice, "Pay By Phone Dialed Back," *Wall Street Journal*, May 4, 2011; T. Team, "American Express and Visa Squeeze PayPal's Crown Jewels," *Forbes*, April 4, 2011; A. Efrati and R. Sidel, "Google Sets Role in Mobile Payment," *Wall Street Journal*, March 28, 2011; T. Bernard and C. Miller, "Swiping Is the Easy Part," *New York Times*, March 23, 2011; D. Aamoth, "Pay Phone," *Time*, February 21, 2011; D. MacMillan, "Turning Smartphones into Cash Registers," *Bloomberg BusinessWeek*, February 14–20, 2011; K. Eaton, "The Race Is On to Make NFC Wireless Credit Card Dreams Come True (and Win Market Share)," *Fast Company*, February 2, 2011; M. Hamblen, "NFC: What You Need to Know," *Computerworld*, January 28, 2011; K. Heussner, "Is Your Next Credit Card Your Cell Phone?" *ABC News*, January 26, 2011; S. Greengard, "Mobile Payment, Please," *Baseline Magazine*, January 26, 2011; E. Zemen, "Will Apple, Google Lead Mobile Payment Revolution?" *InformationWeek*, January 25, 2011; B. Ellis, "The End of Credit Cards Is Coming," *CNNMoney*, January 24, 2011; C. Miller, "Now at Starbucks: Buy a Latte by Waving Your Phone," *New York Times*, January 18, 2011; O. Kharif, "In the Works: A Google Mobile Payment Service?" *Bloomberg BusinessWeek*, January 4, 2011; R. King, "Wells Fargo to Employees: Leave Wallets Home, Pay by Phone," *Bloomberg BusinessWeek*, January 4, 2011; H. Shaughnessy, "Banking Gets Mobile and Social," *Forbes*, November 22, 2010; J. Galante and P. Eichenbaum, "Card Companies Are Wooing Programmers," *Bloomberg BusinessWeek*, November 22–28, 2010; P. Pachal, "U.S. Carriers Create Pay-by-Phone System, for Real This Time," *PC Magazine*, November 16, 2010; T. Claburn, "Web 2.0: Google CEO Sees Android Phones Replacing Credit Cards," *InformationWeek*, November 16, 2010; E. Zeman, "Starbucks Mobile Pay Now in NYC," *InformationWeek*, November 1, 2010; www.iconcessionstand.com, www.paypal.com, accessed April 28, 2011.

Questions

1. Given that you can lose a cell phone as easily as a wallet, which do you feel is a more secure way of carrying your personal data? Support your answer.

2. If mobile computing is the next wave of technology, would you ever feel comfortable with handing a waiter or waitress your cell phone to make a payment at a restaurant the way you currently hand over your credit or debit card? Why or why not?

3. What happens if you lose your NFC-enabled smart phone or it is stolen? How do you protect your personal information?

4. In your opinion, is the mobile wallet a good idea? Why or why not?

CLOSING **CASE 2** > A Paperless Airport

Quantas (www.quantas.com) was running out of room at its large domestic terminal in Sydney, Australia, and needed to develop a new system to reduce frequent backups at its counters. The airline studied customer habits and worked on strategies to eliminate lines. The airline eventually decided to save customers time by eliminating "pain points" in the airport, such as long check-ins, frustrating bag check, and slow boarding lines.

<<< THE PROBLEM

To eliminate these pain points, Quantas decided to invest in technology rather than adding floor space. Accordingly, Quantas built a system around radio-frequency ID (RFID) cards. Top-level frequent flyers received free ID cards that they can flash at a kiosk in the ticketing area. In seconds, the system can find the reservation for that day, assign a seat based on personal preferences if one was not preselected, and check the passenger in. When everything is ready, a beacon illuminates. Paper itineraries, sticky luggage tags, and boarding passes do not enter into the process at all.

<<< THE IT SOLUTION

With kiosks positioned in four V-shaped patterns, it is almost impossible for travelers to bunch up in long lines. There is still an old-fashioned check-in counter, but most of the baggage drop points are self-service.

To check luggage, passengers go to a baggage drop point, flash the frequent-flying card in front of a reader and drop luggage on a conveyor belt. The bag is then automatically weighed and lasers measure its dimensions to make sure it complies with limits.

Top-level frequent flyers have heavy-duty RFID tags called "Q Bag Tags" for their bags that replace paper luggage tags. The technology reads the bag's "identity" as it moves from luggage belts to carts to planes. This process ensures that luggage gets loaded on the same flight as its owner. Other travelers get a paper tag for their bags with an embedded RFID chip. (Customers who do not have top-level frequent flyer status can buy a Q Bag Tag for $51 at Quantas.com or from special vending machines in airports.) Finally, frequent flyers flash the ID card at the gate—no boarding pass needed—and agents there hand the traveler a receipt with the seat number printed on it.

Quantas's new system has created practically paperless airports, eliminated many long lines, and sped up the flying process for passengers from check-in through seating. Quantas is expanding its new system to its stations in New Zealand, which will be the first to incorporate passport information.

<<< THE RESULTS

RFID systems are incredibly useful, but they are expensive. Although the cost of RFID-enabled baggage tags has decreased from more than $1 apiece to less than 20 cents, they are still more expensive than the paper tags currently used by airlines. On the other hand, Quantas notes that the new system could save them money by reducing the cost of reimbursing passengers for lost or delayed luggage. From January through October 2011, U.S. airlines mishandled the bags of about 1.6 million passengers on domestic flights. That figure translates into 1 passenger out of every 287 on domestic flights who arrive without the luggage that person checked.

Quantas will not disclose data on the performance of the new system, such as the percent reduction of mishandled baggage or the reduction in wait times for airport check-in. The company simply states that customer feedback has been "overwhelmingly positive." These superior services may well help Quantas gain market share and help make its operations more successful.

Sources: Compiled from S. McCartney, "The Trump Card at Check-In," *The Wall Street Journal*, December 29, 2011C. ; Swedberg, "Tagsys ICM Airport Technics RFID Bag Tag to Airlines," *RFID Journal*, November 16, 2011; www.quantas.com, accessed March 10, 2012.

Questions

1. What are the possible disadvantages of Quantas's RFID system?
2. How could Quantas measure the value of the RFID system? Provide specific examples of metrics that the airline could use to justify the cost of the system. Please also provide nonquantifiable measures that Quantas could use to justify its system.

Search the Web for "pay-by-phone" applications or for companies that promote mobile, online ordering systems. Ruben and Lisa are most interested in a method to keep customers outside the store from ordering drinks to be picked up by someone else, particularly a minor.

How could they control this? Can you think of any policies or procedures they could put in place to keep this from becoming a problem? Also, can you find any examples of mobile devices being used for restaurants, clubs, or bars? Is there any way to restrict orders to customers currently in the store?

After you do your research, prepare a report for Ruben and Lisa that will help them understand what they may be up against with this mobile ordering system.

SPREADSHEET ACTIVITY: MOBILE SPREADSHEETS

Objective: Spreadsheets are powerful tools, but part of their power comes from the user interface (UI). This activity will use online demonstrations to allow you to experience spreadsheets in a mobile environment.

Chapter Connection: This activity puts wireless spreadsheets into the palm of your hand. While the demonstrations used here are based on spreadsheet tools, the implications of mobile user interface will apply in many situations. While mobile tools are very useful, they are also limited. This activity will help you see the difference in interacting with spreadsheets based on the method used to connect to them.

Activity: Many online tools are available today. Microsoft has now released an online version of its Office Suite, though Google is by far the leader in online document creation. A single account with Google gives users access to e-mail, calendars, documents, YouTube, and much more. While online document creation, editing, and storing offers lots of advantages, there are drawbacks, especially when these tools are used in a mobile environment.

There are three steps to this activity. First, you will create a Microsoft Excel spreadsheet that will track fuel mileage for your company vehicle. This sheet needs columns for the date, odometer reading, gallons pumped, and miles per gallon. The last column will be calculated based on the difference in the previous and current odometer reading and the number of gallons pumped. For this part of the exercise, you need at least five entries to be sure your spreadsheet is working properly.

Once you are satisfied that your spreadsheet is calculating appropriately, create a Google account and log into Google Drive in a Web browser. Upload your spreadsheet, and add five more entries online.

Finally, log into the mobile version of Google Drive on your mobile phone. If you do not have an Internet-enabled phone, search Google for "Opera Mini Demo," and use the demo of Opera's mobile Internet browser. Whether from your phone or the demo browser, add two more entries to your spreadsheet.

Keep a detailed diary of your experience, noting which method worked best. Be sure to explain the advantages and disadvantages of each method of accessing and editing the spreadsheet. Finally, open your Google spreadsheet in a browser, and get the URL to share the document. Add this link to your diary, and submit your document to your professor along with your original Excel spreadsheet.

Deliverable: You will submit both an Excel spreadsheet and a Word document. The spreadsheet should have at least five entries that calculate gas mileage. The document will be the diary detailing each of the three methods of accessing this spreadsheet.

Discussion Questions:

1. What do you think needs to change in the mobile and Web-based environments for them to match the traditional Excel experience? Or do they even need to match?

2. Recently it was reported that Google was going to release an operating system that ran in the "cloud" that would bring us closer to a fully "cloud-based" computing experience. Based on your diary thoughts, what improvements can you see that will need to be made in networks, computer interaction devices, storage speeds, and so on for this to be successful?

Quiz questions are assignable in WileyPLUS, and available on the Book Companion Site at http://www.wiley.com/college/rainer.

DATABASE ACTIVITY: QUERIES I

Objective

In this activity, you will learn how to create a query based on more than one table, with multiple criteria. As you have seen, business questions often involve data from more than one table, so a query that can combine data from multiple tables is more useful than one that cannot.

In the Chapter 6 activity, you selected records from a table by filtering. Sometimes selection criteria are too complex for that approach, especially if more than one table is involved. Or, perhaps you would like to set up a database so a user who is not familiar with Access can accomplish the same thing. Queries let you do that.

CHAPTER CONNECTION

You will see how queries can be useful in a mobile e-commerce situation.

PREREQUISITES

None, although the Chapter 6 activity (Filters) will provide useful background.

Activity

In this activity, which you will find online at http://www.wiley.com/go/rainer/database, you will create queries that combine data from more than one table to find information that, in the database, is spread across all of them.

1. Download and open the **Ch 10 DizzyDonuts** database from http://www.wiley.com/go/rainer/database. It belongs to a chain of donut shops. Much of the company's business comes from people driving or walking by its stores. The company has a "smart phone" application that determines customer location from the phone's GPS data, lets a customer order online and pay by credit card, sends a bar code to the phone as a graphic, and then lets the customer pick up the order by holding the bar code up to a reader at the counter or drive-in window.

   The database you will work with here supports that application. It has five tables: stores, customers, products, orders, and line items. You can see their relationships in the relationship map of the database. (This database resembles the Ch 09 DaffyDonuts database you may have used, plus a new store table with location information to support this app.)

2. The first query will be used to find out how often a given customer uses this service. We know the customer's name, but not his or her number, so we need to use both CustTbl and OrderTbl in this query. To start, click the Create ribbon tab, then Query Design in the Query section.

Usage Hint: In contrast to Design view for most other Access objects, Design view for queries is easy to use and adds important capabilities. Therefore, we will use it rather than a wizard here.

3. The first thing you see there is a Show Table box, similar to the one you may have used in creating the database relationship map in the Chapter 2 activity. You use it to specify which tables you will use in this query. You must include three types of tables:

   - All tables that the query checks to select data to display in response to the query, even if no data from those tables will show up in the reply.
   - All tables that provide data to display in the reply to the query, even if no data from those tables is used in selecting records to display.
   - All tables that sit between any of the others in the database relationship map, because Access needs them to figure out how to connect the others.

Usage Hint: Selecting the wrong tables will cause a query to fail or return erroneous results. If your query has problems, this is one place to check. If the tables are not all connected to each other in the top pane of the query design window, you left one out or (less likely) your database does not have all the necessary table relationships.

   Here, add the Customer and Order tables. You will see a line between them. That means Access does not need any other tables to connect them. Close the Show Table window.

4. Click in the top row of the first column of the query design grid if it is not already selected. Enter Costae or select Costae from the pull-down list under the arrow. When you tab out of that field or click somewhere else, Access will fill in CustTbl as the table name directly underneath it.

Usage Hint: Easier: you can also drag a field name from any table in the upper pane of the design window into the grid. Even easier: double-click a field name in the upper pane and it will appear in the next empty grid column.

By the way, this grid is sometimes referred to as the *Query by Example* or *QBE* grid because you use it to create an example of what you are looking for. The name is not very appropriate; it began at a time when the grid was a real example of data to be found, but it is still around.

5. In the Criteria row of that column, enter "Adam" as the customer name. (The quotation marks are optional. If you leave them off, Access will supply them.) This will be the selection criterion for this query.

Usage Hint (English usage, not Access): *Criteria* is the plural form. Use it only when there are two or more. If you only have one, it is a *criterion*.

6. In the top row of the next three columns, enter Order Date, Order Store and Order Total. Do not enter any selection criteria here. We want to see all of Adam's orders, no matter what date they were on or what store they were at.

7. Click Run, the large red exclamation point near the left of the ribbon, to see the result. It should be correct, but its structure and appearance leave a lot to be desired. If you do the Chapter 11 activity, you will see how to put this result into a better-organized, nicer-looking report.

   If you got an empty table—no matching records—the most likely reason is an error in keying in "Adam" as the selection criterion or entering it in the wrong column. Go back to Design view and check those.

Usage Hint: The table-like results of a query are called a *dynaset*, for "dynamic set." When data in a table change, the dynaset changes dynamically, but records are not rescreened. If changes affect selection criteria, the affected records will not move in or out of the dynaset, but will show the new data. For example, if you select all items priced under $100, then change a price from $99.99 to $109.99, that item will still be displayed with its new, higher price. To update the selection for the new data, rerun the query. This item, which now costs over $100, will no longer be shown.

8. Return to Design view. Change the customer name to "Belina." Run the query again.

9. Close the query, saving it as "CustOrderQry" when prompted.

10. The next query will find all customers who shopped at a given store. Create a new query in Design view. Enter CustTbl and StoreTbl into the upper pane of the query design window. You will see that they are not connected. The database relationship map shows why: They must be linked via the Order table. Reopen the Show Table box if you closed it (near the middle of the Design ribbon) and add OrderTbl to the query. The tables are now connected.

11. Select fields for this query: store city, customer name, order date, and order total.

12. As a selection criterion, enter "Boston" as the store city.

13. Run the query, showing all the orders for the Boston store.

14. Close the query, saving it as "StoreOrderQry" when prompted.

15. The third query can be used to find out who orders expensive products. ("Expensive" is a relative concept. Nothing that a donut shop sells would be considered expensive at an art gallery.) As before, open a new query design window. This time you must connect products and customers. To do this, you will need to show additional tables in the query. Enter them in the upper pane from the Show Table list. You should see a total of four tables here. If you arrange them in a line with the Customer table at one end and the Product table at the other, the tables in that line should be connected from one end to the other.

16. In the first column of the query design grid, enter ProdPrice and a criterion of " > 1.6" (without the quotation marks). Selection criteria can include comparisons, as well as other options. We will get to some of them later here and in future activities.

Usage Hint: Criteria involving currency amounts must be entered as numbers. Access stores currency amounts that way. Specifying Currency data type controls how they are displayed, but does not affect the underlying data. Using a currency symbol in a query criterion will result in an error message. If this happens: Dismiss the message, remove the dollar sign, remove the quotation marks that Access supplied because it thought you entered a character string, and continue.

17. In the next two columns, enter ProdName and CustName. Run the query.

18. Close the query, saving it as "ExpensiveProdQry" when prompted.

19. Make a copy of ExpensiveProdQry and open it in Design view. Add the Store table to the query. Add StoreCity to the first empty column of the query design grid. Enter a selection criterion of "Boston" for it, in the same row as the price criterion. Run the query. The result shows customers who ordered expensive (that is, over $1.60) items from the Boston store.

   Note: Criteria in the same row of the query grid, but in different columns, are combined via an implied "And."

20. Close the query, saving it as "ExpensiveProdStoreQry" when prompted. (Depending on how you created the copy, you may have had a chance to name it earlier.)

21. Make a copy of ExpensiveProdStoreQry, which you just saved, and open it in Design view. Delete the Boston criterion from the grid cell it is in, and re-enter it in the same column, one row down. Run the query. This time, you will see all the customers who ordered expensive products at any store, and in addition all the customers who ordered anything at all from the Boston store.

   Note: Criteria in different rows of the query grid are combined via an implied "Or."

20. Close the query, saving it as "ExpensiveTestQry" when prompted. (Depending on how you created the copy, you may have had a chance to name it earlier.)

21. Close the database.

Deliverable

Your database, with the preceding five queries.

Quiz Questions

1. The relationship between Orders and Products in this database is
   (a) One-to-one
   (b) Many-to-one
   (c) Many-to-many
   (d) One-to-many

2. When criteria are entered on the same row of different columns in the query design grid:
   (a) The query will display result rows in which all criteria are true.
   (b) The query will display result rows in which at least one of the criteria is true.
   (c) The query will display result rows in which at least two of the criteria are true.
   (d) Something else.

3. The table pane of the query design grid should show:
   (a) Only tables whose values are tested by query criteria.
   (b) All tables in the database.
   (c) Only tables whose data we want to see in the query results.
   (d) None of the above answers is correct.

4. True or false: A query must use a minimum of two tables.

Discussion Questions

1. Consider a three-table database of students, grades, and courses, such as your school probably has. Suppose you want to display a student's grades. What would you put in the query design grid? (Make reasonable assumptions about the columns in the three tables.)

2. Suppose you are the director of business planning for Dizzy Donuts. You suspect that order patterns for the morning differ from those in the afternoon. (Access can compare times, though we did not use that here.) What sort of query could you design to help you confirm or deny this suspicion? Draw a sample page of how its results might look. You do not have to use real data from this database.

3. Some database management systems do not treat Currency as a data type when you define a table. Instead, currency amounts are first specified as Number. Currency formatting is available as an option for numeric data, but it is treated as a formatting option like the use of commas to separate groups of three digits. Do you prefer this approach or the Access approach? Why?

11 | Information Systems Within the Organization

LEARNING OBJECTIVES >>>

1. Explain the purpose of transaction processing systems.

2. Explain the types of support information systems can provide for each functional area of the organization.

3. Identify advantages and drawbacks to businesses implementing an enterprise resource planning system.

4. Discuss the three major types of reports generated by the functional area information systems and enterprise resource planning systems, providing examples of each type.

OPENING **CASE** > Henthorn Mower & Engine Service and ADP

© Michael Czosnek/
iStockphoto

Information systems within an organization are not always computer based. Many small businesses still rely on systems where collection, storage, analysis, and distribution of information are all done on paper. For example, paper payrolls include a time card for each employee that each one "punches" every day when arriving and leaving work (data collection). These numbers are manually totaled at the end of each week (analysis) and entered into a ledger for future reference (storage). At the appropriate time, this information will be sent to the accountant (distribution) to determine the amount of pay due to each employee (information).

This process works, but there are many ways this information could be more useful, if it were only in some computer system that would help manage the entire process. Paper systems require significant manual effort and are subject to human error. Computerized information systems are much more reliable and provide many other benefits as well.

For instance, Rickie Star bought his in-laws' mower business in 1978. It now operates under the name of Henthorn Mower & Engine Service, but it remains a small, family-run business (about 12 employees). Like many family-owned businesses, many of the information systems that have developed over time are paper based. Within their organization, the division of responsibilities was initially determined by history, preference, and the "way it has always been." In particular, managing time cards and payroll fell to Rickie's mother-in-law. She spent every Thursday morning going through the manual process outlined above. This process worked fine—that is, until she passed away and the responsibility fell on Rickie to keep up with payroll.

It did not take long for Rickie to realize that he needed a better solution to payroll. Even for his small business, he needed something that was quicker and more reliable so that > > >

RUBY'S CLUB

Each month, Ruben and Lisa sit down to a table of receipts. They know there is a lot of information in there, but they have a terrible time sorting their way through the piles to find it. They know there has to be a better way. This is part of the reason for integrating IT into their remodeled and restructured business. They hope that their new information systems will provide them with more accurate, timely, helpful information so they can go about making decisions.

Specifically, they hope their transaction processing system will capture and collect data on customers' entry and departure times, food and beverage items purchased, bands playing and so on to help them make plans for the future. As you read through this chapter, consider how Ruby's Club could utilize the different information systems presented.

he could spend his time working on other duties. After researching the possible solutions, he decided that the EasyPayNet (https://easynet.adp.com) and ezLaborManager (https://ezlm.adp.com/) solutions from ADP (www.adp.com) were the best for his needs.

His time system moved from paper to the computer in a seamless fashion. Employees now use an electronic clock that scans a time card rather than the old manual clock that "punched" the card. This information is available in real-time (no waiting until Thursday) for Rickie to see who is on time, who is late, and how many hours each employee has worked for each pay period. The system also keeps up with sick days, vacation days, taxes . . . and even cuts the checks to the employees!

For Henthorn Mower & Engine Service, moving its paper-based system to the ADP solutions proved to be worth more than just the time saved by not having to manually calculate payroll. The new IS added a level of reliability and quick access to information that employees had not even realized they were missing.

Sources: Compiled from "Henthorn Mower & Engine Service," *ADP Small Business Services Case Study*, 2011; www.adp.com, https://easynet.adp.com, https://ezlm.adp.com, accessed March 21, 2012.

Questions

1. Describe additional advantages (other than the ones described in this case) of computerizing Henthorn's payroll process.

2. What are some potential disadvantages of computerizing Henthorn's payroll process?

Introduction

Henthorn Mower & Engine Serviced needed a payroll solution and ADP matched the company's requirements. As the opening case demonstrates, "systems within organizations" do not have to be owned by the organization itself. Instead, organizations can deploy very productive information systems that are owned by an external vendor. The important point here is that "systems within an organization" are intended to support internal processes, regardless of who actually owns the systems.

There is an astonishing variety of information systems (IS) that you will learn about in this chapter. IS are everywhere and they affect organizations in countless ways. Who would have thought that an IS could help a large organization like professional baseball become more like a science? Information systems also influence small organizations, as illustrated by the chapter opening case.

It is important for you to have a working knowledge of IS systems within your organization, for a variety of reasons. First, in your job you will be accessing corporate data that are largely supplied by your firm's transaction processing systems and enterprise resource planning systems. Second, you will have a great deal of input into the format and content of the reports that you receive from these systems. Third, you will use the information in these reports to perform your job more productively.

In this chapter, you will see the various systems within the organization. You begin by considering transaction processing systems, the most fundamental information systems within organizations. You continue with the functional area management information systems and then with the enterprise resource planning systems.

11.1 Transaction Processing Systems

Millions (sometimes billions) of transactions occur in large organizations every day. A **transaction** is any business event that generates data worthy of being captured and stored in a database. Examples of transactions are a product manufactured, a service sold, a person hired, and a payroll check generated. In another example, when you are checking out of Walmart, each time the cashier swipes an item across the bar code reader is one transaction.

A **transaction processing system (TPS)** supports the monitoring, collection, storage, and processing of data from the organization's basic business transactions, each of which generates data. The TPS collects data continuously, typically in *real time*—that is, as soon as the data are generated—and it provides the input data for the corporate databases. The TPSs are critical to the success of any enterprise because they support core operations.

In the modern business world, TPSs are inputs to the functional area information systems and business intelligence systems, as well as business operations such as customer relationship management, knowledge management, and e-commerce. TPSs have to handle both high volume and large variations in volume (for example, during peak times) of data efficiently. In addition, they must avoid errors and downtime, record results accurately and securely, and maintain privacy and security. Figure 11.1 shows how TPSs manage data. Consider these examples of how TPSs manage the complexities of transactional data:

- When more than one person or application program can access the database at the same time, the database has to be protected from errors resulting from overlapping updates. The most common error is for the results of one of the updates to be lost.

- When processing a transaction involves more than one computer, the database and all users must be protected against inconsistencies arising from a failure of any component at any time. For example, if an error occurs at some point in an ATM withdrawal, the customer could receive cash while the bank's computer indicates that he did not. (Conversely, the customer might not receive cash while the bank's computer indicates that he did.)

- It must be possible to reverse a transaction in its entirety if it turns out to have been entered in error. It is also necessary to reverse a transaction when a purchased item is returned.

- It may be important to preserve an audit trail. In fact, for certain transactions an audit trail may be legally required.

These and similar issues explain why organizations spend millions of dollars on expensive mainframe computers. In today's business environment, firms must have the dependability, reliability, and processing capacity of these computers to handle their transaction processing loads.

Regardless of the specific data processed by a TPS, the actual process tends to be standard, whether it occurs in a manufacturing firm, a service firm, or a government organization. First, data are collected by people or sensors and are entered into the computer via any input device. Generally speaking, organizations try to automate the TPS data entry as much as possible because of the large volume involved, a process called *source data automation.*

Next, the system processes data in one of two basic ways: batch processing and online processing. In **batch processing**, the firm collects data from transactions as they occur, placing them in groups or *batches*. The system then prepares and processes the batches periodically (say, every night).

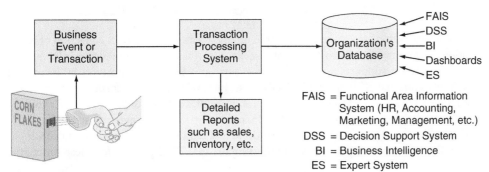

FAIS = Functional Area Information System (HR, Accounting, Marketing, Management, etc.)
DSS = Decision Support System
BI = Business Intelligence
ES = Expert System

Figure 11.1 How transaction processing systems manage data.

In **online transaction processing (OLTP)**, business transactions are processed online as soon as they occur. For example, when you pay for an item at a store, the system records the sale by reducing the inventory on hand by one unit, increasing sales figures for the item by one unit, and increasing the store's cash position by the amount you paid. The system performs these tasks in real time by means of online technologies.

Apply the Concept 11.1

Background This section has shown that transaction processing systems capture data and then automatically send that data on to different functional area systems. Most transaction processing systems are designed based on existing processes in an organization. To better understand how this operates, you should consider the flow of data through the application process for a student.

Activity Visit http://www.wiley.com/go/rainer/applytheconcept and click on the link provided for Apply the Concept 11.1. This will take you to a Web page that describes the process of creating data flow diagrams (DFDs). This Web page uses the example mentioned above (student applications) and it should make a fair amount of sense to you.

After you read over the process of accepting and admitting students and are comfortable with the idea of a DFD, create a DFD for student registration.

Deliverable

Submit your DFD to your professor with a written explanation of each step of the process.

Quiz questions are assignable in WileyPLUS, and available on the Book Companion Site at http://www.wiley.com/college/rainer.

RUBY'S CLUB | **QUESTIONS**

1. How might Ruby's benefit from a TPS that provides an audit trail?
2. Is Ruby' Club subject to inconsistencies? Where might they come from and how could a TPS help protect the club from this problem?
3. Considering the processing methods of OLTP and batch processing, which seems most likely to be used at Ruby's Club?

11.2 Functional Area Information Systems

Each department or functional area within an organization has its own collection of application programs, or information systems. Each of these **functional area information systems** (FAIS) supports a particular functional area in the organization by increasing each area's internal efficiency and effectiveness. FAIS often convey information in a variety of reports, which you will see in Section 11.4. Examples are accounting IS, finance IS, production/operations management (POM) IS, marketing IS, and human resources IS.

As illustrated in Figure 11.1, the FAIS access data from the corporate databases. In the following sections, you will study the support that FAIS provide for these functional areas.

Information Systems for Accounting and Finance

A primary mission of the accounting and finance functional areas is to manage money flows into, within, and out of organizations. This mission is very broad because money is involved in all organizational functions. Therefore, accounting and finance information systems are very diverse and comprehensive. In this section, you focus on certain selected activities of the accounting/finance functional area.

Financial Planning and Budgeting. Appropriate management of financial assets is a major task in financial planning and budgeting. Managers must plan for both acquiring and utilizing resources.

- *Financial and economic forecasting.* Knowledge about the availability and cost of money is a key ingredient for successful financial planning. Cash flow projections are particularly important because they inform organizations what funds they need, when they need them, and how they will acquire them.

  Funds for operating organizations come from multiple sources, including stockholders' investments, bond sales, bank loans, sales of products and services, and income from investments. Decisions concerning funding for ongoing operations and for capital investment can be supported by decision support systems, business intelligence applications (discussed in Chapter 5), and expert systems (discussed in Plug IT In 4). In addition, numerous software packages for conducting economic and financial forecasting are available. Many of these packages can be downloaded from the Internet, some of them for free.

- *Budgeting.* An essential part of the accounting/finance function is the annual budget, which allocates the organization's financial resources among participants and activities. The budget allows management to distribute resources in the way that best supports the organization's mission and goals.

  Several software packages are available to support budget preparation and control and to facilitate communication among participants in the budget process. These packages can reduce the time involved in the budget process. Further, they can automatically monitor exceptions for patterns and trends.

Managing Financial Transactions. Many accounting/finance software packages are integrated with other functional areas. For example, Peachtree by Sage (www.peachtree.com) offers a sales ledger, purchase ledger, cash book, sales order processing, invoicing, stock control, fixed assets register, and more.

Companies involved in electronic commerce need to access customers' financial data (e.g., credit line), inventory levels, and manufacturing databases (to see available capacity, to place orders). For example, Microsoft Dynamics GP (formerly Great Plains Software) offers 50 modules that meet the most common financial, project, distribution, manufacturing, and e-business needs.

Organizations, business processes, and business activities operate with, and manage, financial transactions. Consider these examples:

- *Global stock exchanges.* Financial markets operate in global, 24/7/365, distributed electronic stock exchanges that use the Internet both to buy and sell stocks and to broadcast real-time stock prices.

- *Managing multiple currencies.* Global trade involves financial transactions in different currencies. The conversion ratios of these currencies are constantly in flux. Financial and accounting systems take financial data from different countries and convert the currencies from and to any other currency in seconds. Reports based on these data, which used to take days to generate, now take seconds to produce. These systems manage multiple languages as well.

- *Virtual close.* Companies traditionally closed their books (accounting records) quarterly, usually to meet regulatory requirements. Today, many companies want to be able to close their books at any time, on very short notice. Information systems make it possible to close the books quickly in what is called a *virtual close*. This process provides almost real-time information on the organization's financial health.

- *Expense management automation.* Expense management automation (EMA) refers to systems that automate the data entry and processing of travel and entertainment expenses. EMA systems are Web-based applications that enable companies to quickly and consistently collect expense information, enforce company policies and contracts, and reduce unplanned purchases as well as airline and hotel services. They also allow companies to reimburse their employees more quickly because expense approvals are not delayed by poor documentation.

Investment Management. Organizations invest large amounts of money in stocks, bonds, real estate, and other assets. Managing these investments is a complex task, for several reasons. First, there are literally thousands of investment alternatives and they are dispersed throughout the world. In addition, these investments are subject to complex regulations and tax laws, which vary from one location to another.

Investment decisions require managers to evaluate financial and economic reports provided by diverse institutions, including federal and state agencies, universities, research institutions, and financial services firms. In addition, thousands of Web sites provide financial data, many of them for free.

To monitor, interpret, and analyze the huge amounts of online financial data, financial analysts employ two major types of IT tools: (1) Internet search engines and (2) business intelligence and decision support software.

Control and Auditing. One major reason why organizations go out of business is their inability to forecast and/or secure a sufficient cash flow. Underestimating expenses, overspending, engaging in fraud, and mismanaging financial statements can lead to disaster. Consequently, it is essential that organizations effectively control their finances and financial statements. Let us examine some of the most common forms of financial control.

- *Budgetary control.* Once an organization has finalized its annual budget, it divides those monies into monthly allocations. Managers at various levels monitor departmental expenditures and compare them against the budget and the operational progress of the corporate plans.

- *Auditing.* Auditing has two basic purposes: (1) to monitor how the organization's monies are being spent and (2) to assess the organization's financial health. Internal auditing is performed by the organization's accounting/finance personnel. These employees also prepare for periodic external audits by outside CPA firms.

- *Financial ratio analysis.* Another major accounting/finance function is to monitor the company's financial health by assessing a set of financial ratios. Included here are liquidity ratios (the availability of cash to pay debt), activity ratios (how quickly a firm converts noncash assets to cash assets), debt ratios (measure the firm's ability to repay long-term debt), and profitability ratios (measure the firm's use of its assets and control of its expenses to generate an acceptable rate of return).

Information Systems for Marketing

It is impossible to overestimate the importance of customers to any organization. Therefore, any successful organization must understand its customers' needs and wants and then develop its marketing and advertising strategies around them. Information systems provide numerous types of support to the marketing function. In fact, customer-centric organizations are so important that Chapter 12 (Extending the Organization to Customers) is devoted to this topic.

Information Systems for Production/Operations Management

The POM function in an organization is responsible for the processes that transform inputs into useful outputs as well as for the overall operation of the business. Because of the breadth and variety of POM functions, you see only four here: in-house logistics and materials management, planning production and operation, computer-integrated manufacturing (CIM), and product life cycle management (PLM).

The POM function is also responsible for managing the organization's supply chain. Because supply chain management is vital to the success of modern organizations, Chapter 13 (Extending the Organization Along the Supply Chain) covers this topic in detail.

In-House Logistics and Materials Management.

Logistics management deals with ordering, purchasing, inbound logistics (receiving), and outbound logistics (shipping) activities. Related activities include inventory management and quality control.

INVENTORY MANAGEMENT. As the name suggests, inventory management determines how much inventory to maintain. Both excessive inventory and insufficient inventory create problems. Overstocking can be expensive, because of storage costs and the costs of spoilage and obsolescence. However, keeping insufficient inventory is also expensive, because of last-minute orders and lost sales.

Operations personnel make two basic decisions: when to order and how much to order. Inventory models, such as the economic order quantity (EOQ) model, support these decisions. A large number of commercial inventory software packages that automate the application of these models are available.

Many large companies allow their suppliers to monitor their inventory levels and ship products as they are needed. This strategy, called *vendor-managed inventory* (VMI), eliminates the need for the company to submit purchasing orders.

QUALITY CONTROL. Quality-control systems used by manufacturing units provide information about the quality of incoming material and parts, as well as the quality of in-process semifinished products and finished products. Such systems record the results of all inspections and compare the actual results to established metrics. These systems also generate periodic reports containing information about quality—for example, the percentage of defects and the percentage of necessary rework. Quality control data can be collected by Web-based sensors and interpreted in real time, or they can be stored in a database for future analysis.

Planning Production and Operations.

In many firms, POM planning is supported by IT. POM planning has evolved from material requirements planning (MRP), to manufacturing resource planning (MRP II), to enterprise resource planning (ERP). We briefly discuss MRP and MRP II here, and we examine ERP in detail later in this chapter.

Inventory systems that use an EOQ approach are designed for items for which demand is completely independent—for example, the number of identical personal computers a computer manufacturer will sell. In manufacturing operations, however, the demand for some items is interdependent. Consider, for example, a company that makes three types of chairs, all of which use the same screws and bolts. In this case, the demand for screws and bolts depends on the total demand for all three types of chairs and their shipment schedules. The planning process that integrates production, purchasing, and inventory management of interdependent items is called *material requirements planning* (MRP).

MRP deals only with production scheduling and inventories. More complex planning also involves allocating related resources, such as money and labor. For these cases, more complex, integrated software, called *manufacturing resource planning* (MRP II), is available. MRP II integrates a firm's production, inventory management, purchasing, financing, and labor activities. Thus, MRP II adds functions to a regular MRP system. In fact, MRP II has evolved into enterprise resource planning (ERP).

Computer-Integrated Manufacturing.

Computer-integrated manufacturing (**CIM**; also called *digital manufacturing*) is an approach that integrates various automated factory systems. CIM has three basic goals: (1) to simplify all manufacturing technologies and techniques, (2) to automate as many of the manufacturing processes as possible, and (3) to integrate and coordinate all aspects of design, manufacturing, and related functions via computer systems.

© paci77/iStockphoto

A "Quality Guarantee" requires data collection and analysis throughout production to maintain standards.

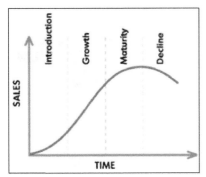

Product life cycle.

Product Life Cycle Management. Even within a single organization, designing and developing new products can be expensive and time consuming. When multiple organizations are involved, the process can become very complex. *Product life cycle management* (PLM) is a business strategy that enables manufacturers to share product-related data that support product design and development and supply chain operations. PLM applies Web-based collaborative technologies to product development. By integrating formerly disparate functions, such as a manufacturing process and the logistics that support it, PLM enables these functions to collaborate, essentially forming a single team that manages the product from its inception through its completion.

Information Systems for Human Resource Management

Initial human resource information system (HRIS) applications dealt primarily with transaction processing systems, such as managing benefits and keeping records of vacation days. As organizational systems have moved to intranets and the Web, however, so have HRIS applications.

Many HRIS applications are delivered via an HR portal. For example, numerous organizations use their Web portals to advertise job openings and conduct online hiring and training. In this section, you consider how organizations are using IT to perform some key HR functions: recruitment, HR maintenance and development, and HR planning and management.

Recruitment. Recruitment involves finding potential employees, evaluating them, and deciding which ones to hire. Some companies are flooded with viable applicants; others have difficulty finding the right people. IT can be helpful in both cases. In addition, IT can assist in related activities such as testing and screening job applicants.

With millions of resumes available online, it is not surprising that companies are trying to find appropriate candidates on the Web, usually with the help of specialized search engines. Companies also advertise hundreds of thousands of jobs on the Web. Online recruiting can reach more candidates, which may bring in better applicants. In addition, the costs of online recruitment are usually lower than traditional recruiting methods such as advertising in newspapers or in trade journals.

Human Resources Development. After employees are recruited, they become part of the corporate human resources pool, which means they must be evaluated and developed. IT provides support for these activities.

Most employees are periodically evaluated by their immediate supervisors. Peers or subordinates may also evaluate other employees. Evaluations are typically digitized and are used to support many decisions, ranging from rewards to transfers to layoffs.

IT also plays an important role in training and retraining. Some of the most innovative developments are taking place in the areas of intelligent computer-aided instruction and the application of multimedia support for instructional activities. For example, companies conduct much of their corporate training over their intranet or via the Web.

Human Resources Planning and Management. Managing human resources in large organizations requires extensive planning and detailed strategy. The following three areas are where IT can provide support:

- *Payroll and employees' records.* The HR department is responsible for payroll preparation. This process is typically automated with paychecks being printed or money being transferred electronically into employees' bank accounts.

- *Benefits administration.* Employees' work contributions to their organizations are rewarded by wages, bonuses, and other benefits. Benefits include health and dental care, pension contributions, wellness centers, and child care centers.

  Managing benefits is a complex task because of the multiple options offered and the tendency of organizations to allow employees to choose and trade off their benefits. In many organizations, employees can access the company portal to self-register for specific benefits.

TABLE 11.1 Activities Supported by Functional Area Information Systems

Accounting and Finance

Financial planning—and cost of money

Budgeting—allocates financial resources among participants and activities

Capital budgeting—financing of asset acquisitions

Managing financial transactions

Handling multiple currencies

Virtual close—ability to close books at any time on short notice

Investment management—managing organizational investments in stocks, bonds, real estate, and other investment vehicles

Budgetary control—monitoring expenditures and comparing against budget

Auditing—ensuring the accuracy and condition of financial health of organization

Payroll

Marketing and Sales

Customer relations—know who customers are and treat them like royalty

Customer profiles and preferences

Sales force automation—using software to automate the business tasks of sales, thereby improving the productivity of salespeople

Production/Operations and Logistics

Inventory management—how much inventory to order, how much inventory to keep, and when to order new inventory

Quality control—controlling for defects in incoming material and defects in goods produced

Materials requirements planning—planning process that integrates production, purchasing, and inventory management of interdependent items (MRP)

Manufacturing resource planning—planning process that integrates an enterprise's production, inventory management, purchasing, financing, and labor activities (MRP II)

Just-in-time systems—principle of production and inventory control in which materials and parts arrive precisely when and where needed for production (JIT)

Computer-integrated manufacturing—manufacturing approach that integrates several computerized systems, such as computer-assisted design (CAD), computer-assisted manufacturing (CAM), MRP, and JIT

Product life cycle management—business strategy that enables manufacturers to collaborate on product design and development efforts, using the Web

Human Resource Management

Recruitment—finding employees, testing them, and deciding which ones to hire

Performance evaluation—periodic evaluation by superiors

Training

Employee records

Benefits administration—retirement, disability, unemployment, etc.

- *Employee relationship management.* In their efforts to better manage employees, companies are developing *employee relationship management* (ERM) applications. A typical ERM application is a call center for employees' problems.

Table 11.1 provides an overview of the activities that the FAIS support. Figure 11.2 diagrams many of the information systems that support these five functional areas.

BEFORE *YOU GO ON . . .*

1. What is a functional area information system? List its major characteristics.

2. How do information systems benefit the finance and accounting functional area?

3. Explain how POM personnel use information systems to perform their jobs more effectively and efficiently.

4. What are the most important HRIS applications?

ACCOUNTING	FINANCE	HUMAN RESOURCES	PRODUCTION/ OPERATIONS	MARKETING	
Profitability Planning	Financial Planning	Employment Planning, Outsourcing	Product Life Cycle Management	Sales Forecasting, Advertising Planning	STRATEGIC
Auditing, Budgeting	Investment Management	Benefits Administration, Performance Evaluation	Quality Control, Inventory Management	Customer Relations, Sales Force Automation	TACTICAL
Payroll, Accounts Payable, Accounts Receivable	Manage Cash, Manage Financial Transactions	Maintain Employee Records	Order Fulfillment, Order Processing	Set Pricing, Profile Customers	OPERATIONAL

Figure 11.2 Examples of information systems supporting the functional areas.

Apply the Concept 11.2

Background Section 11.2 introduces you to the concept of functional area systems. As you can see, every area of business has processes in place that define how data is stored, analyzed, applied, and distributed across the functional area. Inventory management is easy to do in a computer system because it is simply keeping track of your materials and products. However, when you couple inventory management with production and operations management (POM), you have a very effective functional system that supports the internal production line.

Activity Visit http://www.wiley.com/go/rainer/applytheconcept and click on the link provided for Apply the Concept 11.2. This will take you to the homepage for ADP. Then search for their Human Resource Management Systems. HR, like POM, integrates many aspects of dealing with employees. ADP offers systems that integrate services from recruitment of employees to termination and everything in between.

Imagine that you are the Senior HR Manager of a medium-sized organization facing somewhat of an HR crisis. Of your 175 employees, 50 of them are nearing retirement in the next 5 years. This means that your growing business will not only have to deal with the paperwork and plans of retirees, but also search for, hire, and train new employees.

Your current system of spreadsheets has been sufficient until now. There is no way your department can handle the amount of information you will create and process in the next 5 years with a "homemade" spreadsheet system.

Deliverable

Write a business letter to your CEO requesting that she consider purchasing the Human Resource Management System from ADP. Use the following outline:

- Give projections of your shift in employment over the next 5 years (use the data provided earlier).
- Discuss how your current systems are unable to provide support through this time of such significant employment shift.
- Reference information from the ADP site to show how you believe this system will not only provide sufficient support through your upcoming time of turnover but will provide better support into the future.
- Remind your CEO of your employment projections and conclude your request.

  Submit your letter to your professor.

Quiz questions are assignable in WileyPLUS, and available on the Book Companion Site at http://www.wiley.com/college/rainer.

RUBY'S CLUB | QUESTIONS

1. Do you think Ruby's Club is big enough to need a different system for finance, accounting, HR, and marketing? Or, would different views of the club's data suffice for Ruben and Lisa's small business?

2. How might Ruben and Lisa best tackle the difficulty of measuring shrinkage within their club (bartenders pouring more alcohol than the customer paid for)? With an inventory management system or a quality control system?

3. What are some benefits of replacing their old time-card system (they actually still use a card to "clock in and clock out") with a newer HR system that tracks this data in a computer rather than on a card?

11.3 Enterprise Resource Planning Systems

Historically, the functional area information systems were developed independently of one another, resulting in *information silos*. These silos did not communicate well with one another, and this lack of communication and integration made organizations less efficient. This inefficiency was particularly evident in business processes that involve more than one functional area.

Enterprise resource planning (ERP) systems are designed to correct a lack of communication among the functional area IS. ERP systems resolve this problem by tightly integrating the functional area IS via a common database. For this reason, experts credit ERP systems with greatly increasing organizational productivity. **ERP systems** adopt a business process view of the overall organization to integrate the planning, management, and use of all of an organization's resources, employing a common software platform and database.

The major objectives of ERP systems are to tightly integrate the functional areas of the organization and to enable information to flow seamlessly across them. Tight integration means that changes in one functional area are immediately reflected in all other pertinent functional areas. In essence, ERP systems provide the information necessary to control the business processes of the organization.

It is important to understand here that ERP systems are an evolution of FAIS. That is, ERP systems have much the same functionality as FAIS and produce the same reports. ERP systems simply integrate the functions of the various FAIS.

Although some companies have developed their own ERP systems, most organizations use commercially available ERP software. The leading ERP software vendor is SAP (www.sap.com), which features its SAP R/3 package. Other major vendors include Oracle (www.oracle.com) and PeopleSoft (www.peoplesoft.com), now an Oracle company.

(With more than 700 customers, PeopleSoft is the market leader in higher education.) For up-to-date information on ERP software, visit http://erp.ittoolbox.com.

Although ERP systems can be difficult to implement because they are large and complicated, many companies have done so successfully. IT'S About Business 11.1 recounts a successful ERP deployment at Rigaku.

IT'S ABOUT BUSINESS 11.1

Rigaku Implements an ERP System

Rigaku Americas (www.rigaku.com) is the U.S. arm of Rigaku Corporation, a world leader in technologies such as general X-ray diffraction, X-ray spectrometry, and X-ray optics. Many of Rigaku's products are built to custom specifications, and the company prides itself on its close collaboration with customers. The company's products are highly complex, which unfortunately led the company to develop an equally complex organizational chain.

First Rigaku had numerous problems with its information systems, which were antiquated and not very well integrated with one another. Therefore, communication between the company's eight plants was not easy. Data was transferred via e-mails and faxes, and there was no mechanism in place by which orders could be efficiently transferred from plant to plant.

Company executives and managers also had very little insight into finances and interactions with vendors. Because so many of the company's products were custom built, this lack of transparency and lack of easy access made it difficult to quickly and accurately assess costs. Furthermore, the company was carrying too much inventory and shipping many orders late to its customers. These problems led to decreased customer satisfaction.

To put the cherry on the icing, the third-party organization supporting Rigaku's largest information system discontinued support for its product. Although the existing system still worked, Rigaku knew its position was untenable and that it had to make a change.

The company decided it needed to lower costs and improve efficiencies in operations. Rigaku then wanted to translate these efficiencies into increased customer satisfaction and increased profits.

It was clear to Rigaku that in order to achieve these goals, an ERP implementation was necessary. This ERP system would need to be able to take orders, buy materials, and schedule and ship efficiently and effec-tively. The system would also need to improve the company's engineering, purchasing, financing, and labor tracking, as well as its control over production.

© Ragip Candan/iStockphoto

As of mid-2012, Rigaku has had great success in its ERP implementation. In mid-2012, the company had fully deployed its ERP system in seven of its eight plants in the United States, with the eighth plant's deployment currently in progress. The firm's CIO notes that, under the new system, his company is finding it much easier to assess costs accurately. Prior to implementing the ERP system, Rigaku used to need 2 or 3 weeks for its finance department to assess product costs. After the system's deployment, the department can assess costs in just 10 minutes.

After Rigaku's system makeover, its corporate executives now have much better insight into the operations of the business. There are fewer late orders, much-improved inventory holding costs, and better planning by decision makers. These improvements should lead to financial growth, stability, and a bright future for the company going forward.

Sources: Compiled from "To ERP or Not to ERP; In Manufacturing, It Isn't Even a Question," *Aberdeen Group*, 2011; www.rigaku.com, accessed March 15, 2012.

Questions

1. Describe why Rigaku decided to implement an ERP system.

2. Describe the benefits that Rigaku realized after deploying its ERP system.

Evolution of ERP Systems

ERP systems were originally deployed to facilitate business processes associated with manufacturing, such as raw materials management, inventory control, order entry, and distribution. However, these early ERP systems did not extend to other functional areas, such as sales and marketing. They also did not include any customer relationship management (CRM) capabilities that would allow organizations to capture customer-specific information. Further, they did not provide Web-enabled customer service or order fulfillment.

Over time, ERP systems evolved to include administrative, sales, marketing, and human resources processes. Companies now employ an enterprisewide approach to ERP that utilizes the Web and connects all facets of the value chain. These systems are called ERP II.

ERP II Systems

ERP II systems are interorganizational ERP systems that provide Web-enabled links among a company's key business systems—such as inventory and production—and its customers, suppliers, distributors, and others. These links integrate internal-facing ERP applications with the external-focused applications of supply chain management and customer relationship management. Figure 11.3 illustrates the organization and functions of an ERP II system.

The various functions of ERP II systems are now delivered as e-business suites. The major ERP vendors have developed modular, Web-enabled software suites that integrate ERP, customer relationship management, supply chain management, procurement, decision support, enterprise portals, and other business applications and functions. Examples are Oracle's e-Business Suite and SAP's mySAP. The goal of these systems is to enable companies to operate most of their business processes using a single Web-enabled system of integrated software rather than a variety of separate e-business applications.

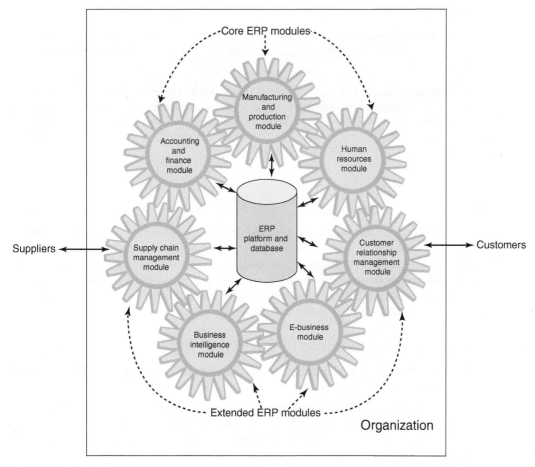

Figure 11.3 ERP II system.

TABLE 11.2 ERP Modules

Core ERP Modules

Financial Management. These modules support accounting, financial reporting, performance management, and corporate governance. They manage accounting data and financial processes such as general ledger, accounts payable, accounts receivable, fixed assets, cash management and forecasting, product-cost accounting, cost-center accounting, asset accounting, tax accounting, credit management, budgeting, and asset management.

Operations Management. These modules manage the various aspects of production planning and execution such as demand forecasting, procurement, inventory management, materials purchasing, shipping, production planning, production scheduling, materials requirements planning, quality control, distribution, transportation, and plant and equipment maintenance.

Human Resource Management. These modules support personnel administration (including workforce planning, employee recruitment, assignment tracking, personnel planning and development, and performance management and reviews), time accounting, payroll, compensation, benefits accounting, and regulatory requirements.

Extended ERP Modules

Customer Relationship Management. (Discussed in detail in Chapter 12.) These modules support all aspects of a customer's relationship with the organization. They help the organization to increase customer loyalty and retention, and thus improve its profitability. They also provide an integrated view of customer data and interactions, enabling organizations to be more responsive to customer needs.

Supply Chain Management. (Discussed in detail in Chapter 13.) These modules manage the information flows between and among stages in a supply chain to maximize supply chain efficiency and effectiveness. They help organizations plan, schedule, control, and optimize the supply chain from the acquisition of raw materials to the receipt of finished goods by customers.

Business Intelligence. (Discussed in detail in Chapter 5.) These modules collect information used throughout the organization, organize it, and apply analytical tools to assist managers with decision making.

E-Business. (Discussed in detail in Chapter 9.) Customers and suppliers demand access to ERP information including order status, inventory levels, and invoice reconciliation. Further, they want this information in a simplified format that can be accessed via the Web. As a result, these modules provide two channels of access into ERP system information—one channel for customers (B2C) and one for suppliers and partners (B2B).

ERP II systems include a variety of modules that are divided into core ERP modules—financial management, operations management, and human resource management—and extended ERP modules—customer relationship management, supply chain management, business intelligence, and e-business. If a system does not have the core ERP modules, then it cannot be called an ERP system. The extended ERP modules, in contrast, are optional. Table 11.2 describes each of these modules.

Benefits and Limitation of ERP Systems

ERP systems can generate significant business benefits for an organization. The major benefits fall into the following categories:

- *Organizational flexibility and agility.* As you have seen, ERP systems break down many former departmental and functional silos of business processes, information systems, and information resources. In this way, they make organizations more flexible, agile, and adaptive. The organizations can therefore react quickly to changing business conditions and capitalize on new business opportunities.

- *Decision support.* ERP systems provide essential information on business performance across functional areas. This information significantly improves managers' ability to make better, more timely decisions.

- *Quality and efficiency.* ERP systems integrate and improve an organization's business processes, resulting in significant improvements in the quality of customer service, production, and distribution.

Despite all of their benefits, ERP systems have drawbacks. The business processes in ERP software are often predefined by the best practices that the ERP vendor has developed. *Best practices* are the most successful solutions or problem-solving methods for achieving a business objective. As a result, companies may need to change existing business processes to fit the predefined business processes of the software. For companies with well-established procedures, this requirement can be a huge problem. It is important to note that best practices, by definition, are appropriate for *most* organizations. However, organizations differ. Therefore, a particular "best practice" might not be the "best" one for your company.

In addition, ERP systems can be extremely complex, expensive, and time-consuming to implement. In fact, the costs and risks of failure in implementing a new ERP system are substantial. Quite a few companies have experienced costly ERP implementation failures. Large losses in revenue, profits, and market share have resulted when core business processes and information systems failed or did not work properly. In many cases, orders and shipments were lost, inventory changes were not recorded correctly, and unreliable inventory levels caused major-stock outs to occur. Companies such as Hershey Foods, Nike, A-DEC, and Connecticut General sustained losses in amounts up to hundreds of millions of dollars. In the case of FoxMeyer Drugs, a $5 billion pharmaceutical wholesaler, a failed ERP implementation caused the company to file for bankruptcy protection.

In almost every ERP implementation failure, the company's business managers and IT professionals underestimated the complexity of the planning, development, and training that were required to prepare for a new ERP system that would fundamentally change their business processes and information systems. Failure to involve affected employees in the planning and development phases and in change management processes, and trying to do too much too fast in the conversion process, were typical causes of unsuccessful ERP projects. Insufficient training in the new work tasks required by the ERP system and the failure to perform proper data conversion and testing for the new system also contributed to unsuccessful implementations. The cases at the end of this chapter highlight many of the difficulties involved in implementing and maintaining ERP systems.

Enterprise Application Integration

For some organizations, ERP systems are inappropriate. This is particularly true for non-manufacturing companies as well as manufacturing companies that find the process of converting from their existing system too difficult, time-consuming, or expensive.

Such companies, however, may still have isolated information systems that need to be connected with one another. To accomplish this task, some of these companies use enterprise application integration. An **enterprise application integration (EAI) system** integrates existing systems by providing layers of software that connect applications together. These layers of software are called *middleware*. In essence, the EAI system allows existing applications to communicate and share data, thereby enabling organizations to use existing applications while eliminating many of the problems caused by isolated information systems.

BEFORE *YOU GO ON . . .*

1. Define ERP and describe its functionalities.
2. What are ERP II systems?
3. Differentiate between core ERP modules and extended ERP modules.
4. List some drawbacks of ERP software.

Apply the Concept 11.3

Background You have seen in this section that enterprise resource planning (ERP) works toward removing silos of information in an organization by implementing a single system to support all functions. One example of this is SAP

Business One. SAP is an industry-leading ERP solution. This activity will have you consider the impact of ERP for small- to medium-sized businesses.

Activity Visit http://www.wiley.com/go/rainer/applytheconcept and click on the link provided for Apply the Concept 11.3. This will take you to a YouTube video titled "SAP-Business-One.wmv" by user "angeltechdotit."

As you watch the video, consider how many departments would have to be contacted to find the information that is presented in just a few short moments. If this organization operated out of silos, the representative would have to take lots of notes, visit multiple departments, and call the customer back at a later time with the answers.

Deliverable

Use Google Docs to create a drawing of the "old" way OEC Computers would have done business. You watched the SAP Business One product in the video, now imagine what it would have been like without that system. Outline the steps that Sophie would have taken after the phone call, estimate the time it would have required for each step, and then total the time of service. You will see a dramatic difference when information is in silos compared to the ERP.

Submit your outline to your professor.

Quiz questions are assignable in WileyPLUS, and available on the Book Companion Site at http://www.wiley.com/college/rainer.

11.4 Reports

All information systems produce reports: transaction processing systems, functional area information systems, ERP systems, customer relationship management systems, business intelligence systems, and so on. We discuss reports here because they are so closely associated with FAIS and ERP systems. However, the important point is that *all* information systems produce reports. These reports generally fall into three categories: routine, ad-hoc (on-demand), and exception.

Routine reports are produced at scheduled intervals. They range from hourly quality control reports to daily reports on absenteeism rates. Although routine reports are extremely valuable to an organization, managers frequently need special information that is not included in these reports. Other times they need the information but at different times ("I need the report today, for the last three days, not for one week").

Such out-of-the routine reports are called **ad-hoc (on-demand) reports.** Ad-hoc reports also can include requests for the following types of information:

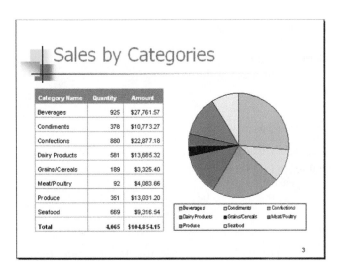

Monthly sales report.

- **Drill-down reports** display a greater level of detail. For example, a manager might examine sales by region and decide to "drill down to more detail" to look at sales by store and then by salesperson.

- **Key-indicator reports** summarize the performance of critical activities. For example, a chief financial officer might want to monitor cash flow and cash on hand.

- **Comparative reports** compare, for example, performances of different business units or of a single unit during different times.

Some managers prefer **exception reports**. Exception reports include only information that falls outside certain threshold standards. To implement *management by exception*, management first creates performance standards. The company then sets up systems to monitor performance (via the incoming data about business transactions such as expenditures), compare actual performance to the standards, and identify exceptions to the standards. The system alerts managers to the exceptions via exception reports.

Let us use sales as an example. First, management establishes sales quotas. The company then implements an FAIS that collects and analyzes all of the sales data. An exception report would identify only those cases where sales fell outside an established threshold—for example, more than 20 percent short of the quota. It would *not* report expenditures that fell *within* the accepted range of standards. By leaving out all "acceptable" performances, exception reports save managers time and help them focus on problem areas.

─── BEFORE *YOU GO ON . . .* ───

1. Compare and contrast the three major types of reports.

2. Compare and contrast the three types of on-demand reports.

Apply the Concept 11.4

Background This section has discussed the different reports you can access from an ERP. These reports truly are the power of an ERP. Getting the right information to the right person at the right time to make the right decision is the purpose for the whole exercise of installing and running an ERP. If you recall from earlier in the text, managers need IT decision support tools because decisions are becoming more complex, there is less time to make decisions, there are more options, and the cost of an incorrect decision is increasing.

Activity Visit YouTube and search for a "Phoebus ERP—Customized Dashboard" by user "kinhvan69." This video will introduce you to the dashboard tool provided by Phoebus and the ability for individual users to customize based on the information they need. This type of dashboard pulls together the many reports you have learned about in this chapter.

You may also access http://www.wiley.com/go/rainer/applytheconcept for a direct link to the video.

Imagine that you are in charge of human resources for a company that manufactures switches for Kia automobiles with this type of dashboard available. What information might you want available?

Deliverable

Sketch out a drawing of your dashboard. You can draw it on paper or build it in a word processor if you want. The main idea is for you to think about what information would be nice for an HR manager to see. What information outside of HR would be helpful for you to see? Anything from production? Anything from sales? What about information within your area?

Submit your sketch to your professor.

Quiz questions are assignable in WileyPLUS, and available on the Book Companion Site at http://www.wiley.com/college/rainer.

RUBY'S CLUB QUESTIONS

1. What types of report do you think Ruben and Lisa will benefit most from: routine, ad-hoc, drill-down, key-indicator, comparative, or exception? Why?

2. What would be some key indicators Ruben and Lisa should look for? Cover charges? Drinks? Food sold? What if they sell more food when there are fewer people and more drinks when there are more people? How could they use this data?

What's in IT for ME?

FOR THE ACCOUNTING MAJOR

Understanding the functions and outputs of TPSs effectively is a major concern of any accountant. It is also necessary to understand the various activities of all functional areas and how they are interconnected. Accounting information systems are a central component in any ERP package. In fact, all large CPA firms actively consult with clients on ERP implementations, using thousands of specially trained accounting majors.

FOR THE FINANCE MAJOR

IT helps financial analysts and managers perform their tasks better. Of particular importance is analyzing cash flows and securing the financing required for smooth operations. In addition, financial applications can support such activities as risk analysis, investment management, and global transactions involving different currencies and fiscal regulations.

Finance activities and modeling are key components of ERP systems. Flows of funds (payments), at the core of most supply chains, must be executed efficiently and effectively. Financial arrangements are especially important along global supply chains, where currency conventions and financial regulations must be considered.

FOR THE MARKETING MAJOR

Marketing and sales expenses are usually targets in a cost-reduction program. Also, sales force automation not only improves salespeoples' productivity (and thus reduces costs), but it also improves customer service.

FOR THE
PRODUCTION/OPERATIONS MANAGEMENT MAJOR

Managing production tasks, materials handling, and inventories in short time intervals, at a low cost, and with high quality is critical for competitiveness. These activities can be achieved only if they are properly supported by IT. In addition, IT can greatly enhance interaction with other functional areas, especially sales. Collaboration in design, manufacturing, and logistics requires knowledge of how modern information systems can be connected.

FOR THE
HUMAN RESOURCES MANAGEMENT MAJOR

Human resources managers can increase their efficiency and effectiveness by using IT for some of their routine functions. Human resources personnel need to understand how information flows between the HR department and the other functional areas. Finally, the integration of functional areas via ERP systems has a major impact on skill requirements and scarcity of employees, which are related to the tasks performed by the HRM department.

FOR THE MIS MAJOR

The MIS function is responsible for the most fundamental information systems in organizations: the transaction processing systems. The TPSs provide the data for the databases. In turn, all other information systems use these data. MIS personnel develop applications that support all levels of the organization (from clerical to executive) and all functional areas. The applications also enable the firm to do business with its partners.

SUMMARY

1. **Explain the purpose of transaction processing systems.**

TPSs monitor, store, collect, and process data generated from all business transactions. These data provide the inputs into the organization's database.

2. **Explain the types of support information systems can provide for each functional area of the organization.**

The major business functional areas are production/operations management, marketing, accounting/finance, and human resources management. Table 11.1 provides an overview of the many activities in each functional area supported by FAIS.

3. **Identify advantages and drawbacks to businesses of implementing an ERP system.**

Enterprise resource planning (ERP) systems integrate the planning, management, and use of all of the organization's resources. The major objective of ERP systems is to tightly integrate the functional areas of the organization. This integration enables information to flow seamlessly across the various functional areas.

The major benefits of ERP systems include the following:

> Because ERP systems integrate organizational resources, they make organizations more flexible, agile, and adaptive. The organizations can therefore react quickly to changing business conditions and capitalize on new business opportunities.

> ERP systems provide essential information on business performance across functional areas. This information significantly improves managers' ability to make better, more timely decisions.

> ERP systems integrate organizational resources, resulting in significant improvements in the quality of customer service, production, and distribution.

The major drawbacks of ERP systems include the following:

> The business processes in ERP software are often predefined by the best practices that the ERP vendor has developed. As a result, companies may need to change existing business processes to fit the predefined business processes of the software. For companies with well-established procedures, this requirement can be a huge problem.

> ERP systems can be extremely complex, expensive, and time-consuming to implement. In fact, the costs and risks of failure in implementing a new ERP system are substantial.

4. **Discuss the three major types of reports generated by the functional area information systems and enterprise resource planning systems, providing examples of each type.**

Routine reports are produced at scheduled intervals. They range from hourly quality control reports to daily reports on absenteeism rates.

Out-of-the routine reports are called *ad-hoc (on-demand) reports*. For example, a chief financial officer might want to monitor cash flow and cash on hand.

Exception reports include only information that falls outside certain threshold standards. An exception report might identify only those cases where sales fell outside an established threshold—for example, more than 20 percent short of the quota.

>>> CHAPTER GLOSSARY

ad-hoc (on-demand) reports Nonroutine reports that often contain special information that is not included in routine reports.

batch processing Transaction processing system (TPS) that processes data in batches at fixed periodic intervals.

comparative reports Reports that compare performances of different business units or times.

computer-integrated manufacturing (CIM) An information system that integrates various automated factory systems; also called *digital manufacturing*.

drill-down reports Reports that show a greater level of detail than is included in routine reports.

enterprise application integration (EAI) system A system that integrates existing systems by providing layers of software that connect applications together.

enterprise resource planning (ERP) systems Information systems that take a business process view of the overall organization to integrate the planning, management, and use of all of an organization's resources, employing a common software platform and database.

ERP II systems Interorganizational ERP systems that provide Web-enabled links among key business systems (such as inventory and production) of a company and its customers, suppliers, distributors, and others.

exception reports Reports that include only information that exceeds certain threshold standards.

functional area information systems (FAIS) Systems that provide information to managers (usually midlevel) in the functional areas, in order to support managerial tasks of planning, organizing, and controlling operations.

key-indicator reports Reports that summarize the performance of critical activities.

online transaction processing (OLTP) Transaction processing system (TPS) that processes data after transactions occur, frequently in real time.

routine reports Reports produced at scheduled intervals.

transaction Any business event that generates data worth capturing and storing in a database.

transaction processing system (TPS) Information system that supports the monitoring, collection, storage, and processing of data from the organization's basic business transactions, each of which generates data.

>>> DISCUSSION QUESTIONS

1. Why is it logical to organize IT applications by functional areas?

2. Describe the role of a TPS in a service organization.

3. Describe the relationship between TPS and FAIS.

4. Discuss how IT facilitates the budgeting process.

5. How can the Internet support investment decisions?

6. Describe the benefits of integrated accounting software packages.

7. Discuss the role that IT plays in support of auditing.

8. Investigate the role of the Web in human resources management.

9. What is the relationship between information silos and enterprise resource planning?

>>> PROBLEM-SOLVING ACTIVITIES

1. Finding a job on the Internet is challenging as there are almost too many places to look. Visit the following sites: www.careerbuilder.com, www.craigslist.org, www.linkedin.com, www.jobcentral.com, and www.monster.com. What does each of these sites provide you as a job seeker?

2. Enter www.sas.com and access *revenue optimization* there. Explain how the software helps in optimizing prices.

3. Enter www.eleapsoftware.com and review the product that helps with online training (training systems). What are the most attractive features of this product?

4. Check out Microsoft Dynamics demos at http://www.wiley.com/go/rainer/problemsolving. View three of the demos in different functional areas of your choice. Prepare a report on each product's capabilities.

5. Examine the capabilities of the following (and similar) financial software packages: Financial Analyzer (from Oracle) and CFO Vision (from SAS Institute). Prepare a report comparing the capabilities of the software packages.

6. Surf the Net and find free accounting software. (Try CNet's software at http://www.wiley.com/go/rainer/problemsolving, www.rkom.com, www.tucows.com, www.passtheshareware.com, and www.freeware-guide.com.) Download the software and try it. Compare the ease of use and usefulness of each software package.

7. Examine the capabilities of the following financial software packages: TekPortal (from www.tekknowledge.com), Financial Analyzer (from www.oracle.com), and Financial Management (from www.sas.com). Prepare a report comparing the capabilities of the software packages.

8. Find Simply Accounting Basic from Sage Software (http://us.simplyaccounting.com). Why is this product recommended for small businesses?

9. Enter www.halogensoftware.com and www.successfactors.com. Examine their software products and compare them.

10. Enter www.iemployee.com and find the support it provides to human resources management activities. View the demos and prepare a report on the capabilities of the products.

>>> COLLABORATION EXERCISE

Background

Transaction processing systems, functional area systems, and enterprise resource planning systems provide much of the basis for decision support within an organization. All of the data often resides in a few databases or data warehouses and is then accessed by the various systems that provide support for making decisions.

Activity

Divide your team into the following positions based on major as much as possible (if you do not have enough majors to divide, then choose by preference): inventory, sales, production, labor, and accounting. Imagine that you are a manufacturing company that sells widgets and that your top salesperson just closed a deal for 10,000 units.

For each of the systems mentioned above (transaction, function, and enterprise), describe the information you think your area would need to capture, store, analyze, and distribute for this transaction.

Once everyone has completed their list of data needs, meet as a team and have a conversation about how similar or different your needs are. Is there any overlap? How would you use the information to make decisions?

Deliverable

Write up a description of the data that is needed by different areas and how important data capture is for providing the correct data points to the enterprise system. Submit your description to your professor.

CLOSING **CASE 1** > Truck Manufacturer Incorporates Information Systems in Trucks

For 105 years, PACCAR has been a manufacturer of Peterbilt, Kenworth, and DAF (in Europe) heavy trucks. The company has turned a handsome profit for around 70 years. However, during the U.S. recession of 2008, PACCAR experienced a 50 percent decrease in sales. Therefore, the company decided to take a risk on a major information technology project.

<<< THE PROBLEM

IT leaders at PACCAR crafted a strategic vision for how electronic systems could change their trucking and freight hauling business, and what their trucks would need to be competitive and turn a profit. They envisioned a navigation system tailored to truckers' needs, plus an onboard electronic network of data-collecting sensors that would warn of performance problems (the diagnostic system). Both of these systems would use pervasive wireless links to send data back to dispatchers, allowing PACCAR to constantly update its customer companies on a truck's location and performance.

As a first step to implementing this vision, IT staffers spoke with employees from all other functional areas of the firm to emphasize the growing importance of in-vehicle electronic systems. Based on these talks, the company's business and IT leaders formed a consensus that PACCAR should develop its electronic systems in house, even though the firm had no expertise in building wireless, consumer electronics, or consumer-friendly computer interfaces.

<<< THE IT SOLUTION

To kick off the project, PACCAR convened a workshop for company design engineers, IT systems developers, and truck parts specialists. The workshop attendees decided their highest priority was to build a smart navigation system.

Then, financial problems hit the company. PACCAR reported revenue of $15 billion in 2008, but that revenue decreased to $8 billion by 2009. PACCAR eventually had to cut 32 percent of its workforce to keep costs in line. The IT department had to reduce its staff as well and was not able to hire new talent in wireless and mobile systems. Furthermore, because of the tough financial climate, the IT department had no research and development budget to create an innovative new system. Adding to these problems, PACCAR knew that in-vehicle electronic systems, a new territory for them, would evolve at a much faster pace than areas where they had deep expertise, such as engine technology.

As a result of these barriers, PACCAR decided to partner with outside organizations. For instance, PACCAR used an automotive system that Microsoft had developed to build an in-cab electronics system. The PACCAR system contained a software development application that third parties could use to develop additional applications for PACCAR. In addition, PACCAR's system enabled high-resolution graphics on a touch screen in the cab of its trucks.

PACCAR's navigation system used Garmin geo-positioning integrated with the driver's user interface and related routing and mapping applications. Truck navigation systems are different from car navigation systems in that truck systems need to track details such as heights of bridges and weight restrictions along a route.

In addition to navigation, the touch screen presents the driver with six "virtual gauges" that display various metrics regarding engine performance. PACCAR plans to add 22 more gauges in the next generation of the system, a change that will require only a software update.

After developing its navigation system, PACCAR turned its attention to its diagnostic system. PACCAR's system uses a modem from SignalSet (www.signalset.com), which automatically links to the strongest wireless signal that the truck can access. In August 2011, PACCAR announced that its diagnostic system was available as an add-on to its trucks. In mid-2012, PACCAR has made the diagnostic system available as a built-in option. The company has kiosks in 1,900 of its dealer showrooms to demonstrate both the navigation and diagnostic systems.

THE RESULTS >>>

PACCAR's electronic systems projects did more than place vital, customer-facing new systems into its products in the middle of a terrible economy. The projects also allowed the 275 PACCAR employees working on the projects gain valuable experience collaborating with external talent.

Having made the leap into customer-facing systems and having now made IT a critical part of its products, PACCAR knows that the pressure will never let up to continually be updating IT systems to keep up with drivers' demands and rival products. Therefore, the company now has a skilled IT staff dedicated to developing products and collaborating with outsiders when they need to.

Sources: Compiled from C. Babcock, "Heavy Truck Maker Revs Up IT Innovation Amid a Brutal Recession," *InformationWeek,* September 19, 2011; "PACCAR Truckerlink Uses Proprietary Cellular Network Technology," *Truckinginfo,* September 16, 2011; "PACCAR Parts Touts Cellular-Based Telematics Fleet Management Service," *Truck Parts and Service,* September 15, 2011; "Kenworth Truck Company Has Introduced the Revolutionary Kenworth NavPlus™, A PACCAR Proprietary Navigation and Infotainment Technology System for Class 5-8 Trucks," *The Street,* March 24, 2010; www.paccar.com, www.kenworth.com, www.peterbilt.com, www.truckerlink.com, www.signalset.com, accessed March 10, 2012.

Questions

1. Why did PACCAR commit such a large amount of resources to electronic systems during the recession?
2. What are the benefits of PACCAR's new navigation system and diagnostic system to truck drivers?
3. What are the benefits to PACCAR of collaborating with outside companies in building new systems?

CLOSING **CASE 2 >** Hilton Embraces Collaboration with Information Technology Partners

THE PROBLEM >>>

Hilton Worldwide (www.hilton.com) accommodates guests in more than 193,000 rooms in 540 hotels. Those hotels are located in 78 countries across six continents. Hilton had experienced years of rapid growth, several mergers, and other business changes, all of which left them with a complex, fragmented information technology strategy that was completely inadequate to their needs. In addition, Hilton was expanding rapidly around the world and had outgrown its ability to support all of its internal technology services. Hilton executives, hotel managers, owners, and customers faced daily problems and inconveniences when trying to accomplish simple tasks, such as accessing Wi-Fi or checking bookings at other properties in the company's portfolio.

<<< **THE IT SOLUTION**

To correct these problems, Hilton adopted a new approach to its technology needs by creating the Hilton Worldwide Innovation Collaborative (HWIC). The mission of the HWIC is to deliver exceptional guest experiences while leveraging the skills, quality, and scale of its technology partners to differentiate Hilton Worldwide brands from the competition. Partnering with technology firms who have experience in implementing systems development best practices, leveraging extensive research and development efforts, and delivering next-generation technology solutions leaves Hilton free to focus on its core competencies without the inconveniences and challenges of a flawed IT system.

Hilton selected five technology partners based on their global expertise and ability to deliver economies of scale in infrastructure, future development, application development, and support services. The Hilton technology partners are Accenture (www.accenture.com), AT&T (www.att.com), IBM (www.ibm.com), Microsoft (www.microsoft.com), and Tata Consultancy Services (TCS; www.tcs.com).

- Accenture provides application development and support services for Hilton's property management systems and multibrand, transactional Web sites. Accenture also supports Hilton with a global service desk.

- AT&T provides a fully managed suite of Wi-Fi and Internet services for Hilton Worldwide. The company also manages and operates Hilton's StayConnected program, which enables guests to access high-speed Internet services in meeting spaces, public areas, and their private hotel rooms.

- IBM hosts and manages the technology platforms that support Hilton's 10 brands, including, global e-mail services, Web hosting, data center management and monitoring, and the central guest reservation system.

- Microsoft allowed Hilton to deploy its SharePoint 2010, Office 2010, Office Communications Server, and Windows 7. Hilton also uses Microsoft's SQL Server and Visual Studio to power its proprietary property management system.

- TCS powers Hilton's corporate suite of applications, including learning management, quality assurance, business intelligence, financial systems, and intranet applications.

<<< **THE RESULTS**

Hilton has benefited greatly from its technology partnerships in three key areas: improved project productivity, enhanced data center efficiency, and greater high-speed Internet access. Specifically, the company's improved project productivity has allowed the hotel giant to accelerate its innovation and be the first to market with new technologies.

In the area of data center efficiency, Hilton has a new Leadership in Energy and Environmental Design (LEED) Gold-certified data center. The data center is an example of Hilton's commitment to sustainability, and includes energy-efficient and redundant power and cooling. These environment-saving technologies also lower the total cost of ownership for technology services. Hilton is using a cloud-computing environment at its data center to enable greater technology flexibility, maintainability, scalability, and overall system security.

Hilton has improved its high-speed Internet access as well. The company has maintained best-in-class Internet performance, reliability, and consistency, while its cost per room is 60 percent of the industry average. Improvements such as these have helped Hilton to considerably grow its customer base, increase confidence in its brands, and lay the foundation for a successful, stable, and growing business in the years ahead.

Sources: Compiled from R. Webb, "Hilton Books IT Partners for Long Stay," *Baseline Magazine*, October 10, 2011; "TCS, Hilton Worldwide Ink Agreement for IT Services," *The Hindu*, December 22, 2010; S. O'Neill, "Hilton CIO: 4 Reasons We're Checking In SharePoint and Office 2010," *CIO*, December 1, 2010; B. De Lollis, "AT&T to Take Over Internet Services in Most Hilton-Brand Hotels," *USA Today*, July 16, 2010; A. Lorden, "Hilton's Innovation Acceleration," *Hospitality Technology*, June 10, 2010; www.hilton.com, accessed March 15, 2012.

Questions

1. Describe the reasons that Hilton decided to collaborate with IT partners rather than develop its own information systems in house.
2. What are the problems associated with collaborating with five large strategic IT partners? Provide specific examples to support your answer.

RUBY'S CLUB — INTERNSHIP ASSIGNMENT

Last week Lisa stayed up late to take data from individual receipts and put them in a spreadsheet. She and Ruben want to see what kind of graphs or charts they might be able to get out of a more sophisticated IS. Although this is just a basic spreadsheet, the principle of taking large amounts of data and analyzing them with a visual aid still applies.

Specifically, this sheet shows entry and departure times for customers. It also lists the number of drinks they purchased. The club owners hope to use this information to know when to run a "special" that might keep customers a little longer and get them to buy one or two more drinks.

Visit http://wiley.com/go/rainer/rubysclub and click on the link provided for Chapter 11. This will provide you with a spreadsheet with lots of information. For this exercise, you will need to use the "Total Number of Hours" and "Total Drinks" columns. Create a scatter plot that shows the number of drinks people buy based on the amount of time they stay at the club. Then make a recommendation as to what hour needs to be the "Happy Hour" that Lisa and Ruben hope will keep their customers in the club! Keep in mind that Ruby's open at 6 PM!

SPREADSHEET ACTIVITY: REGRESSION IN EXCEL

Objective: Microsoft Excel is powerful for more than just keeping up with numbers. With the right add-ins, you can run elaborate statistical analysis. This activity will introduce simple regression within Microsoft Excel.

Chapter Connection: Transaction processing systems are just the beginning. They provide data to many systems throughout an organization. Ultimately, the data they provide are used to plan and forecast for years ahead. This activity ties the spreadsheet tool to the data found in the various systems within the organization.

Activity: Imagine that you are an intern for a local restaurant/bar/club (the focus tends to change as it gets later in the evening). You have been asked to help the owners with a serious problem—managing their supply chain.

Forecasting has always been a problem for them. One week they are booming and another things are dead.

Really, they expect as much because they are in a college town. But there are weekends when people should be in town and the establishment is not and weekends that everyone should be gone and the place is packed.

The owners have put together a spreadsheet for you to use to help them understand their demand and how to better match their food and drink supplies to what the demand will be. For restaurant owners, there is nothing worse than telling customers that the kitchen is out of or throwing away unsold goods that spoiled. They need better forecasting.

Please go to http://www.wiley.com/go/rainer/spreadsheet and click on the videos for Chapter 11. One describes an "Add-In" you may have to install for Excel to run a regression and the other is about regression analysis itself. You will use this tool in Excel to help your employers better understand the situation they are in. Ultimately, you will complete your analysis to determine which variables have the most statistically significant impact on their demand. Finally, you will write a short memo to your employers (your professor) explaining your findings in a way they can understand it.

The spreadsheet you will download has lots of 1's and 0's in it. A "1" means an event was "true." For example, under "Jazz" a "1" would mean that jazz was the genre of music playing that night in the club. A "0" would mean that jazz was not playing that night. Most of the variables are considered independent variables. This means that whether or not jazz was playing is not dependent on any other variables. You use these independent factors to help understand the *dependent* variables that you are most concerned about—cover sales, food sales, and drink sales.

Deliverable: Your work will include a spreadsheet that includes the regression analysis as well as a word document that shows the interpretation of that analysis. The word document will also (based on the interpretation) offer suggestions that will help the employers understand their demand and better schedule their food and drink purchases.

Quiz questions are assignable in WileyPLUS, and available on the Book Companion Site at http://www.wiley.com/college/rainer.

DATABASE ACTIVITY: REPORTS II

Objective

In this activity, you will learn how to create a report that uses a query, rather than tables, as its data source. The Chapter 10 activity gave you the tools to create something like your grade report: the ability to combine data from more than one table, then to select the rows of combined data that you want. A real grade report, however, is formatted nicely and probably has summary calculations such as GPA. This activity adds those capabilities to your toolkit.

CHAPTER CONNECTION

Organizational information systems, such as those this chapter discusses, are a primary source of information for management. The methods used in this activity are how the information is organized and presented to them.

PREREQUISITES

Before starting this activity, you should complete the database activities for Chapter 4 (Reports I) and Chapter 10 (Queries I) activities.

Activity

In this activity, which you will find online at http://www.wiley.com/go/rainer/database, you will combine the selection and table-joining capabilities of queries with the layout and summary capabilities of reports. This creates a powerful tool for presenting data to businesspeople who need to use it.

1. Download the Ch 11 DizzyDonuts database from http://www.wiley.com/go/rainer/database and open it. It is the end product of the Chapter 10 activity, with the queries described there. If you did that activity, you can use what you did there as the basis for this one.

2. Open StoreOrderQry. It shows all the orders placed at the Boston store. Go to Design view and add a column to the query for OrderStatus, because we want to ignore discarded orders in our analysis. Enter "<>Discarded" (without the quotation marks; Access will supply them around the character string part) for "not equal to 'Discarded'" in the Criteria section, on the same row as the store name. Run the query.

3. You will see that the result table is shorter and shows no orders with Discarded status. However, we do not need to display this column. Unnecessary content in user reports is clutter: it gets in the way of focusing quickly on the important parts. Go back to Design view and uncheck the Show box in the OrderStatus column. Rerun the query. It still excludes discarded orders, but no longer reminds us on every line. (If we cared about order status, we could leave that column in, but let us assume we do not.) Close the query, saving your changes.

4. Now click the Create ribbon tab and open the Report Wizard. The Tables/Queries menu in the first step includes both the tables and the queries in the database. We will base our new report on StoreOrderQry. Select it from the menu. Move

CustName, OrderDate, and OrderTotal into the Selected Fields panel. Then click Next.

Usage Hint: If we had left OrderStatus in the query results, we could choose not to move it to Selected Fields here. We would end up with exactly the same report.

5. Organize the report by CustTbl. That will group all the orders of each customer. Click Next twice, because you do not want to add any grouping levels.

6. In the next dialogue box, click Summary Options. Because OrderTotal is the only field that the Report Wizard knows how to summarize, only it will show. (Access can do more, as you may recall from the Chapter 6 activity, but the Wizard cannot.) Check the Sum box to total each customer's orders. Select Detail and Summary at the right. Click OK, then Next.

7. Continue to click Next until the wizard finishes. If you are prompted to name your report, call it OrderSummaryRpt.

8. If you carried out all the above steps properly, the report will have the correct content. Its first few lines should look something like the following. Yours may not look exactly like this, depending on the design it uses. If you named it OrderSummaryRpt in the previous step, that name will show in the header instead of CustTbl.

9. Switch to Report view to make sure you are happy with the results. When you are, close the report. If you did not name it earlier, name it OrderSummaryRpt, renaming it in the navigation pane if necessary. (Right-click on its name for the Rename option.)

10. You realize that this report is just for one city. However, nothing about it identifies that city. Its name is only in the query design. To redo the report to show that go back to step 4, this time moving all the fields into the Selected Fields pane. Organize the report by StoreTbl, and click Next.

11. In the next dialogue box, add a grouping level by customer by selecting CustName and clicking >.

12. Continue as before, inserting a sum on OrderTotal, until you click Finish. Name this report "ImprovedCityRpt" if you are prompted to name it when you create it.

Usage Hint: If your report does not show the fields that should be at the right, revisit the Wizard and choose Landscape format.

13. You now have a report grouped by city. However, there is only one city in it, so that is not ideal. We would rather state the city in the header, with the report body much as it was before. This must be done in Design view, as Layout view does not

This appearance leaves a lot to be desired. So, switch to Layout view, and

(a) Select the label that starts "Summary for 'CustName . . ." and delete it.

(b) Select the sum fields (customer sum and overall sum) and move them to the left, closer to the data they are based on. If your chosen design has the order date and order total at the right, move them over to the left (as in the picture) too.

(c) Edit the report heading to be more descriptive.

(d) Edit the column headings to have meaningful labels, not database field names.

(e) Change the word "Sum" to "Customer Total."

allow moving report elements from one area to another. Change to that view.

14. (Number not used in Access 2010 version of activity, but retained in the exercise for consistency between the two versions; Access 2007 requires another step here.)

15. Edit the report header to read "Customers in City:" (without the quotation marks).

16. Delete the StoreCity column heading. Select the StoreCity data field. In the Home ribbon tab, click Cut (pair of scissors, near the left) or press control-X. Click in the Report Header section of the report design and click Paste (large icon with a

sheet of paper sliding off a clipboard, in the same area) or press control-V. (If you are really good with your mouse or trackpad, you can avoid the cutting and pasting by selecting it and moving it while the mouse pointer is a four-headed arrow.)

17. Click the Format Painter in the Clipboard section of the Home ribbon tab or the Font section of the Format tab. (You may be familiar with it from other parts of Microsoft Office.) Click in the report header to copy its format, then in the StoreCity field you just moved to give it the same format. Move it to the right of the header text.

Usage Hint: If you prefer, click in the report header. Note its font, size and color in the Font section of the ribbon, under either the Home or the Format tab. Then select the StoreCity field and format it the same way. The result will be the same.

18. Format this report as you formatted the previous one. You can do most of the formatting in Layout view if you prefer. Also:

   (a) Drag CustName Header up to remove the space that the store city used to occupy. (This is easiest in Design view.)

   (b) Delete the heading for "StoreCity" in the page header.

   (c) Move all the remaining column headings and data fields to the left, into the space that the city name used to occupy.

   (d) Delete the total at the city level. With just one city, it duplicates the grand total.

19. Close the report. Name it "ImprovedCityRpt."

20. Open StoreOrderQry, change the city to Chicago, and close it, saving when prompted.

21. Open ImprovedCityRpt. It should say "Chicago" in the header and reflect Chicago data.

Deliverable

Your database with the modified query and two reports as described above.

Quiz Questions

1. A report can display data from
   (a) More than one table.
   (b) More than one query.
   (c) A combination of tables and queries.
   (d) All of the above.

2. True or False: When a report is based on a query, the query is rerun with new selection criteria, and the new query result is saved; opening the report will redisplay the original data.

3. Open any Access report (an existing one or a new one you create to play with—it does not matter) in Layout view. Try several Themes (near the left of the Design ribbon). Which of the following do Themes *not* modify?
   (a) Report fonts.
   (b) Report column headings.
   (c) Report font sizes.
   (d) Report colors.

4. True or False: Clicking Remove, as you did in step 14 above, lets you remove a column heading while leaving that column's data in place.

Discussion Questions

1. You are developing an information system for inventory management, which the book discusses in the "In-House Logistics and Materials Management" section of this chapter. You want to identify all items that are at 1.0 to 1.5 times their reorder point for human review. (If an item is below its reorder point, it is already been reordered, or someone decided not to reorder it.) You decide to do this with a query. Its selection criteria will specify these comparisons. Access will then create a report for the purchasing manager. Draw this report, with suitable data columns, groupings, and summaries. Try to put yourself in the purchasing manager's position, asking what information this person needs to make reordering decisions and how that information can best be presented. Make any necessary assumptions about the content of your company's inventory database.

2. Section 4 of this chapter, "Reports," discusses five types of reports: routine, drill-down, key-indicator, comparative, and exception. Give an example of each, not repeating examples from that section, and discuss how a query could be used as the basis for it. If it cannot be, explain why.

3. You work in a university radio station. Your funding comes from several sources: the university, paid memberships, selling merchandise such as logo coffee mugs and soda can holders, and donations. Donations and merchandise sales often come from members, and members often renew year after year. You have a database that stores this information, as well as results of surveys about favorite musicians and music genres. Many, but not all, of the surveys identify the respondent.

   (a) Draw an ERD for this database. If you did not study ER diagramming in Chapter 3, draw an Access relationship map for it. Show its tables, their data fields (columns), and their relationships.

   (b) You want to use this information to help the station raise funds by matching its programming to what its supporters want and in other ways. How could you use query-driven reports to do this? Use your imagination. Be creative. Make any necessary assumptions about the content of the station's database.

12 | Extending the Organization to Customers

LEARNING OBJECTIVES >>>

1. Identify the primary functions of both customer relationship management (CRM) and collaborative CRM.

2. Describe how businesses might utilize applications used in each of the two major components of operational CRM systems.

3. Discuss the benefits of analytical CRM to businesses.

4. Explain the advantages and disadvantages of mobile CRM systems, on-demand CRM systems, and open-source CRM systems.

Have you ever paid attention to the hundreds of little plastic containers in the cosmetics aisle of your grocery store? Or in the pharmaceutical aisle? Or, indeed, every aisle in most stores? When you consider plastic containers of all shapes, sizes, and colors that populate our world, it is really amazing! For some reason, every company feels the need to have a custom-designed container for each of their brands, and for each product within that brand. Now, have you ever wondered whose job it is to make all of these different containers? In fact, the manufacturer of all of the containers you see likely comes from a very small pool of vendors.

One of these vendors is induPlast (www.induplast.it), based in Italy. With around 70 employees, this company manufactures injection-molded plastic containers, which can be customized for patrons. Unfortunately, induPlast began to have trouble providing adequate support to their customers, especially as each had multiple customized products. The problem was that over time, customers' information ended up in different silos of information. This setup made it very difficult for induPlast to track all of the various business dealings it might have with one single customer, leading to deficits in customer relationship management (CRM).

Let's take a hypothetical example (this situation is entirely fictional—the authors of this text are not familiar with specifics regarding induPlast clients). Imagine that Johnson & Johnson (J&J) is a customer of induPlast. J&J has multiple divisions such as skin and hair care, wound care and topicals, oral health care, women's health, over-the-counter medicines, etc. induPlast also has multiple divisions that focus on different product categories such as cosmetics or health care. Without a CRM tool, relationships are developed at the division level of J&J and induPlast rather than between the two companies. Therefore, each division of induPlast looks at each division of the customer company as a separate provider or > > >

© Dmitri Mihhailov/
iStockphoto

RUBY'S CLUB

Ruben and Lisa realize that this generation is much more connected than any before. Facebook, Twitter, MySpace, text messaging, instant messaging, and so on have all connected people anywhere, anytime. They also feel that they need to tap into this social market, but they are not sure how.

They know that many of their customers are on Facebook. However, they think that Facebook is more for personal use and do not want their customers to feel invaded by receiving advertisements from them on Facebook. Twitter seems more popular for business promotions, but they wonder how many of their customers are regulars on Twitter.

As you learn about customer relationship management, consider their dilemma. Maintaining customers is about balance. Communicate at the right time, place, and manner, and Ruben and Lisa can win with their customers. However, if they cross a boundary, they may lose the community atmosphere in their club because of a virtual communication.

customer, rather than as a department of a company with which induPlast has a unified customer relationship.

As you can see, without a CRM system, induPlast has lots of customer data on J&J, but that data is confined to the individual division that gathered it and is not available to other divisions of the company. So, when it comes time to deal with J&J as a whole (not by division), induPlast would have difficulty assimilating all of the different data points in order to gain a unified picture of its customer.

To solve problems similar to this fictional (though possible) example, induPlast needed a CRM that would provide a 360-degree view of each customer. induPlast chose Sugar CRM, an open source tool that would allow the company to streamline its customer information and communication. The company was able to integrate Sugar with its existing systems so that management would have better insight into the manufacturing process. Real-time tracking allowed induPlast to make decisions based on complete and current information rather than based on stale or incomplete data gathered piecemeal from across the company.

The result is that induPlast is now able to monitor trends in the market and customer accounts in real time. As intended, the company now has a 360-degree view of customers across divisions.

CRM tools serve many purposes. In some cases (this case included), they virtually consolidate data. This means that data is still housed in the existing systems where it was gathered, but the CRM makes connections between those systems. In other cases, the CRM completely replaces existing systems and old data is imported into the new system. Whatever the method, the goal of CRM is to provide clean, current information on customers to help management make good decisions.

Sources: www.induplast.it, www.sugarcrm.com, www.jnj.com/connect/healthcare-products/consumer, accessed March 23, 2012.

Questions

1. Why was information stored in "information silos" at induPlast in the first place?
2. Why is a 360-degree view of each customer so important to induPlast?

Introduction

Before the supermarket, the mall, and the automobile, people went to their neighborhood stores to purchase goods. The owner and employees recognized customers by name and knew their preferences and wants. For their part, customers remained loyal to the store and made repeated purchases. Over time, however, this personal customer relationship became impersonal as people moved from farms to cities, consumers became mobile, and supermarkets and department stores were established to achieve economies of scale through mass marketing efforts. Although prices were lower and products were more uniform in quality, the relationship with customers became nameless and impersonal.

The customer relationship has become even more impersonal with the rapid growth of the Internet and the World Wide Web. In today's hypercompetitive marketplace, customers are increasingly powerful. If they are dissatisfied with a product and/or a service from one organization, a competitor is often just one mouse click away. Further, as more and more customers shop on the Web, an enterprise does not even have the opportunity to make a good first impression *in person*.

Customer relationship management (CRM) returns to personal marketing. That is, rather than market to a mass of people or companies, businesses market to each customer individually. By employing this approach, businesses can use information about each customer—for example, previous purchases, needs, and wants—to create offers that customers are more likely to accept. That is, the CRM approach is designed to achieve *customer intimacy*. This CRM approach is enabled by information technology in the form of a variety of CRM systems and applications.

Customer relationship management is not only about the software. Sometimes the problem with managing relationships is simply time and information. Old legacy systems may contain the information, but it may take too long to access it, and the information may not be usable across a variety of applications. The result is reduced time to spend with customers. induPlast is emphasizing a customer-centric approach to its business practices because the company knows that sustainable value is found in long-term customer relationships that extend beyond today's business transaction.

However, you may be asking yourself this: Why should I learn about CRM? As you will see in this chapter, customers are supremely important to *all* organizations. Regardless of the particular job you perform, you will have either a direct or an indirect impact on managing your firm's customers. As you read the What's In IT For Me? feature, you will encounter a number of opportunities in which you can make immediate contributions on your first job. Therefore, it is important that you possess a working knowledge of CRM and CRM systems.

12.1 Defining Customer Relationship Management

Customer relationship management (CRM) is an organizational strategy that is customer focused and customer driven. That is, organizations concentrate on satisfying customers by assessing their requirements for products and services and then providing high-quality, responsive service. CRM is not a process or a technology per se; rather, it is a way of thinking and acting in a customer-centric fashion. The focus of organizations today has shifted from conducting business transactions to managing customer relationships. In general, organizations recognize that customers are the core of a successful enterprise and the success of the enterprise depends on effectively managing relationships with them.

CRM builds sustainable long-term customer relationships that create value for the company as well as for the customer. That is, CRM helps companies acquire new customers, retain existing profitable customers, and grow the relationships with existing customers. This last CRM function is particularly important because repeat customers are the largest generator of revenue for an enterprise. Also, organizations have long understood that getting a customer back after he or she has switched to a competitor is vastly more expensive than keeping that customer satisfied in the first place.

Figure 12.1 depicts the CRM process. The process begins with marketing efforts, where the organization solicits prospects from a target population of potential customers.

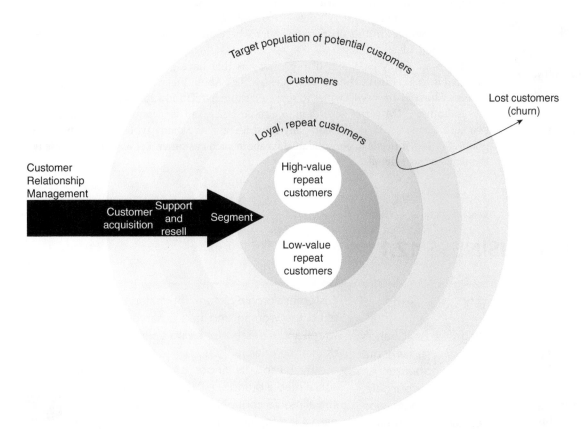

Figure 12.1 The customer relationship management process.

A certain number of prospects will make a purchase, thus becoming customers. Of the organization's customers, a certain number will become repeat customers. The organization then segments its repeat customers into low-value and high-value repeat customers. An organization's overall goal is to maximize the *lifetime value* of a customer, which is that customer's potential revenue stream over a number of years.

The organization inevitably will lose a certain percentage of customers, a process called *customer churn*. The optimal result of the organization's CRM efforts is to maximize the number of high-value repeat customers while minimizing customer churn.

CRM is a simple idea: Treat different customers differently because their needs differ and their value to the company may differ. A successful CRM strategy not only improves customer satisfaction, but it also makes the company's sales and service employees more productive, which in turn generates increased profits. In fact, researchers at the National Quality Research Center at the University of Michigan found that a 1 percent increase in customer satisfaction can lead to as much as a 300 percent increase in a company's market capitalization, defined as the number of shares of the company's stock outstanding multiplied by the price per share of the stock. Put simply, a minor increase in customer satisfaction can lead to a major increase in a company's overall value.

Up to this point, you have been looking at an organization's CRM strategy. It is important to distinguish between a CRM *strategy* and CRM *systems*. Basically, CRM systems are information systems designed to support an organization's CRM strategy. For organizations to pursue excellent relationships with their customers, they need to utilize CRM systems that provide the necessary infrastructure to support those relationships. Because customer service and support are essential to a successful business, organizations must place a great deal of emphasis on both their CRM strategy and their CRM systems.

Broadly speaking, CRM systems can be placed along a continuum, from low-end CRM systems—designed for enterprises with many small customers—to high-end CRM systems—for enterprises with a few large customers. An example of a low-end system is when Amazon uses its CRM system to recommend books to returning customers. An example of a high-end system is when Boeing uses its CRM system to coordinate staff activities in a campaign to sell its new 787 aircraft to Delta Airlines. As you go through the cases and examples in this chapter, consider where on the continuum a particular CRM system would fall.

There are many examples of organizations that have gone beyond what is merely expected in their efforts to be customer-centric. IT's About Business 12.1 illustrates how P.F. Chang's China Bistro used Twitter to score a customer-relationship coup.

Although CRM varies according to circumstances, all successful CRM policies share two basic elements. First, the company must identify the many types of customer touch points. Second, it needs to consolidate data about each customer. Let us examine these two elements in more detail.

Coupon Kiosks are an attempt to build loyalty among customers. (*Source:* © Spencer Grant/ PhotoEdit.)

IT'S ABOUT BUSINESS 12.1

An Instantaneous CRM Effort

While a woman in Florida was sitting in a P.F. Chang's China Bistro restaurant (www.pfchangs.com), she sent out a tweet about her delicious lettuce-wrap appetizer. An employee at P.F. Chang's headquarters in Scottsdale, Arizona, spotted the tweet. He alerted a manager, who immediately called the Florida restaurant. Using the customer's profile picture, the restaurant manager identified the woman and had a server bring her lettuce wraps and a dessert for being an enthusiastic supporter of their company.

By having its finger on the pulse of its social media branding, P.F. Chang's executed a social media coup. Not only did the restaurant earn a fan for life—and one who has an active

Twitter account—but the customer undoubtedly told her friends and co-workers about her lunchtime surprise, praising P.F. Chang's for caring about its customers. Further, in a short time, marketing executives in many organizations were presenting P.F. Chang's and its lettuce wraps in conferences and meetings as an example of intuitive branding.

In the case of P.F. Chang's, social media presented an easy opportunity to make the most of the customer experience and to demonstrate to the organization that there is "gold" in tweets. Regardless of whether organizations have a social media strategy, customers are on Twitter and Facebook, telling the world how they feel about companies, their products, and their services. Whether it is a Facebook group begging Trader Joe's (www.traderjoes.com) to open a store in a certain geographic location or a blogger with a million followers complaining about his or her washing machine, companies ignore social media at their peril.

Sources: Compiled from W. Schuchart, "How P.F. Chang's Turned a Plate of Lettuce Wraps into a Twitter Win," *IT Knowledge Exchange*, March 16, 2011; www.pfchangs.com, accessed March 18, 2012.

Questions

1. Provide two examples of specific actions a company could take to utilize social media in its CRM efforts.

2. Should all organizations include a social media component in their CRM strategy? Why or why not? Support your answer.

Customer Touch Points

Organizations must recognize the numerous and diverse interactions that they have with their customers. These various types of interactions are referred to as **customer touch points**. Traditional customer touch points include telephone contact, direct mailings, and actual physical interactions with customers during their visits to a store. However, organizational CRM systems must manage many additional customer touch points that occur through the use of popular personal technologies. These touch points include e-mail, Web sites, and communications via smart phones (see Figure 12.2).

Data Consolidation

Data consolidation is also critical to an organization's CRM efforts. Customer data must be managed effectively by the organization's CRM systems. In the past, customer data were located in isolated systems in different functional areas across the business. For example, it was not uncommon to find customer data stored in separate databases in the finance, sales, logistics, and marketing departments. Even though all of these data related to the same customer, it was difficult to share them across the various functional areas.

As you saw in Chapter 5, modern, interconnected systems built around a data warehouse now make all customer-related data available to every unit of the business. This complete data set on each customer is called a *360-degree view* of that customer. By accessing this 360-degree view, a company can enhance its relationship with its customers and ultimately make more productive and profitable decisions.

Data consolidation and the 360-degree view of the customer enable the organization's functional areas to readily share information about customers. This information sharing leads to collaborative CRM. **Collaborative CRM systems** provide effective and efficient interactive communication with the customer throughout the entire organization. That is, collaborative CRM systems integrate communications between the organization and its customers in all aspects of marketing, sales, and customer support. Collaborative CRM systems also enable customers to provide direct feedback to the organization. As you read in Chapter 9, Web 2.0 applications such as blogs and Wikis are

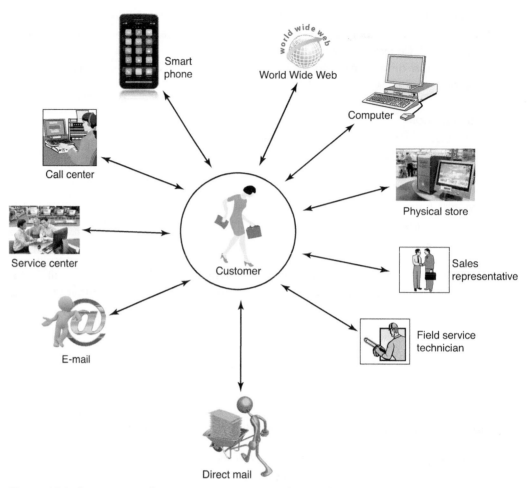

Figure 12.2 Customer touch points. (*Sources:* Smartphone-Oleksiy Mark/Shutterstock; Service center-Media Bakery; Physical store-Media Bakery.)

--- BEFORE *YOU GO ON* ... ---

1. What is the definition of customer relationship management?
2. Why is CRM so important to any organization?
3. Define and provide examples of customer touch points.

very important to companies that value customer input into their product and service offerings as well as into new product development.

A CRM system in an organization contains two major components: operational CRM systems and analytical CRM systems. You learn about these components in the next two sections.

Apply the Concept 12.1

Background This section has introduced the concept of a CRM system and suggested that it is better to focus on relationships than transactions. The idea is that relationships create transactions and therefore if you grow the relationship, you keep the customer!

Activity Visit YouTube and search for the video titled "IBM DB2 Data Warehousing—REI" by user "ibmer5985." You may also go to http://www.wiley.com/go/rainer/applytheconcept and click on the link to the video.

As you watch the video, consider how it makes you feel as a customer to know that your experience is completely unique. Would you feel special knowing that your version of the REI Web site is different from anyone else's?

Now, click on the second link provided. This will take you to the REI homepage. If you see a general page, do you feel cheated? Do you feel like you should create an account, tell the company your preferences, and then go back to the home page to see your custom content?

Deliverable

Write a short e-mail to Julie Derry, the Director of Online Programs for REI, that explains how you feel about their CRM from your customer viewpoint. Watch the YouTube video again if you need help remembering the REI mission statement and what she hopes to accomplish through the CRM.

Submit your email to your professor.

Quiz questions are assignable in WileyPLUS, and available on the Book Companion Site at http://www.wiley.com/college/rainer.

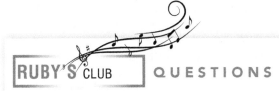

RUBY'S CLUB | QUESTIONS

1. Ruby's Club seeks to maintain customers. If CRM is not a technology but a way of thinking, then what role could technology play to support this way of thinking for Ruben and Lisa?
2. Look at Figure 12.1, the CRM process. Ethically, when should Ruby's Club begin marketing to students: at the beginning of their 4 to 6 years of college or only after they reach the age of 21?
3. If CRM were implemented at Ruby's Club, would Ruben and Lisa need a low-end or high-end system?
4. What do you think are the most common touch points for Ruby's Club customers? Cell phones? Facebook? E-mail? Twitter? Telephone? USPS? Campus flyers?
5. Would Ruben and Lisa have a true 360-degree view of their customers if each order entry area operated on its own database? What would be the problem with having customer data spread over several computers?

12.2 Operational Customer Relationship Management Systems

Operational CRM systems support front-office business processes. Front-office processes are those that directly interact with customers—that is, sales, marketing, and service. The two major components of operational CRM systems are customer-facing applications and customer-touching applications.

Customer-Facing Applications

Customer-facing CRM applications are those applications where an organization's sales, field service, and customer interaction center representatives interact directly with customers. These applications include customer service and support, sales force automation, marketing, and campaign management.

Customer Service and Support. Customer service and support refers to systems that automate service requests, complaints, product returns, and requests for information. Today, organizations have implemented **customer interaction centers (CIC)**, where organizational representatives use multiple communication channels such as the Web, telephone, fax, and face-to-face interactions to support the communication preferences of customers.

One of the most well-known customer interaction centers is the *call center*. A call center is a centralized office used for the purpose of receiving and transmitting a large volume of requests by telephone. Call centers enable companies to respond to a large variety of questions, including product support and complaints.

Organizations use the CIC to create a call list for the sales team, whose members contact sales prospects. This type of interaction is called *outbound telesales*. Customers can communicate directly with the CIC to initiate a sales order, inquire about products and services before placing an order, and obtain information about a transaction that they have already made. These interactions are referred to as *inbound teleservice*.

The CIC also provides the information help desk. The help desk assists customers with their questions concerning products or services and it processes customer complaints. Complaints generate follow-up activities such as quality-control checks, delivery of replacement parts or products, service calls, generation of credit memos, and product returns.

Information technologies are extending the functionality of the traditional CIC to include e-mail and Web interaction. For example, Epicor (www.epicor.com) provides software solutions that combine Web channels, such as automated e-mail reply and Web knowledge bases. The information the software provides is available to CIC representatives and field service personnel. Another technology, live chat, allows customers to connect to a company representative and conduct an instant messaging session. The advantage of live chat over a telephone conversation is the ability to show documents and photos (see www. livechatinc.com and www.websitealive.com). Some companies conduct the chat with a computer rather than a real person using natural language processing.

T'S ABOUT BUSINESS 12.2

Tweet for Immediate Customer Service

In the 1980s and early 1990s, if customers were unhappy with the way they were treated by a business, they would call the manager or write an angry letter via the post office. With the advent of the Internet and online comment forms, angry calls and letters gave way to tersely worded e-mail responses. Soon, these email responses gave way to customer call centers. Now, in mid-2012, customers have Twitter.

Consider this example: A Hotmail user's e-mail account was hacked, leading to spam being forwarded to his entire contact list and him getting locked out of his inbox. To resolve this issue, our anonymous user followed Microsoft's directions (Hotmail is a Microsoft product). He e-mailed its customer service department and received, as promised, an automated response within 24 hours. The response let him know that his problem was being looked into. Then, he heard nothing for the next three days. So, he vented his frustration on Twitter and

© pixelfit/iStockphoto

tagged the message with "@Microsoft" so that anyone searching for tweets about the company would see it. Within 34 minutes, the long silence was broken and a Hotmail program manager contacted him via Facebook. Within 30 minutes, the program manager was able to log the user back into his Hotmail account.

Customer service experts state that it is the public humiliation that sets Twitter complaints apart from other methods of communicating concerns. Many companies now have human resources staff dedicated  to monitoring social media streams, so that they can respond to any angry tweet within 60 minutes. Social media such as Twitter has placed unprecedented power in the hands of customers. Companies beware!

Sources: Compiled from S. Kovach, "Use Twitter to Complain and Get the Customer Service You Deserve," *Business Insider,*

February 3, 2011; "The Customer-Service Express Lane," *Time,* July 26, 2010.

Questions

1. What attributes of Twitter makes the service so valuable for the resolution of customer complaints?
2. List a possible disadvantage of using Twitter to make a complaint about a company.

Social media are now providing methods that customers can use to get faster, better customer service. IT's About Business 12.2 shows how one irritated customer used Twitter to obtain a response to his complaint.

Sales Force Automation. **Sales force automation (SFA)** is the component of an operational CRM system that automatically records all of the components in a sales transaction process. SFA systems include a *contact management system*, which tracks all contacts that have been made with a customer, the purpose of each contact, and any follow-up that might be necessary. This system eliminates duplicated contacts and redundancy, which in turn reduces the risk of irritating customers. SFA also includes a *sales lead tracking system*, which lists potential customers or customers who have purchased related products.

Other elements of an SFA system can include a *sales forecasting system*, which is a mathematical technique for estimating future sales, and a *product knowledge system,* which is a comprehensive source of information regarding products and services. More developed SFA systems also have online product-building features (called *configurators*) that enable customers to model the product to meet their specific needs. For example, you can customize your own running shoe at NikeID (http://nikeid.nike.com). Finally, many of the current SFA systems provide for remote connectivity for the salesperson in the field via Web-based interfaces that can be displayed on smart phones.

Marketing. Thus far you have focused primarily on how sales and customer service personnel can benefit from CRM systems. However, CRM systems have many important applications for an organization's marketing department as well. For example, they enable marketers to identify and target their best customers, to manage marketing campaigns, and to generate quality leads for the sales teams. In addition, CRM marketing applications provide opportunities to sift through volumes of customer data—a process known as data mining—and develop *purchasing profiles*—a snapshot of a consumer's buying habits—that may lead to additional sales through cross-selling, up-selling, and bundling.

Cross-selling is the practice of marketing additional related products to customers based on a previous purchase. This sales approach has been used very successfully by the world's largest online retailer, Amazon (www.amazon.com). For example, if you have purchased several books on Amazon, the next time you visit the Web site, Amazon will provide recommendations of other books you might like to purchase.

Up-selling is a sales strategy whereby the businessperson will provide to customers the opportunity to purchase higher-value related products or services as opposed to or along with the consumer's initial product or service selection. For example, if a customer goes into an electronics store to buy a new television, a salesperson may show him a 1080i high-definition LCD next to non-HD TV in the hope of selling the more expensive set (assuming the customer is willing to pay the extra cost for a sharper picture). Other common examples of up-selling are warranties on electronics purchases and the purchase of a car wash after you purchased gas at the gas station.

Bundling is a form of cross-selling whereby a business sells a group of products or services together at a price that is lower than the combined individual prices of the products. For example, your cable company might offer a bundle price that includes basic cable TV, broadband Internet access, and local telephone service at a lower price than if you acquired each service separately.

Campaign Management. **Campaign management applications** help organizations plan campaigns so that the right messages are sent to the right people through the right channels. Organizations manage their customers very carefully to avoid targeting people who have opted out of receiving marketing communications. Further, companies use these applications to personalize individual messages for each particular customer.

Customer-Touching Applications

Corporations have used manual CRM systems for many years. The term electronic *CRM* (or *e-CRM*) appeared in the mid-1990s, when organizations began using the Internet, the Web, and other electronic touch points (e.g., e-mail, point-of-sale terminals) to manage customer relationships. Customers interact directly with these technologies and applications rather than interact with a company representative as is the case with customer-facing applications. Such applications are called **customer-touching CRM applications** or **electronic CRM (e-CRM) applications**. Using these applications, customers typically are able to help themselves. There are many types of e-CRM applications. Some of the major applications are presented in this section.

Search and Comparison Capabilities. With the vast array of products and services available on the Web, it is often difficult for customers to find what they want. To assist customers, many online stores and malls offer search and comparison capabilities, as do independent comparison Web sites (see www.mysimon.com).

Technical and Other Information and Services. Many organizations offer personalized experiences to induce a customer to make a purchase or to remain loyal. For example, Web sites often allow customers to download product manuals. One example is General Electric's Web site (www.ge.com), which provides detailed technical and maintenance information and sells replacement parts for discontinued models for customers who need to repair outdated home appliances. Another example is Goodyear's Web site (www.goodyear.com), which provides information about tires and their use.

Customized Products and Services. Another customer-touching service that many online vendors use is mass customization, a process in which customers can configure their own products. For example, Dell Computer (www.dell.com) allows customers to configure their own computer systems. The Gap (www.gap.com) allows customers to "mix and match" an entire wardrobe. Web sites such as Hitsquad (www.hitsquad.com) and Surprise (www.surprise.com) allow customers to pick individual music titles from a library and customize a CD, a feature that traditional music stores do not offer.

In addition, customers can now view their account balances or check the shipping status of their orders from their computers or smart phones at any time. If you order books from Amazon, for example, you can look up the anticipated arrival date. Many other companies follow this model and provide similar services (see www.fedex.com and www.ups.com).

Personalized Web Pages. Many organizations permit their customers to create their own personalized Web pages. Customers use these pages to record purchases and preferences, as well as problems and requests. For example, American Airlines generates personalized Web pages for each of approximately 800,000 registered travel-planning customers.

FAQs. Frequently asked questions (FAQs) are a simple tool for answering repetitive customer queries. Customers who find the information they need by using this tool do not need to communicate with an actual person.

E-mail and Automated Response. The most popular tool for customer service is e-mail. Inexpensive and fast, e-mail is used to not only answer inquiries from

Discounts and coupons are also a way to collect shopping data for CRM tools. (*Source:* © Amy Eira/PhotoEdit.)

Starbucks' Loyalty Program Goes Mobile

Starbucks is leveraging mobile phones to improve its much-vaunted loyalty program. In December 2011, the company disclosed that it had successfully handled 26 million transactions via its new mobile payment system, which allows smart phone users to pay for Starbucks' products using their phones. The Starbucks mobile payment app handles between 1 and 2 percent of Starbucks' total sales.

The app is also tied directly to Starbucks' loyalty program. When customers pay for purchases electronically, their accounts are automatically credited and any qualifying discounts are applied. About 3.6 million customers belong to the My Starbucks Rewards program, and 2 million of them have achieved gold status. Starbucks' loyalty members earn one star for each purchase using the company's loyalty card. When loyalty members earn 30 stars, they attain gold status.

Starbucks thinks the success of its mobile loyalty system is the result of convenience. It is a faster and easier way for customers to pay.

Sources: C. Tode, "Starbucks Is Worldwide Leader in Mobile Payment Transactions," *Mobile Commerce Daily*, January 31, 2012; S. Greengard, "Mobile Loyalty Program Scores at Starbucks," *Baseline Magazine*, December 20, 2011; T. Wasserman, "One in Four Starbucks Transactions Now Done Via Card, Including Mobile," *CNN*, December 6, 2011; www.starbucks.com, accessed March 19, 2012.

Questions

1. Do you see any disadvantages to Starbucks' mobile loyalty program? Provide specific examples to support your answer.
2. Refer to Chapter 10's Closing Case 1. How does Starbucks' mobile loyalty program fit in with the concept of the mobile wallet?

---

customers but also to disseminate information, send alerts and product information, and conduct correspondence regarding any topic.

Loyalty Programs. **Loyalty programs** recognize customers who repeatedly use a vendor's products or services. Loyalty programs are appropriate when two conditions are met: a high frequency of repeat purchases and little product customization for each customer. IT's About Business 12.3 illustrates how Starbucks has extended its loyalty program to mobile devices.

The purpose of loyalty programs is not to reward past behavior but to influence future behavior. It is important to note here that the most profitable customers are not necessarily those whose behavior can be influenced the most easily. As one example, most major U.S. airlines provide some "elite" benefits to anyone who flies 25,000 miles with them and their partners over the course of a year. Customers who fly on paid first-class tickets pay many times as much for a given flight as one who flies in discount economy. But, the first-class flyers will reach elite status only 1.5 to 2 times faster than will economy-class passengers. The reason is that, although first-class passengers are far more profitable than discount seekers, they are also less influenced by loyalty programs. Discount flyers respond much more enthusiastically to the benefits of frequent flyer programs. Therefore, airlines award discount flyers more benefits than they offer first-class flyers (relative to their spending).

Perhaps the best-known loyalty programs are the airlines' frequent flyer programs. In addition, casinos use their players' clubs to reward their frequent players and supermarkets use similar programs to reward frequent shoppers. Loyalty programs use a database or data warehouse to keep a record of the points (or miles) a customer has accrued and the rewards to which he or she is entitled. The programs then use analytical tools to mine the data and learn about customer behavior.

Operational CRM systems provide the following benefits:

- Efficient, personalized marketing, sales, and service
- A 360-degree view of each customer
- The ability of sales and service employees to access a complete history of customer interaction with the organization, regardless of the touch point

Another example of an operational CRM system involves Caterpillar, Inc. (www.cat.com), an international manufacturer of industrial equipment. Caterpillar uses its CRM tools to accomplish the following objectives:

- Assist the organization in improving sales and account management by optimizing the information shared by multiple employees and by streamlining existing processes (for example, taking orders using mobile devices)

- Form individualized relationships with customers, with the aim of improving customer satisfaction and maximizing profits
- Identify the most profitable customers and provide them the highest level of service
- Provide employees with the information and processes necessary to know their customers
- Understand and identify customer needs, and effectively build relationships among the company, its customer base, and its distribution partners

BEFORE YOU GO ON . . .

1. Differentiate between customer-facing applications and customer-touching applications.
2. Other than the examples in the book, provide an example of cross-selling, up-selling, and bundling.

Apply the Concept 12.2

Background Section 12.2 has introduced you to the concept of customer-facing and customer-touching CRM applications. Many organizations use a combination of both types of systems to establish, develop, and maintain relationships with consumers. This activity will help you learn to see these systems in action when you encounter a CRM on a Web site or in a brick-and-mortar business.

Activity Visit a physical store where you like to shop (you do not have to buy anything for this exercise) and visit the shop's Web site. Be sure to pick a store that has both an Internet site and a physical store so you can compare both approaches. As you walk through the store, look for cues that could tie a customer to a CRM. Does the business have any customer rewards programs? How does the store use them? Are you a member of these programs? Are there any significant advantages to joining the program?

Is the in-store membership tied to anything online? If so, how? Does it seem that the store has one in-store membership and another online?

Deliverable

List some recommendations for the store you visited on ways it can integrate online and in-store CRM systems. For a good example, visit a Target near you. The photo in Figure 12.3 was taken in a Target in Oxford, Alabama on May 1, 2012. It demonstrates an attempt to bring part of the online customer-touching CRM into the physical store. Are there more ways than simply placing an Internet-enabled touch screen near the products? Once you complete your list, submit it to your professor.

Quiz questions are assignable in WileyPLUS, and available on the Book Companion Site at http://www.wiley.com/college/rainer.

Figure 12.3 Integration of online shopping tools in a physical store. (*Source:* Courtesy of Brad Prince.)

1. Do you think there would there be any legal or ethical issues with up-selling alcoholic beverages? What about cross-selling alcohol with food?

2. Campaign management seems to be the issue Ruben and Lisa are really concerned about. How do they touch their customer on the right touch point, at the right time, in the right way? What examples can you find online that show how other clubs/bars handle campaign management?

3. What type of loyalty club could Ruben and Lisa create? What advantages could they create for their customer with this type of club?

12.3 Analytical Customer Relationship Management Systems

Whereas operational CRM systems support front-office business processes, **analytical CRM systems** analyze customer behavior and perceptions in order to provide actionable business intelligence. For example, analytical CRM systems typically provide information on customer requests and transactions, as well as on customer responses to an organization's marketing, sales, and service initiatives. These systems also create statistical models of customer behavior and the value of customer relationships over time, as well as forecasts about acquiring, retaining, and losing customers. Figure 12.4 illustrates the relationship between operational CRM systems and analytical CRM systems.

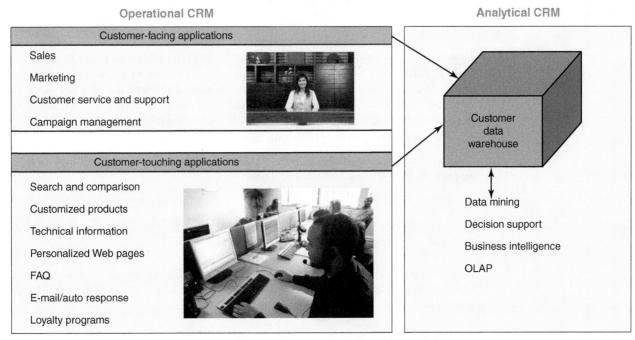

Figure 12.4 The relationship between operational CRM and analytical CRM. (*Source:* Image Source Limited; J-C & D. PRATT/PhotoNonStop/Glow Images.)

Important technologies in analytical CRM systems include data warehouses, data mining, decision support, and other business intelligence technologies (discussed in Chapter 12). Once systems have completed the various analyses, information to the organization is available in the form of reports and digital dashboards.

Analytical CRM systems analyze customer data for a variety of purposes, including these:

- Designing and executing targeted marketing campaigns
- Increasing customer acquisition, cross-selling, and up-selling
- Providing input into decisions relating to products and services (e.g., pricing and product development)
- Providing financial forecasting and customer profitability analysis

BEFORE *YOU GO ON . . .*

1. What is the relationship between operational CRM systems and analytical CRM systems?
2. What are some of the functions of analytical CRM systems?

Apply the Concept 12.3

Background

This section defined analytical CRM as systems that create statistical models of customer behavior and the value of customer relationships over time, as well as forecasts about acquiring, retaining, and losing customers. What that means is the more you shop a Web site, the more it will learn about you. Google is a prime example.

Activity Visit http://www.wiley.com/go/rainer/applytheconcept and click on the link provided for Apply the Concept 12.3. This is a case study that describes how 1-888-Trash-It uses its CRM system to enhance its business analytics. There is also a short video for you to watch. As you watch this, consider the integration and use of data across the organization that helps make better decisions and serve customers.

Now, consider the following scenario. Analytical CRM provides senior management with forecasts and trends model. Based on this model, management decides to run an ad in a local neighborhood for a discounted service for new customers. The week after the ad is run, headquarters uses the GPS location in the trucks to send the closest vehicle to the newest customer to provide efficient and quick service.

Deliverable

Draw a map that shows the locations for the activities in this system and ways this system is making a difference for both the business and the consumer in the scenario described above. At a minimum, you should have activities at headquarters, data at the truck locations, advertisements, and new customers. This will help you see how that a CRM influences many areas of business inside and outside the organization.

Submit your map to your professor.

Quiz questions are assignable in WileyPLUS, and available on the Book Companion Site at http://www.wiley.com/college/rainer.

12.4 Other Types of Customer Relationship Management Systems

Now that you have examined operational and analytical CRM systems, you focus on other types of CRM systems. Three exciting developments in this area are on-demand CRM systems, mobile CRM systems, and open-source CRM systems.

On-Demand CRM Systems

Customer relationship management systems may be implemented as either *on premise* or *on demand*. Traditionally, organizations utilized on-premise CRM systems, meaning that they purchased the systems from a vendor and then installed them on site. This arrangement was expensive, time-consuming, and inflexible. Some organizations, particularly smaller ones, could not justify the cost.

On-demand CRM systems became a solution for the drawbacks of on-premise CRM systems. An **on-demand CRM system** is a CRM system that is hosted by an external vendor in the vendor's data center. This arrangement spares the organization the costs associated with purchasing the system. In addition, because the vendor creates and maintains the system, the organization's employees need to know only how to access and utilize it. The concept of on demand is also known as utility computing (see Plug IT In 2) or software-as-a-service (SaaS; see Plug IT In 3).

Despite their benefits, on-demand CRM systems have potential problems. First, the vendor could prove to be unreliable, in which case the company would have no CRM functionality at all. Second, hosted software is difficult or impossible to modify, and only the vendor can upgrade it. Third, vendor-hosted CRM software may be difficult to integrate with the organization's existing software. Finally, giving strategic customer data to vendors always carries risks.

Salesforce (www.salesforce.com) is the best-known on-demand CRM vendor. The goal of Salesforce is to provide a new business model that allows companies to rent the CRM software instead of buying it. The secret to Salesforce's success appears to be that CRM has common requirements across many customers.

One Salesforce customer is Minneapolis-based Häagen-Dazs (www.haagen-dazs.com). Häagen-Dazs estimated that it would have had to spend $65,000 for a custom-designed database to remain in close contact with its retail franchises. Rather than make this expenditure, the company spent an initial $20,000 to establish service with Salesforce. It now pays $125 per month for 20 users to remotely monitor, via the Web or their smart phones, all the Häagen-Dazs franchises across the United States.

Other vendors also offer on-demand CRM software. The following example demonstrates the advantages that McKesson Specialty (www.mckesson.com) gained from deploying the Oracle on-demand CRM application.

EXAMPLE

McKesson Specialty, a division of the McKesson Corporation (www.mckesson.com), delivers the approaches and solutions needed to ensure success in the evolving specialty pharmaceutical market. The division's services include reimbursement support services for patients and physicians, reimbursement strategies for pharmaceutical manufacturers, specialty distribution and pharmacy services, oncology services, and patient support services including clinical support and patient assistance programs.

McKesson Specialty wanted a CRM system that would enable it to perform the following functions:

- Make sales activities and customer accounts more visible to the corporation.
- Standardize and automate sales and CRM processes.
- Track reported problems, inconsistent processes, and resolution time.

In addition, the system had to be easy to use. McKesson Specialty ultimately implemented Oracle's CRM On Demand application to standardize the sales and marketing systems across all of its product lines. The new system enabled the company to consolidate reporting across product lines and it provided the necessary flexibility to accommodate multiple sales processes. Further, it allowed the organization to monitor and track issues that arose in the resolution process.

In essence, Oracle's CRM On Demand application provided McKesson Specialty with a 360-degree view of customer account information across the entire organization, which has proved to be very useful. In addition, McKesson Specialty was able to deploy the system in less than 90 days.

Sources: Compiled from "McKesson Specialty: Oracle Customer Snapshot," www.oracle.com, accessed August 15, 2011; "McKesson Specialty Standardizes Sales and Marketing Processes and Increases Customer Visibility," http://techrepublic.com, accessed August 15, 2011.

Mobile CRM Systems

A **mobile CRM system** is an interactive CRM system that enables an organization to conduct communications related to sales, marketing, and customer service activities through a mobile medium for the purpose of building and maintaining relationships with its customers. Put simply, mobile CRM systems involve interacting directly with consumers through their own portable devices, such as smart phones. Many forward-thinking companies believe mobile CRM systems hold tremendous promise as an avenue to create a personalized customer relationship that may be accessed anywhere and at any time. In fact, the potential opportunities provided through mobile marketing appear so rich that a host of companies have already identified mobile CRM systems as a cornerstone of their future marketing activities. IT's About Business 12.2 discusses a mobile CRM application at the Hard Rock Hotel and Casino.

Open-Source CRM Systems

As explained in Plug IT In 2, the source code for open-source software is available at no cost to developers or users. An **open-source CRM system**, therefore, is a CRM system whose source code is available to developers and users.

Open-source CRM systems do not provide more or fewer features or functions than other CRM software, and they may be implemented either on premise or on demand. Leading open-source CRM vendors include SugarCRM (www.sugarcrm.com), Concursive (www.concursive.com), and vtiger (www.vtiger.com).

'S ABOUT BUSINESS 12.4

Mobile CRM on a Smart Phone

On busy weekends in Las Vegas, getting a drink at bars and nightclubs can be a full-contact sport. First, you muscle your way through a crowd to get near the bar. Then, you shout your order and hope the bartender hears it correctly. The Hard Rock Hotel and Casino (www.hardrockhotel.com) has developed a unique approach to this problem. In April 2011, the hotel deployed a system that enables customers to use their smart phones to order food and drinks, which are then delivered to their location by a server. The technology, called Kickback, is a product of Kickback Mobile (www.kickbackmobile.com).

To participate, customers download a free app to their smart phones and register with their credit card information. At that point, Kickback uses GPS technology to determine which of the seven Hard Rock venues the customer is visiting and it pushes menu options to the customer's smart phone accordingly. Customers can also use the app for room service.

Kickback offers a number of benefits. For customers, ordering food and drinks at the resort's pool, concert venue, and food and beverage outlets no longer requires trips to the bar. Hard Rock gains full integration with its CRM and point-of-sale systems as well as the capability to track the purchases of big spenders. Hard Rock also hopes to use Kickback to develop and push promotions—for example, a marketing campaign for a particular liquor—based on a customer's preferences, spending habits, and location within the resort.

Kickback uses a technology called geo-fencing, which employs a smart phone's GPS capabilities and location in relation to nearby cellular towers to estimate where a customer is located when he or she places an order. Customers select where the server should deliver the order using a predefined list. They can even purchase food or drinks when they are not at a Hard Rock venue and have the order delivered to friends who are there.

Sources: Compiled from M. Villano, "CRM on a Smart Phone," *CIO,* April 27, 2011; www.hardrockhotel.com, www.kickbackmobile.com, accessed May 9, 2011.

Questions

1. What are the disadvantages of the Kickback mobile CRM application?
2. Identify two additional advantages of the Kickback mobile CRM application.

The benefits of open-source CRM systems include favorable pricing and a wide variety of applications. In addition, these systems are very easy to customize. This is an attractive feature for organizations that need CRM software designed for their specific needs. Finally, updates and bug (software error) fixes for open-source CRM systems occur rapidly and extensive support information is available free of charge.

Like all software, however, open-source CRM systems have certain risks. The most serious risk involves quality control. Because open-source CRM systems are created by a large community of unpaid developers, there sometimes is no central authority that is responsible for overseeing the quality of the product. Further, for best results, companies must have the same information technology platform in place as the platform on which the open-source CRM system was developed.

BEFORE YOU GO ON . . .

1. Define *on-demand CRM.*
2. Define *mobile CRM.*
3. Define *open-source CRM.*

Apply the Concept 12.4

Background This section has outlined the different types of CRM systems—not operational or analytical, but the ways you can actually implement a CRM system. For example, you can purchase industry standard CRM, customized CRM, open-source CRM, on-demand CRM (cloud), and more. In reality, you just about have this many options with any system you plan to implement!

Activity Visit http://www.wiley.com/go/rainer/applytheconcept and click on the links provided for Apply the Concept 12.4. One will take you to a YouTube video describing an on-demand CRM (Salesforce). Another will take you to a video describing an open-source CRM (Sugar CRM). These represent quite extreme approaches. In one instance (Salesforce), the company that is providing the CRM assumes responsibility for all major hardware and software components. In the other, the company buying the CRM assumes all major hardware and software components.

Deliverable

Build a table that illustrates the advantages and disadvantages to each approach. Are they in offerings of the software? Or does this present a more strategic issue of hardware and software ownership? Does one system provide more flexibility than another? Is customization sacrificed for flexibility? What about data security?

Submit your table to your professor.

Quiz questions are assignable in WileyPLUS, and available on the Book Companion Site at http://www.wiley.com/college/rainer.

FOR THE ACCOUNTING MAJOR

CRM systems can help companies establish controls for financial reporting related to interactions with customers in order to support compliance with legislation. For example, the Sarbanes-Oxley Act requires companies to establish and maintain an adequate set of controls for accurate financial reporting that can be audited by a third party. Other sections of the law [302 and 401(b)] have implications for customer activities, including the requirements that sales figures reported for the prior year are correct. Section 409 requires companies to report material changes to financial conditions, such as the loss of a strategic customer or significant customer claims about product quality.

CRM systems can track document flow from a sales opportunity, to a sales order, to an invoice, to an accounting document, thus enabling finance and accounting managers to monitor the entire flow. CRM systems that track sales quotes and orders can be used to incorporate process controls that identify questionable sales transactions. CRM systems can provide exception-alert capabilities to identify instances outside defined parameters that put companies at risk.

FOR THE FINANCE MAJOR

CRM systems allow companies to track marketing expenses, collecting appropriate costs for each individual marketing campaign. These costs can then be matched to corporate initiatives and financial objectives, demonstrating the financial impact of the marketing campaign.

Pricing is another key area that influences financial reporting. For example, what discounts are available? When can a price be overridden? Who approves discounts? CRM systems can put controls into place for these issues.

FOR THE MARKETING MAJOR

CRM systems are an integral part of every marketing professional's work activities. CRM systems contain the consolidated customer data that provide the foundation for making informed marketing decisions. Using this data, marketers develop well-timed and targeted sales campaigns with customized product mixes and established price points that enhance potential sales opportunities and therefore increase revenue. CRM systems also support the development of forecasting models for future sales to existing clients through the use of historical data captured from previous transactions.

FOR THE PRODUCTION/OPERATIONS MANAGEMENT MAJOR

Production is heavily involved in the acquisition of raw materials, conversion, and distribution of finished goods. However, all of these activities are driven by sales. Increases or decreases in demand for goods results in a corresponding increase or decrease in a company's need for raw materials. Integral to a company's demand is forecasting future sales, an important part of CRM systems. Sales forecasts are created through the use of historical data stored in CRM systems.

This information is critically important to a production manager who is placing orders for manufacturing processes. Without an accurate future sales forecast, production managers may face inventory problems (discussed in detail in this chapter). The use of CRM systems for production and operational support is critical to efficiently managing the resources of the company.

FOR THE HUMAN RESOURCES MAJOR

As companies try to enhance their customer relationships, they must recognize that employees who interact with customers are critical to the success of CRM strategies. Essentially, CRM will be successful based on the employees' desire and ability to promote the company and its CRM initiatives. In fact, research analysts have found that customer loyalty is largely based on employees' capabilities and their commitment to the company.

As a result, human resource managers know that if their company desires valued customer relationships, then it needs valued relationships with its employees. Therefore, HR managers are implementing programs to increase employee satisfaction and are providing training for employees so that they can execute CRM strategies.

FOR THE MIS MAJOR

The IT function in the enterprise is responsible for the corporate databases and data warehouse, and the correctness and completeness of the data in them. That is, the IT department provides the data used in a 360-degree view of the customer. Further, IT personnel provide the technologies underlying the customer interaction center.

SUMMARY

1. **Identify the primary functions of both customer relationship management (CRM) and collaborative CRM.**

   Customer relationship management (CRM) is an organizational strategy that is customer focused and customer driven. That is, organizations concentrate on satisfying customers by assessing their requirements for products and services and then providing high-quality, responsive service. CRM functions include acquiring new customers, retaining existing customers, and growing the relationships with existing customers.

   Collaborative CRM is an organizational CRM strategy whereby data consolidation and the 360-degree view of the customer enable the organization's functional areas to readily share information about customers. The functions of collaborative CRM include integrating communications between the organization and its customers in all aspects of marketing, sales, and customer support processes, and enabling customers to provide direct feedback to the organization.

2. **Describe how businesses might utilize applications used in each of the two major components of operational CRM systems.**

Operational CRM systems support the front-office business processes that interact directly with customers (i.e., sales, marketing, and service). The two major components of operational CRM systems are customer-facing applications and customer-touching applications.

Customer-facing CRM applications include customer service and support, sales force automation, marketing, and campaign management. *Customer-touching applications* include search and comparison capabilities, technical and other information and services, customized products and services, personalized Web pages, FAQs, e-mail and automated response, and loyalty programs.

3. **Discuss the benefits of analytical CRM to businesses.**

Analytical CRM systems analyze customer behavior and perceptions in order to provide business intelligence. Organizations use analytical systems for many purposes, including designing and executing targeted marketing campaigns; increasing customer acquisition, cross-selling, and up-selling; providing input into decisions relating to products and services (e.g., pricing and product development); and providing financial forecasting and customer profitability analysis.

4. **Explain the advantages and disadvantages of mobile CRM systems, on-demand CRM systems, and open-source CRM systems.**

On-demand CRM systems are CRM systems hosted by an external vendor in the vendor's data center. Advantages of on-demand CRM systems include lower costs and a need for employees to know only how to access and utilize the software. Drawbacks include possibly unreliable vendors, difficulty in modifying the software, and difficulty in integrating vendor-hosted CRM software with the organization's existing software.

Mobile CRM systems are interactive CRM systems whereby communications related to sales, marketing, and customer service activities are conducted through a mobile medium for the purpose of building and maintaining customer relationships between an organization and its customers. Advantages of mobile CRM systems include convenience for customers and the chance to build a truly personal relationship with customers. A drawback could be difficulty in maintaining customer expectations. That is, the company must be extremely responsive to customer needs in a mobile, near-real-time environment.

Open-source CRM systems are CRM systems whose source code is available to developers and users. The benefits of open-source CRM systems include favorable pricing, a wide variety of applications, easy customization, rapid updates and bug (software error) fixes, and extensive free support information. The major drawback of open-source CRM systems is quality control.

>>> CHAPTER GLOSSARY

analytical CRM systems CRM systems that analyze customer behavior and perceptions in order to provide actionable business intelligence.

bundling A form of cross-selling whereby an enterprise sells a group of products or services together at a lower price than the combined individual price of the products.

campaign management applications CRM applications that help organizations plan marketing campaigns so that the right messages are sent to the right people through the right channels.

collaborative CRM systems CRM systems in which communications between the organization and its customers are integrated across all aspects of marketing, sales, and customer support processes.

cross-selling The practice of marketing additional related products to customers based on a previous purchase.

customer-facing CRM applications Areas where customers directly interact with the organization, including customer service and support, sales force automation, marketing, and campaign management.

customer interaction centers CRM operations where organizational representatives use multiple communication channels to interact with customers in functions such as inbound teleservice and outbound telesales.

customer relationship management (CRM) A customer-focused and customer-driven organizational strategy that concentrates on satisfying customers by addressing their requirements for products and services, and then by providing high-quality, responsive service.

customer-touching CRM applications (or electronic CRM or e-CRM applications) Applications and technologies with which customers interact and typically help themselves.

customer touch points Any interactions between a customer and an organization.

electronic CRM (e-CRM) (see **customer-touching CRM applications**)

loyalty programs Programs that offer rewards to customers to influence future behavior.

mobile CRM system An interactive CRM system where communications related to sales, marketing, and customer service activities are conducted through a mobile medium for the purpose of building and maintaining customer relationships between an organization and its customers.

on-demand CRM system A CRM system that is hosted by an external vendor in the vendor's data center.

open-source CRM system CRM software whose source code is available to developers and users.

operational CRM systems Components of CRM that support the front-office business processes that directly interact with customers (i.e., sales, marketing, and service).

sales force automation The component of an operational CRM system that automatically records all the aspects in a sales transaction process.

up-selling A sales strategy whereby the organizational representative will provide to customers the opportunity to purchase higher-value related products or services as opposed to or along with the consumer's initial product or service selection.

>>> DISCUSSION QUESTIONS

1. How do customer relationship management systems help organizations achieve customer intimacy?

2. What is the relationship between data consolidation and CRM systems?

3. Discuss the relationship between CRM and customer privacy.

4. Distinguish between operational CRM systems and analytical CRM systems.

5. Differentiate between customer-facing CRM applications and customer-touching CRM applications.

6. Explain why Web-based customer interaction centers are critical for successful CRM systems.

7. Why are companies so interested in e-CRM applications?

8. Discuss why it is difficult to justify CRM applications.

9. You are the CIO of a small company with a rapidly growing customer base. Which CRM system would you use: on-premise CRM system, on-demand CRM system, or open-source CRM system? Remember that open-source CRM systems may be implemented either on premise or on demand. Discuss the pros and cons of each type of CRM system for your business.

>>> PROBLEM-SOLVING ACTIVITIES

1. Enter www.anntaylor.com, www.hermes.com, and www.tiffany.com. Compare and contrast the customer service activities offered by these companies on their Web sites. Do you see marked similarities? Differences?

2. Access your university's Web site. Investigate how your university provides for customer relationship management. *Hint:* First decide who your university's customers are.

3. Access www.sugarcrm.com, and take the interactive tour. Prepare a report on SugarCRM's functionality to the class.

4. Enter the Teradata Student Network (http://www.wiley.com/go/rainer/problemsolving), and find the First American Corporation case (by Watson, Wixom, and Goodhue), which focuses on CRM implementation. Answer the questions at the end of the case.

>>> COLLABORATION EXERCISE

Background

Customer relationship management (CRM) tools generally provide information to the marketing department. However, as you have seen in other chapters, the information in one department will affect the activities in another department. For example, when a decision is made about how much to produce over the next quarter, labor is updated, suppliers are updated, and information from that decision is shared with many others who make decisions within the organization so that they can make appropriate plans.

Activity

Visit http://www.wiley.com/go/rainer/collaboration and find the links provided for the Collaboration Exercise for Chapter 12. You will find a list of open-source and proprietary CRM solutions. Look over these and choose one that your team will research.

Imagine that you are an automobile manufacturer. Your vehicles are priced at the lower end of new vehicle prices. The majority of your customers always have a car payment (meaning they trade before they pay one off),

work by the hour, live paycheck to paycheck, and have an average of $10,000 in credit card debt. They like cash rebates, sales, high trade values, and typically give in to "gimmicks" that sell cars.

With this in mind, divide your team into the following positions based on major as much as possible (if you do not have enough majors to divide, then choose by preference): inventory, sales, production, labor, and accounting. Each team member will research the CRM solution from their position (major or functional area) to make note of the information each could use from the CRM.

Once everyone has completed the list of data needs, meet as a team and have a conversation about the type of data you would find useful from a CRM within the context of the automobile manufacturing environment.

Deliverable

Work with your team to write up a summary of the software package you reviewed. Be sure to include the various areas that are supported by this CRM even though it is generally targeted to marketing and sales.

CLOSING **CASE 1 >** A Concierge in Your Pocket

THE PROBLEM >>> Luxury hotels are known for their concierge services that cater discreetly to every guest. Managed by Starwood Hotels & Resorts Worldwide, the SLS Hotel in Beverly Hills, California, is part of the Luxury Collection Hotel brand owned by SBE Entertainment Group LLC. Debuting in 2008 following a $230 million renovation of the former Le Meridien Beverly Hills, the 297-room SLS Hotel is all about delighting the senses. French modern designer Philippe Starck oversaw the $100 million décor. The food is the work of chef Jose Andres, 2011 recipient of the James Beard Foundation's award for most outstanding chef in North America.

Customer service, then, is a hallmark for the SLS Hotel. The hotel's IT manager, Eric Chao, notes that service is all about efficiency, gratification, and particularly, convenience. The last thing a luxury hotel wants is for its guests to feel that they have to work to get service during their stay. In fact, Chao says that many guests at the hotel do not even want to speak directly with any of the hotel's various employees.

Given these high customer expectations, SLS Hotel had to figure out how to discreetly improve the hotel's already sky-high-level service.

THE IT >>>
SOLUTION

To begin solving this issue, the hotel launched a mobile hotel app called GoSLSHotel (www.goslshotel.com), that offers convenient, around-the-clock service at the touch of an icon. Guests who are looking for a late-night snack, an extra bottle of shampoo, or valet service no longer need to pick up their room phone, search for the correct button, and then interact with a hotel employee. They can request any service they need within seconds or minutes just by clicking an icon on their smart phones or computers. SLS Hotel's new app even has a built-in timer. When the "send" button is pressed for an in-room dining order, the order immediately shows up on the kitchen's computer, where orders are timed by different-colored flags.

GoSLSHotel does not only drive better customer service. It also serves to drive business and generate more revenue for the hotel. The first week after the app launched in 2010, it generated 30 service requests (spa, dining reservations, and housekeeping, among others), 15 room-service orders, and 2,500 guest "touches." Two years and many enhancements later, GoSLSHotel is considered such a competitive advantage that the hotel refused to allow Chao to speak about specific revenue numbers. Despite secrecy on the part of the hotel staff, the app's numbers are followed closely. Initially designed as a front-end guest service tool, it now has many functions on the back end as well that track all guest touches, purchases, and requests, and turn this data into reports that help the hotel learn about guest preferences and trends. The app also has a feedback icon that allows guests to register complaints in real time and get them addressed during their stay.

Take the example of Linda, a fictional guest at SLS Hotel. Linda always uses GoSLSHotel to order Dom Perignon champagne in her room on arrival. The hotel might, after five stays, send a bottle of Dom to the room before Linda even arrives. In another example, customers who frequent the hotel's 5,000-square-foot Ciel Spa might receive a discount on their next relaxation massage. The hotel recently promoted free Internet to guests who were willing to "like" SLS Hotel on its Facebook page.

Although GoSLSHotel provides a significant competitive advantage, the security of the mobile app is a major concern for hotel customers. Therefore, SLS Hotel takes great pains to communicate the app's security features to guests, so they will feel comfortable using the app. GoSLSHotel users sign in with their room number and name, and are not required to swipe their credit card for any purchase, thus easing the security fear factor. The hotel states that its app has generated "overwhelmingly positive comments."

THE RESULTS >>> As mentioned above, GoSLSHotel has driven new business, generated additional revenue, and given SLS Hotel a crucial competitive advantage over its competitors. However, the app's return on investment is just as much about the "intangibles" as it is about revenue generation. The level of convenience added by the app generates good customer feelings, which boost the hotel's reputation and ensure future business growth and stability.

Sources: Compiled from E. Savitz, "Rushing Mobile Apps Out Means Ushering Hackers In," *Forbes,* February 26, 2012; E. Savitz, "The Growing Problem of Privacy-Invading Mobile Apps," *Forbes,* February 23, 2012; L. Tucci, "Hotel App Pockets Revenue by Putting Concierge Service in Your Pocket," *SearchCIO.com,* February 23, 2012; P. Dailey, "SLS Hotel Adds Personal Touch to Guest Visits with Custom Mobile App," *Hospitality Technology,* May 13, 2010; "Runtriz Delivering Mobile Guest Facing App for SLS Hotel at Beverly Hills," *Hospitalitynet. com,* February 3, 2010; www.goslshotel.com, accessed March 5, 2012.

Questions

1. Why does GoSLSHotel give the hotel such a competitive advantage? Is this competitive advantage likely to be long-lived? Why or why not?
2. What are the privacy implications of the GoSLSHotel app?

CLOSING **CASE 2** > British Gymnastics

<<< THE PROBLEM

Originally established as the British Amateur Gymnastics Association in 1888, British Gymnastics (www.british-gymnastics.org) is responsible for the promotion, development, and management of gymnastics in the United Kingdom. Its mission is to promote the practice of gymnastics, secure more funding for the sport, improve the quality of coaching, and promote the popularity of gymnastics internationally.

These different organizational missions mean that British Gymnastics needs to efficiently accomplish a wide range of tasks. Among other things, the organization operates 150 to 200 events per year and coaches gymnasts across a broad range of disciplines and abilities. The organization also engages with members and clubs on many levels, including managing membership subscriptions, running courses, distributing awards, and sending out news updates to their membership.

In the past, the organization accomplished all these tasks using either paper-based systems or disparate databases and spreadsheets. This process was slow, expensive to administer, and prone to errors. With London winning the bid to host the 2012 Olympic Games, British Gymnastics realized that updating its membership management system was necessary in order to accommodate an increased public interest in gymnastics and provide more professional and efficient service to its existing members.

British Gymnastics' new member management system automated all of the processes that used to be run manually. Therefore, the organization decided to deploy a customer relationship management (CRM) system to form closer, more targeted relationships with its members.

<<< THE IT SOLUTION

British Gymnastics selected Sage CRM. They chose this product because it was intuitive and browser based, and could be accessed via the Internet without having to install any new software. Sage CRM is also highly customizable, a crucial feature for British gymnastics as their requirements are very different from that of the average commercial environment.

To install the Sage CRM solution, British Gymnastics chose Concentrix (www. concentrix.com), a systems integrator and Sage specialist. This proved to be a good choice, as British Gymnastics was very pleased by the amount of effort Concentrix undertook to understand the organization's particular organizational needs and requirements.

THE RESULTS >>>

One key benefit of the Sage CRM system was its integration with the British Gymnastics Web site. After the integration was completed, users were able to log on to view and update their details, register for events, and renew their membership. Another key benefit of Sage CRM was that it was Web based, so users and managers were able to obtain information and reports from anywhere with an Internet connection. Sage CRM also gave British Gymnastics an efficient way to accommodate growing numbers of members.

In addition to the above front-end benefits, Sage CRM also provided advanced reporting capabilities. These capabilities allowed British Gymnastics to measure and analyze key performance indicators, make informed decisions about operations, and then report on those decisions to their three crucial sources of funds: UK Sport, Sport England, and the UK's Sports Councils.

Finally, Sage CRM stored data on all gymnasts, including their membership and demographic information, the club with which they are associated, their training history, and their list of previously attended events. British Gymnastics can use this information to generate ad hoc reports on, for instance, the success of a particular event or membership mailing.

The Sage CRM system allowed British Gymnastics to accomplish several important goals: to identify community needs and initiate programs to meet these needs; to increase its membership; and to maintain closer relationships with gymnasts at every level of expertise. By meeting these goals, British Gymnastics hopes to secure additional funding with an eye on improving the country's success on an international level.

Sources: Compiled from "Sage CRM and British Gymnastics CRM Case Study," *SageCRM*, 2012; www.british-gymnastics.org, www.sagecrm.com, www.concentrix.com, accessed March 23, 2012.

Questions

1. Why is it so important for British Gymnastics to stay in close touch with its membership?
2. Why do you think British Gymnastics hired Concentrix to install the Sage CRM system? Why did they not just install the system themselves?

RUBY'S CLUB | INTERNSHIP ASSIGNMENT

Excel is a spreadsheet, and it can be used to support CRM efforts. Recently, Ruben and Lisa teamed up with one of their college professors and created a survey to find out about student use of different media. Visit http://www.wiley.com/go/rainer/rubysclub to find the survey results and a video that will describe the data in the spreadsheet.

For your analysis, Ruben and Lisa want you to look specifically for the social networks used by students with three or more free nights a week. Their idea is that if they

can get the people with more free time as customers, those people will become regulars and bring their friends. So Ruben and Lisa want to connect with their potential customers on the right social network and establish loyalty through that channel.

You can accomplish this search by using filters and/or a pivot table. When you are confident that you have found the right target market for Ruben and Lisa, write them a letter describing what you have discovered.

SPREADSHEET ACTIVITY: MAIL MERGE AS CRM

Objective: Customer relationship management (CRM) is very important in today's market. Competition is reaching new frontiers with global companies doing business in rural areas that have traditionally been served by small mom-and-pop companies. How, exactly, can these smaller companies survive without the complex CRM tools available to the "big-box" companies? Although some tools are free (open-source), they do not come with customer support or instruction manuals. It is good to be aware of some of the tasks that CRM tools can help with that can also be accomplished in an Excel spreadsheet. This activity will walk you through the steps of automating and customizing customer engagement based on recent activity.

Chapter Connection: CRM is an excellent use of technology. It is easy to understand because the students are often on the "receiving" end of this particular system. However, students also experience many of its flaws because they receive invitations and coupons that they do not use. This money ends up being wasted because it did not bring its target customer into the store. This activity teaches students how they can utilize a simple spreadsheet to create their own basic CRM. Although it is a very basic function and a poor example of a CRM solution, it does show how simple tools such as Excel and Word can be utilized to create helpful systems.

Activity: A year ago, Dustin was very busy in his shop. That was before Walmart opened its Tire & Lube Express. Now a lot of Dustin's customers have switched to Walmart for the convenience of having their vehicle serviced while they shop. However, Dustin has an idea. He has created a spreadsheet of data from everyone who has brought their car to him on a regular basis. He wants to contact them with a personal letter to try and win back their service.

Dustin wants to thank his customers for past business and draw on their hometown emotions to pull them back to him in spite of Walmart's convenience and lower price. Although he cannot afford an expensive CRM tool, he does remember something about

Microsoft Excel having a mail-merge feature that would allow him to rapidly produce customized letters for the mail.

Visit http://www.wiley.com/go/rainer/spreadsheet and click on the first link provided for Chapter 12. This will take you to Microsoft's Web site and an explanation of how the Mail Merge process works. It is a simple process and it is explained in just a couple of pages. Once you feel comfortable with the concept, visit http://www.wiley.com/go/rainer/spreadsheet again and click on the second link provided. Here you can download the files required for Chapter 12. There will be an Excel spreadsheet and the Word document that Dustin plans to mail out. Your activity is to connect the two such that the letters will be automatically created for multiple customers at one time. After you connect the files, produce a batch of letters ready to send out to customers.

Deliverable: Submit your spreadsheet and Word document, which are linked such that your work can be checked. Your instructor will choose how many letters need to be submitted.

Discussion Questions

1. CRM does not have to be complicated; it is simply an effort to reach out to the customer to develop and/or maintain loyalty. As such, simple tools like Mail Merge can be used to touch customers on a personal basis. In what other ways could this tool be used in place of a more complex and more expensive CRM?

2. What do you think should be the determining factor regarding the type of CRM to use? Given that simple Excel tools can be used to reach customers, why would a company spend lots of time and energy implementing a system that may not reach more customers than the Excel tools would? What creates the "breaking point" of when things need to change?

Quiz questions are assignable in WileyPLUS, and available on the Book Companion Site at http://www.wiley.com/college/rainer.

DATABASE ACTIVITY: QUERIES II

Objective

In this activity, you will learn how to use parameters to simplify entering query selection criteria. When you needed Adam's orders from DizzyDonuts, you entered his name in the query design grid. That is not ideal for casual users. This activity will show you how using query *parameters* avoids this step.

CHAPTER CONNECTION

People who work with customer information must often specify whose information they need to review. Queries can do that, but a customer service agent should not have to modify the query design for each question!

PREREQUISITES

Before starting this activity, you should complete the database activity for Chapter 10 (Queries I).

Activity

In this activity, which you will find online at http://www.wiley.com/go/rainer/database, you will provide a simple interface to enter data for a query. For example, a database user could ask for information on sales between June 1 and August 31 one time, September 1 and 30 another, without needing to alter the query itself.

1. Download and open the Ch 12 DizzyDonuts database from http://www.wiley.com/go/rainer/database. This is a fresh copy of the database you used in the Chapter 10 activity.

2. The first query you developed there was to find out how often a given customer uses the mobile ordering service. This one will be similar. Create a new Query Design with Customer, Order, and Store tables. Enter CustName, StoreCity, OrderDate, and OrderTotal in the grid.

3. In the Chapter 10 activity, you entered "Adam" as the CustName selection criterion. Here, we will use a *parameter* instead. A parameter in Access is a user-entered value that determines what data a query returns. Each time the query

is run, Access will prompt the user to enter a value. No fixed value, Adam or anything else, is built into the query.

To specify that a query will ask for a parameter when it is run, instead of entering the desired value in the Criteria section of the grid, enter a *prompt string* there between square brackets, like this:

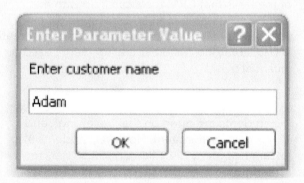

4. Run the query. You will see a dialogue box like this: into which you can enter a customer name. The text above the data entry box is between the brackets in the query design grid. There is a box in which the user can enter any desired parameter value. Enter "Adam," as shown, and click OK. You should see a list of all Adam's orders, with cities, dates, and totals.

Usage Hint: There are a few rules about what you put in a prompt string. It must fit on one line (about 40 characters), it cannot be a field name, and it cannot use "." (period), "!" (exclamation point), "&" (ampersand), "[" or "]" (square brackets).

If your query uses multiple criteria, you can have parameters in several of them. Here, you could look for all the orders from a specific customer (one parameter) after a specific date (a second parameter) at a specific store (a third one).

5. To rerun the query, select Refresh All from the middle of the Home ribbon. (If the icon reads "Refresh," click the down-arrow for other options and select Refresh All.) You will see the dialogue box for entering a parameter value again. Now, enter Belina to see her orders.

Field:	CustName	OrderDate	StoreCity
Table:	CustTbl	OrderTbl	StoreTbl
Sort:			
Show:	☑	☑	☑
Criteria:	[Enter customer name]		

6. Close the query, saving it as CustOrderParamQry.

7. Parameters are not limited to finding exact matches. Any type of comparison that can be done in a query criterion can use parameters. Before Access does the comparison, it gets values for all the parameters in it and replaces the parameter indicators with those values. Entering a parameter value "Adam" is the same as entering "Adam" in the query design grid.

Re-create ExpensiveProdQry from Chapter 10. As the query's only criterion, however, do not use the earlier " > 1.6." Instead, enter " > [Products over what amount?]" (without the quotation marks).

Usage Hint: Comparison operators include, besides ">" for "greater than," these:

< less than

>= greater than or equal to

<= less than or equal to

>< not equal to

= equal to (assumed if no comparison sign is entered)

IN   followed by a list of text strings separated by commas, will match anything in the list

BETWEEN . . . AND . . . does what you would expect. This, by the way, is an example of where you might want to use two parameters in the same criterion—for example, a starting and an ending date when you want all dates between two user-specified limits.

There are more, but this is enough for now. You know enough to understand and use what you will find in a Web search for more in this area.

8. Run this query twice: first with a cutoff of $1.50, then with a cutoff of $5.

Usage Hint: If you use a dollar sign when you enter a currency amount in a parameter entry box, Access is smart enough to ignore it.

9. Close the query, saving it as ExpensiveProdParamQry.

10. Queries can calculate a column based on other data in the same row. This can be data you choose not to show, as long as it comes from a table in the query. Let's create a query to help our staff price out orders for more than one of an item. (In a real store, this would be done electronically, but the query is still a good example.) Open a new query in Design view, select ProdTbl as its data source,

and enter ProdName and ProdPrice into the design grid.

11. In the top row of the first empty column, enter "2*ProdPrice" (without quotation marks), make sure that column's Show box is checked, and run the query. You will see something like this:

ProdName	ProdPrice	Expr1
Plain Donut	$1.19	$2.38
Blueberry Muffin	$1.29	$2.58
Sm Coffee	$1.29	$2.58
Lg Coffee	$1.69	$3.38

The calculated values are in the column where you entered the expression.

12. Return to Design view and look at the expression again. Access changed it in two ways:

   1. Access created the name we saw as its column name, Expr1. It precedes the expression, separated by a colon. If we do not like this name, we can change it. If we know what we want ahead of time, we can enter it when we define the calculated field.

   2. Access put square brackets around the field name. These are only required when there are spaces in the field name, but Access plays it safe and puts them in every time.

13. Change the column name "Expr1" to read "2x."

14. Enter expressions for 3x, 4x, and 5x. (It may be easier to copy and paste the 2x column, then edit its column name and the multiplier in its calculation, than to key in each one from scratch. It is definitely less error-prone.)

15. Run the query to confirm that it works. Then close it, saving it as ProdPriceQry.

This query did not use selection criteria and did not combine tables, but it is still useful. We would not want to store this information in the Product table because it can lead to data errors: When a price changes, someone might forget to update the other columns or might make an error in one of them. (A specialist would say such a table *violates normalization rules* by having columns whose value depends only on other columns of the same table.)

16. It is easier to build complicated expressions with the Expression Builder. Create a new query, using the same two fields from ProdTbl as above. In Design view, click the top row of the first empty column and then Builder in the Query Setup

section of the Design ribbon. The Expression Builder will open. It has two main sections:

- A: a window in which to build an expression.

- B: a series of three areas to select expression elements without keying them in. (Keying them in is always an option, however.) If you click "<< Less," this area is hidden and the button changes to "More >>" so you can display it again.

added $1, a price in whole dollars such as $2.00 would become the next higher dollar amount, in this case $3.00. We do not want that to happen.) With the insertion point between ProdPrice and the right parenthesis of Int, select Operators in Region B. In the middle pane, select either < All > or Arithmetic. In the right pane, double-click the plus sign. It will show up in your expression where the insertion point was. «Expr» shows where it

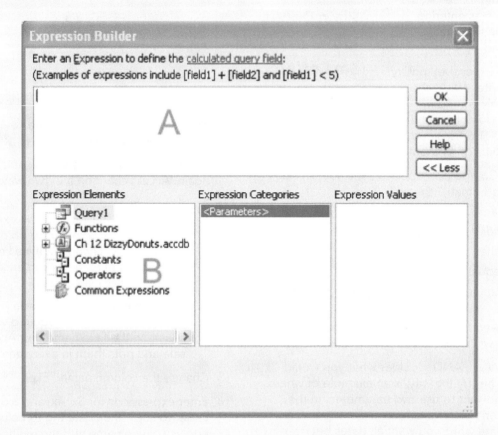

17. We will create an expression to round up each product price to the next whole dollar. Expand Functions in the left pane of the bottom area and select Built-In Functions.

18. In the middle pane, double-click Math as the type of function.

19. In the right pane, double-click Int. The Int function takes the integer part of a number: Given 1.79, it will return 1. It appears in the top pane, with a placeholder for the number.

20. Click the placeholder to select it. Then expand the database name in region B, expand Tables, select ProdTbl in the list of tables that drops down, and double-click ProdPrice in the list of fields for that table in the middle pane. It will replace «Number» in the expression.

21. Because Int gives the integer *below* the price and we want the next whole dollar *above* it, we must add 99¢ to the value it takes the Int of. (If we

needs something to add. Click «Expr» to select it and type "0.99" (without the quotation marks). Then click OK.

Usage Hint: In this case it would probably have been easier to just key in "+0.99" rather than going to the list of operators and then replacing "Expr." However, it's important to know where to find the full process and how to go through it, because it's often the best way to get something done.

22. Back in the design grid, replace the name of this column, which Access has set to its default of Expr1, to "Rounded Up." (It may be easier to do this if you widen the column.)

23. Run the query. It shows 2 for every item priced from $1.01 to $2.00, and so on.

24. The new column would look better formatted as currency. Return to Design view, select the expression, and open the query's Property Sheet

(at the right end of the ribbon, in the Show/Hide section, under the Design tab). Under the General tab of the property sheet, click in the Format row (the second one down). Select Currency formatting from the list.

Usage Hint: You may have read in earlier activities that the Property Sheet is the "go-to place" for most things that do not have ribbon icons. This is an example. We could have used Expression Builder's formatting functions instead, but they are more work.

25. Run the query again to confirm that the formatting is correct, close, and save it. Name it ProdPriceRoundUpQry if you did not do so previously.

Deliverable

Your database, with the above three queries.

Quiz Questions

1. True or False: Access always names calculated fields as Expr1, Expr2, etc.

2. Which of the following is *not* a capability of Access queries?

   (a) Combining data from three tables.

   (b) Choosing all records that have a date field with a value after June 6, 1944.

   (c) Displaying the cosine of a number that the query finds.

   (d) None of the above; Access can do all of them.

3. True or False: You can set the formatting of a calculated field to Currency by clicking the $ sign in the ribbon.

4. A parameter, in the context of an Access query, is

   (a) A characteristic of an Access object on the screen, such as font, height, or color.

   (b) A distance of slightly less than 6 feet, 7 inches, scaled to the window size.

   (c) A query criterion data item that a user can enter.

   (d) The fraction of available RAM that the currently open database is using.

Discussion Questions

1. At the end of every semester, you probably read your grade report online. As you now understand, it is produced by a database query. What are that query's two parameters?

2. If you develop a database in Access, anyone who uses it can see everything in it. In some situations, this is unacceptable. Other database management systems, including some from Microsoft, allow database designers to restrict access to certain rows (for example, only you can see your grade data, other students cannot) or columns (a faculty advisor can see your academic information, but not your medical or financial information). Suppose you are designing a query for a software company's technical support staff. They receive e-mails and phone calls from customers with questions about this company's products. The support staff may need to know something about the customer, such as the version of a product he or she has. Asking would be time-consuming and should not be necessary, because the company already has the information in its customer database. Discuss the row-level and column-level restrictions you might place on a query that they were to use for this purpose. Make any reasonable assumptions about the content and organization of their database.

3. The DizzyDonuts database has a field in the Order table that stores the total amount of each order. This could be calculated each time the order is displayed: a calculated field will multiply price × quantity for each line item, and the Sum function of the report could add them up. When asked why they designed the database this way, the DizzyDonut database designers explained that they wanted to store what orders cost when they are placed, not what they might cost when a report is run later if prices changed in the meantime. Do you agree with their logic? Why or why not?

13 | Extending the Organization Along the Supply Chain

LEARNING OBJECTIVES >>>

1. Describe the three components and the three flows of a supply chain.

2. Identify popular strategies to solving different challenges of supply chains.

3. Explain the utility of each of the three major technologies that supports supply chain management.

OPENING **CASE** > Campus Quilts Partners with UPS to Manage Its Supply Chain

Stephen Chernin/Stringer/Getty Images, Inc.

What do you plan to do with all of the T-shirts you collect in your college years? Store them in a box somewhere? Wear them for the next 30 years? Give them away to someone else? Leigh Lowe of Louisville, Kentucky, has a different alternative for you—why not have a quilt made out of them? Leigh is the owner of a small business that takes T-shirts, ties, baby clothes, sweatshirts, hats, or other memorable clothing items and sews them into pillowcases or quilts. This unique product offering is very time intensive for her to make (taking up to 3 weeks per quilt), but the end product is very personalized and valuable to the customer.

 The supply chain management and logistics for this type of business is different from your typical commercial retailer. In this situation, the supplier of the raw materials and the customer who receives the final product are actually one and the same. Additionally, both the raw materials and the final product are unique and irreplaceable items. Therefore, it is an imperative for Campus Quilts to take the utmost care with the product throughout the product life cycle, from acquiring the raw

materials to delivering the final product. Although Leigh is an incredibly talented quilt maker, she had no experience with protecting the security of irreplaceable items. Therefore, Leigh realized she would need a reliable third-party logistics/supply chain partner to manage this part of the job.

Leigh turned to UPS to handle all of her logistical needs. Campus Quilts has an account with UPS that allows her to initiate and track three separate shipments for each custom product via the Web. The process works like this: The customer initiates the process by placing an order online or by phone. After the customer makes a deposit, Campus Quilts sends a package to the customer that includes information on the product he or she has chosen, design instructions, a prepaid shipping label, and instructions for sending the materials (T-shirts or other memorable clothing) to Campus Quilts. The customers then follow the instructions and ship the raw materials (their T-shirts, hats, etc.) using the > > >

RUBY'S CLUB

Ruben and Lisa always have trouble scheduling their inventory. It is especially difficult in a college town where their customers pour in one week and leave a ghost town behind the next week. It seems that many factors influence their customer base on any given night. Obviously, the school schedule is a big factor, as are community events, athletic events, and more, but how much does each of these influence the number of customers they will have?

More than once Ruben and Lisa have had to throw away perishable goods because they were not able to use all that they had ordered before its expiration date, or they ran out of food when they had more customers than they expected. Neither of these situations is desirable because both mean lost profits.

Ruben and Lisa know they must do a better job of planning. They need to know the key factors that really drive the fluctuations in their customers. They remember some courses about supply chain management, logistics, and statistics, but are not sure how to apply it to their situation in order to determine these key factors. As you learn these concepts, consider their situation. In your final exercise, you will be given some data to analyze in light of this chapter to help Ruben and Lisa make better planning decisions.

prepaid shipping label. Leigh creates the finished product using the raw materials, and then ships the finished quilt back to the consumer (or to the address specified in the order).

Having UPS handle logistics allows Leigh to focus on producing a quality product and expands her potential customer base. Campus Quilts is able to reach customers worldwide via the Web and UPS. Without a shipping solution, her business would be confined to the local area. With a reliable shipping partner, she can expand far beyond her local area. Together, Campus Quilts and UPS provide a seamless customer experience. Customers feel "touched" all the way through the process because they always know where their personal items are—even during shipping. This sense of involve-ment helps customers trust Campus Quilts, brings Leigh closer to her customers, and is leading to a steadily increasing business.

Sources: Compiled from www.campusquilt.com, www.ups.com, accessed March 22, 2012.

Questions

1. Describe why the supply chain for Campus Quilts differs from a "normal" supply chain. Discuss the implications of these differences for Leigh's supply chain management.
2. Why would Leigh's business be confined to her local area without a shipping solution?

13.1 Supply Chains

Modern organizations are increasingly concentrating on their core competencies and on becoming more flexible and agile. To accomplish these objectives, they are relying on other companies to supply necessary goods and services, rather than owning these companies them-selves. Organizations recognize that these suppliers can perform these activities more efficiently and effectively than they themselves can. This trend toward relying on an increasing number of suppliers has led to the concept of supply chains. A **supply chain** refers to the coordinated flow of materials, information, money, and services from raw material suppliers, through factories and warehouses, to the end customers. A supply chain also includes the *organizations* and *pro-cesses* that create and deliver products, information, and services to end customers.

Supply chains improve trust and collaboration among supply chain partners, thus improv-ing supply chain visibility and inventory velocity. **Supply chain visibility** is the ability for all organizations in a supply chain to access or view relevant data on purchased materials as these materials move through their suppliers' production processes and transportation networks to their receiving docks. In addition, organizations can access or view relevant data on outbound goods as they are manufactured, assembled, or stored in inventory, and then shipped through their transportation networks to their customers' receiving docks. The sooner a company can deliver your products and services after receiving the materials required to make them—that is, the higher the *inventory velocity*—the more satisfied the company's customers will be.

Supply chains are a vital component of the overall strategies of many modern organiza-tions. To utilize supply chains efficiently, a business must become tightly integrated with its suppliers, business partners, distributors, and customers. One of the most critical compo-nents of this integration is the use of information systems to facilitate the exchange of infor-mation among the participants in the supply chain.

You might ask why you need to study supply chain management. The answer is that sup-ply chains are critical to modern organizations. Therefore, regardless of your position within an organization, you will be involved with some aspect of your company's supply chain.

The Structure and Components of Supply Chains

The term *supply chain* comes from a picture of how the partnering organizations are linked together. Figure 13.1 illustrates a typical supply chain. Recall that Figure 1.5 also illustrated a supply chain in a slightly different way. Note that the supply chain involves three segments:

1. *Upstream*, where sourcing or procurement from external suppliers occurs. In this segment, supply chain (SC) managers select suppliers to deliver the goods and services

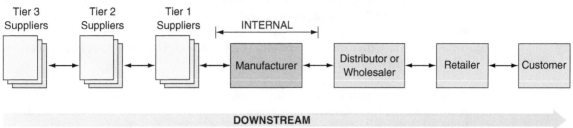

| Tier 3 Suppliers | | Tier 2 Suppliers | | Tier 1 Suppliers | | INTERNAL | | | | |

DOWNSTREAM
Products, Services, Information

Figure 13.1 Generic supply chain.

the company needs to produce its product or service. Further, SC managers develop the pricing, delivery, and payment processes between a company and its suppliers. Included here are processes for managing inventory, receiving and verifying shipments, transferring goods to manufacturing facilities, and authorizing payments to suppliers.

2. *Internal*, where packaging, assembly, or manufacturing takes place. SC managers schedule the activities necessary for production, testing, packaging, and preparing goods for delivery. SC managers also monitor quality levels, production output, and worker productivity.

3. *Downstream*, where distribution takes place, frequently by external distributors. In this segment, SC managers coordinate the receipt of orders from customers, develop a network of warehouses, select carriers to deliver their products to customers, and develop invoicing systems to receive payments from customers.

The flow of information and goods can be bidirectional. For example, damaged or unwanted products can be returned, a process known as *reverse logistics*. Using the retail clothing industry as an example, reverse logistics would involve clothing that customers return, either because the item had defects or because the customer did not like the item.

Tiers of Suppliers. If you look closely at Figure 13.1, you will notice several tiers of suppliers. As the diagram shows, a supplier may have one or more subsuppliers, the subsupplier may have its own subsupplier(s), and so on. For example, with an automobile manufacturer, Tier 3 suppliers produce basic products such as glass, plastic, and rubber. Tier 2 suppliers use these inputs to make windshields, tires, and plastic moldings. Tier 1 suppliers produce integrated components such as dashboards and seat assemblies.

The Flows in the Supply Chain. There are typically three flows in the supply chain: materials, information, and financial. *Material flows* are the physical products: raw materials, supplies, and so forth that flow along the chain. Material flows also include *reverse* flows (or reverse logistics)—returned products, recycled products, and disposal of materials or products. A supply chain thus involves a *product life cycle* approach, from "dirt to dust."

Information flows consist of data that are related to demand, shipments, orders, returns, and schedules, as well as changes in any of these data. Finally, *financial flows* involve money transfers, payments, credit card information and authorization, payment schedules, e-payments, and credit-related data.

Significantly, different supply chains have different numbers and types of flows. For example, in service industries there may be no physical flow of materials, but frequently there is a flow of information, often in the form of documents (physical or electronic copies). In fact, the digitization of software, music, and other content may create a supply chain without any physical flow. Notice, however, that in such a case there are two types of information flows: one that replaces materials flow (for example, digitized software) and one that provides the supporting information (for example, orders and billing). To manage the supply chain an organization must coordinate all of these flows among all of the parties involved in the chain.

BEFORE *YOU GO ON . . .*

1. What is a supply chain?
2. Describe the three segments of a supply chain.
3. Describe the flows in a supply chain.

Apply the Concept 13.1

Background This section has focused on supply chain flows, materials, and "positions" (upstream, internal, and downstream). It is important for you to understand how products move in the supply chain because data moves along with it every step of the way. In fact, the data that travels with materials and products is more important to the efficiency of the operation than the product itself!

Activity Visit http://www.wiley.com/go/rainer/applytheconcept and click on the link provided for Apply the Concept 13.1. This will take you to a YouTube video titled "Module 1: What is Supply Chain Management? (ASU-WPC-SCM)" by user "wpcareyschool."

As you watch the video, imagine the data that would be transferred with each movement of product in the bottled water. Inventory updates, shipment information, quality checks, supplier data, and more would deal just with the bottled water itself. Do not forget that there will be HR information, employee data, machine data, from the internal organization as well as all suppliers!

Deliverable

Build a table that describes the area (upstream, internal, downstream) of the supply chain and provide examples of the data that would be captured at each area. Here is an example of your table.

Supply Chain Area	Materials Needed	Information Flows
Upstream	1. 2. 3.	1. 2. 3.
Internal	1. 2. 3.	1. 2. 3.
Downstream	1. 2. 3.	1. 2. 3.

Submit your table to your professor.

Quiz questions are assignable in WileyPLUS, and available on the Book Companion Site at http://www.wiley.com/college/rainer.

RUBY'S CLUB QUESTIONS

1. Upstream from Ruben and Lisa are grocery providers. What type of information might flow upstream to their suppliers while the materials flow downstream?

2. Ruby's Club has some internal issues to deal with regarding their supplies. The food in the cooler is used in no particular order, and sometimes it goes bad. This situation is not from a lack of customers but, rather, poor planning. What policies could be put in place to help remedy this situation?

13.2 Supply Chain Management

Supply chain management (SCM) is an activity in which the leaders of an organization provide extensive oversight for the partnerships and processes that comprise the supply chain and leverage these relationships to provide an operational advantage. The function of supply chain management is to plan, organize, and optimize the various activities performed along the supply chain. Like other functional areas, SCM utilizes information systems. The goal of SCM systems is to reduce the problems, or friction, along the supply chain. Friction can involve increased time, costs, and inventories as well as decreased customer satisfaction. SCM systems, then, reduce uncertainty and risks by decreasing inventory levels and cycle time while improving business processes and customer service. All of these benefits make the organization more profitable and competitive.

Significantly, SCM systems are a type of interorganizational information system. An **interorganizational information system (IOS)** involves information flows among two or more organizations. By connecting the information systems of business partners, IOSs enable the partners to perform a number of tasks:

- Reduce the costs of routine business transactions
- Improve the quality of the information flow by reducing or eliminating errors
- Compress the cycle time involved in fulfilling business transactions
- Eliminate paper processing and its associated inefficiencies and costs
- Facilitate the transfer and processing of information for users

The Push Model Versus the Pull Model

Many supply chain management systems use the push model. In the **push model**, also known as *make-to-stock*, the production process begins with a forecast, which is simply an educated guess as to customer demand. The forecast must predict which products customers will want as well as the quantity of each product. The company then produces the amount of products in the forecast, typically by using mass production, and sells, or "pushes," those products to consumers.

Unfortunately, these forecasts are often incorrect. Consider, for example, an automobile manufacturer that wants to produce a new car. Marketing managers conduct extensive research, including customer surveys and analyses of competitors' cars, and they provide the results to forecasters. If the forecasters are too high in their prediction—that is, they predict that sales of the new car will be 200,000 and actual customer demand turns out to be 150,000—then the automaker has 50,000 cars in inventory and will incur large carrying costs. Further, the company will probably have to sell the excess cars at a discount.

From the opposite perspective, if the forecasters are too low in their prediction—that is, they predict that sales of the new car will be 150,000 and actual customer demand turns out to be 200,000—then the automaker will probably have to run extra shifts to meet the demand and thus will incur large overtime costs. Further, the company risks losing customers to competitors if the car the customer wants is not available. Using the push model in supply chain management can cause problems, as you see in the next section.

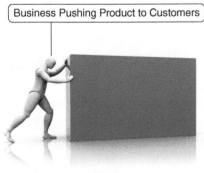
Business Pushing Product to Customers

Push

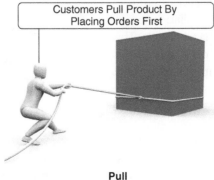
Customers Pull Product By Placing Orders First

Pull

© Milan Zeremski/iStockphoto

To avoid the uncertainties associated with the push model, many companies now use Web-enabled information flows to employ the pull model of supply chain management. In the **pull model**, also known as *make-to-order*, the production process begins with a customer order. Therefore, companies make only what customers want, a process closely aligned with mass customization. "IT's About Business 13.1" shows how Cisco converted from a push model to a pull model.

T's ABOUT BUSINESS 13.1

Cisco Moves From Push Model to Pull Model

Cisco Systems (www.cisco.com) was a very profitable company in the 1990s. Then, the company's stock dropped dramatically when its vaunted inventory forecasting system failed to predict the dot-com bubble's collapse in 2000–2001. The result of this miscalculation was that Cisco's sales decreased by 50 percent, the company lost 25 percent of its customers, and it ultimately had to write off more than $2 billion in inventory. After that experience, Cisco's supply chain managers vowed that the company would never be blindsided again.

Before the dot-com crash, Cisco's supply chain used a push system, where products were made and inventory was built up in anticipation of market demand based on best-guess forecasts. Unfortunately, the push system did not work when demand dropped quickly and severely, as it did during and after the dot-com crash. Cisco knew that it had to create a supply chain system that reacted much more effectively than its push system.

Consequently, Cisco made major information systems investments to transform its push system into a pull system. The pull system enabled Cisco to extract timely data from suppliers and downstream business partners. Cisco optimized its forecasting algorithms by bringing together representatives from its marketing, finance, sales, supply chain, and IT departments, and from key customers. As part of the company's and operations planning process, this group collaborates to create a common view of demand signals. This input drives an agreed-upon plan of action to align manufacturing capacity and inventory deployment, and meet customer service levels. In essence, this group works together with the same data to optimally match supply and demand.

The result was that Cisco did not continue to build inventory that might sit in a warehouse waiting for customers who might never buy it. Therefore, cash was freed up for other purposes. Cisco was confident that it had better visibility into market demand and could manage its way through downturns. Unfortunately, the other shoe fell.

Cisco's supply chain pull system enabled the company to weather the economic recession of 2008 and 2009.

© Lifesizeimages/iStockphoto

During the recession, Cisco reduced its inventory and product manufacturing to prevent filling warehouses with unsold product.

Then, in the last quarter of 2009, an unexpected increase in business demand for core networking infrastructure products caught Cisco and its manufacturing partners off guard. Cisco could not keep up with the sudden increase in orders, resulting in extremely long lead times, back orders, and customer dissatisfaction. Cisco told its customers that its product shortage resulted from a global shortage of raw materials used in the manufacture of key components, such as semiconductors.

Sources: Compiled from L. Walsh, "Cisco Struggling with Product Shortages," *Channel Insider*, January 8, 2010; W. Brandel, "Inventory Optimization Saves Working Capital in Touch Times," *Computerworld*, August 24, 2009; www.cisco.com, accessed May 22, 2011.

Questions

1. Describe the disadvantages of the push system at Cisco.

2. Describe the advantages of the pull system at Cisco.

3. Explain why the pull system enabled Cisco to manage through an economic downturn but seemed to be unable to enable Cisco through an economic recovery.

Not all companies can use the pull model. Automobiles, for example, are far more complicated and more expensive to manufacture than computers, and companies require longer lead times to produce new models. Automobile companies use the pull model, but only for specific automobiles that specific customers order.

Problems Along the Supply Chain

As noted, friction can develop within a supply chain. One major consequence of ineffective supply chains is poor customer service. In some cases, supply chains do not deliver products or services when and where customers—either individuals or businesses—need them. In other cases, the supply chain provides poor-quality products. Other problems associated with friction are high inventory costs and loss of revenues.

The problems along the supply chain arise primarily from two sources: (1) uncertainties and (2) the need to coordinate multiple activities, internal units, and business partners. A major source of supply chain uncertainties is the *demand forecast*. Demand for a product can be influenced by numerous factors such as competition, prices, weather conditions, technological developments, overall economic conditions, and customers' general confidence. Another uncertainty is delivery times, which depend on factors ranging from production machine failures to road construction and traffic jams. In addition, quality problems in materials and parts can create production delays, which also generate supply chain problems.

One of the major challenges that managers face in setting accurate inventory levels throughout the supply chain is known as the bullwhip effect. The **bullwhip effect** refers to erratic shifts in orders up and down the supply chain (see Figure 13.2). Basically, the variables that affect customer demand can become magnified when they are viewed through the eyes of managers at each link in the supply chain. If each distinct entity that makes ordering and inventory decisions places its interests above those of the chain, then stockpiling can occur at as many as seven or eight locations along the chain. Research has shown that in some cases such hoarding has led to as much as a 100-day supply of inventory that is waiting "just in case," versus 10 to 20 days under normal circumstances.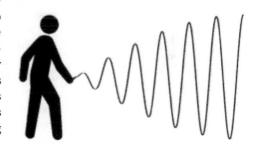

Solutions to Supply Chain Problems

Supply chain problems can be very costly. Therefore, organizations are motivated to find innovative solutions. During the oil crises of the 1970s, for example, Ryder Systems, a large trucking company, purchased a refinery to control the upstream part of the supply chain and to make certain it would have enough gasoline for its trucks. Ryder's decision to purchase a refinery is an example of vertical integration. **Vertical integration** is a business strategy in which a company purchases its upstream suppliers to ensure that its essential supplies are available as soon as they are needed. Ryder later sold the refinery because it could not manage a business it did not understand and because oil became more plentiful.

Ryder's decision to vertically integrate was not the optimal method to manage its supply chain. In the remainder of this section, you will look at some other possible solutions to supply chain problems, many of which are supported by IT.

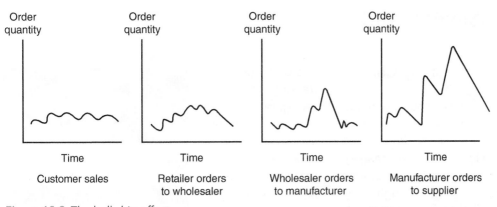

Figure 13.2 The bullwhip effect.

Using Inventories to Solve Supply Chain Problems. Undoubtedly, the most common solution to supply chain problems is *building inventories* as insurance against supply chain uncertainties. As you have learned, some costs are associated with holding too much inventory. Thus, companies make major attempts to optimize and control inventories. IT's About Business 13.2 illustrates how Airbus is using a "smart" supply chain to manage its parts inventory.

A well-known initiative to optimize and control inventories is the **just-in-time (JIT) inventory system**, which attempts to minimize inventories. That is, in a manufacturing process, JIT systems deliver the precise number of parts, called *work-in-process* inventory, to be assembled into a finished product at precisely the right time.

Although JIT offers many benefits, it has certain drawbacks as well. To begin, suppliers are expected to respond instantaneously to requests. As a result, they have to carry more inventory than they otherwise would. The inventory has not gone away in JIT; rather, it has just shifted from customer to supplier. This process can result in an overall improvement if the supplier can spread the increased inventory over several customers, but that is not always possible.

In addition, JIT replaces a few large supply shipments with a large number of smaller ones. This process is less efficient in terms of transportation.

Information Sharing. Another common way to solve supply chain problems, and especially to improve demand forecasts, is *sharing information* along the supply chain. Information sharing can be facilitated by electronic data interchange and extranets, topics you will read about in the next section.

One of the most notable examples of information sharing occurs between large manufacturers and retailers. For example, Walmart provides Procter & Gamble with access to daily sales information from every store for every item P&G makes for Walmart. This access enables P&G to manage the *inventory replenishment* for Walmart's stores. By monitoring inventory levels, P&G knows when inventories fall below the threshold for each product at any Walmart store. These data trigger an immediate shipment.

Information sharing between Walmart and P&G is executed automatically. It is part of a vendor-managed inventory strategy. **Vendor-managed inventory (VMI)** occurs when the supplier, rather than the retailer, manages the entire inventory process for a particular product or group of products. Significantly, P&G has similar agreements with other major retailers. The benefit for P&G is accurate and timely information on consumer demand for its products. Thus, P&G can plan production more accurately, minimizing the bullwhip effect.

BEFORE *YOU GO ON . . .*

1. Differentiate between the push model and the pull model.
2. Describe various problems that can occur along the supply chain.
3. Discuss possible solutions to problems along the supply chain.

S ABOUT BUSINESS 13.2

Airbus Moves to a "Smart Supply Chain"

Supply chain information that was previously generated manually will now increasingly be generated by sensors, RFID tags, meters, GPS, and other devices and systems. What does this mean for supply chain managers? For one thing, it means they will have real-time information on all products moving through their supply chains. Supply chains will therefore need to rely less on labor-based tracking and monitoring, because the new technology will allow shipping containers, trucks, products, and parts to report on their own status.

© Michal Krakowiak/iStockphoto

Airbus is one of the world's largest commercial aircraft manufacturers, producing over half of the world's new aircraft with more than 100 seats per plane. With its suppliers becoming more geographically dispersed, Airbus was finding it increasingly difficult to track parts, components, and other assets as it moved from the warehouses of various suppliers to its 18 different manufacturing sites.

To improve the overall visibility of its supply chain, Airbus created a smart sensing solution capable of detecting any deviations of inbound shipments from their intended path. Here is how the sensing solution works: As parts move from suppliers' warehouses to the Airbus assembly line, they travel in smart containers fitted with RFID tags that hold important information (RFID is discussed in detail in Chapter 10). At each stop along the supply chain, RFID readers communicate with each tag. If shipments end up at the wrong location or do not contain the correct parts, the RFID readers alert employees early so they can fix the problem before it disrupts production.

Airbus's supply chain solution, the largest of its kind in manufacturing, has significantly reduced the incidence and severity of incorrect parts delivery orders, and the costs associated with correcting such problems. Reducing the number of incorrect shipments and deliveries has allowed Airbus to reduce the number of overall travel containers by 8 percent, avoid significant inventory carrying costs, and increase the overall efficiency of its parts flow.

Sources: Compiled from "At Airbus, It's Clear Skies and High Visibility," *The Smarter Supply Chain of the Future* (IBM Corporation), 2012; www.airbus.com, accessed March 22, 2012.

Questions

1. Discuss the value to Airbus of supply chain transparency (i.e., knowing where every part is in real time).

2. What are potential problems with using RFID tags throughout Airbus's parts supply chain?

Apply the Concept 13.2

Background Section 13.2 has shown that managing a supply chain is not a simple task because consumer demand is so uncertain. Although forecasting can get close, actual demand will usually be different from the expected number. As organizations move toward JIT (just-in-time) inventory models, the amount of data shared along the supply chain increases. It must also be shared in a timely fashion to keep organizations flexible and ready to adapt to consumer demand.

Activity Visit http://www.wiley.com/go/rainer/applytheconcept and click on the link provided for Apply the Concept 13.2. It will take you to an article and activity where you will manage a supply chain for beer. This may not sound difficult until you consider that there are serious timing issues because of the perishable supplies. The simulation begins with your supply chain in equilibrium but suddenly shifts. Your job is to get things back in order!

As you work through the simulation, pay attention to how much information needs to be shared across the supply chain to make things work smoothly.

Deliverable

Write a short paragraph explaining your experience. Focus on the data sharing aspect of the simulation. Also, just for fun, let your professor know how well you did in reestablishing equilibrium! (Warning! You may find this a bit addicting. Also be advised that you do not need to have a beer near to play the Near Beer Game.)

Submit your work to your professor.

Quiz questions are assignable in WileyPLUS, and available on the Book Companion Site at http://www.wiley.com/college/rainer.

1. Based on your understanding of Ruby's business model, do you think it is in a push or pull scenario?
2. Do you think Ruby's would begin the bullwhip effect, or do you think it would have problems because someone else started it?
3. Is JIT realistic for Ruby's Club? What about vertical integration? Should Ruby's Club invest in alcohol and grocery distribution businesses?

13.3 Information Technology Support for Supply Chain Management

Clearly, SCM systems are essential to the successful operation of many businesses. As you have seen, these systems—and interorganizational information systems in general—rely on various forms of IT to resolve problems. Three technologies in particular provide support for interorganizational information systems and supply chain management systems: electronic data interchange, extranets, and Web Services. You learn about Web services in Plug IT In 3. You examine the other two technologies in this section.

Electronic Data Interchange (EDI)

Electronic data interchange (EDI) is a communication standard that enables business partners to exchange routine documents, such as purchasing orders, electronically. EDI formats these documents according to agreed-upon standards—for example, data formats. It then transmits messages using a converter, called a *translator*. The message travels over the Internet.

EDI provides many benefits compared with a manual delivery system. To begin, it minimizes data entry errors because each entry is checked by the computer. In addition, the length of the message can be shorter and the messages are secured. EDI also reduces cycle time, increases productivity, enhances customer service, and minimizes paper usage and storage. Figure 13.3 contrasts the process of fulfilling a purchase order with and without EDI.

EDI does have some disadvantages. Business processes must sometimes be restructured to fit EDI requirements. Also, many EDI standards are in use today. As a result, one company might have to use several standards in order to communicate with multiple business partners.

In today's world, where every business has a broadband connection to the Internet and where multimegabyte design files, product photographs, and PDF sales brochures are routinely e-mailed, the value of reducing a structured e-commerce message from a few thousand XML bytes to a few hundred EDI bytes is negligible. As a result, EDI is being replaced by XML-based Web services. (You will learn about XML in Plug IT In 2.)

Extranets

To implement IOSs and SCM systems, a company must connect the intranets of its various business partners to create extranets. **Extranets** link business partners to one another over the Internet by providing access to certain areas of one another's corporate intranets (see Figure 13.4).

The primary goal of extranets is to foster collaboration between and among business partners. An extranet is open to selected business-to-business (B2B) suppliers, customers, and other business partners. These individuals access the extranet through the Internet. Extranets enable people who are located outside a company to work together with the company's internally located employees. An extranet also allows external business partners to

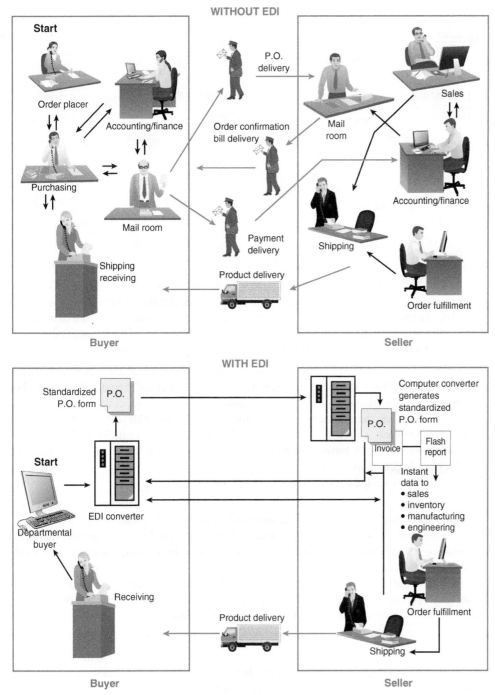

Start

Order placer

Accounting/finance

Purchasing

Mail room

Shipping receiving

P.O. delivery

Order confirmation bill delivery

Payment delivery

Product delivery

Mail room

Sales

Accounting/finance

Shipping

Order fulfillment

Buyer

Seller

WITH EDI

Standardized P.O. form

P.O.

Computer converter generates standardized P.O. form

P.O.

Invoice

Flash report

Instant data to
• sales
• inventory
• manufacturing
• engineering

Start

EDI converter

Departmental buyer

Receiving

Product delivery

Order fulfillment

Shipping

Buyer

Seller

Figure 13.3 Order fulfillment with and without EDI.

enter the corporate intranet, via the Internet, to access data, place orders, check the status of those orders, communicate, and collaborate. It also enables partners to perform self-service activities such as checking inventory levels.

Extranets use virtual private network (VPN) technology to make communication over the Internet more secure. The major benefits of extranets are faster processes and information flow, improved order entry and customer service, lower costs (for example, for communications, travel, and administrative overhead), and an overall improvement in business effectiveness.

There are three major types of extranets. Companies choose a particular type depending on the business partners involved and the purpose of the supply chain. Each type, along with its major business applications, is described in the following subsections.

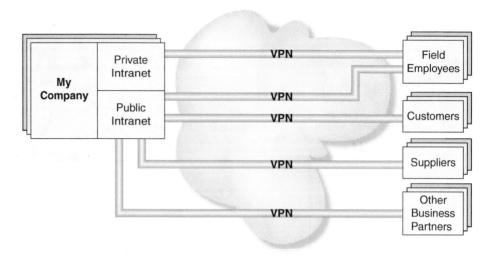

Figure 13.4 The structure of an extranet.

A Company and Its Dealers, Customers, or Suppliers. This type of extranet is centered on a single company. An example is the FedEx extranet, which allows customers to track the status of a delivery. To do so, customers use the Internet to access a database on the FedEx intranet. By enabling a customer to check the location of a package, FedEx saves the cost of having a human operator perform that task over the phone.

An Industry's Extranet. Just as a single company can set up an extranet, the major players in an industry can team up to create an extranet that will benefit all of them. For example, ANXeBusiness (www.anx.com) enables companies to collaborate effectively through a network that provides a secure global medium for B2B information exchange. The ANX Network is used for mission-critical business transactions by leading international organizations in aerospace, automotive, chemical, electronics, financial services, health care, logistics, manufacturing, transportation, and related industries. The network offers customers a reliable extranet and VPN services.

Joint Ventures and Other Business Partnerships. In this type of extranet, the partners in a joint venture use the extranet as a vehicle for communications and collaboration. An example is Bank of America's extranet for commercial loans. The partners involved in making these loans include a lender, a loan broker, an escrow company, and a title company. The extranet connects lenders, loan applicants, and the loan organizer, Bank of America. A similar case is Lending Tree (www.lendingtree.com), a company that provides mortgage quotes for home purchases and sells mortgages online. Lending Tree uses an extranet for its business partners—for example, the lenders.

Portals and Exchanges

As explained in Chapter 4, corporate portals offer a single point of access through a Web browser to critical business information in an organization. In the context of B2B supply chain management, these portals enable companies and their suppliers to collaborate very closely.

The two basic types of corporate portals are procurement (sourcing) portals for a company's suppliers (upstream in the supply chain) and distribution portals for a company's customers (downstream in the supply chain). **Procurement portals** automate the business processes involved in purchasing or procuring products between a single buyer and multiple suppliers. For example, Boeing has deployed a procurement portal called the Boeing Supplier Portal through which it conducts business with its suppliers. **Distribution portals** automate the business processes involved in selling or distributing products from a single supplier to multiple buyers. For example, Dell services its business customers through its distribution portal at http://premier.dell.com.

— BEFORE *YOU GO ON* . . . —

1. Define EDI, and list its major benefits and limitations.

2. Define an extranet, and explain its infrastructure.

3. List and briefly define the major types of extranets.

4. Differentiate between procurement portals and distribution portals.

Apply the Concept 13.3

Background Electronic data interchange (EDI) is defined in this section as a communication standard that enables business partners to exchange routine documents, such as purchasing orders, electronically. You should understand the need for electronic sharing of information if you completed the activity Apply the Concept 13.2. That activity had you managing a supply chain on your own. Imagine doing that with no electronic sharing of data!

Activity Visit http://www.wiley.com/go/rainer/applytheconcept and click on the links provided for Apply the Concept 13.3. You will find a YouTube video titled "What is EDI" by user "hitekequipment." There is also an article that defines EDI and discusses some of its standards.

As you watch the video, pay attention to the important pieces that are necessary to share information between two organizations. Then consider the fact that rarely does a supplier only operate in one supply chain. Suppliers often have multiple customers, which means they are sharing information with many organizations with EDI.

Deliverable

Create a list of the top five reasons EDI needs a standard to operate today. Perhaps it will help you to consider what EDI would be like if there were no standard for everyone to use.

Submit your list to your professor.

Quiz questions are assignable in WileyPLUS, and available on the Book Companion Site at http://www.wiley.com/college/rainer.

RUBY'S CLUB QUESTIONS

1. If Ruby's is not a good candidate for vertical integration, how might information sharing be the answer to its problems? What specific information should be shared with Ruben and Lisa's suppliers to move as close as possible to a JIT system?

2. Would it make sense for alcohol or grocery distributors to allow businesses to connect to them via an extranet to share information and place orders via the Web?

What's in IT for ME

FOR THE ACCOUNTING MAJOR

The cost accountant will play an important role in developing and monitoring the financial accounting information associated with inventory and cost of goods sold. In a supply chain, much of the data for these accounting requirements will flow into the organization from various partners within the chain. It is up to the chief accountant, the comptroller or CFO, to prepare and review this data.

Going further, accounting rules and regulations and the cross-border transfer of data are critical for global trade. Interorganizational information systems can facilitate such trade. Other issues that are important for accountants are taxation and government reports. In addition, creating information systems that rely on EDI requires the attention of accountants. Finally, fraud detection in global settings (for example, transfers of funds) can be facilitated by appropriate controls and auditing.

FOR THE FINANCE MAJOR

In a supply chain, the finance major will be responsible for analyzing the data created and shared among supply chain partners. In many instances, the financial analyst will assume the responsibility for recommending actions to improve supply chain efficiencies and cash flow. This may benefit all the partners in the chain. These recommendations will be based on the development of financial models that incorporate key assumptions such as supply chain partner agreements for pricing. Using extensive financial modeling, the financial analyst helps to manage liquidity in the supply chain.

Many finance-related issues exist in implementing interorganizational information systems. For one thing, establishing EDI and extranet relationships involves structuring payment agreements. Global supply chains may involve complex financial arrangements, which may have legal implications.

FOR THE MARKETING MAJOR

A tremendous amount of useful sales information can be derived from supply chain partners through the supporting information systems. For example, many of the customer support activities take place in the downstream portion of the supply chain. For the marketing manager, an understanding of how the downstream activities of the supply chain relate to prior chain operations is critical.

Furthermore, a tremendous amount of data is fed from the supply chain supporting information systems into the CRM systems that are used by marketers. The information and a complete understanding of its genesis are vital for mixed-model marketing programs.

FOR THE

PRODUCTION/OPERATIONS MANAGEMENT MAJOR

The production/operations management major plays a major role in the supply chain development process. In many organizations, the production/operations management staff members may even lead the supply chain integration process because of their extensive knowledge of the manufacturing components of the organization. Because they are in charge of the procurement, production, materials control, and logistical handling, a comprehensive understanding of the techniques of SCM is vital for the production/operations staff.

The downstream segment of supply chains is where marketing, distribution channels, and customer service are conducted. An understanding of how downstream activities are related to the other segments is critical. Supply chain problems can reduce customer satisfaction and negate marketing efforts. It is essential, then, that marketing professionals understand the nature of such problems and their solutions. Also, learning about CRM, its options, and its implementation is important for designing effective customer services and advertising.

As competition intensifies globally, finding new global markets becomes critical. Use of interorganizational information systems provides an opportunity to improve marketing and sales. Understanding the capabilities of these technologies and their implementation issues will enable the marketing department to excel.

FOR THE

HUMAN RESOURCES MANAGEMENT MAJOR

Supply chains require interactions among employees from partners in the chain. These interactions are the responsibility of the human resources manager. The HR manager must be able to address supply chain issues that relate to staffing, job descriptions, job rotations, and accountability. All of these areas are complex within a supply chain and require the HR function to understand the relationship among partners as well as the movement of resources.

Preparing and training employees to work with business partners (frequently in foreign countries) requires knowledge about how interorganizational information systems operate. Sensitivity to cultural differences and extensive communication and collaboration can be facilitated with IT.

FOR THE MIS MAJOR

The MIS staff will be instrumental in the design and support of information systems—both internal organizational and interorganizational—to underpin the business processes that are part of the supply chain. In this capacity, the MIS staff must have a concise knowledge of the business, the systems, and points of intersection between the two.

SUMMARY

1. Describe the three components and the three flows of a supply chain.

A *supply chain* refers to the flow of materials, information, money, and services from raw material suppliers, through factories and warehouses, to the end customers. A supply chain involves three segments: upstream, where sourcing or procurement from external suppliers occurs; internal, where packaging, assembly, or manufacturing takes place; and downstream, where distribution takes place, frequently by external distributors.

The three flows in the supply chain are *material flows*, which are the physical products, raw materials, supplies, and so forth; *information flows*, which consist of data that are related to demand, shipments, orders, returns, and schedules, as well as changes in any of these data; and *financial flows*, which involve money transfers, payments, credit card information and authorization, payment schedules, e-payments, and credit-related data.

2. Identify popular strategies to solving different challenges of supply chains.

Two major challenges in setting accurate inventory levels throughout a supply chain are the *demand forecast* and the *bullwhip effect*. Demand for a product can be influenced by numerous factors such as competition, prices, weather conditions, technological developments, economic conditions, and customers' general confidence. The bullwhip effect refers to erratic shifts in orders up and down the supply chain.

The most common solution to supply chain problems is *building inventories* as insurance against supply chain uncertainties. Another solution is the *just-in-time* (JIT) inventory system, which delivers the precise number of parts, called work-in-process inventory, to be assembled into a finished product at precisely the right time. The third possible solution is *vendor-managed inventory* (VMI), which occurs when the vendor, rather than the retailer, manages the entire inventory process for a particular product or group of products.

3. Explain the utility of each of the three major technologies that supports supply chain management.

Electronic data interchange (EDI) is a communication standard that enables the electronic transfer of routine documents, such as purchasing orders, between business partners.

Extranets are networks that link business partners to one another over the Internet by providing access to certain areas of one another's corporate intranets. The main goal of extranets is to foster collaboration among business partners.

Corporate portals offer a single point of access through a Web browser to critical business information in an organization. In the context of business-to-business supply chain management, these portals enable companies and their suppliers to collaborate very closely.

>>> CHAPTER GLOSSARY

bullwhip effect Erratic shifts in orders up and down the supply chain.

distribution portals Corporate portals that automate the business processes involved in selling or distributing products from a single supplier to multiple buyers.

electronic data interchange (EDI) A communication standard that enables the electronic transfer of routine documents between business partners.

extranets Link business partners to one another over the Internet by providing access to certain areas of one another's corporate intranets.

interorganizational information system (IOS) An information system that supports information flow among two or more organizations.

just-in-time (JIT) inventory system A system in which a supplier delivers the precise number of parts to be assembled into a finished product at precisely the right time.

procurement portals Corporate portals that automate the business processes involved in purchasing or procuring products between a single buyer and multiple suppliers.

pull model A business model in which the production process begins with a customer order and companies make only what customers want, a process closely aligned with mass customization.

push model A business model in which the production process begins with a forecast, which predicts the products that customers will want as well as the quantity of each product. The company then produces the amount of products in the forecast, typically by using mass production, and sells, or "pushes," those products to consumers.

supply chain Coordinated flow of materials, information, money, and services from raw material suppliers, through factories and warehouses, to the end consumers.

supply chain management An activity in which the leaders of an organization provide extensive oversight for the partnerships and processes that comprise the supply chain and leverage these relationships to provide an operational advantage.

supply chain visibility The ability for all organizations in a supply chain to access or view relevant data on purchased materials as these materials move through their suppliers' production processes.

vendor-managed inventory (VMI) An inventory strategy where the supplier monitors a vendor's inventory for a product or group of products and replenishes products when needed.

vertical integration Strategy of integrating the upstream part of the supply chain with the internal part, typically by purchasing upstream suppliers, in order to ensure timely availability of supplies.

>>> DISCUSSION QUESTIONS

1. Explain how a supply chain approach may be part of a company's overall strategy.

2. Explain the important role that information systems play in supporting a supply chain strategy.

3. Would Rolls-Royce Motorcars (www.rolls-roycemotorcars.com) use a push model or a pull model in its supply chain? Support your answer.

4. Why is planning so important in supply chain management?

>>> PROBLEM-SOLVING ACTIVITIES

1. Enter the Teradata Student Network (at http://www.wiley.com/rainer/go/problemsolving) and find the podcasts that deal with supply chains (by Jill Dyche). Identify the benefits cited in the podcasts.

2. Access www.ups.com and www.fedex.com. Examine some of the IT-supported customer services and tools provided by the two companies. Write a report on how the two companies contribute to supply chain improvements.

3. Enter www.supply-chain.org, www.cio.com, www.findarticles.com, and www.google.com and search for recent information on supply chain management.

4. Surf the Web to find a procurement (sourcing) portal, a distribution portal, and an exchange (other than the examples in this chapter). List the features they have in common and those features that are unique.

>>> COLLABORATION EXERCISE

Background

Supply chain management is very important to organizations because it helps them to manage inventory. Managing inventory is key to reducing costs and increasing profits. However, much of supply chain management also deals with quality, legal contracts, deliveries, production schedules, forecasts, and more.

Activity

Divide into teams and visit local businesses in different industries. Have one group visit a car dealership, gas station, restaurant, auto parts store, doctor's office, or other local businesses that require a supply chain. Visit with the manager and discuss the business's supply chain. Some stores may operate out of a regional warehouse, others may have multiple suppliers. Ask about the products that are shipped, the frequency of the shipping, the information that is shared, and anything else your professor asks you to enquire about.

Deliverable

Draw up a model of the supply chain for the company your team visited. Be sure to include upstream and downstream flows of material, information, and money. Bring your team's work to class and discuss the differences in supply chains for businesses in different industries. Finally, submit your team's supply chain model to your professor.

CLOSING **CASE 1** > Information Technology Helps
Cannondale Manage Its Complex Supply Chain

Cannondale (www.cannondale.com) is a pioneer in the engineering and manufacturing of high-end bicycles, apparel, footwear, and accessories for independent dealers and distributors in more than 66 countries. Cannondale designs, develops, and produces bicycles at its factory in Bedford, Pennsylvania, and it operates subsidiaries in Holland, Switzerland, Japan, and Australia. As a leading custom bicycle manufacturer with an extensive and impressive customer list—including Olympic athletes, professional racing teams, and Tour de France competitors—Cannondale realizes that meeting customer demands and expectations is critical to its success.

<<< **THE PROBLEM**

Cannondale produces more than a hundred different bicycle models annually, 60 percent of which are newly introduced lines. Working in a cyclical business that is affected by market and weather conditions, coupled with the international nature of its business, Cannondale is faced with highly complex and volatile consumer demand. In addition to constantly shifting demand and a rapidly changing product portfolio, Cannondale has a global supply chain that must integrate global manufacturing, assembly, and sales and distribution sites.

Cannondale manufactures both make-to-order and make-to-stock models. Consequently, the company needs to manage a range of product batch sizes, sometimes including one-of-a-kind orders. A typical bicycle requires a 150-day lead time with a 4-week manufacturing window, and some bicycles have more than 250 parts in their bills of materials (BOMs). (A bill of materials specifies the raw materials, assemblies, components, and parts needed to manufacture a final product, along with the quantities of each one.) Cannondale has to manage more than 1 million BOMs and more than 200,000 individual parts. Adding to Cannondale's manufacturing complexity, some of these parts are supplied by specialty vendors who require long lead times and have only limited production capacity. This complexity significantly challenged Cannondale's capacity to quickly deliver complex and custom products to meet its customers' high expectations.

To manage parts availability and varying customer demands, Cannondale's manufacturing operations must be highly flexible. Therefore, the company needed a global system that allowed managers to access all plant inventory levels and supply schedules to better manage shifts in product and customer demand.

Cannondale had been using a legacy material requirements planning system (MRP II) that generated weekly reports. Because Cannondale's manufacturing environment is so dynamic, however, by Tuesday afternoon Monday's reports were so outdated that they were useless. The supply chain team had to substitute parts in order to meet demand, causing an ever-increasing parts flow problem. Cannondale's primary objective was to find an IT solution that would improve the accuracy of the company's parts flow, support the company's need for flexibility, and operate within the confines of its existing business systems—all at an affordable cost.

Cannondale selected the Kinaxis RapidResponse (www.kinaxis.com) system for its integrated demand and supply planning and monitoring. RapidResponse provides users with necessary information in minutes, as opposed to 8 hours with the previous system. RapidResponse generates accurate and detailed supply chain information with an easy-to-use spreadsheet user interface, employing data supplied from the company's existing MRP II systems.

<<< **THE SOLUTION**

RapidResponse has transformed Cannondale's entire supply chain. Buyers, planners, master schedulers, sourcers (people who procure products), product managers, customer service personnel, and financial managers use the system for sales reporting, forecasting, monitoring daily inventory availability, and providing production schedule information to the MRP II and order-processing systems. Supply chain participants located around the world can now instantly simulate, share, and score what-if scenarios to evaluate and select the actions they need to take to respond to changing supply and demand conditions.

Company managers now receive up-to-date visibility of global operations. In addition, the management team uses RapidResponse daily to examine the company's manufacturing backlog. Having access to current information enables the team to compare old forecasts with new ones.

THE RESULTS >>>

Today, Cannondale responds to customer orders quickly, and it has significantly reduced its inventory, with its associated costs. In addition, the company has benefited from higher inventory turns, reductions in safety stock, improvement in cycle times, reduced lead times, and more accurate promise dates. As a result, customer satisfaction has improved. All of these benefits have provided Cannondale with a competitive advantage in a highly competitive industry.

Sources: Compiled from B. Ferrari, "Kinaxis RapidResponse—Much More Than a Planning Application" *Supply Chain Matters*, January 8, 2010; Kinaxis Corporation, "Cannondale Improves Customer Response Times While Reducing Inventory Using RapidResponse," *Kinaxis Customer Spotlight*, 2010; www.kinaxis.com, www.cannondale.com, accessed April 14, 2011.

Questions

1. Describe Cannondale's complex manufacturing environment and identify some of the problems this environment created.
2. Describe the RapidResponse system's impact on Cannondale's global supply chain management.

CLOSING **CASE 2 >** Driving Innovation

THE PROBLEM >>>

With $19.6 billion in annual sales, Kimberly-Clark Corporation (www.kimberly-clark.com) is one of the world's leading manufacturers of family and personal care products. With numerous well-known brands—including Kleenex, Scott, and Huggies—Kimberly-Clark holds the number 1 or number 2 brand share in more than 80 countries. Founded in 1870, today the company employs 57,000 people around the world. In 2011, the company challenged its business support groups, including transportation, to drive cost savings across the organization.

When the company issued this challenge, its transportation group was using a legacy transportation management system (TMS) that had been in place for many years. The group quickly realized that it required a more robust system to deliver the required savings, because the legacy TMS was unable to handle Kimberly-Clark's rapid growth.

THE IT >>> SOLUTION

Kimberly-Clark's transportation group chose JDA Software's (www.jda.com) transportation planning and management system to replace their legacy system.

THE RESULTS >>>

Kimberly-Clark quickly achieved a significant return on their investment in JDA Software's system. The firm saved $8 million in the first year of using the system alone, and continues to save $12 to $14 million per year in freight charges.

The company's centralized planning staff for its North American operations use the system to manage approximately 2,500 shipments a day, which originate from 40 separate locations. The JDA system incorporates business rules that dictate which loads can be automatically processed, eliminating much of the manual work of reviewing and approving daily transportation loads.

Loads that are not particularly complex—for example, shipments with just one pick-up and one drop-off location—are automatically processed by the system, without needing approval from a planner. All loads that are more complex in nature—for instance, because they exceed a certain size or require special handling—must be personally approved by a planner. The system flags any violations of business rules and states why the loads were flagged, so that planners can respond appropriately.

The system enables Kimberly-Clark to automatically process almost 80 percent of its daily transportation loads. Planners estimate that their end-of-day close-out process has been reduced by about 30 minutes to an hour.

Additionally, now that daily loads are managed effectively by the automatic system, planners are able to redirect more of their time to focus on strategic activities. The company estimates that approximately 35 hours per day in manual labor has been eliminated across the company's planning team.

Following this success, Kimberly-Clark is investigating new uses for the JDA system. For example, the company is working on automating the payment of approximately 80 percent of the invoices of the firm's centralized freight approval staff. It also plans to use the system to eliminate duplicate invoices, flag overdue invoices, and reduce the number of steps in the invoice approval process.

Sources: Compiled from "Driving Innovation," *JDA Real Results Magazine*, 2012; www.kimberly-clark.com, www.jda.com, accessed March 24, 2012.

Questions

1. Describe the benefits that Kimberly-Clark received from its implementation of the JDA system.
2. Why did Kimberly-Clark use JDA software rather than simply adding functionality to its existing TMS system?

RUBY'S CLUB | INTERNSHIP ASSIGNMENT

Ruben had last year's sales numbers put into a spreadsheet because he heard about a type of regression analysis that would give him an idea of the impact of different events in the community. However, he does not know how to run this regression or how to use it to plan for the club.

Visit http://www.wiley.com/go/rainer/rubysclub and click on the links for Ruby's Chapter 13. You will find tutorials that will help you learn how to install the Data Analysis Toolpak in Microsoft Excel. Depending on your version of Excel, you may want to search Google for more information. Then click on the second link to download the actual spreadsheet for your analysis.

In the spreadsheet, you will find 1's and 0's. These indicate a "yes" to the item in the column. You will also find a column regarding the type of music played during a particular week. For the analysis to run properly, you will need to divide this into five different columns with 1's and 0's.

Once you interpret your results, write a letter to Ruben and Lisa detailing the impact that outside events have on their sales. Be sure to attach your version of the spreadsheet with analysis included. Submit it to Ruben and Lisa via your professor.

SPREADSHEET ACTIVITY: PROJECT MANAGEMENT IN EXCEL

Objective: Supply chain management is a vital operation for organizations—so much so that if one supplier fails to do its job, the entire operation may be shut down. Microsoft Excel is often used to assist in this basic planning. Logic and algebra can be applied in a spreadsheet to make simple calculations that apply within the supply chain scenario.

Chapter Connection: At one time, Dell realized it had almost perfected the assembly process within its plant. The only way to improve its product was to improve the entire supply chain. So Dell began working with its suppliers to streamline its processes. Although its supply chain system is too complex for a spreadsheet, the principle applies to many situations.

This activity will take a simpler scenario and introduce the concept of planning for the supply chain and using spreadsheet tools to improve the process.

Activity: Mr. Stephens works in construction. Specifically, he builds custom homes. He always gets complaints about his work being late, even though his customers are generally happy with the final product. To try to deal with the complaints and to give his customers a better understanding of when their home will be complete, he wants to build a spreadsheet that will lay out the entire process of building the home, specify the amount of time each part will take, and build in time for bad weather, corrections, and other issues that always arise.

Mr. Stephens compiled the following data for his next construction job. Although he ultimately wants to create a universal spreadsheet, for now he just wants to work on the concept and get it to work for this next job. Use the data and build him a spreadsheet that has the job description in one column and other columns for start date, earliest end date, and latest end date. Unless otherwise noted, these steps are performed in order, and one cannot begin until the previous step is completed.

1. Groundwork will take 3 to 4 days.
2. Footers will take 2 to 3 days.
3. Block work for crawl space will take 7 to 10 days.
4. Foundation will take 3 to 4 days. Lumber should be ordered a week in advance.
5. Remaining frame will take 2 to 3 weeks. Home should be dried-in at this time.
6. Exterior oriented strand board (OSB) and house wrap will take 7 to 10 days.
7. Electrical work may begin at this point. It will take 8 to 12 days to complete the rough-in wiring for the home.
8. Rough-in plumbing work may begin when the exterior OSB is complete. Rough-in plumbing will take 5 to 7 days.
9. Insulation and dry wall may go up at this time when both electrical and plumbing are roughed in. It will take 17 to 21 days to complete the installation of exterior and interior walls insulation as well as the drywall work.
10. Cabinetry and final electrical work may begin at this point. Cabinetry will take 1 to 3 days, and the finish work on electrical items will take 7 to 10 days. Cabinets should be ordered a month in advance.
11. The final plumbing work may begin when the cabinets are complete and will take 3 to 5 days to complete.
12. All work on the rest of the house may begin at this time. Paint, trim, and flooring typically take 2 to 3 weeks.

Given this description from Mr. Stephens, build a spreadsheet that will allow him to demonstrate to his customers how long it takes to build a home. Use a start date of February 1 and allow 2 weeks for weather delays. Given this information, determine the projected end date if everything finishes as early as possible and the projected end date if everything takes as long as possible.

Deliverable: Submit your spreadsheet along with a Word document that answers the questions listed above.

Discussion Questions:

1. Supply chain management is extremely important in today's business environment. Look up some supply chain management tools and compare them to your Excel activity. Discuss the advantages and disadvantages of these systems. What do they provide that the spreadsheet example does not?
2. Given that some refer to supply chains as a web rather than a chain, what type of problems do you see arising from the parent company's need to share information with so many others at the same time? Also, what complications arise from the suppliers needing to share information? Which company should determine the platform and methods of sharing data?

Quiz questions are assignable in WileyPLUS, and available on the Book Companion Site at http://www.wiley.com/college/rainer.

DATABASE ACTIVITY: QUERY BY FORM

Objective

Forms and queries have a two-sided relationship. Forms can be an easy-to-use way to provide the input to a query. Query results can also be used in place of tables to drive forms. In this activity, you will see how a form drives a query, increasing your understanding of both.

CHAPTER CONNECTION

Supply chain integration, as you read in this chapter, is complex. One company's supplier is another company's customer and so on, all the way up to raw material extraction and down to individual end users. The database applications that are needed to manage this supply chain are correspondingly complex. It can take a mix of database features to get the entire job done. This activity shows how two database capabilities interact with each other.

PREREQUISITES

Before starting this activity, you should complete the database activities for Chapter 9 (Forms II) and Chapter 10 (Queries I) activities.

Activity

In this activity, which you will find online at http://www.wiley.com/go/rainer/database, you will take what you know about queries and forms, and combine them to improve the usability of your queries.

1. Download and open the Ch 13 CarlaComputerStores database from http://www.wiley.com/go/rainer/database. (You may be familiar with it from the Chapter 5 activity.) It contains sales data for a chain of computer stores.

2. We will use a querying method called Query By Form, QBF for short. It lets us replace a series of parameter entry dialogue boxes with a single form while allowing us to create a more attractive user interface. To use it, we must create both the query and the form. It is easiest to do this in a few stages.

3. First, we will create the part of the query that returns results, adding criteria later because they will come from a form we have not created yet. We do this so that, when we create the form, we will be able to tell it which query to run. So, start with Query Design in the Other section of the Create ribbon.

Usage Hint: This query-form-query sequence is not strictly necessary. However, methods that do the job in two steps are more complicated, because they require referring to Access objects that do not exist yet.

4. We want this query to tell us which customers ordered products in a chosen category from a chosen store, and exactly what products they ordered. So, first show all five database tables in the upper pane of the query design window. Then, double-click on four fields to enter them into the query design: StoreCity from StoreTbl, ProdCategory from ProductTbl, CustName from CustomerTbl, and ProdDescrip from ProductTbl. Run the query to test it. You should see an unsorted list of all 312 purchases. If you do not,

review the previous steps to find the error. Then close it, saving it as CS_Qry when prompted.

Usage Hint: Testing is a vital part of information system development. Test often. If anything does not work, the reason is usually in what you did since the previous test. You can fix it while what you just did is still fresh in your mind.

5. Now that CS_Qry exists, we can create the form that will activate it. Click the Form Design tool in the Forms section of the Create menu.

6. First, we will create a field to enter the store we want information about. Click the Text Box tool in the Controls section of the Design ribbon. The mouse pointer becomes crosshairs in the form design grid. Drag to create a text-size area somewhere in the upper right part of this grid. (You use the right side to leave room for a label at the left.)

7. The label to the left of the text box will read "Text0." Edit it in place to read "Store City." Its enclosing box will expand to hold its new, longer contents.

8. The text inside the text box reads "Unbound." However, that is not the name of the text box. That says where its data comes from. "Unbound" means it does not come from the database—that is, it has not been "bound" to a database item. We want to give the text box a name so we can refer to it in our query. To do that, open the Property Sheet of the form if it is not already open. (Click the Property Sheet tool in the Tools section of the Design ribbon, or press F4.) Find Name in either the Other or the All tab of the property sheet. Replace it with the name "StoreField."

9. Create another text box named "CatField" in the same way, with its label reading "Product Category." Line up the two fields and labels, one below the other, as closely as you can.

Usage Hint: You can line them up exactly by selecting both boxes and using the tools in the Control Alignment section of the Arrange ribbon. For more precision, open the Property Sheet and set their Left property to any desired value. If you do this while both are selected, they will both take on this value. You can set any desired property of several controls at the same time this way.

10. Enter a form header above the text fields by clicking on Title in the Header/Footer area of the Design ribbon. Enter "Store and Category Search" in the label box. Select the entire box and use the formating tools in the Home ribbon to enlarge the type, make it bold, change its color, and give the label box a light-colored background.

11. Now, we will create the button that starts the search. Make sure Use Control Wizards is

highlighted in the Controls section of the Design ribbon. (Expand that area using the down-pointing triangle with the line above it at the right to see the wizard.) Then click the Button tool. (It is in the top row of controls, fourth from the left.) Drag it over a rectangular area below your text boxes to create the button shape. The wizard will start.

12. We want it to run a query. Select this action from the Miscellaneous category. Click Next.

13. Select the query you created earlier, CS_Qry, from the list of available queries. Click Next.

14. Click "Text" as what you want to see on the button, and enter "Search" into the text field next to that option button. Click Next.

15. Optionally name the button anything you want, and click Finish.

16. To test what you have done so far, switch to Form view and click your button. You should see the same datasheet you saw when you test ran the query in step 4. If you do, the form is finished. Return to it and save it as CS_Qry_Frm. Now, we will continue with the query design.

17. With the query open in Design view, specify a sort order for the data. Click in the Sort row of the StoreCity column in the design grid. Select Ascending from the pull-down menu at the right. Repeat for CustName and ProdCategory. Test again by running the query. You should see all 312 purchases again, but this time they should be sorted.

18. To add a selection to the query, return to Design view and click in the StoreCity column, in the first Criteria row. Next, select the Builder tool from the Query Setup section of the Design ribbon. (Its icon looks like the Use Control Wizards icon.) Your criteria will be based on CS_Qry_Form, so expand the database name, then Forms, then its All Forms sub-folder. Select CS_Qry_Form. In the second column, double-click StoreField.

19. You will see "Forms![CS_QueryForm]![StoreField]" in the upper portion of the dialogue box. This is Access's internal way to identify the form field we want. Click OK. It will appear in the Criteria section of the query design.

Usage Hint: If you know Access well, you can also key criteria directly into the query design grid. For short criteria that can be faster, but it is also more error-prone.

20. To check your work, close the query, saving when prompted. Open CS_Qry_Frm. On the form, enter Chicago into the Store field and click Search. You should get 78 records of Chicago sales. Close the query and enter Miami. You should get a

blank datasheet, because Carla's has no store there. (You will get the same result if you spell "Chicago" wrong.)

Usage Hint: You could have checked your work a bit earlier by running the query directly, without the form. If you do that, you will get a parameter box with an odd-looking prompt string: the name of the form field. It should work, however.

21. Repeat steps 18 and 19 for ProdCategory. Test by entering Denver and Storage into the two form fields. Your query should retrieve ten records.

22. You may want to find data about all Storage sales, or some other category, without regard for city. Enter Storage in the category field, leaving the Store field blank. Run the query. Nothing comes up. You realize the reason: No data records match a blank StoreCity! This must be fixed. You want the query to select a record if either (a) its StoreCity matches what is in the form or (b) if the field in the form is blank. Fortunately, that is not hard.

23. Return to query design view. Click in the StoreCity criterion field and reopen the Expression Builder. Put the insertion point after the field name that is already there. Then either key in the word "Or" or follow Operators > Logical and double-click "Or" in the lower part of the Expression Builder window. You will see the word "Or" appear in the Expression Builder box after the field name. Then select StoreField again, and after it type the words "is null" (without the quotation marks). This means that the query will select a record if it matches what is in the field, OR if the field is null—that is, there is nothing in it. That is exactly what we want.

Usage Hint: Instead of keying in "is null," we could have found the IsNull function in Expression Builder. In this case, the words are so short that keying them in is easier.

24. Modify the CatField test criterion in the same way.

25. Test again: Close the query, enter Storage in the Category field of the form and leave the City field blank. You should see 66 storage sales in all four stores, starting with Alice's purchase of a 1TB disk in Atlanta.

26. Test to confirm that entering a city, but no category, works too.

27. Test to confirm that leaving both blank shows all 312 rows of the full table.

28. Look at the query in Design view. Access has rearranged your criteria, turning them into four and adding two columns that do not show up in the query results. (Their "Show" boxes are unchecked.) It sometimes does this to reduce a complex query to several simpler ones. That is not

a problem. We mention it here only so it does not faze you if you see it.

29. Close your database, saving if prompted.

Deliverable

Your database, with the form and query.

Quiz Questions:

1. True or False? A form is the only way a user can specify search criteria (without opening a query in Design view, which most end users are not up to).

2. How many portable computers did the Atlanta store sell in the period covered by this database? Who bought more than anyone else? How many did this person buy?

3. Look at the Property Sheet of either text box in CS_ Qry_Form. It allows you to specify many properties of these boxes. (Some can be specified through ribbon tools or in other ways as well.) In particular, it lets a form designer choose all of the following *except*

   (a) Font size in points.
   (b) Background color of the box.
   (c) Which sides of the box will show borders.
   (d) Color of the box borders.

4. The condition "IS NULL" in a database query is satisfied if the field in question

   (a) Has a numeric value of 0 (zero).
   (b) Has an incorrect data type—for example, letters where numbers are required.
   (c) Violates validation tests—for example, a month number that is not from 1 to 12.
   (d) Is empty—that is, it contains no data.

Discussion Questions

1. This activity used a form to drive a query. The two can also work together in the opposite direction: using queries as input to a form, where we used only tables until now. Use the form and query you created in this activity to select sales of Display products in all stores. With the query results showing, create a form using the Form tool in the Create ribbon. How does what you created resemble, and how does it differ from, a form you could have created from the tables that underlie this query?

2. In step 25 of the activity, you saw that Access turned your two criteria, each of which contained two elementary conditions combined by OR, into four criteria. Try to figure out the conditions under which each of the four would apply.

3. Query criteria can use hundreds of built-in functions. They are listed under Functions, then Built-In Functions, in the Builder dialogue box. Many of these resemble functions you are familiar with from Excel formulas, including 13 financial functions such as internal rate of return (IRR) and loan payments (PMT) that one might not initially think of when one thinks of database applications. Discuss how a query might use such financial functions.

14 | Acquiring Information Systems and Applications

LEARNING OBJECTIVES >>>

1. Discuss the different cost/benefit analyses that companies must take into account when formulating an IT strategic plan.

2. Discuss the four business decisions that companies must make when they acquire new applications.

3. Enumerate the primary tasks and importance of each of the six processes involved in the systems development life cycle.

4. Describe alternative development methods and tools that augment development methods.

5. Analyze the process of vendor and software selection.

Anniston Orthopaedics

Courtesy of Anniston Orthopaedics Associates

Anniston Orthopaedic Associates, P.A. (AOA), is a surgical group comprised of six physicians who provide services to the Calhoun County area of Alabama. The group had not updated its information systems for several years as of mid-2012. When the federal government initiated a program to incentivize medical practices to migrate to electronic medical records (EMRs), the group's physicians realized that it was time to upgrade their systems. Most of the responsibility for this transition fell on Chad Prince, the group's business administrator.

To transition from paper to EMRs, AOA had to implement a system that would encompass hardware, software, and an upgraded network. In mid-2011, after considering numerous vendors, AOA selected Greenway Medical Technologies' Prime-Suite product as the group's new information system. Making this decision was only the beginning of the process, however.

To run the Greenway PrimeSuite software, AOA would have to upgrade the group's IT infrastructure to match Greenway's

requirements. Therefore, AOA hired IT consultants to install new hardware and set up a new network. This new network brought many needed upgrades, including interoffice e-mail and shared calendars. The staff adjusted well to these changes, but to maintain efficiency for their physicians (critical for maintaining revenue), patient data that was typically recorded on paper charts, such as demographics and vital signs, had to be moved to an electronic format. AOA used third-party software solutions from ChartCapture, Phreesia, and MidMark to gather medical information and have it ready for physicians to electronically review it at the time of the physician–patient encounter.

ChartCapture (www.chartcapture.com) captured paper chart data for AOA and displays images of documents in an intuitive format so that the physician has access to historical records. Phreesia (www.phreesia.com) is a check-in mobile > > >

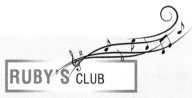

RUBY'S CLUB

It is time for Ruben and Lisa to begin discussing the implementation of the systems they have decided on. Specifically, they need some help determining the best method for developing, implementing, running, and maintaining this mobile ordering system.

They realize that having the idea for a system is only the beginning. They need to know about development methodologies and which ones make the most sense for them. Remember, their strategy is to provide a relaxing, community-type atmosphere, and they think this ordering system will support that mission by making it easier for people to continue with their socializing and not take time away to order drinks and food.

As you read through this chapter, consider the end-of-section questions in light of this case. Although there are more possibilities to think about, these will give you some direction to help develop your final report to them at the end of the chapter.

kiosk system that collects demographics and payment information such as copays, conducts medical questionnaires on wireless touchscreen tablet devices, and enters all of this information into the Greenway PrimeSuite software. MidMark (www.midmark.com) provides vital signs machines that collect blood pressure, heart rate, and temperature and enters these values into discrete fields within the PrimeSuite EMR. During the physician–patient encounter, physicians use speech recognition technology within PrimeSuite to complete medical records for each patient visit.

In addition to upgrading their hardware and software in order to implement Greenway's Prime Suite software, AOA's physicians and staff needed to be trained on how to use the new system. To speed this process along, Chad attended a week of intense training on PrimeSuite that he in turn took back and presented to the practice. All training and upgrades were done in preparation for a phased implementation that would consist of two separate "go-lives." One "go-live" would be for the "practice" side of the office that involved capturing patients' demographics and insurance information, and a second go-live for the "chart" or medical side of the practice, which would involve a full transition to EMR.

 In mid-2012, AOA organized all of its internal workflows around EMRs and is in the process of

training its staff. The first two physicians will begin operating on the new system in April 2012. Two more physicians will join the system in June and the final two will join in August. By moving slowly through the transition, the AOA staff will have time to adjust to the changes and the trainers will have fewer physicians to focus on during the training and go-live process. Thus, as you can see, the process of acquiring new information systems can often involve much more than a simple purchase decision.

Sources: Compiled from interviews with Chad Prince, www.greenwaymedical.com, http://annistonortho.com, accessed May 12, 2011.

Questions

1. Would acquiring a new information system for a small organization be a longer or shorter process than acquiring one at a larger organization? Why do you say that? Support your answer.

2. Why did AOA pick three separate vendors to help implement Greenway's PrimeSuite software application? What are the problems associated with managing four vendors total to implement the group's switch to EMRs? Should AOA have purchased a software application from a company that would manage the entire process? Why or why not?

Introduction

Competitive organizations move as quickly as they can to acquire new information technologies or modify existing ones when they need to improve efficiencies and gain strategic advantage. Today, however, acquisition goes beyond building new systems in-house, and IT resources go beyond software and hardware. The old model in which firms built their own systems is being replaced with a broader perspective of IT resource acquisition that provides companies with a number of options. Thus, companies now must decide which IT tasks will remain in-house, and even whether the entire IT resource should be provided and managed by outside organizations. Regardless of which approach an organization chooses, however, it must be able to manage IT projects adeptly.

Even for a small business, IS upgrades present a complex problem. Small organizations must select vendors based on a number of factors, particularly (1) the ability of the vendor's product(s) to meet the organization's current business needs, (2) the viability of the vendor as a whole (you do not want to sign a contract with someone who might go into bankruptcy), and (3) the relationship between the two companies. After the organization has selected a vendor, the two parties must decide on the contract and clear it with their lawyers. Finally, the organization must acquire the hardware to support the new software. Even for a small business, these decisions are very important because of the lasting impact of this investment. Although the right information systems may not "make or break" the organization, they can definitely help it become more competitive.

In this chapter, you learn about the process of acquiring IT resources from a managerial perspective. This means from *your* perspective, because you will be closely involved in all aspects of acquiring information systems and applications in your organization. In fact, when we mention "users" in this chapter, we are talking about you. You will also study the available options for acquiring IT resources and how to evaluate the options. Finally, you will learn how organizations plan and justify the acquisition of new information systems.

14.1 Planning for and Justifying IT Applications

Organizations must analyze the need for applications and then justify each purchase in terms of costs and benefits. The need for information systems is usually related to organizational planning and to the analysis of its performance vis-à-vis its competitors. The cost–benefit justification must look at the wisdom of investing in a specific IT application versus spending the funds on alternative projects. This chapter focuses on the formal processes of large organizations. Smaller organizations employ less formal processes, or no processes at all. It is important to note that even if a small organization does not have a formal process for planning and justifying IT applications, the steps of a formal process exist for a reason, and they have value. At the very least, decision makers in small organizations should consider each step when they are planning changes in their information systems.

When a company examines its needs and performance, it generates a prioritized list of both existing and potential IT applications, called the **application portfolio**. These are the applications that have to be added, or modified if they already exist.

IT Planning

The planning process for new IT applications begins with analysis of the *organizational strategic plan*, which is illustrated in Figure 14.1. The organization's strategic plan identifies the firm's overall mission, the goals that follow from that mission, and the broad steps required to reach these goals. The strategic planning process modifies the organization's objectives and resources to match its changing markets and opportunities.

The organizational strategic plan and the existing IT architecture provide the inputs in developing the IT strategic plan. The *IT architecture* (see Figure 14.2) delineates the way an organization's information resources should be used to accomplish its mission. It encompasses both the technical and the managerial aspects of information resources. The technical aspects include hardware and operating systems, networking, data management systems, and

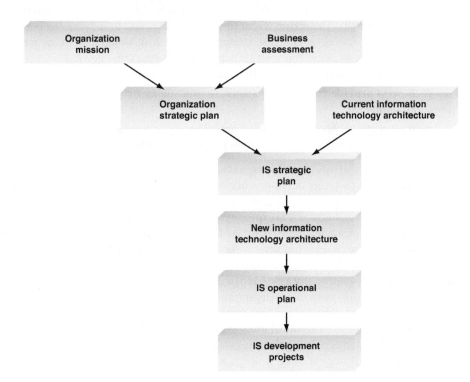

Figure 14.1 Analysis of the organizational strategic plan.

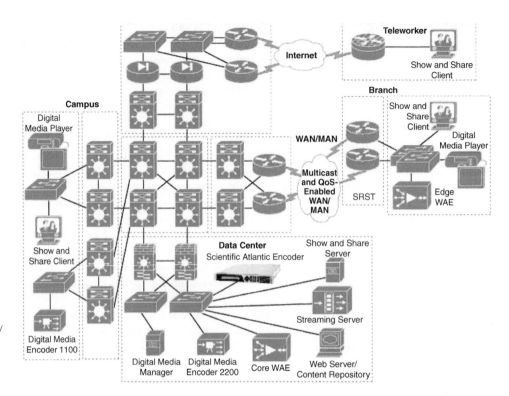

Figure 14.2 IT architecture. (*Source:* http://www.cisco.com/en/US/i/200001-300000/250001-260000/253001-254000/253787.jpg.)

applications software. The managerial aspects specify how the IT department will be managed, how the functional area managers will be involved, and how IT decisions will be made.

The **IT strategic plan** is a set of long-range goals that describe the IT infrastructure and identify the major IT initiatives needed to achieve the organization's goals (see this chapter's Closing Case 2). The IT strategic plan must meet three objectives:

1. *It must be aligned with the organization's strategic plan.* This alignment is critical because the organization's IS have to support the organization's strategies. (Recall the discussion of organizational strategies and information systems in Chapter 2.)

Consider the example of Nordstrom versus Walmart. An application that improves customer service at a small cost would be considered favorably at Nordstrom, but it would be rejected at Walmart. The reason is that the application would fit in favorably (i.e., align) with Nordstrom's service-at-any-cost strategy. However, it would not fit in well with Walmart's low-cost strategy. You see two department stores, same application, same cost and benefits—but different answers to the question "Should we develop the application?"

2. *It must provide for an IT architecture that seamlessly networks users, applications, and databases.*

3. *It must efficiently allocate IS development resources among competing projects so the projects can be completed on time and within budget and still have the required functionality.*

The existing IT architecture is a necessary input into the IT strategic plan because it acts as a constraint on future development efforts. It is not an absolute constraint, however, because the organization can change to a new IT architecture. Companies prefer to avoid this strategy, however, because it is expensive and time-consuming.

Consider this example. You have a Mac (Apple) system and you need a new software application. You search and find several such packages for both Mac and MS Windows. Unfortunately, the best package runs only on Windows. How much better would this package have to be for you to justify a switch to a new system?

One critical component in developing and implementing the IT strategic plan is the **IT steering committee.** This committee, comprised of a group of managers and staff who represent the various organizational units, is created to establish IT priorities and to ensure that the MIS function is meeting the organization's needs. The committee's major tasks are to link corporate strategy with IT strategy, to approve the allocation of resources for the

MIS function, and to establish performance measures for the MIS function and ensure that they are met. The IT steering committee is important to you because it ensures that you get the information systems and applications that you need to do your job.

After a company has agreed on an IT strategic plan, it next develops the **IS operational plan**. This plan consists of a clear set of projects that the IS department and the functional area managers will execute in support of the IT strategic plan. A typical IS operational plan contains the following elements:

- *Mission:* The mission of the IS function (derived from the IT strategy)
- *IS environment:* A summary of the information needs of the functional areas and of the organization as a whole
- *Objectives of the IS function:* The best current estimate of the goals of the IS function
- *Constraints on the IS function:* Technological, financial, personnel, and other resource limitations on the IS function
- *The application portfolio:* A prioritized inventory of present applications and a detailed plan of projects to be developed or continued during the current year
- *Resource allocation and project management:* A listing of how and when who is going to do what

Evaluating and Justifying IT Investment: Benefits, Costs, and Issues

Developing an IT plan is the first step in the acquisition process. Because all companies have limited resources, they must justify investing resources in some areas, including IT, rather than in others. Essentially, justifying IT investment involves calculating the costs, assessing the benefits (values), and comparing the two. This comparison is frequently referred to as cost–benefit analysis. Cost–benefit analysis is not a simple task.

Assessing the Costs. Placing a dollar value on the cost of IT investments is not as simple as it may seem. One of the major challenges that companies face is to allocate fixed costs among different IT projects. *Fixed costs* are those costs that remain the same regardless of any change in the activity level. For IT, fixed costs include infrastructure costs and the costs associated with IT services and IT management. For example, the salary of the IT director is fixed, and adding one more application will not change it.

Another complication is that the costs of a system do not end when the system is installed. Rather, costs for maintaining, debugging, and improving the system can accumulate over many years. This is a critical point because organizations sometimes fail to anticipate these costs when they make the investment.

A dramatic example of unanticipated expenses was the Year 2000 (Y2K) reprogramming projects, which cost organizations worldwide billions of dollars. In the 1960s, computer memory was very expensive. To save money, programmers coded the "year" in the date field 19_ _, instead of _ _ _ _. With the "1" and the "9" hard-coded in the computer program, only the last two digits varied, so computer programs needed less memory. However, this process meant that when the year 2000 rolled around, computers would display the year as 1900. This programming technique could have caused serious problems with financial applications, insurance applications, and countless other apps.

This Y2K example illustrates the point that database design choices tend to affect the organization for a long time. As the 21st century approached, no one still used hardware or software from the 1960s (other than a few legacy applications). Database design choices made in the 1960s, however, were often still in effect.

Assessing the Benefits. Evaluating the benefits of IT projects is typically even more complex than calculating their costs. Benefits may be harder to quantify, especially because many of them are intangible—for example, improved customer or partner relations or improved decision making. As an employee, you will probably be asked for input about the intangible benefits that an IS provides for you.

The fact that organizations use IT for multiple purposes further complicates benefit analysis. In addition, to obtain a return from an IT investment, the company must implement the technology successfully. In reality, many systems are not implemented on time, within budget, or with all the features originally envisioned for them. Also, the proposed system may be "cutting edge." In these cases, there may be no basis for identifying the types of financial payback the company can expect.

Conducting the Cost–Benefit Analysis.

After a company has assessed the costs and benefits of IT investments, it must compare them. You have studied, or will study, cost–benefit analyses in more detail in your finance courses. The point is that real-world business problems do not come in neatly wrapped packages labeled "this is a finance problem" or "this is an IS problem." Rather, business problems span multiple functional areas.

There is no uniform strategy for conducting a cost–benefit analysis. Rather, an organization can perform this task in several ways. Here you see four common approaches: (1) net present value, (2) return on investment, (3) breakeven analysis, and (4) the business case approach.

- Analysts use the *net present value (NPV)* method to convert future values of benefits to their present-value equivalent by "discounting" them at the organization's cost of funds. They can then compare the present value of the future benefits to the cost required to achieve those benefits to determine whether the benefits exceed the costs.

- *Return on investment (ROI)* measures management's effectiveness in generating profits with its available assets. ROI is calculated by dividing the net income generated by a project by the average assets invested in the project. ROI is a percentage, and the higher the percentage return, the better.

- *Breakeven analysis* determines the point at which the cumulative dollar value of the benefits from a project equals the investment made in the project.

- In the *business case approach*, system developers write a business case to justify funding one or more specific applications or projects. IS professionals will be a major source of input when business cases are developed because these cases describe what you do, how you do it, and how a new system could better support you.

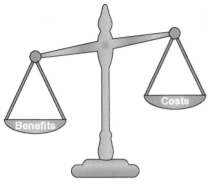

Cost–benefit analysis.

BEFORE YOU GO ON . . .

1. What are some problems associated with assessing the costs of IT?

2. What difficulties accompany the intangible benefits from IT?

3. Describe the NPV, ROI, breakeven analysis, and business case approaches.

Apply the Concept 14.1

Background Part of the initial decision is a cost–benefit analysis. You may not realize it, but you do this all the time. You might want to go to the beach for the weekend, but decide not to because you would have to drive 8 hours each way and would not get to spend much time there. In this case, the cost outweighs the benefits. However, if you could extend your stay another day, the benefits outweigh the costs!

Activity Visit http://www.wiley.com/go/rainer/applytheconcept and click on the link provided for Apply the Concept 14.1. You will read a short article about cost–benefit analysis and be presented with a scenario.

Use Excel to build an analysis tool. Use the numbers provided to build your initial table and make sure your answers match those given. Your spreadsheet will look something like this table.

Costs	Benefits	Payback Time in Months
Cost 1	Benefit 1	Step 1: Total Cost/Total Benefit
Cost 2	Benefit 2	Step 2: Answer above × 12 months
Cost 3	Benefit 3	
Total Cost	Total Benefit per year	

Deliverable

Use the spreadsheet you created to test the following scenarios:

1. Lost time is actually 50 employee days (rather than 40) and the mail shot capacity only doubled (rather than triple).

2. The lost sales through disruption tally is actually $30,000 (rather than $20,000) and the ability to manage the sales effort is only $20,000 (rather than $30,000).

3. Improved customer service and retention total $20,000 (rather than $30,000).

4. Improved efficiency of follow-up is $25,000 (rather than $50,000).

For each scenario, tell whether the payback time has increased or decreased. If the upper management wants no less than 9 months to payback, what is the decision for each of these four scenarios?

   Submit your work to your professor.

Quiz questions are assignable in WileyPLUS, and available on the Book Companion Site at http://www.wiley.com/college/rainer.

RUBY'S CLUB QUESTIONS

1. Based on what you have learned about Ruby's Club in this book, what do you think Ruben and Lisa's strategic plan is? Do you think they could accomplish their plan without the use of technology?

2. If the purpose of this system is to collect orders and serve as the transaction processing system (TPS) for their other information systems, what level of accuracy and reliability do you believe Ruben and Lisa need? At what point does a system failure become a problem to customers?

14.2 Strategies for Acquiring IT Applications

After a company has justified an IT investment, it must then decide how to pursue it. As with cost–benefit analyses, there are several options for acquiring IT applications. To decide on which option to choose, companies must make a series of business decisions. The fundamental decisions are these:

- *How much computer code does the company want to write?* A company can choose to use a totally prewritten application (to write no computer code), to customize a prewritten application (to write some computer code), or to custom-write an entire application (write all new computer code).

- *How will the company pay for the application?* Once the company has decided how much computer code to write, it must decide how to pay for it. With prewritten applications or customized prewritten applications, companies can buy them or lease them. With totally custom applications, companies use internal funding.

- *Where will the application run?* The next decision is whether to run the application on the company's platform or on someone else's platform. In other words, it can employ either a software-as-a-service vendor or an application service provider. (You will examine these options later in this chapter.)

- *Where will the application originate?* Prewritten applications can be open-source software or they can come from a vendor. The company may choose to customize prewritten open-source applications or prewritten proprietary applications from vendors. Further, it may customize applications in-house or outsource the customization. Finally, it can write totally custom applications in-house or outsource this process.

In the following sections, you will find more detail on the variety of ways that companies can acquire applications. A good rule of thumb is that an organization should consider all feasible acquisition methods in light of its own business requirements. You will learn about the following acquisition methods:

- Purchase a prewritten application.
- Customize a prewritten application.
- Lease the application.
- Use application service providers and software-as-a-service vendors.
- Use open-source software.
- Use outsourcing.
- Employ custom development.

Purchase a Prewritten Application

Many commercial software packages contain the standard features required by IT applications. Therefore, purchasing an existing package can be a cost-effective and time-saving strategy compared with custom-developing the application in-house. Nevertheless, a company should carefully consider and plan the buy option to ensure that the selected package contains all of the features necessary to address the company's current and future needs. Otherwise, these packages can quickly become obsolete. Before a company can perform this process, it must decide which features a suitable package must include.

In reality, a single software package can rarely satisfy all of an organization's needs. For this reason, a company sometimes must purchase multiple packages to fulfill different needs. It then must integrate these packages with one another as well as with its existing software. Table 14.1 summarizes the advantages and limitations of the buy option.

TABLE 14.1 Advantages and Limitations of the Buy Option

Advantages

Many different types of off-the-shelf software are available.

Software can be tried out.

The company can save much time by buying rather than building.

The company can know what it is getting before it invests in the product.

The company is not the first and only user.

Purchased software may eliminate the need to hire personnel specifically dedicated to a project.

Disadvantages

Software may not exactly meet the company's needs.

Software may be difficult or impossible to modify, or it may require huge business process changes to implement.

The company will not have control over software improvements and new versions.

Purchased software can be difficult to integrate with existing systems.

Vendors may discontinue a product or go out of business.

Software is controlled by another company with its own priorities and business considerations.

Intimate knowledge in the purchasing company is lacking about how and why the software works as it does.

Customize a Prewritten Application

Customizing existing software is an especially attractive option if the software vendor allows the company to modify the application to meet its needs. However, this option may not be attractive in cases where customization is the only method of providing the necessary flexibility to address the company's needs. It also is not the best strategy when the software is either very expensive or is likely to become obsolete in a short time. Further, customizing a prewritten application can be extremely difficult, particularly for large, complex applications. IT's About Business 14.1 recounts a disastrous effort by Marin County, California, to implement an SAP system.

IT'S ABOUT BUSINESS 14.1

A Disastrous Development Project

In 2004, Marin County in California decided to replace its aging financial management, payroll, and human resources systems with a modern SAP enterprise resource planning (ERP) system. The county solicited proposals from various companies to act as software consultants on the implementation. Thirteen companies, including Oracle, PeopleSoft, and SAP, submitted proposals. In April 2005 the county selected Deloitte Consulting based on the firm's representations concerning its in-depth knowledge of SAP systems and the extensive experience of its consultants.

Lessons From Failures From 2005 to 2009, Marin County paid increasing consulting fees to Deloitte as its staff grappled with serious fiscal problems. Essentially, the staff could not program the SAP system to perform even routine financial functions such as payroll and accounts receivable. A grand jury probe concluded that the system had cost taxpayers $28.6 million as of April 2009.

At that time, Marin County voted to stop the ongoing SAP project, implicitly acknowledging that it had wasted some $30 million on software and related implementation services from Deloitte. The Marin County Information Systems and Technology Group concluded that fixing the Deloitte-installed SAP system would cost nearly 25 percent more over a 10-year period than implementing a new system.

In 2010, Marin County filed a complaint claiming that Deloitte's representations were fraudulent. The complaint alleged that Deloitte used the county's SAP project as a training ground to provide young consultants with public sector SAP experience, at the county's expense.

Further, the complaint charged that Deloitte intentionally failed to disclose its lack of SAP and public sector skills; withheld information about critical project risks; falsely represented to the county that the SAP system was ready to "go live" as originally planned; conducted inadequate testing; and concealed the fact that it had failed to perform necessary testing, thereby ensuring that system defects would remain hidden prior to the go-live date. The county further maintained that, despite the consulting fees it had paid to Deloitte, the system continued to have crippling problems.

Deloitte filed a counterclaim over the county's failure to pay more than $550,000 in fees and interest. In its counterclaim, Deloitte maintained that it had fulfilled all of its obligations under the contract, as evidenced by the fact that all of Deloitte's work was approved by the county officials who were responsible for the project.

In December 2010, Marin County sued Deloitte and two SAP subsidiaries, alleging that Deloitte had "engaged in a pattern of racketeering activity designed to defraud the county of more than $20 million." The county's latest lawsuit also names as a defendant Ernest Culver, a former county employee who served as director on the SAP project. The county alleged that Culver interviewed for jobs at Deloitte and SAP, where he now works in SAP's Public Services division. The county alleges that during the SAP project, Culver "was approving Deloitte's deficient work on the project, approving payments, and causing Marin County to enter into new contracts with Deloitte and SAP Public Services, Inc."

In late December 2011, a judge ruled that Marin County failed to allege sufficient facts to bring a racketeering claim against SAP under the terms of the federal Racketeer Influenced and Corrupt Organizations Act (RICO). However, the judge ruled that Marin County could file an amended complaint. The judge also found that Marin County had alleged sufficient facts to bring a "plausible" bribery claim against SAP with respect to Culver. But, the judge denied SAP's motion to dismiss claims against its SAP America division.

In mid-January 2012, Marin County filed an amended complaint in federal court related to its actions against SAP, Deloitte Consulting, and Ernest Culver. The president of the Marin County Board of Supervisors stated that the board is committed to ensuring accountability for its taxpayers.

Sources: Compiled from C. Kanaracus, "Judge Tosses Racketeering Claims in Marin County Lawsuit Against SAP," *PC World*, December 28, 2011; C. Kanaracus, "Marin County Alleges SAP, Deloitte Engaged in Racketeering," *Computerworld*, February 2, 2011; M. Krigsman, "Understanding Marin County's $30 Million ERP Failure," *ZDNet*, September 2, 2010; C. Kanaracus, "Marin County to Rip and Replace Ailing SAP System," IDG News Service, August 24, 2010; M. Krigsman, "Marin County Sues Deloitte: Alleges Fraud on SAP Project," *ZDNet*, June 3, 2010; J. Vijayan, "Deloitte Hit with $30M Lawsuit over ERP Project," Computerworld, June 3, 2010; T. Claburn, "Deloitte Sued Over Failed SAP Implementation," *InformationWeek*, June 1, 2010; www.co.marin.ca.us, www.deloitte.com, accessed March 14, 2012.

Questions

1. Debate the lawsuit from the point of view of Deloitte and SAP.

2. Debate the lawsuit from the point of view of Marin County.

Lease the Application

Compared with the buy option and the option to develop applications in-house, the lease option can save a company both time and money. Of course, leased packages (like purchased packages) may not exactly fit the company's application requirements. However, as noted, vendor software generally includes the features that are most commonly needed by organizations in a given industry. Again, the company will decide which features are necessary.

It is common for interested companies to apply the 80/20 rule when evaluating vendor software. Put simply, if the software meets 80 percent of the company's needs, then the company should seriously consider changing its business processes so it can utilize the remaining 20 percent. Many times this is a better long-term solution than modifying the vendor software. Otherwise, the company will have to customize the software every time the vendor releases an updated version.

Leasing can be especially attractive to small- to medium-size enterprises (SMEs) that cannot afford major investments in IT software. Large companies may also prefer to lease packages in order to test potential IT solutions before committing to major investments. In addition, a company that does not employ sufficient IT personnel with the appropriate skills for developing custom IT applications may choose to lease instead of developing software in-house. Even those companies that employ in-house experts may not be able to afford the long wait for strategic applications to be developed in-house. Therefore, they lease (or buy) applications from external resources to establish a quicker presence in the market.

Leasing can be executed in one of three ways. The first way is to lease the application from a software developer, install it, and run it on the company's platform. The vendor can assist with the installation and frequently will offer to contract for the support and maintenance of the system. Many conventional applications are leased this way.

The other two options involve leasing an application and running it on the vendor's platform. Organizations can accomplish this process by using an application service provider or a software-as-a-service vendor.

Application Service Providers and Software-as-a-Service Vendors

An **application service provider (ASP)** is an agent or a vendor who assembles the software needed by enterprises and packages the software with services such as development, operations, and maintenance. The customer then accesses these applications via the Internet. Figure 14.3 illustrates the operation of an ASP. Note that the ASP hosts an application and a database for each customer.

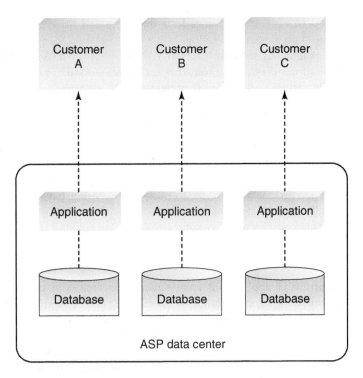

Figure 14.3 Operation of an application service provider (ASP).

Software-as-a-service (SaaS) is a method of delivering software in which a vendor hosts the applications and provides them as a service to customers over a network, typically the Internet. Customers do not own the software; rather, they pay for using it. SaaS eliminates the need for customers to install and run the application on their own computers. Therefore, SaaS customers save the expense (money, time, IT staff) of buying, operating, and maintaining the software. For example, Salesforce (www.salesforce.com), a well-known SaaS provider for customer relationship management (CRM) software solutions, provides these advantages for its customers. Figure 14.4 displays the operation of a SaaS vendor. Note that the vendor hosts an application that multiple customers can use. Further, the vendor hosts a database that is partitioned for each customer to protect the privacy and security of each customer's data.

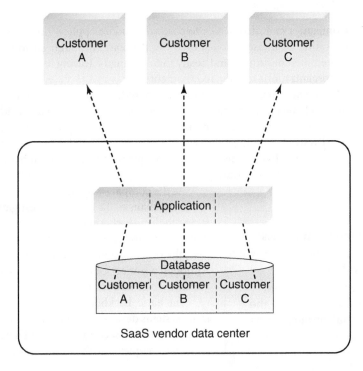

Figure 14.4 Organization of a SaaS provider.

At this point, companies have made the first three decisions and must now decide where to obtain the application. Recall that in general, for prewritten applications, they can use open-source software or obtain the software from a vendor. For customized prewritten applications, they can customize open-source software or customize vendor software. For totally custom applications, they can write the software in-house or outsource this process.

Use Open-Source Software

Organizations obtain a license to implement an open-source software product and either use it as is, customize it, or develop applications with it. Unless the company is one of the few that want to tinker with their source code, open-source applications are, basically, the same as a proprietary application except for licensing, payment, and support. Open-source is really an alternative source of applications rather than a conceptually different development option. (Open-source software is discussed in Plug IT In 2.)

Outsourcing

Acquiring IT applications from outside contractors or external organizations is called **outsourcing**. Keep in mind that outsourcing can be used in many situations. Companies may choose this strategy in certain circumstances. For example, they might want to experiment with new IT technologies without making a substantial up-front investment. They also might use outsourcing to protect their internal networks and to gain access to outside experts. One disadvantage of outsourcing is that a company's valuable corporate data may be under the control of the outsourcing vendor.

Several types of vendors offer services for creating and operating IT systems, including e-commerce applications. Many software companies, from IBM to Oracle, offer a range of outsourcing services for developing, operating, and maintaining IT applications. IT outsourcers, such as EDS, offer a variety of services. Also, the large CPA companies and management consultants—for example, Accenture—offer outsourcing services.

As the trend to outsource is on the rise, so is the trend to relocate these operations offshore, particularly in India and China. *Offshoring* can save money, but it includes risks as well. The risks depend on which services are being offshored. If a company is offshoring application development, then the major risk is poor communication between users and developers.

Custom Development

Companies may also decide to custom-build an application. They can either perform this operation in-house or outsource the process. Although custom development is usually more time-consuming and costly than buying or leasing, it often results in a better fit with the organization's specific requirements.

The development process starts when the IT steering committee (discussed previously in this chapter), having received suggestions for a new system, decides it is worth exploring. These suggestions come from users (who will be you in the near future). Understanding this process will help you get the systems that you will need. Not understanding this process will reduce your chances, because other people who understand it better will make suggestions that use up available resources.

As the company goes through the development process, the mind-set changes. In systems investigation, the organization is trying to decide whether to build something. Everyone knows it may or may not be built. In later stages of the development process, the organization is committed to building the application. Although a project can be cancelled at any time, this change in attitude is still important.

The basic, backbone methodology for custom development is the systems development life cycle (SDLC), which you will read about in the next section. Section 14.4 examines the methodologies that complement the SDLC: prototyping, joint application

BEFORE *YOU GO ON . . .*

1. Describe the four fundamental business decisions that organizations must make when acquiring information systems.

2. Discuss each of the seven development methods in this section with regard to the four business decisions that organizations must make.

development, integrated computer-assisted systems development tools, and rapid application development. You will also consider four other methodologies: agile development, end-user development, component-based development, and object-oriented development.

Apply the Concept 14.2

Background This section has discussed the many possibilities available to acquire information systems. One of the more popular methods today is software-as-a-service (SaaS). This method is popular because it removes the need for the company using the software to maintain the hardware that the software will run on. They simply need an Internet connection to access the software from the host company.

Activity Visit http://www.wiley.com/go/rainer/applytheconcept and click on the links provided for Apply the Concept 14.2. There are two videos linked there that illustrate SaaS. As you watch these videos, think about what hardware is required on both sides of the relationship. Also, consider the legal nature of the relationship given that data will likely reside with the service provider.

Deliverable

Draw an illustration that shows where the software resides, where it can be accessed, and what is required to access the software. Include a few points that discuss the importance of the legal relationship as well.

Quiz questions are assignable in WileyPLUS, and available on the Book Companion Site at http://www.wiley.com/college/rainer.

RUBY'S CLUB QUESTIONS

1. Review Table 14.1 and see if the buy option is truly the best option for Ruben and Lisa's mobile ordering system. Which aspects of the buy option will create the most problems for them?
2. Should Ruben and Lisa consider software-as-a-service as an option for their mobile ordering system, or is the information that they track too sensitive to entrust to another company?

14.3 The Traditional Systems Development Life Cycle

The **systems development life cycle (SDLC)** is the traditional systems development method that organizations use for large-scale IT projects. The SDLC is a structured framework that consists of sequential processes by which information systems are developed. For our purposes (see Figure 14.5), you identify six processes, each of which consists of clearly defined tasks:

- Systems investigation
- Systems analysis
- Systems design
- Programming and testing
- Implementation
- Operation and maintenance

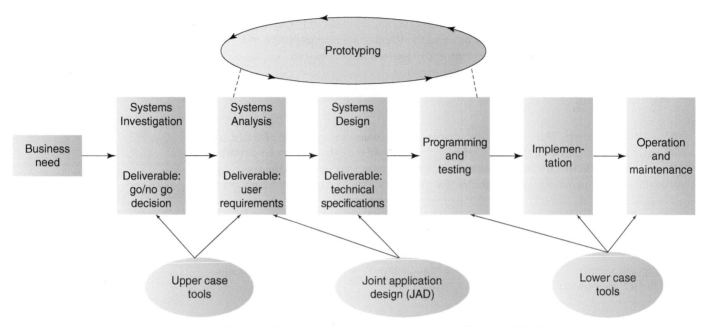

Figure 14.5 A six-stage systems development life cycle (SDLC) with supporting tools.

Other models for the SDLC contain more or fewer than the six stages presented here. The flow of tasks, however, remains largely the same. When problems occur in any phase of the SDLC, developers often must go back to previous phases.

Systems development projects produce desired results through team efforts. Development teams typically include users, systems analysts, programmers, and technical specialists. *Users* are employees from all functional areas and levels of the organization who interact with the system, either directly or indirectly. **Systems analysts** are IS professionals who specialize in analyzing and designing information systems. **Programmers** are IS professionals who either modify existing computer programs or write new programs to satisfy user requirements. **Technical specialists** are experts on a certain type of technology, such as databases or telecommunications. The **systems stakeholders** include everyone who is affected by changes in a company's information systems—for example, users and managers. All stakeholders are typically involved in systems development at various times and in varying degrees. IT's About Business 14.2 shows how Atlassian helps companies apply collaborative software development with large projects.

IT's ABOUT BUSINESS 14.2

Atlassian Helps Manage Large Software Projects

In-house software development was once the sole responsibility of companies' IT departments. Today, the process is also of concern to business managers and executives. Companies' business leaders are now involved in discussions about how well software projects are delivering. These discussions increasingly need to be open and global, as the work of development,

implementation, bug fixes, and upgrades is more divided than ever across different areas of expertise around the world. This process of cross-company discussion around software project development is called collaborative software development.

One example of a company successfully using collaborative software development is Lancôme, a division of L'Oréal that owns brands such as YSL Beauty. In 2010, Lancôme wanted to revamp its Web sites, electronic commerce, and online marketing efforts. In order to do this, the company had to figure out some way to coordinate the work of in-house employees, freelance Web developers, and creative staff in Chicago, India, and elsewhere. The company needed to figure out how to use software to manage its product development and production process.

Rather than assign this task to its overworked IT staff, Lancôme turned to Atlassian (www.atlassian.com). Atlassian sells an online application called Jira, which can track and manage large software projects.

Atlassian helped speed up Lancôme's projects and made each step of the development process visible to anyone on the team. The software also decreased the number of meetings and back-and-forth e-mails required for each project. These benefits translated into more sales on Lancôme's Web sites. After this successful experience, the company is now looking at implementing Jira in other divisions of the company.

Another company that made good use of Atlassian's product is NYSE Euronext. NYSE Euronext wanted to improve its collaboration and speed up the development process of its software projects. The firm also wanted to revamp its Web site and its mobile and e-commerce data products. When NYSE Euronext deployed Atlassian, some employees who used to jealously guard their code did not like the openness and collaboration of the new tools. These employees no longer work at NYSE Euronext. The CIO notes that the firm experienced a lot of attrition among their developers, but that it was "good attrition." Productivity in software development improved from 30 to 50 percent in just the first 6 months.

Research shows that when a company uses one Atlassian product, it will often also end up using another because of its tight integration. For example, a data management firm called Cloudera uses Jira to track bugs. Additionally, all 150 of Cloudera's employees use Atlassian's Confluence collaboration software to share information on sales, personnel issues, business development, and bug reports from Jira.

Atlassian is serious about collaboration and transparency in how people work and how companies are run. It posts an unusually large amount of company information for employees to see on an internal Web site, including financials, sales performance, and pretty much everything except employee salaries.

Atlassian applies different community collaboration rules for different kinds of content. Developer documentation is managed in a wiki where anyone with an account can post or edit content. This process works well for generating code samples and usage examples. For the core product documentation, Atlassian gives editing abilities to some members of the community, but requires those editors to first undergo a vetting process. Furthermore, individuals with editing capabilities are required to sign an agreement detailing their rights and responsibilities. Users that lack editor rights can also post comments on the formal documentation, and the editors are responsible for monitoring those comments to see if there are items that they need to add or change.

Once per quarter, Atlassian hosts its "FedEx Days," which are competitions in which employees compete to produce a product in 24 hours (typically fueled by pizza and beer). Atlassian uses a social event, rather than any promise of monetary reward, to spur innovation and creativity. FedEx the company has nothing to do with this competition, other than to be a source of inspiration. The name of the competition references FedEx's tradition of being the delivery company to choose "when it absolutely, positively has to be there overnight."

Atlassian adopted the trend of pricing Web software so cheaply that small firms are able to purchase their products. Atlassian then grows virally through companies that adopt its software. Atlassian posts all its prices on its Web site—typically $10 per month for up to 10 users for each product and up to $1,000 per month for up to 2,000 users per product. The firm invites customers to sign up with no negotiation necessary. This business model has proved its worth to Atlassian—the company now has 24,000 customers across 138 countries, including Microsoft, Oracle, Facebook, Twitter, LinkedIn, L'Oréal, and NYSE Euronext, and are growing rapidly despite competition from IBM, Microsoft, MindTouch, and Jive. Atlassian's revenue was up more than 40 percent in 2011.

Sources: Compiled from T. Geron, "We're All Coders," *Forbes*, March 12, 2012; D. Carr, "Atlassian Boosts JIRA Social Features, Social Integration," *InformationWeek*, February 22, 2012; D. Carr, "How Social Media Changes Technical Communication," *InformationWeek*, January 4, 2012; D. Carr, "How to Create a New Product in 24 Hours," *InformationWeek*, December 2, 2011; T. Taulli, "Atlassian: $100M+ Business With No Sales People?" *Forbes*, June 14, 2011; www.atlassian.com, accessed March 5, 2012.

Questions

1. Why are collaboration and transparency so important in the software development process?

2. What are potential problems that could arise when using Atlassian to manage software development? Provide specific examples to support your answer.

3. Provide an example of a software development project for which it would not be advisable to use Atlassian.

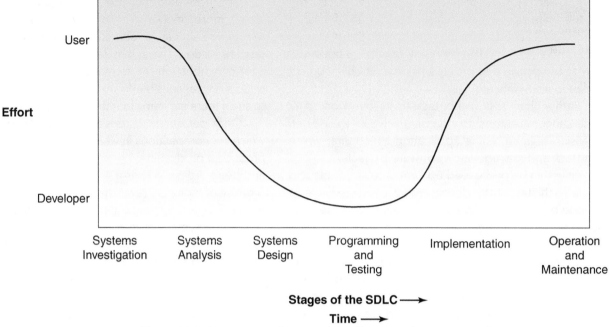

Figure 14.6 Comparison of user and developer involvement over the SDLC.

Figure 14.6 indicates that users have high involvement in the early stages of the SDLC, lower involvement in the programming and testing stage, and higher involvement in the later stages. Table 14.2 discusses the advantages and disadvantages of the SDLC.

TABLE 14.2 Advantages and Disadvantages of System Acquisition Methods

Traditional Systems Development (SDLC)

Advantages

- Forces staff to systematically go through every step in a structured process.
- Enforces quality by maintaining standards.
- Has lower probability of missing important issues in collecting user requirements.

Disadvantages

- May produce excessive documentation.
- Users may be unwilling or unable to study the approved specifications.
- Takes too long to go from the original ideas to a working system.
- Users have trouble describing requirements for a proposed system.

Prototyping

Advantages

- Helps clarify user requirements.
- Helps verify the feasibility of the design.
- Promotes genuine user participation.
- Promotes close working relationship between systems developers and users.
- Works well for ill-defined problems.
- May produce part of the final system.

Disadvantages

- May encourage inadequate problem analysis.
- Not practical with large number of users.
- User may not give up the prototype when the system is completed.
- May generate confusion about whether the system is complete and maintainable.
- System may be built quickly, which may result in lower quality.

Joint Application Design

Advantages

- Involves many users in the development process.
- Saves time.
- Greater user support for new system.
- Improved quality of the new system.
- New system easier to implement.
- New system has lower training costs.

Disadvantages

- Difficult to get all users to attend JAD meeting.
- JAD approach has all the problems associated with any group meeting.

Integrated Computer-Assisted Software Engineering

Advantages

- Can produce systems with a longer effective operational life.
- Can produce systems that closely meet user requirements.
- Can speed up the development process.
- Can produce systems that are more flexible and adaptable to changing business conditions.
- Can produce excellent documentation.

Disadvantages

- Systems often more expensive to build and maintain.
- Require more extensive and accurate definition of user requirements.
- Difficult to customize.

Rapid Application Development

Advantages

- Can speed up systems development.
- Users intensively involved from the start.
- Improves the process of rewriting legacy applications.

Disadvantages

- Produces functional components of final systems, but not final systems.

End-User Development

Advantages

- Bypasses the IS department and avoids delays.
- User controls the application and can change it as needed.
- Directly meets user requirements.
- Increased user acceptance of new system.
- Frees up IT resources.
- May create lower-quality systems.

Disadvantages

- May eventually require maintenance from IS department.
- Documentation may be inadequate.
- Poor quality control.
- System may not have adequate interfaces to existing systems.

Object-Oriented Development

Advantages

- Objects model real-world entities.
- May be able to reuse some computer code.

Disadvantages

- Works best with systems of more limited scope (i.e., with systems that do not have huge numbers of objects).

Systems Investigation

The initial stage in a traditional SDLC is systems investigation. Systems development professionals agree that the more time they invest in (1) understanding the business problem to be solved, (2) specifying the technical options for the systems, and (3) anticipating the problems they are likely to encounter during development, the greater the chances of success. For these reasons, systems investigation addresses *the business problem* (or business opportunity) by means of the feasibility study.

The main task in the systems investigation stage is the feasibility study. Organizations have three basic solutions to any business problem relating to an information system: (1) do nothing and continue to use the existing system unchanged, (2) modify or enhance the existing system, and (3) develop a new system. The **feasibility study** analyzes which of these three solutions best fits the particular business problem. It also provides a rough assessment of the project's technical, economic, and behavioral feasibility, as explained below.

- *Technical feasibility* determines whether the company can develop and/or acquire the hardware, software, and communications components needed to solve the business problem. Technical feasibility also determines whether the organization can use its existing technology to achieve the project's performance objectives.

- *Economic feasibility* determines whether the project is an acceptable financial risk and, if so, whether the organization has the necessary time and money to successfully complete the project. You have already learned about the commonly used methods to determine economic feasibility: NPV, ROI, breakeven analysis, and the business case approach.

- *Behavioral feasibility* addresses the human issues of the systems development project. Clearly, you will be heavily involved in this aspect of the feasibility study.

After the feasibility analysis is completed, a "go/no-go" decision is reached by the steering committee if there is one or by top management in the absence of a committee. The go/no-go decision does not depend solely on the feasibility analysis. Organizations often have more feasible projects than they can fund. Therefore, the firm must prioritize the feasible projects and pursue those with the highest priority. Unfunded feasible projects may not be presented to the IT department at all. These projects therefore contribute to the *hidden backlog*, which are projects that the IT department is not aware of.

If the decision is no-go, then the project either is put on the shelf until conditions are more favorable or is discarded. If the decision is go, then the project proceeds, and the systems analysis phase begins.

Systems Analysis

Once a development project has the necessary approvals from all participants, the systems analysis stage begins. **Systems analysis** is the examination of the business problem that the organization plans to solve with an information system.

The main purpose of the systems analysis stage is to gather information about the existing system in order to determine the requirements for an enhanced system or a new system. The end product of this stage, known as the *deliverable*, is a set of *system requirements*.

Arguably, the most difficult task in systems analysis is to identify the specific requirements that the system must satisfy. These requirements are often called *user requirements*, because users (meaning you) provide them. When the systems developers have accumulated the user requirements for the new system, they proceed to the systems design stage.

Systems Design

Systems design describes how the system will resolve the business problem. The deliverable of the systems design phase is the set of *technical system specifications*, which specifies the following:

- System outputs, inputs, and user interfaces
- Hardware, software, databases, telecommunications, personnel, and procedures
- A blueprint of how these components are integrated

When the system specifications are approved by all participants, they are "frozen." That is, they should not be changed. Adding functions after the project has been initiated causes **scope creep**, which endangers the project's budget and schedule. Because scope creep is expensive, successful project managers place controls on changes requested by users. These controls help to prevent runaway projects.

Programming and Testing

If the organization decides to construct the software in-house, then programming begins. **Programming** involves translating the design specifications into computer code. This process can be lengthy and time-consuming, because writing computer code is as much an art as a science. Large systems development projects can require hundreds of thousands of lines of computer code and hundreds of computer programmers. These large-scale projects employ programming teams. The teams often include functional area users, who help the programmers focus on the business problem.

Thorough and continuous testing occurs throughout the programming stage. Testing is the process that checks to see if the computer code will produce the expected and desired results. It is also intended to detect errors, or bugs, in the computer code.

Implementation

Implementation (or *deployment*) is the process of converting from an old computer system to a new one. The conversion process involves organizational change. Only end users can manage organizational change, not the MIS department. The MIS department typically does not have enough credibility with the business users to manage the change process. Organizations use three major conversion strategies: direct, pilot, and phased.

In a **direct conversion**, the old system is cut off and the new system is turned on at a certain point in time. This type of conversion is the least expensive. It is also the most risky because, if the new system does not work as planned, there is no support from the old system. Because of these risks, few systems are implemented using direct conversion. IT's About Business demonstrates the risks of a direct conversion.

 'S ABOUT BUSINESS 14.3

Virgin America Has Problems Converting to a New Reservation System

Reservation systems are the digital nervous systems of airlines. Among other things, reservation systems store, organize, and calculate flight schedules, prices, and passenger lists. To handle future growth, Virgin America (www.virginamerica.com) changed to a reservations system developed by Sabre Holdings Corporation (www.sabre.com). Sabre Holdings' system enables airlines to enter codeshare agreements, meaning that participating airlines can sell tickets for each other's flights.

Virgin America switched to its new reservations system on October 28, 2011. The airline had informed customers that its Web site would be down for 12 to 24 hours as it transferred 239,000 reservations and

created two million new frequent-flier accounts. But, when the Web site went live again, problems were widespread and persisted for several weeks, disrupting the airline's busy Thanksgiving travel period.

© ansonsaw/iStockphoto

Most Virgin America customers were unable to modify their flights online and many complained that they were overcharged, could not book flights or check in online. Customers also complained that they could not select seats or book flights using frequent-flyer miles. These Web site issues caused long lines at Virgin America ticket counters in airports across the country.

Lessons From IT Failures

To further compound the issue, Web site error messages directed customers to call the airline, but phone lines were clogged with long waits and some calls were disconnected altogether. Virgin America call centers were overwhelmed, despite temporarily doubling their call-center staff.

Fortunately, the airline was able to fix almost all of its Web-related problems by December 1, 2011. They placated their customer base by waiving certain fees and awarding free flights to about 56,000 affected fliers, for a total value of more than $7 million.

Sources: Compiled from B. Mutzabaugh, "Virgin America Dogged by Reservation Glitches," *USA Today*, December 22, 2011; J. Nicas, "Jet Lagged: Web Glitches Still Plague Virgin America,"

The Wall Street Journal, November 23, 2011; H. McCracken, "Virgin America's Web Site Meltdown: Four Weeks and Counting," *Technologizer,* November 22, 2011; www.virginamerica.com, www.sabre.com, accessed March 21, 2012.

Questions

1. What could Virgin America have done to reduce the risks associated with converting its reservation system? Provide several specific examples to support your answer.

2. What are the potential long-term problems for Virgin America that could result from its difficulties converting its system?

A **pilot conversion** introduces the new system in one part of the organization, such as in one plant or one functional area. The new system runs for a period of time and is then assessed. If the assessment confirms that the system is working properly, then the system is implemented in other parts of the organization.

A **phased conversion** introduces components of the new system, such as individual modules, in stages. Each module is assessed. If it works properly, then other modules are introduced, until the entire new system is operational. Large organizations commonly combine the pilot and phased approaches. That is, they execute a phased conversion using a pilot group for each phase.

A fourth strategy is *parallel conversion,* in which the old and new systems operate simultaneously for a time. This strategy is seldom used today. One reason is that parallel conversion is totally impractical when both the old and new systems are online. Imagine that you are finishing an order on Amazon, only to be told, "Before your order can be entered here, you must provide all the same information again, in a different form, and on a different set of screens." The results would be disastrous for Amazon.

Operation and Maintenance

After the new system is implemented, it will operate for a period of time, until (like the old system it replaced) it no longer meets its objectives. Once the new system's operations are stabilized, the company performs audits to assess the system's capabilities and to determine if it is being utilized correctly.

Systems require several types of maintenance. The first type is *debugging* the program, a process that continues throughout the life of the system. The second type is *updating* the system to accommodate changes in business conditions. An example is adjusting to new governmental regulations, such as changes in tax rates. These corrections and upgrades usually do not add any new functions. Instead, they simply help the system to continue meeting its objectives. In contrast, the third type of maintenance *adds new functions* to the existing system without disturbing its operation.

BEFORE YOU GO ON . . .

1. Define *feasibility study.*
2. What is the difference between systems analysis and systems design?
3. Describe structured programming.
4. What are the four conversion methods?

Apply the Concept **14.3**

Background The systems development life cycle uses a very systematic approach where each stage is built from work done at an earlier stage. It is an excellent model to follow, assuming the right decision is made in the feasibility study. The feasibility study looks at three different aspects of the organization. First is technical feasibility (Can it be done?), then financial feasibility (Can we afford it?), and last is behavioral feasibility (Will the people use it?). If the answer to any of these is "No," then the new system must be seriously reconsidered.

Activity Consider the following scenario. A customer pulls up to a gas station and chooses to pay at the pump. After he has swiped his card, he begins pumping gas. While standing at the pump, he is asked if he would like to add a beverage to the gas bill he has already paid. Or, he may choose a $5 credit that would print so he could take inside and redeem for merchandise. If he chooses the beverage, it would simply be added to the bill and a receipt printed. If he chooses the dollar amount, he would take the credit slip into the store and redeem it for goods.

The next time you fill up your car, go inside and speak to the manager about this idea. How did he respond? Do they think it is technically feasible? Would it be financially beneficial to set this up? Would people use it or would customers just pay at the pump and leave?

Deliverable

Build a table that has your assumed answers and the manager's answers. Your table will look like the one below.

Feasibility Area	Personal Thoughts	Manager's Thoughts
Technical		
Financial		
Behavioral		

Quiz questions are assignable in WileyPLUS, and available on the Book Companion Site at http://www.wiley.com/college/rainer.

RUBY'S CLUB QUESTIONS

1. Have Ruben and Lisa already engaged in any stages of the SDLC?
2. Do you think there is enough time to devote to this type of system development?
3. Who should Ruben and Lisa include in their behavioral feasibility analysis? Does anyone outside of Ruby's employment need special consideration?

14.4 Alternative Methods and Tools for Systems Development

Alternative methods for systems development include joint application design, rapid application development, agile development, and end-user development.

Joint Application Design

Joint application design (JAD) is a group-based tool for collecting user requirements and creating system designs. It is most often used within the systems analysis and systems design stages of the SDLC. JAD involves a group meeting attended by the analysts and all of the users. It is basically a group decision-making process that can be conducted manually or via the computer. During this meeting, all users jointly define and agree on the systems requirements. This process saves a tremendous amount of time. Table 14.2 lists the advantages and disadvantages of the JAD process.

Rapid Application Development

Rapid application development (RAD) is a systems development method that can combine JAD, prototyping, and integrated computer-assisted software engineering (ICASE) tools (discussed later in this section) to rapidly produce a high-quality system. In the first RAD stage, developers use JAD sessions to collect system requirements. This strategy ensures that users are intensively involved early on. The development process in RAD is iterative, similar to prototyping. That is, requirements, designs, and the system itself are developed and then undergo a series, or sequence, of improvements. RAD uses ICASE tools to quickly structure requirements and develop prototypes. As the prototypes are developed and refined, users review them in additional JAD sessions. RAD produces the functional components of a final system, rather than prototypes. To understand how RAD functions and how it differs from SDLC, see Figure 14.7. Table 14.2 highlights the advantages and disadvantages of the RAD process.

Agile Development

Agile development is a software development methodology that delivers functionality in rapid iterations, which are usually measured in weeks. To be successful, this methodology requires frequent communication, development, testing, and delivery. Agile development focuses on rapid development and frequent user contact to create software that addresses the needs of business users. This software does not have to include every possible feature the user will require. Rather, it must meet only the user's more important and immediate needs. It can be updated later to introduce additional functions as they become necessary. The core tenet of agile development is to do only what you have to do to be successful right now.

One type of agile development uses the *scrum approach*. A key principle of scrum is that during a project users can change their minds about what they want and need. Scrum acknowledges that a development problem cannot be fully understood or defined from the start. Therefore, scrum focuses on maximizing the development team's ability to deliver iterations quickly and to respond effectively to additional user requirements as they emerge.

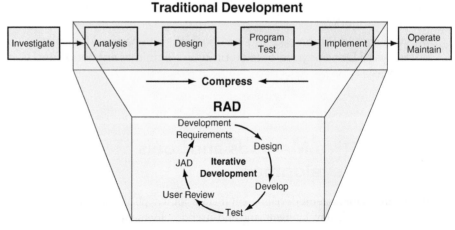

Figure 14.7 A rapid prototyping development process versus SDLC. (*Source:* www.datawarehouse-training.com/Methodologies/rapid-application-development.)

Scrum contains sets of practices and predefined roles. The primary roles are these:

- The *Scrum Master*: maintains the processes (typically replaces a project manager)
- The *Product Owner*: represents the business users and any other stakeholders in the project
- The *Team*: a cross-functional group of about seven people who perform the actual analysis, design, coding, implementation, testing, and so on

Scrum works this way: During each sprint—typically a 2- to 4-week period—the team creates a potentially shippable product increment, such as working and tested software. The set of features that goes into each sprint come from the product backlog, which is a prioritized set of high-level work requirements to be completed.

The sprint planning meeting determines which backlog items will be addressed during a sprint. During this meeting, the Product Owner informs the team of the items in the product backlog that he or she wants completed. The team members then determine how many of these projects they can commit to during the next sprint and they record this information in the sprint backlog.

During a sprint, no one is allowed to change the sprint backlog, which means that the requirements are frozen for the sprint. Each sprint must end on time. If the requirements are not completed for any reason, they are left out and returned to the product backlog. After each sprint is completed, the team demonstrates how to use the software. IT's About Business 14.4 illustrates how GE Healthcare moved from the systems development life cycle to agile development.

S ABOUT BUSINESS 14.4

GE Healthcare Switches from Waterfall to Agile

GE Healthcare (www.gehealthcare.com) is a $17-billion business unit of General Electric (www.ge.com) that manufactures products designed to help clinicians be more productive. These technologies, which range from high-definition CT scanners to diagnostic pharmaceutical devices, are developed by the company's Imaging Solutions unit. Imaging Solutions employs 375 engineers who support 18 high-tech products. Unfortunately, this unit has experienced several difficulties.

First, Imaging Solutions struggled with the predictability of its systems development project execution. The cycle time on projects was too long to begin with (from 12 to 24 months) and often experienced significant delays beyond the already-long cycle time. These long cycle times frequently caused the business to add features beyond the initial user requirements, reflecting concerns that customers could not wait for a new system to have these features. This coping mechanism, in turn, often increased a project's scope, causing further delays and increasing the project cycle time even more. Longer cycle times increase the risk that the user requirements gathered at the beginning of the project will be out-of-date by the time the product reaches the market.

© fStop_Images/iStockphoto

In addition, Imaging Solutions' systems development process followed the systems development life cycle (SDLC) approach. In other words, Imaging Solutions began its process with investigation, systems analysis, and systems design. After completing these steps, the unit then conducted a formal design review. After obtaining the various approvals for the design, the engineers began programming new systems.

Programming at Imaging Solutions typically took several months, after which the development team would release the new system into a test environment to collect user feedback. This point in the process was usually the first time that users came into contact with the new system. After the team accumulated and incorporated user input, it continued the testing effort prior to implementing the new system.

The problem with the SDLC approach was that the system did not have the opportunity to incorporate user-requested modifications until very late in the project cycle. As a result, any significant errors could require the team to change the design completely—in effect, to start over. This approach wasted a great deal of time and effort, and often caused significant delays in projects.

To address these issues, Imaging Solutions replaced its SDLC approach with an agile-based scrum initiative. Scrum (discussed in detail in this chapter) focuses on maximizing the development team's ability to deliver iterations quickly and respond effectively to additional user requirements as they emerge. In contrast to SDLC, agile development involves adding functionality in a series of phases and then testing the product after each phase is completed. The Imaging Solutions unit particularly liked the idea of demonstrating each phase's functionality to users and then receiving immediate feedback. This approach was much more economical and efficient than receiving feedback at the point when the system was nearing completion.

Imaging Solutions launched its move to agile development with a single development team and a pilot project that had a manageable scope and a luxurious 4-month deadline. The project was substantial enough that the team could learn scrum skills while delivering a valuable product, but manageable enough to be a good first test run. The team also established clear criteria by which to measure its success so that team members could objectively evaluate whether they had achieved their goals.

The pilot project was concluded successfully and contained all of the correct features and functionality. The release, however, was one month past the desired roll-out date, so Imaging Solutions is still working on its predictability of delivery.

This pilot project informed Imaging Solutions that the company could adopt agile development, but only with certain limitations. Specifically, the rigors of operating in a regulated industry required it to deploy a hybrid development process that involved more initial planning and testing than would be found in other agile organizations.

Following the resolution of the pilot project, Imaging Solutions formed 10 scrum teams of 7 to 9 people each. Every 2 weeks, the teams met on Wednesday mornings to conduct increment reviews and on Wednesday afternoons to hold their planning meetings for the next increment. This process ensured that teams were sharing knowledge with their fellow team members and were aware of what was being done outside of their own particular team.

To obtain maximum benefits from the agile system, Imaging Solutions had to transform its culture somewhat by modifying the role of managers and individual contributors on scrum teams. For example, Imaging Solutions managers can no longer use a command-and-control style of management and must instead concentrate on assembling empowered teams.

These cultural and process changes have resulted in positive results for Imaging Solutions. Obtaining user feedback early and often has enabled Imaging Solutions to prioritize features correctly. For instance, in one example, the new system helped a team identify a clinical workflow it previously was not aware of. Insights such as this one will continue to allow Imaging Solutions to develop products that will be successful in the market and release those products in a timely manner, thereby growing profitability and credibility as a company.

Sources: Compiled from K. Liang, "What Jobs Are Available for Software Engineers Who Want to Advance Medical Research?" *Forbes*, March 2, 2012; J. Hammond, "Customer-Centric Development: It's Now or Never for IT Shops," *InformationWeek*, April 26, 2011; S. Denning, "Six Common Mistakes That Salesforce.com Didn't Make," *Forbes*, April 18, 2011; A. Deitsch and R. Hughes, "GE Healthcare Goes Agile," *InformationWeek*, December 6, 2010; J. Vijayan, "The Grill: John Burke," *Computerworld*, September 13, 2010; J. Kobelius, "Agile Data Warehousing: Do You Scrum?" *InformationWeek*, July 21, 2010; www.ge.com, www.gehealthcare.com, www.rallydev.com, accessed March 17, 2012.

Questions

1. The health care industry will be in turmoil for a few years to come. Because of the federal government's push for health care providers to maintain electronic health records, many physicians' practices, both large and small, are acquiring new information systems. What risks can you think of that are associated with digitizing such private information? Do you feel more comfortable with your medical records in a paper file on a shelf or in a computer?

2. Search for the phrase *scope creep* and relate your findings. How would this phenomenon cause a problem in the acquisition and implementation of information systems?

End-User Development

End-user development is an approach in which the organization's end users develop their own applications with little or no formal assistance from the IT department. Table 14.2 lists the advantages and disadvantages of end-user development.

Tools for Systems Development

Several tools can be used with various systems development methods. These tools include prototyping, integrated computer-assisted software engineering (ICASE), component-based development, and object-oriented development.

Prototyping. The **prototyping** approach defines an initial list of user requirements, builds a model of the system, and then refines the system in several iterations based on users' feedback. Developers do not try to obtain a complete set of user specifications for the system at the outset, and they do not plan to develop the system all at once. Instead, they quickly develop a smaller version of the system known as a **prototype**. A prototype can take two forms. In some cases, it contains only the components of the new system that are of most interest to the users. In other cases, it is a small-scale working model of the entire system.

Users make suggestions for improving the prototype, based on their experiences with it. The developers then review the prototype with the users and use their suggestions to refine the prototype. This process continues through several iterations until the users approve the system or it becomes apparent that the system cannot meet the users' needs. If the system is viable, then the developers can use the prototype to build the full system. One typical use of prototyping is to develop screens that a user will see and interact with. Table 14.2 describes the advantages and disadvantages of the prototyping approach.

A practical problem with prototyping is that a prototype usually looks more complete than it is. It may not use the real database, it usually does not have the necessary error checking, and it almost never includes the necessary security features. Users who review a prototype that resembles the finished system may not recognize these problems. Consequently, they might have unrealistic expectations about how close the actual system is to completion.

Integrated Computer-Assisted Software Engineering Tools. **Computer-aided software engineering (CASE)** is a group of tools that automate many of the tasks in the SDLC. The tools that are used to automate the early stages of the SDLC (systems investigation, analysis, and design) are called upper CASE tools. The tools used to automate later stages in the SDLC (programming, testing, operation, and maintenance) are called lower CASE tools. CASE tools that provide links between upper CASE and lower CASE tools are called **integrated CASE (ICASE) tools.** Table 14.2 lists the advantages and disadvantages of ICASE tools.

Component-Based Development. **Component-based development** uses standard components to build applications. Components are reusable applications that generally have one specific function, such as a shopping cart, user authentication, or a catalog. Component-based development is closely linked with the idea of Web services and service-oriented architectures, which you see in Plug IT In 3.

Many startup companies are pursuing the idea of component-based application development, or less programming and more assembly. An example of these companies is Ning (www.ning.com), which allows organizations to create, customize, and share their own social network.

Object-Oriented Development. **Object-oriented development** is based on a different view of computer systems than the perception that characterizes traditional development approaches. Traditional approaches can produce a system that performs the original task but may not be suited for handling other tasks. This observation applies even when these other tasks involve the same real-world entities. For example, a billing system will handle billing but probably cannot be adapted to handle mailings for the marketing department or to generate leads for the sales force. This is true even though the billing, marketing, and sales functions all use similar data, including customer names, addresses, and purchases. In contrast, an *object-oriented (OO) system* begins not with the task to be performed but with the aspects of the real world that must be modeled to perform that task. Therefore, in our example, if the firm has a good model of its customers and its interactions with them, then it can use this model equally well for billings, mailings, and sales leads.

The development process for an object-oriented system begins with a feasibility study and an analysis of the existing system. Systems developers identify the *objects* in the new system—the fundamental elements in OO analysis and design. Each object represents a tangible, real-world entity, such as a customer, bank account, student, or course. Objects have *properties*, or *data values*. For example, a customer has an identification number, a name, an address, an account number(s), and so on. Objects also contain the *operations* that can be performed on their properties. For example, operations that can be performed on the customer object may include obtain-account-balance, open-account, withdraw-funds, and so on. Operations are also referred to as *behaviors*.

This approach enables OO analysts to define all the relevant objects needed for the new system, including their properties and operations. The analysts then model how the objects interact to meet the objectives of the new system. In some cases, analysts can reuse existing objects from other applications (or from a library of objects) in the new system. This process saves the analysts the time they otherwise would spend coding these objects. In most cases, however, even with object reuse, some coding will be necessary to customize the objects and their interactions for the new system.

You have studied many methods that can be used to acquire new systems. Table 14.2 provides an overview of the advantages and disadvantages of these methods.

BEFORE YOU GO ON . . .

1. Describe the tools that augment the traditional SDLC.
2. Describe the alternate methods that can be used for systems development, other than the SDLC.

Apply the Concept 14.4

Background Prototyping is a method of systems development that allows an idea to get into a testable form very quickly. Often, ideas can go from discussion to prototype at the dinner table in a simple sketch on a napkin.

Activity Visit http://www.wiley.com/go/rainer/applytheconept and click on the link provided for Apply the Concept 14.4. This will show you a Vimeo video about prototyping.

Imagine that you are an app developer for iPhone apps. At lunch the other day someone mentioned a very cool idea for a new camera app that would allow you to take pictures by opening the app and saying "click" rather than pushing a button. This would also allow you to take remote pictures when you are ready rather than using a timer.

What should this app look like? Draw up a sketch of at least two screens. First, the camera screen, second the options screen. Discuss this with a couple of your friends and see what they think. Try to find someone who has an iPhone and get that person's ideas on your prototype.

Deliverable

Based on your friends' reviews, write up a revision plan for your app. Submit your sketches and your plan for revisions to your professor.

Quiz questions are assignable in WileyPLUS, and available on the Book Companion Site at http://www.wiley.com/college/rainer.

RUBY'S CLUB QUESTIONS

1. Do any of the prototyping methods of development seem to fit well within Ruben and Lisa's needs?
2. After reviewing Table 14.2, which method do you feel is most suited to the needs of this mobile ordering system?

14.5 Vendor and Software Selection

Few organizations, especially small- to medium-size enterprises, have the time, financial resources, or technical expertise required to develop today's complex IT or e-business systems. For this reason, business firms increasingly rely on outside vendors to provide software, hardware, and technical expertise. Consequently, selecting and managing these vendors and their software offerings has become a major aspect of developing an IT application. The following six steps in selecting a software vendor and an application package are useful.

Step 1: Identify Potential Vendors. Companies can identify potential software application vendors through various sources:

- Software catalogs
- Lists provided by hardware vendors
- Technical and trade journals
- Consultants and industry analysts experienced in the application area
- Peers in other companies
- Web searches

These sources often yield so many vendors and packages that the company must use some evaluation criteria to eliminate all but the most promising ones from further consideration. For example, it can eliminate vendors that are too small or have a questionable reputation. Also, it can eliminate packages that do not have the required features or are not compatible with the company's existing hardware and/or software.

Step 2: Determine the Evaluation Criteria. The most difficult and crucial task in evaluating a vendor and a software package is to select a detailed set of evaluation criteria. Some areas in which a customer should develop detailed criteria are these:

- Characteristics of the vendor
- Functional requirements of the system
- Technical requirements that the software must satisfy
- Amount and quality of documentation provided
- Vendor support of the package

These criteria should be set out in a **request for proposal (RFP)**. An RFP is a document that is sent to potential vendors inviting them to submit a proposal that describes their software package and explains how it would meet the company's needs. The RFP provides the vendors with information about the objectives and requirements of the system. Specifically, it describes the environment in which the system will be used, the general criteria that the company will use to evaluate the proposals, and the conditions for submitting proposals. The RFP may also request a list of current users of the package whom the company may contact. Finally, it can require the vendor to demonstrate the package at the company's facilities using specified inputs and data files.

Step 3: Evaluate Vendors and Packages. The responses to an RFP generate massive volumes of information that the company must evaluate. The goal of this evaluation is to determine the gaps between the company's needs (as specified by the requirements) and the capabilities of the vendors and their application packages. Often, the company gives the vendors and packages an overall score by (1) assigning an importance weight to each of the criteria, (2) ranking the vendors on each of the weighted criteria (say 1 to 10), and then (3) multiplying the ranks by the associated weights. The company can then shorten the list of potential suppliers to include only those vendors who achieved the highest overall scores.

Step 4: Choose the Vendor and Package. Once the company has shortened the list of potential suppliers, it can begin negotiations with these vendors to determine how their packages might be modified to remove any discrepancies with the company's IT needs. Thus, one of the most important factors in the decision is the additional development effort that may be required to tailor the system to the company's needs or to integrate it into the company's computing environment. The company must also consider the opinions of both the users and the IT personnel who will have to support the system.

TABLE 14.3 Criteria for Selecting a Software Application Package

Functionality (Does the package do what the organization needs?)

Cost and financial terms

Upgrade policy and cost

Vendor's reputation and availability for help

Vendor's success stories (Visit the vendor's Web site, contact clients.)

System flexibility

Ease of Internet interface

Availability and quality of documentation

Necessary hardware and networking resources

Required training (check if provided by vendor)

Security

Learning (speed of) for developers and users

Graphical presentation

Data handling

System-required hardware

Several methods are commonly used for selecting software. For a list of general criteria, see Table 14.3.

Step 5: Negotiate a Contract. The contract with the software vendor is very important. It specifies both the price of the software and the type and amount of support that the vendor agrees to provide. The contract will be the only recourse if either the system or the vendor does not perform as expected. It is essential, then, that the contract directly references the proposal, because this is the vehicle that the vendor used to document the functionality supported in its system. Furthermore, if the vendor is modifying the software to tailor it to the company's needs, the contract must include detailed specifications (essentially the requirements) of the modifications. Finally, the contract should describe in detail the acceptance tests that the software package must pass.

Contracts are legal documents, and they can be quite tricky. For this reason, companies might need the services of experienced contract negotiators and lawyers. Many organizations employ software-purchasing specialists who assist in negotiations and write or approve the contract. These specialists should be involved in the selection process from the start.

Step 6: Establish a Service-Level Agreement. **Service-level agreements (SLAs)** are formal agreements that specify how work is to be divided between the company and its vendors. These specifications are based on a set of agreed-upon milestones, quality checks, and what-if situations. They describe how quality checks will be made and what is to be done in case of disputes. SLAs accomplish these goals by (1) defining the responsibilities of both partners, (2) providing a framework for designing support services, and (3) allowing the company to retain as much control as possible over its own systems. SLAs include such issues as performance, availability, backup and recovery, upgrades, and hardware and software ownership. For example, the SLA might specify that the application service provider have its system available to the customer 99.9 percent of the time.

BEFORE YOU GO ON . . .

1. List the major steps of selection of a vendor and a software package.
2. Describe a request for proposal (RFP).
3. Explain why SLAs play an important role in systems development.

Apply the Concept 14.5

Background Part of acquiring information systems is determining exactly what you need! When it is decided that there will be a third party involved (in designing or building your system), a request for proposal, or RFP, is often posted. This RFP states all of the expectations of the company, its timeline, and perhaps its budgetary restrictions.

Activity Visit http://www.wiley.com/go/rainer/applytheconcept and click on the link provided for Apply the Concept 14.5. This will take you to a Web site that specializes in helping small and medium-sized enterprises (SME) with planning, documentation, examples, etc. In particular, this page provides an example RFP. Download the sample and review it.

Imagine that you are on the receiving end of the proposal, meaning that you are the company wanting to place a bid for the job. Based on this RFP, what questions might you have? Is there any further information you would need to complete a proposal?

Deliverable

Build out your list of questions and submit them to your professor. Be sure to include discussions of whether you felt the RFP was complete and/or adequate. Considering that this is a sample RFP, do you think the SME Toolkit Web site is doing a good job?

Quiz questions are assignable in WileyPLUS, and available on the Book Companion Site at http://www.wiley.com/college/rainer.

RUBY'S CLUB QUESTIONS

1. What information would Ruben and Lisa need to include in an RFP?
2. Search the Web for SLAs and see if you can find some key words that Ruben and Lisa will need to include in their document.

What's in IT for ME?

FOR THE ACCOUNTING MAJOR

Accounting personnel help perform the cost–benefit analyses on proposed projects. They may also monitor ongoing project costs to keep them within budget. Accounting personnel undoubtedly will find themselves involved with systems development at various points throughout their careers.

FOR THE FINANCE MAJOR

Finance personnel are frequently involved with the financial issues that accompany any large-scale systems development project (for example, budgeting). They also are involved in cost–benefit and risk analyses. To perform these tasks they need to stay abreast of the emerging techniques used to determine project costs and ROI. Finally, because they must manage vast amounts of information, finance departments are also common recipients of new systems.

FOR THE MARKETING MAJOR

In most organizations, marketing, like finance, involves massive amounts of data and information. Like finance, then, marketing is also a hotbed of systems development. Marketing personnel will increasingly find themselves participating on systems development teams. Such involvement increasingly means helping to develop systems, especially Web-based systems that reach out directly from the organization to its customers.

FOR THE

PRODUCTION/OPERATIONS MANAGEMENT MAJOR

Participation on development teams is also a common role for production/ operations people. Manufacturing is becoming increasingly computerized and integrated with other allied systems, from design to logistics to customer support. Production systems interface frequently with marketing, finance, and human resources. In addition, they may be part of a larger, enterprisewide system. Also, many end users in POM either develop their own systems or collaborate with IT personnel on specific applications.

FOR THE

HUMAN RESOURCES MANAGEMENT MAJOR

The human resources department is closely involved with several aspects of the systems acquisitions process. Acquiring new systems may require hiring new employees, changing job descriptions, or terminating employees. Human resources staff perform all of these tasks. Further, if the organization hires consultants for the development project, or outsources it, the human resources department may handle the contracts with these suppliers.

FOR THE MIS MAJOR

Regardless of the approach that the organization adopts for acquiring new systems, the MIS department spearheads it. If the organization chooses either to buy or to lease the application, the MIS department leads in examining the offerings of the various vendors and in negotiating with the vendors. If the organization chooses to develop the application in-house, then the process falls to the MIS department. MIS analysts work closely with users to develop their information requirements. MIS programmers then write the computer code, test it, and implement the new system.

SUMMARY

1. **Discuss the different cost/benefit analyses that companies must take into account when formulating an IT strategic plan.**

   The four common approaches to cost–benefit analysis are these:

   > *The net present value (NPV)* method converts future values of benefits to their present-value equivalent by "discounting" them at the organization's cost of funds. They can then compare the present value of the future benefits to the cost required to achieve those benefits to determine whether the benefits exceed the costs.

   > *Return on investment (ROI)* measures management's effectiveness in generating profits with its available assets. ROI is calculated by dividing net income attributable to a project by the average assets invested in the

   project. ROI is a percentage, and the higher the percentage return, the better.

   > *Breakeven analysis* determines the point at which the cumulative dollar value of the benefits from a project equals the investment made in the project.

   > In the *business case approach,* system developers write a business case to justify funding one or more specific applications or projects.

2. **Discuss the four business decisions that companies must make when they acquire new applications.**

   > *How much computer code does the company want to write?* A company can choose use a totally prewritten application (to write no computer code), to customize a prewritten application (to write some computer code), or to customize an entire application (write all new computer code).

> *How will the company pay for the application?* Once the company has decided how much computer code to write, it must decide how to pay for it. With prewritten applications or customized prewritten applications, companies can buy them or lease them. With totally custom applications, companies use internal funding.

> *Where will the application run?* Companies must now decide where to run the application. The company may run the application on its own platform or run the application on someone else's platform (use either a software-as-a-service vendor or an application service provider).

> *Where will the application originate?* Prewritten applications can be open-source software or come from a vendor. Companies may choose to customize prewritten open-source applications or prewritten proprietary applications from vendors. Companies may customize applications in-house or outsource the customization. They also can write totally custom applications in-house or outsource this process.

3. **Enumerate the primary tasks and importance of each of the six processes involved in the systems development life cycle.**

The six processes are these:

> *Systems investigation:* Addresses the business problem (or business opportunity) by means of the feasibility study; main task in the systems investigation stage is the feasibility study.

> *Systems analysis:* Examines the business problem that the organization plans to solve with an information system; main purpose is to gather information about the existing system in order to determine the requirements for the new system; end product of this stage, known as the "deliverable," is a set of system requirements.

> *Systems design:* Describes how the system will resolve the business problem; deliverable is the set of technical system specifications.

> *Programming and testing:* Programming translates the design specifications into computer code; testing checks to see if the computer code will produce the expected and desired results and detects errors, or bugs, in the computer code; deliverable is the new application.

> *Implementation:* The process of converting from the old system to the new system via three major conversion strategies: direct, pilot, and phased; deliverable is properly working application.

> *Operation and maintenance:* Types of maintenance include debugging, updating, and adding new functions when needed.

4. **Describe alternative development methods and tools that augment development methods.**

These are the *alternative methods*:

> *Joint application design (JAD)* is a group-based tool for collecting user requirements and creating system designs.

> *Rapid application development (RAD)* is a systems development method that can combine JAD, prototyping, and ICASE tools to rapidly produce a high-quality system.

> *Agile development* is a software development methodology that delivers functionality in rapid iterations, which are usually measured in weeks.

> *End-user development* refers to an organization's end users developing their own applications with little or no formal assistance from the IT department.

These are the *tools*:

> The *prototyping* approach defines an initial list of user requirements, builds a model of the system, and then improves the system in several iterations based on users' feedback.

> *Integrated computer-aided software engineering (ICASE)* combines upper CASE tools (automate systems investigation, analysis, and design) and lower CASE tools (programming, testing, operation, and maintenance).

> *Component-based development* uses standard components to build applications. Components are reusable applications that generally have one specific function, such as a shopping cart, user authentication, or a catalog.

> *Object-oriented development* begins with the aspects of the real world that must be modeled to perform that task. Systems developers identify the *objects* in the new system. Each object represents a tangible, real-world entity, such as a customer, bank account, student, or course. Objects have *properties*, or *data values*. Objects also contain the *operations* that can be performed on their properties.

Table 14.2 shows advantages and disadvantages of alternative methods and tools.

5. **Analyze the process of vendor and software selection.**

The process of vendor and software selection is composed of six steps:

> Identify potential vendors.

> Determine evaluation criteria.

> Evaluate vendors and packages.

> Choose the vendor and package.

> Negotiate a contract.

> Establish service-level agreements.

>>> **CHAPTER GLOSSARY**

agile development A software development methodology that delivers functionality in rapid iterations, measured in weeks, requiring frequent communication, development, testing, and delivery.

application portfolio The set of recommended applications resulting from the planning and justification process in application development.

application service provider (ASP) An agent or vendor who assembles the software needed by enterprises and packages them with outsourced development, operations, maintenance, and other services.

component-based development A software development methodology that uses standard components to build applications.

computer-aided software engineering (CASE) Development approach that uses specialized tools to automate many of the tasks in the SDLC; upper CASE tools automate the early stages of the SDLC and lower CASE tools automate the later stages.

direct conversion Implementation process in which the old system is cut off and the new system is turned on at a certain point in time.

end-user development Approach in which the organization's end users develop their own applications with little or no formal assistance from the IT department.

feasibility study Investigation that gauges the probability of success of a proposed project and provides a rough assessment of the project's feasibility.

implementation The process of converting from an old computer system to a new one.

integrated CASE (ICASE) tools CASE tools that provide links between upper CASE and lower CASE tools.

IS operational plan Consists of a clear set of projects that the IS department and the functional area managers will execute in support of the IT strategic plan.

IT steering committee A committee, comprised of a group of managers and staff representing various organizational units, set up to establish IT priorities and to ensure that the MIS function is meeting the needs of the enterprise.

IT strategic plan A set of long-range goals that describe the IT infrastructure and major IT initiatives needed to achieve the goals of the organization.

joint application design (JAD) A group-based tool for collecting user requirements and creating system designs.

object-oriented development A systems development methodology that begins with aspects of the real world that must be modeled to perform a task.

outsourcing Use of outside contractors or external organizations to acquire IT services.

phased conversion Implementation process that introduces components of the new system in stages, until the entire new system is operational.

pilot conversion Implementation process that introduces the new system in one part of the organization on a trial basis; when the new system is working properly, it is introduced in other parts of the organization.

programmers IS professionals who modify existing computer programs or write new computer programs to satisfy user requirements.

programming The translation of a system's design specifications into computer code.

prototype A small-scale working model of an entire system or a model that contains only the components of the new system that are of most interest to the users.

prototyping An approach that defines an initial list of user requirements, builds a prototype system, and then improves the system in several iterations based on users' feedback.

rapid application development (RAD) A development method that uses special tools and an iterative approach to rapidly produce a high-quality system.

request for proposal (RFP) Document that is sent to potential vendors inviting them to submit a proposal describing their software package and how it would meet the company's needs.

scope creep Adding functions to an information system after the project has begun.

service-level agreements (SLAs) Formal agreements regarding the division of work between a company and its vendors.

software-as-a-service (SaaS) A method of delivering software in which a vendor hosts the applications and provides them as a service to customers over a network, typically the Internet.

systems analysis The examination of the business problem that the organization plans to solve with an information system.

systems analysts IS professionals who specialize in analyzing and designing information systems.

systems design Describes how the new system will resolve the business problem.

systems development life cycle (SDLC) Traditional structured framework, used for large IT projects, that consists of sequential processes by which information systems are developed.

systems stakeholders All people who are affected by changes in information systems.

technical specialists Experts on a certain type of technology, such as databases or telecommunications.

>>> DISCUSSION QUESTIONS

1. Discuss the advantages of a lease option over a buy option.

2. Why is it important for all business managers to understand the issues of IT resource acquisition?

3. Why is it important for everyone in business organizations to have a basic understanding of the systems development process?

4. Should prototyping be used on every systems development project? Why or why not?

5. Discuss the various types of feasibility studies. Why are they all needed?

6. Discuss the issue of assessing intangible benefits and the proposed solutions.

7. Discuss the reasons why end-user-developed information systems can be of poor quality. What can be done to improve this situation?

>>> PROBLEM-SOLVING ACTIVITIES

1. Access www.ecommerce-guide.com. Find the product review area. Read reviews of three software payment solutions. Assess them as possible components.

2. Use an Internet search engine to obtain information on CASE and ICASE tools. Select several vendors and compare and contrast their offerings.

3. Access www.ning.com. Observe how the site provides components for you to use to build applications. Build a small application at the site.

4. Enter www-01.ibm.com/software. Find its WebSphere product. Read recent customers' success stories. What makes this software so popular?

5. Enter the Web sites of the Gartner (www.gartner.com), the Yankee Group (www.yankeegroup.com), and CIO (www.cio.com). Search for recent material about ASPs and outsourcing, and prepare a report on your findings.

6. StoreFront (www.storefront.net) is a vendor of e-business software. At its site, the company provides demonstrations illustrating the types of storefronts that it can create for shoppers. The site also provides demonstrations of how the company's software is used to create a store.

   a. Run the StoreFront demonstration to see how this is done.

   b. What features does StoreFront provide?

   c. Does StoreFront support smaller or larger stores?

   d. What other products does StoreFront offer for creating online stores? What types of stores do these products support?

>>> COLLABORATION EXERCISE

Background

System acquisition and implementation is as important to the life of information system as is anything else. The right decision could be made about what is needed, but if the implementation of that system is not successful, the whole exercise is in vain. This chapter has covered many techniques for developing and implementing information systems, all of which apply to different needs and situations.

Activity

If you completed the Collaboration Exercise for Chapter 13, assemble that same group and complete this exercise. If you did not, please review the requirements for that activity. You will visit a local business and learn about its' supply chain management systems.

Once you have done this (no matter if it was for Chapter 13 or not), imagine that this company is going to develop and implement a new supply chain management system. The business has chosen to use the SDLC and has created a team of employees (your team) to layout the plan of attack. For this particular business situation, imagine how the SDLC would play out.

Ultimately, provide feedback as to whether or not the SDLC was the best pick for that business in that industry.

Deliverable

Work with your group to lay out the steps of the SDLC for the project implementation you have learned about. Submit your outline and your recommendation on acquisition methods to your professor.

CLOSING CASE 1 > Tweak or Trash?

Chief Information Officers (CIOs) face a continuing dilemma. When the time comes to upgrade information technology equipment and systems, is it better to repair what you already have by patching and tweaking systems and software to keep them operating, or is it better to replace (a.k.a. trash) your old technology and start with an entirely new system?

<<< THE PROBLEM

The "tweak or trash" problem is extremely complicated. The main directive of every IT department is to ensure uptime and avoid downtime at all costs, which creates a bias toward risk avoidance, and therefore toward tweaking. Usually, tweaking seems to be far less risky than implementing an entirely new system. However, tweaking nurtures a growth of hybrid IT environments in which multiple systems coexist, making system documentation and qualified programmers hard to find. Additionally, tweaking often makes programmers feel that it is safer and cheaper to make tiny patches rather than risk transformational change, which can limit a company's IT capability and result in inefficiencies that cost the company time and money.

In 2000, Accenture (www.accenture.com) was a new company that had only recently gone live to the public. The company had inherited legacy systems from its former parent company and needed to build separate technology capabilities. Accenture had ambitious growth strategies and knew that it needed appropriate IT infrastructure to support that growth.

THE IT >>> SOLUTION

When Accenture started the process of revamping its IT infrastructure in the early 2000s, the company did not consciously pursue a total replacement policy of the systems that were already in place. However, managers generally did not want to be encumbered by old technology. They knew that conflicts between different IT systems could impose huge burdens on performance. Therefore, they consistently got rid of old systems in favor of new systems. In other words, they chose to trash rather than to tweak.

Accenture kicked off the replacement process by first establishing a coherent IT strategy and building its own independent IT capabilities. Then, it concentrated on operating the IT department just as any other business would be operated, with a focus on efficiency. Accenture centralized and standardized its IT function. The company cut its total number of global applications from 600 globally to just 267 and decreased its total number of local applications from 1,500 down to 255. An example of this application-cutting process was Accenture's migration from multiple country-specific platforms to a single global enterprise resource planning (ERP) system from SAP (www.sap.com).

By the middle of the decade, Accenture had its IT function in order and began to address larger changes. These changes included a complete network transformation, which gave the company the bandwidth to construct one of the world's largest high-definition video conferencing networks and enabled it to introduce an entire suite of powerful collaboration tools. These technologies enable Accenture professionals to travel less, thereby saving money and time while providing enormous benefits for family life.

THE RESULTS >>>

Accenture invested a grand total of approximately $1 billion in its IT infrastructure from 2001 to 2011. These investments resulted in $3 billion in savings.

Each of the IT changes that Accenture achieved took time to implement and caused disruption to the business. For example, the company moved to its global SAP platform in a single "big-bang" implementation. The downside risks were huge, but so was the upside potential. When the company implemented SAP successfully, it was able to achieve a "single version of the truth" across its entire global enterprise more quickly than before. (A "single version of the truth" means that everyone in a company operates from the same data and information, at the same time.)

Accenture's internal customers are pleased with the results of the IT transformation. The percentage of "satisfied sponsors" (sponsors being the pool of senior executives who work closely with the IT department on new initiatives) increased from 67 to 92 percent between 2001 and 2011.

Accenture's IT transformation led to a dramatic increase in operational efficiency over a 10-year period. The amount spent on IT in total dropped 22 percent over this period and IT expense as a percentage of Accenture's net revenue decreased by 59 percent. IT expense per employee decreased by 70 percent, even though Accenture had made massive IT investments throughout the decade to equip its professionals with the most advanced technology tools possible.

So, what was the final result of Accenture's decision to trash not tweak? Today, Accenture is a global company with more than 244,000 employees and revenues of over $25 billion.

Sources: Compiled from D. Carr, "Accenture CIO Vision Emphasizes Social, Contextual IT," *InformationWeek*, February 27, 2012; F. Modruson, "Debate: Remaking IT at Accenture," *Baseline Magazine*, February 27, 2012; S. Overby, "5 Things Accenture's CIO Has Learned About Cloud Computing," *CIO*, March 15, 2011; J. King, "The Grill: To Kishore Swaminathan, CIO Means 'Chief Intelligence Officer,'" *Computerworld*, September 15, 2008; "CIO 100 2008 Winner Profile: Accenture," *CIO*, 2008; www.accenture.com, accessed February 28, 2012.

Questions

1. What are the risks associated with throwing out old information systems and replacing them with new information systems? Provide examples to support your answer.
2. Provide examples of a situation in which it would be better for an organization to tweak an existing information system rather than replace it with a new system.

CLOSING **CASE 2** > Putting IT All Together

Chubb Insurance (www.chubb.com) is the 11th largest property and casualty insurer in the United States and has a net worth of $50 billion. The company was among the first to implement enterprise information systems as it emerged in the early 2000s. The problem with its implementations was that they were more ad hoc than guided by an overall vision. Every business unit within the company had its own information systems and information systems plan. Chubb was therefore faced with the task of learning which information systems worked best at a corporate level and which information systems worked best within the smaller business units.

<<< **THE PROBLEM**

Chubb's senior corporate IT leadership determined that the company needed an overall strategic IT plan to gain effectiveness and efficiency in its information systems. After meeting with IT leadership in each of the business units to hear different perspectives on how such a plan could be implemented, Chubb selected Patrick Sullivan to implement the overall strategic plan.

<<< **THE SOLUTION**

Sullivan spent a great deal of time with IT leaders in the different business units, explaining why a "federated architecture" was so important to Chubb. A federated architecture is an IT strategic plan that emphasizes interoperability, information sharing, and clearly distinguished functional responsibilities between information systems in the lines of business and corporate information systems.

Chubb based its federated architecture on The Open Group Architecture Framework (TOGAF). TOGAF is a framework for planning, designing, implementing, and governing an enterprise's information systems.

Sullivan used the following metaphor to describe Chubb's overall IT plan. The overall plan for Chubb's portfolio of applications, he said, was analogous to a city plan. Applications are linked with "city blocks" that represent Chubb's business capabilities (e.g., marketing and sales, claims, etc.). All new information systems projects must obtain a "building permit" to ensure that they are following corporate standards and not duplicating other IT efforts, either at the corporate level or in other business units. If someone wants to use a technology that is nonstandard at Chubb, that person needs to request a "variance."

Business-unit review boards enforce corporate IT standards at Chubb for new applications within each business unit. Each board scrutinizes new applications for certain characteristics, including efficiency, value, a focus on the needs of the business unit, and funding.

The strategic IT plan and federated architecture model have provided many benefits for Chubb. Because Chubb's plan and architecture show how data, technologies, applications,

<<< **THE RESULTS**

and business capabilities fit together, IT leaders in each line of the business can communicate with their non-IT business colleagues about where and how IT is investing in the capabilities they need. This process has led to increased credibility for IT because managers have confidence that Chubb is selecting the correct technologies to match business needs.

The strategic IT plan also helps to identify opportunities to share common tools and processes across lines of business. For example, in 2010, Chubb saved $600,000 by redistributing unused site licenses for software. Using its strategic IT plan and federated architecture, Chubb is able to quickly make decisions about new products that result in large savings and quick launch-to-market time.

Sources: M. Weiss, "One Enterprise Architecture to Rule Them All," *Baseline Magazine*, March 1, 2012; Broderick, M. "Will TOGAF Guarantee Business Success?" *Articles Factory*, November 15, 2011; M. Heller, "Making Enterprise Architecture Matter," CIO, April 27, 2011; www.chubb.com, accessed March 5, 2012.

Questions

1. Review the section in Chapter 1 on Managing Information Resources. Based on your review, which information systems capabilities should Chubb keep at the corporate level? Justify each one.
2. Based on your review, which information systems capabilities should Chubb keep in the business units? Justify each one.

RUBY'S CLUB | INTERNSHIP ASSIGNMENT

Based on your answers to the section discussion questions, write one final report to Ruben and Lisa detailing your suggestions for the development and implementation of their mobile ordering system. If you choose the SDLC, explain why. If you choose for them to have someone else develop the software, defend your position.

Be aware that there is no perfect answer. No situation will be without disadvantages and risks. Be sure to detail the risks so they will be well aware as they move through this process. Finally, submit your report to Ruben and Lisa via you professor.

SPREADSHEET ACTIVITY: IF-THEN STATEMENTS

Objective: This activity will introduce the "if-then" statement within the context of making a decision. It will help students take criteria from a situation and build it into a spreadsheet.

Chapter Connection: Acquiring an information system should be an easy task, right? Wrong! Sometimes the method of acquiring the system is as complex as the system itself. Although most situations would require a much more complicated decision support system, in this situation a spreadsheet formula can help make the decision by using formulas to narrow down the top contenders and provide a score/ranking for the companies under consideration.

Activity: It is time for the university to upgrade its Web site. This decision is very important because it will affect current and potential students, faculty, and the community at large. The university has graded 50 different vendors on 10 criteria and the weight given to each. The 10 criteria and their weights are given below.

1. Customizability (15%)
2. Expandability (15%)
3. Faculty Tutorials (5%)
4. Student Tutorials (5%)

5. Mobile Access (10%)
6. Video Support (10%)
7. File System (5%)
8. Course Migration (15%)
9. Faculty User Interface (10%)
10. Student User Interface (10%)

Visit http://www.wiley.com/go/rainer/spreadsheet and download the spreadsheet provided for Chapter 14. Then create two formulas. One will calculate a final grade based on the weights provided above and the work already done by the university. Once you have the final grade, you will then create an if-then formula to find those vendors that rank worthy of an "A" and those who "fail" to meet the stated criteria. If you are not familiar with if-then statements, please see the Help material in Microsoft Excel under the formulas area of the program. Basically, your statement will say "If the score is greater than a 90, then say 'Yes,' otherwise, "No."

Deliverable: Prepare a written summary of your findings. Is there a clear winner? Or does it depend on what the university favors in the rankings?

Discussion Questions:

1. Acquisition of information systems is a complicated affair. Decisions to build in-house, outsource, or purchase off-the-shelf software can sometimes be the greatest asset or the Achilles heel of a company. Given the complexity, what roles can a spreadsheet play in this process other than the one illustrated by this case?

2. Implementation strategies vary as much as the acquisition decision. Considering products like the Google Spreadsheet Flow Chart, how can spreadsheets assist with the planning of software implementation?

Quiz questions are assignable in WileyPLUS, and available on the Book Companion Site at http://www.wiley.com/college/rainer.

DATABASE ACTIVITY: FORMS III

Objective

In this activity, you will learn how to create a menu interface (a "navigation form" in Access terminology) that will allow users with no training to reach important elements of a system easily. Consider what happens when you launch Access. You get an easy-to-navigate screen that asks questions such as "Do you want to open an existing database, start a blank one, or . . .?" We should design databases for the same ease of entry. Navigation forms are how.

CHAPTER CONNECTION

In this chapter, you read how organizations acquire their information systems. Often, they develop IS internally. The result has to look as professional as if the application had been purchased. That includes interfaces such as you will develop here.

PREREQUISITES

None.

Activity

In this activity, which you will find online at http://www.wiley.com/go/rainer/database, you will take an existing database with

forms and reports, develop menus for using it, and set your database to launch with these menus.

A finished navigation form, which you will end up with at the end of this activity, might look like the figure below. One does not have to be an Access expert, or even an experienced Access user, to use it. Each button is labeled with its function. Such an interface is planned in the System Design stage of the SDLC development process, which you read about in this chapter. Putting it together, as you will do here, is part of the Programming and Testing stage.

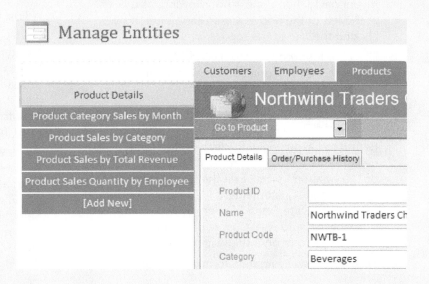

1. Download the Ch 14 DandyDonuts database from http://www.wiley.com/go/rainer/database. (It resembles the donut store databases you may have worked with in earlier activities.) It has four tables: stores, customers, orders, line items (each item in an order), and products. It also includes a few forms and reports. These are not intended as good examples of form or report design. They are there only to so your switchboards will have something to open.

2. To create a navigation form, go to the Create ribbon tab and pull down the list of navigation forms via the triangle to its right. Select the first layout, Horizontal Tabs.

3. You will see a blank navigation form in Design view. The space where the tabs will go, across the top, is empty except for a placeholder that reads "[Add New]."

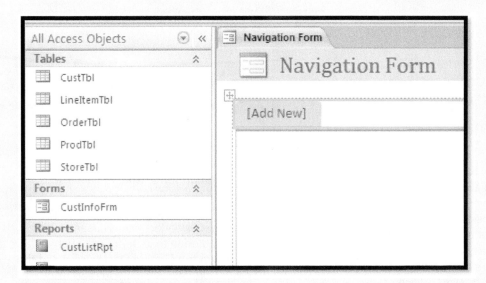

4. If your navigation pane is not showing, as it is at the left of the above screen shot, open it by clicking the >> at the top.

5. Drag the four reports into the Add New area, one at a time. As each one comes in, you will see a tab created for it.

6. Go to Form view. The "[Add New]" has gone away. Click on each tab to see the corresponding report.

7. Return to Layout view. To clean up the form design, edit the top line to read "Reports" instead of "Navigation Form." Edit the four tabs to read, respectively, "Customer List," "Customer Orders," "Orders by Date," and "Orders by Store." You will probably have to widen some of the tabs for the new names to fit on a single line.

8. Save your new navigation form as "Report List."

9. Create a new navigation form, but this time use Vertical Tabs Left layout.

10. Enter CustInfoFrm and your new Report List into the tab area.

11. Change the header of this form to read "Main Menu" and the name "CustInfoFrm" to read "Cust. Info."

12. Confirm in Form view that everything works.

13. Now we will add an "Exit" button to our main menu. Go to Design mode and make sure Use Control Wizards is highlighted in the Controls section of the Design ribbon. (Expand that area using the down-pointing triangle with the line above it at the right to see the wizard.) Then click the Button tool. (It is in the top row of controls, fourth from the left.) Drag it over a rectangular area in the form header, to the right of the words "Main Menu," to create the button shape. The wizard will start.

Usage Hint: You can create buttons in Layout mode, but in that mode, if you try to put them in the navigation tab area, Access will insist on turning them into new tabs. In Design view, you can create freestanding buttons.

14. Choose the Application category, then Quit Application (the only item in it). Click Next.

15. Select Text for the button content type, then enter "Exit" into the text field.

16. Name the button "ExitButton" so you will know what it is later, and click Finish.

17. Adjust the size and location of your button if you wish.

18. Go to Form view and confirm that your new button works. If it does not, the easiest fix is probably to start over rather than figuring out why. If your second attempt to create it fails too, it is time to try to diagnose the problem. Close your form, naming it "Main Menu."

19. Users would like the application to open with this menu, instead of having to open it from the navigation pane. To make this happen, go to the File tab and click Options near the bottom. Select Current Database at the left, then select your main switchboard from the pull-down menu for Display Form. It should look like this:

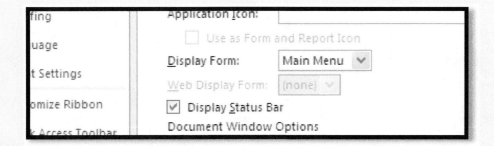

20. Close the database (as you will be told to do for this option to take effect), reopen it, and confirm that it opens with your main menu.

Deliverable

The above database, with its two navigation forms.

Quiz Questions

1. How many tabs can a standard Access navigation form can have?

2. A navigation form can do the following:

   (a) Open a form or a report.

   (b) Open a report or a table.

   (c) Open another navigation form.

   (d) It can do all of the above.

3. True or false: A navigation form is a specialized type of report.

4. When a user clicks a button linked to the Quit Application action,

   (a) The database closes, but Access remains active.

   (b) The computer shuts down.

   (c) Access closes.

   (d) The computer goes into Sleep mode.

Discussion Questions

1. Open the Main Menu navigation form in Design view. Click on Cust. Info. and change something in the customer information form. Then close the navigation form. What happened? Do you think it is a good idea for Access to work this way, or not? Explain why you feel this way.

2. In the second part of this activity, you created the Main Menu navigation form after you created the Reports form. Could you have done this in the other order? If not, why not?

3. Search the Web for images of Access 2007 switchboards. You will find that many look more or less like this, with only cosmetic changes:

   This menu, called a *switchboard*, was created with Access 2007 or an earlier version. Find three such switchboards. In your opinion, are they more attractive and/or easier to use (as far as you can tell by without trying them out) than the navigation forms of Access 2010? Explain why you feel this way. (Paste the three switchboards' images into the answer you submit to your instructor.)

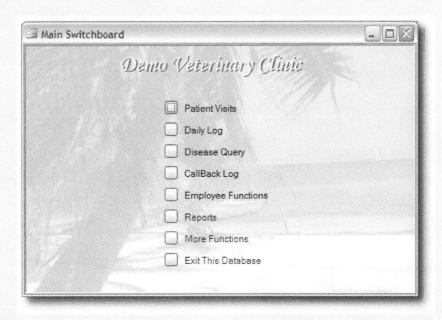

Plug IT In | 1

Business Processes and Business Process Management

LEARNING OBJECTIVES >>>

1. Discuss ways in which information systems enable cross-functional business processes and business processes for a single functional area.

2. Compare and contrast *business process reengineering* and *business process management* to determine the different advantages and disadvantages of each.

PI1.1 Business Processes

A **business process** is an ongoing collection of related activities that create a product or a service of value to the organization, its business partners, and/or its customers. A process has inputs and outputs, and its activities can be measured. Many processes cross functional areas in an organization. For example, product development involves research, design, engineering, manufacturing, marketing, and distribution. Other processes involve only a single functional area. Table PI1.1 identifies the fundamental business processes performed in an organization's functional areas.

TABLE PI1.1 Examples of Business Processes

Accounting Business Processes

- Managing accounts payable
- Managing accounts receivable
- Reconciling bank accounts
- Managing cash receipts

- Managing invoice billings
- Managing petty cash
- Producing month-end close
- Producing virtual close

Finance Business Processes

- Managing account collection
- Managing bank loan applications
- Producing business forecasts
- Applying customer credit approval and credit terms

- Producing property tax assessments
- Managing stock transactions
- Generating financial cash flow reports

Marketing Business Processes

- Managing postsale customer follow-up
- Collecting sales taxes
- Applying copyrights and trademarks
- Using customer satisfaction surveys
- Managing customer service

- Handling customer complaints
- Handling returned goods from customers
- Producing sales leads
- Entering sales orders
- Training sales personnel

Production/Operations Management Business Processes

- Processing bills of materials
- Processing manufacturing change orders
- Managing master parts list and files
- Managing packing, storage, and distribution
- Processing physical inventory
- Managing purchasing

- Managing quality control for finished goods
- Auditing for quality assurance
- Receiving, inspecting, and stocking parts and materials
- Handling shipping and freight claims
- Handling vendor selection, files, and inspections

Human Resources Business Processes

- Applying disability policies
- Managing employee hiring
- Handling employee orientation
- Managing files and records
- Applying health care benefits
- Managing pay and payroll
- Producing performance appraisals and salary adjustments

- Managing resignations and terminations
- Applying training/tuition reimbursement
- Managing travel and entertainment
- Managing workplace rules and guidelines
- Overseeing workplace safety

Management Information Systems Business Processes

- Antivirus control
- Computer security issues incident reporting
- Training computer users
- Computer user/staff training
- Applying disaster recovery procedures

- Applying electronic mail policy
- Generating Internet use policy
- Managing service agreements and emergency services
- Applying user workstation standards
- Managing the use of personal software

Cross-Functional Processes

All of the business processes listed in Table PI1.1 fall within a single functional area of the company. However, many other business processes, such as procurement and fulfillment, cut across multiple functional areas. That is, these processes are **cross-functional**, meaning that no single functional area is responsible for their execution. Rather, multiple functional areas collaborate to perform the process. For a **cross-functional process** to be successfully completed, each functional area must execute its specific process steps in a coordinated, collaborative way. To clarify this point, let us examine the procurement and fulfillment cross-functional processes in more detail.

The *procurement process* includes all of the tasks involved in acquiring needed materials externally from a vendor. Procurement is comprised of five steps that are completed in three different functional areas of the firm: warehouse, purchasing, and accounting.

The process begins when the warehouse recognizes the need to procure materials, perhaps from low inventory levels. The warehouse documents this need with a purchase requisition, which it sends to the purchasing department (step 1). In turn, the purchasing department identifies a suitable vendor, creates a purchase order based on the purchase requisition, and sends the order to the vendor (step 2). When the vendor receives the purchase order, it ships the materials, which are received in the warehouse (step 3). The vendor then sends an invoice, which is received by the accounting department (step 4). Accounting sends payment to the vendor, thereby completing the procurement process (step 5).

The *fulfillment process* is concerned with efficiently processing customer orders. Fulfillment is triggered by a customer purchase order that is received by the sales department. Sales then validates the purchase order and creates a sales order. The sales order communicates data related to the order to other functional areas within the organization, and it tracks the progress of the order. The warehouse prepares and sends the shipment to the customer. Once accounting is notified of the shipment, it creates an invoice and sends it to the customer. The customer then makes a payment, which accounting records.

An organization's business processes can create a competitive advantage if they enable the company to innovate or to execute better than its competitors. They also can be liabilities if they make the company less responsive or less efficient. Consider the airline industry. It has become a competitive necessity for all of the airlines to offer electronic ticket purchases via their Web sites. At the same time, however, these sites must be highly responsive and provide the most current information on flights and prices. An up-to-date, user-friendly site will attract customers and increase revenues. In contrast, a site that provides outdated or inaccurate information will hurt rather than improve business. Figure PI1.1 illustrates the e-ticket purchasing business process.

Figure PI1.1 Business process for ordering e-ticket from airline Web site.

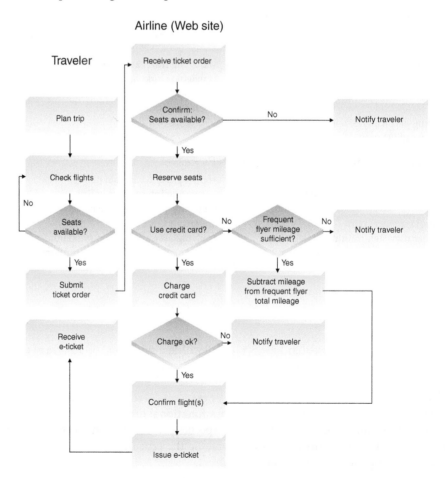

Information Systems and Business Processes

An information system (IS) is an important enabler of business processes in an organization. An IS facilitates communication and coordination among different functional areas, and it allows easy exchange of, and access to, data across processes. Specifically, IS play a vital role in three areas:

- Execute the process
- Capture and store process data
- Monitor process performance

In this section, you will learn about each of these roles. In some cases the role is fully automated—that is, it is performed entirely by the IS. In other cases the IS must rely on the manager's judgment, expertise, and intuition.

Execute the Process. IS helps organizations execute processes efficiently and effectively. IS are typically embedded into the processes and they play a critical role in executing the processes. In other words, an IS and processes are usually intertwined. If the IS does not work, the process cannot be executed. IS help execute processes by informing people when it is time to complete a task, by providing the data necessary to complete the task, and in some cases by providing the means to complete the task.

In the procurement process, for example, the IS generates the purchase requisitions and then informs the purchasing department that action on these requisitions is needed. The accountant will be able to view all shipments received to match an invoice that has been received from a supplier and verify that the invoice is accurate. Without the IS, these steps, and therefore the process, cannot be completed. For example, if the IS is not available, how will the warehouse know which orders are ready to pack and ship?

In the fulfillment process, the IS will inform people in the warehouse that orders are ready for shipment. The IS also provides them with a listing of what materials must be included in the order and where to find those materials in the warehouse.

Capture and Store Process Data. Processes create data such as dates, times, product numbers, quantities, prices, and addresses, as well as who did what, when, and where. IS capture and store these data, commonly referred to as process data or transaction data. Some of these data are generated and automatically captured by the IS. These are data related to who, when, and where an activity is completed. Other data are generated outside the IS and must be entered into it. This data entry can occur in various ways, ranging from manual data entry to automated methods involving data in forms such as bar codes or RFID tags that can be read by machines.

In the fulfillment process, for example, when a customer order is received by mail or over the phone, the person taking the order must enter data such as the name of the customer, what was ordered, and how much was ordered. When a customer order is received via the firm's Web site, then all customer details are captured by the IS. Data such as the name of the person entering the data (who), at which location the person is completing the task (where), and the date and time (when) are automatically included by the IS when it creates the order. The data are updated as the process steps are executed. When the order is shipped, the warehouse will provide data about what and how many products were shipped, and the IS will automatically include data related to who, when, and where.

An important advantage of using an IS compared to a manual system or multiple functional area information systems is that the data need to be entered into the system only once. Further, once they are entered, they are easily accessible to other people in the process and there is no need to reenter them in subsequent steps.

The data captured by the IS can provide immediate feedback. For example, the IS can use the data to create a receipt or to make recommendations for additional or alternate products.

Monitor Process Performance. A third contribution of IS is to help monitor the state of processes. That is, the IS indicates how well a process is executing. The IS performs this role by evaluating information about a process. This information can be created either at the instance level (i.e., a specific task or activity) or the process level (i.e., the process as a whole).

At the instance level, for example, a company might be interested in the state of a particular customer order. Where is the order within the fulfillment process? When was it shipped? Was the complete order shipped? If it has not been shipped, then when can we expect it to be shipped? Or, for the procurement process, when was the purchase order sent to the supplier? What will be the cost of acquiring the material? At the process level, the IS can evaluate how well the procurement process is being executed by calculating the lead time, or the time between sending the purchase order to a vendor and receiving the goods, for each order and each vendor over time.

Not only can the IS help monitor a process, it can also detect problems with the process. The IS performs this role by comparing the information with a standard—that is, what the company expects or desires—to determine if the process is performing within expectations. Management establishes standards based on organizational goals.

If the information provided by the IS indicates that the process is not meeting the standards, then the company assumes that some type of problem exists. Some problems can be routinely and automatically detected by the IS, whereas other problems require a person to review the information and make judgments. For example, the IS can calculate the expected date that a specific order will be shipped and determine whether this date will meet the established standard. Or, the IS can calculate the average time taken to fill all orders over the last month and compare this information to the standard to determine if the process is working as expected.

Monitoring business processes, then, helps detect problems with these processes. Very often these problems are really symptoms of a more fundamental problem. In such cases, the IS can help diagnose the cause of the symptoms by providing managers with additional, detailed information. For example, if the average time to process a customer order appears to be increasing over the previous month, this problem could be a symptom of a more basic problem. A manager can then drill down into the information to diagnose the underlying problem.

To accomplish this, the manager can request a breakdown of the information by type of product, customer, location, employees, day of the week, time of day, and so on. After reviewing this detailed information, the manager might determine that employee turnover in the warehouse has been high over the last month and that the delays are occurring because new employees are not sufficiently familiar with the process. The manager might conclude that this problem will work itself out over time, in which case there is nothing more to be done. Alternatively, the manager could conclude that the new employees are not being adequately trained and supervised. In this case, the company must take actions to correct the problem.

— BEFORE *YOU GO ON* . . . —

1. What is a business process?
2. Describe several business processes carried out at your university.
3. Define a cross-functional business process and provide several examples of such processes.
4. Describe the three roles that information systems play in enabling business processes.

Apply the Concept PI 1.1

Background This Plug IT In defines a *business process* as an ongoing collection of related activities that create a product or a service of value to the organization, its business partners, and/or its customers. Normallly, we do not see everything that goes into a process, we only see the result of the process. For example, if you go into a grocery store, you will see stocked shelves. You do not see the inventory management processes (or the information systems that support those processes) that operate in the background to keep the shelves stocked.

Activity Visit http://www.wiley.com/go/rainer/applytheconcept and click on the link provided for Plug IT In 1.1. This will show you a YouTube video about workflow and business process management.

Next, examine your university's registration system, including the necessary inputs, outputs, and processes to represent your perspective of the system (i.e., the processes that the system must go through to process your registration for classes, the necessary inputs, and the outputs). Note that these may be different from another user's perspective. For example, the registrar may identify different processes that are necessary or relevant to other parts of the registration system that you may not recognize or even need to know about, such as minimum enrollment, course locations, and instructor credentials.

What data/input are required of you? What data/input may be needed from other sources (e.g., things like course credit hours, prerequisites, etc.)? What outputs do you expect from the system? What are the processes necessary to get from the inputs to the desired outputs?

Deliverable

Prepare a diagram that identifies and shows the relationships between

- Necessary input/data from the student (and other sources as necessary to complete the student part of registration)
- Expected/desired outputs of registration
- Processes that are necessary to convert inputs into the expected/desired outputs

Submit your diagram to your professor.

Quiz questions are assignable in WileyPLUS, and available on the Book Companion Site at http://www.wiley.com/college/rainer.

PI1.2 Business Process Reengineering and Business Process Management

Excellence in executing business processes is widely recognized as the underlying basis for all significant measures of competitive performance in an organization. Consider the following measures, for example:

- *Customer satisfaction:* the result of optimizing and aligning business processes to fulfill customers' needs, wants, and desires
- *Cost reduction:* the result of optimizing operations and supplier processes
- *Cycle and fulfillment time:* the result of optimizing the manufacturing and logistics processes
- *Quality:* the result of optimizing the design, development, and production processes
- *Differentiation:* the result of optimizing the marketing and innovation processes
- *Productivity:* the result of optimizing each individual's work processes

The question is this: How does an organization ensure business process excellence?

In their book *Reengineering the Corporation*, first published in 1993, Michael Hammer and James Champy argued that to become more competitive, American businesses needed to radically redesign their business processes to reduce costs and increase quality. The authors further asserted that information technology is the key enabler of such change. This radical redesign, called **business process reengineering (BPR)**, is a strategy for improving the efficiency and effectiveness of an organization's business processes. The key to BPR is for enterprises to examine their business processes from a "clean sheet" perspective and then determine how they can best reconstruct those processes to improve their business functions.

Although some enterprises successfully implemented BPR, many organizations found this strategy too difficult, too radical, and too comprehensive. The impact on employees, on facilities, on existing investments in information systems, and even on organizational culture was overwhelming. Despite the many failures in BPR implementation, however, businesses increasingly began to organize work around business processes rather than individual tasks. The result was a less radical, less disruptive, and more incremental approach, called business process management. **Business process management (BPM)** is a management technique that includes methods and tools to support the design, analysis, implementation, management, and optimization of business processes.

BPM initially helps companies improve profitability by decreasing costs and increasing revenues. Over time, BPM can create a competitive advantage by improving organizational flexibility. For many companies, BPM can provide cost benefits and increase customer satisfaction. In all cases, the company's strategy should drive the BPM effort, as the case of Enterprise illustrates.

> ### BEFORE YOU GO ON . . .
> 1. What is business process reengineering?
> 2. What is business process management?

Enterprise Rent-A-Car (www.enterprise.com) is one of the largest car rental companies in the world. The company's Request Services department processes, approves, and fulfills requests for IT hardware, software, and services from 65,000 Enterprise employees located in 7,000 locations worldwide. Historically, this department had used multiple manual systems to manage this process. As the company expanded, however, this system could no longer keep up with the growing number of IT requests. Determined to improve this process, Enterprise initiated a BPM project and selected a product from Appian (www.appian.com) for this project.

Before Enterprise actually started the project, the company made certain that its strategy was in place. Enterprise recognized that implementing a new process would transform the company's traditional work behaviors. Therefore, the Request Services department engaged key stakeholders—primarily the people who approve IT product and service requests and the people who fulfill these requests—early in the project. The company also educated employees about BPM in general as well as how to use the new Appian system.

After the BPM system was implemented, Enterprise eliminated its manual processes entirely. Its employees now use the Appian system to request IT products and services. Significantly, they now fulfill requests more promptly while making fewer errors than they did with the manual system. In addition, the new process contains business rules that provide appropriate restrictions on fulfillment (e.g., what IT hardware, software, or service an employee is entitled to).

Important components of BPM are process modeling, Web-enabled technologies, and business activity monitoring.

BPM begins with *process modeling,* which is a graphical depiction of all the steps in a process. Process modeling helps employees understand the interactions and dependencies among the people, the information systems they rely on, and the information they require to optimally perform their tasks.

Web-enabled technologies display and retrieve data via a Web browser. They enable an organization to integrate the necessary people and applications into each process.

Business activity monitoring (BAM) is a real-time approach for measuring and managing business processes. Companies use BAM to monitor their business processes, identify failures or exceptions, and address these failures in real time. Further, because BAM tracks process operations and indicates whether they succeed or fail, it creates valuable records of process behaviors that organizations can use to improve their processes.

Sources: Compiled from B. Violino, "BPM Success at Enterprise," *Baseline Magazine,* March 13, 2009; B. Violino, "BPM: Strategy Before Software," *CIO Insight,* March 13, 2009; D. Byron, "Appian BPM at Enterprise: Can Renting BPM Be Like Renting a Car?" www.bpminaction.com, March 24, 2008; "Enterprise Rent-A-Car Goes Live with Appian Enterprise," Appian Press Release, March 24, 2008; www.enterprise.com, accessed March 30, 2009; www.appian.com, accessed March 20, 2011.

Apply the Concept PI1.2

Background This section has shown that reengineering processes is not an easy task. Many organizations attempt but do not complete the redesign. Sometimes, a task could be redesigned, but the resulting difference in process efficiency is not worth the time and energy required to redesign the process. That is something each organization must determine.

Activity Map the activities of a typical senior at college getting ready for school in the morning. You will then reengineer the process to reduce the amount of time necessary to get ready for school. A partial list of activities that the student already does before going to school (and the time required) is presented in the following table. Add any items that may have been left off the list based upon your own experience of getting ready each day (If time permits, you may find it helpful to keep a diary of your morning activities, to get an accurate accounting of the activities.)

Activity	Time Required
Hit snooze bar and sleep in	10 minutes
Shower and wash hair	15 minutes
Blow dry and fix hair	10 minutes
Shave or put on makeup	10 minutes
Prepare and eat breakfast	15 minutes
Take dog out	5 minutes
Feed dog	5 minutes
Wash, dry, put away dishes	5 minutes
Drive to campus and park	15 minutes
Pick out clothes and get dressed	15 minutes
Read newspaper	15 minutes
Brush teeth	5 minutes
Work out	20 minutes
Check e-mail	10 minutes
Check Facebook	20 minutes

Deliverable

Organize and design a plan for getting ready in the morning that will reduce the time necessary. The current model takes almost 3 hours! See if there is anything you can do that would reduce the time for this plan down to around 2 hours. Submit your redesigned "getting ready" process to your professor.

Quiz questions are assignable in WileyPLUS, and available on the Book Companion Site at http://www.wiley.com/college/rainer.

What's in IT for ME?

For All Business Majors

All functional areas of any organization are literally composed of a variety of business processes, as we can see from the examples in this plug-in. Regardless of your major, you will be involved in a variety of business processes from your first day on the job. Some of these processes you will do by yourself, some will involve only your group or department, while others will involve several (or all) functional areas of the organization.

It is important for you to be able to visualize processes, understand the inputs and outputs of each process, and know the "customer" of each process. If you can do these things, you can contribute to making processes more efficient and effective, which often means incorporating information technology in the process. It is also important for you to know how each process fits into your organization's strategy.

SUMMARY

1. **Discuss ways in which information systems enable cross-functional business processes and business processes for a single functional area.**

   A business process is an ongoing collection of related activities that produce a product or a service of value to the organization, its business partners, and/or its customers. Examples of business processes in the functional areas include managing accounts payable, managing accounts receivable, managing after-sale customer follow-up, managing bills of materials, managing manufacturing change orders, applying disability policies, employee hiring, computer user/staff training, and applying Internet use policy. The procurement and fulfillment processes are examples of cross-functional business processes.

2. **Compare and contrast *business process reengineering* and *business process management* to determine the different advantages and disadvantages of each.**

   Business process reengineering (BPR) is a radical redesign of business processes that is intended to improve the efficiency and effectiveness of an organization's business processes. The key to BPR is for enterprises to examine their business processes from a "clean sheet" perspective and then determine how they could best reconstruct those processes to improve their business functions. Because BPR proved difficult to implement, organizations have turned to business process management. Business process management (BPM) is a management technique that includes methods and tools to support the design, analysis, implementation, management, and optimization of business processes.

>>> GLOSSARY

business process A collection of related activities that create a product or a service of value to the organization, its business partners, and/or its customers.

business process management A management technique that includes methods and tools to support the design, analysis, implementation, management, and optimization of business processes.

business process reengineering A radical redesign of a business process that improves its efficiency and effectiveness, often by beginning with a "clean sheet" (from scratch).

cross-functional processes No single functional area is responsible for a process's execution.

>>> DISCUSSION QUESTIONS

1. Consider the student registration business process at your university:

   • Describe the steps necessary for you to register for your classes each semester.

   • Describe how information technology is used (or is not used) in each step of the process.

2. Why is it so difficult for an organization to actually implement business process reengineering?

Plug IT In | 2

Hardware and Software

LEARNING OBJECTIVES >>>

1. Discuss strategic issues that link hardware design to business strategy.
2. Describe different issues associated with the two major types of software.

Introduction

As you begin this Plug IT In, you might be wondering, why do I have to know anything about hardware and software? There are several reasons why it is advantageous to know the basics of hardware and software. First, regardless of your major (and future functional area in an organization), you will be using different types of hardware and software throughout your career. Second, you will have input concerning the hardware and software you will use. In this capacity you will be required to answer many questions, such as "Is my hardware performing adequately for my needs? If not, what types of problems am I experiencing?" "Does my software help me do my job?" "Is this software easy to use?" "Do I need more functionality, and if so, what functionality would be most helpful to me?" Third, you will also have input into decisions when your functional area or organization upgrades or replaces its hardware, as well as input into decisions about the software you need to do your job. MIS employees will act as advisors, but you will provide important input into such decisions. Finally, in some organizations, the budget for hardware and software is allocated to functional areas or departments. In such cases, you might be making hardware and software decisions (at least locally) yourself.

This Plug IT In will help you better understand the hardware and software decisions your organization must make as well as your personal computing decisions. Many of the design principles presented here apply to systems of all sizes, from an enterprisewide system to your home computer system. In addition, the dynamics of innovation and cost that you will see can affect personal as well as corporate hardware decisions.

PI2.1 Introduction to Hardware

Recall from Chapter 1 that the term *hardware* refers to the physical equipment used for the input, processing, output, and storage activities of a computer system. Decisions about hardware focus on three interrelated factors: appropriateness for the task, speed, and cost. The incredibly rapid rate of innovation in the computer industry complicates hardware decisions because computer technologies become obsolete more quickly than other organizational technologies.

The overall trends in hardware are that it becomes smaller, faster, cheaper, and more powerful over time. In fact, these trends are so rapid that they make it difficult to know when to purchase (or upgrade) hardware. This difficulty lies in the fact that companies that delay hardware purchases will, more than likely, be able to buy more powerful hardware for the same amount of money in the future. It is important to note that buying more powerful hardware for the same amount of money in the future is a trade-off. An organization that delays purchasing computer hardware gives up the benefits of whatever it could buy today until the future purchase date arrives.

Hardware consists of the following:

- *Central processing unit (CPU).* Manipulates the data and controls the tasks performed by the other components.
- *Primary storage.* Temporarily stores data and program instructions during processing.
- *Secondary storage.* Stores data and programs for future use.
- *Input technologies.* Accept data and instructions and convert them to a form that the computer can understand.
- *Output technologies.* Present data and information in a form people can understand.
- *Communication technologies.* Provide for the flow of data from external computer networks (e.g., the Internet and intranets) to the CPU, and from the CPU to computer networks.

Strategic Hardware Issues

For most businesspeople the most important issues are what the hardware enables, how it is advancing, and how rapidly it is advancing. In many industries, exploiting computer hardware is a key to achieving competitive advantage. Successful hardware exploitation comes from thoughtful consideration of the following questions:

- How do organizations keep up with the rapid price and performance advancements in hardware? For example, how often should an organization upgrade its computers and storage systems? Will upgrades increase personal and organizational productivity? How can organizations measure such increases?
- How should organizations determine the need for the new hardware infrastructures, such as server farms, virtualization, grid computing, and utility computing? (See Plug IT In 3 for a discussion of these infrastructures.)
- Portable computers and advanced communications technologies have enabled employees to work from home or from anywhere. Will these new work styles benefit employees and the organization? How do organizations manage such new work styles?

Computer Hierarchy

The traditional standard for comparing classes of computers is their processing power. This section presents each class of computers, from the most powerful to the least powerful. It describes both the computers and their roles in modern organizations.

Supercomputers. The term **supercomputer** does not refer to a specific technology. Rather, it indicates the fastest computers available at any given time. At the time of this writing (mid-2012), the fastest supercomputers had speeds exceeding one petaflop (one petaflop is 1,000 trillion floating point operations per second). A floating point operation is an arithmetic operation involving decimals.

Because supercomputers are costly as well as very fast, they are generally used by large organizations to execute computationally demanding tasks involving very large data sets. In contrast to mainframes, which specialize in transaction processing and business applications, supercomputers typically run military and scientific applications. Although they cost millions of dollars, they are also being used for commercial applications where huge amounts of data must be analyzed. For example, large banks use supercomputers to calculate the risks and returns of various investment strategies, and healthcare organizations use them to analyze giant databases of patient data to determine optimal treatments for various diseases.

Mainframe Computers. Although mainframe computers are increasingly viewed as just another type of server, albeit at the high end of the performance and reliability scales, they remain a distinct class of systems differentiated by hardware and software features. **Mainframes** remain popular in large enterprises for extensive computing applications that are accessed by thousands of users at one time. Examples of mainframe applications are airline reservation systems, corporate payroll programs, Web site transaction processing systems (e.g., Amazon and eBay), and student grade calculation and reporting.

Today's mainframes perform at teraflop (trillions of floating point operations per second) speeds and can handle millions of transactions per day. In addition, mainframes provide a secure, robust environment in which to run strategic, mission-critical applications.

Midrange Computers. Larger midrange computers, called **minicomputers**, are relatively small, inexpensive, and compact computers that perform the same functions as mainframe computers, but to a more limited extent. In fact, the lines between minicomputers and mainframes have blurred in both price and performance. Minicomputers are a type of **server**—that is, a computer that supports computer networks and enables users to share files, software, peripheral devices, and other resources. Mainframes are a type of server as well because they provide support for entire enterprise networks.

Microcomputers. **Microcomputers**—also called *micros, personal computers*, or *PCs*—are the smallest and least expensive category of general-purpose computers. It is important to point out that people frequently define a PC as a computer that utilizes the Microsoft Windows operating system. In fact, there are a variety of PCs available, many of which do not use Windows. One well-known example are the Apple Macs, which use the Mac OS X operating system (discussed later in this Plug IT In). The major categories of microcomputers are desktops, thin clients, notebooks and laptops, netbooks and tablets.

Desktop PCs. The *desktop personal computer* is the familiar microcomputer system that has become a standard tool for business and the home. (Desktops are being replaced with portable devices such as laptops, netbooks, and tablets.) A desktop generally includes a central processing unit (CPU)—which you will learn about later—and a separate but connected monitor and keyboard. Modern desktop computers have gigabytes of primary storage, a rewriteable CD-ROM and a DVD drive, and up to a few terabytes of secondary storage.

Thin-Client Systems. Before you address thin-client systems, you need to differentiate between clients and servers. Recall that **servers** are computers that provide a variety of services for clients, including running networks, processing Web sites, processing e-mail, and many other functions. *Clients* are typically computers on which users perform their tasks, such as word processing, spreadsheets, and others.

Thin-client systems are desktop computer systems that do not offer the full functionality of a PC. Compared to PCs, or **fat clients**, thin clients are less complex, particularly because they do not have locally installed software. When thin clients need to run an application, they access it from a server over a network instead of from a local disk drive.

For example, a thin client would not have Microsoft Office installed on it. Thus, thin clients are easier and less expensive to operate and support than PCs. The benefits of thin clients include fast application deployment, centralized management, lower cost of ownership, and easier installation, management, maintenance, and support. The main disadvantage of thin clients is that if the network fails, then users can do very little on their computers. In contrast, if users have fat clients and the network fails, they can still perform some functions because they have software, such as Microsoft Office, installed on their computers.

Laptop and Notebook Computers. **Laptop computers** (or **notebook computers**) are small, easily transportable, lightweight microcomputers that fit easily into a briefcase (Figure PI2.1). Notebooks and laptops are designed to be as convenient and easy to transport as possible. Just as important, they also provide users with access to processing power and data outside an office environment. At the same time, they cost more than desktops for similar functionality.

Netbooks. A **netbook** is a very small, lightweight, low-cost, energy-efficient, portable computer. Netbooks are generally optimized for Internet-based services such as Web browsing and e-mailing.

Tablet Computers. A **tablet computer** (or **tablet**) is a complete computer contained entirely in a flat touch screen that users operate via a stylus, digital pen, or fingertip instead of a keyboard or mouse. Examples of tablets are the Apple iPad 2 (www.apple.com/ipad), the HP Slate (www.hp.com), the Toshiba Thrive (www.toshiba.com), and the Motorola Xoom (www.motorola.com).

Figure PI2.1 Laptop, notebook, and tablet computers.

Laptop computer

Netbook

Motorola Xoom tablet

Apple iPad tablet

T'S PERSONAL: PURCHASING A COMPUTER

One day you will purchase a computer for yourself or your job. When that day comes, it will be important for you to know what to look for. Buying a computer can be very confusing if you just read the box. This Plug-IT-In has explained the major components of a computer in terms of both hardware and software. But there are more things you need to consider when you purchase a computer: what you plan to do with it, where do you plan to use it, and how long you need service from it. To help answer the first question, consider the following questions.

- What do you plan to do with your computer? Just like buying a vehicle, your plans for using the vehicle determine the type of vehicle you will purchase. It is the same with a computer. You need to consider what you currently do with a computer and what you may do before you replace the one under consideration. Although many people just buy as much as they can afford, they may also overpay because they do not consider what they need the computer for.
- Where do you plan to use your computer? If you only plan to use it at home at your desk, then a desktop model will be fine. In general, you can get more computer for your money in a desktop model. However, if you think you may ever want to take the computer with you, then you will need some type of a laptop or tablet computer. When portability is a requirement, you will want to reconsider what you plan to use the computer for because as computers become more portable (smaller) their functionality changes and you want to make sure it will meet your needs.

- How long do you need service from this computer? Most things we purchase today are bought with the intention of being replaced in a few years. The length of service is really more about warranty and availability of repair services. In some cases, purchase decision should be made based on these issues rather than speed because they can extend the life of your computer.

There are always new tips for purchasing computers that often focus on the specs of a computer rather than some of these more aesthetic issues. Specs and recommendations will change, but the issues mentioned above will remain constant.

Input and Output Technologies

Input technologies allow people and other technologies to enter data into a computer. The two main types of input devices are human data-entry devices and source-data automation devices. As their name implies, *human data-entry* devices require a certain amount of human effort to input data. Examples are keyboard, mouse, pointing stick, trackball, joystick, touchscreen, stylus, and voice recognition.

In contrast, *source-data automation* devices input data with minimal human intervention. These technologies speed up data collection, reduce errors, and gather data at the source of a transaction or other event. Bar code readers are an example of source-data automation. Table PI2.1 describes the various input devices.

TABLE PI2.1 Input Devices

Input Device	Description
Human Data-Entry Devices	
Keyboards	Most common input device (for text and numerical data).
Mouse	Handheld device used to point cursor at point on screen, such as an icon; user clicks button on mouse instructing computer to take some action.
Optical mouse	Mouse is not connected to computer by a cable; mouse uses camera chip to take images of surface it passes over, comparing successive images to determine its position.
Trackball	User rotates a ball built into top of device to move cursor (rather than moving entire device such as a mouse).

(continued)

Input Device	Description
Pointing stick	Small button-like device; cursor moves in the direction of the pressure you place on the stick. Located between keys near center of keyboard.
Touchpad (also called a trackpad)	User moves cursor by sliding finger across a sensitized pad and then can tap pad when cursor is in desired position to instruct computer to take action (also called *glide-and-tap pad*).
Graphics tablet	A device that can be used in place of, or in conjunction with, a mouse or trackball; has a flat surface for drawing and a pen or stylus that is programmed to work with the tablet.
Joystick	Joystick moves cursor to desired place on screen; commonly used in workstations that display dynamic graphics and in video games.
Touch screen	Users instruct computer to take some action by touching a particular part of the screen; commonly used in information kiosks such as ATM machines. Touch screens now have gesture controls for browsing through photographs, moving objects around on a screen, flicking to turn the page of a book, and playing video games. For example, see the Apple iPhone.
Stylus	Pen-style device that allows user either to touch parts of a predetermined menu of options or to handwrite information into the computer (as with some PDAs); works with touch-sensitive screens.
Digital pen	Mobile device that digitally captures everything you write; built-in screen confirms that what you write has been saved; also captures sketches, figures, and so on with on-board flash memory.
Wii	A video game console by Nintendo. A distinguishing feature of the Wii is its wireless controller, which can be used as a handheld pointing device and can detect movement in three dimensions.
Microsoft Kinect	Enables users to control and interact with the Xbox 360 without the need to touch a game controller, through a natural interface using gestures and spoken commands.
Web camera (Webcam)	A real-time video camera whose images can be accessed via the Web or instant messaging.
Voice-recognition	Microphone converts analog voice sounds into digital input for computer; critical technology for physically challenged people who cannot use other input devices.

Source-Data Automation Input Devices

Automated teller machine	A device that includes source-data automation input in the form of a magnetic stripe reader; human input via a keyboard; and output via a monitor, printer, and cash dispenser.
Magnetic stripe reader	A device that reads data from a magnetic stripe, usually on the back of a plastic card (for example, credit or debit cards).
Point-of-sale terminals	Computerized cash registers that also may incorporate touch screen technology and bar code scanners to input data such as item sold and price.
Barcode scanners	Devices scan black-and-white bar code lines printed on merchandise labels.
Optical mark reader	Scanner for detecting presence of dark marks on predetermined grid, such as multiple-choice test answer sheets.
Magnetic ink character reader	Read magnetic ink printed on checks that identify the bank, checking account, and check number.
Optical character recognition	Software that converts text into digital form for input into computer.
Sensors	Collect data directly from the environment and input data directly into computer; examples include vehicle airbag activation sensors and radio-frequency identification tags.
Cameras	Digital cameras capture images and convert them into digital files.
Radio Frequency Identification (RFID)	Uses active or passive tags (transmitters) to wirelessly transmit product information to electronic readers.

The output generated by a computer can be transmitted to the user via several output devices and media. These devices include monitors, printers, plotters, and voice. Table PI2.2 describes the various output devices.

Multimedia technology is the computer-based integration of text, sound, still images, animation, and digitized motion video. It usually represents a collection of various input and output technologies. Multimedia merges the capabilities of computers with televisions, VCRs, CD players, DVD players, video and audio recording equipment, and music and gaming technologies. High-quality multimedia processing requires powerful microprocessors and extensive memory capacity, including both primary and secondary storage.

TABLE PI2.2 Output Devices

Output Device	Description
Monitors	
Cathode ray tubes	Video screens on which an electron beam illuminates pixels on display screen.
Liquid crystal display (LCDs)	Flat displays that have liquid crystals between two polarizers to form characters and images on a backlit screen.
Flexible displays	Thin, plastic, bendable computer screens.
Organic light-emitting displays	Displays that are brighter, thinner, lighter, cheaper, faster, and take less power diodes (OLEDs) to run than LCDs.
Retinal scanning displays	Project image directly onto a viewer's retina; used in medicine, air traffic control, and controlling industrial machines.
Heads-up displays	Any transparent display that presents data without requiring that the user look away from his or her usual viewpoint; for example, see Microvision (www.microvision.com).
Printers	
Laser	Use laser beams to write information on photosensitive drums; produce high-resolution text and graphics.
Inkjet	Shoot fine streams of colored ink onto paper; usually less expensive to buy than laser printers but can be more expensive to operate; can offer resolution quality equal to laser printers.
Thermal	Produces a printed image by selectively heating coated thermal paper; when the paper passes over the thermal print head, the coating turns black in the areas where it is heated, producing an image.
Plotters	Use computer-directed pens for creating high-quality images, blueprints, schematics, drawing of new products, and such.
Voice Output	A speaker/headset, which can output sounds of any type; voice output is a software function that uses this equipment.
Electronic Book Reader	A wireless, portable reading device with access to books, blogs, newspapers, and magazines. On-board storage holds hundreds of books.
Amazon Kindle Sony Reader Barnes and Noble Nook	
Pocket Projector	A projector in a handheld device that provides an alternative display method to alleviate the problem of tiny display screens in handheld devices. Pocket projectors will project digital images onto any viewing surface.
Pico Projector	A very small projector incorporated into portable devices, such as the Nikon Coolpix S1000pj camera. Also incorporated into Samsung and LG mobile phones.

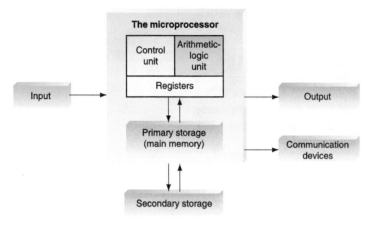

The microprocessor

| Control unit | Arithmetic-logic unit |
| Registers | |

Figure PI2.2 Parts of a microprocessor.

The Central Processing Unit

The **central processing unit (CPU)** performs the actual computation or "number crunching" inside any computer. The CPU is a **microprocessor** (for example, Intel's Core i3, i5, and i7 chips with more to come) made up of millions of microscopic transistors embedded in a circuit on a silicon wafer or *chip*. Hence, microprocessors are commonly referred to as chips.

As shown in Figure PI2.2, the microprocessor has different parts, which perform different functions. The **control unit** sequentially accesses program instructions, decodes them, and controls the flow of data to and from the arithmetic-logic unit, the registers, the caches, primary storage, secondary storage, and various output devices. The **arithmetic-logic unit (ALU)** performs the mathematic calculations and makes logical comparisons. The registers are high-speed storage areas that store very small amounts of data and instructions for short periods.

How the CPU Works. In the CPU, inputs enter and are stored until they are needed. At that point, they are retrieved and processed, and the output is stored and then delivered somewhere. Figure PI2.3 illustrates this process, which works as follows:

- The inputs consist of data and brief instructions about what to do with the data. These instructions come into the CPU from random access memory (RAM). Data might be entered by the user through the keyboard, for example, or read from a data file in another part of the computer. The inputs are stored in registers until they are sent to the next step in the processing.

- Data and instructions travel in the chip via electrical pathways called buses. The size of the bus—analogous to the width of a highway—determines how much information can flow at any time.

- The control unit directs the flow of data and instructions within the chip.

- The ALU receives the data and instructions from the registers and makes the desired computation. These data and instructions have been translated into **binary form**—that is, only 0s and 1s. A "0" or a "1" is called a **bit**. The CPU can process only binary data. All types of data, such as letters, decimal numbers, photographs, music, and so on, can be converted to a binary representation, which can then be processed by the CPU.

- The data in their original form and the instructions are sent to storage registers and then are sent back to a storage place outside the chip, such as the computer's hard drive. Meanwhile, the transformed data go to another register and then on to other parts of the computer (to the monitor for display or to storage, for example).

Figure PI2.3 How the CPU works.

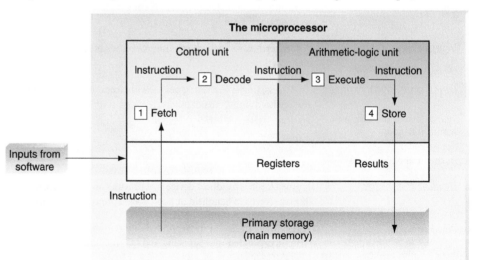

TABLE PI2.3 Comparison of Personal Computer Components and Cost over Time

Year	Chip	RAM	Hard Drive	Monitor	Cost
1997	Pentium II	64 megabytes	4 gigabytes	17-inch	$4,000
2007	Dual-core	1 gigabyte	250 gigabytes	19-inch	$1,700
2012	Quad-core	8 gigabytes	2 terabytes	22-inch	$1,700

Intel offers excellent demonstrations of how CPUs work: (search the web for "Intel" with "Explore the Curriculum" to find their demos).

This cycle of processing, known as a *machine instruction cycle*, occurs billions of times per second.

Advances in Microprocessor Design. Innovations in chip designs are coming at a faster and faster rate, as described by **Moore's law.** In 1965, Gordon Moore, a cofounder of Intel Corporation, predicted that microprocessor complexity would double approximately every 2 years. His prediction has been amazingly accurate.

The advances predicted from Moore's law arise mainly from the following changes:

- Producing increasingly miniaturized transistors.

- Placing multiple processors on a single chip. Chips with more than one processor are called *multicore* chips. For example, the Cell chip, produced by a consortium of Sony, Toshiba, and IBM, contains nine processors. Computers using the Cell chip display very rich graphics. The chip is also used in TV sets and home theaters that can download and show large numbers of high-definition programs. Intel (www.intel.com) and AMD (www.amd.com) offer multicore chips.

- In April 2012, Intel launched its next-generation chips, which employ a three-dimensional (3D) design. The 3D chips require less power than Intel's current chips while improving performance. These chips enhance the performance of all computers. However, they are particularly valuable in handheld devices, because they extend the device's battery life.

In addition to increased speeds and performance, Moore's law has had an impact on costs, as you can see in Table PI2.3.

Computer Memory

The amount and type of memory that a computer possesses has a great deal to do with its general utility. A computer's memory also determines the types of programs that the computer can run, the work it can perform, its speed, and its cost. There are two basic categories of computer memory. The first is *primary storage*. It is called "primary" because it stores small amounts of data and information that will be used immediately by the CPU. The second category is *secondary storage*, which stores much larger amounts of data and information (an entire software program, for example) for extended periods.

Memory Capacity. As you have seen, CPUs process only binary units—0s and 1s—which are translated through computer languages into bits. A particular combination of bits represents a certain alphanumeric character or a simple mathematical operation. Eight bits are needed to represent any one of these characters. This 8-bit string is known as a **byte**. The storage capacity of a computer is measured in bytes. Bits typically are used as units of measure only for telecommunications capacity, as in how many million bits per second can be sent through a particular medium.

The hierarchy of terms used to describe memory capacity is as follows:

- *Kilobyte. Kilo* means "one thousand," so a kilobyte (KB) is approximately 1,000 bytes. Actually, a kilobyte is 1,024 bytes. Computer designers find it convenient to work with powers of 2: 1,024 is 2 to the 10th power, and 1,024 is close enough to 1,000 that for *kilobyte* people use the standard prefix *kilo*, which means exactly 1,000 in familiar units such as the kilogram or kilometer.

- *Megabyte*. Mega means "one million," so a megabyte (MB) is approximately 1 million bytes. Most personal computers have hundreds of megabytes of RAM memory.
- *Gigabyte*. Giga means "one billion," so a gigabyte (GB) is approximately 1 billion bytes.
- *Terabyte*. A terabyte is approximately 1 trillion bytes. The storage capacity of modern personal computers can be several terabytes.
- *Petabyte*. A petabyte is approximately 1,000 terabytes.
- *Exabyte*. An exabyte is approximately 1,000 petabytes.
- *Zettabyte*. A zettabyte is approximately 1,000 exabytes.

To get a feel for these amounts, consider the following example: If your computer has one terabyte of storage capacity on its hard drive (a type of secondary storage), it can store approximately 1 trillion bytes of data. If the average page of text contains about 2,000 bytes, then your hard drive could store approximately 10 percent of all the print collections of the Library of Congress. That same terabyte can store 70 hours of standard-definition compressed video.

Primary Storage. **Primary storage** (or **main memory**, as it is sometimes called), stores three types of information for very brief periods of time: (1) data to be processed by the CPU, (2) instructions for the CPU as to how to process the data, and (3) operating system programs that manage various aspects of the computer's operation. Primary storage takes place in chips mounted on the computer's main circuit board, called the *motherboard*, which are located as close as physically possible to the CPU chip. As with the CPU, all the data and instructions in primary storage have been translated into binary code.

The four main types of primary storage are (1) register, (2) cache memory, (3) random access memory (RAM), and (4) read-only memory (ROM). You learn about each type of primary storage next.

Registers are part of the CPU. They have the least capacity, storing extremely limited amounts of instructions and data only immediately before and after processing.

Cache memory is a type of high-speed memory that enables the computer to temporarily store blocks of data that are used more often and that a processor can access more rapidly than main memory (RAM). Cache memory is physically located closer to the CPU than RAM. Blocks used less often remain in RAM until they are transferred to cache; blocks used infrequently remain in secondary storage. Cache memory is faster than RAM because the instructions travel a shorter distance to the CPU.

Random access memory (RAM) is the part of primary storage that holds a software program and small amounts of data for processing. When you start most software programs on your computer (such as Microsoft Word), the entire program is brought from secondary storage into RAM. As you use the program, small parts of the program's instructions and data are sent into the registers and then to the CPU. Compared with the registers, RAM stores more information and is located farther away from the CPU. However, compared with secondary storage, RAM stores less information and is much closer to the CPU.

RAM is temporary and, in most cases, *volatile*—that is, RAM chips lose their contents if the current is lost or turned off, as from a power surge, brownout, or electrical noise generated by lightning or nearby machines.

Most of us have lost data at one time or another due to a computer "crash" or a power failure. What is usually lost is whatever is in RAM, cache, or the registers at the time, because these types of memory are volatile. Therefore, you need greater security when you are storing certain types of critical data or instructions. Cautious computer users frequently save data to nonvolatile memory (secondary storage). In addition, most modern software applications have autosave functions. Programs stored in secondary storage, even though they are temporarily copied into RAM when they are being used, remain intact because only the copy is lost, not the original.

Read-only memory (ROM) is the place—actually, a type of chip—where certain critical instructions are safeguarded. ROM is nonvolatile, so it retains these instructions when the power to the computer is turned off. The read-only designation means that these instructions

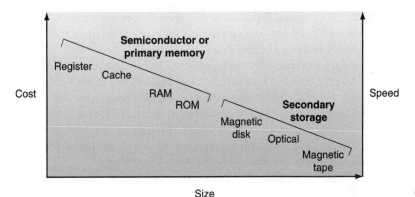

Figure PI2.4 Primary memory compared to secondary storage.

can only be read by the computer and cannot be changed by the user. An example of ROM is the instructions needed to start or "boot" the computer after it has been shut off.

Secondary Storage. **Secondary storage** is designed to store very large amounts of data for extended periods. Secondary storage has the following characteristics:

- It is nonvolatile.
- It takes more time to retrieve data from it than from RAM.
- It is cheaper than primary storage (see Figure PI2.4).
- It can utilize a variety of media, each with its own technology, as you see next.

One secondary storage medium, magnetic tape, is kept on a large open reel or in a smaller cartridge or cassette. Although this is an old technology, it remains popular because it is the cheapest storage medium, and it can handle enormous amounts of data. As a result, many organizations use magnetic tape for archival storage. The downside is that it is the slowest method for retrieving data because all the data are placed on the tape sequentially. Sequential access means that the system might have to run through the majority of the tape before it comes to the desired piece of data.

Magnetic disks (or **hard drives** or **fixed disk drives**) are the most commonly used mass storage devices because of their low cost, high speed, and large storage capacity. Hard disk drives read from, and write to, stacks of rotating (at up to 15,000 rpm) magnetic disk platters mounted in rigid enclosures and sealed against environmental and atmospheric contamination (see Figure PI2.5). These disks are permanently mounted in a unit that may be internal or external to the computer.

Solid state drives (SSDs) are data storage devices that serve the same purpose as a hard drive and store data in memory chips. Where hard drives have moving parts, SSDs do not. SSDs use the same interface with the computer's CPU as hard drives and are therefore a seamless replacement for hard drives. SSDs offer many advantages over hard drives. They use less power, are silent and faster, and produce about one-third the heat of a hard drive. The major disadvantage of SSDs is that they cost more than hard drives.

Unlike magnetic media, **optical storage devices** do not store data via magnetism. Rather, a laser reads the surface of a reflective plastic platter. Optical disk drives are slower than magnetic hard drives, but they are less susceptible to damage from contamination and are less fragile.

Figure PI2.5 Traditional hard drives are less expensive, but solid state drives are faster and are more reliable. (*Sources:* © АлексейБрагин/iStockphoto; © Krzysztof Krzyscin/iStockphoto.)

In addition, optical disks can store a great deal of information, both on a routine basis and when combined into storage systems. Types of optical disks include compact disk read-only memory and digital video disk.

Compact disk *read-only memory* (*CD-ROM*) storage devices feature high capacity, low cost, and high durability. However, because a CD-ROM is a read-only medium, it cannot be written on. *CD-R* can be written to, but once this is done, what was written on it cannot be changed later. That is, CD-R is writeable, which CD-ROM is not, but is not rewriteable, which *CD-RW* (compact disk, rewritable) is. There are applications where not being rewriteable is a plus, because it prevents some types of accidental data destruction. CD-RW adds rewritability to the recordable compact disk market.

The digital video disk (*DVD*) is a 5-inch disk with the capacity to store about 135 minutes of digital video. DVDs can also perform as computer storage disks, providing storage capabilities of 17 gigabytes. DVD players can read current CD-ROMs, but current CD-ROM players cannot read DVDs. The access speed of a DVD drive is faster than that of a typical CD-ROM drive.

A dual-layer *Blu-ray disc* can store 50 gigabytes, almost three times the capacity of a dual-layer DVD. Development of the Blu-ray technology is ongoing, with 10-layered Blu-ray discs being tested.

Flash memory devices (or *memory cards*) are nonvolatile electronic storage devices that contain no moving parts and use 30 times less battery power than hard drives. Flash devices are also smaller and more durable than hard drives. The trade-offs are that flash devices store less data than hard drives. Flash devices are used with digital cameras, handheld and laptop computers, telephones, music players, and video game consoles.

One popular flash memory device is the **thumb drive** (also called *memory stick, jump drive*, or *flash drive*). These devices fit into Universal Serial Bus (USB) ports on personal computers and other devices, and they can store many gigabytes. Thumb drives have replaced magnetic floppy disks for portable storage.

BEFORE YOU GO ON . . .

1. Decisions about hardware focus on what three factors?
2. What are the overall trends in hardware?
3. Define hardware and list the major hardware components.
4. Describe the computer hierarchy from the largest to the smallest computers.
5. Distinguish between human data-input devices and source-data automation.
6. Briefly describe how a microprocessor functions.
7. Distinguish between primary storage and secondary storage.

Apply the Concept PI 2.1

Background Computer hardware *components* have an interesting relationship with software. The physical size of the processor and memory is decreasing while their performance (speed and capacity) are increasing. Other hardware improvements have opened a whole new possibility for computer software. For example, smart phone hardware has created a market for app developers that did not exist just a few years ago. What will be next as processors and memory continue to improve performance and decrease in size?

Activity Visit http://www.wiley.com/go/rainer/applytheconcept and click on the links provided for Apply the Concept for Plug IT In 2.1. This will take you to Wikipedia articles where you can read about the history of computer hardware. You will notice that we are living in a time where innovation is progressing at an amazing speed.

Look up the year that you were born and see what was going on with technology. Then read every 10th year since then and finish by reading the latest entries. For example, if you were born in 1985 and the year now is 2013, you would look up 1985, 1995, 2005, and 2013. You may need to research other places to find more information.

Deliverable

Build a table that discusses the progression of technology since the year you were born. Highlight your favorite findings. Finally, project forward to the close of the next decade (according to the example above, 2015).

Submit your work to your professor.

Quiz questions are assignable in WileyPLUS, and available on the Book Companion Site at http://www.wiley.com/college/rainer.

PI2.2 Introduction to Software

Computer hardware is only as effective as the instructions you give it, and those instructions are contained in **software**. The importance of computer software cannot be overestimated. The first software applications of computers in business were developed in the early 1950s. Software was less costly in computer systems then. Today, software comprises a much larger percentage of the cost of modern computer systems because the price of hardware has dramatically decreased, while the complexity and the price of software have dramatically increased.

The increasing complexity of software also leads to the increased potential for errors or *bugs*. Large applications today can contain millions of lines of computer code, written by hundreds of people over the course of several years. The potential for errors is huge, and testing and *debugging* software is expensive and time-consuming.

Regardless of the overall trends in software—increased complexity, increased cost, and increasing numbers of defects—software has become an everyday feature of our business and personal lives. You begin your examination of software by defining some fundamental concepts. Software consists of **computer programs**, which are sequences of instructions for the computer. The process of writing, or *coding*, programs is called *programming*. Individuals who perform this task are called *programmers*.

Computer programs include **documentation**, which is a written description of the functions of the program. Documentation helps the user operate the computer system, and it helps other programmers understand what the program does and how it accomplishes its purpose. Documentation is vital to the business organization. Without it, if a key programmer or user leaves, the knowledge of how to use the program or how it is designed may be lost as well.

The computer is able to do nothing until it is instructed by software. Although computer hardware is, by design, general purpose, software enables the user to instruct a computer system to perform specific functions that provide business value. The two major types of software are systems software and application software. The relationship among hardware, systems software, and application software is illustrated in Figure PI2.6.

Systems software is a set of instructions that serves primarily as an intermediary between computer hardware and application programs (Figure PI2.7a–c). Systems software provides important self-regulatory functions for computer systems, such as loading itself when the computer is first turned on and providing commonly used sets of instructions for all applications. *Systems programming* refers to both the creation and the maintenance of systems software.

Application software is a set of computer instructions that provide more specific functionality to a user (Figures PI2.8 a–b). That functionality may be broad, such as general word processing, or narrow, such as an organization's payroll program. Essentially, an application program applies a computer to a certain need. *Application programming* refers to both the creation and the modification and improvement of application software. Application software may be proprietary or off the shelf. As you shall see, many different software applications are used by organizations today.

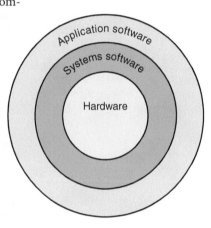

Figure PI2.6 Systems software services as intermediary between hardware and functional applications.

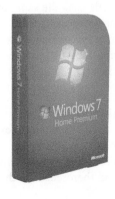

Figure PI2.7a–c System software. (*Source*: © Oliver Leedham/Alamy; © studiomode/Alamy.)

App Store

Figure PI2.8a–b Application software.

Software Issues

The importance of software in computer systems has brought new issues to the forefront for organizational managers. These issues include software defects (bugs), software evaluation and selection, licensing, open systems, and open-source software.

Software Defects. All too often, computer program code is inefficient, poorly designed, and riddled with errors. The Software Engineering Institute (SEI) at Carnegie Mellon University in Pittsburgh defines good software as usable, reliable, defect free, cost effective, and maintainable. As you become increasingly dependent on computers and networks, the risks associated with software defects are getting worse.

The SEI maintains that, on average, professional programmers make between 100 and 150 errors in every 1,000 lines of code they write. Fortunately, the software industry recognizes this problem. Unfortunately, however, the problem is enormous, and the industry is taking only initial steps to resolve it. One critical step is better design and planning at the beginning of the development process (discussed in Chapter 14).

Software Licensing. Although many people routinely copy software, making copies without the manufacturer's explicit permission is illegal. The Business Software Alliance (BSA) is a nonprofit trade association dedicated to promoting a safe and legal digital world. It collects, investigates, and acts on software piracy tips. Most tips come from current and past employees of the offending companies. The Business Software Alliance (BSA) (www.bsa.org) has calculated that software piracy costs software vendors around the world billions of dollars annually.

To protect their investment, software vendors must protect their software from being copied and distributed by individuals and other software companies. A company can copyright its software, which means that the U.S. Copyright Office grants the company the exclusive legal right to reproduce, publish, and sell that software.

As the number of desktop computers continues to increase and businesses continue to decentralize, it becomes more and more difficult for IS managers to supervise their software assets. In fact, a recent survey found that 70 percent of chief information officers (CIOs) are "not confident" that their companies are in compliance with software licensing agreements. For example, one medium-size company was fined $10,000 for Microsoft Exchange mailbox licenses for which the company unknowingly had not paid. Worse, the company was also fined $100,000 for not having the necessary licenses for Autodesk, Inc.'s AutoCAD design software.

To help companies manage their software licenses, new firms have arisen that specialize in tracking software licenses for a fee. Firms such as Express Metrix (www.expressmetrix. com), Insight Technology Solutions and others will track and manage a company's software licenses to ensure that the company is in compliance with U.S. copyright laws.

Open Systems. The concept of **open systems** refers to a model of computing products that work together. To achieve this goal, the same operating system with compatible software must be installed on all the different computers that interact with one another within an organization. A complementary approach is to produce application software that will run across all computer platforms. If hardware, operating systems, and application software are designed as open systems, the user will be able to purchase the best software, called *best of breed*, for the job without worrying whether it will run on particular hardware.

Open-Source Software. There is a trend within the software industry away from proprietary software toward open-source software. **Proprietary software** is software that has been developed by a company and has restrictions on its use, copying, and modification. The company developing such software spends money and time on research and development of its software product and then sells it in the marketplace. The proprietary nature of the software means that the company keeps the source code—the actual computer instructions—private (as Coca-Cola does with its formula).

In contrast, the source code for **open-source software** is available at no cost to developers and users. Open-source software is copyrighted and distributed with license terms ensuring that the source code will always be available.

Open-source software products have worldwide "communities" of developers who write and maintain the code. Inside each community, however, only a small group of developers, called *core developers*, is allowed to modify or submit changes to the code. Other developers submit code to the core developers.

Figure PI2.9 Open-source software. (*Source*: www. blackball.com.)

There are advantages and disadvantages to implementing open-source software in an organization. According to the Open Source Initiative (www.opensource.org), open-source development produces high-quality, reliable, low-cost software (Figure PI2.9). This software is also flexible, meaning that the code can be modified to meet the needs of the user. In many cases, open-source software is more reliable than commercial software. Because the code is available to many developers, more bugs are discovered early and quickly, and they are fixed immediately. Support for open-source software is also available from firms that provide products derived from the software. An example is Red Hat for Linux (www.redhat.com). These firms provide education, training, and technical support for the software for a fee.

Open-source software also has disadvantages, however. The biggest disadvantage is that companies using open-source software are dependent on the continued goodwill of an army of volunteers for enhancements, bug fixes, and so on, even if these companies contract for support. Some companies will not accept this risk, even though as a practical matter the support community for Linux, Apache, or Firefox is not likely to disappear. Further, organizations that do not have in-house technical experts will have to buy maintenance-support contracts from a third party. In addition, questions have arisen concerning the ease of use of open-source software, the amount of time and expense needed to train users, and the compatibility with existing systems or with the systems of business partners.

There are many examples of open-source software, including GNU (GNU's Not UNIX) suite of software (www.gnu.org) developed by the Free Software Foundation (www.fsf. org); Linux operating system (see www.linux.com); Apache Web server (www.apache.org); sendmail SMTP (Send Mail Transport Protocol) e-mail server (www.sendmail.org); Perl programming language (www.perl.org); Firefox 5 browser from Mozilla (www.mozilla. org); and the OpenOffice applications suite (www.openoffice.org). In fact, there are more than 150,000 open-source projects under way on SourceForge (www.sourceforge.net), the popular open-source hosting site.

Linux and Apache are excellent examples of how open-source software is moving to the mainstream. Linux is gaining market share in servers. It now runs on approximately one-fourth of all servers, whereas Microsoft runs on about two-thirds of all servers. Further, almost two-thirds of the world's Web servers now run Apache, compared to one-third for Microsoft.

Many major companies use open-source software. For example, Japan's Shinsei Bank (www.shinseibank.com/english) uses Linux on its servers, SugarCRM (www.sugarcrm. com) for certain customer relationship management tasks, and MySQL (www.mysql.com) open-source database management software. Further, the *Los Angeles Times* uses Alfresco (www.alfresco.com) to manage some of the images and video for the newspaper's Web site.

Systems Software

As noted, systems software is the class of programs that control and support the computer system and its information-processing activities. Systems software also facilitates the programming, testing, and debugging of computer programs. Systems software programs support application software by directing the basic functions of the computer. For example, when the computer is turned on, the initialization program (a systems program) prepares and readies all devices for processing. The major type of systems software with which we are concerned is the operating system.

The **operating system (OS)** is the director of your computer system's operations. It supervises the overall operation of the computer, including monitoring the computer's status, scheduling operations, and managing the input and output processes. The operating system also provides an interface between the user and the hardware.

This user interface hides the complexity of the hardware from the user. That is, you do not have to know how the hardware actually operates. You simply have to know what the hardware will do and what you need to do to obtain desired results.

The ease or difficulty of the interaction between the user and the computer is determined largely by the user interface. The **graphical user interface (GUI)** allows users to exercise direct control of visible objects (such as icons) and actions that replace complex commands.

The next generation of GUI technology will incorporate features such as virtual reality, head-mounted displays, speech input (user commands) and output, pen and gesture recognition, animation, multimedia, artificial intelligence, and cellular/wireless communication capabilities. The new interfaces, called *natural user interfaces* (NUIs), will combine *haptic interfaces*, *social interfaces*, and *touch-enabled gesture-control interfaces.*

A **haptic interface** allows the user to feel a sense of touch by applying forces, vibrations, and/or motions to the user. A **social interface** is a user interface that guides the user through computer applications by using cartoonlike characters, graphics, animation, and voice commands. The cartoonlike characters can be cast as puppets, narrators, guides, inhabitants, or avatars (computer-generated humanlike figures). Social interfaces are hard to do without being corny. For example, most users of Microsoft Office 97 found the assistant "Clippy" so annoying that it was deleted from Office 2003 and later versions.

Motion control gaming consoles are another type of interface. Three major players currently offer this interface: Xbox 360 Kinect, PS3 PlayStation Move, and Nintendo Wii.

- Kinect tracks your movements without a physical controller, has voice recognition, and accommodates multiple players.

- PlayStation Move uses a physical controller with motion-sensing electronics, making it the technological "cross" between Kinect and Wii. Move requires each player to use a wand.

- Wii uses a physical controller. Compared to Kinect and Move, Wii has been on the market longer, has the biggest library of motion-sensing games, and is the least expensive system. However, Wii has the least accurate motion sensing of the three systems, and it is not available in high-definition, whereas Kinect and Move are.

Touch-enabled gesture-control interfaces enable users to browse through photos, "toss" objects around a screen, "flick" to turn the pages of a book, play video games, and watch movies. Examples of this type of interface are Microsoft Surface and the Apple iPhone.

Microsoft Surface is used in casinos such as Harrah's iBar in Las Vegas and in some AT&T stores. The most visible use of Surface, however, was the touch wall used by CNN during the presidential election coverage in 2008.

Well-known desktop operating systems include Microsoft Windows (www.microsoft.com), Apple Mac OS X (www.apple.com), Linux (linux.com), and Google Chrome OS (www.google.com/). As their developers release new versions with new features, they often give the new version a new designation. For example, the latest version of Windows is Windows 7 and the latest version of OS X is Snow Leopard or OS X 10.6.

Application Software

As noted, application software consists of instructions that direct a computer system to perform specific information-processing activities and that provide functionality for users. Because there are so many different uses for computers, there are a correspondingly large number of application software programs.

Application software may be developed in house by the organization's information systems personnel, or it may be commissioned from a software vendor. Alternatively, it can be purchased, leased, or rented from a vendor that develops programs and sells them to many organizations. This "off-the-shelf" software may be a standard package, or it may be customizable. Special-purpose programs or "packages" can be tailored for a specific purpose, such as inventory control or payroll. The term **package** is commonly used for a computer program (or group of programs) that has been developed by a vendor and is available for purchase in a prepackaged form.

TABLE PI2.4 Personal Application Software

Category of Personal Application Software	Major Functions	Examples
Spreadsheets	Use rows and columns to manipulate primarily numerical data; useful for analyzing financial information, and for what-if and goal-seeking analyses	Microsoft Excel Corel Quattro Pro Apple iWork Numbers
Word processing	Allow users to manipulate primarily text with many writing and editing features	Microsoft Word Apple iWork Pages
Desktop publishing	Extend word processing software to allow production of finished, camera-ready documents, which may contain photographs, diagrams, and other images combined with text in different fonts	Microsoft Publisher QuarkXPress
Data management	Allow users to store, retrieve, and manipulate related data	Microsoft Access FileMaker Pro
Presentation	Allows users to create and edit graphically rich information to appear on electronic slides	Microsoft PowerPoint Apple iWork Keynote
Graphics	Allow users to create, store, and display or print charts, graphs, maps, and drawings	Adobe PhotoShop Corel DRAW
Personal information management	Allow users to create and maintain calendars, appointments, to-do lists, and business contacts	IBM Lotus Notes Microsoft Outlook
Personal finance	Allow users to maintain checkbooks, track investments, monitor credit cards, bank, and pay bills electronically	Quicken Microsoft Money
Web authoring	Allow users to design Web sites and publish them on the Web	Microsoft FrontPage Adobe Dreamweaver
Communications	Allow users to communicate with other people over any distance	Novell Groupwise

General-purpose, off-the-shelf application programs designed to help individual users increase their productivity are referred to as **personal application software**. Some of the major types of personal application software are listed in Table PI2.4. *Software suites* combine some of these packages and integrate their functions. Microsoft Office is a well-known example of a software suite.

Speech recognition software is an input technology, rather than strictly an application, that can feed systems software and application software. **Speech recognition software**, or **voice recognition software**, recognizes and interprets human speech, either one word at a time (discrete speech) or in a conversational stream (continuous speech). Advances in processing power, new software algorithms, and better microphones have enabled developers to design extremely accurate voice recognition software. Experts predict that, in the near future, voice recognition systems will likely be built into almost every device, appliance, and machine that people use. Applications for voice recognition technology abound. Consider these examples:

- Call centers are using the technology. The average call-center call costs $5 if it is handled by an employee, but only 50 cents with a self-service, speech-enabled system. The online brokerage firm E-Trade Financial uses Tellme (www.tellme.com) to field about 50,000 calls per day, thereby saving at least $30 million annually.

- Siri (Speech Interpretation and Recognition Interface) is an intelligent personal assistant and knowledge navigator that works as an application on the Apple iPhone 4S. The application uses a natural language user interface to answer questions, make recommendations (for example, recommendations for a nearby seafood restaurant), and perform other actions such as providing directions. Apple claims that the software adapts to the user's individual preferences over time and personalizes results.

- IBM's Embedded ViaVoice software powers GM's OnStar and other dashboard command systems, such as music players and navigational systems.
- Apple's Macintosh OS X and Microsoft's Windows 7 operating system come with built-in voice technology.
- Nuance's Dragon NaturallySpeaking (www.nuance.com) allows for accurate voice-to-text and e-mail dictation.
- Vocera Communications (www.vocera.com) has developed a communicator badge that combines voice recognition with wireless technologies. Among its first customers were medical workers, who use the badge to find medical records or to search through hospital directories by voice to find the right person to help with a patient problem.
- Vox-Tec's (www.voxtec.com) Phraselator, a handheld device about the size of a checkbook, listens to requests for a phrase and then delivers a translation in any of 41 specified languages. It is being used by U.S. troops in Iraq and Afghanistan to provide translations in Arabic and Pashto.

BEFORE YOU GO ON . . .

1. What does the following statement mean? "Hardware is useless without software."
2. What are the differences between systems software and application software?
3. What is open-source software, and what are its advantages? Can you think of any disadvantages?
4. Describe the functions of the operating system.

Apply the Concept PI 2.2

Background Have a look back at Figure PI 2.6. You will notice that hardware is the central component and the OS and applications are then installed on the hardware. Imagine that there is another ring called "input/output hardware" that encircles the entire figure. Given the recent increases in Internet bandwidth and hardware capabilities, many software services are being delivered through the World Wide Web, with minimal hardware requirements. Effectively, this has separated the computer such that the primary hardware and software is receiving inputs from a separate device.

Activity Visit http://www.wiley.com/go/rainer/applytheconcept and click on the link provided for Plug IT In 2.2. This will take you to a Web site that focuses in offering software without hardware. This particular company is called OnLive and it focuses on online gaming and virtual desktops. In the case of the company's online desktop, the software of the desktop is displayed on a mobile device (iPad, iPhone, or other mobile tablet device) while the software actually runs on hardware that is kept at a distance. There will be more on this later in Plug IT In 3.

For this activity, consider the pros and cons of your data processing and data storage taking place on remote hardware. In this case, you are strictly working with the software.

Deliverable

Build a table of advantages and disadvantages. Consider scenarios where you may experience physical losses locally (such as fire or theft)—perhaps your Internet connection is lost, perhaps the server for the software provider fails. Your table will be similar to the following.

Scenario	Advantage	Disadvantage

Quiz questions are assignable in WileyPLUS, and available on the Book Companion Site at http://www.wiley.com/college/rainer.

Hardware

For All Business Majors

The design of computer hardware has profound impacts for businesspeople. Personal and organizational success can depend on an understanding of hardware design and a commitment to knowing where it is going and what opportunities and challenges hardware innovations will bring. Because these innovations are occurring so rapidly, hardware decisions at both the individual level and at the organizational level are difficult.

At the *individual level*, most people who have a home or office computer system and want to upgrade it, or people who are contemplating their first computer purchase, are faced with the decision of *when* to buy as much as *what* to buy and at what cost. At the *organizational level*, these same issues plague IS professionals. However, they are more complex and more costly. Most organizations have many different computer systems in place at the same time. Innovations may come to different classes of computers at different times or rates. Therefore, managers must decide when old hardware *legacy systems* still have a productive role in the organization and when they should be replaced. A legacy system is an old computer system or application that continues to be used, typically because it still functions for the users' needs, even though newer technology is available.

Software

FOR THE ACCOUNTING MAJOR

Accounting application software performs the organization's accounting functions, which are repetitive and high volume. Each business transaction (e.g., a person hired, a paycheck produced, an item sold) produces data that must be captured. After accounting applications capture the data, they manipulate them as necessary. Accounting applications adhere to relatively standardized procedures, handle detailed data, and have a historical focus (i.e., what happened in the past).

FOR THE FINANCE MAJOR

Financial application software provides information about the firm's financial status to persons and groups inside and outside the firm. Financial applications include forecasting, funds management, and control applications. Forecasting applications predict and project the firm's future activity in the economic environment. Funds management applications use cash flow models to analyze expected cash flows. Control applications enable managers to monitor their financial performance, typically by providing information about the budgeting process and performance ratios.

FOR THE MARKETING MAJOR

Marketing application software helps management solve problems that involve marketing the firm's products. Marketing software includes marketing research and marketing intelligence applications. Marketing applications provide information about the firm's products and competitors, its distribution system, its advertising and personal selling activities, and its pricing strategies. Overall, marketing applications help managers develop strategies that combine the four major elements of marketing: product, promotion, place, and price.

FOR THE

PRODUCTION/OPERATIONS MANAGEMENT MAJOR

Managers use production/operations management (POM) applications software for production planning and as part of the physical production system. POM applications include production, inventory, quality, and cost software. These applications help management operate manufacturing facilities and logistics. Materials requirements planning (MRP) software is also widely used in manufacturing. This software identifies which materials will be needed, what quantities will be needed, and the dates on which they will be needed. This information enables managers to be proactive.

FOR THE

HUMAN RESOURCES MANAGEMENT MAJOR

Human resources management application software provides information concerning recruiting and hiring, education and training, maintaining the employee database, termination, and administering benefits. HRM applications include workforce planning, recruiting, workforce management, compensation, benefits, and environmental reporting subsystems (e.g., equal employment opportunity records and analysis, union enrollment, toxic substances, and grievances).

FOR THE MIS MAJOR

If your company decides to develop software itself, the MIS function is responsible for managing this activity. If the company decides to buy software, the MIS function deals with software vendors in analyzing their products. The MIS function is also responsible for upgrading software as vendors release new versions.

SUMMARY

1. **Discuss strategic issues that link hardware design to business strategy.**

   Strategic issues linking hardware design to business strategy encompass these questions: How do organizations keep up with the rapid price/performance advancements in hardware? How often should an organization upgrade its computers and storage systems? How can organizations measure benefits gained from price/performance improvements in hardware?

2. **Differentiate between the two major types of software.**

   Software consists of computer programs (coded instructions) that control the functions of computer hardware.

The two main categories of software are systems software and application software. Systems software manages the hardware resources of the computer system; it functions between the hardware and the application software. Systems software includes the system control programs (operating systems) and system support programs. Application software enables users to perform specific tasks and information-processing activities. Application software may be proprietary or off the shelf.

>>> GLOSSARY

application software The class of computer instructions that directs a computer system to perform specific processing activities and provide functionality for users.

arithmetic-logic unit (ALU) Portion of the CPU that performs the mathematic calculations and makes logical comparisons.

binary form The form in which data and instructions can be read by the CPU—only 0s and 1s.

bit Short for *binary digit* (0s and 1s), the only data that a CPU can process.

byte An 8-bit string of data, needed to represent any one alphanumeric character or simple mathematical operation.

cache memory A type of high-speed memory that enables the computer to temporarily store blocks of data that are used more often and that a processor can access more rapidly than main memory (RAM).

central processing unit (CPU) Hardware that performs the actual computation or "number crunching" inside any computer.

computer programs The sequences of instructions for the computer, which comprise software.

control unit Portion of the CPU that controls the flow of information.

documentation Written description of the functions of a software program.

fat clients Desktop computer systems that offer full functionality.

flash memory devices Nonvolatile electronic storage devices that are compact, are portable, require little power, and contain no moving parts.

graphical user interface (GUI) System software that allows users to have direct control of visible objects (such as icons) and actions, which replace command syntax.

haptic interface Allows the user to feel a sense of touch by applying forces, vibrations, and/or motions to the user.

laptop computers (notebook computers) Small, easily transportable, lightweight microcomputers.

magnetic disks (or hard drives or fixed disk drives) A form of secondary storage on a magnetized disk divided into tracks and sectors that provide addresses for various pieces of data.

magnetic tape A secondary storage medium on a large open reel or in a smaller cartridge or cassette.

mainframes Relatively large computers used in large enterprises for extensive computing applications that are accessed by thousands of users.

microcomputers The smallest and least expensive category of general-purpose computers; also called micros, personal computers, or PCs.

microprocessor The CPU, made up of millions of transistors embedded in a circuit on a silicon wafer or chip.

minicomputers Relatively small, inexpensive, and compact midrange computers that perform the same functions as mainframe computers, but to a more limited extent.

Moore's law Prediction by Gordon Moore, an Intel cofounder, that microprocessor complexity would double approximately every 2 years.

multimedia technology Computer-based integration of text, sound, still images, animation, and digitized full-motion video.

netbook A very small, lightweight, low-cost, energy-efficient, portable computer, typically optimized for Internet-based services such as Web browsing and e-mailing.

notebook computer (see computer)

open-source software Software made available in source code form at no cost to developers.

open systems A model of computing products that work together by use of the same operating system with compatible software on all the different computers that would interact with one another in an organization.

operating system (OS) The main system control program, which supervises the overall operations of the computer, allocates CPU time and main memory to programs, and provides an interface between the user and the hardware.

optical storage devices A form of secondary storage in which a laser reads the surface of a reflective plastic platter.

package Common term for a computer program developed by a vendor and available for purchase in prepackaged form.

personal application software General-purpose, off-the-shelf application programs that support general types of processing, rather than being linked to any specific business function.

primary storage (also called main memory) High-speed storage located directly on the motherboard that stores data to be processed by the CPU, instructions telling the CPU how to process the data, and operating systems programs.

proprietary software Software that has been developed by a company and has restrictions on its use, copying, and modification.

random access memory (RAM) The part of primary storage that holds a software program and small amounts of data when they are brought from secondary storage.

read-only memory (ROM) Type of primary storage where certain critical instructions are safeguarded; the storage is nonvolatile and retains the instructions when the power to the computer is turned off.

registers High-speed storage areas in the CPU that store very small amounts of data and instructions for short periods.

secondary storage Technology that can store very large amounts of data for extended periods.

sequential access Data access in which the computer system must run through data in sequence to locate a particular piece.

server Smaller midrange computers that support networks, enabling users to share files, software, and other network devices.

social interface A user interface that guides the user through computer applications by using cartoonlike characters, graphics, animation, and voice commands.

software A set of computer programs that enable the hardware to process data.

solid state drives (SSDs) Data storage devices that serve the same purpose as a hard drive and store data in memory chips.

speech recognition software (or voice recognition software) Software that recognizes and interprets human speech, either one word at a time (discrete speech) or in a stream (continuous speech).

supercomputer Computers with the most processing power available; used primarily in scientific and military work for computationally demanding tasks on very large data sets.

systems software The class of computer instructions that serve primarily as an intermediary between computer hardware and application programs; provides important self-regulatory functions for computer systems.

tablet computer (or tablet) A complete computer contained entirely in a flat touch screen that uses a stylus, digital pen, or fingertip as an input device instead of a keyboard or mouse.

thin-client systems Desktop computer systems that do not offer the full functionality of a PC.

thumb drive Storage device that fits into the USB port of a personal computer and is used for portable storage.

voice recognition software (see speech recognition software)

>>> DISCUSSION QUESTIONS

1. If you were the CIO of a firm, what factors would you consider when selecting secondary storage media for your company's records (files)?

2. Given that Moore's law has proved itself over the past 2 decades, speculate on what chip capabilities will be in 10 years. What might your desktop PC be able to do?

3. If you were the CIO of a firm, how would you explain the workings, benefits, and limitations of using thin clients as opposed to fat clients?

4. You are the CIO of your company, and you have to develop an application of strategic importance to your firm. What are the advantages and disadvantages of using open-source software?

5. You have to take a programming course, or maybe more than one, in your MIS program. Which programming language(s) would you choose to study? Why? Should you even have to learn a programming language? Why or why not?

>>> PROBLEM-SOLVING ACTIVITIES

1. Access the Web sites of the major chip manufacturers—for example, Intel (www.intel.com), Motorola (www.motorola.com), and Advanced Micro Devices (www.amd.com)—and obtain the latest information regarding new and planned chips. Compare performance and costs across these vendors. Be sure to take a close look at the various multicore chips.

2. Access "The Journey Inside" on Intel's Web site at (http://www.wiley.com/go/rainer/problemsolving). Prepare a presentation of each step in the machine instruction cycle.

3. A great deal of software is available for free over the Internet. Go to http://wiley.com/go/rainer/problemsolving, and observe all the software that is available for free. Choose one software program and download it to your computer. Prepare a brief discussion about the software for your class.

4. Enter the IBM Web site (www.ibm.com) and search on "software." Click on the drop box for "Products" and notice how many software products IBM produces. Is IBM only a hardware company?

5. Compare the following proprietary software packages with their open-source software counterparts, and prepare your comparison for the class:

Proprietary	Open Source
Microsoft Office	Google Docs, OpenOffice
Adobe Photoshop	Picnik.com, Google Picasa

6. Compare the Microsoft Surface interface (http://wiley.com/go/rainer/problemsolving) with Oblong Industries' (http://oblong.com) g-speak spatial operating environment. Demonstrate examples of both interfaces to the class. What are the advantages and disadvantages of each one?

Plug IT In | 3

Cloud Computing

LEARNING OBJECTIVES >>>

1. Describe the evolution of IT infrastructure.
2. Describe the key characteristics and advantages of cloud computing.
3. Identify a use-case-scenario for each of the four types of clouds.
4. Explain the operational model of each of the three types of cloud services.
5. Identify the key benefits of cloud computing.
6. Discuss the concerns and risks associated with cloud computing.
7. Explain the role of Web services in building a firm's IT applications, providing examples.

Because the overall goal of this book is for you to be an informed user of information technology, we devote this Plug IT In to a vital and cutting-edge topic: cloud computing. A working knowledge of cloud computing will enhance your appreciation of what technology can and cannot do for a business. In addition, it will enable you to make an immediate contribution by analyzing how your organization manages its information technology assets.

You will be using these computing resources yourself in your career and you will have input into decisions about how your department and organization can best utilize them. Additionally, cloud computing can be extremely valuable to you if you decide to start your own business.

This Plug IT In defines the cloud as distributed computing services and presents many examples of how the cloud can be used for business purposes. However, the cloud also provides you with personal applications, and this Plug IT In can help you plan for your own use of the cloud. See IT's Personal: "The Cloud" later in this Plug In.

PI 3.1 Introduction

You were introduced to the concept of IT infrastructure in Chapter 1. Recall that an organization's *IT infrastructure* consists of IT components—hardware, software, networks, and databases—and IT services—developing information systems, managing security and risk, and managing data. (It is helpful to review Figure 1.3 here.) The organization's IT infrastructure is the foundation for all of the information systems that the organization uses.

Modern IT infrastructure has evolved through several stages since the early 1950s, when firms first began to apply information technology to business applications. These stages are as follows:

- *Stand-alone mainframes.* Organizations initially used mainframe computers in their engineering and accounting departments. The mainframe was typically housed in a secure area and only MIS personnel had access to it.

- *Mainframe and dumb terminals.* Forcing users to go to wherever the mainframe was located was time-consuming and inefficient. As a result, firms began placing so-called dumb terminals—essentially electronic typewriters with little processing power—in user departments. This arrangement enabled users to input computer programs into the mainframe from their departments, a process called *remote job entry*.

- *Stand-alone personal computers.* In the late 1970s, the first personal computers appeared. The IBM PC's debut in 1981 legitimized the entire personal computer market. Users began bringing personal computers to the workplace to improve their productivity—for example, by using spreadsheet and word processing applications. These computers were not initially supported by the firm's MIS department. However, as the number of personal computers increased dramatically, organizations decided to support personal computers, and they established policies as to which personal computers and software they would support.

- *Local area networks (client/server computing).* When personal computers are networked, individual productivity is substantially increased. For this reason, organizations began to connect personal computers into local area networks (LANs) and then connect these LANs to the mainframe, a type of processing known as *client/server computing*.

- *Enterprise computing.* In the early 1990s, organizations began to use networking standards to integrate different kinds of networks throughout the firm, thereby creating enterprise computing. As the Internet became widespread after 1995, organizations began using the TCP/IP networking protocol to integrate different types of networks. All types of hardware were networked, from mainframes to personal computers to smart phones. Software applications and data could now flow seamlessly throughout the enterprise and between and among organizations.

- *Cloud computing and mobile computing.* Today, organizations and individuals can use the power of cloud computing. As you will see in this Plug IT In, cloud computing provides access to a shared pool of computing resources, including computers, storage, applications, and services, over a network, typically the Internet.

Keep in mind that the computing resources in each stage can be cumulative. For instance, most large firms still use mainframe computers (in addition to all the other types of computing resources) as large servers to manage operations that involve millions of transactions per day.

BEFORE *YOU GO ON . . .*

1. Describe the evolution of the IT infrastructure in organizations.

Apply the Concept PI 3.1

Background This section has shown how computer infrastructure has evolved over time. Early computing models were called "terminal to host" and now a similar model is called "cloud" or "distributed computing." It is helpful to understand how infrastructure models have changed so you can better predict how it may continue to evolve. The rise of mobile computers (smart phones) has driven much computing to servers to lessen the load on the smaller processors.

A key factor to distributed computing is the increasing bandwidth that allows for greater amounts of information to be sent over greater distances at greater speed.

Activity Create two continuums that show the distribution of processing and storage as the models have changed. First, show the location of processing as either distributed (on a central server) or local (on the local machine), then show the location of storage as either distributed or local. As you build these, be sure to discuss the typical bandwidth that was available when these models were used.

Deliverable

Submit your continuum to your professor. It will look something like the following.

Distributed
Processing

Centralized
Processing

Quiz questions are assignable in WileyPLUS, and available on the Book Companion Site at http://www.wiley.com/college/rainer.

PI 3.2 What Is Cloud Computing?

Information technology departments have always been tasked to deliver useful IT applications to business users. Today, however, for a variety of reasons, IT departments are facing increased challenges in delivering useful applications. This section begins with a look at problems that traditional IT departments face in delivering useful applications. In that way, when you learn about cloud computing, you will see how cloud computing can help organizations manage the problems that occur in traditional IT departments. You will also see why so many organizations are utilizing cloud computing. The section continues with a definition of cloud computing and closes with an examination of the essential characteristics of cloud computing.

Problems Facing Traditional IT Departments

Today, the world is experiencing a digital and mobile transformation, with more information available more quickly from more sources than ever before. As a result, businesspeople need IT-enabled services to help them handle this transformation and envision new opportunities.

Before you take a look at cloud computing, let's look at traditional IT departments in organizations and the problems they face. Today, most companies own IT infrastructure (their software, hardware, networks, and data management) and keep them "on premise" in their data centers, the traditional model of the IT function in organizations.

Traditional IT departments spend huge amounts on IT infrastructure and expert staffs to build and maintain complex IT systems. These expenses include software licenses, hardware, and staff training and salaries. Typically, these expenses result in an infrastructure that often is not used to its full capacity. The majority of these expenses are typically applied to maintaining existing IT infrastructure, with the remainder being spent on developing new systems. In addition, companies are being buried in vast amounts of data (which you learned about in Chapter 3). Traditional IT departments are having difficulty capturing, storing, managing, and analyzing all this data. As a result of these problems, traditional IT infrastructures can actually inhibit an organization's ability to respond quickly and appropriately to rapidly changing dynamic environments.

Large organizations can afford comprehensive enterprise software and top IT talent. These companies can buy or build software and install these systems in their data centers. They can enable their applications for use on different devices—desktops, laptops, tablets, and smart phones—and make them accessible to employees wherever they are. These companies can also make their applications available to people outside the organization, such as consultants, contractors, suppliers, customers, and other business partners. Although large companies have these capabilities, their IT departments are often overtaxed and are not able to accomplish all these functions. Further, smaller organizations usually do not have the resources to accomplish these functions.

As you will see in the next section, cloud computing can help organizations manage the problems that traditional IT departments face. The next section defines cloud computing and discusses cloud computing's essential characteristics.

Definition of Cloud Computing

Cloud computing is a type of computing that delivers convenient, on-demand, pay-as-you-go access for multiple customers to a shared pool of configurable computing resources (e.g., servers, networks, storage, applications, and services) that can be rapidly and easily accessed over the Internet. Cloud computing lets customers acquire resources at any time and get rid of them the instant they are no longer needed. The essential *characteristics* of cloud computing are as follows:

Cloud Computing Provides On-Demand Self-Service. A customer can access needed computing resources automatically.

Cloud Computing Encompasses the Characteristics of Grid Computing. Grid computing applies the unused processing resources of many geographically dispersed computers in a network to form a virtual supercomputer.

- Grid computing enables organizations to utilize their computing resources more efficiently.
- Grid computing provides fault tolerance and redundancy, meaning that there is no single point of failure, so the failure of one computer will not stop an application from executing.
- Grid computing makes it easy to "scale up" (add computers) to meet the processing demands of complex applications.
- Grid computing makes it easy to "scale down" (remove computers) if extensive processing is not needed.

Figure PI3.1 A server farm. Notice the ventilation in the racks and ceiling.

Cloud Computing Encompasses the Characteristics of Utility Computing. In **utility computing**, a service provider makes computing resources and infrastructure management available to a customer as needed. The provider then charges the customer for specific usage rather than a flat rate. Utility computing enables companies to efficiently meet fluctuating demands for computing power by lowering the cost of owning hardware infrastructure.

Cloud Computing Utilizes Broad Network Access. The cloud provider's computing resources are available over a network, accessed with a Web browser, and able to be used with any computing device.

Cloud Computing Pools Computing Resources. The cloud computing provider's computing resources are available to serve multiple customers, with resources dynamically assigned and reassigned according to customer demand.

Cloud Computing Often Occurs on Virtualized Servers. Cloud computing providers have placed hundreds or thousands of networked servers inside massive data centers called **server farms** (see Figure PI3.1). Recall that a *server* is a computer that supports networks, enabling users to share files, software, and other network devices. Server farms require massive amounts of electrical power, air-conditioning, backup generators, and security. They also need to be located fairly closely to fiber-optic communications links (see Figure PI3.2).

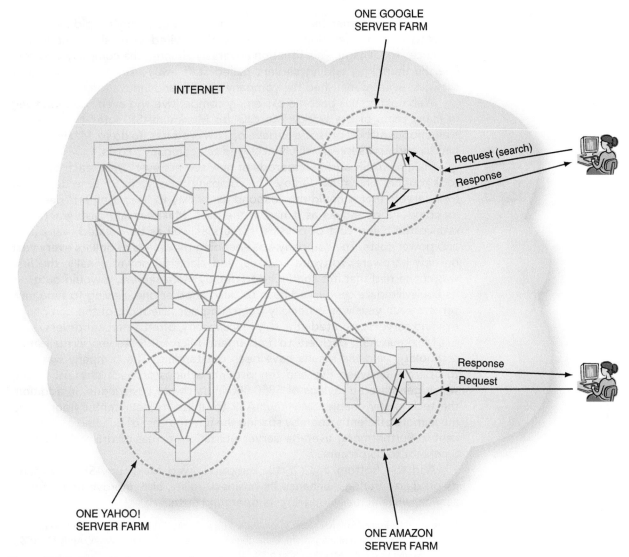

ONE GOOGLE
SERVER FARM

INTERNET

Request (search)

Response

ONE YAHOO!
SERVER FARM

ONE AMAZON
SERVER FARM

Response

Request

Figure PI3.2 Organizational server farms in relation to the Internet.

According to Gartner Inc. (www.gartner.com), a research firm, typical utilization rates on servers range from 5 to 10 percent. That is, most of the time, organizations are using only a small percentage of their total computing capacity. CIOs tolerate this inefficiency to make certain that they can supply enough computing resources to users in case of a spike in demand. To help with this underutilization problem, companies and cloud computing providers are utilizing virtualization.

Server virtualization uses software-based partitions to create multiple virtual servers—called *virtual machines*—on a single physical server. Therefore, each server no longer has to be dedicated to a particular task. This arrangement enables multiple applications to run on a single physical server, with each application running within its own software environment. As a result, virtualization enables companies to increase server utilization. In addition, companies see cost savings in two areas. First, they do not have to buy additional servers to meet peak demand and, second, they reduce their utility costs through reduced energy needs. The following example illustrates the benefits of virtualization for MaximumASP.

EXAMPLE

MaximumASP is a Web-hosting company based in Louisville, Kentucky. Its 35 employees host more than 48,000 domains for customers located in more than 60 countries. MaximumASP prides itself on its innovative offerings and its outstanding customer service. Unfortunately, the company's rapid expansion resulted in a proliferation of servers that required increasing amounts of resources to manage. This situation adversely affected the company's bottom line. Furthermore, adding servers pulled staff away from researching new services, which diminished the company's agility and innovation.

Web hosting has become extremely competitive and even commoditized in many parts of the world. The CIO for MaximumASP notes that there is tremendous market pressure to develop new products. To do so, MaximumASP had to add new servers, which increased the company's costs.

MaximumASP added hundreds of new servers every year, each of which took roughly 4 hours to deploy. The company spent so much time deploying new servers that it could not respond as quickly to its customers' needs or its competitors' moves as it had in the past. MaximumASP also wanted to reduce the rising cost of physical servers as well as the related real estate and power costs. The company was spending thousands of dollars every year on new hardware, software licenses, and electrical power. Finally, the firm was concerned that if it continued to deploy more servers, it would outgrow its Louisville data center and have to build another one. Having to fund new servers each year was especially frustrating because most of the company's existing servers operated at a very low capacity, often 5 percent or less.

MaximumASP decided to implement Microsoft's server virtualization technology, and the results have been outstanding. The company was able to operate between five and ten virtual machines on each physical server, which generated a savings of $350,000 in hardware costs alone. In addition, the technology enabled MaximumASP to utilize its data center floor space much more efficiently, thereby sparing the firm the cost of building a new data center. Furthermore, average server utilization increased dramatically from 5 percent to 65 percent.

And the bottom line? Virtualization allowed MaximumASP to expand its product offerings, enhance its business agility, and improve its customer service, while actually lowering its operating costs.

Sources: "MaximumASP," *Microsoft Virtualization Case Study*, 2011; J. Hoover, "Microsoft Ramps Up Virtualization Management, Management Services," *InformationWeek*, April 28, 2009; www.maximumasp.com, accessed March 19, 2012.

With cloud computing, setting up and maintaining an IT infrastructure need no longer be a challenge for an organization. Businesses do not have to scramble to meet the evolving needs of developing applications. With cloud computing, up-front capital expenses and operational costs are reduced, and infrastructure is better utilized and shared from one project to the next. The difficult tasks of procuring, configuring, and maintaining hardware and software environments are eased to a large degree by using cloud computing. Cloud computing allows enterprises to get their applications up and running faster, with easier manageability and less maintenance, and enables IT to more rapidly adjust IT resources (such as servers, storage, and networking) to meet fluctuating and unpredictable business demand.

Businesses are employing cloud computing for important and innovative work. The next example shows how Amazon has successfully "moved music into the cloud."

EXAMPLE

Amazon, whose online music store competes with Apple's (www.apple.com/icloud), has "moved music into its cloud" to solve two problems. The first problem is that music libraries have typically been scattered. For example, when you bought a new song at home, you could not listen to it at work, at least not without copying it manually. You could buy a song on your phone, but it would not be on your computer until you performed a sync. Moreover, if your music library was large, then you could fit only a portion of the music onto your phone. The second problem is that Amazon wants more people to buy music from its proprietary store, instead of from iTunes.

In March 2011, Amazon released a package of software and services that solved both of these problems. The fundamental idea behind the new package is that your music collection will reside in the cloud. That way, you can conveniently listen to it from any computer—at home, at work, at a friend's—by logging into a special Web page called the Amazon Cloud Player (www.amazon.com/clouddrive).

You can also listen to any of the songs in your music collection on an Android phone without having to copy or sync the music. All your songs are always available everywhere, and they do not take up any storage on your phone itself.

In addition to being accessible from anywhere, the Cloud Player has some other notable perks. It contains a list of your songs, which you can sort and search. You can also drag songs into playlists and play back a song, an album, or a playlist. Plus, you can download songs to your computer. Amazon also provides a free Uploader app that lets you send your existing music files to your online library so that your existing music is also available from anywhere.

The Cloud Player is almost free. To get you started, Amazon offers everyone 5 gigabytes of free space online—enough room for about 1,200 MP3 songs. You can buy additional storage for the price of $1 per gigabyte per year. Although this price might seem insignificant, the service can become expensive if you have a huge music collection—enough to make "pay $15 per month for unlimited music" sites like Rhapsody look appealing.

To attract customers, Amazon is offering incentives. For example, if you buy an album from Amazon's music store, your Cloud Drive storage is increased to 20 gigabytes for the year at no charge. In addition, any songs you buy from Amazon do not count against your storage limit.

Amazon faces tough competition with its Cloud Drive. Many other companies offer similar systems. Apple (www.apple.com/icloud) and Google (http://music.google.com) offer similar services. Also, Rdio (www.rdio.com), Audio Galaxy (www.audiogalaxy.com), Spotify (www.spotify.com), and GrooveShark (www.grooveshark.com) all offer some elements of the Amazon concept for less money.

Sources: Compiled from E. Bott, "How Amazon Has Outsmarted the Music Industry (and Apple)," *ZDNet*, March 30, 2011; D. Pogue, "The Cloud That Rains Music," *New York Times*, March 30, 2011; www.amazon.com/clouddrive, www.apple.com/icloud, http://music.google.com, accessed April 15, 2012.

In the next section, you learn about the various ways in which customers (individuals and organizations) can utilize cloud computing. These types of cloud computing include public clouds, private clouds, hybrid clouds, and vertical clouds.

BEFORE *YOU GO ON . . .*

1. Define cloud computing.
2. Describe the essential characteristics of cloud computing.

Apply the Concept PI 3.2

Background One of the more popular versions of virtual servers is a virtual Web server offered by Web hosting companies. Historically, someone would simply purchase and share space on a server that would host his or her files. However, many people today need dedicated servers so they have guaranteed performance for their consumers.

Activity Visit http://www.wiley.com/go/rainer/applytheconcept and click on the link provided for Apply the Concept 3.2 for Plug IT In 3.2. This will take you to the Web page of a company that provides different levels of virtual servers. Additionally, this company offers mobile reporting tools (also a form of cloud computing) where data are stored and analyzed locally and then distributed to the users over the Internet.

Read over the site and look for all the implementations you find of cloud computing.

Deliverable

Make a list of the ways you see cloud or distributed computing implemented by a company that hosts Web sites. Do any of these look reasonable for personal use?

Quiz questions are assignable in WileyPLUS, and available on the Book Companion Site at http://www.wiley.com/college/rainer.

PI 3.3 Different Types of Clouds

There are three major types of cloud computing, representing different types of exclusive and nonexclusive clouds provided to customers or groups of customers. The three types are public clouds, private clouds, and hybrid clouds. A fourth type of cloud computing is called vertical clouds. (See Figure PI3.3.)

Public Cloud

Public clouds are shared, easily accessible, multicustomer IT infrastructures that are available nonexclusively to any entity in the general public (individuals, groups, and/or organizations). Public cloud vendors provide applications, storage, and other computing resources as services over the Internet. Public cloud services may be free or offered on a pay-per-usage model.

Movirtu provides an example of a public cloud. Sharing mobile phones is a common practice among poor consumers in the developing world. Many customers use their own SIM card and switch it in and out when borrowing a mobile device. But, this practice can compromise privacy, and SIM cards are easy to lose.

Now, millions of impoverished citizens in Africa and Asia will receive mobile phone numbers under a plan developed by the United Nations and a private technology company, Movirtu. Movirtu (www.movirtu.com) is a cloud-based phone service that allows people to manage their own mobile network accounts—phone number, voice mail, texting, etc.—without ever owning a phone or a SIM card. The Movirtu service is priced with lower income users in mind and the mobile network carriers will get a share of the profits.

Movirtu will supply low-cost mobile phone numbers to participants, who can use any mobile device to login with their own number to make and receive calls and access information and services. The main beneficiaries will be women in rural communities in South Asia and sub-Saharan Africa, as they are far less likely than men to own their own phones.

Movirtu will bring the technology to 12 or more markets in the selected regions by early 2013, improving the lives and expanding the earning potential of at least 50 million people. The company selected Madagascar, an island nation off Africa's east coast, as a starting point. The country has an extensive network, but many of its citizens cannot afford to buy a phone. The service became available via a local carrier throughout the island in August 2011.

Private Cloud

Private clouds (also known as *internal clouds* or *corporate clouds*) are IT infrastructures that are accessible only by a single entity or by an exclusive group of related entities that share the same purpose and requirements, such as all the business units within a single organization. With private clouds, IT activities and applications are provided as a service over an intranet within an enterprise. Private clouds are usually private because of the need for system and data security, and for this reason they are behind the corporate firewall.

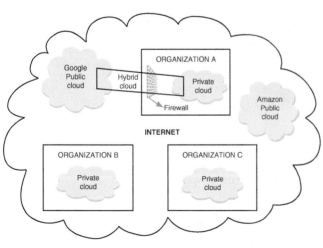

Figure PI3.3

Hybrid Cloud

Hybrid clouds are composed of public and private clouds that remain unique entities but are bound together, offering the benefits of multiple deployment models. Hybrid clouds deliver services based on security requirements, the mission-critical nature of applications, and other company-established policies. For example, customers may need to keep some of their data in a private cloud, for security and privacy reasons, but it may be more economical to keep some other, perhaps less sensitive, data in a public cloud, because the cost of these is generally lower.

Vertical Clouds

It is now possible to build cloud infrastructure and applications for different businesses—the construction, finance, or insurance businesses, for example—thus building vertical clouds (see www.vertical-cloud.com).

┌─ BEFORE *YOU GO ON . . .* ─┐
1. Define *public clouds*.
2. Define *private clouds*.
3. Define *hybrid clouds*.

Apply the Concept PI 3.3

Background This section describes public, private, and hybrid clouds. Specifically, it describes a public cloud used in developing countries to help protect the privacy of mobile phone users.

There are many other public cloud examples. Amazon, Apple, and Google are some of the bigger names in cloud services for personal use. These provide storage for files and access to music and videos. Google also offers document modification in the cloud. Dropbox is a popular file storage and sharing service. In fact, Dropbox integrates so well with different platforms, it may be the most popular storage service available.

Activity Visit http://www.wiley.com/go/rainer/applytheconcept and click on the link provided. It will take you to the home page for Dropbox. You can sign up for a free account that (at the time of this writing) is about 2GB. There are many free services that Dropbox offers such as mobile apps, file sharing, and photo sharing.

First, you will need to sign up for a free account. Next, create a Word document about the services Dropbox provides and upload this document along with a screenshot of the Dropbox Web site. Create a folder named "Plug IT In 3.3" and move the files into the folder. Then share the folder. This should generate a link that will allow you to share the folder with other people by e-mail.

Deliverable

Share the link provided by Dropbox with your professor.

Quiz questions are assignable in WileyPLUS, and available on the Book Companion Site at http://www.wiley.com/college/rainer.

PI 3.4 Cloud Computing Services

Cloud computing providers offer their services according to three service models: infrastructure-as-a-service (IaaS), platform-as-a-service (PaaS), and software-as-a-service (SaaS). These models represent the three types of computing generally required by consumers: infrastructure to run software and store data (IaaS), platforms to develop applications (PaaS), and software applications to process their data (SaaS). Figure PI 3.4 shows the differences between on-premise software, Infrastructure-as-a-Service, Platform-as-a-Service, and Software-as-a-Service.

Note that as you look at the figure from left to right, the customer manages less and less, and the vendor manages more and more.

There are similarities across these three service models: First, customers rent them instead of buying them, shifting IT from a capital expense to an operating expense. Second,

ON-PREMISE SOFTWARE	INFRASTRUCTURE-AS-A-SERVICE	PLATFORM-AS-A-SERVICE	SOFTWARE-AS-A-SERVICE
CUSTOMER MANAGES { Applications, Data, Operating system, Servers, Virtualization, Storage, Networking	**CUSTOMER MANAGES** { Applications, Data, Operating system **VENDOR MANAGES** { Servers, Virtualization, Storage, Networking	**CUSTOMER MANAGES** { Applications, Data **VENDOR MANAGES** { Operating system, Servers, Virtualization, Storage, Networking	**VENDOR MANAGES** { Applications, Data, Operating system, Servers, Virtualization, Storage, Networking
Examples	Amazon, IBM, Google, Microsoft, Rackspace	Mircosoft Windows Azure, Google App Engine, Force.com	Salesforce.com, Google Apps, Dropbox, Apple iCloud, Box.net

Figure PI3.4 Comparison of On-premise software, Infrastructure-as-a-Service, Platform-as-a-Service, and Software-as-a-Service.

vendors are responsible for maintenance, administration, capacity planning, troubleshooting, and backups. Finally, it is usually fast and easy to obtain more computing resources (i.e., scale) from the cloud—e.g., more storage from an IaaS vendor, the ability to handle more PaaS projects, or more seats for users of a SaaS application.

Infrastructure as a Service (IaaS)

With the **infrastructure-as-a-service** (IaaS) model, cloud computing providers offer remotely accessible servers, networks, and storage capacity. (IaaS is also referred to as *hardware-as-a-service*.) IaaS providers supply computing resources on demand from their large pools of such resources located in their data centers.

IaaS customers are often technology companies with IT expertise. They want access to computing power but do not want to be responsible for installing or maintaining it. Companies use the infrastructure to run software or simply to store data.

To deploy their applications, IaaS users install their operating system and their application software on the cloud computing provider's computers. With IaaS, customers can deploy any software on the infrastructure, including different operating systems, applications, or development platforms. The IaaS user is responsible for maintaining their operating system and application software. Cloud providers typically bill IaaS services on a utility computing basis—i.e., cost reflects the amount of resources consumed.

For example, Amazon sells the spare capacity of its vast IT infrastructure to its customers in a cloud environment. These services include its Simple Storage Service (S3) for storing customers' data and its Elastic Compute Cloud (EC2) service for operating their applications. Customers pay only for the amount of storage and computing they use.

Platform as a Service (PaaS)

In the **platform-as-a-service** (PaaS) model, customers rent servers, operating systems, storage, a database, software development technologies such as Java and .NET, and network capacity over the Internet. The PaaS model allows the customer to run existing applications or develop and test new applications.

PaaS offers customers several advantages, which include the following:

- Application developers can develop and run their software solutions on a cloud platform without the cost and complexity of buying and managing the underlying hardware and software layers.
- Underlying computing and storage resources scale automatically to match application demand.

- Operating system features can be upgraded frequently.
- Geographically distributed development teams can work together on software development projects.
- PaaS services can come from diverse sources anywhere in the world.
- Initial and ongoing costs can be reduced by the use of infrastructure services from a single vendor rather than maintaining multiple hardware facilities that often perform duplicate functions or suffer from incompatibility problems.

For example, the city of Miami (www.miamigov.com) is putting PaaS to good use. Miami has built a service that monitors nonemergency 311 requests. City officials and local residents can go to a Web site that pulls up a map of the city with pins in every spot that is tied to a 311 complaint. Before cloud computing, the city would have needed three months to develop the concept, buy new hardware (including backups in case of a hurricane), get a team to install the necessary software, and then build the application. Now that cloud computing is an option, Miami had a working prototype within 8 days and deployed the application shortly thereafter.

Software as a Service (SaaS)

With the **software-as-a-service** (**SaaS**) delivery model, cloud computing vendors provide software that is specific to their customers' requirements. The SaaS model is the largest and it provides a very wide range of software applications. The pricing model for SaaS applications is typically a monthly or yearly flat fee per user.

These applications reside in the cloud instead of on a user's hard drive or in a data center. The host manages the software and the infrastructure that runs this software and that stores data. The customers do not control the software, beyond the usual configuration settings, or the infrastructure, beyond changing the resources they use, such as the amount of disk space required for their data. This process eliminates the need to install and run the application on the cloud user's own computers simplifying maintenance and support.

What makes a SaaS application different from other applications is its ability to scale (i.e., access increased computing resources). This process means that applications can run on as many servers as necessary to meet changing demands. This process is transparent to the cloud computing user.

To reduce the risk of an infrastructure outage, SaaS providers regularly backup all data, across all customers. However, customers can also back up their own data on their own storage hardware.

For example, Flextronics (www.flextronics.com) is using SaaS from Workday for some of its human resources management function. Flextronics is the Singapore-based manufacturer of such electronics as Research in Motion's BlackBerry handsets and Microsoft's motion-sensing Kinect add-on for the Xbox 360 gaming console. The chief information officer of Flextronics knew he was taking risks as he handed over the human resources computing tasks for his 200,000-employee company to Workday (www.workday.com), an outside provider. What would happen, for example, if Workday lost sensitive employee data?

Workday handled Flextronics's human resources processes from tracking employee compensation and benefits to hiring for open positions. By outsourcing to Workday rather than handling HR computing in-house with on-premise IT infrastructure, Flextronics was able to save $100 million in 3 years and employee information remained secure. These expense reductions were critically important at Flextronics, which has an operating margin of only 2.9 percent.

A subset of the SaaS model is the *Desktop-as-a-Service* (DaaS) model. In the DaaS model, a SaaS provider hosts a desktop personal computer software environment, including productivity and collaboration software–spreadsheets, word processing programs, etc. such as Google Apps, Microsoft 365, and other products. The DaaS model means that only a thin client can access all the required software. The DaaS model can be financially advantageous for the consumer. Also, it simplifies deployment and administration of the PC environment. DaaS is also known as a *cloud desktop* or *desktop in the cloud*.

BEFORE YOU GO ON . . .

1. What is infrastructure-as-a-service?
2. What is platform-as-a-service?
3. What is software-as-a-service?

T'S PERSONAL: "THE CLOUD"

This Plug IT In defines the cloud as distributed computing services and presents many examples of how the cloud can be used for both personal and business purposes. This IT's Personal is intended to help you differentiate between the business and personal applications of the cloud and help you plan for your own use of the cloud.

First, you need to understand that there is no single "cloud" but that almost all businesses calls their Internet-based services "cloud services." Basically, anything you do over the Internet that you used to do on a local computer is a form of cloud computing. When you store files on Dropbox, type a document with Google Docs, use iCloud to store purchases or sync documents, or use OnLive on your iPad, you are using cloud-based services intended for personal use.

Infrastructure-as-a-service is an important application of the cloud for personal purposes. Dropbox is one of the most prominent companies in this area. In the past, users had to carry around a USB drive, CD, external hard drive, or (way back in the day) floppy discs to store their personal information. At the time of this writing, a free Dropbox account offers 2 GB of online storage. Not only does this offer you a place to store your files (eliminating the need for personal infrastructure of removable storage), but it provides synchronization across computers and access from mobile devices!

Virtualization is gaining ground. If you have an iPad you should look up the app called "OnLive" and give it a test run. It allows you to log into a virtual computer that is running Windows 7. Here, your iPad is simply providing the input/output and the server is "serving up" a virtual operating system. It is very likely that one day your home computer will be virtual as well.

Software-as-a-service has been a popular option for quite some time. Google Docs have offered Internet-based word processing, spreadsheet, presentation, forms, and drawing tools for quite some time. Recently, Microsoft has moved into the game with their Microsoft Office 365 product. Basically, each of these services allows you to use a computer program without having to install it on your computer or mobile device. You simply access the entire program (and your saved files) over the Internet.

Google recently combined a couple of these cloud services with Google Drive, a service that offers the same services as Dropbox with the addition of their online Google Docs editing and sharing of files. This also crosses over with software-as-a-service because of the added benefit of Google Docs. It is very likely that one day Google will try again with its Chrome Notebook, which would merge virtualization, infrastructure, and software into one cloud-based service. When this happens, all you will need as a consumer is an Internet-connected device and you will be able to store, access, edit, and share your files from the cloud. You will also be able to choose apps to run on your "virtual machine" much the way that today you go through a vendor-approved store to purchase applications for your mobile devices.

So what is the point? Cloud-based services are here to stay. The rise of ubiquitous Internet access has brought a new world of possibilities. As you move into your future, you need to pay close attention to privacy statements and Internet security. Because your files, apps, and editing capability will no longer be stored on a local machine, they are only as safe as the company you have trusted them with makes them. Be sure you choose wisely!

Apply the Concept PI 3.4

Background Software-as-a-service (SaaS) is growing at a very rapid pace. More and more applications are being made available where companies just subscribe to the service rather than purchasing, installing, and maintaining the software. This makes it easier on the purchasing company because it does not have to manage updates, patches, etc. They are all just rolled out by the host/providing company.

Activity Visit http://www.wiley.com/go/rainer/applytheconcept and click on the link provided for Apply the Concept for Plug IT In 3.4. It will take you to a page that shows some industry examples of SaaS. Choose one and learn all you can about it. Research some companies that offer software for purchase that performs the same function. For example, if you choose to read about "Payroll" SaaS, you may also research ADP's Payroll solutions to compare.

Deliverable

Prepare a brief summary of your comparison of the SaaS solution you chose and the one that is installed and run locally. Is there any reason you would pick one over the other?

Quiz questions are assignable in WileyPLUS, and available on the Book Companion Site at http://www.wiley.com/college/rainer.

PI 3.5 Cloud Computing Benefits

Cloud computing offers benefits for individuals and groups. It allows companies to increase the scale and power of their IT and the speed at which it can be deployed and accessed. It eliminates administrative headaches and works across locations, devices, and organizational boundaries.

Cloud computing has changed both business and everyday life—from consumers who use it to access their favorite music to companies that harness its powerful resources. When utilized effectively, cloud computing capabilities offer numerous opportunities to businesses to drive innovation. Organizations are exploiting cloud computing to transform both product and service development and strengthen customer relationships.

Organizations of all sizes, across geographies, and in virtually every industry are using cloud computing as a way to reduce the complexity and costs associated with traditional IT approaches. Nearly half of the respondents in a recent CIO Economic Impact survey indicated that they evaluate cloud computing options first—over traditional IT approaches—before making any new IT investments.

Organizations are not only relying on cloud computing to enhance internal efficiencies, but also to target more strategic business capabilities. IBM predicts that the global cloud computing market will grow 22 percent annually to $241 billion by 2020.

Benefit 1: Making Individuals More Productive

Cloud computing can enable companies to ensure that their employees have access to all the information they need no matter where they are, what device they are using, or whom they are working with.

Cloud computing provides a way for organizations to "hide" some of the complexity of their operations from end users, which can help attract a broader range of consumers. Because complexity is hidden from the end user, a company can expand its product and service sophistication without needing to increase the level of user knowledge to utilize or maintain the product or service.

For example, global contractor Balfour Beatty (www.balfourbeatty.com) is using cloud computing to allow its employees access to the information they needed to do their jobs. The company's design and construction professionals spend much of their time on job sites overseas, where they needed instant and reliable access to cost estimates, photos, blueprints, and other large files. For 10 years, Balfour had been managing uploads and downloads of all these documents with an internal FTP (file transfer protocol) server maintained by its IT department, which was difficult to use and constantly running out of capacity.

Therefore, Balfour turned to Box (www.box.com), a provider of cloud-based content management and file sharing. Balfour employees can now access resources stored on Box via a Web browser located on computers, tablets, and smart phones.

Although the firm had implemented Box to allow easier access to its information, it quickly realized that Box had other advantages as well. With the old system, the IT department had to sign up each new user and create a unique folder for him or her. If a user wanted to invite a collaborator into that folder, the request also had to be routed through IT. With the cloud-based solution, users could administer their own accounts and digital properties, saving valuable time. Overall, the Box cloud-based solution significantly improved productivity at Balfour.

Benefit 2: Facilitating Collaboration

Cloud computing enables groups and communities to work together in ways that were previously not possible. Cloud computing facilitates external collaboration with business partners and customers, which can lead to improvements in productivity and increased innovation. Cloud-based platforms can bring together disparate groups of people who can collaborate and share resources, information, and processes.

For example, to improve knowledge capture and sharing among its 90,000 employees, CSC (www.csc.com), is using Jive's cloud-based collaboration software. CSC's first step was an experiment to see if people would be receptive to working with the software. Jive was made available to all employees, an approach that would have been prohibitively expensive if CSC had needed to buy all the hardware and software licenses itself. People could use Jive to, among other things, pose a question to the entire company, visit and contribute to digital forums like "Where Have We Done This Before?" and "Excel Power Tips," and set up new communities as needed.

During the initial 20-week experiment, more than 25,000 people registered for the new cloud-based resource, called C3. They created more than 2,100 groups and logged as many as 150,000 activities per month. Those results persuaded CSC to make C3 permanent. The company chief information officer noted that the results had been "stunning." He said that C3 is now the standard for how CSC collaborates.

Benefit 3: Mining Insights from Data

Analytics is one of the most popular cloud computing applications. Companies today gather massive amounts of data, and cloud providers are providing the hardware and software algorithms to help businesses perform sophisticated analyses of this data.

For example, restaurant owners can use Aloha Restaurant Guard, a cloud-based service from Radiant Systems, to reduce shrinkage. Shrinkage, a polite term for employee theft, is a serious problem in the food service industry. It is also a difficult problem to solve, because it is difficult for restaurant owners to closely monitor servers and bartenders in their busy work environments.

Enter Radiant Systems (www.radiantsystems.com), a company that supplies the Aloha point-of-sale system to thousands of restaurants and keeps their data. Radiant realized that the huge amounts of transaction data that it kept for each customer could be analyzed for suspicious patterns, such as a volume of large tips far above average for bartenders on a Friday night. When this pattern occurs, it is likely that the bartender is not charging people for drinks in hopes of getting a big tip.

Using data from all of its customers, Radiant developed a set of algorithms to detect many types of shrinkage and bundled them into a product called Aloha Restaurant Guard (ARG). ARG generates a weekly set of reports on suspicious activity by site and by employee. These reports are sent to restaurant owners and managers, who use them to take corrective action. The results can be surprising and dramatic. According to Radiant, one casual dining restaurant saw a profit increase of $20,000 to $40,000 per year after using ARG to detect employee theft. The restaurant owner did not have to buy or install any new software, hire IT people, or alter his IT infrastructure in any way.

Benefit 4: Reduce Costs

Cloud computing can help an organization reduce fixed IT costs by enabling a shift from capital expenses to operational expenses. IT capital expenses—which typically include enterprise software licenses, servers and networking equipment, and other costs—tend to be more expensive than routine IT operating expenses. With cloud computing applications, there is no need to buy hardware, build and install software, or pay dedicated software licensing fees. By adopting cloud computing services, an organization can shift costs from capital to operational—or from fixed to variable. The organization pays only for the computing resources it needs, only when it needs them. This pay-for-use model provides greater flexibility and eliminates the need for significant capital expenditures.

Consider Etsy (www.etsy.com), an online marketplace for handmade goods. In addition to bringing buyers and sellers together, Etsy provides recommendations for buyers. The company rents hundreds of Amazon servers every night to cost-effectively analyze data from the 1 billion monthly views of its Web site. When Etsy's engineers come to work in the morning, they have a wealth of data showing what types of clothes, furniture, and jewelry appeal to what types of people. Etsy has used this information to create product recommendation systems that let people rank their interest in a series of products. Etsy then creates a list of products that they might like. Consumers can also grant Etsy permission to search through their Facebook accounts and find products that their friends might like as gifts. The cost flexibility afforded by cloud computing provides Etsy access to tools and computing power that have, in the past, been affordable only for larger retailers.

Benefit 5: Expand Scope of Business Operations

Cloud computing allows organizations to use the amount of computing resources they need, without any limitations. Therefore, companies utilizing cloud computing are able to increase the scope of their business operations.

Consider Netflix (www.netflix.com), an Internet subscription service for movies and television shows. Because the company streams many movies and shows on demand, it faces large surges of capacity at peak times. As Netflix began to outgrow its data center capabilities (on-premise IT), the company decided to move its Web site and streaming service from a traditional data center implementation to a cloud computing environment. This move allowed Netflix to manage peak demands more efficiently and effectively, providing a better customer experience. As a result, Netflix was able to grow and expand its customer base without having to build and support the larger data center that they would have needed to meet company requirements.

Benefit 6: Respond Quickly to Market Changes

The ability to quickly respond to rapidly changing customer needs is a critically important strategic goal for organizations. Therefore, companies are continuously seeking ways to improve their agility in adjusting to market demands. Cloud computing enables businesses to rapidly adjust business processes, products, and services to meet the changing needs of the market. Furthermore, cloud computing facilitates rapid prototyping and innovation, and speeds time to market for new products.

For example, ActiveVideo (www.activevideo.com) recognized cloud computing's potential to enhance their market adaptability when they created CloudTV, a cloud-based platform that unifies all forms of content—Web, television, mobile, social, video-on-demand, etc.—onto any video screen. Content and applications from Web content creators, television networks, advertisers, and other media entities can be quickly developed for CloudTV using standard Web tools. CloudTV leverages content stored and processed in the cloud to significantly expand the reach and availability of Web-based user experiences, and allow operators to quickly deploy a consistent user interface across diverse set top boxes and connected devices. The CloudTV approach of placing the intelligence in the network, rather than in the device, enables content creators, service providers, and consumer electronics manufacturers to create new television experiences for their viewers.

Benefit 7: Customize Products and Services

Because of its expanded computing power and capacity, cloud computing can store massive amounts of information about user preferences, which can then serve to enable customization of a service or a product. This context-driven variability allows businesses to offer personal experiences to users by having the service or production adapt to subtle changes in user-defined context. As a result, the company's customers are more likely to enjoy their personally customized experience, and are more likely to become return customers.

A good example of a product that has effectively made use of cloud computing's user preference storage is Siri, the Apple iPhone 4S cloud-based natural language "intelligent assistant." Siri allows users to send messages, schedule meetings, place phone calls, locate restaurants, and much more. And while other phones have some voice recognition features, Siri effectively "learns your voice." Siri uses artificial intelligence and a growing base of knowledge about the user, including his or her location and frequent contacts, to understand not only what users say, but what they actually mean. Siri leverages cloud computing to enable individualized, context-relevant customer experiences.

— BEFORE *YOU GO ON* . . . —

1. Describe several benefits that cloud computing can offer organizations. Provide a specific example of each benefit you discuss.

Apply the Concept PI 3.5

Background This section has outlined the benefits that are driving many organizations to use cloud computing. Productivity, cost reduction, collaboration, more robust data mining, flexibility, and scope expansion are just the beginning. Cloud computing is a powerful tool that is changing the way we do business today.

Activity Search the Web for a company that offers cloud computing services of some kind. Then look for customer testimonials. Read them over and see if these customers indicate the same benefits that we have discussed in the book.

Deliverable

Write a paragraph about the company you have learned about, what that company does with cloud computing, and which benefits parallel what you have read about in the book.

Submit your work to your professor.

Quiz questions are assignable in WileyPLUS, and available on the Book Companion Site at http://www.wiley.com/college/rainer.

PI 3.6 Concerns and Risks with Cloud Computing

Even though Gartner predicts that cloud computing will grow at an annual rate of 19 percent through the year 2015, cloud computing will still account for less than 5 percent of total worldwide IT spending that year. Why is this percentage so low? The reason is that there are serious concerns with cloud computing. These concerns fall into the areas of legacy IT systems, cost, reliability, security, and regulations.

Concern 1: Legacy IT Systems

Historically, organizational IT systems have accumulated a diversity of hardware, operating systems, and applications (together called "legacy spaghetti"). These systems are not easily transferable to the cloud because they must first be untangled and simplified. Furthermore, many IT professionals have vested interests in various legacy systems and are unwilling to allow them to be exchanged for cloud computing.

Concern 2: Cost

There are widespread debates over the comparative cost of cloud computing. A 2009 McKinsey case study involving an anonymous client concluded that putting the client's entire data center in the cloud would increase costs by 144 percent. On the other hand, a 2010 Microsoft report concluded that it would be cheaper for all organizations to move to cloud computing.

Whatever the truth, this focus on cost is irrelevant for two reasons. First, most companies do not spend massive amounts of money on information technologies. Gartner estimates that for S&P 500 companies, all IT-related costs account for less than 5 percent of revenue on average. Therefore, even large percentage-wise changes in the IT budget will not make an overall budget difference to most firms.

Secondly, over time, the economics of building and operating an IT infrastructure will favor cloud computing. Cloud providers purchase massive amounts of technology infrastructure (e.g., hardware and bandwidth), because they can obtain better prices by buying in bulk. Because they also buy technology all the time, they can take continual advantage of computing cost declines predicted by Moore's Law. Amazon Web Services, for example, reduced its prices a dozen times between 2008 and 2012.

Concern 3: Reliability

Many skeptics state that cloud computing is not as reliable as a well-managed, on-premise IT infrastructure. The cloud's reliability was called into question in April 2011, when large parts of Amazon's Web Services infrastructure went down for as long as three days (see example below). This outage was a major blow to many companies that used the service. Although the outage was serious, it affected only one of Amazon's U.S. data centers. Amazon had also explicitly advised its customers to design their IT architectures to withstand a service interruption. Other cloud companies have learned from Amazon's experience and are all improving the redundancy and reliability of their offerings.

EXAMPLE

Amazon Web Services (AWS; http://aws.amazon.com), the Amazon cloud, is designed with backups to the backups' backups to prevent -hosted Web sites and applications from failing. Despite all of these safety measures, however, in April 2011 Amazon's cloud crashed, taking with it Reddit (www.reddit.com), Quora (www.quora.com), FourSquare (www.foursquare.com), ProPublica (www.propublica.org), parts of the New York Times (www.nytimes.com), and about 70 other Web sites. The massive outage raised questions about the reliability of Amazon Web Services and of the cloud itself.

Lessons From IT Failures

Thousands of companies use Amazon Web Services (AWS) to run their Web sites through a service called Elastic Compute Cloud (EC2). Rather than hosting their sites on their own servers, these customers essentially rent some of Amazon's unused server capacity. EC2 is hosted in five regions: Virginia, California, Ireland, Tokyo, and Singapore. Within each region are multiple "availability zones," and within each availability zone are multiple "locations" or data centers.

Amazon assured its customers that its method of linking together many different data centers would protect its customers from isolated failures. It promised to keep customers' sites up and running 99.95 percent of the year, or it would reduce their monthly bills by 10 percent. Based on these claims, customers could be down a maximum of just 4.4 hours in a year. In fact, during the outage, some customers' Web sites were down for days.

The crash occurred at Amazon's Virginia data center, located in one of the company's East Coast availability zones. Amazon claimed that a "networking event" caused a domino effect across other availability zones in that region, which in turn caused many of its storage volumes to create backups of themselves. That process filled up Amazon's available storage capacity and prevented some Web sites from accessing their data. Amazon did not reveal what the "networking event" was.

Web sites like Quora and Reddit were able to come back online in "read-only" mode, but users were not able to post new content for many hours. Many experts blamed Amazon's customers themselves, asserting that their Web sites should have spread their processing out among multiple geographical regions to take full advantage of Amazon's backup systems. In fact, sites like Reddit were simply following the instructions that Amazon provided in its service agreement. The agreement states that hosting in a single region should be sufficient. Furthermore, some smaller companies were not able to afford the resources needed to duplicate their infrastructure in data centers all over the world.

Sources: Compiled from C. Brooks, "A Crack in the Cloud: Why the Amazon Outage Caught So Many by Surprise," *SearchCloudComputing.com*, April 27, 2011; D. Goldman, "Why Amazon's Cloud Titanic Went Down," *CNN Money*, April 22, 2011; J. Brodkin, "Amazon EC2 Outage Calls 'Availability Zones' into Question," *CIO*, April 21, 2011; http://aws.amazon.com, accessed May 21, 2011.

Concern 4: Privacy

Privacy advocates have criticized cloud computing for the ease with which cloud computing providers control, and thus lawfully or unlawfully monitor, the communication and data stored between the user and the host company. For example, the secret NSA program, working with AT&T and Verizon, used cloud computing to record over 10 million phone calls between American citizens. Instances such as these raise concerns among privacy advocates.

Using a cloud computing provider complicates data privacy because of the extent to which cloud processing and cloud storage are used to implement cloud services. The point is that customer data may not remain on the same system or in the same data center. This situation can lead to legal concerns over jurisdiction.

There have been efforts (e.g., US-EU Safe Harbor) to integrate the legal environment. (US-EU Safe Harbor is a streamlined process for U.S. companies to comply with the European Union directive on the protection of personal data.) However, providers such as Amazon still cater to major markets (typically the United States and the European Union) by deploying local infrastructure and allowing customers to select "availability zones." Cloud computing poses privacy concerns because the service provider may access the data that is on the cloud at any point in time. They could accidentally or deliberately alter or even delete some information.

Concern 5: Security

The security of cloud computing is frequently questioned. The effectiveness and efficiency of traditional security mechanisms are being reconsidered as the characteristics of cloud computing can differ widely from those of traditional IT architectures. Security issues include sensitive data access, data segregation (among customers), privacy, error exploitation, recovery, accountability, malicious insiders, and account control.

The relative security of cloud computing services is a contentious issue that may be delaying its adoption. Security issues are due in large part to the private and public sectors' unease surrounding the external management of security-based services. It is the very nature of cloud computing-based services, private or public, that promote external management of provided services. This situation provides great incentive to cloud computing service providers to prioritize building and maintaining strong security services.

Another security issue is controlling who is able to do and see what (see our discussion of least privilege in Chapter 7). Many organizations exercise least privilege controls effectively with their on-premise IT infrastructures. Some cloud computing environments, in contrast, cannot exercise least privilege controls effectively. This problem occurs because cloud computing environments were originally designed for individuals or groups, not for hierarchical organizations in which some people have both the right and the responsibility to exercise control over others. Cloud computing vendors are working to incorporate administrative, least-privilege functionality into their products, and many have already done so.

Security experts note that the best approach for excellent security is to constantly monitor the threat landscape; buy or build the best technologies to protect devices and networks; and hire and retain top digital security specialists. Cloud computing vendors are better able to do these things than all but the very largest and most security-conscious organizations.

Concern 6: The Regulatory and Legal Environment

There are numerous legal and regulatory barriers to cloud computing, and many have to do with data access and transport. For example, the European Union prohibits consumers' data from being transferred to non-member countries without prior consent and approval. Companies outside the EU can overcome this restriction by demonstrating that they provide a "safe harbor" for data. Some countries, such as Germany, have even more restrictive data export laws, and it is not yet clear (as of mid-2012) if the safe harbor process will satisfy them. Cloud computing vendors are aware of these regulations and laws and are working to modify their offerings so that they can assure customers and regulators that data entrusted to them is secure enough to meet all applicable regulations and laws.

In order to obtain compliance with regulations including the Federal Information Security Management Act (FISMA), the Health Insurance Portability and Accountability Act (HIPAA), and the Sarbanes-Oxley Act (SOX) in the United States, the Data Protection Directive in the European Union, and the credit card industry's Payment Card Industry's Data Security Standard (PCI DSS), cloud computing customers may have to adopt hybrid deployment modes that are typically more expensive and may offer restricted benefits. This process is how, for example, Google is able to "manage and meet additional government policy requirements beyond FISMA" and Rackspace (www.rackspace.com) is able to claim PCI compliance.

> **BEFORE** *YOU GO ON . . .*
> 1. Describe the privacy and security risks associated with cloud computing.
> 2. Describe the risks of cloud computing involved with adhering to regulatory guidelines.

Apply the Concept PI 3.6

Background This section has shown how, even though cloud computing offers many benefits, the risks outweigh the benefits for some. The statistics given early on that cloud computing will remain a small portion of IT spending shows that there are very legitimate concerns.

Activity Visit http://www.wiley.com/go/rainer/applytheconcept and click on the link provided for Plug IT In 3.6. This will take you to an article that exposes some of the risks of cloud computing for senior managers to consider. As you read the article, see if you can organize their thoughts according to the concerns presented in this section: legacy systems, costs, reliability, security, privacy, and regulatory and legal environment.

Deliverable

Summarize your findings for your professor. Are there any concerns brought up in this article that are not brought up in the chapter? Are there any discussed in the chapter that are not brought up in the article? Submit your summary to your professor.

Quiz questions are assignable in WileyPLUS, and available on the Book Companion Site at http://www.wiley.com/college/rainer.

PI 3.7 Web Services and Service-Oriented Architecture

As you have seen so far in this Plug IT In cloud computing can deliver a variety of functionality to users in the form of services. (Think Infrastructure-as-a-Service, Platform-as-a-Service, and Software-as-a-Service.) Therefore, in this section you will learn about Web services and service-oriented architecture.

Web services are applications delivered over the Internet (the cloud) that MIS professionals can select and combine through almost any device, from personal computers to mobile phones. By using a set of shared standards, or protocols, these applications permit different systems to "talk" with one another—that is, to share data and services—without requiring human beings to translate the conversations. Web services have great potential because they can be used in a variety of environments: over the Internet, on an intranet inside a corporate firewall, on an extranet set up by business partners. Web services perform a wide variety of tasks, from automating business processes to integrating components of an enterprisewide system to streamlining online buying and selling.

Web services provide numerous benefits for organizations, including the following:

- The organization can utilize the existing Internet infrastructure without having to implement any new technologies.

- Organizational personnel can access remote or local data without having to understand the complexities of this process.

- The organization can create new applications quickly and easily.

The collection of Web services that are used to build a firm's IT applications constitutes a **service-oriented architecture**. Business processes are accomplished by executing a series of these services. The Web services can be reused across an organization in other applications. For example, a Web service that checks a consumer's credit could be used with a service that processes a mortgage application or a credit card application.

Web services are based on four key protocols: XML, SOAP, WSDL, and UDDI.

Extensible markup language (XML) is a computer language that makes it easier to exchange data among a variety of applications and to validate and interpret these data. XML is a more powerful and flexible markup language than **hypertext markup language (HTML)**.

HTML is a page-description language for specifying how text, graphics, video, and sound are placed on a Web page document. HTML was originally designed to create and link static documents composed largely of text. Today, however, the Web is much more

(a) html

```
<!DOCTYPE HTML PUBLIC "-//W3C//DTD XHTML 1.0 Transitional//EN" http://www.wiley.com/college/gisslen/0470179961/video/
video111
<html xmlns="http://www.wiley.com/college/rainer/0470179061/video/video111.html"><head>
<meta http-equiv="content-Type" content="text/html; charset=ISO-8859-1">
<title>CSS Text Wrapper</title>
<link type="text/css" rel="stylesheet" href="css/stylesheet.css">
</head><body id="examples">

<div id="container">
        <div class="wrapper">
                <div class="ex">
                        <script type="text/javascript">shapewrapp
er("15","7.5,141,145|22.5,89,89|37.5,68,69|52.5,46,50|67.5,3
height: 15px; width: 39px;"></div><div style="float: left; clear: left; height: 15px; width: 27px;"></div><div style="float:
15px; width: 4px;"></div><div style="float: left; clear: left; height: 15px; width: 6px;"></div><div style="float:
right; cle
width: 43px;"></div><div style="float: left; clear: left; height: 15px; width: 57px;"></div><div style="float: right; clear:
                        <span style="font-size: 13px;" class="c">
```

(b) XML

```
<feature numbered="no" xml:id="c08-fea-0001">
    <titleGroup>
        <title type="featureName">OPENING CASE</title>
        <title type="main">Tiger Tans and Gifts</title>
    </titleGroup>
    <section xml:id="c08-sec-0002">
        <p>
            <blockFixed onlyChannels="print" type="graphic">
                <mediaResource alt="p0310" copyright="John Wiley &amp; Sons, Inc." eRights="yes"
                    href="urn:x-wiley:9781118443590:media:rainer9781118443590c08:p0310" pRights="yes"/>
            </blockFixed>
            Lisa Keiling owns & tanning salon in Wedowee, Alabama, that does very well from January to May....
        </p>
    </section>
</feature>
```

Figure PI3.5 a) Screenshot of an HTML wrapper. This wrapper gives instructions on how to open a video associated with this book. b) Example of XML tagging done on Ch.8 of this book.

social and interactive, and many Web pages have multimedia elements, such as images, audio, and video. Third-party plug-in applications such as Flash, Silverlight, and Java have been required to integrate these rich media into Web pages. However, these add-ons require additional programming and require a great deal of computer processing.

The next evolution of HTML, called **HTML5**, solves this problem by making it possible to embed images, audio, and video directly into a document without the add-ons. HTML5 also makes it easier for Web pages to function across different display devices, including mobile devices as well as desktops. HTML5 also supports the storage of data offline for apps that run over the Web. Web pages will execute more quickly, and look like smart phone apps.

HTML5 is used in a number of Internet platforms, including Apple's Safari browsers, Google Chrome, and Firefox browsers. Google's Gmail and Google Reader also use HTML5. Web sites listed as "iPad ready" are using HTML5 extensively. Examples of such sites include CNN, *The New York Times*, and CBS.

Whereas HTML is limited to describing how data should be presented in the form of Web pages, XML can perform presentation, communication, and storage of data. For example, in XML a number is not simply a number. The XML tag specifies whether the number represents a price, a date, or a ZIP code. Consider this example of XML, which identifies the contact information for Jane Smith.

```
<contact-info>
<name>Jane Smith</name>
<company>AT&amp;T</company>
<phone>(212) 555-4567</phone>
</contact-info>
```

Simple object access protocol (*SOAP*) is a set of rules that define how messages can be exchanged among different network systems and applications through the use of XML. These rules establish a common protocol that allows different Web services to interoperate. For example, Visual Basic clients can use SOAP to access a Java server. SOAP runs on all hardware and software systems.

The *Web services description language* (*WSDL*) is used to create the XML document that describes the tasks performed by the various Web services. Tools such as VisualStudio .Net automate the process of accessing the WSDL, reading it, and coding the application to reference the specific Web service.

Universal description, discovery, and integration (*UDDI*) allows MIS professionals to search for needed Web services by creating public or private searchable directories of these services. In other words, UDDI is the registry of descriptions of Web services.

Examples of Web services abound. The next example shows how Yelp uses Amazon Web Services successfully.

── BEFORE *YOU GO ON . . .* ──

1. Describe the function of Web services.
2. Describe the function of service-oriented architectures.

EXAMPLE Yelp

Yelp was founded in 2004 with the main goal of helping people connect with great local businesses. The Yelp community is best known for sharing in-depth reviews and insights on all types of local businesses. Yelp has gone from being based in one city only (San Francisco), to becoming an international phenomenon spanning 8 countries and nearly 50 cities. As of November 2011, Yelp had almost 50 million unique visitors to its site. In total, "yelpers" have posted more than 14 million reviews.

Yelp has established a loyal consumer following, due in large part to the fact that the company is vigilant in protecting the user from suspect content. Yelp uses an automated review filter to identify suspicious content and minimize exposure to the consumer. The site also features a wide range of other features that help people discover new businesses (lists, special offers, and events), and communicate with each other. Additionally, business owners and managers are able to set up free accounts to post special offers, upload photos, and message customers.

The company has also focused on developing mobile apps and has been voted into the iTunes Apps Hall of Fame. Yelp apps are also available for Android, Blackberry, and Windows 7 devices.

Local search advertising makes up the majority of Yelp's revenue stream. The search ads are colored light orange and clearly labeled "Sponsored Results." Paying advertisers are not allowed to change or re-order their reviews.

Yelp originally depended upon giant RAIDs (redundant arrays of independent disks, a type of enterprise storage) to store their customer posts, along with a single local instance of Hadoop (a type of database; see Chapter 3). Because they were running out of hard drive space and capacity, Yelp decided to use Amazon Web Services. They implemented Amazon Simple Storage Service (Amazon S3) and Amazon Elastic MapReduce. They were then able to replace their RAID storage technology with Amazon S3 and immediately transfer all Hadoop jobs to Amazon Elastic MapReduce.

Yelp uses Amazon S3 to store daily logs and photos, generating around 100GB of posts per day. The company also uses Amazon Elastic MapReduce to process customer posts. Each day, Yelp runs approximately 200 Elastic MapReduce jobs, processing 3 terabytes of data. Features powered by Amazon Elastic MapReduce include:

- People Who Viewed This Also Viewed
- Review highlights
- Auto complete as users type on search
- Search spelling suggestions
- Top searches
- Ads

Using Amazon Elastic MapReduce, Yelp was able to save $55,000 in upfront hardware costs and was able to get up and running in a matter of days. However, the opportunity cost is most important to Yelp. The company says that with AWS, its developers can now do things they could not do before, and focus their energies on other challenges.

Sources: C. Babcock, "Cloud Success Stories," InformationWeek, February 6, 2012; N. Hemsoth, "Elastic MapReduce Lead Traces Big Data Clouds," datanami, November 4, 2011;

"Yelp," Amazon Web Services Case Study, http://aws.amazon.com, accessed May 5, 2012; www.yelp.com <http://www.yelp.com> , accessed May 5, 2012.

Apply the Concept PI 3.7

Background Apple has never allowed Adobe Flash to run on its iPhones, iPads, or iPods. For a while, this was a very controversial point and opened the door for some competition to create "flash-ready" mobile devices. However, lately a new technology, mentioned in this section, has quieted the critics some. That technology is HTML5.

HTML5 is the next version of code that is the basis for coding and displaying Web pages. The big improvement of HTML5 over HTML4 is that it has the ability to display video and other graphics without using "plug-ins" like Adobe Flash. This allows video to play quicker without the need for the periodic updates.

Activity Visit http://www.wiley.com/go/rainer/applytheconcept and click on the links provided for Plug IT In 3.7. The first is a letter written by the late Steve Jobs (former Apple CEO) discussing the reasons why his company did not allow Flash to run on their mobile devices.

The second link is for a company that designed an HTML5 video player that will run on any browser. It uses a "fall back" methodology where it tries to play a video in HTML5 first, Flash second, and other plug-ins third; last, it provides a download link to the video to make it available.

Think about the state of technology and why it is important to understand where things will be in 5 years rather than just using everything as is today. Preparation and planning are paramount in IT.

Do you remember what Henry Ford (founder of Ford Motor Company) said? "If I had asked people what they wanted, they would have said faster horses."

Deliverable

Develop your own list of 5 reasons why it is important to have a solid understanding of the direction of technology and where it will be in 5 years.

Quiz questions are assignable in WileyPLUS, and available on the Book Companion Site at http://www.wiley.com/college/rainer.

What's in **IT** for ME?

For All Business Majors

As with hardware (Plug IT In 2), the design of enterprise IT architectures has profound impacts for businesspeople. Personal and organizational success can depend on an understanding of cloud computing and a commitment to knowing the opportunities and challenges they will bring.

At the organizational level, cloud computing has the potential to make the organization function more efficiently and effectively, while still saving the organization money. Web services and SOA make the organization more flexible when deploying new IT applications.

At the individual level, you might very well be utilizing cloud computing yourself if you decide to start your own business. Remember that cloud computing provides start-up companies with world-class IT capabilities at a very low cost.

SUMMARY

1. **Describe the evolution of IT infrastructure.**

   The IT infrastructure in organizations has evolved through these stages:

   - The stand-alone mainframe
   - Mainframe and dumb terminals
   - Stand-alone personal computers
   - Local area networks (client/server computing)
   - Enterprise computing
   - Cloud computing and mobile computing

2. **Describe the key characteristics and advantages of cloud computing.**

   Cloud computing is a type of computing that delivers convenient, on-demand, pay-as-you-go access for multiple customers to a shared pool of configurable computing resources (e.g., servers, networks, storage, applications, and services) that can be rapidly and easily accessed over the Internet. The essential *characteristics* of cloud computing include the following:

   - Cloud computing provides on-demand self-service.
   - Cloud computing includes the characteristics of grid computing.
   - Cloud computing includes the characteristics of utility computing.
   - Cloud computing utilizes broad network access.
   - Cloud computing pools computing resources.
   - Cloud computing typically occurs on virtualized servers.

3. **Identify a use-case-scenario for each of the four types of clouds.**

   Public clouds are shared, easily accessible, multi-customer IT infrastructures that are available non-exclusively to any entity in the public (individuals, groups, and/or organizations). *Private clouds* (also known as *internal clouds* or *corporate clouds*) are IT infrastructures that are accessible only by a single entity, or by an exclusive group of related entities that share the same purpose and requirements, such as all the business units within a single organization. *Hybrid clouds* are composed of public and private clouds that remain unique entities but are bound together, offering the benefits of multiple deployment models. *Vertical clouds* serve specific industries.

4. **Explain the operational model of each of the three types of cloud services.**

With the *Infrastructure-as-a-Service* (IaaS) model, cloud computing providers offer remotely accessible servers, networks, and storage capacity. In the *Platform-as-a-Service* (PaaS) model, customers rent servers, operating systems, storage, a database, software development technologies such as Java and .NET, and network capacity over the Internet. With the *software-as-a-service* (SaaS) delivery model, cloud computing vendors provide software that is specific to their customers' requirements.

5. **Identify the key benefits of cloud computing.**

The benefits of cloud computing include making individuals more productive; facilitating collaboration; mining insights from data; developing and hosting applications; cost flexibility; business scalability; improved utilization of hardware; market adaptability; and product and service customization.

6. **Discuss the concerns and risks associated with cloud computing.**

Cloud computing does raise concerns and have risks, which include legacy spaghetti, cost, reliability, privacy, security, and the regulatory and legal environment.

7. **Explain the role of Web services in building a firm's IT applications, providing examples.**

Web services are applications delivered over the Internet that MIS professionals can select and combine through almost any device, from personal computers to mobile phones. A *service-oriented architecture* makes it possible to for MIS professionals to construct business applications using Web services.

>>> GLOSSARY

cloud computing A technology in which tasks are performed by computers physically removed from the user and accessed over a network, in particular the Internet.

Extensible markup language (XML) A computer language that makes it easier to exchange data among a variety of applications and to validate and interpret these data.

grid computing A technology that applies the unused processing resources of many geographically dispersed computers in a network to form a virtual supercomputer.

Hybrid clouds Clouds composed of public and private clouds that remain unique entities but are bound together, offering the benefits of multiple deployment models.

HTML5 A page-description language that makes it possible to embed images, audio, and video directly into a document without add-ons. Also makes it easier for Web pages to function across different display devices, including mobile devices as well as desktops. Supports the storage of data offline.

hypertext markup language (HTML) A page-description language for specifying how text, graphics, video, and sound are placed on a Web page document.

infrastructure-as-a-service (IaaS) model Cloud computing providers offer remotely accessible servers, networks, and storage capacity.

platform-as-a-service (PaaS) model Customers rent servers, operating systems, storage, a database, software development technologies such as Java and .NET, and network capacity over the Internet.

Private clouds (also known as *internal clouds* or *corporate clouds*) IT infrastructures that are accessible only by a single entity or by an exclusive group of related entities that share the same purpose and requirements, such as all the business units within a single organization.

Public clouds Shared, easily accessible, multicustomer IT infrastructures that are available nonexclusively to any entity in the general public (individuals, groups, and/or organizations).

server farms Massive data centers, which may contain hundreds of thousands of networked computer servers.

server virtualization A technology that uses software-based partitions to create multiple virtual servers (called *virtual machines*) on a single physical server.

service-oriented architecture An IT architecture that makes it possible to construct business applications using Web services.

software-as-a-service (SaaS) delivery model Cloud computing vendors provide software that is specific to their customers' requirements.

utility computing A technology whereby a service provider makes computing resources and infrastructure management available to a customer as needed.

Web services Applications delivered over the Internet that IT developers can select and combine through almost any device, from personal computers to mobile phones.

>>> DISCUSSION QUESTIONS

1. What is the value of server farms and virtualization to any large organization?

2. If you were the chief information officer (CIO) of a firm, how would you explain the workings, benefits, and limitations of cloud computing?

3. What is the value of cloud computing to a small organization?

4. What is the value of cloud computing to an entrepreneur who is starting a business?

>>> PROBLEM-SOLVING ACTIVITIES

1. Investigate the status of cloud computing by researching the offerings of the following leading vendors. Note any inhibitors to cloud computing.

   - Dell (see e.g., http://www.wiley.com/go/rainer/problemsolving)
   - Oracle (see e.g., http://www.wiley.com/go/rainer/problemsolving)
   - IBM (see e.g., http://www.wiley.com/go/rainer/problemsolving)
   - Amazon (see e.g., http://www.wiley.com/go/rainer/problemsolving)
   - Microsoft (see e.g., http://www.wiley.com/go/rainer/problemsolving)
   - Google (see e.g., http://www.wiley.com/go/rainer/problemsolving)

Plug IT In | 4

Intelligent Systems

LEARNING OBJECTIVES >>>

1. Explain the potential value and the potential limitations of artificial intelligence.
2. Provide examples of the benefits, applications, and limitations of expert systems.
3. Provide examples of the use of neural networks.
4. Provide examples of the use of fuzzy logic.
5. Describe the situations in which genetic algorithms would be most useful.
6. Describe the use case for several major types of intelligent agents.

PI4.1 Introduction to Intelligent Systems

This Plug IT In focuses on information systems that can make decisions by themselves. These systems are called intelligent systems. The major categories of intelligent systems are expert systems, neural networks, fuzzy logic, genetic algorithms, and intelligent agents. You learn about each of these systems in the following sections.

Intelligent systems is a term that describes the various commercial applications of artificial intelligence. **Artificial intelligence (AI)** is a subfield of computer science that is concerned with studying the thought processes of humans and re-creating the effects of those processes via machines, such as computers and robots.

One well-publicized definition of AI is "behavior by a machine that, if performed by a human being, would be considered *intelligent*." This definition raises the question, What is *intelligent behavior*? The following capabilities are considered to be signs of intelligence: learning or understanding from experience, making sense of ambiguous or contradictory messages, and responding quickly and successfully to new situations.

The ultimate goal of AI is to build machines that will mimic human intelligence. A widely used test to determine whether a computer exhibits intelligent behavior was designed by Alan Turing, a British AI pioneer. The **Turing test** proposes that a man (or a woman) and a computer both pretend to be women (or men), and a human interviewer has to identify which is which. Based on this standard, the intelligent systems exemplified in commercial AI products are far from exhibiting any significant intelligence.

We can better understand the potential value of AI by contrasting it with natural (human) intelligence. AI has several important commercial advantages over natural intelligence, but it also displays some limitations, as outlined in Table PI4.1.

Artificial Intelligence brings computers closer to processing information like a human. (*Source:* © Luis Alonso Ocana/Age Fotostock America, Inc.)

Intelligent systems show up in a number of places, some of them surprising, as the following examples illustrate:

- A good session player is hard to find, but UJAM (www.ujam.com) is always ready to rock. This Web app doubles as a studio band and a recording studio. It analyzes a melody and then produces sophisticated harmonies, bass lines, drum tracks, horn parts, and more.

  Before UJAM can produce accompaniment, the app must figure out which notes the user is singing or playing. Once ujam recognizes them, its algorithms use a mix of statistical techniques and programmed musical rules to search for chords to match the tune.

- To the human eye, an X-ray is a murky puzzle. But to a machine, an X-ray—or a computed tomography (CT) scan or a magnetic resonance imaging (MRI) scan—is a dense data field that can be assessed down to the pixel level. AI techniques are being applied very aggressively in the field of medical imaging.

  New software gathers high-resolution image data from multiple sources—X-rays, MRI scans, ultrasounds, CT scans—and then groups together biological structures that share hard-to-detect similarities. For instance, the software can examine several

TABLE PI4.1 Comparison of the Capabilities of Natural vs. Artificial Intelligence

Capabilities	Natural Intelligence	Artificial Intelligence
Preservation of knowledge	Perishable from an organizational point of view	Permanent
Duplication and dissemination of knowledge	Difficult, expensive, takes time	Easy, fast, and inexpensive once in a computer
Total cost of knowledge	Can be erratic and inconsistent, incomplete at times	Consistent and thorough
Documentability of process and knowledge	Difficult, expensive	Fairly easy, inexpensive
Creativity	Can be very high	Low, uninspired
Use of sensory experiences limited	Direct and rich in possibilities	Must be interpreted first, limited
Recognizing patterns and relationships	Fast, easy to explain	Machine learning still not as good as people in most cases, but in some cases better
Reasoning	Making use of wide context of experiences	Good only in narrow, focused, and stable domains

images of the same breast to measure tissue density. The software then color codes tissues with similar densities so humans can see the pattern as well.

The software finds and indexes pixels that share certain properties, even if they are far apart in one image or in a different image altogether. This process enables medical personnel to identify hidden features of diffuse structures as well as features within a region of tissue.

- A human brain receives visual information from two eyes. Google's AI system receives visual information from billions of smart phone camera lenses. The company collects these images from users of Google Goggles (www.google.com/mobile/goggles), a mobile service that lets users run Web searches by taking pictures. Snap a bar code, and Goggles will shop for the item's best price. Take a picture of a book, and it will link users to, for instance, a Wikipedia page about the book's author. Photograph the Eiffel Tower, and Goggles will give you historical background on the landmark.

  The software behind Goggles coordinates the efforts of multiple object-specific recognition databases. There is a database for text, one for landmarks, one for corporate logos, and so on. When an image arrives, Goggles transmits it to each of these databases, which in turn use a variety of visual-recognition techniques to identify potential matches and compute confidence scores. Goggles then applies its own algorithm to decide which result(s), if any, go back to the user. Goggles' next category? Identifying plants.

- Building a model to run a major railroad is a complex task. One of the nation's largest freight carriers, Norfolk Southern (www.nscorp.com), uses an intelligent system, the Princeton Locomotive and Shop Management System (PLASMA), to manage its huge operation. PLASMA uses algorithms to analyze the railroad's operations by tracking thousands of variables to predict the impact of changes in fleet size, maintenance policies, transit time, and other factors. The key breakthrough was refining PLASMA so that it could mimic the complex behavior of the company's dispatch center in Atlanta, Georgia. PLASMA examines vast amounts of historical data from the railroad's databases. It then uses this analysis to model the dispatch center's collective human decision making and suggest improvements.

- Today we have much to keep up with while we are driving, such as GPS devices, touch-screen media and climate controls, text messages (that we should not answer while driving), phone calls, and of course oncoming traffic! Add a stressful day on the job, fatigue, irritability, or sickness, and you have the recipe for disaster!

  Artificial intelligence could change all of this. Google is testing a car that drives itself and learns as it drives. Although it ultimately may not be necessary to put a vehicle on "autopilot" for long periods of time, it could be helpful in either congested, bumper-to-bumper traffic or in rural areas where there is very little traffic. In these situations, it could be useful to have a computer monitoring 360 degrees of surroundings while the driver checks e-mail, places a phone call, or takes care of other business while on the road.

BEFORE *YOU GO ON . . .*

1. What is artificial intelligence?
2. Differentiate between artificial and human intelligence.

Apply the Concept PI 4.1

Background This section introduced you to a few applications of artificial intelligence. One of those was the Google self-driving car. This is a very interesting situation where technology can greatly enhance the safety of motorist, pedestrians, and passengers. However, there are also significant risks posed by turning over the keys to the computer.

Activity Visit http://www.wiley.com/go/rainer/applytheconcept and click on the link provided for Plug IT In 4.1. This will show you a YouTube video that introduces the Google self-driving car. Although this is very exciting, it can also be very scary! While you are watching the video, imagine the advantages and disadvantages of this type of intelligent system. Would it be best as a "pilot" or just a very helpful "copilot"?

Deliverable

Build a table that shows both the advantages and disadvantages for different scenarios as shown in the example table below.

Advantages	Disadvantages
Tired driver	
Distracted driver (texting)	
Sick/stressed-out driver	
Ambulance driver	
School bus driver	
Soccer mom, mini van driver	

Quiz questions are assignable in WileyPLUS, and available on the Book Companion Site at http://www.wiley.com/college/rainer.

PI4.2 Expert Systems

When an organization has to make a complex decision or solve a problem, it often turns to experts for advice. These experts have specific knowledge and experience in the problem area. They can offer alternative solutions and predict how likely the proposed solutions are to succeed. At the same time, they can calculate the costs that the organization may incur if it does not resolve the problem. Companies engage experts for advice on such matters as mergers and acquisitions, advertising strategy, and purchasing equipment. The more unstructured the situation, the more specialized and expensive is the advice.

Expertise refers to the extensive, task-specific knowledge acquired from training, reading, and experience. This knowledge enables experts to make better and faster decisions than nonexperts in solving complex problems. Expertise takes a long time (often many years) to acquire, and it is distributed unevenly across organizations.

Expert systems (ESs) are computer systems that attempt to mimic human experts by applying expertise in a specific domain. ESs can either *support* decision makers or completely *replace* them. ESs are the most widely applied and commercially successful intelligent system. A fascinating example of an ES is IBM's Watson.

EXAMPLE   IBM's Watson

In the last decade, question-answering systems have become increasingly important for companies dealing with vast amounts of information. Legal firms, for example, need to quickly sift through case law to find a useful precedent or citation. Help-desk workers often have to access enormous databases of product information to find an answer for customers on the line. In situations like these, speed is typically of the essence.

Since 2007, IBM scientists have been developing what they expected to be the world's most advanced question-answering system, known as Watson. Their goal was to program Watson so that it could understand a question posed in everyday human language, or *natural language,* and come up with a precise, factual, correct answer. That is, Watson's capabilities must surpass those of search engines like Google and Bing, which merely point to a document where a user might find a suitable answer. Watson has to give the correct answer itself.

The IBM team input millions of documents into Watson to build up its knowledge base—including books, reference manuals, any sort of dictionary, encyclopedias, novels, plays, the Bible, and many other information sources. Watson is not connected to the Internet. It "knows" only what has been input into its knowledge base.

Watson uses more than a hundred algorithms at the same time to analyze a question in different ways, generating hundreds of possible solutions. Another set of algorithms ranks these answers according to plausibility. In essence, Watson thinks in probabilities.

In mid-2011, IBM was training Watson in medicine by inputting medical textbooks and journals. The team plans on linking Watson to the electronic health records that the federal government requires hospitals to maintain. In addition, medical students are sending sample questions to Watson to help train it.

When Watson appeared as a contestant on the television show *Jeopardy!*, it had to produce only one correct answer to each question. The medical Watson offers several possible diagnoses, ranked in order of its confidence in the diagnoses. The IBM team learned that physicians want to see a list of options. Further, being presented with more than one choice might help doctors move away from "anchoring," or being too attached to a particular diagnosis. The medical Watson will have a diagnosis application and a treatment application.

IBM envisions several uses for medical Watson:

- Allowing a doctor to connect to Watson by speaking into a handheld device, using speech-recognition technology and cloud computing
- Serving as a repository for the most advanced research in cancer and other fields
- Providing an always-available second opinion

Medical Watson does have competition. Isabel Healthcare (www.isabelhealthcare.com) offers Isabel, a private medical database that is already being used by several multihospital health systems. Isabel is purported to perform roughly the same functions as the medical Watson system.

Sources: Compiled from J. Fitzgerald, "IBM Watson Supercomputer Graduates from 'Jeopardy!' to Medicine," *Huffington Post,* May 21, 2011; C. Thompson, "What Is I.B.M.'s Watson?" *New York Times,* June 14, 2010; www.ibm.com/innovation/us/watson/index.html, accessed May 27, 2011.

ESs are also used by human resources management to analyze applicants for available positions. These systems assign "scores" to candidates, lessening the workload for HR managers in the hiring process. Human HR managers actually make the final decision, but the ES provides useful information and recommendations.

The previous examples demonstrated the usefulness of ESs in a relatively narrow domain. Overall, however, ESs may not be as helpful as users would like. Consider the Microsoft Windows troubleshooting software located in the "Help" section in the taskbar menu. Microsoft has designed its ES to provide solutions, advice, and suggestions to common errors users encounter in its operating systems. We have all found that, in some cases, the assistance provided by the help section is not particularly useful.

Typically, an ES is decision-making software that can reach a level of performance comparable to a human expert in certain specialized problem areas. Essentially, an ES transfers expertise from a domain expert (or other source) to the computer. This knowledge is then stored in the computer. Users can call on the computer for specific advice as needed. The computer can make inferences and arrive at conclusions. Then, like a human expert, it offers advice or recommendations. In addition, it can explain the logic behind the advice. Because ESs can integrate and manipulate so much data, they sometimes perform better than any single expert can.

An often overlooked benefit of ESs is that they can be embedded in larger systems. For example, credit card issuers use ESs to process credit card applications.

The transfer of expertise from an expert to a computer and then to the user involves four activities:

- *Knowledge acquisition.* Knowledge is acquired from domain experts or from documented sources.
- *Knowledge representation.* Acquired knowledge is organized as rules or frames (object oriented) and stored electronically in a knowledge base.
- *Knowledge inferencing.* The computer is programmed so that it can make inferences based on the stored knowledge.
- *Knowledge transfer.* The inferenced expertise is transferred to the user in the form of a recommendation.

The Components of Expert Systems

An ES contains the following components: knowledge base, inference engine, user interface, blackboard (workplace), and explanation subsystem (justifier). In the future, ESs will include a knowledge-refining component as well. You learn about these components below. In addition, Figure PI4.1 diagrams the relationships among these components.

The *knowledge base* contains knowledge necessary for understanding, formulating, and solving problems. It is comprised of two basic elements: (1) *facts*, such as the problem situation, and (2) *rules* that direct the use of knowledge to solve specific problems in a particular domain.

The *inference engine* is essentially a computer program that provides a methodology for reasoning and formulating conclusions. It enables the system to make inferences based on the stored knowledge. The inference engine is considered the "brain" of the ES.

The following is an example of a medical ES for lung cancer treatment:

IF lung capacity is high

AND X-ray results are positive

AND patient has fever

AND patient has coughing

THEN surgery is necessary.

IF tumor has spread OR contraindications to surgery exist

THEN surgery cannot be performed.

The *user interface* enables users to communicate with the computer. That communication can best be carried out in a natural language, usually a question-and-answer format. In some cases, it is supplemented by graphics. The dialogue between the user and the computer triggers the inference engine to match the problem symptoms with the knowledge contained in the knowledge base and then generate advice.

The *blackboard* is an area of working memory set aside for the description of a current problem, as specified by the input data. It is a kind of database.

A unique feature of an ES is its ability to *explain* its recommendations. It performs this function in a subsystem called the *explanation subsystem* or *justifier*. The explanation subsystem interactively answers questions such as the following: *Why* did the ES ask a certain question? *How* did the ES reach a particular conclusion? *What* is the plan to reach the solution?

Human experts have a *knowledge-refining* system—that is, they can analyze their own performance, learn from it, and improve it for future consultations. This type of evaluation is also necessary in computerized learning so that the program will be able to improve by analyzing the reasons for its success or failure. Unfortunately, such a component is not available in commercial ESs at the moment. However, it is being developed in experimental systems.

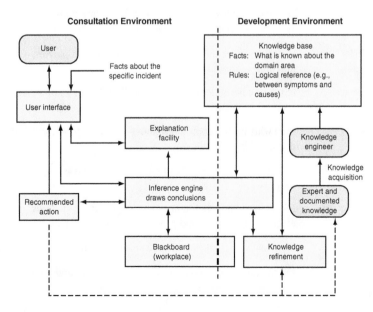

Figure PI4.1 Structure and process of an expert system.

Category	Problem Addressed
Interpretation	Inferring situation descriptions from observations
Prediction	Inferring likely consequences of given situations
Diagnosis	Inferring system malfunctions from observations
Design	Configuring objects under constraints
Planning	Developing plans to achieve goal(s)
Monitoring	Comparing observations to plans, flagging exceptions
Debugging	Prescribing remedies for malfunctions
Repair	Executing a plan to administer a prescribed remedy
Instruction	Diagnosing, debugging, and correcting system performance
Control	Interpreting, predicting, repairing, and monitoring systems behavior

Applications, Benefits, and Limitations of Expert Systems

Today, ESs are found in all types of organizations. They are especially useful in ten generic categories, which are displayed in Table PI4.2.

During the past few years, thousands of organizations worldwide have successfully applied ES technology to problems ranging from AIDS research to analyzing dust in mines. ESs have become so popular because they provide a large number of capabilities and benefits. Table PI4.3 lists the major benefits of ESs.

TABLE PI4.3 Benefits of Expert Systems

Benefit	Description
Increased output and productivity	ESs can configure components for each custom order, increasing production capabilities.
Increased quality	ESs can provide consistent advice and reduce error rates.
Capture and dissemination of scarce expertise	Expertise from anywhere in the world can be obtained and used.
Operation in hazardous environments	Sensors can collect information that an ES interprets, enabling human workers to avoid hot, humid, or toxic environments.
Accessibility to knowledge and help desks	ESs can increase the productivity of help-desk employees, or even automate this function.
Reliability	ESs do not become tired or bored, call in sick, or go on strike. They consistently pay attention to details.
Ability to work with incomplete or uncertain information	Even with an answer of "Don't know," an ES can produce an answer, although it may not be a definite one.
Provision of training	The explanation facility of an ES can serve as a teaching device and knowledge base for novices.
Enhancement of decision-making and problem-solving capabilities	ESs allow the integration of expert judgment into analysis (for example, diagnosis of machine and problem-malfunction and even medical diagnosis).
Decreased decision-making time	ESs usually can make faster decisions than humans working alone.
Reduced downtime	ESs can quickly diagnose machine malfunctions and prescribe repairs.

Despite all of these benefits, ESs present some problems as well. The difficulties involved with using ESs include the following:

- Transferring domain expertise from experts to the ES can be difficult because these experts cannot always explain how they know what they know. Often they are not aware of their complete reasoning process.

- Even if the domain experts can explain their entire reasoning process, automating that process may not be possible. The process may be either too complex, requiring too many rules, or too vague.

- In some contexts, there may be a potential liability from the use of ESs. Humans are known to make errors from time to time, but they are generally "off the hook" if they take reasonable care and apply generally accepted methods. An organization that chooses to use an ES, however, may lack this legal protection if problems arise later. The usual example is medical treatment, but this issue can arise if someone is harmed financially by a business decision driven by an ES.

— BEFORE *YOU GO ON* . . . —

1. What is an expert system?
2. Describe the benefits and limitations of using expert systems.

Apply the Concept PI 4.2

Background In the old days, expertise was transferred from a master to an apprentice by years of training. Only when all the tricks of the trade were mastered was the apprentice ready to go perform on his or her own. We still use similar methods today for doctors when they participate in a residency program under the guidance of the resident doctor.

This is different in nonlife-threatening situations. In some cases, being able to make an expert decision is simply a matter of having access to the experts' knowledge and experiences. If this can be captured in a computer-based information system, then this can be distributed to others to use this information to make similar decisions.

Although this sounds great, there are many challenges to obtaining this expertise. In some cases, it is the expertise that makes the employee special and valuable! To give this up would remove the need of the organization to keep the individual employee, right?

Activity The knowledge base consists facts and rules. In this activity, you will experience the difficulty of obtaining facts and turning them into rules. Consider the job of getting dressed. That may seem easy to you, but you will interview a friend and ask a series of questions to determine how to advise someone on getting dressed. Some of the questions you will ask should revolve around plans, weather, protocol (what is expected where the person is going), wardrobe, preferences, etc.

Deliverable

Develop ten facts and rules that a computer system could use to make a decision on how to get dressed. Submit your list to your professor.

Quiz questions are assignable in WileyPLUS, and available on the Book Companion Site at http://www.wiley.com/college/rainer.

PI4.3 Neural Networks

A **neural network** is a system of programs and data structures that simulates the underlying concepts of the biological brain. A neural network usually involves a large number of processors operating in parallel, each with its own small sphere of knowledge and access to data in its local memory (see Figure PI4.2). Typically, a neural network is initially "trained" or fed large amounts of data and rules about data relationships.

Neural networks are particularly adept at recognizing subtle, hidden, and newly emerging patterns within complex data, as well as interpreting incomplete inputs. Neural networks can help users solve a wide range of problems, from airline security to infectious disease control. They have become the standard for combating fraud in the credit card, health care, and telecom industries, and they are playing an increasingly important role in today's stepped-up international efforts to prevent money laundering.

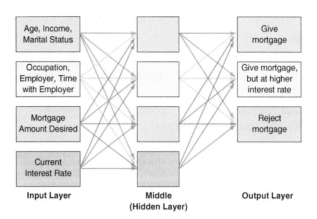

Figure PI4.2 Neural network.

Neural networks are used in a variety of ways, as illustrated by the following examples.

- The Bruce nuclear facility in Ontario, Canada, has eight nuclear reactors, making it the largest such facility in North America and the second largest in the world. The company uses a neural network in its checkpoint X-ray screening system to detect weapons concealed in personal belongings. The system also identifies biologically dangerous liquids.

- Neural networks are used in research on diseases such as Alzheimer's disease, Parkinson's disease, and epilepsy. Researchers build robots with simulated rat brains that mimic the rats' neural activity. The researchers can study brain function and the brain's reaction to stimuli.

- Neural networks are used to forecast the performance of stock index futures, currencies, natural gas and oil stocks, T-bond futures, gold stocks, and other major investments.

- Neural networks are used to detect fraud in credit card transactions and insurance claims, to fight crime, and to gauge customer satisfaction.

Figure PI4.2 illustrates how a neural network would process a typical mortgage application. Note that the network has three levels of interconnected nodes (similar to the human brain): an input layer, a middle or hidden layer, and an output layer. As you train the neural network, the strengths, or *weights*, of the connections change. In our example, the input nodes are age, income, occupation, marital status, employer, length of time with that employer, amount of mortgage desired, and current interest rate. The neural network has already been trained with data input from many successful and unsuccessful mortgage applications. That is, the neural network has established a pattern as to which input variables are necessary for a successful mortgage application. Interestingly, the neural network can adjust as both mortgage amounts and interest rates increase or decrease.

BEFORE YOU GO ON . . .

1. What are neural networks?
2. Describe how neural networks function.

Apply the Concept PI 4.3

Background This section describes a neural network as one that operates much like a human brain. Our minds are able to analyze and sometimes predict and make decisions much quicker than computers. It resembles our learning processes. Imagine yourself as a child learning to walk. Each stand and each fall made connections in your brain that helped you learn to eventually walk.

Activity Visit http://www.wiley.com/go/rainer/applytheconcept and click on the link for Plug IT In 4.3. This will show you a YouTube video that demonstrates a neural network in which a car learns to drive itself around a road. Watch this demo and be amazed at how this system learns over time. It seems that the car is constantly crashing, then all of a sudden it makes it all the way around the track.

Imagine what other applications could use this type of technology where systems are built to learn how to navigate tricky scenarios like the stock market, gold futures, and even predicting crime!

Build a list of possible applications of neural networks. Research the Web if you need some help. For example, imagine the trial and error we have gone through with medical care and the treatment of various diseases. Can we learn from each other the way a computer-based neural network operates? Submit your list of possible applications to your professor.

Quiz questions are assignable in WileyPLUS, and available on the Book Companion Site at http://www.wiley.com/college/rainer.

PI4.4 Fuzzy Logic

Fuzzy logic is a branch of mathematics that deals with uncertainties by simulating the process of human reasoning. The rationale behind fuzzy logic is that decision making is not always a matter of black and white, true or false. It often involves gray areas where the term *maybe* is more appropriate.

A computer programmed to use fuzzy logic defines in precise terms subjective concepts that humans do not define precisely. For example, for the concept *income*, terms such as *high* and *moderate* are subjective and imprecise. Using fuzzy logic, however, a computer could define "high" incomes as those exceeding $200,000 per year and "moderate" incomes as those ranging from $150,000 to $200,000 per year. A loan officer at a bank might use these fuzzy values when considering a loan application.

Fuzzy logic has also been used in financial analysis and the manufacture of antilock brakes. In accounting and finance, fuzzy logic allows you to analyze information with imprecise values, such as intangible assets like goodwill. Google uses fuzzy logic to find answers to your search terms because your perception of a topic often influences how you phrase your query, therefore determining the relevance of the Web pages that Google delivers to you.

> **BEFORE** *YOU GO ON . . .*
> 1. What is fuzzy logic?
> 2. Give some examples of where fuzzy logic is used.

Apply the Concept PI 4.4

Background Fuzzy logic allows computers to use our vague descriptions as data points. Although we may describe a house as big or small, the computer will assign specific data ranges to "big" homes and "small" homes so that a house under 1000 square feet is "small" and anything bigger is "big." Fuzzy logic, then, can be used to let computer systems analyze and consider options where "fuzzy" descriptions are the best we can come up with.

Activity Imagine that you are going to use fuzzy logic to design a formula that will help determine if people are at risk for having an accident while texting. What variables would you use? What categories would you create for each criteria? Come up with at least five variables that each have three categories. For example, you may use "comfort with texting" as a variable and have measurements such as the following:

"Uncomfortable" (sends less than 100 messages a month)

"Somewhat comfortable" (sends 101–500 messages a month)

"Very comfortable" (sends more than 501 messages a month)

Develop your list of criteria that would predict whether a person would have an accident while texting. Submit your fuzzy logic information to your professor.

Quiz questions are assignable in WileyPLUS, and available on the Book Companion Site at http://www.wiley.com/college/rainer.

PI4.5 Genetic Algorithms

An algorithm is a method for solving a problem expressed as a finite sequence of steps. A **genetic algorithm** is an approach that mimics the evolutionary, survival-of-the-fittest process to generate increasingly better solutions to a problem. That is, a genetic algorithm is an optimizing process that finds the combination of inputs that produces the best outputs. Genetic algorithms have three functional characteristics:

- *Selection* (survival of the fittest). The key to selection is to give preference to better and better outcomes
- *Crossover.* The process of combining portions of good outcomes in the hope of creating an even better outcome
- *Mutation.* The process of randomly trying combinations and evaluating the success (or failure) of an outcome

Genetic algorithms are best suited to decision-making environments in which thousands or millions of solutions are possible. Genetic algorithms can find and evaluate solutions intelligently, and they can process many more possibilities more thoroughly and faster than a human can. Users do have to tell the genetic algorithm what constitutes a "good" solution. Good solutions could be low cost or high return, or any number of other results. Let us look at some examples:

- Boeing uses genetic algorithms in its design of aircraft parts such as the fan blades on its 777 jet. Rolls Royce and Honda also use genetic algorithms in their design processes.
- Retailers such as Marks and Spencer, a British chain that has 320 stores, use genetic algorithms to manage their inventories more effectively and also to optimize their store displays.
- Air Liquide, a producer of industrial gases, uses genetic algorithms to find optimal production schedules and distribution points in its supply chain. The company has 40 plants and 8,000 client sites and must consider factors such as power prices and customer demand projections, as well as the power costs and efficiency of each plant.

┌─ **BEFORE** *YOU GO ON . . .* ─┐

1. What is a genetic algorithm?
2. Give examples of the use of genetic algorithms.

Apply the Concept PI 4.5

Background Genetic algorithms are used to calculate possible outcomes of hundreds (or thousands) of scenarios over time. This is different from other forms of artificial intelligence because it attempts to predict how things will change in the long term based on criteria set forth in the algorithm.

Activity Visit http://www.wiley.com/go/rainer/applytheconcept and click on the link provided for Plug IT In 4.5. This will take you to a page where you can see a genetic algorithm in action. You get to change variables on "plants" and "eaters" and see how things evolve differently over time.

Run this algorithm with different variables at least five times. Write down your initial settings and the outcome.

Deliverable

Put your results into a table and submit this to your professor with a description of how this exercise has helped you to better understand genetic algorithms and the effect of variance in initial settings.

Quiz questions are assignable in WileyPLUS, and available on the Book Companion Site at http://www.wiley.com/college/rainer.

PI4.6 Intelligent Agents

An **intelligent agent** is a software program that assists you, or acts on your behalf, in performing repetitive computer-related tasks. Behind the scenes, intelligent agents often use ISs such as ESs and fuzzy logic to create their seemingly intelligent behavior.

You may be familiar with an early type of intelligent agent: the paper clip ("Clippy") that popped up in early versions of Microsoft Word. For example, if your document appeared as

Lessons From IT Failures

though it were going to be a business letter—that is, you type in a date, name, and address—the animated paper clip would offer helpful suggestions on how to proceed. Users objected so strenuously to this primitive intelligent agent that Microsoft deleted it from subsequent versions.

There are many intelligent agents—also called *bots*—for a wide variety of tasks. You can view the many different types of available agents by visiting BotSpot (www.botspot.com), for example. The following sections examine three types of agents: information agents, monitoring-and-surveillance agents, and user or personal agents.

Information Agents

Information agents are a type of intelligent agent that searches for information of some kind and displays it to the users. The best-known information agents are buyer agents. A **buyer agent** (or **shopping bot**) is an intelligent agent on a Web site that helps customers find the products and services they need. There are many examples of information agents. Here are a few illustrative cases:

- The information agents for Amazon display lists of books and other products that customers might like, based on past purchases.

- Google and Ask.com use information agents to find information, and not just when you request it. Google, for example, sends Googlebots out to surf all the Web sites in Google's index. These bots copy individual pages to Google's repository, where Google software indexes them. This process means that when you perform a Google search, the search engine builds a list of all the pages that contain the key words you specify and presents them to you in PageRank order. Google's PageRank algorithm sorts Web pages based on the number of links on the Web that point to each page. That is, the more links on the Web that point to a particular page, the higher the likelihood that Web site will be on the list.

- The Federal Electronic Research and Review Extraction Tool (FERRET) was developed jointly by the Census Bureau and the Bureau of Labor Statistics. You can use FERRET to find information on employment, health care, education, race and ethnicity, health insurance, housing, income and poverty, aging, and marriage and the family.

Monitoring-and-Surveillance Agents

Monitoring-and-surveillance agents (or **predictive agents**) are intelligent agents that constantly observe and report on some item of interest. There are many examples of predictive agents. Consider the following:

- Allstate Insurance uses monitoring-and-surveillance agents to manage its large computer networks 24/7/365. Every 5 seconds, the agent measures 1,200 data points. It can predict a system crash 45 minutes before it happens. The agent also watches for electronic attacks to detect them early so they can be stopped.

- Monitoring-and-surveillance agents can watch your competitors and notify you of price changes and special offers.

- These agents can monitor Internet sites, discussion groups, and mailing lists for stock manipulations, insider trading, and rumors that might affect stock prices.

- These agents can monitor Web sites for updated information on topics of your choice, such as price changes on desired products (e.g., airline tickets).

User Agents

User agents (or **personal agents**) are intelligent agents that take action on your behalf. Let us look at what these agents can do (or will be able to do shortly):

- Check your e-mail, sort it according to your priority rules, and alert you when high-value e-mails appear in your in-box.

- Automatically fill out forms on the Web for you. They will also store your information for future use.

┌─ BEFORE *YOU GO ON* . . . ─┐

1. Define *intelligent agents, information agents, monitoring-and-surveillance agents,* and *user agents.*

2. Explain the uses of each type of intelligent agent.

Apply the Concept PI 4.6

Background Information agents are a type of intelligent agent that searches for information or products and displays it to the users. The best-known information agents are buyer agents. A buyer agent, also called a shopping bot, is an intelligent agent on the Web that helps customers find products and services.

Activity Let us assume the big game is coming up this weekend and you have invited a group of friends over to watch it at your apartment. However, last evening, your TV went black. So you need to shop for a new TV quickly. You have heard about Web sites that can help you find the best deals, so you decide to try one out. You have at the most about $450 to spend and you think you want an LCD screen.

Because a lot of people are coming, you would like a big screen, at least 40 inches, so everybody can see. Visit http://www.wiley.com/go/rainer/applytheconcept and click on the link provided for Plug IT In 4.6. It will take you to Shopzilla's Web site where you can put in the criteria described above and shop many sites at one time.

Compare your results here to those you may find on Google's shopping site (or any other shopping site you may find).

Deliverable

After you work through the activity described above, submit your top five choices to your professor. Also, describe your experience with the buyer agent.

Quiz questions are assignable in WileyPLUS, and available on the Book Companion Site at http://www.wiley.com/college/rainer.

What's in IT for ME?

FOR THE ACCOUNTING MAJOR

Intelligent systems are used extensively in auditing to uncover irregularities. They are also used to uncover and prevent fraud. Today's CPAs use intelligent systems for many of their duties, ranging from risk analysis to cost control. Accounting personnel also use intelligent agents for several mundane tasks such as managing accounts and monitoring employees' Internet use.

FOR THE FINANCE MAJOR

People have been using computers for decades to solve financial problems. Innovative intelligent applications have been developed for activities such as making stock market decisions, refinancing bonds, assessing debt risks, analyzing financial conditions, predicting business failures, forecasting financial trends, and investing in global markets. In many cases, intelligent systems can facilitate the use of spreadsheets and other computerized systems used in finance. In addition, intelligent systems can help to reduce fraud in credit cards, stocks, and other financial services.

FOR THE MARKETING MAJOR

Marketing personnel utilize intelligent systems in many applications, from allocating advertising budgets to evaluating alternative routings of salespeople. New marketing approaches such as targeted marketing and marketing transaction databases are heavily dependent on IT in general and on intelligent systems in particular. Intelligent systems are particularly useful in mining customer databases and predicting customer behavior. Successful applications are visible in almost every area of marketing and sales, from analyzing the success of one-to-one advertising to supporting customer help desks. With the increased importance of customer service, the use of intelligent agents is becoming critical for providing fast response.

FOR THE

PRODUCTION/OPERATIONS MANAGEMENT MAJOR

Intelligent systems support complex operations and production decisions, from inventory to production planning. Many of the early expert systems were developed in the production/operations management field for tasks ranging from diagnosing machine failures and prescribing repairs to complex production scheduling and inventory control. Some companies, such as DuPont and Kodak, have deployed hundreds of expert systems in the planning, organizing, and control of their operational systems.

FOR THE

HUMAN RESOURCES MANAGEMENT MAJOR

Human resources personnel use intelligent systems for many applications. For example, these systems can find resumes of applicants posted on the Web and sort them to match needed skills. Expert systems are used in evaluating candidates (tests, interviews). HR personnel use intelligent systems to train and support employees in managing their fringe benefits. In addition, they use neural computing to predict employee job performance and to predict labor needs.

FOR THE MIS MAJOR

The MIS function develops (or acquires) and maintains the organization's various intelligent systems, as well as the data and models that these systems use. In addition, MIS staffers sometimes interact with subject-area experts to capture the expertise used in ESs.

SUMMARY

1. **Explain the potential value and the potential limitations of artificial intelligence.**

   Table PI4.1 differentiates between artificial and human intelligence on a number of characteristics.

2. **Provide examples of the benefits, applications, and limitations of expert systems.**

   Expert systems are computer systems that attempt to mimic human experts by applying expertise in a specific domain. Tables PI4.2 and PI4.3 offer examples of expert systems.

3. **Provide examples of the use of neural networks.**

   A neural network is a system of programs and data structures that simulate the underlying concepts of the human brain. Neural networks are used to detect weapons concealed in personal belongings, in research on various diseases, for financial forecasting, to detect fraud in credit card transactions, to fight crime, and many other applications.

4. **Provide examples of the use of fuzzy logic.**

   Fuzzy logic is a branch of mathematics that deals with uncertainties by simulating the process of human reasoning. Fuzzy logic is used in financial analysis, the manufacture of antilock brakes, measuring intangible assets like goodwill, and finding responses to search terms in Google.

5. **Describe the situations in which genetic algorithms would be most useful.**

   A genetic algorithm is an intelligent system that mimics the evolutionary, survival-of-the-fittest process to generate increasingly better solutions to a problem. Genetic algorithms are used to design aircraft parts such as fan blades, to manage inventories more effectively, to optimize store displays, and to find optimal production schedules and distribution points.

6. **Describe the use case for several major types of intelligent agents.**

   An intelligent agent is a software program that assists you, or acts on your behalf, in performing repetitive, computer-related tasks. Intelligent agents are used to display lists of books or other products that customers might like, based on past purchases; to find information; to manage and monitor large computer networks 24/7/365; to detect electronic attacks early so they can be stopped; to watch competitors and send notices of price changes and special offers; to monitor Internet sites, discussion groups, and mailing lists for stock manipulations, insider trading, and rumors that might impact stock prices; to check e-mail, sort it according to established priority rules, and alert recipients when high-value e-mails appear in their inbox; and to automatically fill out forms on the Web.

>>> GLOSSARY

artificial intelligence A subfield of computer science that is concerned with studying the thought processes of humans and re-creating the effects of those processes via machines, such as computers.

buyer agent (or shopping bot) An intelligent agent on a Web site that helps customers find products and services that they need.

expert systems (ESs) Computer systems that attempt to mimic human experts by applying expertise in a specific domain.

fuzzy logic A branch of mathematics that deals with uncertainties by simulating the process of human reasoning.

genetic algorithm An approach that mimics the evolutionary, survival-of-the-fittest process to generate increasingly better solutions to a problem.

information agent A type of intelligent agent that searches for information of some kind and displays it to the users.

intelligent agent A software program that assists you, or acts on your behalf, in performing repetitive, computer-related tasks.

intelligent systems A term that describes the various commercial applications of artificial intelligence.

monitoring-and-surveillance agents (or predictive agents) Intelligent agents that constantly observe and report on some item of interest.

neural network A system of programs and data structures that simulates the underlying concepts of the human brain.

personal agents (see **user agents**)

predictive agents (see **monitoring-and-surveillance agents**)

shopping bot (see **buyer agent**)

Turing test A test in which a man and a computer both pretend to be women (or men), and the human interviewer has to decide which is which.

user agents (or personal agents) Intelligent agents that take action on your behalf.

>>> **DISCUSSION QUESTIONS**

1. Explain how your university could employ an expert system in its admission process. Could it apply a neural network to this process? What might be the outcome if a student were denied admission to the university and the student's parents discovered that an expert system had been involved in the admissions process?

2. One difference between a conventional business intelligence system and an expert system is that the former can explain a *how* question, whereas the latter can explain a *how* and a *why* question. Discuss the implications of this statement.

>>> **PROBLEM-SOLVING ACTIVITIES**

1. You have decided to purchase a new video camcorder. To purchase it as inexpensively as possible and still get the features you want, you use a shopping bot. Visit several of the shopping bot Web sites that perform price comparisons for you. Begin with MySimon (www.mysimon.com), BizRate.com (www.bizrate.com), and Google Product Search (www.google.com/prdhp). Compare these shopping bots in terms of their ease of use, number of product offerings, speed in obtaining information, thoroughness of information offered about products and sellers, and price selection. Which site or sites would you use, and why? Which camcorder would you select and why? How helpful were these sites in making your decision?

2. Access the Web site MyMajors (www.mymajors.com). This site contains a rule-based expert system to help students find majors. The expert system has more than 300 rules and 15,000 possible conclusions. The site ranks majors according to the likelihood that a student will succeed in them, and it provides 6 possible majors from among 60 alternative majors that a student might consider. Take the quiz and see if you are in the "right major" as defined by the expert system. You must register to take the quiz.

3. Access Exsys (www.exsys.com) and click on "Corvid Demo." Provide your e-mail address and click on the link for "Student–Needed for a Class." Try the various demos, and report your results to the class.

Plug IT In | 5

Project Management

LEARNING OBJECTIVES >>>

1. Explain the relationship between the triple constraints on projects.

2. Describe the five phases of the project management process.

3. Review how each of the nine processes of the Project Management Body of Knowledge is necessary in order to ensure smooth project deployment.

PI5.1 Project Management for Information Systems Projects

Projects are short-term efforts to create a specific business-related outcome. These outcomes may take the form of products or services. In the context of information systems (IS), many of the resource investments made by organizations are in the form of projects. For example, Home Depot (www.homedepot.com) recently engaged in an IS project to develop an inventory management system. The objectives of the project were to improve inventory turnover, reduce product stock-outs, and integrate more tightly with supply chain partners. The outcome was to lower companywide costs by carrying less physical inventory.

Almost every organization that utilizes information technology to support business processes engages in some form of IS project management. **IS project management** is a directed effort to plan, organize, and manage resources to bring about the successful achievement of specific IS goals. All projects, whether they are IS projects or not, are constrained by the same three factors, known as the **triple constraints of project management**: time, cost, and scope. *Time* refers to the window of opportunity in which a project must be completed to provide a benefit to the organization. *Cost* is the actual amount of resources, including cash and labor that an organization can commit to completing a project. *Scope* refers to the processes that ensure that the project includes all the work required—and only the work required—to complete the project successfully. For an IS project to be successful, the organization must allow an adequate amount of time, provide an appropriate amount of resources, and carefully define what is and is not included in the project.

The triple constraints are related and involve trade-offs. For example, scope can often be increased by using additional time and incurring increased costs. Cost and/or time can often be saved by reducing scope. For a given scope, time can sometimes be saved by increasing cost. The following example illustrates how Charter Communications successfully deployed project management software.

BEFORE *YOU GO ON . . .*

1. What is a project?
2. What is the triple constraint of any project?

Example **Charter Communications Relies on IT Project Management Software**

In today's turbulent economic times, managers are having difficulty justifying spending money on IT projects when resources are so scarce. At Charter Communications (www.charter.com), a telecommunications firm that provides telephone, cable, and high-speed Internet service, the company's response to these funding requests was simple: If a project makes money or saves more money than it costs, then do it.

In the highly competitive telecommunications industry, Charter faced mounting pressures from competitors and customers alike. Comcast Cable (www.comcast.com) and Time Warner Cable (www.timewarnercable.com) are the largest competitors in the cable television/telecommunications market. Because they are better financed, Comcast and Time Warner are able to engage in aggressive acquisitions and mergers. Each company has consolidated a significant share of the markets in which Charter operates. Therefore, Charter has less potential revenue. To compound this problem, Charter has a restricted cash flow resulting from its highly leveraged position (the company has more than $21 billion of debt on its balance sheet).

Further, Charter has experienced difficulties addressing customer-related issues. In fact, Charter received so many customer complaints that the Better Business Bureau (www.bbb.org) issued a warning notice to consumers regarding the company's poor customer service. Finally, on March 27, 2009, Charter filed for Chapter 11 bankruptcy.

Charter responded to these challenges by adopting an ambitious goal: to win, and subsequently retain, customers in the hypercompetitive communications environment. To accomplish this goal, Charter is investing heavily in new information technology. This technology is intended to support the company's customer services operations, with the aim of providing superb service. Charter executives retained the services of CA Technologies (www.ca.com), a consulting firm specializing in IT project management, to help Charter develop a comprehensive project management system that the company could use to assess potential return on investment for proposed IT projects. CA delivered a project management system known as Clarity. Clarity replaced Charter's previous system, which consisted only of spreadsheets and PowerPoint-driven dashboards.

Clarity enables Charter to evaluate projects under consideration and to manage the projects already in process. Because Charter deployed the Clarity system, its record of completing projects on time and within budget has improved noticeably. Clarity has become a principal tool that Charter uses to eliminate the detrimental cost overruns that have contributed to its recent financial struggles. Further, controlling costs has enabled Charter to allocate additional resources toward much needed customer service improvements.

Sources: Compiled from "Charter Communications Files for Chapter 11 Bankruptcy," *Associated Press*, March 28, 2009; D. Gardner, "Charter Communications to Seek Financial Protection," *InformationWeek*, February 12, 2009; Y. Adegoke, "Wall Street on Charter Communications Bankruptcy Watch," *Reuters*, Jan 16, 2009; "Charter Communications Maximizes Its Investment in New Technology with Improved Project Management," *Computer Associates Success Story*; www.ca.com, accessed August 11, 2011.

Questions

1. What were Charter's business problems that led the company to deploy the Clarity project management software?
2. What results did Charter see from using the Clarity software?

Apply the Concept PI 5.1

Background This section describes how software is used to support project management. The planning, communication, coordination, measurement, data collection, and many more tools are offered by project management software.

Activity Visit http://www.wiley.com/go/rainer/applytheconcept and click on the link provided for Plug IT In 5.1. This will take you to a Web site that sells project management software. You will be able to click on links that will show you tours, customer success stores, pictures, and demos of the software. As you look around on the site, pick out 10 advantages you find of using project management software. Then put them in a rank order of your perception of how IT can help projects be more successful.

Deliverable

Submit your lists to your professor and explain why you have chosen these 10 as your top 10 reasons to use project management software.

Quiz questions are assignable in WileyPLUS, and available on the Book Companion Site at http://www.wiley.com/college/rainer.

PI5.2 The Project Management Process

The traditional approach to project management divides every project into five distinct phases: initiation, planning, execution, monitoring and control, and completion (see Figure PI5.1). These phases are sequential, and we discuss them in order.

Project Initiation

The first phase in the management of a process is to clearly define the problem that the project is intended to solve and the goals that it is to achieve. In this phase, it is also necessary to identify and secure the resources necessary for the project, analyze the costs and benefits of the project, and identify potential risks.

In an IS project, a user's business problem or need typically initiates a project that can solve the problem and meet the need. The user must clearly define the problem so that the IS team can understand it. The user must also define the benefits he or she expects to gain from successful completion of the IS project.

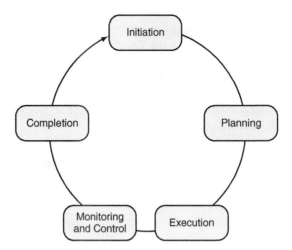

Figure PI5.1 The project management process.

Project Planning

As the term *planning* suggests, in this phase, every project objective and every activity associated with that objective must be identified and sequenced. This phase is critically important to avoid scope creep once the project gets underway. **Scope creep** refers to uncontrolled changes in a project's scope. This phenomenon can occur when the scope of a project is not properly defined, documented, or controlled. It is generally considered a negative occurrence that is to be avoided.

In an IS project, users often contribute to scope creep when they ask for additional features or functionality after the project is underway. This situation often leads to the project being overtime and over budget.

Many tools assist developers in sequencing these activities, including dependence diagrams, such as the program evaluation and review technique (PERT), the critical path method (CPM), and a timeline diagram called the Gantt chart. Project managers use these tools to ensure that activities are performed in a logical sequence. As the project progresses, project managers also employ these tools to evaluate whether the project is on schedule and, if not, where the delays are occurring and what the managers must do to correct them.

Project Execution

In this phase, the work defined in the project management plan is performed to accomplish the project's requirements. Execution coordinates people and resources, and it integrates and performs project activities in accordance with the plan.

Users may be involved in project execution. For example, in an IS project, users often evaluate prototypes so that they can provide meaningful feedback to the IS team.

Project Monitoring and Control

The purpose of monitoring and control is to determine whether the project is progressing as planned. This phase consists of three steps: (1) monitoring ongoing project activities (where we are); (2) comparing project variables (cost, effort, time, resources, etc.) with the actual plan (where we should be); and (3) identifying corrective actions (how do we get on track again).

Project Completion

The project is completed when it is formally accepted by the organization. All activities are finalized and all contracts are fulfilled and settled. In addition, all files are archived and all lessons learned are documented.

Project Management Failure

Many times IT projects fail to achieve their desired results. In fact, analysts have found that only 29 percent of all IS projects are completed on time, within budget, and with all the features and functions originally specified. Further, between 30 and 40 percent of all IS software development projects are *runaway projects*, meaning they are so far over budget and past deadline that they must be abandoned, typically with large monetary loss. IS projects do not deliver their potential value for a number of reasons, including these:

- Lack of sufficient planning at the start of a project
- Difficulties with technology compatibility (that is, new technology may not work with existing technology)
- Lack of commitment by management to providing the necessary resources
- Poorly defined project scope
- Lack of sufficient time to complete the project

— BEFORE *YOU GO ON . . .* —

1. What are the five phases of the project management process?
2. What are the major causes of project failure?

Apply the Concept PI 5.2

Background As you have seen in this section, project management is a complicated task. Multiple people, multiple activities, and multiple opinions about the "right" way to handle the project always make it difficult for the one who is actually managing things.

Activity Visit http://www.wiley.com/go/rainer/applytheconcept and click on the link provided for Plug IT In 5.2. The article linked tells about Hershey's and the difficulties the company faced when implementing a new IT project. In fact, it cost the company over $100 million in sales because the ordering system did not function properly.

After reading the article, search the Web to see what else you can find about this story.

Deliverable

Build a list of five failures and five successes from this story. If you find them in another article than the one linked here, please submit a link to that article along with your work.

Quiz questions are assignable in WileyPLUS, and available on the Book Companion Site at http://www.wiley.com/college/rainer.

PI5.3 The Project Management Body of Knowledge

The **Project Management Body of Knowledge** (**PMBOK**) is a collection of processes and knowledge areas generally accepted as best practice within the project management discipline. As an internationally recognized standard, it provides the fundamentals of project management, regardless of the type of project (e.g., construction, software, engineering, automotive, etc.). The purpose of the PMBOK is to provide and promote a common vocabulary within the project management profession for discussing, writing, and applying project management concepts.

The PMBOK recognizes five basic process groups and nine knowledge areas typical of almost all projects. You learned about the five basic process groups in the previous section:

- Initiation
- Planning
- Execution
- Monitoring and control
- Completion

Processes overlap and interact throughout a project. Processes are described in terms of inputs (documents, plans, designs), tools and techniques, and outputs (documents, products). The nine knowledge areas of the PMBOK are these:

- *Project Integration Management.* Project integration management includes those processes required to ensure that all the project's components are properly coordinated. The project plan development processes, project plan execution processes, and integrated change control processes are all included in this area of knowledge. Each process has expected inputs and outputs and plus the appropriate tools and techniques to support the change of inputs to outputs.

- *Project Scope Management.* Project scope management defines the processes that limit and control the work included in a project. Scope creep is a serious problem that often causes projects to go over time and over budget. These processes ensure that all the work of the project is included and properly accounted for.

- *Project Time Management.* Proper sequencing is vital to timely project completion. When the amount of time needed is established, it takes excellent scheduling skills and tools to manage the activities to complete project milestones and the project itself within the allotted time. Different tools are available to assist with this process, such as Gantt charts, milestone charts, and network charts. Each tool helps managers see the big picture and stay in control of the project's progression.

- *Project Cost Management.* Resource planning and cost estimation are equally vital to time management. These two processes cannot exist independently of each other. Resource cost management is difficult to estimate and even more difficult to manage when unforeseen events take place. Early in a project, managers may project a budget range and then fine-tune it as the project progresses.

- *Project Quality Management.* Every project needs a set of processes ensuring that project outcomes meet the needs for which the project was executed. Quality planning, assurance, and control are included in this area. There are many quality management models to consider, such as the Deming Prize, TQM, and Six Sigma. These all aim to help organizations produce quality products the first time they try. There are also many paradigms applicable to this area of knowledge, such as "Zero Defects" and "DTRTRTFT" (Do the right thing right the first time). These paradigms are meant to inspire organizations to operate at higher quality levels.

- *Project Human Resource Management.* People can be the major headache or the major asset of any project. People with differing skill sets are required at various times during a project and their individual skills have to be used effectively for the project to succeed. This area of knowledge includes concepts such as staffing decisions; team management; and organizational culture, style, and structure.

- *Project Communications Management.* A vast amount of communication is necessary in successful projects. Information must be collected, disseminated, stored, and destroyed at the appropriate time. This area of knowledge contains the processes to perform these functions. Often, organizations investigate personality styles to determine their most effective communicators. Choosing the right person to be a leader can make all the difference in the success of a project.

- *Project Risk Management.* All projects face risk. With organizational success, jobs, careers, and livelihoods on the line, it is a good idea to minimize the risk of projects as much as feasible. Therefore, risk management must be an integral part of any project because things do not always happen as planned. The risk management process includes identification of risks, quantitative and qualitative analysis, risk response planning, and risk monitoring.

- *Project Procurement Management.* No matter how good the idea behind a project, without funding it will never be more than a good idea. The accumulated knowledge related to project procurement management encompasses processes of solicitation, selection, contractual agreements, and closeout processes.

─ **BEFORE** *YOU GO ON* . . . ─

1. What is the Project Management Body of Knowledge and why is it important to organizations?

2. What part of the PMBOK do you think is most important? Can a project succeed without all the parts?

Apply the Concept PI 5.3

Background Project management has been shown to be an important part of implementing any new system. As you saw from the Hershey's case in Plug IT In 5.2, projects can get out of hand very quickly (if you did not complete it, visit http://www.wiley.com/go/rainer/applytheconcept and click on the link for that Plug IT In 5.2 to read the article). There are many stories you could read that would demonstrate just how quickly projects can go awry. (For additional reading, search for FBI Virtual Case File Project and Denver Airport Baggage System).

Activity Visit http://www.wiley.com/go/rainer/applytheconcept and click on the link provided for Plug IT In 5.3. You will find an article that compares the waterfall approach to project management to a more agile method of project management. Read over the article and develop for yourself a few key points that would help you determine when to use one method over another.

Deliverable

Using your key points to consider, present three examples of IT projects for each method (waterfall vs. agile development) and tell why they fit better under that method than the other.

Quiz questions are assignable in WileyPLUS, and available on the Book Companion Site at http://www.wiley.com/college/rainer.

What's in IT for ME?

For All Business Majors

Regardless of the functional area in organizations, each of you will be on project teams beginning very early in your careers. These projects will be critical to your organization's success. Therefore, it is critical that all majors understand the project management process so that you can make immediate contributions to your project teams.

SUMMARY

1. **Explain the relationship between the triple constraints on projects.**

   Projects are short-term efforts to create a specific business-related outcome. *IS project management* is a directed effort to plan, organize, and manage resources to bring about the successful achievement of specific IS goals. All projects, whether they are IS projects or not, are constrained by the same three factors, known as the *triple constraints of project management*: time, cost, and scope. *Time* refers to the window of opportunity in which a project must be completed to provide a benefit to the organization. *Cost* is the actual amount of resources, including cash and labor, that an organization can commit to completing a project. *Scope* refers to the processes that ensure that the project includes all the work required—and only the work required—to complete the project successfully.

2. **Describe the five phases of the project management process.**

   Project initiation clearly defines the problem that the project is intended to solve and the goals that it is to achieve. In *project planning,* every project objective and every activity associated with that objective must be identified and sequenced. In the *project execution* phase, the work defined in the project management plan is performed to accomplish the project's requirements. The purpose of the *monitoring and control phase* is to determine whether the progress is progressing as planned. The *project completion* phase is when the project is formally accepted by the organization.

3. **Review how each of the nine processes of the Project Management Body of Knowledge is necessary in order to ensure smooth project deployment.**

IS projects do not deliver their potential value for a number of reasons, including lack of sufficient planning at the start of a project; difficulties with technology compatibility (that is, new technology may not work with existing technology); lack of commitment by management in providing the necessary resources; poorly defined project scope; and lack of sufficient time to complete the project.

>>> GLOSSARY

IS project management A directed effort to plan, organize, and manage resources to bring about the successful achievement of specific IS goals.

project Short-term effort to create a specific business-related outcome.

Project Management Body of Knowledge (PMBOK) A collection of processes and knowledge areas generally

accepted as best practice within the project management discipline.

scope creep Uncontrolled changes in a project's scope.

triple constraints of project management Time, cost, and scope.

>>> DISCUSSION QUESTIONS

1. You manage the department that will use a system being developed on a large project. After carefully reviewing the requirements definition document, you are positive that there are missing, ambiguous, inaccurate, and unclear requirements. The project manager is pressuring you for your sign-off because he has already received sign-offs from all of your coworkers. If you fail to sign off on the requirements, you are going to put the entire project at risk because the timeframe is not negotiable. What should you do? Why? Support your answer.

2. You have been hired as a consultant to build an employee payroll system for a startup restaurant. Before you even have a chance to interview them, the two owners decided to independently come up with a list of their business requirements. When you combine their two lists, you have the following list:

   - All employees must have a unique employee ID.
   - The system must track employee hours worked based on employees' last names.

   - Employees must be scheduled to work a minimum of 8 hours per day.
   - Employee payroll is calculated by multiplying the employees' hours worked by $7.25.
   - Managers must be scheduled to work morning shifts.
   - Employees cannot be scheduled to work more than 8 hours per day.
   - Servers cannot be scheduled to work morning, afternoon, or evening shifts.
   - The system must allow managers to change and delete employees from the system.
     a. Highlight potential issues with the list.
     b. Add requirements that you think should be there but are not.
     c. What do you tell the owners when you derive your new list?

>>> PROBLEM-SOLVING ACTIVITIES

1. Apply each of the five project management processes of the PMBOK to the following massive project. Then, discuss each process with regard to that project. Finally,

use a search engine to find out where the project stands now. Would this be considered a runaway project? Why or why not?

CLOSING CASE > Britain's National Health System

Established in 1948, the National Health Service (NHS) in the United Kingdom (UK) is the largest health care organization in Europe. Controlled by the British government, it is also a vast bureaucracy, employing more than 1 million workers and providing a full range of health care services to the country's 60 million citizens.

The inspiration to digitize this huge bureaucracy first surfaced in 2001. At that time, much of the NHS was paper based and severely lagging in its use of technology, largely because of years of underinvestment. Hospitals throughout the UK were dealing with multiple vendors, many of them small to midsize UK software companies. Predictably, the NHS had become a hodgepodge of incompatible systems from different suppliers, with differing levels of functionality. The NHS had created silos of information that were not shared, or even sharable.

In an attempt to resolve these problems, in 2002 the British government initiated the National Program for Information Technology (NPIT), which includes England, Northern Ireland, and Wales (but not Scotland). The overall objective of the NPIT was to build a single, electronic health care record for every individual. In effect, this record would be a comprehensive, lifelong history of a patient's health care information, regardless of where, when, and by whom he or she was treated. In addition, the NPIT would provide health care professionals with access to a national data repository. Finally, it would support the NHS in collecting and analyzing information and monitoring health trends to make the best use of clinical and other resources.

A major obstacle for the NPIT was the sheer size of England's health care system. For example, in one year, the system served some 52 million people; it dealt with 325 million consultations in primary care, 13 million outpatient consultations, and 4 million emergency admissions; and it issued 617 million prescriptions.

The NPIT is a 10-year project designed to build new information systems to (1) connect more than 100,000 doctors, 380,000 nurses, and 50,000 other health care professionals; (2) allow for the electronic storage and retrieval of patient medical records; (3) permit patients to set up appointments via their computers; and (4) let doctors electronically transmit prescriptions to local pharmacies.

Specifically, the information systems that the NHS is attempting to deliver include the following:

- *The National Spine.* The National Spine is a database at the heart of the NPIT. The Spine encompasses individual electronic NHS lifelong care records for every patient in England, securely accessible by the patients and their health providers. The Spine will enable patients and providers to securely access integrated patient data, prescription ordering, proactive decision support, and best-practice reference data.

- *Choose and Book.* Choose and Book provides convenience for patients in electronically selecting the date, place, and time of their appointments.

- *N3.* The N3 national network is a massive, secure, broadband, virtual private network that provides the IT infrastructure and broadband connectivity for the NHS so that it can share patient information with various organizations. The N3 supports Choose and Book, electronic prescriptions, and electronic transfer of patient information.

The NHS first had McKinsey and Company conduct a study of the UK health care system. McKinsey concluded that the project was too large for any one vendor to act as prime contractor for all of it. Consequently, the NHS divided England into five regions—London, Eastern, Northeast, Northwest, and Southern—each with about 12 million people. Each of the five regions would be serviced by a prime IT vendor, known as a Local Service Provider (LSP).

The vendor-selection process was conducted with great secrecy. Unfortunately, the secrecy led to most frontline health care providers being excluded from the vendor selection process. The NHS offered 10-year service contracts to the LSPs for the five regions, each worth about $2 billion.

The LSPs are responsible for developing and integrating information systems at a local level. The LSPs are also responsible for implementing clinical and administrative applications, which support the delivery of patient care and enable trusts to exchange data with the National

Spine. (A trust is a regional health care agency that administers England's national health care programs). In addition, the LSPs provide the data centers to run all the applications.

Significantly, all of the NHS's contracts with the LSPs stipulated that vendors would not be paid until they delivered working systems. Because the vendors were the prime contractors, this stipulation also meant that the subcontractors would not be paid until they delivered working systems.

Accenture was named LSP for two regions. Computer Sciences Corporation (CSC), British Telecom (BT), and a Fujitsu-led alliance were named LSPs for the other three regions. BT was also given the contract to build both the N3 network and the National Spine. Atos Origin was chosen to provide Choose and Book.

As previously explained, the LSPs were to act as prime contractors for their respective regions, and they were able to choose their own software vendors and subcontractors. BT and the Fujitsu group selected IDX (now part of GE Healthcare), an established health care services and software provider, to develop health records software. Accenture and CSC chose iSoft, a U.K.-based supplier of health care software, for that function.

Developing this software presented many challenges. Both iSoft and IDX had to write some of the software from scratch. The difficulty was that the programmers and systems developers did not comprehend some of the terminology used by the British health system and, more important, how the British health system actually operated.

Compounding these problems was the decision by Accenture and CSC to select iSoft as its clinical and administrative software vendor. These companies were depending on iSoft's Lorenzo application suite, which at that time was still in development. However, iSoft seriously underestimated the time and effort necessary to develop the Lorenzo suite. As a result, under the collect-on-implementation contract that the LSPs had signed with the NHS, neither Accenture nor iSoft could generate revenue. In a catch-22 situation, this lack of revenue left iSoft short of the cash it needed to finish developmental work on Lorenzo.

The ongoing delay of Lorenzo left Accenture and CSC in a quandary. Should they continue to wait for Lorenzo, or should they lock into older, existing applications? Accenture opted to wait and use Lorenzo. In contrast, CSC chose to implement iSoft's existing line of products.

While waiting for Lorenzo, Accenture worked with general practitioners, as opposed to CSC, which focused almost entirely on hospitals. Accenture's problem was that the general practitioner implementation was extremely difficult because there are so many of them and the NHS had given them an option called GP Systems of Choice. This option stipulated that the doctors did not have to follow Accenture's lead in selecting a system but could, instead, choose on their own. This choice, in turn, further complicated the transfer of more than 10 years of data from old systems to the Spine-compliant systems being provided by Accenture. Typically, it cost about $9,000 and took 6 months to transfer the data of each practitioner.

Meanwhile, there were concerns with GE Healthcare's IDX as well. Fujitsu and BT had agreed to develop a Common Solution Program, meaning that the two LSPs would develop common applications for two of England's regions. Because of time delays at IDX, Fujitsu and BT replaced the firm with Cerner, a U.S. health care IT company. This replacement caused additional time delays for the project.

The NPIT was originally budgeted at $12 billion, but that figure has risen to $24 billion as a result of the many problems encountered in developing the NPIT. By mid-2007, the NHS had delivered some of the program's key elements. For example, 1 million patient referrals to specialist care were made through Choose and Book and 97 percent of doctors' offices were connected to the N3 network.

However, many deliverables of the project have been delayed. In addition, the N3 network experienced more than a hundred failures in 2006. One network outage disrupted mission-critical computer services such as patient administration systems for 3 days.

Lessons From IT Failures

Another problem was that the project has little support among health care workers. This problem stemmed from excluding frontline health care professionals in the early phases of the project. Therefore, it fell largely to the vendors and the bureaucrats to create the system. Physicians complained that the system focused too much on administrative needs and not enough on clinicians' concerns. A survey conducted in 2006 showed that only 38 percent of British general practitioners and nurses believed that the project was an important priority for the NHS, and only 13 percent believed that the project represented a good use of NHS resources.

The NHS policy to pay vendors only on delivery of working systems was shortsighted because the policy provided no flexibility to deal with vendors that encountered unexpected problems. In late 2006, Accenture announced that it was walking away from its contract with the NHS. Accenture did not say why it was exiting the project, but the company had set aside some $500 million to cover losses from its work in England.

As of mid-2007, the NHS itself had run short of funding, resulting in huge layoffs, possible closings of hospitals, and reductions in services. These problems were so serious that they prompted the British government to initiate an effort to bring costs under control. Some experts estimate that it will take another $15 billion (over the $24 billion already spent) to get the NPIT initiative fully functional.

Plug IT In | 6

Protecting Your Information Assets

LEARNING OBJECTIVES >>>

1. Explain why it is critical that you protect your information assets.
2. Identify the various behavioral actions you can take to protect your information assets.
3. Identify the various computer-based actions you can take to protect your information assets.

PI6.1 How to Protect Your Assets: The Basics

We travel on our jobs, we work from home, and we access the Internet from home and from our favorite hot spots for personal reasons—shopping, ordering products, planning trips, gathering information, staying in touch with friends and family via e-mail. Unfortunately, every time we use our computers or access the Internet, we risk exposing both professional and personal information to people looking to steal or exploit that information. Therefore, we have prepared Plug IT In 6 to explain how you can protect your information assets when you are computing at home or while you are traveling.

Figure PI6.1 Two types of actions can protect your information assets.

It is important to note that, when you are at work or when you access your university's network from home or on the road, it is hoped you have the advantage of "industrial-strength" information security that your university's IS department has implemented. In all other cases, however, you are on your own and it is your responsibility to protect yourself. Protecting yourself is becoming even more critical because organized crime is increasingly turning its attention to home users. As businesses improve their information security, consumers become the next logical target. According to Symantec (www.symantec.com), which manufactures the Norton Internet security products, if you connected an unprotected personal computer to the Internet in 2003, it would have been attacked within 15 minutes. Today, that same computer will be attacked within seconds.

You can take two types of actions to protect your information assets: behavioral actions and computer-based actions (see Figure PI6.1). Behavioral actions are those actions that do not specifically involve a computer. Computer-based actions relate to safe computing. If you take both types of actions, you will protect your information and greatly reduce your exposure to fraud and identity theft.

 ## Apply the Concept PI 6.1

Background If you knew all the tricks the thieves would use at the grocery store, you would know how to fend them off. The same is true online, although it is often much more difficult to know when you have left yourself vulnerable. Sometimes the best way to know what goes on is a simple tracking activity.

Activity Spend one hour online. Keep up with every bit of information you put on the computer: user names, passwords, preferences you may complete, Web sites you may give your e-mail address to, etc. If you visit a site and they know who you are, make note of that. Visit your junk mail at the end of the hour and see how many messages have been denied since you began the activity.

Deliverable

Compile your diary of events to submit to your professor. Determine for yourself if you feel safe or unsafe because of behavioral or technical issues (or both!).

Quiz questions are assignable in WileyPLUS, and available on the Book Companion Site at http://www.wiley.com/college/rainer.

PI6.2 Behavioral Actions to Protect Your Information Assets

You should take certain behavioral actions to protect your information assets. We discuss these actions in this section.

General Behavioral Actions

You should never provide personal information to strangers in any format—physical, verbal, or electronic. As discussed in Chapter 4, you are vulnerable to social engineering attacks at home as well as at work. Therefore, it is critical that you be on your guard at all times. For example, always verify that you are talking to authorized personnel before you provide personal information over the telephone. To accomplish this, you should hang up and call back the person or company, at a number that you obtain independently of the phone call. If the call is fraudulent, then the number the caller gives you will also be fraudulent. Credit card companies usually print their numbers on the back of their cards and/or on every statement. Further, you can find telephone numbers on your credit card company's Web site.

A critically important behavioral action that you can take is to protect your Social Security number. Unfortunately, far too many organizations use your Social Security number to uniquely identify you. When you are asked to provide this number, ask why you cannot substitute some other combination of nine numbers and letters. If the person asking for your Social Security number—for example, someone at your physician's office—is not responsive, then ask to speak with a supervisor. *Remember:* You have to take the initiative here.

The good news is that the use of Social Security numbers for identification has rapidly decreased. For example, the federal Social Security Number Protection Act of 2007 places restrictions on the use of Social Security numbers for identification purposes. The bad news is that you might have to remember many more identifiers. However, your information security would improve.

Another critical consideration involves your use of credit cards. Securing your credit cards is important because fraudulent credit card use is so widespread. One security measure that you can take is to use credit cards with your picture on them. Although cashiers probably cannot read your signature on the back of your card, they can certainly compare your picture to your face. For example, Bank of America will place your picture on several of its credit cards for free. To access this service, visit www.bankofamerica.com/creditcards and click on "Security Features" on the left-hand column. Also, do not sign the back of your credit cards. Instead, write "Photo ID Required" on the back.

You may also want to use virtual credit cards, which offer you the option of shopping online with a disposable credit card number. For no extra charge, you sign up at your credit card provider's Web site and typically download software onto your computer. When you are ready to shop, you receive a randomly generated substitute 16-digit number that you can use at the online store. The number can be used only once or, in some cases, repeatedly, but only at the same store. The card number can also be used to buy goods and services over the phone and through the mail, although it cannot be used for in-store purchases that require a traditional plastic card. Two card issuers that offer virtual cards are Citibank and Discover. (Recall our discussion of virtual credit cards in Chapter 7.)

Also, pay very close attention to your credit card billing cycles. You should know, to within a day or two, when your credit card bills are due. If a bill does not arrive when expected, call your credit card company immediately. If your credit card is stolen and is being used fraudulently, the first thing the thief does is change the address on the account so that you do not receive the bill. Fortunately, you can view your credit card bills online. Further, most credit card issuers offer the option to receive your credit card bills via e-mail. This process eliminates postal mail theft as a problem. In addition, when you write checks to pay any of your accounts, particularly your credit card accounts, do not write your complete card number on the "For" line of your check. Instead, write only the last four digits.

Another important action is to limit your use of debit cards. Debit cards are linked to your bank account, meaning that a person who steals your debit card and personal identification number (PIN) can clean out your bank account. In contrast, your liability with credit cards is usually zero (or a small amount). Instead, your credit card company bears the liability for fraudulent charges, provided that you notify the company within 60 days of the theft.

Do not use a personal mailbox at your home or apartment for anything other than catalogs and magazines. Use a private mailbox or a P.O. (Post Office) box. It is far too easy for thieves to steal mail from home mailboxes when no one is at home for much of the day. Think about the wealth of information that could be stolen from your mailbox: credit card statements, bank statements, investment statements, and so on.

When you discard mail or old records, use a cross-cut or confetti shredder to cut them up. Recall our discussion of dumpster diving in Chapter 4. A single-cut shredder is not sufficient because, with enough time, a thief can reassemble the strips.

Another security option is to sign up with a company that provides proactive protection of your personal information. Examples of such companies are LifeLock (www.lifelock.com), TrustedID (www.trustedid.com), and CardCops (www.cardcops.com).

LifeLock and TrustedID allow customers to lock their credit files so that new lines of credit cannot be opened unless customers first unlock their existing files. Locking credit files means that merchants and banks must have verbal or written permission from customers before opening new credit in their names. Ordinarily, the locking process involves sending registered mail to each of the three major credit agencies every 90 days. These three agencies are Equifax (www.equifax.com), Experian (www.experian.com), and TransUnion (www.transunion.com). LifeLock and TrustedID perform this service for you, and thus proactively monitor your various credit files.

CardCops provides an early warning service that notifies its customers that the company has found their personal information circulating on the Internet. It also collects compromised data on the Internet and makes it available to its customers and to merchants.

A paper shredder is a simple, but effective tool to use to protect your identity
(Source: discpicture/Shutterstock)

What to Do in the Event of Identity Theft

Identity theft is on the rise, with more than 11 million victims reported in the United States in 2010. If you follow the behavioral and computer-based actions recommended in this Plug IT In, you will greatly reduce, but not eliminate, the chances that your identity will be stolen. If your identity is stolen despite these precautions, you should follow these steps to recover:

- First, get a lawyer.
- Get organized. Keep a file with all your paperwork, including the names, addresses, and phone numbers of everyone you contact about this crime.
- File a detailed police report. Send copies of this report to creditors and other agencies that may require proof of the crime.
- Get the name and phone number of your police investigator and give it to your creditors.
- In all communications about this crime, use certified, return-receipt mail. Report that you are the victim of ID theft to the fraud divisions of all three credit reporting agencies: Equifax, Experian, and TransUnion. In addition, call the Social Security fraud line number. Because of the increased incidence of identity theft, federal law now gives you the right to have one free credit report per year. If you request your free annual credit report from each of the three agencies, you will receive one free report every four months.
- Be sure to obtain your unique case number from each credit agency and ask each agency to send you your credit report.
- Tell each agency to issue a fraud alert. The fraud alert requires mortgage brokers, car dealers, credit card companies, and other lenders to scrutinize anyone who opens an account in your name for 90 days.
- Obtain the document that you need to file a long-term fraud alert, which lasts for 7 years and can be canceled at any time.
- Ask the credit agencies for the names and phone numbers of lenders with whom fraudulent accounts have been opened.
- Point out all entries generated from fraud to each agency. Ask each agency to remove the specified fraudulent entries.
- Instruct each agency to notify anyone who received your report in the 6 six months that you are disputing the information.
- Californians can order a "credit freeze" with all three major credit agencies. This freeze requires lenders, retailers, utilities, and other businesses to obtain special access to your credit report through a PIN-based system. It also helps prevent anyone from getting any new loans or credit in your name. Similar legislation has been introduced in other states.
- Call your credit card companies directly.
- Change all your credit cards immediately. Get replacements with new account numbers and close your old accounts.

- Be alert for change-of-address forms in your mail. The U.S. Postal Service must send notifications to your old and new addresses. If someone tries to change your mailing address, it is a major indication that you have been victimized.

- Fill out fraud affidavits for creditors. The Federal Trade Commission (FTC) provides a form (search the web for "FTC fraud affidavit form") that many creditors accept.

- If debt collectors demand payment of fraudulent accounts, write down the name of the company as well as the collector's name, address, and phone number. Tell the collector that you are the victim of identity theft. Send the collection agency a certified letter with a completed FTC form. If this does not work, refer the agency to your lawyer.

In addition to these behavioral actions, the computer-based actions we discuss in the next section will further help you protect yourself.

Apply the Concept PI 6.2

Background Education is extremely important in being able to determine if something on the Web is legitimate or not. This section teaches you how to respond if your identity has been stolen. One way this could happen is via phishing. Phishing is when a thief sends an e-mail that looks legitimate and asks you to send user name and login information so he/she can update it. Once you send that information, your account (and possibly your identity) is no longer secure.

Activity Visit http://www.wiley.com/go/rainer/applytheconcept and click on the link provided for Plug IT In 6.2. This will take you to a page on Chase's Web site that gives examples of false e-mails. Read over these e-mails and develop for yourself five clues that these messages may be fraudulent. Also, prepare a statement of best practices when you receiving these phishing emails.

Deliverable

Submit your list of five clues and your statement of best practices to your professor.

Quiz questions are assignable in WileyPLUS, and available on the Book Companion Site at http://www.wiley.com/college/rainer.

PI6.3 Computer-Based Actions to Protect Your Information Assets

You can take many computer-based actions to increase the security of your information. We first discuss how to determine where persons who use your computer have visited on the Internet. Next, we briefly explain how to access social networking sites safely.

We then consider how to determine if your computer is infected with malicious software (malware) and what actions to take to prevent such infections. Next, we discuss how to protect your portable devices—for example, laptops and flash drives—and the information they contain. We follow with discussions of other valuable computer-based actions, how to protect your privacy when using the Internet and e-mail, how to recover from a disaster, and how to protect yourself when computing wirelessly.

We also thoroughly discuss Microsoft Windows 7 and provide a section on Microsoft's Internet Explorer 8, because this browser has added security features. We do not discuss other operating systems and browsers because of space limitations.

Determining Where People Have Visited on the Internet Using Your Computer

At home, you may have a single computer or several computers connected to a network. Although you may practice "safe computing," other people who use your computer might not. For example, you might have roommates who use your computer. Their friends could be using your computer as well. You cannot be certain that these individuals take the same safety precautions that you do. You can, however, identify the Internet sites that anyone who uses your computer has visited. To accomplish this task, check the browser history. It is important to note that all modern browsers have a "private browsing" mode in which the viewing history is not recorded. If someone uses private browsing on your computer, then you will not be able to check that person's browser history.

The Dangers of Social Networking Sites

You should never post personal information about yourself or your family in chat rooms or on social networking sites. In fact, you should access these Web sites and review any entries that you have made. The reason for these precautions is that potential employers are now searching these Web sites for information about you. Well-known social networking sites include MySpace, Friendster, Xanga, YouTube, Facebook, and Flickr.

Social Media operates on openness, but safety is in maintaining some privacy.
(Source: Jure Porenta/Shutterstock)

The good news is that social networking Web sites have added features to give us more control over our information. The bad news is that the privacy settings are not always easy to find and use. Your first decision is whether to make your profile publicly available or to keep it more private. More than 33 percent of adult users allow everyone to see their profiles. In contrast, some 60 percent restrict access in some way.

All of the major social networking sites give you control over public accessibility, but they have different mechanisms for doing so. With MySpace, for example, the full profiles of users age 18 and older are available to everyone on the Internet by default. You can make your MySpace profile private by following these steps:

- Click on "Account Settings."
- Click on "Privacy Settings."
- Click on "Change Settings."
- Click on "Who Can View My Profile."
- Now, customize who gets to see what on your profile.

In contrast, on Facebook the default is a private profile, where users decide what information is publicly available. To make privacy adjustments on Facebook, follow these steps:

- Click on "Settings."
- Click on "Privacy Settings."
- Work with the options you find there.

If you want to keep a low profile on Facebook, it is a good idea to look at the "Applications" section in Privacy Settings. You may have shielded parts of your profile from public access, but that does not mean that you have done the same for Facebook applications that have access to much of your same data by default. For a full explanation of Facebook's privacy settings, see www.facebook.com/privacy/explanation.php.

On LinkedIn, most people want public profiles, and that is the default. The information that LinkedIn users share tends to be professional credentials, not details of their social lives, so there is less need for privacy. If you want additional privacy on LinkedIn, follow these steps:

- Click on "Account & Settings" from your home page.
- Scroll down to adjust your privacy settings.

One company, Reputation Defender (www.reputationdefender.com), will search out all information about you on the Internet and present it to you in the form of a report. Then, at your command, it will "destroy all inaccurate, inappropriate, hurtful, and slanderous information about you."

Determining if Your Computer Is Infected

There are several signs to look for if you think your computer system is infected with malicious software or malware (discussed in Chapter 4), including the following:

- Your computer shuts down unexpectedly by itself.
- Your computer refuses to start normally.

- Running the DOS CHKDSK (**CH**ECK **D**ISK) command shows that less than 655,360 (640 kilobytes) bytes are available. To run the CHKDSK command, follow these steps:
  - Click on "Start."
  - Click on "All Programs."
  - Click on "Accessories."
  - Click on "Command Prompt."
  - Type in "CHKDSK" and hit Enter.
- Your computer exhibits erratic behavior, exhibiting some or all of these characteristics:
  - Your system unexpectedly runs out of memory on your computer's hard drive.
  - Your system continually runs out of main memory (RAM).
  - Programs take longer to load than normal.
  - Programs act erratically.
  - Your monitor displays strange graphics or messages.
  - Your system displays an unusually high number of error messages.

Your e-mail program sends messages to all the contacts in your address book without your knowledge or permission.

If you note any or all of these signs, then your computer might be infected with malware. You can then take the computer-based actions discussed later in this chapter to rid your computer of this software. However, taking the actions discussed in the next section will reduce your chances of being infected in the first place.

Computer Actions to Prevent Malware Infections

Many of the actions we discuss in this section are commonsense, but surprisingly large numbers of people do not pay attention to them. Taking these steps will help you prevent a malware infection of your computer system. We begin by considering actions that you must *never* take with your computer.

Never open unrequested attachments to e-mail files, even if they are from people you know and trust. Their computers may have been compromised without their knowledge, in which case the e-mail could be a phishing attack. Recall from Chapter 4 that a phishing attack involves tricking people into visiting a phony Web site and, once there, providing confidential information.

Never open attachments or Web links in e-mails from people you do not know. These attachments can infect your system with a worm or virus. Similarly, these Web links can be a phishing attack that can infect your system with a Trojan horse, turning your computer into a zombie or bot (short for robot). As we saw in Chapter 4, when this occurs your computer is no longer under your control.

Never accept files transferred to you during Internet chat or instant messaging sessions. These files are usually not from people you know and they can infect your system with malware.

Never download any files or software over the Internet from Web sites that you do not know. Never download files or software that you have not requested.

Test Your System. It is a good idea to test your system. Several Web sites provide free security tests. These tests send different types of messages to your computer to evaluate how well your system is protected from a variety of attacks. Free testing Web sites include Shields Up! (www.grc.com), Symantec Security Check (http://security.norton.com), and McAfee My SecurityStatus (search "McAfee My SecurityStatus" on the web)).

Microsoft provides a valuable scanning tool called the Microsoft Baseline Analyzer. This tool scans Windows-based computers for common security problems and generates individual security reports for each computer that it scans. The Baseline Analyzer can be downloaded for free. You can also run free malware scans on your computer. Several companies, including the following, will scan your computer to identify viruses, worms, and other malware, and offer suggestions about how to clean your system if it is infected:

- Trend Micro (search the Web for "Trend Micro HouseCall")
- Panda Software (http://www.pandasecurity.com/usa)

Install a Security Suite on Your Computer. Security suites are software packages that contain a variety of security products, such as anti-malware software, spam protection, e-mail fraud protection, spyware detection, intrusion detection, and monitoring software. These suites provide a great deal of functionality in one package. There is a question of whether the individual functions in a security suite can match the combined functions of a group of individual products. Therefore, we discuss individual products in the next sections.

Well-known security suites include the following, but there are many others:

- ZoneAlarm Security Suite (www.zonelabs.com)
- McAfee Internet Security Suite (www.mcafee.com)
- Norton Internet Security (www.symantec.com)
- PC-cillin Internet Security (www.trendmicro.com)

Install an Anti-Malware Product on Your Computer. You should install an anti-malware product on your computer and use it, ideally at least once per week. Remember that every time you scan your computer for malware with your anti-malware product, you must update your malware definitions before you scan. Typically, anti-malware product vendors automatically update your malware definitions over the Web.

There are free anti-malware products and commercial anti-malware products. In general, the free products are adequate, but the commercial products offer more functionality. An excellent resource offering a great deal of information on free anti-malware products, as well as many other security products, is www.thefreecountry.com. Go to Security > Free Antivirus Software to see their list of anti-malware products.

Well-known commercial anti-malware products include the following, but there are many others:

- Norton Anti-malware (www.symantec.com)
- PC-cillin (www.trendmicro.com)
- VirusScan (www.mcafee.com)

Install a Firewall on Your Computer. A personal firewall is software installed on your home computer that controls communications to and from your computer by permitting or denying communications based on your security settings. A personal firewall usually will protect only the computer on which the software is installed. Nevertheless, firewalls perform essential functions.

Essentially, firewalls should make your computer invisible. This means that your firewall should not respond to Internet requests to ports (i.e., communications links to your computer) that are not used for common Internet use. In effect, your computer operates in stealth mode on the Internet.

Firewalls also should alert you to suspicious behavior. They should tell you when a program or connection is attempting to do something you have not instructed it to do, such as download software or run a program such as ActiveX. ActiveX (by Microsoft), which can execute programs downloaded from Internet Explorer, can be exploited by attackers trying to compromise your computer. To manage ActiveX in Internet Explorer, follow these steps:

- Click on "Start."
- Click on "My Computer."
- Click on "Control Panel."
- Click on "Security Center."
- Click on "Internet Options."
- Click on the "Security" tab.
- Click on the button that says "Custom level. . . ."
- Scroll down and choose the following:
  - The button for "Download signed ActiveX controls"
  - The button for "Download unsigned ActiveX controls"

Firewalls should block outbound connections that you do not initiate. Your firewall should not let your computer access the Internet on its own. If your computer tries to access the Internet by itself, this is a sure sign that it is infected with malware.

As with anti-malware programs, firewall products can be either free or commercially produced. Again, the free products are adequate, but the commercial products offer more functionality. For a list of free firewall software search "about.com free firewalls".

Many companies offer commercial firewall software. These are some of the best-known commercial firewall products:

- ZoneAlarm Security Suite (www.zonelabs.com)
- Norton Internet Security (www.symantec.com)
- PC-cillin Internet Security (www.trendmicro.com)
- McAfee Internet Security (www.mcafee.com)
- F-Secure Internet Security (www.f-secure.com)
- Panda Platinum Internet Security (www.pandasoftware.com)

It is a good idea to test your firewall. However, it is best to use only those test Web sites that are run by actual firewall or security software companies. A good firewall test site is the McAfee HackerWatch site at www.hackerwatch.org/probe. The HackerWatch site allows you to do a basic probe test on your computer to see if your firewall is blocking ports that may be vulnerable.

Install an Antispyware Product on Your Computer. As with anti-malware products and firewalls, free antispyware products are adequate, but commercial antispyware products offer more functionality. Free antispyware products include these:

- Ad-Aware SE Personal (www.lavasoft.com)
- Spybot Search&Destroy (www.safer-networking.org)

Well-known commercial antispyware products include the following, but there are many others:

- CounterSpy (www.sunbeltsoftware.com)
- Spy Sweeper (www.webroot.com)
- Ad-Aware (www.lavasoft.com)
- SpyCatcher (www.tenebril.com)

  Several companies offer free spyware scans:

- Spy Audit (www.webroot.com)
- Zonelabs (www.zonelabs.com)
- Norton (www.symantec.com)

Install Monitoring Software on Your Computer. Monitoring software logs keystrokes, e-mails, applications, windows, Web sites, Internet connections, passwords, chat conversations, Web cams, and even screenshots. Companies that offer monitoring software include the following:

- SpyAgent (www.spytech-web.com)
- SpyBuddy (www.exploreanywhere.com)
- WinSpy (www.win-spy.com)
- SpectorSoft (www.spectorsoft.com)

Install Content-Filtering Software on Your Computer. Content-filtering software performs many functions. It can block access to undesirable Web sites, and it can record and view all of the Web sites that you or other users have visited. It can also record both sides of chat conversations from AOL Instant Messenger (AIM and AIM Triton), Yahoo! Messenger, and MSN Messenger.

Content-filtering software provides many filter categories, thus enabling you to selectively filter content. Companies that offer this software include the following:

- Cybersitter (www.cybersitter.com)
- NetNanny (www.netnanny.com)
- CyberSpy (www.cyberspyware.com)

Internet Explorer's Content Advisor utility allows you to block access to Web sites that meet specified criteria and to set your own tolerance levels for various types of Internet content. To activate and configure Content Advisor, follow these steps:

- Click on "My Computer."
- Click on "Control Panel."
- Click on "Security Center."
- Click on "Internet Options."
- When the Internet Options dialog box appears, select the Content Tab.
- Click on the "Enable" button.
- You will see 13 categories. For each category, you can move the slide bar for increased restriction.
- After you have set the slide bar for each category, click "OK."

You can also block selected Web sites. To accomplish this, follow these steps:

- Click on "My Computer."
- Click on "Control Panel."
- Click on "Security Center."
- Click on "Internet Options."
- When the Internet Options dialog box appears, select the Content Tab.
- Click on the "Enable" button.
- Click the Approved Sites tab.
- Enter the Web sites you wish to block, and click "Never."
- Click "OK."

Install Antispam Software on Your Computer. Antispam software helps you to control spam. Well-known commercial antispam products include the following, but there are many others:

- Cloudmark (www.cloudmark.com)
- MailFrontier Desktop (www.sonicwall.com/)
- SpamKiller (www.mcafee.com)
- Norton Antispam (www.symantec.com)
- SpamGourmet (www.spamgourmet.com)
- SpamAssassin (http://spamassassin.org)

You might also want to set up multiple free e-mail accounts, such as accounts on Hotmail and Gmail. Then, as you surf the Internet and are asked for your e-mail address, you can use one of these accounts rather than your home or business e-mail account. When your free e-mail accounts are full of spam, you can close them and open new accounts.

Install Proactive Intrusion Detection and Prevention Software on Your Computer. Recall from Chapter 4 that anti-malware software is reactive in nature, thereby leaving you vulnerable to zero-day attacks. For this reason, it is important to add proactive intrusion detection and prevention software to your defenses. One such product is Prevx (www.prevx.com). You can download and install Prevx for free, and it will scan your computer for malicious software. If it finds any, it will activate a free 30-day clean-up account and remove the malware from your computer. Once this period runs out, Prevx will continue to scan incoming programs and protect your computer from them. However, if you subsequently get infected and want to continue using Prevx, you must pay for one year of protection.

Manage Patches. You should download and install all software patches immediately—for example, patches for Windows. Companies typically release patches to repair security problems. If you do not download and install patches quickly, your computer will be extremely vulnerable to attack. Microsoft provides an automatic method that checks for and downloads any new patches. To enable Automatic Update in Windows XP, follow these steps:

- Right click on "Start."
- Click on "Explore."
- Scroll down and click on "Control Panel."
- Click on "System."
- Click on the "Automatic Updates" tab at the top of the box.
- You can now configure when you want to download and install updates.

  To open the Microsoft Update window in Windows XP, follow these steps:

- Click on "Start."
- Click on "All Programs."
- Click on "Windows Update."

If you click the "Express" button, your system will be scanned and you will be notified if any new updates are available. You can then review suggested updates and install them.

Use a Browser Other Than Internet Explorer. You might consider using a browser other than Internet Explorer, such as Firefox (www.mozilla.org), Opera (www.opera.com), Safari from Apple (www.apple.com/safari/download), or Google Chrome (www.google.com/chrome). These browsers are not impregnable, but they are less prominent, and hackers, at least so far, have paid less attention to them. Even if you decide to use a browser other than Internet Explorer, however, you should still implement all of the security measures we have discussed.

You should also keep your browser updated. Microsoft released Internet Explorer 9 (IE9) in March 2011. As we discuss later in this Plug IT In, IE9 has added security features.

Use an Operating System Other Than Windows. The two main alternatives to Windows 7 and Vista are Apple's Mac OS X and Linux. These two operating systems are not invulnerable, but they are both based on UNIX, which makes them inherently more secure than any version of Windows. (UNIX is an operating system developed by AT&T in the 1960s and 1970s that usually runs on servers rather than on desktops.) In addition, Linux and Mac OS X have smaller market shares than Windows and thus are less attractive targets for malware.

Protecting Your Portable Devices and Information

Theft or loss of laptops, notebook computers, tablets, personal digital assistants, BlackBerrys, and thumb drives, as well as the data contained on these devices, is a significant problem. You can take many proactive steps to protect portable devices and their data, including prevent the theft, use two-factor authentication, and encrypt your data. You can also take reactive steps after a theft or loss has occurred. We consider all of these actions in this section.

Before we discuss these steps, there are two commonsense precautions that many people forget. First, keep your laptop in an inconspicuous container. Laptop cases with your company logo simply draw the attention of thieves. Second, do not leave your laptop unattended in plain view—for example, in your car where it can be seen; instead, lock it in the trunk of your vehicle.

One strategy to prevent the theft of a portable device is to use alarms. Laptop security systems operate by detecting motion, analyzing the motion to determine whether a threat exists, and, if it does, implementing responses. These alarms are battery powered, are independent of the computer operating system, and operate whether the laptop is on or off. If a laptop armed with a security system is carried beyond a perimeter specified by the user, then the alarm assumes the laptop is being stolen. It can then prevent access to the operating system, secure passwords, and encryption keys and can sound an audible alarm. One company that provides laptop security systems is Absolute Software's LoJack for Laptops (www.absolute.com).

Two-factor authentication means that you must have two forms of identification to access your laptop or notebook. The first authentication factor uses a token or biometrics. The second factor is your personal password. A token generates a one-time password that you must enter within a specified time limit. This password typically consists of six digits, which appear on the token's LCD screen. Companies offering tokens for two-factor authentication include Authenex (www.authenex.com), Kensington (www.kensington.com), and SecuriKey (www.securikey.com).

Fingerprints are the biometric used for two-factor authentication, by incorporating fingerprint readers into the laptop itself. See IBM (www.ibm.com) and Microsoft (www.microsoft.com). You can also use fingerprint authentication on your thumb drive with the SanDisk Cruzer (www.sandisk.com), the Lexar JumpDrive TouchGuard (www.lexar.com), the Sony MicroVault (www.sony.net), and the Kanguru Bio Slider (www.kanguru.com).

Data encryption provides additional protection by turning data into meaningless symbols that can be deciphered only by an authorized person. You can encrypt some or all of the data on your computer by using Windows XP's built-in encryption, folder-based encryption, or full-disk encryption.

Windows XP's Encrypting File System allows you to encrypt files or folders. Follow these steps:

- Right-click on the file or folder.
- Click on "Sharing and Security."
- Click the "General" tab at the top.
- Click the "Advanced" tab.
- Check the box labeled "Encrypt Contents to Secure Data."
- Click "OK."

Beachhead Solutions (www.beachheadsolutions.com) and Credant (www.credant.com) also provide applications that allow you to encrypt files and folders.

Another step you can take to improve your security is to encrypt your entire hard drive, including your applications. See Mobile Armor (www.mobilearmor.com), the Kanguru Wizard (www.kanguru.com), and the PCKey (www.kensington.com).

If your laptop is lost or stolen, you can use laptop tracing tools or device reset/remote kill tools. For example, the XTool Computer Tracker (www.computersecurity.com), PC PhoneHome (www.pcphonehome.com), and LaptopLocate (www.laptoplocate.net) provide transmitters that secretly send a signal to their respective company control centers via telephone or the Internet. This signal enables the company, with the help of the local authorities, Internet service providers, and telephone companies, to track your computer's location.

You can also use device reset/remote kill tools to automatically eliminate specified data on a lost or stolen laptop to prevent it from being compromised or misused. The solution works even when other security software or encryption methods fail. Examples of companies providing these solutions are McAfee (www.trustdigital.com) and Beachhead Solutions (www.beachheadsolutions.com).

Internet Explorer 9

Internet Explorer 9 (IE9) offers multiple, interrelated security features to help defend your computer against malicious software as well as safeguards to help ensure that your personal information does not fall into the hands of fraudulent or deceptive Web site operators. Together with Windows Defender, the security features in IE9 are an improvement over the security features of previous versions of Windows and Internet Explorer. IE9 has been improved so that it limits the amount of damage that malware can do if it is able to penetrate your system. Further, IE9 includes several features designed to thwart attackers' efforts to trick you into entering personal data on inappropriate Web sites. We discuss these features in this section.

Protected Mode. In Protected Mode, IE9 cannot modify any of your files and settings without your consent. Protected Mode requires you to confirm any activity that tries to place any software on your computer or to start another program. This feature also makes you aware of what a Web site is trying to do, giving you the opportunity to prevent it and to verify the trustworthiness of the site.

ActiveX Opt-In. ActiveX Opt-In automatically disables all but a small group of well-known, preapproved controls. Therefore, if a Web site tries to use an ActiveX control that you have not used before, IE9 displays a notice in the Information Bar. This notification enables you to permit or deny access when you are viewing unfamiliar Web sites.

Fix My Settings. Because most users simply accept the default setting on the applications they install and use, IE9 is shipped with security settings that provide the maximum level of usability while maintaining strict security control. Fix My Settings is a feature that alerts you when you might be browsing with unsafe settings on your computer. It does so by displaying a warning in the Information Bar as long as your settings remain unsafe. You can quickly reset your security settings to the Medium-High default level by clicking the Fix My Settings option in the Information Bar. If you close your browser and it reopens with unsafe settings, you will see a notification page reminding you to correct your settings before you visit any Web sites.

Widows Defender. Widows Defender protects you against spyware and thus helps prevent malware from penetrating your system by piggybacking on spyware. This is a common mechanism by which malware is distributed and installed silently on the systems of unsuspecting users.

Personal Data Safeguards. IE9 provides the Security Status Bar, located next to the Address Bar, which helps you quickly differentiate authentic Web sites from suspicious or malicious ones. This feature enhances your access to digital certificate information that helps you validate the trustworthiness of Web sites.

The Security Status Bar provides prominent, color-coded visual cues that indicate whether a Web site is safe and trustworthy. Earlier versions of Internet Explorer placed a gold padlock icon in the lower right corner of the browser window to designate the trust and security levels of the Web site. IE9 displays the padlock more prominently. You can also view a Web site's digital certificate information with a single click on the padlock icon. If IE9 detects any irregularities in the Web site's certificate information, then it displays the padlock icon on a red background.

The Security Status Bar also supports new Extended Validation (EV) certificates that offer stronger identification of secure Web sites such as banking sites. These sites have undergone a comprehensive verification process to ensure that their identity is that of the real business entity. IE9 highlights these validated Web sites with a green-shaded address bar and it prominently displays the associated business's name.

IE9 also provides an Address Bar in every window. This requirement helps ensure that you will be able to learn more about the true source of any information that you are seeing.

Phishing Filter. The Phishing Filter is an opt-in feature that maintains a list of potentially dangerous Web sites by scanning for suspicious Web site characteristics. The filter denotes known phishing sites by turning the Address Bar red. It then navigates users away from that page and displays a warning message about the potential for a phishing attack. For suspicious Web sites—meaning that a page has certain suspicious characteristics—the filter displays a yellow Address Bar. Finally, it identifies acceptable Web sites by displaying the standard white Address Bar.

Delete Browsing History. IE9 provides a Delete Browsing History option for one-click cleanup so that you can easily and quickly erase all personal information stored in the browser. This feature is particularly important when you use a friend's computer or computers in public environments such as libraries, schools, conference centers, and hotel business centers.

InPrivate. IE9 has a new security application called InPrivate, which features InPrivate Browsing and InPrivate Blocking. InPrivate Browsing helps prevent your browser from retaining your browsing history, temporary Internet files, cookies, and user names and passwords, thus leaving no evidence of your browsing or search history. Today, Web sites increasingly access content from multiple sources, providing tremendous value to consumers. However, users may not be aware that some content, images, and advertisements are being provided from third-party Web sites, or that these sites can potentially track the users' behavior. *InPrivate Blocking* enables users to block the information that third-party Web sites can potentially use to track your browsing history.

Domain Highlighting. This feature in IE9 helps you to see the real Web address of the Web sites you visit. It accomplishes this task by highlighting the actual domain you are visiting in the address bar. This process helps you avoid deceptive or phishing Web sites that use misleading Web addresses to trick you.

SmartScreen Filter. This feature helps protect you from online phishing attacks, fraud, and spoofed or malicious Web sites.

Add-on Manager. This feature lets you disable or allow Web browser add-ons and delete unwanted ActiveX controls.

Cross-site Scripting Filter. This feature can help prevent attacks from phishing and fraudulent Web sites that might attempt to steal your personal and financial information.

A 128-Bit Secure Connection for Using Secure Web Sites. This feature helps IE9 create an encrypted connection with Web sites operated by banks, online stores, medical sites, and other organizations that handle sensitive customer information.

Other Actions That You Can Take on Your Computer

You can take some other actions on your computer for added protection. These consist of detecting worms and Trojan horses, turning off peer-to-peer file sharing, looking for new and unusual files, detecting spoofed (fake) Web sites, and adjusting the privacy settings on your computer.

How to Detect a Worm. Worms are malicious programs that perform unwanted actions on your computer (see Chapter 4). They exhibit several characteristics that you can watch for:

- Your system exhibits unexplained hard disk activity.
- Your system connects to the Internet by itself without any action on your part.
- Your system seems to be short on available memory.
- Your family, friends, or colleagues notify you that they have received an odd e-mail message from you, that they are sure you did not send.

Ordinarily, your anti-malware software should detect and remove worms. However, if your computer is currently infected with a worm, you may not be able to delete that file. In this case, you will have to reboot (start up) your system from a bootable disk and then delete the worm file from the Command Prompt. (Follow the steps for "How to Look for New and Unusual Files," which follows, to find the worm file.) Normally, when you reboot your system, the worm file should no longer be present.

How to Detect a Trojan Horse. Trojan horses are malicious programs disguised as, or embedded within, legitimate software (see Chapter 4). You can determine if your computer is infected with a Trojan horse by following the steps listed here. These steps will enable you to see if your computer is "listening" for instructions from another computer. They are based on the DOS-based utility program called Netstat (part of Windows).

- Close all running applications, and reboot your computer.
- When your computer restarts, do *not* establish a dial-up Internet connection. It is okay to let your computer access the Internet via a broadband connection (for example, cable or DSL modem).

The Trojan horse virus is named for the Trojan Horse offered to Troy by Greece during the Trojan War. It was part of a plan to destroy the city.

(Source: Travel Library Limited/ SuperStock)

- Open the DOS window:
  - Click on "Start."
  - Click on "All Programs."
  - Click on "Accessories."
  - Click on "Command Prompt."
- In the DOS window, type the following and press Enter:
  netstat –an>>c:\netstat.txt
- Close the DOS window and
  - Click on "Start."
  - Click on "All Programs."
  - Click on "Accessories."
  - Click on "Notepad."
- In Notepad, click on "File" and then on "Open."
- In the box provided, type:
  c:\netstat.txt
- Click "Open."
- You will see a number of active connections in a Listening state. Each active connection will have a local address. The local address will be in a form like this: 0.0.0.0.xxxxx (where the x's refer to a sequence of numbers).
- If a Trojan horse is present, your system will be listening for one of the addresses listed here:
  - Back Orifice   0.0.0.0.31337 or 0.0.0.0.31338
  - Deep Throat   0.0.0.0.2140 or 0.0.0.0.3150
  - NetBus   0.0.0.0.12345 or 0.0.0.0.12346
  - Remote Grab   0.0.0.0.7000

How to Detect Fake Web Sites. A fake Web site is typically created to look like a well-known, legitimate site with a slightly different or confusing URL. The attacker tries to trick people into going to the spoofed site and providing valuable information by sending out e-mail messages and hoping that some users will not notice the incorrect URL. (We discussed this attack, known as phishing, in Chapter 4.) Products that help detect fake Web sites include the SpoofStick, the Verification Engine, and McAfee's SiteAdvisor. These products are not definitive solutions, but they are helpful.

The SpoofStick (www.spoofstick.com) helps users detect fake Web sites by prominently displaying a new toolbar in your browser that shows you which site you are actually surfing. For example, if you go to Amazon's Web site, the SpoofStick toolbar says, "You're on amazon.com." However, if you go to a fake Web site that pretends to be Amazon, the SpoofStick toolbar shows the actual IP address of the Web site you are surfing, saying for example, "You're on 137.65.23.117."

Similarly, the Verification Engine (www.vengine.com) enables you to verify that the site you are visiting or are directed to via e-mail can be trusted. If you move your mouse to the logo brand or image you want to verify, the Verification Engine will authenticate the trust credentials of the site you are surfing. In addition, during a secure communications session with Internet Explorer, you can move your mouse over the padlock to verify that (1) the padlock is genuine and not a fraudulent graphic and (2) the site uses a secure sockets layer (SSL) certificate (discussed in Chapter 4) that contains the correct information about the company to which you are connected. McAfee's SiteAdvisor (www.siteadvisor.com) sticks a green, yellow, or red safety logo next to search results on Google, Yahoo!, and MSN. It also puts a color-coded button in the Internet Explorer toolbar. Mousing over the button displays details as to why the Web site is good or bad. SiteAdvisor also scores Web sites based on the excessive use of pop-up advertisements, how much spam the Web site will generate if you reveal your e-mail address, and whether the site spreads spyware and adware.

Protecting Your Privacy

In today's hostile Internet environment, you must use strong passwords (discussed in Chapter 4) and adjust the privacy settings on your computer. You may also wish to protect your privacy by surfing the Web and e-mailing anonymously. In this section we discuss these actions.

Use Strong Passwords. You can use the Secure Password Generator at PCTools to create strong passwords. The Generator lets you select the number and type of characters in your password.

Remembering multiple passwords is difficult. You can use free software such as Password Safe or Roboform (www.roboform.com) to help you remember your passwords and maintain them securely.

How to Adjust Your Privacy Settings on Your Computer. Windows 7 allows you to select the level of privacy that you want when using your computer. Here are the steps to follow to adjust your privacy settings:

- Click on "My Computer."
- Click on "Control Panel."
- Click on "Security Center."
- Click on "Internet Options."
- Click on the "Privacy" tab at the top.
- Adjust the slide bar.
- Manipulate the slide bar to determine the level of privacy you desire.
- You will see an explanation of what each level means as you use the slide bar.
- The levels of privacy and their meanings are
  - Lowest (Accept All Cookies)
    - All cookies will be saved on this computer.
    - Existing cookies on this computer can be read by the Web sites that created them.
  - Low
    - Restricts third-party cookies that do not have a compact privacy policy.
    - Restricts third-party cookies that use personally identifiable information without your implicit consent.
  - Medium
    - Blocks third-party cookies that do not have a compact privacy policy.
    - Blocks third-party cookies that use personally identifiable information without your implicit consent.
    - Restricts first-party cookies that use personally identifiable information without your implicit consent.
  - Medium High
    - Blocks third-party cookies that do not have a compact privacy policy.
    - Blocks third-party cookies that use personally identifiable information without your explicit consent.
    - Blocks first-party cookies that use personally identifiable information without your explicit consent.
  - High
    - Blocks cookies that do not have a compact privacy policy.
    - Blocks cookies that use personally identifiable information without your explicit consent.

- ○ Very High (Block All Cookies)
  - ◉ Cookies from all Web sites will be blocked.
  - ◉ Existing cookies on your computer cannot be read by Web sites.

Note: A first-party cookie either originates on, or is sent to, the Web site you are currently viewing. These cookies are commonly used to store information, such as your preferences when visiting that site. In contrast, a third-party cookie either originates on, or is sent to, a different Web site from the one you are currently viewing. Third-party Web sites usually provide some content on the Web site you are viewing. For example, many sites rely on advertising from third-party Web sites, which frequently use cookies. A common use for third-party cookies is to track your browsing history for advertising or other marketing purposes.

How to Surf the Web Anonymously. Many users worry that knowledge of their IP addresses is enough for outsiders to connect their online activities to their "real-world" identities. Depending on his or her technical, physical, and legal access, a determined party (such as a government prosecutor) may be able to do so, especially if he or she is assisted by the records of the ISP that has assigned the Internet Protocol (IP) address. To protect their privacy against this type of activity, many people surf the Web and e-mail anonymously.

Surfing the Web anonymously means that you do not make your IP address or any other personally identifiable information available to the Web sites that you are visiting. There are two ways to surf the Web anonymously: You can use an anonymizer Web site as a proxy server, or you can use an anonymizer as a permanent proxy server in your Web browser.

A *proxy server* is a computer to which you connect, which in turn connects to the Web site you wish to visit. You remain anonymous because only the information on the proxy server is visible to outsiders.

For example, consider Anonymouse (http://anonymouse.org). When you access this site, you can click on a link called "Your calling card without Anonymouse." You will see the information that is available to any Web site you visit when you surf normally.

If you want to surf anonymously, enter the URL of the site you want to visit on the Anonymouse Web site where it says "Enter URL." For example, suppose you wish to visit www.amazon.com. You enter this URL where indicated on the Anonymouse Web site. When the Amazon Web site opens on your computer, the URL will look like this: http://anonymouse. org/cgi-bin/anon-www.cgi/http://www.amazon.com/gp/homepage.html/102-8701104-7307331. You are now anonymous at Amazon because Anonymouse is a proxy server for you, so Amazon sees only the information from Anonymouse. Keep in mind that although anonymous surfing is more secure than regular surfing, it is also typically slower. Other anonymizers include Anonymize (www.anonymize.net), Anonymizer (www.anonymizer. com), IDZap (www.idzap.com), Ultimate Privacy (www.ultimate-anonymity.com), and GhostSurf Platinum.

Another way to surf the Web anonymously is to use an anonymizer as a permanent proxy server on your computer. Here are the steps to take to do this:

- Click on My "Computer."
- Click on "Control Panel."
- Click on "Security Center."
- Click on "Internet Options."
- Select the "Connections" tab.
- Click on "LAN Settings."
- When the Local Area Network (LAN) Settings dialog box opens, check the "Use a Proxy Server for Your LAN" option.
- Enter the anonymizer's Web address in the Address field (it is your choice of which anonymizer you wish to use).
- Enter 8080 in the Port box.
- Click "OK."

How to E-Mail Anonymously. The reasons for anonymous e-mail are the same as those for surfing the Web anonymously. Basically, you want to protect your privacy. When you e-mail anonymously, your e-mail messages cannot be tracked back to you personally, to your location, or to your computer. Essentially, your e-mail messages are sent through another server belonging to a company—known as a *re-mailer*—that provides anonymous e-mail services. The recipient of your e-mail sees only the re-mailer's header on your message. In addition, the re-mailer encrypts your messages so that if they are intercepted, they cannot be read. One possible drawback to utilizing a re-mailer is that your intended recipients might not open your e-mail because they will not know it is from you.

Leading commercial re-mailers include CryptoHeaven (www.cryptoheaven.com), Ultimate Privacy (www.ultimate-anonymity.com), and Hushmail (www.hushmail.com). The commercial version of Pretty Good Privacy (PGP) is available at www.pgp.com.

In addition, several free products for anonymous e-mailing and encryption are widely available. For example, the free, open-source version of Pretty Good Privacy, called Open PGP, is available at www.pgpi.org. For a list of these free products and a review of each one, visit http://netsecurity.about.com/. The Outlook e-mail client that comes with Microsoft Office also allows you to encrypt outgoing e-mail messages. This product is based on public key technology (discussed in Chapter 4), so you must download and purchase a digital certificate. The first time you send an encrypted message, Microsoft takes you through the steps necessary to obtain your digital certificate.

The steps necessary to use e-mail encryption in Outlook are as follows:

- Open Outlook and compose your message.
- Click the "Options" button.
- When the Message Options window opens, click the "Security Settings" button.
- The Security Properties window now opens.
- Check the "Encrypt" message contents and attachments checkbox.
- For the time being, you should *not* check the "Add digital signature to this message" checkbox because you first need to install a digital certificate.
- Click "OK" in the Security Properties dialog box.
- You should now be returned to your message.
- Choose an address to send the message to.
- Click the "Send" button.
- You see the "Welcome to Secure E-mail" window.
- Click the "Get Digital ID" . . . button.
- You now are taken to a Microsoft Web site with links to two digital certificate providers: GeoTrust and VeriSign.
- You have to register for the digital certificate at each provider; you need access to your e-mail (and your telephone for GeoTrust).
- After the registration process, you click an installation button to install the digital certificate.
- When you start the installation, Microsoft may display a Potential Scripting Violation warning; click "Yes" to continue.
- Once you get the digital certificate installed, you can click "Send" in Microsoft Outlook.
- You may encounter problems if the people you are sending encrypted messages to do not have digital certificates; also, some e-mail systems may not accept encrypted messages because antivirus scanners cannot scan encrypted e-mail.

Thawte (www.thawte.com) offers a free personal digital e-mail certificate.

It is a good idea to periodically check the trusted certificate authorities that are configured in your browser and verify that those companies can be trusted. In Internet Explorer, follow these steps:

- Click on "Start."
- Right-click on "Explore."

- Click on "Control Panel."
- Click on "Security Center."
- Click on "Internet Options."
- Click on the "Content" tab.
- Click on the "Certificates" button.
- Click on the "Intermediate Certification Authorities" tab and check that the companies listed can be trusted.
- Click on the "Trusted Publishers" tab and check that the companies listed can be trusted.

Erasing Your Google Search History. If you have signed up for Google's Personalized Search, then you can follow these steps to erase your search history. First you sign in to your Google account at www.google.com/psearch. You can examine the Search History page and choose days on the calendar to see every search you have made since you created your Google account. Click on the Remove Items button. Remember, however, that even after you remove items from your computer, logs and backups will still exist on Google's servers. To prevent Google from collecting this information in the future, select items such as "Web," "Images," and "News" about which you do not want data collected, and then press the "Pause" button.

Preparing for Personal Disasters

Disasters are not limited to businesses. You can experience disasters at home, such as fires and floods. Therefore, you should take certain steps to protect your information assets, whether they are stored on your computer (digital form) or in another form (hard copy). First and foremost, you should have a safety deposit box at your bank for your important papers. You should also have a fireproof safe at home where you can store other important papers. You should make a regular backup of your key files and keep these backups in the safe as well. You might also want to encrypt your backup files if they contain sensitive information.

Restoring Backup Files

You can use the Windows Backup utility to restore the backup copies to your hard disk. This is how you launch Backup in Windows 7:

- Click "Start."
- Click "All Programs."
- Click "Accessories."
- Click "System Tools."
- Click "Backup."

Windows 7 has a utility called Windows System Restore. This utility automatically restores key system files to the state they were in before you had problems. (*Note:* System Restore affects your system files, not your data files.) System Restore creates a "mirror" of key system files and settings—called a restore point—every 10 hours, whenever you install a new piece of software, or whenever you manually instruct it to do so. When your system encounters a problem, such as being infected with a virus or worm, you can revert to a restore point before the problem occurred, thereby putting your system back in working order.

To use System Restore:

- Click "Start."
- Click "All Programs."
- Click "Accessories."
- Click "System Tools."
- Click "System Restore."
- When the System Restore window opens, choose the "Restore My Computer To An Earlier Time" Option.

- Click "Next."
- When the "Select A Restore Point" screen appears, you will see a calendar showing the current month. Any date highlighted in bold contains a restore point. Select a restore point from before the problem appeared, and click "Next."
- When the confirmation screen appears, click "Next."

Wireless Security

Many home users have implemented a wireless local area network. The security considerations for wireless networks are greater than those for wired networks. The reason for this is simple. If you are wirelessly computing and communicating, then you are broadcasting, and therefore by definition, you are nonsecure. The most common reason for intruders to connect to a nonsecure wireless network is to gain access to the Internet. Intruders might also connect in order to use your network as a base for spamming or for other unethical or illegal activities. Finally, they may do so to gain access to your sensitive personal information.

Unfortunately, recent studies have indicated that three-fourths of all home wireless users have not activated any security features to protect their information. Unless you take the steps we discuss here, your information assets are extremely vulnerable.

Hide Your Service Set Identifier (SSID). Your wireless router, which connects your home network with your ISP, comes with a default SSID that is the same for thousands or millions of routers made by the manufacturer. Therefore, an attacker can search for wireless networks by looking for a relatively small number of default SSIDs. For this reason, you should (1) change your default SSID to a unique SSID and (2) configure your wireless home network to stop broadcasting the SSID. A step-by-step guide to perform these security measures is available online (just search "about.com change default SSID").

Use Encryption. To avoid broadcasting in the clear, you must use encryption with your wireless home network. Wireless equivalent protocol (WEP) is an old protocol that is now very easy to crack and therefore should not be used. Instead, you should use Wi-Fi Protected Access (WPA2), which is the second generation of WPA. WPA2 is much stronger than WEP and will protect your encryption against attackers. (*Note:* Your wireless router must support WPA2. Otherwise, use WPA rather than WEP.) In addition, you should use a strong passphrase of at least 20 random characters on your router. (Chapter 4 provides specific instructions for creating strong passphrases.)

Filter Out Media Access Control (MAC) Addresses. Every piece of networking hardware has a unique identification number called a media access control (MAC) address that looks like this: 00-00-00-00-00-00. (This MAC address is only an example.) You should compile the MAC address of all computers on your home wireless network. Then, instruct your router to connect only with those computers, and deny access to all other computers attempting to connect with your network.

To find the MAC address of your computer, follow these steps:

- Click on "Start."
- Click on "All Programs."
- Click on "Accessories."
- Click on "Command Prompt."
- At the cursor, type "ipconfig/all."
- Hit "Enter."
- The MAC address will be the Physical Address.

Limit Internet Protocol (IP) Addresses. You should instruct your router to allow only a certain number of IP addresses to connect to your network. Ideally, the number of IP addresses will be the same as the number of computers on your network.

Sniff Out Intruders. A variety of wireless intrusion detection systems will monitor your wireless network for intruders, alert you when are on your network, display their IP addresses and their activity, and even inform them that you know that they are there.

Commercial products include the Internet Security Systems (www.iss.net) wireless scanner and AirDefense Personal (www.airdefense.net). AirSnare is a free wireless intrusion detection system.

Using a Public Hotspot. When you travel, keep in mind that most public wireless providers and hotspots employ no security measures at all. As a result, everything you send and receive is in the clear and has no encryption. Many intruders go to public hotspots and listen in on the wireless computing and communications taking place there. If you must compute wirelessly at a public hotspot, you should take several precautions before you connect.

- Use virtual private networking (VPN) technology to connect to your organization's network (discussed in Chapter 4).
- Use Remote Desktop to connect to a computer that is running at your home.
- Configure the Windows firewall to be "on with no exceptions."
- Only use Web sites that use secure sockets layer (SSL) for any financial or personal transactions.

Test Your Wireless Network. After you have finished all the necessary steps to protect your wireless home network, it is a good idea to test the network for vulnerabilities. A free Wi-Fi vulnerability scanner has been created by eEye and is available for download (just search "eEye download" for the link). This tool scans your vicinity looking for wireless devices to test. When you run it, it generates a detailed report that outlines all of the security problems it finds.

Wireless Security Software. For extra security, you can purchase wireless security programs. Trend Micro (www.trendmicro.com) has added Wi-Fi Intrusion Detection to PC-cillin, which also includes a personal firewall, antivirus software, and antispyware software. The software warns you when an unknown user tries to access your wireless network.

Zonelabs (www.zonelabs.com) has a product called Zone-Alarm Wireless Security that automatically detects wireless networks and helps secure them.

McAfee (www.mcafee.com) provides a free scan to check the security of the wireless network connection that you are using. The scan works only with Internet Explorer. Go to www.mcafee.com, click the section for home users, and look under Free Services for McAfee Wi-Fi scan.

BEFORE YOU GO ON . . .

1. Why is it so important for you to protect yourself?
2. What are the two types of action that you can take to protect yourself?

Apply the Concept PI 6.3

Background Although computer-based actions are extremely important to the security of a computer, they all begin with the decision to protect your information assets. There are many, many tools available to you to help protect your information. It would be a good idea to become familiar with the many tools available (many of which are presented in this chapter).

Activity Visit http://www.wiley.com/go/rainer/applytheconcept and click on the link provided for Plug IT In 6.3. This will take you to a McAfee product Web site called "Site Advisor." Look for the "how it works" link at the top of the page. You will see that this simple tool makes it easy for you to be more aware of the security level of the sites you are visiting.

Download and install this tool and browse the Web for 30 minutes or so. Visit the sites you routinely go to and write down the security rating each is given by McAfee. After going over your list of sites, does this make you want to change any of your habits?

Deliverable

Submit your list to your professor along with any resulting behavioral changes you plan to make.

Quiz questions are assignable in WileyPLUS, and available on the Book Companion Site at http://www.wiley.com/college/rainer.

SUMMARY

1. **Explain why it is critical that you protect your information assets.**

   We live in a digital world. Unfortunately, every time we use our computers or access the Internet, we risk exposing both professional and personal information to people looking to steal or exploit that information. It is your responsibility to protect yourself in our hostile, digital environment. Protecting yourself is becoming even more critical because organized crime is increasingly turning its attention to home users. As businesses improve their information security, consumers become the next logical target.

2. **Identify the various behavioral actions you can take to protect your information assets.**

   - Do not provide personal information to strangers in any format (physical, verbal, or electronic).
   - Protect your Social Security number.
   - Use credit cards with your picture on them.
   - Do not sign the back of your credit cards. Instead, write "Photo ID Required."
   - Pay very close attention to your credit card billing cycles.
   - Limit your use of debit cards.
   - Do not use a personal mailbox at your home for anything other than catalogs and magazines.
   - Use a cross-cut, or confetti, shredder.
   - Sign up with a company that provides proactive protection of your personal information.

3. **Identify the various computer-based actions you can take to protect your information assets.**

   - Check to see where anyone who may have used your computer has visited on the Internet.
   - Never post personal information about yourself or your family in chat rooms or on social networking sites. Use the privacy features provided by social networking sites to limit public access to your profile.
   - Never open unrequested attachments to e-mail files, even those from people you know and trust.
   - Never open attachments or Web links in e-mails from people you do not know.
   - Never accept files transferred to you during Internet chat or instant messaging sessions.
   - Never download any files or software over the Internet from Web sites that you do not know.
   - Never download files or software that you have not requested.
   - Test your system.
   - Run free malware scans on your computer.
   - Have an anti-malware product on your computer, and use it (ideally at least once per week).
   - Have a firewall on your computer.
   - Have an antispyware product on your computer.
   - Have monitoring software on your computer.
   - Have content-filtering software on your computer.
   - Have antispam software on your computer.
   - Have proactive intrusion detection and prevention software on your computer.
   - Manage patches.
   - Use a browser other than Internet Explorer.
   - Use a laptop security system.
   - Use two-factor authentication.
   - Use encryption.
   - Use laptop-tracing tools or device reset/remote kill tools.
   - Look for new and unusual files.
   - Detect fake Web sites.
   - Use strong passwords.
   - Surf the Web anonymously.
   - E-mail anonymously.
   - Adjust the privacy settings on your computer.
   - Erase your Google search history.
   - Personal disaster preparation: backup, backup, backup!
   - Wireless security
     - Hide your service set identifier (SSID).
     - Use encryption.
     - Filter out media access control (MAC) addresses.
     - Limit IP addresses.
     - Sniff out intruders.
     - Change the default administrator password on your wireless router to something not easily guessed.
     - Use VPN technology to connect to your organization's network.
     - Use Remote Desktop to connect to a computer that is running at your home.
     - Configure Windows firewall to be "on with no exceptions."
     - Only use Web sites that use SSL for any financial or personal transactions.
     - Use wireless security programs.

>>> DISCUSSION QUESTIONS

1. Why is it so important for you to protect your information assets? Can you assume that your organization's MIS department will do it for you?

2. Discuss the differences between behavioral actions that you should take and computer-based actions that you should take.

>>> PROBLEM-SOLVING ACTIVITIES

1. Using one product suggested in this Plug IT In or a product you find, do the following:
   - Test or scan your computer for malware.
   - Test your firewall.
   - Scan your computer for spyware.

2. Follow the steps in this Plug IT In to see if you have a Trojan horse on your computer.

Photo Credits

Chapter Opener Photos:

Chapter opener 1 © Abel Mitja Varela/iStockphoto
Chapter opener 2 © Abel Mitja Varela/iStockphoto
Chapter opener 3 Stephen Swintek/Stone +/Getty Images, Inc.
Chapter opener 4 © Oleksiy Mark/iStockphoto
Chapter opener 5 © Henrik Jonsson/iStockphoto
Chapter opener 6 © Boris Yankov/iStockphoto
Chapter opener 7 Epoxydude/Getty Images, Inc.
Chapter opener 8 © kizilkayaphotos/iStockphoto
Chapter opener 9 Rubberball/Mike Kemp/Getty Images, Inc.
Chapter opener 10 © Martin McCarthy/iStockphoto
Chapter opener 11 © Helder Almeida/iStockphoto
Chapter opener 12 ©Kohlerphoto/iStockphoto
Chapter opener 13 © Louis-Paul St-Onge/iStockphoto
Chapter opener 14 © londoneye/iStockphoto

Icons:

What's in IT for ME? © Skip ODonnell/iStockphoto
Fingers crossed hand gesture © Johnny Chih-Chung Chang/iStockphoto
Computer mouse © adisa/iStockphoto
Music notes © linearcurves/iStockphoto
Apply the Concept/girl using laptop © Selahattain BAYRAM/iStockphoto
Mobile phone with apps © pictafolio/iStockphoto
Abstract wave background © Marina Strizhak
Buttons- Svjatogor/Shutterstock & VectorForever/Shutterstock
Globe © chudo-yudo/Shutterstock
Student Activity/boy on computer Lane Oatey/Getty Image, Inc.
Student Activity/sitting girl with laptop © Voon Nam Fook/iStockphoto

Index

Page numbers in **bold** indicate end of chapter glossary terms.
Page number in *italics* indicate figures.
Page numbers followed by "t" indicate tables.